The Nitrian Principality

East Central and Eastern Europe in the Middle Ages, 450–1450

General Editors

Florin Curta and Dušan Zupka

VOLUME 68

The titles published in this series are listed at *brill.com/ecee*

The Nitrian Principality

The Beginnings of Medieval Slovakia

By

Ján Steinhübel

Translated by

David McLean

BRILL

LEIDEN | BOSTON

Cover illustration: Reconstruction of the Great Moravian hillfort Ducové – Kostolec (Slovakia). Designed by Viktória Kyjovská ©.

This publication originated at the Institute of History of the Slovak Academy of Sciences, where the author works. The English edition, elaborated and supplemented, was prepared as part of the VEGA project "Monarchic Power in the Middle Ages" (VEGA 2/0129/18: Panovnícka moc v stredoveku).

Library of Congress Cataloging-in-Publication Data
Names: Steinhübel, Ján, author.
Title: The Nitrian Principality : the beginnings of medieval Slovakia / by
  Ján Steinhübel ; translated by David McLean.
Other titles: Nitrianské kniežatstvo. English
Description: Leiden ; Boston : Brill, [2021] | Series: East Central and
  Eastern Europe in the Middle Ages, 1450-1450, 1872-8103 ; volume 68 |
  Includes bibliographical references and indexes.
Identifiers: LCCN 2020037599 (print) | LCCN 2020037600 (ebook) |
  ISBN 9789004437821 (hardback) | ISBN 9789004438637 (ebook)
Subjects: LCSH: Nitriansky kraj (Slovakia)—History. |
  Slovakia—History—To 1526.
Classification: LCC DB3000.N57 S7413 2021 (print) | LCC DB3000.N57
  (ebook) | DDC 943.73/3022—dc23
LC record available at https://lccn.loc.gov/2020037599
LC ebook record available at https://lccn.loc.gov/2020037600

Typeface for the Latin, Greek, and Cyrillic scripts: "Brill". See and download: brill.com/brill-typeface.

ISSN 1872-8103
ISBN 978-90-04-43782-1 (hardback)
ISBN 978-90-04-43863-7 (e-book)

Copyright 2021 by Koninklijke Brill NV, Leiden, The Netherlands.
Koninklijke Brill NV incorporates the imprints Brill, Brill Hes & De Graaf, Brill Nijhoff, Brill Rodopi, Brill Sense, Hotei Publishing, mentis Verlag, Verlag Ferdinand Schöningh and Wilhelm Fink Verlag.
All rights reserved. No part of this publication may be reproduced, translated, stored in a retrieval system, or transmitted in any form or by any means, electronic, mechanical, photocopying, recording or otherwise, without prior written permission from the publisher. Requests for re-use and/or translations must be addressed to Koninklijke Brill NV via brill.com or copyright.com.

This book is printed on acid-free paper and produced in a sustainable manner.

Contents

List of Illustrations VII
Abbreviations VIII

Introduction 1

1 Quadia and Suebia 5

2 From the Arrival of the Slavs Up through Samo's Realm 22

3 Avar Domination 57

4 Fall of the Avar Khaganate 78

5 Nitria the Independent Principality (805–833) 110

6 Pribina and Kocel in Pannonia 138

7 The Mojmírs in Nitria 181

8 The Moravian Fight for Independence (861–871) 197

9 Svätopluk's Realm 210

10 Great Moravia and the Magyars 239

11 After the Downfall of Great Moravia 255

12 Tales about Svätopluk 269

13 Hungarian Principalities 300

14 Nitria in the Emerging Árpád State 324

15 Between Hungary and Poland (1001–1029) 380

16 The Escape and Return of Four Árpáds (1029–1048) 417

17 Kings against Princes, Princes against Kings (1048–1077)   440

18 The Last Princes (1077–1108)   465

19 Árpád Nitria – Hungarian and Slavic   487

20 The End of the Nitrian Principality (1108–1110)   515

Conclusion: Nitria and Slovakia   526
Maps   536

Bibliography   541
Index of Names   639
Index of Places   658

Illustrations

1 Division of Pannonia among Franconian Marches – Peter Rybár   536
2 Transdanubia – Peter Rybár   537
3 Great Moravia – Peter Rybár   538
4 Kingdom of Hungary – Peter Rybár   539
5 The Nitrian Principality – Peter Rybár   540

Abbreviations

ÁMF	Az Árpád-kori Magyarország történeti földrajza
Ann. Altah. maior.	Annales Altahenses maiores
Ann. Bert.	Annales Bertiniani
Ann. Fuld.	Annales Fuldenses
Ann. Hildesh.	Annales Hildesheimenses
Ann. reg. Franc.	Annales regni Francorum
AO	Codex diplom. hungaricus Andegavensis. Anjoukori okmánytár
ÁÚO	Codex diplom. Arpadianus continuatus. Árpádkori új okmánytár
CDB	Codex diplomaticus et epistolaris regni Bohemiae I
CDES	Codex diplomaticus et epistolaris Slovaciae
CDH	Codex diplomaticus Hungariae ecclesiasticus ac civilis
Df	Diplomatikai fényképgyűjtemény
DHA	Diplomata Hungariae antiquissima
Dl	Diplomatikai levéltár
FRB	Fontes rerum Bohemicarum
HO	Codex diplomaticus patrius hungaricus. Hazai okmánytár
Chron. Hung. comp. saec. XIV.	Chronicon Hungarici compositio saeculi XIV.
MEF	Magyarország egyházi földleírása a XIV. század elején a pápai tizedjegyzékek alapján feltüntetve
MES	Monumenta ecclesiae Strigoniensis
MHDC	Monumenta historica ducatus Carinthiae
MMFH	Magnae Moraviae fontes historici
Mon. Vat.	Monumenta Vaticana Hungariae historiam regni Hungariae illustrantia
MPH	Monumenta Poloniae historica
MT	Magyarország története
RDES	Regesta diplomatica nec non epistolaria Slovaciae
SRH	Scriptores rerum Hungaricarum tempore ducum regumque stirpis Arpadianae gestarum
UHS	Urkundenbuch des Herzogthums Steiermark
ŽM	Žitije Mefodija
ŽK	Žitije Konstantina

Introduction

European nations and states have medieval foundations. At the beginning of their histories are the Barbarian *gentes*, that is the tribes or nations which stirred during the period of great migration and completely changed Europe.[1] These were primarily Germanic and Slavic tribes, which initially under pressure from the Huns, later driven by the desire for Roman wealth and new settlements, covered Europe with their kingdoms and principalities, constantly collided into one another and into the remnants of the antique world. Many of them started a history that still endures today and gave their name and historical foundation to today's nations and states.

The Gothic historian Jordanes knew that *different nations ... do not have a common perception of one suffering.*[2] Therefore, a nation did have a *common perception of one suffering*, that is, a history permeated by the dominant feeling for all times – suffering. Daily life was already full of suffering, but to a great measure it grew mainly during the ceaseless wars. Victories and reverses alternated with long marches or a settled life on old land or new, recently conquered and occupied territories. These were strong stimuli, which constantly, mostly painfully, pressed on people. If they were able to survive this pressure, which they felt as a common suffering, then it brought them together and hardened them; if it was too destructive, then it broke them apart. They well

---

1 Reinhard Wenskus, *Stammesbildung und Verfassung. Das Werden der frühmittelalterlichen gentes* (Cologne – Graz 1961). Benedykt Zientara. *Świt narodów europejskich. Powstawanie świadomości narodowej na obszarze Europy pokarolińskej*, (Warszawa 1996), pp. 13–34. Dušan Třeštík, "Moderne Nation, hochmittelalterliche politische Nation, frühmittelalterliche gens und unsere genetische Software. Der Fall Mittelaurapa," in *Mittelalterliche nationes-neuzeitliche Nationen. Probleme der Nationenbildung in Europa*, ed. Almut Bues, Rex Rexheuser, (Wiesbaden 1995), pp. 169–181. Dušan Třeštík, "Moderní národ, politický národ vrcholného středověku, raně středověký gens a naše genetické software," in Dušan Třeštík. *Mysliti dějiny* (Praha – Litomyšl 1999), pp. 108–120. Dušan Třeštík, "Počátky českého politického myšlení," in *Dějiny politického myšlení II/1. Politické myšlení raného křesťanství a středověku*, editors Vilém Herold, Ivan Müller, Aleš Havlíček (Praha 2011), pp. 404–446. Karol Modzelewski, *Barbarzyńska Europa* (Warszawa 2004). Ivo Štefan, "Etnicita v raném středověku aneb pátrání po původu kabátu, který se už nenosí," in *"Neslované" o počátcích Slovanů*, editor Przemysław Urbańczyk (Praha 2011), pp. 103–110. Ján Steinhübel, *Kapitoly z najstarších českých dejín 531–1004* (Kraków 2012) pp. 8–28. Miroslav Lysý, *Moravania, Mojmírovci a Franská ríša. Štúdie k etnogenéze, politickým inštitúciám a ústavnému zriadeniu na území Slovenska vo včasnom stredoveku* (Bratislava 2014) pp. 13–43.
2 *Illic concursus factus est gentium variarum ... nec quae unius passioni conpaterentur.* Jordanes, *De origine actibusque Getharum* L 261.

remembered such accumulated suffering and mentioned it often.[3] Its *common perception* brought them together and unified them. This common and enduring experience, filled with strong feelings, good and bad, was imprinted on their imaginations, thinking and eventually into similar characters, and thus also mutual understanding. This was their history, a painful historical pressure that weighed on them and ground them into one common form.

Sometimes the nation divided into two or more parts, or, in contrast, joined together and mixed with another nation, or it took in part of another nation.[4] In this way a new nation could emerge. Two opposites, a natural generational continuity and artificial historical disruption, that is discontinuity, mutually complemented one another in the history of a nation.

A nation is an idea. Its basis is an ideal image that *we* are a nation, *we* have a name,[5] and *we* know our national story.[6] This at least a little bit historical and rational (or only posing as historical and rational) ideal[7] turns inward and relates the self to a strong irrational mixture of feelings (mutual attachment of fellow tribesmen, the feeling of exclusivity, pride in common victories achieved, sorrow over what was lost, suffering from injustices and defeats they have suffered), which provides it with a motivational force. Thanks to the irrational content, this idea (which often grows into a desire) necessitates attention and persists. The will to be a nation is thus a continuity of the idea of a nation.

A contemporary medieval *gens* was able to be exceptionally cohesive. Tribal cohesiveness was determined by the law of likeness and unlikeness. What was kindred was acceptable, friendly and good. What was different was unacceptable, unfriendly and dangerous. They understood that which was like and rejected that which was different. A person who was born and grew up amidst the tribe heard and knew from the start the myth of its origin, enjoyed listening to or speaking about the glory of ancestors and their heroic acts, worshipped

---

3   Mircea Eliade, *Mýtus o věčném návratu. Archetypy a opakování* (Praha 2003), pp. 65–69 [English *The Myth of the Eternal Return: Cosmos and History*, trans. Willard R. Trask (Princeton, 1971)].

4   Herwig Wolfram, "Einleitung oder Überlegungen zur origo gentis," in *Typen der Ethnogenese unter besonderer Berücksochtigung der Bayern. Teil I*, ed. Herwig Wolfram and Walter Pohl (Wien 1990), pp. 19–33. Peter Bystický, *Sťahovanie národov (454–568). Ostrogóti, Gepidi, Longobardi a Slovania* (Bratislava 2008), pp. 8–9, 16, 32–33, 38–39, 42, 43, 50, 74, 78, 92, 99–101, 109, 122, 163–164.

5   Regarding the names of Germanic tribes, see Wenskus, *Stammesbildung*, pp. 59–82. Regarding Slavic tribal names, see Steinhübel, *Kapitoly*, pp. 32–35.

6   Jan Assmann, *Kultura a paměť. Písmo, vzpomínka a politická identita v rozvinutých kultúrach staroveku* (Praha 2001), p. 117 [Original *Kultur und Gedächtnis* (Frankfurt a. M. 1988)].

7   Assmann, *Kultura a paměť*, pp. 125–126. Bystický, *Sťahovanie*, pp. 79–83.

the tribe's gods and attended the common tribal and religious centre, where decisions important for the entire tribe were made.⁸ He didn't merely perceive all of this but also imbued it with strong feelings. The people in his tribe were like him. He knew them and knew that they think and feel as he does. Therefore, he understood them and loved them. This mutual understanding, supplemented by strong feelings, bound them together. Early medieval man thus loved his tribe or nation, and he could hardly imagine a life outside of it. Foreigners who belonged to another nation and who had not undergone all of this with him, were unknown, incomprehensible and suspicious. Furthermore, if they spoke a different or even incomprehensible language and had different customs, religion, way of life and appearance, the mutual distaste grew. The Bohemian chronicler Cosmas of Prague emphasized this: *Indeed, human nature is such that every one of us, regardless from which country, loves his own (suam) more than a foreign (alienam) nation (gentem).*⁹ The opposition of we and they was extraordinarily strong and even insurmountable.¹⁰ This was the cause of tension and constant wars.

Each barbarian nation (*gens*, in other words *natio* or *populus*, Slavic *językъ*¹¹) lived a traditional way of life. All who were born into it or otherwise affiliated with it were provided with the favour of the gods, protection, justice and all rights, mainly ownership of land, livestock and slaves and a vote in the council. A council, common law and a religious cult maintained the *peace*, that is the traditional cycle of life, stability of the nation and organization of this world, which was governed by their gods. This was their certainty and stability; in

---

8   Ján Steinhübel, "Slovanský 'gens' a jeho stred. Kniežací hrad, pohanská svätyňa, snem a trh," *Byzantinoslovaca* V (2014), pp. 142–159.

9   *Cosmae Pragensis Chronica Boemorum* II 23, herausgegeben von Bertold Bretholz, Monumenta Germaniae historica, Scriptores rerum Germanicarum nova series II (Berolini 1923), p. 116.

10 Steinhübel, *Kapitoly*, pp. 18–23. Ján Steinhübel, "Veľká Morava a slovanský svet", *Monumentorum tutela* 28 (2018), pp. 7–14. Regarding different scales of the contrast of us and them, see Juraj Šedivý, "Chápanie etník v nemeckých kronikách a obraz starých Maďarov na prelome 1. a 2. tisícročia," *Historický časopis* 44 (1996), no. 3, pp. 353–382.

11 Isidore of Seville, *Etymologiae* IX 2 (1, 89–135). Fritz Lošek, "Ethnische und politische Terminologie bei Iordanes und Einhard," in *Typen der Ethnogenese unter besonderer Berücksichtigung der Bayern. Teil I. Berichte des Symposions der Kommission für Frühmittelalterforschung, 27. bis 30. Oktober 1986, Stift Zwettl, Niederösterreich*, ed. Herwig Wolfram and Walter Pohl (Wien 1990), pp. 147–152. Hagen Schulze, *Štát a národ v európskych dejinách* (Praha 2003), pp. 99–100 [Orig. *Staat und Nation in der Europäischen Geschichte* (München 1994)]. Lysý, *Moravania*, pp. 21–41. Steinhübel, "Veľká Morava a slovanský svet", pp. 10–12.

their understanding *liberty*, – traditional protocol, held by all free men, who lived according to it, subjugated themselves to it and unanimously fulfilled it.[12] We call a nation which lived according to the old barbarian *liberty* (with a small dose of imprecision) a tribe. Tribal clannishness was replaced by the state and pagan gods by the one God. The state was stronger than the fellowship of the fellow tribesmen, and the Christian God was much more powerful than the old tribal gods. The state stabilized the nation and very effectively secured its independence. However, it abolished its old *liberty*.

Nations that survived the barbarian period acquired a great hardiness. They gave shape to medieval Europe and turned into historical nations. Historical nations and states have a strong historical-legal foundation, territory within old, historically justifiable and hard to doubt borders, an antique name and a history which begins *from ancient times (ab antiquo)*.

12 Wenskus, *Stammesbildung*, pp. 38–44, 299–335, 429–462, 573–575. Dušan Třeštík, "Mír a dobrý rok. Česká státní ideologie mezi křesťanstvím a pohanstvím," *Folia historica Bohemica* 12, 1988, pp. 23–45. Třeštík, "Moderne Nation", pp. 171–173. Třeštík, "Moderní národ," pp. 109–112. Dušan Třeštík, *Počátky Přemyslovců. Vstup Čechů do dějin (530–935)* (Praha 1997), pp. 59–63, 302–311. Dušan Třeštík, "Počátky přemyslovské státnosti mezi křesťanstvím a pohanstvím," in *Stát, státnost a rituály přemyslovského věku. Problémy, názory, otázky*, ed. Martin Wihoda, Demeter Malaťák (Brno 2006), pp. 29–34, 39–41. Dušan Třeštík, "Gens Bohemanorum – kmen Čechů," in *Přemyslovci. Budování českého státu*, ed. Petr Sommer, Dušan Třeštík, Josef Žemlička (Praha 2009), pp. 137–139, 144–148. Třeštík, "Počátky českého politického myšlení," pp. 406–408, 418–421, 425–426. Zientara, *Świt narodów europejskich*, pp. 13–34. Hans Hattenhauer, *Evropské dějiny práva* (Praha 1998, pp. 1–44, 134–145. Modzelewski, *Barbarzyńska Europa*, pp. 49–116, 205–425, 457–458. Vladimír Procházka, "Organisace kultu a kmenové zřízení polabsko – pobaltských Slovanů," in *Vznik a počátky Slovanů* II (1958), pp. 145–168. Vladimír Procházka, "Sněmovnictví a soudnictví polabsko – pobaltských Slovanů," in *Vznik a počátky Slovanů* III (1960), pp. 83–122. Piotr Boroń, *Słowiańskie wiece plemienne* (Katowice 1999). Martin Golema, *Stredoveká literatúra a indoeurópske mytologické dedičstvo. Prítomnosť trojfunkčnej indoeurópskej ideológie v literatúre, mytológii a folklóre stredovekých Slovanov* (Banská Bystrica 2006), pp. 200–206. Rastislav Kožiak, "*Conversio Gentum* a christianizácia vo včasnom stredoveku," *Ružomberský historický zborník* I (2007), pp. 99–103.

CHAPTER 1

Quadia and Suebia

1   The Quadi and Their Neighbours

From the beginning of our epoch Moravia, the Transdanubian part of Lower Austria and much later the south-west part of Slovakia, belonged to the Quadi, a Suebian tribe.[1] In the mountains of today's central Slovakia lived the Celtic Cotins and to the south of them, probably in the Ipeľ River region, the Illyrean Osians.[2] In the eastern vicinity of these two tribes lived the Anartes. This was evidently a Celtic tribe; therefore, Caesar clearly differentiated them from the neighbouring Dacians, whose settlements began in what is now the Zemplín region.[3]

During the Marcomannic Wars (166–180) the Hasdings, a Vandal tribe, settled in the north-eastern part of the Carpathian Basin. The Hasdings, who were led there by kings Raus and Raptus, conquered at the end of 171 or early 172 the Dacian Costobocs and took their settlements in the upper Tisza River region and became allies of the Romans.[4] According to findings of Vandal grey ceramics, we know that their settlements reached even into today's eastern Slovakia, to the Zemplín, Abov and Šariš regions.[5] In addition to the upper

---

1   Oldřich Pelikán, *Slovensko a rímske impérium* (Bratislava 1960), pp. 34–100. Josef Dobiáš, *Dějiny československého území před vystoupením Slovanů* (Praha 1964), pp. 149–299.
2   Pelikán, *Slovensko*, pp. 34–41, 74. Dobiáš, *Dějiny*, pp. 8–9, 19–21, 67–69, 164, 206, 221, 244–245.
3   Dobiáš, *Dějiny*, pp. 23, 34–36, 57, 71–73, 150.
4   *Cassii Dionis Cocceiani Historia Romana* LXXI 11, 12. Endre Tóth, "Dacia római tartomány," in *Erdély története I. A kezdetektől 1606-ig*, ed. László Makkai, András Mócsy (Budapest 1986), p. 69. Endre Tóth, "Dazien als römische Provinz," in *Kurze Geschichte Siebenbürgens*, ed. Béla Köpeczi (Budapest 1990), p. 39. Jerzy Strzelczyk, *Wandalowie i ich afrykańskie państwo* (Warszawa 1992), pp. 57–61. Hermann Schreiber, *Die Vandalen. Siegeszug und Untergang eines germanischen Volkes* (Bern – München 1993), pp. 73–78.
5   The Vandals were bearers of the Przeworsk culture. They made very perfect grey ceramics turned on a wheel and decorated them with stamped, smoothing patterns, pressed on using a toothed wheel. They left behind settlements (Seňa, Peder, Šebastovce, Blažice, Michalovce), pottery ovens (Blažice, Bohdanovce, Beregszurány), burial mounds with urn graves (Zemplín) and wealthy gravesites (Cejkov, Ostrovany). Mária Lamiová-Schmiedlová, "Römerzeitliche Siedlungskeramik in der Südostslowakei," *Slovenská archeológia* 17 (1969), no. 2, pp. 404–458. Mária Lamiová-Schmiedlová, "K otázke proveniencie mincí z doby rímskej na východnom Slovensku," *Slovenská numizmatika* 9 (1986), pp. 134–142. Titus Kolník, "Prehľad a stav bádania o dobe rímskej a sťahovaní národov," *Slovenská archeológia* 19 (1971), no. 2, pp. 525–529. Bohuslav Chropovský, "Slovensko v protohistorickom období," in *Dejiny*

Tisza River region, which until then belonged to the Dacians, they also seized the settlements of the mentioned Anartes people to the west. At the end of the Marcomannic Wars, Emperor Marcus Aurelius resettled in Pannonia the Cotins and the Osians, who before then lived in the region to the east of the Quadi.[6] The Quadi took over the abandoned settlements of the Osians and Cotins and thus became neighbours of the Sarmatians, who between the years 15–20 CE occupied the entire region between the Danube and Tisza rivers,[7] and the Vandals, who also penetrated from the upper Tisza River region into the valley of the Hornád River.

In 271 the Gepids became the southern neighbour of the Vandals, when under the leadership of King Fastida they settled on the rivers Crasna (Tisza), Barcău and Crişul Alb in the north-west surroundings of the Roman province of Dacia, which at this same time fell into the hands of the Visigoths.[8]

2   Two Quadian Kingdoms

In the mid-4th century Quadia was split into two kingdoms. The kingdom that lay on the northern side of the Danube opposite Brigetio (today's Szőny, Hungary) was ruled by King Viduari. The eastern kingdom, which to the south bordered with the Sarmatia, was ruled by the father of Prince Arahari. Both kings had several Quadian principalities subjugated under them. The eastern Quadian king also ruled over Transiugitans, residing perhaps in the mountains of central Slovakia, and Sarmatian Prince Usafer obeyed him as well. If the power of the eastern Quadian king also extended to the neighbouring tribes, then the range of his kingdom had to correspond to this power. Eastern Quadia thus could not have been small; its territory ended only at the borders of the equally powerful barbarian kingdoms to the south of Sarmatia and to the east of the Vandal kingdom. Thus, everything not taken by the Romans, Sarmatians

---

    Slovenska I (Bratislava 1986), p. 58. *Atlas Slovenskej socialistickej republiky, IX. Vývoj osídlenia a územnej organizácie*, map 9: Titus Kolník, "Osídlenie v dobe rímskej", p. 108. Strzelczyk, *Wandalowie*, pp. 61–79. Bohuslav Novotný, *Slovom a mečom. Slovensko v rímskej dobe* (Martin 1995), pp. 83–92.

6 Dobiáš, *Dějiny*, pp. 221, 270–271.
7 Dobiáš, *Dějiny*, p. 150.
8 István Bóna, "Az 'Erdelyi emberek'. A gótok Erdélyben," in *Erdély története I*, ed. Makkai, Mócsy, pp. 108–134. István Bóna, "'Die Waldmenschen'. Die Goten in Siebenbürgen," in *Kurze Geschichte Siebenbürgens*, ed. Köpeczi, pp. 66–77. Herwig Wolfram, *Die Goten. Von den Anfängen bis zur Mitte des sechsten Jahrhunderts. Entwurf einer historischen Ethnographie*, (München 1990), pp. 65–66.

and Vandal Hasdings in the north of the Carpathian Basin belonged to the Quadi.

At the end of winter in 358 *the Sarmatians and Quadi, adjacent neighbours, together undertook smaller marauding raids into Pannonia and Moesia.* In early spring of 358 Emperor Constantius II (337–361) crossed the Danube with a large army, perhaps near Bononia (modern Bonoštor in Serbia), and attacked the Sarmatians. The Quadi came to the aid of the Sarmatians, who had lost the battle with the Romans and were on the run. Most of the Quadi fell, and only the portion that *escaped through the well-known mountains (per notos colles)* were saved. The Roman army followed them and wanted to enter the *kingdoms of the Quadi (ad Quadorum regna)*. The Quadi, in order to prevent the ravaging of their territory, sued for peace. The mountains which the escaping Quadi knew well separated the Sarmatians from the Quadi. These could only be the Cserhát Mountains, enclosing the Sarmatian plain to the north in the area between the Danube and Tisza rivers, on which the mentioned battle played out.

The Sarmatian Prince Zizai and the subjugated Sarmatian princes Rumo, Zinafer and Fragiled were the first to capitulate to the emperor. Then Arahari, who *led the Transiugitans and part of the Quadi*, and Usafer, leading *some of the Sarmatians*, surrendered together. The emperor divided Arahari and Usafer, who *were closely linked together by a common boundary and savageness*, from one another. First *the matter of Arahari and the Quadi was investigated.* After making peace with Arahari, *Usafer was admitted on request. Arahari wilfully objected against this and said that peace, which he deserves, should also apply to Usafer as his ally, although in a lower position and accustomed to obeying his orders.* The emperor rejected this, however, and rid Usafer's Sarmatians of their Quadian overlord: *The Sarmatians ultimately received a command to free themselves out from under the foreign power, because they were always clients of the Romans.* Usafer subjected himself to Zizai, whom the emperor designated as the new Sarmatian king.

Afterwards, the Romans departed Sarmatia, heading to Brigetio, where they again crossed the Danube and entered the centre of Viduari's kingdom. Then *their Prince Vitrodor, son of King Viduari, vassal Prince Agilimund and other nobles and judges administering to various tribes, as they watched the army in the lap of their kingdom and native ground, threw themselves at the feet of the soldiers* and accepted the same peace conditions as the Sarmatians and the eastern Quadi.[9] The emperor no longer approached the Quadi in Moravia,

---

9 *Ammiani Marcellini Rerum gestarum libri qui supersunt* XVII 12. We use the edition of *Ammiani Marcellini Rerum gestarum libri qui supersunt*, recensuit Carolus Upson Clark (Berolini 1910, 1915). Archaeological discoveries also signal the presence of the Quadi in central Slovakia.

because the Quadian capitulation *in the lap of the kingdom* (*in gremio regni*) also included them.

3 Roman Kelemantia and Quadian Nitra

The great Roman fortress and legion settlement, the town of Brigetio (today part of the city of Komárom, Hungary), had a smaller forward fortress (castellum) on the opposite side of the Danube. Opposite Brigetio (in today's Iža, near Komárno, Slovakia) lay the settlement Kelemantia, about which Claudius Ptolemy had already written. In the time of the Marcomannic Wars the Romans built a large wooden-earthen camp on this site, which they then converted into a stone wall fortress.[10] The old settlement at Kelemantia gave its name to the new Roman fortress, just as the Roman camp in Trenčín was given the name Laugaricio according to the local Quadian (or Celtic) settlement, which Ptolemy mentions as Leukaristos.

If the emperor set forth against the settlement of Viduari's kingdom from Brigetio, then after crossing the Danube he entered into Kelemantia, from which a road led that ran along the valley of the rivers Nitra, Bebrava and Svinica to the valley of the Váh River and thus linked Kelemantia with Laugaricio. Ptolemy names on this road the *towns* (*póleis*) of Kelemantia, Singoné, Arsikua, Parienna, Setovia, Asanka, Karrodunon and Leukaristos.[11] We can look for one of them in Nitra, which lay at the halfway point between Kelemantia and Laugaricio and from the end of the 1st century was a major Quadian settlement. Archaeologists have discovered eight Quadian settlements in Nitra and

Atlas Slovenskej socialistickej republiky (Bratislava 1982), XI. Vývoj osídlenia a územnej organizácie, map 9. Kolník, *Osídlenie v dobe rímskej*, p. 108.

10 Bedřich Svoboda, "K dějinám římskeho kastelu na Leányváru u Iže, okres Komárno," *Slovenská archeológia* 10, 1962, no. 2, pp. 379–424. László Borhy – Klára Kuzmová – Ján Rajtár – Emese Számadó, *Kelemantia – Brigetio. Po stopách Rimanov na Dunaji* (Iža 2001). Klára Kuzmová – Ján Rajtár, "Rímsky kastel v Iži – hraničná pevnosť na Dunaji," in *Rímsky kastel v Iži. Výskum 1978–2008. Zborník príspevkov k 30. výročiu archeologického výskumu*, ed. Klára Kuzmová, Ján Rajtár, pp. 11–38. Vladimír Turčan et al., *Archeologické pamiatky* (Bratislava 2009), pp. 82–87. Ján Rajtár, "Stĺp Marca Aurelia a archeologické doklady o rímskych výpravách proti Kvádom," in *Stĺp Marca Aurelia a stredné Podunajsko. Zborník Slovenského národného múzea, Archeológia supplementum 8*, ed. Vladimír Turčan (Bratislava 2014), pp. 113–115.

11 *Claudii Ptolemaei Geographia* II 11, 28–30. *Antické písemné prameny k dějinám střední Evropy*, vybrali a přeložili Dagmar Bartoňková a Irena Radová (Praha 2010), pp. 47–48. J. Zbořil, "Ptolemaiova východná Germánia," *Historický sborník Matice slovenskej* 5 (1947), pp. 261–295. Vojtěch Ondrouch, "Územie Československa v geografii Klaudia Ptolemaia," *Naša veda* 5 (1958), pp. 14–22.

its surroundings (Chrenová I, II, III, Mikov dvor, Janíkovce, Dolné Krškany, Ivanka and Párovské Háje). Their largest blossoming occurred in the period of concluding Commodus's peace, in the year 182, up to the new great attack of the Germanic tribes in Pannonia and the neighbouring provinces in 233. They benefited from the great economic prosperity of Pannonia in the first half of the third century, which was accompanied by a great importing of Roman products, primarily ceramics (terra sigillata). The Quadian settlements in Nitra and its surroundings endured until the fifth century.[12]

Beneath the northern wing of the bishop's palace at Nitra Castle lies the remains of the foundations of a stone-wall building with an uneven, mortared removed floor, partially sunk into the rocky underbed. The builders of the giant fortifications (bulwark I) that protected the Great Moravian castle used stone from this building. They used most of this stone on the external stone wall of the ramparts for the eastern courtyard of the castle, thus not far from its source. In this same place, directly under the bulwark and in two skeletal graves, which the bulwark covered on this site, the remnants of mortar from this extinct building were found. The walled building, the remains of which lay beneath the bishop's palace, was thus already in ruins at the time of construction of the Great Moravian ramparts and served as a welcome source of building stone. It was therefore older than the ramparts.[13] With respect to the

12   Karol Pieta, "Osídlenie z doby rímskej a sťahovania národov v Nitre," in *Nitra. Príspevky k najstarším dejinám mesta*, ed. Karol Pieta (Nitra 1993), pp. 74–93. *Dejiny Nitry. Od najstarších čias po súčasnosť*, ed. Gabriel Fusek – Marián Róbert Zemene (Nitra 1998), pp. 72–79. Jaroslava Ruttkayová, "Nitra a okolie v rímskej dobe," in *Dávne dejiny Nitry a okolia vo svetle najnovších archeologických nálezov*, ed. Matej Ruttkay (Nitra 2005), pp. 45–49.

13   The archaeologists who found the north-eastern part of the foundations of this building assumed that it had been built in the first half of the 9th century. Peter Bednár, "Nitriansky hrad v 9. storočí a jeho význam v sídliskovej štruktúre veľkomoravskej Nitry," in *Svätopluk 894–1994. Materiály z konferencie organizovanej Archeologickým ústavom SAV v Nitre v spolupráci so Slovenskou historickou spoločnosťou pri SAV v spolupráci so Slovenskou historickou spoločnosťou pri SAV*, ed. Richard Marsina – Alexander Ruttkay (Nitra 1997), pp. 19–22. Peter Bednár, *Nitriansky hrad v 9. až 13. storočí. Autoreferát dizertácie na získanie vedeckej hodnosti kandidáta historických vied* (Nitra 1998), p. 9. Peter Bednár, "Die Entwicklung der Befestigung der Nitraer Burg im 9.–12. Jahrhundert," in *Frühmittelalterlicher Burgenbau in Mittel- und Osteuropa*, ed. Joachim Henning – Alexander Tivadar Ruttkay (Bonn 1998), p. 372. Peter Bednár, "Sídlisková štruktúra Nitry v 9. storočí," in *Velká Morava mezi východem a západem. Sborník příspěvků z mezinárodní vědecké konference Uherské Hradiště, Staré Město 28. 9.–1. 10. 1999*, ed. Luděk Galuška, Pavel Kouřil, Zdeněk Měřínský. *Spisy Archeologického ústavu AV ČR Brno* 17 (2001), p. 31. Peter Bednár, "Nitra v 9. storočí. K problematike lokalizácie kniežacieho sídla a Pribinovho kostola," in *Nitra v slovenských dejinách*, ed. Richard Marsina (Martin 2002), p. 90. Peter Bednár, "Nitriansky hrad v 9. storočí," in *Bojná. Hospodárske a politické centrum Nitrianskeho kniežatstva*, ed. Karol Pieta – Alexander Ruttkay – Matej Ruttkay (Nitra 2007), pp. 207, 209, 212, 213. Peter

permanentness of walled constructions, the stonewall building standing at the peak of the Nitra Castle hill ceased to serve and fell apart only a long time after its construction. It had to have been much older than the Great Moravian rampart; it could thus not have been built shortly before construction of the rampart, and decidedly not in the 9th century. In previous centuries, however, the local Slavs did not build walled buildings and hardly ever hired foreign builders. Therefore, it must have originated even before the arrival of the Slavs to Nitra and could be the work of ancient Roman builders, like other ancient constructions on the north side of the Danube.[14]

Bednár, "Počiatky Nitrianskeho hradu," in *Kolíska kresťanstva na Slovensku. Nitriansky hrad a katedrála sv. Emeráma v premenách času*, ed. Viliam Judák, Peter Bednár, Jozef Medvecký (Bratislava 2011), p. 118. Peter Bednár, "Palác a vnútorná zástavba," in *Kolíska kresťanstva*, ed. Judák, Bednár, Medvecký, p. 180. Peter Bednár, "Nitriansky hrad v 9. storočí," in *Bojná. Hospodárske a politické centrum Nitrianskeho kniežatstva*, editori Karol Pieta, Alexander Ruttkay, Matej Ruttkay (Nitra 2007), pp. 207–209. Peter Bednár, "Nitra v časoch pôsobenia sv. Konštantína-Cyrila a sv. Metoda," in *Bratia, ktorí menili svet – Konštantín a Metod. Príspevky z konferencie*, eds. Branislav Panis, Matej Ruttkay, Vladimír Turčan (Bratislava 2012), pp. 148–152. Archaeologists did not explain, however, how a walled construction could after the short time of 20–40 years fall apart and get into the building materials for the stone walls of the rampart, the origin of which, even with respect to the dating of this construction to the first half of the 9th century, they set at approximately the middle of the 9th century. Changes in the dating of the stone wall building, the remnants of whose foundations lie beneath the northern wing of the bishop's palace, in today's kitchen, are testimony to the uncertainty of archaeologists. They at first placed it in the 13th to 14th centuries. Peter Bednár – Ivan Staník, "Archeologický a stavebno-historický výskum národnej kultúrnej pamiatky Nitra-Hrad," *AVANS v r. 1991* (Nitra 1992), p. 22. They then dated it to the 11th to 12th centuries. *Dejiny Nitry*, ed. Fusek – Zemene, p. 137. The newest dating to the first half of the 9th century is also unlikely. If this walled construction was older than the double-layered rampart, which the stones from its walls and fragments of mortar beneath the rampart suggest, then this doesn't mean that it was older by only several decades. Equally good, indeed even better, it could be older by several centuries. We have a similar, but opposite case of incorrect dating at Devín. The foundations of the walled construction, which for a long time were considered to be Roman, thanks to new research have been shown to be from a Great Moravian church. *Pramene k dejinám osídlenia Slovenska z konca 5. až z 13. storočia I/1*, ed. Darina Bialeková (Nitra 1989), pp. 26–28. Veronika Plachá – Jana Hlavicová – Igor Keller, *Slovanský Devín* (Bratislava 1990), pp. 89–94. Tatiana Štefanovičová et al., *Najstaršie dejiny Bratislavy* (Bratislava 1993), pp. 308–310.

14 At the end of the Marcomannic Wars a Roman fortress kept watch over the territory of Quadia. When Emperor Marcus Aurelius travelled well beyond the Danube in 179–180, *The Quadi and Marcomans sent a message to Marcus, because 20 thousand soldiers in a walled fortress (en teichesin ontes) did not permit them to even pasture or plough fields, or to do anything other than without a feeling of fear. Furthermore, even the soldiers took in defectors and many of their prisoners, and themselves did not suffer from want, in the end they had baths and everything they needed, sufficiently. And so the Quadi, no longer*

Long-distance roads, which on the banks of the Danube left the seats of the legions of Vindobona, Carnuntum and Brigetio, continued through Quadian territory. Along them stood walled military and trading stations and settlements, which served the Romans or which the Romans built for friendly Quadian allies educated in Roman comforts.[15] The walled buildings, of which we know only a

---

able to bear the presence of these fortresses (epiteichismon), decided collectively to relocate to Semnones. Antoninus (= Marcus Aurelius), however, first learned of their plan and by obstruction of the mountain passes prevented them from doing so. Cassi Dionis Cocceiani Historia Romana LXXI 20. Antické písemné prameny k dějinám střední Evropy, translations Bartoňková, Radová, p. 64. In year 182 emperor Commodus concluded peace with the Quadi and Marcomans *and abandoned all fortresses in their country beyond a demarcated border line.* Cassii Dionis Cocceiani Historia Romana LXXII 2. *Antické písemné prameny k dějinám střední Evropy,* translations Bartoňková, Radová, pp. 64–65. Traces of temporary Roman camps on Quadian territory, where the Roman army was settled at the end of the Marcomannic Wars, were discovered by aerial survey again in the surroundings of Iža, two near Radvan and two near Mužla. Others can be assumed to be in Jatov, Veľký Kýr, Nemčice, Záhorská Ves and in Suchohrad. Such Roman camps were also in southern Moravia and to the north of Upper Austria. Ján Rajtár, "Limes romanus a rímske opevnenia na Slovensku," *Pamiatky a múzeá* 1996, no. 3, pp. 21–22. Ján Rajtár, "Kastel v Iži – hraničná pevnosť na Dunaji," *Pamiatky a múzeá* 2000, no. 3, pp. 36–37. Balázs Komoróczy, "Das römische temporäre Lager in Modřice (Bez. Brno-venkov)," in *Zwischen Rom und dem Barbaricum. Festschrift für Titus Kolník zum 70. Geburtstag,* ed. Klára Kuzmová – Karol Pieta – Ján Rajtár (Nitra 2002), pp. 129–135.

15 A branch of the Amber Road, emerging from Vindobona, was controlled on Quadian territory by military stations, one of which was in Niederleis and another in Oberleiser Berg, a fortress in Mušov, at the confluence of the Thaya and Svratka rivers, and ultimately the military station at Olomouc. The Romans built them during the Marcomannic Wars and departed shortly after concluding peace in 182. Kurt Genser, *Der österreichische Donaulimes in der Römerzeit. Ein Forschungsbericht. Der römische Limes in Österreich,* Heft 33 (Wien 1986), pp. 685–727. Radoslav Hošek, "Zum römischen castellum Mušov," in *Gentes, Reges und Rom. Auseinandersetzung – Anerkennung – Anpassung. Festschrift für Jaroslaw Tejral zum 65. Geburtstag,* ed. Jan Bouzek – Herwig Friesinger – Karol Pieta – Balázs Komoróczy. *Spisy Archeologického ústavu AV ČR Brno* 16, (2000), pp. 77–78. Claus von Carnap-Bornheim, "Freund oder Feind? Überlegungen und Thesen zum König von Mušov," in *Gentes, Reges und Rom,* ed. Bouzek, Friesinger, Komoróczy, pp. 59–65. Jiří Musil, "Römische Wehranlagen und Baumaterial nördlichder mittleren Donau," in *Gentes, Reges und Rom,* ed. Bouzek, Friesinger, Komoróczy, pp. 87–94. Radoslav Hošek, "Die Römer in Nordmittelmähren," in *Zwischen Rom und dem Barbaricum,* ed. Kuzmová – Pieta – Rajtár, pp. 127–128. The Amber Road crossed the Danube under the watch of a well-defended military station at Devín, which the Romans built perhaps in the first half of the 2nd century and expanded with new buildings in the mid-3rd century and in the second half of the 4th century. Štefanovičová et al., *Najstaršie dejiny Bratislavy,* pp. 242–250. Karol Pieta – Veronika Plachá, "Nové objavy na rímskom Devíne," *Pamiatky a múzeá* 2000, no. 3, pp. 6–9. Drahoslav Hulínek, "Prví rímski legionári na Slovensku. Rímania na Devínskom hrade," *Historická revue* 26, 2015, no. 6, pp. 23–28. The Amber Road ran alongside Quadian settlements in Stupava, where the Romans, perhaps at the same time, built a military

few, stood deep in Quadian interior.[16] The road from Carnuntum to Bratislava,[17] which passed along the base of the Little Carpathians and to the area along the Váh River, also passed through the unfortified station in Pác, which was built in the 4th century in the midst of a large Quadian settlement.[18] In the 4th century an unfortified walled settlement, either a Roman commercial

station at Devín. Genser, *Der römische Limes in Österreich*, pp. 728–746. Ivan Staník – Vladimír Turčan, "Rímska stanica v Stupave," *Pamiatky a múzeá* 2000, no. 3, pp. 22–26. In the vicinity of the Amber Road, in Dúbravka, near Bratislava, an unfortified walled farmstead originated in the first half of the 3rd century, which could belong to some unknown Quadi accustomed to the Roman way of life. Štefanovičová et al., *Najstaršie dejiny Bratislavy*, pp. 250–255. Kristián Elschek, "Rímsko-germánska vidiecka usadlosť s kúpeľom v Bratislave-Dúbravke," *Pamiatky a múzeá* 2000, no. 3, pp. 27–29. The station in Stillfried could control the intersection of both roads at the crossing of the Morava River. Dobiáš, *Dějiny*, pp. 215, 280, 328. Carnuntum also had an advance military station in Bratislava, which the Romans built perhaps simultaneously along with the one at Devín. Štefanovičová et al., *Najstaršie dejiny Bratislavy*, pp. 212–213, 236–242. In the period of Emperor Valentinian I (364–375) the Romans built a guard tower on the northern bank of the Danube. *Ammiani Marcellini Rerum gestarum libri qui supersunt* XXIX 6. One Roman tower stood about 2 km to the east of Kelemantia and others east of the mouth of the Hron River, in Chľaba, Szob and in Nógrádverőce. Sándor Soproni, *Der spätrömische Limes zwischen Esztergom und Szentendre. Das Verteidigungssystem der Provinz Valeria im 4. Jahrhundert* (Budapest 1978), pp. 76–78.

16 František Křížek, "Limes romanus na Žitném ostrově," *Bratislava, časopis pro výzkum Slovenska a Podkarpatské Rusi* 10 (1936), no. 4, pp. 429–432. František Křížek, "Das Problem der römischen Grenzen am nordpannonischen Limes," in *Limes Romanus Konferenz Nitra*, ed. Točík, pp. 49–61. Vojtěch, Ondrouch, *Limes romanus na Slovensku* (Bratislava, 1938), pp. 21–32. Pelikán, *Slovensko*, pp. 101–134. Dobiáš, *Dějiny*, pp. 214–215, 280–281, 327–329. Titus Kolník, "Römische Stationen im slowakischen Abschnitt des nordpannonischen Limesvorlandes," *Archeologické rozhledy* 38, 1986, pp. 314–434, 467–474. Novotný, *Slovom a mečom*, pp. 115–130. Rajtár, "Limes romanus," pp. 18–23. Vladimír Turčan, *Rímske pamiatky na Slovensku* (Bratislava 2000).

17 The Celtic oppidum on the territory of Bratislava still had Roman buildings. Andrej Vrtel – Branislav Lesák – Jozef Kováč – Ivan Staník, "Neskorolaténske osídlenie na nádvorí paláca Bratislavského hradu," in *Bratislavský hrad, dejiny, výskum a obnova. Kolektívna monografia prednášok z konferencie konanej v dňoch 22.–23. 9. 2014 na Bratislavskom hrade*, ed. Margaréta Musilová, Peter Barta, Angelika Herucová (Bratislava 2014), pp. 44–71. Margaréta Musilová – Jana Minaroviech, "Hypotetická rekonštrukcia Rímskej stavby I a skladu amfor v Zimnej jazdiarni na Bratislavskom hrade," in *Bratislavský hrad, dejiny, výskum a obnova*, ed. Musilová, Barta, Herucová, pp. 72–95. Margaréta Musilová, "Najnovšie objavy na Bratislavskom hrade. Stopy antického Ríma v Bratislave," *Historická revue* 26 (2015), no. 6, pp. 8–15.

18 Titus Kolník, "Cífer-Pác. Stanica z mladšej doby rímskej," in *III. medzinárodný kongres slovanskej archeológie, Bratislava 7.–14. september 1975* (Nitra 1975). Titus Kolník, "Cífer-Pác – záhada na pokračovanie. Germánska rezidencia alebo rímska vojenská stanica?" *Pamiatky a múzeá* (2000), no. 3, pp. 41–44. Vladimír Varsik, "Život v rímskom štýle. Germánske panské sídlo v Cíferi-Páci," *Historická revue* 26 (2015), no. 6, pp. 48–53.

station or more the settlement of an advance Quadian representative befriending the Romans, developed in the Quadian settlement located in Veľký Kýr (not far from Nitra).[19]

The Quadi evidently began to penetrate into the territory abandoned by the Osians and Cotins immediately after the Marcomannic Wars. Soon they ruled central Slovakia and reached eastward to the border of the realm of the Vandal Hasdings; thus, the centre of the Quadi was shifted from Moravia to southwest Slovakia.

Nitra was a known Quadian settlement from end of the first up to the fifth centuries. It could have been the seat of the Quadian king, friendly with the Romans, who was accustomed to the Roman way of life and wanted a comfortable walled seat built in *the Roman way*. He had it built on the highest point of the Nitra Castle hill, which stood in the centre of Quadia and exactly at the halfway point between Kelemantia and Laugaricio, that is *in the lap of the kingdom*.[20] Here the Quadian King Viduari and his son and successor Vitrodor, as well as their royal predecessors and successors, could reside. Quadian kings found a new seat near the Nitra River, probably in Nitra itself. Then the Romans began building its counterweight, the monumental fortified Kelemantia.

---

19   Titus Kolník, "Ausgrabungen auf der römischen Station in Milanovce in den Jahren 1956–1957," in: *Limes Romanus Konferenz Nitra*, ed. Anton Točík (Bratislava 1959), pp. 27–48. Titus Kolník assumes that the Romans during the Marcomannic Wars could have built a temporary marching camp or a permanent military station in Nitra, too. Titus Kolník, "Bola v Nitre rímska stanica?" in *Nitra. Príspevky k najstarším dejinám mesta*, ed. Karol Pieta (Nitra 1993), pp. 94–95. The walled construction in Nitra, the foundations of which lie beneath the bishop's palace, did not have to be a Roman station, just as the walled construction near Veľký Kýr probably wasn't, but a significant Quadian settlement built *in the Roman way*. In 357 the Roman army attacked the territory of the Alamans: *they crossed over the Menus River* (Main) ... *built fires and burned down the residential houses, all of which were built with great care in the Roman way* (*domicilia cuncta curentius rito Romano constructa*). *Ammiani Marcellini Rerum gestarum libri qui supersunt* XVII 1, 7.

20   Since we thus far have no archaeological records showing a more significant settlement of the castle hill in the Roman period and in the Migration Period, archaeologists consider our opinion that a walled construction stood directly on the castle hill during the Roman period as very improbable. Bednár, *Nitra v časoch pôsobenia sv. Konštantína-Cyrila a sv. Metoda*, pp. 151. Archaeologists assume that after the violent end of the powerful centres of the Celts and Dacians around the turn of the epochs, the castle deteriorated for at least eight centuries. The burned remnants of homes and fortifications were covered by grass and forest. The castle remained abandoned and unsettled up to the end of the 8th century. Archaeologists do not completely exclude our opinion regarding the walled construction from the Roman period on the Nitra Castle hill, but they assume such a construction more in some of the nearby Germanic settlements on the terraces of the Nitra River or at a larger distance from Nitra. Peter Bednár, "Počiatky Nitrianskeho hradu," in *Kolíska kresťanstva*, ed. Judák, Bednár, Medvecký, pp. 114, 116.

Of all the Roman border fortifications, Brigetio and the advance fortress of Kelemantia on the Quadian bank of the Danube had the best reach into the seat of the Quadian kings. The threat of rapid military encroachment into the centre of Quadia could have discouraged the Quadi from attacks on Roman Pannonia. Kelemantia was the largest Roman fortress on the entire territory of the Quadi. It kept Quadian Nitra in check and stood on the road of Quadian attacks that came directly from the centre of Quadia.

At the end of summer 375 Emperor Valentinian I, after vast preparations and reinforcing of the entire Quadian border, unexpectedly crossed the Danube at Aquincum (today in Budapest, Hungary) and *passed along the other side to the territory of the Quadi. They, meanwhile, tracked his arrival from the mountain slopes, where they usually headed with their families in the confusion and uncertainty of events, but they were struck in wonder at the view of the emperor's battle emblems in their country, because they had absolutely not counted on this.* Emperor Valentinian marched up the Sarmatian bank of the Danube to the eastern, upper part of Quadia and probably desolated the valley of the Ipeľ River. He then returned by this same path to Aquincum, where he remained until the autumn. He visited Sabaria (today's Szombathely, Hungary) and from there again set off for the Danubian border. When he had supplemented the garrisons of the border fortresses, he settled in Brigetio, where he planned to spend the winter. Death, which found Valentinian there in November of 375,[21] prevented him from starting preparations for an attack from Brigetio and Kelemantia to the north into the centre of Quadia, along the Nitra River.

4   Hunimund's Kingdom

In the year 375 the Huns invaded the eastern European steppes and subjugated the Alans and the Ostrogoths. The Visigoths retreated from them over the Danube into Roman Thrace.[22] The Vandals refused to accept Hun domination, and together with the Alans and part of the Suebs (the Quadi) they withdrew to the west in 406.[23] The Gepids, who recognized Hun domination,

---

21   *Ammiani Marcellini Rerum gestarum libri qui supersunt* XXX 5, 6.
22   *Ammiani Marcellini Rerum gestarum libri qui supersunt* XXXI 3–16.
23   The Vandals and their allies reached the Rhine in December 406, conquered the Franks and flooded into Gaul. In October 409 they entered Spain and in 429 poured into Africa. Dobiáš, *Dějiny*, pp. 303–304, 315–316. László Várady, *Das letzte Jahrhundert Pannoniens (376–476)* (Budapest 1969), pp. 182–187. Wilfried Menghin, "Die Völkerwanderungszeit im Karpatenbecken," in *Germanen, Hunen und Awaren. Schätze der Völkerwanderungszeit. Die Archäologie des 5. und 6. Jahrhunderts an der mittleren Donau und der östlich-merowingische*

took with their permission the larger part of the abandoned Vandalian settlements on the upper Tisza and Szamos (Someş) rivers.[24] The basin of the lower and central Hornád also belonged to the Vandals; there, however, Gepid graves are completely lacking. If the Gepids did not enter the valley of the Hornád, then after the departure of the Vandals only the Suebs could have penetrated there, because no other known tribe from the interior of the Carpathian Basin entered the areas of the Vandals. The Gepids and Suebs, who from the south and west divided the empire of the Vandals from other territories of the Carpathian Basin, thus shared the abandoned Vandalian territory. The Suebs acquired the valley of the central and lower Hornád. They were separated from the Gepids, to whom the territories of the Zemplín (in modern Slovakia) and Szabolcs (in modern Hungary) belonged, by the Zemplínske and Slanské hills, which played the same role here as the Little and White Carpathians played in the west. The Suebs, like the Gepids, Ostrogoths, Heruls, Rugians and Scirs, acknowledged the rule of the Huns and fought on their side in the Battle at Catalaunian Plains in year 451.[25]

Gepid King Ardarich and his allies – the Suebs, Heruls and part of the Scirs and Rugians – in 454 defeated the Huns and their allies – the Ostrogoths, Alans and the other part of the Scirs and Rugians – in a battle on the River Nedao in Pannonia and broke up the Hun empire.[26] After the victory *the Gepids forcefully took from the Huns their settlements, and as the victors they occupied all of Dacia.*[27] The Gepids expanded their empire up to the borders of Byzantium

---

Reihengräberkreis (Nürnberg 1987), pp. 18–20. Schreiber, *Die Vandalen*, pp. 85–95. István Bóna, "A hunok," in *Erdély története I*, ed. Makkai, Mócsy, p. 135. István Bóna, "Die Hunen," in *Kurze Geschichte Siebenbürgens*, ed. Köpeczi, p. 78. Strzelczyk, *Wandalowie*, pp. 79–99.

24 Rich Gepidian graves from the 5th century come from the upper basin of the Crasna and Barcău rivers (Şimleul Silvaniei, Tăuteni) and on the upper Tisza (Kisvárda, Rétközberencs-Paradomb, Tiszadob-Ókenez, Oros, Tiszalők, Székely, Vencsellő, Zalkod, Gáva, Gelénes, Barabás-Bagolyvár, Brestov of Mukačevo). Péter Németh, "Frühgepidische Gräberfunde an der oberen Theiss," in *Germanen, Hunen und Awaren*, ed. Menghin, Springer, Warners, pp. 219–222. Bóna, "Die Hunen", p. 77.

25 Paulus Diaconus, *Historia Romanorum* XIV 2–6. We use the edition *Eutropii Breviarium ab urbe condita cum versionibus Graecis et Pauli Landolfi que additamentis*, recensuit et adnotavit Hans Droysen. Monumenta Germaniae historica, Auctorum antiquissimorum, Tom II (Berolini 1879). Jordanes, *De origine actibusque Getharum* XXXVI 191. Peter Bystrický, "Politická situácia strednej Európy po rozpade ríše Hunov," *Historický časopis* 49 (2001), no. 2, pp. 202–203.

26 Jordanes, *De origine actibusque Getharum* L 259–263. Várady, *Das letzte Jahrhundert Pannoniens*, pp. 324–328. Wolfram, *Die Goten*, pp. 259–260. Bystrický, "Politická situácia," pp. 204–207.

27 *Nam Gepidi Hunnorum sibi sedes viribus vindicantes totius Daciae fines velut victores ... potiti.* Jordanes, *De origine actibusque Getharum* L 264.

on the Danube, into Transylvania and Oltenia (Lesser Wallachia).[28] The Ostrogoths, led by King Valamer and his brothers and co-kings Theodemir and Vidimer, then came immediately to the Carpathian Basin and occupied Pannonia, which had been granted to them by Byzantine Emperor Marcian.[29] The Rugians, under the leader of their King Flaccitheus, settled in a part of Lower Austria, north of the Danube. The seat of the Rugian kings was in what is today Krems, Austria.[30] Their north-eastern neighbours became the Heruls, who *had long had their seat beyond the Danube*,[31] and from there they raided into Noricum and Pannonia.[32] The Herulian empire, which included the southern basin of the Morava River up to the confluence with the Danube, neighboured on the south-west with Rugiland, to the south with Roman Noricum and Ostrogoth Pannonia and to the east with the Suebs realm, from which it was separated by the Little and White Carpathians.[33] The Heruls occupied and ruled over southern Moravia, the eastern part of Lower Austrian Weinviertel and the Slovak Záhorie region. They also subjugated the remnants of the Suebs (the former Quadi), who had remained here even after the departure of part of their fellow tribesman to the west in year 406.[34]

28   Jordanes, *De origine actibusque Getharum* V 33–34, XII 74, XXII 114. Dezső Csallányi, *Archäologische Denkmäler der Gepiden im Mitteldonaubecken (454–568 u. Z.)* (Budapest, 1961). István Bóna, "A gepidák királysága," in *Erdély története I*, ed. Makkai, Mócsy, pp. 138–159. István Bóna, "Das Königreich der Gepiden (455–567)," in *Kurze Geschichte Siebenbürgens*, ed. Köpeczi, pp. 80–90. See note 29.

29   Jordanes, *De origine actibusque Getharum* L 264, 268. Paulus Diaconus, *Historia Romanorum* XV 11. Várady, *Das letzte Jahrhundert Pannoniens*, pp. 328–332. Herwig Wolfram, *Die Geburt Mitteleuropas* (Wien 1987), p. 37. Wolfram, *Die Goten*, pp. 260–263. Jerzy Strzelczyk, "Gótok Közép-Európában," *Századok* 122 (1988), no. 5–6, pp. 753–768. Bystrický, *Politická situácia*, pp. 206–209.

30   Rugian settlements lay on the northern bank of the Danube in lower Austria, between Krems and Korneuburg, and spread northward up to the Manhart Mountains. Jaroslav Tejral, *Morava na sklonku antiky* (Praha 1982), pp. 193–194. Wolfram, *Die Geburt*, p. 63.

31   *hyper men Istron ek palaiou ókun*. Procopios, *De bello Gothico* II 14. We use the edition Procopios, *De bello Gothico*, addenda et corrigenda adiecit Gerhard Wirth. *Procopii Caesariensis Opera omnia II*, recensuit Jacob Haury (Leipzig 1963).

32   Eugippius, *Vita Severini* 24. We use the edition Eugippius, *Das Leben des heiligen Severin*. Einführung, Übersetzung und Erläuterungen von Rudolf Noll (Berlin 1963).

33   Dobiáš, *Dějiny*, pp. 306, 316–317. Tejral, *Morava*, pp. 194–196. Wolfram, *Die Geburt*, p. 69. The Heruls settled between the Marcomans and the Quadi: *Marcomanni gens, + manni gens, Heruli gens, Quadi gens*. *Iulii Honorii Cosmographia* 26, in *Geographi latini minores*, collegit Alexander Riese (Heilbronnae 1878), p. 40. The Heruls neighboured on the west with the Bohemian Marcomans and on the east with the Suebs (the former Quadi), who after 406 had remained in Slovakia. The unknown *manni gens* could have neighboured with the Heruls on the north and settled northern Moravia.

34   The Heruls subjugated *all surrounding barbarians*. Procopios, *De bello Gothico* II 14. The remnants of the Suebs, who remained in the Morava River valley after year 406, also had to subjugate themselves to them. Regarding the Suebs and Heruls in Moravia, see Jaroslav

Since the Herulian realm originated in the area along the Morava River, that is in the western half of ancient Suebian (Quadian) territory, Suebia (*Suavia*), which was ruled by King Hunimund, had to be satisfied with the part of Suebian territory east of the Little and White Carpathians.[35] The Scirs settled in the northern part of the area between the Danube and Tisza rivers, in the vicinity of the Ostrogoths, Suebs, Gepids and Sarmatians.[36] The kingdom

[35] Tejral, "Probleme der Völkerwanderungszeit nördlich der mittleren Donau," in *Germanen, Hunnen und Awaren*, ed. Menghin, Springer, Wamers, pp. 351–356, 361–382. The extent of the Heruls empire in the Morava River valley corresponded to the later range of the Longobard empire on the north side of the Danube, because the Longobards, after their triumph over the Heruls in 508, occupied their settlements, which the Heruls had to abandon, and they joined the territory subjugated by them to their empire. See chapter 2, note 7.

[35] Smaller burial sites and individual graves, more rarely also traces of dwellings and settlements not far from Bratislava (Ivanka pri Dunaji, Čataj, Cífer), from the Váh basin (Slovenské Pravno, Pobedim, Krakovany-Stráže, Veľké Kosťolany, Siladice, Abrahám, Čierny Brod), from the basin of the Nitra River (Kšinná, Výčapy-Opatovce, Nitra-Lužianky, Nitra-Párovské Háje, Nitra-Chrenová, Nitra-Mikov dvor, Lipová-Ondrochov, Kostolný Sek, Nitriansky Hrádok, Vlkas, Hul, Bešeňov, Dvory nad Žitavou, Iža pri Komárne), from along the Hron basin (Banská Bystrica-Selce, Banská Bystrica-Sásová, Levice, Kalná nad Hronom, Šarovce, Sikenica-Veľký Pesek, Bíňa, Kamenín, Štúrovo), from the Ipeľ basin (Dolné Semerovce, Prša) and from the Hornád River basin (Košice, Čaňa, Haniska, Kapušany), which we can date to the 5th century, contain in various representations ceramics of the Danube River and eastern Germanic character and jewellery, primarily brooches of several types. The urn grave, characteristic for the Roman period, changed into the burying of a body unburned. Kolník, "Prehľad a stav bádania," pp. 534–548. Bohuslav Novotný, "Nové nálezy z doby sťahovania národov na Slovensku," *Zborník FFUK Musaica* 17 (1984), pp. 111–117. Novotný, *Slovom a mečom*, pp. 139–141. Karol Pieta, "Die Slowakei im 5. Jahrhundert," in *Germanen, Hunnen und Awaren*, ed. Menghin, Springer, Wamers, pp. 385–417. Karol Pieta, "Osídlenie z doby rímskej a sťahovania národov v Nitre," in *Nitra. Príspevky k najstarším dejinám mesta* (Nitra 1993), pp. 78–90. *Atlas Slovenskej socialistickej republiky. IX. Vývoj osídlenia a územnej organizácie*, "mapa č. 10, Darina Bialeková, Osídlenie v 5.–8. stor.," p. 109. Some researchers ascribe this archaeological monument to the Ostrogoths. Tatiana Štefanovičová, *Osudy starých Slovanov* (Martin 1989), pp. 16–17. Chropovský, "Slovensko v protohistorickom období," pp. 59–60. The mentioned archaeological finds belonged most probably to the Suebs, who at the time of Hun domination (in the first half of the 5th century) accepted among them the scattered fractions of other Germanic tribes and some Huns. Anthropological research of graves in Krakovany-Stráže, Kapušany, Bešeňová and in Levice has demonstrated in several graves the presence of Mongolian symbols and deliberate deformation of skulls, a Hun custom, which several members of allies and subjugated tribes also copied. Emanuel Vlček, "Antropologický materiál z období stěhování národů na Slovensku," *Slovenská archeológia* 5 (1957), no. 2, pp. 402–434.

[36] The Scirs settled near the Danube. See note 42. In 468 the Scirs invaded Valamer's part of the Ostrogoth empire, which lay between the unknown rivers *Scaniunga* and *Aqua nigra*. Valamer's younger brother Theodemir ruled in the part of Pannonia *iuxta lacum Pelsois* and the younger Vidimer between them. Jordanes, *De origine actibusque Getharum* L 268.

of the Sarmatians lay on the lower Tisza up to its entry to the Danube, south of the kingdom of the Scirs.[37]

In 454 the Suebs battled on the victorious side of the anti-Hun coalition.[38] The military victory and fall of the Hun empire brought them political independence and perhaps even more territorial growth of their empire, just as their alliance with the Gepids. Suebia, which lay on what is today Slovak territory, bordered on the west with the Herulian empire,[39] on the south, along the Danube, with the Ostrogoth empire[40] and also touched the kingdom of Scirs settlements near the Danube in the eastern vicinity of the Ostrogoth empire. To the east it reached up to the border of the Gepidian kingdom in the Zemplínske and Slanské hills. Thus, it took up the entire north-west part of the Carpathian Basin.

If the Suebs settled on the Slovak side of the Danube, then we cannot look for the seat of the Scirs there. If the Suebs neighboured on the west with the Heruls, then the Scirs could not have settled only in the western part of the Slovak Danubian region, that is between them, as assumed by Josef Dobiáš. Dobiáš, *Dějiny*, p. 304. The seats of the Scirs could lie opposite the one-time Aquincum, from the Danube to the east up to the border of the Gepid kingdom. Wolfram, *Die Geburt*, pp. 37–38.

37 Wolfram, *Die Geburt*, pp. 37–38. Uncovered Sarmatian burial sites and settlements (Kiskundorozsma-Kistemplomtanya, Kiskundorozsna-Kenyérvágódomb, Szentes-Sárgapart, Szeged-Szöreg, Sándorfalva-Eperjes, Tápé-Maljadok, Csongrád-Berzsenyi utca, Csongrád-Kaserne) lay along both sides of the Tisza between Csongrád and the Szeged. Gabriella Vörös, "Spätsarmatische Siedlungen und Gräberfelder in der Tiefebene Südostungarns," in *Germanen, Hunen und Awaren*, ed. Menghin, Springher, Wamers, pp. 133–148. The Sarmatian empire reached south up to the Danube, where it bordered with the Byzantine Empire. In the period of King Babaj the town of Singidunum (Belgrade), lying over the Danube, which was conquered by Byzantium, also belonged to the Sarmatians. And to the west the Sarmatian empire reached up to the Danube, which separated them here from the Ostrogoths. In 471 Theodorich, son of Ostrogoth King Theodemir, crossed with his army over the Danube and was on Sarmatian territory. See note 47.

38 Jordanes, *De origine actibusque Getharum* L 261. Várady, *Das letzte Jahrhundert Pannoniens*, pp. 326–328, 333, 399. Bystrický, *Politická situácia*, p. 205. The significant participation of the Suebs in the Battle of the Catalaunian Plains and at the Nedao River, as well as the position of Suebian King Hunimund at the head of a great anti-Goths coalition in 469, contradicts the opinion of Josef Dobiáš on the significant decline of their numbers, powerful importance and limitation of their settlement only to the eastern part of the Slovak Danubian region. Dobiáš, *Dějiny*, p. 304.

39 See note 33.

40 All of Pannonia belonged to the Ostrogoths. The Danube was the northern border of their empire: *Gothi ... accipientesque Pannoniam, quae longo porrecta planitiae habet ... a septentrione Danubium*. Jordanes, *De origine actibusque Getharum* L 264. When Ostrogoth King Theodemir wanted to attack the neighbouring Suebs in the winter of 469/470, he had to cross the frozen Danube. Jordanes, *De origine actibusque Getharum* LV 280.

The Suebs excelled as foot soldiers. They were also courageous in the large battle at the Nedao River, *where it was evident ... The Suebs as foot soldiers ... scrambled to the front,*[41] and even in later wars with the Ostrogoths. The Suebs had King Hunimund (*ipsum regem Hunimundum*). In 468 Hunimund (*Hunimundus Suavorum dux*) passed through Goth territory with the Suebian army to Roman Dalmatia. On the return journey he stole unguarded Goth herds of livestock. However, he suffered defeat at the hand of Valamer's brother Theodemir in a battle on the shore of the Neusiedler See and fell into captivity along with his entire army. Hunimund had to conclude an alliance with Theodemir. Hunimund, whom Theodemir freed along with his warriors, set forth, however, against the Ostrogoths of the neighbouring Scirs, *who at that time were settled over the Danube and lived in peace with the Goths*.[42] The Scirian King Edika attacked Valamer's territory. Ostrogoth King Valamer fell in the battle, but the enraged Ostrogoths completely slaughtered the Scirs.

Hunimund then allied with Herulian King Alarich and with Scirian King Edika against Valamer's successor, Theodemir. Sarmatian Kings Beuka and Babaj also joined the alliance, as did Gepidian and Rugian troops, and Byzantine Emperor Leo I also supported them. In 469 the alliance raided Pannonia and camped by the Bolia River (today's Ipeľ in Slovakia). The Ostrogoths unexpectedly attacked the alliance camp and in a bloody battle completely destroyed the enemy army. Edika fell in battle, and his kingdom disintegrated.[43] Edika's older son Hunvulf (Hunulf) with part of the Scirs entered into services of the Byzantine emperor, and the younger son Odovakar (Odoacar) with the second part departed for Italy, where in 476 he took over power in Rome. A number of Herulians and Rugians departed with both brothers.[44]

Suebian King Hunimund, head of the defeated anti-Goth coalition, soon experienced another destructive blow. In the winter of 469/470 victorious Ostrogoth King Theodemir unexpectedly crossed the frozen Danube and completely disrupted Hunimund's kingdom. Hunimund and a portion of his nation headed up the Danube far to the west to the Alamans.[45] The rest of the

---

41 *ubi cernere erat ... Suavum pede ... praesumere.* Jordanes, *De origine actibusque Getharum* L 261.

42 *Scirorum gentem incitans, qui tunc super Danubium consedebant et cum Gothis pacifice morabantur.* Jordanes, *De origine actibusque Getharum* LIII 275.

43 Jordanes, *De origine actibusque Getharum* LIII–LIV 273–279. Priscus, *Fragmenta historiae Byzantinae*, fragm. 35. Paulus Diaconus, *Historia Romanorum* XV 12, Wolfram, *Die Geburt*, p. 40. Wolfram, *Die Goten*, pp. 264–267. Bystrický, *Politická situácia*, pp. 209–213.

44 Paulus Diaconus, *Historia Romanorum* XV 8–10, Wolfram, *Die Geburt*, p. 40. Bystrický, *Politická situácia*, pp. 213–215.

45 Jordanes, *De origine actibusque Getharum* LV 280–281. Friedrich Lotter, "Die germanischen Stämmesverbände im Umkreis des Ostalpen-Mitteldonau-Raumes nach der literarischen

Suebs, who still remained on the territory of Slovakia, decimated by defeat and abandoned by their last king, must have been easy pickings for the rising Slavs. The first Slavs occupied the territory of Slovakia from the north, through the Carpathian passes, and their settlements stretched to the south of the Danube. We can date the oldest archaeological evidence on their presence in Slovakia to the end of the 5th century.[46]

In 471 Sarmatian King Babaj triumphed over Byzantium commander Camundos and occupied the Byzantine border town of Singidunum (today's Belgrade). In 472 Theodorich (Theudarichi), son of Ostrogoth King Theodemir, without his father's knowledge, took an army of six thousand, crossed the Danube and attacked the Sarmatian empire. He attacked and killed King Babaj,

---

Überlieferung zum Zeitalter Severins," in *Die Bayern und ihre Nachbarn. Berichte des Symposions der Kommision für Frühmittelalterforschung 25. bis 28. Oktober 1982, Stift Zwettl, Niederösterreich, Teil 1*, ed. Hewig Wolfram und Andreas Schwarcz, Dph 179 (1985), pp. 45–47. Wolfram, *Die Geburt*, p. 40. Wolfram, *Die Goten*, p. 267. Hans J. Hummer, "The fluidity of barbarian identity: the ethnogenesis of Alemanni and Suebi, AD 200–500," *Early Medieval Europe* 7 (1998), no. 1, pp. 18–27. Cassiodor, from whom Jordanes took the report on the history of the Goths, had a very poor notion of the geographic position of Hunimund's country and mistakenly identified it with the Alamans, where Hunimund ran to along with a portion of his Suebs immediately after this defeat. Cassiodor's mistake is understandable, because the Alamans not only accepted Hunimund's Suebs among them, but also got their name. Cassiodor wrote his unpreserved History of the Goths in the years 526–533, and by then it was no longer known how the Alamans became the Suebs. Jordanes, copying from Cassiodor, called Alamania *regio Suavorum*. According to Gregory of Tours *Suebi id est Alamani*. The Life of St. Gall also mentions both names for one tribe: *Alamanniam vel Sueviam nominemus. Nam duo sint vocabula, unam gentem signifi cantia, priori nomine nos appelant circumpositae gentes, quae Latinum habent sermonem; sequenti usus nos nuncupat barbarorum.* Jordanes, *De origine actibusque Getarum* LV 280. Gregorius Turoensis, *Historiarum libri decem* II 2. Walahfrid Strabo, *Vita sancti Galli*, Prolog. Dieter Geuenich – Hagen Keller, "Alamannen, Alamanien, alamanisch im frühen Mittelalter. Möglichkeiten und Schwierigkeiten des Historikers beim Versuch der Eingrenzung," in *Die Bayern und ihre Nachbarn. Berichte des Symposions der Kommission für Frühmittelalterforschung 25. bis 28. Oktober 1982, Stift Zwettl, Niederösterreich, 1. Teil*, ed. Herwig Wolfram, Andreas Schwarcz, Dph 179 (1985), pp. 139–140, 146. Bystrický, *Politická situácia*, pp. 215–216.

46 Gabriel Fusek, "Archeologické doklady k najstaršiemu slovanskému osídleniu Slovenska," *Slavica Slovaca* 28 (1993), no. 1–2, pp. 30–35. Gabriel Fusek, *Slovensko vo včasnoslovanskom období* (Nitra 1994), pp. 93, 118. Gabriel Fusek, "Pôvodné alebo prisťahovalé obyvateľstvo? Príspevok k vypovedacím možnostiam archeologických prameňov o počiatkoch slovanského osídlenia Slovenska," in *Historická Olomouc 12. Sborník příspěvků ze sympozia Historická Olomouc XII., zaměřeného k problematice zakladatelských mýtů a mýtů "počátků" ve světle kritiky pramenů, Muzeum umění Olomouc-sál Beseda, 6.–7. října 1998* (Olomouc 2001), pp. 71–89. Gabriel Fusek – Jozef Zábojník, "Príspevok do diskusie o počiatkoch slovanského osídlenia Slovenska," *Slovenská archeológia* 51 (2003), no. 2, pp. 319–340.

captured his family, looted his property and triumphantly returned to his father. He then ruled Singidunum and rid it of Sarmatians. He did not return it to Byzantium, however, but incorporated it in the Ostrogoth empire. The remnants of the Sarmatians retired to Byzantine territory.[47]

After extinction of the Scirian kingdom in 469 and the Sarmatians in 472, the Gepidian kingdom reached the Danube on the west and touched Ostrogoth Pannonia.[48] Perhaps at this time, possibly under pressure from the Slavs, the Gepids left the upper Tisza River region.[49]

The Suebs, who had fled to the Alamans, were so numerous that they managed to instil their name on the Alamans. Thus, not many Suebs remained in the region north of the Danube. The rest of the Suebs, those who did not join Hunimund and remained in their old settlements for however short a time and perhaps under pressure from the arriving Slavs, eventually departed to Pannonia, which had been abandoned by the Ostrogoths in 473.[50]

47 Jordanes, *De origine actibusque Getarum* LV 282. Wolfram, *Die Goten*, pp. 267–268.
48 The expansion of the Gepidian kingdom up to the Danubian border of Ostrogoth and then Longobardian Pannonia is demonstrated by Gepidian burial sites on both banks of the central and lower Tisza (Szentes-Berekhát, Szentes-Kökényzug, Szentes-Nagyhegy, Hódmezővásárhely-Kishomok, Hódmezővásárhely-Gorza, Békésszentandrás-Mogyoróshalom, Kétegyháza-Homokbánya, Kétegyháza-Argyelánföld and others). Gepidische Reihengräber im Theiß-Maros-Gebiet, in *Germanen, Hunen und Awaren*, pg. 233–253. And according to Procopius, the Gepids and Longobards were neighbours. Procopios, *De bello Gothico* III 34.
49 Rich Gepidian finds from the one-time Vandalian territory on the upper Tisza end in the 5th century and do not extend into the 6th century. See note 24.
50 The Pannonian Suebs were later subjugated to the Longobard King Wacho (510–540): *Eo tempore inclinavit Wacho Suavos sub regno Langobardorum. Origo gentis Langobardorum* 4. We use the edition *Origo gentis Langobardorum*, edidit Georgius Waitz, Scriptores rerum Langobardicarum et Italicarum saec. VI–IX ex Monumentis Germaniae historicis recusi (Hannoverae 1878), pp. 1–6. *Eodemque tempore Waccho super Suavos irruit eosque dominio subiugavit.* Paulus Diaconus, *Historia Langobardorum* I 21. We use the edition *Pauli Historia Langobardorum*, edentibus Ludwig Bethmann – Georgius Waitz, Scriptores rerum Langobardicarum et Italicarum saec. VI–IX ex Monumentis Germaniae historicis recusi (Hannoverae 1878), pp. 12–187. These remaining Suebs, together with the Longobards, moved to Italy in 568. Paulus Diaconus, *Historia Langobardorum* II 26. *Chronicon Gotharum* 4. We use the edition *Historia Langobardorum codicis Gothani*, edidit Georgius Waitz, Scriptores rerum Langobardicarum et Italicarum saec. VI–IX ex Monumentis Germaniae historicis recusi (Hannoverae 1878), pp. 7–11. Tejral, *Morava*, p. 196. The Suebs who came under Longobard rule could no longer live in their original settlements in Slovakia and there accepted the sovereignty of Longobard King Wacho; therefore, we do not find any traces of Longobard domination on Slovak territory (with the exception of the Záhorie), and in the period of Wacho this territory already belonged to the Slavs.

CHAPTER 2

From the Arrival of the Slavs Up through Samo's Realm

1   The Slavs in the Vicinity of the Gepids and Longobards

In the autumn of 473 Ostrogoth King Theodemir, along with his son Theodorich and their nation, departed Pannonia and moved to Byzantine Moesia. Theodemir's younger brother Vidimer led a smaller part of the Ostrogoths through Noricum to Italy, and after Vidimer's death, his son, also named Vidimer, from Italy to the Visigoths in southern Gaul. In 488 the Ostrogoths, under the leadership of King Theodorich the Great, left Moesia and headed to Italy.[1]

After the disappearance of the kingdoms of the Scirs, Suebs, Sarmatians and eventually even the Pannonian Ostrogoths, the Heruls became the crucial force on the middle Danube: *Over time they managed to outdo in power and number of people all the surrounding barbarians; they attacked them and gradually conquered, ravished and plundered them.*[2] Initially, the Rugians succeeded in the shadow of the Herulian empire. Rugian King Feva, also known as Feletheus, made use of the removal of the last Roman emperor in year 476 and the ascension of Odoacer's rule in Italy, which brought an end to Roman rule over Noricum ripense (Noricum along the river), and joined to his own empire the eastern part of this last Roman province on the Danube, from Lorch up through the Vienna Woods.[3] Odoacer, however, wrecked the Rugian empire with two campaigns in 487 and 488.[4]

In 489 the Longobards, with their King Gudeoch, came to the defeated Rugiland, where they lived under Herulian domination, ruled by Gudeoch's son Claffo: *In the end they conquered the Longobards, who were Christians, and imposed a fine on them; they did the same with other tribes … And when*

---

1   Jordanes, *De origine actibusque Getarum* LVI 283–285. Paulus Diaconus, *Historia Romanorum* XV 12–18, Wolfram, *Die Geburt*, pp. 41, 72. Wolfram, *Die Goten*, pp. 268–281. Bystrický, "Politická situácia," pp. 216–221.
2   Procopios, *De bello Gothico* II 14. Wolfram, *Die Geburt*, pp. 69–70. Bystrický, "Politická situácia," pp. 221–222.
3   Wolfram, *Die Geburt*, p. 64. Eugippius, *Vita Severini* 27, 28, 30, 31.
4   Eugippius, *Vita Severini* 44. *Origo gentis Langobardorum* 3. Paulus Diaconus, *Historia Langobardorum* I 19. Wolfram, *Die Geburt*, pp. 64–65. Bystrický, *Politická situácia*, p. 219.

Anastasius I Dicorus took possession of the rule over the Romans (in 491), *they no longer had anyone to turn against; they lay down their weapons and behaved peacefully and passed three years in this period of peace.*[5] In year 505 Longobard King Tato, son of Claffo, withdrew along with his nation from immediate reach of Herulian power at Tullnerfeld[6] and in 508 with a new force conquered the attacking Herulians. Herulian King Rodulph fell in battle, and his empire ceased to exist. The victorious Longobards became lords over all the territories which until then had been controlled by the Heruls, that is Moravia, Rugiland and northern Pannonia up to the lower current of the Drava River.[7] From modern Slovakia, only today's Záhorie region belonged to their empire.[8] The

5   *Origo gentis Langobardorum* 3. Paulus Diaconus, *Historia Langobardorum* I 19. Wolfram, *Die Geburt*, p. 70.
6   *Egressi quoque Longobardi de Rugiland habitaverunt in campis latentibus, qui sermone barbarico feld appelatur.* Paulus Diaconus, *Historia Langobardorum* I 20. *redierunt Langobardi in campis filda. Origo gentis Langobardorum* 4. *Chronicon Gothanum* 4. The *field*, to which the Longobards retreated was Tullnerfeld on the southern bank of the Danube in Lower Austria. Horst Adler, "Das 'feld' bei Paulus Diaconus," *Archeologia Austriaca*, Beiheft 14, Teil 2 (1976), pp. 256–282. Wolfram, *Die Geburt*, p. 70.
7   Procopios, *De bello Gothico* II 14. *Origo gentis Langobardorum* 4. Paulus Diaconus, *Historia Langobardorum* I 20. Wolfram, *Die Geburt*, pp. 69–72. The Longobards took possession of northern Pannonia only up to the lower Drava immediately after their victory over the Heruls, and not in 526, as follows from the mistaken report Origo gentis Langobardorum and Paul the Deacon, that Pannonia belonged to the Longobards for 42 years (568–42 = 526). Dušan Třeštík, "Příchod prvních Slovanů do českých zemí v letech 510–530," *Český časopis historický* 94 (1996), no. 2, pp. 262–263. Dušan Třeštík, *Počátky Přemyslovců. Vstup Čechů do dějin (530–935)* (Praha 1997), pp. 33–34. In 508 the Longobards ruled the lands of the Herulian kingdom. The territory of the Longobardian Kingdom thus overlapped with the lands of the extinct Herulian Kingdom. And the Longobards certainly inherited the border with Slavic territory in Slovakia in the Little and White Carpathians and on the Danube from the Herulian Kingdom. Longobard finds, see: "Die Langobarden," in *Germanen, Hunnen und Awaren*, ed. Menghin, Springer, Wamers, pg. 545–585. István Bóna – János Cseh – Margit Nagy – Péter Tomka – Ágnes Tóth, *Hunok – Gepidák – Langobardok. Történeti régészeti tézisek és címszavak* (Szeged 1993), pp. 115–162. The presence of the Longobards in Moravia only until 568 is also evidenced by the burial site in Lužice, near Hodonín. Zdeněk Klanica, "Die südmährischen Slawen und andere Ethnika im archäologischen Material des 6.–8. Jahrhunderts," in *Interaktionen der mitteleuropäischen Slawen und anderen Ethnika im 6.–10. Jahrhundert, Symposium Nové Vozokany 3.–7. Oktober 1983*, ed. Peter Šalkovský (Nitra 1984), pp. 139–142. Archaeologists have uncovered 27 Longobard burial sites in Moravia. The first safely Longobard settlement object is the floor plan of a rectangular cottage, embedded into the ground, uncovered in Podolí near Brno. Miloš Čižmář, "Langobardský sídlištní objekt z Podolí, okr. Brno-venkov. K problematice langobardských sídlišť na Moravě," *Archeologické rozhledy* 49 (1997), pp. 634–642. Lubomír Peške, "Osteologické nálezy z langobardského sídliště v Podolí (okr. Brno-venkov)," *Archeologické rozhledy* 49 (1997), pp. 643–644.
8   A Longobard grave in Zohor and two burial sites not far from Devínská Nová Ves (10 graves with weapons at the site Devínske Jazero and 3 graves with weapons at the Topoliny site)

Longobard kingdom was separated from Slavic territories in Slovakia by a border along the Little and White Carpathians and on the Danube, which both the Longobards and Slavs mutually respected.[9] The Longobard kingdom bordered on the east, along the Danube, with the Gepids, which after the extinction of the Scirs and the Sarmatians obtained both banks of the middle and lower Tisza up to the Danubian border of Pannonia, and in year 536 also Sirmium (modern-day Sremska Mitrovica, in Serbia).[10]

Not even the Gepids, like the Heruls and then the Longobards, however, touched the land of the destroyed Suebian realm, because it was evidently taken over by Slavs shortly after Hunimund's defeat. The territorial outline, which old *Suavia* imprinted on the map of the world at that time, did not disappear. It was filled anew by the Slavs and became the outline of Slavic territory in the north-west of the Carpathian Basin.

2   A Third Force

In contrast to Moravia, where the Longobards lived along with the Slavs who had entered there through the Moravian gate,[11] contemporary Slovakia (with

---

are testimony that the Záhorie region also belonged to the Longobard empire. Ľudmila Kraskovská, "Nálezy z doby sťahovania národov na západnom Slovensku," *Archeologické rozhledy* 15 (1963), pp. 693–700, 709. Ľudmila Kraskovská, "Hroby z doby sťahovania národov pri Devínskom Jazere," *Archeologické rozhledy* 20 (1968), pp. 209–212. Jaroslav Tejral, "K langobardskému odkazu v archeologických prameneh na území Československa," *Slovenská archeológia* 23 (1975), no. 2, p. 401. *Archeologická topografia Bratislavy*, ed. Belo Polla, Adrián Vallašek (Bratislava 1991), pp. 36–39. Štefanovičová et al. *Najstaršie dejiny Bratislavy*, pp. 267–269.

9   Darina Bialeková, "Nové včasnoslovanské nálezy na juhozápadnom Slovensku," *Slovenská archeológia* 10 (1962), no. 1, p. 135. Štefanovičová, *Osudy starých Slovanov*, p. 29.

10   "Gepiden," in *Germanen, Hunnen und Awaren*, ed. Menghin, Springer, Wamers, pp. 199–253. Bóna – Cseh – Nagy – Tomka – Tóth, *Hunok – Gepidák – Langobardok*, pp. 52–101.

11   The Longobards penetrated into Moravia after the destruction of the Herulian Kingdom in 508. They did not settle the whole of it, however. Longobard skeleton graves and burial sites occur in Lower Austria and continue through southern Moravia up to Němčice nad Hanou and Lužice near Hodonín, where they reach the western bank of the Morava River. Longobard graves in Zohor and near Devínská Nová Ves in the Slovak Záhorie indicate that the eastern bank of the lower Morava River (and perhaps also the middle, though this could be without Longobard settlements, certainly belonged to the Longobard Kingdom). The Slavs lived not only in northern and north-west Moravia, where Longobard settlers did not get to, but reached deeply into lands settled by the Longobard. Slavic settlements and urn graves with ceramics of the Prague type occur on both banks of the middle Morava, to the lower flow of the Thaya, stretch to the vicinity of Brno and to the Záhorie up to the western edge of Bratislava. We do not find them in south-western Moravia and

the exception of today's Záhorie region) did not belong to any Germanic empire. In the ceaseless contest taking place within the Carpathian Basin the local Slavs represented a third force, whose help the enemy Longobards and Gepids had to seek out.

At some point in the final years of the reign of Longobard King Wacho (510–540), who had taken the throne by the murder of his uncle Tato, his son Walthari was born. Dramatic events then followed, as described by Procopius: *Longobard King Vakes (= Wacho) had a nephew name Risiulf, who by law was to become the king's successor upon the death of Vakes. Vakes, however, made up his mind that his own son should be named leader, and thus without reason accused Risiulf and punished him by banishment. Risiulf left home immediately along with several men and escaped to the Warini, but his two sons remained there. Vakes then bribed these barbarians to kill Risiulf. One of Risiulf's sons died of illness and the second, named Ildiges* (= Hildigis), *escaped to the Slavs. Shortly after Vakes became ill and departed this world; his son Valdarus* (= Walthari) *then took over rule of the Longobards*.[12]

---

in Lower Austria (with the exception of finds in Unterrohrbach near Stockerau). Tejral, *K langobardskému odkazu*, pp. 431–446. Jaroslav Tejral, "K otázce doby stěhování národů a počátků slovanského osídlení na Moravě," in *IV. medzinárodný kongres slovanskej archeológie, Sofia 15.–22. septembra 1980, zborník referátov ČSSR*, (Nitra 1980), pp. 177–182. Tejral, *Probleme der Völkerwanderungszeit*, pp. 356–361. Zdeněk Klanica, *Počátky slovanského osídlení našich zemí* (Praha 1986), pp. 45 (map), 58–60, 214–215. Fusek, *Slovensko vo včasnoslovanskom období*, pp. 91–94, 103, 124 (map), 176–177, 211–212, 214. Třeštík, "Příchod," pp. 22–23. Dagmar Jelínková, "Morava v časně slovanském období," in *Staroslovanská Morava*, uspořádal Bohuslav Klíma (Brno 2000), pp. 42–54. Luděk Galuška, "K problematice nejstaršího slovanského osídlení východní Moravy," *Pravěk, Nová řada* 10 (Brno 2000), pp. 119–132.

12   Procopios, *De bello Gothico* III 35. Risiulf could not have gone into exile around 512, as Dušan Třeštík writes. Třeštík, "Příchod," pp. 263. Třeštík, *Počátky*, pp. 34. Around 512 Wacho did not yet have his son Walthari, who was the reason he later banished Risiulf. Walthari was born only in the final years of Wacho's reign, thus before the year 540, and when Wacho died he was still a minor and Audoin ruled on his behalf. If Walthari had been born as early as around 512, then in the year of Wacho's death he would have been 28 years old. He would thus not have been a minor. According to Longobard tradition, which we know from later sources, Hildigis was the son of the murdered king Tato. He was thus Wacho's cousin, because Wacho was the son of Tato's brother Unichis. Origo gentis Langobardorum 4. Paul the Deacon copied from Origo gentis Langobardorum and an unknown author the Chronicon Gothanum. Paulus Diaconus, *Historia Langobardorum* I 21. *Chronicon Gotharum* 4. Třeštík, "Příchod," p. 268. According to Paul the Deacon, the fleeing of Hildigis preceded the conflict with King Wacho: *Hildigis, son of Tato, set forth against Wacho; however, he was overwhelmed by Wacho's primacy, he took refuge with the Gepids and there, as an exile, remained to the end of his life. For this reason the Gepids from that point on were antagonistic towards the Longobards.* Paulus Diaconus, *Historia Langobardorum* I 21.

After the removal of Risiulf, his two sons remained at home in Pannonia. Since one of them died soon after, the succession of young Walthari was threatened only by the second of Risiulf's sons, Hildigis, who was saved by his escape to the mentioned Slavs. Walthari (540–547) was still a minor; thus his guardian Audoin ruled on his behalf, and after Walthari's sudden death, he seized the Longobard throne and then reigned up to year 565.[13] Audoin feared Hildigis, who had not given up his claims to the Longobard throne and relied on Gepidian help. Therefore, in 547 he concluded an alliance with Emperor Justinian, who again had an interest in Sirmium, which had belonged since 536 to the Gepids. Emperor Justinian gifted Noricum mediterraneum (landlocked Noricum, the southern part of Noricum) and the part of Pannonia along the Sava River lying south of the lower Drava to the Longobards.[14] The Gepids, threatened by the new Longobard-Byzantine alliance, responded by allying themselves with the Slavs in the northern Carpathian Basin, where Hildigis was then living.

In 548 a Slavic army passed through Gepidian territory, crossed the Danube to the south and devastated Byzantium territory up to the town of Epidamnos (Durrës, in modern Albania).[15] In 549 war broke out between the Longobards and the Gepids. Then Hildigis took his Longobard retinue and *many Slavs* and came to the Gepid King Thurisind (546–560). He hoped that Audoin would lose the war, and that he would then obtain the Longobard throne. Thurisind, however, was under threat of attack from the great Byzantium army, and therefore he rapidly concluded peace with Audoin, thus dashing Hildigis's hopes. Audoin requested the handing over of Hildigis, but Thurisind refused, and Hildigis returned to the Slavs.[16]

In January 550 a Slavic force of three-thousand on horseback crossed the Danube. It barged into Thrace, and after crossing the Maritsa River it split into two parts. The larger force looted Thrace and the smaller force burst into Illyria. In both provinces the Slavs defeated the Byzantine troops, overran several fortresses and the town of Toperos on the shore of the Aegean Sea. They enslaved or slaughtered the inhabitants and cruelly tortured them. They returned home with thousands of slaves.[17]

---

13   Procopios, *De bello Gothico* III 35. Paulus Diaconus, *Historia Langobardorum* I 22.
14   Procopios, *De bello Gothico* III 33. Třeštík, "Příchod," pp. 256, 269–270. Třeštík, *Počátky*, pp. 26, 41.
15   Procopios, *De bello Gothico* III 29. Třeštík, "Příchod," pp. 270. Třeštík, *Počátky*, pp. 41–42.
16   Procopios, *De bello Gothico* III 34, 35. Třeštík, "Příchod," pp. 270–271. Třeštík, *Počátky*, pp. 41–42.
17   Procopios, *De bello Gothico* III 38. Třeštík, "Příchod," pp. 271–272. Třeštík, *Počátky*, pp. 42–43.

In March 550 the Longobard and Gepidian armies again faced one another. Before the decisive battle, however, both armies panicked; they turned and fled, and the abandoned kings concluded a two-year armistice.[18] In the summer of 550 *an unprecedented number of Slavs* again crossed the Danube and headed for Thessaloniki. Ostrogoth King Totila was responsible for this Slavic attack. Totila paid the Slavs a great deal of money to invade the Balkans and engage the Byzantine army there, thus easing his own situation in Italy. When the Slavs learned about the strong Byzantine forces of commander Germanus that were gathering in Serdica (today Sofia, Bulgaria), they turned off into Dalmatia and joined with a second Slavic army which had also crossed the Danube.

Probably at the same time, Hildigis battled with six thousand Slavic horsemen as Totila's ally against the Byzantine army in the region of Venice. After leaving Italy, Hildigis returned via the lower Danubian border of the Gepid kingdom again north to the Slavs. He didn't remain there for long, however, and together with 30 Longobards came to Constantinople (today Istanbul) and entered into the service of Emperor Justinian. In the meantime the Slavic army in the Balkans divided into three parts and remained on Byzantine territory for the entire winter. In the subsequent year the Slavs defeated a strong Byzantine army not far from Adrianopolis (modern Edirne, Turkey) and ravaged the land up to the Long Walls. After the defeat of one of its brigades, the Slavs returned home.[19]

At this time the Gepidian king Thurisind was preparing a new war with the Longobards. Since the Slavs had no intention of breaching the existing neutrality and ending up in a war with the neighbouring Longobards, Thurisind turned with a request for help against the Longobards to the distant Kutrigurs roaming the steppes beyond the Azov Sea, between the lower Dnieper and the lower Don. Since the 12 thousand Kutrigurian riders came too quickly, a year before the end of the cease fire, Thurisind led them across the Danube to plunder Byzantine territory. Justinian then hired the enemy Utigurs and set them against the Kutrigurs. In the fall of 551 the Utigurs, together with two thousand Crimean Goths, known as the Tetraxites, crossed the Don and delivered a smashing defeat to the Kutrigurs while also breaking up the Kutrigurian army, which abandoned its plundering of Byzantine territory and hurried home.[20]

---

18   Procopios, *De bello Gothico* IV 18. Třeštík, "Příchod," p. 271. Třeštík, *Počátky*, p. 42.
19   Procopios, *De bello Gothico* III 35, 40, IV 27. Třeštík, "Příchod," pp. 272–273. Třeštík, *Počátky*, pp. 43–44.
20   Procopios, *De bello Gothico* IV 18, 19. Třeštík, "Příchod," pp. 272–273. Třeštík, *Počátky*, pp. 43–44. Peter Bystrický, "Slovanské a bulharské vpády na Balkán do roku 559," *Historický časopis* 51 (2003), no. 3, pp. 397–398.

By the end of 551 a *great many Slavs broke into Illyria and caused indescribable terror there*. This was the Gepidian response to the new alliance between Justinian and Audoin. The small Byzantine force was not capable of thwarting the Slavs in their plundering and murdering or even their returning with innumerable slaves *and even hit them at the crossing of the Danube River, or otherwise attacked them, because the Gepids provided them with protection for a fee and led them to the other side for a high sum: the payoff was always one golden stater for every head. The emperor expressed dissatisfaction, because he no longer had the possibility of preventing them from further crossing the Danube on looting excursions through the Roman* (= Byzantine) *Empire or from returning with a gigantic haul; therefore he considered it necessary to conclude a treaty with the Gepidian tribes.*[21]

Justinian first made peace and an alliance with the Gepids and did so despite the fact that his alliance agreement with the Longobards was still valid. In March of 552 the cease fire ended, and another Longobard-Gepid war began. Justinian had to satisfy his obligation as an ally towards the Longobards and so he sent them an army to help against the Gepids, whom he claimed, *that after negotiating an agreement guided some Slavs across the Danube to the detriment of the Romans*. This wasn't true, but Justinian had to somehow justify his behaviour. The Longobard army, together with a small Byzantine force, invaded Gepidian territory. The bloody battle, won by the Longobards, completely exhausted both sides. Upon concluding peace, Audoin, supported by Justinian, again demanded that Thurisind hand over Hildigis, who at the beginning of the war departed from Constantinople and again made it to the Gepids. Hildigis evidently took part in the war, because he wanted to contribute to Audoin's defeat and thus get to the Longobard throne. Thurisind, who like Audoin was also a usurper, replied with a counter request. In return for Hildigis he wanted Ostrogotha, the son of the former Gepidian King Elemund, whom Thurisind had removed in 546. In the end they both withdrew these requests, which contravened the law of hospitality. Hildigis and Ostrogotha, however, were too heavy a burden on the relations of the Longobard and Gepidian king, and so they were both wilfully executed.[22]

---

21 Procopios, *De bello Gothico* IV 25. Třeštík, "Příchod," p. 273. Třeštík, *Počátky*, pp. 44–45.
22 Procopios, *De bello Gothico* IV 25, 27. Třeštík, "Příchod," pp. 273–274. Třeštík, *Počátky*, pp. 45–46. Johannes Irmscher, "Die Slawen und das Justinianische Reich," in *Rapports du IIIe Congrès International d'Archéologie Slave, Tome 2*, éditeur Bohuslav Chropovský (Bratislava 1980), pp. 157–169.

3   The Oldest Slovakia

Procopius's report on the Slavic raids through Gepidian territory to the Byzantine Empire are clear proof of the multitude and military strength of the Slavs in the north of the Carpathian Basin. The Slavs, who respected their Germanic neighbours and were able to set forth both on foot and horseback on large looting raids to the Byzantine Empire, must have also had a sufficiently large territory. If Moravia belonged to the Longobard empire and the upper Tisza region in the north-west of the Carpathian Basin lay too far from the Longobard empire, then Hildigis escaped to those Slavs to whom the north-western part of the Carpathian Basin belonged; that is, to Slovak territory. Although they received Hildigis, enemy of Longobard King Audoin, on their territory and even put him at the head of a Slavic campaign to Italy in the summer of 550, the Slavs were not willing to support him militarily against Audoin. Likewise, the Slavic alliance with the Gepids was not aimed against the neighbouring Longobards, but against the distant Byzantines. The Slavs did not want war with the Longobards, because in contrast to distant Byzantium, they had a long border with the Longobard kingdom along the Danube and in the Little and White Carpathian Mountains. The Slavs in Slovakia, who were neighbours with the Longobard and Gepidian kingdoms, had one common military command, which concluded an alliance with the Gepids and the Ostrogoths and assembled for large campaigns.[23] Only a large and strong tribe (*gens*) with vast territory could gain recognition of the powerful Germanic neighbours, and a large army with several thousand horse soldiers could campaign to distant Byzantine and far away Italy. However, we cannot imagine the tribal centre of these Slavs, to which Hildigis escaped and where Thurisind and Totila directed their appeals for attacks on the Byzantine Empire, however, as a princely seat, because according to Procopius *these tribes, namely the Slavs and Antes, are not ruled by a single man, but for a long time have lived in a democracy, and therefore they negotiate their matters both favourable and unfavourable, together. These barbarian tribes have had all the same other customs for a long time.*[24] And the Slavs, to whom the north-west part of the Carpathian Basin then belonged, thus discussed and ratified all important decisions. They thus acted *commonly*, that is in one location, most probably in Nitra itself, which later became the seat of a principality.

---

23   Třeštík, "Příchod," pp. 274–277. Třeštík, *Počátky*, pp. 46–49. Dušan Třeštík, *Vznik Velké Moravy. Moravané, Čechové a střední Evropa v letech 791–871* (Praha 2001), pp. 17–19. Bystrický, "Slovanské a bulharské vpády," pp. 394–397, 399–401.
24   Procopios, *De bello Gothico* III 14.

4   The Slavs in the Avar Khaganate

In 558 the nomadic Avars became the lords of the Black Sea steppes. They subjugated the Bulgarian Kutrigurs and Utigurs, who wandered the steppes near the Azov Sea[25] and smashed the Slavic Antes. According to Byzantine historian Menander, the Avars *ravaged the land of the Antes and didn't stop hauling people and plunder away from there*.[26] Then several Slavic tribes joined with the Avars or fell under their dominion. One of them had the name Dulebs.

The traditional Longobard-Gepidian conflict came to a head in 567. Victory in war inclined toward the side of the Gepids; therefore, Longobard King Alboin did not hesitate to ally with the Avars. Gepidian King Cunimund fell in battle, and the Avars destroyed and occupied his kingdom. In the following year the Longobard Kingdom ceased to exist. Alboin relinquished Pannonia to the Avars, and at the beginning of April 568 relocated with his nation to Italy.[27] After the departure of the Longobards, the Moravian Slavs were able to occupy southern Moravia, the Záhorie, Weinviertel and Rugiland.

The Avars did not come alone to the Carpathian Basin. In addition to the Bulgarian Kutrigurs, they also dragged with them subjugated or allied Slavic tribes, among them the already mentioned Dulebs.[28] These Slavs got into Pannonia, from where they penetrated into the Alpine valleys of the Drava and Mur up to Landlocked Noricum (*Noricum Mediterraneum*), which then acquired the name Carantania.[29] In 592 Bavarian King Tassilo I (591–609)

---

25   Henryk Łowmiański, *Początki Polski. Z dziejów Słowian w I tysiącleciu n. e. II* (Warszawa 1964), pp. 343–346. František Hýbl, *Dějiny národa bulharského I* (Praha 1930), pp. 57–58. Alexander Avenarius, *Die Awaren in Europa* (Amsterdam – Bratislava 1974), pp. 47–51. Walter Pohl, *Die Awaren. Ein Steppenvolk in Mitteleuropa 567–822 n. Chr.* (München 1988), pp. 21–27, 39–40.

26   Menandros, fragment 6. *Pramene k dejinám Veľkej Moravy*, ed. Peter Ratkoš (Bratislava 1968), pp. 39–40. Łowmiański, Początky Polski II, p. 344, Note 1047. Avenarius, *Die Awaren*, pp. 50–55.

27   Paulus Diaconus, *Historia Langobardorum* I 27. Wolfram, *Die Geburt*, p. 81. Pohl, *Die Awaren*, pp. 50–57. István Bóna, "Az Avar uralom századai," in *Erdély története I*, ed. Makkai, Mócsy, pp. 159–177. István Bóna, "Die Awarenzeit," in *Kurze Geschichte Siebenbürgens*, ed. Köpeczi, pp. 90–97.

28   Avenarius, *Die Awaren*, pp. 75, 193–217. Pohl, *Die Awaren*, pp. 113–114.

29   Bogo Grafenauer, "Nekaj vprašaj iz dobe naseljevanja južnih Slovanov," *Zgodovinski časopis* 4 (1950), pp. 23–126. Aleš Žužek assumes that the Slavs settled the eastern Alps from the upper Danube territory of Lower and Upper Austria, from southern Moravia and southwestern Slovakia. Aleš Žužek, "Naselitiv Slovanov v vzhodnoalpski prostor." *Zgodovinski časopis* 61 (2007), pp. 261–287. Peter Štih, *The Middle Ages between the Eastern Alps and the Northern Adriatic. Select Papers on Slovene Historiography and Medieval History*. East Central and Eastern Europe in the Middle Ages 450–1450. General Editor Florin Curta,

attacked the Carantanian Slavs, and when he did so again in 595, the Avars came to their assistance and destroyed the entire two thousand-strong Bavarian army. The Avars then immediately afterwards pushed through all of Bavaria and attacked Thuringia.[30]

In 602 the Longobards, together with the Avars and Slavs, ravaged Byzantine Istria. In July and August of 603 Slavs that had been sent in by the Avar Khagan helped Longobard King Agilulf in the sieging and conquering of Cremona.[31] These were evidently Slavs from Pannonia, which of all the lands of the khaganate lay closest to Italy and Istria.

The Avar-Byzantine wars in years 578–582, 592–602, 610, 619, 623 and 626 were accompanied by Slavic forays over the lower Danubian border into Byzantine provinces.[32] Then, when the Slavs with Avar help occupied the eastern Alps, other Slavic allies of the Avars, who lived above the lower Danube to the south of the Avar empire, that is *Slavs beyond the river, who were referred to as Avars* or *Slavs also called Avars*, crossed the Danubian border of the khaganate, invaded the Balkans and conquered Dalmatia from Byzantium, with the exception of the coastal towns and islands.[33]

The southern lands of the khaganate remained Slavic even after the departure of a portion of the Slavs to Dalmatia. At the head of the Slavic tribe, which under the rule of Avar khagan Bajan settled on the lower Tisza (in today's Bačka and Banat) and ruled over the entire lower Danubian border of the

Leiden – Boston 2010, pp. 87–107. Stefan Eichert, "Zentralisierungsprocesse bei den frühmittelalterlichen Karantanen," in *Zentralisierungsprocesse und Herrschaftsbildung im frühmittelalterlichen Ostmitteleuropa*, herausgegeben von Przemysław Sikora. Studien zur Archäologie Europas 23, herausgegeben von Joachim Henning, Felix Biermann, Jiří Macháček, Bonn 2014, pp. 18–20.

30 Paulus Diaconus, *Historia Langobardorum* IV 7, 10–11. Třeštík, *Vznik*, pp. 22–23. Eichert, "Zentralisierungsprocesse bei den frühmittelalterlichen Karantanen," p. 20.
31 Paulus Diaconus, *Historia Langobardorum* IV 24, 28.
32 *Theophylacti Simocattae Historiae* I 6–7, VI 3–4, 6–9, 11, VII 2, 5, 10, 11, 15, VIII 2, 3, 4. Georgios Th. Kardaras, *To Byzantio kai oi Abaroi* (Athhna 2010), pp. 37–136, 244–246. Martin Hurbanič, "Vpády Avarov na balkánske územia Východorímskej ríše v rokoch 582–626," *Historický časopis* 63 (2015), no. 3, pp. 387–404. Avar attacks on Balkan towns could not take place without the participation and support of the increasingly more aggressive Slavs. In these wars the more the failure of the nomadic way of battle grew, the authority of the Avars declined, and the Slavic way of battle was employed, and so the military importance of the Slavs grew. Hurbanič, "Vpády Avarov na balkánske územia Východorímskej ríše," pp. 401–403.
33 Constantine Porphyrogenitus *De administrando imperio* 29, edidit Gyula Moravcsik (Washington 1967), pp. 122–139. Konstantinos Porfyrogenetos, *De administrando imperio* 29, *Magnae Moraviae fontes historici III. Diplomata, epistolae, textus historici varii*, curaverunt Dagmar Bartoňková, Lubomír Havlík, Jaroslav Ludvíkovský, Radoslav Večerka (Brno 1969), pp. 384–387.

khaganate with Byzantium, was Ardagast. Ardagast's Slavs did not avoid Avar wars. In 584 Ardagast, together with the Avars, sacked Byzantine lands up to Constantinople and protected their own land from Byzantine counter-attack in the spring of 594.[34] The Slavic tribe to the south of the Avar Khaganate, which they knew well in Byzantium as an unpleasant neighbour and militarily capable antagonist, is clear proof of the abundance and military prowess of the Slavs within the Avar empire.

A nearly contemporary Frankish chronicler, originally by mistake but now traditionally called Fredegar, wrote about the military obligations of the Slavs in the service of the Avar Khaganate: *The Vinidi (= Slavs) had been the befulci (cannon-fodder) of the Huns (= Avars) for a long time; so that when the Huns with their army attacked any tribe, the Huns put the army for the defence of their camps, while the Vinidi had to fight; if they were victorious, then the Hun dashed out in order to grab the plunder; if, however, the Vinidi were defeated, they again rallied with the help of the Huns. The Huns called them befulci because when forming in battle a double battle formation, they marched in front of the Huns.*[35]

For an entire century, Pannonia alone, which the Longobards relinquished to them, and the territory of the former Gepidian kingdom in the Tisza River region and Transylvania, was sufficient for the Avars in the Carpathian Basin. The khaganate, and Pannonia in particular, was full of Slavs, which the Avars had pulled in from the east in the years 567–568 or that khagan Bajan had drawn in under his rule from the wide surroundings of the khaganate.[36] These were thus other Slavs than those who had for an entire century been settled under the Western Carpathians and in the subsequent century were to be independent neighbours of the Avars.[37] Slovak territory in the north of the

---

34 *Theophylacti Simocattae Historiae* I 7, VI 6–7.
35 *Chronicarum quae dicuntur Fredegarii Scholastici libri IV cum continuationibus* IV 48. *Monumenta Germaniae historica inde ab anno Christi quingentesimo usque ad annum millesimum et quingentesimum. Scriptorum rerum Merovingicarum tomus II. Fredegarii et aliorum chronica. Vitae sanctorum*, edidit Bruno Krusch (Hannoverae 1888), pp. 144–145. *Magnae Moraviae fontes historici I. Annales et chronicae*, curaverunt Dagmar Bartoňková, David Kalhous, Jiří K. Kroupa, Zdeněk Měřínský, Anna Žáková (Praha 2019), pp. 2–3.
36 Zlata Čilinská, "K otázke príchodu Antov na stredný Dunaj," *Sborník prací Filosofické fakulty Brněnské university* E 34–35, 1989–1990, pp. 19–25. Třeštík, *Počátky*, p. 442. Třeštík, *Vznik*, pp. 22–23.
37 We do not have archaeological proof of the presence of the khaganate in Slovakia for all the centuries from the arrival of the Avars to the Carpathian Basin. "Grabfunde der frühen Awarenzeit," in *Germanen, Hunen und Awaren*, ed. Menghin, Springer, Wamers, pp. 255–269. An exception may be gravesite 9 and horse rider graves 10, 19, 23 and 32 from Komárno (Robotnícka štvrť) and graves 85 and 452 from nearby Holiar, dated before the middle of

Carpathian Basin still did not belong to the Avars, just as it had not belonged to previous Germanic kingdoms.

5 Slavic Rebellion and Slavic Principalities

The Slavs in the khaganate withstood with difficulty the domination of the Avars, the annual wintering of the Avars in their settlements and the taxes they had to hand over to the Avars. When a second generation of Slavic-Avar half-castes grew up, those who grew out of the violent wintering of Avars in Slavic settlements, the tension in the khaganate resulted in a great explosion. The Slavs prepared their rebellion against the Avars, and in 623 it was begun by these same half-castes.[38] The rich graves of their Avar enemies close to Lake

---

the 7th century. The burial site in Robotnícka štvrt in Komárno is the oldest of 8 Komárno burial sites from the Avar period. Archaeologists have examined 33 graves in it; others (perhaps the bigger part) were destroyed. Finds from the mentioned five graves, especially metal pressings from silver plate in graves 19 and 23, date this burial site to the 1st half of the 7th century. Anton Točík, *Slawisch-awarisches Gräberfeld in Holiare* (Bratislava 1968), pp. 3, 6–23, 26. Alexander Trugly, "Pohrebisko z doby Avarskej ríše v Komárne-Robotníckej štvrti," *Spravodaj Oblastného podunajského múzea v Komárne* 2 (1982), pp. 9–10, 14–15, 17, 22–23, 24–27, 29, 32, 33, 35, 37, 38, 40. Jozef Zábojník, "Soziale Problematik der Gräberfelder des nördlichen und nordwestlichen Randgebietes des Awarischen Kaganats," *Slovenská archeológia* 43 (1995), no. 2, pp. 285, 286, 300. Jozef Zábojník, "Das Awarische Kaganat und die Slawen an seiner nördlichen Peripherie (Probleme der Archäologischen Abgrenzung)," *Slovenská archeológia* 47 (1999), no. 1, pp. 156, 166. Zlata Čilinská places the beginnings of burials in the large burial site in Želovce to approximately the period of the 630s. Jozef Zábojník, however, does not date any graves from Želovce before the middle of the 7th century. Zlata Čilinská, *Frühmittelalterliches Gräberfeld in Želovce* (Bratislava 1973), p. 10. Zlata Zlata Čilinská, *Slovania a Avarský kaganát. Výpoveď staroslovanského pohrebiska v Želovciach* (Bratislava 1992), pp. 32, 79. Zábojník, "Soziale Problematik," pp. 332–336. The beginnings of burials in the large burial site in Devínska Nová Ves at first were cautiously dated to the period of origin of Samo's realm. Jan Eisner, *Devínska Nová Ves. Slovanské pohřebiště* (Bratislava 1952), pp. 347–348. Erwin Keller – Volker Bierbrauer, "Beiträge zum awarenzeitlichen Gräberfeld von Devínska Nová Ves," *Slovenská archeológia* 13 (1965), no. 2, pp. 378–380. Jozef Zábojník dates only a solitary grave site uncovered in Vlašič's field before the middle of the 7th century. He dates horse rider graves 124 and 131 with ornamentation pressed from silver plate up to the 3rd quarter of the 7th century and horse rider grave 79 with the same ornamentation up to the 4th quarter of the 7th century. Zábojník, "Soziale Problematik," pp. 289, 293.

38 Chronicarum quae dicuntur Fredegar Scholastici IV 48, ed. Bruno Krusch, pp. 144–145. *MMFH I*, pp. 2–3. Třeštík, *Počátky*, pp. 51, 442. Třeštík, *Vznik*, pp. 26–27. Kornél Bakay and Vladimír Turčan have already written about the Slavic rebellion in Pannonia. See note 39. Lysý, *Moravania*, pp. 53–55. The anti-Avar rebellion of the Slavs on the territory of the khaganate broke out in 623, when a large Avar military with the khagan at the head was

Balaton also fell victim to the insurgents, as well as those at the burial sites of Káptalantóti, Zamárdi, Halimba, Gyönk-Vásártér and on the Danubian island of Csepel.[39] They also robbed the graves at the oldest Avar burial site, in Komárno.[40] The explosion ripped through the western part of the khaganate and quickly set the disaffected Slavic tribes into motion, which in a very short time altered Central Europe and the northern Balkan.

Russian chronicler Nestor wrote of the old tradition on the dispersal of the Slavs from the Danube (primarily from Pannonia): *After a long time the Slavs settled along the Danube, where there is now Hungarian and Bulgarian land. And from these Slavs they spread over the earth and named themselves (according to) where they settled, at which place. When they came, they settled on the river with the name Morava, and were called the Moravians; and the other were called Czechs. And these Slavs are also the White Croats and Sorbs and Carantanians.*[41] The Russian chronicler, or perhaps his Bohemian original, mistakenly considered the tradition on the dispersal of the Danubian Slavs, which probably got to Kiev from Bohemia, as a report on the original dispersal of all Slavs and the Danube for the ancient Slavic homeland.[42] Therefore, their original count, which ended with the Carantanians, is expanded by all other known Slavic tribes, which could not, however, have originated from the Danube.

---

in Byzantine Thrace and before the ramparts of Constantinople. It could only return to the khaganate after the concluding of an Avar-Byzantine peace treaty at the turn of the years 623/624. Pohl, *Die Awaren*, pp. 245–248. Martin Hurbanič, "Byzancia a Avarský kaganát v rokoch 623–624," *Historický časopis* 55 (2007), no. 2, pp. 229–248. Martin Hurbanič, *Posledná vojna antiky. Avarský útok na Konštantinopol roku 626 v historických súvislostiach* (Prešov 2009), pp. 101–113.

39 Kornél Bakay, "Az avarkori időrendjéről. Újabb avar temetők a Balaton környékén," *Somogyi Múzeumok Közleményei* 1 (1973), pp. 5–86. Vladimír Turčan, "K otázke najstaršieho slovanského osídlenia juhozápadného Slovenska a vzťahu Slovanov a Avarov," *Zborník Slovenského národného múzea* 78 (1984), *História* 24, pp. 143–145.

40 Trugly, "Pohrebisko," p. 24.

41 *Povesť vremennych let*, MMFH I, pp. 191–192. Radoslav Katičić, "Die Ethnogenesen in der Avaria," in *Typen der Ethnogenese unter besonderer Berücksichtigung der Bayer, Teil 1. Berichte des Symposions der Kommission für Frühmittelalterforschung, 27. Bis 30. Oktober 1986, Stift Zwettl, Niederösterreich*, ed. Herwig Wolfram, Walter Pohl (Wien 1990), pp. 127–128. Alexander Avenarius, "Začiatky Slovanov na strednom Dunaji. Autochtonistická teória vo svetle súčasného bádania," *Historický časopis* 40 (1992), no. 1, pp. 1–16.

42 Boris Nikolajevič Florja, "Skazanie o preloženii knig na slavjanskij jazyk. Istočniki vremja i mesto napisanija," *Byzantinoslavica* 46 (1985), pp. 121–130. Třeštík, *Počátky*, pp. 50–51, 442–443. Třeštík, *Vznik*, pp. 26–27. Třeštík, *Mýty*, pp. 94–96. The opinion of Dušan Třeštík on the other, smaller migration of the Slavs that left Pannonia, climaxed in the great anti-Avar rebellion and led to the origin of several tribal principalities, some of which are linked to Samo's realm, is convincing and cogent. That's why we accept it in nearly its full range.

In the extensive work of educated Byzantine Emperor Constantine Porphyrogenitus we read how under the rule of emperor Heraclius (610–640) a portion of the Croats left Great, or White Croatia (in the territory of Lower Silesia and both Lusatias), and part of the Sorbs (Serbs) from White Serbia (near the Saale on the middle Elbe) in the south. Emperor Constantine learned of this migration of the Croats and Serbs from two old Slavic stories, Croatian and Serbian, which he modified and included in his work. The Croats came to Dalmatia, where other Slavs had lived since the second half of the 6th century. The Croats *went to Dalmatia and found the Avars* (= Slavs) *as the owners of this land. They battled between themselves over this for several years. The Croats won; they slaughtered a part of the Avars, but they forced others to surrender. Since then this country has been occupied by the Croats.* The Croats also remembered the names of the seven brothers who led them to Dalmatia. These were Kloukas, Lobelos, Kosentzis, Mouchlo, Chrobatos, Touga and Bouga. One of them, perhaps the fifth Croat brother (*Chrobatos*), whose name had the same root, was the first Croatian prince in Dalmatia. Afterwards, still in the time of emperor Heraclius, his son Porga succeeded him.[43]

A portion of the Croats, shortly after arriving in Dalmatia, separated from their fellow tribesmen and conquered the southern part of Pannonia, more exactly one of the four late-Roman provinces on Pannonian territory, Savia, settled from the second half of the 6th century by Slavs. They established a principality here: *From those Croats who settled in Dalmatia a certain portion separated and took over Illyria and Pannonia; and these had an independent leader, who maintained friendly relations with the leader of Croatia, although only through dispatches.* The seat of the Savian Principality was Sisak, in antique form Siscia, the former capital of Roman Savia.[44]

---

43 Constantine Porphyrogenitus De administrando imperio 30–32, ed. Moravcsik, pp. 138–161. MMFH III, pp. 387–391. Gerard Labuda, *Pierwsze państwo słowiańskie państwo Samona* (Poznań 1949), pp. 194–262. Bogo Grafenauer, "Prilog kritici izvještaja Konstantina Porfirogeneta o doseljenju Hrvata," *Historijski zbornik* 5 (1952), pp. 1–56. Pohl, *Die Awaren*, pp. 261–266. The names Touga and Bouga are Turkish male names first of Avar origin. Touga and Bouga thus were not sisters, as Constantine Porphyrogenitus writes, but brothers. Jooseppi Julius Mikkola, "Avarica," *Archiv für slavische Philologie* 41 (1927), pp. 158–160. Třeštík, *Počátky*, p. 492.

44 Constantine Porphyrogenitus De administrando imperio 30, ed. Moravcsik, pp. 138–147. MMFH III, pg. 388. Annales regni Francorum inde ab a. 741. usque ad a. 829. qui dicuntur Annales Laurissenses maiores et Einhardi, post editionem G. H. Pertzii recognovit Fridericus Kurze. Scriptores rerum Germanicarum in usum scholarum ex Monumentis Germaniae historicis separatim editi (Hannoverae 1895), p. 158. Annales regni Francorum ad a. 822, MMFH I, p. 29. Wolfram, *Die Geburt*, pp. 269–272, 355–357, 360, 379, 428. Concilium Spalatense, Magnae Moraviae fontes historici IV. Leges, textus iuridici,

The non-Slavic names of the mentioned seven Croatian brothers and Croatian Prince Porga[45] demonstrate the variegated ethnic mix in the khaganate and not the distant Slavs along the Elbe and Oder rivers. The Croats and Serbs did not come to the Balkans from the Elbe and Oder, as Constantine Porphyrogenitus writes, but directly from the territory of the khaganate. Constantine Porphyrogenitus, who wrote his work in the middle of the 10th century, knew about the Croats on the middle Oder, which then belonged to the Bohemian Principality, to Prince Boleslaus I and Boleslaus II, and about the Serbs from the Elbe, subjugated to the Saxon margrave, and by mistake located them there, perhaps according to the Croatian and Serb stories, and original settlements of the Balkan Croats and Serbs. Both Croatian and Serbian branches, however, were already divided from one another in Pannonia, one moved to the north-west and the other to the south.[46]

The Croats came not only to Dalmatia and Savia, but also to the territory of the former Roman province of Noricum Mediterraneum, settled from the second half of the 6th century by Slavs. Here, in the eastern Alps, on the upper parts of the Drava, Mur and Enns rivers, the Carantanian Principality originated after the arrival of the Croats. Around year 665 Arnefrit, son of Friulian Prince Lupus, escaped after his father's death from the anger of the Longobard king *to the tribe of the Slavs to Carnuntum, which was incorrectly called Carantania (ad Sclavorum gentem in Carnuntum, quod corrupte vocitant Carantanum)*.[47] The Carantanians (*Carontani*) are mentioned around the year 700 by in the anonymous Ravenna Cosmography.[48] The first known Carantanian Prince was

---

suplementa, curaverunt Dagmar Bartoňková, Karel Kaderka, Lubomír Havlík, Jaroslav Ludvíkovský, Josef Vašica, Radoslav Večerka (Brno 1971), p. 126. Emperor Diocletianus (284–305) divided Pannonia into four smaller provinces. One of them was Savia. The Drava River then became the border. To the north of it lay Pannonia Prima and on the south side Savia. Wolfram, *Die Geburt*, p. 73. Herwig Wolfram, *Salzburg, Bayern, Österreich. Die Conversio Bagoariorum et Carantanorum und die Quellen ihrer Zeit, Mitteilungen des Instituts für Österreichische Geschichtsforschung, Ergänzungsband 31* (Wien – München 1995), pp. 68–71.

45 The seven Croatian brothers and the prince of Porga have Turkish names. Mikkola, "Avarica," pp. 158–160. Otto Kronsteiner, "Gab es unter den Alpenslawen eine kroatische ethnische Gruppe?," *Österreichische Namenforschung* 6 (1978), p. 155.

46 Třeštík, *Počátky*, pp. 50–51, 442–443. Třeštík, *Vznik*, pp. 26–27. Dušan Třeštík, *Mýty kmene Čechů (7.–10. století). Tři studie ke "starým pověstem českým"* (Praha 2003), pp. 78–98.

47 Paulus Diaconus, *Historia Langobardorum* V 22.

48 *Kosmograph von Ravenna IV 37, Eine Erdschreibung um das Jahr 700*, ed. Joseph Schnetz, Itineraria Romana II, Leipzig 1940, pp. 75–76. Regarding the older history of Carantania, see Wolfram, *Die Geburt*, pp. 341–346. Wolfram, *Salzburg, Bayern, Österreich*, pp. 71–81. Třeštík, *Vznik*, pp. 38–52. Peter Štih, *The Middle Ages between the Eastern Alps and the*

Valuk (before 631–after 663).[49] Although he was a Slav, he had, like the seven Croatian brothers, a Turkish name.[50] And he could thus have come from the territory of the khaganate, more specifically from Pannonia.

The Croatian part in the origin of the Carantanian Principality also rests in the name of the Carantanian *kosezi*, which recalls the name *Kosentzes*, which was the name of the third Croatian brother. The *kosezi* or *kasezi* were free warriors, settled on princely (later ducal) land, who elected and installed the Carantanian princes. Even several centuries after the loss of Carantanian independence they still had ownership rights, courts and a military organization, which were closely linked with the Carantanian prince.[51] And the Carantanian Principality was thus established by Slavic-Avar half-castes, more exactly the

---

Northern Adriatic. Select Papers on Slovene Historiography and Medieval History (Leiden – Boston 2010), pp. 108–122, 173–176.

49 Bulgarian Prince Alciok (*Alciocus*), who together with 9-thousand Bulgarians and their families were chased out of Pannonia and into Bavaria by the Avars in 631, found refuge in the principality of Valuk. When the Bavarians on the command of Dagobert murdered the majority of Bulgarians, Alciok took refuge with the remaining 700 Bulgarians *in marca Vinedorum*, that is, to Carantania, where *he lived with Valuk, Prince of the Vinidi, for many years with them* (*cum Wallucum ducem Winedorum annis plurimis vixit cum suis*). Chronicarum quae dicuntur Fredegarii Scholastici IV 72, ed. Krusch, s. 157. *MMFH I*, pp. 5–6. In year 663 *the prince of the Bulgarians named Alzek* (*Vulgarum dux Alzeco nomine*) departed to the Longobard King Grimuald (662–671). Paulus Diaconus, *Historia Langobardorum* V 29. Henryk Łowmiański, *Początki Polski. Z dziejów Słowian w I tysiącleciu n. e. IV* (Warszawa 1970), pp. 242–243. Pohl, *Die Awaren*, pp. 175, 188, 223, 268–270. Štih, *The Middle Ages between the Eastern Alps and the Northern Adriatic*, pp. 108–115. *Conversio Bagoariorum et Carantanorum. Das Weißbuch der Salzburger Kirche über die erfolgreiche Mission in Karantanien und Pannonien mit Zusätzen und Ergenzungen.* Herausgegeben, übersetzt, kommentiert und um die Epistola Theotmari wie um Gesammelte Schriften zum Thema ergänzt von Herwig Wolfram (Ljubljana/Laibach 2012), pp. 115–117. Valuk, who kept Alciok (identical with Alzek) with him for *many years*, ruled even before his arrival in 631 and died only after his departure, that is, after 663. Stefan Eichert, "Zentralisierungsprocesse bei den frühmittelalterlichen Karantanen," pp. 20–28.

50 Otto Kronsteiner, *Die alpenslawischen Personennamen*, Österreichische Namenforschung, Sonderreihe 2 (1975), p. 26. Kronsteiner, "Gab es unter den Alpenslawen," p. 144. Pohl, *Die Awaren*, p. 270. Wolfram, *Salzburg, Bayern, Österreich*, pp. 50–51. *Conversio*, ed. Wolfram, p. 122. Valuk or his predecessors brought a part of the Croatian tribe from Pannonia to Carantania around year 623. If Valuk, like Alciok, was the prince of the Carantanian Croats who came to Carantania from Pannonia, then both could understand one another.

51 Bogo Grafenauer, *Ustoličevanie koroških vojvod in država karantanskih Slovencev*. Slovenska akademija znanosti in umetnosti, Razred za zgodovinske in družbene vede, Dela 7 (Ljubljana 1952), pp. 478–505. Bogo Grafenauer, "Deset let proučevania koroških vojvod, kosezov in država karantanskih Slovencev," *Zgodovinski časopis* 16 (1962), pp. 176–210. Bogo Grafenauer, "Razvoj in struktura države karantanskih Slovanov od VII. do IX. stoletja," *Jugoslovenski istorijski časopis* 3 (1963), pp. 19–30. Bogo Grafenauer, "Ustoličevanie koroških vojvod in vojvodski prestol," *Zgodovinski časopis* 24 (1970), pp. 112–122. Třeštík,

portion of the Croats[52] who had departed from neighbouring Pannonia. The Croats in Carantania and in Savia, however, were unable to imprint the local Slavs and their land with their name, as they did in Dalmatia, which became Croatia, and Dalmatian Slavs became Croats.[53]

The basin of the upper Sava belonged to Carniola. The Ravenna Cosmography, written around the year 700, mentions it as *patria quae dicitur Carneola* or *patria Carnech*, or *Carnich patria* and even *patria Carnium*.[54] The word *patria* (country) had in medieval times a wide, but stable meaning. It indicated counties, dukedoms, principalities, kingdoms and empires, that is small and large tribal territories and states, as well as their administrative parts and provinces. If Slavic Carniola was a *patria*, then it must have been a kind of principality[55] like neighbouring Carantania, Croatia and Savia.

The Serbs also got territory in the Balkan (more specifically the eastern part of the former Roman province of Dalmatia), settled even before them by other Slavs, from emperor Heraclius. This was half of the Serb tribe which Prince Serb brought to the Balkans, one of two brothers, who after their father's death took possession of rule over the Serbs. Serb princes, similarly as Croatian and Carantanian princes, inherited rule from father to son: *Then, when their Prince*

Počátky, pp. 344–346, 543. Třeštík, *Vznik*, pp. 49–51. Štih, *The Middle Ages between the Eastern Alps and the Northern Adriatic*, pp. 157–161, 168.

52 Kronsteiner, "Gab es unter den Alpenslawen," pp. 144–157. Ljudmil Hauptmann, "Karantanska Hrvatska," in *Zbornik kralja Tomislava* (Zagreb 1925), pp. 297–317. Otto Kronsteiner, *Staroslovenska družba in obred na knežjem kamnu* (Ljubljana 1954), pp. 75–126. Stjepan Antoljak, "Hrvati u Karantaniji. Prilog seobi Hrvata iz Dalmacije u prekosavske krajeve u 7. stoljecu," *Godišen zbornik na Filozofskot fakultet na Univerzitetot vo Skopje, Istorisko-filološki oddel* 9 (1956), pp. 15–38. Bogo Grafenauer, "Hrvati u Karantaniji," *Historijski zbornik* 11–12 (1958–1959), pp. 207–231. Henryk Łowmiański, *Początki Polski. Z dziejów Słowian w I tysiącleciu n. e. III* (Warszawa 1967), pp. 455–456. *Conversio*, ed. Wolfram, pp. 121–122. Wolfram, *Salzburg, Bayern, Österreich*, pp. 50–51. Pohl, *Die Awaren*, pp. 263–264. Evidence of the Croats in Carinthia is also a reference to the Kroatengau. Wolfram, *Die Geburt*, pp. 343, 394, 409, 469.

53 The first proof on the name of the Croats is in a document from 4 March 852. The letter was issued by *Tirpimirus dux Chroatorum*, to whom the *regnum Chroatorum* belonged. *Priručnik izvora hrvatske historije I/1*, napsao i uredio Ferdo Šišic (Zagreb 1914), n. 6/a, p. 193.

54 *Kosmograph von Ravenna* IV 21, 22, 37–38, ed. Schnetz, pp. 58, 75–76. *Conversio*, ed. Wolfram, pp. 76–77. Štih, *The Middle Ages between the Eastern Alps and the Northern Adriatic*, pp. 123–128.

55 Thomas Eichenberger, *Patria. Studien zur Bedeutung des Wortes im Mittelealter (6.–12. Jh.)*, Nationes 9 (Sigmaringen 1991). Peter Štih, "Carniola, patria Sclavorum," *Österreichische Osthefte* 37 (1995), Heft 4, pp. 856–858.

Serb died ..., his son ruled according to succession and then grandchild and so on, the princes from his family.[56]

The other part of the Serbs, who were led by Prince Dervan, or his predecessor, perhaps identical with the mentioned brother of Prince Serb, came at this same time to the Saale River and on the middle Elbe, that is to so-called White Serbia. Dervan's Serbs, similarly as their fellow Balkan tribesmen, to whom the Byzantine emperor had granted new territory, could have gotten new settlements on the Saale River, on the frontier of the Frankish empire, from then Frankish King Chlothar II. From that point *they belonged to the Kingdom of the Franks.* They took advantage, however, of the first opportunity and in 631 departed the territory which they had received several years earlier from the Frankish king, and concluded an alliance with Samo.[57]

One of the Slavic tribes that left Pannonia and found new territory was named the Bohemians (Czechs). The story on the origin of the Bohemians, like the Croatian story, tells of seven brothers. One of them was named Čech, and he led his nation to the Říp mountain, which stood in the centre of a new homeland. Just as the Croats and Serbs were mistaken after several centuries of tradition, when they sought their original homeland in the distant northwest, on the middle Oder and middle Elbe, where the other part of their tribe settled, so errored the Czechs, who sought their original settlements far to the south-east, in Croatia. The starting point of the Bohemian migration was not in Croatian, but halfway between the Croats and the Bohemians, in Pannonia, from where the Croats and Serbs also departed. Nestor and the German version of the story about Čech not only tell of the arrival of the Bohemians from the Danube, who then gave their name to all Slavs in the Bohemian basin, but they also tell of a significant change of the material culture, which had its origins in Pannonia.[58]

---

56 Constantine Porphyrogenitus *De administrando imperio* 31–33, ed. Moravcsik, pp. 146–163. *MMFH III*, pp. 389–392. Třeštík, *Mýty*, pp. 81–82.
57 After the Slavic victory near Wogastisburg in 631 *Dervan, prince of the Sorbs, who were from the Slavic line and had for a long time belonged to the Kingdom of the Franks, joined with his people to the kingdom of Samo. Chronicarum quae dicuntur Fredegarii Scholastici* IV 68, ed. Krusch, pp. 154–155. *MMFH I*, p. 5. If in 631 Dervan's Sorbs *had for a long time (iam olem) belonged to the King of the Franks*, then they had to have come to the middle Elbe and Saale, that is to White Serbia, at least several years earlier.
58 Třeštík, *Počátky*, pp. 50–51, 442–443. Třeštík, *Vznik*, pp. 26–27. Třeštík, *Mýty*, pp. 57–98. Dušan Třeštík, "Od příchodu Slovanů k 'říši' českých Boleslavů," in *Přemyslovci. Budování českého státu*, ed. Petr Sommer, Dušan Třeštík, Josef Žemlička (Praha 2009), pp. 69–71. Třeštík, "Počátky českého politického myšlení," pp. 409–412. Jiří Zeman, "K problematice časné slovanské kultury ve střední Evropě," *Památky archeologické* 70 (1979), pp. 113–130. Not only did the Croats and Bohemians have a story about the origin of their nation

The anti-Avar rebels, who established a wide and continuous band of principalities around a turbulent Pannonia, could not avoid the Slavic territory to its neighbouring north. That's why two Slavic principalities, separated from Pannonia by the watery barrier of the middle Danube, one Nitrian and the other Moravian, could originate right at the time of the great anti-Avar rebellion, just like Carantania, Carniola, Savia, Croatia and other principalities lying in the wide surrounding of Avarian Pannonia. And according to the mentioned old tradition written by Nestor, a part of the Danubian Slavs, more specifically a part of the Slavic rebels who came from beyond the Danube, *settled on the river with the name Morava and called itself Morava*. This was the beginning of the Moravian Principality.

Nearly the entire cultivated Slavic world knew that Constantine (Cyril) and Methodius worked in Moravia, bringing the Slavic script and writing the first books in the Slavic language. Moravia could therefore not be missing from a tradition on the dispersal of the Danubian Slavs. Nitria (Nitraland) then belonged to Moravia and later to the Hungarian Kingdom. It was hidden away and less significant from a Slavic-wide point of view; therefore, the beginning of the Nitrian Principality did not get included in this Slavic-wide tradition.

The Croats in the western Balkan established not one large principality, but two neighbouring ones. Dalmatia and Savia existed up to then, and after the arrival of the Croats they further remained two different Slavic territories. And the other two principalities lying in the vicinity of hot Pannonia, one Nitrian and the other Moravian, were established by similar Slavic-Avar cross-breeds, such as the already mentioned Croats. Just as in the south, one large principality could not arise on the middle Danube either. The same as in the western Balkan, here, too, Pannonian rebels also found two different Slavic territories. Thus, they proceeded the same as the Croats had. Two different Slavic territories became two different principalities, not only in Dalmatia and Savia, but also on the middle Danube. The territorial base of Moravia and Nitria were two different Slavic territories, which before had belonged to different German kingdoms.

We can trace the historic differentiation of Nitria and Moravia from the early times of the great migration of nations. The Herulian Kingdom, lying in the basin of the Morava River, was separated from the realm of the Suebs, to which the territory of contemporary Slovakia belonged, by the Little and White Carpathians. The Little and White Carpathians remained the border even after the arrival of the Slavs, and in the years 508–568 they separated the Longobard

---

and the beginning of its history, but the Longobards and Angles did, too. Modzelewski, *Barbarzyńska Europa*, pp. 59–66.

Kingdom, to which Moravia belonged, from the Slavic territory in Slovakia. And the Moravian Slavs, to whom the entire Morava River basin with their abandoned Longobard settlements remained after the departure of the Longobards in year 568, had to run into and respect this border. First as a border of the Longobard Kingdom, in whose interior they lived, and after 568 as the border of two different Slavic territories. Moravia and Nitria eventually inherited the border in the Little and White Carpathians, and it remained their mutual border even after the origin of the common Great Moravian state in 833.

6 Samo's Realm

The Slavic principalities near the middle Danube initially formed a common realm. One of the domestic princes could not become their common leader. This would have sparked natural jealousy and mutual disputes. Therefore, a capable foreigner came in handy, the Frankish merchant Samo. He had distinguished himself in leading wars; therefore, *they appointed him as king over themselves*. Samo ruled the Slavs for 35 years (623–658).[59] If *under his rule the Vinidi led many battles against the Huns*, then Samo's realm bordered the Avar Khaganate and contained the entire Slavic space on the middle Danube. Only such a vast space could offer the large military force needed for the *Vinidi to*

---

[59] Krzysztof Polek, "'Państwo Samona' w nowych badaniach archeologicznych i historicznych," in *Cognitioni gestorum. Studia z dziejów średniowiecza dedykowane profesorowi Jerzemu Strzelczykowi*, redakcja Darius A. Sikorski, Andrzej M. Wyrwa (Poznań – Warszawa 2006), pp. 41–51. The Slavs were mutually disagreeing because they often chose foreigners as their rulers. Peter Bystrický, "Samova ríša a prepožičiavanie vlády cudzincom," in Dušan Kováč et al., *Slovenské dejiny v dejinách Európy. Vybrané kapitoly* (Bratislava 2015), pp. 251–254. Slavic disunion is mentioned in the *Taktika strategiká*, also called the *Strategikon*, which (later at the turn of the 6th to 7th centuries) was written by an unknown Byzantine author called Pseudo-Mauricius: *The nations of the Slavs and Antes live in the same way and have the same customs. They are both independent, absolutely refusing to be enslaved or ruled ... Owing to their lack of rule and their ill feeling toward one another, they are not acquainted with an order of battle. They are also not prepared to fight a battle standing in close order or to present themselves on open or level ground.... When a difference of opinion prevails among them, either they come to no agreement at all or when some of them do come to an agreement, the others quickly go against what was decided. They are always at odds with each other, and nobody is willing to yield to another ... Because they have many chieftains who disagree among themselves, it is recommended to obtain some of them by coaxing, or by gifts, and mainly those who are near the borders, and to attack the others so that war with all of them does not permit them to unify or rule by an individual.* Pseudo-Maurikios, *Strategikon* XXI 5, Pramene, ed. Ratkoš, pp. 44–46.

always overpower the Huns.⁶⁰ If Samo's realm contained the entire free Slavic space between the Avar and the Frankish realms, then not only did Moravia and Nitria belong to it, but also the north-western part of Pannonia, Rugiland and the eastern part of Noricum on the river (Noricum ripense), that is the whole territory between the lower Rába in the east and the lower Enns in the west, which touched Carantania in the south. The lower Enns was the eastern border of Bavaria, and Avar settlements ended near the lower Rába.⁶¹ Samo increased the power of his realm by an alliance with the Bohemians and in 631 also with distant Dervan's Sorbs.⁶²

Crucial political and military events connected with the shifting of large tribes, which broke up the old and after which created a new balance of power in this large area, usually played out in a short period of perhaps one or two years. After the Battle of Nedao in 454, the Hun kingdom quickly fell, and a new Germanic kingdom rapidly arose on its territory. And the Battle of Bolia in 469 and the events of the following year in 470 and then in 473 likewise rapidly destroyed all the barbarian kingdoms lying between the Herulian and the Gepidian kingdoms. The freed space was immediately filled by the Heruls and probably by Slavs, too, who occupied what is today Slovakia. The destruction of the Herulian Kingdom by the Longobards and the origin of a great Longobard Kingdom on its territory was an event of perhaps only a single year, 508. Not quite an entire year (from 567 to spring 568) was sufficient for the Gepid and Longobard kingdoms to cease to exist in the Carpathian Basin and their territory to be taken over by the Avars. The events around year 623 also occurred equally fast. The anti-Avar rebellion, the departure of the Croats, Sorbs, Bohemians, part of the Dulebs and other Slavs from hot Pannonia on the west, north and south, the origin of new Slavic principalities and Samo's realm all played out in a very short time, perhaps of only two or three years. A new balance of power originated, and this brought peace. Pannonia (without Savia), or at least the predominant part of it, remained a part of the khaganate,

---

60   *Chronicarum quae dicuntur Fredegarii Scholastici* IV 48, ed. Krusch, pp. 144–145. *MMFH I*, pp. 2–3. Labuda, *Pierwsze państwo słowiańskie*, pg. 148–193.

61   Jaroslava Ruttkayová, "K problematike osídlenia severozápadného pomedzia Avarského kaganátu," in *K problematike osídlenia stredodunajskej oblasti vo včasnom stredoveku*, ed. Zlata Čilinská (Nitra 1991), pp. 193–196. Zábojník, *Das Awarische Kaganat und die Slawen*, pp. 156–157.

62   The annual devastation of Thuringia by Samo's Slavs in the years 631–634 and the alliance of Samo with the Sorb Prince Dervan demonstrates that the Bohemians were also Samo's allies. Without the Bohemians, the allying with the Elbe River Sorbs would have been impossible, and Thuringia would have been too distant, beyond Samo's military reach. *Chronicarum quae dicuntur Fredegarii Scholastici* IV 68, 74, 75, 77, ed. Krusch, pp. 154–155, 158–159. *MMFH I*, pp. 3–7.

and Samo's realm lay on territory which had never belonged to the Avars before then. The peace was bilaterally accepted and thus stable, and it enabled the Avars to turn their entire attention to the opposite side. In 626 a huge Avar army, in which there were many Slavs, set off against Constantinople.[63] This would not have been possible if the war had continued between Samo and the Avar empire and with it the shift of Slavic tribes across all of Pannonia. Everything important thus occurred in a very short period of time, in 623–624, at the latest in the first half of the 620s, and definitely before year 626.

When Slavic rebels abandoned the hotbed of the rebellion, the Avars continued to bury their dead at their damaged burial sites.[64] They ceased to bury their dead in Komárno, however,[65] because the local Avar bridgehead ceased to exist at the time of the origin of Samo's realm. In 626, when it was all over and peace again reigned between the Avars and the Slavs, the Avar khagan could launch himself into a new great adventure. The Slavic rebels were pleased to have the occupied territories on which they established principalities, and the Avars laid siege to Constantinople while additional *people who were of no harm*, the Bulgarian Kutrigurs, came to Pannonia.[66]

7 The Intersection of Long-Distance Roads

Two ancient trade routes and military roads of European importance, the Amber Road[67] and the Danube Road, passed through Samo's realm. The routes crossed at the confluence of the Morava and Danube rivers, where there was a crossing over the great flow of the Danube. This crossroads attracted merchants, who came to the Slavs to make large trades. Samo was one of them. As

63 Pohl, *Die Awaren*, pp. 248–255. Kardaras, *To Byzantio kai oi Abaroi*, pp. 123–126. Martin Hurbanič, "Avarské vojsko počas obliehania Konštantinopola," *Vojenská história* 11 (2007), no. 3, pp. 16–38. Martin Hurbanič, "Obrana Konštantinopola počas avarského útoku roku 626," *Vojenská história* 12 (2008), no. 1, pp. 3–27. Martin Hurbanič, "Historické súvislosti a príčiny avarského útoku na Konštantinopol roku 626," *Vojenská história* 12 (2008), no. 3, pp. 3–23. Hurbanič, *Posledná vojna antiky*, pp. 137–234. Martin Hurbanič, *História a mýtus. Avarský útok na Konštantinopol roku 626 v legendách* (Prešov 2010).
64 See note 39.
65 Archaeologists did not find in even one of 33 graves at the Komárno-Robotnícká štvrt any cast bronze metal work or beads in the shape of melon seeds, characteristic for the later Avar period. Trugly, "Pohrebisko," p. 26.
66 Třeštík, *Vznik*, p. 26.
67 McCormick, *Narodziny Europy*, pp. 356–369. Martina Škutová, "Neskoroantické cesty v Karpatskej kotline na príklade úseku z Itineraria Burdigalense," *Byzantinoslovaca* V (2014), pp. 21–22.

a successful military leader and Slavic ruler he certainly valued not only the profitable trade but also the strategic position of this crossroad, which even under the Romans was guarded by a large fortress and the city of Carnuntum[68] and its forward position at Devín.

In 375 Roman Emperor Valentinian built and renovated the Roman fortresses on the northern border of Pannonia. Then the Romans built several wooden and stone walled buildings at Devín and fortified the site with a bulwark, which is still partially preserved today.[69] At the time of the anti-Avar rebellion new residents came to Devín and its nearest surroundings, and they began to bury their dead in Devínská Nová Ves and do so together with the local Slavs, to whom Devín had belonged since year 568 when the Longobards abandoned it. The Avar customs of the new residents of Devín and its surroundings indicate that they came from the khaganate. These were the numerous anti-Avar rebels who departed Pannonia and settled among the Slavs who had long before settled in the area of Devín and blended in with them. They interchanged their Slavic and Avar customs and material culture, and therefore at their common burial ground in Devínská Nová Ves the oldest skeletal graves alternate with smaller urn graves, and Slavic weapons, accessories, ornaments, ceramics and funereal practices are often mixed in these same graves with those of nomads.[70]

Devín stood exactly at the interface of the three parts of Samo's realm: Moravia, Nitria and the north-west part of Pannonia, that is beyond the centre and crucial influence of only one of several tribes which recognized him as their common ruler. The Danube and the Little Carpathians covered the Devín fortress against direct Avar attack from Pannonia. Thus, Devín had for the Slavic ruler a more suitable location than the alternative Carnuntum or another place on the open plain south of the Danube. At the same time it was close to restless Pannonia, and from it Samo could promptly intervene into the relations of the khaganate.[71] Evidently, it was here that Dagobert's emis-

---

68 Ann. reg. Franc. ad a. 805, rec. Kurze, pp. 119–120. *MMFH I*, p. 23.
69 Vojtěch Ondrouch, *Limes Romanus na Slovensku* (Bratislava 1938), pp. 25–26. Ján Dekan, "Výskum na Devíne v roku 1950," *Archeologické rozhledy* 3 (1951), pp. 167–168. Veronika Plachá – Karol Pieta, "Römerzeitliche Besiedlung von Bratislava – Devín," *Archeologické rozhledy* 38 (1986), no. 4, pp. 339–357. Veronika Plachá – Jana Hlavicová – Igor Keller, *Slovanský Devín* (Bratislava 1990), pp. 16–17, 85–88. Štefanovičová et al., *Najstaršie dejiny Bratislavy*, pg. 242–250.
70 Keller – Bierbrauer, "Beiträge," pp. 377–380, 393.
71 Matúš Kučera has already pointed out the great importance of the Bratislava gate for Samo's realm. Matúš Kučera, "Problémy vzniku a vývoja feudalizmu na Slovensku," *Historický časopis* 22 (1974), no. 4, pp. 554–556. Matúš Kučera, "Typológia včasnostredovekého štátu na strednom Dunaji," *Československý časopis historický* 27 (1979), no. 6, pp. 870–874. Matúš Kučera, *Postavy veľkomoravskej histórie* (Martin 1986), pp. 37–40, 49–50. He

sary Sicharius looked for Samo, and from where he also had to ignominiously depart. Dagobert's Austrasians wanted to come there in 631, join with the Alamans and Longobards, and enclose the Devín fortress, just as the eastern Frankish King Louis the German managed to do later, in August of 864.

Samo, however, could not remain in only one place. In order to maintain control over his people and territory, he had to move around all the tribal principalities and for shorter or longer periods of time settle in their centres. We can look for one of them in Nitra, another somewhere in Moravia as well as in the former Rugiland. He also had to stay for at least some time on the margins of the realm, where it was necessary to withstand the pressure of the Avars and Franks.

8 Wogastisburg

At the point where the Enns River enters into the Danube stood two Roman fortresses. On the western, that is the Bavarian side, stood Lorch (Roman Lauriacum), which was a Bavarian border fortress until 791.[72] On the eastern

> rightfully looks here for Samo's main seat, which, however, he incorrectly identifies with Wogastisburg. Archaeological findings, more exactly burial sites from the side surroundings of Bratislava and weapons of western origin to which he emphatically refers, only date to the time after the end of Samo's realm. Only a smaller portion of the graves from the burial sites in Devínská Nová Ves may come from the period of Samo. Erwin Keller – Volker Bierbrauer, "Beiträge zum awarenzeitlichen Gräberfeld von Devínska Nová Ves," *Slovenská archeológia* 13 (1965), no. 2, pp. 377–380, 393. Jozef Zábojník, "K výskytu predmetov západného pôvodu na pohrebiskách z obdobia avarskej ríše v Dunajskej kotline," *Slovenská archeológia* 26 (1978), no. 1, pp. 193–214. Jozef Zábojník, "Soziale Problematik der Gräberfelder des nördlichen und nordwestlichen Randgebietes des Awarischen Kaganats," *Slovenská archeológia* 43 (1995), no. 2, pp. 205–344. Jozef Zábojník, *Slovensko a Avarský kaganát* (Bratislava 2004), pp. 78–84. Kučera's far-reaching derivations from the oldest known record of the name of Bratislava Castle *Brezalauspurc*, primarily from the ending -*purc* that is burg, which he considers as a merchant settlement, or a *burgus*, are also mistaken. Kučera, "Typológia," pp. 874–881. Kučera, *Postavy*, pp. 41–45. Burg in the 7th century was a castle. Marie Bláhová, "Terminologie sídlišť v pramenech doby merovejské. Exkurs: Několik poznámek k problematice Fredegarova castrum Wogastisburc," *Z pomocných věd historických IV, Acta Universitatis Carolinae, Philologica et Historica* 5 (1980), pp. 39–44. Bratislava in the period of Samo could have been sought out by merchants; however, the suffix -*purc* in the later records of the castle name is not proof of this.

72   *Ann. reg. Franc.* ad a. 791, rec. Kurze, pp. 86–89. Hardt, "Die Donau," pp. 111–112. In 696 Salzburg Bishop Rupert floated down the Danube and pulled up at Lorch. He went no further and then returned to Salzburg. *Gesta sancti Hrodberti confessoris* 5, edidit W. Levison. Monumenta Germaniae historica, Scriptores rerum Merovingicarum Tomus VI. Passiones vitaeque sanctorum aevi Merovingici, ediderunt B. Krusch et W. Levison (Hannoverae

side, in today's Albing (near the small town of Sankt Pantaleon), stood another Roman fortress whose name has not been preserved.[73] In addition to the Danube Road, it also guarded the opposite valley of the Aist River, along which the road north to Bohemia led.[74] If the road to the valley of the Aist River, which in the 9th century was still known as *Agasta*,[75] emerged directly from the former Roman fortress standing in today's Albing, directly opposite the mouth of the Aist, then the fortress would have taken its name from this river.

And other Roman fortresses standing on the south bank of the Danube bore the names of rivers that flowed into the Danube from the north. Castra Regina (Regensburg, *Reganesburg*) stood on the south bank of the Danube and took its name from the Reganus River (Regen), which flowed into the Danube from the north directly opposite the fortress.[76] Near the confluence of the Inn (Aenus) with the Danube stood the fortresses Boiodurum and Batavis (Passau). However, the Romans didn't name either of them after the Inn River. They named Boiodurum after the Boioduria River, identified with the Ilz River, which flows from the former Boiohaema and into the Danube opposite Passau, Germany. A road emerged here, called the Golden Road in medieval times, which went across the Danube, through the valley of the Ilz River and its outflow into the Ohe through the Bohemian Forest (Šumava) and into Bohemia.[77] Esztergom, lying on the south bank of the Danube, got the German name Gran

---

et Lipsiae 1913), p. 159. In 713 or 714 the Avars crossed the Enns and devastated Bavarian Lorch. Pohl, *Die Awaren*, p. 284.

73 The Romans built this fortress in the period of the Marcomannic Wars. Its stone walls, 1.80 metres thick and reinforced towers, enclosed a rectangle of 568 × 412 metres. It was the seat of a legion (legio II Italica). We do not know its antique name. The fortress was originally endangered, because under the rule of emperor Commodus (180–192) or Septimius Severus (193–211) the legionnaires abandoned it and departed to neighbouring Lauriacum. The late-Roman bricks testify that the fortress was again revived under the rule of Valentinian I (364–375). *Tabula Imperii Romani. Castra Regina, Vindobona, Carnuntum, M – 33*, připravili Pavel Oliva, Jan Burian, Zdenka Nemeškalová-Jiroudková, Jan Tejral (Praha 1986), p. 75. Genser, *Der österreichische Donaulimes*, pp. 165–179.

74 Dobiáš, *Dějiny*, pp. 144, 220, 325, 326.

75 *infra duo flumina, id est inter Agastam et Narinam, a locis videlicet ubi ipsa in Danubium fluunt, usque ad loca, ubi de venis in amnes dirivantur, et ita usque in Nortuualt in hanc partem silve sine termini conclusione ... et circa Agasta*. MMFH III, Diplomata 22, pp. 42–43. In Bulgaria is the Ogosta River, which flows into the Danube between Kozloduy and Oryahovo.

76 *Tabula Imperii Romani, M – 33*, ed. Oliva, Burian, Nemeškalová – Jiroutková, Tejral, pp. 33–34. Dobiáš, *Dějiny*, p. 326.

77 *Tabula Imperii Romani, M – 33*, ed. Oliva, Burian, Nemeškalová – Jiroutková, Tejral, pp. 25, 27–28. Dobiáš, *Dějiny*, pp. 326–327. František Kubů – Petr Zavřel, "Terénní průzkum starých komunikací na příkladu Zlaté stezky," *Archaeologia historica* 23 (1998), pp. 35–57. The Boioduria River, that is the Duria river of the Boii, recalls with its name another

from the River Hron (Gran), which flowed into the Danube from the north.[78] Roads emerged from the mentioned fortresses which headed into the valleys of the opposite side. Therefore, they took their names according to these rivers and not according to the rivers on which they lay.

The Agasta fortress, which a Frankish chronicler recorded as *Wogastisburc*, became a Slavic border castle, which protected the primary western entry point into Samo's realm.[79] Wogastisburg was a former Roman fortress which stood on the eastern bank of the Enns River, flowing into the Danube. The name of Samo's castle had a Germanic form, which could have been given only by the neighbouring Bavarians. It stood near Bavaria or directly by its eastern border, which was formed by the lower arm of the Enns River. It thus stood on the western edge of Samo's realm and guarded the road which led down the Danube to its interior.

Wogastisburg is testimony to the fact that Samo's realm had castles which were in no way different than the castles Samo knew in the Frankish kingdom. These were former Roman fortresses (Wogastisburg, Devín) or wooden

---

river, the Duria, probably identical with the Váh. *G. Plinii Secundi Naturalis historia* IV 80. *Slovensko na úsvite dejín*, ed. Škoviera, pp. 18–19.

78 György Györffy, *Az Árpád-kori Magyarország törtéteti földrajza II* (Budapest 1987), pp. 237–250. Mainz (Mogontiacum), which lay on the left bank of the Rhine, was named after the Main River (Moenus), which entered the Rhine on the opposite bank.

79 Vincent Sedlák convincingly showed that Wogastisburg got its name according to the river *Agasta*, that is it stood *in its immediate vicinity*. He correctly emphasized that *it is not necessary to consider Wogastisburg as a Slavic castle built by the Slavs, only as a castle used by Slavs*. He was unable to find its exact position, however. Vincent Sedlák, "Historicko-spoločenský vývin Slovanov v dunajsko-karpatskej oblasti (so zreteľom na predkov Slovákov)," *Slavica Slovaca* 27 (1992), no. 2, pp. 180–181. We don't know of any fortress on the northern side of the Danube where the Aist discharges into the Danube which could be the sought-after Wogastisburg. Aist Castle (Alt Aist), mentioned in years 1161 and 1170 as *castrum Agist*, is too new and stuck in the mountains north of Mauthausen. Thus, it could not be the sought for Wogastisburg. *Urkundenbuch des Landes ob der Enns I*, herausgegeben vom Verwaltungs-Ausschuss des Museums Francisco-Carolinum zu Linz (Wien 1853), n. 234, p. 343. Karl Lechner, *Die Babenberger. Markgrafen und Herzoge von Österreich 976–1246* (Wien – Köln – Weimar 1992), pp. 263, 396. Sedlák, "Historicko-spoločenský vývin," p. 181. If Wogastisburg stood on the road of the approaching Dagobert's army, then it guarded an old Roman road which runs along the south bank of the Danube. It therefore had to stand on the south bank, like neighbouring Lorch. Peter Bystrický allows that Wogastisburg could lie not only on the Danube opposite the outflow of the Aist River, but also in northern Bavaria, in the Frankenwald region. Bystrický, "Samova ríša," pp. 258–259. Václav Vaněček has also looked for Wogastisburg in this area. Václav Vaněček, "Souvislost Velké Moravy se slovanským svazem Sámovým? (Ke vzniku státu na Moravě)," *Právněhistorické studie* 9 (1963), pp. 217–218. Herwig Wolfram looks for Wogastisburg in the vicinity of Cheb and the centre of Samo's realm in Bohemia. *Conversio*, ed. Wolfram, p. 116.

castles with a palisade rampart. Samo, too, could have had a *castle fortified with beams*, as was built by his contemporary, Thuringian Prince Radulf.[80] And certainly not just one. Indeed, Samo's realm was much larger than Radulf's little Thuringia. If Wogastisburg guarded the Danube Road and the main entry point from the Frankish kingdom to Samo's realm, then the Danubian entrance to Avar Pannonia must have had similar defence. On the bank of the Danube, which (from the mouth of the Rába up to the bend near Vác) separated Samo's realm from that of the Avars, there was no place more important than the border castle focused against the khaganate, the destroyed Avar bridgehead in Komárno, which controlled not only the important river crossing but also the shortest comfortable road north to Nitra.[81]

9 The Nibelung Road

In 631 Frankish King Dagobert assembled a large Austrasia army in the centre of Austrasia, in Metz[82] and sent it to the east against Samo's realm. If Dagobert's Austrasians were headed east, to the centre of Samo's realm, they set off towards the middle Rhine, which they crossed near Worms. They could get from Metz to Worms through Saarbrücken and Kaiserlautern.[83] If the Austrasians passed through Worms, then they went by road to Pförring, where there was a ferry over the Danube.[84] From there they continued to Regensburg and further to Platting or straight from Pförring to Platting. The road from Worms to Pförring was for the most part an old Roman road, which linked the Roman

---

80 *castrum lignis monitum in quodam montem. Chronicarum quae dicuntur Fredegarii Scholastici* IV 87, ed. Krusch, pp. 164–165. *MMFH I*, p. 8.

81 Ján Dekan, "K problémom slovanského osídlenia na Slovensku," *Historica Slovaca* VI–VII (1948–1949), p. 62.

82 Metz was a centre of Austrasia. Dagobert's son Sigibert, who in 633 became the Austrasian king, was based in Metz. In 641 the entire Austrasian military assembled there. *Chronicarum quae dicuntur Fredegarii Scholastici* IV 75, 87, ed. Krusch, pp. 158–159, 164–165. *MMFH I*, pp. 7–8. Metz was a great favourite of Dagobert. Metz bishop Arnulf was his favourite advisor. *Chronicarum quae dicuntur Fredegarii Scholastici* IV 58, ed. Krusch, pp. 149–150. *MMFH I*, p. 3.

83 Karl Weller, "Die Nibelungenstrasse," *Zeitschrift für deutsches Altertum und deutsche Literatur* 70 (1933), pp. 52, 54–55.

84 From Worms the road went to Ladenburg, Wimpfen, Ohringen and after Westernach it divided. The southern branch went through Ellwangen and the northern through Crailsheim and Weissenburg. Both branches joined in Kösching and the road continued to Pförring, where it crossed over the Danube. Weller, "Die Nibelungenstrasse," pp. 52–54. The ferry across the Danube at Pförring and near Mehring is mentioned in "The Song of the Nibelungs".

fortresses on the Upper German limes, which ran along the Neckar and Altmühl rivers.[85] From Pförring the road went along the south bank of the Danube all the way to Pannonia.

The road from Worms to Pförring and further along the south bank of the Danube to Pannonia was the Nibelung Road.[86] In 406 the Vandals, Suebs and Alans moved along this road, and on 31 December 406 they crossed the frozen Rhine, ravaged Worms and burst into Gaul.[87] The Huns passed along this road to Worms in 436 against the Burgundy Kingdom.[88] In 451 Attila passed along it through Passau to the Rhine, though he did not cross the Rhine at Worms or even Mainz, but in Koblenz, and on 7 April 451 he conquered Metz. He then encircled Orléans, which he lay siege to until 14 June.[89]

At the beginning of 791 Charlemagne left Worms and set off for Regensburg. If he departed Worms for Regensburg, then he undoubtedly came along the mentioned Nibelung Road. Charlemagne and his Franks joined the Bavarians in Regensburg, and together they moved on to the border area of Lorch, where they awaited the Saxons and Frisians, who were led by Count Theodorich and his highest chamberlain Meginfred. The Saxons and Frisians assembled somewhere in Saxony or Thuringia, passed through Sorb territory, crossed the Nakléřovský Pass and travelled through the whole of Bohemia. Along the road other Slavic tribes joined them,[90] probably Sorbs and Bohemians.[91] In order to get to Lorch, where Charlemagne awaited them, they had to go up the Vltava and Malše rivers, cross the Bohemian border and then move down the Aist River to descend to the Danube.[92] However, they did not enter Lorch,

---

85 Weller, "Die Nibelungenstrasse," pp. 52–58. Reinhard Wolters, Římané v Germánii (Praha 2002), pp. 74–76.
86 Weller, "Die Nibelungenstrasse," pp. 49–66.
87 Weller, "Die Nibelungenstrasse," p. 57. Jerzy Strzelczyk, Wandalowie i ich afrikańskie państwo (Warszawa 1992), pp. 65, 83–86.
88 In 413 Burgundy became foederati of the Romans, and they received from them a seat on the left-hand bank of the Rhine with a centre in Worms. Strassburg, Mainz and Speyer also belonged to them. Weller, "Die Nibelungenstrasse," pp. 57–58. Achim Leube, "Die Burgunden bis zum Untergang ihres Reiches an der oberen Rhône im Jahre 534," in Die Germanen 2, ausgearbeitet unter Leitung von Bruno Krüger, pp. 373–376.
89 Weller, "Die Nibelungenstrasse," p. 58. Dobiáš, Dějiny, p. 314, note 28.
90 Annales Alamanici ad a. 790, MMFH I, pp. 14–15.
91 Třeštík, Vznik, pp. 61–63.
92 Hartmut Hoffmann has already anticipated the march of the Saxons and Frisians through Bohemia directly to Lorch. Hartmut Hoffmann, Böhmen und das deutsche Reich im hohen Mittelalter, Jahrbuch für Geschichte Mittel- und Ostdeutschlands 18, 1969, p. 4. Even in the early Roman period and then in medieval times a road led from the confluence of the Enns with the Danube through the valley of the Aist River to the north into Bohemia. Dobiáš, Dějiny, pp. 144, 220, 325, 326. Josef Vítěslav Šimák, Pronikání Němců do

but remained on the north bank of the river.[93] On 20 August the royal court at which Meginfred testified sat in the military camp at Lorch.[94] Charlemagne's army soon after crossed the border near the mouth of the Enns and headed for the interior of the khaganate, the Franks on the southern bank of the Danube and the Saxons and Frisians on the northern bank. Bavarian boats floated down river. When they reached the mouth of the Rába into the Danube, Charlemagne *decided that he would return through Sabaria* [today Szombathely, Hungary]. *He commanded the other military units, at whose head he placed Theodoric and Meginfred, to return via the Bohemia* (per Beehaimos) *by the road along which they came.* Charlemagne *headed back to Bavaria with his untouched Frankish army. The Saxons and Frisians returned home with Theodorich and Meginfred through Bohemia, as they were ordered.*[95]

In 803 emperor Charlemagne and his army set off for Regensburg. The emperor with a smaller escort *headed to Bavaria, going ... through the Hircanum Forest ... he left the other armies to move over the open roads* (per apertiores vias).[96] The Hircanian Forest, that is the Fichtel Mountains, could only be reached by travelling up the valley of the Main River along the Royal Road. This road began in Metz and headed through Trier to Mainz, where it crossed

---

Čech kolonisací ve 13. a 14. století (Praha 1938), pp. 558–559. Dušan Třeštík doubts that this road would have been suitable for an army in 791. Třeštík, *Vznik*, pp. 59–60, 233, note 38. The road from southern Bohemia directly to the mouth of the Enns perhaps was unsuitable for a large army, but for a smaller army, which the Saxons and Frisians sent in 791, it could have been sufficient, however.

93 According to Dušan Třeštík, they turned through Gmünd pass to the valley of the Kamp River, and at the mouth of the Kamp they reached the north bank of the Danube. They didn't come to Lorch. Only Meginfrid, one of its two leaders, was to be in Lorch in order to decide on the next step. Třeštík, *Vznik*, pp. 57–63. If Charlemagne *then proceeded along the south bank of the Danube; the Saxons, however, moved in a similar way together with some Franks and the largest part of the Frisians along the north side of the Danube until they reached the place where the forementioned Avars had prepared fortifications; thus, on the south side of the Danube near Comagenan Mount (ad Cumeoberg), that is from the other bank at the place which is called Kamp (Camp) and where the river which flows into the Danube there is so named*, then all the armies made the journey down the Danube from Lorch up to the Avar fortress together. They could not, therefore, have met only after the mouth of the Kamp River, where the first Avar fortress was located. *Ann. reg. Franc.* ad a. 791, rec. Kurze, pp. 88–89. *MMFH I*, pp. 19, 20–21. Charlemagne's Franks joined with the Bavarians in Regensburg and the Saxons and Frisians joined with them near Lorch.

94 *Die Traditionen des Hochstiftes Freising, Band I*, herausgegeben von Theodor Bitterauf. Quellen und Erörterungen zur bayerischen Geschichte, Neue Folge 4 (München 1908), no. 142, pp. 146–147, n. 143a, pp. 147–148.

95 *Ann. reg. Franc.* ad a. 791, rec. Kurze, pp. 86–91. *MMFH I*, pp. 19, 20–21. Wolfram, *Österreichische Geschichte 378–907*, pp. 155–156, 235–236. Třeštík, *Vznik*, pp. 57–61.

96 *Annales Mettenses priores* ad a. 803, *MMFH I*, p. 34.

the Rhine and continued to the valley of the Main to Frankfurt, Würzburg and Forchheim, and from there through the Fichtel Mountains to the valley of the Ohře River up to the centre of Bohemia.[97] The emperor stopped in the Fichtel Mountains, where he arranged a hunt. He then turned off towards Regensburg, where he met with his army. While Charlemagne remained in Bavaria, his army headed down the Danube to Pannonia. When it returned, the emperor stood at its front in Regensburg and *passed through Alamania and through the town of Worms, in winter he came to the royal seat in Aachen*.[98] If Charlemagne's army passed *through Alamania and through the town of Worms*, then it marched along the Nibelung Road. If it marched *along more open roads*, as was the Royal Road in the valley of the Main, then the Nibelung Road was more suitable for the march of the large army than the Royal Road.

In 805 Charlemagne sent three armies *to the country of the Slavs which is called Bohemia*. One of them was led by Charlemagne's son Charles. The emperor *ordered* (him) *to head to the east of the land of the Franks or Germans in order to penetrate the Hircanian Forest (Hircano saltu) and attack the already mentioned Slavs*.[99] If Charles went through East Francia and then through the Fichtel Mountains and penetrated into Bohemia, then he went along the mentioned Royal Road.[100] Several other roads split off from the Royal Road in the valley of the Main. From Frankfurt the road headed north-east through Fulda to Thuringia, to Erfurt,[101] from Würzburg there was a shorter turnoff to Hallstadt and from Forchheim a side road went south-east through Premberg (Pfreimt) to Regensburg. Erfurt, Hallstadt, Forchheim, Premberg and Regensburg lay there where these roads drew near to the eastern border of Charlemagne's kingdom. Royal emissaries were seated in them whom Charlemagne directed to watch over merchants, so that they did not bring any weapons and armour over the border.[102]

---

97 Josef Bubeník, "K raně středověkému osídlení severozápadních Čech, jeho strukturám a centrům," *Studia mediaevalia Pragensia* 1 (1988), p. 55. Michal Lutovský – Naďa Profantová, *Sámova říše* (Praha 1995), p. 80.
98 *Annales Mettenses priores* ad a. 803, MMFH I, p. 34.
99 *Annales Mettenses priores* ad a. 805, MMFH I, p. 35.
100 Třeštík, *Vznik*, pp. 71–80, 84–85.
101 Labuda, *Pierwsze państwo*, p. 279.
102 *Capitulare missorum* VII, MMFH IV, pp. 23–24. Matthias Hardt, "Die Donau als Verkehrs- und Kommunikationsweg zwischen der ostfränkischen Residenz Regensburg und den Zentren an der mittleren Donau im 9. Jahrhundert," in *Flüsse und Flusstäler als Wirtschafts- und Kommunikationswege*, ed. Stephan Freund, Mathias Hardt, Petra Wiegel (Bonn 2007), pp. 110–111. The merchants who travelled to the Slavs through Forchheim, Premberg and Regensburg were under the watch (either personally or with the help of his people) of Nordgau Count and Bavarian Prefect Audulf (799–818). Steinhübel, *Kapitoly*,

The Nibelung Road was used for military purposes more frequently than the Royal Road. The armies of emperor Louis the Pious and his sons, who battled one another for power, passed along the road from Worms to the Danube and back several times from 838–841.[103] The Crusaders also passed along the road from the Rhine to Regensburg and from there down the Danube. The Crusades that passed through Germany in 1096 departed from Cologne. They first set off up the Rhine and then turned off to Regensburg. Most of them got to Regensburg via the Nibelung Road, while some went through the valley of the Main.[104]

In 1146 construction of a stone bridge was completed in Regensburg. The Danube crossing at Pförring thus lost importance at that time, as did the road from Worms through Ladenburg, Wimpfen, Ohringen and Pförring to the Danube. More popular was the road that went from Worms to the valley of the Main, through Miltenberg and Würzburg, where it turned off for Nuremberg and from there to Regensburg.[105] French King Louis VII, who in June 1147 assembled an army of Crusaders in Metz, set off for Regensburg by this then new road. By the end of June he crossed the Rhine at Worms, entered the Main Valley, passed through Würzburg and descended to the Danube, which he crossed on the new Regensburg bridge. In Regensburg, German Crusaders joined with him under the leadership of German King Conrad III. They then marched together down the Danube to Hungary, the Balkans and further to Damascus.[106]

If the army which Dagobert assembled in 631 was made up of Austrasians, then its starting point had to be Metz. If the Nibelung Road was then more suitable for the march of a large army than the Royal Road, then Dagobert's army crossed the Rhine at Worms and moved east along the Nibelung Road. If the Austrasian army was headed for the centre of Samo's realm, then Samo had to protect the main western entry point to his kingdom, which was on the Danube. He could not send his army to Bohemia and leave his own kingdom

---

p. 75, note 314, 315. So that Audulf could have the merchants under his care in all three towns, Forchheim, Premberg and Regensburg (and thus also the valley of the Main with the Danube) must have been linked by a road.

103 Weller, "Die Nibelungenstrasse," pp. 61–62.
104 Steven Runciman, *Dzieje wypraw krzyżowych 1* (Warszawa 1997), pp. 119–137, 140 [Original *A History of the Crusades. Vol. I. The First Crusade* (Cambridge 1951)]. Only Folkmar's army passed through Bohemia and came to Nitra, where it was massacred by the Hungarians. Runciman, *Dzieje wypraw krzyżowych 1*, pp. 130, 133.
105 Weller, "Die Nibelungenstrasse," pp. 63–64.
106 Weller, "Die Nibelungenstrasse," p. 64. Steven Runciman, *Dzieje wypraw krzyżowych 2* (Warszawa 1997), pp. 234–236, 253 [Original *A History of the Crusades, Vol 2. The Kingdom of Jerusalem and the Frankish East* (Cambridge 1952)].

unprotected at many more important places. That's why we cannot search for Wogastisburg in Bohemia.[107] Therefore, Dagobert's army could not after crossing the Rhine have marched along the Royal Road to Bohemia.

Dagobert's Austrasians marched the same road as Charlemagne's Franks in 791 and 803, that is along the Nibelung Road. They crossed the Rhine in Worms, and they passed along this road to Pförring, where they crossed the Danube and could enter into do Regensburg. They then passed down the south bank of the Danube up to Wogastisburg Castle (*ad castro Wogastisburc*).[108] If Samo placed the crucial part of his army at Wogastisburg and Dagobert hurled his strongest army at it, then Wogastisburg guarded the primary entry from the Frankish kingdom into Samo's realm.[109] And this was on the old Roman road that ran along the south bank of the Danube. Since Bavaria recognized Frankish domination, the eastern edge of the Frankish kingdom was at the eastern border of Bavaria, that is at Enns.

10 Austrasians, Alamanni and Longobards

Simultaneously with Dagobert's Austrasians, the Alamans and Longobards also marched against Samo's realm. If the *Slavs at these and other places prepared for this*, then they expected attacks from several sides. Thus, the Austrasians,

---

[107] Several archaeologists and historians look for (with a varying dose of care) Wogastisburg on the hill Rubín near the Ohře River. Josef Bubeník, "K opevnění vrchu Rubína u Podbořan (osada Dolánky, obec Podbořany, okres Louny) v době hradištní," *Archeologické rozhledy* 47 (1995), pp. 128–151. Josef Bubeník, "Die Besiedlung des südöstlichen Vorfeldes des Berges Rubin in der Burgwallzeit und ihre Chronologie. Ausgrabung in den Jahren 1984–1991," *Památky archeologické* 88 (1997), pp. 56–106. Josef Bubeník, "Hradiště Rubín u Podbořan v severozápadních Čechách v raném středověku," in *Na prahu poznání českých dějin. Sborník prací k poctě Jiřího Slámy. Studia mediaevalia Pragensia* 7 (2006), pp. 21–37. Lutovský – Profantová, *Sámova říše*, pp. 60, 75–83. Jiří Sláma, "K problému historické interpretace archeologických výzkumů staroslovanských hradišť v Čechách," *Archeologie ve středních Čechách* 5 (2001), svazek 2, pp. 533–535. Zdeněk Měřínský, *České země od příchodu Slovanů po Velkou Moravu I* (Praha 2002), pp. 208–215. Třeštík, *Vznik*, pp. 29–30. If the core of Samo's realm was where later the core of Mojmír's Great Moravian state was located, and if none of the many eastern Frankish campaigns which (at the start of 846) attacked the Moravians did not pass through Bohemia (and not even at a time when the Bohemians belonged to Great Moravia in the time of Svätopluk's rule), then not even the Frankish army, which attacked Samo's realm and focused on its centre, passed through Bohemia. All went down the Danube.

[108] *Chronicarum quae dicuntur Fredegarii Scholastici* IV 68, ed. Krusch, p. 155. *MMFH I*, p. 5.

[109] Wogastisburg was a border castle of Samo's realm. Labuda, *Pierwsze państwo słowiańskie*, pp. 125–126. Lutovský – Profantová, *Sámova říše*, p. 79.

Alamanni and Longobards each attacked a different part of Samo's realm individually.[110]

The Alamans, who were based on the upper Rhine and upper Danube, certainly marched down the Danube. From Regensburg up to the border town of Lorch they came along the same road as the Austrasians. The Austrasians took over care of adjacent Wogastisburg, which was full of Slavic soldiers, and the Alamanni headed to the interior of Samo's realm.

If Samo was expecting an attack from several sides, then the Longobards invaded Samo's realm at a completely different place than Dagobert's Austrasians and Chrodobert's Alamanni. Therefore, they could not have passed through the Bavarian Alps and joined Dagobert's army by the Danube and then take the same route as it did. And they could not have gone even along the Amber Road through Pannonia, because this belonged to the Avar Khaganate. The Longobards thus selected the shortest road. They went from Friuli through Carantania and from there, through Semmering, got into the valley of the Leitha and could reach the Danube near Carnuntum.[111] They struck the south-eastern end of Samo's realm, into the Viennese Basin, where they *triumphed* and also *led away with them a very large number of Slavic captives*. If the Longobard army could freely pass through Carantania, then Carantanian Prince Valuk was an ally of Longobard King Arioald.[112]

The Austrasians wanted, in the case of victory, to march to the interior of Samo's realm. Since they were the main military force, they went the main direction, that is down the Danube and directly to the centre of Samo's realm, where they wanted, together with the Alamanni and Longobards, to encircle Samo. Dagobert's Austrasian army, marching down the Danube, entered into Lorch, the easternmost fortress of Dagobert's kingdom. It then crossed the Enns and circumvented neighbouring Wogastisburg, which stood in its path. There *they fortified against very numerous brigades of Vinidi* within its old Roman walls.

---

110 Lutovský – Profantová, *Sámova říše*, p. 79.
111 The road which led from Longobard Friuli through Carinthia, left Carinthia in Semmering. Peter Csendes, *Die Strassen Niederösterreichs im Früh- und Hochmittelalter*. Dissertationen der Universität Wien 33 (Wien 1969), pp. 242–244. Michael McCormick, *Narodziny Europy. Korzenie gospodarki europejskiej 300–900* (Warszawa 2007), p. 359 [Original *Origins of the European Economy. Communications and Commerce AD 300-900* (Cambridge 2001)].
112 *Chronicarum quae dicuntur Fredegarii Scholastici* IV 68, ed. Krusch, p. 155. MMFH I, pp. 4–5. Harald Krahwinkler, *Friaul im Frühmittelalter. Geschichte einer Region vom Ende des fünften bis zum Ende des zehnten Jahrhunderts* (Wien – Köln – Weimar 1992), pp. 45–46, 49–50. Wolfram, *Salzburg, Bayern, Österreich*, pp. 43–44, 50–51.

If the Alamanni divided and did not come together with Dagobert's main army against Wogastisburg, then Samo was not in this fortress; otherwise they would have enclosed him with their combined forces. Samo was not with his army concentrated in Wogastisburg, the same as Dagobert did not go at the head of his Austrasians. In the opposite case, the Frankish chronicler would have clearly noted their presence at the head of battling armies, just as he mentioned Prince Chrodobert at the head of the Alamannian army. After all, the chronicler could not mention only a lower leader and then leave out the highest, if the highest had been present in the army.

After three days of battle near Wogastisburg, the Austrasians suffered an overwhelming defeat and headed home in shame. After the defeat of the Austrasians, Chrodobert's Alamannian army had to stop its march to the interior of Samo's realm. Although *they achieved victory in the country to which they came*, it had to rapidly pull back. And the Longobards, although *they triumphed*, ultimately had to withdraw. Samo's Slavs then forayed several times through the territory of their Bohemian allies up to faraway Thuringia.

Samo's attacks against the Thuringians and other parts of the Frankish kingdom helped the Sorbs. Sorb Prince Dervan, whose principality neighboured with the Bohemians and Thuringians, rid himself of his dependence on Dagobert and joined with Samo.[113]

11   The End of Samo's Realm

In 631 *great tension occurred in Pannonia*. A dispute over the new khagan flared up between the Avars and the Pannonian Bulgarians, more specifically the Bulgar Kutrigurs. First, they asked that the new khagan be an Avar, while the others wanted a Bulgarian. Since they didn't agree, a battle erupted. The Avars triumphed, and nine thousand Bulgarian men had to leave Pannonia with their families. Samo did not take advantage of the Bulgarian insurrection in Pannonia to attack the khaganate, and the expelled Bulgarians could not find a place to attack his realm. They had to fall back to Bavaria and then to Carantania.[114] Likewise, Samo could rely on his Avar neighbour. Therefore, he

---

113   Steinhübel, *Kapitoly*, pp. 34, 46, 48–49, 104.
114   See note 49. If Alciok set off to Bratislava, then he had to pass through Samo's realm. Samo was the first who could take in Alciok and his Bulgarians. However, he was at war with Dagobert; so, he did not want to also ruffle the Avars. Therefore, he could not offer Alciok a place of refuge and only allowed him to freely pass through his realm, obviously, up the Danube. Carinthian Prince Valuk, who ultimately leaned towards Alciok escaping from Bavaria, did not pay any heed to the Avars or Bavarians or even Samo. If Valuk

could force a split with Frankish King Dagobert to the point of open war and did not have to fear an unexpected Avar attack from the opposite side.

In 658 Samo died, and his realm collapsed soon after. The Slavs, who had been settled in Slovakia and maintained independence for two centuries, could have still lived with the neighbouring Avars in peace for several years after the collapse of Samo's realm. Avar power, however, grew uncontrollably in the last two decades of the 7th century, and all the principalities that had before then made up Samo's realm, as well as other Slavic principalities around the circumference of Avar Pannonia, felt it.

---

was subject to Samo, then in the case of Alciok he could not act completely the opposite as Samo. Thus, Valuk's principality did not belong to Samo's realm. If Valuk permitted the Longobard army to pass through Carinthia against Samo, then he was an ally of the Longobards.

CHAPTER 3

Avar Domination

1   The New Ascension of the Avar Khaganate

In the years 679–681 the Bulgarians came to the lower Danube. In a similar way as the Croatians in Dalmatia, the Bulgarians subjugated the Slavic tribe of *Seven lines*, settled in Lower Moesia and in Dobruja, and established a Bulgarian Khaganate there.[1] At the same time a new ascent of the Avar Khaganate began, accompanied by a change of material culture on its territory. The burying of unburned bodies and graves with horses and equipment expanded. The belts of men and horse tackle were decorated with cast bronze armour, very often gilded, more rarely silvered, sometimes wholly from silver. The pottery wheel and gently silted clay enabled the production of fine ceramics. The change of material culture occurred not only in Transdanubia, in the Tisza River region and in Transylvania, but also reached into today's Slavonia, Slovakia and Moravia,[2] which is testimony to the expansion of Avar power in the surrounding Slavic principalities.

---

1 Vasil Nikolov Zlatarski, *Istorija na bălgarskata dăržava prez srednite vekove I/1* (Sofija 1970), pp. 176–213. Avenarius, *Die Awaren*, pp. 176–178. Genoveva Cankova-Petkova, "L'état bulgare, les Slaves et Byzance," in *Rapports du IIIe Congrés International d'Archéologie Slave, Tome 2*, éditeur Bohuslav Chropovský (Bratislava 1980), pp. 73–77. Petăr Ch. Petrov, *Obrazuvane na bălgarskata dăržava* (Sofija 1981), pp. 179–285. Pohl, *Die Awaren*, pp. 277–282. Panajot Panajotov, *Srednovekovna bălgarska istorija* (Gabrovo 1992), pp. 37–40. Uwe Fiedler, "Die Slawen im Bulgarenreich und im Awarenkhaganat. Versuch eines Vergleichs," in *Ethnische und kulturelle Verhältnisse an der mittleren Donau vom 6. bis zum 11. Jahrhundert, Symposium, Nitra 6. bis 10. November 1994*, ed. Darina Bialeková, Jozef Zábojník (Bratislava 1996), pp. 195–214.

2 *Magyarország története. Elözmények és magyar történet 1242-ig I/1* (Budapest 1987), pp. 320, 325–336. Pohl, *Die Awaren*, pp. 282–292. Jozef Zábojník, "Soziale Problematik der Gräberfelder des nördlichen und nordwestlichen Randgebietes des Awarischen Kaganats," *Slovenská archeológia* 43 (1995), no. 2, pp. 205–344. Jozef Zábojník, "Materiálna kultúra nálezísk z obdobia Avarského kaganátu na Slovensku (Stav, možnosti a perspektívy štúdia)," in *Slovensko a európsky juhovýchod. Medzikultúrne vzťahy a kontexty. Zborník k životnému jubileu Tatiany Štefanovičovej*, ed. Alexander Avenarius – Zuzana Ševčíková (Bratislava 1999), pp. 189–222. Martin Odler, "Avarské sídliská v strednej Európe: problémová bilancia," *Studia mediævalia Pragensia* 11 (2012), pp. 17–96.

The Avar Khaganate was no longer a restless, nomadic realm. Settled agriculture became predominate in it.[3] The khagan shifted his seat from the steppes of the Tisza River region to among the settled agricultural population of Pannonia[4] and turned his attention to its surroundings. The Avars ceased going on large marauding raids and began to subjugate Slavic principalities around the edges of Pannonia.

2   Carniola and Savia

In 663 Longobard King Grimoald summoned the Avars against the insurgent Friulian Prince Lupo.[5] The Avars penetrated from Pannonia into Friuli undoubtedly along the Amber Road, which stretched through Carniola. In approximately 705, 720 and 737 Carniolan Slavs burst into Friuli and battled with Friulian princes Ferdulf and Pemmo. Friulian Prince Ratchis prepared a retort. In 738 he set off *to Carniola, homeland of the Slavs* (*in Carniolam, Sclavorum patriam*), where he ravaged and killed.[6] In 788 the Avars, certainly passing through Carniola, again and for the last time attacked the *March of Friuli*

---

3   Alexander Avenarius, "Stepné národy v Európe: charakter a vývoj avarskej spoločnosti," *Historický časopis* 36 (1988), no. 2, pp. 155–157.
4   In year 795 a great Avar hoard, *which Friuli Duke Erik, when he sacked the royal seat of the Huns, which is called the hrink, brought in this year to the king of Pannonia (de Pannonia)*. Annales regni Francorum (Annales qui dicuntur Einhardi) ad a. 796, rec. Kurze, p. 99, MMFH I, pp. 19–20. *But Friuli Duke Erik sent his people with Vojnomir's Slavs to Pannonia (in Pannonias), ransacked the hrink, the nation of the Avars ...... the treasure of previous kings gathered for many centuries and sent it to his lord, King Charlemagne at his palace in Aachen.* Annales regni Francorum (Annales Laurissenses maiores) ad a. 796, rec. Kurze, p. 98, MMFH I, pp. 21–22. Annales Mettenses priores ad a. 796, MMFH I, p. 33. *And Charles's son Pepin marched in 796 to Pannonia (in Pannoniam) and after the retreat of the Avar army beyond the Tisza, he utterly destroyed their ruling seat, which, as has been said, is called the hrink, among the Longobards, however, the campus, and captured almost all the property of the Huns.* Ann. reg. Franc. (Einhardi) ad a. 796, rec. Kurze, p. 99, MMFH I, p. 20. *The king ... sent his son Pepin, the king of Italy, with an army to Pannonia (in Pannonias) ... Pepin with his army settled in the hrink ... with joy he saw in the palace in Aachen his son Pepin returning from Pannonia (e Pannonia) and bringing the part of the treasure which remained.* Ann. reg. Franc. (Laurissenses maiores) ad a. 796, rec. Kurze, p. 98, 100, MMFH I, pp. 21–22.... *he says Pannonia, rid of all residents and the place in which the ruling settlement of the khaganate was located, is such a desert that there is no trace of human habitation in it.* Einhardi Vita Karoli Magni 13, MMFH II, pp. 21–22.
5   Pauli Historia Langobardorum V 19–21, ed. Bethmann, Waitz, pp. 151–152.
6   Pauli Historia Langobardorum VI 24, 45, 51, 52 ed. Bethmann, Waitz, pp. 172–173, 180, 182–183. Peter Štih, "Die Ostgrenze Italiens im Frühmittelalter," in *Grenze und Differenz im früher Mittelalter*, ed. Walter Pohl, Helmut Reimitz (Wien 2000), pp. 32–33.

(*marcam Foroiuliensem*).⁷ Carniola, which connected Pannonia with Italy, was an open country for the Avars. An advance fortress (*uualum*),⁸ had been built in Carniola, which was capable of stopping an enemy army approaching against the khaganate on the Amber Road and ensuring Avar domination over the Carniolans. The Carniolans were dependent on the khaganate; they had to tolerate a fortified Avar position on their land and hold their *patriam*, that is the tribal principality; however, they did have a significant measure of independence with it.

The Savian Principality, which was separated from the khaganate by the wetlands of the lower Drava River, recognized Avar domination. Cast bronze armour from local skeleton graves of Velika Gorica, Samatovci, Zagreb-Kruge, Osijek, Dalj, Brodski Drenovac, Sisak, Čadjavica and Brestovac are evidence of Avar domination.⁹ The princes of Savia recognized their dependence on the Avar khagan until year 797.¹⁰

3 Devín and Mikulčice, Komárno and Nitra

The Avars penetrated into the territory of what was formerly Samo's realm. First they crossed the lower Rába and took the territory up to the Vienna Woods. Avar burial sites in this part of Pannonia are numerous, but not even

7   *Ann. reg. Franc. (Einhardi)* ad a. 788, rec. Kurze, p. 83.
8   *Epistolae variorum Carolo Magno regnante scriptae*, edidit Ernst Dümmler, Monumenta Germaniae Historica, Epistolae IV (Berolini 1895), no. 20, p. 528. See chapter 4, note 15.
9   Viktor Hoffiller, "Starohrvatsko groblje u Velikoj Gorici," *Vjesnik Hrvatskoga arheološkoga društva nove serije sveska* 10 (1908–1909), pp. 120–134. Paul Reinecke, "Die archäologische Hinterlassenschaft der Awaren," *Germania* 12 (1928), pp. 94–98. Andreas Alföldi, "Zur historischen Bestimmung der Awarenfunde," *Eurasia septentrionalis antiqua* 9 (1934), pp. 285–307. Tibor Horváth, "Az üllői és kiskörösi avar temető," *Archaeologia Hungarica* 19 (1935), p. 79. Helmut Preidel, "Zur Frage des Aufenthaltes von Awaren in den Sudetenländern," *Südostdeutsche Forschungen* 4 (1939), p. 400. Nandor Fettich, "Der Fund von Čadjavica," *Vjesnik Hrvatskoga arheološkoga društva nova serije sveska* 22–23 (1941–1942), pp. 55–61. Jan Eisner, *Devínska Nová Ves. Slovanské pohřebiště* (Bratislava 1952), p. 225. *Historija naroda Jugoslavije I* (Zagreb 1953), pp. 180–181. Adela Horvat, "O Sisku u starohrvatsko doba na temelju pisanih izvora i arheoloških nalaza," *Starohrvatska prosvjeta* 3 (1954), no. 2, pp. 93–104. Ksenija Vinski-Gasparini – Slavenka Ercegović, "Ranosrednjovjekovno groblje u Brodskom Drenovcu," *Vjesnik Arheološkog muzeja u Zagrebu* 3 (1958), no. 1, pp. 129–161. Mirko Bulat, "Neki nalazi ranog srednjeg vijeka iz Osijeka," *Starohrvatska Prosvjeta* 3 (1968), no. 10, pp. 11–21. Zdenko Vinski, "O postojanju radionica nekita starohrvatskog doba u Sisku," *Vjesnik Arheološkog muzeja u Zagrebu* 3 (1970), no. 4, pp. 45–92. Marija Šmalcelj, "Privlaka – 'Gole njive' (opčina Vinkovci) – nekropola 7–9 stoljeca – sistematska iskopavanja," *Arheološki Pregled* 15 (1973), pp. 117–119. MT I/I, pp. 320 (map), 335.
10 See chapter 4, note 37.

the largest of them, uncovered in Simmering (Vienna – Csokorgasse, 705 uncovered graves, only 4 of them horse riders),[11] achieved the size of the burial sites which archaeologists uncovered in Devínská Nová Ves, and the number of horse rider graves isn't even close to being equal. At the same time or shortly after, Nitria (Nitraland) came next in line. Since it lay near the centre of Avar power, a great many of the mentioned burial sites remained on its territory. Then the Avars could go beyond the Vienna Woods and rule the eastern part of the former Noricum ripense up to the Enns River[12] and with it also the onetime Rugiland. The Avar fortress on the edge of the Vienna Woods controlled entry to Pannonia and the fortress over the Kamp River (near Krems, where long before them Rugian kings were based), ruled the former Rugiland (the southern part of the Lower Austrian Waldviertel and the south-western part of the Weinviertel), in the middle of which it lay.[13] Moravia also fell into dependence on the khaganate.

The Enns is mentioned as a border river as early as the end of the 7th century. In 696 Salzburg Bishop Rupert set off on a journey by boat down the Danube. He travelled to Lorch, which was located at the confluence of the Danube with the Enns. He went no further, but instead turned around and headed back to Salzburg.[14] In 713 or 714 the Avars crossed the Enns and ravaged Bavarian Lorch.[15] The completion of Rupert's journey in Lorch and the Avar attack over the Enns at the border town Lorch dates the mentioned ascent of Avar power to the period of 680s or 690s.

The western border of the Avar Khaganate was on the lower Enns, which divided it from Bavaria in the Alps of Lower Austria, at the ridge of the Fischbach Alps and on the Karawanks, beyond which lay Carantania, and in the Julian Alps, where it bordered with Friuli, which belonged to the Longobard Kingdom. This was therefore distant from the marginal Avar burial sites near the Vienna Woods, in the surroundings of Sabaria (Szombathely), on the Zala and Sava rivers. Not even the northern border of the Avar Khaganate could have been in

---

11   Jarmila Justová, *Dolnorakouské Podunají v raném středověku. Slovanská archeologie k jeho osídlení v 6.–11. století* (Praha 1990), pp. 53–66, 70–71, 76–79, 80–81, 84–91, 255.
12   In the 8th century the lower flow of the Enns was the border between the Avar Khaganate and Bavaria. In 791 Charlemagne lay out a military camp on its western bank, from where he marched against the Avars: *Ac sic inchoato itinere prima castra super Anesum posita sunt; nam is fluvius inter Baioariorum atque Hunorum terminos medius currens certus duorum regnorum limes habebatur. Ann. reg. Franc. (Einhardi)* ad a. 791, rec. Kurze, s. 89. *MMFH I*, pp. 18–19. Pohl, *Die Awaren*, pp. 308–312.
13   Charlemagne conquered both of these Avar fortresses in 791. *Ann. reg. Franc.* ad a. 791, rec. Kurze, pp. 88–89. *MMFH I*, pp. 19–21.
14   *Gesta sancti Hrodberti confessoris* 5, ed. Levison, p. 159.
15   Pohl, *Die Awaren*, p. 284.

the middle of the Danubian Lowland, where the northernmost skeletal burial sites with Avar material culture lay, as is assumed by archaeologists,[16] but it was further north, evidently somewhere in the Carpathians. Thus, the whole of Nitria and all of Moravia belonged to the Avar Khaganate, and likewise all of Savia and Carniola, as well as Carantania, which belonged to Bavaria after year 741 or 742.

After the fall of Samo's realm, the Avars ruled Devín and its surroundings, and Avar graves began to be added to the burial site in Devínska Nová Ves. All 94 horse rider graves in Devínska Nová Ves (nearly as many as in Komárno) are from the period after the arrival of the Avars.[17] To differentiate which of the examined 866 graves in Devínska Nová Ves and the 262 (only 3 of which are horse riders) in nearby Záhorská Bystrica[18] belonged to the Slavs and which to the Avars is impossible. Such a high number of graves with a large representation of horse riders is exceptional for the whole of Slavic territory in the north-western surrounding of the khaganate, which the Avars ruled after the disappearance of Samo's realm. In the middle of the village of Devín the grave of an Avar warrior with a sabre, an axe and two arrow shafts was uncovered. His belt was decorated with bronze armour of Merovingian origin, which has been dated to the last quarter of the 7th century. We do not know whether it was a lone grave or belonged to a larger burial site.[19]

---

16   Jozef Zábojník, "Das Awarische Kaganat und die Slawen an seiner nördlichen Peripherie (Probleme der archäologischen Abgrenzung)," *Slovenská archeológia* 47 (1998), no. 1, pp. 153–173. Jozef Zábojník, "Problematika včasného stredoveku na Slovensku," *Historický časopis* 58 (2010), no. 2, p. 224. Discoveries of skeletal horsemen graves with typical Avar equipment cannot be the only criterion for membership to the Avar Khaganate. To connect with one line the places of all the distant finds typical for a given culture and to thus determine the territorial range and borders of a kingdom which the bearers of this culture were able to create and rule over a long period is too simple and deceptive an opinion. If the Avar Khaganate by far exceeded the reach of Avar culture documented by archaeological finds to the west, then it equally could have also extended to the north and to other sides.

17   Erwin Keller – Volker Bierbrauer, "Beiträge zum awarenzeitlichen Gräberfeld von Devínska Nová Ves," *Slovenská archeológia* 13 (1965), no. 2, pp. 377–397. Vladimír Mináč, "O osídlení Bratislavskej brány v 7. a 8. storočí," *Zborník Slovenského národného múzea* 72 (1978), *História* 18, pp. 61–81. Štefanovičová et al., *Najstaršie dejiny Bratislavy*, pp. 280–292. *Pramene I/1*, ed. Bialeková, p. 31.

18   Ľudmila Kraskovská, *Slovansko-avarské pohrebisko pri Záhorskej Bystrici* (Bratislava 1972). *Pramene I/1*, ed. Bialeková, p. 40. Štefanovičová et al., *Najstaršie dejiny Bratislavy*, pg. 285, 290–291. Jozef Zábojník, *Slovensko a avarský kaganát* (Bratislava 2004), pp. 79–81, 83–84.

19   Štefanovičová et al., *Najstaršie dejiny Bratislavy*, pp. 286–287. Zábojník, *Soziale Problematik*, pp. 211, 288. Before then this grave was considered to be Longobard. Plachá – Hlavicová – Keller, *Slovanský Devín*, pp. 18–19, fig. 21, 22. Zábojník, *Slovensko a avarský kaganát*, p. 79.

The Moravians responded to the Avar occupation of Devín with the construction of a new fortress. They fortified one of the islands on the Morava River in Mikulčice. They dug into the firmly embedded gravel and placed four to five lines of thick oak posts closely together and thus built a perhaps 5-metre high palisade wall, which on the backside leaned against an earthen bulwark reinforced with a wooden construction. This castle, which could then be the seat of Moravian principalities, spread over an area of about 4-ha and on the north-west side had perhaps a large 3-ha ravelin fortified with a simple palisade. A settlement was located in the ravelin with irregular lines of log cabins and narrow streets.[20]

At the turn of the 7th to 8th century a hilltop settlement was established on Zelená Hora near Vyškov and also at Staré Zámky in Brno-Líšeň, both fortified with a palisade. A palisade also protected the settlement at Povel, near Olomouc, lying on a moderate hillock. Settlements in Uherské Hradiště (Ostrov svatého Jiří), in Staré Město (Na Valách) and in Pohansko near Břeclav could have had a palisade fortification in the second half of the 8th century.[21]

---

20 Josef Poulík, *Mikulčice. Sídlo a pevnost knížat velkomoravských* (Praha 1975), pp. 130–133, 137, tab. 26, 75, 76, 79. Josef Poulík, "Svědectví výzkumů a pramenů archeologických o Velké Moravě," in Josef Poulík – Bohuslav Chropovský et al., *Velká Morava a počátky československé státnosti* (Praha – Bratislava 1985), pp. 20, 37, 56. Klanica, *Počátky*, pp. 180–193. Zdeněk Klanica, "Zur Periodisierung vorgroßmährischer Funde aus Mikulčice," in *Studien zum Burgwall von Mikulčice, Band 1*, ed. Falko Daim, Lumír Poláček (Brno 1995), pp. 379–469. Rudolf Procházka, "Charakteristika opevňovacích konstrukcí předvelkomoravských a velkomoravských hradišť," in *Pravěké a slovanské osídlení Moravy. Sborník k 80. narozeninám Josefa Poulíka*, (Brno 1990), pp. 283–306.

21 Čeněk Staňa, "Diskusní příspěvky z Mezinárodního kongresu slovanské archeologie, Warszawa 1965," *Přehled výzkumů Archeologického ústavu ČSAV*, Brno 1966, 1967, pp. 60–64. Čeněk Staňa, "Velkomoravské hradiště Staré Zámky u Líšně. Stavebný vývoj," in *Monumentorum tutela-ochrana pamiatok* 8 (1972), pp. 112–114. Čeněk Staňa, "Pustiměřský hrad," *Archaeologia historica* 18 (1993), pp. 181–184. Čeněk Staňa, "Archäologische Erforschung mährischer Höhenburgwälle," in *Frühmittelalterliche Machtzentren in Mitteleuropa. Mährjährige Grabungen und ihre Auswertung*, ed. Čeněk Staňa, Lumír Poláček (Brno 1996), pp. 275–278. Pavel J. Michna – Miloslav Pojsl, *Románský palác na olomouckém hradě. Archeologie a památková obnova* (Brno 1988), pp. 22–23. Josef Bláha, "Předběžná zpráva o objevu předvelkomoravského ústředí v Olomouci," *Archaeologia historica* 13 (1988), pp. 165–168. Josef Bláha, "Topografie a otázka kontinuity raně středověkého ústředí v Olomouci," in *Přemyslovský stát kolem roku 1000. Na pamět' knížete Boleslava II. († 7. února 999)*, uspořádali Luboš Polanský, Jiří Sláma, Dušan Třeštík (Praha 2000), pp. 183–184. Josef Bláha, "Komunikace, topografie a importy ve středověku a raném novověku (7.–17. století) na území města Olomouce," *Archaeologia historica* 23 (1998), pp. 136–139. Josef Poulík, "K otázce vzniku předvelkomoravských hradišť," *Slovenská archeologia* 36 (1988), no. 1, pp. 189–216. Zdeněk Měřínský, "Die Zentren Großmährens," in *Velká Morava mezi východem a západem. Sborník příspěvků z mezinárodní vědecké konference Uherské*

In the 6th and 7th centuries several Slavic settlements were located on the territory of today's town of Nitra.[22] In the 8th century foreigners also arrived to Nitra from the west. Frankish weapons and items from the Merovingian Age were found in a disturbed burial site near the southern edge of Nitra-Dolné mesto: a sword, a spearhead, an arrowhead, a shield boss, a bronze belt buckle, glass beads from a necklace and three receptacles.[23] This indicates the presence of foreigners from the Frankish kingdom, who not only passed through Nitra but also lived and buried their dead there.

Nitra's castle hill with its steep rocky slopes, projecting upward in the centre of a lowland and protected on all sides by a river, was all but predetermined to be the seat of a principality. The palisade, traces of which archaeologists found on the edge of the western slope of the castle hill, is younger, however, than the palisade in Mikulčice or in Povel at Olomouc, or in Staré Zámky near Brno-Líšeň. Archaeologists place its origin at the turn of the 8th to the 9th century.[24]

Hradiště, Staré Město 28. 9.–1. 10. 1999, ed. Luděk Galuška, Pavel Kouřil, Zdeněk Měřínsky. *Spisy Archeologického ústavu AV ČR Brno* 17 (2001), pp. 297–298, 300–301.

22 Archaeologists examined the remains of a Slavic settlement from the 6th and 7th centuries at Mikov dvor in Dolné Krškany, in the barracks under Zobor Hill, near the Church of St. Stephen in Párovce, by the stadium not far from the Hotel Olympia in Chrenová and at Šindolka. At Biovet in Dolné Krškany a smaller burned burial site was found, and in the Mier plant in Dolné Krškany 53 skeletal graves were surveyed. Juraj Bárta, "Pohrebište zo staršej doby hradištnej v Dol. Krškanoch pri Nitre," *Archeologické rozhledy* 5 (1953), pp. 167–171, 190, 191. Bohuslav Chropovský, "Nálezy keramiky pražského typu v Nitre," *Sborník prací Filosofické fakulty Brněnské university* 20 (E 16), (Brno 1971), pp. 147–149. Bohuslav Chropovský – Gabriel Fusek, "Výsledky výskumov na stavenisku športového areálu v Nitre," *Študijné zvesti Archeologického ústavu SAV* 24 (1988), pp. 153–154. Gabriel Fusek, "Včasnostredoveké sídlisko v Nitre na Mikovom dvore," *Slovenská archeológia* 39 (1991), pp. 289–330. Gabriel Fusek, *Slovensko vo včasnoslovanskom období* (Nitra 1994), pp. 220–231. Gabriel Fusek, "Príchod prvých Slovanov do Nitry," in *Nitra v slovenských dejinách*, ed. Richard Marsina (Martin 2002), pp. 79–80.
23 M. U. Kasparek, "Fränkische Gräber aus Neutra, Slowakei," *Karpaten-Jahrbuch* 7 (München 1956). *Dejiny Nitry*, ed. G. Fusek, M. R. Zemene, pp. 88–89.
24 Peter Bednár, "Siedma sezóna výskumu Nitrianskeho hradu," *AVANS v r. 1994* (Nitra 1996), p. 30. Peter Bednár, "Nitriansky hrad v 9. storočí a jeho význam v sídliskovej štruktúre veľkomoravskej Nitry," in *Svätopluk 894–1994. Materiály z konferencie organizovanej Archeologickým ústavom SAV v Nitre v spolupráci so Slovenskou historickou spoločnosťou pri SAV, Nitra 3.–6. október 1994*, ed. Richard Marsina, A. Ruttkay (Nitra 1997), pp. 19, 21, 22. Peter Bednár, "Die Entwicklung der Befestigung der Nitraer Burg im 9.–12. Jahrhundert," in *Frühmittelalterlicher Burgenbau in Mittel- und Osteuropa*, ed. Joachim Henning, Alexander Tivadar Ruttkay (Bonn 1998), pp. 371–372. Peter Bednár, *Nitriansky hrad v 9. až 13. storočí. Autoreferát dizertácie na získanie vedeckej hodnosti kandidáta historických vied* (Nitra 1998), p. 8. *Dejiny Nitry*, ed. Fusek, Zemene, p. 101. Peter Bednár – Marián Samuel, "Nitriansky hrad na prelome tisícročí," in *Slovensko vo včasnom stredoveku*,

Still in the 7th century, Slav peasants worked with a wooden plough wheel, which merely scarified the soil. An iron ploughshare was the only exception. In the 8th century the Slavic tracing wheel had an iron ploughshare and an iron tiller.[25] This more accomplished tilling tool improved the ploughing of soil, and this began to provide greater yields. Princes could be encircled by professional warriors who lived at the expense of peasants. Even a small group of professionals, well-armed and well-prepared for battle and fully dependent on the generosity of their princes and unconditionally devoted to him, meant a crucial strengthening of princely power.

The most important seat of the Moravian princely retinue was in Mikulčice, where archaeologists found 60 iron and bronze spurs with hooks at the end of the sides, sometimes inlaid with copper or silver. The hooks served for catching the straps, by which the spur was secured to the shoes, always on only one leg. The hooked spurs were worn by horse soldiers in Moravia from the second half of the 7th century to the end of the 8th century. They lived in the close vicinity of their prince, in the Mikulčice ravelin, where according to estimates of archaeologists, some 200 to 250 spacious log cabins stood with hard-packed clay tiles, which may correspond to the number of the closest princely retinue.[26] In addition, 4 hooked spurs (3 of them made of bronze) found in Uherské Hradiště also belonged to Moravian horse riders (3 of them were found on Ostrov svatého Jiří 3 and in 1 spur in Sady (at the site Sady II). Seven hooked spurs come from Staré Zámky in Brno-Líšeň, 1 spur is from Zelená hora near Vyškov, 1 spur from Břeclav-Pohansko, 2 spurs from Dolní Věstenice, 1 spur from Mutěníce, 4 spurs from Povel near Olomouc (2 of them are bronze), 1 spur from Podbranč in Myjava and 2 spurs from Devínska Nová Ves.[27]

editori Alexander Ruttkay, Matej Ruttkay, Peter Šalkovský (Nitra 2002), pp. 150–151. Peter Bednár – Michal Šimkovic, "Opevnenie Nitrianskeho hradu," in *Kolíska kresťanstva*, ed. Judák, Bednár, Medvecký, pp. 134, 136.

25 Magdaléna Beranová, *Zemědělství starých Slovanů* (Praha 1980), pp. 168–169, 174–192.

26 Poulík, *Mikulčice*, pp. 42–45, 135–136. Poulík, *Svědectví*, pp. 13–20, 56, 60–61. Blanka Kavánová, "Slovanské ostruhy na území Československa," *Studie Archeologického ústavu ČSAV* 4 (1976), no. 3. Klanica, "Die südmährischen Slawen," pp. 139–150. Klanica, *Počátky*, pp. 92, 94–102, 104. Naďa Profantová, "K nálezům ostruh z konce 7.–9. stol. v Čechách," *Mediaevalia archaeologica Bohemica 1993*, *Památky archeologické*, Supplementum 2 (1994), pp. 60–71, 82–85.

27 Poulík, "Svědectví," pp. 13–17. Josef Poulík, "K otázce vzniku předvelkomoravských hradišť," *Slovenská archeológia* 36 (1988), p. 204. Robert Snášil, "Specializovaná řemesla z ostrovního hradiska v Uherském Hradišti a jejich přínos pro další poznání společenské diferenciace 8.–9. století," in *13. Mikulovské sympozium* (Praha 1984), pp. 157–160. Staňa, "Velkomoravské hradiště Staré Zámky u Líšně," p. 114. Blanka Kavánová, "Slovanské pohřebiště v Mutěnicích, okr. Hodonín," *Archeologické rozhledy* 34 (1982), no. 5, pp. 512, 514, 515, 518. Bláha, "Předběžná správa," pp. 160–162, 167. *Pramene I/2*, ed. Bialeková,

AVAR DOMINATION 65

Hooked spurs found at several locations east of the Little and White Carpathians suggest the presence of the princely mounted warriors in the 8th century in Nitria as well.[28] However, we don't have such large finds of hooked spurs from its territory as have come from Moravian Mikulčice. From Nitra itself (from the site beneath Zobor) we have only 1 spur,[29] 4 spurs from Bojná (3 are from Bojná I, the Valy site and 1 from Bojná III, Žihľavník site),[30] 3 spurs from Pobedim,[31] 2 spurs from Klátova Nová Ves (1 iron and 1 bronze),[32] 3 from Molpír (in Smolenice),[33] 1 spur from Neštich (in Svätý Jur),[34] 1 spur from Trenčianske Bohuslavice,[35] 1 spur from Dubnica nad Váhom,[36] 2 spurs from Dolné Věstenice,[37] 1 spur from Krivín (in Rybník),[38] 1 spur from Kalamárka (in

     p. 307. In graves 104 and 116 at the burial site in Devínska Nová Ves were two damaged spurs, whose hooks were not preserved. Ján Eisner also mistakenly assigned the find from grave 79 to these two spurs. Eisner, *Devínska Nová Ves*, pp. 25, 35, 39, 304, Fig. 13, 15, 17. Miriam Jakubčinová, "Ostrohy s háčikmi z Bojnej," in *Bojná 2. Nové výsledky výskumov včasnostredovekých hradísk*, editori Karol Pieta, Zbigniew Robak (Nitra 2015), pp. 93–94, 95–96, 99, 100, 101, 102. The spurs from the burial site in Devínska Nová Ves come from the west, just as 5 saxons and 4 spears from graves 95, 124, 412, 524, 616, 633, 777 and 840 at this same burial site. Kraskovská, *Slovansko-avarské pohrebisko pri Záhorskej Bystrici*, p. 80. *Pramene I/1*, ed. Bialeková, p. 31. The spur from grave 140 from the burial site in Záhorská Bystrica is Roman. Kraskovská, *Slovansko-avarské pohrebisko pri Záhorskej Bystrici*, pp. 32, 80–81, 137, 165. *Pramene I/1*, ed. Bialeková, p. 40.
28 Jakubčinová, "Ostrohy s háčikmi," pp. 91–107.
29 Anton Točík – Vojtech Budinský-Krička, "Z archeologických zbierok na Slovensku," *Zborník Slovenského národného múzea* 81 (1987), *História* 27, p. 85. Jakabčinová, "Ostrohy s háčikmi," pp. 93, 97, 98, 99, 100, 104.
30 Jakubčinová, "Ostrohy s háčikmi," pp. 91–92, 95, 97, 98, 99, 100, 102.
31 Darina Bialeková, "Sporen von slawischen Fundplätzen in Pobedim (Typologie und Datierung)," *Slovenská archeológia* 25 (1977), no. 1, pp. 103–160. *Pramene I/2*, ed. Bialeková, pp. 402–403. *Významné slovanské náleziská na Slovensku*, editor Bohuslav Chropovský (Bratislava 1978), pp. 162–165. Jakubčinová, "Ostrohy s háčikmi," pp. 95, 96, 97, 98, 100–101, 104.
32 Jakubčinová, "Ostrohy s háčikmi," pp. 94, 95, 98, 100, 103.
33 Sigrid Dušek, "Ostroha s háčikmi zo Smoleníc," in *Zborník prác Ľudmile Kraskovskej (k životnému jubileu)* (Bratislava 1984), pp. 159–162. Vladimír Turčan, "Ďalšie slovanské nálezy zo Smoleníc-Molpíra," *Zborník Slovenského národného múzea* 88 (1994), *Archeológia* 4, p. 75. Vladimír Turčan, "Nové nálezy ostrôh zo Smoleníc-Molpíra," *Zborník Slovenského národného múzea* 89 (1995), *Archeológia* 5, pp. 77–82. Jakubčinová, "Ostrohy s háčikmi," pp. 95, 96, 97, 98, 99. 101, 105.
34 Vladimír Turčan, "Príspevok k poznaniu včasnostredovekého osídlenia Sv. Jura pri Bratislave," *Zborník Slovenského národného múzea* 94 (2000), *Archeológia* 10, pp. 129, 131, 134. Jakubčinová, "Ostrohy s háčikmi," pp. 96, 98, 101, 105.
35 Jakubčinová, "Ostrohy s háčikmi," pp. 97, 98, 101, 105.
36 Jakubčinová, "Ostrohy s háčikmi," pp. 97, 98, 100, 103.
37 Jakubčinová, "Ostrohy s háčikmi," pp. 98, 99, 100,
38 Jakubčinová, "Ostrohy s háčikmi," pp. 95, 98, 99, 101, 104.

Detva),[39] 2 spurs from Ostrá skala (in Vyšný Kubín) in Orava[40] and 2 spurs from Čingov (Hradisko I in Spišské Tomášovce-Smižany).[41]

The seat of Avar power in Nitria was not in Nitra, but in Komárno, which belonged among the most significant Avar centres in the khaganate. The Avar cavalry elite were based in Komárno and remained there up to the fall of the khaganate. Avar riders left graves with horses, weapons, richly decorated belts and horse harnesses. From the more than 240 graves examined in Komárno, 103 were cavalry graves. The Komárno Avars even put horses into the graves of the most important women (15 of them belonged to women). The representation of cavalry graves at burial sites in Komárno (up to 42%) is much higher than in other burial sites of southern Slovakia and the whole of the Carpathian Basin.[42] Nearly all the men buried in 5 burial sites and in 2 single graves in Komárno were thus cavalry warriors in the army of the Avar prince, who could have ruled all of Nitria from Komárno. The remaining 58% of the buried were women, children and other family members. The Avars had a similar settlement as that in Komárno, although smaller, in the vicinity of Žitavská Tôn (part of Radvaň nad Dunajom, near the mouth of the Žitava River into the Danube), where out of 83 richly furnished skeletal graves, more than one-quarter (22, or 29%), were cavalry graves.[43]

In the last decades of the 7th century the Avars settled only along the Danubian bank, where after them, aside from the mentioned burial sites at

39 Jakubčinová, "Ostrohy s háčikmi," pp. 97, 98, 99, 100, 103.
40 Turčan, "Nové nálezy ostrôh zo Smoleníc," p. 79. Vladimír Turčan, "Nové včasnostredoveké nálezy z Oravy," in *Zborník na počesť Dariny Bialekovej*, ed. Gabriel Fusek (Nitra 2004), pp. 427–428, 430. Jakubčinová, "Ostrohy s háčikmi," pp. 95, 98,
41 Július Béreš – Sanica Staššíková-Štukovská, "Výskum slovanského hradiska v Spišských Tomášovciach," *AVANS v r. 1978* (Nitra 1980), p. 44. Jakubčinová, "Ostrohy s háčikmi," pp. 93, 95, 98–99. Distant Brekov in the east, from where we know of 1 spur, already lay outside the territory of Nitria. *Významné slovanské náleziská*, ed. Chropovský, p. 40. *Pramene I/2*, ed. Bialeková, p. 307. Jakubčinová, "Ostrohy s háčikmi," pp. 96, 98, 99, 101, 105.
42 Priska Ratimorská, "Jazdecký hrob z 8. storočia v Komárne," *AVANS v r. 1978* (Nitra 1980), pp. 228–229. Zlata Čilinská, "Dve pohrebiská z 8.–9. storočia v Komárne," *Slovenská archeológia* 30 (1982), no. 2, pp. 347–393. Trugly, "Pohrebisko," pp. 5–48. Alexander Trugly, "Gräberfeld aus der Zeit des Awarischen Reiches bei der Schiffswert in Komárno," *Slovenská archeológia* 35 (1987), no. 2, pp. 251–344. Alexander Trugly, "Gräberfeld aus der Zeit des Awarischen Reiches bei der Schiffswert in Komárno II (1987–1989)," *Slovenská archeológia* 41 (1993), no. 2, pp. 191–237. Zábojník, *Slovensko a avarský kaganát*, pp. 36, 93–96.
43 Vojtech Budinský-Krička, "Pohrebisko z neskorej doby avarskej v Žitavskej Tôni na Slovensku," *Slovenská archeológia* 4 (1956), no. 1, pp. 5–131. Zlata Čilinská, "Slovansko-avarské pohrebisko v Žitavskej Tôni," *Slovenská archeológia* 11 (1963), no. 1, pp. 87–120. Jozef Zábojník, "Zur horizontalen Stratigraphie des Gräberfeldes in Radvaň nad Dunajom-Žitavská Tôň," *Slovenská archeológia* 33 (1985), no. 2, pp. 329–346. Zábojník, *Slovensko a avarský kaganát*, pp. 106–107.

Komárno and the Žitava River, others were also found: Holiare, Bodza, Veľký Meder, Virt and Štúrovo. The abundant burial sites with Avar weapons, cast bronze armour and cavalry graves increased in the 8th century. They expanded on the Danubian Lowland: Obid, Szob, Nové Zámky, Veľké Kosihy, Vojnice, Dvory nad Žitavou, Bešeňov, Šaľa, Čierny Brod, Bernolákovo, Čataj and Pác; penetrated into the area along the Ipeľ River: Vyškovce, Malá Čalomija, Želovce, Balassagyarmat, Szécsény and Prša; and got into the valleys of both the Sajó River: Sajószentpéter, Edelény and Miskolc (Vezér út), and the Hornád River: Böcs, Kechnec, Valaliky, Šebastovce, Barca and Lemešany.[44]

Devín maintained the importance it had in the period of Samo's realm during the period of Avar rule, exactly as Komárno, seat of an important Avar viceroy. The Avars of Devín penetrated into the valley of the Morava River, and got under their control new tribal centres of the Moravians in Mikulčice and its broader surroundings, while in Mistelbach, Schönkirchen-Reysenhofene, Hevlín and in Dolní Dunajovice they left smaller burial sites and solitary graves.[45]

At the end of the 7th century two centres of Avar power emerged on the northern bank of the Danube – Komárno and Devín. Avars from Komárno ruled Nitria, while Moravia was subject to Avars from Devín. Mikulčice was independent from Devín just as Nitra was from Komárno. The Avars preserved the distinctness of Nitria and Moravia; each was ruled from a different centre. The number of archaeological finds with cast bronze armour from the territory

---

44   Dezső Csallányi, *Archäologische Denkmäler der Awarenzeit in Mitteleuropa* (Budapest 1956), pp. 83, 163. Ján Dekan, "Vývoj a stav archeologického výskumu doby predveľkomoravskej," *Slovenská archeológia* 19 (1971), no. 2, pp. 559–580. Éva Sz. Garam, "A böcsi későavarkori lelet és köre," *Archaeologiai Értesítő* 108 (1981), no. 1, pp. 34–51. Jozef Zábojník, "Seriation von Gürtelbeschlaggarnituren aus dem Gebiet der Slowakei und Österreichs (Beitrag zur Chronologie der Zeit des Awarischen Kaganats)," in *K problematike osídlenia stredodunajskej oblasti vo včasnom stredoveku*, responsible editor Zlata Čilinská (Nitra 1991), pp. 219–321. Jozef Zábojník, "Soziale Problematik der Gräberfelder des nördlichen und nordwestlichen Randgebietes des Awarischen Kaganats," *Slovenská archeológia* 43 (1995), no. 2, pp. 205–344. Jozef Zábojník, "Zum Vorkommen der Reitergräber auf Gräberfeldern aus der Zeit des Awarischen Kaganats," in *Ethnische und kulturelle Verhältnisse*, ed. Bialeková, Zábojník, pp. 179–193. Zábojník, "Das Awarische Kaganat und die Slawen an seiner nördlichen Peripherie," pp. 153–173. Zábojník, "Materiálna kultúra," pp. 189–222. Zábojník, "Slovensko a avarský kaganát," pp. 76–117.

45   Zdeněk Klanica, *Předvelkomoravské pohřebiště v Dolních Dunajovicích* (Praha 1972). Zábojník, *Slovensko a avarský kaganát*, pp. 75, 106, 126, 152, 202. Justová, *Dolnorakouské Podunají*, pp. 53, 56, 58, 60–66, 74, 76, 78–79, 84–91, 93, 95–98, 101–102, 104–107, 115, 118, 226, 234, 243, 250. Zdeněk Měřínský – Eva Zumpfe, "Obchodní cesty na jižní Moravě a v Dolním Rakousku do doby vrcholného středověku," *Archeologia historica* 23 (1998), pp. 176–177.

of Bratislava to the valley of the Hornád River is several times greater than in the neighbouring region on the Morava River, where they are only found in the lower basin of the Morava and the Thaya rivers. This is evidence that Nitria, lying in the Carpathian Basin, had to be more dependent on the khaganate than Moravia, to the north-west and more distant from the Avar centre in Pannonia.

4   The Tudunate

The Avars were ruled by a khagan and other high dignitaries subordinate to the khagan: the jugur, tudun and kapkhan, who were at the same time khagan-appointed viceroys in the individual parts of the Avar Khaganate.[46] In 782 Frankish King Charlemagne called an empire-wide diet, to which also came *Avars sent by the khagan and jugur*.[47] In the war between the Avar chieftains in 795, which weakened the Avar Khaganate, the jugur lost his life along with the khagan.[48] The khagan's seat, the *hrink*, filled with treasures, lay in Pannonia. If the khagan had his seat in Pannonia, then his co-ruler the jugur[49] had his seat in the other part of the khaganate – in the Tisza River region. An unusually rich burial site in Hortobágy-Árkus[50] indicates that perhaps there we can look for the jugur's seat.

A third Avar ruler, a *tudun, which in the nation and country of the Avars had great power*, administered the part of the Avar empire *with a territory and with its people* or *with its people and homeland*.[51] The tudun was a *prince from*

---

46   Avenarius, "Stepné národy," p. 156.
47   The Khagan decided in the most important matters together with the jugur: *Avari … missi a cagano et iugurro. Ann. reg. Franc. (Laurissenses maiores)* ad a. 782, rec. Kurze, p. 60. *legatos … quos ad se Caganus et Iugurus principes Hunorum velut pacis causa miserunt. Ann. reg. Franc. (Einhardi)* ad a. 782, rec. Kurze, p. 61.
48   *civili bello fatigatis inter se principibus, spoliavit, chagan sive iuguro intestina clade addictis et a suis occisis. Ann. reg. Franc. (Laurissenses maiores)* ad a. 796, rec. Kurze, p. 98. MMFH I, p. 21. *Cagan et Iugurro principibus Hunorum civili bello et intestina clade a suis occisis … Annales Fuldenses* ad a. 796, post editionem G. H. Pertii recognovit Fridericus Kurze, Scriptores rerum Germanicarum in usum scholarum ex Monumentis Germaniae historicis recusi (Hannoverae 1891), p. 351.
49   Pohl, *Die Awaren*, pp. 293–300.
50   István Bóna, "Die Awaren. Ein asiatisches Reitervolk an der Mittleren Donau," in *Awaren in Europa. Schätze eines asiatischen Reitervolkes, 6.–8. Jahrhundert. Ausstellungskatalog* (Frankfurt/Main 1985), pp. 5–19.
51   *Ibi etiam venerunt missi tudun, qui in gente et regno Avarorum magnam potestatem habebat; qui dixerunt, quod idem tudun cum terra et populo suo se regi dedere vellet et eius ordinatione christianam fidem suscipere vellet. Ann. reg. Franc. (Ann. Lauriss. mai.)* ad a. 795,

Pannonia (*dux de Pannonia*);[52] thus, the khagan shared rule in Pannonia with the tudun.

And the *kapkhan, prince of the Huns*, was based in the middle *of his people*.[53] The last (or penultimate) tudun and the last kapkhan negotiated in years 795, 796 and 805 directly with Charlemagne and were baptized on the territory of his empire.[54] The dependencies of the tudun and the kapkhan had to lie in the west, more exactly in the north-west part of the khaganate, which bordered the Frankish Empire. The tudun *had great power*, which must have corresponded to a relatively large territory. His territory, which lay in Pannonia and at the same time bordered the Frankish Empire, had to touch on the west the

rec. Kurze, s. 96. *MMFH I*, p. 21.... *venerunt ad eum legati de Pannonia unius ex primoribus Hunorum, qui apud suos tudun vocabatur, is et suum adventum et se christianum fieri velle promisit. Ann. reg. Franc.* (*Ann. q. d. Einhardi*) ad a. 795, rec. Kurze, s. 97. *Ann. Fuld.* ad a. 795, rec. Kurze, p. 13. *In eodem anno tudun secundum pollicitationem suam cum magna parte Avarorum ad regem venit, se cum populo suo et patria regi dedit; ipse et populus baptizatus est et honorifice muneribus donati redierunt. Ann. reg. Franc.* (*Ann. Lauriss. mai.*) ad a. 796, rec. Kurze, s. 98. *MMFH I*, p. 21. *Tudun etiam ille, de quo superius mentio facta est, fidem dictis suis adhibens ibidem ad regem evenit ibique cum omnibus, qui secum venerant, baptizatus ac remuneratus post datum servandae fidei sacramentum domum rediit. Ann. reg. Franc.* (*Ann. q. d. Einhardi*) ad a. 796, rec. Kurze, s. 101. *Ann. Fuld.* ad a. 796, rec. Kurze, s. 13.

52 *Rotanus dux de Pannonia. Annales Alamannici* ad a. 795, Monumenta Germaniae historica, Scriptores I, edidit Georgius Heinricus Pertz (Hannoverae et Lipsiae 1826), p. 47. *de terra Avarorum regulus quidam nomine Todanus ... cum comitibus suis. Annales Laureshamenses* ad a. 795, Monumenta Germaniae historica, Scriptores I, edidit Georgius Heinricus Pertz (Hannoverae et Lipsiae 1826), p. 36. *Chronicon Moissiacense* ad a. 795, Monumenta Germaniae historica, Scriptores I, edidit Georgius Heinricus Pertz (Hannoverae et Lipsiae 1826), p. 302. A tudun had in the Avar Khaganate a similar position as Hungarian *horka* in the 10th century. István Bóna, "'Cundpald fecit'. Der Kelch von Petőháza und die Anfänge der bairisch-fränkischen Awarenmission in Pannonien," *Acta Archaeologica Academiae Scientiarum Hungungaricae* 18 (1966), pp. 319–321. Other authors also emphasize the special position of the tudun, who had in his power a portion of the Avar empire. Avenarius, *Die Awaren*, p. 183. Pohl, *Die Awaren*, pp. 300–301. Péter Váczy, *A magyar történelem korai századaiból* (Budapest 1994), pp. 39–40. Mänän-Tudun is known from the Secret History of the Mongols (§ 46). Pavel Poucha, *Die Geheime Geschichte der Mongolen als Geschichtsquelle und Literaturdenkmal. Ein Beitrag zu ihrer Erklärung, ČSAV Archiv orientální, supplementa IV* (Praha 1956), pp. 70, 105–108.

53 *capcanus, princeps Hunorum, propter necessitatem populi sui ... in pristinis sedibus esse non poterat.... erat enim capcanus christianus nomine Theodorus ... Qui rediens ad populum suum ... Ann. reg. Franc.* ad a. 805, rec. Kurze, pp. 119–120. *MMFH I*, p. 23. *Ann. Fuld.* ad a. 805, rec. Kurze, p. 16. *MMFH I*, p. 69. Gyula Moravcsik, *Byzantinoturcica 2. Sprachreste der Türkvölker in den byzantinischen Quellen* (Budapest 1943), pp. 140–141. Pohl, *Die Awaren*, pp. 302–304. The Secret History of the Mongols (§ 239) mentions a Mongolian tribe called the *Quabqanas*. Poucha, *Die Geheime Geschichte der Mongolen*, pp. 67, 75.

54 See chapter 4, notes 18, 20, 21, 54, 64.

border of the Enns River and to the east to extend into the Pannonian interior, where the internal border was formed by the lower part of the Rába. The tudun's territory between the lower Enns and the lower Rába later fell under the Bavarian Eastern (Avar) March.[55] If the tudun *had great power*, then Moravia, controlled from Devín, must have been subject to him, and probably also a kapkhan, who at the time of disintegration of the khaganate was in the in tow of tudun's policy.[56]

The khagan, as the highest ruler, could not have had a smaller territory than the tudun or any other lower worthy; therefore, the larger part of Pannonia, bordered by the lower flow of the Rába, the eastern edge of Carantania, the Danube and the Drava, which later fell to the Carantanian March, must have belonged to him,[57] and with it eastern Slavonia with Sirmium, which was later occupied by the Bulgarians. Savia and Carniola, contiguous to the khagan's territory from the south, acknowledged his rule.

The last kapkhan, before he moved with his Avars and with the permission of Charlemagne in 805 to the region between Carnuntum and Sabaria, used to dwell *in earlier settlements (in pristinis sedibus)*,[58] which lay in the western part of the Avar empire. Since the khagan and the tudun had divided Pannonia, there was no longer a place there for the kapkhan. The kapkhan and his Avars could then settle only in the surroundings of Nitria. The kapkhan was the Avar viceroy who settled in Komárno and Nitria was subjugated to him.[59] If the

---

55 See pp. 83, 94–95.
56 See pp. 94–95.
57 See pp. 82–85.
58 See chapter 4, note 64.
59 Dušan Třeštík has already linked the Avar centre in Komárno with Kapkhan Theodor and his Avars. He thus linked to the opinion of Naďa Profantová regarding the crucial participation of south Moravian power centres in a unified Nitria and for pushing Avar power out of its southern part in the period of the Avar wars. Marie Bláhová – Jan Frolík – Naďa Profantová, *Velké dějiny zemí Koruny české I. Do roku 1197* (Praha 1999), pp. 188, 190. Třeštík, *Vznik*, pp. 69–70, 109, 112, 127. Since Avar graves extend up to Nitra itself, Naďa Profantová assumes that at the end of the 8th century there was only a little space in Nitria for any Slavic tribes. Nitria was thus formed by Moravians at the expense of the Avars. Naďa Profantová – Martin Profant, "Archeologie a historie aneb 'jak vykopávat' dějiny?" in *Dějiny ve věku nejistot. Sborník k příležitosti 70. narozenin Dušana Třeštíka*, ed. Jan Klápště, Eva Plešková, Josef Žemlička (Praha 2003), pp. 244–245. The relationship of Nitria to the Avars recalls the relation between Judea and the Romans in the years 41 and 44–66. After removal of the Judean ethnarch Archelaus in the year 6 CE, Judea and with the subordinates Samaria and Edom became a Roman province. Representatives of Roman power, called procurators, did not settle in its capital city in Jerusalem, but on the Judean coast, in the port town of Caesarea Maritima. Caesarea and other coastal towns and some also in the Judean and Samarian interior had abundant hellenized residents, who were anti-Judaic and supported Roman power. Michael Grant, *Židé v římském světě*

kapkhan was subject to the tudun, then the tudun had the whole of the northwestern part of the Avar Khaganate under his power, that is the territory of Samo's former realm.

The tudun took over not only Samo's former territory but also Samo's former seat. Evidence of this lies in the large burial site at Devínská Nová Ves, with 866 examined graves, 94 of them cavalry graves, the size of which no other such site the entire territory of the tudunate can match. Only Komárno, where the kapkhan was based, has a larger number of horsemen graves. The Komárno burial sites had, however, a total of 3.5-times fewer graves than the site at Devínská Nová Ves. The tudun, like Samo and the Romans before him, must have valued the advantageous position of Devín, from which all part of his tudunate were well within reach.

If the khagan, tudun and kapkhan divided the western part of the Avar Khaganate, then the jugur was based in the east. The jugur was the khagan's co-ruler; therefore, his dependency had to lie in the vicinity of the khagan's Pannonia. The jugur ruled the area around the Tisza River and the southern Obotrites on the lower Tisza,[60] and the Slavs on the upper Tisza were also subject to him.[61] An additional Avar viceroy could have been settled in the more distant and smaller Transylvania, divided from the Tisza River region by the Biharian Mountains.

The Avar Khaganate was perhaps divided into four major distinct parts, to which Slavic principalities, Nitria included, belonged. Nitria was subject to the kapkhan, who in turn was subordinate to the tudun and the tudun to the khagan.

A song about the Avar victory of King Pepin in 796 recalls how the *ruling khagan ... with leading tarkhans* (*cacanus rex ... cum Tarcanis primatibus*) submitted to Pepin, son of Charlemagne.[62] The tarkhans were leading Avar magnates. Similarly as the tarkhans in the army of the Bulgarian khagan[63] the Avar tarkhans were also leaders of military units in the army of the Avar khagan

---

(Praha 2003), pp. 93–95, 103–106 [Original *Jews in the Roman World* (London 1973)]. The relationship of Caesarea – Jerusalem is a thus very distant but appropriate analogy of the relation of Komárno – Nitra.

60 See chapter 4, note 81, chapter 5, notes 15, 16.

61 Avar finds are missing from the upper Tisza River region. The population that was settled there was therefore undoubtedly Slavic.

62 *cacanus rex ... cum Tarcanis primatibus*. *Carmen de Pippini regis victoria Avarica a. 796* 10, *MMFH II*, p. 15. Pohl, *Die Awaren*, pp. 301–302. Poucha, *Die Geheime Geschichte der Mongolen*, pp. 83, 153.

63 See chapter 4, note 78. Zoltán Gombocz, "Árpádkori török személyneveink VII," *Magyar Nyelv* 11 (1915), pp. 433–439. Andreas Alföldi, "A tarchan méltóságnév eredete," *Magyar Nyelv* 28 (1932) pp. 205–220. Moravcsik, *Byzantinoturcica* 2, pp. 94, 102, 253.

and representatives of khaganate power. In 796 the khagan and his tarkhans submitted to Pepin and handed over their sons as hostages.

Iron armour belts, iron falers decorated with silver plate and other iron decorations of horse harnesses, bony combs and other decorative items from the west are scattered in graves from the 7th and 8th centuries throughout the whole Carpathian Basin;[64] however, finds of Merovingian weapons are concentrated in the south-western part of the Avar Khaganate, on territories which previously belonged to Samo's realm. At burial sites in north-western Pannonia, between the lower Rába and the Vienna Woods archaeologists found 2 swords and 21 saxes.[65] At burial sites spaced around Bratislava and up to the valley of the Hornád, including the mentioned finds in Nitra, archaeologists found 2 swords, 7 saxes, 2 spears, 7 arrow shafts, 1 square pike and 1 shield boss.[66] In the valley of the lower Morava River they dug up 2 swords, 5 saxes, 5 spears and 3 spurs.[67] From other territories of the Avar Khaganate we know

---

64   Frauke Stein, "Awarisch-merowingische Beziehungen, ein Beitrag zur absoluten Chronologie der awarenzeitlichen Funde," *Študijné zvesti Archeologického ústavu SAV* 16 (1968), pp. 233–244. Jozef Zábojník, "K výskytu predmetov západného pôvodu na pohrebiskách z obdobia Avarskej ríše v Dunajskej kotline," *Slovenská archeológia* 26 (1978), no. 1, pp. 197–209.

65   Merovingian weapons in the burial sites Vienna-Csokorgasse: 11 saxes (graves 40, 106, 112, 117, 257, 426, 460, 480, 514, 604), Vienna-Liesing: 3 saxes (graves 16, 22, horseman grave 1), 1 sword-spatha (horseman grave 3), Mödling: 1 short sword (grave 93), Münchendorf: 1 sax (grave 38), Zwölfaxing I: 1 sax (grave 3), Traiskirchen: 1 sax, Brunn a. d. Schneebergbahn: 1 sax (missing), Čunovo: 1 sax (grave 127), Mosonszentjános: 1 sax, Hédervár: 1 sax. Stein, "Awarisch-merowingische Beziehungen," pp. 239–240. Zábojník, "K výskytu predmetov západného pôvodu," pg. 193–195, 197. Justová, *Dolnorakouské Podunají*, pp. 91–93.

66   In addition to Nitra itself (see note 23) Merovingian weapons were also found at an additional 7 burial sites in Nitria: in Bernolákovo 1 sax and 1 spearhead of the Egling type (horseman grave 53), in Komárno 2 saxes (horseman grave 78 at Lodenica and grave 24 on Hadovská cesta), in Štúrovo 1 sax (grave 208), in Szob 1 twisted shaft (an arrow shaft with a curved neck, horseman grave 125), in Želovce 1 backsword (grave 124), 1 sax (grave 311), 4 twisted arrow shafts (graves 219, 733, 748, 787) and 1 twisted square pike (grave 758), in Valalíky 1 twisted arrow shaft (grave 10) and 2 saxes. Zábojník, "K výskytu predmetov západného pôvodu," pp. 193–197. Trugly, "Gräberfeld aus der Zeit des Awarischen Reiches bei der Schiffswert in Komárno," pp. 267–268, 319. Ľubomír Mihok – Marta Soláriková – Alojz Hollý – Zlata Čilinská, "Archeometalurgický výskum sečných zbraní z pohrebiska v Želovciach," in *K problematike osídlenia stredodunajskej oblasti vo včasnom stredoveku*, ed. Čilinská, pp. 67–101.

67   At the burial site in Devínska Nová Ves archaeologists found 5 saxes (horseman graves 124, 412, 524, 633, 840), 1 spearhead of the Egling type (horseman grave 616) and 2 spearheads of Pfullingen type (grave 777, horseman grave 95), at the burial site in Mistelbach 2 swords (grave B, horseman grave 48), 1 spearhead (grave A) and 1 spearhead of the Pfullingen type (grave 28). Eisner, *Devínska Nová Ves*, pp. 30–31, 41–42, 94–95, 119–120, 137, 139–140, 163, 180, 289–292, fig. 19, 28, 47, 65, 71, 73, 84, 85. Stein, "Awarisch-merowingische Beziehungen,"

only 1 Longobard spatha, 1 sax and 1 spear.[68] These 55 finds of western weapons indicate that the tudunate held a commercial and political alliance with the neighbouring Frankish empire and significantly differed from the other territory of the Avar empire, from where we have only 3 such finds.

The Slavs had predominance in the tudunate. They undoubtedly surrounded the tudun (as Samo had previously) and co-determined his policies. The different interests of the tudun and the khagan was manifested in years 795 and 796, when the tudun did not hesitate to join with the Franks against the khagan.

5   Carantania

By ruling the Danube up to the Enns and Carniola up through the Karawanks and the Julian Alps, the Avars surrounded Carantania. This alpine principality was surrounded by the Avars for about 60 years, but it avoided the fate that fell on the other Slavic principalities lying on the perimeter of Avar Pannonia.

To the south-west, in the Carnic Alps, Carantania bordered with Friuli. In 663 the Avars allied with Longobard King Grimoald (662–671) and helped defeat of the rebellious Friulian Prince Lupus. His son Arnefrit escaped from Grimoald to Carantania. He returned with a Slavic brigade to conquer Friuli, but he died in the battle.[69] Then the Carantanians attacked the town of Cividale. The new Friulian Prince Wechtari, installed by Grimoald, surprised them, however, and triumphed over them.[70] In the war over Friuli the Carantanians battled on the opposite side as the Avars; thus, they were independent from the Avar Khaganate.

In perhaps 740 a group of Slavs, undoubtedly Carantanian, invaded the valley of the Salzach River, where they marauded the Bavarian monastery

---

pp. 239, 244. Zábojník, "K výskytu predmetov západného pôvodu," pp. 193–194, 196–197. Justová, *Dolnorakouské Podunají*, p. 93.

68   A Longobard spatha from a burial site in Pécs (grave 30) and a spearhead which archaeologists found at a burial site in Csepel (horseman grave 5), the Avars could have seized in Friuli in 663. *Pauli Historia Langobardorum* VI 19–21, ed. Bethmann, Waitz, pp. 151–152. The only sax which got to the interior of the khaganate comes from the burial site Üllő II (grave 77). Stein, "Awarisch-merowingische Beziehungen," pp. 234, 239. Zábojník, "K výskytu predmetov západného pôvodu," pp. 195–197, 206–207.

69   *Arnefrit ... fugiit ad Sclavorum gentem in Carnuntum, quod corrupte vocitant Carantanum*. *Pauli Historia Langobardorum* v 22, ed. Bethmann, Waitz, pp. 152. Štih, *The Middle Ages between the Eastern Alps and the Northern Adriatic*, pp. 198–201, 206.

70   *Pauli Historia Langobardorum* v 23, ed. Bethmann, Waitz, pp. 152–153. Štih, *The Middle Ages between the Eastern Alps and the Northern Adriatic*, pp. 202–203.

at Bischofshofen.[71] The only good approach from Carantania directly to the monastery opened in the valley of the upper Enns, which belonged to the Carantanians. The Bavarians could easily move along this road and penetrate into Carantania, and they established the monastery as the jumping-off point of their influence. The Carantanians didn't like seeing it in their vicinity and thus destroyed the monastery, which was troubling them. Then Bavarian Duke Odilo (737–748) decided that he would take the gap that Carantanian formed between his principality and the khaganate. Perhaps simultaneously with the repair of the monastery in 741 or in the following year of 742 Odilo subjugated Carinthia and requested that Carinthian Prince Borut hand over his son Gorazd and nephew Hotimir as hostages.

Carantania was small, independent and unfriendly toward Bavaria, and although it extended deep into Avar territory, it could not threaten the Avars at all. However, when the Carantanian wedge that pushed into the territory of the Avar empire became a part of the Bavarian principality and the Frankish Empire, the Avars felt threatened and attacked in order to conquer Carantania for themselves: *The Huns (= Avars) began to pursue with difficulty these Carantanians with enemy attacks. And their Prince at that time was named Borut, who let the Bavarians know the Hun military was setting forth against him. And he beseeched them to come and help him. They quickly took up arms, defeated the Huns and secured the Carantanians and subjected them and likewise their neighbours to the service of the kings.*[72]

Conversio reversed the sequence of events. The Bavarians first *secured the Carantanians and subjected them to the service of the kings* and only then did they beat back the attack of the Avars. The Bavarians defended the Carantanians because they belonged to them. Shortly after beating back the Avar attack, Borut supported the Bavarian prince militarily. In the summer of 743 Slavs, certainly Carantanian, fought at the battle of Lech on the side of Prince Odilo against the Franks.[73] The Avar attack against Carantania clearly shows us in what way the Avars subjected neighbouring Slavic principalities, that is Nitria, Moravia, Carniola and Savia, which did not receive effective foreign help.

---

71   Wolfram, *Salzburg, Bayern, Österreich*, pp. 47, 75, 347. Třeštík, *Vznik*, p. 41.
72   *Conversio* 4, ed. Wolfram, pp. 64–65, 117–119. Wolfram, *Salzburg, Bayern, Österreich*, pp. 45–46. Třeštík, *Vznik*, pp. 38–41. The Carinthians attacked the Bavarian monastery; then they were enemies of the Bavarians and hardly would have asked the enemy Bavarians for assistance. The Bavarians went to defend Carantania because it belonged to them.
73   *Annales Mettenses priores* ad a. 743, primum recognovit B. de Simson, Scriptores rerum Germanicarum in usum scholarum ex Monumentis Germaniae historicis editi (Hannoverae et Lipsiae 1905), p. 33. Wolfram, *Salzburg, Bayern, Österreich*, p. 277. *Conversio*, ed. Wolfram, pp. 117–119. Třeštík, *Vznik*, p. 41.

Borut's son Gorazd (749–752) was a Christian, but he never tried to Christianize his nation. Until his successor Hotimir (752–769) received from Bishop Vergilius of Salzburg a group of missionaries led by chorbishop Modestus: *When those came to Carantania, they consecrated the Church of St. Mary there and another at the castle Liburnia (in Liburnia civitate) or in Undrima (ad Undrimas) and in a great many other places.*[74] The Church of St. Mary stood not far from Krnski Grad, in today's Maria Saal, Austria. Liburnia (today Sankt Peter in Holz) was ancient Teurnia (Tiburnia), where as early as in 591 was a bishopric, which was the religious centre or the Roman province of Noricum mediterraneum.[75] Undrima lay on the upper Mur River, near Knittelfeld.[76]

The consecrating of three churches by chorbishop Modestus is the only proof of the work of the Salzburg mission in Carantania for the entire 30 years from the time it belonged to Bavaria and to the Frankish empire. If the unknown author of Conversio also speaks about other churches than about the three named ones, then he is exaggerating. If he truly knew of others, then he would certainly have named them. He would certainly have not left out such important documents on the credits of the Salzburg missionaries for the conversion of Carantania, such as the names of additional consecrated churches and even *in ... a great many other places*.

The location of the three named churches was not random. They stood in the middle of the small principalities into which Carantania was then divided. Little Carantania, where the Church of St. Mary stood, lay on the Drava River, in the area of the ancient city of Virunum. The Liburnian Principality, to which the second church belonged, covered the area of the ancient cities of Teurnia and Aguntum on the upper Drava. The principality served by the church

---

74 *Conversio* 5, ed. Wolfram, pp. 64–67, 119–120. *MMFH III*, p. 301. Stefan Eichert, "Kirchen des 8. bis 10. Jahrhunderts in Kärnten und ihre Bedeutung für die Archäologie der Karantanen," in *Frühmittelalterliche Kirchen als archäologische und historische Quelle*, ed. Lumír Poláček, Jana Mařiková-Kubková. *Internationale Tagungen in Mikulčice, Band VIII* (Brno 2010), pp. 219–232. Kurt Karpf, "Kirchen in Karantanien vor und nach Einführung der Grafschaftsverfassung (828)," in *Frühmittelalterliche Kirchen als archäologische und historische Quelle*, ed. Poláček, Mařiková-Kubková, pp. 233–242.

75 Franz Glaser, "Teurnia – civitas Tiburnia," in *"Castellum, civitas, urbs" – Zentren und Eliten im frühmittelalterlichen Ostmitteleuropa – Centres and Elites in Early Medieval East-Central Europe*, ed. Orsolya Heinrich-Tamáska, Hajnalka Herold, Péter Straub und Tivadar Vida, *Castellum Pannonicum Pelsonense* 6 (Budapest – Leipzig – Keszthely – Rahden/Westf. 2015), pp. 11–26. Michael Huber, "Tiburnia – Liburnia – Lurn: Philologische Beobachtungen zu einem alten Namensproblem," in *"Castellum, civitas, urbs"*, ed. Heinrich-Tamáska, Herold, Straub, Vida, pp. 27–34.

76 *Conversio*, ed. Wolfram, pp. 126–129. Wolfram, *Salzburg, Bayern, Österreich*, pp. 27–28, 119–128, 280–282.

ad Undrimas was part of the Mur Basin and the upper Enns. We can assume there were other small principalities on the central Mur, in the area of the ancient town of Flavia Solva. This was the most distant from Salzburg, and Modestus and his missionaries did not consecrate a church there that Conversio could name.[77] In the middle of Little Carantania, near the ruins of the Noricum capital city of Virunum, stood the seat of the Carantanian Principality of Krnski grad (Karnburg, civitas Carantana).[78]

A rebellion swept aside Modestus's mission. This was obviously Bavarian Duke Tassilo III (748–788), who in years 763 and 765 suppressed two rebellions of the Carinthians against Bavarian rule. In 769 Hotimir died, and the Carinthians rebelled again. Tassilo conquered the Carantanians only after a

[77] Andrej Pleterski differentiates only three small principalities in Carantania: Little Carantania, Liburnia and probably a principality on the middle Mur in the area of the former Roman town of Flavia Solva. He translates the conjunction *seu* in the report on the consecration of three Carantanian churches as *natačneje* (= that is). The words *et aliam in Liburnia civitate seu ad Undrimas* acquire in his translation a different meaning: *in neko drugo na poročju Liburnije, natačneje v Undrimach* (= and others in the district of Liburnija, that is, in Undrima). According to Andrej Pleterski, Modestus's mission consecrated only two churches, the Church of St. Mary near Krnski Grad and the church in Undrima, which belonged to the Liburnia district. The Liburnia Principality belonged likewise not only to the most upper part of the Drava, but also to the upper Mur, where Undrima lay. Andrej Pleterski, "Mitska stvarnost koroških knežjich kamnov," *Zgodovinski časopis* 50 (1996), no. 4 (105), pp. 520–528. Andrej Pleterski, "Modestuskirchen und Conversio," in *Slovenija in sosednje dežele med antiko in karolinško dobo. Začetki slovenske etnogeneze I*, ed. Rajko Bratož (Ljubljana 2000), pp. 425–476. The churches consecrated by Modestus and his missionaries stood in the most important towns of Carantania. They were the main and then only churches of the small principalities into which Carantania was divided. The main church could not have stood at the opposite and upper ends of the principalities; it had to be within comfortable reach of the principality castle, just as the main Carantanian Church of St. Mary stood near Krnski Grad. Therefore, the church *ad Undrimas*, if it were the main church of the Liburnian Principality, then it must have stood near the Liburnia Castle, and not by Knittelfeld. But if it stood near Knittelfeld, that is, far away from Liburnia Castle, then it could not have been the main church of the Liburnian Principality. In both cases, however, we can count on a small principality on the upper Mur and the upper Enns, different from the Liburnian Principality. If the Undrima church did stand near Knittelfeld, then it was the main church of this small principality. If Undrima lay near the Liburnia Castle, which is not likely, however, then the assumed principality on the upper Mur and upper Enns would not have its own church, just as other principalities which we assume to be on the middle Mur didn't have one.

[78] Pleterski, "Mitska stvarnost," pp. 482–485. Wolfram, *Salzburg, Bayern, Österreich*, pp. 119, 281. *Conversio*, ed. Wolfram, pp. 110–112. Štih, *The Middle Ages between the Eastern Alps and the Northern Adriatic*, pp. 110–112. Eichert, "Zentralisierungsprocesse bei den frühmittelalterlichen Karantanen," pp. 28–52.

great military excursion in 772[79] and he appointed Valtunk as prince (772–788). Valtunk cooperated with Bishop Vergilius of Salzburg (748–785), who sent the missionaries to Carantania.[80] Among the Salzburg missionaries one Ingo stood out; he had been sent to Carantania by Vergilius's successor Arno (785–836, archbishop from 798).[81]

79 *Conversio* 5, ed. Wolfram, pp. 66–67, 131–132. *Tassilo Carenthaniam subiugavit, et Theodo filius eius Romae baptizatus est. Annales Admuntenses* ad a. 772, edidit Wilhelmus von Wattenbach, Monumenta Germaniae historica, Scriptores 9 (Hannoverae 1851), p. 572. *Adrianus papa factus est. Karolus in Saxoniam, conquesivit Erespurc et Irminsul eorum destrixit. Tassilo Carintanos vicit. Annales Iuvavenses maximi* ad a. 772, edidit Harry Bresslau, Monumenta Germaniae historica XXX, 2 (Lipsiae 1934), p. 732. *Carolus in Saxonia, conquesivit Erespurc et Irmisul et Tassilo Carentanos. Adrianus papa factus est. Annales sancti Emmerami Ratisponensis maiores* ad a. 772, edidit Harry Bresslau, Monumenta Germaniae historica, Scriptores XXX, 2 (Lipsiae 1934), p. 733. Wolfram, *Salzburg, Bayern, Österreich*, pp. 283–284. Třeštík, *Vznik*, p. 46.
80 *Conversio* 5, ed. Wolfram, pp. 66–67, 130–132. Wolfram, *Salzburg, Bayern, Österreich*, pp. 283–285.
81 *Conversio* 7, ed. Wolfram, pp. 68–69, 151–157. Wolfram, *Salzburg, Bayern, Österreich*, pp. 287–289. Třeštík, *Vznik*, pp. 46–47, 226. Támas Nótári, *A salzburgi historiográfia kezdetei* (Szeged 2007), pp. 242–254.

CHAPTER 4

Fall of the Avar Khaganate

1   Charlemagne's War against the Khaganate

Charlemagne conquered the Longobard kingdom in the year 774[1] and in 776 suppressed an uprising of Friulian Duke Hrodgaud. Hrodgaud fell in the battle, and Friuli, one of the nullified Longobard principalities, became a border march focused against the Avars.[2] In 788 the March of Friuli expanded its territory by Byzantine Istria.[3]

In 788 Charlemagne renewed Frankish dominion over Bavaria. He removed the last Bavarian duke from the Agilolfing line, his nephew Tassilo III, and sent him with his son to a monastery and exiled his loyal magnates.[4] Charlemagne abolished the principality, appointed his brother-in-law Gerold as the Bavarian prefect[5] and installed his own counts throughout all of Bavaria.[6] Tassilo's allies, the Avars, were left without a response to his fall. After fending off an Avar attack into Bavaria and the March of Friuli, the Bavarians and Franks invaded Avar territory beyond the Enns, winning the battle in the fields at Ybbs and rebutting another Avar attack into Bavaria.[7]

---

1   *Ann. reg. Franc.* (*Ann. Lauriss. mai.*, *Ann. Einhardi*) ad a. 773, 774. rec. Kurze, pp. 34–41.
2   *Ann. reg. Franc.* (*Ann. Lauriss. mai.*, *Ann. Einhardi*) ad a. 776, rec. Kurze, pp. 42–45. Krahwinkler, *Friaul*, pp. 119–143.
3   Wolfram, *Die Geburt*, pp. 256–257. Krahwinkler, *Friaul*, pp. 179, 199–201. Harald Krahwinkler, … in loco qui dicitur Riziano … Zbor v Rižani pri Kopru leta 804. Die Versammlung in Rižana/Risano bei Koper/Capodistra im Jahre 804 (Koper 2004), pp. 17–20, 27–29, 111–114, 122–124.
4   *Ann. reg. Franc.* (*Ann. Lauriss. mai.*, *Ann. Einhardi*) ad a. 788, rec. Kurze, pp. 80–85. Wolfram, *Die Geburt*, pp. 105–106. Nótári, *A salzburgi historiográfia kezdetei*, pp. 87–119.
5   Margrave Gerold was the brother of Charles's deceased wife Hildegard. Richter – Kohl, *Annalen* II/1, p. 106. James Bruce Ross, "Two Neglected Paladins of Charlemagne: Erich of Friuli and Gerold of Bavaria," *Speculum* 20 (1945), p. 233. Michael Mitterauer, *Karolingische Markgrafen in Südosten. Fränkische Reichsaristokratie und bayerischer Stammesadel im österreichischen Raum*, Archiv für österreichische Geschichte 123 (1963), pp. 8–26. Wolfram, *Die Geburt*, p. 189.
6   *Tassilo tamen postmodum ad regem evocatus neque redire permissus, neque provincia, quam tenebat, ulterius duci, sed comitibus ad regendum commissa est. Einhardi Vita Karoli Magni* 11, curavit Reinholdus Rau, Quellen zur karolingischen Reichsgeschichte 1. Teil, neubearbeitet Reinholdus Rau. Augewählte Quellen zur deutschen Geschichte des Mittelalters, ed. Rudolf Buchner, Band 5, Darmstadt 1980, pp. 180–181. Mitterauer, *Karolingische Markgrafen*, pp. 80–81.
7   *Ann. reg. Franc.* (*Ann. Lauriss. mai.*, *Ann. Einhardi*) ad a. 788, rec. Kurze, pp. 82–84.

On the eastern edge of Bavaria lay the Carantanian Principality and Traungau County. Because they bordered the Avar Empire, Charlemagne transformed them, as he had done 12 years earlier with Friuli, into border marches focused against the Avars: *After all of this, King Charlemagne himself came personally to Regensburg and appointed the border or marches (marcas) of the Bavarians, so that under God's power they could be safe against the mentioned Avars.*[8] Carantania could not avoid the change of administration in 788. The king had to depose not only Bavarian Duke Tassilo, but also his protector, the last Carantanian Prince Valtunk, whom Tassilo had installed after putting down the last anti-Bavarian rebellion of the Carantanians in 772.[9] Valtunk had to depart from the scene similarly as Tassilo's Bavarian magnates, and Valtunk's Carinthia faced a similar fate as Hrodgaud's Friuli. Both became border marches of Charlemagne's empire against the Avars. Even Conversio, which in the 3rd through 5th chapters describes Carantania in detail, ends the rule of the domestic Carantanian principalities with Valtunk.[10] Thus, Bavarian prefect Gerold I became margrave of the Avar and Carantanian Marches and took part in the subsequent wars against the Avars.[11]

In 790 Charlemagne began to negotiate with the Avars. Discussions broke down, however, on disputes about the common borders of the Frankish and Avar realms,[12] and this led to another war. Charlemagne assembled a huge army in Regensburg the following year and moved with it into a military camp on the border at Lorch. Freising Bishop Atto, Salzburg Bishop Arno and Charlemagne's brother-in-law Gerold I were all at the camp, too.[13] The

---

[8] *Post haec omnia domnus Carolus per semet ipsum ad Reganesburg pervenit et ibi fines vel marcas Baioariorum diposuit, quomodo salvas Domino protegere contra iamdictos Avaros esse potuissent. Ann. reg. Franc. (Ann. Lauriss.)* ad a. 788, rec. Kurze, p. 84. The plural *marcas Baioariorum* clearly states that Charlemagne appointed not one, but at least two Bavarian border marches against the Avars. *Rex autem in Baioariam profectus eandem provinciam cum suis terminis ordinavit atque disposuit. Ann. reg. Franc. (Ann. Einhardi)* ad a. 788, rec. Kurze, p. 85.

[9] Ernst Klebel, "Der Einbau Karantaniens in das Ostfränkische und Deutsche Reich," *Carinthia* I, 150 (Klagenfurt 1960), pp. 670–671. Třeštík, *Vznik*, p. 46.

[10] *Conversio* 5, ed. Wolfram, pp. 66–67. *MMFH III*, p. 302. *Conversio Bagoariorum et Carantanorum*, edidit Milko Kos, Rozprave znanstvenega drušstva v Ljubljani 11, Historični odsek 3 (Ljubljana 1936), pp. 38–39.

[11] *Notkeri Gesta Karoli* I 34, *MMFH II*, p. 40. Gerold, as the border margrave, fought against the Avars and fell in battle. See note 50.

[12] *Ann. reg. Franc. (Ann. Einhardi)* ad a. 790, rec. Kurze, p. 87.

[13] *Ann. reg. Franc. (Ann. Lauriss. mai., Ann. Einhardi)* ad a. 791, rec. Kurze, pp. 86–89. Richter – Kohl, *Annalen II/1*, p. 106. Wolfram, *Die Geburt*, pp. 189, 255.

Saxon and Frisian army, led by Count Theodorich and his highest chamberlain Meginfrid, moved against the Avars through Bohemia.[14]

Charlemagne's son Pepin (King of Italy since 781) was the first to attack the Avars, from the territory of the March of Friuli. On 23 August 791 Pepin conquered a forward Avar fortress in neighbouring Carniola and along with it the territory on which it lay and returned home victorious.[15] After 20 August, Charlemagne crossed the Bavarian border on the Enns and headed down the right bank of the Danube. The Saxons and Frisians crossed the Bohemian border to the valley of the Kamp River and on the left-hand bank of the Danube. Bavarian boats floated down the Danube. They first destroyed the advanced Avar fortresses, one above the Kamp River and a second, reinforced with a strong bulwark, on the edge of the Vienna Woods. After passing beyond the Vienna Woods, the Frankish army entered into Pannonia and continued in its expedition up to the Rába River. They came along its banks up to its confluence with the Danube, but due to unfavourable autumn weather and a plague among the horses, at the beginning of November they had to return through Sabaria (Szombathely) and along the south bank of the Danube to Bavaria and through Bohemia to Saxony.[16]

Both armies set off against two different parts of the Avar Khaganate. The southern army of Pepin advanced through Carniola directly against khaganate territory. The northern army of Charlemagne headed down the Danube through the territory of the tudun from its western edge to the Enns up to the confluence of the Rába with the Danube at its opposite end. Both

---

14   Třeštík, *Vznik*, pp. 57–63.
15   Pepin *introvit in Illyricum et inde in Pannonia, partibus Avariae in Hunorum confinia residendum, perexerunt infra fines ipsorum X. Calend. Septembris* (= 23. 8. 791). *Annales Laureshamenses* ad a. 791. *Annales Moissiacenses* ad a. 791, edidit Georgius Heinricus Pertz, Monumenta Germaniae historica, Scriptores I (Hannoverae et Lipsiae 1826), pp. 34, 299. *Regesten und Urkunden der ersten Karolinger II*, gesammelt und bearbeitet Theodor Sickel (Wien 1867), n. 132, p. 54. Gottlieb von Ankershofen, *Handbuch der Geschichte des Herzogthumes Kärnten im Mittelalter im Mittelalter bis zur Vereinigung mit den österreichischen Fürstentümern*, II. Band, 1. Heft 476–1122 (Klagenfurt 1851), p. 120. August Dimitz, *Geschichte Krains von der ältesten Zeit bis auf das Jahr 1813. Mit besonderer Rücksicht auf Culturentwicklung. Erster Theil: Von der Urzeit bis zum Tode Kaiser Friedrichs III. (1493)* (Laibach 1874), p. 108. *Erläuterungen zum historischen Atlas der österreichischen Alpenländer. I. Abteilung: Die Landgerichtskarte, 4. Teil: Kärnten, Krain, Görz und Istrien* von August von Jaksch, Martin Wutte, Ludmil Hauptmann, Anton Mell und Hans Pirchegger, 2. *Heft: Kärnten (Nachtrag), Krain und Istrien*, Wien 1929, pp. 338–341. Bogo Grafenauer, *Zgodovina slovenskega naroda I* (Ljubljana 1964), p. 406. Pohl, *Die Awaren*, p. 316. Krahwinkler, *Friaul*, pp. 148–149. Štih, *Die Ostgrenze Italiens*, pp. 20, 26.
16   *Ann. reg. Franc.* (*Ann. Lauriss. mai., Ann. Einhardi*) ad a. 791, rec. Kurze, pp. 86–91. *MMFH I*, pp. 18–19. Wolfram, *Die Geburt*, p. 256. Třeštík, *Vznik*, pp. 56–59.

campaigns, Pepin's and Charlemagne's, ended with the same result. They conquered not only the forward Avar fortresses but also the territories on the road to Pannonia. Charlemagne could then assign the territory between the Enns and the Vienna Woods to the Avar (later called the Eastern) March, the basis of which was Bavarian Traungau. The March of Friuli on the south again acquired Carniola, conquered by Pepin. The subsequent anti-Avar campaigns of King of Italy Pepin and Friulian Margrave Erik now had a free path to Pannonia through Carniola.

Dissent within the khaganate, which climaxed with the murder of the khagan and the jugur, undermined its ability to defend itself. The tudun, who wanted to get out from under the khagan's rule, took advantage of this. Therefore, *envoys of the tudun, who had great power in the nation and in the realm of the Avars*, sought out Charlemagne in 795, to whom *these said that this tudun wants to subject his territory and his people to the king and on his order he wants to accept the Christian faith*.[17]

2   The Slav Vojnomir

In this same year Friulian Margrave Erik took advantage of the weakening of the khaganate: *He sent his people with the Slav Vojnomir (cum Wonomyro Sclavo), sacked the hrink of the Avar nation ... and sent the spoils of the previous rulers, gathered in the course of many centuries, to King Charlemagne at the palace in Aachen.*[18] How could a Friulian margrave hand over the leadership of his army to a Slav? What was Vojnomir seeking in the services of the Friulian margrave? Vojnomir set off in 795 with Erik's military to Pannonia against the Avars, similarly as Svätopluk had led Carloman's Bavarian army into Moravia against Slavomir in 871. Svätopluk could reliably lead the Bavarian army against the rebels in Moravia. He knew Slavomir well, because he was a relative of his, and he was able to fully move in Moravia, because he was himself a Moravian. Vojnomir was equally well known in Pannonia; that is, with complete certainty he came from Pannonia, because he knew where to go and how to strike at the khagan's seat.[19] That's why he alone could lead a campaign whose leadership belonged to the Friulian margrave.

17   *Ann. reg. Franc.* (*Ann. Lauriss. mai.*) ad a. 795, 796, rec. Kurze, pp. 96, 98. *MMFH I*, p. 21. Wolfram, *Die Geburt*, pp. 257–258. Třeštík, *Vznik*, pp. 63–65.
18   *Ann. reg. Franc.* (*Ann. Lauriss. mai.*, *Ann. Einhardi*) ad a. 796, rec. Kurze, s. 98, 99. *MMFH I*, pp. 20, 21. Pohl, *Die Awaren*, p. 319. Třeštík, *Počátky*, p. 265. Třeštík, *Vznik*, pp. 65–66.
19   The Longobard Hildigis became the leader of the Slavic campaign to Italy in year 550 evidently because he knew the local relations. Regarding the khagan's seat in Pannonia,

In the meantime, by the end of 795 Charlemagne released Erik's messengers, who had brought the Avar treasure to him; he received the tudun along with a large train of followers: *The tudun, as promised and with a large portion of Avars, came to the king with his people and submitted his homeland to the king; he and his people were baptised and returned honoured with gifts.*[20] In addition to the tudun the kapkhan also became a Christian, baptised under the name Theodor, and he ruled his Avars until his death in 805.[21] In the battle against the khagan, who remained a pagan until 805,[22] he certainly stood on the side of the tudun and obviously received baptism together with him.

3 The Division of Pannonia among the Frankish Border Marches and Bishoprics

In 796 Charlemagne sent his son, Italian King Pepin, to Pannonia (*in Pannonias*) at the head of an Italian and Bavarian army. When Pepin entered into the khaganate part of Pannonia, *Ingomer* (*Unguimeri*) ... *from the line of the Avars* appealed to the khagan and his influential wife the khatun for capitulation. A part of the Avars, evidently the part which came on the khagan's order from the Tisza River region, withdrew back across the Tisza. Pepin ransacked and disrupted the khagan's residential hrink. The khagan and his tarkhans surrendered to Pepin and handed their sons to him as hostages. Pepin then made camp on the bank of the Danube and there, certainly acting on the will of his father, he decided on the division of Pannonia between the border marches and the bishoprics.[23] The remaining part of the khaganate, that is, the lower

---

see chapter 3, note 4. József Szentpéteri, "Cartographia avarica. Kartographische Bemerkungen von ADAM bis Bajan," in *Ethnische und kulturelle Verhältnisse an der mittleren Donau vom 6. bis zum 11. Jahrhundert, Symposium Nitra 6. bis 10. November 1994*, ed. Darina Bialeková, Jozef Zábojník (Bratislava 1996), pp. 154–159.

20 *Ann. reg. Franc.* (*Ann. Lauriss. mai.*) ad a. 796, rec. Kurze, p. 98. MMFH I, pg. 21. *Conversio* 6, ed. Wolfram, pp. 46–47, MMFH III, pg. 303–304. Wolfram, *Die Geburt*, p. 258. Třeštík, *Vznik*, p. 66.
21 See notes 64, 65.
22 See note 63.
23 Ann. reg. Franc. (Ann. Lauriss. mai., Ann. Einhardi) ad a. 796, rec. Kurze, pp. 98–100, MMFH I, pg. 20, 22. *Carmen de Pippini regis victoria Avarica a. 796*, MMFH II, pp. 13–15. *Conversio* 6, ed. Wolfram, pp. 46–47, MMFH III, p. 304. Ernst Dümmler, "Über die südöstlichen Marken des Fränkischen Reiches unter den Karolingern (795–907)," *Archiv für Kunde österreichischer Geschichtsquellen* 10 (1853), pp. 3–5. Josef Cibulka, *Velkomoravský kostel v Modré u Velehradu a začátky křesťanství na Moravě* (Praha 1958), pp. 167–168, 174–175. Franz Zagiba, *Das Geistesleben der Slawen im frühen Mittelalter* (Wien – Köln – Graz 1971), p. 61. Wolfram, *Die Geburt*, p. 258. Třeštík, *Vznik*, pp. 66–67.

Pannonian part of Transdanubia to the south and east from the Rábca and the lower Rába up to the Drava and to the Danube went to the Carantanian March.[24] The Friulian margrave retained its claim to the Savian Principality,[25] which recognized the hegemony of the khaganate but did not join in with capitulation to the khaganate. The entire tudunate, which extended into the interior of Pannonia up to the lower Rába and the Rábca rivers fell to the Avar March. For several years following, however, the Avar March did not cross the Enns River and was limited to Traungau County. The oldest names of this marches are Avaria (*Avaria* of year 811),[26] the province of the Avars (*provintia Avarorum* of year 823, 832, 833, 836)[27] and the land of the Avars (*terra Avarorum* of year 831).[28] After year 836 this naming expired and was replaced by others that better described its role.

Pepin *called a dignified gathering of several bishops* to his military camp on the bank of the Danube. The ecclesiastical assembly was chaired by Aquileia Patriarch Paulino[29] and among the bishops present there, we know only the name of Salzburg Bishop Arno.[30] The Danubian synod resolved the question of Christianization and church administration of the conquered territory.[31] Pepin, obviously on the basis of a recommendation of the synod, which had to be in agreement with the dividing of Pannonia among the border marches, *assigned the part of Lower Pannonia near Lake Pleso* (Balaton), *beyond the river which is called the Rába, and up to the Drava River and to the place where the*

---

24 See notes 34, 36, 56.
25 Charlemagne also subjugated (*ita perdomuit, ut eas tributarias effi ceret*), among other nations and territories, *both Pannonias* (*utraque Pannoniam*), that is, also lower Pannonian Savia. Einhardi Vita Karoli Magni 15, MMFH II, p. 23. In 818 the Savian prince Ljudevit complained about the unjust rule of Friulian Margrave Cadolah. Ann. reg. Franc. ad a. 818, rec. Kurze, p. 149. MMFH I, pp. 26–27. Anonymi Vita Hludovici 31, MMFH II, p. 28.
26 MMFH III, Diplomata 5, p. 20.
27 Urkundenbuch des Landes ob der Enns II, Wien 1856, no. 5, p. 8. Codex diplomaticus Hungariae ecclesiasticus ac civilis I, studio et opera Georgii Fejér (Budae 1829), p. 156. MMFH III, Diplomata 12, 13, 15, pp. 30–31, 31–33, 34–35. Lubomír Havlík, Staří Slované v rakouském Podunají v době od 6. do 12. století. Rozpravy ČSAV, ročník 73, sešit 9 (Praha 1963), pp. 62–63.
28 MMFH III, Diplomata 11, p. 29.
29 Conventus episcoporum ad ripas Danubii, MMFH IV, pp. 18–20. MMFH III, Epistolae 2, p. 137. Conversio, ed. Wolfram, p. 107. Pepin's military camp on the bank of the Danube is also recalled in the Song on King Pepin's Victory Over the Avars: *Rex accintus Dei virtute Pippinus, rex catholicus, castra figit super flumen Danubium, hostibus accingens totum undique presidia.* Carmen de Pippini regis victoria Avarica a. 796 5, MMFH II, p. 14. Wolfram, Salzburg, Bayern, Österreich, pp. 285–287.
30 MMFH III, Epistolae 3, p. 138. Cibulka, Velkomoravský kostel, pp. 174–175.
31 László Veszprémy, "Mint békák a mocsárban. Püspökök gyűlése a Duna mellett 796-ban," Aetas 19 (2004), no. 2, pp. 53–71.

Drava flows into the Danube, to where his power reached ... to Arno, the bishop of Salzburg.[32] The thus-designated diocese of the Salzburg Bishop coincided with the Carinthian march: *Similarly, Bishop Arno, the successor of Vergilius in the Salzburg bench ..., sanctifying priests from all sides and sending them to Slavinia, that is to the lands of Cariantania and also Lower Pannonia (in Sclaviniam, in partes videlicet Quarantanas atque inferioris Pannoniae), to the princes and to the counts (ducibus atque comitibus), as Vergilius did before.*[33] From the elevating of the Salzburg bishopric to an archbishopric in year 798 chorbishop Theodorich directed the work of the Salzburg mission in the Carantanian parts of the diocese: *Then on the command of the emperor* (correctly of the king) *Salzburg Archbishop Arno ordained Theodorich as bishop, whom Arno and Count Gerold alone accompanied to Slavinia (in Sclaviniam) and delivered into the hands of the princes (in manus principum), entrusted to the bishop of the land of the Carinthians (regionem Carantanorum) and its boundary lands near the western flow of the Drava River up to the place where the Drava pours into the Danube River.*[34] Gerold, who administered not only to the Bavaria and the Avar March, but was also the margrave of Carantania, accompanied, together with Salzburg Archbishop Arno, chorbishop Theodorich to the land of his Carantanian March, which stretched eastward up to the confluence of the Drava with the Danube. The Transdanubian part of Lower Pannonia also belonged to it, and the name Carantania was transferred to the whole large territory. Even a document from Charlemagne in 811 labels Carantania as Transdanubian territory, to which the Aquileian patriarch made a claim *provintia Karantanorum*[35] and a description of Germania in the Anglo-Saxon

32 *partem Pannoniae circa lacum Pellissa inferioris, ultra fluvium, qui dicitur Hrapa, et sic usque ad Dravum fluvium et eo, usque ubi Dravus fluit in Danubium, prout potestatem habuit, praenominavit ... Arnoni Iuvavensium episcopo. Conversio* 6, ed. Wolfram, pp. 68–69, 150. MMFH III, p. 304.

33 *Conversio* 7, ed. Wolfram, pp. 68–69. MMFH III, pp. 304–305. On 20 April 798 Salzburg Bishop Arno was ordained as Archbishop. Nótari, *A salzburgi historiográfia kezdetei*, pp. 119–132.

34 *Conversio* 8, ed. Wolfram, pp. 70–71, 158–162. MMFH III, pp. 306–307. Theodorich became chorbishop in year 798 or 799 after the elevation of Arno to archbishop and before the death of Margrave Gerold I. Bavarian Slavinia was not only Carantania, but also the Eastern March. In 837 the Salzburg archbishop got property *in Sclauinia* from the Bavarian King Louis the German, at a place called *Ipusa* (= Ybbs) on both banks of the River *Ipusa*. MMFH III, Diplomata 16, pp. 36–37. In 893 Kremsmünster Abbey got from East Francia King Arnulf of Carantania property which he had confiscated from brothers Wilhelm and Engelschalk lying *ad Eporespurch* (near Mautern), *ad Cambe* (= Kamp), *ad Persiniccham* (= Perschling) and other places *in Baioariae scilicet atque Sclaviniae*. MMFH III, Diplomata 48, pp. 80–81.

35 See note 56.

translation of Orosius's work Historia mundi from Alfred the Great *land Carendre*.³⁶

The division of Pannonia between the Frankish border marches and the bishoprics in 796, which sorted the interior division of the Avar empire, was still premature, because the khagan and the tudun and with them the entire structure of the khaganate remained further in place. By an early decision, however, many future disputes between the margraves and the bishops were avoided. They were unable to mutually cross their claims in the future, because they had to have them clearly defined, in a duly set time and with recognized borders.

The later author of Conversio knew that the Salzburg chorbishop and the missionaries who worked in Carantania and in the Salzburg part of Pannonia belonged *to the hands of the princes* or *to the princes and also the counts*, because they needed protection and powerful support of the Carantanian counts as well as the small principalities and then counts in the Salzburg part of Pannonia and later also the Pannonian princes Pribina and Kocel. The Pannonian part of the Salzburg diocese was, however, safe for Bavarian missionaries only after the end of the Slavic-Avar conflicts in 811; thus, they could not have operated there from 796, as Conversio tells us. Arno and Gerold could in 798 or 799 delegate Theodorich and the mission in the Pannonian part of the Salzburg diocese; he, however, had to limit his work up to year 811 only to Carantania.

The splitting of the Salzburg part of Pannonia enables us to determine the territorial share of the neighbouring diocese. The Passau bishop got church administration of Upper Pannonia belonging to the Avar March and with the missionary rights to Moravia and Nitria, that is the entire territory of the tudunate. Church administration of the Pannonian territory south of the Drava River, that is the Savian Principality belonging under the Friulian Margrave, fell to the Aquilean patriarch.

4 Vojnomir, Prince of Savia

After Pepin's departure *from Pannonia (ex Pannonia)*, the Avars were resolved to continue in the war. Therefore, in 797 Pepin and Erik again set out for Pannonia: *Erik triumphed over the Vandals* (= Avars), *Pepin over the Slavs*. Pepin again marched at the head of the Bavarian and Italian militaries: *Pepin, along*

---

36 *Orosius* I/1, MMFH III, pp. 338–340.

with the Bavarians and with some Longobards (triumphed) *over the Slavs, devastated the territory and returned in peace to their father lord King Charles.*[37]

Pepin's army was at the very least equal to Erik's. Pepin was the king of Italy and Erik only its margrave. Pepin could therefore not have a smaller army than his direct subordinate Erik. The Slavs whom Pepin attacked were thus an equally serious adversary as the Pannonian Avars against whom Erik marched. The Slav territory which lay in the direction of Pepin's attack, and whose size, number of warriors and political and military organization could at least approximately compare with that of the Avar part of Pannonia, was the Slavic principality on the middle Sava with its centre in Sisak. Pepin thus crossed the eastern border of the March of Friuli and set off down the Sava to Sisak, from which he certainly removed a prince loyal to the Avars. However, he did not abolish his principality. In addition, he had to respect the local relations; he therefore could not place just anyone in Sisak. He had to select a new prince who would be a guarantee of loyalty to him from the local princely family line. Just as East Francia King Louis the German, present in 846 with his military in Moravia, could place onto the Moravian Principality only a member of the local princely line of the Mojmír family and put there Mojmír's nephew Rastislav, in whom he then saw a guarantee of loyalty, so Pepin, if he wanted to have his own man on the princely seat of Sisak, then he had to choose from among the members of the Sisak princely family.[38] The Friulian sovereignty over Savia that followed[39] is evidence that Pepin actually found such a person, and this was certainly Vojnomir, who came from Pannonia and had distinguished himself in Erik's service.

---

[37] *Ericus victoriam in Uuandalos, Pippinus super Sclauos.* Annales Alamanici (*Codex Modoectiensis*) ad a. 797, MMFH I, pp. 14–15. *Pippinus cum Baguariis et quosdam de Langobardis super Sclauos terram devastavit et cum pace reversus est ad patrem suum dominum regem Karolum.* Annales Alamanici (*Codex Turicensis*) ad a. 797, MMFH I, pp. 14–15. Henryk Łowmiański, *Początki Polski. Z dziejów Słowian w I tysiącleciu n. e. IV* (Warszawa 1970), p. 265. Třeštík, *Počátky*, p. 266.

[38] The Bavarian expedition, led by Eichstadt Bishop Otgar, Count Palatine Hruodolt and Ernest, son of Margrave Ernest, exiled in 857 from the Bohemian Prince Slavitech. East Francia King Louis the German put Slavitech's brother, who *handed over, came to the king and was in place of his brother name prince* into Slavitech's castle. Ann. Fuld. ad a. 857, rec. Kurze, s. 47. MMFH I, p. 76. Louis the German thus could not hand over Slavitech's principality to any of his own people, but only to a member of the existing princely line.

[39] See note 25.

Vojnomir's labelling as *Sclavus* is not unique. People labelled as *Saxo*,[40] *Wasco*,[41] *Sarracenus*,[42] *Gothus*,[43] *Langobardus*,[44] *Nordmannus*,[45] *Iudeus*[46] and

40   In 743 Carloman, brother of Frankish King Pepin the Short, marched on the Saxon castle Hochseeburg (between Halle and Eislebenom), in which *Saxon Dietrich* (*Theodericus Saxo*) was seated. Dietrich had to subjugate himself to Carloman: *Carlomannus solus in Saxoniam profectus est et castrum, quod dicitur Hohseoburg, et in eo Theodericum Saxonem, illius loci primarium, in dedicionem accepit*. In the following year Carloman and Pepin again marched into Saxony and they took Dietrich captive. *Ann. reg. Franc.* (*Ann. Lauriss. mai., Ann. Einhardi*) ad a. 743, 744, rec. Kurze, pp. 4–5.

41   After the defeat of the Aquitaine rebellion of 769, the last Aquitanian duke, Hunald II, escaped *to the Basque Lupus* (*ad Luponem Wasconem*). *Ann. Reg. Franc.* (*Ann. Lauriss. mai.*) ad a. 769, rec. Kurze, p. 30. Lupus was the Duke of Gascony: *Erat tunc Wasconum dux Lupus nomine*, who recognized Frankish domination and gave Hunald to Charlemagne. *Ann. Reg. Franc.* (*Ann. Einhardi*) ad a. 769, rec. Kurze, p. 31. *Einhardi Vita Karoli Magni* 5, cur. Rau, pp. 170–173. In 819 *the Basque Lupus Centulli* (*Lupus Centulli Wasco*) suffered defeat from Berengar, the Count of Toulouse, and Warin, the Count of Auvergne. His brother Garsando fell in the battle. If Lupo Centulli led a war with two Aquitanian counts, and neighbouring Toulouse County was even larger than the defeated Gascony, then it could not have been any smaller than the Principality of Gascony. *Ann. reg. Franc.* ad a. 819, rec. Kurze, pp. 150–152. *Anonymi Vita Hludowici imperatoris* 32, cur. Rau, pp. 308–309.

42   In 777 Sulayman al-Kalbi, Amirate in Zaragoza, Kasim, son of one-time caliph's viceroy in Cordoba Yusuf al-Fihri and Yusuf's son-in-law Hasan ibn Jahjá came to Paderborn: *Sarraceni de partibus Hispaniae, hi sunt Ibin al Arabi et filius Deiuzefi, qui et latine Ioseph nominatur, similiter et gener eius*, or also: *Sarracenus quidam nomine Ibin al Arabi cum aliis Sarracenis sociis suis* and asked Charlemagne for help against the Cordoba Amir Abd ar-Rahman I. Charlemagne in the following year crossed the Pyrenees with a great army and unsuccessfully laid siege to Zaragoza. On the journey back the Basques attacked, and on 15 August 778 they destroyed the rear guard of his military in the Pyrenees pass Roncesvalles. *Ann. reg. Franc.* (*Ann. Lauriss. mai., Ann. Einhardi*) ad a. 777–778, rec. Kurze, pp. 48–51, 53. In 797 Barcelona viceroy Zaid accepted Frankish rule: *Barcinona ... per Zatum Sarracenum, qui tunc eam invaserat, regi redita est*. Or also: *Barcinona ... per Zatun praefectum ipsius nobis est reddita*. In this same year Charlemagne received in his court in Aachen Abdallah, son of former Cordoba Amirate Abd ar-Rahman I (756–788). Abdallah had been exiled from Cordoba by his brother, Cordoba amirate Hisham I (788–796): *Abdellam Sarracenum, filium Ibin-Maugae regis, qui a fratre regno pulsus in Mauritania exulabat, ipso semetipsum commendante suscepit*. In November 797 Charlemagne's son Louis (after 781 the Aquitanian king) took the Saracen Abdallah on an expedition to Spain: *Inde iterum ... Hludowicum ad Aquitaniam remisit, cum quo et Abdellam Sarracenum ire iussit, qui postea, ut ipse voluit, in Hispaniam ductus et illorum fidei, quibus se credere non dubitavit, commissus est. Ann. reg. Franc.* (*Ann. Lauriss. mai., Ann. Einhardi*) ad a. 797, rec. Kurze, pp. 100–103. In 799 Hassan, viceroy of Huesca, recognized Frankish rule: *Azan Sarracenus, praefectus Oscae, claves urbis cum aliis donis regi misit, promittens eam se dediturum, si oportunitas eveniret. Ann. reg. Franc.* (*Ann. Lauriss. mai., Ann. Einhardi*) ad a. 799, rec. Kurze, pp. 108–109.

43   In 826 Emperor Louis the Pious was betrayed by his courtier Aizo, who departed the emperor's court and called for a rebellion on the eastern edge of the Spanish March. Aizo, welcomed by the inhabitants, seized the town of Osona (today Vic, north of Barcelona). He

Britto[47] were princes, dukes, amirs, viceroys, counts, important political emigrants and emissaries, thus important members of their own tribe or nation, who lived or found themselves in direct reach of Frankish politics. Not one of them was a sovereign monarch. The mentioned Vojnomir was also such a significant

    then demolished the nearby town of Roda, occupied and fortified the surroundings of the castle and asked for help from the Cordoba amirate Abd ar-Rahman II against the expected Frankish counterattack. In the following year Aizo, with the help of Saracens, subjugated additional towns and castles. *Ann. reg. Franc.* ad a. 826–827, rec. Kurze, pp. 170, 172–173. *Anonymi Vita Hludovici imperatoris* 40–41, curavit Reinholdus Rau. Quellen zur karolingischen Reichsgeschichte 1. Teil, neubearbeitet Reinholdus Rau. Ausgewählte Quellen zur deutschen Geschichte des Mittelalters, ed. Rudolf Buchner, Band 5 (Berlin 1955), pp. 324, 326. The Annals of Fulda tell of Aizo's Gothic origin: *Aizo Gothus de palatio fugiens. Ann. Fuld.* ad a. 826, rec. Kurze, p. 20.

44   In years 775–776 the last Friulian duke of Longobard origin, Hrodgaud (*Hrodgaudus Langobardus*), rebelled against Charlemagne. Ann. reg. Franc. (Ann. Lauriss. mai., Ann. Einhardi) ad a. 775–776, rec. Kurze, pp. 42–43. In 792 *to the credit of the Longobard Ferdulf (per Fardulfum Langobardum)* a conspiracy against Charlemagne was discovered. *Ann. reg. Franc.* (*Ann. Einhardi*) ad a. 792, rec. Kurze, pp. 91, 93. In 811 Charlemagne sent a delegation to Constantinople, led to by Haido, Bishop of Basel, Count Hugo of Tours and *the Longobard Aio of Friuli (Aio Langobardus de Foro Iuli)*. Aio was *comes*, that is a count, certainly in some of the counties which were then assigned to the March of Friuli. *Ann. reg. Franc.* ad a. 811, rec. Kurze, pp. 133–134. Krahwinkler, *Friaul*, pp. 47, 64, 123, 134, 137–141, 146, 148, 181–185, 196, 202, 210, 223, 251, 275, 294. If Aio was *de Foro Iuli*, then he was a prince later in the Friulian Principality, in the central principality of the March of Friuli. He was then directly subordinate to then Friulian Margrave Cadolah II (802–819).

45   In 782 at an imperial conference near the source of the Lippe River, even couriers of Danish King Siegfried came: *The Normans, couriers of King Siegfried, namely Halfdan with his seconds (Nordmanni missi Sigifridi regis, id est Halptani cum sociis suis). Ann. reg. Franc.* (*Ann. Lauriss. mai.*) ad a. 782, rec. Kurze, p. 60.

46   In 797 Charlemagne sent a delegation to the caliph Harun ar-Rashid, which was led by the *Jew Isaac (Isaac Iudeus)*. In October 801 Isaac returned with rich gifts from the caliph, among which was even an elephant. *Ann. reg. Franc.* ad a. 801, rec. Kurze, p. 116.

47   *The Breton Salaün (Salomon Britto)*, cousin of Duke Erispoe of Brittany (*Respogius*), in 852 for his loyalty got a third of Brittany from the West Francia King Charles the Bald. After several years of common rule, a rupture occurred between the cousins. In November 857 *Bretonnians Salaün and Almaro (a Salomone et Almaro Brittonibus)* killed Erispoe, and Breton Salomon became the Duke of Brittany (857–874). *Annales Bertiniani* ad a. 852, 857, 861, 862, 863, 864, 867, 868, 869, 873, 874, recensuit Georgius Waitz. Scriptores rerum Germanicarum in usum scholarum ex Monumentis Germaniae historicis recusi (Hannoverae 1883), pp. 41, 48, 55, 57–58, 61, 72, 87–88, 97, 107, 124, 125. *Annales Bertiniani*, curavit Reinholdus Rau, Quellen zur karolingischen Reichsgeschichte, 2. Teil, neubearbeitet Reinholdus Rau. Ausgewählte Quellen zur deutschen Geschichte des Mittelalters, herausgegeben von Rudolf Buchner (Berlin 1966), pp. 82, 94, 106, 110, 116, 138, 166, 184, 202, 230, 234. Wolfram, *Salzburg, Bayern, Österreich*, pp. 169–171.

person,[48] undoubtedly of princely origin. His leadership capability and high position in Erik's service are testimony of this. If he was put into the service of the Friulians, he had to have come from Savia, which lay in the sphere of interest of the March of Friuli. If Vojnomir had come from northern Pannonia, which was an immediate part of the khaganate, then he would have offered his services to the Bavarian prefect and the margraves of the Avar and Carinthian Marches Gerold I, because Pannonian territory north of the Drava River fell not to Erik's March, but to Gerold's Marches. Vojnomir was thus obviously a member of the Sisak princely family, which believed in the victory of Frankish arms. Savia thus accepted Vojnomir as its prince in 797, and he recognized the dominion of the Friulian margrave.

5   War against the Tudunate

With the exception of Charlemagne's autumn march in 791, all other anti-Avar campaigns up to 797 came from Italy, directly against the khaganate, and the tudunate remained untouched. The tudun, on whom Charlemagne had counted as an ally, disappointed him. He broke away from the khaganate and became the independent ruler of a small realm, and the alliance with the Frankish king had thus served its purpose and then ended. He decidedly had no intention of battling alongside the Franks, as Charlemagne undoubtedly expected him to do. Therefore, in 796, when he had rid himself of dependence on the khaganate, he abandoned Charlemagne.[49]

The tudun felt the force of Frankish weapons only three years later, when the anti-Avar campaigns changed direction. In 799 the Bavarian prefect and margrave of the Avar and Carantanian Marches, Gerold I, set off to war. He undoubtedly headed from Bavaria down the Danube to the territory of the neighbouring tudunate. In the battle which took place on 1 September 799, *Gerold, prefect of Bavaria, was killed somehow while in Pannonia, when he arranged his*

---

48   We can compare the case *cum Wonomyro Sclavo* with the case *Abdellam Sarracenum*. The Saracen Abdallah came from an emirate family in Cordoba; similarly, the Slav Vojnomir was of a Slavic princely line. Both had to leave their countries and seek help and offer their services in the neighbouring Frankish Empire. Because their cases were alike, the Royal Frankish Annals labeled both of them important political emigrants in the same way. At the time of his presence in the Frankish Empire neither Vojnomir (year 795) nor Abdallah (year 797) were prince and emir, respectively. Only later did Vojnomir become a prince in Sisak. However, Abdallah never did become the Cordoba emir.

49   *Tudun ... sed in promissa fidelitate diu manere noluit nec multo post perfi diae suae poenas dedit. Ann. reg. Franc. (Ann. Einhardi)* ad a. 796, rec. Kurze, p. 101.

military for battle against the Huns and did so with only two (men), *who accompanied him when circumventing* (the military) *and encouraging individuals. Otherwise, this war was for the Franks almost bloodless, and it had a very successful ending, even though due its mightiness, it dragged on rather long.*[50]

After Gerold's death, Charlemagne divided administration of the border marches from the administration of Bavaria. Audulf (799–818), the margrave of the Bavarian Northern March (Nordgau), became the Bavarian prefect.[51] King Charles (from the year 800 emperor) appointed Goteram (799–802) as margrave of the Avar and Carantanian March,[52] and he, together with Friulian Margrave Cadolah I, fell in a battle with the Avars *near Guntio's Castle* (*ad castellum Guntionis*) in 802.[53] Only the military expedition that Charlemagne sent from Bavaria in 803 forced the tudun to recognize Frankish rule.

50   Einhardi Vita Karoli Magni 13, MMFH II, p. 22. Ann. reg. Franc. (Ann. Lauriss. mai., Ann. Einhardi) ad a. 799, rec. Kurze, pp. 108–109. *Reginonis abbatis Prumiensis Chronicon cum continuatione Treverensi*, post editionem G. H. Perzii recognovit Fridericus Kurze, Scriptores rerum Germanicarum in usum scholarum ex Monumentis Germaniae historicis recusi (Hannoverae 1890), p. 61. MMFH III, Epistolae 11, p. 140. Dümmler, *Über die südöstlichen Marken*, p. 7. Ross, *Two Neglected Paladins*, pp. 225–228.

51   *Capitulare missorum* VII, MMFH IV, p. 24. Dümmler, *Über die südöstlichen Marken*, p. 16. *Conversio*, ed. Wolfram, pp. 167–170, 262–263, 266, 267. Wolfram, *Die Geburt*, pp. 194–195, 209, 270.

52   See note 98.

53   *Cadaloc et Goterhammus seu ceteri multi interfecti fuerunt ad castellum Guntionis. Annales sancti Emmerami Ratisponensis maiores* ad a. 802, edidit Georgius Heinricus Pertz, Monumenta Germaniae historica, Scriptores I (Hannoverae et Lipsiae 1826), p. 93. Friulian Margrave Cadolah I (799–802) was the successor of Margrave Erik. If Cadolah (*Cadaloc*), who died in 802, had been an ordinary count, that is of lower standing than Margrave Goteram (*Goterhammus*), as Herwig Wolfram assumes, then the St. Emmeram annals could not have named him as the first, even before Goteram. Wolfram, *Die Geburt*, p. 259. Wolfram, *Salzburg, Bayern, Österreich*, pp. 302–303. *Conversio*, ed. Wolfram, p. 168. Cadolah thus had to be at the very least equal to Goteram and his march had to lie in the Avar surroundings. If Goteram administered the Avar and Carinthian Marches, then Cadolah could have only been the Friulian margrave. In the crypt of the Church of St. Rupert in Traismauer lays the skeleton of perhaps a 30-year-old man, who was fatally injured by an arrow with an iron three-wing point. This arrowhead today lies near the pelvic bone of the deceased. The skeleton probably belongs to Margrave Goteram. The crypt belonged originally to the Carolingian church from the beginning of the 9th century itself, obviously the Church of St. Martin, where Pribina was later baptised. Justová, *Dolnorakouské Podunají*, pp. 150–152. Herwig Wolfram, *Österreichische Geschichte 378–907. Grenzen und Räume. Geschichte Österreichs vor seiner Entstehung* (Wien 1995), pp. 239–240. Some researchers identify Guntio's Castle with Köszeg, (Kysek, Güns). István Lelkes looks for it on the hill Óház, near Kőszeg (in today's Hungary), on which ramparts are preserved. István Lelkes, *Kőszeg* (Budapest 1960), pp. 7–36. Walter Steinhauser, Endre Tóth, Herwig Wolfram, Walter Pohl and Béla Miklós Szőke reject the identification of Guntio's Castle with Köszeg. Walter Steinhauser, "Die Ortsnamen des

The expedition in 803 set off (like those in the years 799 and 802) from Bavaria against the neighbouring tudunate. Emperor Charlemagne *waited for the arrival of soldiers returning from Pannonia. When they arrived, he came to Regensburg to meet them. The tudun, prince of Pannonia (Zodan princeps Pannoniae), came there with him and surrendered to the emperor. In this representation there were also many Slavs and Huns and with all whom they ruled, they surrendered to the emperor's dominion.*[54]

Many Slavs and Huns who *ruled (possidebant)* came with the tudun, that is subordinate Slavic principalities, and the Avar kapkhan Theodor, dependent on the tudun, along with his court. The Slavs, named in first place before the Avars, had primacy in the tudun's breakaway realm. The most important Slavs in the whole tudunate were undoubtedly the Moravians. The mentioned *many Slavs*, who came along with the tudun to Regensburg, were Slavic princes dependent on the tudun, primarily from Moravia and Nitria.

6 Dispute over the Diocese Border between Salzburg and Aquileia

From Regensburg the emperor set off for Salzburg, where he confirmed Pepin's appointment of Pannonian territory to the Salzburg diocese and thus also to both neighbouring dioceses: *Then in year 803 Emperor Charles entered Bavaria and in the month of October came to Salzburg and again emphasizing the mentioned appointing of his son, from official power and in the presence of many of his loyal followers he confirmed and permitted that it remain intact forever.*[55]

The dissatisfaction of Aquileia with this decision grew into a great dispute after the death of Aquilean patriarch Paulino. His successor Ursus (802–807) appealed to the testimony of old synodal records, according to which the *provincia Karantana*, that is, Carantania, fell to the Aquilean patriarch even

---

Burgenlandes als siedlungsgeschichtliche Quelle," *Mitteilungen des Instituts für österreichische Geschichtsforschung* 45 (1931), pp. 319–320. Endre Tóth, "Die karolingische Burg von Sabaria-Szombathely," *Folia Archaeologica* 29 (1978), pp. 178–179. Wolfram, *Die Geburt*, pp. 520–521. Herwig Wolfram, "Der Raum der Güssinger Herrschaft in der Karolingerzeit," *Wissenschaftliche Arbeiten aus dem Burgenland*, Heft 79 (1989), p. 6. Pohl, *Die Awaren*, p. 321. Béla Miklós Szőke, *The Carolingian age in the Carpathian basin* (Budapest 2014), p. 16. If Margrave Cadolah and Goteram led their expeditions against the tudunate, then Guntionis Castle, near which the battle with Avars was fought, lay on its territory. Therefore, it cannot be identical with Kőszeg lying on the territory of the Carantanian March and the Salzburg diocese, which did not belong to the tudunate.

54   *Ann. reg. Franc.* ad a. 803, MMFH I, p. 22. *Annales Mettenses priores* ad a. 803, MMFH I, p. 34. Třeštík, *Vznik*, pp. 67–68.
55   *Conversio* 6, ed. Wolfram, pp. 68–69. MMFH III, p. 304.

before the arrival of the Longobards to Italy. Therefore, he requested for himself the entire territory of the Carantanian March assigned to Salzburg. Arno, who referred to the decisions of Popes Zacharias, Stephen II and Paul, defended his rights before the emperor. According to the decision of Charlemagne from 18 June 811, the Drava River remained the border of the two ecclesiastical provinces.[56]

7 Dispute over Dalmatia

Charlemagne had already got into a dispute with the Byzantine Empire regarding rule over Istria in 788. The dispute was ratcheted up when Friulian Margrave Erik made a claim on Dalmatia, where the Croatian principality and the coastal Latin cities lay, which along with Venice fell to the Byzantine emperor. However, immediately in year 799, as he entered into Dalmatia, more exactly to Liburnia, which lay on its north-western edge, in the vicinity of Istria, he met with antagonism and fell in battle: *Erik, Duke of Friuli … was near the town of Tersatto in Liburnia overwhelmed by the machinations of the town residents.*[57] In 803 Charlemagne recognized Byzantine rule over Venice and the Dalmatian coast and made peace with Byzantine Emperor Nikephoros I (802–811). Then the Croats recognized the sovereignty of the Friulian margrave.[58]

The new open conflict with Byzantium over Venice and the Dalmatian coastal towns broke out at the turn of the years 805/806[59] and lasted until 812,

---

56 *Drauus fluuius qui per mediam illam prouinciam currit, terminus ambarum dyo[ce]seon esset et ripa australi ad Aquilegiensis ecclesie rectorem, ab aquilonali uero ripa ad Juuauensis ecclesie presulem pars ipsius prouincie pertineret.* Monumenta historica ducatus Carinthiae III. Die kärtner Geschichtsquellen 811–1202, herausgegeben von August von Jaksch (Klagenfurt 1904), no. 1, p. 2. Cibulka, *Velkomoravský kostel*, pp. 173–174. František Dvorník, *Byzantské misie u Slovanů* (Praha 1970), p. 42. Wolfram, *Die Geburt*, pp. 265–266. Herwig Wolfram, "Karantanija med vzhodom in zahodom, Obri, Bavarci in Longobardi v 8. in 9. stoletju," *Zgodovinski časopis* 45 (1991), pp. 180–181. Krahwinkler, *Friaul*, pp. 166–168. The narrow strip of Carantanian territory from the Drava south to the Carnic Alps and the Karawanks, which divided Carantania from neighbouring Friuli and Carniola, remained under the administration of the Aquileian patriarch. The Drava River was the northern border of the March of Friuli and the narrow strip of Carantanian territory south of the Drava belonged under the administration of the Friulian margrave. If the border between the Friuli and Carantanian Marches did not take into consideration the territorial integrity of Carantania, then Carantania was no longer an individual principality.

57 *Ann. reg. Franc.* (*Ann. Lauriss. mai.*, *Annales Einhardi*) ad a. 799, rec. Kurze, pp. 108, 109. *Einhardi Vita Karoli Magni* 13, MMFH II, p. 22.

58 *Ann. reg. Franc.* ad a. 802, 803, rec. Kurze, pp. 117–118. Třeštík, *Vznik*, p. 91.

59 *Ann. reg. Franc.* ad a. 806, rec. Kurze, pp. 120–121, 122. Krahwinkler, *Friaul*, p. 180.

when Emperor Charlemagne gave up the claim to these towns. The peace that Charlemagne concluded in 812 with Emperor Michael I (811–820) confirmed the result of the previous wars, in which Charlemagne subjugated *Istria and Liburnia, as well as Dalmatia with the exception of the coastal towns, which he permitted Constantinople Emperor to have out of friendship and an agreement concluded with him.*[60]

8 *infestationes Sclavorum*

In 805 the Slavs attacked the Avars. The khagan, who did not hang on to even the last remnants of power, abandoned his seat in the Pannonian interior, never to return there. Charlemagne's biographer Einhard could write: *The place where the monarchal court of the khagan had been located was left so abandoned that there was hardly a trace of human habitation there.*[61] Small Slavic principalities then ruled over the residual khaganate, and it thus became *Sclavinia*. The khagan lost the *ancient honour, which the khagan of the Huns brandished*, and retired to the Fischa River (in today's Austria), on the territory of the collapsing tudunate, where on 21 September 805 he accepted baptism and the name Abraham: *In this year the khagan (paganus) was baptised Abraham on the 11th day before the October calends.*[62] The khagan did the same thing the tudun had done 10 years before. He subjugated himself to Charlemagne, accepted baptism and obtained Charlemagne's support. At the time of Abraham's baptism the kapkhan presented himself to the emperor: *The kapkhan (cabuanus) came to Lord Charles and near the Fischa the khagan was baptised Abraham.*[63] The Nitrian Slavs surrounded the kapkhan: *Soon after the kapkhan, prince of the Huns (capcanus princeps Hunorum), due to a lack of* (support) *of his people came to the emperor with the request that he be given space for living between Sabaria and Carnuntum, because due to attacks of the Slavs (infestationes Sclavorum) he cannot live in his previous settlements. The emperor graciously received him;*

---

60 *Einhardi Vita Karoli Magni* 15, MMFH II, p. 23. *Ann. reg. Franc.* ad a. 809, 810, 811, 812, 813, rec. Kurze, pp. 127, 130, 132–134, 136, 137. Krahwinkler, *Friaul*, pp. 180–181.
61 *Einhardi Vita Karoli Magni* 13, MMFH II, pp. 21–22.
62 *Annales Iuvavenses maiores* ad a. 805, edidit Georgius Heinricus Pertz, Monumenta Germaniae historica, Scriptores I (Hannoverae et Lipsiae 1826), p. 87.
63 *Annales sancti Emmerami Ratisponensis maiores* ad a. 805, ed. Pertz, p. 93. Khagan Abraham accepted baptism *super Fiskaha*. Fiskaha did not have to refer to the Fischa River, but the Fischamend (the ancient Aequinoctium), because St. Emmeram's Annals do not mention such a river.

kapkhan Theodor was a Christian, and satisfying his request, he bestowed gifts on him and permitted him to return.[64]

Theodor died soon after, and Abraham asked the emperor about renewal of the khaganate: *When he returned to his people, he died after a short time. And the khagan (caganus) sent one of his best (optimatibus), requesting ancient honour (honorem antiquam), which the khagan wielded with the Huns. The emperor expressed consent with his request and ordered that the khagan be again considered the head of the whole country according to long custom.*[65] If Abraham in September 805 was staying near the Fischa River outside the territory of his khaganate and asked the emperor about its renewal, then he had to have lost his khaganate shortly before. Despite the emperor's command, he could hardly have again taken hold of it, because he could not defeat the Slavs by himself. He was simply left with the title khagan and with it rule over the Upper Pannonia Avars, among whom were also those who had then just lost their kapkhan.

The tudunate, which had recognized Frankish dominion in 795, peacefully survived all the events that shook the khagan's part of Pannonia up to 799. Only in 805 did the Slavs begin to attack the Avars. The tudunate, which in 805 could not hold off the attacks of its own Slavs, mainly Moravian and Nitrian, then collapsed. The Slavs attacked in particular the centres of Avar power on their territory, Devín and Komárno. The tudun lost Devín and had to seek refuge to the south of his broken tudunate, certainly as far as possible from the attacking Moravians and as close as possible to Bavaria, from where he could expect help.

If the khagan found refuge on the eastern side of the Vienna Woods at the end of summer 805, and if the emperor there and at that same time assigned

---

64 *Ann. reg. Franc.* ad a. 805, rec. Kurze, pp. 119–120. *MMFH I*, p. 23. Naďa Profantová and Dušan Třeštík assume that the southern Moravian centres of power played a crucial part in unifying Nitria and dislodging Theodor's Avars from their centre in Komárno and from the whole of southern Nitria at the time of the Avar wars. Bláhová – Frolík – Profantová, *Velké dějiny zemí Koruny české I*, pp. 188, 190. Třeštík, *Vznik*, pp. 112, 127. Profantová – Profant, *Archeologie a historie*, pp. 244–245. If the Moravians, according to Dušan Třeštík (*Vznik*, pp. 290–291), were unable before 855 to cross the Thaya and dominate the less settled territory between the Thaya and the Danube, which lay in the close vicinity of the Moravian centre in Mikulčice and was a natural part of Moravia, then how could they at the beginning of the 9th century take interest and find the power for crossing the Little and White Carpathans and attack down the valley of the Váh and against distant Komárno? The weakened Avars in the southern part of Nitria were attacked by the Nitrian Slavs themselves, who must have considered them as intruders in their territory and had to have a much greater interest in reaching the Danube near Komárno than the neighbouring Moravians, who according to D. Třeštík did not reach the bank of the Danube in today's Lower Austria for another 50 years.

65 *Ann. reg. Franc.* ad a. 805, rec. Kurze, p. 120. *MMFH I*, p. 23.

new settlements to the kapkhan and his Avars, then the tudun, who like the khagan and kapkhan had to retreat from Slavic attacks, could have settled on the opposite side, that is between the Vienna Woods and the Enns. From year 805 only the southern part of the broken tudunate remained a part of the Avar (Eastern) March. However, the margrave of the Eastern March and the Passau bishops still made a claim to the entire territory of the former tudunate, that is to Moravia and Nitria,[66] exactly according to the decision which was made in Pepin's military camp on the bank of the Danube in 796.

Avar settlements in Upper Pannonia are also mentioned by the donations of brothers Wirut, Gisilmar and Wentilmar for the St. Emmeram Abbey in Regensburg from year 808. The borders of the abbey property began near the Wolfsbach stream (*Eoluepah*) and from there stretched to the Wiesah (*Uisaha*) and further to Winterbach (*Uuinterpah*) and then headed towards two mounds (*ad duos tumulos*) and to the place of the Avars (*loca Avarorum*).[67] The kapkhan's Avars settled several *towns* and not the entire associated territory *between Sabaria and Carnunutum*. To the south the settlements of the kapkhan's Avars could only stretch to Sabaria (Szombathely), but Sabaria itself no longer belonged to them. They had to end near the upper flow of the Zöbernbach and on the Spratzbach and Rábca rivers, which in these locations, together with the lower flow of the Rába to the east, formed the border between the former tudunate and the remnants of the khaganate, which ultimately became the border between Upper Pannonia, belonging to the Avar March and the Passau diocese, and Lower Pannonia belonging to the Carantanian March and the Salzburg diocese.

Only some *places* (*loca*) belonged to the Upper Pannonian Avars, surrounded by Slavs. Thus, there were only a few Avars who had been led by kapkhan Theodor to Upper Pannonia, and likewise there must have only been a few of them *in previous settlements* (*in pristinis sedibus*). That's why they were able to so easily leave and occupy new areas and do so on territories which already had some of their residents. Until the summer of 805 the kapkhan's Avars lived in Komárno and sporadically at other important places in the southern part of Nitria, just as later in Upper Pannonia. They lived on territories associated with settlements of Slavs, who had the same weapons and decorations as the Avars and likewise buried their dead unburned. If the kapkhan's Avars had

---

66 See pp. 124–126, 181–182.
67 *Urkundenbuch des Burgenlandes und der angrenzenden Gebiete der Komitate Wieselburg, Ödenburg und Eisenburg. Band 1: Die Urkunden von 808 bis 1270*, ed. Hans Wagner (Graz – Köln 1955), no. 1, p. 1. *MMFH III*, Diplomata 3, p. 19. (regest), Ágnes Cs. Sós, *Die slawische Bevölkerung, Westungarns im 9. Jahrhundert. Müncher Beiträge zur Vor- und Frühgeschichte* 22 (München 1973), pp. 10–11.

inhabited the whole of the southern Nitria and all skeleton graves with Avar weapons and cast bronze armour belonged to them, then hardly all or at least a major portion of them would have fit into new sporadic settlements between Carnuntum and Sabaria. If there had been so many that they lived over the whole southern part of Nitria, then they would have certainly been able to more effectively defend against a Slavic attack. The Slavs would not have been able in such a short time (at the end of summer 805) to chase them over the Danube; Slavic attacks against it would have lasted several years, just as against the Avars in the remains of the Lower Pannonian khaganate.

Certainly Slavic princes from the neighbouring principalities of Nitria and Savia and the khagan, perhaps even with the tudun, from the territory of the Avar March, interfered in the mutual battles of small Slavic principalities and Avar tarkhans in the remnants of the khaganate, which continued and flared up completely after the khagan's escape. The Frankish Empire was unable for several years to settle or suppress the tussles between the Slavs and Avars. By the end of 805 the imperial diet in Thionville forbade merchants to export weapons through the eastern border of the Frankish Empire *to the country of the Slavs and Avars*. Then margrave of the Avar March, Werinhar, checked on merchants who in Lorch crossed the border of secured imperial territory to the Enns and departed for trade to the dangerous east.[68] In 807 Charlemagne issued an order on military preparedness of the Saxons for the case of war against the Sorbs, Bohemians, Spanish or Avar lands.[69] The attacks of the Slavs reached such a dimension that they caused an ethnic shift and the extinction of Avar settlements in the predominant part of Pannonia: *Then the Slavs, when the Huns were expelled from there, arrived and began to settle various regions in these parts of the Danube.*[70]

In this restless period khagan Abraham, died and his successor became *canizauci princeps Avarum*.[71] The word *canizauci* is made up of two parts. The first part *can* is clear – this is the title khan or khagan. The second part – *izauci* – is unclear. If this was a part of a title, then it would be in the first place, as the kap in Theodorich's title kapkhan (*capcanus*) and tar in the title tarkhan (*tarcanus*). If *izauci* comes after the title, then it is an actual name. We can therefore assume that *canizauci* = Khan Izauki = Khagan Isaac. The family

---

68 *Capitulare missorum* VII, *MMFH* IV, pp. 23–24. *Codex diplomaticus et epistolaris Slovaciae* 1, ad edendum praeparavit Richard Marsina (Bratislava 1971), no. 1, p. 3. Pohl, *Die Awaren*, p. 323.
69 CDES 1, ed. Marsina, no. 2, pp. 3–4.
70 *Conversio* 6, ed. Wolfram, pp. 66–67. *MMFH* III, p. 303.
71 See note 72. Dümmler, *Über die südöstlichen Marken*, p. 9.

of the khagan thus accepted during their baptism a pair of biblical names: Abraham and Isaac.

Peace was restored only after the military campaign that Charlemagne sent in year 811 *to Pannonia to end the disputes of the Huns and Slavs.* Everyone who ended up within reach of the emperor's military in Pannonia came with it to Aachen and there awaited the arrival of Charlemagne: *His arrival in Aachen was awaited by those who had come from Pannonia, Khagan Isaac, prince of the Avars* (canizauci princeps Avarum), *and the tudun and other powers* (primores) *and the Slavic princes* (duces Sclavorum) *living around the Danube, who got into the presence of the emperor on the order of leaders of the brigades that were sent to Pannonia.*[72]

The khagan and the tudun came from the territory of the Avar March, each with his own accompaniment of magnates. From the territory of the former Lower Pannonian khaganate came Slavic princes. The situation in Pannonia fully engaged the Frankish campaign, and it did not cross its border. Leaders of the Pannonian campaign were unable to reach the northern bank of the Danube and could not command the princes in Moravia and in Nitria. These,

---

72   *Imperator ... in tres partes regni sui totidem exercitus misit ... alterum in Pannonias ad controversias Hunorum et Sclavorum finiendas ... Qui omnes rebus prospere gestis incolomes regressi sunt ... Fuerunt etiam Aquis adventum eius expectandes, qui de Pannonia venerunt, canizauci princeps Avarum et tudun et alii primores ac duces Sclavorum circa Danubium habitantium, qui a ducibus copiarum, que in Pannoniam missae fuerunt, ad praesentiam principis iussi venerunt.* Ann. reg. Franc. ad a. 811, rec. Kurze, pp. 134–135. *MMFH I*, p. 44. The military campaign headed *in Pannonias*. The Slavic princes who came with the Frankish military do Aachen came from Pannonia: *qui de Pannonia venerunt* and they came to the emperor *a ducibus copiarum quae in Pannoniam missae fuerunt.* Therefore, the princes of the Transdanubian Slavs could not have been among them, as is assumed by Lubomír Havlík and Matúš Kučera. Lubomír Havlík, "Velká Morava a Franská říše," *Historické štúdie* 8 (1963), p. 136. Matúš Kučera, *Postavy veľkomoravskej histórie* (Martin 1986), p. 79. *Living around the Danube* (circa Danubium habitantium) doesn't mean on both sides of the Danube. The Danube forms and arch around the whole of Transdanubia, flowed around the settlements of Transdanubian Avars and the Slavs. The situation in Pannonia engaged the Frankish campaign and did not cross its border. Leaders of the Pannonian campaign thus could not command the princes in Moravia and in Nitra. Not a single Frankish campaign, which would have compelled their obedience, touched their territory. In the opinion of Dušan Třeštík the Slavic princes, who in the year 811 appeared before the emperor, settled in Pannonia and soon in the south, where Pepin attacked in 797. Třeštík, *Vznik*, pp. 86–88. If, however, these princes were settled in southern Pannonia, that is on the territory of Savia, then they would not be said to live *around the Danube*, because the Danube bends only around northern Pannonia. But today's eastern Slavonia and Sirmium do lay near the Danube; however, Frankish power did not extend there in 811. Slavic princes who settled *around the Danube*, were thus settled in northern Pannonia, that is in Transdanubia.

together with the tudun, had bowed down to Charlemagne since 803; however, in 805 they got rid of tudun hegemony and thus also any obligations towards the Frankish empire that would fall to them from it. The *Slavic princes* who in 811 visited the emperor *came from Pannonia* and not from the north side of the Danube.

The *Divisio imperii* (817) mentions the Upper Pannonian Avars[73] and the presence of the Avar delegation at the imperial diet in Frankfurt in 822 is the last known political appearance and last written report on the Avars.[74]

9   The Bulgarian Offensive into the Tisza River Region

If during the internal war of 795 not only the khagan died but also the khagan's subordinate, the jugur, who ruled in the Tisza River region, then a split afflicted not only the khagan's Pannonia, but also the jugur's Tisza River region. If in September 805 the Avar khagan had to head west before the attacks of the Slavs, to the territory of the expanding Eastern March and ask for the protection of Charlemagne, then departure to the east, to the Tisza River region, was no longer possible. We learn who destroyed the eastern part of the Avar Empire from the report which got into the Suidae Lexicon at the end of the 10th century: *The Bulgarians destroyed these Avars with their full force. Krum asked the captured Avars: What do you think, why did your leader die and all* (the people)? *And they replied to him: Mutual slanders spread and led the virtuous and rational to destruction. Then the unjust and the thieves became the judges. This led to drunkenness, because everyone turned into drunks from all the wine. Then there was corruption. Everyone could be bought and sold, and they lied to one another. Our destruction started from this.*[75] The invasion into the Tisza River region at the expense of the subverted Avar Realm was led by Bulgarian Khagan Krum

---

73   *Divisio imperii* II, *MMFH IV*, pp. 31–32. *CDES I*, ed. Marsina, no. 3, pp. 4–5. The emperor's army marching in the year 820 through Transdanubia against Sisak Prince Ljudevit (Louis) did not meet any resistance here. Transdanubia was a peaceful country. *Ann. reg. Franc.* ad a. 820, rec. Kurze, p. 153. *MMFH I*, p. 29.

74   *Ann. reg. Franc.* ad a. 822, rec. Kurze, p. 159. *MMFH I*, p. 30. A grave that archaeologists uncovered in Sopronkőhida dates from these times. Béla Miklós Szőke, "Archäologische Angaben zu den ethnischen Verhältnissen Pannoniens am Anfang der Karolingerzeit," in *Zborník na počesť Dariny Bialekovej*, ed. Gabriel Fusek (Nitra 2004), pp. 371–382.

75   Teréz Olajos, *A IX. századi avar töténelem görög nyelvű forrásai* (Szeged 2001), pp. 26–43. Samu Szádeczky-Kardoss, *Az avar történelem forrásai 557-tól 806-ig* (Budapest 1998), 138. §, pp. 304–306. Zlatarski, *Istorija na bălgarskata dăržava I/1*, pp. 321–322. Pohl, *Die Awaren*, pp. 327–328.

(802–814) even before he turned against Byzantium at the end of 808.[76] He got Avar Tisza River region under his rule perhaps at this same time and perhaps in cooperation with the Slavs, who in 805 attacked the Avars in Pannonia.[77] The Bulgarian presence in the Tisza River region is evidenced by a gravestone inscription in Pliska, which recalls that Bulgarian Tarkhan Onegavon, under the rule of Krum's successor Omurtag (814–831), drowned in the Tisza River.[78] After the fall of Avar power, the Bulgarians ruled the entire south-eastern part of the Carpathian Basin. On the west it buttressed against the Danubian border of the Carantanian March and to the north-west drew near to the Nitrian Principality.

Bulgarian Khagan Omurtag immediately at the beginning of his rule concluded a 30-year peace with Byzantium[79] and turned his attention to the west and north-west, where the Slavic tribes which had thrown off Avar rule were located. In 818, or shortly before then, the Timochans broke away *from the society of the Bulgarians* (*a Bulgarorum societate*), leaving their settlement on the Timok River and settling on the border of the Frankish Empire.[80] The southern Obotrites, called the *Praedenecenti*, or *Bandits*, who neighboured Omurtag's kingdom but did not belong to it, also tried to ally with Emperor Louis. The Obotrites *as neighbours of the Bulgarians occupied Dacia up to the Danube*, that is today's Banat and Bačka. They settled exactly where the Slavs of Ardagast had lived long before. They were obviously their distant descendants. Emissaries from the southern Obotrites appeared before Emperor Louis the Pious at the end of autumn 818 in Herstal. Emissaries from the Croatian Prince Borna, the Timochans and the Savian Prince Ljudevit (Louis) also came there.[81]

---

76   In 807 Byzantine emperor Nikephoros I marched against the Bulgarians. Unrest in the military, however, forced him to stop in Adrianopolis (modern Edirne, Turkey) and then turn back. At the end of 808 Khagan Krum attacked the valley of the Struma River, defeated the local Byzantine military and took away 1100 gold talents. In the spring of 809 he took over Serdika. Krum's successor Omortag ended the war with Byzantium in 814. Zlatarski, *Istorija na bălgarskata dăržava I/1*, pp. 321–364, 526–538, 552–563. Hýbl, *Dějiny národa bulharského I*, pp. 72–75. Panajotov, *Srednevekovna bălgarska istorija*, pp. 57–62, 65. Andreas Schwarcz, "Pannonien im 9. Jahrhundert und die Anfänge der direkten Beziehungen zwischen dem Ostfränkischen Reich und den Bulgaren," in *Grenze und Differenz in frühen Mittelalter*, ed. Pohl, Reimitz, pp. 100–101.
77   Zlatarski, *Istorija na bălgarskata dăržava I/1*, p. 248.
78   Zlatarski, *Istorija na bălgarskata dăržava I/1*, pp. 405, 423. Třeštík, *Vznik*, pp. 104–106.
79   Zlatarski, *Istorija na bălgarskata dăržava I/1*, pp. 383–391, 563–576.
80   *Ann. reg. Franc.* ad a. 818, rec. Kurze, p. 149. *MMFH I*, pp. 26–27. Predrag Komatina, "The Slavs of the Mid-Danube Basin and the Bulgarian Expansion," in *Zbornik radova Vizantološkog instituta* 47 (2010), pp. 55–59, 66, 67, 68, 73, 77.
81   *Ann. reg. Franc.* ad a. 818, 822, 824, rec. Kurze, pp. 149, 158, 165–166. *MMFH I*, pg. 26–27, 29–31. Alexander Avenarius, "K problematike avarsko-slovanského vzťahu na dolnom

An anonymous Bavarian geographer, who wrote his work perhaps 10 years after the subjugation of Nitria by the Moravians, mentions, aside from the duplicitous Moravians, only the Bulgars (*Vulgarii*) immediately over the Danubian border of the East Francia Empire. This anonymous informant found no other independent nation or tribe among them.[82] A description of Germania, which Anglo-Saxon King Alfred the Great (871–900) added to the Anglo-Saxon translation of the work of Paulus Orosius, also mentions lands and nations bordering with the Moravians (who also subjugated Nitria from 833): *and to the south of them, on the other side of the Danube, is the country Carantania (land Carendre), south of the mountains called the Alps ... Then to the east of the country of the Carantanians (Carendran londe), from that side of the barren land (westenne), is the country of the Bulgarians (Pulgara land). And to the east of them is the country of the Greeks.*[83] The mentioned Carantania is not only the territory of the former Carantanian Principality in the eastern Alps, but the whole of the Carantanian and Eastern March along with their Pannonian part on the east. The barren lands which lay between the Carantania and Bulgaria is the area between the Danube and Tisza rivers. The Eastern Francia and Bulgarian realms were separated not only by the Danube, which was north and eastern border of both Bavarian border marches, but also the barren territory between the Danube and Tisza rivers.

10 Margraves of the Avar and Carantanian Marches

After Goteram, the mentioned Werinhar (*Warnarius*, 802–after 806) became the margrave of the Avar and Carantanian Marches.[84] We know nothing for certain about Werinhar's successor Alberic (after 806–before 818).[85] Margrave Gotofrid (before 818–up to 823) unjustifiably appropriated several properties of the Passau bishopric on the territory of the Avar March. Immediately upon becoming the bishop of Passau in 818 Reginhar asked that the bishopric's

---

Dunaji v 6.–7. storočí," *Slovanské štúdie* 11 (1971), pp. 241–242. Třeštík, *Vznik*, pp. 92, 101–104. Komatina, "The Slavs of the Mid-Danube Basin," pp. 55–57, 68–69, 73, 74, 77.

82   *Descriptio civitatum et regionum ad septentrionalem plagam Danubii*, MMFH III, pp. 285–287.
83   *Orosius I/1*, MMFH III, pp. 338–340.
84   See note 68. *Conversio*, ed. Wolfram, pp. 168, 263, 264. Wolfram, *Die Geburt*, p. 264. Wolfram, *Salzburg, Bayern, Österreich*, pp. 298, 301.
85   *Conversio*, ed. Wolfram, pp. 168, 169. Wolfram, *Die Geburt*, p. 264. Wolfram, *Salzburg, Bayern, Österreich*, p. 302.

property be returned. Reginhar won the dispute with Gotofrid and in 823 had his property confirmed by an imperial document.[86]

Margrave Gerold II (before 826–828), nephew of Gerold I and uncle of Louis the German,[87] was the first one of the counts of the Avar March. In Gerold's original county, between the Enns and the Vienna Woods, Emperor Charlemagne gifted in 811, at Gerald's request, Niederaltaich Abbey near the mouth of the stream Pielach (*Bielaha*) into the Danube.[88] In 815 the new emperor, Louis the Pious, sent Count Gerold, together with Italian King Bernhard, to see the Pope in Rome.[89] Count Gerold became margrave only after Gotofrid, that is only after year 823. He is first securely documented as margrave in 826.[90] In 827 Margrave Gerold II ordered his subordinate, Traungau Count Wilhelm, to research and agree on the exact definition of the borders between the parishes in Buchenau and neighbouring Slavic village on the territory of Wilhelm's county.[91] Gerold II, again as count, is mentioned in a donation document for the Kremsmünster Abbey from 22 March 828. Then, on the request of Bavarian King Louis the German and Count Gerold, Emperor Louis the Pious with his son Lothar gifted to Kremsmünster Abbey lands in the area of Grunzvitigau near the Traisen River on the territory of Gerold's own county between the Enns and the Vienna Woods. The Slavs who were settled on the gifted lands became serfs of this abbey. The tax which before then had been handed over to Count Gerold fell to the abbey. The border of the new abbey property was demarcated by envoys of Count Gerold.[92]

Margraves Goteram, Werinhar, Alberik, Gotofrid and Gerold II *administered the eastern part* (*orientalem procurabant plagam*),[93] which was made up of the Avar (East) and Carantanian Marches. Both further remained Bavarian border marches. In 817 Emperor Louis the Pious at an imperial diet in Aachen stated his will to divide the rule in the empire between his sons after his death. Louis the German was to get Bavaria, including both marches: *Likewise, we want Louis to get Bavaria, Carantanians, the Bohemians and Avars and also the Slavs, who are from the eastern part of Bavaria* (*Avaros atque Sclaves, qui*

---

86 *MMFH III*, Diplomata 7, pp. 20–22. *Conversio*, ed. Wolfram, pp. 168, 169. Wolfram, *Die Geburt*, pp. 264, 270. Wolfram, *Salzburg, Bayern, Österreich*, pp. 300–302, 308.
87 *Conversio*, ed. Wolfram, pp. 168, 169, 172, 175, 176, 184, 262, 264, 290, 291. Wolfram, *Die Geburt*, pp. 195–196, 264, 273. Wolfram, *Salzburg, Bayern, Österreich*, pp. 56, 188, 300–302, 308–310, 368.
88 *MMFH III*, Diplomata 5, p. 20 (regest).
89 *Ann. reg. Franc.* ad a. 815, rec. Kurze, p. 142.
90 See chapter 5, note 17.
91 *MMFH III*, Diplomata 8, pp. 23–24, Wolfram, *Die Geburt*, p. 352.
92 *MMFH III*, Diplomata 9, pp. 24–26. Wolfram, *Die Geburt*, pp. 233, 275.
93 See note 98.

ab orientali parte Baioariae sunt), and in addition to this we give to his servitude two Dominican settlements in Nordgau: Luttraifa, Ingolstatd.[94] The eastern part of Bavaria, where the Avars and Slavs lived, is the Avar March. The name Carantanians (*Carentanos*) indicates all of the Carantanian March and with it the Lower Pannonian part, as in the document of Charlemagne from the year 811.[95] From the *Divisio imperii* of Emperor Louis the Pious it clearly follows that these were two different marches, even though under the administration of a common margrave.

11 Four Transdanubian Principalities

The baptism of the Carantanians and the history of the Carantanian Principality are found in the 3rd through 5th chapters and then the 7th chapter of Conversio. The rule of domestic Carantanian princes ends with Prince Valtunk at the end of the 5th chapter. In the 6th and then in the 8th through 14th chapters, Conversio deals with the Lower Pannonian part of Transdanubia, highlighting the credit to the Salzburg church and defending the right of the Salzburg archbishop on this territory. Chapters 6 and 7 have been put in reverse order, because the 7th chapter still deals with Carantania and the 6th chapter tells of Pannonia.[96] At the beginning of the 6th chapter, which was originally the 7th chapter, the unknown author clearly defines the whole of his further discussion (ending only with the 14th and final chapter) on the Salzburg part of Pannonia: *Now, however, we consider the need to speak about how the Huns were chased away from here, how the Slavs began to settle and how that part of Pannonia was connected to the Salzburg diocese.*[97]

The 10th chapter of Conversio states that *on the territory from which the Huns* (*terram, unde ille expulsi sunt Huni*) *were expelled*, that is in the Salzburg part of Transdanubia, four Slavic princes ruled, who recognized the sovereignty of the emperor and were freely subjected to the Carantanian margrave: *Then the first margrave appointed by the emperor is Margrave Goteram, the second Werinhar, the third Alberik, the fourth Gotofrid, the fifth Gerold. Meanwhile, however, the mentioned counts administered to the eastern part, some princes* (*aliqui duces*) *settled in that country belonging to the already mentioned* (Salzburg) *seat. These were the mentioned counts subordinated to the service of the emperor, and their*

---

94   *Divisio imperii* 11, MMFH IV, pp. 31–32. CDES I, ed. Marsina, no. 3, pp. 4–5.
95   See note 56.
96   *Conversio*, ed. Wolfram, pp. 49–50. Wolfram, *Salzburg, Bayern, Österreich*, pp. 287–288.
97   *Conversio* 6, ed. Wolfram, pp. 66–69. MMFH III, p. 303.

names are Pribislav, Semika, Stojmír, Edgar (Priwizlauga, Cemicas, Ztoimar, Etgar).[98]

If the author of Conversio put Pribislav, Semika, Stojmír and Edgar into the 10th chapter, then he certainly took them to be princes of Lower Pannonia. The later error regarding their Carantanian origin came about by a mistaken comment in a short scrap from the Conversio called the Excerptum de Karentanis, which an unknown author wrote at the end of the 12th or early 13th century. He wrote about them as Carantanian princes (*duces Carantanorum*).[99]

---

98   *Postquam ergo Karolus imperator Hunis reiectis ... coeperunt populi sive Sclavi vel Bagoarii inhabitare terram, unde illi expulsi sunt Huni, et multiplicari. Tunc primus ab imperatore constitutus est confinii comes Goterammus, secundus Werinharius, tertius Albricus, quartus Gotafridus, quintus Geroldus. Interim vero dum praedicti comites orientalem procurabant plagam, aliqui duces habitaverunt in illis partibus ad iam dictam sedem pertinentibus. Qui comitibus praefatis subditi fuerunt ad servitium imperatoris; quorum nomina sunt Priwizlauga, Cemicas, Ztoimar, Etgar.* Conversio 10, ed. Wolfram, pp. 72–73. MMFH III, pp. 308–310.

99   Conversio, ed. Wolfram, pp. 82–83, 214, 217. Conversio, ed. Kos, pp. 107–109, 140. MMFH III, pp. 434–435. Several historians place Pribislav, Semik, Stojmír and Edgar as the last four Carinthian princes, who ruled up to year 828, or perhaps only to 820. Ankershofen, *Handbuch II/1*, pp. 142–143, 321. Dümmler, *Über die südöstlichen Marken*, pp. 18–19. Dimitz, *Geschichte Krains I*, p. 123. Hans Pirchegger, "Karantanien und Unterpannonien zur Karolingerzeit," *Mitteilungen des österreichischen Instituts für Geschichtsforschung* 33 (1912), pp. 277, 305. August von Jaksch, *Geschichte Kärntens bis 1333 I* (Klagenfurt 1928), pp. 73, 85. Josip Mal, *Probleme aus der Frühgeschichte der Slowenen* (Ljubljana 1939), p. 70. Kos, *Conversio*, pp. 70–71. Milko Kos, *Zgodovina Slovencev od naselitve do petnajstega stoletja* (Ljubljana 1955), pp. 100, 108. Grafenauer, *Ustoličevanje koroških vojvod*, pp. 512–513, 533, 549–550. *Historija naroda Jugoslavije I* (Zagreb 1953), p. 148. Grafenauer, *Zgodovina I*, pp. 401–402. Bogo Grafenauer, *Zgodovina slovenskega naroda II* (Ljubljana 1965), p. 5. Bogo Grafenauer, "Großmähren, Unterpannonien und Karantanien," in *Das Großmährische Reich. Tagung der wissenschaftlichen Konferenz des Archäologischen Instituts der Tschechoslowakischen Akademie der Wissenschaften, Brno – Nitra 1.–4. 10. 1963*, Praha 1966, p. 382. Klebel, "Der Einbau Karantaniens," p. 671. Gotbert Moro, "Zur politischen Stellung Karantaniens im fränkischen und deutschen Reich," *Südost-Forschungen* 22 (1963), pp. 83–86. Mitterauer, "Karolingische Markgrafen," p. 7. Lubomír Havlík, "Panonie ve světle franských pramenů s novějším řešením některých otázek," *Slavia Antiqua* 17 (1970), p. 1. Lubomír E. Havlík, *Slovanské státní útvary raného středověku* (Praha 1987), p. 85. Łowmiański, *Początki Polski IV*, p. 254. Conversio, ed. Wolfram, pp. 115, 126–127, 153. Herwig Wolfram, "Der Zeitpunkt der Einführung der Grafschaftsverfassung in Karantanien," in *Veröffentlichungen des Steiermärkischen Landesarchiv 12. Siedlung, Macht und Wirtschaft. Festschrift Fritz Posch zum 70. Geburtstag*, herausgegeben von Gerhard Pferschy (Graz 1981), pp. 313–317. Wolfram, *Die Geburt*, pp. 282, 345. Wolfram, *Karantanija*, pp. 181–182. Wolfram, *Salzburg, Bayern, Österreich*, pp. 288, 298, 304–310. Třeštík, *Vznik*, pp. 87–88. Štih, *The Middle Ages between the Eastern Alps and the Northern Adriatic*, p. 134. Ernst Dümmler and Hans Pirchegger do not exclude the possibility of the rule of these four princes in Lower Pannonia between the Rába and the Drava. Hynek Bulín consider

The unknown author of the Excerpt, however, did not understand under Carantania only the territory of the former Carantanian Principality in the eastern Alps. If in the previous section he writes about Methodius, who *was exiled from the Carantanian lands (fugatus a Karentanis partibus)*,[100] then under the name Carantania he understood the whole of the Carantanian March, even with its Lower Pannonian part, where Methodius actually worked for a short time.[101] Thus, Carantania was also so understood by Alfred the Great in his translation of Orosius's work,[102] Emperor Louis the Pious in the *Divisio imperii* from 817,[103] Charlemagne in a document from 811[104] and eventually Conversio, too, with the installation of chorbishop Theodorich.[105] The four mentioned princes thus ruled in the Lower Pannonian part of the Carantanian March. The 10th chapter of Conversio names five margraves in numerical order and by numbering them emphasises their chronological order. The names of the four princes are not ordered and their sequence is thus not chronological. In no case can we see in their ordering a dynastic succession, a single family line in a single principality. All written sources recall Slavic princes in Transdanubia after the fall of the Avar Khaganate in plural numbers,[106] which excludes the rule of a single princely line. Pribislav, Semika, Stojmír and Edgar were thus contemporaries and representatives of four princely lines, which were divided in the Lower Pannonian part of Transdanubia. Their principalities were subjected to the Carantanian Margrave and administered ecclesiastically by the Salzburg seat. Conversio thus knows one entire generation of Transdanubian princes, their exact number and their names.

---

these four princes as *princes of the Slavs living around the Danube*, who in year 811 *came from Pannonia*. Hynek Bulín, "Aux origines des formations étatiques des Slaves du moyen Danube au IXe siècle," in *Europe aux IXe–XIe siècles* (Varsovie 1968), pp. 160–161.

100 *Conversio*, ed. Wolfram, pp. 82–83, 214, 216. *Conversio*, ed. Kos, pp. 107–109, 140. *MMFH III*, pp. 434–435.
101 *Žitije Konstantina* 15, *MMFH II*, p. 105.
102 *MMFH III*, p. 338.
103 See note 94.
104 See note 56.
105 See note 34.
106 Arno sent his missionaries not only to the Carantanian *counts (comitibus)*, but also to the *princes (ducibus)* in Salzburg's Lower Pannonia. See note 33. In 811 *duces Sclavorum* came from Pannonia to the emperor. See note 72. In 827 the Bulgarians disembarked on the northern bank of the Drava, attacked the *Slavs settled in Pannonia* and chased away their *princes (ducibus)*. See chapter 5, note 12.

12 The Rebellion of Prince Ljudevit

Croatia and Savia were subjected to Friulian Margrave Cadolah II (802–819). At the beginning Prince Borna ruled over only the Guduscans, the people settled near the Gacka River in the middle of Croatia. He was thus only one of the several smaller Croatian princes. Cadolah, however, assigned Borna as his viceroy for the whole of Dalmatia, and he subjected all the other Croatian princes to him, including Borna's uncle Ljudemysl.[107] Borna thus became Prince of Dalmatia and Liburnia (*Borna dux Dalmatiae atque Liburniae*).[108] Because Liburnia belonged to Dalmatia, he was simply the Prince of Dalmatia (*Borna ... dux Dalmatiae*).[109] Further, however, he was also prince of the Guduscans (*legati ... Bornae ducis Guduscanorum*).[110] The seat of the main Croatian prince was Nin (antique Nona), which in the middle of the 9th century became the seat of a bishop.[111]

Prince Borna along with his principality accepted Christianity. The report on the baptism of the Croats under the rule of Prince Borna (*Porinos*) was preserved by Constantine Porphyrogenitus: *The Croats ... asked for a sacred baptism from Rome. And bishops were sent, and they baptised them during the reign of Porina, their ruler.*[112]

Borna was loyal to the Friulian Margrave Cadolah, and with his support threatened Latin cities on the Dalmatian coast, which recognized the sovereignty of the Byzantine Empire. In early 817 Emperor Louis the Pious in Aachen listened to the complaint of Byzantine Emperor Leo V *because of the affairs of Dalmatia* (*pro Dalmatinorum causa*), which Nikephoros, an emissary of the Byzantine Emperor, had previously delivered. Shortly after, *Cadolah, in whose charge the border area belonged* came briefly to Aachen and began to negotiate with Nikephoros, who awaited his arrival. The Byzantine complaint *related to a great many, both Roman and Slavic*, that is the Latin cities on the Dalmatian coast and the Croatian Slavs. Since a decision could be made only in the presence of their representatives, Emperor Louis sent Cadolah and Nikephoros

---

107 See notes 110, 132. Třeštík, *Vznik*, pp. 97–101.
108 See note 129.
109 *Ann. reg. Franc.* ad a. 819, rec. Kurze, pp. 150–151. MMFH I, pp. 27–28. *Anonymi Vita Hludowici imperatoris* 32, MMFH II, p. 29.
110 *Ann. reg. Franc.* ad a. 818, rec. Kurze, p. 149. MMFH I, pp. 26–27.
111 Dvorník, *Byzantské misie*, pp. 42–46.
112 *Constantine Porphyrogenitus De administrando imperio* 30, ed. Moravcsik, pp. 144–145. MMFH III, pg. 389. Ján Steinhübel, "Moravania, Chorváti a Bulhari v plánoch pápežskej kúrie (860–880)," in *Bratia, ktorí menili svet – Konštantín a Metod. Príspevky z konferencie (Bratislava 21. februára 2013)*, eds. Branislav Panis, Matej Ruttkay, Vladimír Turčan (Bratislava 2012), pp. 158–159.

together with Albgar, nephew of Unruoch, *to Dalmatia (ad Dalmatiam)*.[113] In this same year Louis the Pious received in Ingelheim additional emissaries from Leo V with the same complaint as was brought in January by Nikephoros.[114]

At the end of autumn 818 emissaries from the southern Obotrites, Croatian Prince Borna, the Timochans and Savian Prince Ljudevit (Louis) appeared before Emperor Louis the Pious in Herstal.[115] Ljudevit was the Prince of Lower Pannonia[116] and had his seat in the castle at Sisak (antique Siscia).[117] Ljudevit, who wanted to be rid of the foreign rule, accused Margrave Cadolah *of cruelty and vainglory*.[118] The emperor had only a little sympathy for the complaint of the Prince of Sisak, which he heard in Herstal. Ljudevit had rebelled and activated the entire western Balkan. Immediately after his return from an unsuccessful campaign, which in July 819 moved from Italy against Ljudevit, Margrave Cadolah died and the *neighbouring tribes (vicinas iuxta se gentes)*, primarily the Carniolans of the upper Sava[119] and part of the Carantanians on the upper Drava, who allowed Ljudevit's brigades into their lands, joined in the rebellion. The Timochans, who the previous year had settled in the eastern vicinity of Ljudevit's principality on territory belonging to the Frankish Empire, also joined in.[120] At the beginning of the war, Ljudevit's father-in-law Dramagos deserted him and left to join Borna. The new Friulian margrave Baldric

---

113   *Ann. reg. Franc.* ad a. 817, rec. Kurze, pp. 145–146. *MMFH I*, p. 26. These events are also mentioned in an anonymous biography of Emperor Louis. It reveals that the complaint which the Byzantine Emperor's emissary Nikephoros had brought to Aachen *was about the borders of the Dalmatians, Romans and Slavs (erat de finibus Dalmatorum, Romanorum et Sclavorum)*. Since their representatives were not present in Aachen and not even *the administrator of the borders Cadolah (Chadalo finium preafectus)* was there, the dispute could not be judged. Cadolah in the end arrived to Aachen. And thus *Albgar was sent to Dalmatia with Cadolah, duke of this border region (cum Chadalo earundem finium principe), for appeasement and settlement of this*. Anonymi Vita Hludowici imperatoris 27, *MMFH II*, pp. 27–28.

114   *Ann. reg. Franc.* ad a. 817, rec. Kurze, p. 146.

115   *Ann. reg. Franc.* ad a. 818, 822, 824, rec. Kurze, pp. 149, 158–159, 165–166. *MMFH I*, pp. 26–27, 29–31. Alexander Avenarius, "K problematike avarsko-slovanského vzťahu na dolnom Dunaji v 6.–7. storočí," *Slovanské štúdie* 11 (1971), pp. 241–242. Třeštík, *Vznik*, pp. 92, 101–104. Komatina, *The Slavs of the Mid-Danube Basin*, pp. 55–57, 68–69, 73, 74, 77.

116   *Liudewiti ducis Pannoniae inferioris. Ann. reg. Franc.* ad a. 818, rec. Kurze, p. 149. *MMFH I*, p. 27. *Liuteviti rectoris inferioris Pannoniae.* Anonymi Vita Hludowici imperatoris 31, *MMFH II*, p. 28.

117   See notes 126, 127, 131.

118   *Ann. reg. Franc.* ad a. 818, rec. Kurze, p. 149. *MMFH I*, p. 27. Anonymi Vita Hludowici imperatoris 31, *MMFH II*, p. 28.

119   See notes 124, 125.

120   *Ann. reg. Franc.* ad a. 819, rec. Kurze, pp. 150–151. *MMFH I*, p. 27. Anonymi Vita Hludowici imperatoris 32, *MMFH II*, p. 29.

(819–828) still in 819 *entered the country of the Carantanians, which was under his administration (Carantanorum regionem, que ad ipsum curam pertinebat), and met there the army of Ljudevit marching along the Drava River, which he attacked with a small brigade, and when he slaughtered and beaten back a great many, he expelled it from the province.*[121]

Ljudevit battled not only against the Frankish army, but also against Croatian Prince Borna, who remained loyal to the Friulian margrave. Immediately after Ljudevit's failure in Carantania in 819, Borna attacked the Savian Principality *with large brigades (cum magnis copiis)*. At the beginning of the battle, which took place along the Kupa River, the Guduscans betrayed Borna, and Ljudevit's father-in-law Dragamos, who fought on Borna's side, died in battle. Borna lost, but he was able to withdraw under the protection of *his retinue (praetorianorum suorum)*. He returned to Dalmatia and again subjugated the Guduscans.

In December 819 Ljudevit moved into Croatia *with a strong army (cum valida manu)*. Borna *closed all of his in castles (castellis)* and continually agitated and attacked *Ljudevit's brigades (Liudewiti copias)*. Borna's castles withstood Ljudevit's devastating attacks, and in a devastating war led by Borna, Ljudevit lost some 3-thousand soldiers and more than 300 horses.[122]

In the early spring of 820 two imperial armies, approaching against Ljudevit from Italy, ran into opposition in the Julian Alps and in Carantania. Only a third of the military wending its way *through Bavaria and Upper Pannonia (per Baioariam et Pannoniam superiorem)* did not meet with opposition.[123] After the desolation of Ljudevit's principality by the imperial armies *the Carniolans, who live by the Sava River (Carniolenses, qui circa Savum fluvium habitant) and almost neighbour with the Friulians, surrendered to Baldric; a portion of the Carantanians (pars Carantanorum), which fell from us on the side of Ljudevit, tried to do the same*.[124] That is, the *Carniolans (Carniolenses) and some of the Carinthians (quidam Carantanorum), who had joined with Ljudevit, surrendered to our Duke Baldric*.[125] Thus, only a small portion of the Carantanians joined in the rebellion of Sisak Prince Ljudevit.

The Drava River divided the Salzburg diocese from the Aquileia diocese. Since the diocese territory of the Aquileia patriarch was the March of Friuli and the Carantanian March belonged to the Salzburg diocese, the Drava River

---

121 *Ann. reg. Franc.* ad a. 819, rec. Kurze, p. 151. MMFH I, pp. 27–28. *Anonymi Vita Hludowici imperatoris* 32, MMFH II, p. 29.

122 *Ann. reg. Franc.* ad a. 819, rec. Kurze, pp. 150–151. MMFH I, pp. 27–28. *Anonymi Vita Hludowici imperatoris* 32, MMFH II, pp. 29–30.

123 *Ann. reg. Franc.* ad a. 820, rec. Kurze, pp. 152–153. MMFH I, p. 29.

124 *Ann. reg. Franc.* ad a. 820, rec. Kurze, p. 153. MMFH I, p. 29.

125 *Anonymi Vita Hludowici imperatoris* 33. MMFH II, p. 30.

was also the border between both marches, and a narrow strip of Carantanian land south of the Drava belonged (perhaps since 788, when Carantania ceased to be a principality) under the rule of the Friulian margrave. Thus, only a part of the Carantanians who lived under the cruel rule of the Friulian margrave joined in Ljudevit's rebellion. Perhaps Carantanians on the northern bank of the Drava also joined with him, but the whole of Carantania did not rebel. The campaign of the Friulian margrave in 819 and the imperial army in the spring of 820, which marched through Carantania, operated only in the valley of the Drava. Gotofrid, margrave of the Avar and Carantania Marches, did not take part in this war at all, because the rebellion was not aimed against him, and he had nothing to do with it.

Prince Ljudevit, facing three imperial armies that sacked his principality in the spring of 820, closed himself into his castle at Sisak above the confluence of the Kupa and Sava rivers and did not go out of it at all: *He and his people only remained in the castle fortress (munitione tantum castelli), which he had built on a steep hill (in arduo monte)*.[126] That is, *Ljudevit hid himself in the heights of a castle (castelli cuiusdam altitudine)*.[127] Borna's and Ljudevit's castles were stone wall fortresses. Grado patriarch Fortunatus, who encouraged Ljudevit in his opposition to the emperor, sent him *craftsmen and masons for reinforcing his castles (ad castella sua munienda)*.[128]

Borna died in 821. The Croats selected his nephew Ladislas as his successor: *In the meantime Borna, Prince of Dalmatia as well as Liburnia, died and at the request of the people (populo), as well as with the consent of the emperor, his nephew of name Ladislas (Ladasclaus) is set as his successor.*[129] The Croatian prince was chosen by the whole tribe of Croatians. Even the Carantanian prince was elected by all free Carantanians: *Then when Borut died, the Bavarians sent Gorazd ... back to the Slavs at their request and they made a prince of him.*[130] The Sisak princes, among certainly also Ljudevit, undoubtedly went through the same tribal election. We don't know, however, what name the tribe to which Ljudevit's principality on the middle Sava belonged.

Before the next attack of the imperial army (in the summer of 822) *Ljudevit left Sisak Castle (Siscia civitate)* and escaped to the Serbs. The Serbian prince who received Ljudevit was very careless. At a time when the imperial army was still in Savia, Ljudevit treacherously murdered his host and *took control of*

---

126 *Ann. reg. Franc.* ad a. 820, rec. Kurze, p. 153.
127 *Anonymi Vita Hludowici imperatoris* 33, MMFH II, p. 30.
128 *Ann. reg. Franc.* ad a. 821, rec. Kurze, p. 155.
129 *Ann. reg. Franc.* ad a. 821, rec. Kurze, p. 155.
130 *Conversio* 4, ed. Wolfram, pp. 42–43. MMFH III, p. 300.

his castle (civitatem eius).[131] In the following year Ljudevit fled from Serbia to Croatia to Borna's uncle Ljudemysl, who after a short time did away with him.[132] Ljudevit and Borna had castles, large armies and did not move around without *their retinue (praetorianorum suorum)*.[133] Borna's and Ljudevit's princely power, resting on their armies, castles and princely retinue, was already the power of an arising state.[134] The principalities of Mojmír in Moravia and Pribina's Nitria were also just such principalities, as was Carantania up to year 788.

---

131 *Ann. reg. Franc.* ad a. 822, rec. Kurze, p. 158. *MMFH I*, p. 29. *Anonymi Vita Hludowici imperatoris* 35, *MMFH II*, p. 30.

132 *Ann. reg. Franc.* ad a. 823, rec. Kurze, p. 161. *MMFH I*, p. 30. *Anonymi Vita Hludovici imperatoris* 36, *MMFH II*, p. 31.

133 *Borna ... auxilio tamen praetorianorum suorum protectus evasit. Ann. reg. Franc.* ad a. 819, rec. Kurze, p. 151. *MMFH I*, p. 28. *Sed Borna ... suorum tamen iutus auxilio domestico discrimen imminens tutus evasit. Anonymi Vita Hludovici imperatoris* 32, *MMFH II*, p. 29. Štih, *The Middle Ages between the Eastern Alps and the Northern Adriatic*, pp. 181–183.

134 Denis Evgenevič Alimov, "Politija Borny: *Gentes* i *Herrschaft* v Dalmacii v pervoj četverti IX veka," *Peterburgskije slavjanskije u balkanskije issledovanija* (2011), N° 1 (9), pp. 101–142.

CHAPTER 5

Nitria the Independent Principality (805–833)

1   Morava and Nitrava

Mojmír's Moravia took its name from the Morava River. The name of this river (*Marus*) is mentioned as early as in Pliny the Elder and Tacitus.[1] If Methodius had the title of Moravian Archbishop, then his episcopal seat could have also been called Moravia, as was written in the Second Life of Naum: *Methodius ... was released from blessed Pope Hadrian, he departed ... to the castle Morava (vъ grad Moravu), which he got as Archbishop.*[2] The titles of bishops and archbishops were indicated according to the town or castle of their seat and only exceptionally according to the name of the land which they administered to, because several bishoprics could lie in one land (for example, in Bavaria) or several regions could belong to a single bishopric (for example, to the Salzburg diocese). We can identify Morava Castle with the princely seat of Mojmír in today's Mikulčice.[3]

Morava Castle, the princely castle of the House of the Mojmírs, took its name from the Morava River, which flowed around it on both sides, and also gave its name to the entire country that the Mojmírs ruled over. The name of the Nitra River, too, at that time the *Nitrava*, was taken by the princely castle built on a hill in its meander.[4] Using a simple analogy, we can fill in the name of Pribina's principality:

---

1   C. Plinius Secundus, *Naturalis historia* 4, 80–81, in *Griechische und lateinische Quellen zur Frühgeschichte Mitteleuropas bis zur Mitte des 1. Jahrtausends u. Z.*, ed. Joachim Herrmann, *1. Teil: von Homer bis Plutarch* (Berlin 1988), pp. 326–327. Dobiáš, *Dějiny*, pp. 7, 11.
2   *II. Žitije Nauma*, MMFH II, p. 254.
3   Lubomír E. Havlík, *Morava v 9.–10. století. K problematice politického postavení, sociální a vládní struktury a organizace* (Praha 1978), pp. 18–19. Lubomír E. Havlík, *Kronika o Velké Moravě* (Brno 1993), pp. 142, 150, 156–157. Lubomír E. Havlík, *Svatopluk Veliký, král Moravanů a Slovanů* (Brno 1994), pp. 34–38. Róbert Snášil, "Grad Morava," in *Velká Morava mezi východem a západem. Sborník příspěvků z mezinárodní vědecké konference Uherské Hradiště, Staré Město 28. 9.–1. 10. 1999*, ed. Luděk Galuška, Pavel Kouřil, Zdeněk Měřínský, *Spisy Archeologického ústavu AV ČR Brno* 17 (2001), pp. 355–364.
4   *Conversio* 11, ed. Wolfram, pp. 74–75. Peter Bednár – Ivan Staník, "Archeologický a stavebnohistorický výskum národnej kultúrnej pamiatky Nitra Hrad," *AVANS v r. 1991* (Nitra 1992), pp. 21–22. Peter Bednár – Ivan Staník, "Archeologický a stavebno-historický výskum Nitrianskeho hradu v rokoch 1988–1991," in *Nitra. Príspevky k najstarším dejinám mesta*, ed. Karol Pieta (Nitra 1993), pp. 127–141. Peter Bednár, "Die Nitraer Burg im 9.–12. Jahrhundert," in *4. Castrum bene-Konferenz, 10–13. Oktober 1994* (Visegrád 1994), pp. 18–19. Peter Bednár, "Zisťovací výskum

river:	MORAVA	NITRAVA
castle:	[MORAVA]	NITRAVA
principality:	MORAVA	[NITRAVA]

Just as the land and *Morava* castle took their name from the *Morava* River, thus, the *Nitrava* River gave its name to the princely castle on its meander and to the entire country ruled from there by the Princes of *Nitrava*. Pribina's principality in Slovakia was thus named *Nitrava*.

2 The Moravians and Nitravians

In July 817 Emperor Louis the Pious decided how it would be necessary to divide the rule of his empire after his death. Bavaria and together with it the Carantanian March (*Carentanos*), the Bohemians (*Beheimos*)[5] and the Eastern March (*Avaros atque Sclaves, qui ab orientali parte Baioariae sunt*) would go to Louis the German.[6] The Moravians, whom emperor Louis the Pious left out of this *Divisio imperii*, then became out of the reach of Frankish power. In 822, however, the Moravians came to the imperial diet that the emperor had called to Frankfurt am Main. At the diet the emperor *heard delegations of all the eastern Slavs, that is the Obotrites, Sorbs, Veletes, Bohemians, Moravians, Predenecentes* (= southern Obotrites) *and Avars settled in Pannonia*. All of these delegations came before the emperor *with gifts* (*cum muneribus*).[7] The

---

na južnom nádvorí Nitrianskeho hradu," *AVANS v r. 1993* (Nitra 1995), pp. 31–33. Peter Bednár, "Nitriansky hrad v 9. storočí," *Pamiatky a múzeá* 3 (1995), pp. 65–67. Peter Bednár, "Siedma sezóna výskumu Nitrianskeho hradu," *AVANS v r. 1994* (Nitra 1996), pp. 29–31. Peter Bednár, "Nitriansky hrad v 9. storočí a jeho význam v sídliskovej štruktúre veľkomoravskej Nitry," in *Svätopluk 894–1994*, ed. Marsina, Ruttkay, pp. 19–32. *Dejiny Nitry*, ed. Fusek, Zemene, pp. 97–108. Peter Bednár, "Die Entwicklung der Befestigung der Nitraer Burg im 9.–12. Jahrhundert," in *Frühmittelalterlicher Burgenbau in Mittel- und Osteuropa*, ed. Joachim Henning, Alexander Tivadar Ruttkay (Bonn 1998), pp. 371–382. Peter Bednár, *Nitriansky hrad v 9. až 13. storočí. Autoreferát dizertácie na získanie vedeckej hodnosti kandidáta historických vied* (Nitra 1998). Peter Bednár, "Sídlisková štruktúra Nitry v 9. storočí," in *Velká Morava mezi východem a západem*, ed. Galuška, Kouřil, Měřínsky, pp. 29–39. Bednár, "Nitra v 9. storočí," pp. 88–98. Gertrúda Brezinová – Marián Samuel, "Osídlenie hradného kopca v praveku a včasnej dobe dejinnej," in *Kolíska kresťanstva*, ed. Judák, Bednár, Medvecký, pp. 96–100. Peter Bednár – Michal Šimkovic, "Opevnenie Nitrianskeho hradu," in *Kolíska kresťanstva*, ed. Judák, Bednár, Medvecký, pp. 134, 136.

5   The Bohemians, too, came to the attention of Charlemagne, who compelled them to pay tribute by two military campaigns in 805 and 806. Třeštík, *Počátky*, pp. 69–73.
6   See chapter 4, note 94.
7   *Ann. reg. Franc.* ad a. 822, rec. Kurze, p. 159. *MMFH I*, p. 30.

Moravians thus ended up in the same dependency on the Frankish Empire as the other Slavs present in Frankfurt. The Frankish Empire collected taxes from them and intervened in their inter-dynastic disputes.[8]

In 833 Moravian Prince Mojmír routed Pribina from Nitra and connected Nitria to Moravia. Some ten years after the conquest of Nitria by the Moravians, an unknown Bavarian author compiled the Description of the Castles and Lands on the North Side of the Danube, in which he named the Slavic tribes on the eastern borders of the new East Francia Kingdom.[9] Both Transdanubian principalities were considered as Moravian, but they could be differentiated. The difference between them appeared in a deviation in the naming. He called the nearer group the *Marharii* and the more distant, who were still considered as an individual *populus* or people, that is a nation, he called the *Merehani*.[10] And he also counted the castles that belonged to them: *In Bohemia are 15 castles. The Moravians (Marharii) have 11 castles. The Bulgarians have a vast territory and plentiful people owning 5 castles, and because there is so many of them, they are not accustomed to having castles. A people exist which are called the Moravians (Merehanos), and these have 30 castles. These are the lands which are along our borders.*[11]

The Nitrian Slavs, however, could not have been called Moravians before 833, because the Morava River, according to which the Moravians and their principality got their name, did not pass through Nitria. The princely castle and the Principality of *Nitravia* took their name from the *Nitrava* River. Therefore, if we may continue in the Morava–Nitrava analogy, we arrive at another Moravian–Nitravian analogy. Just as the residents of the Principality of Moravia (*Morava*) were the Moravians, the residents of the Principality of Nitravia (*Nitrava*) could be exactly the Nitravians. The Bohemians, Sorbs, Croats, Obotrites, Dulebs and other tribes took their name from time immemorial, preserved it even after division into two (or three) smaller tribes and it remained to them even after occupying new territory. The assumed Nitravians, like the Moravians, however,

---

8 *Ann. reg. Franc.* ad a. 812, 817, 818, 819, 821, 822, 823, 824, 826, rec. Kurze, pp. 137, 147, 149–150, 157, 159, 160, 162, 165–166, 169. *Anonymi Vita Hludovici imperatoris* 36, cur. Rau, p. 316. Třeštík, *Počátky*, p. 270. The gift which the Moravians delivered to the emperor in Frankfurt was, according to Miroslav Lysý, an expression of dependence. The dependency of the Moravians on the neighbouring empire originated only after their baptism in 831. Lysý, *Moravania*, pp. 169–171, 182–183.

9 Třeštík, *Počátky*, pp. 477–479.

10 Třeštík, *Vznik*, pp. 131–135.

11 *Descriptio civitatum et regionum ad septentrionalem plagam Danubii*, MMFH III, pp. 285–287. Erwin Herrmann, *Slawisch-germanische Beziehungen im südostdeutschen Raum von der Spätantike bis zum Ungarnsturm. Ein Quellenbuch mit Erläuterungen*. Veröffentlichungen des Collegium Carolinum 17 (München 1965), pp. 212–221.

belonged among those tribes which according to the word of Russian chronicler Nestor *were called by their names* (according to), *where they settled, on which location*. A Slavic tribe could get the name Nitravians only after they were settled under the Western Carpathians and their new centre was found near the Nitria River.

A pair of related tribes were also the Carantanians (*Carantani*) and the Carniolans (*Carniolenses*). Paul the Deacon, The Royal Frankish Annals and The Life of Emperor Louis clearly differentiates them from one another. Their relatedness is not only seen in a common archaeological culture but also their rapid fusion after unification in 828.[12] After the fall of the March of Friuli in 828, Carniola became a part of Carantania, one of several Carantanian counties.[13] From that point we don't find the name *Carniolenses* in any written sources.[14] After 828 the Carniolans became Carantanians, just as the Nitravians after Mojmír's victory over Pribina in 833 (also) became Moravians.

In 822 delegations *of all the eastern Slavs* came to Frankfurt, that is all the Slavic tribes which were settled beyond the eastern borders of the Frankish Empire and had the obligation on the appeal of the Frankish king and emperor to come *with gifts* to the imperial diet. However, we don't see the Nitravian (Nitrian) Slavs in the list of these *eastern Slavs*. If the Nitravians were not at the imperial diet, then the powerful influence of the neighbouring Frankish rulers,

---

12   See chapter 3, notes 6, 7, chapter 4, notes 119, 124, 125. Timotej Knific, "Carniola in the early Middle Ages," *Balcanoslavica* 5 (1976), pp. 111–121. Klaus Bertels, "Carantania. Beobachtungen zur politisch-geographischen Terminologie und zur Geschichte des Landes und seiner Bevölkerung im frühen Mittelalter," *Carinthia I*, 177 (1987), pp. 113–121. Wolfram, "Karantanija med vzhodom in zahodom," pp. 182–184. Wolfram, *Salzburg, Bayern, Österreich*, pp. 82–84. Štih, "Carniola, patria Sclavorum," pp. 845–861. Štih, *The Middle Ages between the Eastern Alps and the Northern Adriatic*, pp. 123–135, 140–143, 154–156.

13   *Ann. reg. Franc.* ad a. 828, rec. Kurze, p. 174. *MMFH I*, p. 52. In 838 Carniolan Count Salacho took in the fleeing Pribina and reconciled him with his direct superior, Margrave of the Eastern and Carinthian March Ratbod. *Conversio* 10, ed. Wolfram, pp. 52–53, 126, 129. *MMFH III*, p. 311. Wolfram, *Salzburg, Bayern, Österreich*, pp. 83, 306, 310, 312, 320, 322. See note 27.

14   Carniola was again recalled in two imperial donations from 973 as a border march of the Carantanian Principality, which was administered by Margrave Popo. According to the first document, from 30 June 973, the gifted property lay *in comitatu Poponis comitis, quod Carniola vocatur et quod vulgo Creina marcha appellatur*. According to the second, from 23 November 973, *in regione vulgari vocabulo Chreine et in marcha et in comitatu Poponis comitis*. *Monumenta historica ducatus Carinthiae III. Die kärntner Geschichtsquellen 811–1202*, ed. August von Jaksch (Klagenfurt 1904), no. 135, p. 54. Wolfram, *Salzburg, Bayern, Österreich*, pp. 83–84. The name *Carniola* also endured in the subsequent centuries; however, we never find the name *Carniolenses* after 828. Štih, *The Middle Ages between the Eastern Alps and the Northern Adriatic*, pp. 128–135.

which stretched beyond the mentioned Moravians and the Avars of Upper Pannonia, did not then reach Nitravia (Nitria, Nitraland).

The Principality of *Nitrava* at the time of its independence lay outside the attention of the contemporary administrators; thus, they did not record even the name of the assumed Nitravians. After 833 the differentiation of the Nitravians from the Moravians lost meaning, just as the differentiation of the Carniolans from the Carantanians did after 828. Therefore, all written sources know only the Moravians. Only the mentioned anonymous geographer differentiated dual Moravians. One of them (the *Merehani*) are actually the sought-after Nitravians.

3 Bulgarian Attack into Transdanubia

Shortly after suppressing a rebellion in Savia, Emperor Louis the Pious had to deal with the Bulgarian threat on the Pannonian borders of his empire. Emissaries of the southern Obotrites, who attempted to form an alliance with the Frankish empire, came to the imperial diet in Frankfurt in 822.[15] In 824 they complained in Aachen about the enemy Bulgarians. They didn't get help from the emperor in time, however, and had to subject themselves to the Bulgarian khagan.[16] Khagan Omurtag then for two years (824–826) appealed to Emperor Louis for an agreement on the setting of the borders between their realms. Louis obviously feared Omurtag's territorial demands; perhaps that's why he left his appeal without a clear response. When in 826 Louis got an ultimatum from Omurtag linked with the threat of a military attack, he sent his Count Palatine Bertric to the Carantanian March (*in Carantanorum provinciam*) to locate Friulian Margrave Baldric and Gerold II, Margrave of the Avar and Carantanian March and responsible for defence of the Pannonian borders, and verified the rumour of the murder or exiling of Omurtag. Bertric learned nothing for certain, and Louis again did not reply to the Bulgarian ultimatum. In May 826 both margraves got to the imperial diet in Ingelheim, where they assured the emperor about peace on Bulgarian territory.[17]

Ultimately, after thorough military preparations, which he managed to keep in secret, Khagan Omurtag unexpectedly attacked. The surprised and

---

15 *Ann. reg. Franc.* ad a. 822, rec. Kurze, p. 159. *MMFH I*, pp. 29–30.
16 *Ann. reg. Franc.* ad a. 824, rec. Kurze, pp. 165–166. *MMFH I*, pp. 30–31. Třeštík, *Vznik*, pp. 103–106.
17 *Ann. reg. Franc.* ad a. 824, 825, 826, rec. Kurze, p. 164, 167, 168–169. *MMFH I*, pp. 30–32. Schwarcz, "Pannonien," pp. 102–103.

unprepared defence of both border marches completely failed. As soon as the Bulgarians crossed the border of Louis's empire in 827, the Savian Principality (Principality of Sisak) fell away from it. Savian Prince Ratmir, or his unknown predecessor, shook off Frankish rule, which made it easier for the Bulgarians to navigate the Drava to the interior of Frankish Pannonia: *the Bulgarian army devastated the border region of Upper Pannonia without any retaliation*.[18] Upper Pannonia in the understanding of the Frankish Annals (unlike later from Conversio) covered the entirety of Transdanubia, separated from the Savian Principality, to which Lower Pannonia belonged, by the Drava River. The Bulgarian army that came by boat up the Drava thus landed on its northern bank. The Bulgarians attacked and occupied the Transdanubian principalities lying along the northern bank of the Drava, forced the domestic Slavic princes out of them and put Bulgarian administrators in their place: *And the Bulgarians also sent an army along the Drava (per Dravum) on boats and devastated by sword and by fire the Slavs settled in Pannonia and chased away their princes (ducibus) and set Bulgarian administrators (rectores) over them*.[19]

18   *Ann. reg. Franc.* ad a. 828, rec. Kurze, p. 174. *MMFH I*, p. 52. Einhard knew both Pannonias (*utramque Pannoniam*). *Einhardi Vita Karoli Magni* 15, *MMFH II*, p. 23. The Royal Frankish Annals refer to the entire Transdanubia up to the Drava on the south as Upper Pannonia: *per Pannoniam superiorem, terminos Pannoniae superioris* and Ljudevit's (Louis's) Principality of Savia as Lower Pannonia: *Liudewiti ducis Pannoniae inferioris. Ann. reg. Franc.* ad a. 818, 820, 828, rec. Kurze, p. 149, 152–153, 174. *MMFH I*, pp. 27, 28–29, 32. Conversio writes about the Salzburg part of Transdanubia as about Lower Pannonia: *de inferiori Pannonia, in plagis Pannoniae inferioris, partem Pannoniae circa lacum Pellisse inferioris, inferioris Pannoniae, aliquam inferioris Pannoniae in beneficium partem circa fluvium, qui dicitur Sala. Conversio* 3, 6, 7, 11, ed. Wolfram, pp. 62–63, 66–67, 68–69, 74–75. *MMFH III*, pp. 298, 302, 304, 305, 312. The Royal Frankish Annals contain records from the years 741–829, most of which are from the 8th century. Their author could differentiate two parts of Pannonia, divided by the Drava River. The Principality of Savia, considered as Lower Pannonia, and Transdanubia, which belonged directly to the Avar Khaganate, was for him Upper Pannonia. This differentiation did not lose its persistence, and we find it in the earliest records of these annals. The younger Conversio needed with the name Lower Pannonia to distinguish the Salzburg diocese territory from that of Passau. This emerged from the situation which arose after the fall of Avar power, by the partitioning of Pannonia between the border marches and the bishoprics. If, according to the document of King Louis the German from 1 May 859 *Tulln lies in the land of Pannonia* (*Tullina situs in regione Pannonia*), then afterwards the entire county between the Vienna Woods and the lower Enns, in which Tulln lay, was counted as Pannonia, more specifically as Upper Pannonia. *MMFH III*, Diplomata 25, pp. 48–50.

19   *Ann. reg. Franc.* ad a. 827, rec. Kurze, p. 173. *MMFH I*, p. 52. If the Bulgarians crossed the Drava and occupied the southern part of Transdanubia, then they must have had a free crossing through the territory of Savia. The Bulgarians marched *per Dravum*, that is they already had the lower Danube up to the confluence with the Drava firmly under their power. They did not install their own administrator in Savia, but they enabled a rebellion.

Bulgar Khagan Omurtag thus wanted to expand his own realm even over the southern part of Transdanubia.

4 Pribina's Church in Nitra and the Events of 828

Pribina, although a pagan, had a church built in Nitra, which was consecrated by Salzburg archbishop Adalram (821–836) himself.[20] When did Adalram come to Nitra and why him specifically?

In February 828 Emperor Louis the Pious called an imperial diet to Aachen, which dealt with the situation in Pannonia.[21] Upon its assessment everyone was certainly aware how exceptionally the military strength of Pribina's principality had grown in value. An alliance with Pribina could significantly contribute to the success of the anti-Bulgarian campaign then being prepared. This was also the main reason for the arrival of the Salzburg Archbishop Adalram, a future participant in the anti-Bulgarian campaign, to Pribina's princely court in Nitra. Pribina also had to feel threatened by the expansiveness of neighbouring Bulgaria; therefore, he obviously came to an agreement very quickly with Adalram. And on this occasion he found time for the consecration of a church.[22]

Adalram's diplomatic mission ensured a prepared attack against the Bulgarians in Transdanubia from the northern side. Adalram returned to Bavaria and the emperor, obviously pleased with the results of his visit in Nitra,

---

The local prince, whom Louis the Pious had installed in Sisak after the exiling of Louis in 822, was overthrown or joined forces with the Bulgarians. If he joined the Bulgarians, then he was identical with Ratimír mentioned in 838 or was his unknown predecessor.

20 *Cui quondam Adalrammus archiepiscopus ultra Danubium in sua proprietate loco vocato Nitrava consecravit ecclesiam. Conversio* 11, ed. Wolfram, pp. 74–75. *MMFH III*, p. 312. According to Herwig Wolfram, Archbishop Adalram consecrated a church in Nitra for Pribina's wife and his son Kocel even before 821. Conversio, ed. Wolfram, pp. 51, 186, 319. Herwig Wolfram, "The Bavarian Mission to Pannonia in the 9th century," in Pavel Kouřil et al., *The Cyril and Methodius Mission and Europe – 1150 Years Since the Arrival of the Thessaloniki Brothers in Great Moravia* (Brno 2014), p. 30.

21 Ann. reg. Franc. ad a. 828, rec. Kurze, p. 174.

22 In 915 Veronian Bishop Nother II came to Prague with the delegation of Italian King Berengar II. The diplomatic mission of the Veronian Bishop in Prague climaxed the formation of the Italian-Bavarian-Bohemian-Hungarian alliance. The Veronian Bishop on this occasion also performed the tonsuring of Vaclav, son of then Bohemian Prince Vratislaus I. Dušan Třeštík, "Václav a Berengár. Politické pozadí postřižin sv. Václava roku 915." *Český časopis historický* 89 (1992), no. 5–6, pp. 643–644, 647–649, 660. Třeštík, *Počátky*, pp. 360–361. Adalram's mission in Nitra in 828 thus had an analogue in Nother's mission in Prague in 915.

handed over leadership of the war to his youngest son (from 826 Bavarian king) Louis the German. Louis the German conquered back the lost part of Transdanubia in 828.[23] Because the victorious Bavarian king was battling over the diocesan territory of Salzburg, he was certainly accompanied by Salzburg Archbishop Adalram.[24]

At the diet in Ingelheim Margraves Baldric and Gerold II assured the emperor about peace on the Frankish-Bulgarian borders. The Bulgarian invasion in the following year, however, showed how neglected the defence of their marches were. Therefore, at the next imperial diet in Aachen, in February 828, the emperor ordered extensive reorganization of the border marches: *Baldric, the Friulian duke, when due to his cowardice the Bulgarian army plundered the borders of Upper Pannonia (terminos Pannoniae superioris) without retribution, was stripped of the rank (honoribus) he had, and the march that he held was divided among four counts (inter quattuor comites divisa est).*[25] The Friulian margrave was left with only Friuli itself (between the Julian Alps and the Livenza River), which together with other counties of Istria belonged further to Italy.[26] Carantania recorded a territorial gain. Carniolan County on the upper Sava was added to several Carantanian counties.[27] In addition to this, Carantania got back the narrow strip of Carantanian territory on the southern bank of the Drava (aside from a small run beyond the Tarvisio pass around Villach,

---

23 *Imperator Iunio mense ad Ingilinheim villam venit ibique per aliquot dies placitum habuit; in quo cum de filiis suis Hlothario et Pippino cum exercitu ad marcam Hispanicam mittentis consilium inisset.* Ann. reg. Franc. ad a. 828, rec. Kurze, p. 174. In June in Ingelheim the emperor also decided on a campaign of his youngest son Louis the German against the Bulgarians: *Hlotarius cum exercitu ad marcam Hispanicam missus est, similiter et Hludovicus iuvenis contra Bulgaros.* Ann. Fuld. ad a. 828, rec. Kurze, p. 25. MMFH I, p. 88. Cibulka, *Velkomoravský kostel*, pp. 253–254.

24 Cibulka, *Velkomoravský kostel*, pp. 252–257. Dvorník, *Byzantské misie*, p. 94, 322. Josef Cibulka assumed that Archbishop Adalram turned away from Upper Pannonia in 828 to Nitra in order to consecrate the church there. He went their either alone or with part of the military, which could proceed through Nitria to the upper Tisza against Bulgaria. Cibulka, *Velkomoravský kostel*, p. 254.

25 Ann. reg. Franc. ad a. 828, rec. Kurze, p. 174. MMFH I, p. 52.

26 Wolfram, *Die Geburt*, p. 273. Krahwinkler, *Friaul*, pp. 193–197.

27 If Ratbod marched in 838 against Savian Prince Ratimír, then Carniola, through which he undoubtedly passed, must have then already belonged to his Carantania. Carniolan Count Salacho in 838 appeased Pribina with his own superior Carantanian Margrave Ratbod. See note 36. The Carniolan county belonged to Carantania up until year 1077. Dimitz, *Geschichte Krains I*, pp. 126–127. Victor Hasenöhrl, "Deutschlands südöstliche Marken im 10., 11. und 12. Jahrhundert," *Archiv für österreichische Geschichte* 82 (1895), pp. 518–532. *Erläuterungen I. Abt., 4. Teil, 2. Heft,* pp. 343–375. Karl Brunner, *Österreichische Geschichte 907–1156. Herzogtümer und Marken. Von Ungarnsturm bis ins 12. Jahrhundert* (Wien 1994), pp. 334–335.

which remained to Friuli) administered up to then by the Friulian margrave.[28] This narrow strip of land fell to one of the Carantanian counties, which lay in southern Carantania in the basin of the Carantanian part of the Drava River. Thus the four counts, among whom Baldric's March of Friuli was divided, were the Friulian count, the Istrian, the Carniolan count and the count seated on the Carantanian Drava, either in Krnski Grad (Carnburg, civitas Carantana) or now in Moosburg.

In 827 both margraves faltered; therefore, in February 828 the emperor had to remove not only Baldric, but also Gerold, and he named Ratbod as the new margrave of the Avar and Carantanian Marches after the removal of Gerold. In 828 Gerold II lost the title of margrave; however, he further remained a count in his county between the Enns and the Vienna Woods. On 22 March 828 at the request of Bavarian King Louis the German and Count Gerold (*Geroldi comitis*) the emperor gifted to the Kremsmünster Abbey property *in pago Grunzwiti* near the Traisen River. The tax that the local Slavs were then paying to the count (*ad partem comitis solvebatur*) went instead to the abbey. Couriers of Count Gerold (*missi Geroldi comitis*) staked out the borders of the property of the gifted abbey.[29] In the winter of 831/832 Emperor Louis the Pious sent two bishops to Rome and *the most illustrious Count Gerold (Geroldum illustrissimum comitem)* to get confirmation from the pope of the title of archbishop and a pallium for the newly elected Hamburg Archbishop Ansgar.[30]

After the expulsion of the Bulgarians and their administrators from Transdanubia in the summer of 828, the victorious Bavarian king did not permit the restoring of rule to the domestic Slavic princes on the freed territory. He filled their emptied places with military leaders: *After them, however, the mentioned territory, by donation of the king (dato regum) got into the hands of dukes of Bavaria (duces Bagoarii) named Helmwin, Albgar and Pabo as a county (in comitatum). When that happened (His ita peractis)*, Ratbod took over defence of the

---

28   A small strip beyond the pass between Tarvisio and Arnoldstein, in the vicinity of Villach, remained a monument to the rule of the Friulian Margrave in the Aquileia part of Carinthia, which the Friulian count held until 1077. *Erläuterungen zum Historischen Atlas der österreichischen Alpenländer, herausgegeben von Kaiserliche Akademie der Wissenschaften in Wien. I. Abteilung: Die Landesgerichtskarte, 4. Teil: Kärnten, Krain, Görz und Istrien* von August von Jaksch, Martin Wutte, Anton Kaspret und Anton Mell, *1. Heft: Kärnten, Görz und Gradisca* (Wien 1914), pp. 227–243. *Erläuterungen I. Abt., 4. Teil, 2. Heft*, pp. 307–308.

29   *MMFH III*, Diplomata 9, pg. 24–26.

30   *Rimberti Vita Anskarii* 13, curaverunt Werner Trillmich et Rudolf Buchner. Quellen des 9. und 11. Jahrhunderts zur Geschichte der Hamburgischen Kirche und des Reiches, neu übertragen von Werner Trillmich (Berlin 1961), pp. 46–47.

borders.[31] Helmwin, Albgar and Pabo were *dukes of Bavaria*, military leaders of the Bavarian army,[32] who marched against the Bulgarians with their King Louis the German. The king rewarded their loyalty and service in the victorious war. They acquired the administration of the conquered territory, and they became the first generation of Transdanubian counts.

If three counties originated in the Carantanian part of Transdanubia in 828, then one of the four principalities missed out on the transformation into a county. One of the four Transdanubian principalities mentioned in Conversio was based beyond the reach of the Bulgarian invasion and the subsequent anti-Bulgarian campaign of Louis the German. He did not have to run from the Bulgarians; he remained loyal to the Bavarian king, and he obviously joined his side in the battle against the Bulgarians, and so the king left him in place.

Louis the German, on the basis of a decision of the emperor, just then (*His ita peractis*), that is in 828, handed over administration of the Bavarian border marches to the new Margrave Ratbod (828–854). The neighbouring Savian Principality also passed under the dominion of Ratbod. Savian Prince Ratimir, however, with the support of the Bulgarian Khagan Omurtag, rejected Frankish rule until 838.[33]

The deed of donation of Louis the German from 15 September 844 mentions the border of two counties, Ratbod's and Richard's (*Radpoti et Rihharii comitatus*), which were located in the vicinity of the stream Zöbern (*Seuira*).[34] This border divided not only the two mentioned counties but also the Eastern March from the Carantanian March and Passau's Upper Pannonia from Salzburg's Lower Pannonia. The sequence of both counties is certainly not random, and the deed may list them in order, first Ratbod's and then Richard's county, only according to their distance from Louis's royal seat of Regensburg. East Francia King Louis the German issued it near Roding (*Actum ad Rotachin*), perhaps 35 km north-east from Regensburg. Since Upper Pannonia was closer to Regensburg than Lower Pannonia, the first named Ratbod's county was identified with Upper Pannonia and the following Richard's county lay only beyond

---

31   *Conversio* 10, ed. Wolfram, pp. 72–73, *MMFH III*, p. 310.
32   *with the dukes of the brigades* (*a ducibus copiarum*), which were sent to Pannonia in 811, Avar and Slavic princes from Pannonia came to emperor Charlemagne to Aachen. See chapter 4, note 72. In 819 Obotrite Prince Slavomir was presented before Charlemagne *with the dukes of Saxony* (*a ducibus Saxonum*), that is the dukes of the Saxon military. *Anonymi Vita Hludowici imperatoris* 31, *MMFH II*, p. 28. They were the same military dukes as the *dukes of Bavaria* (*duces Bagoarii*), who marched with King Louis the German at the head of the Bavarian army to Pannonia in 828, expelled the Bulgarians from there and then took over administration of the conquered territory from their king.
33   *Conversio* 10, ed. Wolfram, pp. 74–75. *MMFH III*, p. 311.
34   See note 134.

this, in more distant Lower Pannonia. Richard's county, which lay to the south, on the Lower Pannonian side of this border, was one of the mentioned three counties that originated in 828 in the Lower Danubian part of Transdanubia. Richard already belonged to the second generation of Transdanubian counts. Ratbod's county, lying north of this border, was Upper Pannonia. Ratbod, margrave of the Eastern and Carantanian Marches, was thus simultaneously also an Upper Pannonian count, exactly as before Margrave Gerold II was simultaneously the count between the Enns and the Vienna Woods and Aribo was later margrave of the Eastern March and the Count of Traungau at the same time.[35] The margrave was thus also the local count of this county, in which he had his seat. Upper Pannonia was Ratbod's county seat. In 828, when Ratbod became not only margrave but also the local Upper Pannonian count, then Isaac's Upper Pannonian khaganate had to expire, and Upper Pannonia became the third county of the Eastern March.[36]

5 Saint Emmeram

Not only does the archbishop's consecration testify to the importance of Pribina's church in Nitra, but the recording of this event in Conversio itself does, too. The record on the consecration of the Nitrian church is the only one in this entire extensive text which transgresses the strong framework of his work, the precisely defined range of the diocesan territory of Salzburg. If the unknown author, who in 870 advocated the right of the Salzburg archbishop on the territory of his diocese, primarily, however, his endangered right to Lower Pannonia,[37] he did not forget after forty years to mention an event which no longer had anything in common with the mission of his text; thus, this event had to be an exceptionally important and worthy moment for the history of the Salzburg archbishopric. Adalram, that is, did not consecrate in Nitra only a small, unimportant church, but a properly walled construction (*consecravit*

---

[35] See note 173. Zibermayr, *Noricum, Baiern und Östereich*, pg. 310–315. Karl Lechner, *Die Babenberger. Markgrafen und Herzogen von Österreich 976–1246* (Wien – Köln – Weimar 1992), p. 27.

[36] *Conversio*, ed. Wolfram, pp. 114, 170, 172. Wolfram, *Die Geburt*, p. 275.

[37] The unknown author wrote Conversio according to the dating in the conclusion of his work 75 years after the assigning of Pannonian territory to the Salzburg diocese, that is in year 870. The Salzburg archbishop undoubtedly had this defence of the rights and claims of the Salzburg archbishopric with him at the synod, which in Regensburg in the fall of 870 judged the captured Archbishop Methodius. *Conversio* 14, ed. Wolfram, pp. 78–81, 202.

ecclesiam)³⁸ for the first and significant Christian congregation directly in the seat of a still pagan principality. But where did these Christians come from in Pribina's Nitra?

At a later time Pribina's son Kocel gifted three properties from his inheritance (*de hereditate mea*) to the Abbey of St. Emmeram in Regensburg. The first property lay in Strumingen (*ad Stromogin*), the second in Rennersdorf (*in villa nuncupante Reginuuartesdorf*), both near Haibach, and the third in Rosdorf (*in Rosdorf*) near Aschach.³⁹ Kocel's inheritance lying on the southern bank of the upper Austrian Danube between Haibach and Aschach (west of Linz) was located in the midst of extensive properties of the Bavarian Wilhelm family of counts, whose location we know from the donation of Pribina's contemporary, Traungau Count Wilhelm I (821–853). In 833 Wilhelm donated his property in the villages of Schönering (*Sconheringa*, west of Linz), Kematen (*Cheminatum*, south-west of Wels) and Puchham (*Purcheim*, south-east of Eferding) to the Abbey of St. Emmeram in Regensburg.⁴⁰ In 834 this abbey got property in Perschling (*Bersnicha*) from Wilhelm.⁴¹ In addition to this, Wilhelm also owned a great deal of property on the norther bank of the Danube between the mouths of the Aist and Naarn rivers (*inter Agastam et Nardinam*) up through the Northern Forest (*Nortuualt*), from which they flowed. He lent a portion of these lands into the use his wife Engilrada, and after her death, Wilhelm then donated them to the Abbey of St. Emmeram together with all the property that he had in Rosdorf (*ad Rosdorf*, near Aschach). On 18 January 853 King Louis the German confirmed Wilhelm's donation in a document.⁴² Kocel could have only inherited his Traungau property from his mother, who remains unknown to us. Since it lay in the middle of Wilhelm's great estates, we can assume that Kocel's mother came from Wilhelm's family, and the property that Kocel inherited from her was originally her dowry taken from Wilhelms's family estates.⁴³

---

38   Otto Ritz, "Svätý Emmeram, patrón nitrianskeho kostola," in *Ríša Veľkomoravská, sborník vedeckých prác*, sostavil Ján Stanislav (Praha – Bratislava 1933), pp. 93–95.
39   *MMFH III*, Diplomata 26, pp. 50–51. *Die Traditionen des Hochstiftes Regensburg und des Klosters S. Emmeram*, herausgegeben von Josef Widemann. *Quellen und Erörterungen zur bayerischen Geschichte*, Neue Folge 8 (München 1943), no. 37, p. 43.
40   *MMFH III*, Diplomata 26, no. 26, pp. 32–33.
41   *MMFH III*, Diplomata 26, no. 27, pp. 33–34.
42   *MMFH III*, Diplomata 22, pp. 42–45. Mitterauer, *Karolingische Markgrafen*, pp. 104–106.
43   *Conversio*, ed. Wolfram, pp. 185–186, 280, 319–320. Herwig Wolfram, "Überlegungen zur politischen Situation der Slawen im heutigen Oberösterreich (8.–10. Jahrhundert)," in *Baiern und Slawen in Oberösterreich. Probleme der Landnahme und Besiedlung. Symposion 16. November 1978, Schriftenreihe des OÖ. Musealvereins-Gesellschaft für Landeskunde*, Band 10 (Linz 1980), pp. 21–23. Wolfram, *Salzburg, Bayern, Österreich*, p. 312. Wilhelm was not margrave of the Eastern March, as Oskar von Mitis writes. Oskar von Mitis,

We can date Kocel's donation for the Regensburg Abbey of St. Emmeram to the time when he was a *comes*, that is one of the counts in the Pannonian Principality that his father Pribina administered (perhaps 840–861).[44] The first among the witnesses of Kocel's donation was margrave of the Eastern and Carantanian Marches and Upper Pannonian Count Ratbod (*Ratpot comis*). We can thus date Kocel's donation to before Ratbod's removal in 854.[45] The donation of Count Kocel in time and content associates with a similar donation of his relative on his mother's side of Count Wilhelm I for this same Regensburg Abbey of St. Emmeram, which East Francia King Louis the German confirmed by his royal deed from 18 January 853. Both relatives, Kocel and Wilhelm, probably together in January 853 or only shortly before donated to this same abbey.

Evidence of the Bavarian origin of Pribina's wife is not only her Traungau dowry but also the Bavarian name of her son Kocel.[46] We know its original Bavarian form Gozil from two documents of Pope John VIII from 873 to Prince Kocel (*Gozili comiti*).[47] In other Latin sources the form is Chozil, Chezil, Chezul.

"Die Herkunft des Ostmarkgrafen Wilhelm," *Mitteilungen des Instituts für österreichische Geschichtsforschung* 58 (1950), pp. 534–549. Only administration of County Traungau, one of three counties that made up the Eastern March, belonged to Wilhelm I. The Margrave of the Eastern March in Wilhelm's time was Ratbod (828–854).

44 Sometime before 850 Kocel came into administration of Blatenian County and was a count until the death of his father in 861, when he became the Prince of Pannonia. See chapter 6, note 155, 156, 157, 158.

45 See chapter 7, note 20, 22. Mitterauer, "Karolingische Markgrafen," p. 88.

46 *Conversio*, ed. Wolfram, pp. 185–186, 280, 319–320. Daniel Rapant has already written about the German origin of Pribina's wife, and Peter Ratkoš is also inclined towards his opinion. Daniel Rapant, "Pribynov kostolík v Nitre," *Elán* 12, november–december 1941, no. 3–4, pp. 18–21. Daniel Rapant, "Ešte raz o Pribynovom nitrianskom kostolíku," *Elán* 13, marec 1943, no. 7, p. 5. Peter Ratkoš, "Kristianizácia Veľkej Moravy pred misiou Cyrila a Metoda," *Historický časopis* 19 (1971), no. 1, pp. 76–77.

47 *MMFH III*, Diplomata 53, 54, pp. 171–172. The name Gozil (Cozzol, Cozzilo, Cocili, Gozzili, Gozili, Gozzele) is found several times among the testimonies in donations for the Abbey of St. Emmeram in Regensburg from the 9th, 11th and 12th centuries. *Die Traditionen des Hochstifts Regensburg*, ed. Widemann, no. 19, 30, 288, 359, 628, 663, 915, pp. 25, 38, 231, 256, 312, 324, 452. Three Dukes of Lower Lorraine had the name Gozelo (Gozilo, Gozzilo, Gozzelo, Cozelo). Lower Lorraine Duke Gozelo I (1023–1044) also became a duke of Upper Lorraine (1033–1044). His middle son Gozelo II was also a duke of Lower Lorraine (1044–1046). Lower Lorraine Duke Gozelo III (1069–1076) is also known under the name Gottfried III. Lamperti monachi Hirsfeldensis annales, editionis quam paraverat Oswald Holder-Egger textum denuo imprimendum curavit Wolfgang Dietrich Fritz, neu übersetzt von Adolf Schmidt, erläutert von Wolfgang Dietrich Fritz, Augewählte Quellen zur deutschen Geschichte des Mittelalters VII, herausgegeben von Rudolf Buchner (Berlin 1957), pp. 42, 44, 122, 202, 280, 292, 316, 320, 348, 350, 398. Wipo, *Gesta Chuonradi II. imperatoris* I, XXXV; *Annales Sangallenses maiores* ad a. 1037; *Chronicon Herimanni Augiensis* ad a. 1037; *Chronicon Suevicum universale* ad a. 1037, *Wiponis opera*,

Similarly, Ptuj Count Gozwin is written as Chozwin (Chozivin).[48] Composite names beginning with Goz- (Gozhard, Gozbert, Gozbald, Gozmar, Gozlen, Gozlind, Gozpirin, Gozfrid, Gozolf, Gozrad, Gozhelm) or ending with -goz (Helmgoz, Megingoz, Adalgoz, Albgoz, Giselgoz, Ratgoz/Rotgoz, Ruadgoz, Hruodgoz) were very much favoured in Bavaria.

Pribina thus had a church built in Nitra which was to serve his Christian wife and her entourage. If he just then married, he was certainly still young and obviously had become the Nitrian Prince only short before then. We can thus date the beginning of Pribina's princely rule and his wedding to shortly before the consecration of his church by Salzburg Archbishop Adalram.

Kocel inherited not only property in Traungau from his mother but also veneration for the Bavarian St. Emmeram. As is evident from the donations of Count Wilhelm from years 833, 834 and 853, veneration towards this saint was very strong in Wilhelm's family. Kocel's mother, who came from this family, also brought veneration for St. Emmeram to Nitra, and she cultivated it in her son. When Kocel, probably in 853, endowed this same Abbey St. Emmeram as his relative Wilhelm, he did so out of common family veneration to its patron and to the memory of his mother, who was no longer alive.[49] Certainly, he was

---

herausgegeben von Harry Bresslau. Scriptores rerum Germanicarum in usum scholarum ex Monumentis Germaniae historicis separatim editi (Hannoverae et Lipsiae 1915), pp. 12, 56, 93, 99, 102. *Allgemeine Deutsche Biographie*, 9. Band (Leipzig 1879), pp. 531–532. *Lexikon des Mittelalters IV* (München – Zürich 1989), p. 1615.

48   See chapter 6, note 110. The name Gozwin occurs very frequently among the witnesses in the donations from the 9th, 11th and 12th centuries for Regensburg's Abbey of St. Emmeram. *Die Traditionen des Hochstifts Regensburg*, ed. Widemann, no. 17, 200, 576, 599, 600, 625, 783, 791, 792, 822, 854, 855, 867, 880, 894, 897, 903, 917, 920, 926, 960, 1035, 1046, pp. 22, 148, 150, 300, 306, 307, 310, 364–365, 371, 373, 393, 413, 419, 427, 436, 439, 444, 454, 455, 459, 484, 528.

49   At the time of Kocel's donation, his mother was no longer alive. If she had been alive, her property would not yet have been Kocel's inheritance, and Kocel could not have donated part of it to the abbey. The opinions of Václav Chaloupecký and György Györffy on the earlier origin of St. Emmeram patronage in Nitra bypasses the answer to a fundamental question: To whom was Pribina's church consecrated, if not to St. Emmeram? Václav Mencl also accepted Chaloupecký's opinion on the Bohemian origin of St. Emmeram patronage in Nitra in the second half of the 10th century. Václav Chaloupecký, "Sv. Svorád," *Prúdy* 6 (1922), pp. 544–553. Václav Chaloupecký, "Radla – Anastázius, druh Vojtěchův, organizátor uherské církve," *Bratislava, časopis Učenej společnosti Šafaříkovy* I (1927), no. 2, pp. 218–219. Václav Mencl, *Stredoveká architektúra na Slovensku. Kniha prvá: Stavebné umenie na Slovensku od najstarších čias až do konca doby románskej* (Praha – Prešov 1937), pp. 57–58. According to Györffy, veneration of St. Emmeram was brought to Nitra by Gisela, the wife of Saint Stephen, who in the last years of rule of his father Géza, became the Prince of Nitra. Görgy Györffy, *István király és műve* (Budapest 1977), pp. 115–116. *MT I/1*, p. 748. Nitra in the period of Christianization of Hungary in 972 belonged to the most significant of

also thinking of his native Nitra, where St. Emmeram protected his most tender childhood.

6 Dispute over the Diocese Border between Salzburg and Passau

Adalram came to Nitra at a time when his dispute with the Passau bishopric over the diocese border in Pannonia was at its peak. The common border of the Passau and Salzburg diocese in Pannonia had been set earlier by King of Italy Pepin, son of Charlemagne, in 796. With Pepin's decision, the Salzburg diocese acquired only Lower Pannonia. Upper Pannonia, lying between the Vienna Woods and the lower Rába, went with missionary rights in both Transdanubian principalities to the neighbouring Passau bishopric.

Salzburg Archbishops Arno (785–798–820) and Adalram, however, did not recognize the right of the Passau bishopric to Upper Pannonia. Before Bavarian King Louis the German *Archbishop Adalram said that his predecessor Arno had this area and that he preached and preached there*. Without Upper Pannonia, Passau lost direct contiguity with Nitria, because his claim on the missionary work in the Nitria also followed from the claim of the Salzburg bishop to Upper Pannonia. The consecration of the church at the princely court in Nitra is among the Adalram's major intrusions into the diocesan and missionary rights of the Passau bishopric. Passau bishop Reginhar (818–838) however, had no intention of giving up Upper Pannonia: *Bishop Reginhar said that this region should belong to the Passau diocese*. The dispute between Reginhar and Adalram *over the region which lies beyond the Comagenan Mount* (*super parrochia, que adiacet ultra Comagenos montes*), that is beyond the Vienna Woods, ended in November 829. Bavarian King Louis the German in a document from 18 November confirmed the old diocese border. Upper Pannonia with a border on the Spratzbach (*Spraza*) and the Rábca (*alia Spraza*) up to its confluence with the Rába (*Rapa*) remained to Passau. Adalrám did not convince the

---

Árpád's castles. The building, or more the renovation of the castle church in Nitra, could not have awaited until the arrival of Gisela to Nitra in 996. St. Emmeram patrocinium, then the only castle patrocinium in Nitra, is thus older than György Györffy assumes it to be. Václav Chaloupecký is not correct either, because there was no patrocinium of St. Emmeram in Prague. Třeštík, *Počátky*, pp. 405–412. St. Emmeram was a favourite saint in the 9th century; his veneration peaked during the rule of East Francia King and Emperor Arnulf (887–899). In the 10th century his favour was lost, and by the end of this century his cult ceased to spread. S. Stolz, "Emmeram (Haimhramnus)," in *Lexikon des Mittelalters III* (München und Zürich 1986), pp. 1888–1889. Ján Lukačka, "K problému kontinuity kresťanstva na území Slovenska v 10. storočí," *Studia historica Tyrnaviensia* 3 (2003), p. 38.

king and had to be satisfied with the original range of the Salzburg diocese in Pannonia *from the western bank of the above-mentioned waters to the east and south ... just as his predecessor Arno had*.[50] Along with confirmation of the diocese rights of the Passau bishop to Upper Pannonia was also the renewal of his missionary right to adjacent Nitria.[51]

7   Baptism of the Moravians

In 831 Passau Bishop Reginhar *baptised all the Moravians*. This short report is also contained in the much later Records on Passau Bishops.[52] Contemporary

---

50   MMFH III, Diplomata 107, pp. 119–121. CDES I, ed. Marsina, no. 5, p. 7. Cibulka, *Veľkomoravský kostel*, pp. 262–265. The document of Louis the German is false from a diplomatic point of view; however, no one has stated any serious doubts about its contents. Marsina, "Štúdie k slovenskému diplomatáru I," pp. 77–78. Louis the German set the borders of Adalram's diocese toward Reginhar's *just as his predecessor Arno had* (*sicut Arno antecessor eius habuit*), so that he renewed the original partitioned Pannonia from Arno's time. The border dividing Pannonia between Salzburg and Passau, described in Louis's document, is actually Pepin's work from 796. Louis thus did not set the new border; he only renewed the validity of the old borders, which divided not only both diocese but also the Eastern March from the Carantanian March, and before then the territory of the tudunate from the actual khaganate.

51   If Nitria had after 829 remained in the sphere of the Salzburg archbishopric, then the Bavarian bishops, who in 900 protested against the consecration of the Moravian archbishop and three bishops subordinated to him, one of which was undoubtedly based in Nitra (see chapter 9, note 93), would have had to protest not only against the interference in the rights of the Passau Bishop by reducing his diocese, but also against a smaller Salzburg diocese. If East Francia King Louis the German in 867 sent the Passau bishop and his priests to Bulgaria, which bordered with Nitria to the south-east, and not the Salzburg archbishop, whose diocese bordered directly on the east with Bulgaria, then Nitria was undoubtedly considered as belonging to the Passau diocese. Ratkoš, "Kristianizácia," pp. 77–78.

52   *Anno Domini 831. Reginharius episcopus Matavorum baptizat omnes Moravos. Notae de episcopis Pataviensibus* ad a. 831, *Magnae Moraviae fontes historici IV, leges, textus iuridici, supplementa,* curaverunt Dagmar Bartoňková, Karel Kaderka, Lubomír Havlík, Jaroslav Ludvíkovský, Josef Vašica, Radoslav Večerka (Brno 1971), p. 407. Zdeněk R. Dittrich, *Christianity in Great-Moravia. Bijdragen van het Instituut voor middeleeuwse Geschiedenis der Rijksuniversiteit te Utrecht 33* (Groningen 1962), pp. 61–65. Łowmiański, *Początki Polski IV*, pp. 249–250, 312–317. Boris Nikolajevič Florja, "Prinjatie christianstva v Velikoj Moravii, Čechii i Poľše," in *Prinjatie christianstva narodami Centraľnoj i Jugo-Vostočnoj Evropy i kreščenie Rusi*, ed. Gennadij G. Litavrin (Moskva 1988), p. 124. Ján Steinhübel, "Štyri veľkomoravské biskupstvá," *Slovanské štúdie* 1 (1994), pp. 21–24. Ján Steinhübel, "Die Großmährischen Bistümer zur Zeit Mojmirs II.," *Bohemia* 37 (1996), Heft 1, pp. 2–6. Třeštík, *Vznik*, pp. 117–121. Piotr Boroń, "Wiece słowiańskie a decyzja o przyjęciu chrześcijaństwa – możliwości poznawcze," in *Zborník z konferencie Pohanstvo a kresťanstvo usporiadanej*

commentators do not mention Reginhar's Moravian mission of 831. The Royal Frankish Annals (Annales regni Francorum) end in 829 and the Annals of Fulda (Annales Fuldenses) begin only in 838. The Annals of Sankt Bertin (Annales Bertiniani), which also recorded events during these years, also do not have a report on the baptism of the Moravians. From 829–843 they namely focus their attention on the war between the sons of Louis the Pious and on events internal to the empire, which led to its disintegration into three parts.[53] The Slavs beyond the eastern border of the Frankish Empire temporarily ended up outside of their attention. For the Passau bishopric, however, the baptism of the Moravians in 831 was an event of major importance; therefore, knowledge of it could not be lacking in Passau. Therefore, it's no accident that in the entire text called the Records on the Passau Bishops (Notae de episcopis Pataviensibus) the record of baptism of the Moravians by Bishop Reginhar is the only one from all 18 records on 18 Passau bishops, beginning with Urolf (804–806) and ending with Altman (1065–1091), that is dated with the exact year.[54]

The consecrating of the Nitrian church by Salzburg Bishop Adalram in 828 and the baptism of the Moravians by Passau Bishop Reginhar in 831 demonstrate that the church administration of Moravia belonged to Passau and that Nitria temporarily ended up in the missionary sphere of Salzburg. The different ecclesiastical administrative allegiance clearly demonstrates that Moravia and Nitria (Nitravia) were still in these years two distinct principalities independent of one another.[55]

[ ] 5.–6. II. 2003 v Banskej Bystrici (Bratislava 2004), pp. 95–102. Vladimír Vavřínek, *Cyril a Metoděj mezi Konstantinopolí a Římem* (Praha 2013), pp. 99–101.

53 Ernst Dümmler, *Geschichte des Ostfrankischen Reiches I* (Leipzig 1887), pp. 41–205. Łowmiański, *Początki Polski IV*, pp. 313–315.

54 *Notae de episcopis Pataviensibus*, recensuit Georgius Waitz, Monumenta Germaniae historica, Scriptores 25 (Hannoverae 1880), pp. 623–624.

55 Pavol Jozef Šafárik, Jonáš Záborský and František Víťazoslav Sasinek already thought that Pribina, who had his seat in Nitra, was subservient to the great Prince Mojmír. According to Šafárik, Mojmír I established around 826 two bishoprics, one in Olomouc and the other in Nitra. In 830, *Pribina, the Nitrian Prince, stubborn and fervently inclined to paganism, opposing the plans of the grand prince, was expelled by Mojmír from his principality and exiled* (oddílný, k pohanstwí urputně lpiej a záměrům welikého knížete protiwný kníže nitranský Pribina byl od Mojmira panstwí sweho zbawen a z wlasti wypowězen). Pavel Josef Šafařík, *Slowanské starožitnosti. Oddíl dějepisný* (w Praze 1837), p. 799. According to Záborský, Pribina was *an appanaged prince of the Váh River region (povážsky údelný kňaz), who was at odds with the great Prince Mojmír I and was from year 828 exiled from Nitra because he was against the introduction of Christianity* (ťahal prsty s velikým kňazom Mojmírom I. a bol od neho o. r. 828 z Nitry vyhnaný preto, že sa protivil zavedeniu kresťanstva). Pribina's territory was given the name of the *Váh Principality* (povážske kniežatstvo), which was justified by a document of the Prague bishopric, in which the *provincia Wag* is mentioned. Jonáš

8 Pribina between Paganism and Christianity

At the time of Pribina's wedding, his future baptism was evidently counted on in Bavaria. Wilhelm's family, however, could not directly pressure Pribina, as they did not have such authority; they were merely lords in the Traungau County. Pribina, knowing the relations in his principality, could not act rashly, because he would not be accepting baptism and a new faith only for himself but for his entire principality. That is exactly what Borna and his Croats did and what Mojmír was then preparing to do with his Moravians. Pribina could only break the opposition of his people to the new and completely foreign religion gradually. At the time of the wedding what was most important was that the good relations of the count's and the prince's families continue, and mainly that in the war being prepared against the Bulgarians the Nitrian prince stand on the side of the Bavarians. Pribina only had to promise the Count of Traungau the

Záborský, *Dejiny kráľovstva uhorského od počiatku do časov Žigmundových* (Bratislava 2012, Manuscript 1875), pp. 24–25. According to Sasinek, Moravian Prince Samomír (740–787) acquired the Nitrian Principality from the Avars. Other Moravian princes were Samoslav, Hormidor and Mojmír I, to whom Pribina was subordinated: *Pribina, Nitrian Prince, ruled over Slovakia at that time; but because this perhaps with Gerold II, Count of the Eastern March, plotted against his sovereign Mojmír, was stripped of his title and was exiled from the country (Nad Slovenskom vtedy panoval Privina, knieža nitrianske; poneváč ale tento snad s Geroldom II., grófom Východnej marky, pletichy proti svojmu nadvladárovi Mojmírovi snoval, bol hodnosti zbavený a z vlasti vypovedaný)*. František Víťazoslav Sasinek, *Dejiny drievnych národov na území terajšieho Uhorska* (Skalica 1867), pp. 158–159. Several contemporary historians are of a similar opinion. According to Zdeněk Radslav Dittrich, Pribina's principality was a part of the Moravian state as an appanaged principality, and Pribina was Mojmír's relative, probably a cousin or brother. Dittrich, *Christianity*, pp. 67–72. Jan Sieklicki considers Pribina to be a member of Mojmír's line, installed in subordinate Nitria and dependent on Mojmír, and whom Mojmír later sent into exile. Jan Sieklicki, "Quidam Priwina," *Slavia Occidentalis* 22 (1962), pp. 115–146. Jan Sieklicki, "Privina exulatus", *Pamietnik Słowiański* 17 (1967), pp. 162–163. Hynek Bulín writes about Pribina as about a Moravian magnate and Mojmír's lieutenant. Hynek Bulín, "Aux origines des formations étatiques des Slaves de moyen Danube au IXe siècle," in *L'Europe aux IXe–XIe siècles* (Varsovie 1968), p. 178. According ot Dušan Třeštík, Pribina was only one of several small Moravian princes who were subjugated to Mojmír. Mojmír, who asserted his power over the princes of Moravia, sent Pribina into exile. Dušan Třeštík, "Vozniknovenie slavjanskich gosudarstv v srednem Podunave," in *Rannefeodaľnye gosudarstva i narodnosti. Južnye i zapadnye slavjane VI–XII vv.* (Moskva 1991), pp. 83–84. Dušan Třeštík, "Křest českých knížat roku 845 a christianizace Slovanů," *Český časopis historický* 92 (1994), no. 3, p. 439. Třeštík, *Počátky*, p. 271. According to a further expanded opinion of Dušan Třeštík, the Moravians established Nitra only at the end of the 820s or early 830s and Pribina, whom they installed there, was soon after, no later than the spring of 832, was simply exiled by Mojmír from the country. Třeštík, *Vznik*, pp. 109–112, 131, 135. Dušan Třeštík, "K poměru archeologie a historie," *Archeologické rozhledy* 53 (2001), pp. 357–361.

conditions for the Christian life of his close relative (perhaps his sister); thus, the building of the church in pagan Nitra, which he could fulfil immediately after the wedding.[56] Count Wilhelm certainly knew Pribina very well. He knew that the young prince was favourably inclined towards Christians and that he could rely on the strong influence of his young relative, her Bavarian train and other Christian foreigners who were welcome in Nitra.

Pribina's son Kocel was born in Nitria.[57] Nitrian Prince Pribina satisfied his wife not only in the choice of a Bavarian name for his son, but he also fulfilled her other wish: she could have Kocel baptised immediately after his birth.[58] If Kocel had not been baptised before the escape from Nitria, undoubtedly in the Nitra Church of St. Emmeram, then Pribina would later have not gone alone to be baptised in Traismauer,[59] but together with his son. Conversio, who also knows Kocel as Pribina's companion in Bavarian exile,[60] would certainly have not forgotten to emphasize this. Kocel was thus a Christian before his father. Pribina accepted baptism in Traismauer not only without his Christian wife, but also without his Christian son.

The baptism of the neighbouring Moravians in 831 increased the pressure for Christianisation of the Nitrian (Nitravian) Principality and could have speeded up Pribina's final decision on the path to Christianity. Pribina could not and obviously did not want to remain a pagan forever. However, he did not manage to accept baptism and begin the Christianization of the Nitrian Principality.

9   The Conquest of Nitria by the Moravians

The wars and battles with the Avars lasted twenty years (791–811), and neither the Moravians nor the Nitrians (Nitravians) were able to elude war-time events.

---

56   Pribina could have begun to build the church even before the wedding, immediately after he agreed with the family of his bride.
57   If Kocel was already an adult before 850 and so mature that he administered to the county (see note 44), then he was born in the princely court in Nitra. Miloš Weingart, "Pribina, Kocel' a Nitra v zrkadle prameňov doby cyrilometodskej," in *Ríša veľkomoravská*, ed. Stanislav, p. 330. *Conversio*, ed. Wolfram, pp. 13, 128.
58   Clotilde, the Christian wife of Frankish King Clovis I, also had her first-born son Ingomer baptised when Clovis was still a pagan, that is before 496, and then the second born Clovis. *Gregorii episcopi Turonensis Historiarum libri decem* II 29. Pribina's wife could have urged Pribina to accept baptism, just as Clotilde urged Clovis to do so: *The queen, however, continually urged the king to know the true God and to stop worshiping idols*. *Gregorii episcopi Turonensis Historiarum libri decem* II 30.
59   *Conversio* 10, ed. Wolfram, pp. 50–53. *MMFH III*, p. 311.
60   *Conversio* 10, ed. Wolfram, pp. 52–53. *MMFH III*, p. 311.

The Moravian and Nitrian princes, ancestors of Mojmír and Pribina, were surrounded by a strong military presence (just as Croatian Prince Borna and Savian Prince Ljudevit). During the ceaseless wars it grew in size, battle experience and professional quality. When peace came, the opportunity for invasion and war plunder at the expense of the khaganate ended. For the Moravian and Nitrian princes, however, a substantial brigade remained that was accustomed to war and which could not survive on resources just from home. Both principalities were poised on the margin of their economic possibilities. An agricultural society which was barely able to support itself suddenly stood before the task of supporting a great number of people who needed good food, expensive weapons, good horses and clothing. Only a more extensive territory with a larger agricultural population could support all the warriors without regular spoils of war. Territorial expansion was a starting point. He who was stronger could attack. He could chase off a neighbouring prince, destroy and chase away his retinue and subjugate his principality.[61] Moravia and Nitria ended up facing a mutual confrontation. The Moravians were stronger. They had to wait for the right time for their attack, however. That came only when the neighbouring Frankish Empire was busy with an internal war between the sons of Emperor Louis the Pious[62] and could not strike against Moravian Prince Mojmír as before against Ljudevit in Sisak.

In 829 the Bulgarians once more and for the last time attacked the southern margin of Transdanubia: *The Bulgarians took boats along the Drava River (per Dravum fluvium) and burned several of our villages near the river.*[63] The Bulgarian attack headed again to the northern bank of the Drava, because the southern bank belonged to Bulgarian ally Ratimir. With this attack the Bulgarians could no longer take the occupied part of Transdanubia and were limited only to plundering along the bank. In 831 Khagan Omurtag died, and his successor Malamir no longer continued the war. After the retreat of the Bulgarian threat, the Franks no longer needed to have a reliable ally in Nitria, but a dependent principality, like Moravia had been since 822. And that's why

---

61 Anežka Merhautová – Dušan Třeštík, *Románske umění v Čechách a na Moravě* (Praha 1983), pp. 47–51. The Moravians ruled over the Amber Road from Devín in the south up to the Moravian Gate to the north. It had a large market in its main castle. *Kitábu l-a láki nnáfísati li-bni Rusta*, MMFH III, p. 347. Ján Pauliny, *Arabské správy o Slovanoch (9.–12. storočie)* (Bratislava 1999), p. 99. Dušan Třeštík, "'Trh Moravanov' – ústřední trh staré Moravy," *Československý časopis historický* 21 (1973), no. 6, pp. 876–890. Třeštík, *Počátky*, pp. 289, 294–295. Martin Wihoda, *Morava v době knížecí 906–1197* (Praha 2010), pp. 92–94. The large marketplace brought profit to the prince. And with growing income, his power grew, as well. Pribina's Nitra had no such market.

62 Ernst Dümmler, *Geschichte des Ostfränkischen Reiches I* (Leipzig 1887), pp. 41–205.

63 *Ann. Fuld.* ad a. 829, rec. Kurze, pp. 25–26. MMFH I, p. 70.

they did not undertake anything against Mojmír's attack, which brought Nitria the same political dependence on the Frankish empire and to a certain ecclesiastical subordination as Moravia had felt since 822 and 831.

Year 833 was for Emperor Louis the Pious the worst of all his years of rule. His second wife Judith wanted for her only and the emperor's youngest son Charles the Bald the largest share of the divided Frankish empire. The empress was able to influence her husband. The emperor's consent with her requests, which broke the agreement on the future division of rule of the Frankish empire from 817, evoked a great rebellion of the three oldest of the emperor's sons: Lothair, Pepin of Aquitaine and Louis the German. Louis the Pious learned of the rebellions immediately after arrival to Aachen at the beginning of 833. The oldest son Lothair led a military expedition against his father, bringing along Pope Gregory IV to act as an arbitrator. His rebelling sons came to Worms before the start of Lent (= 26 February) and there they called a synod from 13 April to 1 June. Most of the Frankish bishops gathered in Worms remained loyal to Emperor Louis and stood against the pope, who stood on the side of Louis's sons. Emperor Louis conceded that the pope act as a mediator between him and his sons. On the Rotfeld near Colmar (in Alsace), where both militaries were camped against one another, the pope came on 24 June to the emperor's camp. While they negotiated together, the majority of the emperor's army moved into the camp of his sons. On 30 June the betrayed emperor had to give in to his sons. Rotfeld got a new name that day *Lügenfeld* (*Campus mentitus*) or the *Field of Lies*. Deposed and humiliated Louis ended up in October 833 in the Abbey of Saint-Médard de Soissons, and Lothair became emperor. Lothair's brothers, Pepin of Aquitaine and Louis the German, however, felt threatened by their brother's imperial rule. Therefore, they compelled him to pull back to Italy, and by the beginning of 834 they helped their father return to the throne.[64]

Two Frankish armies stood in the first half of 833 against one another and could not interfere in the events on the borders of the Frankish Empire. This brought an exceptional advantage to Prince Mojmír. Not even his relations with Count Wilhelm, who obviously ended up in this war on the side of then-Bavarian king Louis the German, could help Pribina, who remained alone against the stronger Mojmír. Moravia lay further from the centre of the Avar Empire than Nitria, protruding to the east. Avar dominion had pressed less on the Moravians in the past than on neighbouring Nitria. The Mojmír family

---

[64] Johann Friedrich Böhmer, *Regesta imperii I. Die Regesten des Kaiserreichs unter den Karolingern 751–918*, ed. Engelbert Mühlbacher and Johann Lechner, 1. Band, III. Abteilung (Innsbruck 1908), pp. 362–372.

more easily shook free of Avar dominance and began to build their own state. They thus had a head start, which was crucial for their ascendency. Mojmír's Moravia did not have to have in 833 significant territorial and military ascendency over Pribina's Nitria. Mojmír, however, sat much more firmly on the princely throne. His princely power was so strong that in 831 he could begin the Christianization of his principality. Pribina was still only preparing for such an eventuality.[65]

For Mojmír to triumph over Pribina, he did not have to overmatch him in the size of his principality or even the number of soldiers. He triumphed because his princely power was more secure than Pribina's. Mojmír certainly prepared his attack against Pribina thoroughly and obviously combined it with some of his domestic antagonists.

In 833 Mojmír unleashed a similar war as the one Ljudevit had unleashed 14 years earlier in Borna's Dalmatia. The invaded Borna then lost the battle, and victorious Ljudevit in December 819 *burst into Dalmatia with a strong force and by sword and fire ransacked everything.*[66] Mojmír and Pribina were in 833 equal antagonists as Ljudevit and Borna in years 819–820. Besieged Borna, however, unlike Pribina, could rely on an alliance with Emperor Louis the Pious. In January 820 *Borna complained about Ljudevit's behaviour obtained from the emperor great military corps, which was capable of destroying his country.*[67] Therefore, Prince Ljudevit was unable to subjugate Croatia in the way that Mojmír subjugated neighbouring Nitria.

10   *Priwina exulatus*

Regarding Pribina's exile we have only a single sentence: *During this time Pribina, exiled (exulatus) by Mojmír, Prince of the Moravians, came across the*

---

65   If a pagan prince married a Christian wife, then usually in a very short time he accepted baptism and with his entire principality. Polish Prince Mieszko did so in 965 when he married Bohemian Dobravka, as did Hungarian Prince Géza in 972 when he married Transylvanian Sarolt, and Russian Prince Vladimir in 988, who took Byzantine Princess Anna as his wife. Györffy, *István király*, pp. 80–81. Pribina, married to a Bavarian, obviously had the same idea as Mieszko, Géza and Vladimír. His princely power, however, was not so strong that he was able to assert his will as they and his Moravian antagonist Mojmír did.

66   *At Liudewitus occasionem nanctus cum valida manu Decembrio mense Dalmatiam ingressus, ferro et igni cuncta devastat. Ann. reg. Franc.* ad a. 819, rec. Kurze, p. 151. *MMFH I*, p. 28. The same is written in the *Anonymi Vita Hludowici imperatoris* 32, *MMFH II*, p. 29.

67   *Quo tempore Borna de infestatione Ljudeviti conquestus, magnas ab imperatore suscepit adiutorii copias, quae terram illius atterere possent. Anonymi Vita Hludowici imperatoris* 33, *MMFH II*, p. 30.

Danube (supra Danubium) to Radbod.[68] What can we say about Pribina's exile? Why and mainly how in Pribina's time did one withdraw into exile?

In the neighbouring Frankish Empire those accused and convicted of treason, murder, adultery, kidnapping of another's bride were sent into exile and for killing in self-defence into temporary exile.[69] In 786 a *dangerous conspiracy (valida coniuratio)* against Charlemagne was uncovered: *Its authors partly had one hand cut off, partly remained with uninterrupted members, all were expelled into exile (exilio deportati sunt).*[70] In 788 Charlemagne sentenced deposed Bavarian Duke Tassilo. He was under threat of a death sentence, but he was given mercy by the king. Tassilo ended up in a monastery and *several Bavarians who wanted to endure as enemies of the Lord King Charles were sent into exile (missi sunt in exilio).*[71] They had to leave for various towns of Charlemagne's empire: *And the Bavarians who in their treachery and deceit were participants and agreed were found out and confined in exile in various towns (exilio per diversa loca religantur).*[72] In 790 *Chorso, Duke of Toulouse, was cheated by a crafty Basque by the name of Adeleric (dolo cuiusdam Wasconis, Adelerici nomine), shackled with the manacles of an oath, and thus became independent of him.* The dispute over the validity of Chorso's oath got before the Aquitanian kingdom, which was presided over by Aquitanian King Louis the Pious. Since they did not know what to do with Alderic, he had to get to Worms in the following year, where he answered to Louis's father, Frankish King Charlemagne. Adeleric in the presence of both kings was unable to defend himself and thus *was irrevocably ordered into exile (inrevocabili est exilio deportatus).*[73] In 857 *Count Richard (was) sent into exile (exilio [mis]sus)*, because he had rebelled against Margrave Carloman.[74]

The East Francia bishops gathered in Mainz on 3 October 852 resolved: *Albgis, who publicly kidnapped the wife of Patrick, and took her to the most distant ends of the kingdom, to the yet crude Christianity of the Moravian nation and sullied the church of Christ with the sin of adultery, with common council we order that on the command of the king be sent into exile (in exilium missus) ...*[75] The Frankish penal system ordered the punishment which the bishops requested

---

68   *Conversio* 10, ed. Wolfram, pp. 50–51. *MMFH III*, pp. 310–311. Třeštík, *Vznik*, pp. 112, 275–276.
69   Sieklicki, "Privina exulatus", p. 165.
70   *Einhardi Vita Karoli Magni* 20, ed. Buchner, pp. 192–193.
71   *Ann. reg. Franc* (*Ann. Lauriss. mai., Ann. Einhardi*) ad a. 788, rec. Kurze, pp. 80–83.
72   *Ann. reg. Franc* (*Ann. Einhardi*) ad a. 788, rec. Kurze, pp. 81, 83.
73   *Anonymi Vita Hludowici imperatoris* 5, ed. Buchner, pp. 264–267.
74   See chapter 6, note 135.
75   *Decreta synodi Moguntiensis*, *MMFH IV*, pp. 34–35. Cibulka, *Velkomoravský kostel*, pp. 279–281.

for Albgis: *If anyone commits adultery ..., let him be penitent for seven years or surely let him be ordered into exile (exilio destinetur) and let him perform many alms.*[76] Or similarly: *If anyone commits adultery ..., let him be penitent for ten years, five of them on bread and water or surely let him be ordered into exile (in exilio destinet) and let him perform many alms.*[77]

The last of the Wilhelms were also exiles among the Moravians. The bold Engelschalk, who kidnapped the unmarried daughter of King Arnulf, *moved temporarily among the Moravians as an exile (ad tempus se Maravos exul contulit)*. Engelschalk soon got mercy from the king and in 893 (perhaps in March) became margrave of the Eastern March. His cousin Ruodpert, *hiding among the Moravians as an exile (Maravanis exul delatiscens)*, did not survive his exile. In 893 Svätopluk not only had him killed, but also his entire retinue.[78]

If the Frankish king or emperor had to send someone powerful, capable of raising opposition, into exile for treason or insurrection, or a neighbouring independent prince, such as Obotrite Prince Slavomir (*Sclaomir Abodritorum rex*), for example, then he had to send the military against him. In 819 Emperor Louis the Pious sent the military of the Saxons and the Eastern Franks against Obotrite Prince Slavomir, *to punish him for treachery (ob cuius perfidiam ulciscendam)*. The emperor's army captured Slavomir and took him *with the prominent among his tribe (cum primores populi sui)* to Aachen. There they *accused [him] of many crimes, and he could not answer the reproaches with a reasonable defence, he was sentenced to exile (exilio condempnatus est)*.[79] In other words, when he was accused of rebellion and did not want to defend himself against the reproaches, he was sent into exile *(exilio est deportatus)*.[80]

In 819 a similar event played out at the opposite end of Louis's empire: *In a similar way Lupus Centulli the Basque (Wasco), who in this year clashed in battle (proelio conflixit) with Counts Berengar of Toulouse and Warin of Auvergne, in which he lost a brother Garsand, a person of exceptionally mad bravado, and himself, if escaping had not saved him, was nearly annihilated. When he came into the presence of the emperor and was terribly accused of treason by the mentioned Counts, he could not clear his name and was sent into exile for life (ipse temporali est exilio deportatus)*.[81] If *some Basque Lupus Centulli* was bold enough to launch to open war with Frankish power, then the whole of Gascony

---

76   *Poenitentiale Hubertense* IX, *Die Bußordnungen der abendländischen Kirche nebst einer rechtsgechichtlichen Einleitung*, ed. F. W. H. Wasserschleben (Halle 1851), p. 378.
77   *Poenitentiale Merseburgense* 24, *Die Bußordnungen*, ed. F. W. H. Wasserschleben, p. 431.
78   *Ann. Fuld.* ad a. 893, rec. Kurze, p. 122. *MMFH I*, p. 102.
79   *Ann. reg. Franc.* ad a. 819, rec. Kurze, pp. 149–150.
80   *Anonymi Vita Hludowici imperatoris* 31, ed. Buchner, pp. 308–309. *MMFH II*, p. 28.
81   *Ann. reg. Franc.* ad a. 819, rec. Kurze, p. 150.

stood behind him. If both Aquitaine counts *rising in rebellion* (*in rebellionem adsurgens*) ... *fell in battle* (*proelio lacessivit*), then shortly before he could have seized the principality in Gascony. For the emperor's biographer, as for the emperor himself, this was, however, only *some Basque* (*quidam Wasco*), a usurper, which he could not consider as a duke. Since he was unable to defend himself before the emperor, *he was sentenced to exile* (*exilio est dampnatus*).[82]

The Magyars, who in July 900, in alliance with the Moravians, attacked Braslav's Pannonian Principality, *ordered an innumerable number of them, however, into exile* (*exilio deputaverunt*). War had preceded the exile of *innumerable* Pannonians: *indeed, they themselves attacked them and took some into captivity, killed others, others died imprisoned of hunger and thirst, an innumerable number, however, they ordered into exile and forced the noble men and honourable women into slavery, ... they saw the entire country pillaged.*[83] The reason for exile of the Pannonians in 900, as well as Pribina in 833, was the military attack and permanent occupation of the Pannonian Principality by the Magyars and the Nitrian Principality by the Moravians.

Mojmír could not simply send or order Pribina into exile. Pribina, based in Nitra, was thus the prince of all of Nitria; he ruled castles, could stand at the forefront of an army and was surrounded by a princely retinue, with which (*cum suis*) he then left into exile. Pribina was *exulatus* up through defeat in the war, as was Slavomir *exilio condempnatus est* or *exilio est deportatus*, Lupus Centulli *ipse tempore est exilio deportatus* or *exilio est dampnatus* and the Pannonians *exilio deputaverunt*, after their military humbling.

If Mojmír wanted to exile Pribina, then he had to attack him militarily. And he could have captured him, as Emperor Louis in 819 attacked and captured the Obotrite Prince Slavomir and the Basque rebel Lupus Centulli and like the Magyars, in alliance with the Moravians in 900, attacked the Pannonians and captured many. Pribina was not ordered or sentenced or sent into exile as the royal or imperial court did in the neighbouring Frankish Empire. Pribina was *exiled* without a court, before which he could defend himself. Mojmír could have captured Pribina in war and could have taken him back to Moravia with him; he could not, however, judge him as a rebel or traitor, because he was not his subordinate. Mojmír exiled Pribina, just as the victor exiled a defeated enemy, or an already captured one, or only an escaping and pursued one. The Frankish royal or imperial courts did not know the pure and simple *exulatus* of the kind Pribina lived, because this was not a court. And the Magyars, who in 900 *ordered into exile* captured Pannonians, certainly did not stand them

---

82 *Anonymi Vita Hludowici imperatoris* 32, ed. Buchner, pp. 308–309.
83 See chapter 10, note 30.

NITRIA THE INDEPENDENT PRINCIPALITY (805–833)

before any court. The Bavarian bishops who recorded this event used the concept of *exilio deputaverunt*, whose foundation was departure into exile on the basis of a court decision, a little unsuitably. Conversio, unlike the letter from the Bavarian bishops, is exact in regard to Pribina's exile, which was beyond the reach of Frankish law; he states it correctly: Pribina was only *exulatus*. And the Pannonians exiled by the Magyars were actually only *exulati*.

With Sorbian Prince Čestibor, son of Bohemian Prince Vistrach, who after his father's death exiled his brother Slavitach, *was in exile (exulabat)* until 857. Slavitach's brother was *expelled from the homeland (patria pulsus)*.[84] By the end of 896 the Moravians requested of Emperor Arnulf, that *their refugees of expulsion (exules eorum profugi) be accepted*.[85] The exiles of the Moravians, Vistrach's son and Pribina, were welcomed over the border of their own homeland and found there a mutual refuge, where they became a constant danger for those who exiled them. At the next opportunity these *exules* could return to their homeland, expel their antagonists and take their place.

Mojmír attacked Pribina in a similar way that Margrave Ratbot attacked Ratimir five years earlier: *And in the time Louis, King of the Bavarians, sent Ratbot with many soldiers to expel (ad exterminandum) Prince Ratimir. He, not trusting his ability to defend himself, escaped (fugam iniit) together with his people, who thus evaded death.* Ratbot struck at the most convenient time, when Ratimír *did not trust his ability to defend himself*, that is when he had lost support of his own people. And Pribina himself, who only shortly before retired to Ratimír and joined him, in a crucial moment left him and through the Carniolan Count Salacho willingly came to terms with the enemy Ratbot.[86] Ratimír lost Savia similarly as Pribina had lost Nitria five years earlier. Pribina and Ratimír escaped together *with their people (cum suis)*,[87] that is with the part of their princely retinue that survived the attack of the Moravians and the Bavarians. There was one major difference between the exiling of Ratimír and Pribina, however. Margrave Ratbot considered Ratimír's principality as a part of the wide Bavarian border area that he administered. In his opinion, as well as according to the author of Conversio, it lay in the borderlands of the Frankish Empire and belonged to the system of his south-eastern marches. Ratimír, whom Ratbot had expelled beyond the empire's borders, was thus *exterminandus*. If Ratimir's Savia had not belonged to the borders of the extensive Ratbot's holdings and the Frankish Empire, then Ratimír would not have

---

84 *Ann. Fuld.* ad a. 857, rec. Kurze, p. 47. *MMFH I*, p. 76.
85 *Ann. Fuld.* ad a. 897, rec. Kurze, p. 131. *MMFH I*, p. 123.
86 *Conversio* 10, ed. Wolfram, pp. 74–75, 176, 184. *MMFH III*, p. 311.
87 See notes 60, 86.

been *exterminandus*. Conversio would have labelled him with the broader term *expulsus*, as he labelled the Romans, Goths and Gepids, who were *expelled* (*expulerunt*), and the Huns *expelled* (*expulsos*), or who *were expelled* (*expulsi sunt*) from Pannonia.[88]

We have a great many reports of such expulsions. In 827 the Bulgarians *by expulsion* (*expulsis*) of Slavic princes took over parts Transdanubia.[89] In 857 the Bavarian army marched against the Bohemians, *expelling* (*expulso*) Prince Slavitach from his castle.[90] In 861 Margrave Carloman *expelled* (*expulit*) all of his antagonists from the territory of his marches.[91] At that time one of the Carantanian Counts, Pabo, was also *expelled* (*expulsus*).[92] In 871 Slavomir promised the Moravians that he would fight against Margraves Engelschalk and Wilhelm and *forcefully expel* (*expellere*) *them from their captured castles*,[93] and in 884 the sons of Wilhelm and Engelschalk *expelled* (*expellebant*) Margrave Aribo from the Eastern March.[94] The nation of the Magyars *was expelled* (*expulsa est*) from their original seats by the Pechenegs.[95]

If Pribina would have simply run away from Mojmír, he would have been *expulsus*. If he were *exulatus*, then Mojmír would have first captured him and only later expelled him, as the Magyars in 900 captured and expelled *innumerable* Pannonians. If Pribina got to Margrave Ratbot *over the Danube* (*supra Danubium*), then he did not escape from Nitria to the east or the south-east, as far as possible from the reach of the attacking Moravians, but departed for exile in a south-westerly direction, that is through territory occupied and ruled by Mojmír. Mojmír thus captured Pribina and then permitted him to leave by the shortest road to the Eastern March. He let him depart not only with his family, but with a portion of his princely retinue. Mojmír needed to get rid of people loyal to Pribina, so he expelled them together with Pribina.

Nitrian Prince Pribina ended up similarly as the appanaged Nitrian Prince Svätopluk II would 66 years later, after *a very difficult dispute* (*discordia gravissima*) with his brother, Moravian Prince Mojmír II. Mojmír II triumphed in this war and imprisoned Svätopluk *and his people* (*suumque populum*), that is his princely retinue, at some castle. While a Bavarian expedition freed Svätopluk

---

88 Conversio 3, 6, ed. Wolfram, pp. 62–63, 66–67. MMFH III, p. 298, 303. Sieklicki, "Privina exulatus", pp. 163–164.
89 Ann. reg. Franc. ad a. 827, rec. Kurze, p. 173. MMFH I, p. 52.
90 Ann. Fuld. ad a. 857, rec. Kurze, p. 47. MMFH I, p. 76.
91 Ann. Fuld. ad a. 861, p. 55. MMFH I, pp. 77–78.
92 See chapter 8, note 5.
93 Ann. Fuld. ad a. 871, rec. Kurze, pp. 73–74. MMFH I, pp. 103–104.
94 Ann. Fuld. ad a. 884, MMFH I, pp. 94–95.
95 Reginonis abbatis Prumiensis Chronicon ad a. 889, rec. Kurze, pp. 131–132. MMFH I, p. 121.

and his train and took them away with them,[96] Mojmír simply expelled the captured Pribina and his loyalists to Bavarian exile.

The concept of *exulatus* stands exactly in the middle between *expulsus* (a special case of which is *exterminandus*) and the concept of *exilio deportatus* (*condempnatus, dampnatus, missus, destinetur*). There are three methods of exile: 1. the Romans, Goths, Gepids and Huns were expelled. Ratimír was also only expelled; 2. Pribina was captured and expelled; 3. Slavomir was captured, sentenced and ordered into exile.

96   *Ann. Fuld.* ad a. 898–899, rec. Kurze, pp. 131–133. *MMFH I*, pp. 106–109.

CHAPTER 6

Pribina and Kocel in Pannonia

1 Pribina's Baptism

Pribina fled to Ratbot, the Margrave of the Eastern and Carantanian Marches, who very willingly received him: *He immediately introduced him to our lord King Louis and at his command was instructed in the faith and baptised in the church of St. Martin in a place named Traismauer (Treisma), namely in the court belonging to the Salzburg seat.*[1] Ratbot and Louis the German were together in

---

1 *Conversio* 10, ed. Wolfram, pp. 72–73. *MMFH III*, p. 311. Pribina *was instructed in the faith*, that is he became a catechumen, only on the command of Louis the German in 833 and not on the occasion of his wedding, as Dušan Třeštík assumes. From Pribina's wedding and consecrating of the church, which according to Třeštík were simultaneous with the beginning of Pribina's catechumenate, up to Pribina's baptism in Traismauer in 833, several years passed. This is, however, too long a time for a catechumenate. Therefore, its commencement, and thus also the consecration of the Nitra church, shift approximately to year 832, by which causes doubt regarding the currently recognized dating of Adalram's presence in Nitra by year 828. Třeštík, *Vznik*, pp. 114–117, 122–126. If Pribina had already been a catechumen in Nitra, then in 833 Louis the German would have only ordered a baptism and done so immediately after Pribina's arrival in Regensburg. Instruction in the faith in Traismauer would have thus been pointless. If despite this we wanted to assume that Pribina became a catechumen while still the Prince of Nitria, then more probably on the occasion of the baptism of his son and not before the wedding and building of the Nitra church. And this leads to the necessity to shift the building of Pribina's church up to year 832, as Dušan Třeštík does. Vladimír Vavřínek also opposes the hypothesis on Pribina's catechumenate in Nitra. Vavřínek, *Cyril a Metoděj*, p. 103. Pribina, although he was a pagan, had a Christian family (wife, son, brother-in-law), and in exile he lived only among Christians. This was sufficient guarantee of his future Christian life; thus, he did not need a long preparation for baptism. In addition to this, he had important princely origins. The East Francia king (and obviously Pribina himself) thus undoubtedly desired that he become a Christian as soon as possible, in the shortest possible time and without delay. Pribina's Traismauer catechumenate was thus short, obviously equally short as the catechumenate of 14 Bohemian princes who received baptism on 13 January 845, shortly after their arrival to Regensburg. Louis the German *commanded (iussit)* the baptism of the Bohemian princes. *Ann. Fuld.* ad a. 845, rec. Kurze, p. 35. *MMFH I*, p. 71. He commanded not the princes but his bishop, who performed this uncommon baptism. Třeštík, *Počátky*, pp. 85–86. Similarly, Pribina was instructed and baptised *on his command (suo iussu)*. The Bavarian king did not command Pribina; he, like the mentioned Bohemian princes, *desiring the Christian religion*, certainly requested baptism. He commanded the baptising priest, perhaps the Salzburg archbishop himself, to whom the mentioned court in Traismauer belonged. Frankish King Clovis I, who had himself baptised in 496, either was not a catechumen, or only very shortly before baptism. Gregory of Tours, who wrote of Clovis's baptism,

Regensburg in February, March and May of 833.[2] At this very time Pribina came to Regensburg together with Ratbot. Ratbot acted *immediately* (*statim*). Thus, there was hardly any gap in time between Pribina's arrival to Ratbot and his introduction to the king. Therefore, we can date Pribina's fleeing from Nitria to Ratbot, and thus also the rule of Mojmír I over Nitria, to the first half of 833.[3]

The imperial army vanquished Sisak Prince Ljudevit and thus prevented the origin of a strong Slavic state in the western Balkan. From 829, however, the Frankish empire suffered internal military conflicts. Therefore, it had to leave Mojmír's victory in neighbouring Nitria and the origin of a larger Slavic state on the middle Danube unnoticed. Only after the peace treaty in Verdun in 843, by which brothers Lothair, Charles the Bald and Louis the German decided on the division of their father's empire, did the internal wars end and the attention of the East Francia King Louis the German turn to the east.

2 *quidam Priwina*

Pribina was only the Prince of Nitria for five or six years. When he came to Margrave Ratbot in 833, he was then only *some Pribina* (*quidam Priwina*), *exiled by Mojmír, Prince of the Moravians*.[4] At the time of Mojmír's attack Pribina was still a prince, the same as Mojmír himself; he became *quidam* only after the defeat in war, when he lost his principality and had to leave for abroad. The unknown author who wrote Conversio only ten years after Pribina's death knew Pribina's story only after his arrival to Ratbot in 833. Pribina, before around 840 when he took hold of his new fief in Blatengrad (Mosapurc; present-day Zalavár in Hungary) and administration of the Pannonian Principality, was for him *some Pribina*, a new person with an adventurous life, of which there were in this ever-unstable space more than enough. The wheel of their fortune turned rapidly; they were always on the road and seeking a new *opportunity* (*occasione*).[5] Conversio doesn't mention Pribina's previous short princely rule

---

did not mention any catechumenate at all. *Gregorii episcopi Turonensis Historiarum libri decem* II 31.

2 Milko Kos, "K historii kniežaťa Pribinu a jeho doby," in *Ríša Veľkomoravská*, ed. Stanislav, pp. 54–55.

3 And according to Herwig Wolfram, Radbot introduced Pribina in Regensburg to his king in the 1st half of 833. Wolfram, *Salzburg, Bayern, Österreich*, pp. 311–312.

4 *Conversio* 10, ed. Wolfram, pp. 72–73. *MMFH III*, pp. 310–311.

5 Around 840 Pribina found his new opportunity, when he acquired a fief on the Zala River from Louis the German: *When, however, in the meantime an opportunity (occasione) arose, at the request of those loyal to the mentioned king* ... *Conversio* 11, ed. Wolfram, pp. 74–75. *MMFH III*, p. 312. We know of more people with a fate similar to that of Pribina. Herwig

over Nitria. The well-known and often mentioned sentence tells only about Pribina's property *Nitrava*, where Adalram consecrated a church.

For the unknown author of Conversio, Samo, Virgil and Methodius, were also *quidam*. Conversio mentions the older history of the Carantanians, when *some Slav by the name of Samo, living in Carantania, was the prince of this nation (Samo nomine quidam Sclavus manens in Quarantanis fuit dux gentis illius)*.[6] Vergilius, who before year 745 undertook the administration Salzburg bishopric (ordained in 767), was only *some man wise and well learned from the island of Ireland by the name of Vergilius (vir quidam sapiens et bene doctus de Hibernia insula nomine Virgilius)*.[7] In 869 *some Greek by the name of Methodius (quidam Graecus Methodius nomine)* tried to take hold of church administration in Kocel's Pannonia.[8] According to Venetian chronicler John the Deacon in 879 *some Slav by the name of Branimir (quidam Sclavus nomine Brenamir)* murdered Croatian Prince Zdeslav and seized hold of his principality.[9] Such a *quidam Sclavus* was also a member of the Hevellian princely family, Tugumir, who was captured by German King Henry the Fowler. Tugumir, who was released from captivity in 939, returned to Brenna (Brandenburg an der Havel) and became the Hevellian prince.[10] Samo, Vergilius, Pribina, Methodius, Branimír and Tugumir were people with an unsettled life; they risked a lot a achieved a lot, winning and losing, once climbing to the top, then falling down. When they were down and began completely anew, they were nobodies; each of them was only *quidam*.[11] In 623, 745, 840, 869, 879 and 939 they were lucky, and they took advantage of their new *opportunity* and became somebodies.

Wolfram, "Ljudevit und Priwina (ein institutioneller Vergleich)," in *Interaktionen der mitteleuropäischen Slawen und anderen Ethnika im 6.–10. Jahrhundert* (Nitra 1984), pp. 291–296. Třeštík, *Počátky*, pp. 77–78.

6   Conversio 4, ed. Wolfram, pp. 64–65. *MMFH III*, p. 299.
7   Conversio 2, ed. Wolfram, pp. 62–63. *MMFH III*, p. 297.
8   Conversio 12, ed. Wolfram, pp. 78–79. *MMFH III*, p. 318.
9   *La Cronaca Veneziana del Diacono Giovanni. Cronache Veneziane antichissime pubblicate a cura di Giovanni Monticolo. Volume I.* (Roma 1890), p. 126. Nada Klaić, *Povijest Hrvata u ranom srednjem vijeku* (Zagreb 1971), pp. 250–251.
10   *Fuit autem quidam Slavus a rege Heinrico relictus, qui iure gentis paterna successione dominus esset eorum qui dicuntur Heveldi, dictus Tugumir. Hic pecunia multa captus et maiori promissione persuasus, professus est se prodere regionem. Unde quasi occulte elapsus, venit in urbem quae dicitur Brennaburg, a populoque agnitus et ut dominus susceptus, in brevi quae promisit inplevit. Widukindi Rerum gestarum Saxonicarum libri tres* II 21, recognovit Georgius Waitz. Scriptores rerum Germanicarum in usum scholarum ex Monumentis Germaniae historicis recusi (Hannoverae 1882), p. 58.
11   The label *quidam* for Pribina applies only for the period of his exile in years 833–perhaps 840, when he was not a prince, not to the period of his rule in Nitra, as Jan Sieklicki

In the autumn of 861 *some Pabo (Pabo quidam) exiled from Carantania by Carloman, took refuge in Salzburg.*[12] Pabo and others with him had joined with Carantanian counts and rebelled (*seditio Pabonis cum sociis comitibus*) against Carloman in 857.[13] Pabo stood at the forefront of the rebelling Carantanian counts; thus, he was one of them. He was one of the several Carantanian counts, until Carloman exiled him four years later. When he then came to Salzburg, he was only *quidam*, that is, a refugee who had lost his county, the same as Pribina, who had lost his principality.

In 833 Pribina went from being the Nitrian Prince to merely *some Pribina*, who sought asylum and help, first with Margrave Ratbot and then with Bulgarian Khagan Presian I. Thus, he tried out two possibilities which might enable him to return to the princely seat in Nitra. Both failed, however. Ratbot was employed by the rebellion of Savian Prince Ratimír, and Presian conquered Macedonia from Byzantium and led the war with the Serbs.[14] Pribina did not have a third option. There was no third person in the vicinity of his lost Nitria to whom he could turn to with hope. Therefore, after departing Bulgaria in 838 he had to meekly return through Savia and Carniola to Margrave Ratbot. Thus, between Great Moravia and Bulgaria no other significant independent principalities or tribes lay where Pribina could take refuge after departing from Bulgaria.

The territories of the Frankish and Bulgarian empires had reached the maximum of their expanse. Frankish King Charlemagne had conquered Pannonia, and Bulgarian Khagans Krum and Omurtag had subjugated the eastern part of the Avar empire (Transylvania and the Tisza River regions). The northwestern part of the Carpathian Basin, which was not ruled by either the Franks or Bulgarians, belonged to the Nitrian Principality. The Cserhát and Bükk Mountains divided it from the Bulgarian Tisza River region and the Danube from the Bavarian border march.

---

assumes. Sieklicki, "Quidam Priwina," pp. 132, 144. Equally, it does not apply even to the period of his second princely rule, when he took over Blatengrad, perhaps in the year 840.
12   See chapter 8, note 5.
13   See note 135.
14   Zlatarski, *Istorija na bălgarskata dăržava* I/1, pp. 430–442. Hýbl, *Dějiny národa bulharského I*, p. 84. *Historija naroda Jugoslavije I*, pp. 249–250, 287. Panajotov, *Srednovekovna bălgarska istorija*, pp. 70–71.

3 The Pannonian Principality

Around 840 Louis the German divided the Carantanian March into two parts. Carantania itself he left further to Margrave Ratbot, and he handed over administration of the Pannonian part of the march to Pribina. Blatengrad (Mosaburg, Marsh Castle, Zalavár), which lay in the centre of Pribina's extensive fief in the basin of the lower Zala River, became the administrative seat of the new principality: *The king granted a fief (in beneficium) in one part of Lower Pannonia around the Zala River to Pribina. He then began to settle there and to build a fortress in one wood and the wetlands of the Zala River and from all sides to gather people and to greatly expand on that territory.*[15]

A Bulgarian legend about Velika Bishop Clement recalls Pribina's son and successor Kocel as the leader of all of Pannonia.[16] Pribina and Kocel's principality, however, could not have covered all of Pannonia. Upper Pannonia belonged to the Eastern March and south of the Drava was the Savian Principality. The range of Pribina's new principality thus did not exceed the Salzburg part of Pannonia. In the Life of Constantine Kocel is the Pannonian Prince.[17] The Annals of Fulda and Regino know only the name Pannonia for a principality administered after Kocel's death by Carantanian Margrave Arnulf (876–887) and Savian Prince Braslav (896–900). Arnulf *administered Pannonia. Svätopluk marauded in Arnulf's holdings, invaded Pannonia, led an enemy army into Pannonia,*[18] *the emperor ... entrusted Pannonia with Mosaburg Castle to the protection of Prince Braslav.*[19] Pribina's, Kocel's, Arnulf's and Braslav's principality had the name according to the country in which it lay, the Pannonian Principality.

4 Roman Towns and Fortresses

Pribina's new principality had, unlike his original one, a wealthy ancient past. Slavic-Carolingian Pannonia continued in the tracks of Roman Pannonia. Four legions stationed in the fortresses along the Danubian border are testimony that Pannonia was primarily of military importance for the Roman Empire.

---

15 *Conversio* 11, ed. Wolfram, pp. 74–75, 183–185. *Conversio*, ed. Kos, pp. 77–78, 136. *MMFH III*, p. 312. East Francia King Louis the German clearly recalls Pribina's princely title in his document from 20 February 860: *Briuuinus fidelis dux noster ... in suo ducatu.* See note 82.
16 *Život sv. Klimenta (Legenda bulharská)* 15. *MMFH II*, p. 211.
17 *ŽK* 15, *MMFH II*, p. 105.
18 *Ann. Fuld.* ad a. 884, rec. Kurze, pp. 111–112. *MMFH I*, pp. 95–97.
19 *Ann. Fuld.* ad a. 896, rec. Kurze, p. 130. *MMFH I*, p. 105.

After departure of the Roman legions and parts of the Roman population, the barbarians took an interest in the Roman fortresses. Longobard King Audoin expanded the Longobard kingdom in 547 to the southern part of Pannonia along the Sava River: *In relation to the Longobards, Emperor Justinian gifted them the city of Noricum, fortresses in Pannonia and many other areas, and in addition to this gave them significant sums of money.*[20] The solid walls of the antique fortresses also served Slavic princes. The seat of Savian princes was Sisak Castle, antique Siscia, on a steep hill above the confluence of the Kupa and the Sava rivers. Patriarch Fortunatus of Grado sent to Savian Prince Ljudevit *craftsmen and masons for the reinforcing of his castles (ad castella sua munienda).*[21] Ljudevit's antagonist, Croatian Prince Borna, in 819 *closed all of his castles (castellis).*[22] Ljudevit, before the predominance of three imperial armies which in the spring of 820 scourged his principality, holed up in the Sisak *castle fortress (munitione castelli).*[23] Savian and Croatian princes did not have to build wooden-earthen castles, like those we know from the Danube and north to the Baltic. The castles of Ljudevit and Borna were walled fortresses of antique origin (*castella*), the legacy of the Romans and Byzantines.

Slavic castles were missing not only in the Balkans, but also in Transdanubia. With the exception of Pribina's princely seat of Blatengrad (Mosapurc, Zalavár), his Pannonian Principality did not have castles similar to Great Moravia. However, former Roman fortresses still stood there in the 9th century: *Thus, for a long time the Romans ruled the lands south of the Danube on the territory of Lower Pannonia and around the borders, and they themselves built for their own defence castles and fortresses (civitates et munitiones) and many other buildings, as can still be seen today (sicut adhuc apparet).*[24]

The oldest Roman towns and fortresses originated on the Amber Road, and written sources from the 9th century document their continuing settlement. Shortly before the beginning of our common era, the Romans occupied the Illyrian seat in Ptuj, lying at the crossing of the Amber Road over the Drava River, and there they built a vast military camp, by which grew the civilian

---

20 Procopios, *De bello Gothico* III 33. See chapter 2, note 14. Wolfram, *Die Geburt*, pp. 79–80. Messengers of the Gepids reprimanded the emperor for gifting the Franks, Heruls and Longobards a lot of towns and territory. Procopios, *De bello Gothico* III 34.

21 *Ann. reg. Franc.* ad a. 821, rec. Kurze, p. 155. Wolfram, *Die Geburt*, pp. 269, 428. *Conversio*, ed. Wolfram, p. 205. Šišić, *Geschichte der Kroaten I*, p. 63. See chapter 4, note 128.

22 *Ann. reg. Franc.* ad a. 819, rec. Kurze, p. 151. MMFH I, p. 28. Anonymi Vita Hludowici imperatoris 32, MMFH II, pg. 29. See chapter 4, note 122.

23 *Ann. reg. Franc.* ad a. 820, rec. Kurze, p. 153. *Anonymi Vita Hludowici imperatoris* 33, MMFH II, p. 30. See chapter 4, notes 126, 127.

24 *Conversio* 6, ed. Wolfram, pp. 66–67, 145–147. *Conversio*, ed. Kos, pp. 47–49, 131. MMFH III, pp. 302–303.

town of Poetovio.[25] Two roads led out of the town, up the Drava to Virunum, and down the Drava to Mursa (today Osijek, Croatia) and Sirmium (today Sremska Mitrovica, Serbia) and an important road along Lake Balaton through Gorsium (Tác, Hungary) to Aquincum.[26] Further testimony of the endurance of Ptuj are the two churches which the Salzburg bishop consecrated there, the first (*ad Bettobiam*) around year 855[27] and the second in 874, when Count Gozwin settled in Ptuj (*ad Bettowe*).[28] Sabaria (Szombathely), mentioned in 791, 805 and 860 (*Sabaria*),[29] originated as a Roman military camp. On its site, under the rule of Emperor Claudius (41–54), veterans of the 15th legion, based in Carnuntum, founded the town of Colonia Claudia Sabaria. After the division of Pannonia into four smaller provinces by Emperor Diocletian (284–305), the viceroy and civil administration of one of the four Pannonian provinces were based in Sabaria.[30] The ramparts and the tower of Roman Scarbantia (Sopron, Hungary) protected, after modifications, the seat of the Hungarian borderland county, and after reconstruction in the 13th century served for the defence of the medieval town and to a large extent still stand today.[31] From 859 Sopron

25 Josip Klemenc, *Ptujski grad v kasni antiki* (Ljubljana 1950). Iva Mikl-Curk, "Poetovio," *Das Altertum* 9 (1963), pp. 84–97. Balduin Saria, "Pettau. Entstehung und Entwicklung einer Siedlung im deutsch-slowenischen Grenzraum," *Zeitschrift des Historischen Vereines für Steiermark*, Sonderband 10 (1965), pp. 6–14. Pavol Valachovič, "Hospodárske a sociálne problémy miest v Panónii v 4.–5. storočí," *Historický časopis* 30 (1982), no. 3, p. 388. *Pannonia régészeti kézikönyve*, ed. András Mócsy – Jenő Fitz (Budapest 1990), pp. 86–87.
26 Andreas Graf, *Übersicht der antiken Geographie Pannoniens, Dissertationes Pannonicae Musei nationalis hungarici* I 5 (Budapest 1936), p. 42. *Zgodovina Slovencev* (Ljubljana 1979), p. 73. Grafenauer, *Zgodovina slovenskega naroda I*, p. 143. *Pannonia régészeti kézikönyve*, ed. Mócsy – Fitz, pp. 115–124.
27 *Conversio* 11, ed. Wolfram, pp. 76–77, 205. *MMFH III*, pp. 315–316. See chapter 6, note 110.
28 See chapter 6, note 111.
29 See chapter 4, notes 16, 64, chapter 6, note 137.
30 Valachovič, *Hospodárske a sociálne problémy*, p. 387. Gyula J. Hajnóczi, *Pannónia római rómjai* (Budapest 1987), pp. 63–71. *Pannonia régészeti kézikönyve*, ed. Mócsy – Fitz, pp. 62, 119, 121–122, 217, 219.
31 Klára Póczy, *Scarbantia. A római kori Sopron* (Budapest 1977). Hajnóczi, *Pannónia*, pp. 51–61. János Gömöri, *Castrum Supron. Sopron vára és környéke az Árpad-korban* (Sopron 2002), pp. 11–23. The one-time Roman fortresses in Britain – Eboracum (York), Deva (Chester), Isca (Caerleon), Verulamium (St. Albans), Londinium (London) – several centuries after the fall of Roman power still served in the wars of the Anglo-Saxons against the Danes. In 866 the Danes took over York, and they beat back an Anglo-Saxon attack from behind stone ramparts from Roman times. York became the centre Danelaw, Danish territory in Britain. In 892 the Danes unexpectedly took over Chester (ancient Colonia Devana), and up to the spring of 893 they resisted from behind the ramparts of the Roman fortress the attack of Mercian Lord Aethelred, son-in-law of King Alfred the Great, who in the end chased the Danes away. Aethelred repaired the fortifications in Chester in 907 in order to resist the threat of Norwegian attacks from the Irish Sea.

(*Odinburch*) neighboured the property of Passau chorbishop Alberic.[32] At the turnoff from Scarbantia to Vindobona lay Aquis (Baden). In the 9th century the royal court of *Padun*, mentioned in year 869, was located in it.[33]

At the crossing of the Amber Road with the Danube, which connected the border towns and fortresses, stood the seat of the legion and the seat of the Roman viceroy for the administration of Upper Pannonia: Carnuntum (between today's Bad Deutsch-Altenburg and Petronell, Austria), mentioned in year 805.[34] The massive remains of the Roman fortress still stand today in Carnuntum.[35] To the west of Carnuntum lay Aequinoctium (Fischamend), where in 805 (*Fiskaha*) Khagan Abraham was baptised,[36] and the seat of a legion, Vindobona (Vienna), mentioned in 881 (*ad Weniam*).[37] And on the edge of the Vienna Woods, where there was an Avar fortress that Charlemagne conquered in 791,[38] stood Asturis (Klosterneuburg).[39]

The seat of a legion, Brigetio, and together with it smaller Danubian fortresses, disappeared with the end of the Roman *limes*.[40] Arrabona (Győr) originated under the rule of Tiberius (14–37) and became the most important military point between Carnuntum and Brigetio. Its company formed the brigades of several Pannonian legions. A town that originated from a military seat

---

The city ramparts of Chester from the 14th century stand atop the Roman walls. Holger Arbman, *Vikingové* (Praha 1969), p. 46. Josef Polišenský, *Dějiny Británie* (Praha 1982), p. 25. Peter Brent, *Sága Vikingov* (Bratislava 1982), pp. 21, 64.

32   *MMFH III*, Diplomata 27, p. 52.
33   *MMFH III*, Diplomata 35, p. 65.
34   See chapter 4, note 64.
35   Erich Swoboda, *Carnuntum, seine Geschichte und seine Denkmäler* (Graz – Köln 1958). Kurt Genser, *Der österreichische Donaulimes in der Römerzeit. Der römische Limes in Österreich*, Heft 33 (Wien 1986), pp. 574–684. Manfred Kandler – Hermann Vetters, *Der römische Limes in Österreich. Ein Führer* (Wien 1989), pp. 202–230.
36   See chapter 4, note 63. Genser, *Der österreichische Donaulimes*, pp. 548–557. Kandler – Vetters, *Der römische Limes in Österreich*, pp. 192–199.
37   *Annales Iuvavenses maximi* ad a. 881, *MMFH I*, p. 115. Roman walled buildings were not only found in medieval Vienna, but they were also found in Mauer and Mauerbach, near Vienna. Karl Oettinger, *Das Werden Wiens* (Wien 1951), pp. 7–15. Justová, *Dolnorakouské Podunají*, pp. 149–150. Genser, *Der österreischische Donaulimes*, pp. 430–531. Kandler – Vetters, *Der römische Limes in Österreich*, pp. 177–187.
38   See chapter 4, note 16.
39   Genser, *Der österreichische Donaulimes*, pp. 402–429. Kandler – Vetters, *Der römische Limes in Österreich*, pp. 167–177.
40   Sándor Soproni, *Die letzten Jahrzehnte des pannonischen Limes*, Münchner Beiträge zur Vor- und Frühgeschichte 38 (München 1985), pp. 55–58. Hajnóczy, *Pannonia*, pp. 86–89. *Pannonia régészeti kézikönyve*, ed. Mócsy, Fitz, pp. 62, 89–90, 98, 216.

(*canabae*) was a large trading centre.[41] Győr was a major Hungarian fortress, guarding the western entrance to the interior of Hungary at the narrowest place between the Danubian arms and the Moson marsh (Hanság). It was the castle seat of one of the first Hungarian counties and from year 1009 an episcopal seat.[42]

In the time of Emperor Trajan (98–117) the Roman fortress Solva originated in Esztergom, the tribal centre of the Pannonian Azali tribe. A military centre (*canabae*) grew up alongside the fortress (*castellum*), which was inhabited by one military cohort (*Cohors I. Ulpia Pannoniorum*). A burial site from the 4th and 5th centuries on the eastern edge of the ancient settlement is proof of the settlement of Solva even after the fall of the Pannonian *limes*.[43] The Slavs named the former Roman fortress Striegom,[44] because it guarded an important crossing over the Danube into Nitria. Esztergom was the seat of Hungarian Prince Géza (971–997) and his son Stephen I (997–1038). In the year 1000 it became the seat of the Esztergom archbishop and later Esztergom County.[45]

Halfway along the road between Esztergom and Pilismarót, on the top of Hideglelőskerest, the Romans built in the time of Emperor Valentinian I (364–375) a fortress of unknown name.[46] Under the rule of Emperor Diocletian (284–305) the Romans built a fortress (*castellum*) on the Kishegy hill in Pilismarót and called it Castra ad Herculem.[47] In the first half of the 4th cen-

41   Dénes Gábler, "Győr a rómaiak korában," in *Győr. Várostörténeti tanulmányok* (Győr 1971), pp. 19–48. Soproni, *Die letzten Jahrzehnte*, pp. 82–83. *Pannonia régészeti kézikönyve*, ed. Mócsy, Fitz, p. 98.

42   On 23 August 1009 King Stephen I issued *at Győr Castle* (*in ciuitate Iauryana*) the deed of foundation for the Pécs bishopric. *DHA I*, ed. Györffy, no. 8, p. 58. Györffy, *István király*, p. 182. Gyula Kristó, *A vármegyek kialakulása Magyarországon* (Budapest 1988), pp. 262–267. In 1030 Emperor Conrad II had to stop a campaign against Hungary near Győr. The Hungarian army first retreated to Győr, then pursued the emperor reatreating from Hungary and occupied Vienna. See chapter 16, note 2. Alfréd Lengyel, "A középkori Győr," in *Győr. Várostörténeti tanulmányok* (Győr 1971), pp. 79–108.

43   Sándor Soproni, "Der spätrömische Limes zwischen Visegrád und Esztergom," in *Limes Romanus Konferenz Nitra*, ed. Anton Točík (Bratislava 1959), p. 135. Sándor Soproni, *Der spätrömische Limes zwischen Esztergom und Szentendre. Das Verteidigungssystem der Provinz Valeria im 4. Jahrhundert* (Budapest 1978), pp. 15–26, 86, 158, 167, 194, 205, Tafel 2. Soproni, *Die letzten Jahrzehnte*, pp. 60–61. *Pannónia régészeti kézikönyve*, ed. Mócsy, Fitz, pp. 60, 95, 98, 99, 109, 110.

44   Ján Stanislav, *Slovenský juh v stredoveku II* (Turčiansky Sv. Martin 1948), pp. 380–382.

45   See chapter 14, notes 15, 21, 102, 232, 233, chapter 15, notes 94, 95.

46   Soproni, *Der spätrömische Limes zwischen Visegrád und Esztergom*, pp. 137, 139. Soproni, *Der spätrömische Limes zwischen Esztergom und Szentendre*, pp. 26–29, 87, 88, 93, 98–99, 120, 157, 162, 166, 180, 188, 201, 205, Tafel 9, 10.

47   Soproni, *Der spätrömische Limes zwischen Visegrád und Esztergom*, pp. 134, 136, 139–140. Soproni, *Der spätrömische Limes zwischen Esztergom und Szentendre*, pp. 12–13, 16, 28–48,

tury the Roman fortress (*castellum*) Pone Navata was built on the Sibrik hill;[48] the Slavs later gave it the name Vyšehrad. Vyšehrad (Visegrád) was the seat of one of the oldest castle counties in Hungary.[49] Vyšehrad on Sibrik remained a county castle up to the 13th century, when a new castle on the neighbouring Fellegvár hill took its name and was further one of the main royal castles of Hungary.[50] Solva, Hideglelöskereszt, Castra ad Herculem and Pone Navata, unlike other Pannonian fortresses, stood on hills. The fortress Gardellaca (Tokod, 8 km south of Esztergom), which originated under the rule of Emperor Constantine II (337–361) as a fortified supply station, was in the 5th century a refuge for the Pannonian population.[51]

Other Danubian fortresses also had a Hungarian continuation: Aquincum and Alta Ripa. Alta Ripa was a Roman predecessor of the Tolna County castle.[52] Aquincum (Old Buda or Óbuda, part of modern Budapest), besides being the seat of a legion, was also the seat of the Roman viceroy of Lower Pannonia. The oppidum on Gellért Hill was a tribal centre of the Celtic Eravisci.[53] The remnants of walls and building of antique Aquincum are today still testimony of its former size.[54] Anonymus considered the Roman buildings in Óbuda as Attila's town: *Prince Árpád and all of his chieftains with all of their Magyar soldiers entered into the town of King Attila and saw all the royal palaces, some disintegrated to the foundations, some not, and marvelled excessively*

77–78, 87, 92–93, 97–99, 100–102, 119, 130, 137, 166, 168, 171, 179, 180, 189, 191, 194, 205–206, Tafel 8–50. Soproni, *Die letzten Jahrzehnte*, pp. 62–63. Sós, *Die slawische Bevölkerung*, p. 156. Hajnóczi, *Pannónia*, pp. 86–87, 89.

48 Soproni, *Der spätrömische Limes zwischen Visegrád und Esztergom*, pp. 131–134, 140. Soproni, *Der spätrömische Limes zwischen Esztergom und Szentendre*, pp. 12–13, 33, 51–61, 72, 76, 87, 92–94, 99–101, 103, 104, 107, 109, 119, 130, 154, 157, 160–163, 166, 177, 180, 191, 194, 196, 205, Tafel 54–66. Soproni, *Die letzten Jahrzehnte*, pp. 31–35, 44–48, 63–64. Sós, *Die slawische Bevölkerung*, pp. 154–156, Tafel 26. Hajnóczi, *Pannónia*, pp. 91–92.

49 DHA I, ed. Györffy, no. 8, pp. 49–53. *Chronici Hungarici compositio saeculi XIV*. II 133, SRH I, p. 408. Györffy, ÁMF IV, pp. 583–585, 705–712. Kristó, *A vármegyek*, pp. 251–254. Gyula Kristó, "Néhány vármegye kialakulásának kérdéséhez," *Századok* 136 (2002), no. 2, pp. 477–483. Attila Zsoldos, "Visegrád vármegye és utódai," *Történelmi Szemle* 40 (1998), no. 1–2, pp. 1–17.

50 Györffy, ÁMF IV, pp. 583–585, 705–712.

51 Soproni, *Der spätrömische Limes zwischen Esztergom und Szentendre*, pp. 48, 170–171, 177, 199. András Mócsy, *Die spätrömische Festung und Gräberfeld von Tokod* (Budapest 1981), pp. 42–45. Hajnóczi, *Pannónia*, pp. 88–89.

52 Soproni, *Der spätrömische Limes zwischen Esztergom und Szentendre*, pp. 161–162, 167, 169, 177, 179, 181.

53 *Budapest története I* (Budapest 1973), pp. 75–76.

54 *Budapest története I*, pp. 83–184. Hajnóczi, *Pannónia*, pp. 95–139.

*at all of those stone buildings.*⁵⁵ Aside from Árpád, another Magyar Prince, named Kurszán (Kuszal), also lived in Attila's town (*Etzilburg*). Kurszán's castle in Óbuda can be identified with the Roman amphitheatre, which became a fortress.⁵⁶

In the interior of Pannonia stood Floriana (Csákvár), Mursella (Kisárpás), fortresses in Györszentmárton, Somlóvásárhely, Tüskevár (perhaps antique Mogentiana)⁵⁷ and the massively fortified Vincentia (Környe), Valcum (Fenékpuszta), Tricciana (Ságvár) and Iovia (Alsóheténypuszta near Kapospula).⁵⁸ Among them the towns of Gorsium and Sopianae (at modern Pécs) stood out. Gorsium (Tác-Fövenypuszta) grew on the site of a military camp destroyed during the Marcomannic Wars. It later was given the new name of Herculia, and it perished after the fall of Roman power.⁵⁹ The centrepoint of settlement was brought 15 km to the north, where Székesfehérvár (Alba Regia, Stoličný Belehrad, Weissenburg) originated, the seat of one of the oldest Hungarian counties and the royal court.⁶⁰ Sopianae (Pécs, Päťkostolie,

---

55 *dux Arpad et omnes sui primates cum omnibus militibus Hungarie intraverunt in civitatem Atthile regis. Et viderunt omnia palatia regalia, quedam destructa usque ad fundamentum, quedam non, et ammirabantur ultra modum omnia illa edifi cia lapidea.* Anonymi Belae notarii *Gesta Hungarorum* 46, SRH I, p. 94. MMFH I, pp. 232–233. Transylvanian Prince Gyula I *qui civitatem magnam in Erdelw in venatione sua inverat, que iam pridem a Romanis constituta fuerat. Chron. Hung. comp. saec. XIV.* II 30, SRH I, pg. 290–291.

56 See chapter 13, notes 51, 52.

57 Attila Kiss, "A tüskevári római telep 1961–1063 évi feltárása," *Veszprém megyei múzeumok közleményei* 6 (1967), p. 37. Soproni, *Der spätrömische Limes zwischen Esztergom und Szentendre*, pp. 101, 144, 175, 197, 199. *Pannonia régészeti kézikönyve*, ed. Mócsy, Fitz, pp. 62, 122, 231.

58 Edit Baja Thomas, *Römische Villen in Pannonien. Beiträge zur pannonischen Siedlungsgeschichte* (Budapest 1964), pp. 60–68, 243–244, 270, 271–273, 274–282, 288–289, 297–299. *Magyarország régészeti topográfiája 1*, főszerkesztő László Gerevich. *Veszprém megye régészeti topográfi ája*, ed. Károly Sági. *A keszthelyi és tapolcai jarás*, írta Kornél Bakay, Nándor Kalicz, Károly Sági (Budapest 1966), pp. 82–87. Károly Sági, "Das Problem der pannonischen Romanisation im Spiegel der völkerwanderungszeitlichen Geschichte von Fénékpuszta," *Acta Antiqua Academiae Scietiarum Hungaricae* 18 (1970), pp. 147–196. Ferenc Fülep, *Sopianae* (Budapest 1984). Hajnóczi, *Pannónia római romjai*, pp. 78–85, 89, 152–162. *Pannonia régészeti kézikönyve*, ed. Mócsy, Fitz, pp. 235–236, 262–263. The late-Roman fortresses Iovia (Kapospula-Alsóheténypuszta) and Tricciana (Ságvár) date from the 4th century and resemble the fortresses Valcum (Fénékpuszta) and Vincentia (Környe). Thomas, *Römische Villen*, pp. 243–299. Sági, Das Problem der pannonischen Romanisation, pp. 147–196. Soproni, *Der spätrömische Limes zwischen Esztergom und Szentendre*, pp. 138, 173. Soproni, *Die letzten Jahrzehnte*, pp. 19, 21–23. Hajnóczi, *Pannónia*, pp. 84–85, 152–153.

59 Jenő Fitz, *Gorsium* (Székesfehérvár 1983). Hajnóczi, *Pannónia*, pp. 144–151.

60 Arnold Marosi, "Volt-e Székesfehérvárott római telep?" *Századok* 69 (1935), pp. 266–269. *atque Albam civitates ... in comitatu Albensis civitatis.* DHA I, ed. Györffy, no. 8, p. 52. Györffy, ÁMF II, pp. 326–327, 363–382. Kristó, *A vármegyék*, pp. 243–247.

Fünfkirchen) was the seat of the civil administration of one of the four Roman Pannonian provinces – Valeria. In the 2nd half of the 4th century in the vicinity of an existing burial site they built a *cella trichora*, which in the 9th century was repaired and again painted.[61] Around year 855 the Salzburg archbishop consecrated a church in Pécs (*ad Quinque basilicas*) on the wishes of the Pannonian Prince Pribina.[62] In 1009 the Pécs bishopric was established.[63]

As in Pannonia, in neighbouring Noricum ripense several fortresses of fallen Roman power endured. In the Eastern March, the eastern part of which belonged to the former Noricum ripense and Carolingian Upper Pannonia, Bavarian colonists gave the names *Mauer-* or *-mauer* to several walled fortresses, which the Romans had left behind: Traismauer, Zeiselmauer, Mauer near Amstetten in the county below the Enns River, while Wildungsmauer near Petronell, Mauer near Vienna and Mauerbach near Vienna in Upper Pannonia still today have Roman buildings in the their medieval core. And the seats of the Margraves of Lorch, Traismauer, Sankt Pölten, Tulln and Mautern were originally the Roman border fortresses of Lauriacum, Augustianis, Aelium Cetium, Comagena and Favianis, respectively. We find parts of their walls today in the medieval town buildings and fortifications.[64] In Oberranna today stands the southern rampart of the small Roman camp Stanacum. The Roman tower in Bacharnsdorf, Austria, for the most part still stands today to a height of 9.4 metres. From the Roman military camp Favianis, which was swallowed up by medieval Mautern, part of the north-west and eastern part of the ramparts with three towers are still preserved. The medieval town of Traismauer grew up within the ramparts of Roman Augustianis. Both semi-circular towers of the city gate (called the Vienna Gate), the tower in the south-western corner and another tower on the north side of the extinct Roman ramparts in Traismauer are of Roman origin. Tulln can boast its preserved tower of the Roma camp Comagena, which in medieval times served as a storeroom for salt. In Zeiselmauer (Cannabiaca?) stands the remains of Roman ramparts with corner towers and a partially preserved large burgus (tower) in the north-west corner of the local Roman camp.[65]

---

61   Ferenc Fülep, *Sopianae. Die Stadt Pécs zur Römerzeit* (Budapest 1975). Hajnóczi, *Pannónia*, pp. 154–162. Thomas, *Römische Villen*, pp. 243–244, 270, 271–273, 274–282, 288–289, 297–299. Ferenc Fülep, "Neuere Ausgrabungen in der Cella Trichora von Pécs," *Acta Archaeologica Academiae Scientiarum Hungaricae* 11 (1959), pp. 415–416. Fülep, *Sopianae*, pp. 30–32. Sós, *Die Slawische Bevölkerung*, pp. 146–148. Tamás Fedeles – László Koszta, *Pécs (Fünfkirchen). Das Bistum und die Bischofsstadt im Mittelalter* (Wien 2011), pp. 32–38.
62   *Conversio* 11, ed. Wolfram, pp. 76–77, 205. *MMFH III*, pp. 315–316. Fedeles – Koszta, *Pécs*, pp. 9–11.
63   *DHA I*, ed. Györffy, no. 9/I, II, pp. 54–59. Fedeles – Koszta, *Pécs*, pp. 22–31.
64   Justová, *Dolnorakouské Podunají*, pp. 11, 128–129, 149–150, 243, 257.
65   Hansjörg Ubl, *Der spätrömische Burgus von Zeiselmauer. Grabung und Restaurierung, Studien zu den Militärgrenzen Roms II* (Köln – Bonn 1977), pp. 251–262. Kurt Genser, *Der*

Huns, Ostrogoths, Heruls, Longobards and Avars did not destroy all the settlements of ancient Pannonia. The unknown author of Conversio saw *castles and fortresses and many other buildings*, which were once there, built by the Romans. Several of them were occupied by Slavs and became the construction beginnings of later medieval castles and towns.

5   Valcum

In the 4th century the Romans built the massive fortress Valcum near the mouth of the Zala River into Lake Balaton (today Fenékpuszta), protected by water and wetlands. Walls 2.6 metres thick with 40 circular towers and two gates enclosed a rectangle measuring 392 × 348 metres. Tricciana, Iovia and Vincentia were all similar fortresses.[66] Valcum had a thickly settled countryside around it, with tens of Roman villas in its broad surroundings.[67]

A full three centuries after the fall of Roman power its Latin inhabitants still lived in the fortress. Their extensive burial sites from the 5th through 8th centuries in neighbouring Keszthely and the wider surroundings differed notably from the burial sites of their barbarian neighbours. The graves were without offerings, and the jewellery was decorated with Christian symbols.[68] Within

---

österreichische Donaulimes in der Römerzeit. Der römische Limes in Österreich, Heft 33 (Wien 1986), pp. 38–43, 264–266, 271–327, 356–396. Manfred Kandler – Hermann Vetters, *Der römische Limes in Österreich. Ein Führer* (Wien 1989), pp. 73–74, 130–140, 142–146, 153–165. Verena Gassner – Stefan Groh – Sonja Jilek – Alice Kaltenberger – Wolfgang Putsek – Roman Sauer – Herma Stiglitz – Heinrich Zabehlický, *Das Kastell Mautern-Favianis. Der römische Limes in Österreich*, Heft 39 (Wien 2000).

66   See note 58.
67   Thomas, *Römische Villen*, pp. 14–124.
68   Ilona Kovrig, "Megjegyzések a Keszthely kultúra kérdéséhez," *Archaeologiai Értesitő* 85 (1958), pp. 66–74. Ilona Kovrig, "Újabb kutatások a keszthely avarkori temetőben," *Archaeologiai Értesitő* 87 (1960), pp. 136–168. *Magyarország régészeti topográfiája 1*, főszerkesztő Sági. *A keszthelyi és tapolcai járás*, írta Bakay, Kalicz, Sági, pp. 76–96. István Erdélyi, *Die Kunst der Awaren* (Budapest 1966), Tafel 43. Attila Kiss, "Keszthely kultúra a Pannónia Római kontinuitás kérdésében," *Archaeologiai Értestő* 95 (1968), pp. 93–101. László Barkóczi, "A 6th century cemetery from Keszthely-Fenékpuszta," *Acta Archaeologica Scientiarum Hungaricae* 20 (1968), pp. 289–291. Gyula László, *Steppenvölker und Germanen* (Budapest 1970), p. 51. Arnulf Kollautz, *Denkmäler byzantinischen Christentums aus der Awarenzeit der Donauländer* (Amsterdam 1970), pp. 19–20. Robert Müller, "Über die Herkunft und das Ethnikum der Keszthely-Kultur," in *Ethnische und kulturelle Verhältnisse an der mittleren Donau vom 6. bis zum 11. Jahrhundert*, ed. Darina Bialeková, Jozef Zábojník (Bratislava 1996), pp. 75–82. Robert Müller, "Die Bevölkerung von Fenékpuszta in der Frühawarenzeit," in *Christentum in Pannonien im ersten Jahrtausend. Internationale Tagung im Balaton Museum in Keszthely vom 6. bis 9. November 2000*, ed. Robert Müller,

the fortress, near the northern gate, stood a large three-aisled basilica with an extended apse, and another three-aisle basilica was located by the eastern rampart, near the north-eastern corner of the fortress. Valcum was a refuge for Pannonian Christians still in the first third of the 7th century. The fortress was ultimately besieged and destroyed by unknown conquerors.[69] This could have been at the time of the Slavic rebellion against the Avars, which broke out in Pannonia in perhaps 623, or it became a victim of the war which blazed in 631 between the Avars and the Pannonian Bulgarians. Up until the end of the 8th century the destroyed fortress lay wide open and empty. People settled in its surroundings; however, they still lived rather divided from their neighbours.

The former Roman fortress revived in the 9th century. Slavic settlement within its walls is evidenced by the cemetery in front of the southern rampart, where burials were done up to the start of the 10th century. Slavs established other settlements in neighbouring Zalavár and Keszthely. In the 9th century we already find the isolated Keszthely culture in this area. After the baptism of the Slavs, the Latin Christians lost their reason to live separated and accepted assimilation. However, the remnants of the walls of the old fortress were still protruding from the ground in the 18th century.[70]

Zalai Múzeum 11 (Zalaegerszeg 2002), pp. 93–101. Péter Straub, "Eine frühchristliche Taubenfibel mit christlichem Symbol von Keszthely-Fenékpuszta," in *Christentum in Pannonien im ersten Jahrtausend*, ed. Müller, pp. 103–111. Falko Daim, "Pilgeramulette und Frauenschmuck? Zu den Scheibenfibeln der frühen Keszthely-Kultur," in *Christentum in Pannonien im ersten Jahrtausend*, ed. Müller, pp. 113–132. Franz Glaser, "Die Bildmotive der Scheibenfibeln aus Keszthely," in *Christentum in Pannonien im ersten Jahrtausend*, ed. Müller, pp. 145–152. Tivadar Vida, "Heidnische und christliche Elemente der awarenzeitlichen Glaubenswelt, Amulette in der Awarenzeit," in *Christentum in Pannonien im ersten Jahrtausend*, ed. Müller, pp. 179–209.

[69] Müller, "Die Bevölkerung von Fenékpuszta in der Frühawarenzeit," pp. 93–101.

[70] Károly Sági, "Die spätrömische Bevölkerung der Umgebung von Keszthely," *Acta Archaeologica Academiae Scientiarum Hungaricae* 12 (1960), pp. 187–256. Károly Sági, "Die zweite altchristliche Basilica von Fenékpuszta," *Acta Antiqua Academiae Scientiarum Hungaricae* 9 (1961), pp. 397–460. Károly Sági, "A Balaton szerepe Fenékpuszta, Keszthely és Zalavár IV–IX. századi történetének alakulásában," *Antik Tanulmányok* 15 (1968), pp. 15–46. Sági, "Das Problem de pannonischen Romanisation," pp. 147–196. István Bóna, "Beiträge zu den ethnischen Verhältnissen des 6.–7. Jahrhunderts in Westungarn," *Alba Regia* 2–3 (1961–1962), pp. 49–68. Nándor Fettich, *Das awarenzeitliche Gräberfeld von Pilismarót-Basaharc* (Budapest 1965), pp. 13–19. Ágnes Cs. Sós, "Das frühmittelalterliche Gräberfeld von Keszthely-Fenékpuszta," *Acta Archaeologica Academiae Scientiarum Hungariae* 13 (1961), pp. 247–305. Sós, *Die slawische Bevölkerung*, pp. 127–144. *Magyarország régészeti topográfiája* 1, főszerkesztő Gerevich, *Veszprém megye régészeti topográfiája*, ed. Sági, *A keszthelyi és tapolcai járás*, írta Bakay, Kalicz, Sági, pp. 83–87. Hajnóczi, *Pannónia*, p. 79. Dorottya Gáspár, "Donatio Iustiniani," in *Christentum in Pannonien im ersten Jahrtausend*, ed. Müller, pp. 79–83. See note 58.

6   Pannonian Churches

The land near the mouth of the Zala into Lake Balaton did not lose its exceptional position. In the 840s Pribina fortified one of the islands near the Zala River (today Várziget or Castle Island) and picked up on the old Christian traditions of this region.[71] Pribina's new princely seat got the name Blatengrad. On 24 January 850 Salzburg Archbishop Liupram ceremonially consecrated the first of Pribina's churches in Blatengrad and consecrated it as St. Mary, Mother of God.[72] On this occasion 32 important people went to Blatengrad: *Present here were Chezil, Unzat, Chotemir, Liutemir, Zcurben, Siliz, Wlkina, Witemir, Trebiz, Brisnuz, Zuemir, Zeska, Crimisin, Goimer, Zistilo, Amalrih, Altwart, Wellehelm, Fridepercht, Scrot, Gunther, another Gunther, Arfrid, Nidrih, Isanpero, Rato, Deotrih, Madalperht, Engilhast, Waltker, Deotpald.*[73]

The names of Slavic and Bavarian witnesses of the ceremonial consecrating of the first and main church of Blatengrad are not mixed up on the list, but clearly designated. Their order is not random. The first was Pribina's son Kocel (*Chezil*). After Kocel another 14 Slavs follow. Who were these Slavs, who were evidently given precedence over the following 17 Bavarians in Pribina's princely court?

Pribina had come to Pannonia *with his own people* (*cum suis*), that is with a part of his own Nitrian retinue, which accompanied him on his long road from Nitra to Blatengrad. We have before us the names of Pribina's train, those who survived the attack of the Moravians in 833 and did not remain in the

---

71   Béla Miklós Szőke, "Christliche Denkmäler in Pannonien aus der Karolingerzeit," in: "*Christentum in Pannonien im ersten Jahrtausend*," ed. Muller, pp. 250–266. Béla Miklós Szőke, "Mosaburg/Zalavár und Pannonien in der Karolingerzeit," *Antaeus* 31–32 (2010), pp. 9–52. Béla Miklós Szőke, "Beziehungen zwischen Keszthely-Fenékpuszta und Mosaburg/Zalavár in der Karolingerzeit," in *Keszthely-Fenékpuszta im Kontext spätantiker Kontinuitätsforschung zwischen Noricum und Moesia. Castellum Pannonicum Pelsonense, Bd. II.*, ed. Orsolya Heinrich-Tamáska (Budapest – Leipzig – Kesthely – Rahden Westf. 2011), pp. 509–540. Szőke, *The Carolingian age in the Carpathian basin*, pp. 55–56, 58.

72   *Conversio* 11, ed. Wolfram, pp. 74–75, 204. *MMFH III*, pp. 312–313. Blatengrad (Zalavár) and Keszthely survived the Magyar incursions and lived to see the origin of the Kingdom of Hungary. In the years 1019 and 1024 King Stephen I gifted substantial properties to the Benedictine Abbey of St. Adrian in Zalavár, which included, among others, the tithe in the village Keszthely (*Kestel*). *DHA I*, ed. Györffy, no. 14, 17, pp. 86–92, 98–102. Szőke, *The Carolingian age in the Carpathian basin*, pp. 66.

73   *Conversio* 11, ed. Wolfram, pp. 74–75, 188–190. *Conversio*, ed. Kos, pp. 80–81, 136. *MMFH III*, pp. 312–313. Ján Stanislav considered the Slavic names on this list as Western Slavic, aside from the names Liutemir, Goimer and Zistilo. Ján Stanislav, "Pribinovi veľmoži," *Linguistica Slovaca* I–II (1939–1940), pp. 118–150.

conquered Nitria. They accompanied their prince on his entire journey and lived to see this celebration.

Archbishop Liupram installed Pribina's priest Dominik in the main church of Blatengrad, elevated him to the position of presbyter and ceded to him clerical administration for the whole of Pribina's principality.[74] After Dominik's death Liupram appointed the priest Swarnagal as presbyter and after him Altfrid. Archbishop Adalvin (859–873) elevated Altfrid to archipresbyter, and after Altfrid's death, Rihpald became the archipresbyter.[75] The Blatengrad archipresbyteriate covered the whole of the Lower Pannonian part of the Salzburg diocese.

Louis the German gifted two great properties to Pribina. In 846 he gifted to Pribina 100 manses of land which lay directly on the western border of Blatengrad fief, on the Válicka River (*Valchau*), which flows into the Zala.[76] In 847 he *granted to him ownership of everything which he previously had in the fief*,[77] that is the already mentioned *one part of Lower Pannonia around the river called Zala*.[78] Pribina owned a vast and contiguous territory, from which King Louis detached property of the Salzburg bishopric.[79]

A portion of Pribina's new property in the Zala Basin went into the ownership of his son Kocel, because at the end of January 850 he gifted two new churches and led their priests Sandrat and Ermperht into the holdings of church lands. Both churches and their lands remained in Kocel's ownership.[80] In 852 the Salzburg archbishop consecrated the Church of St. Rupert in Zalabér (*ad Salapiugin*) and immediately got it, along with its property, and took over its ownership from Pribina.[81] Prince Pribina also endowed an abbey in Lower Altaich *from his own ownership, which he had in his principality (de sua*

---

74 *Conversio* 11, 12, ed. Wolfram, pp. 33, 74–75, 76–79, 187–188, 196. *Conversio*, ed. Kos, pp. 79–80, 136. MMFH *III*, p. 313. Milko Kos, "K histórii kniežaťa Pribinu a jeho doby," in *Ríša Veľkomoravská*, ed. Stanislav, pp. 58–61. Wolfram, *Die Geburt*, pp. 278–279. Szőke, *The Carolingian age in the Carpathian basin*, pp. 63, 67.

75 *Conversio* 12, ed. Wolfram, pp. 76–79, 196–197. *Conversio*, ed. Kos, pp. 80–82, 138–139. MMFH *III*, p. 318. Kos, "K histórii kniežaťa Pribinu," p. 61. Wolfram, *Die Geburt*, p. 280. Szőke, *The Carolingian age in the Carpathian basin*, pp. 78–81, 91.

76 CDES *I*, ed. Marsina, no. 6, p. 7. MMFH *III*, Diplomata 20, pp. 40–41.

77 *Conversio* 12, ed. Wolfram, pp. 76–77, 191–196. *Conversio*, ed. Kos, pp. 90–92, 137. MMFH *III*, pp. 316–317, Diplomata 21, pp. 41–42. CDES *I*, ed. Marsina, no. 7, p. 7.

78 See note 14.

79 See note 77. Szőke, *The Carolingian age in the Carpathian basin*, pp. 59–61.

80 *Conversio* 11, ed. Wolfram, pp. 74–75, 203, 205, 209, 211. MMFH *III*, pp. 313–314. Szőke, *The Carolingian age in the Carpathian basin*, pp. 67–68.

81 *Conversio* 11, ed. Wolfram, pp. 74–77, 195, 209–210, 212. *Conversio*, ed. Kos, pp. 82, 137. MMFH *III*, p. 314. Szőke, *The Carolingian age in the Carpathian basin*, p. 76.

proprietate in suo ducatu quicquid habuit). In February 860 he granted lands in Zalabér (*Salapiugiti*) to it,[82] and on 21 March 861 the Freising bishop acquired the settlement *Wampaldi* near Lake Balaton (*Pilozsvve*) from Kocel.[83] The settlement of *Ortahu*, where on 1 January 865 the Salzburg archbishop consecrated the Church of St. Michael, also lay on Kocel's property.[84] The property *Ruginesfeld* on the western edge of the Pannonian Principality also belonged to Prince Kocel.[85] Arnulf, who took over rule in Blatengrad after the death of Prince Kocel, gifted to Deacon Gundbat property with the Church of St. John the Evangelist *ad Quartinaha* near the Blatenian Lake (*Bilisasseo*, Balaton, Marsh Lake) and with attachments on the Zala (*Sala*) and Válicka (*Velih*) rivers.[86] Soon after, Deacon Gundbat, with the consent of Arnulf, swapped it with the Regensburg bishopric for property on the Rába River, which Prince Kocel had gifted to the bishopric.[87]

The donations of Pribina and Kocel and then their successor Arnulf are related to lands in the Zala Basin which they owned from 846 and 847. Kocel, or his father Pribina, also acquired other properties. Some (possibly all) of them lying on the Rába, Prince Kocel bestowed on the Regensburg bishop.

The donation of King Louis the German to other territories of the Pannonian Principality demonstrates that it further remained royal property. Pribina, Kocel, Arnulf and ultimately Braslav were only entrusted with its administration. The Salzburg archbishopric got the oldest land ownership in the Pannonian Principality from the king. Louis the German exempted it from the large donation for Pribina in 847.[88] The Salzburg archbishopric obtained abundant properties in Pribina's principality from King Louis on 20 November 860, and among them were lands in the mentioned Zalabér (*Salapiugin*) and *Chuartinahu*,[89] which is the mentioned *Quartinaha* near Lake Balaton.

---

82 *CDES I*, ed. Marsina, no. 10, p. 9. *MMFH III*, Diplomata 28, pp. 53–55.
83 *CDES I*, ed. Marsina, no. 11, p. 10. *MMFH III*, Diplomata 31, p. 61.
84 See note 175.
85 See note 120.
86 *Conversio* 13, ed. Wolfram, pp. 78–79, 141, 208, 212–213. *Conversio*, ed. Kos, pp. 99–100, 139. *MMFH III*, pp. 320–322. Klebel, "Die Ostgrenze," p. 372. Thomas von Bogyay, "Die Kirchenorte der Conversio Bagoariorum et Carantanorum. Methoden und Möglichkeiten ihrer Lokalisierung," *Südost-Forschungen* 19 (1960), pp. 61–62. Bogyay, "Die Salzburger Mission," pp. 284–285. Havlík, *Panonie*, p. 16.
87 *CDES I*, ed. Marsina, no. 27, p. 21. *MMFH III*, Diplomata 38, pp. 68–69.
88 See note 77.
89 *ad Salapiugin et ecclesiam ad Chuartinahu*. *MMFH III*, Diplomata 30, pp. 57–61. See notes 81, 82.

In addition to the mentioned Church of St. Mary, Mother of God[90] two other churches were built in Pribina's Blatengrad. In 852, immediately after returning from Zalabér, Archbishop Liupram sent to Blatengrad at Pribina's request *masters from Salzburg, masons and painters, smiths and carpenters*, who *within Pribina's castle (infra civitatem Priwinae)* built the Church of St. Adrian.[91] If Pribina also had *masons (murarios)* in Blatengrad, then he was building a stone church. The Salzburg archbishop consecrated another Blatengrad church to John the Baptist.[92]

---

90   Béla Miklós Szőke, "Eine Kirchenfamilie von Mosapurc/Zalavár (Ungarn). Neue Ergebnisse zur Kirchenarchäologie in Pannonien," in *Kirchenarchäologie heute. Fragestellungen – Methoden – Ergebnisse*, ed. *Niklot Krohnund und Alemannisches Institut Freiburg im Breisgau e. V.* (Darmstadt 2010), pp. 569–574. Ágnes Ritoók, "The Benedictine Monastery of Zala/Zalavár (Hungary)," *Kultúrne dejiny* 5 (2014), no. 1, pp. 19–47.

91   *Conversio* 11, ed. Wolfram, pp. 54–55, 135. *MMFH III*, pp. 314–315. Endre Tóth, "Szent Adorján és Zalavár," *Századok* 133 (1999), no. 1, pp. 3–40. Szőke, "Eine Kirchenfamilie," pp. 574–580. Szőke, *The Carolingian age in the Carpathian basin*, pp. 60, 82–90.

92   *Item in eadem civitate ecclesia sancti Iohannis baptistę constat dedicata. Conversio* 11, ed. Wolfram, pp. 76–77, 205. *MMFH III*, p. 315. On the Zalavár island Récéskút, which lay near Pribina's castle, stood a large stone three-aisle basilica. Szőke, *The Carolingian age in the Carpathian basin*, pp. 69–70. Aladár Radnóti, who discovered the foundations of this basilica in 1946, considered it to be Pribina's church from the mid-9th century. Dezső Dercsényi agreed with this opinion. Thomas von Bogyay also dated the basilica to the 9th century and identified it with Pribina's Church of St. John the Baptist. Aladár Radnóti, "Une église du haut moyen age a Zalavár," *Études Slaves et Roumaines* I, (1948), pp. 27–28. Dezső Dercsényi, "L'église de Pribina a Zalavár," *Etudes Slaves et Roumaines* I (1948), pp. 85–100. Thomas von Bogyay, "Mosapurc und Zalavár. Eine Auswertung der archäologischen Funde der schriftlichen Quellen," *Südost-Forschungen* 14 (1955), pp. 393–394. Ágnes Cs. Sós assumed the remains of two older churches beneath the foundations of the three-aisle basilica on Récéskút. She explained the origin of the older wooden church with the arrival of the Salzburg mission to Transdanubia at the end of the 8th century. She ascribed the building of the second church of wood and stone to Pribina. She dates the stone basilica to the 11th century. Ágnes Cs. Sós, "Über die Fragen des frühmittelalterlichen Kirchenbaues in Mosapurc-Zalavár," *Annales Instituti Slavici* 1/2 (1966), pp. 66–69. Ágnes Cs. Sós, "Bericht über die Ergebnisse der Ausgrabung von Zalavár-Récéskút in den Jahren 1961–1963," *Acta Archaeologica Academiae Scientiarum Hungaricae* 21 (1969), pp. 54–55, 60–84, 92–103. Sós, *Die slawische Bevölkerung*, pp. 93–127, Tafel 4–16, 18–19, 22–25, 27. Tatiana Štefanovičová, who refuted Sós's theory on the existence of two older churches, convincingly defended the original dating of the stone basilica. Tatiana Štefanovičová, *Bratislavský hrad v 9.–12. storočí* (Bratislava 1975), pp. 70–73. Tatiana Štefanovičová, "K niektorým otázkam stavebnej techniky a proveniencie veľkomoravskej architektúry," *Zborník Filozofickej fakulty Univerzity Komenského, Historica* 26 (1975), pp. 29–37. In the 9th century Blatengrad was the princely seat and ecclesiastical centre of the entire Pannonian Principality. In the 11th century Zalavár no longer had this importance; therefore, the building of a large stone basilica corresponds well to the period of Pribina's building activities in the mid-9th century. Since the Church of St. John the Baptist stood together with the Church of St. Mary,

Aside from Pribina's Blatengrad, the Salzburg archbishop consecrated an additional 13 churches.[93] We only know of or can only assume where at least some of them approximately stood. Salzburg Archbishop Adalram consecrated 12 churches in 11 different locations under the rule of Pannonian Prince Kocel.[94] We know only one of them: Ablanc. We can search for the church

[93] Mother of God, and with the Church of St. Adrian, directly *in eadem civitate*, that is within Pribina's Blatengrad, archaeologists have most recently been looking for it directly on the island Vársziget, where both mentioned churches stood. Approximately ten metres west of the Church of St. Adrian archaeologists uncovered (in 2007–2009) the rectangular ground plan of a wooden building. Since it had an east-west orientation, like all churches, then they consider it to be a church and have identified it with the Church of St. John the Baptist. Szőke, "Eine Kirchenfamilie," pp. 580–581. Szőke, *The Carolingian age in the Carpathian basin*, pp. 64–65. The mentioned wooden building had a vestibule along the whole length of the south side. Churches, however, have their vestibule (narthex) on the shorter western side, there where they have their main entrance. Therefore, its identification with a church is not convincing. Tatiana Štefanovičová, "Blatnohrad. Osudy Pribinu a Koceľa po opustení Nitrianska," *Historická revue* 25 (2014), no. 12, pp. 75–76. Two neighbouring island rises, Várziget and Récéskút, could be in a similar relation as the two rises on which stood Great Moravian Nitra, that is as the Nitra castle hill (with the later Upper Town) and the rise of the Lower Town. The settlement on Récéskút could be a ravelin and thus also a part of Blatengrad. In this case the large three-aisle basilica on Récéskút, which is by its dimension and walled construction a building comparable with both large Blatengrad churches, could be the third Blatengrad church, consecrated to John the Baptist. The wooden building could belong to the Church of St. Adrian, which stood nearby. The Blatengrad presbyter could have been based in it and later the archipresbyter.

[93] *et foris civitatem in Dudleipin, in Ussitin* (= Wisitindorf), *ad Businiza, ad Bettobiam* (= Ptuj), *ad Stepiliperc, ad Lindoveschirichun, ad Keisi* (= Kysek), *ad Wiedhereschirichun, ad Isangrimeschirichun, ad Beatuseschirichun, ad Quinque Basilicas* (= Pécs), *temporibus Liuprammi ecclesiae dedicatae sunt; et ad Otachareschirichun, et ad Paldmunteschirichun, ceterisque locis, ubi Priwina et sui voluerunt populi. Conversio* 11, ed. Wolfram, pp. 76–77, 205–206, 209, 210–211. *Conversio* ed. Kos, pp. 85–89, 137. *MMFH III*, pp. 315–316. Bogyay, "Die Kirchenorte," pp. 61–63. Havlík, "Panonie," pp. 13–14. Szőke, *The Carolingian age in the Carpathian basin*, pp. 76–78. If the author of Conversio also knew other churches consecrated by Liupram in Pannonia, then he would have gladly supplemented the list of Pannonian churches and certainly have named them. If he did not name other churches, then not only did he not know of them, but he probably could not have known of them, because there were none. The words *and in other places* are a common aggrandization by which the author of Conversio wanted to impress the reader and have on him the biggest effect possible. Using the same words, he exaggerated the result of the mission a hundred years before in Carinthia, where Chorbishop Modest, aside from the three named churches, supposedly consecrated others *in a great many other places*. See chapter 3, note 74.

[94] Salzburgh Archbishop Adalvín on 26 December 864 *in proprietate Wittimaris dedicavit ecclesiam in honore sancti Stephani protomartiris*. On 1 January 865 *ad Ortahu consecravit ecclesiam in honore sancti Michaelis archangeli in proprietate Chezilonis*. On 13 January *ad Weride in honore sancti Pauli apostoli ... dedicavit ecclesiam*. On 14 January *ad Spizzun in honore sanctae Margaretae virginis ecclesiam dedicavit. Ad Termperhc dedicavit*

ad Ablanza in the present day village of Abláncz, lying near the like-named stream, which flows into the Rábca River on the south side.[95] The Rábca River separated the Pannonia Principality from the Eastern March.[96]

The churches in Ptuj (*ad Bettobiam*), Dudleba (*in Dudleipin*), Wisitindorf (*in Ussitin*) and in Köszeg (*ad Keisi*) together with the property of Pribina's priest Dominik *Brunnaron*,[97] the church in Ablanc and Kocel's property *in loco Ruginesfeld*[98] indicate the range of Pribina's principality to the west, where it reached *mons Predel*,[99] that is the Pannonian-Carinthian border in the foothills of the alps, and on the north-west, where the Rábca River bordered with the Eastern March. The range of Pribina's principality on the south-east is marked by the church *ad Quinque Basilicas*, that is in Pécs.[100] Here it ended on the Drava River, beyond which lay Savia, and on the Danube, where it bordered with Bulgaria.

Some churches remained in the ownership of Pribina's magnates. On Vitemír's property (*in proprietate Wittimaris*) near Blatengrad the Salzburg archbishop consecrated at the end of 864 the Church of St. Stephen the First Martyr.[101] In January 865 he consecrated the Church of St. Peter on Unzat's

---

ecclesiam in honore sancti Laurentii. Ad Fizkere eodem anno dedicavit ecclesiam. Et singulis proprium dedit presbyterum ecclesiis. Sequenti quoque tempore veniens iterum in illam partem ... in locum qui dicitur Cella, proprium videlicet Unzatonis, ibique apta fuit ecclesia consecrandi. Quam dedicavit in honore sancti Petri principis apostolorum, constituitque ibi proprium presbyterum. Ecclesiam vero Ztardach dedicavit in honore sancti Stephani. Item in Weride ecclesia dedicata floret in honore sancti Petri principis apostolorum. Postea vero tres consecravit ecclesias, unam ad Quartinaha in honore sancti Iohannis euangelistae, alteram ad Muzziliheschirichun, tertiam ad Ablanza, quibus constituit proprios presbyteros. Conversio 13, ed. Wolfram, pp. 78–79, 206–208, 209, 210, 211, 212–213. Conversio, ed. Kos, pp. 97–100, 139–140. MMFH III, pp. 319–320. Regarding the location of these churches, see also Pirchegger, "Karantanien und Unterpannonien," p. 286. Klebel, "Die Ostgrenze," pp. 372–377. Bogyay, "Die Kirchenorte," pp. 58–67. Bogyay, "Die Salzburger Mission," pp. 284–285, 287–288. Havlík, "Panonie," pp. 18–19. Szőke, *The Carolingian age in the Carpathian basin*, pp. 76, 78.

95 See notes 128, 129, 130, 131.
96 See notes 133, 134, 136, 139. See chapter 5, note 50.
97 See note 134.
98 See note 120.
99 See note 154.
100 Conversio 11, ed. Wolfram, pp. 76–77, 205, 211. Conversio, ed. Kos, pp. 88, 137. MMFH III, pp. 315–316. Bogyay, "Die Kirchenorte," p. 54. Bogyay, "Die Salzburger Mission," pp. 288–289. Sós, *Die slawische Bevölkerung*, p. 148. Fedeles – Koszta, *Pécs*, pp. 9–11.
101 Conversio 13, ed. Wolfram, pp. 78–79, 206. Conversio, ed. Kos, pp. 97, 99–100, 139. MMFH III, pp. 319, 320. Near the edge of Lake Balaton, approximately 600 metres north-west from Castle Island, there was at the site Zalaszabar – Borjúállás an island, on which in the 2nd half of the 9th century and the beginning of the 10th century a pallisade-fortified court,

property (*proprium videlicet Unzatonis*) called *Cella*.[102] Pribina, Kocel, Unzat and Vitemír were owners of old settlements (Blatengrad, Salapiugin, Ortahu, Cella), which they obtained by royal donation (Pribina in years 846 and 847), a princely donation from Pribina (Kocel, Unzat, Vitemír) or inheritance (Kocel), and established their own churches within them.

Like Unzat, Vitemír and other Slavic magnates, Lindolf, Wiedheri, Isangrim, Beatus, Otachar, Paldmund and Muzzili all had property in the Pannonian Principality with their own churches. The churches which belonged to these seven Bavarians took their names: *Lindolveschirichun, Wiedhereschirichun, Isangrimeschirichun, Beatuseschirichun, Otachareschirichun, Paldmunteschirichun, Muzziliheschirichun*.[103] The churches named according to their Bavarian owners also gave their names to new settlements that grew up around them. The settlements in which the churches owned by the mentioned Slavs stood originated and got their names long before these men became their owners and long before the church was built; therefore, they did not take the name of their Slavic owner and got along without being labeled with the meaningful form of the German *-chirichun* (= church). The Bavarians built churches for their newly colonized settlements. Conversio has this to say about the Bavarian colonization in Pannonia: *nations, whether Slavic or Bavarian, began to settle the land, from which the Huns* (= Avars) *had been expelled, and to multiply*.[104]

Conversio, who at the end of his lists of various churches also names the ownership of the churches of seven Bavarians, immediately adds that the Salzburg archbishop consecrated them there *where Pribina and his people wanted* (*ubi Priwina et sui voluerunt populi*).[105] The mentioned Bavarians were thus Pribina's people. Thus, like the important Slavs, they, too were support for Pribina's rule in Pannonia.

Bavarian administration of the then Carantanian part of Pannonia did not end with the origin of Pribina's Pannonian Principality. Pribina had to take

---

25 × 32 m in size, was located. In the corner of the courtyard stood a wooden house, in the centre a wooden single-aisle church and a cemetery. Robert Müller and other researchers regard this as Vitemír's seat, with the Church of St. Stephen the First Martyr. Robert Müller, "Karoling udvarház és temetője," in *Honfoglalás és régészet* (Budapest 1994), pp. 91–98. Szőke, *The Carolingian age in the Carpathian basin*, pp. 71–75, 77. Ruttkay, "Dvorce v 9. až 13. storočí," pp. 143–145.

102 See note 101. Unzat and Vitemír were present in January 850 at the consecration of the Church of Mary, Mother of God in Blatengrad. See note 73.
103 See note 93, 94. Szőke, *The Carolingian age in the Carpathian basin*, pp. 76, 77.
104 *coeperunt populi sive Sclavi vel Bagoarii inhabitare terram, unde illi expulsi sunt Huni, et multiplicari*. Conversio 10, ed. Wolfram, pp. 72–73, 166. Conversio, ed. Kos, pp. 68–69, 135. *MMFH III*, p. 309.
105 See note 93.

into his services the local representatives of Bavarian power, who further remained in the places where Louis the German had put them in 828. Pribina, if he wanted to get along well with King Louis, could not simply replace them with his own people. They had made decisions here for 12 years; they knew the local relations, and the new prince needed their services. The Bavarians, who in the 850s and 860s colonized and enhanced their Pannonian estates, already belonged to a younger generation of representatives of Carolingian Pannonia, who around 840 entered into the service of Pribina. However, we don't find even one of them among the 17 Bavarian witnesses present on 24 January 850 in Blatengrad, as we would by simple analogy look for them there. The 17 Bavarians present at the consecrating of the first Blatengrad church came in the accompaniment of Salzburg Archbishop Liupram. At least three of them, Gunther, Arfrid and Rato, were Liupram's fief-tenants.[106]

Three counties and one small principality,[107] whose direct superior was the Carantanian margrave, were combined into one common principality in approximately 840. Pribina's new principality, however, with respect to its geographical position and historical circumstances, was further subjected to the Carantanian margrave, similarly as the neighbouring Savian Principality. We have a wealth of written reports about the Pannonian Principality. If we want to know the position and territorial range of the three counties and the small principality and to find the names of at least some of the princes and counts who in roughly year 840 were subject to Margrave Ratbot and his predecessor and then to Prince Pribina and his successor, then we cannot rely on clear and direct reports.

7   Ptuj County

First on the road from Carantania via the valley of the Drava to Pannonia lay Ptuj (Pettau). This road crossed the Amber Road in Ptuj and branched out to all of Pannonia. In the 7th century Slavs settled in Ptuj. The extensive Slavic burial ground in Ptuj dates from the 9th and 10th centuries.[108] In the 850s Pribina had a church built and consecrated *ad Bettobiam*, that is in Ptuj.[109] Thus, Ptuj belonged to Pribina's and Kocel's Pannonian Principality. In 874 Salzburg

---

106   *Conversio*, ed. Kos, p. 81. *Conversio*, ed. Wolfram, p. 190.
107   See pp. 118–119.
108   Josip Korošec, *Staroslovansko grobišče na Ptujskom gradu*. Razred za zgodovinske in družbene vede SAZU, Dela 1 (Ljubljana 1950). Franjo Ivaniček, *Staroslovenska nekropola u Ptuju*. Razred za zgodovinske in družbene vede SAZU, Dela 5 (Ljubljana 1951).
109   *Conversio* 11, ed. Wolfram, pp. 76–77, 205, 206. *MMFH III*, pp. 315–316.

Archbishop Thietmar consecrated *ad Bettowe*, that is in Ptuj, the church of Count Gozwin (*Gozwini comitis*).[110] Ptuj Count Gozwin was subjugated at this time to Pannonian Prince Kocel.

Ptuj Castle was the centre of the Ptuj County, later the Ptuj March also called the Drava March. In the 10th and 11th centuries Ptuj Land was a border county and defensive march of the Carantanian Duchy against Hungary.[111] It was a small country on the middle Drava and its feeder rivers the Dravinja and Pesnica. To the west it stretched to the old Noricum-Pannonian border in the alpine foothills of the Kozjak and Pohorje; the northern border was formed by the Mur River; on the south it extended to the mountain Macelj and to the east up to Medžumurje (Muraköz).[112]

Around the year 980 Count Rachwin administered Ptuj Land. In 980 Emperor Otto II bestowed on Count Wilhelm in Ptuj Land *in the county of count Rachwin* (*in comitatu Rachvuini comitis*) property which on the north neighboured with the property of Margrave Markwart and on the south touched the border of neighbouring Savinja County administered by Count Wilhelm.[113] In

---

110   *Diotmarus archiepiscopus ecclesiam ad Petowa Chozivini comitis consecravit. Annales Iuvavenses maximi* ad a. 874, MMFH IV, p. 383. *Dietmarus ecclesiam ad Petowe Gozwizi comitis consecravit. Annales sancti Rudberti Salisburgenses* ad a. 874, MMFH IV, p. 402. *Dietmarus archiepiscopus ecclesiam ad Bettowe Gozwini comitis consecravit. Auctarium Gartense* ad a. 874, MMFH IV, p. 425. Dvorník, *Byzantské misie*, p. 167.

111   In 977 Ptuj belonged to the Carantanian Principality. In years 977, 982 and 984 the emperor confirmed to the Salzburg archbishop, in addition to other lands, also the ownership *ad Pettouiam ecclesiam cum decima et duas partes ciuitatis cum bannis, theloneis et insuper tertiam partem ciuitatis qua proprietas fuit Carentani eique diiudicatum erat eo quod reus maiestatis criminatus est constare, exceptis illis rebus que suae uxori concessas fuere, id est in supcriori ciuitate in orientali parte ciuitatis curtilem locum ubi noua ecclesia incepta est, atque* [*in*] *inferiori ciuitate in occidentali parte ciuitas ipsius illa curtilia loca in potestate tunc habuit, cum hobis C et uineis X in Zistanesfeld* (= Ptujsko polje) *firmamus ad prefatam monasterium sicut acerui duo prope Trauum* (= Drava) *positi sunt ex summitate termini qui Uuagreini tendit usque dum Treuuina* (= Dravinja) *fluit in amnem Traum*. MHDC III, ed. Jaksch, no. 147, 154, 159, pp. 59–61, 65, 67. *Urkundenbuch des Herzogthums Steiermark. Band I: 798–1192*, bearbeitet von Joseph von Zahn (Graz 1875), no. 27, 30, 31, pp. 32–33, 36–38. These imperial confirmations originated on the basis of an older forgery, which the forger dated to year 885, and he prepared it shortly before the issuing of the imperial deed from year 997. MMFH III, Diplomata 110, pp. 123–127. UHS I, ed. Zahn, no. 9, pp. 12–14. MHDC III, ed. Jaksch, no. 62, p. 24.

112   For the territorial range of Ptuj, see Hasenöhrl, "Deutschlands südöstliche Marken," pp. 510–512. *Erläuterungen I. Abt., 1. Teil*, pp. 265–304. *Zgodovina Slovencev* (Ljubljana 1979), p. 161 (map). Bogo Grafenauer, *Zgodovina slovenskega naroda II* (Ljubljana 1965), pp. 200–202 (map).

113   *ab orientali parte montis iamdicti Doberich montium quorum nomina sunt Stenniz, Frezniz, et ipsius montis iamdicti ac inde que ad usque idem comitatus conuenit ac tangit comitatum, qui dicitur Sovuina. Monumenta historica ducatus Carinthiae I. Die Gurker*

985, on the appeal of Carinthian Duke Henry I, Count Rachwin also obtained property from the emperor on the territory of Ptuj Land.[114]

We have more numerous reports on the Ptuj March from the end of the 11th century.[115] After the loss of Styria (year 1000), Savinja (1025), Trentino (1027), Verona, Friuli, Istria and Carniola (1077), only the Ptuj March remained to the Carantanian Principality. The Ptuj March was separated from Carantania by the *Drava forest* (*Trawalt*), the forested alpine foothills of Kozjak and Pohorje, which constrict it from both sides of the Drava River and offers it only a narrow passage.[116] This position also gave Ptuj another name: *The march beyond the forest* (*Marchia trans siluam*).[117] The last Ptuj Margrave, Bernhard

---

Geschichtsquellen, herausgegeben von August von Jaksch (Klagenfurt 1896), no. 9, p. 48. UHS I, ed. Zahn, no. 29, pp. 35–36.

114 *ob interventu Henrici Karintinorum ducis cuidam fideli nostro Rachuuin nominato de nostra proprietate dedimus quindecim mansos regales in uilla Razuuai* (= Razvanje) *dicta sitos si ibi inveniatur, si autem ibi inveniri non possint, in proximis uillis ubi suppleri ualennt, tollendos, et in pago Zitelinesfeld* (= Ptujsko polje) *uocato ac comitatv prefati Rachuini comitis iacentes, atque eosdem quindecim mansos regales cum omnibus utensilibus ad eos rite pertinentibus.* UHS I, ed. Zahn, no. 32, pp. 39–40. Hasenöhrl, "Deutschlands südöstliche Marken," p. 507. *Erläuterungen I. Abt.*, 4. *Teil*, 2. *Heft*, p. 374. The village Razvanje lies perhaps 6 km south of Maribor.

115 Abbot Vencelin († 1117) obtained for the monastery of St. Paul from the Istrian Margrave Engelbert (1107–1123), son of Engelbert von Sponheim, the whole of his inherited share in the Ptuj March: *in marchia Pitouensi totam que se contingebat, hereditas portionem, hoc est curtim et ecclesiam Razwei* (= Razvanje) *cum subscriptis Razwei, Circuniz* (= Cirkulane), *Celniz* (= Selnica), *Zegonewoz* (= Zelkoves), *Pabenpotoch, Pozengazelo* (= Polskava), *Dragotsoy* (= Trakoščan), *Dobrenga* (= Dobrovce), *Riesitz* (= Rotšica), *Vulpingepotoch, Ztiplina, Boratsowe* (= Borovci), *Zegoinezelo, Noblitwitz, Pribissendorf.* MHDC III, ed. Jaksch, no. 539, pp. 218–219. UHS I, ed. Zahn, no. 132, pp. 143–144.

116 UHS I, ed. Zahn, no. 197, p. 205.

117 In 1091 Engelbert I von Sponheim gifted to the Carantanian Abbey of St. Paul *in Marchia trans siluam uineas duas, ultra Traum* (= Drava) *uillam Ruoste* (= Ruše) *et heremum huic contiguam Redimlic* (= Lovrenc na Pohorju) *dictam ubi etiam aliquot Christo militaturos se uiuente instituit.* MHDC III, ed. Jaksch, no. 496, pp. 192–194. UHS I, ed. Zahn, no. 86, p. 100. He gifted other property in these places to the Abbey of St. Paul in 1093 *Weriant de Grez* (= Slovenj Gradec) *duos mansos siluam apud Celniz* (= Selnica), *Ludwich Ludwici filius duas hobas et quartam partam vectigalium in Vuostric* (= Bistrica pri Fali) *et ut homines ecclesie qui eadem bona incoluit communionem habeant in saltu adiacente a torrente Vodmunt* (= Vindenava) *dicto usque ad torrentem Gemniz* (= Kamnica) *pascendo, venando et omni utilitate.* UHS I, ed. Zahn, no. 87, pp. 100–101. Another donation for the Abbey of St. Paul around 1100 calls Ptuj simply the *Marka* (*Marchia*). The sons of Engelbert von Sponheim, Hartvik, Sigfrid, Bernhard and Heinrich, bestowed on this abbey *in Marchia* properties in the villages *Razwei* (= Razvanje), *Hunoldindorf, Ramestein, Gamniz* (= Kamnica), *Zubilink, Legindorf, Radewan* and *Brunne*. MHDC III, ed. Jaksch, no. 500, pp. 197–198. UHS I, no. 89, pp. 103–105. Carinthian Duke Henry IV (1122–1123), son of Engelbert von Sponheim, gifted to the Abbey of St. Paul *in marchia Transsiluana* properties in Kamnica (*Camnitz*) and in

von Sponheim (1122–1147)[118] married Kunigunde, sister of Styrian Margrave Leopold the Strong (1122–1129). For the case of a childless marriage he determined as his primary heir and successor Leopold's son Ottokar II. Bernhard died in 1147 on a Crusade of King Conrad III of Germany. He found death on 16 November in a battle with the Turks near Laodicea in Asia Minor. The Carantanian Sponheims were left with nothing after the death of Bernhard. Ottokar II inherited Ptuj Land and connected it to Styria.[119] The Ptuj March ended with the death of the last margrave and connection to Styria.

Which of the three Transdanubian counts named in Conversio was Gozwin's predecessor and administered the Ptuj County from year 828? The order in which they are named in Conversio cannot be random. Since they were contemporaries and were equals in relation to the superior Carantanian Margrave, they are not put in chronological order or even based on the level of their social standing. The order in which the unknown author wrote them could have come only from gradual geographic distance of their counties in the direction from Salzburg, where Conversio originated. Ptuj Land lay on the western edge of Pannonia as the first of the three Transdanubian counties on the road from Carantania. Thus, Helmwin, who in 828 replaced the last Ptuj prince exiled by the Bulgarians, became the Ptuj count, the first of the recorded trio. Ptuj

---

Pesnica (*Peznitza*). *UHS I*, ed. J. Zahn, n. 226, pg. 238. Kunigunde, wife of Ptuj Margrave Bernhard von Sponheim, gave around year 1145 *iuxta Brunne in Marchia eisdem claustricolis Victrigensibus* (= Viktring) *villam unam que Lonch* (= Deutschlandsberg) *dicitur*. *UHS I*, no. 237, pp. 244–245. In 1146 Bernhard and Kunigunde mortgaged their castle Denia (*Dithenia*) in the Friulian Patriarchate of Aquileia to Pelegrin for 30 talents of silver and 2 parts of the tithes of the parishes Konjice (*Cuonowiz*), Slivnice (*Scliuniz*) and Hoče (*Choz*). *UHS I*, ed. Zahn, no. 253, pp. 261–262. Hasenöhrl, *Deutschlands südöstliche Marken*, pp. 507–508.

[118] Bernhard's father Engelbert I von Sponheim married Hedwig, the sister of Henry III, the last Carantanian duke from the Eppenstein line. After the death of Henry III in 1122, the Sponheim family inherited the Carantanian Principality. Engelbert's son Henry IV (1122–1123) became the duke and another son Bernhard acquired the Ptuj March. The rule of the Sponheims in Carantania ended with the death of Ulrich III in 1269. August von Jaksch, *Geschichte Kärntens bis 1335 I* (Klagenfurt 1928), pp. 248–395. August von Jaksch, *Geschichte Kärntens bis 1335 II* (Klagenfurt 1929), pp. 1–60. Grafenauer, *Zgodovina II*, pp. 215, 340–365. Ptuj Margrave Bernhard established an abbey in Viktring in 1140. *Iohannis abbatis Victoriensis Liber certarum historiarum, Liber I. Rec. D*, ed. Schneider, p. 121. *MHDC III*, ed. Jaksch, no. 749, pp. 290–291.

[119] *MHDC III*, ed. Jaksch, no. 856, 857, 858, 861, pp. 334–335, 336. *Iohannis abbatis Victoriensis Liber certarum historiarum, Liber I. Rec. D*, ed. Schneider, pp. 122–123. Hasenöhrl, *Deutschlands südöstliche Marken*, pp. 508–509. Jaksch, *Geschichte Kärntens I*, pp. 276–279. Fritz Posch, "Die Anfänge der Steiermark," in *Österreich im Hochmittelalter (907–1246)*, herausgegeben von der Kommission für die Geschichte Österreichs bei der Österreichischen Akademie der Wissenschaften (Wien 1991), pp. 117–118.

Count Helmwin (from 828), Gozwin (around 874) and Rachwin (before 980–after 985) have similar names, and perhaps we have before us counts of a single family line. The history of the Ptuj princes, counts and margraves and their small county on the middle Drava began with the fall of Avar power at the turn of the 8th and 9th centuries and ended in 1147.

8   Dudlebian County

Dudlebian County (*comitatus Dudleipa*) is mentioned in a donation document of East Francia King Arnulf from 891. Arnulf gifted to the Salzburg archbishop *in the lands of the Slavs, a county by the name of Dudlebia* (*Dudleipa*), property of *Ruginesfeld*, which was once owned by Prince Kocel (*Chocil dux*), the former Reginger's fief near the Gnasbach (*Knesaha*) stream, the former Lorio's fief near Lafnitz (*ad Lauentam*) and the former fief of Erinbert's soldier Isaac (*Ysaac*) near Pinka (*ad Peiniccaham*).[120] The Pinka and Lafnitz rivers and the Gnasbach stream determine for us the position of Dudlebian County on the western edge of the Carantanian part of Pannonia, approximately the territory of the later Vas County (Vas vármegye). The old Pannonian border in the Fischbach Alps bordered Dudlebia (Dudlebland) on the west and separated it from Carantania. To the south, where the Gnasbach stream entered into the Mur River, it bordered with Ptuj Land and on the Drava River with Savia, to the east with Lower Pannonia and on the north it had to respect the border of Upper Pannonia on the Rábca. On this territory (perhaps in Radkersburg) lay Dudleba with Pribina's church (*Dudleipin*) and with the curia of the Salzburg archbishop (*Tuddleipin*).[121]

---

120   In partibus Sclauiniensibus vero in comitatu Dudleipa vocato in loco Ruginesfeld, sicut Chocil dux quondam inibi ad opus suum habere visus est valuti Reginger in eodem comitatu iuxta aquam, que dicitur Knesaha, in beneficium habebat; ad Lauentam quoque, sicut Lorio in beneficium habuerat, ad Peiniccaham ergo, sicut Ysaac miles Erinberti in beneficium tenuit. MMFH III, Diplomata 111, pp. 127–129. UHS I, ed. Zahn, no. 10, p. 14. Pirchegger, "Karantanien und Unterpannonien," pp. 284, 294, 296, 307, 318, 319.

121   *Conversio* 11, ed. Wolfram, pp. 76–77, 184, 205, 206. MMFH III, pp. 315–316. The archbishop acquired the court in Dudleba to his ownership in 860. MMFH III, Diplomata 30, p. 60. We don't know the exact position of Dudleba; in no case, however, did it lay in the surroundings of Graz and Lipnica, near antique Flavia Solva, where Ljudmil Hauptmann and Milko Kos looked for it. Ljudmil Hauptmann, "Politische Umwälzungen unter den Slowenen vom Ende des sechsten Jahrhunderts bis zur Mitte des neunten," *Mitteilungen des österreichischen Instituts für Geschitsforschung* 36 (1915), p. 234. Ljudmil Hauptman, "Mejna grofija Spodnjepanonska," *Razprave Znanstvenega društva za humanistične vede* 1 (Ljubljana 1923), p. 311. *Conversio*, ed. Kos, p. 86. Kos, *Zgodovina Slovencev*, p. 41. Pribina's

The axis of the entire country was the Amber Road, which headed from Ptuj in the direction to Sabaria (Szombathely) and from there to Upper Pannonia to Sopron and Carnuntum. Dudlebian County lay as the second along the road from Carantania to Pannonia. The road from Carantania led first along the Drava Valley to Ptuj and from there by the Amber Road north to Dudlebian County.

Dudlebian County was the territory of the Slavic Dudlebs, who under Avar rule were taken away from their original settlements in Volhynia. The Avars took the Dudlebs with them, along with other Slavs, in year 567–568 all the way to Pannonia,[122] where they had a difficult life: *These Obri (= Avars) battled with the Slavs and plagued the Dudlebs, who were also Slavs, and committed violence on the Dudlebian women. If an Obrin wanted to travel, he didn't harness a horse or ox, but ordered 3 or 4 or 5 women to be harnessed to a cart to carry the Obri. And thus they troubled the Dudlebs. Because the Obri were large in body and proud of mind. And God condemned them, and they all died and not one Obrin remained.*[123]

A portion of the Dudlebs left at the time of the great anti-Avar rebellion of the Slavs and the origin of Samo's realm out of Avar reach far to the north-west up to the southern Bohemia, but the second part of the Dudlebs remained in Pannonia.[124] The Dudlebs, like other Slavs who shook up Avarian rule, attacked the Avars in years 805–811. Their small principality took up nearly the entire south-western quarter of Transdanubia. In 827 the Bulgarians expelled

and Kocel's principality, to which Dudlebia (Dudlebland) belonged, did not extend beyond the western Pannonian border and did not reach the middle Mur to Carantania. The territorial integrity of Carantania had to remain untouched upon the origin of Pribina's principality. We don't know the exact position of Kocel's property *Ruginesfeld*, but the Reginger, Lorio and Isaac estates near the Gnasbach stream, by the rivers Lafnitz and Pivka clearly puts the position of Dudlebian County in Pannonia for us, to the east of Carantania.

122   See chapter 2, note 28.
123   *Povesť vremennych let*, MMFH I, pp. 188–191. Bohumila Zástěrová, "Avaři a Dudlebové v svědectví Pověsti vremennych let," *Vznik a počátky Slovanů* III (1960), pp. 15–37. Alexander Avenarius, "Byzantská a západoslovanská zložka v Povesti vremennych let," *Slovanské štúdie* 14 (1973), pp. 165–186. Avenarius, *Die Awaren in Europa*, pp. 193–217. Arnulf Kollautz, "Nestors Quelle über die Unterdrückung der Duleben durch die Obri (Awaren)," *Die Welt der Slawen* 27, Neue Folge 6 (1982), pp. 307–320. Pohl, *Die Awaren*, pp. 113–114, 118.
124   Třeštík, *Počátky*, pp. 53, 66, 443. The Dudlebs penetrated into neighbouring Carinthia from their Pannonian seat, to the basin of the middle Mur, and established settlements there which later bore their name. Jakob Kelemina, "Nekaj o Dulebih na Slovenskem," *Časopis za zgodovino in narodopisje* 20 (1925), pp. 144–154. Jakob Kelemina, "Nove dulebske študije," *Časopis za zgodovino in narodopisje* 21 (1926), pp. 57–75. Fritz Posch, "Die Dudleben in der Steiermark," *Blätter für Heimatkunde* 66 (1992), pp. 21–25.

the last Dudlebian prince. His place in the following year, after expulsion of the Bulgarians by Bavarian King Louis the German, was occupied by Count Albgar, the second of the three Transdanubian counts recorded in Conversio.

Around 840, Dudlebian County became a part of Pribina's principality. On his territory in Dudleba (*in Dudleipin*),[125] in Wisitindorf (*in Ussitin*)[126] and in Köszeg (*ad Keisi*)[127] Pribina had churches built and consecrated during the 850s. The stream Ablanc (Abláncz, *rivulus Oblanch*, mentioned in 1255) flowed into the border river Rábca from the south.[128] In its valley (*vallis Ablanch* 1233, 1255)[129] today still lies the village Ablanc (*terra Oblanch* 1255, 1257, *terra Ablanhc* 1299,[130] *villa Ablanch* 1279[131]). Here, *ad Ablanza*, on the northern border of his principality, Pribina's son Kocel established another church after 865.[132]

---

125   *Conversio* 11, ed. Wolfram, pp. 76–77, 205, 206. MMFH III, pp. 315–316. The Salzburg archbishop used one yard in Dudleba (*ad Tuddleipin*) as a fief, which came into his ownership in 860. See note 144.

126   *Conversio* 11, ed. Wolfram, pp. 76–77, 205, 206. *Conversio*, ed. Kos, pp. 86–87. MMFH III, pp. 315–316. In 864 the Salzburg archbishop obtained *ad Wisitindorf*, that is in Wisitindorf, 8 estates into his ownership. See note 145.

127   *Conversio* 11, ed. Wolfram, pp. 76–77, 205, 206. *Conversio*, ed. Kos, pp. 88, 137. MMFH III, pp. 315–316. The Salzburg archbishop here used as a fief a curia belonging to the local church (*ecclesiam ad Kensi*), which he acquired into his ownership in 860. MMFH III, Diplomata 30, pp. 63–65. See note 144. The church in Köszeg (*ecclesiam ad Gensi*) also mentions in the same association the forgery from the 10th century, reporting to year 885. MMFH III, Diplomata 110, p. 123. Bogyay, "Die Kirchenorte," p. 62. The *Kensi* in the donation document for the Salzburg archbishop from 860 and the *Keisi* mentioned in Conversio are exactly as the *Chuartinahu* in the mentioned donation document and the *Quartinaha* known from Conversio is the same place. See note 89. The compiler of the document and the author of Conversio were two different people, and they wrote with a 10-year time gap. Therefore, the small deviation in the written names of the same location is completely understandable.

128   *iuxta rivulum Oblanch ... ad rivulum Oblanch. Urkundenbuch des Burgenlandes und der angrenzenden Gebiete der Komitate Wieselburg, Ödenburg und Eisenburg I*, bearbeitet von Hans Wagner (Graz – Köln 1955), no. 347, pp. 238–239.

129   *in vallem quandam Ablanch nomine. Urkundenbuch des Burgenlandes. Band I*, ed. Wagner, no. 201, 202, pp. 150–151. *vallem que ozy Oblanch nominatur. Urkundenbuch des Burgenlandes I*, ed. Wagner, no. 347, p. 239.

130   *terra Oblanch, terram Oblanch. Urkundenbuch des Burgenlandes I*, ed. Wagner, no. 346, 347, 361, 362, pg. 238–239, 246, 262. *in terris Ablanhc vocatis. Urkundenbuch des Burgenlandes und der angrenzenden Gebiete der Komitate Wieselburg, Ödenburg und Eisenburg. Band II. Die Urkunden von 1271 bis 1301*, bearbeitet von Irmtraut Lindeck-Pozza (Graz – Köln 1965), no. 471, p. 328.

131   *cum altere parte villae Ablanch. Urkundenbuch des Burgenlandes* II, ed. Lindeck-Pozza, no. 193, p. 140.

132   *Conversio* 13, ed. Wolfram, pp. 78–79, 208. *Conversio*, ed. Kos, pp. 100, 140. MMFH III, p. 322. Thomas von Bogyay, "Kontinuitätsprobleme im karolingischen Unterpannonien,

We know the names of other Dudlebian counts from the royal land donations lying near the common border of Upper Pannonia and Dudlebian County. The rivers Spratzbach (*Spraza*), Rábca (*alia Spraza*) and the upper flow of the Zöbern–Sabaria stream (*Sabaria, Seuira*) together with the surrounding mountains, formed the border, which stretched not very far to the northern bank of the Zöbern stream (*Seuira*). This border is mentioned in the document of Louis the German from 829 as the diocese border of Passau and Salzburg.[133] To the north of this border lay Upper Pannonia, which belonged to the Eastern March, and to the south side Dudlebian County, to which the south-western part of Lower Pannonia also belonged.

Directly on this border, west of Köszeg, lay the property *Brunnaron* (today Pilgersdorf or Lebenbrun), which Pribina's priest Dominik (from 850 the Blatengrad presbyter) acquired in 844. Dominik's *Brunnaron* property lay on the border of two counties, Ratbot's and Richard's, and also touched the Zöbern stream (*iuxta rivolum qui vocatur Seuira in marca, ubi Radpoti et Rihharii comitatus confinuit*).[134] Ratbot's Upper Pannonian county in these places, in the vicinity of the Zöbern stream, neighboured only with Dudlebian territory; thus, Richard could only be the Dudlebian count. Count Richard in 857 became involved in the revolt of Pabo and other counts in neighbouring Carantania against Margrave Carloman, who then plundered the lands of the

---

Methodios Wirken in Mosapurc im Lichte der Quellen und Funde," *Das östliche Mitteleuropa in Geschichte und Gegenwart*, Abb. 2 (Wiesbaden 1966), p. 64. Bogyay, "Die Kirchenorte," pp. 57–58. Sós, *Die slawische Bevölkerung*, pp. 33, 37. Ján Stanislav, *Slovenský juh v stredoveku I* (Turčiansky Sv. Martin 1948), p. 8.

133 See notes 135, 137, 140, chapter 5, note 50. Regarding the names of these rivers and streams, see also Peter Wiesinger, "Antik-romanische Kontinuitäten im Donauraum von Ober- und Niederösterreich am Beispiel der Gewässer-, Berg- und Siedlungsnamen," in *Typen der Ethnogenese unter besonderer Berücksichtigung der Bayern, Teil 1, Berichte des Symposions der Kommission für Frühmittelalterforschung, 27. bis 30. Oktober 1986, Stift Zwettl, Niederösterreich*, ed. Herwig Wolfram, Walter Pohl (Wien 1990), pp. 291–293.

134 *MMFH III*, Diplomata 18, pp. 37–38. Pirchegger, *Karantanien und Unterpannonien*, p. 291. Klebel, *Die Ostgrenze*, p. 370. *Conversio*, ed. Kos, pp. 79–80. Milko Kos, "K histórii kniežaťa Pribinu a jeho doby," in *Ríša Veľkomoravská*, ed. Stanislav, p. 60. Tóth, "Zu den historischen Problemen," pp. 104, 107. *Conversio*, ed Wolfram, pp. 130–131, 187–188. Wolfram, *Die Geburt*, pp. 278–279. The priest Dominik established here the church mentioned in the donation for the Salzburg archbishop from 860: *ad ecclesiam Minigonis presbiteri*. *MMFH III*, Diplomata 30, pg. 59. Minigo is short for Dominicus. Brunnaron, Ablanca and Köszeg lay near the border of Pribina's and Kocel's Lower Pannonian principalities, with Upper Pannonia belonging to the Eastern March. *Seuira*, that is Zöberbach between Deutsch-Gerisdorf and Lockenhaus (west of Köszeg in Burgenland) flows into the stream *Sabaria*, that is into the Sabaria stream (Güns, Gyöngyös).

Carantanan rebels and crushed their insurrection. Richard was deposed and ended up in exile.[135]

Near the mentioned border in 860 the Abbey of St. Michael in Matsee acquired from King Louis the German 20 settlements, which began at the Sabaria ford (*Sabariae vadum*), from where they stretched *inter Sprazam et Savariam*, that is between the Rábca and the Sabaria stream (Güns, Gyöngyös) up to the border with the hills *Wachreini, Wangariorum marcha* and *Witinisberc*. The property lay in Odolric's county (*in comitatu Odolrici*).[136] In that same year Count Odolric also circumvented the new property of the Salzburg archbishop, Sabaria Castle and the settlement Pinkava (*Sabariam civitatem et Peinihhaa*), and led the archbishop into ownership.[137] We can identify Odolric's county, in which the Sabaria and Pinkava lay[138] and which stretched north up to the Upper Pannonian border, only with the Dudlebian County.

On the Dudlebia-Upper Pannonia border also lay the property of the Kremsmünster Abbey. The abbey obtained it from Louis the German and also King Carloman confirm its ownership in 877. The abbey property lay along the Spratzbach (*iuxta fluvium qui dicitur Spraza*) from the place called *Benninvuanc*, where a spring flows into the Spratzbach, then *inter duas Sprazas* that is between the Spratzbach and the Thalbach up past through their confluence.[139] The gifted property lay on the southern edge of Upper Pannonia and also touched the border of neighbouring Dudlebia. Therefore, when marking its borders, both local counts, Upper Pannonian Arathot and Dudlebian Ernest (*a duobus comitibus Arathoto et Ernusto circumequitatum fuerat*), had to be circumvented.[140]

---

135 *Excerpta Aventini ex Annalibus Iuvavensibus antiquis derivati* ad a. 857, MMFH *I*, pp. 382–383. Mitterauer, "Karolingische Markgrafen," pp. 118, 139.

136 *consistentes in comitatu Odolrici, id est mansos XX in loco qui dicitur Sauariae et inde inter Sprazam et Sauariam in summitatem montis et inde per circuitum in aquilonem usque in illum locum qui dicitur Uuachreini et inde usque in summitatem illius montis qui dicitur Uuangariorum marcha et inde usque in rummum montem qui dicitur Uuitinesberc.* MMFH *III*, Diplomata 29, pp. 55–57.

137 *Tradimus itaque ad praedictam casam dei Sabariam civitatem et Peinihhaa, sicut Odolricus comes noster et missus de ipsis rebus eas circuivit ceterique nostri fi deles et praedictum venerabilem archiepiscopum de ipsis rebus vestavit.* MMFH *III*, Diplomata 30, pp. 57–58.

138 Pinkava (Pinkafeld) lies on the Pinka River. Heinrich Koller, "Fluß und Ort 'Peinihhaa'," *Burgenländisches Heimatblatt* 26 (1964), pp. 61–70.

139 MMFH *III*, Diplomata 37, pp. 66–68. The streams Spratzbach and Thalbach meet near the village of Blumau (not far from Landsee) on the border of Burgenland with Lower Austria in the region named Bucklige Welt and they form the Rábca River, equally called in year 860 the *Spraza* and in 829 *alia Spraza*. See note 137, chapter 5, note 44.

140 Carloman issued this confirmation document in Ranshofen (*actum Ranterdorf*) on the Inn River, south of Passau. From the viewpoint of the issuer of the document, the Upper

We thus know the names of several Dudlebian counts. Count Albgar acceded in 828 in the place of the last Dudlebian prince. His successors were Count Richard (before 844–857), Count Odolric (around 860) and Count Ernest (before 877). We can no longer find the names of the other counts.

Sabaria (modern Szombathely), which a royal document from 860 labelled as *civitas*, was the most important settlement in all of Dudlebian County. In 791 the anti-Avar campaign of Charlemagne returned *through Sabaria (per Sabariam)*.[141] In 805 Kapkhan Theodor settled with his Avars on the territory between Sabaria and Carnuntum *(inter Sabariam et Carnuntum)*.[142] Since in the south of Upper Pannonia, which was to accept Theodor's Avars, there was no significant point of the kind there was to the north in Carnuntum, the emperor marked the southern edge of their new Upper Pannonian settlements with historically important Sabaria, although this lay on its southern edge, that is on the territory of Lower Pannonia.

In the 9th century a small round castle grew up in the middle of the dead antique town. Its stone wall ramparts, two metres thick, enclosed a circle with a diameter of approximately 40 metres and an area of 1,390 m². The castle was a Carolingian construction. It stood throughout medieval times, and in the 14th century a square tower was added on the external side. This small Carolingian castle was obviously the mentioned Sabaria *civitas*, which could have been the county seat.[143]

Pannonian county was closer to him and Dudlebian County more distant. Therefore, the first name Arathot could be the Upper Pannonian count, and the second Ernest we can consider as the Dudlebian count. Michael Mitterauer considers the name Arathotus as the full name of Arbo. Mitterauer, "Karolingische Markgrafen," pp. 164–166. Arbo (or Aribo) was Margrave of the Eastern March and local count in Traungau. See note 173. Margrave Aribo could not be identical with Count Arathot, because as the Trangau count he could not have moved around the territory in Upper Pannonia. The local counts only moved around the gifted property in their own counties. And Wilhelm II, who was a count in the area from the Enns to the Vienna Woods in 865–871 and Margrave of the Eastern March, went around the property of Kremsmünster Abbey on the north side of the Danube from Schmida (*Smidaha*) to Wagram (*Wachrein*). Kremsmünster Abbey had to have got this property from King Louis the German before the death of Wilhelm II in the spring of 871, and Carloman confirmed this donation in that same document from year 877 as the property on the Spratzbach.

141 See chapter 4, note 16.
142 See chapter 4, note 64.
143 Endre Tóth, "Die karolingische Burg von Sabaria-Szombathely," *Folia Archaeologica* 29 (1978), pp. 151–182. Erika P. Hajmási, "Szombathely középkori várának kutatástöténete és a külső várfal nyomvonalának meghatározása néhany ponton," *Savaria* 20 (1991) no. 1, pp. 39–51. Existing literature writes about Richard, Odolric and Ernest as the Sabarian counts. Zibermayr, *Noricum, Baiern und Österreich*, pp. 300–301, 304. Mitterauer, "Karolingische Markgrafen," pp. 86, 118, 139, 160, 204–205. Tóth, "Zu den historischen

In 860 the Salzburg archbishop acquired on Dudlebian territory, in addition to the mentioned Sabaria and Pinkafeld, also a feudal curia near the church of presbyter Minigo in Kundpoldesdorf, on the Rábca at the Sabarian ford in Pinkafeld, by the church in Köszeg, by the church in Safenbach, in Nestelbach, again in the Rabnitz in Dudleba.[144] In 864 eight settlements (*mansos integros VIII*) on the Lafnitz in Wisitindorf were added to them.[145]

Aside from Ruginesfeld property mentioned in 891, Kocel also owned property on the Rába River, which he donated to the bishopric in Regensburg.[146] The Abbey of St. Emmeram in Regensburg also owned 30 settlements (*hobas XXX*)

Problemen," pp. 106, 107, 117. Tóth, "Die karolingische Burg," pp. 175, 179. *Conversio*, ed. Wolfram, pp. 114, 149, 172, 173, 182, 190, 264–265, 281, 343. Wolfram, *Die Geburt*, pp. 277, 279, 284, 583. Szőke, *The Carolingian age in the Carpathian basin*, pp. 48–49. These authors consider Sabarian County as a part of Upper Pannonia and the Eastern March. In their opinion, Upper Pannonia had two counties separated by the Rábca River, and the north one of them already began on the lower Enns and ended at the lower Rába and did not respect the old Pannonian border in the Vienna Woods. We cannot agree with this opinion. The Eastern March, even with the border of Upper Pannonia, did not exceed the diocesan territory of the Passau bishopric, which ended at the lower Rába and the Rábca. Sabaria and all of Sabarian County with it already belonged to the Salzburg diocese and were also a part of Pribina's principality, which belonged fully to Lower Pannonia. We don't have even the smallest report that the Sabarian part of Pribina's and Kocel's principality and the Salzburg diocese belonged to Upper Pannonia and to the Eastern March. The County of Sabaria, which these authors place south of the Semmering and Wechsel mountains and the Rábca River, on the east up to the Rába and Marcal and on the west to the valley of the upper Rába, we can identify with the Dudlebian County, which reached to the south up to the Gnasbach Valley, where near its confluence with the Mur it neighboured with Ptuj. Medžumurje (Muraköz), which did not belong to neighbouring Ptuj (see note 112), could have belonged to Dudlebia.

144   *Insuper etiam tradimus ibi istas curtes in proprium, quae antea ibi in benefi cium fuerunt ex alicuius dato sive ex alterius cuiuslibet parte ibi antea benefi ciatae fuissent, quarum haec sunt nomina: ... ad ecclesiam Minigonis presbyteri, ad Kundpoldesdorf, ad Rapam, ad siccam Sabariam, item ad Peinicahu, ... ecclesiam ad Kensi, ... ecclesiam ad Sabnizam, ad Nezilinpah, item ad Rapam, ad Tuddleipin* ... *MMFH III*, Diplomata 30, pp. 57–61. The property *ad siccam Sabariam* is not identical with Sabaria. Tóth, "Zu den historischen Problemen," pp. 105–112. The property *ad Rapam* did not lay on the Rába, but on the Rábca. Tóth, "Zu den historischen Problemen," p. 112.

145   *ad Labenza, ad Wisitindorf. MMFH III*, Diplomata 33, pp. 63–65.

146   The Regensburg bishop Ambrich handed over these properties for lifetime use to Deacon Gundbat with an exchange for his property in Quartinaha (see note 86): *Econtra Cundbertusaduocatus consentiente domino suo episcopo tradidit de rebvs s. Emmerami ante nominato Gundbatoni venerabili diacono, quod Chezil dux quondam pro remedio anime suae ad predictum sanctum condonavit iuxta amnem qui dicitur Raba*. Bishop Ambrich in addition to this, permitted Deacon Gundbat: *vt mancipia sancti Emmerami, quae vltra Rabam fuga lapsa sunt, inquirat et capiat et in easdem res ecclesiae constituat. MMFH III*, Diplomata 38, pp. 68–69.

on the Rába, which Abbot Hitto swapped in 883 with the Regensburg bishop for a lifetime pension of the abbey in Mondsee.[147]

Dudlebian County lay in the old western Pannonian iron region. In the earlier period of the La Téne culture, the whole of western Pannonia, lying along the Amber Road from Emona (Ljubljana) up through Carnuntum, belonged to the kingdom Noricum.[148] The Noricum kingdom, wealthy in iron ore, was a great producer of iron. Metallurgy and iron production were in the hands of the Celtic Taurisci.[149] Under the rule of Emperor Claudius (41–54) Noricum became a Roman province, and the Romans connected the area along the Amber Road with the towns of Emona, Poetovio, Salla, Sabaria, Scarbantia and Carnuntum to Pannonia.[150] The Slavs continued in the tradition of metallurgy and iron production from domestic stores of iron ore. Hungarian archaeologists found in Köszegfalva a battery of metallurgical furnaces similar to the Slavic furnaces on the territories of the Czech lands and Slovakia.[151]

The territory of the former Dudlebian County became a significant iron-producing region in the Kingdom of Hungary.[152] The Hungarian king had the whole of domestic iron production under his control. His monopoly was guarded by Vasvár (Castrum Ferreum, Eisenburg), which was a royal warehouse and royal distribution centre for Hungarian iron.[153] Only the eastern part of the

147 Abbot Hitto handed over *proprietatam suam quam habuit in oriente iuxta fluvium qui vocatur Raba id est hobas XXX, in manum Ambrichonis venerabilis episcopi et advocati eius Gundperti.* MMFH III, Diplomata 39, pp. 69–71.
148 Pavel Oliva, *Pannonie a počátky krize římskeho imperia* (Praha 1959), p. 91. Endre Tóth, "Pannonia és Noricum közös határának a kialakulása," *Antik tanulmányok* 24 (1977), no. 2, pp. 192–200. *Pannonia*, ed. Mócsy, Fitz, pp. 53–54.
149 Alphons Barb, "Spuren alter Eisengewinnung im heutigen Burgenland," *Wiener praehistorische Zeitschrift* 24 (1937), pp. 152–154. Jan Filip, *Keltové ve střední Evropě* (Praha 1956), pp. 27–28, 32, 34. Oliva, *Pannonie*, pp. 132–133. Radomír Pleiner, "Die Eisenverhüttung in der 'Germania Magna' zur römischen Kaiserzeit," *45. Bericht der Römisch-Germanischen Kommission 1964* (Berlin 1965), pp. 11–86.
150 Erich Polaschek, "Noricum," *Realencyklopädie der classischen Altertumswissenschaft* XVII 11 (1936), pp. 980–982. Oliva, *Pannonie*, p. 91. Endre Tóth, "Megjegyzések Pannonia provincia kialakulásának kérdéséhez," *Archaeologiai Értesítő* 108 (1981), pp. 13–33.
151 Gusztáv Heckenast – Gyula Nováki – Gábor Vastagh – Endre Zolttay, *A Magyarországi vaskohászat története a korai középkorban. A honfoglalástól a XIII. század közepéig*, (Budapest 1968), pp. 44–51, 74–76. Matúš Kučera, *Slovensko po páde Veľkej Moravy Štúdie o hospodárskom a sociálnom vývine v 9.–13. storočí* (Bratislava 1974), p. 229. *Dějiny hutníctví železa v Československu I*, ed. Jaroslav Purš (Praha 1984), p. 41.
152 Heckenast – Nováki – Vastagh – Zoltay, *A Magyarországi vaskohászat története*, pp. 40–59, 62–69, 74–76, 120–130, 137–146, 158. Gyula Nováki, "Archäologische Denkmäler der Eisenverhüttung in Nordostungarn aus dem X.–XII. Jahrhundert," *Acta Archaeologica Academiae Scientiarum Hungaricae* 21 (1969), Fasciculi 3–4, pp. 299–331.
153 Kučera, *Slovensko po páde Veľkej Moravy*, p. 230. *Dějiny hutníctví I*, ed. Purš, p. 62.

then Dudlebia belonged to the Iron Castle County; Hungary lost the territory to the west of the Lafnitz River in 1043. Up to that year, the ridge of the Fischbach Alps, then called *mons Predel*, which divided the basin of the middle Mur from the basin of the upper Rába and was also the original border of Carolingian Pannonia with Carantania, formed the Hungarian border. Hungarian King Samuel Aba had to relinquish the territory of the old Pannonian border in the Fischbach Alps up to the Lafnitz River in order to meet the peace conditions of King Henry III.[154]

9 Blatenian County

During Pribina's period of rule of the Pannonian Principality his son Kocel was a count. Count Kocel issued two donation documents, the first as the *Chozil humilimus comes* before 859[155] and the second as the *comes de Slauis nomine Chezul* on 21 March 861.[156] He had to have already been a count in 850, because in the list of witnesses of the ceremonial consecrating of the first Blatengrad church, he is in the first, most honoured position,[157] and on this occasion

---

154 Fritz Posch, "Die deutsch-ungarische Grenzentwicklung im 10. und 11. Jahrhundert auf dem Boden der heutigen Steiermark," *Südost-Foschungen* 22 (1963), pp. 126–139. The territory between the Lafnitz and the Fischback Alps, which Samuel Aba had to relinquish, was acquired by the Carantanian March, the Ottonian border march on the middle Mur, the basis of the later March of Styria. We cannot confuse it with the Carolingian Carantanian March. Posch, "Die deutsch-ungarische Grenzentwicklung," pp. 127, 128, 139. Posch, "Die Anfämge der Steiermark," pp. 105–112. Hasenöhrl, "Deutschlands südöstliche Marken," pp. 482–506. In 970, when the Carantanian March was administered by its first known margrave Markwart (before 970–up through 980), the emperor gifted to the Salzburg archbishop property *in comitatu Marchuuardi marchionis nostri*. UHS I, ed. Zahn, no. 25, pp. 29–31. Markwart also had property in neighbouring Ptuj in 980. See note 113.

155 *Chozil humilimus comes* CDES I, ed. Marsina, no. 9, pp. 8–9. MMFH III, Diplomata 26, pp. 50–51.

156 CDES I, ed. Marsina, no. 11, p. 10. MMFH III, Diplomata 31, p. 61. In 873 Pope John VIII sent Kocel 2 letters which he addressed to *Gozili comiti* and *Tozili comiti*. CDES I, ed. Marsina, no. 19, 21, pp. 16, 17. MMFH III, Epistolae 53, 54, pp. 171–172. The address of both letters is a characteristic of the office of Pope John VIII. The pope did not address Kocel as count. The address *comiti* had nothing in common with his position in the administrative organization of East Francia. In 880 he likewise addressed Svätopluk: *Dilecto filio Sfentopulcho glorioso comiti*. CDES I, ed. Marsina, no. 30, p. 23. MMFH III, Epistolae 90, pp. 197–208.

157 *Conversio* 11, ed. Wolfram, pp. 74–75, 184, 185, 198–200. *Conversio*, ed. Kos, pp. 81, 136. MMFH III, pp. 312–313. See note 44. Kocel could not have been the Dudlebian count, because Dudlebian territory was at that time administered by Count Richard (before 844–857) and then Count Odolric (around 860). Ptujland was again too small for the successor to the Pannonian princely seat, and it was administered by counts of Bavarian origin

he had the present Salzburg archbishop consecrate the church of the priest Sandrat and the church of the priest Ermperht, and he himself gifted them; he went around church property and guided both priests to them.[158] Bypassing granted property in the presence of witnesses, by which its borders were determined directly on site, was among the obligations of the local count. Traungau Count Wilhelm performed this obligation on the territory of his counties in 827[159] and Dudlebian Count Odolric did so in 860.[160]

Pribina's fief, on which the seat Blatengrad stood, did not cover the entire basin of the Zala. The territory on the Válicka River, which came into Pribina's ownership in 846, bordered it, but did not belong to it and did not form a whole with it. The border that passed between them could have been the border of two counties. On the western side of this border, in Dudlebia, lay property on the Válicka River and on the eastern side, in Kocel's county, a more extensive Blatengrad fiefdom.

The location of Pribina's Blatengrad estate (his property from year 847) determines the territorial range of Kocel's county to the west. If there were only three counties in southern Transdanubia, and two of them (Dudlebia and Ptuj Land) took up the western part of the Pannonian Principality, then the entire south-east must have belonged to the third count. Kocel's county thus stretched to the east all the way to the Danube, beyond which lay Bulgaria, and in the south the Drava River divided it from Savia. Its northern border, beyond which we can assume was the last of the four extinct Transdanubian principalities, lay somewhere in the Bakon Forest. Kocel's county took up the whole of the south-eastern part of Transdanubia around Blatengrad and Pécs, approximately in range of the later castle counts of Somogy, Tolna, Baranya and the eastern part of the Zala County.

The most significant and undoubtedly also the seat castle of the third Transdanubian count was Blatengrad. The German form of its name *Mosapurc* or *Mosaburg* and the Latin *Urbs paludarum* corresponds to the Slavic *Blatьnskъ kostel* (Marsh castle), as it was written in the early 10th century by the monk Chrabr.[161] Blatengrad stood *in the swamps of the Zala River (in palude*

(Helmwin, Gozwin, Rachwin), among whom Kocel did not engage with and did not even belong.

158 *Conversio* 11, ed. Wolfram, pp. 74–75, 205, 209, 211. *Conversio*, ed. Kos, pp. 82, 136. *MMFH III*, pp. 313–314. Bogyay, *Die Kirchenorte*, p. 62. Szőke, *The Carolingian age in the Carpathian basin*, pp. 67–68.
159 See chapter 4, note 91.
160 See note 138.
161 *Conversio* 13, ed. Wolfram, pp. 78–79, 208. *Conversio*, ed. Kos, pp. 78, 97, 139. *MMFH III*, p. 319. *Pannoniam cum urbe Paludarum. Ann. Fuld.* ad a. 896, rec. Kurze p. 130. *MMFH I*,

Salae fluminis)[162] and near the large Blatenian Lake (Blatenské jazero, Balaton, Marsh Lake). The whole lower part of the Drava also had wide, swampy banks. For the imperial army marching in the spring of 820 through Transdanubia against Sisak Prince Ljudevit *the Drava River ... was also an obstacle which had to be got around.* This army *at the crossing of the Drava River for the unhealthy land and poor water was heavily afflicted with stomach complaints and no small part of it died from this illness.*[163] The confluence of the Drava with the Danube created a widely flooded land called the Mursa Lake, named after the town Mursa (today Osijek) on its southern bank.[164] The mud, swamps and great many blind river branches reached north up to Kalocsa.[165] The water, mud and swamps surrounded the country on the south-east of Transdanubia, and in Pribina's age they formed its dominant natural feature. And they named it as they named Blatenian Lake (Balaton, Plattensee) and the seat Blatengrad.

In 827 Blatenia (Blatenland), thanks to its position, became the first victim of the attack of Bulgarians moving against the current of the Drava River. The last Blatenian prince was replaced by a Bulgarian administrator. The campaign of Louis the German in the following year expelled the Bulgarians and a place for the last domestic Slavic prince was freed up for Count Pabo, the last of the trio of first Transdanubian counts named in Conversio.[166] Conversio didn't know the circumstances of the origin of the Pannonian Principality; he only ambiguously writes how it happened: *When, however, in the meantime some opportunity (occasione) arose, upon the appeal of the mentioned king.*[167] The opportunity which the unknown author of Conversio no longer remembered could be the death of Blatenian Count Pabo (or one of his successors),[168] which freed a place for Pribina and Kocel. Aside from Blatenian County, the

---

p. 105.... въ врѣмена ... Коцелѣ, кнѧза Блатьньска костелѣ. Чрьноризца Храбра Сказаније о писменехъ 9, MMFH III, p. 371. Havlík, *Územní rozsah*, p. 68. Ján Stanislav, *Dejiny slovenského jazyka I* (Bratislava 1956), p. 155.

162 See note 14. The wide swamps and mud were the dominant feature of the whole country on the lower Zala and near the south-western end of Lake Balaton, where the centre of the country was located long before the arrival of Pribina. They gave the name not only to the lake and Pribina's fortress but also the county administered from there.
163 Ann. reg. Franc. ad a. 820, rec. Kurze, p. 153. MMFH I, p. 29.
164 *eo tenus, ubi Ister oritur amnis vel stagnus dilatatur Morsianus.* Jordanes, *De origine actibusque Getharum* V, 30. *a ... laco qui appellatur Mursiano.* Jordawnes, *De origine actibusque Getharum* V, 35. Łowmiański, *Początki Polski II*, pp. 257–260. Třeštík, *Počátky*, pp. 25–27.
165 Hungarian King Louis II drowned in the swamps near Mohács in 1526.
166 See chapter 5, note 31.
167 *Conversio* 11, ed. Wolfram, pp. 74–75, 183. *Conversio*, ed. Kos, pp. 78, 136. MMFH III, p. 312.
168 Milko Kos puts the arrival of Pribina to Pannonia around year 840. *Conversio*, ed. Kos, p. 78. We will also observe this dating.

Ptuj and Dudlebian counties to the west and the last of the original four small Slavic principalities lying in the north-east of Transdanubia were subjected to Pribina's rule. Pribina's Pannonian Principality inherited them after Carantanian Pannonia.

10   Edgar's Principality

After the fall of the Avar Khaganate, four small Slavic principalities remained in Transdanubia. We already know the location of Ptuj Land, Dudlebia and Blatenia in southern Transdanubia, and we can look for the fourth principality only in the distant north-east, north of Blatenia and east of Upper Pannonia. Which of the four Transdanubian princes named in Conversio (Pribislav, Semika, Stojmír and Edgar) ruled in these regions?

The order of the four principalities is not random. The geographical viewpoint of Salzburg determined it, the gradual distance of their principalities from this diocesan centre. From the viewpoint of the unknown author of Conversio, writing in Salzburg, the first on the road to the interior of Pannonia lay Ptuj Land, then Dudlebia, beyond it Blatenia and the most distant was the anonymous principality in north-west Transdanubia.[169] If we know the order of the four princes as well as the order of their principalities in the direction from Salzburg, then we can assign Ptuj Land to Prince Pribislav, Dudlebia to Prince Semika, Blatenia to Prince Stojmír and the north-eastern part of Transdanubia to Prince Edgar.

Prince Edgar (*Etgar*) had a name of Anglo-Saxon origin, which one of the most significant Anglos-Saxon kings in Britain, Edgar the Peaceful (959–975), bore.[170] However, we come across this name in Transdanubia in the 850s in the German form of *Otachar*. The Salzburg archbishop consecrated then on the property of one of Pribina's retinue the church *Otachareschirichun*[171]

---

169 From a geographical viewpoint of Salzburg, the territory in north-east Transdanubia was the last, to the end of its diocese itself.

170 Charter of Edgar to Ely. In: *An Anglo-Saxon Reader*, edited by Alfred J. Wyatt (Cambridge 1947), pp. 119–121. C. P. Wormald, "Edgar, Kg. v. Mercien und Northumbrien 957–975, Kg. v. England 959–975," in *Lexikon des Mittelalters III* (München – Zürich 1986), pp. 1570–1571. This name also belonged to Edgar, bishop in Lindisse (perhaps 693–716) and London Bishop Edgar (768–773). Pius Bonifacius Gams, *Series episcoporum ecclesiae catholicae quotquot innotuerunt a beato Petro apostolo* (Leipzig 1931), pp. 191, 193. Edgar Etheling (*1052, † about 1130), grandson of King Edmund II, was to accede to the throne after the death of Edward the Confessor († 1066). N. P. Brovks, "Edgar' the Aetheling," in *Lexicon des Mittelalters III*, p. 1571.

171 See note 93.

named after its owner. While the name of the Slavic prince still preserved its Anglo-Saxon form, the owner of the church was a Bavarian and still had the name in German form. We know the German forms Otgar, Otkar, Odacar, Otker, Otachar, Otakar, Otakir primarily from Bavaria and Carinthia.[172] At the beginning of the 10th century Count Otakar (*Otachar*) administered the county Leoben on the upper Mur.[173]

In 827 the Bulgarians invaded against the current of the Drava River into Pannonia, ravaged and occupied the principalities of the Transdanubian Slavs along the left-hand bank of the Drava. Transdanubian princes Pribislav, Semika and Stojmír could not handle the defence of their own territory and could only return to their locations after the expulsion of the Bulgarians in 828. Louis the German, who at the head of the Bavarian campaign expelled the

---

[172] As early as the start of the 8th century a Bishop Otkar worked in Bavaria. Albert Hauck, *Kirchengeschichte Deutschlands I* (Leipzig 1898), pp. 361, 367. Otgar was archbishop in Mainz (826–847). Albert Hauck, *Kirchengeschichte Deutschlands II* (Leipzig 1900), pp. 185, 224, 510, 523, 565, 608, 624, 672, 714, 731, 747. Otgar, bishop in Eichstädt (847–881), took part in 857 in the campaigns against the Bohemians. *Ann. Fuld.* ad a. 857, rec. Kurze, p. 47. *MMFH I*, p. 76. Hauck, *Kirchengeschichte II*, pp. 624, 694, 710. In 860 Abbot Otgar (*Otgarius abba*) obtained for his abbey in Niederalteich property from Pribina. *CDES I*, ed. Marsina, no. 27, p. 21. *MMFH III*, Diplomata 38, pp. 68–69. In the confirmation document of Deacon Gundbat from the 880s the name Otachar is among the witnesses. *CDES I*, ed. Marsina, no. 34, pp. 26–27. Count Odacar (*Odacar comes*) was a vassal of King of Lotharingia Zwentibold (895–900). Otgar was a bishop in Speyer (960–970). Albert Hauck, *Kirchengeschichte Deutschlands III* (Leipzig 1936), p. 234. Gams, *Series episcoporum*, p. 314. Donation documents and legal property testimonies for the Salzburg archbishop from years 925, 927, 928, 931 and 935 on the territory of Carinthian Principality name witnesses with the name Otakar (*Otachar, Otker*) 6-times. *UHS I*, ed. Zahn, no. 14, 18, 20, 21, pp. 17–18, 21–23, 24–26. *MHDC III*, ed. Jaksch, no. 89, 91, 94, pp. 33–34, 36–37. Lists of witnesses in donation documents and legal property testimonies from lands of the Styrian March in the following 11th and 12th centuries list this name very often. See edition *UHS I*, ed. Zahn and *MHDC III*, ed. Jaksch, which contain many examples of this name.

[173] Otakar's line came from Steyer Castle on the Enns in Traungau County. His brother Aribo was count in Traungau and margrave of the Eastern March. *MMFH III*, Diplomata 42, 43, 44, 45, 47, 54, 55, pp. 72–78, 79–80, 88–90. *Ann. Fuld.* ad a. 884, 898, rec. Kurze, pp. 110–112, 132. *MMFH I*, pp. 94–96, 107. In 904 Otakar's son Aribo (*Arpo*) acquired property in his father's county Leoben from King Louis the Child. *UHS I*, ed. Zahn, no. 13, pp. 16–17. *Erläuterungen I. Abt., 4. Teil, 1. Heft*, p. 53. The following generations of the Traungau line very much favoured the name Otakar. Otakar II was count in Chiemgau (923–959) and Otakar III, aside from county Chiemgau, acquired in 1056 administration of the Carantanian March (on the middle Mur, from then also called the Styria March, 1056–1059). Ankershofen, *Handbuch II/I*, p. 831, *Regesten und Urkunden* 27, 28, 29a, pp. 76–77. *UHS I*, ed. Zahn, no. 65, 66, pp. 74–76. Grafenauer, *Zgodovina II*, p. 420. Styrian margraves and from year 1180 dukes were Otakar IV (1082–1122), Otakar V (1129–1164), Otakar VI (1164–1192). Posch, *Die Anfänge der Steiermark*, pp. 104–125.

Bulgarians, handed over administration of the liberated territory to his counts. The free places in three Slavic principalities in southern Transdanubia were occupied by three Bavarian counts: Helmwin, Albgar and Pabo. Helmwin got Ptuj Land, Albgar Dudlebia and Pabo Blatenia. The fourth Slavic principality lay in north-eastern Transdanubia outside the military reach of the Bulgarians. Louis's campaign there in the following year had no work to do. Prince Edgar did not have to run away from the Bulgarians and in 828 could alone join Louis and contribute to the defeat of the Bulgarians. Therefore, he could remain in his place even after the great reorganization of the Bavarian border region and after the origin of counties in his vicinity.

Anglo-Saxon names penetrated into Bavaria thanks to the Anglo-Saxon missionaries.[174] The Anglo-Saxon name of a Slavic prince is thus testimony about the close ties of his family with some significant Bavarian magnate lines, which could also ensure him favour of the Bavarian king, and thus also political survival. Edgar and his followers could further rule in his principality, freely subjugated to the Carantanian margrave and from approximately year 840 to Prince Pribina.

Written sources of the 9th century, which tell of history, political-administrative divisions, ecclesiastical organization, settlements and property relations of Carolingian Pannonia, do not notice the territory of Edgar's principality at all. The fates of north-eastern Transdanubia in the 9th century are cloaked in great silence, which contrasts with the rich reports on the southern and north-western parts of Transdanubia.

Salzburg Archbishop Adalvin consecrated on 1 January 865 on Kocel's property *ad Ortahu* the Church of St. Michael Archangel.[175] We must search for *Ortahu* with the Church of St. Michael either in one of the four mentioned Kocel properties (the Blatenian property on the lower Zala, on the Valicka, on the Rába and the property in Ruginesfeld), or we can consider it as a fifth Kocel property in an unknown location of the Pannonian Principality. However, we can hardly identify *Ortahu* with Veszprém, where the episcopal temple consecrated to Michael the Archangel stands.[176] The Veszprém bishopric originated

---

174 Cibulka, *Velkomoravský kostel*, pp. 127–129.
175 *ad Ortahu consecravit ecclesiam in honore sancti Michaelis archangeli in proprietate Chezilonis. Conversio* 13, ed. Wolfram, pp. 56–57, 210. *MMFH III*, p. 319.
176 Thomas von Bogyay on the basis of the patron name of St. Michael and etymological analysis of the name Ortahu identified Ortahu with Veszprém, where today the episcopal St. Michael's Cathedral stands. Bogyay, *Die Kirchenorte*, pp. 58–59, 67–70. Thomas von Bogyay, "Kontinuitätsprobleme im karolingischen Unterpannonien, Methodios Wirken in Mosapurc im Lichte der Quellen und Funde," *Das östliche Mitteleuropa in Geschichte und Gegenwart*, Abb. 2 (Wiesbaden 1966), p. 66. Bogyay, "Die Salzburger Mission in Pannonien,"

under the rule of Hungarian Prince Géza (971–997). Its beginning is associated with the arrival of the mission of Bishop Bruno from St. Gallen to Hungary in 972, who baptised Prince Géza and other Árpáds. Géza's younger brother took the name Michael during the baptism after the Archangel Michael, who also became the patron of the simultaneously established Veszprém bishopric.[177]

Géza's wife Sarolt was based in Veszprém,[178] and she came from the Christian family of Transylvanian Prince Gyula I. Gyula accepted baptism in 953[179] and immediately could have had built for this in his princely seat of Gyulafehérvár (today Alba Iulia, Romania) a church consecrated to St. Michael, which was later elevated to an episcopal cathedral.[180] The Archangel Michael accompanied Gyula's daughter Sarolt from birth and was thus very close to her. When she married Árpád Prince Géza and settled in Veszprém, she took care that the Veszprém episcopal cathedral, established shortly afterward, be consecrated to the Archangel Michael. St. Michael in Veszprém is thus the patron saint of the Árpáds. The Veszprém bishopric did not inherit it from older pre-Hungarian times. The patrocinium of St. Michael the Archangel was not anything unusual in the time of the Árpáds;[181] Árpád Veszprém was not the only place where a church with this consecration stood.[182]

---

pp. 287–288. Thomas von Bogyay rejected the objections made by Katalin H. Gyürky, Péter Váczy, Endre Tóth and István Bóna against the identification of Ortahu with Veszprém. Katalin H. Gyürky, "Die St. Georg – Kapelle in der Burg von Veszprém, Bericht über die Ausgrabungen im Jahre 1957 und ihre wissenschaftliche Ergebnisse," *Acta Archaeologica Academiae Scientiarum Hungariae* 15 (1963), p. 366. Péter Váczy, "Karolingische Kunst in Pannonien. Der Cundpald-Kelch. Évolution générale et dévelopements régionaux en l'histoire de l'art." *Actes du XXIIe Congrés international de l'histoire de l'art, Tome II* (Budapest 1972), p. 328. Tóth, "Zu den historischen Problemen," pp. 117–118. István Bóna, "A népvándorláskor és a korai középkor története Magyarországon," in *Magyarország története. Előzmények magyar történet 1242-ig I/2*, főszerkesztő György Székely (Budapest 1984), p. 1602. Jenő Gutheil, Herwig Wolfram and András Uzsoki accepted the opinion of Thomas von Bogyay on the identification of Ortahu with Veszprém, and most recently Dušan Třeštík rejected it. Jenő Gutheil, *Az Árpád-kori Veszprém* (Veszprém 1977), p. 24, 27. Conversio ed. Wolfram, pp. 140–141. András Uzsoki, "A veszprémi püspökség szent Mihály patrociniuma," in *Egyházak a változó világban. A nemzetközi egyháztörténeti konferencia előadásai, Esztergom 1991 május 29–31*, ed. István Bárdos, Margit Beke (Tatabánya 1992), p. 87. Třeštík, *Vznik*, p. 292.

177 See pp. 329–332.
178 See pp. 329–331.
179 See chapter 13, note 26.
180 See chapter 13, notes 27, 28.
181 Tóth, "Zu den historischen Problemen," p. 118.
182 Sándor Török, "Mi volt a neve a három kabar törzsnek?" *Századok* 116 (1982), no. 5, pp. 993, 1042–1045, 1058–1059. András Mező, *Patrocíniumok a középkori Magyarországon* (Budapest 2003), pp. 278–308.

An older rotunda stood in the vicinity of the cathedral. A small fragment of it is preserved on the south-east wall of the round aisle with traces of a rounded apse on the east side. It was consecrate to George, like the younger octagonal chapel which was built in the 13th century exactly in its place.[183] The Rotunda of St. George was already very ancient at the time when Emeric, the son of Stephen, the first king of Hungary, visited it: *St. Emeric ... entered into the most hoary and ancient (vetustissimam et antiquissimam) church, which was built in the Veszprém Castle (in Besprimiensi civitate) to honour Christ's dearest George.*[184] If the Veszprém Church of St. George was the most hoary and most ancient evidently among all Hungarian churches which stood in the time of Prince Emeric († 1031), then it was older than the neighbouring episcopal Cathedral of St. Michael. Since in the previous pagan period no one built a round church, the rotunda had to stand in the 9th century and serve the Veszprém Christians even after occupation of Transdanubia by the Magyars. St. George was a favourite in the 9th century in Bavaria, primarily in the Regensburg diocese, but we don't find him among the patrocinia of Pribina's and Kocel's churches in Pannonia, known from Conversio, as we do over the whole territory of the Bavarian border marches. If the Veszprém rotunda is safely not a Carolingian building[185] and its patrocinium is not of Bavarian origin, and if it really was already standing in the 9th century, then we can consider it to be of Great Moravian origin.

Even the name Veszprém, derived from the Slavic personal name of Bezpriem, has an old pre-Hungarian origin.[186] Veszprém in the 9th century hardly had

---

183 Gyürky, "Die St. Georgs-Kapelle," pp. 341–408. *Magyarország régészeti topográfiája 2*, főszerkesztő László Gerevich, *Veszprém megye régészeti topográfiája*, ed. István Éri. *A veszprémi járás*; írta István Éri, Márta Kelemen, Péter Németh, István Torma (Budapest 1969), pp. 227–230. Sós, *Die slawische Bevölkerung*, pp. 149–153. Vera Gervers-Molnár, A középkori Magyarország rotundái (Budapest 1972), pp. 10, 28, 30, 61, 62, 103. Mező, *Patrocíniumok*, pp. 113–114.

184 *Legenda sancti Emmerici ducis* 4, SRH II, pp. 453–454.

185 See note 180. Regarding the spread of the cult of St. George in the 9th–11th centuries, see Jiří Sláma, "Svatojiřské kostely na raně středověkých hradištích v Čechách," *Archeologické rozhledy* 29 (1977), no. 2, pp. 269–280. Ratkoš, "Kristianizácia," p. 78.

186 Stanislav, *Slovenský juh v stredoveku I*, pp. 74–75, Stanislav, *Slovenský juh v stredoveku II*, pp. 569–571. Archaelogical finds document the old pre-Hungarian settlement of Veszprém. *Magyarország régészeti topográfiája 2*, ed. Gerevich, *Veszprém megye régészeti topográfiája*, ed. Éri, *A veszprémi járás*; írta Éri, Kelemen, Németh, Torma, pp. 224–256. Veszprém Castle bore its name undoubtedly in 997, when rebellious Prince Koppány besieged it: *Illis forte diebus urbem, que vulgo Bresprem vocatur obsederant. Legenda minor sancti Stephani regis* 3, SRH II, p. 395. According to György Györffy, Stephen I named his nephew Bezprim as the first Veszprém count, or district administrator, who gave the settlement his own name. György Györffy, "A magyar nemzetségtől a vármegyéig, a törzstől

two different names: Bezpriem and Ortahu. Ortahu took its name from a river or stream by which it lay, just as *Knesaha*, *Peiniccaha*[187] or *Peinihhaa*,[188] *Fiskaha*,[189] *Quartinaha*[190] or *Chuartinahu* had.[191] The endings -aha and -ahu come from the Germanic ahwa = water. We don't know that the Séd, flowing below Veszprém Castle, had the name Ortahu in the 9th century. Thus, we don't know where Ortahu lay, certainly not, however, in Veszprém.

All known or approximately known places with churches mentioned in Conversio lay on the territory of the three counties in southern Transdanubia. However, we cannot look for even one of the numerous churches whose position remains unknown in north-eastern Transdanubia. If the Pannonian princes and their people founded churches in these regions, then they could not have avoided Esztergom, Győr, Székesfehérvár, Veszprém, Buda and Visegrád, which have an ancient settlement tradition and exceptional standing in the originating Hungarian state. In the future centres of the Kingdom of Hungary and its ecclesiastical organization, which were already settled in the period of the Roman province, some with a solid stone building and fortifications, the Salzburg archbishop in the 9th century did not consecrate even one of the mentioned 32 churches. It is as if Conversio, who protects the interests of the Salzburg archbishop, completely forgot this most outlying corner of its diocese, hidden beyond the lower Rába and the Bakon Forest.

North-eastern Transdanubia is recalled by Hungarian chroniclers, who tell of the conquest of this land by the Magyars. Hungarian chroniclers also

az országig," *Századok* 92 (1958), no. 1–4, p. 589. Györffy, *István király*, pp. 88, 176, 231, 276, 283. György Györffy, *König Stephan der Heilige* (Budapest 1988), p. 165. *MT I/I*, pp. 807–808. Bezprim was the son of the future Polish Prince Boleslaw the Brave, and his mother was the oldest daughter of Hungarian Prince Géza, who shortly after the wedding Boleslaw was expelled back to Hungary. Bezprim was born in 987. *Thietmari Merseburgensis episcopi Chronicon* IV, 58 (37), post editionem Ioh. M. Lappenbergii recognovit Fridericus Kurze. Scriptores rerum Germanicarum in usum scholarum ex Monumentis Germaniae historicis recusi. (Hannoverae 1889), p. 96. *Thietmari Merseburgensis episcopi Chronicon* IV, 37, curavit Werner Trillmich. Ausgewählte Quellen zur deutsche Geschichte des Mittelalters, Band 9, herausgegeben von Rudolf Buchner, Berlin 1960, p. 174. Szabolcs de Vajay, "Geysa von Ungarn. Familie und Verwandschaft," *Südostforschungen* 21 (München 1962), pp. 58, 69, 73, 88–89. Mór Wertner, *Az Árpádok családi története* (Nagy Becskereken 1892), pp. 33–35. Veszprém hardly got its name only after the rule of Stephen I from the minor figure Bezprim. Vajay, *Großfürst Geysa*, pp. 88–89.

187 See note 120.
188 See note 138.
189 See chapter 4, note 63.
190 *Conversio* 13, Wolfram, pp. 78–79, 141, 208, 212–213. *Conversio* ed. Kos, pp. 99–100, 139. *MMFH III*, pp. 320–322. *MMFH III*, Diplomata 38, p. 68. See note 86.
191 *MMFH III*, Diplomata 30, pp. 59–60. See note 89.

added to their stories a portion of the local tradition, which preserved the memory of the rule of Svätopluk and a memory on the opposition of the Great Moravian military, with whom Árpád's Magyars met near these places.[192] The Great Moravia tradition which the chroniclers found in the anonymous northeast was a belated response to dramatic events, which in the first centuries of Hungarian history still remained in the tales of the domestic population. This explains not only the silence of the Carolingian sources of the 9th century but also the additional fate of Edgar's principality.

Conversio originated in 870,[193] when Prince Kocel ruled over the Salzburg part of Transdanubia. North-eastern Transdanubia at the time of origin of Conversio was already out of reach of the Salzburg archbishop and beyond the borders of Kocel's principality. How long was this territory under Carolingian dominion? When did Great Moravia cross its borders on the Danube and acquire this territory?

---

192 See pp. 282–299.
193 An unknown author wrote Conversio according to the dating in the conclusion of his work 75 years after the assigning of the Pannonian territory to the Salzburg diocese. *Conversio* 14, ed. Wolfram, pp. 25, 26–27, 78–81, 202. *Conversio*, ed. Kos, pp. 13, 101–105, 140. *MMFH III*, p. 322.

CHAPTER 7

The Mojmírs in Nitria

1   Christianization

In 833 Mojmír opened the conquered and still then pagan Nitria to the Christian mission. Certainly to those who two years before had baptised his Moravia, that is the Passau mission. The common ecclesiastical administration of both principalities was important for the political unity of Mojmír's enlarged state.[1] From those times *the bishop of the city Passau, in whose diocese live the people of that country from the beginning of their baptism* (that is from years 831 and 833), *came there without any obstacles, whenever he was requested or the obligation led him, and he took part with his own and with the locals (cum suis et etiam ibi) at a synodial gathering; and he did all that was needed in his own power, and no one stood in opposition to him.*[2]

Bavarian bishops established archipresbyterates on the marginal territories of their dioceses. An archpresbyter was a representative of the bishop and the closest representative of priests and missionaries who operated there. The establishing of an archpresbyterate in Moravia and after Pribina's expulsion in Nitra, too, was probably handled by Passau Bishop Reginhar (818–838).[3] He undoubtedly cooperated with Prince Mojmír on this. Thus, archpresbyters and priests from Great Moravia appointed by him attended the mentioned synodial gathering of the Passau bishop. These were the *Latin and Frankish archpriests with priests and disciples*, for whom Constantine and Methodius later must

---

[1] The only proof that the Salzburg archbishop considered Pribina's Nitria as his missionary territory is the consecrating of the church in Nitra in 828. Moravia, which was the missionary territory of the Passau bishop, became in 831 a direct component of the Passau diocese. After conquering Nitria, Mojmír took care that it was baptised. He certainly handed over this work to Passau Bishop Reginhar and his priests, who worked in Moravia. Nitria, like Moravia, also became a part of this diocese, from which it was baptised, that is from Passau.

[2] *MMFH III*, Epistolae 109, pp. 234–235. Heinz Dopsch, "Passau als Zentrum der Slawenmission. Ein Beitrag zur Frage des 'Grossmährischen Reiches'," *Südostdeutsches Archiv* 28–29 (1985), pp. 5–28. Steinhübel, "Štyri veľkomoravské biskupstvá," p. 24. Steinhübel, "Die Grossmährischen Bistümer," pp. 2–3. Lysý, *Moravania*, pp. 182–183.

[3] Vladimír Vavřínek, "Die Christianisation und Kirchenorganisation Grossmährens," *Historica* 7 (1963), pp. 25–26. Vavřínek, *Cyril a Metoděj*, p. 105. Dvorník, *Byzantské misie*, pp. 96, 130.

have had to handle disputes on church dogma.[4] The Church of St. Emmeram, built by Prince Pribina, could have become Nitra's archpresbyterate church.

Proof of the success of the Bavarian missionaries are two churches that archaeologists have found, one at Devín[5] and the other on Bratislava's castle hill.[6] The oldest Bratislava church was consecrated to the Most Holy Saviour. This patrocinium is testimony of the link between Bratislava (then known as Preslava) with the Abbey of the Most Holy Saviour in Kremsmünster, which Bavarian Duke Tassilo founded in 777.[7]

The Most Holy Saviour was in the 9th through the 11th centuries a typical missionary patrocinium. If this patrocinium was in Bratislava, which stood directly at the entry point from the Eastern March into Nitria, then Bratislava was the first castle in the Nitrian Principality which the Bavarian missionaries consecrated. They could not have gone around Bratislava, and when they passed through it, they certainly stopped in it. In March 828 Frankish King and Emperor Louis the Pious gifted to Kremsmünster Abbey land in Grunzvitigau in the Eastern March. Kremsmünster monks built *a church and other buildings* on their new land, which lay halfway between Kremsmünster and Bratislava.[8] It was these monks who could have brought Christianity to Bratislava (similarly as in the mentioned Grunzvitigau) and could have shared in the establishing and construction of the Bratislava castle church.

Kremsmünster lay in the middle of Bavarian county Traungau. The St. Emmeram patrocinum of Pribina's church in Nitra, which was consecrated

---

4   ŽK 15, *MMFH II*, pp. 102–103. Steinhübel, "Štyri veľkomoravské biskupstvá," p. 24. Steinhübel, "Die Grossmährischen Bistümer," pp. 5–6.

5   Veronika Plachá – Jana Hlavicová – Igor Kelller, *Slovanský Devín* (Bratislava 1990), pp. 100–102. Martin Illáš, "Predrománsky kostol na Devíne," *Historický zborník* 21 (2011), no. 1, pp. 19–39. Alexander T, Ruttkay, "Najstaršie sakrálne stavby na Slovensku ako odraz christianizácie a budovania kresťanských inštitúcií v 9.–11. storočí," in *Bratia, ktorí menili svet*, ed. Panis, Ruttkay, Turčan, pp. 86–87. Ján Steinhübel, "Moravania, Chorváti a Bulhari v plánoch pápežskej kúrie," in *Bratia, ktorí menili svet*, ed. Panis, Ruttkay, Turčan, p. 162. Andrej Botek, *Veľkomoravské kostoly na Slovensku a odraz ich tradície v neskoršom období* (Bratislava 2014), pp. 80–91.

6   Tatiana Štefanovičová – Andrej Fiala, "Veľkomoravská bazilika, kostol sv. Salvátora a pohrebisko na Bratislavskom hrade," *Historica, zborník FFUK* (Bratislava 1967), pp. 151–216. Tatiana Štefanovičová, *Bratislavský hrad v 9.–12. storočí* (Bratislava 1975), pp. 57–62. Andrej Fiala, "Výtvarný prejav staroslovanskej baziliky na Bratislavskom hrade," in *Byzantská kultúra a Slovensko. Zborník SNM. Archeológia*, supplementum 2, ed. Vladimír Turčan (Bratislava 2007), pp. 103–114. Ruttkay, "Najstaršie sakrálne stavby na Slovensku," p. 86. Botek, *Veľkomoravské kostoly*, pp. 65–80.

7   *MMFH III*, Diplomata 1, 2, pp. 15–19. Wolfram, *Salzburg, Bayern, Österreich*, pp. 356–379.

8   *MMFH III*, Diplomata 9, pp. 24–27. Herwig Wolfram, *Österreichische Geschichte 378–907. Grenzen und Räume. Geschichte Österreichs vor seiner Entstehung* (Wien 1995), pp. 89, 120–121, 133–135, 310, 361, 364, 406, Note 375, p. 420, Note 354.

in 828 by Salzburg Archbishop Adalram, also has its origins in county Traungau. Bratislava was the first castle on the road from Bavaria and the Eastern March to Nitra and to the whole of the Nitrian Principality. Thanks to this position it could not have lagged behind Nitra in the accepting of Christianity. Therefore, the Bratislava Church of the Most Holy Saviour could rank among the oldest churches in all of Nitria.

2   The End of Rule of Mojmír I and the Accession of Rastislav

In the opinion of the East Frankish king, the Moravians belonged *to the most distant ends of the kingdom*, thus, they were a marginal component of his empire.[9] Other Slavic tribes that settled immediately beyond the empire's borders on the lower Elbe, Saale, Šumava and middle Danube were given the same attention. Like Carantanian Prince Borut, who handed over his son Gorazd and nephew Hotimír to the Bavarian duke, Mojmír I, too, could send, among other hostages, his nephew and successor Rastislav to Regensburg.[10]

At the end of Mojmír's rule, the Moravians wanted to rid themselves of independence on the neighbouring empire. East Frankish King Louis the German attacked the Moravians *for their efforts at defection* (*defectionem molientes*) in August 846: *Here he arranged and settled everything according to his own considerations and he appointed Rastislav, nephew of Mojmír, as the prince.*[11] Rastislav could have obtained Louis's trust during his stay in Bavaria, from where Louis could have taken him to Moravia with him. Louis thus knew Rastislav well and trusted him.

In August 846 Pribina's hope for a return to Nitria ended. If Louis didn't want to anger the Moravians too much, then he could not take over Nitria and return it to Pribina. He satisfied Pribina at least somewhat with donations in Pannonia. Still in November of this same year he gifted him property on the Valicka River[12] and in the following year an entire fief on the lower Zala,[13] by which he even more tightly attached him to his new principality.

Bulgarian Khagan Boris (852–889) began his rule with an attack on Frankish territory. He allied himself with domestic antagonists of King Louis the German; he accepted gifts from them, and in 853 the Bulgarian military in

---

9   *Decreta synodi Mogutiensis*, MMFH IV, pp. 34–35. Třeštík, *Vznik*, p. 154.
10 Cibulka, *Veľkomoravský kostel*, p. 278. Kučera, *Postavy*, p. 91. Třeštík, *Vznik*, p. 154.
11 *Ann. Fuld.* ad a. 846, rec Kurze, p. 36. MMFH I, pp. 71–72. Lysý, *Moravania*, pp. 171–181.
12 See chapter 6, note 76.
13 See chapter 6, note 77.

alliance with Slavs attacked Louis's empire.[14] Louis the German was able to repulse the attack of the Bulgarians and the Slavs allied with them.[15] The allies of the Bulgarians were obviously those Slavs whose messengers were in Mainz together with the Bulgarians in October 852[16] and in 845 in Paderborn.[17] Together with the Bulgarian messengers, emissaries of the southern Obotrites and other Slavs from the Tisza River basin, who recognized the rule of the Bulgarian khagan, they appeared before the East Frankish king.[18]

Great Moravian Prince Rastislav was at the beginning a peaceful neighbour to the east of Louis's empire, and attentive Frankish chroniclers wrote nothing about Rastislav and his land for several years. He came to their attention only when he ceased making allowances for the interests of the East Frankish empire. In 852 Rastislav offered asylum to a leading Frankish refugee, Albgis, whom King Louis had condemned at a synod in Mainz for the kidnapping of another's wife.[19] In 854 he openly supported the rebellion of Margrave Ratbot of the Eastern and Carantanian Marches. Louis the German recalled Ratbot five years later: *He abandoned us with all of his forces and also breached an oath of loyalty with all faithlessness.*[20] If Ratbot rebelled against Louis the German and allied himself with Rastislav, then he had to abandon Pribina, who until his death remained loyal to King Louis[21] and was enemy to Rastislav. King Louis deposed Ratbot, but Rastislav remained obstinate.[22] Therefore, so that his Bohemian allies could not come to his aid, in March 855 a smaller Bavarian army led by Ernest, one of the Bavarians counts, fell upon the Bohemians.[23] Perhaps by the end of summer 855 Louis the German rushed with a large army into Moravia and unsuccessfully laid siege to Rastislav in his fortress (probably in Mikulčice) and ravaged the surrounding countryside. Upon retreat he lost a

---

14   *Bulgari, sociatis sibi Sclavis et, ut fertur, a nostris muneribus invitati, adversus Lodowicus Germaniae regem acriter permoventur, sed Domino pugnante vincuntur.* Ann. Bert. ad a. 853, rec. Waitz, p. 43. MMFH I, p. 52.
15   See note 14.
16   Ann. Fuld. ad a. 852, rec. Kurze, p. 42. MMFH I, p. 74.
17   Ann. Fuld. ad a. 845, rec. Kurze, p. 35. MMFH I, p. 71.
18   Lubomír E. Havlík, "Bulgaria and Moravia between Byzantium, the Franks and Rome," Paleobulgarica 13 (1989), no. 1, p. 8. Třeštík, Vznik, pp. 162–163.
19   See note 9.
20   MMFH III, Diplomata 25, pp. 48–50.
21   Třeštík, Vznik, p. 163.
22   *Rantopot comes plagis orientalibus terminum dimisit. Rastislao carmulam fecit.* Excerpta Aventini ex Annalibus Iuvavensibus antiquis derivati ad a. 854, MMFH I, p. 382. Třeštík, Vznik, pp. 163, 302.
23   MMFH III, Diplomata 23, pp. 45–46. Ann. Bert. ad a. 855, rec. Waitz, p. 46. MMFH I, p. 52. Třeštík, Vznik, pp. 163–164.

large part of his military and could not prevent Rastislav's counterattack into the Eastern March.[24]

In 854–855 the Moravians managed to succeed at what they had unsuccessfully tried to do in 846. The success of the anti-Frank uprising of the Moravians was a breaking point in the relations of Great Moravia toward the East Frankish empire. While there are no reports on the Frankish-Moravian conflicts previous to this, from this point on they occur regularly. The change of Rastislav's policies to being anti-Frank is testimony of the rising power of Great Moravia, which became the most resolute antagonist on the eastern border of the Franks.

After beating back the Bulgarian attack into East Francia, Trpimir I, Prince of the Dalmatian Croats and an ally of Louis the German, attacked the Bulgarians. Then Khagan Boris, after several years (854–860) of unsuccessful battles, concluded peace with Trpimir.[25] Rastislav was able to take advantage of the Bulgarians being busy in the war with the Croatians in order to expand his own state to the east with additional territory of the Carpathian Basin interior, which the Bulgarians had an interest in. The Croatian-Bulgarian peace, concluded in 860, helped to end the old animosity of the Bulgarians and the Franks.

During the Frankish-Moravian wars at the time of Rastislav's and later Svätopluk's rule, the Bohemians were allies of the Moravians and they fought on the side of the Moravians from year 846 onward.[26] Bohemian Prince Vistrach for *many years*, perhaps from 846, rebelled against the Franks, and his son Slavitah continued in this antagonism.[27] In 857 Slavitah and Rastislav countered an attack from Bavaria and the Eastern March. Slavitah did not defend his castle and had to save himself by fleeing to Rastislav in Moravia.[28]

---

24   *Ann. Fuld.* ad a. 855, rec. Kurze, pp. 45–46. *MMFH I*, p. 75. *Herimanni Augiensis Chronicon* ad a. 855, *MMFH I*, p. 160.
25   Constantine Porphyrogenitus, *De administarando imperio* 31, ed. Moravcsik, pp. 150–151. Ferdinand von Šišić, *Geschichte der Kroaten I* (Zagreb 1917), pp. 80–81. Zlatarski, "Veľká Morava a Bulharsko," p. 278. Vasil Nikolov Zlatarski, *Istorija na bălgarskata dăržava prez srednite vekove I/2*, Sofija 1971, p. 10. Vjakoslav Klaić, *Povijest Hrvata od najstărijich vremena do svršetka XIX stoljeća I* (Zagreb 1972), pp. 76–77.
26   *Ann. Fuld.* ad a. 846, rec. Kurze, p. 36. *MMFH I*, pp. 71–72. Třeštík, *Vznik*, pg. 151–155.
27   *Ann. Fuld.* ad a. 857, rec. Kurze, p. 47. *MMFH I*, p. 76. *Excerpta Aventini ex Ann. Iuvav. ant.* ad a. 857, *MMFH I*, pp. 382–383. Steinhübel, *Kapitoly*, pp. 60–63.
28   Třeštík, *Vznik*, pp. 170–173. Steinhübel, Kapitoly, pp. 63–65.

3   Nitrian Prince Svätopluk

Under the rule of Great Moravian Prince Rastislav (846–870) his nephew Svätopluk became the appanaged prince of Nitria (Nitraland). The Annals of Fulda mention the Nitrian Principality as a *regnum Zuentibaldi*, that is the country in which Svätopluk ruled. This country of Svätopluk is clearly differentiated from Rastislav's Moravia.[29] The Roman Curia knew well of two different Great Moravian principalities, of Rastislav's and Svätopluk's. Pope Hadrian II addressed in 869 a letter *Gloria in excelsis* to Rastislav, Svätopluk and Kocel, whose principalities were under papal decision to create Methodius's archdiocese.[30] The Roman Curia and office learned of the important position of Svätopluk from Methodius, who together with his brother in June 867 left Moravia, and by the end of the year were being welcomed by Pope Hadrian in Rome.[31]

Svätopluk already ruled in Nitria at the time of Methodius's departure from Moravia. If he had such power that in three years he was able to turn against Rastislav, then we must look for the beginning of his rule in Nitria in earlier times. If Rastislav and Svätopluk together sent a deputation to Constantinople to Emperor Michael III at this time, that is in 862 (or 863), he was not only the Nitrian Prince but also Rastislav's co-ruler.[32] Svätopluk was not one of those small second-level princes with whom Rastislav only *consulted* on sending a deputation, so that he later *sent* the deputation himself. Svätopluk had the same role as Rastislav in this whole event. It was he who not only advised but also took advice and mainly who sent. Rastislav and Svätopluk *sent* the deputation to Constantinople together and addressed the emperor: *Rastislav, a Slavic prince, with Svätopluk sent from Moravia to Emperor Michael, saying this* ...[33] Svätopluk was thus the Nitrian Prince and Rastislav's co-ruler at the latest by the beginning of the 860s, but probably in the 850s. And like Rastislav he certainly consulted *with his princes*,[34] who lived under his rule in Nitria.

29   *Ann. Fuld.* ad a. 869, rec. Kurze, p. 69. *MMFH I*, p. 83. For the meaning of the word *regnum* in the medieval period, see František Graus, "Rex – dux Moraviae," in *Sborník prací filosofické fakulty Brněnské university. Řada historická* IX, C 7 (1960), pp. 181–190. Hans-Werner Goetz, "Regnum. Zum politischen Denken der Karolingerzeit," in *Zeitschrift für Rechtsgeschichte. Germanische Abteilung* 104 (1987), pp. 110–147. Lysý, *Moravania*, pg. 107–112.
30   ŽM 8, *MMFH II*, pp. 147–148.
31   ŽK 15–18, *MMFH II*, pp. 105–115. ŽM 5–7, *MMFH II*, pp. 145–147. Třeštík, *Počátky*, pp. 276–278.
32   Richard Marsina, "Svätopluk, legenda a skutočnosť," in *Svätopluk 894–1994. Materiály z konferencie organizovanej Archeologickým ústavom SAV v Nitre v spolupráci so Slovenskou historickou spoločnosťou pri SAV, Nitra 3.–6. október 1994*, ed. Richard Marsina, Alexander Ruttkay (Nitra 1997), pp. 156–157. Třeštík, *Vznik*, p. 195.
33   ŽM 5, *MMFH II*, pp. 143–144.
34   ŽK 14, *MMFH II*, p. 98.

The East Frankish king needed an equally matched replacement for Rastislav, whom he removed in 846. Therefore, his young nephew and prospective successor Svätopluk obviously went to replace him. This stay left its mark on Svätopluk's upbringing, which was manifested in his later sticking to the Latin liturgy. Since Rastislav obeyed the East Frankish king for several years, Svätopluk could return home. More exactly, the East Frankish king delivered Svätopluk, who had been raised in his own court and well orientated in the surroundings of the East Frankish empire, to Rastislav, and he had to satisfy him with princely appanage and co-rule. The East Frankish king thus strengthened the dualism of Mojmír's state, which was its great weak point. Later disagreements and conflicts between the main Moravian prince and the Nitrian prince beneath him were a welcome opportunity for divisive intervention of the neighbouring Carolingian power.

According to Chronicle of the Priest of Duklja, Svätopluk ruled for 40 years and 4 (possibly only 3) months.[35] If Svätopluk died in 894, then 894−40 = 854. If we take into account Duklja's day of Svätopluk's death, 17 March, and to the mentioned 40 years and 4 (or 3) months, then Svätopluk would have begun to rule in 853. Since he became the Great Moravian prince only in 871, then 853 may be the beginning of his previous rule in Nitria.[36] The Chronicle of the Priest of Duklja originated only in the 2nd half of 12th-century Duklja (a Serbian principality on the territory of Montenegro). Svätopluk's rule in Duklja

---

35   *Regnavit praeterea rex sanctissimus XL annos et menses quatuor ... et septima decima die intrante mense martio mortuus est sepultus que est in ecclesia sanctae Marie in civitate Dioclitana honorofice cum magnis exequiis. Presbyteri Diocleatis regum Sclavorum* IX, MMFH I, p. 245. *I potom blaženi kralj kraljeva lit četrdeset i miseci tri s voljom [onoga] ki sve može.... I sedminade [se]te dan umri, na devet miseca marča i pogreben bi i crikvi blažene Marije u gradu Dokoliji s velikim počtenjem.* Lubomír E. Havlík, *Dukljanská kronika a Dalmatská legenda* (Praha 1976), pp. 82, 43–44. Marsina, "Svätopluk, legenda a skutočnosť," p. 156. The recollection on Svätopluk could have gotten to the western Balkan with Moravian emigration, which Constantine Porphyrogenitus mentions: *and the Turks* (= Hungarians) *came and utterly ruined them and possessed their country, in which even now thei live. And those of the folk who were left were scattered and fied for refuge to the adjacent nations, to the Bulgarians and Turks and Croats and to the rest of the nations.* Constantine Porphyrogenitus, *De administrando imperio* 41, ed. Moravcsik, pp. 180–181. Konstantinos Porfyrogennétos, *De administrando imperio* 41, MMFH III, pp. 399–400.

36   Václav Richter imagined that a rebellion broke out in Nitria in 846, which the Moravians had conquered even before 822. Then East Frankish King Louis the German interfered and not only appointed Rastislav to rule in Moravia, but at the same time also Svätopluk in Nitra. Václav Richter, "Die Anfänge der grossmährischen Architektur," in *Magna Moravia. Spisy University J. E. Purkyně v Brně, Filosofická fakulta* 102 (Praha 1965), p. 134. And according to Matúš Kučera, Louis the German handed over rule in Nitria to Svätopluk in 846, and furthermore, Svätopluk allegedly was from that moment also king. Matúš Kučera, *Kráľ Svätopluk (830?–846–894)* (Martin 2010), pp. 31–32, 37–38.

is invented, but Duklja's length of Svätopluk's rule somewhat mysteriously is not in conflict with known and reliably documented Great Moravian history, and it seems that it importantly and suitably adds to it.

Svätopluk as a major Moravian captive in the court of East Frankish King Louis the German was a guarantee of peace and obedience of the Moravians towards the neighbouring empire. When Svätopluk returned home, perhaps in 853, the Moravians began to be rebellious, and in 854 they supported the revolt of Margrave Ratbot.

4 Castles in Moravia and in Nitria

Meanwhile, in August 846 the East Frankish king *arranged and settled everything according to his own consideration* in Moravia; in the summer of 855 he was not successful. He clashed with Rastislav, who was *fortified by ... a very strong wall*.[37] The Moravians in the peaceful period from 846–854 expanded the Morava Castle (in today's Mikulčice) from the original 4 hectares to 7.2 in a south-westerly direction and thoroughly rebuilt it. The wooden palisades were replaced by a massive rampart. A new 3.5 m thick stone wall built from mortar from dried deposited stones rested on a clay escarpment braced by a wooden chamber construction. The entire fortification, perhaps 9 m wide at the base and at least as high, protected the channel and arms of the Morava River from all sides.[38] Other Moravian castles also got (either then or sometimes later) a massive wooden-earthen escarpment with a facing stone wall. The most important of these were Pohansko near Břeclav,[39] Staré Zámky in Brno-Líšeň,[40] Zelená hora near Vyškov, Znojmo, Rajhrad, Mařín and Podbranč.[41] The large

---

37 *firmissimo ... vallo munitum. Ann. Fuld.* ad a. 855, rec. Kurze, p. 45. *MMFH I*, p. 75.
38 According to the oldest opinion of Josef Poulík, the massive fortifications at Mikulčice originated in year 800. Poulik, *Mikulčice*, pp. 48, 52–54. Michal Lutovský, *Encyklopedie slovanské archeologie v Čechách, na Moravě a ve Slezsku* (Praha 2001), pp. 184–186. Archaeologists on the basis of new studies consider the massive Great Moravian rampart as younger. They more probably built it *only in the late 9th century*. Lumír Poláček, "Mikulčice 60 rokov po svojom objave," *Historická revue* 25 (2014), no. 12, pp. 35–36.
39 Petr Dresler – Renáta Přichystalová, "Břeclav – Pohansko. Veľkomoravské hradisko," *Historická revue* 25 (2014), no. 12, pp. 45–50.
40 Čeněk Staňa, "Velkomoravské hradiště Staré Zámky u Líšně. Stavební vývoj," *Monumenta tutela. Ochrana pamiatok* 8 (1972), pp. 115–119, 124–126, 134–135.
41 Čeněk Staňa, "Pustiměřský hrad," *Archaeologica historica* 18 (1993), p. 184. Staňa, "Archäologische Erforschung mährischer Höhenburgwälle," pp. 267–281. Viera Drahošová, "Podbranč-Starý hrad," *Záhorie* IV (1995), no. 4, pp. 18–19. Bohuslav Klíma, "Archeologický výskum MU na velkomoravském výšinném hradišti sv. Hypolita ve Znojmě," in *Velká*

settlement Uherské Hradiště (Ostrov svatého Jiří) and Staré Město (Na Valách) were further protected by only a light palisade fortification. The massive rampart with the facing stone wall stood only in certain places.[42] At the end of the 8th century the older fortified settlement of Povel, near Olomouc, died out, and a new Olomouc Castle grew at a distance in the ravelin of the later Přemyslid castle.[43] In the south, the forward Devín Castle was protected by an old late-Roman bulwark, which the Moravians could only fortify and supplement with a palisade.[44]

Some time at the beginning of Svätopluk's rule of Nitria the castle in Nitra was thoroughly rebuilt. The older palisade was replaced with a massive rampart (bulwark 1), braced with a wooden grating construction and reinforced on the exterior and interior side with a wall of broken stones piled without mortar, 110–150 cm thick. The Great Moravian rampart was 5 metres thick.[45] Stone

---

Morava mezi východem a západem, ed. Galuška, Kouřil, Měřínsky, pp. 229–240. Bohuslav Klíma, "Objev části velkomoravského pohřebiště pod středověkým až novověkým hřbitovem u kostela sv. Hypolita ve Znojmě-Hradišti," in *Zborník na počesť Dariny Bialekovej*, ed. Gabriel Fusek (Nitra 2004), pp. 179–190. Zdeněk Měřínsky, "Die Zentren Großmährens," in *Velká Morava mezi východem a západem*, ed. Galuška, Kouřil, Měřínsky, pp. 297–304. Lutovský, *Encyklopedie*, pp. 35, 38, 148, 220–221, 280–282, 375–376.

42   Vilém Hrubý, *Staré Město. Velkomoravský Velehrad* (Praha 1965), pp. 214–233. Luděk Galuška, "Velkomoravská hradba v Uherském Hradišti – Rybárnách," *Archeologické rozhledy* 58 (2006), pp. 486–510. Luděk Galuška, "Die großmährische Siedlungsagglomeration Staré Město – Uherské Hradiště und das Problem ihrer Gliederung anhand der Befestigungen," in *Burg – Vorburg – Suburbium. Zur Problematik der Nebenareale frühmittelalterlicher Zentren. Internationale Tagungen in Mikulčice VII*, herausgegeben von Ivana Boháčová und Lumír Poláček (Brno 2008), pp. 169–178. Luděk Galuška, "Veligrad Veľkej Moravy. Sídelná aglomerácia Staré Město – Uherské Hradiště," *Historická revue* 25 (2014), no. 12, pp. 39–44. Lutovský, *Encyklopedie*, pp. 307–308.

43   Bláha, *Topografie*, pp. 184–187. Josef Bláha, "Archeologické poznatky vývoju a významu Olomouce," in *Velká Morava mezi východem a západem*, ed. Galuška, Kouřil, Měřínsky, pp. 41–68.

44   *Pramene I/1*, ed. Bialeková, pp. 26, 32–33. *Pramene I/2*, ed. Bialeková, p. 307. Plachá – Hlavicová – Keller, *Slovanský Devín*, pp. 77–89. Štefanovičová et al., *Najstaršie dejiny Bratislavy*, pp. 308–320. Vladimír Turčan et al., *Veľkomoravské hradiská* (Bratislava 2012), pp. 22–31.

45   This double-layered rampart covered two pit-houses in the eastern courtyard of the castle and three skeletal graves from the 8th or possibly the 9th century (two ended up under the fortifications on the edge of the eastern courtyard and one underneath the western fortification on the western edge of the southern courtyard). Later graves, which lay immediately by the internal and external wall of the double-layered rampart and respected its course, were sunk at the time when the rampart still stood, according to their furnishings, perhaps from the mid-9th century to the first half of the 10th century. Two graves were discovered in the casemate of the south-eastern bastion in the close vicinity of the interior stone wall of the rampart and four others at the opposite end of the castle, on

from the ruins of the mentioned (perhaps antique) walled building, whose remains lay beneath the northern wing of the bishop's palace, were placed into both stone walls.[46]

The Nitrian Principality had, in addition to Nitra, other castles that were protected by a wide earthen-wood rampart, reinforced (aside from Ostrá Skala, which was protected by its inaccessible position and perhaps also Bratislava) by a facing wall made of stacked quarry stone. A palisade stood atop the rampart.[47] Bratislava (then called Preslava) protected the south-western entry point to Nitria via the Danube.[48] The southern Danubian border was also

---

the narrow area between the exterior stone wall of the rampart and the marginal steep western slope. Most important for dating the ramparts is one of the two mentioned graves in the casemate (grave 1/91), which according to earrings with a tubular necklace can be dated to the middle, at the latest, however, to the second third of the 9th century. Peter Bednár – Ivan Staník, "Archeologický a stavebno-historický výskum Nitrianskeho hradu v rokoch 1988–1991," in *Nitra. Príspevky k najstarším dejinám mesta*, ed. Karol Pieta (Nitra 1993), pp. 129–131. Bednár, "Nitriansky hrad v 9. storočí a jeho význam v sídliskovej štruktúre veľkomoravskej Nitry," in *Svätopluk 894–1994*, ed. Marsina, Ruttkay, pg. 20–21, 28–31. Bednár, "Die Entwicklung," pp. 371–379. Bednár *Nitriansky hrad v 9. až 13. storočí. Autoreferát dizertácie*, pp. 9–11. Bednár, "Sídlisková štruktúra," pp. 31–32. *Dejiny Nitry*, ed. Fusek, Zemene, pp. 99–102. Bednár, "Nitriansky hrad v 9. storočí," in *Bojná*, ed. Pieta, Ruttkay, Ruttkay, pp. 205–216, F 83. Bednár – Samuel, "Nitriansky hrad na prelome tisícročí," in *Slovensko vo včasnom stredoveku*, ed. Ruttkay, Ruttkay, Šalkovský, pp. 150–152. Turčan et al., *Veľkomoravské hradiská*, pp. 66–79. Bednár – Šimkovic, "Opevnenie Nitrianskeho hradu," in *Kolíska kresťanstva*, ed. Judák, Bednár, Medvecký, pp. 136–138. Ruttkay, "Mocenské centrá Nitrianskeho kniežatstva," in *Bratia, ktorí menili svet*, ed. Panis, Ruttkay, Turčan, pp. 134–137. Matej Ruttkay – Peter Bednár, "Nitra. Významné mocenské centrum Veľkej Moravy," *Historická revue* 25 (2014), no. 12, pp. 51–57.

46   See chapter 1, note 13.

47   Peter Šalkovský, "K vývoju a štruktúre slovanského osídlenia v hornatých oblastiach Slovenska," in *IV. medzinárodný kongres slovanskej archeológie, Sofia, 15.–22. 9. 1980, zborník referátov ČSSR* (Nitra 1980), pp. 168, 170. Štefanovičová, *Osudy starých Slovanov*, pp. 70–77. Darina Bialeková, "Zur Datierung archäologischer Quellen vom Ende des 8. bis Mitte des 9. Jh. im nördlichen Teil des Karpatenbeckens," in *Ethnische und kulturelle Verhältnisse*, ed. Bialeková, Zábojník, pp. 249–256. Darina Bialeková, "Das Gebiet der Slowakei vom Zusammenbruch des awarischen Kaganats bis zur Entstehung Großmährens," in *Central Europe in 8th–10th Centuries. International Scientific Conference, Bratislava, October 2–4, 1995*, ed. Dušan Čaplovič, Ján Doruľa, Bratislava 1997, pp. 31–39.

48   They reinforced the oldest rampart with wooden chambers of size 110 × 150 cm. It was not possible to determine the original width of the rampart, and no traces of a facing stone wall were found. Štefanovičová, *Bratislavský hrad v 9.–12. storočí*, pp. 21–35, 47, 50–57. *Pramene I/1*, ed. Bialeková, pp. 21–22. Štefanovičová et al., *Najstaršie dejiny Bratislavy*, pp. 295–305. Tatiana Štefanovičová – Joachim Henning – Matej Ruttkay, "Možnosti prezentácie veľkomoravských archeologických pamiatok na Bratislavskom hrade," in *Bojná*, ed. Pieta, Ruttkay, Ruttkay, pp. 237–246, F 76–81. Ruttkay, "Mocenské centrá

guarded by Mužla.[49] On the eastern edge of the Little Carpathians, aside from the already mentioned Bratislava, stood Neštich (near Svätý Jur)[50] and Molpír (near Smolenice).[51] Along the road from Nitra north to Vistulia (Vistulaland) stood Prievidza-Hradec,[52] Vyšehrad[53] and Ostrá Skala in Orava.[54] The valley

Nitrianskeho kniežatstva," in *Bratia, ktorí menili svet*, ed. Panis, Ruttkay, Turčan, p. 129. Turčan et al., *Veľkomoravské hradiská*, pp. 32–37.

[49] Milan Hanuliak – Ivan Kuzma – Peter Šalkovský, *Mužla-Čenkov I. Osídlenie z 9.–12. storočia* (Nitra 1993). Milan Hanuliak, "Methodik der Bearbeitung der Keramikkollektion aus Mužľa-Čenkov und ihre Ergebnisse," in *Slawische Keramik in Mitteleuropa vom 8. bis zum 11. Jahrhundert – Terminologie und Beschreibung. Internationale Tagungen in Mikulčice 2*, ed. Lumír Poláček (Brno 1995), p. 45. Turčan et al., *Veľkomoravské hradiská*, pp. 62–65. Milan Hanuliak, "Opevnené sídlisko v Mužle – Čenkove," in *Hradiská – svedkovia dávnych čias. Zborník odborných príspevkov o hradiskách a ich obyvateľoch*, redaktor a editor Peter Jenčík, Víťazoslav Struhár (Dolná Mariková 2015), pp. 163–173, 267.

[50] Zdeněk Farkaš, "Ojedinelé nálezy zo Svätého Jura," *AVANS v r. 1993* (Nitra 1995), p. 40. Turčan, "Príspevok," in *Zborník SNM* 94 (2000), *Archeológia* 10, pp. 123–136. Turčan et al., *Archeologické pamiatky*, pp. 38–41. Turčan et al., *Veľkomoravské hradiská*, pp. 104–107. Július Vavák, "Včasnostredoveké hrady na juhozápade Malých Karpát," in *Hradiská – svedkovia dávnych čias*, ed. Jenčík, Struhár, pp. 103–106, 110–111. Július Vavák, *Pevnosť v Malých Karpatoch. Vznik, význam a úloha výšinného centra vo Svätom Jure* (Pezinok 2019), pp. 55–115, 135–138.

[51] Slavs were also settled in the hill-fort from the Hallstatt period at Molpír, which guarded the road through the Little Carpathians to Moravia. *Významné slovanské náleziská*, ed. Chropovský, pp. 187–189. Sigrid Dušek, "Veľkomoravské pohrebisko v Smoleniciach," *Slovenská archeológia* 27 (1979), no. 3, p. 372. Dušek, "Ostroha s háčikmi," in *Zborník prác Ľudmile Kraskovskej*, ed. Studeníková, Zachar, pp. 159–162. *Pramene I/2*, ed. Bialeková, pp. 453–454. Turčan, "Ďalšie slovanské nálezy," *Zborník SNM* 88 (1994), *Archeológia* 4, pp. 75–84. Turčan, "Nové nálezy ostrôh," *Zborník SNM* 89 (1995), *Archeológia* 5, pp. 77–82. Turčan et al., *Archeologické pamiatky*, pp. 46–51. Turčan et al., *Veľkomoravské hradiská*, pp. 98–103.

[52] The Slavs began to use the small Hradec in Prievidza, fortified by a rampart, at the end of the 8th century. Darina Bialeková – Karol Pieta, "Zisťovací výskum v Hradci, okres Prievidza," *Slovenská archeológia* 12 (1964), no. 3, pp. 447–466. *Významné slovanské náleziská na Slovensku*, ed. Bohuslav Chropovský (Bratislava 1978), pp. 83–84. *Pramene II*, ed. Bialeková, pp. 116–117.

[53] Marta Remiášová, "Zisťovací výskum na lokalite Vyšehrad," in *Horná Nitra* 6 (1974), pp. 236–244. Marta Remiášová, "Archeologický výskum na hradisku Vyšehrad," *AVANS v r. 1974* (Nitra 1975), pp. 91–92. Marta Remiášová, "Archeologický výskum na hradisku Vyšehrad v r. 1975," *AVANS v r. 1975* (Nitra 1976), pp. 189–190. Marta Remiášová, "Pokračovanie výskumu na lokalite Vyšehrad," *AVANS v r. 1976* (Nitra 1978), pp. 205–206. Marta Remiášová, "Pokračovanie výskumu hradiska Vyšehrad," *AVANS v r. 1978* (Nitra 1980), pp. 231–233. Marta Remiášová, "Hradisko Vyšehrad," *Horná Nitra* 9 (1980), pp. 13–29. *Významné slovanské náleziská*, ed. Chropovský, pp. 144–146. *Pramene II*, ed. Bialeková, p. 57. Turčan et al., *Veľkomoravské hradiská*, pp. 80–83.

[54] Pavol Čaplovič, "Sídlisko z doby rímskej a slovanskej na Ostrej Skale nad Vyšným Kubínom," *AVANS v r. 1975* (Nitra 1976), pp. 78–82. Pavol Čaplovič, "Osídlenie Ostrej Skaly

of the Váh was ruled from Majcichov,[55] Pobedim,[56] Ducové,[57] Trenčín[58] and

[55] nad Vyšným Kubínom," *AVANS v r. 1977* (Nitra 1978), pp. 72–73. Pavol Čaplovič, *Orava v praveku vo včasnej dobe dejinnej a na začiatku stredoveku* (Martin 1987), p. 239. *Pramene k dejinám osídlenia Slovenska z konca 5. až z 13. storočia II, Stredoslovenský kraj*, ed. Darina Bialeková (Nitra 1992), p. 22. Turčan et al., *Veľkomoravské hradiská*, pp. 108–111. *Významné slovanské náleziská*, ed. Chropovský, pp. 123–124. *Pramene I/2*, ed. Bialeková, p. 445. Tatiana Štefanovičová, "Archäologische Quellen über die Besiedlung der Slowakei im 6.–8. Jahrhundert (Zustand und Perspektiven)," *Slovenský národopis* 38 (1990), no. 3, p. 407. Eva Fottová – Joachim Henning – Matej Ruttkay, "Archeologický výskum včasnostredovekého hradiska v Majcichove," in *Bojná*, ed. Pieta, Ruttkay, Ruttkay, pp. 217–236, F 63–70. Turčan et al. *Veľkomoravské hradiská*, pp. 54–61.

[56] Darina Bialeková, "Výskum slovanského hradiska v Pobedime v rokoch 1959–1962," *Archeologické rozhledy* 15 (1963), pp. 316, 349–364, 369–372. Darina Bialeková, "Výskum slovanského hradiska v Pobedime roku 1964," *Archeologické rozhledy* 17 (1965), pp. 516, 530–538. Darina Bialeková, "Výskum slovanského hradiska v Pobedime, okres Trenčín," *Archeologické rozhledy* 24 (1972), pp. 121–129. Darina Bialeková, "Archeologický výskum a prieskum v Pobedime v roku 1975," *AVANS v r. 1975* (Nitra 1976), pp. 43–46. Darina Bialeková, "Pobedim. Slovanské hradisko a sídliská z 9. storočia," in *III. medzinárodný kongres slovanskej archeológie, Bratislava 7.–14. september 1975* (Nitra 1975). *Významné slovanské náleziská na Slovensku*, ed. Chropovský, pp. 159–167. *Pramene I/2*, ed. Bialeková, pp. 401–408. Darina Bialeková, "Zu Bautechnik der Befestigungsmauer des Burgwalls in Pobedim, Bezirk Trenčín," in *Frühmittelalterlicher Burgenbau in Mittel- und Osteuropa*, ed. Joachim Henning, Alexander Ruttkay (Bonn 1998), pp. 383–390. Turčan et al. *Veľkomoravské hradiská*, pp. 84–89.

[57] Alexander Ruttkay, "Výskum včasnostredovekého opevneného sídla v Ducovom, okres Trnava," *Archeologické rozhledy* 24 (1972), pp. 130–139, 217–220. Alexander Ruttkay, "Ducové. Veľkomoravský veľmožský dvorec a včasnostredoveké pohrebisko," in *III. medzinárodný kongres slovanskej archeológie, Bratislava 7.–14. september 1975* (Nitra 1975). Alexander Ruttkay, "Výsledky výskumu v Ducovom na Kostolci v rokoch 1968–1972 a 1975," *AVANS v r. 1975* (Nitra 1976), pp. 190–196. Alexander Ruttkay, "Dvorce v 9. až 13. storočí," in *Slovensko vo včasnom stredoveku*, ed. Ruttkay, Ruttkay, Šalkovský (Nitra 2002), pp. 135–143. *Významné slovanské náleziská na Slovensku*, ed. Chropovský, pp. 63–72. *Pramene I/2*, ed. Bialeková, pp. 446–447. Alexander T. Ruttkay, "Významné archeologické lokality z včasného stredoveku v oblasti Považského Inovca," in *Bojná*, ed. Pieta, Ruttkay, Ruttkay, pp. 191–201, F 58. Turčan et al., *Archeologické pamiatky*, pp. 52–59. Turčan et al., *Veľkomoravské hradiská*, pp. 46–53.

[58] The fortifications around the location Čerešňový sad cover the highest place at Trenčín Castle. The local rampart was the same as the rampart in Pobedim. Štefan Pozdišovský, "Zisťovací výskum na Čerešňovom sade v Trenčíne v roku 1957," *Informačné správy okresného múzea v Trenčíne* 4 (1958), pp. 49–56. Ján Vavruš, "Hradisko a hrad v Trenčíne, jeho význam a postavenie v dejinnom vývoji," in *Slovensko a európsky juhovýchod. Medzikultúrne vzťahy a kontexty. Zborník k životnému jubileu Tatiany Štefanovičovej*, ed. Alexander Avenarius, Zuzana Ševčíková (Bratislava 1999), pp. 385–388. Tamara Nešporová, "Druhá sezóna výskumu na Brezine," *AVANS v r. 1987* (Nitra 1988), pp. 118–119. *Pramene I/2*, ed. Bialeková, pp. 413–414. Tomáš Michalík, "Počiatky Trenčianskeho hradu. Včasnostredoveké hradisko v Trenčíne," in *Hradiská – svedkovia dávnych čias II. Zborník odborných príspevkov o hradiskách a ich obyvateľoch*, zostavovatelia Peter Jenčík, Zuzana Staneková, Dolná Mariková 2019, pp. 155–164.

Divinka, near Žilina.[59] Along the road which ran through the Považský Inovec Mountains and connected the area along the Váh with the upper Nitra, stood Bojná.[60] Pobedim, Majcichov and Bojná had at the beginning only light palisade fortifications. They got their massive ramparts, which were later destroyed by fire, only in the last years of Svätopluk's Great Moravian rule (according to the most recent dendrochronological dating).[61] The castles at Starý Tekov,[62]

---

59 *Významné slovanské náleziská na Slovensku*, ed. Chropovský, pp. 58–59. *Pramene II*, ed. Bialeková, p. 187. Gabriel Fusek, "Hradisko Veľký vrch v Divinke," in *Hradiská – svedkovia dávnych čias*, ed. Jenčík, Struhár, pp. 147–161, 262–263. On the hill Mesciská in Pružina, in the middle of the Strážovské vrchy Mountains, stood a castle which we can consider to be Great Moravian. Archaeologists found there a great many iron objects which they dated to the 2nd half of the 9th century. Turčan et al., *Veľkomoravské hradiská*, pp. 94–97. Lucia Kováčová – Branislav Kovár – Peter Milo, "Hradisko Pružina – Mesciská a jeho okolie," in *Hradiská – svedkovia dávnych čias. Zborník odborných príspevkov o hradiskách a ich obyvateľoch*, ed. Jenčík, Struhár, pp. 175–185, 264–265, 268.

60 Karol Pieta – Alexander Ruttkay, "Bojná – mocenské a christianizačné centrum Nitrianskeho kniežatstva," in *Bojná*, ed. Pieta, Ruttkay, Ruttkay, pp. 21–36, F 1–53. Karol Pieta, "Hradiská Bojná II a Bojná III. Významné sídlo z doby sťahovania národov a opevnenia z 9. storočia," in *Bojná*, ed. Pieta, Ruttkay, Ruttkay, pp. 173–190, F 54–57. Turčan et al., *Archeologické pamiatky*, pp. 64–69. Turčan et al., *Veľkomoravské hradiská*, pp. 16–21. Peter Šalkovský, "K územným 'zoskupeniam' slovanských hradov vo včasnom stredoveku," in *Hradiská – svedkovia dávnych čias II*, ed. Jenčík, Staneková, pp. 225–226.

61 According to the latest dendrochronological dating the massive fortifications at Majcichov, Pobedim and Bojná only originated sometime around the years 892–893. Ruttkay, "Mocenské centrá," in *Bratia, ktorí menili svet*, ed. Panis, Ruttkay, Turčan, pp. 123–126, 128–129. Turčan et al., *Veľkomoravské hradiská*, pp. 17–18, 60–61, 86–87. According to the oldest dating, the massive rampart of Pobedim and Majcichov is much older and was burned still before the mid-9th century. Darina Bialeková, "Výskum slovanského hradiska v Pobedime v rokoch 1959–1962," *Archeologické rozhledy* 15 (1963), pp. 316, 349–364, 369–372. Darina Bialeková, "Výskum slovanského hradiska v Pobedime r. 1964," *Archeologické rozhledy* 17 (1965), pp. 516, 530–538. Dagmar Bialeková, "Výskum slovanského hradiska v Pobedime, okr. Trenčín," *Archeologické rozhledy* 24 (1972), pp. 121–129. Darina Bialeková, "Archeologický výskum a prieskum v Pobedime v roku 1975," *AVANS v r. 1975* (Nitra 1976), pp. 43–46. The dating of the massive fortifications of Great Moravian castles to the mentioned later period, which archaeologists determined using dendrochronology, brings up the question of whether wood from later repair or reconstruction of the ramparts (and thus better preserved) were not selected for the dating. Peter Šalkovský, "Počiatky, rozmach, premeny a zánik hradov západných Slovanov," *Byzantinoslovaca* v (2014), pp. 107–108. Dendrochronology shifts the dating of the massive fortifications with the frontal stone wall to a later period not only for Great Moravian castles but also those of other Central European Slavs. Luděk Kos, "Raně středověké fortifikace s čelní kamennou plentou ve střední Evropě," *Studia mediævalia Pragensia* 11 (2012), pp. 117–175.

62 Alois Habovštiak – Ľubomír Juck, "Starý Tekov v praveku a stredoveku," *Vlastivedný časopis* 23 (1974), pp. 168–176. *Významné slovanské náleziská na Slovensku*, ed. Chropovský, pp. 193–195. *Pramene I/1*, ed. Bialeková, pp. 165–166. Šalkovský, "Hradiská na Pohroní," in *Slovensko vo včasnom stredoveku*, ed. Ruttkay, Ruttkay, Šalkovský, p. 125.

Zvolen-Môťová,[63] Kalamárka near Detva,[64] Čingov (Hradisko I at the interface of Spišské Tomášovce and Smižany) on the northern bank of the Hornád[65] and Šarišské Sokolovce (Hradová hura) also had massive earthen-wooden ramparts with a facing stone wall during Great Moravia.[66] Čingov (Hradisko I), whose

63 Marta Mácelová, "Príspevok k stredovekému osídleniu Zvolena," *Archaeologia historica* 14 (1989), pp. 171–180. Marta Mácelová, "K počiatkom osídlenia Zvolena v stredoveku," *Archaeologia historica* 18 (1993), pp. 69–74. Marta Mácelová, "Môťovský hrádok vo svetle archeologického výskumu," in *Zvolen 1243–2008. Zborník príspevkov z vedeckých konferencií*, ed. Júlia Ragačová, Pavol Maliniak (Zvolen 2008), pp. 25–27. Marta Mácelová, *Slovania vo Zvolenskej kotline* (Kraków 2013), pp. 12, 13, 14–15, 28, 29–34, 71, 73, 81. *Zvolen. Monografia k 750. výročiu obnovenia mestských práv*, ed. Viera Vaníková (Zvolen 1993), pp. 37–38. *Pramene II*, ed. Bialeková, p. 174. Šalkovský, "Hradiská na Pohroní," in *Slovensko vo včasnom stredoveku*, ed. Ruttkay, Ruttkay, Šalkovský, pp. 125, 129, 130. Turčan et al., *Veľkomoravské hradiská*, pp. 116–119. Noémi Beljak Pažinová – Ján Beljak, "Fortifikácie na sútoku Hrona a Slatiny," in *Hradiská – svedkovia dávnych čias II*, ed. Jenčík, Staneková, pp. 14–15.
64 Peter Šalkovský, *Hradisko v Detve* (Nitra 1994). Peter Šalkovský, "Frühmittelalterlicher Burgwall bei Detva," *Slovenská archeológia* 42 (1994), no. 1, pp. 110–142. Peter Šalkovský, "Slovanské hradisko pri Detve – príspevok k rekonštrukcii dejín stredného Slovenska v 9.–11. storočí," in *Svätopluk 894–1994*, ed. Marsina, Ruttkay, pp. 213–219. Šalkovský, "Hradiská na Pohroní," in *Slovensko vo včasnom stredoveku*, ed. Ruttkay, Ruttkay, Šalkovský, pp. 125, 129, 131. Peter Šalkovský, *Detva. Praveké a včasnohistorické hradisko k dávnym dejinám Slovenska, Archeologické pamätníky Slovenska 10* (Nitra 2009). Mácelová, *Slovania vo Zvolenskej kotline*, pp. 27, 29–30. Turčan et al., *Veľkomoravské hradiská*, pp. 42–45.
65 Július Béreš – Peter Šalkovský, "Výskum slovanského hradiska v Spišských Tomášovciach," *AVANS v r. 1977* (Nitra 1978), pp. 36–38. Július Béreš – Danica Štukovská, "Výskum slovanského hradiska v Spišských Tomášovciach," *AVANS v r. 1978* (Nitra 1980), pp. 42–46. František Javorský, "Výskumy a prieskumy výskumnej expedície v okrese Spišská Nová Ves," *AVANS v r. 1977* (Nitra 1978), pp. 103–120. František Javorský, "Záchranný výskum na hradisku I v Smižanoch," *AVANS v r. 1978* (Nitra 1980), pp. 131–135. Gabriel Lukáč, "K počiatkom stredovekého osídlenia Spiša (do konca 12. stor.)," *Archaeologia historica* 18 (1993), pp. 9–18. Peter Šalkovský, "Dávna pevnosť na Spiši. Slovanské hradisko v Slovenskom raji," *Historická revue* 7 (1996), no. 2, pp. 2–3. *Pramene k dejinám osídlenia Slovenska z konca 5. až z 13. storočia III, Východné Slovensko*, ed. Július Bereš (Nitra 2008), pp. 237–238, 250. Danica Staššíková-Štukovská – Peter Šalkovský – Július Béreš – Eva Hajnalová – Eva Hušťaková – Zuzana Krempaská – František Javorský, "Včasnostredoveké Hradisko I Spišské Tomášovce – Smižany – 1. etapa spracovania," *Zborník Slovenského národného múzea* 100 (2006), *Archeológia* 16, pp. 187–234. Turčan et al., *Veľkomoravské hradiská*, pp. 38–40.
66 Vojtech Budinský-Krička, "Slovanské osídlenie na severovýchodnom Slovensku," *Slovenská archeológia* 9 (1961), no. 1–2, pp. 359–360. Vojtech Budinský-Krička, "Pokusný výskum na slovanskom hradisku v Šarišských Sokolovciach, okres Prešov," *Nové obzory* 9 (1967), pp. 164–185. Július Béreš, "Výsledky doterajšieho výskumu slovanského hradiska v Šarišských Sokolovciach," *Nové obzory* 16 (1974), pp. 113–131. *Významné slovanské náleziská na Slovensku*, ed. Chropovský, pp. 205–207. *Pramene k dejinám osídlenia Slovenska z konca 5. až z 13. storočia III, Východné Slovensko*, ed. Béreš, pp. 182–183.

rampart was destroyed by fire, was converted into an unfortified settlement. Its role was taken over still during the Great Moravian period by the newer and smaller Čingov Castle (Hradisko II in Smižany), which was built on the opposite bank of the Hornád, on a rocky promontory protruding from the Čingov hill, approximately a thousand metres away to the south-west.[67]

A code of laws compiled for the Moravians mentions *soldiers* (*ratnychъ*) ... *returning to their own country and castle* (*vъ svoju zemlju i gradъ*)....[68] Soldiers, that is free Moravians, who served in the military, were thus linked to their own castle. The administration of a defined district was based at these castles, and a church stood here which was the main church in the entire hill-fort's district. With it was a priest subject first to the Passau bishopric, later to the Moravian archbishop or (from year 880) to the Nitra bishop. In 873 Methodius, released from a Bavarian prison, gained possession of the Moravian archbishopric: *When Svätopluk received him with all the Moravians, he handed over to him all the churches and clerics at all the castles.*[69] The Great Moravian ecclesiastical organization copied not only the dualism of the state but also its castle system.

An Arabian report on the Slavs, which Persian scholar Ibn Rustah included in his own work, mentions a market in the seat of Great Moravian Prince Svätopluk: *And the town* (*l-madínatu*), *in which they were based, is called Dž.r.wáb and they have a market* (*súkun*) *in it three days each month, at which they buy and sell.*[70] It was at this market in 886 where Methodius's pupils were

---

67   Július Béreš – Peter Šalkovský, "Výskum slovanského hradiska v Spišských Tomášovciach," *AVANS v r. 1977* (Nitra 1978), pp. 36–38. Július Béreš – Danica Štukovská, "Výskum slovanského hradiska v Spišských Tomášovciach," *AVANS v r. 1978* (Nitra 1980), pp. 42–46. František Javorský, "Záchranný výskum na Hradisku I v Smižanoch," *AVANS v r. 1978* (Nitra 1980), pp. 131–135. Peter Šalkovský, "K vývoju a štruktúre slovanského osídlenia v hornatých oblastiach Slovenska," in *IV. medzinárodný kongres slovanskej archeológie, Sofia 15.–22. septembra 1980, zborník referátov ČSSR* (Nitra 1980), pp. 168, 170. Peter Šalkovský, "Dávna pevnosť na Spiši. Slovanské hradisko v Slovenskom raji," *Historická revue* 7 (1996), no. 2, pp. 2–3. *Pramene I/2*, ed. Bialeková, pp. 401–408, 445. *Pramene II*, ed. Bialeková, p. 22. Gabriel Lukáč, "K počiatkom stredovekého osídlenia Spiša (do konca 12. stor.)," *Archaeologia historica* 18 (1993), pp. 9–18. *Pramene III*, ed. Béreš, pp. 238–239. Turčan et al., *Veľkomoravské hradiská*, pp. 40–41. Peter Šalkovský, "K územným 'zoskupeniam' slovanských hradov vo včasnom stredoveku," in *Hradiská – svedkovia dávnych čias II*, ed. Jenčík, Staneková, pp. 229–231.

68   *ZSL* 21, *MMFH IV*, p. 190. Leon Sokolovský, "Grad – španstvo – stolica – župa. Príspevok k terminológii dejín správy," *Slovenská archivistika* 16 (1981), no. 2, p. 94.

69   *ŽM* 10, *MMFH II*, p. 154.

70   *Kitábu l-a láki n-náfísati li-bni Rusta*, *MMFH III*, p. 347. Pauliny, *Arabské správy*, p. 99. This was the primary market of the Moravians. Dušan Třeštík, "'Trh Moravanov' – ústřední trh staré Moravy," *Československý časopis historický* 21 (1973), no. 6, pp. 876–890. Třeštík, *Počátky*, pp. 289, 294–295. Wihoda, *Morava v době knížecí*, pp. 92–94.

sold into slavery.[71] Merchants who arrived at the market had to pay a customs fee. The Raffelstetten customs tariff (perhaps in 904) set the duty *as was very justly paid during the times of Louis and Carloman and other kings*. The duty was collected from merchants, who traded in salt, slaves, horses, cattle and foodstuffs in several towns in the Eastern March and also went *to the market of the Moravians (ad mercatum Marahorum)*.[72]

[71] *Žitije Nauma I*, MMFH II, p. 178. Třeštík, "Trh Moravanov", p. 890. Michael McCormick, *Narodziny Europy*, pp. 198–199, 727–729. Martin Wihoda, "Großmähren und seine Stellung in der Gechichte," in *Zentralisierungsprozesse und Herrschaftsbildung im frühmittelalterlichen Ostmitteleuropa*, ed. Przemyslaw Sikora, pp. 74–78.

[72] *If they wanted, however, to go to the market of the Moravians, according to a merchant's estimates at this time one solidus was paid per boat and then could freely travel; upon return, however, they are not compelled to pay anything by law. Merchants, that is Jews and other merchants, from wherever they came, from this country or other countries, let them pay a just custom from slaves as well as other items, as always under the times of the previous kings. Inquisitio de theloneis* 8, 9, MMFH IV, p. 119. Luděk Galuška, "O otrocích na Velké Moravě a okovech ze Starého Města," in *Dějiny ve věku nejistot. Sborník k příležitosti 70. narozenin Dušana Třeštíka*, ed. Jan Klápště, Eva Plešková, Josef Žemlička (Praha 2003), pp. 75–86. On the means of payment in the Mojmirid principality see the study: Matej Harvát, "… *iactitant se magnitudine pecuniae*. Otázka platobných prostriedkov na mojmírovskej Morave," in *Acta historica Neosoliensia* 22, 2019, no. 1, pp. 4–28.

CHAPTER 8

The Moravian Fight for Independence (861–871)

1   Pribina's Death

In July 858 Louis the German suddenly called off an extensive campaign planning to attack the Moravians, Sorbs and Obotrites and Linones, because he received the appeal of rebels who wanted a change on the West Francia throne and stood at the front of a rebellion against his brother Charles the Bald.[1] He did not obtain his brother's throne; however, he was surprised by a rebellion in Bavaria. At the head of the rebellion stood Ernest, one of the most significant of Bavarian magnates, Margrave of the Bavarian Northern March (Nordgau) and *first among the king's friends*.[2] Louis the German abandoned the battle in West Francia and in April 861 returned to Bavaria. He suppressed the insurgency and summoned to Regensburg a court, which removed and punished Margrave Ernest and his relatives involved in the rebellion, who ended up in the grasp of the king's rage.[3]

Louis's oldest son Carloman, margrave of the Eastern and Carantanian Marches (856–863), was Ernest's son-in-law. Similarly as Ratbot seven years before, Carloman, too, allied with Rastislav against his own father and in 861 in the full reach of power removed counts loyal to Louis the German: *And Carloman, the oldest of the king's sons, tried to make a change. He expelled the commanders to whom care of the Pannonian and the Carantanian border areas (Pannonici limitis et Carantani) were entrusted and organized the march (marcam) with his own people. And this led the thought of the king to the suspected insurrection.*[4] In the autumn of 861 one of the exiled Carantanian counts, Pabo, fled to Salzburg.[5]

---

1   *Ann. Fuld.* ad a. 858, rec. Kurze, p. 49. Třeštík, *Vznik*, pp. 175–177.
2   *Ernustus dux partium illarum et inter amicos regis primus* led the campaign against the Bohemians in 849. *Ann. Fuld.* ad a. 849, rec. Kurze, p. 38. MMFH I, pp. 72–73.
3   *Ann. Fuld.* ad a. 861, rec. Kurze, p. 55.
4   *Ann. Fuld.* ad a. 861, rec. Kurze, p. 55. MMFH I, pp. 77–78.
5   Count Pabo is already known from the donation document for Pribina's priest Dominik from 844. See chapter 6, note 134. In 847 he was in Regensburg, among the witness in the presence of whom Louis the German gifted to Pribina the Blatengrad (*Mosapurc*) fief, which he until then had only held in tenendum. See chapter 6, note 77. In 857 the counts in Carantania rebelled against Carloman. Pabo stood at the head of the rebels, and Dudlebian Count Richard joined with them. See chapter 6, note 135. Carloman eventually expelled the restless count in 861: *Pabo quidam a Karinthia per Karolmannum eiectus Salzburge consedit. Annales sancti*

Carloman replaced the entire administration of his marches and together with Rastislav prepared an open military attack. Pannonian Prince Pribina stood in the path of approach of both allies. Carloman needed a reliable base for the prepared attack into Bavaria; therefore, he wanted to rid himself of Pribina, just as he had rid himself of counts loyal to King Louis. The Pannonian Principality took up the predominant part of Transdanubia, and its area was equal to Carloman's Carantania. Pribina's military strength must have corresponded to the territorial range and exceptionally exposed position of his principality. Carloman thus could not simply expel him, as he had *expelled* (*expulit*) Pabo and the other inconvenient counts from Carantania and the Eastern March. He could only remove Pribina with a large military attack and by conquering fortresses such as Blatengrad itself. Carloman left this work to his Moravian ally.

Pribina had been an antagonist of the Moravians from the time when they expelled him from Nitria. Rastislav certainly did not like to see him in his nearby surroundings. He had a free hand; he wasn't bound to a different side, so he could strike at Pribina with full force. While Carloman chased Louis's counts out of Carinthia and the Eastern March, the Moravians attacked the neighbouring Pannonian Principality, and they killed Pribina in battle.[6] Pabo's mentioned escape to Salzburg helps us date the common act of Carloman and Rastislav more exactly. Pribina, who was still prince on 21 March 861,[7] died in the summer or fall of 861.[8]

Rudberti Salisburgenses ad a. 861, MMFH IV, p. 402, MHDC III, ed. Jaksch, no. 28, p. 12. *Papo a Karlomanno expulsus a Karentana Salzpurch seder cepit. Auctarium Gartense* ad a. 861, MMFH IV, p. 425, MHDC III, ed. Jaksch, no. 28, p. 12. This Pabo was one of the Carantanian counts (before 844–861) and is not the same as Count Pabo mentioned in the 10th chapter of the Conversio, whose county lay in Transdanubia. See chapter 5, note 31, chapter 6, note 166.

6 *Priwina, quem Maravi occiderunt. Conversio* 13, ed. Wolfram, pp. 78–79. *Conversio*, ed. Kos, p. 96. MMFH III, p. 319. Bavarian chronicler Johannes Aventinus, who knew the no longer preserved source of this information, wrote: *Rastislaus Venedorum regulus (qui ut supra diximus se clientelam Carolmanni dicarat) adversus Brynnonem amicum Ludovici, itidem Sclavorum, qui Danubii oram aquilonarem tum incolebant, ducem, hostili animo cum exercitu procedit, eundem praelio superatum occidit. Ioannis Aventini Annales Boiorum* IV, XIV 43, MMFH I, p. 394. Aventinus incorrectly connected two different events: 1. the expulsion of Pribina from Nitria in 833: ... *adversus Brynnonem, itidem Sclavorum, qui Danubii oram aquilonarem tum incolebant, ducem, hostili animo cum exercitu procedit, eundem praelio superatum* ... 2. Pribina's death in battle with Rastislav in 861: *Rastislaus Venedorum regulus ... adversus Brynnonem amicum Ludovici ... hostili animo cum exercitu procedit, eundem praelio ... occidit.*

7 Pribina's son and successor, Kocel, was on 21 March 861 still only a count (*comes*) CDES I, ed. Marsina, no. 11, p. 10. MMFH III, Diplomata 31, p. 61. See chapter 6, note 156. Thus, Pribina must have then still be the Pannonian Prince.

8 Milko Kos assumed that on 21 March 861 Pribina was dead and that he died sometime between 20 February 860, when he visited King Louis in Regensburg, and 21 March 861, when his son Kocel was already on a visit in Regensburg. *Conversio*, ed. Kos, pp. 96–97.

Rastislav immediately at the beginning brought the war to the territory of his antagonists. He attacked not only in Transdanubia but still in this same year, together will Carloman, he fell upon Bavarian territory: *Carloman, son of Louis, king of Germania, allied with Rastislav, prince of the Veneti, broke away from his father and with the help of Rastislav took over a large part his father's empire up to the Inn River.*[9] The conquered part of the Bavarian territory is testimony that the aim of both allies was a territorial invasion. While Rastislav undertook the battle into Bavaria on behalf of his ally, he followed the territorial interests of his own state in the battle in Transdanubia. Rastislav wasn't satisfied with only the removal of Pribina and common plundering, but he did not depart from Transdanubia. The attack against Pribina, the military presence of the Moravians in Transdanubia and other events on the middle Danube in 861 determined the circumstances and date Great Moravia's territorial gains in north-eastern Transdanubia.

In the summer or autumn of 861 Pribina defended the Pannonian Principality, which he had got into his administration from Louis the German, similarly as in 833 he defended Nitria.[10] He lost the battle with the Moravians the second time, too. Not only did he die in the battle, but he then could have also lost a portion of territory on the north-east part of his principality, which Rastislav attached to Great Moravia. In 862 Louis the German rapidly and in good faith settled with his son Carloman. Because he had to hurry north, where the Danes were plundering and where he was preparing a campaign against the Obotrites,[11] he could not intervene militarily against Carloman and Rastislav and acknowledged the results of the rebellion: *Carloman, son of Louis, king of Germania, when his father ceded to him the part of the empire which he had*

Kos, "K histórii kniežaťa Pribinu," pp. 62–64. Ján Dekan, who in the question of Pribina's death convincingly argues with Milko Kos, puts Pribina's death *in the summer months of 861, perhaps in August – with respect to the time of Pabo's fleeing*. Ján Dekan, *Začiatky slovenských dejín a Ríša veľkomoravská. Slovenské dejiny II* (Bratislava 1951), pp. 68–69. Herwig Wolfram and Dušan Třeštík also accepted the wrongful opinion of Milko Kos. *Conversio*, ed. Wolfram, p. 139. Wolfram, *Die Geburt*, p. 280. Wolfram, *Salzburg, Bayern Österreich*, pp. 315, 327. *Conversio*, ed. Wolfram, pp. 198, 199. Třeštík, *Vznik*, p. 177. George Kruger (Georgius Crugerius) in his work Sacri pulveres, which he published in Litomyšl, in the years 1669–1676, wrote that the Moravians killed Pribina on 6 July. Tomáš J. Pešina from Čechorod in his work Mars Moravicus, published in Prague in 1677, wrote that Rastislav then ruled over northern Pannonia. Lubomír E. Havlík, *Kronika o Velké Moravě* (Brno 1993), p. 107.

9 *Ann. Bert.* ad a. 861, rec. Kurze, p. 55. *MMFH I*, p. 53.
10 The similarity of both events confused Johannes Aventinus, who regarded two different reports with similar contents as correct regarding this same even and in his chronicle simply combined them. See note 6.
11 *Ann. Fuld.* ad a. 862, rec. Kurze, p. 56. *Ann. Bert.* ad a. 862, rec. Kurze, pp. 59–60. *MMFH I*, pp. 53–54.

previously taken, and when he promised that he would take nothing more without his father's permission, he concluded peace with his father.[12] Thus, Carloman, with his father's permission, kept the conquered Bavarian territory, while the north-eastern part of Transdanubia remained in Rastislav's hands.

2   Alliance of Louis the German with the Bulgarians and Carloman's Fall

While Louis the German battled in the north against the Obotrites, the Danes and Magyars (*Ungri*) attacked his kingdom, and Carloman, again with the help of Rastislav, rebelled against him.[13] Louis returned to Bavaria, where accusations aimed against his son rained down upon him.[14] The angry king prepared his retaliation. The war against Carloman and Rastislav began in the following year, in 863: *Louis remained in Bavaria for nearly a year, warily directing activities against the Moravian opponents as well as against his son.*[15] In the summer of 863 East Frankish King Louis the German allied with Bulgarian Khagan Boris (852–889) against the Moravians, who supported the rebellion of Margrave Carloman.[16] The threat of Bulgarian attack caused Rastislav to detach himself from Carloman. Rastislav expected an attack from two sides; therefore he asked Carloman for help, but in vain. *Rastislav deserted and forced away* Carloman. Louis the German asked his brother, West Francia King Charles II the Bald, not to receive the abandoned Carloman.[17]

On 3 September 863 Byzantine strategist Petronas defeated the army of Amir Omar of Meletine, which had attacked Byzantine territory to the east of Asia Minor. With the victory over the Arabs, Byzantine forces secured the eastern border and turned their attention in the opposite direction, to neighbouring Bulgaria.[18] Boris could not withstand Byzantine pressure and agreed with baptism.[19]

---

12   Ann. Bert. ad a. 862, rec. Kurze, p. 58. MMFH I, p. 53.
13   Ann. Bert. ad a. 862, rec. Kurze, pp. 59–60. MMFH I, pp. 53–54.
14   Ann. Fuld. ad a. 863, rec. Kurze, pp. 56–57. MMFH I, p. 78.
15   Ann. Xant. ad a. 863, MMFH I, p. 46.
16   Ann. Fuld. ad a. 863, rec. Kurze, p. 56. MMFH I, p. 79.
17   Ann. Bert. ad a. 863, rec. Kurze, p. 62. MMFH I, p. 55.
18   Tadeusz Wasilewski, "Studia nad dziejami panowania cesarza Michala III. (842–867). Cz. II: Przewrót państwowy w 851/852 r. i ofenzywa w Azji Mniejszej przeciwko Arabom," *Przegląd Historiczny* 61 (1970), 4, pp. 369–373. Márton Tösér, "Arab-bizánci harcok a IX. század második felében. A porsoni ütközet, 863, szeptember 3.," *Hadtörténelmi Közlémenyek* 116 (2003), 2. szám, pp. 525–531. *Dějiny Byzance*, ed. Bohumila Zástěrová (Praha 1992), p. 139.
19   George Harmatolos wrote about how Byzantine Emperor Michael III marched against the Bulgarians and compelled them to accept Christianity: *Then Michael marched with*

Louis the German, seeing that Bulgarian aid was not coming, rapidly changed his military plan. He left Rastislav in peace and unexpectedly turned against his own son: *In the meantime the king, when he had gathered his forces, as if preparing to take on Rastislav, prince of the Moravian Slavs, with the help of the Bulgarians arriving from the east, as was rumoured, in reality, however, marched into Carantania preparing to conquer his son.*[20] But Louis the German didn't have to battle against Carloman. Count Gundakar, the leader of Carloman's military, betrayed his ruler and came with his army to the side of Louis, who had secretly promised him the title of Carantanian margrave in advance. Carloman surrendered without a fight.[21]

After Carloman's capture, Louis separated administration of the Eastern March from Carantania. Gundakar became the Carantanian margrave (863–865) and Werinhar got administration of the Eastern March (863–865).

3 The Battle over Illyricum

At this same time the struggle on the middle Danube took on yet another dimension. In the 860s the battle over ecclesiastical orientation of the entire space between the East Francia and the Byzantine Empire climaxed. The Bavarian clergy, supported by Louis the German, the Roman Pope and the Patriarch of Constantinople, entered into a struggle over the extensive territory on the middle and lower Danube, which was divided mainly between Great Moravia and Bulgaria. The papal curia planned to revive the old *Illyricum*, a late antique church province with its seat in Sirmium, which would, as it had before, be directly ruled by the pope. Pope Nicholas I energetically reclaimed it

---

Caesar Bardo against Bulgarian ruler Michael (= Boris), *since he learned that the Bulgarian people were dying of famine. Only when the Bulgarians came to know this, terror stricken by the rumbling, they fled. Since they had lost any hope of victory even before the battle, they requested the acceptance of Christianity and subjected themselves to the emperor and the Romans.* Russian chronicler Nestor also mentioned this event: *Emperor Michael marched along the banks and along the seaside against the Bulgarians. The Bulgarians, seeing that they cannot possibly oppose him, requested that they be baptised and subjected to the Greeks. The emperor baptised their duke and all the boyars and concluded peace with the Bulgarians.* Povest' vremennych let 14 (6366), MMFH I, pp. 190–191. Michael III campaigned against the Bulgarians in 854 or 855 and not in 864. Thus, this campaign is not at all associated with Boris's baptism. Wasilewski, "Studia nad dziejami," pp. 369–373.

20 *Interea rex collecto exercitu specie quidem quasi Rastizen Margensium Sclavorum ducem cum auxilio Bulgarorum ab oriente venientum, ut fama fuit, domaturus, re autem vera ad Carantanos filium expugnaturus accessit.* Ann. Fuld. ad a. 863, rec. Kurze, p. 56. MMFH I, p. 79. MHDC III, ed. Jaksch, no. 30, p. 15. Třeštík, *Vznik*, p. 183.

21 Ann. Fuld. ad a. 863, rec. Kurze, pp. 56–57. MMFH I, p. 79.

and met with understandable opposition from Patriarch Photios and Emperor Michael III.[22]

In 861–863 Rastislav also entered into this dispute. Great Moravia belonged to the Passau diocese. The Passau bishopric was not limited only to pastoral activities but was also a tool of political influence of the East Frankish empire; therefore, Rastislav decided to change the ecclesiastical orientation of his land. The years 861–864 are the beginning of Rastislav's independent church policy. An emissary to the pope, to the Byzantine emperor, and the arrival and working of the Byzantine mission are the beginning of implementation of a plan for an independent Slavic ecclesiastical province, independent from Bavarian bishops.

4   Baptism of the Bulgarians

Despite the failure of Bulgarian help against the Moravians at the end of summer in 863, Louis the German still valued his friendship with the Bulgarians. Therefore, in the following year he agreed to a meeting with Boris in Tulln an der Donau: *The true king had in mind to depart to Tulln and then to confirm peace with the ruler of the Bulgarians and to steer Rastislav for good or bad to obedience.* At the same time preparations for Boris's baptism were also starting.[23] In the summer of 864 Louis the German marched to the east with a large military force against Rastislav. On the way he stopped in Tulln, where he met with Khagan Boris: *Louis, King of Germania, marched militarily to meet the Bulgarian khagan by the name of [Boris], who promised that he wants to become a Christian, from there he intended to proceed further in order to put the march of the Vinidi in order, if convinced that fortune smiles upon him.*[24]

---

22 František Dvorník, "Metodova diecéza a boj o Illyricum," in *Ríša Veľkomoravská*, ed. Stanislav, pp. 190–195.

23 *fidelis rex dispositum habeat venit Tullinam et deinde pacem cum rege Vulgarorum confirmare et Rastitium aut nolendo sibi oboedientem facere.* The letter of Pope Nicholas I recalls not only the Frankish-Bulgarian peace, but also preparation for baptism of the Bulgarian monarch: *christianissimus rex speret, quod ipse rex Vulgarorum ad fidem velit converti et iam multi ex ipsis Christiani facti sint.* MMFH III, Epistolae 23, pp. 146–147. Třeštík, *Vznik*, pp. 184–185.

24 *Hludovicus rex Germaniae hostiliter obviam Bulgarorum cagano ... nomine, qui se christianum fieri velle promiserat, pergit; inde ad componendam Winidorum marcam, si se prosperari viderit, perrectus.* Ann. Bert. ad a. 864, rec. Kurze, p. 72. MMFH I, pp. 54–55. Třeštík, *Vznik*, pp. 185–186.

If Boris *promised that he wants to become a Christian*, then this was a promise which he gave to the Byzantine emperor. The Annales Bertiniani make no mention of Boris promising something to the East Frankish king. The author of the annals only wrote that Boris made such a promise. We don't learn about to whom he made it in the Annales Bertiniani. If we were to admit that he made this promise to Louis the German at the meeting in Tulln, this doesn't mean at all that he wanted Louis's missionaries to baptise him. The author of the annals obviously didn't consider it worth mentioning that the Bulgarian khagan, with whom the East Frankish king was allied, decided to convert from paganism and that baptism awaited him. An alliance with a near Christian was for the reputation of a Christian king better than a shameful alliance with a pagan.

Bulgarian Khagan Boris received baptism in 866.[25] A bishop sent by the Constantinople patriarch baptised him. Boris's godfather was Byzantine Emperor Michael III himself; therefore, Boris took the name Michael.[26] The Bulgarian khagan became a Christian prince. The bishop and priests whom Constantinople patriarch Photios had sent to Bulgaria not only baptised Boris but began to baptize his nation as well.[27] Still in this same year Boris suppressed

---

25   The Annales Bertiniani mention that Boris received baptism in 866. In the previous year he was still only considering baptism: *Rex Bulgarorum, qui praecedente anno, Deo inspirante et signis atque affictionibus in populo regni sui monente, christianus fieri meditatus fuerat, sacrum baptisma suscepit.* Ann. Bert. ad a. 866, MMFH IV, p. 374. The Annales Bertiniani mention: *The king of the Bulgarians ... accepted holy baptism.* Who baptised Boris is not mentioned, just as to whom Boris two or three years earlier *promised that he wants to become a Christian*. The Annals do not tell us that Boris's baptism was Byzantine and that Boris's previous promise was given to the Byzantine emperor.

26   André Vaillant – Michel Lascaris, "L' date de l' conversion des Bulgares," *Revue des études* 13 (1933), pp. 5–15. Dvorník, *Byzantské misie*, pp. 140–141. Lubomír E. Havlík, "Bulgaria and Moravia between Byzantium, the Franks and Rome," *Palaeobulgarica* 13 (1989), no. 1, p. 10.

27   Several researchers put Boris's baptism in year 865, or even 864. Ernst Dümmler, *Geschichte des Ostfränkischen Reiches II* (Leipzig 1865), pp. 85–86. Vasil Nikolov Zlatarski, *Istorija na bǎlgarskata dǎržava I/2* (Sofija 1971), pp. 55–209, 351–391. Zlatarski, "Veľká Morava a Bulharsko v IX. storočí", p. 284. František Hýbl, *Dějiny národa bulharského I* (Praha 1930), pp. 85–87. František Dvorník, "Byzancia a Veľká Morava," in *Ríša Veľkomoravská*, ed. Stanislav, pp. 125–134. Dvorník, *Byzantské misie*, pp. 72–73, 115–118, 140–141, 328. František Dvorník, *Fotiovo schizma. Historie a legenda* (Olomouc 2008), pp. 115–116. Vaillant – Lascaris, L' date de l' conversion des Bulgares, pp. 5–15. Petǎr Ch. Petrov, "Za godinata na nalagane christinstvoto v Bǎlgarija," *Izvestija na Instytut za bǎlgarskata istorija* 14–15 (1964), pp. 569–589. Havlík, "Bulgaria and Moravia between Byzantium, the Franks and Rome," pp. 9–10. István Lórand Magyar, "'Quaestio bulgarica' (A kereszténység felvétele Bulgárában)," *Századok* 116, 1982, no. 5, p. 848. Gennadij G. Litavrin, "Vvedenije christianstva v Bolgarii (IX–načalo X v.)," in *Prinjatije christianstva narodami Centraľnoj i Jugo-Vostočnoj Evropy i kreščenie Rusi*, otvetstvennyj redaktor Gennadij G. Litavrin

an anti-Christianity rebellion of the boyars.[28] The battle for authority over the Bulgarian church (863–870) was won in 870 by the Constantinople patriarch against the efforts of the Pope and the Frankish clergy.[29]

5   The Devín Peace

After taking leave of Boris, King Louis had to remain in Tulln a bit longer, *in order to put the March of the Vinidi in order*.[30] The Eastern March, then called the *March of the Vinidi* or the *March against the Vinidi*,[31] felt the effects of the attack of the Moravians. Carloman's ally Rastislav in 861 fell on his antagonists along the entire length of the Danubian border, and Carloman expelled the inconvenient counts and administrators loyal to King Louis. The presence of the king and his military in Tulln in the summer of 864 was a necessity. He had to renew administration of the country, the security of the borders and the shaken authority of royal power so that the Eastern March again became a reliable jumping off point against the Slavs to the east.

(Moskva 1998), pp. 41–45. Zástěrová et al., *Dějiny Byzance*, pp. 144–145. Sergej Arkaďjevič Ivanov, *Byzantské misie aneb je možné udělat z "barbara" křesťana?* (Červený kostelec 2012), pp. 156–158. According to Tadeusz Wasilewski and Dušan Třeštík, Boris in 864 or even 863 became the emperor's catechumen and received baptism only in 866. Tadeusz Wasilewski, "Data chrztu Bulgarii," *Pamiętnik Słowiański* 18 (1968), pp. 115–129. Tadeusz Wasilewski, *Byzancium i Słowianie w IX wieku. Studium z dziejów stosunków politycznych i kulturalnych* (Warszawa 1972), pp. 122–126. Tadeusz Wasilewski, *Bălgarija i Vizantija IX–XV vek* (Sofija 1997), pp. 31–47. Třeštík, *Vznik*, p. 185. Vasil Gjuzelev also puts Boris's baptism in year 866. Vasil Gjuzelev, *Knjaz Boris Părvi* (Sofija 1969), pp. 141–143.

28   *Ann. Bert.* ad a. 866, rec. Kurze, pp. 85–86. *MMFH I*, pp. 56–57. *MMFH IV*, pp. 374–375. *Responsa Nicolai papae I. ad consulta Bulgarorum* 17, *MMFH IV*, pp. 58–59.

29   Zlatarski, *Istorija na bălgarskata dăržava I/2*, pp. 507–509. Hýbl, *Dějiny národa bulharského I*, pp. 89–90. *Dějiny Byzance*, ed. Zástěrová, pp. 146–147. Alexander Avenarius, *Byzantská kultúra v slovanskom prostredí v VI.-XII. storočí. K problému recepcie a transformácie* (Bratislava 1992), p. 144. Alexander Avenarius, *Die byzantinische Kultur und die Slawen. Zum Problem der Rezeption und Transformation (6. bis 12. Jahrhundert)*. Veröffentlichungen des Instituts für österreichische Geschichtsforschung, Band 35 (Wien – München 2000), p. 154. Steinhübel, *Moravania, Chorváti a Bulhari*, pp. 163–166.

30   See note 24.

31   *Winidorum marcam.* See note 24. *in marca adversus Winidos. Ann. Bert.* ad a. 866, rec. Kurze, p. 82. *MMFH I*, p. 55. *in marcha contra Winidos. Ann. Bert.* ad a. 873, rec. Kurze, p. 124. *MMFH I*, p. 60. *duo fratres, Willihalmus et Engilscalchus, terminum regni Baiowariorum in oriente a rege, id est seniore Hludowico, concessum contra Maravanos tenuerunt. Ann. Fuld.* ad a. 884, rec. Kurze, p. 110. *MMFH I*, p. 94. *in Sclauinia. MMFH III*, Diplomata 16, p. 36. *in aliis Baioriae scilicet atque Sclavinie locis vel terminis. MMFH III*, Diplomata 48, p. 81.

Rastislav, obviously from 858, when he began to openly ally with Carloman,[32] gave preference to Devín over the main princely seat in Mikulčice. He ceased staying covered in the deep Moravian interior and began to remain at Devín. From there he could immediately and very readily intervene into situations in the wider border region of the empire on the opposite side of the Danube, either on behalf of his ally Carloman or in his own interest.

Rastislav not only attacked from Devín, but prepared there to defend it, especially from the summer of 863, when Louis the German allied with the Bulgarians and captured Carloman. Rastislav waited on the East Frankish king and his large army directly on the borders; he had no intention of letting him into the country. He closed himself in at Devín and wanted to stop Louis's progress there. In August 864 Louis left Tulln, crossed the Danube and surrounded Rastislav's fortress standing above the confluence of the Morava and Danube rivers.[33] If Rastislav remained at Devín and did not retreat from Louis's army to the interior, then the defence of Devín was well prepared.

Both antagonists saved their forces. Rastislav *had no intention of battling with the king's armies and in addition was convinced that there was no chance of escape for him*, and Louis again didn't want to drive his people against the Devín ramparts, risk great losses and camp for a long time in an enemy land, exposed to ceaseless assaults from the interior and strongly fortified surroundings of Devín. No easy victory awaited him as the year before in Carantania. Rastislav was protected by the entire fortified system of the Bratislava gate; he had behind him a land untouched by war prepared to defend and give aid to the besieged prince. Louis the German had unpleasant memories of the last great campaign against the Moravians in 855, when he besieged Rastislav, who was *protected by reportedly the strongest bulwark*. Even then he did not conquer the fortress; he didn't dare attack it and be exposed to ceaseless attacks. He had to retreat with losses and without a result. Louis the German had to come to a compromise beneath Devín. Both antagonists avoided an open collision and came to an agreement. Rastislav *gave up the hostages, of the kind and in the numbers commanded by the king, and aside from this and guaranteed with all of his best (optimatibus) vow, that he would maintain loyalty to the king for all time*,[34] and Louis the German pulled back.

And this time Rastislav again protected his country from war. From year 855 up to 869 the interior of Great Moravia did not suffer any enemy plundering. Since no war had taken place, there could be no talk about the victor or the

---

32 Třeštík, *Vznik*, pp. 176–177.
33 *Ann. Fuld.* ad a. 864, rec. Kurze, p. 62. *MMFH I*, p. 79.
34 *Ann. Fuld.* ad a. 864, rec. Kurze, p. 62. *MMFH I*, pp. 79–80. Lysý, *Moravania*, pp. 190–193.

defeated and the situation of Rastislav, who was closed up in Devín fortress was not so precarious that he had to prostrate himself before Louis. The East Frankish king could not act at all from the position of a victor, so he had to be satisfied only with a formal promise of loyalty. He was unable to touch the independence of Great Moravia and force it into a more significant retreat. The compromise Devín peace ended a period of wars (861–864) but did not change their results. Rastislav had to conclude peace and cease threatening Bavaria and its border march, but the main result of his three-year struggle was that he did not surrender. The Devín peace did not disrupt the military power of Great Moravia; it did not thwart the further working of the Byzantine mission or the plans for an independent Great Moravian church, and it did not affect even Rastislav's territorial conquest in north-eastern Transdanubia. The August campaign of Louis the German remained stopped under Devín; it did not continue into Great Moravia's interior and did not conquer even one of Rastislav's fortresses and did not launch even one common round of plundering. In August 864 the Moravians were now three years the rulers of north-eastern Transdanubia and remained there further, until the arrival of the Magyars (Hungarians). Rastislav ceased with attacks into neighbouring territories of the East Frankish empire, but he did not take the promise he'd made completely seriously.[35] Malcontents in the East Frankish empire in the subsequent years sought an ally in him against their own king.

6   Carloman's Return

In 865 Louis the German divided rule in the East Francia empire between his sons Carloman, Louis and Charles, though he did not confer the title of king on them. Carloman acquired Bavaria;[36] thus, all the marginal territories of the Bavarian kingdom were subjugated to him. Louis and Carloman immediately ran into opposition from Margrave Werinhar (Warnar) in the Eastern March (*in marca adversus Winidos*). Werinhar, however, was unable to get Rastislav on his side, and his rebellion rapidly fell apart. Still in 865 King Louis deposed Margrave Werinhar[37] and handed the Eastern March to Wilhelm II and to

---

[35]   The Annals of Fulda emphasize that Rastislav *did not keep at all* the promised loyalty. See note 34.
[36]   *Erchanberti Breviarum regum Francorum*, MMFH *I*, p. 63.
[37]   *Ann. Fuld.* ad a. 865, rec. Kurze, p. 63. MMFH *I*, p. 80. Because Rastislav did not accept Werinhar's appeal, Louis the German suppressed his rebellion *in marca adversus Winidos* in this same year without a fight. *Ann. Bert.* ad a. 866, rec. Kurze, p. 84. MMFH *I*, p. 55.

Engelschalk I (865–871), the sons of the former Traungau Count Wilhelm I.[38] Obviously, Carloman's one-time betrayer, Carantanian margrave Gundakar, whom Carloman after his return to power in Carantania certainly could not bear, took part in Werinhar's rebellion. Gundakar ran away to the Moravians and entered into the service of Prince Rastislav.[39]

In 866 the king's middle son, Louis, unhappy with the division of the property, prepared a rebellion in Saxony and Thuringia; he got the deposed Werinhar on his side as well as other malcontents. He sent Henry, the leader of his forces, to Rastislav to request an alliance with him and suggested *that he come to plunder Bavaria*. Louis the German left the defence of Bavaria and the Eastern March to his oldest son Carloman and came himself to Frankfurt, where he gathered a great number of his backers and easily suppressed the rebellion of his middle son.[40] Rastislav correctly estimated the weak forces of the insurgents and therefore did not accept any offer for an unsuitable alliance. He maintained the Devín peace and did not repeat the attack on Bavaria from five years before.

7 Svätopluk's Betrayal

In August 869 East Frankish King Louis the German gathered his empire's entire three armies against the Slavs. The army of the Thuringians and the Saxons mustered against the Sorbs along the River Elbe (Labe), who were also aided by the Bohemians, was led by his middle son Louis. The king sent his oldest son Carloman with the Bavarian army against Svätopluk, leaving himself the Franks and Alamans against Rastislav. Because he became ill, his youngest son Charles took over leadership of the Franks and Alamans. Charles looted and burned in Moravia and got as far as *to Rastislav's unimaginable fortress*, with all probability identifed with Mikulčice. At the same time his brother pillaged Svätopluk's Nitria: *Carloman with fire and sword no less despoiled the country of Svätopluk (regnum Zventibaldi), nephew of Rastislav*.[41] Charles and Carloman then proceeded especially against each of the two principalities that were combined in 833 to form Great Moravia.

---

38 See note 31.
39 *Ann. Fuld.* ad a. 869, rec. Kurze, pp. 67–68. *MMFH I*, p. 82.
40 *Ann. Bert.* ad a. 866, rec. Kurze, pp. 82, 84–85. *MMFH I*, pp. 55–56. *Ann. Fuld.* ad a. 866, rec. Kurze, pp. 64–65. *MMFH I*, pp. 80–81.
41 *Ann. Fuld.* ad a. 869, rec. Kurze, pp. 68–69. *MMFH I*, pp. 82–84.

In the following year of 870 Svätopluk began to betray Rastislav. Behind Rastislav's back and against his wishes he agreed with then Bavarian administrator Carloman: *Svätopluk, nephew of Rastislav, seeing to his own benefit, delivered himself to Carloman together with the country (una cum regno) he held.* Svätopluk's separate peace with Carloman infuriated Rastislav. Rastislav desired his nephew's death. Svätopluk, however, was able to avoid the hired killers and he himself captured Rastislav, who had followed him into a prepared trap. He then handed over the captured Rastislav to Carloman. Svätopluk, however, did not acquire Rastislav's princely seat. Carloman was faster. He attacked Rastislav's Moravia (*regnum illius*), where the castles (*civitates et castella*) subjugated themselves to him. And he handed over the *organizing of the country* (*ordinato regno*) to the margraves of the Eastern March, Wilhelm II and Engelschalk I, sons of mentioned Traungau Count Wilhelm I. In 871 Svätopluk also lost Nitria. Both margraves accused him of treason, and he ended up in a Bavarian prison.[42]

8 Slavomir

Svätopluk's relative Slavomir became his successor: *The Slavs, however, the Moravians (Sclavi autem Marahenses), assuming the death of their prince, put at the head (in principem constituunt) a former presbyter, a relative of this prince by the name of Slavomir (Sclagamarum), threathening him with death, if he did not accept the principality (ducatum) over them.*[43] If Svätopluk was until then the Nitrian prince, then only Nitria (Nitravia) could have considered Svätopluk's purported death as the death of *its prince* (*ducem suum*). If Moravia was in the hands of the mentioned margraves and Slavomir was Svätopluk's successor as the Nitrian (Nitravian) prince, then Slavomir's princely seat must have been in Svätopluk's Nitra.[44] The *Sclavi autem Marahenses*, who *set* Slavomir as their prince, were thus Svätopluk's Nitrians (Nitravians), who (especially to foreign observers) appeared to be a component of the Moravians.

Many malcontents from Moravia certainly moved to Nitria and surrounded Slavomir and placed on him the hope of liberating Moravia. Wilhelm and Engelschalk had to beat back Slavomir's attacks from Nitria against the Bavarian garrison forces at Moravian castles.

---

42   *Ann. Fuld.* ad a. 870–871, rec. Kurze, pp. 70–74. *MMFH I*, pp. 84–87. *Ann. Bert.* ad a. 870, rec. Kurze, p. 109. *MMFH I*, p. 59. Lysý, *Moravania*, pp. 102–103.
43   *Ann. Fuld.* ad a. 871, rec. Kurze, p. 74. *MMFH I*, p. 86.
44   Kučera, *Postavy*, pp. 172–173. Lysý, *Moravania*, pp. 104–106.

Carloman wanted to conquer Slavomir and also subdue Nitria. Therefore, he believed in Svätopluk, who promised him that he would conquer Slavomir. He released him from captivity and sent him with a great Bavarian force into Moravia. According to Carloman's plan, Svätopluk, after defeating Slavomir, should again take over rule of his Nitria and live in peace with the margraves in Moravia and acknowledge their sovereignty. However, Svätopluk *entered into old Rastislav's castle*, secretly allied with Slavomir and destroyed Carloman's army, which he himself had led there. Both margraves died,[45] and Nitria was again joined with Moravia under the common rule of Prince Svätopluk (871–894).

---

45 *Ann. Fuld.* ad a. 871, rec. Kurze, pp. 73–74. *MMFH I*, pp. 86–87. *Ann. Bert.* ad a. 871, rec. Kurze, p. 117. *MMFH I*, pp. 59–60.

CHAPTER 9

Svätopluk's Realm

1   Svätopluk and Bořivoj

In October 871 *the Moravian Slavs (Sclavi Marahenses) arranged a wedding, bringing the daughter of some prince from Bohemia (cuiusdam ducis filiam de Behemis)*. The wedding train was imposing, made up of mounted soldiers from Moravia. On the road back they were surprised by a Frankish military brigade. The Moravians, along with the bride, managed to escape; however, *644 horses with reigns and saddles and the same number of shields, which the escaping had left behind* fell into hands of the Franks.[1] The Moravians certainly managed to save at least a portion of their horses and arms; thus, we can assume a rounded number of up to a thousand riders. Only Svätopluk, who not long before had sat on the Great Moravian princely seat, could have assembled, armed, equipped and sent such a large contingent of mounted Moravians over the border. Only he could have been the groom for a Bohemian prince's daughter, whom we can identify with his wife Svätožízňa.

The names of both spouses *Zuuentibald, Uengizizna* are recorded alongside one another among the names of other then-living monarchs and their wives in the list which is a part of the Book of Brotherhood of St. Peter's Abbey in Salzburg.[2] Both names are written alongside one another in the margin of the Gospel Book of Cividale: *Szuentiepulc, Szuentezizna*.[3]

With a political wedding, Svätopluk at the start of his rule immediately linked himself to the most important princely line in Bohemia, which was undoubtedly the Přemyslids. He would hardly have expressed interest in a bride from a less important family. The Přemyslid Bořivoj was then 19 years old and

---

1   *Ann. Fuld.* ad a. 871, rec. Kurze, pp. 74–75. *MMFH I*, pp. 87–88. If the wedding train was so close to the borders that the Bavarians could attack them, then it went along the road that passed through Gmünd pass. Třeštík, *Vznik*, p. 233, note 37. One road went through the Gmünd pass to the Thaya River, that is to Moravia, and the other road down the Kamp River to the Danube, that is to Rugiland. Regarding the path through the border crossing in the Gmünd pass, see Šimák, *Pronikání Němců*, pp. 559–560. Czendes, *Die Strassen Niederösterreichs*, pp. 79–80, 163–164, 190–191. Naďa Profantová, "Přínos archeologie k poznání českých dějin devátého století," *Studia mediaevalia Pragensia* 2 (1991), p. 49.
2   *Liber confraternitatum salisburgensis vetustior Ordo ducum vivorum cum coniugibus et liberis.* *MMFH III*, p. 335.
3   *Evangelium de Cividale, MMFH III*, p. 332.

later died in 888 as a 36-year-old.[4] Considering his age, he could have been Svätožízna's brother. We cannot seriously consider any other blood relations. Svätopluk would hardly have later made Bořivoj his own representative in Bohemia, if he were only some more distant relative. A close family relation was politically the most advantageous. Their father (perhaps Hostivít, who is mentioned by Cosmas) was still alive in October 871 and was a prince, because the Annals of Fulda mention the bride as *the daughter* (not sister) *of some Bohemian prince*. Thus, a father gave away his daughter, not a brother his sister.

In May of 872 the King of East Francia, Louis the German, sent an army against the Moravians and the Bohemians. Bořivoj (*Goriwei*), together with five other Bohemian princes, battled against this Frankish incursion moving into Bohemian territory.[5] He had taken his father's place on the princely seat only shortly before then. His new relations with the powerful Svätopluk ensured him political ascendency. The Bohemian princes suffered a bitter defeat in the battle. Svätopluk's victory over Louis's army and over Carloman's follow up campaign in Moravia,[6] however, significantly reduced the consequences of the Bohemian setback.

2   Kocel and the *Pannonian Diocese*

In 873 Kocel, in cooperation with the pope, tried for a final time to extricate the Pannonian Principality from the power of the Salzburg archbishop. Pope John VIII turned to both of Kocel's superiors. He warned the Eastern Frankish King Louis the German that *the Pannonian diocese has long been counted among the privileges of the Apostolic seat*.[7] He requested of Bavarian administrator Carloman, who was Kocel's immediate superior: *And so after returning and renewal of our Pannonian bishopric, allow us to recall our brother Methodius,*

---

4   Třeštík, *Počátky*, pp. 177–178, 188–195. Jiří Sláma convincingly shows that Bořivoj and Svätopluk could not have been related by blood. However, he doesn't doubt Svätopluk's wedding with a Přemyslid bride in October 871. Jiří Sláma, "K údajnému moravskému původu knížete Bořivoje," in *Velká Morava mezi východem a západem*, ed. Galuška, Kouřil, Měřínsky, pp. 349–353. František Palacký has already written about the wedding of Bořivoj's sister with Svätopluk in the fall of 871. František Palacký, *Dějiny národu českého w Čechách a w Moravě I/1. Od prvowěkosti až do roku 1125* (W Praze 1876), pp. 147–148.
5   *Ann. Fuld.* ad a. 872, rec. Kurze, p. 76. MMFH I, pp. 89–90. Třeštík, *Počátky*, pp. 181–188.
6   *Ann. Fuld.* ad a. 872, rec. Kurze, pp. 75–76. MMFH I, pp. 88–90. *Ann. Bert.* ad a. 872, rec. Kurze, p. 119. MMFH I, p. 60.
7   MMFH III, Epistolae 46, pp. 159–160.

to be there appointed to the Apostolic seat, and according to the ancient custom to freely perform the duties of a bishop.[8]

The pope tried to make the new ecclesiastical province as large as possible. Therefore, he also wrote to Serbian Prince Mutimir in Ras: *Therefore, I recall to you that you observe the custom of your predecessors, and to the extent you can, try to return to the Pannonian diocese.*[9] In 873 Bavarian bishops had to release Archbishop Methodius from captivity; however, they warned Kocel: *If you keep him near you, you'll not rid yourself of us so easily.*[10] The Pannonian Principality remained a part of the Salzburg diocese.

Two letters, dated 14 May 873, which Pope John VIII sent to Prince Kocel,[11] are the last reports we have on Kocel. After Kocel's death, Carloman, administrator of the Bavarial kingdom, handed over administration of the Pannonian Principality to his son Arnulf.[12]

3 Peace in Forchheim

In 874 Svätopluk concluded through his emissaries peace in Forchheim with the East Frankish King Louis the German.[13] Svätopluk was willing to promise loyalty and to pay tribute for the peace he needed to build and expand his realm. The tribute that the Moravians began to hand over each year,[14] was a burden, but thanks to it the Prince of the Moravians could *live in peace* with his neighbours, who were stronger than he was, and he could *peacefully act*, that is, gradually subject all his other neighbours, who were weaker. The presence of Bohemian emissaries together with Moravians in Forchheim is evidence that the Bohemian Prince Bořivoj acted in cooperation with Svätopluk, that he was his ally.[15] Peace with Eastern Frankish kingdom freed Svätopluk's hands, and the alliance with the Bohemians added strength for extensive invasions into the surrounding Slavic principalities.

---

8   *MMFH III*, Epistolae 47, p. 161.
9   *MMFH III*, Epistolae 55, pp. 173–174. Dvorník, *Byzantské misie*, pp. 57–58, 168.
10 ŽM 10, *MMFH II*, p. 153.
11 *MMFH III*, Epistolae 53, 54, pp. 171–173. *CDES I*, ed. R. Marsina, no. 19, 21, pp. 16, 17. Dvorník, *Byzantské misie*, pp. 166–168.
12 See notes 45, 46, 47. Szőke, *The Carolingian age in the Carpathian Basin*, pp. 98–102.
13 *Ann. Fuld.* ad a. 874, rec. Kurze, pp. 82–83. *MMFH I*, pp. 91–92. Lysý, *Moravania*, pp. 195–200.
14 This was the same tribute that Svätopluk agreed on with Arnulf in 890. See note 74.
15 Třeštík, *Počátky*, pp. 334–338.

4 Great Moravia along the Tisza River

The Life of Methodius mentions two wars of Svätopluk against pagans. First, he subjugated a powerful principality on the upper Vistula (Wiśla). The prince who ruled the Vistulians was *very strong* and was probably based in Kraków. Then, as he yielded to Svätopluk, he had to accept baptism from Moravian Archbishop Methodius.[16]

Immediately after the victory over the Vistulian Principality Svätopluk led another war. Methodius's biography emphasizes its difficult course: *Another time, when Svätopluk battled with pagans without the smallest success and was waiting, the mass, that is the service of St. Peter, was approaching, and* (Methodius) *went to him and said: If you promise me that you and your soldiers will spend St. Peter's Day* (29 June) *with me, I believe that God will soon return them to you. Which also happened.*[17]

Methodius's biographer did not write the name of the subjugated pagan tribe that put up such a great and initially also successful opposition to Svätopluk. Svätopluk, shortly after subjugating the Vistulians, could have attacked either the Croats on the middle Oder and on the Spree (in Lower Silesia and in both Lusatias) or the Slavs in the Tisza River region. Due to their position between the Morava and Vistulians (in Upper Silesia) he subjugated the Opolans at the same time as the Vistulians, or a bit later,[18] and he never led such a war against the Bohemians and the Sorbs along the Elbe River, and he conquered Pannonia, which had not been pagan or a newly Christianized country for a long time, in years 882–884. The Croats, who were divided into Silesians, Trebovans, Bobrans, Dadosezans, Milcens and Lusatians,[19] could

---

16   ŽM 11, *MMFH II*, p. 156.
17   ŽM 11, *MMFH II*, p. 156.
18   The Opolans probably belonged to the Vistulan principality. Widajewicz, *Państwo Wiślan*, pp. 59–60. Łowmiański, *Początki Polski IV*, p. 476.
19   Havlík, "Územní rozsah," pp. 43–46. Lubomír Havlík, "Tři kapitoly z nejstarších česko-polských vztahů," *Slovanské historické studie* 4 (1961), pp. 21–27, 49–50, 61–62. Łowmiański, *Początki Polski IV*, pp. 477–478. Steinhübel, *Kapitoly*, pp. 55, 56–58, 111. The Sorbs inhabited the *territory lying between the Elbe and the Sala* (campos inter Albim et Salam interiacentes). Ann. reg. Franc. (Ann. Einhardi) ad a. 782, rec. Kurze, p. 61. Thus, the Žirmuntes, Nižans, Koledicians, Neleticians, Suslians, Škudicians and Glomucians belonged to him, but no longer the Lusatians and Milcens, who were settled to the east of the Elbe, more exactly east of the Black Elster and its flow into the Pulsnitz up to the lower Bobrava and its flow into the Kwisa and together with the Silesians, Trebovans, Bobrans and the Dadosezans belonged to the Croatian tribes, who neighboured with the Sorbs. Constantine Porphyrogenitus, *De administrando imperio* 31, 32, ed. Moravcsik, pp. 147–161. Konstantinos Porfyrogenetos, *De administrando imperio*, *MMFH III*, pp. 389–391.

hardly have put up such great opposition, greater than the before then *very strong* Vistulian prince. This was left to the Slavs along the Tisza, who were subjugated to Bulgarian dominion and could have, with Bulgarian help, put up such opposition that Svätopluk had to wait at the beginning *with the smallest success*.[20] Svätopluk in the end triumphed and expanded his realm all the way to the lower Danube.

Methodius's pupils Clement, Naum and Angelarius, upon escape from Moravia in 886, arrived to the territory of neighbouring Bulgaria only after crossing the lower Danube, beyond which lay the nearest Bulgarian town, Belgrade (today in Serbia), where they were received by the Bulgarian viceroy.[21] And according to Constantine Porphyrogenitus, Svätopluk's Great Moravia lay immediately beyond Belgrade and Sirmium, and the rivers Timiş, Tutis (perhaps the Bega), Maros (Mureş), Körös and Tisza flowed through it. The Danube divided it from neighbouring Bulgaria. The lower Danube border of Svätopluk's realm, occupied by the Magyars at the time of Constantine Porphyrogenitus, began at Trajan's Bridge, which stood at the Iron Gates near Turnu Severin. The Danubian Trajan's Bridge stood *at the start of Turkey*, that is there where the Danubian border with the Magyars of the occupied Great Moravian area along the Tisza River, later the Hungarian state border. Three days travel from there lay the border-area, Belgrade, and another two days travel from Belgrade lay Sirmium, near the Danubian border.[22] The distance from the Iron Gates to Belgrade is actually about one-third longer than the distance between Belgrade and Sirmium. According to the mentioned rivers and according to the position of the three border points, Svätopluk's realm included in the south the entire territory of later Banat and Bačka. We can look for its eastern border in the Bihor Mountains (Muntii Apuseni). They were a major obstacle that could stop Svätopluk's expansion.[23] After Svätopluk's conquest, only Transylvania remained to the Bulgarians in the Carpathian Basin. The Bulgarians certainly helped the attacked Slavs and did not reconcile with the loss of the region around the Tisza. Testimony of this is Bulgaria's devastating counterattack in 882.[24]

---

20   Henryk Łowmiański has already identified Viching's *neophita gens* with the Slavs along the Tisza. We accept his opinion. Łowmiański, *Początky Polski IV*, p. 477.
21   *Život sv. Klimenta* XVI 47, *MMFH II*, p. 233.
22   Constantine Porphyrogenitus, *De administrando imperio* 40, ed. Moravcsik, pp. 176–179. Konstantinos Porfyrogenetos, *De administrando imperio*, *MMFH III*, pp. 396–397. Havlík, "Územní rozsah," pp. 63–67. Hadrian Daicoviciu, *Dákové* (Praha 1973), pp. 225–226.
23   The border which passed through the Apuseni Mountains divided Biharia from Transylvania. See chapter 13, notes 7, 8, 21, 22.
24   *Ann. Fuld.* ad a. 884, rec. Kurze, p. 112. *MMFH I*, p. 96.

Constantine Porphyrogenitus differentiates Moravia and Great Moravia. He refers to Svätopluk's area around the Tisza as Great or unbaptized Moravia and the original territory of the Moravians on the middle Danube only as Moravia.[25] Great or unbaptized Moravia means distant Moravia,[26] distant from the actual, original Moravia. The exiled pupils and followers of Methodius, who wanted to get to neighbouring Bulgaria, passed through here.[27]

5   The Nitra Bishopric

In 880, on Svätopluk's request and on the decision of Pope John VIII, Nitra became the seat of the second Great Moravian bishopric. The Nitra bishopric is clear proof of the importance of Nitra as a centre of one of two Great Moravian principalities. It shows us that the appanaged princes, such as Svätopluk I during Rastislav's rule and Svätopluk II under the rule of his brother Mojmír II, were based in Nitra. If Svätopluk in 880 had to decide where to put the second Great Moravian bishopric, then he could not get around Nitra, which even after Pribina's expulsion did not lose the importance of a princely seat. In June of 880 John VIII wrote to Svätopluk: *And the priest with the name of Wiching, whom you sent to us, we ordained as the chosen bishop of the holy Nitra church. We commanded him to obey his archbishop in everything, as is taught in the sacred canons.*[28] The subjugated position of the Nitrian bishopric towards the Moravian archbishop followed from the subjugated position of the Nitrian Principality to the Moravian Principality. The Great Moravian church thus exactly copied the asymmetrical dualism of the Great Moravian state.

The Nitra bishopric took over the old St. Emmeram patrocinum.[29] The Church of St. Emmeram, which Pribina had built, thus became the bishopric cathedral in 880.[30] In the archaeological layer which is younger than the

---

25   Constantine Porphyrogenitus, *De administrando imperio* 13, 40, 41, 42, ed. Moravcsik, pp. 64–65,176–183. Konstantinos Porfyrogenetos, *De administrando imperio* 13, 40, 41, 42, MMFH III, pp. 384, 396, 398–401.
26   Avenarius, *Byzantská kultúra*, p. 50. Avenarius, *Die byzantinische Kultur*, pp. 52–53.
27   See chapter 9, note 21.
28   MMFH III, Epistolae 90, p. 205. CDES I, ed. Marsina, no. 30, p. 24.
29   Peter Bednár – Zuzana Poláková, "Katedrála sv. Emeráma," in *Kolíska kresťanstva*, ed. Judák, Bednár, Medvecký, pp. 184–195.
30   If Pribina's church and later Wiching's episcopal cathedral were two different churches, then there were two different patrons at Nitra's castle. In addition to St. Emmeram, which Pribina's wife brought to Nitra, also the bishopric's patron, which the Árpád bishopric would later take over. There are two different patrons for the older small church and the newer bishopric or archbishopric cathredral, in Veszprém (St. George and St. Michael)

massive Great Moravian rampart of Nitra Castle (bulwark I), sporadically even in the filling of the younger earthen-wooden rampart with the grated construction from the 10th century (bulwark II) and in a large amount also in the wide earthen-wooden rampart with the chamber construction, built perhaps in the middle of the 11th century (bulwark III), blocks of white limestone, the remnants of a fine white mortar and fragments of well smoothed plaster, some even with the remnants of paintings, as well as several other architectural articles, were found. They were found primarily near today's churches. Worked limestone blocks are also found in the walls of the Romanesque rampart from the end of the 11th century or the beginning of the 12th century and mainly in the walls of the late-Romanesque church with the horseshoe apse from the 13th century. They originally belonged to a splendid building, probably a church, which stood at the top of the castle hill. Because they bear a significant Frankish construction and creative influence, they may come from Pribina's church, which later could have been included in the construction of the oldest bishopric cathedral. Traces of fire found in the construction remains could be from the same fire which overwhelmed the mentioned Great Moravian rampart.[31]

Wiching became the bishop of *sancte ecclesie Nitrensis*. Thus, the name Nitria was shortened to Nitra even before the establishing of the Nitra bishopric. Approximately one century later the bishop of Passau, Pilgrim (971–991), had a forgery made which also mentions the Nitrian bishopric.[32] Pilgrim, or the forger entrusted by him, did not take into consideration the then shortened name of Nitra and wrote it in the old and no longer used form *Nitrauensis*. He thus had an old source before him, which he'd sought in the episcopal archive,

---

and in Esztergom (St. Stephen and St. Adalbert). The Árpád bishopric cathedral in Nitra is consecrated to St. Emmeram, the same as the previous Great Moravian cathedral, which was the continuation of Pribina's church. And the Árpád bishopric cathedral in Alba Iulia took on the patron name of St. Michael from the older pre-Árpád rotunda which stood on its site. See chapter 13, note 28.

31 Bednár – Staník, "Archeologický a stavebnohistorický výskum hradu v rokoch 1988–1991," pp. 131–132. Bednár, "Nitriansky hrad v 9. storočí," pp. 21–22, 32. Bednár, "Die Entwicklung," pp. 376–377. Bednár, *Nitriansky hrad v 9. až 13. storočí. Autoreferát dizertácie*, pp. 11–13. Bednár, "Sídlisková štruktúra," pp. 31–32. Bednár, "Nitra v 9. storočí," pp. 90–92. Bednár, "Nitriansky hrad v 9. storočí," in *Bojná*, ed. Pieta, Ruttkay, Ruttkay, pp. 210, 213. Bednár, "Počiatky Nitrianskeho hradu," in *Kolíska kresťanstva*, ed. Judák, Bednár, Medvecký, p. 119. Bednár – Poláková, "Katedrála sv. Emeráma," in *Kolíska kresťanstva*, ed. Judák, Bednár, Medvecký, pp. 186–188. *Dejiny Nitry*, ed. Fusek, Zemene, p. 102.

32 *MMFH III*, Epistolae 122, p. 255. *CDES I*, ed. Marsina, no. 4, p. 5. Steinhübel, "Štyri veľkomoravské biskupstvá," pp. 28–29, 38. Steinhübel, "Die Großmährischen Bistümer," pp. 11, 21.

and copied the mention of Nitria from it. Pilgrim would certainly not have compiled his forgeries without looking through and using the archive. In the mentioned old source he could also find the name of Alcuin of Nitrava. Pilgrim added the title of bishop to his name: *Alchuuino sancte Nitrauensis ecclesie ... episcopis*. Alcuin, if in fact he really did live and work in Nitra, was not a bishop, because he could have only been so after Wiching's departure, more exactly only after 899, when the Great Moravian church got new bishops, among them certainly a Nitra bishop.[33] At that time, however, it would not have been a bishop *Nitrauensis ecclesie*, but only a *Nitrensis ecclesie*, like Wiching. Alcuin, if he is not fully invented, thus could have been an older Nitrian archipresbyter, subordinated to the Passau bishopric. This was perhaps in the time of Mojmír I or Rastislav, when the name of Nitra was still in the form Nitria.[34]

The territory conquered by Svätopluk within the Carpathian Basin, particularly in the area around the Tisza River, lay far from Methodius's Moravian diocese, even beyond Wiching's Nitrian diocese, which separated it from Moravia. Therefore, the Christian mission on what was distant territory for the Moravian archbishopric, had to come from Nitra. Wiching became the bishop of Nitra in 880. His first episcopal task, which he got immediately after being ordained and returning from Rome, could have been missionary work in the extensive area around the Tisza River, which Constantine Porphyrogenitus called *Great Moravia, the unbaptised part*.[35] Thus, the Bavarian bishops 20 years later could write that the pope did not send Wiching after ordination to the territory claimed by the Passau bishopric, to which Nitra, in addition to Moravia, also belonged,[36] but *to a certain nation turned from the faith (in quandam*

---

33   See note 113.
34   Branislav Varsik assumed that the change of Nitria to Nitra is the result of Hungarianization and the new form *Nitrensis* got into text from year 880 only with its description in the 12th century. He thus assumes the change of the name later by a scribe according to the actual state. Branislav Varsik, "K vzniku dnešného slovenského názvu Nitra," in Branislav Varsik, *Zo slovenského stredoveku. Výber historických štúdií a článkov z rokov 1946–1968* (Bratislava 1972), pp. 147–155. Scribes, however, were not accustomed to updating the texts of older documents by altering old names of castles, towns and villages according to their latest form. Indeed, they would have had to laboriously verify them. Therefore, it is much more probable that the old form of *Nitrauensis* is written from an old source, which Pilgrim found in the episcopal archive. The name of Nitra thus was not shortened by the Hungarians, but by the Slavs, namely in the 9th century. The Slavs did not take the shortened form Nitra, in Hungarian Nyitra, from the Hungarians but the Hungarians from the Slavs.
35   Constantine Porphyrogenitus, *De administrando imperio* 40, ed. Moravcsik, pp. 176–177. Konstantinos Porfyrogenetos, De administrando imperio 40, MMFH III, p. 396.
36   If Nitria had belonged for the entire 9th century to the Salzburg diocese, then in 900 not only would the Passau bishopric have complained about the reduction of its diocese, but

neophitam gentem), which the prince subjugated by war and made Christians from pagans.[37] Immediately after ordination and probably only shorly after stopping in Nitra, Wiching went to work in the extensive newly connected and still unbaptised area around the Tisza River, which directly neighboured with his Nitrian diocese. The pope didn't send him there, however; it was Svätopluk. This small, but important difference, however, somehow evaded the Bavarian bishops 20 years later. The Bavarian bishops, so that in their document from year 900 they did not have to acknowledge the existence of the Nitra bishopric,

---

[37] also the Salzburg archbishop. Conversio, too, defends the right of the Salzburg archbishop only in the Pannonian Principality, against its prepared inclusion into Methodius's archdiocese. The Salzburg archbishop did not in this document apply any claims at all on Nitria, which undoubtedly fell to Methodius's archdiocese at the time of its origin; thus, it did not belong to his diocese. See chapter 5, note 51.

MMFH III, Epistolae 109, pp. 237–238. Ernst Dümmler, Jan Dąbrowski and Gerard Labuda identified Wiching's *neophita gens* with Nitria. Dümmler, "Über die südostlichen Marken," pp. 40–41. Ernst Dümmler, *Geschichte des Ostfrankischen Reiches II* (Leipzig 1887), p. 179. Jan Dąbrowski, "Studia nad początkami państwa polskiego," *Rocznik Krakowski* 34 (1957–1959), no. 1, pp. 10–12. Gerard Labuda, "Kraków biskupi przed rokiem 1000. Przyczynek do dyskusji nad dziejami misji metodianskiej w Polsce," *Studia Historyczne* 27 (1984), no. 3 (106), pp. 384–385. Gerard Labuda, *Studia nad początkami państwa polskiego II* (Poznań 1988), pp. 143–145. According to Gerard Labuda, not one of the four bishops ordained in 899 by the papal legates was a Nitra bishop. He placed all four only in Moravia. However, even in modern times the Moravians never had such a dense episcopal organization, and for the entire Middle Ages a single bishopric sufficed. Labuda does not explain why the Nitra bishopric would have remained unoccupied and where such a strong need arose at the end of the 9th century to concentrate as many as four bishoprics on the territory of Moravia. Dušan Třeštík accepted the opinion that the *neophita gens* is actually Nitria and the more recently also Miroslav Lysý. Třeštík, *Vznik*, pp. 115–116, 278–279. Lysý, *Moravania*, pp. 91, 96–101. If three bishops could ordain a fourth, then a church province with four bishops was in the case of death of any of them capable of itself ordaining his successor. Therefore, even Poland in year 1000 got four bishops and not three or five. See chapter 14, notes 227, 228. If the Great Moravian church in the time of Mojmír II had, aside from four Moravian bishoprics, also a Nitra bishop, then it would have had a total of 5 bishoprics, which would have been above the scope of the desired self-sufficiency. Thus, they ordained four bishops for the whole of Mojmír II's state, that is also for Nitra. In addition to this, no one could consider Nitria in the time of arrival of Bishop Wiching to Nitra in 880 as unbaptised, because a second Christian generation was already living there and a third was being born. If, despite this, the Bavarian bishops considered Nitria in 880 as unbaptised, then this would have also applied for Moravia, because both principalities accepted Christianity at the same time, Moravia in 831 and Nitria after the exile of Pribina in 833. The Bavarian bishops well knew that Wiching was the bishop of Nitra. If they did not consider Nitria as a part of the Passau diocese, then nothing would prevent them writing that Wiching was the bishop of Nitra. They were silent, however, on the name of Nitra and mentioned only Wiching's episcopal station, which they skillfully connected with another territory on which Wiching also worked.

linked Wiching's episcopal title with another territory lying beyond the borders of their then immediate interest.[38]

Wiching came from Swabia and became friends with Svätopluk probably during Svätopluk's involuntary stay in Bavarian captivity nine years earlier.[39] Wiching was an opponent of Moravian Archbishop Methodius.[40] A lot of the old antagonism of both Great Moravian principalities was brought into their relations, which were the relations of the Slavic and the Latin side in the Great Moravian church. In 880, when each of them got their own diocese, their mutual rivalry had to enter into the relationship of their bishops.

6 Zobor Abbey

The first Nitra bishop, Wiching, was originally a Benedictine monk and probably the abbot of some abbey in the south of the East Frankish kingdom. Therefore, it was he who could have convinced Svätopluk to establish a Benedictine abbey on Zobor hill, which stood over his bishopric seat. Evidence on the beginning of the abbey in this period comes not only from the Zobor report on Svätopluk recorded by Cosmas, but mainly the abbey patrocinium of St. Hippolytus.[41]

---

38 Karol Potkański and Józef Widajewicz identified Wiching's *neophita gens* with the Vistulans. Thus, ecclesiastical adminstration of the Vistulans, in addition to the Nitra bishopric, must have been in Wiching's hands. Karol Potkański, "Kraków przed Piastami," *Rozprawy Akademii umiejetnosci* 35 (1898), p. 187. Józef Widajewicz, *Kraków i Poważe v dokumencie biskupstwa praskiego z 1086 roku* (Poznań 1938), pp. 78–80. Józef Widajewicz, *Państwo Wiślan* (Kraków 1947), pp. 71–74. Józef Widajewicz, "Prohor i Prokulf, najdawniejsi biskupi krakowscy," *Nasza przeszłość* IV (1948), pp. 27–30. Methodius negotiated directly with the Vistulian prince. If archbishop Methodius was interested in the baptism of the Vistulian prince and his country, then he would hardly have sent Wiching to do this work. Therefore, we cannot identify Wiching's *neophita gens* with the Vistulans.

39 Dvorník, *Byzantské misie*, p. 172.

40 Dvorník, *Byzantské misie*, pp. 177–179, 181–183, 196–205.

41 See chapter 12, note 7. Lajos J. Csóka, *Szent Benedek fiainak világtörténete különös tekintettel Magyarországra I* (Budapest 1969), p. 248. Alexander Ruttkay – Michal Slivka, "Cirkevné inštitúcie a ich úloha v sídliskovom a hospodárskom vývoji Slovenska v stredoveku," *Archaeologia historica* 10 (1985), p. 335. Michal Slivka, "Najstarší kláštor na Slovensku," *Historická revue* 2 (1991), no. 7, pp. 4–5. Michal Slivka, "Doterajšie poznatky z dejín a kultúry kresťanstva na Slovensku (4.–15. stor.)," *Studia archaeologica slovaca mediaevalia* III–IV (2000–2001), pp. 29–30. The Zobor patronage of St. Hippolytus and perhaps also the first Zobor monks could have come from the Abbey of Sankt Pölten in the Eastern March. Bavarian missionaries came from this abbey, established around 800 and consecrated to Hippolytus, to nearby Moravia and to Nitria. Wolfram, *Die Geburt*, pp. 163, 191, 254, 265, 277, 360. Testimony about this is the Church of St. Hippolytus, which stood

The abbey was certainly not built on Zobor by coincidence. Slavic and non-Slavic tribes had great respect for a dominant peak shrouded in myth, which stood over their land, such as Říp Mount (in Bohemia), Silesian Mount (Ślęża) or the Saxon Eresburg. This was a mythical centre of the tribe and the place of pagan celebrations. It was holy for the whole tribe, because long ago their history began there. A strengthening state, fortified by Christianity, built there a monastery or at least a church. The old pagan cult was thus covered by a new, Christian one. Thus, it was tied to the holy and unifying tradition of the tribe, and at the same time suppressed its pagan content.[42] What Eresburg was for the Saxons, Říp for the Bohemians, Silesian Mount for the Oder Croats, Zobor could be for the Slavic tribe to which Nitria belonged.[43]

7   Svätopluk in Pannonia

On 28 August 876 East Frankish King Louis the German died. According to an agreement made in 865, Louis's empire was divided among his sons. The oldest of them, Carloman, became the King of Bavaria: *Carloman got Bavaria, Pannonia and Carantania (Carnutum), which is erroneously called Karantanum, as well as the lands of the Slavs – the Bohemians and Moravians (regna Sclavorum, Behemensium et Marahensium)*.[44] Then Carloman handed Carantania over to his son Arnulf.[45] Carantanian margrave and Pannonian Prince Arnulf (876–887) was towards his father, Bavarian King Carloman, in the same position as Margrave Aribo, who starting in 871 administered the Eastern March.

in Znojmo in Great Moravia. Its foundations, which archaeologists excavated at the highest point of the Great Moravian castle, belonged undoubtedly to the 9th century, perhaps even to the time of Prince Mojmír I. A local monastery and the monastery church, which stands on over the foundations of an earlier but also Great Moravian rotunda, also has the patron name of St. Hippolytus. Klíma, "Archeologický výskum MU na velkomoravském výšinném hradišti sv. Hypolita ve Znojmě," pp. 232–238.

42   Třeštík, *Mýty*, pp. 71–77, 87, 92.
43   Ján Steinhübel, "Slovanský 'gens' a jeho stred. Kniežací hrad, pohanská svätyňa a trh." *Byzantinoslovaca* V, 2014, pp. 142–159.
44   *Reginonis abbatis Prumiensis Chronicon cum continuatione Treverensi*, ad a. 876, recognovit Fridericus Kurze, Scriptores rerum Germanicarum in usum scholarum ex Monumentis Germaniae historicis recusi (Hannoverae 1890), p. 112. *MMFH I*, p. 120, *MHDC III*, ed. Jaksch, no. 40, p. 15.
45   *Reginonis Chron.* ad a 876, rec. Kurze, p. 112. *MMFH I*, p. 120. *Concessit autem idem rex Arnulfo Carantanum, quod ei pater iam pridem concesserat, in quo situm est castrum munitissimum, quod palude inpenetrabili locus vallatus difficillimum adeuntibus preberat accessum. Reginonis Chron.* ad a. 880, rec. Kurze, p. 117.

This arrangement of the Bavarian border region and the peace that had reigned there since 874 was interrupted by the maturing sons Wilhelm and Engelschalk, who considered the Eastern March as their inheritance. They threatened Aribo: *Or Count Aribo will die by a sharpened sword, if he does not depart from the county of their parents, or they themselves.* Aribo, however, had no intention of abandoning the Eastern March to the Wilhelms. Therefore, he concluded an alliance with Great Moravian Prince Svätopluk and entrusted his own son Isanrich to him. The Wilhelms, however, assembled their army in 882 and gradually forced Aribo out and seized the Eastern March.

Svätopluk had to stifle his anger until Moravian envoys had departed a court meeting of Charles III in Worms in November 882. In that same year, thus immediately after the return of his envoys, he attacked the Wilhelms. Svätopluk managed to capture Werinhar, the middle of Engelschalk's three sons, and his relative Count Vezzilo and had both cruelly mutilated. He immediately attacked the Wilhelm properties lying near the Danube and ravaged them for the whole year.

The sons of Wilhelm and Engelschalk escaped to Carantanian Margrave and Pannonian Prince Arnulf in 883 and became vassals to him. Svätopluk sent a message to Arnulf: *You are supporting my enemies, if you don't let them go, do not count on my friendship with you.* He also blamed him for the attack of the Bulgarians, *who in the previous year devastated his realm,* and reproached him: *Your people are planning schemes on my life and my realm, allied with the Bulgarians. I want you to confirm on your oath that this is not true.*[46] Arnulf refused both requests. Svätopluk in a short time assembled his military from the whole of his realm, sacked Arnulf's Pannonia and remained there for the whole year. He returned home in the spring of 884. In this same year he again assembled a large army and repeated the devastating attack: *He had so many people on this campaign that his army could be seen arriving in one place from sunrise to sunset. He plundered Arnulf's holdings for twelve days with such a number of people.*

With two campaigns Svätopluk thoroughly annihilated Frankish power in Transdanubia and shifted the border of his realm up to the Drava River and the Vienna Woods. The physical liquidation of the representatives of Arnulf's administration did not stop even with their servants, whom Svätopluk's soldiers murdered along with their families: *They killed the servants with their children and captured some of the important people (primoribus) and murdered others,*

---

46 Ann. Fuld. ad a. 884, rec. Kurze, pp. 110–112. *MMFH I*, pp. 94–96. Wolfram, *Die Geburt*, p. 289.

and what is even more atrocious, they let them go with hands cut off, tongues cut out and genitalia mutilated.

After returning from the second Pannonian campaign Svätopluk *sent a certain portion of his army over the Danube* and thus secured power over the conquered Pannonian territory with his military units. Then Megingoz and Pabo, the oldest sons of Wilhelm and Engelschalk, *took with them several Pannonians* and marched against Svätopluk's brigades. The campaign ended unhappily: *Megingoz and Pabo ended their life in a river called the Rába, the brother of Count Berthold was captured by the Slavs along with many others.*[47]

8 Three Invasions of Mojmírs

Tension in the relations of Great Moravia and the Pannonian Principality climaxed in the years 883–884. With the arrival of Pribina to Blatengrad (around 840), Nitrian political emigration came to power in the Pannonian Principality, which determined the sharp anti-Moravian course of Pribina's rule. The response was the attack of the Moravians in 861. In that year the Moravians repeated what they had succeeded at in 833 in Nitria, and again at the expense of luckless Pribina. Pribina did not survive the second attack of the Moravians. In 861 he not only lost a piece of land in the north-eastern part of the Pannonian Principality, which Rastislav appended to Great Moravia, but he lost his life, too. Both attacks against Pribina, Mojmír's and Rastislav's, did not vary from the attack of a third, Svätopluk's. Svätopluk's extermination campaigns in years 883–884 fell upon the second generation of Pribina's princely retinue, the descendants of Nitrian emigrants who, after Kocel's death, entered into the service of the new Pannonian Prince, Arnulf, and in 883–884 together with the Wilhelms defended Arnulf's Pannonia against Svätopluk's attack. Their opposition, just as in the previous years 833 and 861, was, however, unsuccessful this time, too. All three Moravian attacks against Pribina and his faithful and against his principalities, Nitria and Pannonia, were a repetition of the old Mojmír policy, which followed one goal – territorial conquest and physical extermination of an antagonist who doubted their legitimacy on the conquered territory. Pribina's princely line could namely at the right moment and with Frankish help claim the old right to the princely seat in Nitra.

---

47 Ann. Fuld. ad a. 884, rec. Kurze, pp. 112–113. *MMFH I*, pp. 95–98.

9 Peace at Comagenan Mount

In the autumn of 884 Svätopluk met with Emperor Charles III (also called Charles the Fat): *The emperor had a meeting with Svätopluk on the borders of Bavarians and the Slavs (in terminis Noricorum et Sclavorum)*. The border between Svätopluk's and Charles's realms became the Vienna Woods: *The emperor marched through Bavaria to the east, and when he came to the vicinity of the river at Tulln at the Comagen Mount (monte Comiano) led the meeting. In addition to others, Prince Svätopluk came here with his princely retinue (Zwentibaldus dux cum principibus suis); he became a vassal (homo), as is the custom, by the hand of the emperor (per manus imperatoris). He confirmed loyalty to him with an oath and that so long as Charles will live, he will never come to his kingdom with an enemy army.*[48] The aim of Svätopluk's offensive was thus not only Arnulf's Pannonian Principality in southern Transdanubia, but also Upper Pannonia, which he could have still occupied during the attack on the Wilhelms in the Eastern March at the end of 882.[49]

If we count the time from the exiling of Aribo by the Wilhelm in 882, the war lasted two and a half years, as is stated in the Annals of Fulda. Arnulf lost Pannonia and only Carantania remained to him. And at the end in 885 he also made peace with Svätopluk.[50]

10 Bohemia in Svätopluk's Realm

Perhaps in the break between the attack on the Eastern March against the Wilhelms and the first invasion into Arnulf's Pannonia, that is in the spring of 883, Svätopluk subjugated the Bohemians: *Because the Bohemians (Behemi), too, abandoned their long preserved loyalty, and Svätopluk, convincing that attaching another country (regni) added to him no small power, swelled with haughty pride and rebelled against Arnulf.*[51] Svätopluk *through force (per vim) subjugated all the Bohemian princes.*[52] One of them, Prince Bořivoj, not only recognized Moravian supremacy but together with his closest retinue received

---

48 *Ann. Fuld.* ad a. 884, rec. Kurze, p. 101, 113. *MMFH I*, pg. 93, 98. Wolfram, *Die Geburt*, pp. 289–290. Sós, *Die slawische Bevölkerung*, pp. 48–63. Lysý, *Moravania*, pp. 210–221.
49 Ján Steinhübel, "Veľká Morava a bavorské pohraničie v rokoch 871–901," *Byzantinoslovaca* I (2006), pp. 146–150.
50 *Ann. Fuld.* ad a. 885, rec. Kurze, p. 114. *MMFH I*, p. 99.
51 See chapter 9, note 57.
52 See chapter 9, note 114.

baptism in Moravia from the hand of Archbishop Methodius.[53] He became Svätopluk's representative in Bohemia, and the other Bohemian princes were subjected to him.[54]

The Bohemians, however, did not want to be subjected to Moravian hegemony. When Svätopluk was busy with the first Pannonian campaign and the subsequent year-long stay in Pannonia, they rebelled. Bořivoj had to escape to Moravia. Shortly after this, evidently during the break between the two large Pannonian campaigns, that is in the spring or summer of 884, Svätopluk suppressed the rebellion and put Bořivoj back in Bohemia.[55] Bořivoj settled in central Bohemia, from where he was within equal reach of all the other Bohemian principalities.

After annexing the Bohemians, Svätopluk subjugated the Sorbs along the Elbe, who *annually paid tribute (cenzus)* to him.[56] Svätopluk's realm moved up to the Saale River that divided the Sorbs from Thuringia.

Bořivoj died in 888, and rule in Bohemia on behalf of Bořivoj's young sons went to Svätopluk himself, their relative and the supreme ruler. Even East Frankish King Arnulf had to recognize Svätopluk's rule in Bohemia in 890: *King Arnulf granted to Svätopluk, king of the Moravian Slavs, a principality of the Bohemiand (ducatum Behemensium), which until then had been ruled by a prince (principem) from his own blood line and nation and maintained the promised fealty to the Frankish King.*[57]

---

53 *Kristiánova legenda. Život a umučení svatého Václava a jeho báby svaté Ludmily (Legenda Christiani. Vita et pasio sancti Wenceslai et sancte Ludmile ave eius)* 2, edidit Jaroslav Ludvíkovský, Praha 1978, pp. 18–21. *MMFH II*, pp. 193–195. Dušan Třeštík, "Bořivoj a Svatopluk – vznik českého státu a Velká Morava," in Poulík, Chropovský et al., *Velká Morava a počátky československé státnosti*, pp. 273–301. Třeštík, *Počátky*, pp. 312–347. Bořivoj's baptism at Svätopluk's court established godparent relations, which strengthened Svätopluk's and Bořivoj's family. Třeštík, "Bořivoj a Svatopluk," pp. 287–288. Třeštík, *Počátky*, p. 335.

54 Třeštík, "Bořivoj a Svatopluk," p. 288. Třeštík, "Počátky," pp. 335–336. Just as Svätopluk elevated Bořivoj over the other Bohemian princes, Friulian Margrave Cadolah II appointed one of the small Croatian princes, Borna, as his viceroy for the whole of Croatian Dalmatia and subjected the other Croatian princes to him. See chapter 5, note 18.

55 *Kristiánova legenda* 2, ed. Ludvíkovský, pp. 21–25. *MMFH II*, pp. 195–197. Třeštík, "Bořivoj a Svatopluk," pp. 282–284, 289. Třeštík, "Počátky," pp. 331–334, 336–337.

56 *Thietmari Merseburgensis episcopi Chronicon* VI 60 (VII 39), post editionem Ioh. M. Lappenbergii recognovit Fridericus Kurze. Scriptores rerum Germanicarum in usum scholarum ex Monumentis Germaniae historicis recusi (Hannoverae 1889), pp. 190–191. *MMFH I*, pp. 150–151.

57 *Reginonis Chron.* ad a. 890, rec. Kurze, p. 134. *MMFH I*, pp. 137–138. Třeštík, *Počátky*, pg. 188–193.

Bořivoj left two sons behind, the older of which, Spytihněv, died in 915[58] and the younger, Vratislaus, on 13 February 921.[59] The Old Church Slavonic Prologue of St. Ludmila mentions the 33 years of Vratislaus's rule: *And the father's place was taken by his son Vratislaus. He then, ruling for thirty-three years, rested in the Lord.*[60] The Prologue of St. Ludmila is an abstract from the original St. Ludmila legend, which got to Russia by means of the Sázava Monastery (that is, before year 1096). The Prologue has, compared to the Latin legend Fuit in provincia Bohemorum and the Legenda Christiani, several surprisingly precise pieces of information, which could not be the result of Russian modification, but must have been of Bohemian origin. It writes of the Sorbian origin of Ludmila: *Blessed Ludmila was from a Sorbian country, daughter of a Sorbian prince.* It mentions the princely court in Tetín, in which Ludmila had her home: *they surrounded the doors with weapons. And they broke down the doors and went into her home.* It knows the exact location of her grave in Tetín *under the castle wall* and the name of the church to which they took her remains: *in the Church of St. George.*[61] The exact knowledge of Bohemian topography and the family relations of the princess Ľudmila and truthfulness of the other information in the Prologue also make the 33 years of rule of not only Vratislaus but of both of Bořivoj's and Ludmila's sons trustworthy. The unknown writer of the legend left out the older brother Spytihněv, though he could not leave out the years of his rule. Therefore, he simply added them to the younger Vratislaus, whom he left to rule immediately after his father's death. From Bořivoj's death through the death of Vratislaus was a period of 33 years.

Since the Prologue, or perhaps the unknown Bohemian writer of legend who wrote its Slavonic original, left out Prince Spytihněv and left Vratislaus to rule immediately from Bořivoj's death, he also had to add all the years of Spytihněv rule to the six years of Vratislaus's rule (915–921). Their sum could reach the 33 years which the Prologue mentions as the years of Vratislaus's rule. Since they

---

58   Třeštík, *Počátky*, pp. 109, 176, 194–195, 205.
59   Třeštík, *Počátky*, pp. 109, 176, 194, 205.
60   *Proložní legendy o sv. Lidmile a o sv. Václavu*, vydal N. J. Serebrjanskij, in *Sborník staroslovanských literárních památek o sv. Václavu a sv. Lidmile*, uspořádal Josef Vajs (Praha 1929) p. 64. *Proložní legenda o sv. Ludmile. Na úsvitu křesťanství*, uspořádal Václav Chaloupecký (Praha 1942), p. 253. Rogov – Bláhová – Konzal, *Staroslověnské legendy*, pp. 273, 280. Třeštík, *Počátky*, pp. 177–178.
61   *Proložní legendy o sv. Lidmile a o sv. Václavu*, vydal N. J. Serebrjanskij, in *Sborník staroslovanských literárních památek o sv. Václavu a sv. Lidmile*, ed. Vajs, pp. 64–65. *Na úsvitu křesťanství*, ed. Chaloupecký, pp. 253–254. Rogov – Bláhová – Konzal, *Staroslověnské legendy*, pp. 262, 276, 284–285. Třeštík, *Počátky*, pp. 148–153. Václav Chaloupecký, "Prameny X. století legendy Kristiánovi o svatém Václavu a svaté Ludmile," in *Svatováclavský sborník. Na památku 1000. výročí smrti knížete Václava Svatého II* 2 (Praha 1939), pp. 17–18.

are identical with the 33 years which the St. Ludmila legend, Fuit in provincia Bohemorum and the Legenda Christiani mention as the length of Vratislaus's life,[62] Vratislaus was born in the same year that his father died. If we then subtract 33 years of Vratislaus's life from the year of his death, we get not only the year of his birth, but also the year of Bořivoj's death: 921 − 33 = 888. Bořivoj thus died in 888, and since he lived to be 36 years old, he was born in 852. Spytihněv was thus born in 875, as he died in 915 as a 40-year-old.[63]

Svätopluk in his Bohemian policy favoured the Přemyslid line, because the duke of their family line was the main Bohemian prince, and from the small Přemyslid principality in central Bohemia they were able to best rule the whole of Bohemia. In the fall of 871 he married the daughter of a Přemyslid prince, and in years 883 and 884 the Bohemians had to acknowledge Moravian sovereignty. Prince Bořivoj became Svätopluk's representative for the whole of Bohemia, and after Bořivoj's death in 888, Svätopluk himself sat in Bořivoj's place and began to rule in Bohemia directly, without the Přemyslids.

11 Peace at Omundesberg

Emperor Charles III the Fat in November 887 had to abandon rule in the East Frankish kingdom to his son Arnulf.[64] The new East Frankish King Arnulf (887–899) gave the station he held then, that of Carantanian Margrave, to Ruodpert (887–893), the son of Wilhelm II[65] and also elevated the other Wilhelms, who from 882 were under his protection.

In March of 890 Arnulf met with Svätopluk *in a place which was informally called Omundesberg (Omuntesperch)*. Svätopluk attempted to turn Arnulf's interest away from Great Moravia. Therefore, he very willingly delivered to him a papal request and urgently advised him to visit Rome and turn the whole of

---

62   *Kristiánova legenda*, ed. Ludvíkovský, pp. 28–29. *Fuit in provincia Boemorum* 3, *Prameny X. století*, ed. Chaloupecký, p. 460. *Na úsvitu křesťanství*, ed. Chaloupecký, p. 61. Třeštík, *Počátky*, pp. 177–178.
63   Třeštík, *Počátky*, pp. 176–178.
64   *Ann. Fuld.* ad a. 887, rec. Kurze, p. 106. Ernst Dümmler, *Geschichte des Ostfränkisches Reiches II. Ludvig der Deutsche vom Koblenzer Frieden bis zu seinem Tode (860–876)* (Berlin 1887), pp. 287–303.
65   Ruodpert is mentioned in 889 as *terminalis comes*. *Monumenta Germaniae historica, Diplomata regum Germaniae ex stirpe Karolinorum 3. Die Urkunden Arnolfs*, herausgegeben von Paul Kehr, Berlin 1940, no. 63. According to a document from 892, Ruodpert administered the Carinthian March: *in comitatu Ruodperti in regno Carantano*. *Monumenta Germaniae historica. Diplomata regum Germaniae ex stirpe Karolinorum 3. Die Urkunden Arnolfs*, ed. Kehr, no. 109.

his attention to Italy. Svätopluk promised loyalty to Arnulf, promised to deliver tribute to him, and Arnulf recognized Svätopluk's rule in Bohemia.[66]

Under the Omundesberg hill lay Omundesdorf, through which Charlemegne passed in 791: *Lord Charles headed ... to Pannonia beyond Omundesdorf* (*ultra Omundesthorf*).[67] Charlemagne marched along the old Roman road down the southern bank of the Danube. In Omundesdorf, which lay on it, the former region known as Noricum ripense came to an end, and immediately beyond it began Pannonia. Arnulf, unlike Charles, came only to Omundesberg and did not enter into Pannonia, which then belonged to Svätopluk. According to the Annals of Fulda, Carolingian Pannonia began at the Enns River;[68] therefore, in 890 Arnulf, too, *marched to Pannonia*. It was enough to cross the Enns. According to the older Annales Maximiniani, which mention the campaign of Charlemagne in 791, Pannonia began, in line with antique borders, only in the Vienna Woods. Omundesdorf and Omundesberg stood on the Danubian road to Pannonia, on the edge of the Vienna Woods, beyond which began Pannonia[69] and which separated Svätopluk's realm from that of Arnulf. Svätopluk and Arnulf met somewhere in the foothills of the Vienna Woods, approximately where six years earlier Svätopluk had met with Charles III.

In 890 the same was decided in Omundesberg as was decided in Forchheim in 874, that is loyalty, tribute and peace. Svätopluk was again bound to assemble every year the agreed amount of livestock and deliver it to the neighbouring empire. The Annals of Fulda mention the meeting at Omundesberg, but aside from mention of the papal appeal that Svätopluk mediated for Arnulf, they say nothing else. They reveal, however, that the papal request that Arnulf go to Italy to help Rome was *among others* (*inter alia*); thus it was not the only reason for the meeting.[70] From Regino we know that Arnulf in 890 *granted Bohemia to Svätopluk*.[71] The year 890 is testimony that this compromise was made in Omundesberg. There was no other suitable opportunity for this important decision of Arnulf in the mentioned year. Svätopluk had already ruled

---

66   *Ann. Fuld.* ad a. 890, rec. Kurze, p. 118. *MMFH I*, pp. 99–100. *Reginonis Chron.* ad a. 890, rec. Kurze, p. 134. *MMFH I*, pp. 122–123. Steinhübel, "Veľká Morava a bavorské pohraničie," pp. 150–153. See chapter 9, notes 54, 74.
67   *Annales Maximiniani* ad a. 791, *MMFH I*, p. 42.
68   See chapter 5, note 18.
69   Ján Dekan identified Omundesberg with the peak Amandhegy standing near Pannonhalma. Dekan, *Slovenské dejiny II*, pp. 173–175. If Pannonia lay only beyond Omundesdorf, that is beyond Omundesberg, then Omundesberg could not have lay deep within Pannonia. Therefore, we cannot identify Amandhegy, lying in the interior of Pannonia, with Omundesberg.
70   *Ann. Fuld.* ad a. 890, rec. Kurze, p. 118. *MMFH I*, pg. 99–100.
71   *Reginonis Chron.* ad a. 890, rec. Kurze, p. 134. *MMFH I*, pg. 122–123.

in Bohemia for two years, and Arnulf could no longer change this; he gave up only his formal claim to Bohemia.[72]

Regino doesn't mention the papal appeal and the Annals of Fulda do not mention the granting of Bohemia. Neither mentions Svätopluk's commitment to pay tribute. They are silent on more than this, however. Arnulf and Svätopluk called a *general diet* (*generale conventum*); thus, they negotiated not only old breached obligations but everything that burdened their relationship. If they wanted to conclude peace, then they had to resolve primarily all the territorial disputes. Bohemia wasn't the only disputed territory between the two realms. Pannonia was the most important lost territory for Arnulf. The Pannonian Principality was the first and long-term base of Arnulf's ascent. Unlike Charles the Fat, who in 884 gave it up easily at Arnulf's expense, Arnulf had a soft spot for it, very close relations, and this was his *once happy Pannonia*.[73] Thus, in March 890, as in the autumn of 884, Pannonia was the primary focus of decisions made on the edge of the Vienna Woods.

If Arnulf gave up Bohemia, then he expected a similar concession from Svätopluk. Svätopluk did withdraw from Pannonia, but not fully. He drew back from an unsecured and unfriendly Pannonian Principality in southern Transdanubia. Northern Transdanubia, which was very advantageously contiguous with the territorial core of the Great Moravian state, that is Upper Pannonia between the Vienna Woods and the lower course of the Rába (northwestern Transdanubia), which he took in 882, and Lower Pannonian territory beyond the Bakony Forest and the lower Rába (north-eastern Transdanubia), which the Moravians had torn away from the Pannonian Principality in 861, remained in his possession.

Arnulf and Svätopluk settled all disputes, concluded peace and began to satisfy the peace conditions. In 891 Aribo, Margrave of the Eastern March, sent a letter to East Frankish King Arnulf, in which he wrote how *all Moravians* were gathering livestock as payment or an allowance, literally an *easement* (*servitium*), to which Svätopluk was bound in the previous year.[74] The Pannonian

---

72   Třeštík, *Počátky*, pp. 190–192.
73   *quondam Pannonia felix*. *Ann. Fuld.* ad a. 884, rec. Kurze, p. 111. *MMFH I*, p. 95.
74   Peter Ratkoš, "Cenný prírastok k prameňom o Veľkej Morave," *Slovenská archivistika* 11 (1976), no. 2, pp. 178–179. *Slovenská archivistika* 15 (1980), no. 1, p. 210. Třeštík, *Počátky*, pp. 288–289. Ondřej Zavadil, Dopis markrabího Ariba králi Arnulfovi, Mediaevalia historica Bohemica 11 (Praha 2007), pp. 7–17. In 831 Passau Bishop Reginhar baptised *all the Moravians* (*omnes Moravos*) and in 891 *all the Moravians* (*omnes Marahoni*) gathered livestock as the tribute intended for the East Frankish king. The baptism of the Moravians in 831 is mentioned in the *Notae de episcopis Pataviensibus* ad a. 831, *MMFH IV*, p. 407. Łowmiański, *Początki Polski IV*, pp. 249–250, 312–317. Třeštík, *Vznik*, pp. 117–121, 127–130.

Principality that Svätopluk had occupied in years 883–884 he returned in 890 to the East Frankish king. Testimony of this is the donation of King Arnulf on the territory of one of his three counties in the following year. In 891 King Arnulf could donate three properties in the Pannonian Principality to the Salzburg bishopric. The gifted lands lay *in the county called Dudlebia* on the rivers Pinka and Lafnitz and on the Gnasbach stream.[75] Dudlebian County was one of the three counties that made up the Pannonian Principality. If Dudlebia did not belong to Svätopluk, then not even little Ptuj Land, a separated territory of Dudlebia stuck at the south-western end of the Pannonian Principality, could have belonged to him. Svätopluk did not keep even Blatenia (Blatenland) with the seat at Blatengrad, because the western half of the Pannonian Principality as a territorial concession would hardly have sufficed for Arnulf. If Svätopluk kept in possession Bohemia and Upper Pannonia, then he had to let go of all of the Pannonian Principality, all three of its counties. This is the only way he could have satisfied Arnulf at least a little bit and conclude peace with him.

12 Svätopluk's Last War in Pannonia and the Destruction of the Wilhelms

In 891, Arnulf, undoubtedly during a stay in Bavaria, dispatched messengers to the Moravians *for the renewal of peace (pro renovanda pace)*. Since no one had breached the previous year's peace treaty, it was not necessary to renew anything. Arnulf thus wanted to change the concluded treaty, which he considered as disadvantageous.[76] Svätopluk rejected the new and undoubtedly less advantageous peace proposals that Arnulf's messengers submitted. Thus, a new antagonism began. In summer of 891 a devastating incursion of Danish Vikings surprised Arnulf; therefore, he could not march against the Moravians immediately. Svätopluk thus gained time. In November Arnulf defeated the

---

75 Arnulf's donation in 891 on the territory of the Pannonian Principality is at variance with affiliation of the Pannonian Principality, which took up the whole of southern Transdanubia, to Svätopluk's realm in the years 884–894. Ernst Dümmler noticed this variance. According to Dümmler, Svätopluk took only the eastern part of the Pannonian Principality, which then for 10 years did not continuously belong to his realm, and the western part, where the county *Dudleipa* lay, remained to Arnulf. Lubomír Havlík accepted this opinion. Ernst Dümmler, "Die südöstlichen Marken des fränkischen Reiches unter den Karolingern," *Archiv für Kunde österreichischer Geschichtsquellen* 10 (1853), pp. 48–49. Havlík, "Územní rozsah," p. 71.

76 *Ann. Fuld.* ad a. 891, rec. Kurze, p. 119. *MMFH I*, p. 100. Dekan, *Začiatky slovenských dejín*, pp. 177–178.

Vikings[77] and could again turn his attention to the east. At the end of February or early March of 892 he set off for the eastern border of Bavaria, where he wanted to meet with Svätopluk. But Svätopluk was not interested in his new proposals and could not be bothered to meet him at all. The angry Arnulf ended his journey in Carantania, where in Hengstfeld he met with Savian Prince Braslav and together with him thought through and planned a campaign against Svätopluk.

In July 892 Arnulf, together with an army of Franks, Bavarians and Alamans, attacked Great Moravia along with Prince Braslav and Magyar forces and marauded there for four weeks.[78] The war certainly ended the handing over of the agreed tribute to the empire and again opened the Pannonian Principality to the Moravians, who penetrated there and attacked its territory. Arnulf did not obtain anything; therefore, he began to negotiate with Bulgarian Prince Vladimir on a salt blockade of Svätopluk's realm. Arnulf's emissaries in September 892 had to go around the Pannonian Principality *for the snares of Prince Svätopluk*. They floated down the Sava to Bulgaria through Braslav's Savian Principality, and in May 893 returned by the same route.[79] If they avoided the Pannonian Principality, then Svätopluk's *snares (insidias)* must have been waiting for them there. If Arnulf's people had to travel through Braslav's Savia in the years 892 and 893, then Svätopluk no longer felt bound by the agreements concluded in Omundesberg, which Arnulf breached, and again penetrated into the southern Transdanubia. In August 893 Arnulf attacked Svätopluk's realm, where he ran into similar *snares (insidias)*, as had awaited Arnulf's people in the previous year in Pannonia.[80] This attack by Arnulf was obviously a response to the military presence of Moravians in the Pannonian Principality.

In the meantime Engelschalk's audacious son Engelschalk kidnapped Arnulf's unmarried daughter and, like Albgis 40 years before, he had to depart in exile for Moravia. Engelschalk was in Moravia for only a short time, because the king *soon after* pardoned him and perhaps in March 893 elevated him to Margrave of the Eastern March (*marchensis in Oriente*). Margrave Engelschalk II *haughtily marched against the Bavarian magnates* and completely antagonized them. Still in that same year, however, he lost everything. When he visited the royal palace in Regensburg, his Bavarian adversaries seized him and then blinded him. Engelschalk's cousin, Carantanian Margrave

---

77   *Ann. Fuld.* ad a. 891, rec. Kurze, p. 119.
78   *Ann, Fuld.* ad a. 892, rec. Kurze, pp. 120–121. *MMFH I*, pp. 100–101.
79   *Ann. Fuld.* ad a. 892, rec. Kurze, pp. 121–122. *MMFH I*, p. 101.
80   *Ann. Fuld.* ad a. 893, rec. Kurze, p. 122. *MMFH I*, p. 102. *Ann. Alaman.* ad a. 893, *MMFH I*, p. 15. *Annales Laubacenses* ad a. 893, *MMFH I*, p. 125.

Ruodpert, had to leave for exile with the Moravians. Engelschalk's brother Wilhelm, who through emissaries requested help from Svätopluk, was accused of treason and it cost him his head.[81] King Arnulf confiscated Engelschalk's and Wilhelm's property, which was the country they owned between the Enns and the Vienna Woods.[82]

After the fall of the last of the Wilhelms, Aribo returned to the Eastern March, and Arnulf's relative Liutpold (893–907), who was a margrave in Nordgau, became the new Carantanian margrave.[83] Liutpold and Aribo became the most powerful Bavarian magnates and undoubtedly stood at the forefront of anti-Wilhelm opposition, which in 893 carried them to the peak of Bavarian politics.

Ruodpert, who lost his position in Bavaria, was worthless to Svätopluk and became a victim of an old revenge. The deposed Carantanian margrave, *hiding among the Moravians as an exile, was killed with very many others by the unscrupulous intention of the prince.*[84] Svätopluk thus on this last occasion avenged the Wilhelms in an equally bloody way as 10 years before.

Svätopluk died in 894,[85] and his successor, Mojmír II, gave up the aggressive intentions in the Pannonian Principality. The Pannonian Principality, which again belonged to the Bavarian borderlands, was invaded and cruelly despoiled by the Magyars.

In the autumn of 894 the Moravians concluded a peace with the Bavarians.[86] Mojmír with the greatest probability acknowledged and confirmed what his father had agreed upon with Arnulf four years before at Omundesberg, that is he recognized Bavarian sovereignty over the Pannonian Principality. From Svätopluk's territorial acquisitions in Pannonia, only Upper Pannonia now remained to Mojmír, which he then lost in January 901.

---

81   *Ann. Fuld.* ad a. 893, rec. Kurze, p. 122. *MMFH I*, p. 102. *Ann. Alaman.* ad a. 893, *MMFH I*, p. 15. *Ann. Laub.* ad a. 893, *MMFH I*, p. 125.
82   King Arnulf donated the confiscated property to Kremsmünster Abbey on 22 October 893. *MMFH III*, Diplomata 48, pp. 80–81.
83   Mitterauer, "Karolingische Markgrafen," pp. 189–190, 236–237. Wolfram, *Die Geburt*, p. 306. Wolfram, *Salzburg, Bayern, Österreich*, p. 321. *Conversio*, ed. Wolfram, p. 266.
84   *Ann. Fuld.* ad a. 893, rec. Kurze, p. 122. *MMFH I*, p. 102. *Ann. Alaman.* ad a. 893, *MMFH I*, p. 15. *Ann. Laub.* ad a. 893, *MMFH I*, p. 125. Mitterauer, "Karolingische Markgrafen," pp. 180–181. Wolfram, *Die Geburt*, p. 305. Wolfram, *Salzburg, Bayern, Österreich*, p. 321.
85   *Ann. Fuld.* ad a. 894, rec. Kurze, p. 125. *MMFH I*, p. 103. *Reginonis Chron.* ad a. 894, rec. Kurze, p. 143. *MMFH I*, p. 124. Havlík, *Kronika o Velké Moravě*, pp. 230–233.
86   *Ann. Fuld.* ad a. 894, rec. Kurze, p. 125. *MMFH I*, p. 103. Havlík, "Územní rozsah," p. 72. Havlík, "Pannonie," p. 33.

13   Bohemians and Bavarians against the Moravians

In July 895 *all the princes of the Bohemians (duces Boemanorum), which Prince Svätopluk had recently by force torn away from the bondage and rule of the Bavarian nation and usurped and the principals (primores) of which were Spytihněv and Vratislaus (Spitignewo, Witizla)*, came to Regensburg and sought assistance there against the Moravians, who did not want to lose the Bohemians.[87] Prince Spytihněv took with him to Regensburg not only the smaller and subjugated Bohemian principalities but also his seven-year-old brother Vratislaus. Vratislaus was his successor and could not be absent from Regensburg, because the Bohemian-Bavarian alliance was also concluded for the period of his future rule. Vratislaus's presence during the concluding of the alliance was a guarantee of its duration even after Spytihněv's death. Like his brother, he also had a higher position than the other Bohemian principalities. Spytihněv and Vratislaus were *primores* among the Bohemian princes.

With the secession of the Bohemians the neighbouring Sorbs lost their territorial link with the Moravians. In 897 Sorbian emissaries visited emperor Arnulf, delivering gifts to him.[88] Their dependence on Great Moravia was now a thing of the past.

In 897 the Bohemians again asked Arnulf for help: *Princes of the Bohemian people (gentis Behemitarum duces) came to Emperor Arnulf ... and asked him for help as well as his support against the enemy Moravians, who often, as they stated, very cruelly suppressed them.* Through the entire autumn of 897 Arnulf waited in northern Bavaria, prepared to help the Bohemians in the case of a Moravian attack.[89]

Mojmír II was on his mother's side half Přemyslid. Perhaps that is why Bohemia was so very important to him. Only up to the war between Mojmír II and his brother Svätopluk II in the years 898–899, linked with the Bavarian attacks against Mojmír's realm, did Mojmír's intervention into Bohemia cease.

---

87   *Ann. Fuld.* ad a. 895, rec. Kurze, p. 126. *MMFH I*, pp. 103–104. Since Vratislaus was still a minor in 895 and could not be Spytihněv's co-ruler, Jiří Sláma and Dušan Třeštík reject his identification with Vitislaus, who came together with Spytihněv to Regensburg. Jiří Sláma, "Vratislav I. a sv. Václav," *Archelogické rozhledy* 42 (1990), pp. 296–298. Třeštík, *Počátky*, pp. 100, 188, 193, 350, 445, 454. Jiří Sláma looks for Vitislaus's principality in northwestern Bohemia, where archaeologists have found a larger number of hill-forts. Jiří Sláma, "Vitislav (ui utizla)," in *Seminář a jeho hosté. Sborník prací k 60. narozeninám doc. dr. Rostislava Nového*, ed. Zdeněk Hojda, Jiří Pešek, Blanka Zilynská (Praha 1992), p. 17.
88   *Ann. Fuld.* ad a. 897, rec. Kurze, p. 131. *MMFH I*, p. 106.
89   *Ann. Fuld.* ad a. 897, rec. Kurze, p. 131. *MMFH I*, p. 106.

14 Mojmír II and Svätopluk II – *Disagreement and a Very Difficult Dispute*

Before his death Svätopluk divided rule in the land between his sons. Both sons got their own principality. The younger, Svätopluk II, with the greatest probability was granted the Nitrian Principality and was subjected to his older brother Mojmír II.

In 899 Svätopluk was still only a *boy* (*puer*),[90] that is, not an adult. There must have been a large age difference between him and his brother Mojmír. They probably did not have the same mother. The mother of Mojmír II could have been the Bohemian Princess Svätožízňa, whom his father married in October of 871. According to a much later report from Bavarian chronicler Aventinus from the 16th century, Svätopluk I in 885 married Arnulf's sister Gisela.[91] If Aventinus was right, then Svätopluk II could very well have come from this marriage and was thus Arnulf's nephew.

Four years after his father's death, Svätopluk II, instigated and supported by Margrave Aribo, rebelled against his brother: *Then, however, in the year of our Lord 898 disagreement arose between both brothers from the Moravian nation, Mojmír and Svätopluk, and their people (eorumque populum) and a very difficult dispute occurred (dissensio atque discordia gravissima), and to such a measure that if one could have gotten to the other and captured him, he would have sentenced him to death.*[92] Emperor Arnulf sent help to the Nitrian Prince in the form of Bavarian Duke Liutpold and Margrave of the Eastern March Aribo, who devastated the land with a large Bavarian army. Shortly after, the emperor temporarily deposed Aribo, citing his guilt in fomenting mischief in Great Moravia. In the winter, at the start of 899, the Bavarians repeated the devastating campaign; however, they could not prevent the defeat of Svätopluk. Mojmír imprisoned his disobedient brother *and his people* (*suumque populum*) at some castle, from where he was shortly after freed by a third Bavarian campaign: *The Bavarians again boldly crossed the border of the Moravians, and they looted whatever they could and by plundering they liberated the boy Svätopluk, son of former Prince Svätopluk, and his people from captivity of the castle in which they*

---

90 See note 93.
91 *Aventini Annales Boiorum* IV, XIX 27, *MMFH I*, p. 409.
92 *Ann. Fuld.* ad a. 898, rec. Kurze, pp. 131–132. *MMFH I*, pp. 106–107. Constantine Porphyrogenitus wrote about the sons of Svätopluk I: *between them a feud and a rupture arose and they started an internal war one against one another.* Constantine Porphyrogenitus, *De administrando imperio* 41, ed. Moravcsik, pp. 180–181. Konstantinos Porfyrogennétos, *De administrando imperio* 41, *MMFH III*, pp. 399–400.

were held and burned the castle (civitatem) itself and out of mercy took them with them to the ends of their homeland.[93]

If Princes Mojmír II and Svätopluk II had *people* who were *theirs*, and if together with Svätopluk *his people* were also imprisoned in a castle, then these *people* were the princely retinue, which accompanied the prince, were loyal to him and shared his fate.

In the meantime, however, Mojmír II concluded an alliance with Aribo's son Isanrich, who after his father's removal temporarily took over administration of the Eastern March. Margrave Isanrich paid no regard to the authority of the then very ill East Frankish King and Emperor Arnulf and stood up to the army with which Arnulf surrounded his seat at Mautern. After a short siege, however, Isanrich surrendered and was taken captive. On the trip to Regensburg he managed to free himself of Arnulf's capture and escape to the Moravians. Immediately after the Moravians invaded the Eastern March, took it over and handed it over to their allies.[94] Isanrich, however, did not acquire the entire Eastern March, because its Upper Pannonian part had already belonged to Great Moravia since year 882,[95] and the Bavarians held county Traungau to the west of Enns. From his seat at the castle in Mautern he ruled, with Moravian help, only its central county, between the Enns and the Vienna Woods.

Right at this time (year 899) papal emissaries came to Moravia and consecrated there a new Moravian archbishop and three bishops subjugated to him. One of the newly ordained bishops undoubtedly came to Nitra.[96]

---

93   *Ann. Fuld.* ad a. 898–899, rec. Kurze, pp. 131–133. *MMFH I*, pp. 106–109.
94   *Ann. Fuld.* ad a. 899, rec. Kurze, pp. 132–133. *MMFH I*, pp. 108–109.
95   See p. 223.
96   We have to look for the other two bishoprics on the territory that Mojmír II still had in his power and that the Passau bishopric considered as part of its diocese. Therefore, in line with the later and rather unreliable knowledge of Passau Bishop Pilgrim (971–991), we can look for one of them in Upper Pannonia (perhaps in Sopron), which then belonged to Great Moravia, and the other in Mautern, where Margrave Isanrich settled; he had been put in Mautern in 899 by the Moravians and with Moravian help stayed here until 901. Steinhübel, "Štyri veľkomoravské biskupstvá," pp. 28–38. Steinhübel, "Die Grossmährischen Bistümer," pp. 11–22. See note 31. Not only Upper Pannonia but the whole of the norther Transdanubia could have belonged to the diocese of the Upper Pannonian bishopric, by which it would have achieved adequate size. This opinion, despite the fact that it well explains the anger of the Passau bishop and may depend on one of Pilgrim's falsifications, has a weak foundation. The area around the Tisza River, where in 896 with the consent of the Moravians a portion of the Magyars settled, still belonged to the realm of Mojmír II. The local Moravians, who *took in* the Magyars had not yet departed from there. And this territory undoubtedly needed a bishop. Thus, the opinion of Richard Marsina, who seeks the third bishopric in ancient Veszprém and the fourth in Feldebrő (near Eger), is more probable. Richard Marsina, "Cirkevná organizácia na Veľkej Morave," in *Velká*

15 The Princes and Their Retinues, Freedom and Servitude

The Mojmírs, who ruled the Moravians, had the Slavic title of *knɛzь* (*kъnɛzь*).[97] Rastislav was a *moravьskyj kъnɛzь*[98] or a *kъnɛzь slovьnьskъ*.[99] The Life of Methodius refers to Svätopluk as a *knɛzь*,[100] that is a prince. And the Prologue to the life of Constantine and Methodius tells clearly of Svätopluk's princely title, when it mentions that archbishop Methodius *settled in the land of Moravia ... by prince Svätopluk* (*pri Svɛtopolьca knɛzy*). *The Greek emperor was Vasilij* (= Basil I) *and the Bulgarian from God* (ruled) *Prince* (*knɛzь*) *Boris. A king* (ruled) *the German people* (*kralь nѣmečьskymь ljudemь*).[101] In the Slavonic text of the

---

Morava mezi východem a západem, ed. Galuška, Kořil, Měřínský, pp. 294–295. Veszprém in the time of the Hungarian Prince Géza became the seat of the first Hungarian bishopric, which could connect not only to the enduring continuity of Great Moravian Christianity (see pp. 179–180), but also in the tracks shortly lasting (899–900) Great Moravian bishopric. The whole northern Transdanubia, that is also Upper Pannonia, which belonged to the Passau diocese, could have been assigned to the Great Moravian bishopric with its seat in Veszprém. The fourth bishop could be the Great Moravian forerunner of the Eger bishop, assigned in 1009. Thus, it could have based in Eger or perhaps in nearby Feldebrő, or we can look for it in another place, perhaps in an unknown centre of the Tisza River area of Great Moravia; if as a consequence of the events of 896, it did not shift to the mentioned Eger, or to another castle in the southern foothills of the Bükk Mountains or the Matra Mountains. Steinhübel, "Veľká Morava a bavorské pohraničie," pp. 155–158. Passau Bishop Richarius could consider the Tisza River area, which could be the diocese of the fourth Great Moravian bishopric, as the easternmost part of his diocese. His interest certainly did not end in the Nitria. He also wanted to include the territory beyond its eastern and south-eastern borders, attached to Great Moravia by Svätopluk. Indeed in year 867, on the invitation of Bulgarian Prince Boris, his predecessor Hermanarich came there and wanted to work there. *Ann. Fuld.* ad a. 867, rec. Kurze, pp. 65–66. *MMFH I*. p. 81.

97 Piotr Boroń, *Kniaziowie, królowie, carowie ... Tytuły i nazwy władców słowiańskich we wczesnym średniowieczu* (Katowice 2010), pp. 78–81, 116–119. Bohumil Vykypěl, *Studie k šlechtickým titulům v germánských, slovanských a baltských jazycích* (Praha 2011), pp. 128–133. Ján Steinhübel, "Bol alebo nebol Svätopluk kráľom?" *Historický časopis* 61 (2013), no. 4, pp. 671–696. Ján Steinhübel, "Slovanské 'gentes' a ich vladykovia, kniežatá a kagani od sťahovania národov po Svätopluka," in Dušan Kováč et al., *Slovenské dejiny v dejinách Európy. Vybrané kapitoly* (Bratislava 2015), pp. 267–273, 284. Lysý, *Moravania*, pp. 227–247. For the last attempt to defend the royal title for Svätopluk, see Martin Homza, "O kráľovskom titule Svätopluka I. († 894)," *Historický časopis* 61 (2013), no. 4, pp. 655–669. Martin Homza, "K argumentácii o kráľovskom titule Svätopluka I. († 894)," in Martin Homza et al., *Svätopluk v európskom písomníctve. Štúdie z dejín svätoplukovskej legendy* (Bratislava 2013), pp. 142–161.
98 ŽK 14, *MMFH II*, p. 98.
99 ŽM 5, *MMFH II*, p. 143.
100 *Svɛtopъlkъ knɛzь. ŽM* 10, *MMFH II*, p. 154. The dying Methodius *preached the blessing of the emperor and the prince* (*knɛzɛ*). *ŽM* 17, *MMFH II*, pp. 161–162.
101 *Proložnoje žitije Konstantina i Mefodija*, *MMFH II*, p. 166.

code of laws which Archbishop Methodius compiled in Great Moravia during Svätopluk's period of rule the term *knѧzь*, or prince, is mentioned.[102] Likewise, Methodius's admonition *reproach to rulers*, mentions a *knѧzъ* and *kъnѧzѧ*.[103]

According to contemporary Arab reports on the Slavs, which at the beginning of the 10th century Persian scholar Ibn Rusta put into his great historical-geographical work, *S.w.j.tb.l.k*, that is Svätopluk, was the *main head (ra'ísu r-ru'asá'i)*,[104] that is a *prince of the princes*. In the autumn of 884 *Prince Svätopluk with his princes (Zwentibaldus dux cum principibus suis)* swore to Emperor Charles III the Fat peace at Comagen Mount (Kaumberg).[105] Similarly, his predecessor Rastislaus, *with all of his best (cum universis optimatibus suis)*, that is with his small princes, swore in August 864 to East Frankish King Louis the German the Devín peace.[106] The Moravian decided on the fate of the state along with his subjugated Nitrian prince together with all the small, secondary princes and with the free Moravians. Regarding the delegation to the Byzantine emperor in 862 *Rastislav, the Moravian prince ... consulted with his princes and with the Moravians*.[107] Svätopluk proceeded the same way, when in 873 he received Archbishop Methodius and *with all the Moravians*.[108] When Svätopluk handed over the state that he ruled in 880 to the papal patronate, the pope praised him: *You have chosen the blessed Peter ... and his deputy as a patron ... together with your lofty and faithful men and with the entire population of your country*, that is together with the princes and free Moravians.[109] Margrave of

102   ZSL 2, 3, 4, MMFH IV, pp. 178, 180, 181.
103   *Vladykam zemlę božie slovo velitь*, MMFH IV, p. 201.
104   *Kitábu l-aláki n-náfísati li-bni Rusta*, MMFH III, pp. 346–347. Ján Pauliny, *Arabské správy o Slovanoch (9.–12. storočie)* (Bratislava 1999), p. 99. Třeštík, *Počátky*, pp. 289, 294–295. Later al-Marwazí also mentioned Svätopluk: *And their greatest head (ra`ísuhumu l-akbaru) is called Svätopluk (S.wít) ... Kitábu tabá'i`i l-hajawáni li-Šarafi z-Zamáni Táhiri Marwazíi* 14, MMFH III, p. 433. Pauliny, *Arabské správy*, p. 140. Steinhübel, "Slovanské 'gentes' a ich vladykovia, kniežatá a kagani," pp. 280–284.
105   See note 48.
106   See chapter 8, note 34.
107   See chapter 7, note 33.
108   ŽM 10, MMFH II, pp. 153–154. Polish Prince Boleslaw the Brave also consulted with his subjugated princes *(coram principibus suis)*. *Thietmari Chronicon* VIII (VII) 9, rec. Kurze, p. 109. *Thietmari Chronicon* VII 9, cur. Trillmich, pp. 362–363. Łowmiański, *Początky Polski IV*, p. 118.
109   MMFH III, Epistolae 90, p. 205. CDES I, ed. Marsina, no. 30, p. 24. Polish Prince Boleslaw the Brave before his death in 1025 *assembled all of his princes (principibus) and friends, from everywhere by his side. Galli Chronicon* I 16, MPH I, ed. Bielowski, p. 411. Boleslaw the Brave *loved his princes (duces) and counts (comites) and leaders (principes) and brothers or sons. Galli Chronicon* I 13, MPH I, ed. Bielowski, p. 408. And Russian Prince Vladimir *loved the retinue, considering with them the adminstration of the land and in wars and in organizing the country. Latopis Nestora* 45, year 6504 (996), MPH I, ed. Bielowski, pp. 672–673.

the Eastern March, Aribo, in 891 sent a letter to East Frankish King Arnulf, in which he wrote, as *all Moravians* assembled livestock as tribute or an allowance, literally *service (servitium)*, to which Svätopluk promised to Arnulf in the previous year. Aribo emphasizes that the Moravians are acting freely *without any domination of the prominent (cum nulli dominationi proceres)*. The princes, literally *the prominent (proceres)*, did not have any rule or power over free Moravians, literally *domination (dominatio)*. If all the Moravians assembled and handed over tribute from their own livestock freely, then they must have agreed to Svätopluk's obligation at a common meeting.[110]

Both principalities, Moravia and Nitria, which made up Mojmír's state in 833, were divided into several smaller principalities. Later, the emerging Bohemian and Hungarian states had this sort of two-level princely subordination.[111] Small principalities, more closely or only freely subordinated to the main Přemyslid and Árpád prince, were abolished in Bohemia only by Boleslaus I and in Hungary by Stephen I.

The Moravian-Nitrian dualism of Mojmír's state was also manifested in its large territorial expansion. Svätopluk subdued and ruled the Vistulans, Bohemians and Sorbs along the Elbe River from the territory of Moravia itself. The Moravian bishop had the responsibility of baptising these tribes in his care. The natural point of departure for Great Moravian offensives into nearly the entire Carpathian Basin, that is Transdanubia and the land along the Tisza, was the Nitrian Principality. Svätopluk entrusted the Christian mission on these territories, if they were not yet baptised, to the Nitrian bishopric.

Professional horse soldiers lived in the vicinity of a prince. An Arab report on the Slavs mentions, how Svätopluk equipped them all: *This ruler (l-maliki) has riding animals (dawábbun) ... And has excellent armour, solid and valuable.*[112] Svätopluk also had a large, probably thousand-plus member, fully equipped cavalry brigade, which in October 871 led the daughter of the Bohemian prince to Moravia.[113] Even Princes Mojmír II and Svätopluk II had their own *people (populum)*, a princely retinue that accompanied them everywhere they went.

110 Peter Ratkoš, "Cenný prírastok k prameňom o Veľkej Morave," *Slovenská archivistika* 11 (1976), no. 2, pp. 178–179. *Slovenská archivistika* 15 (1980), no. 1, p. 210. Třeštík, *Počátky*, pp. 288–289.
111 Steinhübel, *Kapitoly*, pp. 53–56. Miroslav Lysý, "Druhostupňové kniežatá na Morave v 9. storočí," *Byzantinoslovaca* V (2014), pp. 123–127.
112 *Kitábu l-a láki n-náfisati li-bni Rusta*, MMFH III, p. 347. Pauliny, *Arabské správy*, p. 99. Třeštík, *Počátky*, pp. 289–291. Even later al-Marwazí recalled the same: *And their ruler (l-maliki) has riding animals (dawábbun) ... Kitábu tabá'i'i l-hajawáni li-Šarafi z-Zamáni Táhiri Marwazíi* 14, MMFH III, p. 433. Pauliny, *Arabské správy*, p. 140.
113 Ann. Fuld. ad a. 871, rec. Kurze, pp. 74–75. MMFH I, pp. 87–88.

Professional princely warriors needed expensive weapons and equipment, good horses and an abundance of food and clothing. In order for the prince to meet these demands, they worked for him, whether freely or not, settled on their own or on princely land and regularly provided him with exactly determined services and products. We know of such a service organization in Árpád Hungary, Přemyslid Bohemia and in Piast Poland. Although we don't have direct proof of a service organization in Great Moravia, the large, several-thousand strong retinue of Svätopluk certainly needed one.[114]

Among the free Moravians who attended tribal-wide assemblies, the magnates stood out. They were wealthy and shared significantly in administration of the state or at the princely court or at castles. Svätopluk's *kind of associate, a great rich man and advisor*, who got into a dispute with Archbishop Methodius due to marriage with his godmother, had such a position and influence that other princes, in order to not lose his favour, questioned Methodius's efforts to divorce him from this marriage, which was unacceptable to the church.[115]

At the opposite end of society stood the serfs, settled on princely land and the land of magnates, and slaves, who could be bought and sold.[116]

[114] Třeštík, *Počátky*, pp. 291–292, 295–296.
[115] ŽM 11, 17, *MMFH II*, pp. 156–157, 162. Lubomír Havlík, "Velká Morava v kontextu evropských a obecných dějin," in Poulík – Chropovský et al., *Velká Morava a počátky československé státnosti*, pg. 200. Třeštík, *Počátky*, pp. 287, 293.
[116] ŽM 17, *MMFH II*, pp. 162. Havlík, "Velká Morava v kontextu evropských a obecných dějin," p. 201. Třeštík, *Počátky*, p. 287.

CHAPTER 10

Great Moravia and the Magyars

1   Levedia and Etelköz

Until the middle of the 9th century, Magyar tribes wandered through the Onogur Steppes between the Don and the Dnieper rivers on the western edge of the Khazar empire. A part of the Bulgarian Onogurs expanded the Magyar tribal alliance and also gave it its name. That's why the Slavs called the Magyar tribes Ogri, Ugri or Ungri, the Greeks called them Ongroii and Latin sources referred to them as Ungri, Ungari, Ungarii, later Hungari, Hungarii.[1] At the head of each of the seven Magyar tribes (*geneai*) – Nyék, Megyer, Kürt-Gyarmat, Tarján, Jenő, Kér and Keszi – were commanders or *voivodes* (*vojévodoi*). The first among them was Levedi (*Lebedias*), after whom the old Magyar settlements, called Levedia, were named.[2]

After defeat at the hands of the Pechenegs, the Magyars (Hungarians) departed to the west to Etelköz (the region between the Dnieper, the Carpathians and the Danubian delta). Thus, they rid themselves of dependence on the Khazar empire and selected as their grand prince (*archont*) Árpád, son of one of the tribal voivodes, Álmos: *Before this Árpád, the Turks* (= Hungarians) *never had another prince and since then until today the prince of Turkey* (= Hungary) *comes from this line*.[3] Three Khazar tribes joined the Magyars departing to Etelköz: *It is necessary to know that the so-called Kabars come from a generation of Khazars. However, it happened that among them a rebellion broke out against their ruler, and a civil war started, in which their earlier ruler triumphed. Some of them were slaughtered; others, however, ran away and settled with the Turks in the land of the Pechenegs* (= in Etelköz, which was later occupied by the Pechenegs). *They befriended one another and were called the Kabars.*

---

1   Alexander Avenarius, "Prabulhari v prameňoch 6.–7. storočia," *Slovanské štúdie* 8 (1966), pp. 185–204. Henryk Łowmiański, *Początki Polski. Z dziejów Słowian w I tysiącleciu n. e. V* (Warszawa 1973), pp. 53–71. *MT I/1*, pp. 481–498. Antal Bartha, *A magyar nép őstörténete* (Budapest 1988), pp. 203–205, 215, 233–234. András Róna-Tas, *A honfoglaló magyar nép. Bevezetés a korai történelem ismeretébe* (Budapest 1997), pp. 217–221.
2   Constantine Porphyrogenitus, *De administrando imperio* 38, 40, ed. Moravcsik, pp. 170–179. Konstantinos Porfyrogenetos, *De administrando imperio* 38, 40. *Az Árpád-kori magyar történet bizánci forrásai*, ed. Gyula Moravcsik (Budapest 1988), pp. 42–44, 46–47. *MMFH III*, p. 394.
3   Constantine Porphyrogenitus, *De administrando imperio* 38, ed. Moravcsik, pp. 170–175. Konstantinos Porfyrogenetos, *De administrando imperio* 38. *Az Árpád-kori magyar történet bizánci forrásai*, ed. Moravcsik, pp. 43–45.

In consequence of this, these Turks learned the speech of the Khazars and still today use this language, but they also know the other speech of the Turks.[4] The Khazars, like the Bulgarian Onogurs, speak a Turkish language. A monument to this Magyar-Turkish bilingualism is perhaps three hundred words of Turkish origin, among them several personal names in Hungarian.[5]

Alongside Árpád with a second intertribal principality stood Kuszal,[6] who in leadership of the tribal alliance obviously represented the only recently joined Kabars. One of both prince was called a *kende* (kündü) and a second a *gyula*, or military leader. According to Ibn Rusta *The Magyars (l-Madžgharíjatu) are a tribe of Turks and their chieftain goes on campaigns with perhaps 20-thousand riders. He is called a kende (k.n.dah) and this name is an emblem of their ruler, because the name of the man who has ruling power over them is the gyula (dž.lah), and all Magyars obey the commands of this chieftain, called a gyula, relating to an attack, defence and other matters.*[7] Gardízí also took up this report: *Their chieftain has 20-thousand riders. And they call this chieftain the kende (k.n.de),*

---

4   Constantine Porphyrogenitus, *De administrando imperio* 39, ed. Moravcsik, pp. 174–175. Konstantinos Porfyrogenetos, *De administrando imperio* 39. *Az Árpád-kori magyar történet bizánci forrásai*, ed. Moravcsik, p. 46. MMFH III, p. 394.

5   Lajos Ligeti, "A magyar nyelv török kapcsolatai és ami körulöttük van," *Magyar Nyelv* 72 (1976), pp. 11–27. Lajos Ligeti, "A magyar nyelv török kapcsolatai a honfoglalás előtt és az Árpád-korban" (Budapest 1986). Antal Bartha, *Hungarian society in the 9th and 10th centuries* (Budapest 1975), pp. 49–54. Bartha, *A magyar nép*, pp. 198, 215, 230–232, 248, 261, 285. István Fodor, "Altungarn, Bulgarotürken und Ostslawen in Südrußland," *Archeologische Beiträge. Acta Antiqua et Archaeologica* 20 (Szeged 1977), pp. 7–64. István Fodor, "On Magyar-Bulgar-Turkish Contacts," in *Chuvash Studies*, ed. András Róna-Tas (Budapest 1982), pp. 45–81. István Fodor, "Zur Problematik der Ankunft der Ungarn im Karpatenbecken und ihrer Fortlaufenden Besiedlung," in *Interaktionen der mitteleuropäischen Slawen und anderen Ethnika im 6.–10 Jahrhundert. Symposium Nové Vozokany 3.–7. Oktober 1983*, ed. Peter Šalkovský (Nitra 1984), pp. 99–100.

6   Róna-Tas, *A honfoglaló*, pp. 262, 270–272, 302.

7   Ibn Rusta, *Kitábu l-a'láki n-náfísati*, MMFH III, pp. 343–344. The Magyars took the names of both stations, the kündü and the gyula, from the Turkic Onogurs and Khazars still in Levedia. The lündürkagan was the third of the four highest titles of the Khazar empire. *Ibn Fadlan's Reisebericht*, herausgegeben von Ahmed Zeki Velidî Togan, *Archiv für die Kunde des Morgenlandes* 24 (1939), no. 3, pp. 98–100, 260. Dezső Pais, "A gyula és a kündüh," *Magyar Nyelv* 27 (1931), pp. 172–174. Bartha, *Hungarian society*, p. 59. Bartha, *A magyar nép*, pp. 347–349. Peter Benjamin Golden, *Khazar Studies. An Historico-Philological Inquiry into the Origins of the Khazars I* (Budapest 1980), pp. 191, 200–201. Pohl, *Die Awaren*, pp. 294–296. Róna-Tas, *A honfoglaló*, pp. 193, 259, 269–272, 333. Gyula was a Bulgarian personal name. Khan Asparuh, who in the years 679–681 led a portion of Bulgarians on the lower Danube, came from the Bulgarian Dulo line. Hýbl, *Dějiny národa bulharského* I, pp. 61, 63. Petr Dobrev, *Prabălgarite. Proizchod, ezik, kultura* (Sofija 1991), pp. 95–96, 162, 168. Róna-Tas, *A honfoglaló*, pp. 63, 188. The Onogurs, a part of whom joined with the Magyars, also belonged to the Bulgarians. The Magyars, along with Turkish words, also took several personal names from the Onogurs and

and this is the name of their greatest ruler. The chieftain, who administers affairs, is called a gyula (dž.le). The Magyars do what the gyula commands them to do.[8] Since the title of *gyula* was in second position, it did not belong to Árpád. Árpád was the kende; therefore, *this name is an emblem of their ruler*, more exactly *this is the name of their greatest ruler*. Kurszán, mentioned in second place with concluding the Magyar-Byzantine alliance against the Bulgarians in 894 was thus after Árpád,[9] had in order the second title of *gyula*.[10]

Etelköz began to threaten the states lying along the Danube. In 862 the Magyars (*Ungri*) pillaged in the East Frankish Empire.[11] In 881 the Magyars and the Kabars invaded the Eastern March. The Bavarians met them in two battles. They battled with the Magyars (*cum Ungaris*) near Vienna and near

---

the Khazars, and the names Kündür and Dulo became or already then were at the same time titles of kündü and gyula.

[8] Gardízí, *Kitábe zajnu l-achbár*, MMFH III, p. 425. Dezső Pais, "Gyila, Julus," *Magyar Nyelv* 31 (1935), pp. 53–54. Moravcsik, *Byzantinoturcica* 2, pp. 109, 279.

[9] See note 13.

[10] Attila Zsoldos, *The Legaci of Saint Stephen* (Budapest 2004), pp. 20–22, 26–27, 31–32. According to Hungarian chroniclers and Anonymus, Kurszán's father was called Kündü: *nuncium nomine Kusid filium Kund. Chronici Hungarici compositio saeculi XIV.* 11 28, SRH I, p. 288. *Cund cuius filius Kusyd. Chron. Hung. comp. saec. XIV.* 11 30, SRH I, p. 291. *Quorum VII virorum nomina hec fuerunt: Almus pater Arpad, Eleud pater Zobolsu, a quo genus Saac descendit, Cundu pater Curzan, Ound pater Ete, a quo genus Calan et Colsoy descendit, Tosu pater Lelu, Huba, a quo genus Zemera descendit, VII-us Tuhutum pater Horca, cuius filii fuerunt Gyula et Zombor, a quibus genus Moglout descendit, ut inferius dicetur.* Anonymi (P. magistri) *Gesta Hungarorum* 6, SRH I, p. 41. *Cundulec patri Cursan.* Anonymi (P. magistri) *Gesta Hungarorum* 46, SRH I, p. 95. According to György Györffy, Kündü (*Cundu*) is not the name of Kurszán's father but is Kurszán's title. Kurszán had the title of kende (kündü) and Árpád the title gyula. György Györffy, *Krónikáing és a magyar őstörténet* (Budapest 1948), pp. 110–111. György Györffy, *Tanulmányok a magyar állam eredetéről* (Budapest 1959), pp. 127–160. Györffy, *István király*, pp. 28–29, 32. MT I/1, pp. 592–593, 596, 616–618. Györffy, *König Stephan*, pp. 26, 34, 52. György Györffy, *Pest-Buda kialakulása. Budapest története a honfoglalástól az Árpád-kor végi székvárossá alakulásig* (Budapest 1997), pp. 65–66, 69–72. Kündü was not only a personal name but also the intertribal title kende. The names Álmos, Előd, Kündü, Ond, Tas, Tetény and Horka, mentioned by Anonymus, however, certainly are not titles but the names of fathers of the names seven Magyar voivodes and princes. Therefore, the name Kündü, which is mentioned among them, is not in this case the title of kende, but a personal name. Just as Gyula I and his brother Zombor did not have the title *horka*, because that belonged to Bulcsú (see note 39), but they were Horka's sons, just as Kurszán was not kündü (kende) but was the son of Kündü. According to other historians Kurszán had the title Gyula and Árpád was kündü (kende). Gyula Kristó, *Levedi törzsszövetségétől Szent István államáig. Elvek és utak* (Budapest 1980), pp. 218–228. Gyula Kristó, "A 10. századi Erdély politikai történetéhez," *Századok* 122 (1988), no. 1–2, p. 16. Károly Czeglédy, *Magyar őstörténeti tanulmányok.* Budapest Oriental Reprints, Series A 2 (Budapest 1985), pp. 126–128.

[11] *Ann. Bert.* ad a. 862, rec. Kurze, p. 60. MMFH I, p. 54.

Kullmitzberg with the Kabars (*cum Cowaris*).[12] The Magyars and the Kabars thus represented two only loosely associated and clearly distinguished parts of the tribal alliance. If kende Árpád, who came from a voivode line of one of the seven Magyar tribes, was prince of the Magyars, then gyula Kurszán was prince of three Kabarian tribes.

2 The Magyars in the Tisza River Region

In 894 the Magyars cruelly ravaged the Pannonian Principality. Still in this same year Byzantine leader Niketas Skleros *met with their chieftains Árpád and Kursan* and gave them rich gifts from Emperor Leo the Wise and concluded an alliance with them against the Bulgarians.[13] Thus, the Magyars became involved in the Bulgarian-Byzantine war (894–896), at the end of which they lost Etelköz, from which their old enemy the Pechenegs forced them out. The Magyars, weakened by defeat in Bulgaria and retreating from the Pechenegs, still in the first half of 896 concluded an agreement with the Moravians, according to which they could cross the Carpathians and enter into the area around the Tisza River.[14] The Moravians *took no small number of Magyars to them*,[15] thus, not all of them. The larger portion of Magyars remained beyond the Carpathians even after 896, on the territory of what was later Galicia.[16]

12   *Primum bellum cum Ungariis ad Weniam. Secundum bellum cum Cowaris ad Culmite. Annales Iuvavenses maximi* ad a. 881, MMFH I, p. 115.
13   *Georgius Monachus Continuatus, Az Árpád-kori magyar történet bizánci forrásai*, ed. Moravcsik, pp. 59–60.
14   *Ann. Fuld.* ad a. 895, 896, rec. Kurze, pp. 126–127, 129–130. MMFH I, pp. 103–105. Ivan A. Božilov, "Kăm chronologijata na bălgaro-madžarskata vojna pri car Simeon (894–896 g.)," *Voennoistoričeski sbornik* 40, 1971, no. 6, pp. 20–33. Dušan Třeštík, "Pád Velké Moravy," in *Typologie raně feudálních slovanských států. Sborník příspěvků z mezinárodní konference k tématu "Vznik a rozvoj slovanských raně feudálních států a národností ve střední a jihovýchodní Evropě", konané ve dnech 18.–20. listopadu 1986 v Praze* (Praha 1987), pp. 29–33, 48–51. Sándor László Tóth, "Az etelközi magyar-besenyő háború," *Századok* 122 (1988), no. 4, pp. 541–576.
15   MMFH III, Epistolae 109, pp. 241–242. CDES I, ed. Marsina, no. 39, p. 34.
16   Vladimír P. Šušarin, "Russko-vengerskije otnošenija v IX v.," in *Meždunarodnyje svjazi Rosii do XVII v.* (Moskva 1961), pp. 131–179. Třeštík, "Pád Velké Moravy," pp. 32–33. The finds of Magyar graves Sudovaja Višnja and Krilos near Galicia and Przemyśl testify to the longer stay of the Magyars in Galicia. Andrzej Koperski – Michal Parczewski, "Das althungarische Reitergrab von Przemyśl (Südpolen)," *Acta Archaeologica Academiae Scientiarum Hungaricae* 30 (1978), pp. 213–229. Andrzej Koperski – Michal Parczewski, "Wczesnośredniowieczny grób Węgra-koczownika z Przemyśla," *Acta Archaeologica Carpatica* 18 (1978), pp. 151–199. Andrzej Koperski, "Cmentarzysko staromadziarskie w Przemyślu," *Prace i Materiały Muzeum Archeologocznego i Etnograficznego w Łodzi* 29

The Moravians *took in* a part of the weakened Magyars. In this way the Magyars became federates of the Moravians and occupied the then thinly settled steppe region of the Tisza River, which suited their flocks.

A monument to the agreement closed between the Magyars and the Moravians may be the story of the white horse with the gilded saddle and reigns which Árpád sent to Svätopluk, for which he wanted territory, grass and water from him. Svätopluk's gifts had great meaning for the Magyars, because *if they then have land, grass and water, they have everything*, that is, an entire country from which the gifted land, grass and water came.[17]

At the time of arrival of the Magyars, Svätopluk had already been dead for two years, so he certainly did not close any agreement with Árpád, and talk about the exchange of land for a white horse could have only come up later.[18] Only later tradition or perhaps only after a Hungarian chronicler, who at the end of the 11th century wrote this story in his Gesta Ungarorum vetera (The Deeds of the Hungarians), needed to assign to Magyar Prince Árpád an important monarchal opposite, from which Árpád would obtain territory with all legal force.

The Moravians let the Magyars have *the land between the Danube and the Tisza*, or *the land that spreads between the Danube and the Tisza*, in which a Prince Salan, an invention of Anonymus, ruled, based *in the castle Alpár by the Tisza*, as well as *in the place which is called Titel ... at the princely court*. If *Prince Salan sent to Prince Árpád ... two bottles full of Danube water and a basket from the best grasses from the sands of Alpár*, received from him 12 white horses and other gifts and was most powerful of all the princes, who stood against the Magyars,[19] then he is identical with the chronicler's Svätopluk, who gave Árpád land, grass and water and got a white horse from him.[20] The country which Salan lost in the battle with the Magyars is that *wasteland (westenne)* between the Danube and the Tisza, which according to Anglo-Saxon map-maker Alfred the Great separated the East Frankish realm from Bulgaria.[21]

The Tisza River region, even with Magyars there, still remained for several years a part of Mojmír's realm, and the Moravians and their military forces certainly remained there. The Magyars then for *many years* (896–900) battled

---

(1982), pp. 261–267. Michal Parczewski, *Początki kształtowania sie polsko-ruskiej rubieży etnicznej w Karpatach. U źródeł rozpadu Słowiańszczyzny na odłam wschodni i zachodni* (Kraków 1991), pp. 40–41. Róna-Tas, *A honfoglaló magyar nép*, pp. 103–104.

17   *Chron. Hung. comp. saec. XIV.* II 28, SRH I, p. 289.
18   Třeštík, "Pád Velké Moravy," pp. 69–73. Györffy, "Formation," p. 33.
19   See chapter 13, notes 43, 46.
20   See notes 17, 18.
21   *Orosius* I/1, MMFH III, pp. 338, 340.

as Mojmír's ally or directly in the Moravian military and *always threatened the Bavarians*.[22]

3 The Magyars in Pannonia

The larger portion of the Magyars remained beyond the Carpathians even after 896. Evidence of this are the burial sites of Magyar nomads directly in the centres of the future Galician principality in Przemyśl and in Galicia.[23] The Magyar tribes settled from 896 on both sides of the Carpathians. The Magyars who crossed the Carpathians only in later years and found the Tisza region occupied had to seek another territory. They threatened primarily the neighbouring Pannonian Principality, administration and defence of which was handed over by East Frankish King and Emperor Arnulf to Savian Prince Braslav in 896.[24] Two vassal principalities, the Pannonian and Savian, allied under the rule of Prince Braslav, about whose loyalty Arnulf did not have to doubt, should have been a barrier against the dangerous Magyars.

Arnulf, in order to protect the easternmost part of his realm, sent rich gifts to the Magyars and appealed to them to depart for Lombardy,[25] where his antagonist, King Berengar I of Italy, ruled. Bavarian bishops wrote to the pope: *Since they still threaten our Christians* (= belonging under the authority of the Salzburg archbishopric), *settled far away from us* (= far from Bavaria, that is in Pannonia), *and they harassed them with striking persecution, we did not give them money or any valuables, though only woven garments, so that we subjugate their savageness them and achieve that they have peace from their persecution.* The Moravians explained to the pope the Bavarian ransom for the safety of Pannonia as Bavarian bribery and manipulating the Magyars to attack into Italy: *The mentioned Slavs accused us of dishonouring the faith with the Magyars and that we for a dog or wolf and other most godless and pagan objects swore and made peace and that we gave them money to leave for Italy.*[26]

In August of 899 the Magyars went around Braslav's principality and invaded Italy by the southern route from the River Sava. On 24 September in a battle near Brent they destroyed the 20-thousand member army of King Berengar,

---

22 MMFH III, Epistolae 109, p. 241.
23 See note 16.
24 *Ann. Fuld.* ad a. 896, rec. Kurze, p. 130. MMFH I, p. 105.
25 Třeštík, "Pád Velké Moravy," pp. 34–35. Dušan Třeštík, "Großmähren, Passau und die Ungarn um das Jahr 900. Zu den neuen Zweifeln an der Authentizität des Briefes der bayerischen Bischöfe an Papst Johann IX. aus dem Jahr 900," *Byzantinoslavica* LIV (1998), pp. 154–157.
26 MMFH III, Epistolae 109, pp. 240–241.

and until the end of June 900 they marauded throughout all of Lombardy. They didn't remain there long, however, as was desired by Arnulf, who in the midst of these events died (on 29 November 899). The Magyars made peace with Berengar and headed back.[27] On 29 June they tried to conquer Venice, which did not belong to Berengar's realm, but without success.[28]

The Magyars did not return to the Tisza, but in an alliance with the Moravians they plundered and occupied the Pannonian Principality in southern Transdanubia: *They then returned by this route, by which they entered, devastating the larger part of Pannonia.*[29] If the Magyars were on 29 June near Venice, then they could have invaded Pannonia at the beginning of July. Bavarian bishops in their letter to the pope in the middle of July 900 ascribed blame for the whole of this cataclysm on the Moravians: *They themselves took in no small number of Magyars and as is their custom, they shaved the heads of their improper Christians and sent them to our Christians; indeed, they themselves attacked them and took one into captivity and killed another and others they imprisoned and killed by hunger and thirst; uncountable numbers again they ordered into exile and they flung noble men and honourable women into slavery; they destroyed sacred temples, so that in all of Pannonia, our largest province, not a single church is to be seen, as the bishops you appointed can tell, if they wanted to admit how many days passed and they saw the entire countryside looted.*[30]

The participation of the Moravians in the Magyar plundering of the Pannonian Principality in July of 900 was a response to the three-week Bavarian-Bohemian marauding of Moravia in the spring of this same year.[31] Proof of the Moravian alliance with the Magyars is the finding of one denar of Italian King Berengar I (888–924), minted in 894–895, and two endorsed denars of Emperor Lampert (894–898) directly in Mikulčice, in graves 35 metres apart, north-west of the foundations of a large three-aisle basilica, immediately by the enclosure of a Great Moravian cemetery. They testify to the presence

---

27 Ann. Fuld. ad a. 900, rec. Kurze, p. 134. *MMFH I*, pp. 109–110. Johannes Diaconus, *Chronicon Venetum*, Albinus Franciscus Gombos, *Catalogus fontium historiae Hungaricae aevo ducum et regum ex stirpe Arpad descendentium ab anno Christi 800 usque ad annum 1301. II* (Budapest 1937), p. 1313. *Liudprandi Antapodosis* II 7–15, Liudprandi episcopi Cremonensis opera omnia ex Monumentis Germaniae historicis fecit Georgius Heinricus Pertz (Hannoverae 1839), pp. 42–46. Dümmler, *Geschichte des Ostfränkischen Reiches II*, pp. 507–510. Vajay, *Der Eintritt*, pp. 29–31. *MT I/1*, pp. 598–601. Třeštík, "Großmähren, Passau und die Ungarn," pp. 155–156.

28 Johannes Diaconus, *Chronicon Venetum*, Gombos, *Catalogus II*, p. 1313. Třeštík, "Großmähren, Passau und die Ungarn," pp. 156–157.

29 Ann. Fuld. ad a. 900, rec. Kurze, p. 134. *MMFH I*, pp. 109–110.

30 *MMFH III*, Epistolae 109, pp. 241–242. Třeštík, "Großmähren, Passau und die Ungarn," pp. 156–159.

31 Ann. Fuld. ad a. 900, rec. Kurze, p. 134, *MMFH I*, pp. 109–110.

of Magyar warriors in Mojmír's princely seat after the return from Lombardy in the summer of 900. Since they were pagan, they were buried outside the wall of the Christian cemetery.[32] Thanks to this Magyar-Moravian alliance, the papal legatees – archbishop John, bishops Benedict and Daniel – could return from Moravia to Italy through the despoiled Bavarian part of Pannonia, which was occupied by the Magyars, precisely at this time: *The bishops appointed by you ... passed through and saw the entire devastated country.*[33]

The horka Bulcsú (also called Vérbulcsú) acquired the former Pannonian Principality, conquered in July of 900: *he drew near to Zala and to the Balaton Lake*[34] and *around Balaton Lake, as it is called, he set up his tents.*[35] From there Bulcsú led plundering excursions into Byzantium,[36] in 942 to Italy and to Spain[37] and in 954 and 955 to Germany.[38] Since the title of *horka*, like the

---

32   Taťána Kučerovská, "Die Zahlungsmittel in Mähren im 9. und 10. Jahrhundert," in *Rapports du IIIe Congrès International d'Archéologie Slave*, Tome 2, ed. Chropovský, pp. 216–229. Třeštík, "Pád Velké Moravy," pp. 33–34, 51–52. László Kovács, *Münzen aus der ungarischen Landnahmezeit. Archäologische Untersuchung der arabischen, byzantinischen, westeuropäischen und römischen Münzen aus dem Karpatenbecken des 10. Jahrhunderts, Fontes Archaeologici Hungariae* (Budapest 1989), p. 112. Pavel Kouřil, "Staří Maďaři a Morava z pohledu archeologie," in *Dějiny ve věku nejistot*, ed. Klápště, Plešková, Žemlička, pp. 112, 114.

33   *prout episcopi a vobis destinati, si fateri velint, enarrare possunt, quantos dies transierunt et totam terram* (= Pannonia) *desolatam viderunt. MMFH III*, Epistolae 109, pp. 241–242.

34   *Septimi siquidem exercitus Werbulchu dux est dictus. Hic in Zala, circa lacum Boloton descendisse perhibetur. Simonis de Keza Gesta Hungarorum* II 33, *SRH I*, p. 167.

35   *Sextus capitaneus Werbulchu nomen habuit, qui circa Balatim sua thabernacula fixisse probatur. Chron. Hung. comp. saec. XIV.* II 33, *SRH I*, p. 292.

36   Bulcsú, although he concluded an alliance with God (= accepted baptism), and then many times with all of his people marched against the Romans. Ioannes Skylitzes 5, *Az Árpád-kori magyar történet bizanci forrásai*, ed. Moravcsik, p. 86.

37   In the spring of 942 the Magyars invaded Italy. Italian King Hugo purchased peace from them and sent them through the south of France to Spain. *Liudprandi Antapodosis* V 19, ed. Pertz, p. 142. In Spain they attacked an Arab fortress and in July 942 they laid siege to the town of Lleida. According to a report written by Ibn Hajján, Bulcsú was certainly among the seven Magyar commanders: [w].l.h.w.d.y = Vulšudi, that is Bulcsú. Károly Czeglédy, "Új arab forrás a magyarok 942 évi spanyolországi kalandozásról," *Magyar Nyelv* 75 (1979), pp. 273–282. Károly Czeglédy, "Még egyszer a magyarok 942 évi spanyolországi kalandozásáról," *Magyar Nyelv* 77 (1981), pp. 419–423. György Györffy, "A 942. évi magyar vezérnévsor kérdéséhez," *Magyar Nyelv* 76 (1980), pp. 308–317. György Györffy, "Új arab forrás a magyarok 942. évi kalandozásáról," *Magyar Nyelv* 77 (1981), pp. 511–512. György Györffy, *Krónikáink és a magyar őstörténet. Régi kérdések – új válaszok* (Budapest 1993), pp. 225–230. István Elter, "Néhány megjegyzés Ibn Hayyánnak a magyarok 942. évi spanyolországi kalandozásáról szóló tudósításához," *Magyar Nyelv* 77 (1981), pp. 413–419. István Elter, "A magyar kalandozáskor arab forrásai," in *A honfoglaláskor írott forrásai*, ed. László Kovács, László Veszprémy, (Budapest 1996), pp. 173–180.

38   *MT I/1*, pp. 687–701. See chapter 13, note 74.

gyula and the head prince, as well as other Hungarian principalities was inheritable, Bulcsú's father Kál was already the horka and prince in the southern Transdanubia: *It is necessary to know that the Karchas Bulcsú is the son of Karchas Kál and that Kál is a personal name, karchas* (= horka) *however, the title as gylas* (= gyula), *which is a position higher than the karchas*.[39]

Kál, also called Bogat,[40] together with Árpád's oldest son Tarhos (Tarkachu), called Durszak (*Dursac*), led in years 921–922 a campaign into Italy.[41] Bogat, that is Kál, led the Magyar military into Italy obviously in the years 899–900. Horka Kál could have stood at the head of this part of the Magyars, which came from beyond the Carpathians only in year 898 or 899. Therefore, there was no longer room for them in the Tisza River region; they accepted (certainly also with many fighters from the Tisza River region) Arnulf's appeal to leave for Lombardy. After Arnulf's death, however, they returned and occupied southern Transdanubia.

In the late autumn of the year 900 the Magyars ravaged the Bavarian border county of Traungau, and they spared the territory of Mojmír's ally, Margrave Isanrich, between the Enns and the Vienna Woods, *and they returned with what they stole from where they came, to their own in Pannonia*. After the withdrawal of the main Magyar military, a smaller Magyar force attacked *from the northern side of the Danube* into Traungau. Margrave Liutpold with Passau Bishop Richard attacked the plundering Magyars and defeated them in a battle near

---

39   Constantine Porphyrogenitus, *De administrando imperio* 40, ed. Moravcsik, pp. 178–179. Konstantinos Porfyrogenetos, *De administrando imperio* 40, *Az Árpád-kori magyar történet bizánci forrásai*, ed. Moravcsik, p. 49. *MMFH III*, p. 398. László Rásonyi Nagy – Dezső Pais, "Kál és társai," *Magyar Nyelv* 25 (1929), pp. 121–128. Moravcsik, *Byzantinoturcica* 2, p. 139. Bulcsú, who died only in 955 namely by a premature death (see chapter 13, note 74), could not have been the prince in the south of Transdanubia for a full 55 years. Bulcsú inherited this principality from his father Kál, just as after him he inherited the intertribal title of *horka*.

40   Bulcsú's father Kál also had a second name, Bogat: *Bulsuu filius Bogat. Anonymi (P. magistri) Gesta Hungarorum* 39, 41, *SRH I*, pp. 82, 86. *Bulsuu vir sanguinis filius Bogat. Anonymi (P. magistri) Gesta Hungarorum* 53, *SRH I*, p. 107. Prince Géza–Deviux also had two names, as did his wife Sarolt–Beleknegini and her brother, Transylvanian Gyula II–Prokuj. *Thietmari Chronicon* IX (VIII) 4, rec. Kurze, p. 241. *Thietmari Chronicon* VIII 4, cur. Trillmich, pp. 442–445.

41   *Inter agendum contigit, Hungarios Veronam his ignorantibus advenisse; quorum duo reges, Dursac et Bugat, amicissimi Berengario fuerant ... rogavit Berengarius Hungarios, ut si se amarent, super inimicos suos irruerent. Liutprandi Antapodosis* II 61–62, ed. Pertz, pp. 63–64. *MMFH I*, pp. 135–136. *MT I/1*, pp. 663–664. And Kál-Bogat's son horka Bulcsú led a campaign to Italy in 942. See note 37. Just as Bogat is identical with horka Kál (see note 40), then the first and thus more important of both names *reges* may be identical with the main Hungarian prince, who was then the oldest son of Árpád, Tarhos. See chapter 13, note 60.

Linz on 20 November. Some 1200 of them died in battle or drowned in the Danube.[42]

4   Alliance of the Moravians and Bavarians against the Magyars

In December or at the end of November of 900 the Moravian-Magyar alliance ended. The Magyar attack against the Moravians was not led by horka Kál from the south, but came from the east, from Árpád's territory, in line with the telling of the Hungarian chroniclers, according to whom the Magyars crossed the Danube near Pest and Szob and in a battle near Bánhida defeated the Moravian army.[43] The Moravians lost north-eastern Transdanubia. If the Magyars attacked from the Tisza River region, then their Tisza settlements, which they had gotten four years earlier from the Moravians, were suddenly crowded. This was undoubtedly because they had received among them other tribesmen from beyond the Carpathians. The Moravians who until then were settled in the Tisza River region and secured it for Mojmír's realm mainly felt the brunt of the Magyar attack. Constantine Porphyrogenitus and Naum's biography tell of the conquering and plundering of the Great Moravian Tisza River region, the capturing and expelling of the local Moravians by the Magyars and the escape of Moravian emigration from this territory to neighbouring Bulgaria and Croatia.[44]

The Magyars came into the Carpathian Basin in three waves. *No small number of Magyars*, led by kende Árpád, in the first half of 896 became allies of the Moravians and with their consent they migrated to the Great Moravian Tisza River region. The Magyars, led from beyond the Carpathians in 899 by horka Kál, plundered and occupied Braslav's Pannonian Principality in southern Transdanubia in July of 900 in alliance with the Moravians. At the end of autumn in 900 gyula Kurszán could enter into the Tisza River region with his Kabars. The Magyars needed more territory; therefore, they expelled the allied

---

42   *Ann. Fuld.* ad a. 900, rec. Kurze, pp. 134–135. *MMFH I*, pp. 110–111. Vajay, Der Eintritt, pp. 33–34.
43   See chapter 12, notes 58, 59, 62.
44   Constantine Porphyrogenitus, *De administrando imperio* 38, 40, 41, ed. Moravcsik, pp. 172–181. Konstantinos Porfyrogenetos, *De administrando imperio* 38, 40, 41. *MMFH III*, pp. 393, 396, 399–400. I. Žitije Nauma, *MMFH II*, pp. 178–179. Constantine Porphyrogenitus and the Life of Naum write only about the conquering of Great Moravia's Tisza River region, which the Danube separated from Bulgaria near Belgrade. The direction of escape of the Moravians clearly tells about the position of the land from which they ran.

Moravians from the Tisza region and conquered north-western Transdanubia from them.

Mojmír II abandoned all battles with the Bavarians. At a general diet in Regensburg in January 901 Prince Mojmír and Margrave Isanrich reconciled with East Frankish King Louis the Child. Mojmír gave up his influence in the Eastern March and concluded an anti-Magyar alliance with the Bavarians.[45]

The peace treaty had to also include the withdrawal from Upper Pannonia, which Svätopluk had attached to his realm nearly twenty years before. In 903 and 905 Bavarian properties are mentioned on its territory.[46] The peace and the anti-Magyar alliance of Bavarians with the Moravians also had to relate to the Bohemian princes, who from 895 were allies of the Bavarians and recognized Bavarian sovereignty. In this way the Moravians and Bohemians ended six years of antagonism and renewed their traditional alliance.

On 11 April 901 the Magyar army, plundering Carantania, suffered a defeat.[47] In 902 the Magyars fell upon the Moravians, whom the Bavarians then came to help. The Magyars triumphed over the allied Bavarian military, but they suffered defeat from the Moravians and had to retreat.[48] In 903 the Magyars attacked the Bavarians.[49] The Rafelstetten customs tariff testifies to the still unchanged relations on the middle Danube and about the uninterrupted use of long-distance roads in the Eastern March and in Moravia.[50] The antagonism of the Bavarians and Magyars, however, was just then ratcheted up by the deceitful murder of gyula Kurszán (Kuszal). The Bavarians invited him to a banquet in 904 and proceeded to slaughter him and his entire entourage.[51]

---

45 *Ann. Fuld.* ad a. 901, rec. Kurze, p. 135. *MMFH I*, p. 111. *Chronicon Suevicum universale* ad a. 900, *MMFH I*, p. 158.
46 *MMFH III*, Diplomata 54, 56, pp. 88–89, 91. Havlík, "K otázce karolinské kolonizace," pp. 63, 65. The inclusion of Upper Pannonia to Great Moravia is also indicated by archaeological finds in the circle of the Slavic hill-fort in Pitten. At the burial site in Pitten, a Great Moravian axe and silver, raisin-like earrings were found and not far from there, in Wartmannstetten, Great Moravian jewellery was found in several graves of the local burial site. Justová, *Dolnorakouské Podunají*, pp. 184–186, 204–205.
47 *Ann. Fuld.* ad a. 901, rec. Kurze, p. 135. *MMFH I*, p. 111. *Herimanni Augiensis Chronicon* ad a. 901, *MMFH I*, pp. 111, 165. Vajay, Sz.: Der Eintritt, pg. 33–34.
48 *Ungarii Marahenses petunt, pugnaque victi terga verterunt. Herimanni Augiensis Chronicon* ad a. 902. *MMFH I*, p. 112, 165. *Et bellum in Maraha cum Ungaris et patria vincta. Annales Alamanici* ad a. 902, *MMFH I*, pp. 14–15. *Ungarii a Maruis occiduntur. Chronicon Suevicum universale*, *MMFH I*, p. 158. Vajay, *Der Eintritt*, pp. 33–34. Třeštík, *Pád Velké Moravy*, pp. 36, 54–55. Dušan Třeštík, "Kdy zanikla Velká Morava?" *Studia mediaevalia Pragensia* 2 (1991), pp. 20–23.
49 Vajay, *Der Eintritt*, pp. 20–23.
50 *Inquisitio de theloneis*, *MMFH IV*, pp. 114–119. CDES 1, ed. Marsina, no. 41, pp. 37–38.
51 Vajay, *Der Eintritt*, pp. 33–35, 37–38.

5 Saxon Expansion, the Fall of the Mojmír Line and the Magyar-Slavic Alliance

In 897 the Sorbs subjected themselves to Emperor Arnulf;[52] they recognized their dependency on the East Frankish empire and became a border component of the Saxon duchy, which was ruled by Duke Otto (880–912). Not everyone agreed, however. The Sorbian Glomucians, thanks to the more distant position of their settlements, remained further free and felt Saxon expansion only in 906. The Saxon attack against the Glomucians, who were settled beyond the subjugated Sorbs, was led some time in the spring of 906 by Otto's son, Henry the Fowler. The Glomucians were unable to answer the Saxons.[53]

The Moravians also felt the cruelty of military defeat at the same time as the Glomucians. Regino mentions the Magyar invasion into Great Moravia, when he writes about its sad fate after the death of Svätopluk: *His sons unhappily administered his realm for a short time, while everything was depopulated to the foundations by the Magyars.*[54] The Magyars defeated, robbed and burned the primary seat of the Mojmírs in Mikulčice. Evidence of this are traces of a fire and primarily the many arrows which the Magyars fired at the defences. Archaeologists have found some 59 arrowheads, the rhombic and deltoid shape of which was characteristic for the Magyars, who also overran Strachotín, Staré Zámky near Líšeň and perhaps even Pohansko near Břeclav, Zelená Hora and

---

52 *Ann. Fuld.* ad a. 897, rec. Kurze, p. 131. *MMFH I*, p. 106.

53 *Widukindi monachi Corbiensis Rerum gestarum Saxonicarum libri tres* I 17, *MMFH I*, p. 138. *MMFH IV*, p. 388. *Thietmari Chronicon* I 3, rec. Kurze, p. 3. *Thietmari Chron.*I 3, cur. Trillmich, pp. 6–7. Lothar Dralle and after him Dušan Třeštík assume that shortly before year 906 the Saxons crossed the border of Saxony on the Saale River and subjugated the neighbouring Sorbs, by which they freed up the road for attack against the distant Glomucian tribe. Lothar Dralle, "Zur Vorgeschichte und Hintergründen der Ostpolitik Heinrichs I.," in *Europa Slavica – Europa Orientalis. Festschrift für Herbert Ludat zum 70. Geburtstag*, herausgegeben von Klaus-Detlev Grothusen, Klaus Zernack (Berlin 1980), p. 113. Dušan Třeštík, "Václav a Berengar. Politické pozadí postřižin sv. Václava roku 915," *Český časopis historický* 89 (1992), no. 5–6, p. 657. Třeštík, *Počátky*, p. 357. If Saxon chronicler Widukind recorded in detail the Saxon attack against the Glomucians, then he would undoubtedly have also mentioned the same important attack against the Sorbs. If the Sorbs were subjugated just before the Glomucians, they would have joined in the summer of 906 the same as the Glomucians with the Magyars in order to rid themselves of Saxon rule. Therefore, the assumption that the Saxon attack against the Sorbs occurred right before the attack against the Glomucians is not likely.

54 *Circa haec etiam tempora Zuentibolch rex Marahensium Sclavorum, vir inter suos prudentissimus et callidissimus, diem clausit extremum; cuius regnum filii eius pauco tempore infeliciter tenuerunt, Ungaris omnia usque ad solum depopulantibus. Reginonis Chron.* ad a. 894, rec. Kurze, p. 143. *MMFH I*, p. 124.

GREAT MORAVIA AND THE MAGYARS 251

other Moravian castles. Arrow shafts from Magyar arrows and traces of a large fire have also been found there.[55]

The Magyar invasion that disrupted the core of Mojmír's Moravia and destroyed the Mojmír line needs to be dated before 908, the year in which Regino wrote his chronicle.[56] Benedictine Ruotger from Cologne also left a report on the Magyar attack against the Moravians in the Life of St. Bruno, which he wrote in 966–967. In it Ruotger describes the state in which he found Germany, when Henry I the Fowler took over rule in 919: *He found all the towns of the kingdom shaken and terribly desolated by the constant invasions of neighbours as well as the very serious conflicts between citizens, even relatives. Indeed, from one side the wild nation of the Danes, powerful on land and sea, expanded, and from the other side the excessively raging, rabid Slavic barbarians.*[57] Ruotger knew that after the victory of the Saxons over the Slavic Glomucians in 906 a series of nearly annual Magyar campaigns followed over the whole of German territory: *likewise the cruelty of the Magyars followed, crossing the border of the Moravians (terminos Marahensium), which shortly before had been taken (usurped) by criminal will, scourged with sword and fire most of the provinces of his kingdom.*[58] The first was Saxony, to which the Magyars still in June 906

---

55 Pavel Kouřil, "Staří Maďaři a Morava z pohledu archeologie," in *Dějiny ve věku nejistot. Sborník k příležitosti 70. narozenin Dušana Třeštíka*, uspořádali Jan Klápště, Eva Plešková, Josef Žemlička (Praha 2003), pp. 110–146. Pavel Kouřil, "Archeologické doklady nomádského vlivu a zásahu na území Moravy v závěru 9. a v 10. století," in *Bitka pri Bratislave v roku 907*, ed. Štefanovičová, Hulínek, pp. 116–121. Marian Mazuch, "Výzkumy severního podhradí hradiště Valy u Mikulčic: k otázce násilného zániku velkomoravských mocenských center na počátku 10. věku," in *Mezi raným a vrcholným středověkem. Pavlu Kouřilovi k šedesátým narozeninám přátelé, kolegové, žáci*, uspořádali Jiří Doležal, Matin Wihoda (Brno 2012), pp. 137–159. The Magyars also conquered and burned Znojmo (The Castle of St. Hyppolitus) in the middle of the 10th century. Klíma, "Archeologický výzkum MU," pp. 229–230. Kouřil, "Staří Maďaři a Morava," pp. 124–126.
56 Regino finished writing his chronicle in 908. He writes about this in the introduction to his work. Reginonis Chron. rec. Kurze, p. 1. Třeštík, "Pád Velké Moravy," p. 56. Třeštík, "Kdy zanikla Velká Morava?" p. 23.
57 See note 65.
58 *cum ipse omnia regni spacia et continuis finitimorum incursionibus et gravissimis inter cives etiam et cognatos dissensionibus concussa et atrociter vexata repererit. Hinc etenim saeva Danorum gens terra marique potens, inde centifi da Sclavorum rabies barbarorum frendens inhorruit; Ungrorum nihilominus insecuta crudelitas, transgressa terminos Marahensium, quos sibi non longe ante impia usurpavit licentia, plerasque provintias regni eius ferro et igne longe lateque vastavit. Ruotgeri Vita Brunonis* 3, MMFH II, p. 184. Abbot Folkuin (965–990) took Ruotger's report and wrote it into the history of his abbey in Lobbes: *Quorum insantiata crudelitas sub Heinrico rege transgressa terminos Marahensium, quo sibi non longe ante impia usurpavit licentia, plerasque provincias regni eius ferro et igne longe lateque vastavit. Folcuini Gesta abbatum Lobiensium seu Chronicon Lobiense* 25,

and then in August 908 brought the Glomucians. In 909 the Magyars invaded Swabia, in 910 Swabia and Franconia; in 911 a large Magyar campaign ravaged Bavaria, Franconia, Swabia and Upper Burgundy. In 912 Franconia and Thuringia followed. In 913 they invaded Burgundy and on the return journey they marauded in Swabia. In 915 the Magyars devastated Thuringia and Saxony and destroyed Bremen. In 917 they invaded Swabia, where they burned Basel and continued their marauding up to Upper Burgundy and Upper Lorraine. In 919 they desolated Saxony and from there they fell upon Lorraine.[59]

Mojmír's state fell at the time defined by the Saxon-Glomucian war in the spring of 906 and the marauding invasion of the Magyars into Saxony in June of 906, with which the mentioned Magyar attacks on imperial territory began. When Henry the Fowler plundered the territory of the Glomucians, the Magyars had just then triumphed over the Moravians. The Glomucians, who desired a reprisal, could very quickly connect with them. Their emissaries did not have to travel to distant Pannonia. They sought the Magyars in much closer Moravia and concluded an alliance with them.[60]

Saxon expansion also angered the Bohemians. The Glomucian emissaries, who were in a hurry to meet the Magyars as soon as possible in Moravia, had a free road through neighbouring Bohemia. The Bohemians immediately joined in with the anti-Saxon alliance and freed up the Magyar's path through their territory.[61] Thus, they ended their 11 years of dependence on the Bavarians, who were further enemies of the Magyars. The Stodorans (Hevells) also entered into the anti-Saxon alliance, which was confirmed by the wedding of

---

MMFH II, p. 45. Lubomír E. Havlík puts the Hungarian attack against the Moravians mentioned by Ruotger and Folkuin only in the years 924–925. Havlík, *Morava v 9. a 10. století*, pp. 98–100. Lubomír E. Havlík, "Velká Morava v kontextu evropských a obecných dějín," in Poulík – Chropovský et al., *Velká Morava a počátky československé státnosti*, pp. 196–197. Lubomír E. Havlík, "Slované a Maďaři ve středním Podunají v IX.–X. století," in *Současný stav a úkoly československé hungaristiky* (Brno 1985), pp. 73–74. Lubomír E. Havlík, "Mähren und die Ungarn am Ende des 9. und am Anfang des 10. Jahrhunderts," in *Baiern, Ungarn und Slawen im Donauraum*, (Linz 1991), pp. 117–118. Havlík, *Kronika o Velké Moravě*, pp. 262–264. Dušan Třeštík, who sets the fall of Great Moravia in the years 905–906, convincingly refuted the opinion of Lubomír E. Havlík. Třeštík, "Pád Velké Moravy," pp. 57–58. Třeštík, "Kdy zanikla Velká Morava?" pp. 9–27. In the evaluation of Ruotger's and Folkuin's report we clearly lean toward the opinion of Dušan Třeštík.

59   Vajay, *Der Eintritt*, pp. 47–61. *MT I/1*, pp. 658–663.
60   *Widukindi monachi Corbiensis Rerum gestarum Saxonicarum libri tres* I 17, 20, *MMFH I*, pp. 138, 139. *MMFH IV*, pp. 388, 389. *Thietmari Chron.* I 3, rec. Kurze, p. 3. *Thietmari Chron.* I 3, cur. Trillmich, pp. 6–7. *Ungari fines Saxoniae VIII Kal. Iulii depopulati sunt, multosque interfecerunt. Annalista Saxo* ad a. 906, *MMFH IV*, p. 400.
61   The Magyars marched from Moravia to Saxony through Bohemia and not through Silesia. Gerard Labuda, *Fragmenty dziejów Słowiańscyzny zachódniej* (Poznań 1960), p. 248.

Drahomíra, daughter of the Stodoran prince, with Vratislaus, the younger brother of Bohemian Prince Spytihněv I, in this same year of 906.[62] The Magyars thus did not remain long in Moravia and did not continue with sacking the whole of its territory.[63] As soon as they had destroyed the Mojmír line, they hurried off to Saxony, which they invaded and began to devastate on 24 June 906.[64] According to Ruotger this was the *no less attacking brutality of the Magyars, crossing the border of the Moravians, which shortly before had been taken by criminal will*; that is the incoming Magyar invasion passing through defeated Moravia, so that from 906 to 919, in which the mentioned Henry the Fowler became the German king, *they scourged with sword and fire most of the provinces of his kingdom*.[65]

In 908 the Glomucians again brought in the Magyar military, which fell on Saxony and Thuringia. In a battle with the Magyars on 3 August 908 Thuringian Duke Burkhard, Würzburg Bishop Rudolf, Count Egino and many Saxons and Thuringian soldiers fell. The Magyars took advantage of the defeat of the Saxons and Thuringians and plundered their territory.[66]

---

62   Dušan Třeštík, "Václav a Berengár. Politické pozadí postřižin sv. Václava roku 915," *Český časopis historický* 89 (1992), no. 5–6, pp. 657–658. Třeštík, *Počátky*, pp. 357, 401–402. This ant-Saxon alliance at the beginning did not rest on Bavaria, as Dušan Třeštík writes, because the Bavarians were enemies of the Magyars until 914. See chapter 11, notes 14, 15, 20, 24. The Bohemians thus in 906 rid themselves of dependence on Bavaria, which they had acknowledge in July of 895.

63   Northern Moravia and partially also Velehrad (Staré Město in Uherské Hradiště) avoided destruction. Luděk Galuška, *Slované. Doteky předků* (Brno 2004), pp. 134–135, 138–139. Luděk Galuška, "Bylo povědomí o Svatoplukově Moravě, Veligradu a Metodějově arcibiskupství na Moravě 10.–12. století skutečně věcí neznámou?" in *Od knížat ke králům. Sborník u příležitosti 60. narozenin Josefa Žemličky*, uspořádali Eva Doležalová, Robert Šimůnek (Praha 2007), pp. 53–54.

64   *Widukindi Rerum gestarum Saxonicarum* I 17, 20, MMFH I, p. 138, 139. MMFH IV, pg. 388, 389. *Annalista Saxo* ad a. 906, MMFH IV, p. 400. See chapter 1, notes 48.

65   *cum ipse omnia regni spacia et continuis finitimorum incursionibus et gravissimus inter cives etiam et cognatos dissensionibus concussa et atrociter vexata repererit. Hinc etenim saeva Danorum gens terra marique potens, inde centifida Sclavorum rabies barbarorum frendens inhorruit; Ungrorum nihilominus insecuta crudelitas, transgressa terminos Marahensium, quos sibi non longe ante impia usurpavit licentia, plerasque provintias regni eius ferro et igne longe lateque vastavit. Ruotgeri Vita Brunonis* 3, MMFH II, p. 184. Abbot Folkuin (965–990) incorporated Ruotger's report into the history of his abbey in Lobbes. *Folcuini Gesta abbatum Lobiensium seu Chronicon Lobiense* 25, MMFH II, p. 45. And the Bavarians in 899 *terminos Maravorum confidenter interato intrantes et quaecumque poterant direpiendo populati sunt. Ann. Fuld.* ad a. 899, MMFH I, p. 108. Ruotger's *terminos Marahensium* and *terminos Maravorum* in the Annals of Fulda are the same. Both indicate the land of the Moravians. Třeštík, "Kdy zanikla Velká Morava?", p. 13.

66   *Annalista Saxo* ad a. 908, MMFH IV, p. 400. *Annales Alamanici* ad a. 908, Gombos, *Catalogus I*, p. 91.

The Magyar attack against the Moravians in 906 obviously did not differ from the invasion into Saxony and Thuringia in 906 and 908. In 906 the Magyars invaded the territories of the enemy Mojmírs, and similarly as in 902 they ran this time into opposition, too. Just as Bavarian Duke Liutpold died with several Bavarian bishops and counts and with the entire army a year later in a great battle with the Magyars beneath Bratislava, and another year later during the defence of Saxony and Thuringia Duke Burkhard died with other leaders and many soldiers, exactly in this way Mojmír II and his military could have died in the defense of their country. This was the end of the Mojmírs, mentioned by Regino.

After plundering Saxony in the summer of 906 the Magyars returned to Pannonia and to the Tisza River region obviously by the same path from which they had come. Certainly, however, they did not decide to remain in Moravia, because there there are no Magyar graves found there. They are likewise missing from this period on Slovak territory.

CHAPTER 11

After the Downfall of Great Moravia

1   Mojmírids's Legacy

With the fall of the Mojmír line, the dynastic connection of the two principalities, Moravia and Nitria, which formed the core of the Great Moravian state, ended. Since Moravia and Nitria lay between the Bohemians and their Magyar allies, on the path that the Magyars took to enemy Saxony in 906, 908 and 915, they could not have been missing from the broad Slavic-Magyar alliance aimed against the Saxons. In 906 the Bavarian-Moravian and Bavarian-Bohemian alliance ended. The Bohemians and the Moravians, however, further remained allies, not however against the Magyars, as before, but with the Magyars against the Saxons.

Allied warriors often went around borders to the territory of their allies. In 869 and 880 Bohemian allies set forth to the Sorbs in order to attack Thuringia together.[1] In the following years the Bohemians secured Sorbia for the Great Moravian empire.[2] The Moravians in 896 settled their Magyar allies in the Tisza River region, then together with them battled against the Bavarians[3] and *took* them to their main castle.[4] In July 900 Bavarian bishops complained that the Moravians *took in no small number of Magyars*.[5] If the allied Bohemians in the period of Great Moravia arrived to neighbouring Sorbia, then after the fall

---

1   *Ann. Fuld.* ad a. 869, 880, rec. Kurze, pp. 67, 95. MMFH I, pp. 81–82, 92.
2   Steinhübel, *Kapitoly*, p. 71.
3   See pp. 242–248.
4   The alliance of the Moravians with the Magyars is documented by a denar of Italian King Berengar I (888–915), minted in 894–895, and two endorsed denar of Emperor Lampert (894–898) found in graves just 35 metres to the north-west of the three-aisle basilica in Mikulčice. They testify to the presence of Magyar warriors in the main Great Moravian castle after the return from Longobardy in the summer of year 900. Since they were pagans, they were buried outside the enclosure of the Christian cemetery. Taťána Kučerovská, "Die Zahlungsmittel in Mähren im 9. und 10. Jahrhundert," in *Rapports du IIIe Congrès International d'Archéologie Slave, Tome 2*, éditeur Bohuslav Chropovský (Bratislava 1980), pp. 216–229. Třeštík, "Pád Velké Moravy," pp. 33–34, 51–52. László Kovács, *Münzen aus der ungarischen Landnahmezeit. Archäologische Untersuchung der arabischen, byzantinischen, westeuropäischen und römischen Münzen aus der Karpatenbecken des 10. Jahrhunderts. Fontes Archaeologici Hungariae* (Budapest 1989), p. 112. Kouřil, "Staří Maďaři a Morava," pp. 112, 114. Kouřil, "Archeologické doklady," pp. 127–128.
5   *Ipsi Ungarorum non modicam multitudinem ad se sumpserunt.* MMFH III, Epistolae 109, pp. 241–242. CDES I, ed. Marsina, no. 39, p. 34.

of the Mojmírs, they could thus have also come to Moravia and to Nitria. If the Moravians in 896 *took in* the allied Magyars, then a decade later the Moravians and Nitrians could have also accepted allied Bohemians. The Magyars, who later took over Nitria, met with the *Bohemians (Boemis) ... in the lands of Nitria (in partibus Nittriae)*.[6]

Decisions on Mojmír's dynasty's legacy could have also been made in the scope of the Bohemian-Moravian alliance. Just as after Bořivoj's death in 888 the nearest relative of his minor sons, Great Moravian Prince Svätopluk, took over rule in Bohemia,[7] then after the death of Mojmír II in 906 the Přemyslids inherited rule over Moravia and Nitria on the basis of this same relation. Since the military force of the Bohemians was not sufficient for the extensive territorial annexation, Bohemian Princes Spytihněv I (895–915) and Vratislaus I (915–921) could exert their influence in Moravia and in Nitria and send their warriors there, only if the Moravians and Nitrians wanted them.

Two eastern Slavic tribes (the Sloviens and Krivichians) and two Finnish tribes (the Chuds and the Vesians) invited the Swedish Varangians, called Russians, into their country: *And they went over the sea to the Varangians, to the Russians; because that's what they called the Vrangian Russians ... And the Chuds, Sloviens, Krivichians and the Vesians told the Russians: Our land is large and abundant in everything, but there is no order in it; so come to execute princely power and rule* (knjažiť i volodieti) *over us*. Just as the Varangians, led by Rurik and his brothers Sineus and Truvor, came in 856 to Ladoga, Beloozersk and Izborsk,[8] thus the Bohemians could also after the extinction of the Mojmír

---

6   *Simonis de Keza Gesta Hungarorum* II 32, SRH I, pp. 166–167. MMFH I, pp. 279–280. *Chron. Hung. comp. saec. XIV*. 32, SRH I, pp. 291–292. MMFH I, pp. 310–311.
7   Třeštík, *Počátky*, pp. 190–192. See pp. 210–211, 223–226.
8   *Latopis Nestora* 15, year 6370 (862), MPH I, ed. Bielowski, pg. 564–565. Two years later, in 858, Sineus and Truvor died, and Rurik, to whom rule over the entire territory of four tribes remained, moved from Ladoga to the south to Il'mensk Lake, where he established Novgorod (today's Gorodishche). Steinhübel, "Slovanské 'gentes' a ich vladykovia, kniežatá a kagani," pp. 273–278. The Swedish Varangians, who came to Slavic and Finnish principalities and settled in their primary castles, did not attach them to Sweden. Thus, not even the Bohemian warriors, who after the extinction of the Mojmírs could have come to Moravia and to Nitria, and the number of which could not be great with respect to the existing possibilities of the Přemyslids, did not connect Moravia and Nitria to Bohemia. They did not form a large realm, as is presented by Václav Chaloupecký. Václav Chaloupecký, "Počátky státu českého a polského," in *Dějiny lidstva od pravěku k dnešku 3. Základy středověku* (v Praze 1937), pp. 596–599. Chaloupecký, *Prameny X. století*, pp. 194–205, 218–222. Václav Chaloupecký, "Kníže svatý Václav," *Český časopis historický* 47 (1946), pp. 32–36. In 906 there were several small principalities in Bohemia, and Sweden in 856 was decidedly broken up into several small kingdoms. This, however, did not prevent Swedish and Bohemian warriors from departing for abroad.

line in 906 get to Moravia and to Nitria. They did not come, however, *to execute princely power and to rule*; they could only come there as allies.

The Magyars regarded the Glomucians and the Bohemians and along with the Bohemians, the Moravians and Nitrians, who opened up the road to rich plunder, as their allies. The Magyars could have taken over Nitria only in 906. Since they were nomads and were attracted by plunder, they regarded the rich Saxon prey as more significant than the territory of neighbouring Nitria. As a reward for the open road to rich Saxony, they recognized Nitria as an ally and left it alone.

2   4 July 907

The Bavarians, who were still enemies of the Magyars, wanted to turn around the situation on the middle Danube, which occurred after the fall of the allied Mojmírs in 906, and win back the territory in Pannonia, which they had lost in 900. Árpád died in 907.[9] The Bavarians obviously considered the death of the chief Magyar prince as an opportunity to attack the Magyars. A large Bavarian army led by Luitpold headed down the Danube. The Magyar army that awaited the Bavarians could have been led by two Hungarian princes who ruled the part of Pannonia occupied by the Magyars and in the case of a Bavarian victory would have lost a lot. The first was Árpád's oldest son Tarhosh, also known under the name of Dursak, who in addition to the fact that he was the main Magyar Prince (907–through 922), divided up with his three younger brothers Árpád's domain, which covered the area between the rivers Danube, the lower Tisza and the Zagyva and northern Transdanubia.[10] The second was Kál, also known as Bogat (*Bugat*), who ruled in southern Transdanubia, in the principality formerly belonging to Pribina, Kocel, Arnulf and Braslav.[11] Both princes led a Magyar military which in 921–922 ravaged Italy.[12]

The Bavarians came all the way to Preslava Castle (today's Bratislava). The castle on the left bank of the Danube, however, was no longer interesting to them; they remained on Pannonian territory, on the right bank of the river,[13]

---

9   *anno dominice incarnationis DCCCCVII dux Arpad migravit de hoc seculo.* Anonymi (*P. magistri*) *Gesta Hungarorum* 52, SRH I, p. 106. Wertner Mór, *Az Árpádok családi története* (Nagy-Becskereken 1892), pp. 17–20.
10   See pp. 310–313.
11   See pp. 246–248, 313.
12   *Liutprandi Antapodosis* II 61–62, ed. Pertz, pp. 63–64.
13   The Bavarians did not need to get to the independent castle on the northern bank of the Danube. Herwig Wolfram and Maximilian Dieseberger convincingly write that

and here on 4 July 907 they ran into the Magyars: *The worst war was near Preslava castle (ad Brezalauspurc) on the fourth day of July.*[14] The Magyars pulverized the large Bavarian army. Military leaders, Margrave Luitpold, Salzburg Archbishop Thietmar, Freising Bishop Udo, Säben Bishop Zacharias, two other bishops and several Bavarian counts all died along with their soldiers.[15]

---

the battlefield *ad Brezalauspurc* could have been and was to the south, that is on the Pannonian bank of the Danube, where the Magyars could much better develop their method of battle than on the northern bank. Maximilian Dieseberger, "Baiern, das Ostfränkische Reich und die Ungarn bis zur Schlacht von Pressburg 862–907," in *Schicksalsjahr 907. Die Schlacht bei Pressburg und das frühmittelalterliche Niederösterreich. Katalog zur Ausstellung des Niederösterreichischen Landesarchivs*, ed. Roman Zehetmayer (St. Pölten 2007), p. 41. In 1189 Emperor Frederick Barbarossa with his Crusaders camped *apud Brezburc in cam[po Firfelt] in introitu Vngarie*. CDES *I*, ed. Marsina, no. 100, p. 94. The Vierfeld field lay between Kittsee and Petržalka. If this field, although it was on the opposite side of the Danube, lay *apud Brezburc*, and if on this field the great Crusader's army could have camped in 1189, then this could have been the battlefield in 907. Wolfram, *Österreichische Geschichte 378–907*, pp. 272, 435, Note 356. Dušan Třeštík assumes that the campaign led by Margrave Luitpold headed to Great Moravian territory to the southwest of Slovakia, where the main Hungarian forces obviously were located. Třeštík, "Pád Velké Moravy," p. 37. The Magyar army was on Great Moravian territory in 906, when it destroyed the Mojmírs. In the summer of 906 it was already in Saxony. Why would the main Magyar army have remained in Slovakia after returning from Saxony?

14   *Bellum pessimum fecit ad Brezalauspurc IIII nonas Iulii. Annales Iuvavenses maximi* ad a. 907, MMFH *I*, p. 115. Regarding Great Moravia Bratislava, see Tatiana Štefanovičová, *Bratislavský hrad v 9.–12. storočí* (Bratislava 1975). *Archeologická topografia Bratislavy*, ed. Bello Polla, Adrián Vallašek (Bratislava 1991), pp. 60–66. Štefanovičová et al. *Najstaršie dejiny Bratislavy*, pp. 295–305. Tatiana Štefanovičová – Joachim Henning – Matej Ruttkay, "Možnosti prezentácieveľkomoravských archeologických pamiatok na Bratislavskom hrade," in *Bojná*, ed. Pieta, Ruttkay, Ruttkay, pp. 237–246.

15   *Ditmarus Salzburgensis episcopus occiditur ab Ungaris cum Utone et Zacharia aliisque duobus episcopis. Annales Admuntenses* ad a. 906 (correctly 907), MMFH *I*, p. 208. (*Interfectio Boiorum*) *ad Braslavespurch. Excerpta Aventini ex Annalibus Iuvavensibus antiquis derivati* ad a. 907, MMFH *I*, p. 383. *Baiovariorum omnis exercitus ab Ungaris occiditur. Annales Alamanici* (*Codices Turiciensis et Sirmodianus*) ad a. 907, MMFH *IV*, p. 369. MMFH *I*, pp. 14–15. *Item bellum Baguariorum cum Ungaris insuperabile, atque Liutpaldus dux et eorum supersticiosa superbia occisa, paucique christianorum evaserunt, interremptis multis episcopis comitibusque. Annales Alamanici* (*Codices Modoetiensis et Veronensis*) ad a. 907, MMFH *IV*, p. 370. MMFH *I*, pp. 14–15. *Baioariorum omnis exercitus ab Agarenis occiditur. Annales Sangallenses maiores* ad a. 908 (correctly 907), MMFH *IV*, p. 386. MMFH *I*, p. 130. *Ungari bellum contra Bauworios inexsuperabile fecerunt et Liutbaldus dux eorum comitesque atque episcopos quam plurimos, illorumque supersticiosa superbia crudeliter occisa est. Annales Laubacenses* ad a. 908 (correctly 907), MMFH *IV*, p. 387. MMFH *I*, p. 126. *Liutboldus occiditur. Chronicon Suevicum universale* ad a. 906 (correctly 907), MMFH *IV*, p. 394. MMFH *I*, p. 158. *Bawari ab Ungaris occiduntur, et Lipoldus dux, pater Arnulfi ducis. Annales sancti Rudberti Salisburgenses* ad a. 907, MMFH *IV*, p. 402. MMFH *I*, p. 257. *Bawarii cum Ungariis congressi multa cede prostrati sunt; in qua congressione Liutbaldus dux occisus est, cui filius*

Some of them could have died later as a result of wounds.[16] If all the other Bavarian bishops, Passau's Burchard (903–915), Regensburg's Tuto (893–930) and Eichstädt's Erkenbald (884–916), lived still longer after 907, thus, the two unnamed Bavarian bishops, who according to Admont's Annals died together with the three named,[17] could not have been proper bishops. Therefore, one of the two unknown bishops killed by the Hungarians could be Passau chorbishop Madalvin, mentioned in 903 in Upper Pannonia.[18]

The mentioned Slavic allies of the Magyars did not interfere in the battle, because these Slavs were allied with the Magyars not against the Bavarians but against the Saxons. The Magyars attacked the Saxons together with the Glomucians, Bohemians and other Slavs, and against the Bavarians (up to 913) they attacked without these allies. Not even the Moravians entered into

suus Arnolfus in ducatum successit. Reginonis Chronicon. (Adalberti) continuatio Reginonis ad a. 907, rec. Kurze, p. 154. *Baarii ab Ungaris occiduntur, et Liupoldus pater Arnolfi ducis ab eis occiditur. Auctarium Gartense* ad a. 908, MMFH IV. p. 425. MMFH I, p. 303. Reindel, *Die bayerischen Liutpoldinger*, no. 45, pp. 71–75. Albinus Franciscus Gombos, *Catalogus fontium historiae Hungaricae aevo ducum et regum ex stirpe Arpad descendentium ab anno Christi DCCC usque ad annum MCCCI*. I (Budapestini 1937), pp. 89, 91, 124, 140, 146, 168, 212, 216, 314, 346–348, 453, 524, 676–677, 754. 781. Vajay, *Der Eintritt*, pp. 41–43. Wolfram, *Österreichische Geschichte 378–907*, pp. 272–273. István Bóna, *A magyarok és Európa a 9–10. században* (Budapest 2000), p. 34. *Egy elfeledett diadal. A 907. évi pozsonyi csata*, ed. Béla Gyula Torma, László Veszprémy (Budapest 2008). Ján Turmair Aventinus left a similar but very late and unreliable report on the defeat of the Bavarians. According to Aventinus *for three days the battle raged in bad weather. Ioannis Aventini Annales Boiorum* IV, XXI 18–21, MMFH IV, pp. 437–439. MMFH I, pp. 418–421. Aventinus compiled a similar description of the battle in 907 and dated to the 9th to 11th of August according to similar descriptions of a battle on the Lech River in 955. On 9 August 955 German King Otto I came to the aid of besieged Augsburg, and on 10 August destroyed the Magyar military and on 11 August had their leaders Bulcsú, Lehel and Sur hanged. Dümmler, "Über die südöstlichen Marken," pp. 72–73, 82–85. Ernst Dümmler, *Geschichte des Ostfränkischen Reiches III* (Leipzig 1888), p. 548. Mária Vyvíjalová, "Bitka pri Bratislave roku 907. Príspevok ku kritickému prehodnoteniu prameňov," *Študijné zvesti Archeologického ústavu Slovenskej akadémie vied* 21 (1985), pp. 226–234. László Veszprémy, "Eine wechselvolle Rezeptionsgeschichte. Die Pressburger Schlacht aus Sicht der Ungarn," in *Schicksalsjahr 907*, ed. Zehetmayer, pp. 99–102. László Veszprémy, "Aventinus híradása a magyarok 907. évi győzelméről. Csata Pozsonynál," *Történelmi Szemle* 49 (2007), no. 1, pp. 1–17.

16 According to necrological records, which, however, are not necessarily accurate, Säben Bishop Zacharias died on 5 July and Frisian Bishop Udo on 6 July. The Magyars reportedly killed Salzburg Archbishop Thietmar only on 21 July. Gombos, *Catalogus II*, p. 1676. Dümmler, "Über die südöstlichen Marken," pp. 72–73. Albert Hauck, *Kirchengeschichte Deutschlands II* (Leipzig 1935), pp. 815–817. Peter Ratkoš, "Vzťahy naddunajských Slovanov a starých Maďarov v rokoch 881–1018," *Historický časopis* 35 (1987), no. 6, p. 807.

17 *Ditmarus Salzburgensis episcopus occiditur ab Ungaris cum Utone et Zacharia aliisque duobus episcopis. Annales Admuntenses* ad a. 906 (correctly 907), MMFH I, pg. 208.

18 MMFH III, Diplomata 27, p. 52.

the battle,[19] because plague in the previous year had undoubtedly exhausted them, and the entire Magyar-Slavic alliance to which they were connected, was aimed not against the Bavarians, but against the Saxons.

After the victory near Bratislava, the Magyars ruled the territory of the Eastern March up to the Enns River[20] and they attacked into Bavaria continually until 913.[21]

3   The Bavarians between the Magyars and the Saxons

After the death of Margrave Luitpold, his older son Arnulf became the Duke of Bavaria (907–937).[22] Arnulf was *duke of the Bavarians and also the adjacent lands*.[23] Since the Eastern March ceased to exist in July 907 and the Bohemians abandoned the Bavarians in 906, only Carantania remained of the *adjacent lands*. The younger brother of Arnulf, Bertold (907–937), who after Arnulf's death would become the Duke of Bavaria (937–947), became the Carantanian margrave.

The first years of Arnulf's rule in Bavaria were filled with Magyar invasions. In 909 the Magyars poured into Swabia. On the journey back, on 11 August, one Magyar unit suffered a defeat in Rott, at Pocking, at the hands of the Bavarians. In 910 the Magyars invaded Bavaria, Swabia and Franconia, and on 12 June in a battle near Augsburg, they destroyed the Swab army and on 22 June they defeated the Franks. The Magyar brigade that ravaged Bavaria on the journey

---

19   Třeštík, "Kdy zanikla Velká Morava," p. 23.

20   Vajay, *Der Eintritt*, pp. 43–45. Karl Lechner, *Die Babenberger. Markgrafen und Herzoge von Österreich 976–1246* (Wien – Köln – Weimar 1992), pp. 26–27. Karl Brunner, "Der österreichische Donauraum zur Zeit der Magyarherrschaft," in *Österreich im Hochmittelalter (907–1246)*. Herausgegeben von Kommision für die Geschichte Österreichs der Österreichischen Akademie der Wissenschaften (Wien 1991), pp. 54–61. Karl Brunner, *Österreichische Geschichte 907–1156. Herzogtümer und Marken. Vom Ungarnsturm bis ins 12. Jahrhundert* (Wien 1994), pp. 58–60, 81.

21   See note 11.

22   *Liutbaldus dux occisus est, cui filius suus Arnolfus in ducatum successit. Reginonis Chron. (Adalberti) continuatio Reginonis*, ad a. 907, rec. Kurze, p. 154. Kurt Reindel, *Die bayerischen Liutpoldinger 893–989. Sammlung und Erläuterung der Quellen.* Quellen und Erörterungen zur bayerischen Geschichte. Herausgegeben von der Kommission für bayerische Landesgeschichte bei der Bayerischen Akademie der Wissenschaft. Neue Folge 11 (München 1953), no. 46, pp. 71–75. Brunner, "Der fränkische Fürstentitel," p. 243.

23   Duke Arnulf issued a document with the title *Arnolfus divina ordinante providentia dux Baioariorum et etiam adiacentium regionum*. Reindel, *Die bayerischen Liutpoldinger*, p. 78. Brunner, "Der fränkische Fürstentitel," p. 243, note 64. Třeštík, *Počátky*, pp. 356–357.

back defeated the Bavarians near Neuching. In 911 the Magyars sacked Bavaria, Franconia and Swabia and entered Upper Burgundy. In 913 Duke Arnulf with the help of the Swabs defeated near the Inn River the Magyar army that had plundered southern Germany and northern Burgundy.[24]

Arnulf, besieged by Duke of Franconia and German King Conrad I (911–918), fled in 914 *to the Magyars* and concluded an alliance with them.[25] Arnulf was the son-in-law and ally of Italian King Berengar I (888–924, from 915 emperor), who had invited the Magyars against his antagonists back in 904.[26] The forming of an Italian-Bavarian-Magyar-Bohemian alliance was concluded in 915 by the mission of Veronian Bishop Nother II, who came to Prague with Arnulf and Berengar's messengers.[27] In this same year the Bohemians took part in the Magyar incursions into Saxony.[28]

Arnulf remained in Carantania, close to both strong allies, his emperor father-in-law Berengar and mainly the Magyars.[29] In 916 Arnulf returned to Bavaria and occupied Regensburg, but only briefly; however, under pressure of the royal army, he again retreated to the Magyars.[30] In 917 he again returned to Bavaria and without greater effort took over Regensburg, where the enthusiastic Bavarians welcomed him.[31] During an unsuccessful campaign against Arnulf, Conrad I was wounded, and as a result he died on 23 December 918.[32]

---

24   Reindel, *Die bayerischen Liutpoldinger*, no. 50–51, pp. 93–98, no. 54, pp. 103–106. Vajay, *Der Eintritt*, pp. 48–52. *MT I*/1, pp. 661–662. Karl Brunner, "Der österreichische Donauraum zur Zeit der Magyarherrschaft," in *Österreich im Hochmittelalater (907–1246)*. Herausgegeben von Kommision für die Geschichte Österreichs der Österreichischen Akademie der Wissenschaften (Wien 1991), pp. 54–55. Brunner, *Österreichische Geschichte 907–1156*, pp. 53–54.

25   Reindel, *Die bayerischen Liutpoldinger*, no. 55, pp. 107–111.

26   Italian King Berengar I paid off and invited the Magyars against his antagonist King Louis of Provence of Lower Burgundy, later Holy Roman Emperor Louis III. The Magyars from June 904 to July 905 plundered in Longobardy. Louis fell into captivity and on 21 July 905 was blinded. Krahwinkler, *Friaul*, p. 287.

27   Třeštík, "Václav a Berengár," pp. 642, 657–660. Třeštík, *Počátky*, pp. 357–361, 401–402.

28   *In diebus illis inmanissima persecutio Saxoniam oppressit, cum hinc Dani et Sclavi, inde Behemi et Ungri laniaret ecclesias. Tunc parrochia Hammaburgensis a Sclavis, et Bremensis Ungrorum impetu demolita est. Magistri Adami Bremensis Gesta Hammaburgensis ecclesiae pontificum* I 52, ed. Trillmich, pp. 224–225. *MMFH I*, p. 167. Vajay, *Der Eintritt*, pp. 55–56. Dralle, "Zur Vorgeschichte," p. 114.

29   Třeštík, *Počátky*, p. 360.

30   Reindel, *Die bayerischen Liutpoldinger*, no. 56–57, pp. 111–114.

31   Reindel, *Die bayerischen Liutpoldinger*, no. 58, pp. 114–116. Třeštík, *Počátky*, pp. 358–359.

32   Widukindi Rerum gestarum Saxonicarum libri tres I 25, rec. Waitz, p. 22. Reindel, *Die bayerischen Liutpoldinger*, no. 60, pp. 118–119.

In May of 919 the Franks and Saxons elected Saxon Duke Henry the Fowler as king. Swabian Duke Burchard II and Bavarian Duke Arnulf rejected the election of a new king. Burchard, threatened by Upper Burgundy King Rudolf II, however, needed Henry's military power; therefore, by the end of 919 he subjugated himself to Henry and recognized him as king.[33] Arnulf was more powerful than Burchard and obviously also counted on his allies; therefore, he remained in opposition.

4   End of the Broad Anti-Saxon Alliance

With the election of the Saxon duke as king in 919, any attack against the Saxons became an attack against the entire realm. The power of King Henry I the Fowler (919–936) grew quickly. Those from the anti-Saxony alliance who bordered directly on his kingdom had to reassess their enemy stance towards Henry. This began to break up the cohesiveness of the entire anti-Saxony alliance.

In the following year, the dispute of Bavarian Duke Arnulf with King Henry fully broke out. The Bohemians saw that Henry was much more powerful than the year before, when he was only a Saxon duke. They undoubtedly knew that if Arnulf loses, then they, as Arnulf's allies and long-time enemies of the Saxons, would very quickly feel the growing military force of Henry's entire kingdom. Bohemian Prince Vratislaus I obviously wanted to avoid an open collision with the powerful German king; therefore, he abandoned Arnulf and did not support him in the expected confrontation. When Henry attacked Regensburg in 920, Arnulf defended himself without allies.[34]

If the Bohemians at the crucial moment stepped aside from their Bavarian ally, then the Bavarian-Bohemian alliance fell apart. If they ceased being enemies with the Saxons, who were the target of Magyar or Magyar-Slav (and Magyar-Bohemian) incursions, then the Bohemian-Magyar alliance also ended. Both alliances aimed against the Saxons fell apart, and thus the entire anti-Saxon grouping also disintegrated. The alliance agreement of the Magyars with the Bohemians and other Slavs was no longer binding. As soon as the Magyars ceased considering the Bohemians, Moravians and Nitrians as allies, without hesitation they seized neighbouring Nitria and immediately attacked Moravia and Bohemia.

---

33   *Widukindi Rerum gestarum Saxonicarum* I 26, 27, rec. Waitz, p. 23. Reindel, *Die bayerischen Liutpoldinger*, no. 61, pp. 119–131.

34   Reindel, *Die bayerischen Liutpoldinger*, no. 61, pp. 119–131.

5 The Magyars in Nitria, Princes Tas and Lehel

The Magyars came across not only the Nitrians in Nitria, who are referred to by a Hungarian chronicler as the *Messianis*),[35] but they also ran into the Bohemians there. According to Hungarian chronicler Simon of Kéza, Magyar Prince Lehel (Lél) and his warriors settled in Nitria: *Lehel thus was the leader of the sixth army. He, at first living around Hlohovec, then after extermination of the Messians and Bohemians (exinde Messianis et Boemis exstirpatis), was eventually said to be more often settled in the regions of Nitra (in partibus Nittriae).*[36] Lehel, who died a premature death in 955 during the best years of his life,[37] obviously was not the first Magyar prince in Nitria, but very probably inherited the Nitrian Principality from his father Tas.[38] In 920 Lehel's father Tas could have become the first Magyar prince in Nitria.

Archaeological research has indirectly confirmed the dating of the rule of Nitria by the Magyars to year 920. From the 26 oldest Magyar burial sites or individual graves from south Slovakia (except the Zemplín region, which certainly no longer belonged to the Nitrian Principality) and the adjacent southern Novohrad, northern Borsod, southern Abov and the Tokaj regions: Vojnice, Bešeňov, Čakajovce, Horné Obdokovce, Horné Saliby, Hlohovec, Iža, Dolný Peter, Miskolc-Repülőtér, Veľké Kostoľany, Košúty, Zemianska Olča, Veľký Kýr, Hurbanovo-Bohatá, Prša, Piliny-Leshegy, Sóshartyán-Zúdótető, Sereď, Mudroňovo, Szob-Kiserdő, Tvrdošovce, Tokaj and Červeník come nearly 80 endorsed coins of different origin,[39] which date for us the presence of their

---

35 See pp. 491–493.
36 *Simonis de Keza Gesta Hungarorum* II 32, SRH I, pp. 166–167. MMFH I, pp. 279–280. A later Hungarian chronicler, who in the 14th century took up and altered an older chronicler's text, mistakenly identified the Messians with the Bohemians: *Leel ..., qui Messianos scilicet Bohemicos ... expulit ... Chron. Hung. comp. saec. XIV.* II 32, SRH I, pp. 291–292. MMFH I, pp. 310–311. We don't have to seriously deal with whether the Bohemians and with them some Nitrians were *exstirpatis* or Lehel, more probably, however, his father Tas, only expelled (*expulit*) them. Neither of them is an authentic statement; both chroniclers chose according to their literary taste.
37 *Widukindi Rerum gestarum Saxonicarum* III 44, rec. Waitz, pp. 71–73.
38 According to Anonymus *Tas [was]the father of Lehel* and *Lehel the son of Tas*. *Anonymi (P. magistri) Gesta Hungarorum* 6, 21, 39, 41, 53, SRH I, pp. 41, 61, 63, 82, 85, 86, 107.
39 Kovács, *Münzen aus der ungarischen Landnahmezeit*, pp. 17–77. When dating a grave using coins, the youngest coin found in the grave is crucial. We have to also considered the distance in time from the issuing of the coin into circulation after its placement in the grave. The territory for which we took these finds into consideration is that of the Nitrian Principality in the 11th century. If Árpád's Nitria was a continuation of Great Moravian

Magyar owners on this territory. We cannot date even one of the mentioned Magyar graves to the first two decades of the 10th century.[40]

Hlohovec Castle, whose surroundings were occupied by Lehel and his Magyars according to a Hungarian chronicler, is also mentioned by the Zobor document from year 1113.[41] It was built on the site of an older castle, of which archaeologists have found only minor traces.[42] The presence of the first Magyars in Hlohovec is documented in a horserider grave in the castle park dated by an endorsed dirham of Samanid Amir Nasr ibn Ahmed (914–943), which they minted in Samarkand in the years 918–919.[43] In addition to the mentioned coin, a gilded pointed forged sheath made from silver sheet metal with rich vegetative ornamentation, a woven silver neck guard, two decorated silver bracelets and silver earrings were found in the grave.[44]

Princes Tas and Lehel did not have to occupy all of Nitria with their soldiers in order to rule it. The oldest Magyar horserider graves that we can date to the 2nd quarter of the 10th century according to the coins found, do not extend beyond the northern line of Hlohovec – Nitra – Levice – Krupina – Lučenec – Rimavská Sobota – Turňa – Michaľany.[45] Magyar horse brigades thus had the centre of the land with Nitra under their control. The northern parts of Nitria, there where Tas and Lehel's Magyars did not penetrate, recognized the superiority of the mentioned Magyar princes and did so without direct control, because Tas and then Lehel had Nitra in their power, to which the whole of Nitria had long before then been subjugated.

Nitria, then its naturally defined and historical sustained territorial range could also be taken from it.

40 Gabriel Nevizánsky, "K významu a vypovedacej schopnosti mincí v staromaďarských hroboch," *Slovenská numizmatika* 6 (1980), pp. 121–130. Ján Vavruš, *Nové pohľady na interpretáciu pohrebísk 10. storočia z juhozápadného Slovenska* (Unpublished dissertation) (Bratislava 2000).

41 *Golgoc, Golguz*. DHA I, ed. Györffy, no. 142/I, pp. 393–394. CDES I, ed. Marsina, no. 69, p. 66.

42 *Pramene I/2*, ed. Bialeková, p. 439.

43 Kovács, *Münzen aus der ungarischen Landnahmezeit*, p. 28.

44 *Významné slovanské náleziská na Slovensku*, ed. Chropovský, pp. 76–77. *Pramene I/2*, ed. Bialeková, pp. 438–440.

45 Alexander Ruttkay, "Problematika historického vývoja na území Slovenska v 10.–13. storočí z hľadiska archeologického bádania," in Poulík – Chropovský et al., *Veľká Morava a počátky československé státnosti*, p. 157. Milan Hanuliak, "Gräberfelder der slawischen Population im 10. Jahrhundert im Gebiet der Westslowakei," *Slovenská archeológia* 40 (1992), no. 2, pp. 280–281.

6 Bohemia in 920-922

According to a Hungarian chronicler, the Magyars, after occupying Nitria, also invaded Moravia and Bohemia: *The Magyars ... cruelly plundered Moravia and Bohemia, where at this time Prince Vratislaus was seen to rule. From there they victoriously returned, making peace with the mentioned prince, and rested for one year.*[46] Simon of Kéza wrote about these events: *When they afterwards settled in occupied Pannonia, they ultimately despoiled all the property of Moravia and Bohemia, killing their Prince Vratislaus in battle.*[47] Russian chronicler Nestor confirms the report of the Hungarian chroniclers: *And the Magyars began to battle ... And they began to battle against the Moravians and Bohemians (na Moravu i na Čechy).*[48] A report on the Magyar attack against the Moravians and Bohemians was thus already in the old Gesta Ungarorum, whose author was Nestor's contemporary.

Bohemian Prince Vratislaus I died on 13 February 921. He was only 33 years old when he died, and he left two minor sons behind.[49] He thus died young, and this led to suspicions that his death was not natural, but a violent one, that he really died in a battle with the Magyars, as is mentioned by Simon of Kéza.[50] February of 921 could be that time in which the Magyars, after the end of the Bohemian-Magyar alliance and after the subsequent conquering of Nitria, invaded *Moravia and Bohemia*.[51] Perhaps it was then that the Magyars conquered and burned the Moravian castles that they did not manage to destroy in 906.[52] We can then consider Vratislaus's death *in battle* with the Magyars

---

46 *Hungari ... Moraviam et Bohemiam, in quibus eo tempore dux Vratizlaus regnare videbatur, crudeliter. Exinde cum victoria redeuntes treugis ordinatis cum prefato duce uno anno quieverunt. Chron. Hung. comp. saec. XIV.* II 54, SRH I, p. 304.
47 *Cum autem residissent Pannonia occupata, tandem Moraviam et Boemiam bonis omnibus spoliarunt Waratizlao eorum duce in praelio interfecto. Simonis de Keza Gesta Hungarorum* II 34, SRH I, p. 167.
48 *Latopis Nestora* 19, year 6406 (898), MPH I, ed. Bielowski, p. 568. MMFH I, p. 194.
49 Třeštík, *Počátky*, pp. 109, 176-178, 194, 205.
50 Naďa Profantová consideres this to be a real possibility. Bláhová – Frolík – Profantová, *Velké dějiny zemí Koruny české I*, pp. 268-269.
51 Up until 920 the Magyars and Bohemians were allies. When this alliance broke apart in 920, the Magyars immediately attacked the former ally first in Nitria and in the following year (perhaps in February) on its own territory. Twenty years before the Magyars and Moravians were similar allies. Still in the summer and autum of 900 the Magyars and Moravians allied against the Bavarians, but as early as in the late autumn of this same year the Magyars attacked their own ally.
52 Kouřil, "Staří Maďari a Morava," pp. 110-146. The Magyars conquered and burned the Znojmo hill-fort of St. Hyppolitus in the mid-10th century. Klíma, "Archeologický výskum MU na velkomoravském výšinném hradišti sv. Hypolita ve Znojmě," pp. 229-230.

either as a chronicler's literary license, by which he wanted to emphasize the Magyar victory, or as a real event, which would explain why Vratislaus died at such a young age.

Arnulf beat back Henry's attack on Regensburg in 920.[53] At the start of summer in 921 German king and Saxon Duke Henry I attacked Regensburg again with a large army. Arnulf, who had no allies,[54] willingly concluded a compromising peace with Henry and opened the gates of Regensburg to him.[55] The Regensburg peace agreement also certainly related to Bohemia. If in the following year the Bavarian duke marched to Bohemia, then King Henry acknowledged Bohemia as a Bavarian holding. The Bohemians, allies until recently, had after 15 years again fall into dependence on Bavaria and through Bavaria also to Henry's realm, to which Arnulf's Bavaria undoubtedly belonged after 921.

After Vratislaus's death, the princess Drahomíra took over rule in Bohemia on behalf of Vratislaus's minor son Wenceslaus (*perhaps 907), and she certainly did not consent with the position of the Bohemians as decided by the two most powerful men in the neighbouring realm. Drahomíra, resolute to put up opposition to Arnulf (and perhaps also Henry), ordered the murder on 15 September 921 of Princess Ludmila, who was willing (and under the influence of archipresbyter Pavel, who lingered in her presence) to subjugate to the Regensburg conditions and thus come to terms with the loss of Bohemian independence. She then expelled Bavarian priests who welcomed Bohemian dependence on Bavaria.[56] Arnulf, who marched to Bohemia in 922,[57] wanted

---

Kouřil, "Staří Maďari a Morava," pp. 124–126. The Magyars horserider grave in Gnadendorf (near Mistelbach) is among the oldest Magyar graves on on the north side of the middle Danube. Ernst Lauermann: "Ein landnahmezeitliches Reitergrab aus Gnadendorf," *Archäologie Österreichs* 11 (2000) no. 2, pp. 34–35. Ernst Lauermann, "Ein frühungarischer Reiter aus Gnadendorf, Niederösterreich," in *Schicksalsjahr 907*, ed. Zehetmayer, pp. 92–98. This is a rare find of a Hungarian grave on the territory which originally belonged to the Moravians.

53 Reindel, *Die bayerischen Liutpoldinger*, p. 130.
54 Arnulf was lacking not only Bohemian but also Magyar allies. The Magyars gave preference to Italian King and Emperor Berengar I. Magyar Princes Tarhos (*Dursac*) and Kál (*Bugat*), who *were very friendly towards Berengar* (*amicissimi Berengario fuerant*), came in 921 to Verona, where *Berengar asked the Magyars that if they love him* (*ut si se amarent*), *to fall upon his enemies. Liutprandi Antapodosis* II 61–62. Liutprandi episcopi Cremonensis opera omnia, ed. Pertz, pp. 63–64. *MMFH I*, pp. 135–136. Vajay, *Der Eintritt*, pp. 64–65. *MT I/1*, pp. 654, 663–664.
55 Widukindi *Rerum gestarum Saxonicarum* I 27, rec. Waitz, p. 23. Reindel, *Die bayerischen Liutpoldinger*, no. 61, pp. 119–131.
56 Třeštík, *Počátky*, pp. 369–374.
57 Josef Pekař, "Svatý Václav," in *Svatováclavský sborník. Na památku 1000. výročí smrti knížete Václava Svatého I. Kníže Václav Svatý a jeho doba*, ed. Karel Guth, Jan Kapras,

to renew the relations of Bohemia to Bavaria (and thus to the entire empire to which Bavaria belonged), as applied from 895–906. He managed to do this only in 929, when he came to Bohemia together with Henry.[58]

7 Saxon Victories over the Slavs and Magyars

In 924 *The Magyars again passed through the whole of Saxony* and this time pillaged without their former Slavic allies. Princess Drahomíra, who ruled until 924 or 925, obviously very willingly allowed them to pass through Bohemian territory. The Saxons managed to capture *some of the Magyar princes*. German King Henry rejected the rich ransom the Magyars offered him for their prince and released him only when they concluded a 9-year peace with him.[59]

Henry thoroughly enjoyed nine peaceful years. He built castles and prepared a military, with which in 928–932 he subjugated the Slavic tribes beyond the Saale River and the lower Elbe. The Magyars did not breach the peace and did not support the Slavs militarily. The Slavs defended themselves, but in the end they fell to the assault of Henry's military.[60] When in 933 the peace agreement ended, Stodorians and others, the Luticians, Glomucians, Obotrites, the Milcens and Lusatians lived under the rule of the Saxon margrave and they no longer counted on Magyar help.[61] When in 933 the Magyars invaded

---

Antonín Novák, Karel Stloukal, *Národní výbor pro oslavu svatováclavského tisíciletí* (Praha 1934), pp. 37–38. Reindel, *Die bayerischen Liutpoldinger*, no. 62, pp. 131–132. Dralle, "Zu Vorgeschichte," pp. 118–124. Třeštík, *Počátky*, p. 374.

[58] *Widukindi Rerum gestarum Saxonicarum* I 35, rec. Waitz, p. 29. Novotný, *České dějiny* I/1, p. 468. František M. Bartoš, "Kníže Václav Svatý u Vidukinda," in *Svatováclavský sborník I. Kníže Václav Svatý a jeho doba*, ed. Guth, Kapras, Novák, Stloukal, pp. 833–841. Reindel, *Die bayerischen Liutpoldinger*, no. 76, pp. 148–150. Gerad Labuda, *Fragmenty dziejów Słowiańscyzny zachódniej* (Poznań 1960), pp. 253, 254–260. Zdeněk Fiala, "Dva kritické příspěvky ke starým dějinám českým," *Sborník historický* 9 (1962), pp. 24–26.

[59] *quendam ex principibus Ungariorum*. *Widukindi Rerum gestarum Saxonicarum* I 32, rec. Waitz, p. 26. *Thietmari Chronicon* I 15 (8), rec. Kurze, pp. 10–11. *Thietmari Chronicon* I 15, cur. Trillmich, pp. 20–21.

[60] *Widukindi Rerum gestarum Saxonicarum* I 35–36, rec. Waitz, pp. 28–31. *Annales Hildesheimenses* ad a. 932, contulit cum Codice Parisiensi Georgius Waitz, Scriptores rerum Germanicarum in usum scholarum ex Monumentis Germaniae historicis recusi (Hannoverae 1878), p. 20. *Thietmari Chronicon* I 10 (6), 16 (9), rec. Kurze, pp. 7–8, 11 *Thietmari Chronicon* I 10, 16, cur. Trillmich, pp. 14–15, 20–21. Labuda, *Fragmenty dziejów Słowiańscyzny zachódniej*, pp. 251–263. *Die Slawen in Deutschland*, ed. Herrmann, pp. 336–337.

[61] The rebellion of the Lutician Ratars in 936, to which the Obotrites joined in, and then a new rebellion of the Obotrites, Stodolans and Luticians in 939–940 had no Magyar

Saxony and Thuringia, they revived their old friendship with the Glomucians and invited them to again join forces and march against their conquerors. The Glomucians, who knew that King Henry was well prepared for war, rejected the appeal of the Magyars and in a sign of defiance gave them a *fattened dog*. The caution of the Glomucians was a wise choice. In a battle near Riade Henry triumphed, and 36,000 Magyars died.[62]

support. *Widukindi Rerum gestarum Saxonicarum* II 4, 20–21, rec. Waitz, pp. 39–40, 47–48. *Die Slawen in Deutschland*, ed. Herrmann, pp. 337–339.

62   *Widukindi Rerum gestarum Saxonicarum* I 38, rec. Waitz, pp. 32–33. *Liutprandi Antapodosis* II 25–31, ed. Pertz, pp. 50–53. Labuda, *Fragmenty dziejów Słowiańscyzny zachódniej*, pp. 263–270.

CHAPTER 12

Tales about Svätopluk

1   Svätopluk in the Narratives of His Contemporaries

The Moravians liked to talk about Svätopluk's victories: *The more Moravia began to expand on all sides and to overcome enemies without hesitation, the more they always talked about it.*[1] Methodius's biographer did not write any more about the stories of the Moravians; he did capture, however, the beginning of an epic tradition about glorious periods of the nation and its greatest ruler, the development and sources of which we can trace in the work of chroniclers for a full 400 years.

Foreign merchants also visited Svätopluk's country, and especially the large market in his princely seat. In their telling, Svätopluk was *grand and known*. One of them wrote a report in Arabic on the Slavs, in which he also mentioned Svätopluk: *Grand and known among them is one who is called the head of heads, and they call him S.w.j.tb.l.k.* This report got as far as to distant Isfahán, into the hands of Persian scholar Ibn Rust, and he included it in his work at the beginning of the 10th century.[2] Tales about Svätopluk's fame and the size of his land even reached Constantinople. In the mid-10th century, Byzantine Emperor and scholar Constantine Porphyrogenitus took an interest in *Great Moravia, namely the country of Svätopluk* and in his work left a reference about Svätopluk's military glory: *It is necessary to know that Moravian Prince Svätopluk was valiant and feared in the nations neighbouring with him.*[3] A contemporary of Emperor Constantine, Cremona Bishop Liudprand, wrote about Arnulf as about the most powerful king and mentioned that *Svätopluk, Prince of the Moravians, took heart and became an antagonist to him.*[4]

The motif of monarchal wisdom was also connected with Svätopluk. West Frankish chronicler Regino wrote: *Svätopluk, king of the Moravian Slavs, a man among the wisest and a spirit most astute, lived his last day.*[5] And the mentioned

---

1   ŽM 10, *MMFH II*, p. 154.
2   *Kitábu l-a láki n-nafísati li-bni Rusta* 2, *MMFH III*, pp. 346–347, Pauliny, *Arabské správy o Slovanoch*, p. 99. Łowmiański, *Początki Polski II*, pp. 152–153. Steinhübel, "Slovanské 'gentes' a ich vladykovia, kniežatá a kagani," pp. 280–284.
3   Constantine Porphyrogenitus, *De administrando imperio* 13, 41, ed. Moravcsik, pp. 64, 65, 180–181. Konstantinos Porfyrogenetos, *De administrando imperio* 13, 41, *MMFH III*, pp. 384, 398.
4   *Liudprandi Antapodosis* I 13, *MMFH I*, pp. 145–146.
5   *Reginonis Chron.* ad a. 894, rec. Kurze, p. 143. *MMFH I*, p. 124.

Constantine Porphyrogenitus in a story about three rods set Svätopluk up as an example of a wise monarch.[6]

2 The Nitrian and Zobor Tale

In 1099 Bohemian chronicler Cosmas travelled through Slovakia to Esztergom and noticed that Svätopluk *is generally spoken about* and for his chronicle captured in brief and elaborated two tales, which told of Svätopluk's military and Svätopluk's military camp. Thus, they were a commemoration on the old military glory. The first legend connected this memory with the motif of monarchal immortality: *Svätopluk (Zuatopluk), king of Moravia, as is generally said (sicut vulgo dicitur), disappeared amidst his military and was never seen again.* That is, he didn't die and may again reappear at any time. While this first tale was generally spread in Nitria, another tale was expressly local, linked to Zobor Abbey. It told of Svätopluk, who left a military camp and marched to the Zobor hermits: *Svätopluk, king of Moravia ... turned around ... led by sorrow, in the middle of the dark night, when no one knew of it, sat on a horse and coming through his camp, ran off to the place located on the side of the mountain Zobor, where three hermits built with his support and help a church in a large forest, inaccessible to people. We he got there in the hidden place of this forest, he killed his horse and buried his sword in the ground. And when the light of day came, he arrived at the hermits, who didn't see who he was. His head was shaved, and he was dressed in a hermit's garments and as long as he lived he remained unknown to all. When, however, he saw that death was upon him, he told the monks who he was and died immediately after.*[7]

Cosmas, as a man in the service of an ecclesiastical order (the future dean of the Prague chapter), used the rare opportunity, and on the road to or from Esztergom, where on 14 June 1099 he was ordained as a priest by archbishop Serafin,[8] he visited the oldest monastery in Slovakia. The legend that swirled around Zobor Abbey interested Cosmas very much, because he wrote it with

---

6   Constantine Porphyrogenitus, *De administrando imperio* 41, ed. Moravcsik, pp. 180–181. Konstantinos Porfyrogenetos, *De administrando imperio* 41, MMFH III, pp. 398–399.

7   *Cosmae Pragensis Chronica Bohemorum* I 14 ad a. 894, herausgegeben von Bertold Bretholz, Monumenta Germaniae historica, Scriptores rerum Germanicarum nova series II (Berolini 1923), pp. 32–34. MMFH I, pp. 199–200, Matúš Kučera, "O historickom vedomí Slovákov v stredoveku," *Historický časopis* 25 (1977), no. 2, p. 229. Eugen Pauliny, *Slovesnosť a kultúrny jazyk Veľkej Moravy* (Bratislava 1964), pp. 41–50.

8   *Cosmae Pragensis Chronica Boemorum* III 9, ed. Bretholz, p. 169. Dušan Třeštík, *Kosmova kronika. Studie k počátkům českého dějepisectví a politického myšlení* (Praha 1968), pp. 42–43.

great care and with several details. He devoted only one sentence in his chronicle to the Nitrian tale, although it was generally widespread.

3 Tale of the Hungarian King-Hermit Solomon

At the same time another very similar tale was widespread about the penitence of Hungarian King Solomon: *When, however, he got to one large forest, he told his people to stop for a moment and desired that the horses be rested. He alone put down his shield and pretending that he will immediately return, he left into the dark depths of the forest. Meanwhile, it didn't occur to any of his people; he distanced himself from them and was no longer to be seen. Broken in spirit and afflicted by so many great failures, he was visited by the redemptive Holy Spirit, so that after these hardships he no longer ceased, even from his own will, to launch into another battle against the most just truth of God, but feeling how the highest merciful hand of God punishes him, he mourned at the memory of his acts and because human justice may judge him, with a despondent heart he remorsefully regretted his sins. Happy that anxiety that compels one to improve! Because all that is really needed is that he whom the world hates be loved by God. And the noble body of King Solomon, raised in royal pleasures, lay in the dust and ashes of suffering, and he who previously battled for earthly things, now sought only heavenly things. The entire rest of his life he spent in pilgrimages and prayers, in fasts and vigils, in toils and adorations of the Lord. Once more, in the time of King Coloman, he was seen in Hungary, but he very rapidly slipped away and was no longer seen.*[9]

The deposed Hungarian King Solomon in March 1087 took part in a campaign of the Pechenegs on Byzantine territory and fell in battle.[10] A Hungarian chronicler, however, instead of a reliable report about the time and circumstances of Solomon's death, just as with other Hungarian kings, wrote very willingly this legend in order to emphasize (similarly as Cosmas with Svätopluk) the opposite, with his previous life, when he still *battled against the most just*

---

9   *Chron. Hung. comp. saec. XIV.* II 136, SRH I, pp. 410–411. *Legendy a kroniky koruny uherské*, translation Dagmar Bartoňková, Jana Nechutová, ed. Richard Pražák (Praha 1988), pp. 359–360.
10 Anna Komnene, *Alexias* 3, *Az Árpád-kori magyar történet bizanci forrásai*, ed. Moravcsik, pp. 103–105. *Chron. Hung. comp. saec. XIV.* II 134–135, SRH I, pp. 409–410. MT I/2, pp. 928–929. According to the Zagreb Chronicle, Solomon was buried in the Istrian town of Pula. *Chronicon Zagrabiense* 6, SRH I, p. 208.

of God's truth.[11] Both chroniclers, Bohemian and Hungarian, wanted to demonstrate in the monarchal story the power and importance of penance.

Both tales, about the Moravian king and the Hungarian king, are very similar. Svätopluk *ran off to the place ... in a large forest inaccessible to people*; Solomon *he left into the dark depths of the forest*. Svätopluk *killed his horse and buried his sword in the ground*; Solomon *put down his shield*. Svätopluk *turned around ... led by sorrow*, Solomon *mourned at the memory of his acts ... with a despondent heart he remorsefully regretted his sins*. Svätopluk's *head was shaved, and he was dressed in a hermit's garments and as long as he lived he remained unknown to all*; Solomon *the entire rest of his life he spent in pilgrimages and prayers, in fasts and vigils, in toils and adorations of the Lord*.

The story about the king-hermit rapidly spread. Under the rule of King Coloman, when Solomon had been dead for eight years, he reportedly was seen: *Once more, in the time of King Coloman, he was seen in Hungary, but he very rapidly slipped away and was no longer seen*. Exactly as with Svätopluk, who *disappeared ... and was never seen again*. Solomon gained veneration after death and enjoyed it for the whole 12th century. He was even capable of competing with the growing cult of King Ladislas. While Ladislas achieved canonization in 1192, Solomon's memory had to retreat.[12] Veneration towards Solomon endured through the entire 12th century, and the memory of Svätopluk lived in the oral tradition for several centuries, although neither of them was ever a hermit.[13]

4   Hungarian Chronicles

Cosmas knew two tales about Svätopluk in 1099. At this time the oldest Hungarian chronicler ended his work, the now lost Gesta Ungarorum or The

---

[11]   Solomon battled against his cousins Géza I and Ladislas I. Svätopluk battled against Arnulf.

[12]   Georgius Pray, *Dissertationes Historico-Criticae de Sanctis Salomone rege et Emerico duce Hungariae* (Posonii 1774). Gyula Kristó, *Az Árpád-dinasztia szentjei és legendáik*, in Gyula Kristó, *Tanulmányok az Árpád-korról* (Budapest 1983), pp. 367–368. Martin Homza, *Stredoveké korene svätoplukovskej tradície u Slovákov (čierna a biela svätoplukovská legenda)*, in Martin Homza et al., *Svätopluk v európskom písomníctve*, pp. 108–117.

[13]   An example of a king who after death became a successful figure of hagiography is Lotharingian King Zwentibold (895–900), the godson of Great Moravian Prince Svätopluk I. The centre of the Zwentibold cult became the monastery in the Dutch town of Susteren, in which relics of Zwentibold and allegedly his burial site are located. Ľubica Štrbáková, *Svätopluk Lotrinský († 900), krstný syn Svätopluka I., ako postava historická a hagiografická*, in Homza, et al., *Svätopluk v európskom písomníctve*, pp. 177, 180, 212–229.

Deeds of the Hungarians. Their text, with greater or smaller changes, was taken by later Hungarian chroniclers and most fully preserved in the Chronicum Pictum (in chapters 6, 23, 26–27, 41, 58–59, 63–65, 68–141).[14] The original Gesta Ungarorum, labelled as the Gesta Ungarorum vetera, probably began with a description of the Scythians[15] and the arrival of the Magyars to Pannonia, by which they understood the whole future Hungary, their victory over Svätopluk, and they continued with the history of the oldest Hungarian princes and kings.

The unknown chronicler could not have written the Gesta Ungarorum vetera before the year 1083, because it consistently labels Stephen I and his son Emeric as saints.[16] In addition he mistakenly labels the Pechenegs, who on the invitation of deposed King Solomon invaded Hungary in 1085 and Byzantium territory in 1087, as the Cumans.[17] Confusing the former Pechenegs, whom they knew well in Hungary, with the Cumans was possible only after year 1091. On 29 April 1091 an allied Cuman and Byzantine army defeated and destroyed the Pechenegs in a battle near Levounion (near the mouth of the Maritsa River). The Cumans (Polovtsi, Kipchak) immediately after invaded their seats east of the Carpathans in Moldova and of the steppes of the Black Sea,[18] and still in this same year they invaded Hungary for the first time and sacked Transylvania and the Tisza River region.[19] The oldest Hungarian chronicler wrote in great detail about the extensive Cuman plundering in Hungary in 1091, which only ended with the victory of King Ladislas I. He also considered the previous Pecheneg invasions of 1085 and 1087 under the impression of these events. The Gesta Ungarorum vetera thus could not have originated before year 1091. Therefore, because it originated only in the last decade of the 11th century, it

---

14   Györffy, *Krónikáink*, pp. 92–96. János Horváth, *Árpád-kori latin nyelvű irodalmunk stílusproblémái* (Budapest 1954), pp. 293–294.

15   Bálint Hóman, "Szkitia leírása a Gesta Ungarorumban," *Magyar Könyvszemle* 1930, pp. 243–263. Gyula Kristó, "Az Exordia Scythica. Regino és a magyar krónikák," *Filológiai Közlöny* 16 (1970), pp. 106–115.

16   *Chron. Hung. comp. saec. XIV.* II 28, 30, 38, 41, 53, 63–67, 69, 70, 72, 86, SRH I, pp. 290, 291, 295, 297, 303, 311–323, 325, 344. References to Ladislas's piousness and holiness are an interporlation of the original text Gesta Ungarorum vetera from the times after Ladislas's canonization in 1192. *Chron. Hung. comp. saec. XIV.* II 124, 131 139, 140, 141, 143, SRH I, pp. 394, 403–406, 417–421. Hungarian chroniclers label Ladislas as saintly (beatus, sanctus, gloriosus) very inconsistently. Simon of Kéza has no mention of Ladislas's saintliness. The Buda Chronicle and the Chronicon Pictum usually write Ladislas's name without this attribute. The Zagreb Chronicle has these attributes consistent with each use of the names of Stephen, Emeric and Ladislas.

17   *Chron. Hung. comp. saec. XIV.* II 134–135, SRH I, pp. 409–410. MT I/2, p. 928.

18   Karl Krumbacher, *Geschichte der byzantinischen Literatur von Justinian bis zum Ende des Oströmischen Reichs* (München 1897), p. 1017. *Dějiny Byzance*, ed. Zástěrová, p. 252.

19   *Chron. Hung. comp. saec. XIV.* II 137, SRH I, pp. 411–412. MT I/2, pp. 935–937.

is an unreliable source for the beginnings of Hungarian history, the period of Saint Stephen and the following decades. It contains several inaccuracies and errors up through the decade of the 1080s.[20] The Gesta Ungarorum vetera thus originated at the time of educated Hungarian King Coloman (1095–1116). Coloman, who in his youth prepared to be a bishop, had a substantial education and a reputation as a bookworm.[21] He was certainly very interested in this chronicle, and it was undoubtedly written on his initiative.

There are two different reports about Bishop Coloman in the Hungarian Chronicles which show us the reach of the Gesta Ungarorum vetera text. According to the first (in the 140th chapter of the Chronicon Pictum), referring to year 1095, King Ladislas I decided that his older nephew Coloman will be the bishop in Eger. Coloman, however, wanted to be king; therefore, he ran off to Poland, from where he returned after Ladislas's death. Another author wrote the second report referring to year 1114 (in the 152nd chapter of the Chronicon Pictum): *This Coloman, as some say (sicut quidam dicunt), was the Bishop of Várad, and only because his brothers died before him, with the Pope's permission, he was admitted to rule. The Hungarians called him Könyves Kálmán (Cunues*

20 Several historians place the origin of Gesta Ungarorum vetera into older times. Sándor Domanovszky assumes their origin around year 1060. Bálint Hóman sees their origin in the time of Ladislas I. György Györffy accepted the opinion on the origin of Gesta Ungarorum vetera around 1060, then later abandoned it. János Horváth considered their compiler to be Bishop Nicholas, who was a notary of Andrew I. József Gerics put their origin immediately after 1067. Elemér Mályusz places the period of their origin at the beginning of Solomon's rule. Sándor Domanovszky, *Kézai Simon mester krónikája* (Budapest 1906), pp. 128–130. Bálint Hóman, *A Szent László-kori Gesta Ungarorum és XII–XIII. századi leszármazói* (Budapest 1925), pp. 50–54. Györffy, *Krónikáink*, pp. 5, 89–91. Horváth, *Árpád-kori latin nyelvü irodalmunk stílusproblémái*, pp. 306–312. József Gerics, *Legkorábbi Gesta-szekésztéseink keletkezésrendjének problémái* (Budapest 1961), pp. 79–84. Elemér Mályusz, *A Thuróczy-krónika és forrásai* (Budapest 1967), pp. 34–35.

21 Pope Urban II wrote to Coloman on 27 July 1096: *Retulit enim nobis venerabilis filius noster Odilo Sancti Aegydii abbas strenuitatem vestram preter secularem, qua precellis, industriam scripturis etiam ecclesiasticis eruditam*. DHA I, ed. Györffy, no. 109, p. 317. The Polish Gallus Anonymus also mentions Coloman's education: *Inde rediens Bolezlavus cum rege Ungarorum Colomano super reges universos suo tempore degentes litterali scientia erudito*. *Galli Chronicon* II 29, MPH I, ed. Bielowski, p. 448. Raimund F. Kaindl, Marian Plezia, Gyula Kristó and György Györffy all put the origin of Gesta Ungarorum vetera in the period of King Coloman. Raimund F. Kaindl, *Beiträge zur ältesten ungarischen Geschichte* (Wien 1893), pp. 52–53. Marian Plezia, "Ungarische Beziehungen des ältesten polnischen Chronisten," *Acta Antiqua* 7 (1959), pp. 291–294. Gyula Kristó, *A történeti és politikai gondolkodás elemeinek fejlödése krónika-irodalmunkban* (Budapest 1968), p. 9. Györffy, "Az Árpád-kori magyar krónikák," pp. 392–395.

Calman), *because he had books, according to which he as bishop performed canonical hours.*[22]

The report on Várad Bishop Coloman contradicts the report on the preparation of Coloman as the Eger bishop; thus, undoubtedly they are from two different authors. If one person had written all of this, then he would have had a troubling dilemma before him. In order to remove the confusion, he would have certainly synchronized both reports or would have selected only one of them. Therefore, between these two contradictory reports we can search for the end of the text Gesta Ungarorum vetera and the beginning of the work of their first continuator.

The introductory chapter strictly assess Coloman's rule. *In his time many crimes were committed, as will be shown in the future.* And immediately the first sentence of the following chapter emphasizes Coloman's ugly and repulsive appearance and bad character.[23] This malicious introduction could not have been written by the author of the Gesta Ungarorum vetera, who was Coloman's contemporary and stayed close to him. It can come only from the period after 1131, when Béla II, whom Coloman had blinded when he was a small child along with his father Álmos, came to the Hungarian throne.[24] The Gesta Ungarorum vetera thus reaches up to the end of the rule of Ladislas I, that is to year 1095. If its unknown author was a chaplain and scribe of Ladslas I and later Bishop Koppány,[25] who died when he accompanied King Coloman on the unhappy

---

22 *Chron. Hung. comp. saec. XIV.* II 140–142, 152, SRH I, pp. 419–420, 432–433. Simon of Kéza writes *Qunwes enim Kalman est vocatus* and leaves out the whole previous sentence about Coloman's position as the Bishop of Várad and with introduction of the words *sicut quidam dicunt*. *Simonis de Keza Gesta Hungarorum* II 64, SRH I, p. 182. The Zagreb Chronicle mentioned King Coloman as a former bishop of Várad: *Colomanus rex, qui fuit episcopus Waradiensis*. It is silent on the plans of King Ladislas I to make Coloman the Bishop of Eger. *Chronicon Zagrabiense* 10, SRH I, p. 209.
23 *Chron. Hung. comp. saec. XIV.* II 142, 143, SRH I, p. 421.
24 *Chron. Hung. comp. saec. XIV.* II 150, SRH I, pp. 429–430. The Buda Chronicle in its 142nd chapter assesses Coloman's rule the same as the Chronicon Pictum, with a brief sentence on the many crimes in the period of his rule. Aside from the short report on the blinding of Béla II, the Buda Chronicle says nothing about the events of Coloman's rule and his successors. With the exception of the short 142nd chapter, it is silent about the years 1095–1162; it thus left out the text of all the continuations of the Gesta Ungarorum vetera from the 12th century and continues directly with the text of Magister Ákos. Simon of Kéza also left out of his work the text continuing the Gesta Ungarorum vetera from the 12th century, mentioning from the whole of Coloman's rule only the annexation of the Croatian kingdom to Hungary. *Simonis de Keza Gesta Hungarorum* 64, SRH I, pp. 182–183.
25 Ubul Kállay, "Kopán krónikája," *Turul* 33 (1915), pp. 21–23. Györffy, "Az Árpád-kori magyar krónikák," p. 393. DHA I, ed. Györffy, no. 85, 88, 96, 151, pp. 261, 268, 285, 412. Bishop Koppány (Cupan) could be identical with Vencelin's great-grandson Koppány. *Chron. Hung. comp. saec. XIV.* II 64, SRH I, p. 314. Kállay, "Kopán krónikája," pp. 21–22. Koppány

campaign in Russia in April of 1099,[26] then we can place the origin of Gesta Ungarorum vetera into the first years of Coloman's rule, that is to 1095–1099.

An unknown contemporary of Béla II (1131–1141) wrote not only the mentioned malicious introduction about King Coloman, but as he himself stated (*as will be shown in the following*), the entire subsequent text. He did not save on words of praise about his own King Béla II.[27] In the 12th century several short continuations, which told the events of Hungarian history up to year 1152, were attached to the original Gesta Ungarorum vetera text.[28]

Under the rule of King Stephen V (1270–1272), Magister Ákos (1254–1272), Provost of Buda, supplemented the Gesta Ungarorum vetera and their continuation with chapters on the old Hungarian princes and on the origin of the Hungarian noble families, modified their content in places and completed and added the period of years 1162–1272. His work became the foundation for Hungarian chronicles of the 14th century (Chronicon Pictum, the Buda Chronicle) and in a shortened form got into the chronicle of Simon of Kéza.[29] Ten years after the death of Magister Ákos, Simon of Kéza began to write the history of the Huns;[30] he added to it a history according to the chronicle of

could perhaps be the Veszprém bishop, because he owned a village in the county Zala in the Veszprém diocese. *DHA I*, ed. Györffy, no. 151, p. 412. He could have been the successor of Veszprém Bishop Cosmas.

26 *Chron. Hung. comp. saec. XIV.* II 145, *SRH I*, pp. 423–426. *Latopis Nestora* 82, 83, year 6605 (1097), *MPH I*, ed. Bielowski, pp. 802–804. Elemér Mályusz, *Johannes de Thurocz Chronica Hungarorum II. Commentarii, 1. Ab initiis usque ad annum 1301*, composuit Elemér Mályusz, adiuvante Julio Kristó, Budapest 1988, pp. 414–416.

27 *Chron. Hung. comp. saec. XIV.* II 160. *SRH I*, pp. 446–447. He only wrote about Béla's rule in the conclusion of the text, probably after Béla's death; he wrote that Béla liked to revel in excessive drinking of wine. *Chron. Hung. comp. saec. XIV.* II 162, *SRH I*, pg. 452.

28 Researchers do not have a unified opinion about where in the Hungarian chronicle the original text of the Gesta Ungarorum vetera ends and their continuations begin. Gerics, *Legkorábbi Gesta-szerkésztéseink*, pp. 84–112. Mályusz, *A Thuróczy-krónika és forrásai*, pp. 39–42. Kristó, *A történeti és politikai gondolkodás*, p. 10. Richard Marsina, "Stredoveké uhorské rozprávacie pramene a slovenské dejiny," *Zborník Slovenského národného múzea* 78, *História* 24 (1984), pp. 171–173.

29 Györffy, *Krónikáink*, pp. 152–180. Györffy, "Az Árpad-kori magyar krónikák," pp. 395–409. Mályusz, *A Thuróczy-krónika és forrásai*, pp. 46–51. Elemér Mályusz, *Az V. Istán-kori Gesta* (Budapest 1971). Marsina, "Stredoveké uhorské rozprávacie pramene," p. 176.

30 Imre Madzar, "A hun krónika szerzője," *Töténeti Szemle* 11 (1922), pp. 75–103. Bálint Hóman, *A magyar hún-hagyomány és hún-monda* (Máriabesnyő – Gödöllő 2010), pp. 93–112. Horváth, *Árpádkori latinnyelvű irodalmunk stílusproblémai*, pp. 350–359. János Horváth, "A hun történet és szerzője," *Irodalomtörténeti Közlemények* 67 (1963), pp. 446–476. Mályusz, *A Thuróczy-krónika és forrásai*, pp. 51–54. Jenő Szűcs, *Nation und Geschichte. Studien* (Budapest 1981), pp. 275–295. Györffy, "Az Árpád-kori magyar krónikák," pp. 396–400, 406. Michal Jakliński, *Hunovie. Historia i tradycja* (Sandomierz 2011), pp. 127–143.

Magister Ákos, supplemented by the period of rule of Ladislas IV and two of his own supplements: *De nobilibus advenis* and *De udvornicis*. Thus, the chronicles of Simon of Kéza originated in the years 1272–1285.[31]

In the 14th century two related groups of Hungarian chronicles originated (Chronici hungarici compositio saeculi XIV). The Chronicon Pictum, which belongs to the second group of Hungarian chronicles of the 14th century, took over Simon's history of the Huns but left out the second part of his chronicles, including both supplements. It lifted the entire history of Hungary in full from Magister Ákos and took it up through to the 14th century.[32] The first group of Hungarian chronicles, to which the Buda Chronicle belongs, is briefer.[33]

5 Tales of Villagers and Songs of the Igrics

Hungarian chroniclers were also interested in domestic historical traditions, which were spread by word-of-mouth. Anonymus, who wrote his work around the year 1200, heard the stories of villagers and the songs of igrics (minstrels); he noticed, however, only those which addressed *heroic acts and wars of the Magyars*. Since *he found them in no historiographic codex*, he also considered these as unsuitable and immediately in the introduction of his work rejected them: *If the very noble nation of the Magyars heard about the first beginnings of their origin and about all of their courageous acts from the false stories of villagers or from the prattling songs of minstrels only as in a dream, it would be very unsuitable and not sufficiently dignified.*[34] In the 42nd chapter, where he writes about the military excursions of Lehel, Bulcsú and Botond, he briefly also mentions one of the village tale: *So long as it is about their military excursions and courageous acts, if you don't want to believe what is written on these pages,*

---

31   József Gerics, "Adalékok a Kézai Krónika problémainak megoldásához," *Annales Universitatis Scientiarum Budapestinensis*, Sectio Historica 1 (1957), pp. 106–134. *Legendy a kroniky koruny uherské*, ed. Pražák, pp. 304–339.

32   Györffy, "Krónikáink," pp. 152–180. Horváth, *Árpádkori latinnyelvű irodalmunk stíluspro-blémai*, pp. 305–315. Mályusz, *A Thuróczy-krónika és forrásai*, pp. 61–66. Gyula Kristó, "Anjou-kori krónikáink," *Századok* 101 (1967), no. 4, pg. 457–504. Gyula Kristó, "A Képes Krónika szerzője és szövege," in *Képes Krónika* (Budapest 1986), pp. 459–516. Marsina, "Stredoveké uhorské rozprávacie pramene," pp. 177–179. *Legendy a kroniky*, ed. Pražák, pp. 340–372.

33   *Chron. Hung. comp. saec. XIV.* I 23, SRH I, pp. 280–281. MMFH I, pp. 306–309.

34   *Et si tam nobilissima gens Hungarie primordia sue generationis et forcia queque facta sua ex falsis fabulis rusticorum vel a garrulo cantu ioculatorum quasi sompniando audiret, valde indecorum et satis indecens esset. Anonymi Belae regis notarii Gesta Hungarorum* Prologus, SRH I, p. 34.

believe the prattlings song of the igrics and the false stories of villagers, who still today don't let us fall into forgetting the heroic acts and wars of the Magyars. Some in the end tell how they allegedly came all the way to Constantinople, and how Botond broke open the golden gate of Constantinople with an axe. I didn't find them in any historical codex; I heard lies from the false stories of villagers, and that's why I don't have in mind to write about them in the present work.[35]

The story about Botond was a response to a Magyar excursion, which in April 958 plundered Byzantine territory. The chronicle of Simon of Kéza, as well as the Buda Chronicle and the Chronicon Pictum include the event as a true one with many details. The Hungarian hero (*rectus Hungarus*) Botond with one blow of an axe slashed a large opening in the armoured gate of Constantinople, through which a five-year-old child could easily pass, and immediately afterwards he triumphed in battle over a certain huge Greek warrior.[36] If Anonymus says that the story about Botond he *found in no historigraphic codex*, then it could not have been in the older Gesta Ungarorum vetera. Thus, the first to write it was Magister Ákos, whose work was the common model of the mentioned later chronicles.

Not even the story about Magyar commander Lehel, who after a lost battle on the Lech River fell into German captivity and ended up on the gallows, escaped the attention of Magister Ákos. Before his execution he reportedly asked the emperor for his trumpet to play one last time. But when he got it in his hands, he broke it over the emperor's head. According to his pagan faith (*fides Sciticorum*) the murdered would have to serve him in the other world. Simon of Kéza read the story of Lehel in Ákos's chronicle and also knew it from oral sources: *Some, however,... speak mythically (Quidam vero ... fabulose asseverant).* Simon mentioned this tale only briefly, because he considered it to be untrue: *This tale (fabula) goes against all probability, and anyone who believes it is characterized by a frivolous mind.*[37] The Buda Chronicle and the Chronicon Pictum copied it from Magister Ákos without the smallest doubt and with all the details.[38]

---

35   Quorum etiam bella et fortia quoque facta sua, si scriptis presentis pagine non vultis, credite garrulis cantibus ioculatorum et falsis fabulis rusticorum, qui fortia facta et bella Hungarorum usque in hodiernum diem oblivioni non tradunt. Sed quidam dicunt eos ivisse usque ad Constantinopolim et portam auream Constantinopolis Botondium cum dolabro suo incidisse. Sed ego, quia in nullo codice hystoriographorum inveni, nisi ex falsis fabulis rusticorum audivi, ideo ad presens opus scribere non proposui. Anonymi Belae regis notarii Gesta Hungarorum 42, SRH I, p. 87.

36   Simonis de Keza Gesta Hungarorum 42, SRH I, pp. 171–172. Chron. Hung. comp. saec. XIV. II 62, SRH I, pp. 310–311.

37   Simonis de Keza Gesta Hungarorum II 40, SRH I, p. 169.

38   Chron Hung. comp. saec. XIV. II 60, SRH I, pp. 307–308.

6 The Transformation of the Slavic Tradition into a Hungarian One

Equally significant historical events, such as Svätopluk's military victories, happened even following the destruction of his realm by the Magyars. According to Russian chronicler Nestor *The Hungarians ... coming from the east, poured through the large mountains, which they called the Hungarian Mountains, and at the beginning to battle against those living here ... the Slavs. Because the Slavs lived here first ... And then the Hungarians ... they inherited this land and settled together with the Slavs, subjugating them beneath themselves; and from there they called it Hungarian territory.* These were the *Slavs who settled by the Danube, which the Hungarians subjugated.*[39]

The first Magyars from the beginning did not mix with the Slavs. Their small burial sites and individual scattered graves lay separated from those of the Slavs. Since the Magyars were still nomadic, they didn't have fixed settlements and abodes, and they left us only their graves.[40] Defeat on the Lech River in 955 brought a major change in the Magyar-Slavic relationship. The Magyars had to abandon their nomadic life and begin to settle among the Slavs. They buried their dead in common gravesites, where it is no longer possible to distinguish Magyars and Slavs. The common material culture, which we know from jewellery, offerings, work tools and weapons put into graves, got the name Bijelo Brdo culture according to finds at Bijelo Brdo near Osijek in Slavonia. The ethnically and culturally mixed Bijelo Brdo burial sites are scattered in the Tisza River region, Transdanubia, in south-western Slovakia, in Slavonia and reach even into Carantania and Serbia.[41] The Magyars thus did not live separated in Hungary, but as the Russian chronicler writes, *together with the Slavs.*

Co-habitation and ethnic assimilation are not avoided without cultural interaction. And so the Magyars began to adopt Slavic tales, whose content and tendencies they altered. This source of original tales peaked in the Hungarian chronicler's editing, which had the heroics of the Magyar fighters and Árpád's leaders stand out fully.

Hungarian chronicler Simon of Kéza knew the Song of the Nibelungs, which celebrates the courage of King Gunther and his Burgundians in the battle with the Huns. This is the apotheosis of German heroism. Simon of Kéza, however, denied the German heroism and changed it fully to shame: *This is about that*

---

39   *Latopis Nestora* 19, year 6406 (898), MPH I, ed. Bielowski, p. 568. MMFH I, pp. 190–191.
40   See chapter 11, notes 39, 40, 45.
41   Zdeněk Váňa, "Maďaři a Slované ve světle archeologických nálezů X.–XII. století," *Slovenská archeológia* 2 (1954), no. 1, pp. 51–104. Jan Eisner, "Slované a Maďaři v archeologii," *Slavia antiqua* 7 (1960), pp. 189–210. Kučera, *Slovensko po páde Veľkej Moravy*, pp. 57–59.

battle which the Huns still today call the battle of Krimhild. So much German blood was spilled in this battle that if the Germans had not out of shame made secret of it and wanted to tell everything fully, that for many days drink the water of the Danube could not be drunk, not by people or livestock, because the river from the Sicambria up through the city of Potentia was flooded in blood.[42] An original Slavic tradition about Svätopluk and his country got into the Hungarian chronicles in just such a tendentiously changed form.

7 The Biharia Tale

The mentioned alteration also happened to the story that told how the Prince Moravec (*Morout*) took Biharia, and how his grandson defended the Biharian Principality and Castle Bihar against the Magyars.[43] Svätopluk conquered Biharia and the entire Tisza River region from the Bulgarians. Constantine Porphyrogenitus called this specific territory Great Moravia.[44] No one any longer recalled after three centuries the real name of the lord who connected this country to the Moravian realm. Therefore, he got the name Moravec, according to the nation he ruled over. Moravec's grandson *was called Menumorout by the Magyars* (*dictus est ab Hungaris*), thus the Magyars gave him the name Menumorout; this wasn't in the original tale. The story of Biharian Prince Moravec is a monument to the Great Moravian period of this land.

Around the year 1200 Anonymus heard the Biharia tale and selected from it only a small number of details that he considered suitable; he added something of what the Magyars said and invented a detailed description of the gradual and fearless occupation of the Biharian Principality and Bihar Castle by Árpád's warriors. Prince *Menumorout*, who was based at Bihar Castle, *became alarmed more than he should have*, and his soldiers after fruitless opposition *opened the castle and came out barefoot, meekly beseeching*. He then *fell into the greatest fear* and handed over the whole of his principality to Árpád.[45] The

---

42   Simonis de Keza Gesta Hungarorum I 19, SRH I, p. 162.
43   Anonymi Belae regis notarii Gesta Hungarorum 11, 19, 20, 28, 50, 51, 52, SRH I, pp. 49, 59–62, 70, 101–106, MMFH I, pp. 216, 221–223, 235–237. Lubomír Havlík, "Moravské a české tradice v uherských kronikách," *Slovanský přehled* 5 (1969), pp. 338–339. Kučera, "O historickom vedomí," pp. 227–228. Regarding the origin of the name Menumorout, see Györffy, *Krónikáink*, pp. 17–21.
44   Constantine Porphyrogenitus, *De administrando imperio* 38, 40, 41, ed. Moravcsik, pp. 172–173, 176–181, Konstantinos Porfyrogenetos, *De administrando imperio* 38, 40, 41, MMFH III, pp. 393, 396–400. Havlík, "Územní rozsah," pp. 63–67.
45   See note 43.

wedding of Árpád's son Zoltán with the daughter of the mentioned Biharian prince mentioned by Anonymus could be a reflection of the contract between the Moravians and the Magyars, according to which a portion of the Magyars could in 896 settle in the Great Moravian Tisza River regions.[46]

8   The Magyars and Slavs in Transdanubia

Hungarian chroniclers also described the Magyar invasions into Transdanubia. According to Anonymus, Árpád and his magnates decided to subjugate Pannonian territory up to the Drava River and to attack the Carantanians. He describes in detail the story of an invented expedition, the march of which is connected with various places, most of them geographical. He names mountains, rivers, smaller rivers and other waters.[47] All of the geographical names that Anonymus uses to mark the march of Árpád and his fellow warriors are located in the north-eastern part of Transdanubia. The second part of Árpád's military, which was led by Usubu, in addition to Veszprém (*Bezprem*), also conquered Vasvár (*Castrum ferreum*) and Baranya (*Borona*).[48] Árpád and his fighters conquered territory up to the Carantanian border and to the Rába and Rábca rivers.[49] Anonymus doesn't mention the territory of Upper Pannonia lying beyond these rivers at all, but immediately tells about the invasions in Carantania.[50] He fully leaves out the historical ground and presents to the reader brilliant victories of Árpád that never actually occurred.[51]

The long-enduring Slavic settlement in Transdanubia is documented by the abundant Slavic names of towns, villages and settlements in the vicinity of Magyar place names.[52] The Transdanubia Slavs, although in a minor-

---

46   See chapter 10, notes 14, 15, 17, 18.
47   *Anonymi Belae regis notarii Gesta Hungarorum* 44, 46, 47, 48, 49, 50, 51, SRH I, pp. 88–105. MMFH I, pp. 232–236.
48   *Anonymi Belae regis notarii Gesta Hungarorum* 47, 48, 49, SRH I, pp. 95–99.
49   *usque ad Rabam et Rabuceam venerunt. Anonymi Belae regis notarii Gesta Hungarorum* 50, SRH I, p. 100. MMFH I, p. 233. Upper Pannonia lay beyond the Rába and Rábca.
50   *Anonymi Belae regis notarii Gesta Hungarorum* 50, SRH I, p. 100. MMFH I, pp. 233–234.
51   *Anonymi Belae regis notarii Gesta Hungarorum* 46, 50, 51, SRH I, pp. 94, 100–101, 103. MMFH I, pp. 232–236. Anonymus's story about the successful rule of the new territory and the conquered Pannonia by the Magyars recalls the Old Testament book of Joseph. Peter Ratkoš, "Anonymove Gesta Hungarorum a ich pramenná hodnota," *Historický časopis* 31 (1983), no. 6, pp. 835–836.
52   Stanislav, *Slovenský juh I*, pp. 71–85. Ján Stanislav, *Dejiny slovenského jazyka I* (Bratislava 1956), pp. 169–180, 212–232. István Kniezsa, "Charakteristik der slowakischen Ortsnamen in Ungarn," *Studia Slavica* 9 (1963), pp. 27–44. Sós, *Die slawische Bevölkerung*,

ity, lived alongside the Magyars for several centuries.[53] The property register of Bakonybél Abbey from year 1086 contains 220 names, the majority of the vassals of this abbey who lived in villages on the territory of the Veszprém committee. Several of them were Slavs. Among the privates (*liberi*) were *Iuan* and *Grossus Yuan*. In the village Bakonykoppány (*Cupan*) lived horsemen (*equites*) *Keca, Dobron, Mutina* and ploughmen (*aratores*) *Yuan*, his son *Poscuba, Zaztou, Ratun, Woiadi*. In Kajar (*Kyar*) lived horsemen *Vgrin, Petyr, Lada* and ploughman *Rodoan*. In Kethellak (*Ketelloca*) lived horseman *Yuan*. Among the smiths (*fabri*) was *Bodin*, the carpenters (*dolatores*) were *Duda* and *Bodin*. *Nemka, son of Turwoj* (*filius Turuuoi*) had property in the village Sár (*Sar*), who gifted the abbey also with planters *Gneuku, Nouuoi, Zlaucu, Benata, Pazman* and his son *Milozt, Trinsin, Vranis, Vrbas*. A fake supplement to this register contains the names *Zagordi, Kuna, Keta* and *Boguta*.[54] Slavic and Magyar vassals of Bakonybél Abbey lived in common villages. Their names are not divided in the register but are mixed together.

Slavs lived in the village, later the small town of Tata (in the Transdanubian part of Komárno County). That's why, in addition to the naming *Tata, Thata* and *Tatha*, they called it *Tota* (year 1221, 1231) or *Thotha* (1268).[55] Slovaks still lived there together with Magyars in the 15th century. In 1459 it was *oppidum Tata hungaricale et slauonicale*, in 1472 *Thoth*, 1489 *Tata Tothwaros dicta*.[56]

9   Transdanubian Tales

Just as the Magyars *did not let* the heroic acts of their ancestors *fall into oblivion*, the Slavs also didn't lose interest in their past. The historical tradition of

---

pp. 71–82. We don't know the story of mutual assimilation that proceeded in Transdanubia in favour of the Magyars. Certainly, however, it required the co-habitation of several generations to overcome the social, employment and religious differences.

53   Similarly, the remains of the numerous islands of settlement in contemporary Hungary, which the great colonization wave of Slovaks created in the first half of the 18th century, has endured despite the progressive assimilation up to today. Alexej Leonidovič Petrov, *Příspěvky k historické demografii Slovenska v 18.–19. století* (Praha 1928), pp. 238–304. Ján Svetoň, *Slováci v Maďarsku, Príspevky k otázke štatistickej maďarizácie* (Bratislava 1942), pp. 92–173. Ján Svetoň, *Slováci v európskom zahraničí* (Bratislava 1943), pp. 16–46.

54   DHA I, ed. Györffy, no. 84, pp. 253–255. Stanislav, *Slovenský juh I*, pp. 76–77.

55   Dezső Csánki, *Magyarország történelmi földrajza a Hunyadiak korában III* (Budapest 1897), p. 491. György Györffy, *Az Árpad-kori Magyarország történeti földrajza III* (Budapest 1987), pp. 485–489.

56   Csánki, *Magyarország történeti földrajza III*, pp. 491–492.

Slavic origin, about which Anonymus was silent, was taken up by Hungarian chroniclers in a very complicated and tenditiously form and added into their own works. The most expansive was written by Simon of Kéza: *Then arose Svätopluk, son of Morot, a former prince in Polonia* (= in Pannonia) ...[57] *However, Magyars on the Ung River lured Svätopluk away with a variety of presents; they then sent messengers to appraise the situation. After sizing up Svätopluk's ill-equipped host, they suddenly fell upon him by the Rakus River near Bánhida, slaughtering him and all his men in a certain town whose ruins are still visible. As a result the Magyars succeeded as overlords of the above-mentioned peoples of Pannonia. Another tradition recounts that it was not Svätopluk but his father Morot whom the Magyars found ruling in Pannonia on their second entry. The basis for this story seems to be that Morot was the better-known name, but being old and weak he was resting in his castle called Bezprem* (Veszprém), *and when he heard of the disaster which had overwhelmed his son, he was so grief-stricken that he forthwith ended his life. The son, however, was new to the throne.*[58] In another place he continues: *And then after the death of Svätopluk, as is spoken of above ... they crossed the Danube in Pest and at the ford Zub* (= Szob) *and there they conquered a castle in the vicinity of Danube, in which the soldiers of Svätopluk who were saved by fleeing when their lord died. It was there afterwards they killed, among others, the very decrepit Morot's relative and still today speak mythically that this was Morot himself.*[59]

We can hardly consider both mentioned battles as real. No story and the complex transformation associated with it can have any direct historical

---

57   See notes 58, 71.
58   *Surrexit tandem Zvataplug filius Morot, princeps quidam in Polonia, qui Bracta subiugando Bulgaris Messianisque imperabat, incipiens similiter in Pannonia post Hunnorum exterminium dominari. Hunc quidem Hungari de fluvio Hung variis muneribus allectum et nunciis explorantes, considerata militia illius immunita, ipsum Zvataplug irruptione subita prope fluvium Racus iuxta Banhida, in quodam oppido, cuius interrupta adhuc eminent, cum tota militia peremerunt, et sic Pannoniae populis, qui superius sunt notati, inceperunt dominari. Tradunt quidam, quod Hungari Morot, non Zvataplug in secundo eorum reditu in Pannonia reperissent principantem. Hoc idcirco esse habetur, quia Morot eius nomine maior erat, sed confectus senio repausabat in castro, quod Bezprem nominatur. Audito infortunio, quod filio acciderat, morte subita ob dolorem finivit vitam suam. Filius vero in dominando novus erat.* Simonis de Keza Gesta Hungarorum I 23, SRH I, pp. 163–164. MMFH I, pp. 277–278.
59   *Tandemque Zuataplug interempto, quemadmodum superius est naratum ... Danubium in Pest et in portu Zub transierunt, ubi castrum quoddam circa Danubium, in quo erant milites Zuataplug recollecti, qui fuere erepti per fugam, quando dominus ipsorum interienrat, expugnarunt. In quo quidem affinem Morot nimis vetulum cum aliis perimentes, usque hodie fabulose Morot ipsum fuisse asseverant.* Simonis de Keza Gesta Hungarorum II 26, SRH I, p. 165. MMFH I, p. 279.

value after more than 200 or 300 years of oral tradition, particularly after a brief and tenditious chronicler's editing. Before us we have a literary-artistic monument, a creative reproduction of the very distant past, the real corresponding value of which we can uncover only by a thorough analysis and a broad comparative study. In no case, however, can we look to it for exact historical details. After several generations of oral tradition, no one could have remembered them.

The Hungarian chronicler wanted to celebrate the arrival of Árpád's Magyars; therefore, he elaborated old tales to satisfy this aim. The chronicle records and clearly emphasises the Magyar victory and the defeat of Svätopluk or Moravec, from which Morot was derived. This emphasis, together with the change from Moravec > Morot is either the editing of the chronicler or the transformation of the original tale in the Magyar environment. What, however, was the original form of the old tradition?

The oldest Hungarian chroniclers knew two genres of domestic oral epic: the songs of minstrels and village tales. Anonymus did not believe *the prattling songs of minstrels and the false stories of the villagers*; he did not acknowledge them and refused to write about them. The chronicle of Simon of Kéza, who does not avoid oral tradition, is full of contradictions which enable us to differentiate three original sources:

1. The tale of the battle by the river Rakus (Rákos) connected the memory on Svätopluk and the memory of the opposition of the Moravian military and its defeat with the mysterious castle ruins standing on the bank of this river: *the Magyars ... suddenly fell upon Svätopluk by the river Rakus near Bánhida, slaughtering him and all his men in a certain town whose ruins are still visible.*

2. The Veszprém tale is the most ample of all: *Morot ..., being old and weak, he was resting in his castle called Bezprem, and when he heard of the disaster which had overwhelmed his son, he was so grief-stricken that he forthwith ended his life. The son, however, was new to the throne.* The Veszprém tale preserved the memory of the famous ruler Moravec. It connected the defeat of Moravec's military with his inexperienced son, whom the Hungarian chronicler identified with Svätopluk. The tale ascribes to Veszprém Castle the importance of Moravec's seat.

3. A tale from Pilis linked the memory to a great lord Moravec and a monument to the opposition of the Moravian military and its defeat with a castle that guarded the crossing over the Danube. The Magyars crossed the Danube at the Szob ford and they conquered this castle, and Moravec, who defended it, fell in battle. Opposite Szob, on the other side of the Danube, on the edge of the Pilis Mountains, where Moravec's castle stood, lies the village of Pilismarót (Pilišské Moravce). Archaeologists have there uncovered the foundations of

the Roman fortress Castra ad Herculem[60] and in the neighbouring village of Basaharc 266 graves from the 8th and 9th centuries.[61]

Since the chronicler learned from the Veszprém tale that Moravec died in Veszprém, and since he could not have died in two places, he modified the telling of the Pilis story and wrote that Morot's relative died there. Thus, the Magyars *crossed the Danube ... at the ford Zub and there they conquered a castle in the vicinity of Danube, in which the soldiers of Svätopluk who were saved by fleeing when their lord died. It was there afterwards they killed, among others, the very decrepit Morot's relative and still today speak mythically that this was Morot himself.*

The Pilis tale, unlike that of Veszprém, did not link the memory to the opposition of Moravec's military with Moravec's son, but directly with Moravec, who died defending his own castle: *and still today speak mythically that this was Morot himself.* The original tale thus doesn't tell about the fleeing of Svätopluk's army from the battlefield to the castle,[62] or even about an aged relative of Moravec. The Hungarian chronicler modified the original content of the Pilis tale so that it harmonized with the content of the previous tale and linked them into a single associated story. The fleeing of soldiers from the battlefield, where they left the dead Svätopluk, to the castle made from this final tale a free continuation of the first tale coming from the area of Bánhida, and the exchange of Moravec for his relative removed the conflict with the Veszprém tale about the place of Moravec's death.

Cosmas and Hungarian chroniclers captured a Great Moravian tradition each on the territory of the other and with a great distance in time. They met, however, with the same genre of oral tradition. These were local tales which they elaborated in similar ways. Svätopluk's mysterious disappearance in the midst of his army and Svätopluk's eremitism on Zobor were originally two independent tales, which Cosmas freely combined and supplemented with Svätopluk's sorrow and penitence for his rebellion against his own lord, who was emperor

---

60 Soproni, "Der spätrömische Limes zwischen Visegrád und Esztergom," pp. 134–136, 139–140. Soproni, *Der spätrömische Limes zwischen Esztergom und Szentendre*, pp. 12–13, 16, 28, 29–48, 65, 77–78, 87, 92–93, 97–99, 100–102, 105, 119, 130, 157, 166, 168, 175, 179, 180, 189, 191, 194, 205–206, Tab. 8–50. Soproni, *Die letzten Jahrzehnte*, pp. 62–63. Hajnóczi, *Pannónia*, pp. 86–87, 89.

61 Nandor Fettich, *Das awarenzeitliche Gräberfeld von Pilismarót-Basaharc* (Budapest 1965).

62 If Svätopluk died near the Rákos River *and with his entire military (cum tota militia peremerunt)*, then Svätopluk's soldiers could not have fled the battlefield and gathered in a castle near the Danube. The fleeing of Svätopluk's soldiers from the battlefield to the castle is thus the modification of a chronicler who wanted to connect the conflicting content of the tales. Thus, the chronicler did not manage to thoroughly remove the mutual conflicts in their content.

Arnulf. Svätopluk's death in the battle near the Rakus River, Moravec's death from sorrow in Veszprém Castle and his death near the gate of the castle above the Danube ford were the same story. Just as Cosmas connected the two tales from neighbouring Nitria and supplemented them with moral explanations, Hungarian chronicle editors connected three Transdanubian tales and added to them the motif about Kriemhild known from the *Song of the Nibelungs* and antique Bactria (*Bracta*) mentioned in the Alexandreid.[63] Hungarian chroniclers, like Bohemian chronicler Cosmas, were unable to efface the difference of the original tales and the mutual conflicts in their content; therefore, we can distinguish them in the chronicle texts.

The Hungarian chronicler also knew the tale emblazoned by the ruins near Bánhida: *by the river Rakus near Bánhida ... in a certain town whose ruins are still visible*. In the little town of Környe, perhaps 5 km south-west of Bánhida (today a part of Tatabánya), archaeologists found the foundations of the Roman fort of Vincentia. Its thick walls with round towers enclose a rectangle of size 150 × 210 metres. It is very similar to the fortress in Fenékpuszta. And Vincentia survived the fall of Roman power and for some time served the last generations of the Pannonian population.[64] Eventually, however, it lost its last residents, and after several centuries no one recalled its origin. The old abandoned fortress, *whose ruins are still visible* (*cuius interrupta adhuc eminent*), however, made a massive impression. Its walls stood out in the landscape and engaged the imagination of people. People in the surrounding countryside told a tale about the mysterious fortress, linking it with the memory of Svätopluk's rule, under whom their entire country once belonged. The tale of the battle at Svätopluk's fortress on the Rakus was the result of multiple syncretization of historical and non-historical themes. It recalled the real name of the strongest Great Moravian monarch. They thus recorded it earlier than the similar Pilis story and in content the different Veszprém tale.

Slovaks also lived in the vicinity of the old ruins at the time when the story about Svätopluk was in circulation there. A neighbouring village, later the small town of Tata, was initially Slovak. And it was still partially Slovak even in 15th century.[65] The original tale thus circulated in the local Slovak environment. Therefore, the form of the name *Zvataplug* in Hungarian chronicles is

---

63 See note 72.
64 Ágnes Salamon, "Über die ethnischen und historischen Beziehungen des Gräberfelds von Környe (VI. Jh.)," *Acta Archaeologica Academiae Scientiarum Hungaricae* 21 (1969), pp. 273–279. Ágnes Salamon – István Erdélyi, *Das völkerwanderungszeitliche Gräberfeld von Környe* (Budapest 1971). Soproni, *Der spätrömische Limes zwischen Esztergom und Szentendre*, p. 144. Hajnóczi, *Pannónia*, pp. 88–89.
65 See note 56.

also of domestic, Slovak origin. They also wrote it thus in neighbouring Slavic countries: *Zuatopluk* (Cosmas) and *Svatopelek* (Letopis popa Dukljanina).[66] Period Frankish chronicles don't know of a battle near Bánhida at all, and they write Svätopluk's name itself with the old nasal vowel: *Zuentibald, Zwentibaldus* (Annals of Fulda, Herimann's Chronicle), *Zuentibolch* (Regino), *Centibaldus* (Liudprand).[67]

In addition to the Great Moravian Svätopluk, Hungarian chronicles also mention a Bohemian Prince Svätopluk (1107–1109, before then a subordinate prince in Olomouc 1095–1107). They wrote his name with the nasal vowel *Sentepolug*.[68] Slavic dialects, from which the Slovak and Czech languages gradually developed, no longer had any nasal vowels at the end of the 11th century.[69] Cosmas and the unknown author of the old Hungarian chronicle known as the Gesta Ungarorum vetera knew Svätopluk's name directly from narratives that circulated in Slavic environments at the end of the 11th century. Therefore, they heard them and recorded them without nasal vowels. The later author, who later continued the old Hungarian chronicle, however, recorded the name of Bohemian Svätopluk with the nasal vowel. Words of Slavic origin, which the non-Slavic language environment (German, Latin, Magyar) still took before their disappearance, preserved the nasal vowel.[70] And the name Svätopluk got

---

66 *Presbyteri Diocleatis Regnum Sclavorum* 9, MMFH I, pp. 239–241, 243.
67 The name Zwentibold in several variations was from the 9th to 11th centuries also spread in Germany. Eduard Hlawitschka, "Die Verbreitung des Namens Zwentibold in frühdeutscher Zeit," in *Personengeschichtliche Beobachtungen und Erwägungen. Festschrift für Herbert Kolb zu seinem 65. Geburtstag* (Bern – Frankfurt am Main – New York – Paris 1989), pp. 264–292.
68 *Chron. Hung. comp. saec. XIV.* II 122, 140, SRH I, pp. 391, 418.
69 Ján Stanislav, *Dejiny slovenského jazyka I* (Bratislava 1958), pp. 364–367. Rudolf Krajčovič, *Náčrt dejín slovenského jazyka* (Bratislava 1971), pp. 55–57.
70 Stanislav, Dejiny slovenského jazyka I, p. 365. See note 67. Some historians exclude the presence of Svätopluk's name *Zvataplug* or *Zvatapolug* in the Gesta Ungarorum vetera, namely only because it doesn't have a nasal vowel, just as the Hungarian chroniclers have the name of Bohemian Prince Svätopluk recorded as *Sentepolug*. János Melich, "Szvatopluk," *Magyar Nyelv* 18 (1922), pp. 110–114. Bálint Hóman, *A Szent László-kori Gesta Ungarorum és XII–XIII. századi leszármazói* (Budapest 1925), pp. 24, 70. György Györffy, *Krónikáink*, pp. 20, 105. György Györffy, "Formation d'états au IXe siécle suivant les 'Gesta Hungarorum' du notaire anonyme," in *Nouvelles études historiques publiées á l' occasion du XIIe Congrés International des Sciences Historiques par la Commission Nationale des Historiens Hongrois I* (Budapest 1965), p. 33. György Györffy, "Die Erinnerung an das Grossmährische Fürstentum in der mittelalterlichen Überlieferung Ungarns," *Acta Archaeologica Academiae Scientiarum Hungaricae* 17 (1965), p. 44. *Chronica Hungarorum II. Commentarii 1. Ab initiis usque ad annum 1301*, composuit Elemér Mályus, Budapest 1988, pg. 198. However, the author of Gesta Ungarorum vetera did not record the nasal vowel name *Sentepolug*, but someone else, first their continuer in the 12th century,

into the non-Slavic languages even before the disappearance of nasal vowels; therefore, Frankish and German chroniclers, as well as the unknown continuer of the Gesta Ungarorum vetera, wrote it with the nasal vowel.

10 Svätopluk and the Hun History of Simon of Kéza

Simon of Kéza put the story about the battle near the Rakus River, linked with the Veszprém tale, at the end of the first part of his chronicle, which is called the Hun Chronicle. He linked the start of Svätopluk's rule with the extinction of Attila's realm: *Then, when the sons of Attila nearly died in the Krumhelt battle with the Scythian nation, Pannonia remained for ten years without a king, and the Slavs, Greeks, Germans and Mesians remained in it and the Valachs, who served Attila during his life as his serfs, migrated in. Then Svätopluk, son of Morot, a former prince in Polonia* (= in Pannonia), *who after subjugation of Bracta ruled the Bulgarians and the Mesians, similarly seizing to rule after the eradication of the Huns in Pannonia.*[71]

who came from another, non-Slavic environment. Despite this, the tale of the battle of the Magyars with Svätopluk near the Rákos could have come from a Slavic environment. The Gesta Ungarorum vetera took Svätopluk's name from this Slavic, more exact Slovak environment, without the nasal vowel, which by the end of the 11th century was foreign to the then Slavic dialect from which Slovak evolved. Dušan Třeštík also took the opinion on the absence of Svätopluk's name in the original text of Gesta Ungarorum vetera. Třeštík, "Pád Velké Moravy," pp. 70–73. The mention of a Bohemian Prince Svatopluk (1107–1109) in the battle near Mogyoród in 1074 (see note 68) is the result of a later mistaken interference into the text of the Gesta Ungarorum vetera. Svatopluk of Bohemia was not even born in 1074. And the placing of the report on the rule of Prague by Bohemian Prince Svatopluk to the last year of rule of Ladislas I († 1095) is a chronologically incorrect interpolation of the original text of the Gesta Ungarorum vetera. These mistakes could not have been made by the unknown author of the Gesta Ungarorum vetera at the end of the 11th century, or even their direct continuer and contemporary of Bohemian Prince Svatopluk at the beginning of the 12th century, who would be able to correctly order the Bohemian Svatopluk chronologically, but a later continuer or even Magister Ákos in the 13th century.

71 *Postquam autem filii Ethelae in praelio Crunhelt cum gente Scitica fere quasi deperissent, Pannonia extitit X annis sine rege, Sclavis tantummodo, Graecis, Teutonicis, Messianis et Ulahis advenis remanentibus in eadem, qui vivente Ethela populari servitio sibi serviebant. Surrexit tandem Zvataplug filius Morot, princeps quidam in Polonia, qui Bracta subiugando Bulgaris Messianisque imperabat, incipiens similiter in Pannonia post Hunnorum exterminium dominari.* Simonis de Keza Gesta Hungarorum I 23, SRH I, p. 163. Later Hungarian chroniclers also took this learned construction of Simon. *Chron. Hung. comp. saec. XIV.* I 23, SRH I, pp. 280–281. Svätopluk was not a prince *in Polonia*, but *in Pannonia*, as is stated in the Buda Chronicle, in which *in Pononia* is written. The Gesta Ungarorum vetera, which does not write about the Huns and the end of Attila's realm, could mention only

Bracta is ancient Bactria, a country on the upper Amu Darya River with its capital city of Bactra (today Balkh). Under the rule of King Cyrus it became a *satrapia* (an administrative unit) of the Persian Empire. In 329 BCE Alexander the Great joined it to his own empire and two years later married Roxana, daughter of Bactrian magnate Oxyartes. Medieval stories about Alexander the Great and Alexander's conquests were very widespread. Knowledge of these stories helped Simon of Kéza with the writing of Hun history. According to Simon of Kéza, Attila was not only served by the Pannonian nations of the Slavs, Greeks, Germans, Mesians and Vlachs, but he also subjugated Egypt, Assyria and Africa. The chronicler simply added Alexander's conquests to Attila's empire. Thus Bactria, too, belonged to the subjugated kingdom, and Bactrian Princess Micolt (*Bractanorum regis filiam Micolt*) became Attila's wife.[72] With the ruling of the former Hun Pannonia by Svätopluk, where the nations previously subjugated to Attila lived, Svätopluk's realm became the inheritance of Attila's empire in the imagination of the Hungarian chronicler. That's why he also ascribed the conquest of distant Bactria (*Bracta*), the location of which he

---

[72] Svätopluk's rule in Pannonia (*Zvataplug ... princeps quidam in P[an]onia*). The whole other text is a chronicler's construction of Simon of Kéza and belongs (with the exception of the mention of Morot) to his Hun history. If Pannonia belonged originally to Attila and after the fall of his empire was 10 years without a ruler, then Svätopluk could not have seized it already as the ruler of Pannonia. Simon's construction got into conflict with the original information in the Gesta Ungarorum vetera, and therefore Simon of Kéza changed the original information *Panonia* (or *Pannonia*) to *Polonia*, that is Poland. The anonymous legend of the suffering of St. Adalbert also has Polonia in place of Pannonia: *Episcopus ... tellure in brevi recedens in Pannoniam. Passio sancti Adalberti martyris* 1, MPH I, ed. Bielowski, p. 152. Václav Chaloupecký, "Radla – Anastasius, druh Vojtěchův, organisátor uherské církve," in Bratislava, časopis učené společnosti Šafaříkovy I (1927), p. 217. Simonis de Keza Gesta Hungarorum I 17, 18, SRH I, pp. 160–161. Chron. Hung. comp. saec. XIV. I 17, 18, SRH I, pp. 275–276. Attila's real wife was ther Germanic Hildigo, whom Jordanes recalls in his work De origine actibusque Getarum (chap. 49) as *Ildico*. Thanks to the sound similarity, Simon of Kéza could exchange her with Micolt or Míkal (in Vulgate Michol), the wife of Israeli King David (1. S 18, 27–28; 19, 11–13). Sándor Eckhardt, "Micolt", *Magyar Nyelv* 26 (1930), pp. 167–170. However, the Hungarian chronicler exchanged not only the names but also the Germanic origin of Attila's wife for Bactrian. The Hungarian chronicler not only confused Attila with Alexander the Great (and also partially with Svätopluk), but also confused their wives. Micolt (originally Ildico) was confused with Roxana, who came from Bactria. That's why Micolt as a Bactrian princess could become Attila's wife. Therefore, he confused Attila's empire with that of Alexander and with the later Svätopluk's realm. Thanks to this syncretic confusion, Svätopluk, in the imagination of Simon of Kéza, could have subjugated Bracta, that is Bactria. Lubomír E. Havlík allowed her identity of Bracta with Prague. We have to exclude this possibility, because Prague does not fit at all in Hun history. Lubomír E. Havlík, "Moesie a listy pasovského biskupa Pilgrima," *Jižní Morava* 8 (1972), p. 8. This study is a valuable contribution on the origin of the name *Messiani*.

could not have known, to Svätopluk. For the Hungarian chronicler Svätopluk already belonged to the distant past and was for him of the same magnitude as Attila and Alexander the Great.

The Chronicon Pictum, and with it the entire second group of Hungarian chroniclers of the 14th century, took Simon's Hun history and both Transdanubian tales with it but left out the second part of Simon's chronicle. It copied the whole of Hungarian history completely from Magister Ákos and took it up to the 14th century.[73] That's why the Pilis tale, which Simon put into the second part of his chronicle, is missing from the Chronicon Pictum. The first group of Hungarian chroniclers of the 14th century, to which the Buda Chronicle belongs, has in places a shortened text and from the three Transdanubian tales records only the battle near the Rakus River.[74]

11 Dicunt, Tradunt, Asseverant

The chronicler introduced the Veszprém and Pilis tales with the words *Tradunt quidam, quod* and *usque hodie fabulose ... asseverant*. The words *dicunt, tradunt* and *asseverant* are synonyms. They introduce several chronicler reports which belong to the ancient or at least distant past. The chroniclers didn't know them from immediate experience, and therefore they appealed to the older written version or to the old oral tradition.

Anonymus knew the story about Botond from the stories of villagers and begins it with the words *Sed quidam dicunt*.[75] Simon of Kéza introduced the story about Lehel with the words *Quidam vero ... fabulose asseverant, quod*; however, he rejects the story (*fabula*) as untrue of how Magyar commander Lehel before his execution struck the emperor in the head with a trumpet and killed him.[76] Simon of Kéza also knew the Pilis tale from oral tradition and introduces it with the same words as the tale about Lehel: *Usque hodie fabulose ... asseverant*. The Veszprém tale also had its origin in the oral tradition. The words *Tradunt quidam, quod* in its introduction, however, do not come from Simon of Kéza; for his chronicle the term *asseverant* is typical.[77] The introductory words to the Veszprém tale come from Magister Ákos, and we also find them at another place in Ákos's chronicle.[78] Magister Ákos wrote the Veszprém tale and

---

[73] See note 32.
[74] See note 33.
[75] See note 35.
[76] *Simonis de Keza Gesta Hungarorum* II 40, SRH I, p. 169.
[77] *Simonis de Keza Gesta Hungarorum* II 26, 40, 55, SRH I, pp. 165, 169, 178.
[78] *Chron. Hung. comp. saec. XIV.* I 23, II 87, SRH I, pp. 282, 344.

linked it with the battle by the Rakus River. Simon of Kéza took his version and supplemented it with the Pilis tale.

More often, however, the chroniclers evoked with the introductory words *dicunt, tradunt* and *asseverant* not the oral tradition but an older written source, the content of which they either accepted or that they used to polemicize. The Hungarian chronicles contain in the part coming from Magister Ákos a falsified genealogy of the Árpád kings, which rejected the direct genealogy of the Vazul line and convinces us that the brothers Levente, Andrew and Béla were the sons of Vazul's older brother Ladislas the Bald and his Russian wife. The Gesta Ungarorum vetera could no longer state this, because in the 11th century it was still in living memory that Kings Andrew I (1046–1060) and Béla I (1060–1063) were Vazul's sons.[79] Thanks to the great distance in time, Magister Ákos, whose opinion was taken up by other Hungarian chronicles, could deny Vazul's fatherhood: *Some say (Tradunt quidam) that these three brothers were the sons of Prince Vazul from one girl from the Tatun line and not from the legitimate marriage and that their nobleness should come from this connection with Tatun. But this is certainly a false and only invented fable, because they were really from this noble line, because they were the sons of Ladislas the Bald, who took his wife from Russia. The three brothers were born from this marriage.*[80]

The mentioned *quidam*, with which magister Ákos polemicizes, are the Gesta Ungarorum vetera, which served him as a prototype. Magister Ákos could not pass over the report of Gesta Ungarorum vetera on Vazul's fatherhood in silence and leave it without comment. If his new interpretation was in conflict with it, then he had to come to terms with its controversies. Simon of Kéza also took Ákos's interpretation but used other introductory words: *Quidam autem ... asseverant*.[81] The Veszprém tale and the denial of Vazul's fatherhood beginning with the introductory words *Tradunt quidam* are Ákos's interpolation of the original text of the Gesta Ungarorum vetera.

The Gesta Ungarorum vetera and their continuer introduced five events with the word *dicunt* or *dicitur*. These were Levente's burial *near the village Taksony, on that side of the Danube, where, as is said (dicitur), his grandfather Taksony was buried according to pagan custom*,[82] a betrayal in the Hungarian military (*Et ut dicitur*) and the pope's anathema before the Battle of Menfő

---

79 See pp. 346–347.
80 *Chron. Hung. comp. saec. XIV.* II 87, SRH I, p. 344.
81 *Simonis de Keza Gesta Hungarorum* II 55, SRH I, p. 173. Since Simon of Kéza and the chronicles of the 14th century addressed the opinion denying Vazul's fatherhood of the future Hungarian kings, their common model, the unpreserved chronicle of Magister Ákos, must have contained it.
82 *Chron. Hung. comp. saec. XIV.* II 86, SRH I, p. 344.

(*ut dicitur*),[83] the test by sword and crown that Andrew I used to prepare Prince Béla (*Dicunt alii, quod*)[84] and the originally determined King Coloman as the Várad bishop (*sicut quidam dicunt*).[85]

The Gesta Ungarorum vetera and their first continuer used the introductory word *dicunt* or *dicitur*; Magister Ákos used *tradunt*, and Simon of Kéza *asseverant*. If, then, the word *dicunt* or *dicitur* introduces the chronicler's report, then the Gesta Ungarorum vetera recorded it first, and later chroniclers took it from there with this introductory word. If the word *tradunt* introduces it, then Magister Ákos wrote it first, and it wasn't in the Gesta Ungarorum vetera at all. However, later chronicles, which took Ákos's text, have it along with this introductory word. If the chronicler's report has the introductory word *asseverant*, then it was written for the first time by Simon of Kéza. His predecessors, the Gesta Ungarorum vetera and Magister Ákos, could not have had it. If we find a report introduced with this word in the later chronicles, then they certainly took it from Simon of Kéza and not from the older Ákos or even older Gesta Ungarorum vetera. Therefore, the Pilis tale, begun with the word *asseverant*, is only first recorded by Simon of Kéza, and Magister Ákos was the first to write down the Veszprém tale with the word *tradunt*. The story about the battle by the Rakus does not have such an introductory word; however it contains the name *Zvataplug*, just like the Nitrian and Zobor tales captured by Cosmas in 1099. The story about Svätopluk's battle with the Magyars near the Rákos River had to then be recorded by a contemporary of Cosmas, who in Hungary was the author of the lost Gesta Ungarorum vetera. From there it got into the other Hungarian chronicles.

12 How Svätopluk Became Moravec

The stoary about the battle *at some place* near the Rakus River, which got into the Gesta Ungarorum vetera at the end of the 11th century, as well as both tales which Cosmas described in neighbouring Nitria in 1099, still recalled Svätopluk's name. The Biharia tale, which Anonymus recorded around year 1200, no longer knew the name of Svätopluk and spoke about Moravec (*Morout*). The Veszprém tale, which Magister Ákos wrote down in 1270–1272 and the Pilis tale that Simon of Kéza recorded in years 1282–1285 told about Moravec (*Morot*) and his son.

---

83   *Chron. Hung. comp. saec. XIV.* II 76, SRH I, pp. 331–332.
84   *Chron. Hung. comp. saec. XIV.* II 92, SRH I, pp. 353–355.
85   *Chron. Hung. comp. saec. XIV.* II 152, SRH I, pp. 432–433.

Between the story about the battle near the Rakus and the Veszprém and Pilis tales, or more exactly between their written presentation, is a time difference of nearly two centuries, which caused a difference in the naming of the Great Moravian ruler. Svätopluk's name fell from memory in the course of the 12th century, and the reputable ruler was named according to the nation that he led, that is Moravec (Magyar Marót, in the Hungarian chronicles *Morot*).[86]

Magister Ákos knew the original name of this monarch – Svätopluk – from the story of the battle near the Rakus recorded in the Gesta Ungarorum vetera and did not know how to fit it in with the telling of the Veszprém tale about Moravec. He did not conceal his quandary: *Some say that the Magyars supposedly ... found in Pannonia a leader Morot and not Svätopluk*. He resolved the apparent conflict between what *some say*, that is what was told in the Veszprém tale (Moravec/Morot), and his knowledge from the Gesta Ungarorum vetera (Svätopluk), not realizing that this was the same person. That's why he identified Svätopluk with Morot's son and at the same time attempted to explain why *some say* about Morot, and not about Svätopluk: *This supposition comes from the fact that Morot's name was greater than his*. The Veszprém tale ascribes the defeat not to Morot, as it doesn't fit with his fame and greatness, but to his inexperienced son. Magister Ákos gave the name of this Morot's son as Svätopluk. Svätopluk, ruler of a great realm, who seized rule in Pannonia only *after eradication of the Huns*, is, however, identical with old Moravec > Morot in the Veszprém and Pilis tales and not with Morot's inexperienced son, as is assumed by Magister Ákos. The familial father/Morot–son/Svätopluk relationship is a chronicler's construction, which should have spanned the conflict with the doubly named ancient monarch.

Simon of Kéza added the Pilis tale to his chronicle. He wanted to remove the conflicts in its content with the content of the previous two tales; therefore, he thought up the fleeing of Svätopluk's soldiers from the battlefield to the castle at the Danube ford (despite the fact that Svätopluk died on the battlefield *and with his entire army*), and he replaced Morot, who according to the original tale fell in defense of this castle, with his invented relative.

The stories that Hungarian chroniclers knew are a later response to the historical events of the 9th century and have a common historical core, which is the memory of the rule of a famous Moravian ruler and memory of the opposition and defeat of the Great Moravian army by the Magyars. North-eastern Transdanubia and neighbouring Nitria were the starting points of the victorious Svätopluk's conquests. Svätopluk assembled a huge army there, about which the Annals of Fulda give us a reliable report. He defeated his strongest

---

86   Kučera, "O historickom vedomí," pp. 227–228.

antagonists – the East Frankish empire and Bulgaria – several times, and in these wars he conquered and unified under his rule almost the entire territory of the Carpathian Basin. He destroyed Bulgarian and Frankish power and put Great Moravian forces on the conquered territory. A monument to these events lived for a long time in the figure of a famous ruler, who took as his name the name of his country. Moravec is the personification of his country, its ancient glory and size. In 900 the Magyars conquered and occupied Transdanubia. The invasion of foreign raiders and the loss of their own state is a terrible cataclysm in the life of every nation. The generation that grew up in the time of Svätopluk's victories felt the recoil of the threat of military defeats, plundering and foreign rule. This shock remained in the awareness of the nation and in subsequent generations evoked the image of a monarch dying of sorrow over the annihilation of his military and the misfortune of his country. The famous and great Moravec (*Morot eius nomine maior est*), who died of sorrow, personified the misfortune of the nation.

13 A Heroic Death

The image of great and tragic events is subject to heroic idealization in the memory of subsequent generations. Roland died a heroic death, when in his last battle he killed a great many Saracens.[87] In 436 the Huns destroyed the Burgundy realm on the central Rhine. Some 20,000 Burgundians died in the battle, including King Gunther, his brother and the entire royal train. The heroic song on the death of King Gunther and his realm circulated among the Germans for several centuries and became the foundation for the Eddaic song *Atlakviða*. The ending of this epic tradition is the Song of the Nibelungs, which hyperbolizes the heroism of King Gunther and his Burgundians.[88]

The dominant mythical period of British history is that of King Arthur, the central figure of an extensive epic cycle, the historical basis of which is memory of the British Prince Arthur (*Arthurus dux bellorum*), who in the battle near

---

87 *Das altfranzösische Rolandslied* 1320–2396, ed. Edmund Stengel (Heilbronn 1878), pp. 48–86. Viktor Maximovič Žirmunskij, *O hrdinském eposu (slovanském a středoasijském)* (Praha 1984), p. 38.

88 *Die Germanen, Geschichte und Kultur der germanische Stämme in Mitteleuropa, Band 2*, ed. Bruno Krüger (Berlin 1983), pp. 373–376. *Die Edda, Göttersagen und Spruchweisheiten der Germanen*, nach der Heldenschrift des Brynjolfur Sveinsson, ed. Karl Simrock (Berlin 1987), pp. 244–250. *Warnliedar. Band I: Kriemhilt und Meister Kuonrat*, von Henrik Becker (Leipzig 1993), pp. 51–69. *Píseň o Nibelunzích*, translation Jindřich Pokorný (Praha 1974), pp. 294–358.

Mount Badon for a longer time stopped the penetration of the Anglo-Saxons into Britain. The story of Arthur, recorded at the beginning of the 9th century in the Nennius's chronicle Historia Britonum, lived in the telling of the domestic Celtic population, also took on fairy tale motifs and ultimately became the subject of an extensive epic elaboration in the work of Bishop Geoffrey of Monmouth Historia regum Britanniae (in the mid-12th century). King Arthur in the elaboration of Geoffrey of Monmouth and other English writers is the embodiment of chivalric honour.[89] At the conclusion of the Arthurian cycle a final battle and the immortality of the great British king are advanced. The fatally wounded king departs for the island of Avalon, from where he will return when things will be at their worst in Britain. His sword Excalibur rests in the sea, where the last knight threw it on Arthur's command. The Pilis tale and the story of the battle near Bánhida also contain the motif of a final battle. The motif of the immortality of the monarch is the basis of the Nitrian tale about Svätopluk's mysterious disappearance in the middle of his own army, recorded by Cosmas.

The Vikings, led by Olaf Tryggvesson, the future king of Norway, attacked and pillaged Britain in 991 and invaded Essex. Essex Ealdorman Byrhtnoth assembled a Saxon army from the whole of Essex, refused to pay Olaf the desired ransom and decided to stand in defence of the country. The heroism of Byrhtnoth and his Saxons in the battle near Maldon was celebrated by an unknown Anglo-Saxon poet, whose verses are still preserved today. The Saxons did not withstand the attack of the Vikings. Byrhtnoth was wounded by a spear but battled on, until he finally fell in battle. The Saxons did not care about their own lives, and they battled to the end in a hopeless situation.[90]

The story about the destruction of Ryazan by Batu Khan is a hyperbolization of Russian heroism. It celebrates the heroic defence of the Ryazan region and the city of Ryazan against the Tatars in 1237: *And the Ryazans marched out against the unbelieving Batu Khan and they met with him on the border of the Ryazan principality. And they rushed at him and began to fight firmly and sturdily*

---

[89] Geoffrey of Monmouth, *The History of the Kings of Britain*, translated with an introduction by Lewis Thorpe (Nottingham 1976), pp. 212–261. Geoffrey z Monmouthu, *Dějiny britských králů*, translation Jana Fuksová (Praha 2010), pp. 5–15, 143–144, 148–177, 181–186, 204. Thomas Malory, *Artušova smrt'*, translation Eduard Castiglione (Bratislava 1979). Thomas Malory, *Artušova smrt*, translation Jan Caha (Praha 1997). Bernhard Brink, *Geschichte der Englischen Litteratur I* (Strassburg 1899), pp. 158–160, 166, 200–203, 210–211, 222–224, 283–284, 391–406. George K. Anderson, *Staroanglická a stredoanglická literatúra od počiatku až do roku 1485*, in *Dějiny anglické literatury I*, editor-in-chief Hardin Craig (Praha 1963), pp. 41, 73–74, 86–94, 99, 113, 191–196.

[90] *An Anglo-Saxon Reader*, edited by Alfred J. Wyatt (Cambridge University 1947), pp. 188–197, 278–282. Brink, *Geschichte der Englischen Litteratur I*, pp. 110–114.

and this was a very cruel, terrible attack. Many of the strong Batu regiments fell there, and Batu Khan was shocked when he saw how bravely and resolutely the Ryazan soldiers fought ... one Ryazan native battled there with a thousand and two with tens of thousands. Ryazan Grand Prince Yuriy Ingvarevich died in the battle along with his brothers and the entire army: *All died there to the last man, and together they drank from the fatal goblet. Not one of them left the field, and all lay killed together on it.*[91]

Not even the Transdanubian tales about Svätopluk/Moravec, which speak about the defence against foreign raiders, could avoid heroic idealization. The great ruler defended his realms against the Magyar raid and fell *with a whole army* in open battle or in the midst of defence of his castle. We can only assume the larger heroic hyperbolization of Svätopluk, because the rumours were oral tradition, and no one wrote them down permanently in the original form, and they were only preserved for us in a very scant form. Hungarian chroniclers who mediated them for us left out everything that would contradict the celebrated acquisition of the new homeland by the Magyars in the Carpathian Basin.

14 A Syncretic Source

Great events of a national past, memorable places and the figures of heroes and kings were subjected to a complex transformation. Through long years of tradition people forgot the original associations or varying origins of historical memories. Local narrators synchronized them and creatively linked them to new mutual associations and causal relations. And they often added a mythical and fairy tale motif to them. This connection – syncretism – is a result of the archaic thinking that transforms the national past into a story. Even the figure of the famous ruler Svätopluk > Moravec, who defends his country and does not survive the extinction of his realm, is the result of a multiple syncretization:

---

91   *Izbornik. Povesti drevnej Rusi*, ed. Lev Alexandrovič Dmitrijev, Natal'ja Vladimirovna Ponyrko, D. S. Lichačev, (Moskva 1987), pp. 154–163, 416–417. Vladimir Vladimirovič Kuskov, *Istorija drevnerusskoj literatury* (Moskva 1989), pp. 129–132. Apollon G. Kuzmin, "Letopisnye izvestija o razorenii Rjazani Batyem," *Vestnik Moskovskogo universiteta* (1963), no. 2, pp. 55–70. *Slovo o pluku Igorovom a ďalšie staroruské historické povesti*, translation Helena Križanová-Bryndzová (Bratislava 1986), pp. 43–44. About the heroic idealisation in epic creation of the Turkish and Mongol nations, writes Jeleazar Mojsejevič Meletinskij, *Proischoždenie geroičeskogo eposa* (Moskva 1963), pp. 199, 316, 340, 349–350, 354, 368–369, 431–432, 434–435.

1. Its historical model is Svätopluk,[92] the strongest among the Great Moravian princes, whose power was felt by all of his neighbours. The stories connected the whole Great Moravian period with this one ruler. They didn't know other princes and they brought the period of their rule to Svätopluk > Moravec, who ruled immediately *after annhilation of the Huns in Pannonia*, up to the extinction of their realm.

2. The death of a great ruler and the extinction of his realm was merged in the memory of a nation into one event. Svätopluk, although he died at the peak of his power and did not survive to see the end of his nation, is depicted as its defender. The original archetype of the first and third Transdanubian tales contains an ancient motif. The monarch did not die a natural death, but in the middle of the army during the defense of his castle and country. The acts and death of a great ruler had to correspond to the rules of heroic ethics, which determined the behaviour and fates of heroes and kings of epic production of many nations.

3. The tales that Cosmas and the unknown author of the Gesta Ungarorum vetera wrote in the 11th century know the name Svätopluk. It then fell into oblivion, and later narrators of the 12th and 13th century connected the figure of the great ruler with the name of his realm. Thus originated the name Moravec, in the Magyar environment Marót and in the Hungarian chronicle Morot.

4. The other form of Moravec was determined by local syncretism. The memory of the great monarch lived in several places, where it was connected with major local features: the ruins of the fortress on the bank of the Rákos (*Rakus*) River near Bánhida, Veszprém Castle, the extinct castle above the Danube ford on the edge of the Pilis Mountains.

The memory of Great Moravia, the rule of its strongest ruler and the Magyar invasion lost in the course of several generations its historically real content and became a tale, the development and final form of which was determined by two contrary sources:

1. The results of multiple syncretization was a fabular collapse of the historical core of the tale: Moravec (Svätopluk), who ruled immediately *after annihilating the Huns in Pannonia*, created a great realm, defended it against an enemy raid and fell in battle while defending his own castle, personified the

---

92 Under the rule of Rastislav, Svätopluk ruled in Nitria, which separated the Great Moravian part of Transdanubia from Rastislav's Moravia. Svätopluk was thus closer to this territory than his uncle in Moravia. Magyar invasions and the war with his brother Svätopluk II filled the period of rule of Mojmír II in the years 898–899. The glorious age of the country is thus linked with Svätopluk.

ancient size and misfortune of the nation. The contracting of historical and non-historical motifs in the figure of a great ruler is not at all unique. Thus was fashioned the image of heroes and kings who stand at the beginning of history and at the centre of historical memory of their nations.[93]

2. In the Great Moravian part of Transdanubia a cycle of several local stories with a common historical core originated. The place of origin left a mark on their content. The details, which did not belong to the wide collective experience of the nation, were easily subject to changes or being lost from memory, and local invented motifs were added. With this variable part of their content local narrators creatively improvised. Therefore, the individual Transdanubian tales are mutually contradictory: Svätopluk > Moravec was based at and died at several places; he died from sorrow, fell in battle, his son fell in battle; an inexperience son ruled after the death of the father.

15   Six Tales

In 900 the Magyars conquered the Tisza River region from the Moravians and the Great Moravian part of Transdanubia and in 906 Great Moravia disintegrated. The nation which grew up in the period of Svätopluk's victories and created the core of his large armies, suddenly underwent the extinction of its own state. Svätopluk's victories contrasted with the subsequent calamity of the Magyar invasion. This was a great experience and one filled with suffering.

---

93   An example of the contraction of historical and non-historical motifs are several Old Testament figures connected with the beginning of a great period of Israeli history: Abraham, Moses, Joshua, Solomon and others. Solomon, whom the Old Testament recalls as the historical figure of an Israeli king (*1. Kings* 1–11, *1. Chron* 28–29, *2. Chron* 1–9), in the course of centuries was altered into the hero of the Jewish apocrypha and Islamic myths. Solomon's wisdom as a ruler, about which the Old Testament writes (*1. Kings* 3, 1–28, 5, 9–14, *2. Chron* 1, 7–12), grew to fairy tale dimensions. According to Solomon's legacy, which is obviously an older, today unknown Jewish model reworked by Christians, Solomon got power from God, with which he conquered all demons of the desert and the sea. They had to listen to his commands and with their help build Jerusalem. For his love for women, however, he succumbed to demons and lost all power. Solomon obtained wide favour in Islamic religious folklore and ended up even in the dynastic legend of the Ethiopian kings. Miloš Bič, *Ze světa Starého zákona II* (Praha 1989), p. 638. *Quran*, surah 21, 78–82, surah 27, 15–45, surah 34, 11–13, surah 38, 29–39. Abú al-Hasan al-Kisáí, *Kniha o počiatku a konci a rozprávania o prorokoch (islamské mýty a legendy)*, translation Ján Pauliny (Bratislava 1980), pp. 124–155. Abu l-Hasan 'Alí al-Mas'údí, *Rýžoviště zlata a doly drahokamů*, translation Ivan Hrbek (Praha 1983), p. 59. The motif of monarchal wisdom in the work of Constantine Porphyrogenitus and chronicler Regino is also connected with Svätopluk.

Everyone, the entire last Great Moravian generation, experienced the glory and subsequent pain; therefore, they were embedded into the national memory.

Large events of national history, glorious or tragic, are an unforgettable experience, which become the basis of a vast epic creation. King Arthur, the Nibelungs, Prince Marko, Miloš Kobilić, David of Sasun, Manas and other heroes were the centrepoint of the historical memory of their nations. The Great Moravia tradition did not become the basis of a vast domestic epic creation, which could lead to the origin of a written epic. Its traces are scanty. In five chronicles we can differentiate six old tales in chronological order:

1. Tale of the battle near the Rakus River (1095–1099) Gesta Ungarorum vetera
2. Nitrian tale (1099) Cosmas
3. Zobor tale (1099) Cosmas
4. Biharia tale (around 1200) Anonymus
5. Veszprém tale (1270–1272) Magister Ákos
6. Pilis tale (1282–1285) Simon of Kéza.

The question of the origin (*origo gentis*)[94] did not satisfy to an educated chronicler or even a common peasant (*fabulae rusticorum*); Magyars and Slovaks in medieval Hungary had to answer it. The memory of Svätopluk, later Moravec, which were linked in Transdanubia with the memory of opposition and defeat of the Great Moravian army by the Magyars, were memories about the Great Moravian origin of the Slovaks. Methodius's biographer recorded the beginning of this old memory in the 9th century, and we can follow its continuity in six stories which circulated in the former Great Moravian territory at the end of the 13th century.

---

94 Třeštík, *Kosmova kronika*, pp. 85–90.

CHAPTER 13

Hungarian Principalities

The Hungarian chronicler Anonymus wrote about the conquering of the Carpathian Basin by the Magyars three centuries after the fact. The invented Slavic, Bulgarian and Valachian princes, who lost their principalities and their lives in battles with Árpád's victorious warriors, as well as the detailed descriptions of battles full of heroism, military glory and great Magyar victories are not important for us. They are the fruits of Anonymus's imagination and have no historical value.[1] However, the existence of his work and with it the many details that recorded the range of the old principalities that he put into the invented descriptions of their conquering and occupation, is worthy of attention.

1   Ung

According to Anonymus, the Magyars, after crossing the Carpathians, entered into the territory of a principality centred on the castle at Ung (Uzhhorod), to which the castles at Mukačevo (Munkács), Boržava (Borzsova) and Zemplín all belonged. The Magyars, led by Árpád's father Álmos, *descended into the country Ung (ad partes Hung). When they got there, they named the town that they first occupied as Mukačevo (Muncas) ... Then the Slavs, the residents of that land,... were subject of Prince Salan ... Then Prince Álmos and his magnates ... came on horseback to the castle Ung (ad castrum Hung), in order to conquer it. And when they had camped around the ramparts, then the count of this castle, by the name of Laborec, who was labeled as a duca in their language (comes eiusdem castri nomine Loborcy, qui in lingua eorum duca vocabatur), ran off, hurrying to Zemplín Castle (ad castrum Zemlum). The prince's warriors followed him, caught up to him by a river, and at this same site they hanged him and from this day forward they called that river by the name Laborec. Then Prince Álmos and his soldiers went into the castle Ung ...* Álmos's son Árpád *sent his army and occupied the entire territory, which spread between the Tisza and the Bodrog up to Ugocsa (totam terram, que est inter Thisciam et Budrug usque ad Vgosam), and with all residents. He surrounded castle Boržava (castrum Borsoa), and when he conquered it on the third day of battle, he broke down its ramparts, gave the*

---

[1] Ratkoš, "Anonymove Gesta Hungarorum," pp. 832–840.

soldiers of Prince Salan whom he found there manacles of iron and commanded that they be taken to Castle Ung.[2]

The Principality of Ung, which according to Anonymus was run by a count (*župan*), more exactly a *duca*, that is Prince Laborec, should have belonged to the fabular Salan's realm. It took up the territory of the later castle counties Zemplín (without Szerencs), Ung and Boržava (and with the territory of Kisvárda on the left-hand bank of the Tisza, to the north of the later Szabolcs seat, which no longer belonged to the later Boržava seat).[3] Its northern border conformed with the Hungary-Russia border on the main ridge of the Carpathian Mountains. That's why Salan's realm, as recorded by Anonymus, reached *up to the border of the Russians*.[4]

Stephen I transformed the Principality of Ung into a castle county, but he did not change its territorial range. In 1085 deposed Hungarian King Solomon was living with Pecheneg Khagan Cselgü on the territory of the later Moldova: *He promised him that if he helps him against Ladislas, he will hand to him the province of Transylvania and take his daughter as his wife.* Prince Kutesk (= Cselgü), *seduced by false hope, bursting with a great many Cumans* (= Pechenegs) *into Hungary, marched up to the province of the castles of Ung and Boržava* (*usque in provinciam castrorum Vng et Borsua*).[5] All of the events on the conquering of the Principality of Ung by Álmos and Árpád, its previous subjection to the distant Prince Salan and the name of Prince Laborec of Ung himself are all inventions of Anonymus.[6] However, he did capture its oldest territorial range truthfully. An older Hungarian chronicler, according to whom Ung County

---

2   Anonymi (P. magistri) *Gesta Hungarorum* 13, 14, SRH I, pp. 51–53. Loránd Benkő, *Név és történelem. Tanulmányok az Árpád-korról* (Budapest 1998), pp. 35–36. The Slavs of Ung addressed their prince with the Latin title *duca*, just as by the end of the 6th century the Slavic chief on the Wallachian territory of Mužok had a similarly Latin title – *rega*. Theofylaktos Simokattes, *Oikumeniké historia* VI 9. For opinions on the Byzantine or Bulgarian origin of the title *duca*, see Benkő, *Név*, p. 108. In 1214 the pristald (bailiff) of the Biharian count had the name Duka: *per pristaldum nomine Ducam. Regestrum Varadinense examinum ferri candentis ordine chronologico digestum descripta effigie editionis a. 1550 illustrata sumptibusque capituli Varadinensis lat. rit.* curis et laboribus Joannis Karácsonyi et Samuelis Borovsky editum (Budapest 1903), no. 96 (322), p. 187.
3   The northern part of the Szabolcs seat around Kisvárda originally belonged to Boržava County. Györffy, ÁMF I, pg. 520–522. Péter Németh, *Borsova határvármegye kialakulása. A Kisvárdai Vármúzeum kiadványi* 5 (Debrecen 1975). Kristó, *A vármegyék*, pp. 421–426. If the Kisvárda area belonged to Boržava County, then before then it had to belong to the oldest Ung County, from which Boržava County was split off.
4   See note 43.
5   *Chron. Hung. comp. saec. XIV.* II 134, SRH I, p. 408.
6   Anonymus derived the name of Prince Laborec from the Laborec River. Benkő, *Név*, pp. 15, 19.

still belonged to the eastern territory of the later Boržava County in 1085, confirmed Anonymus's knowledge of the size of the older Ung County and its princely forerunner.

2   Biharia

At the time of arrival of the Magyars, according to Anonymus, Prince Menumorout, who inherited rule of Biharia from his Uncle Morout, was based at Bihar Castle. Princes Morout and Menumorout, as well as Anonymus's description of the conquering of Biharia by Árpád's warriors, are a literary fiction, but from Anonymus's rich geographical data we can deduce the territorial range of the Biharian Principality, and in the names of both princes the memory that Biharia once belonged to the Great Moravian Empire: *Thus the territory which lies between the Tisza and the Igfon forest, which lies near Transylvania, from the river Maros up to the river Szamos, was allegedly occupied by Prince Morout, whose nephew was called Menumorout by the Magyars because he had many lovers.*[7] The southern border of Biharia did not lie on the Maros (Mureș) River, as Anonymus writes, but north of this river, at the watershed of the Maros and Körös rivers.[8]

To Biharia belonged on the north-east the *territory from the river Szamos up through the Nyírség frontier and up to the Meszes Gates* (*terram a fluvio Zomus usque ad confi nium Nyr et usque ad portam Mezesynam*), which according to Anonymus, Árpád's messengers requested from Biharian Prince Menumorout. Castle Szatmár (Satu Mare, *castrum Zotmar*), lying in the middle of the mentioned territory, also belonged to Biharia. A company of Menumorout's soldiers reportedly defended Szatmár Castle against the attack of Árpád's warriors for three days. After the fall of Szatmár, the Magyar commanders *subjugated many peoples from the forest of Nyírség up to the Omsó-ér River* (*magnum sibi populum subiugaverunt a silvis Nyr usque ad Umusoer*) and without opposition came all the way to Zilah (Zalău, *ad Zyloc*), *because Prince Menumorout and his people did not have the courage to battle with them*, and they ended their campaign

---

7   *Anonymi (P. magistri) Gesta Hungarorum* 11, SRH I, p. 49.
8   South of Biharia lay the Marosvár Principality, later Csanád County, to which the entire floodplain of the Maros (Mureș), that is also its northern bank, belonged. See pp. 307–308, 358. Likewise, not even the Szamos (Someș) River was the border, because according to Anonymus's telling, both banks and the entire basin of the lower and middle Szamos and with the castle Szatmár on the northern bank of this river, that is, the entire territory of the oldest Szatmár County belonged to Biharia. See note 10.

at the Biharia-Transylvania border *at the Meszes* (Mezeş) *Gates* (*in porta Mezesina*).[9] Biharia thus reached to the basin of the Kraszna, the lower and middle Szamos (Someş) and the upper Tisza rivers. The whole of this north-eastern part of the Biharian Principality, from the south-eastern border of the oldest Ung County up to the north-eastern border of Transylvania, was ruled, according to Anonymus, by Árpád's warriors in consequence of conquering Szatmár Castle, which was therefore also its centre. Anonymus thus captured the range of the oldest Szatmár County.[10]

The Kabars settled in Biharia: *On that territory reportedly lived nations, who were called the Kabars* (*gentes, qui dicuntur Cozar*).[11] Three Kabar tribes still had in the time of Constantine Porphyrogenetius (in 948) one common prince: *They have one prince, three tribes of Kabars, which still today exist*. The Kabars showed themselves in war to be the strongest and most courageous among the eight tribes and in war they battled at the front;[12] therefore, the second most important Magyar prince after Árpád was certainly the Kabar Prince Kurszán, and therefore Kurszán and his successors had the title of *gyula*, the second highest title in the tribal federation.[13] Gyula Kurszán was the Kabar prince up to year 904.[14] We do not know the names of his successors, who also inherited the supra-tribal title of *gyula*.

In the battle near Kemej in 1074 four Bihar County brigades battled against Hungarian King Solomon.[15] The Biharian Principality thus consisted of four

---

9   *Anonymi (P. magistri) Gesta Hungarorum* 19, 20, 21, SRH I, pp. 59–63.
10   The entire north-western part of the Transylvania diocese, which overlapped northern and the north-western border Transylvania, belonged to the oldest Szatmár County. Regarding Szatmár County and other castle counties, which were divided from them, see Kristó, *A vármegyék*, pp. 487–497. Gyula Kristó, "Néhány vármegye kialakulásának kérdéséhez," *Századok* 136 (2002), no. 2, pp. 473–475. The oldest Szatmár County, similarly as the mentioned Ung County, included the territory of several later smaller castle counties.
11   *Anonymi (P. magistri) Gesta Hungarorum* 11, SRH I, p. 49.
12   Constantine Porphyrogenitus, *De administrando imperio* 39, ed. Moravcsik, pp. 174–175. Konstantinos Porfyrogenetos, *De administrando imperio* 39, *Az Árpád-kori magyar történet bizánci forrásai*, ed. Moravcsik, p. 46. MMFH III, p. 394. The three Kabar tribes had one common prince. Thus, only one of the Hungarian principalities belonged to them, namely the Biharian Principality. The Kabars therefore could not also have had Nitria in addition to Biharia, as is assumed by György Györffy. György Györffy, "Az Árpád-kori szolgálónépek kérdéséhez," *Történelmi Szemle* 15 (1972), p. 281. Györffy, *István király*, pp. 35, 41, 202. Györffy, *König Stephan*, p. 35. MT I/1, pp. 622–624, 659, 690, 696.
13   See p. 150.
14   Vajay, *Der Eintrit*, pp. 33–35, 37–38.
15   *Chron. Hung. comp. saec. XVI.* II 117, SRH I, p. 384.

castle counties.[16] Their historical basis could be the territory of the three Kabar tribes and the adjacent Principality of Ung. Three castle counties originated from the three Kabar tribal territories. Szabolcs County (without Kisvárda, which belonged to the later Boržava County) belonged to the Eger diocese and had its seat at Castle Szabolcs.[17] Bihar County included the whole of the Bihar diocese and the neighbouring enclave of the Eger diocese at Féher-Körös (Crişul Alb) (later the Bihar, Békés and Zaránd seat).[18] Szatmár County (on the territory of the later seats of Ugoča, Maramaros (Maramureş), Szatmár, Közép-Szolnok and Kraszna) had belonged, from an unknown time, to the Transylvania diocese, not, however, to Transylvania.[19] The fourth Biharian county was not Kabar, but Slavic, and originated with the transformation of the Ung Principality to Ung County (*provincia castrorum Ung et Borsua*).[20]

---

16 Gyula Kristó, *A XI. századi hercegség története Magyarországon* (Budapest 1974), p. 85. Kristó, *A vármegyék*, pp. 197–200.
17 Kristó, *A vármegyék*, pp. 418–421.
18 Attila Zsoldos, "Bihar megye korai története," in *Nagyvárad és Bihar a korai középkorban. Tanulmányok Biharország történetéről 1* (Nagyvárad 2014), pp. 167–190. Békes County was detached from Bihar County earlier than Zaránd County. In 1203 Békés was already a special castle county, but the territory of castle Zaránd still belonged to Bihar County: *duas partes tributorum totius comitatus Byhoriensis tam circa Byhar quam circa Zarand ... et in comitatu de Bebes tam in villis quam in foris exigutur*. *Chronicon Varadiense* 16, SRH I, p. 211. Kristó, *A vármegyék*, pp. 480–482. Boglárka Weisz, "A 15. századi váradi vámper Árpád-kori gyökerei," in *Nagyvárad és Bihar a korai középkorban*, pp. 147–165. In 1214 Zaránd County no longer existed: *dato pristaldo nomine Dyonisio filio Ompud, de provincia Zaránd, de villa Vosian*. *Regestrum Varadinense*, ed. Karácsonyi, Borovszky, no. 97 (323), p. 188. Zaránd County (*comitatum de Zarand*) is also mentioned by Anonymus. *Anonymi (P. magistri) Gesta Hungarorum* 52, SRH I, p. 106. It thus became independent in the period of Anonymus, that is very shortly after 1203. Zaránd was until the start of the 13th century a part of Bihar County; however, it did not belong to the Bihar (Várad) bishopric, but to Eger. Tivadar Ortvay, *Magyarország egyházi földleírása a XIV. század elején a pápai tizedjegyzékek alapján feltüntetve I* (Budapest 1891), pp. 116, 118–120, 129–131, 175–177. Tivadar Ortvay, *Magyarország egyházi földleírása a XIV. század elején a pápai tizedjegyzékek alapján feltüntetve II* (Budapest 1892), p. 517. Béla Kovács, *Az egri egyházmegye története 1596-ig* (Eger 1987), pp. 27–28, 48–49. Kristó, *A vármegyék*, pp. 470–474. See chapter 15, note 38.
19 Ortvay, MEF II, pp. 627, 650, 665–669. Tivadar Ortvay – László Hrubant, *Az Erdélyi egyházmegye a XIV-ik század elején. Mérték 1 : 600 000. Photolitographie und Schnellpressendruck des k. k. militär-geographischen Instituts in Wien* (Wien 1888). If Szatmár County did not belong to neighbouring Transylvania, which lay beyond the Meszes Gates, then it belonged to Biharia. Up to year 1299 even Maramaros belonged to the Transylvania diocese. See chapter 20, note 4.
20 *Chron. Hung. comp. saec. XIV.* II 134, SRH I, p. 408.

3 Transylvania

Transylvania was ruled up to year 1003 by a princely family which traced its origin from Tetény (*Tuhutum*), one of Árpád's commanders. According to Anonymus, *Tuhutum ... marched beyond the forest (ultra silvas) in an eastern direction against Prince Gelou of the Valachs. Transylvanian Prince Gelou (dux Ultrasilvanus) ... assembled his army and set out on a journey very quickly against Tuhutum, in order to prevent his passing through the Meszes Gates (per portas Mezesinas). Tuhutum, however, passed through the forest in a single day and arrived at the Almas River (ad fluvium Almas).* Prince Gelou, his defeat in battle at the Almas (Almaș) River and subsequent attempt to flee *to his castle lying near the Szamos River (ad castrum suum iuxta fluvium Zomus positum)*, his death *by the Capus River (iuxta fluvium Copus)* and the promise of loyalty by the residents of Transylvania to Tetény *at that site which is called Esculeu*,[21] are likewise a literary fictions, just as Princes Laborec and Menumorout and their stories, but we can rely on Anonymus's testimony regarding the border between Biharia and Transylvania at the Meszes Gates and on the ridge of the surrounding mountains.

In 1085 the Pechenegs marched through northern Transylvania and *broke through the barriers near the upper part of the Meszes Gates, invaded Hungary and mercilessly despoiled the entire province of Nyírség up to Bihar Castle.*[22] To the north the upper basin of the Szamos belonged to Transylvania. The Meszes Gates divided it from the central and lower basin, which together with the

---

21   *Anonymi (P. magistri) Gesta Hungarorum* 24–27, SRH I, pp. 65–68.
22   *superiori parte porte Mezes ruptis indaginibus irruperunt in Hungariam totamque provinciam Nyr usque civitatem Byhor crudeliter depredantes. Chron. Hung. comp. saec. XIV.* II 102, SRH I, p. 366. According to a Hungarian chronicler, the Pechenegs entered *into Hungary (in Hungariam)* only after crossing the Transylvania-Biharia border at the Meszes Gates. Thus, Hungary existed, in a narrow sense of the word, in which Biharia was a part, but not Transylvania. A donation for the abbey in Hronský Beňadik from year 1075 mentions the extensive abbey properties first on the north side of the Danube and then in the Tisza River region. From the view of the abbey that lay on the territory of Nitria and which prepared this document, and from the view of its founder and donor, Hungarian King Géza I, who until recently was the subordinate Nitrian Prince (1063–1074), the properties in the Tisza River region *scilicet in Meler, Sapi, Pelu, Sagi, Alpar, Chonu et Fizeg* (Millér, Pelli in the Szolnok seat, Sáp, Ság, Alpár, Csany, in the Csongrád seat, Füzegy on the middle Zagyva in southern Novohrad) lay *in Hungary (in Hungaria).* DHA I, ed. Györffy, no. 73, p. 218. CDES I, ed. Marsina, no. 58, p. 57. Richard Marsina, "Štúdie k Slovenskému diplomatáru 1. Druhá časť: Obdobie od roku 1000 do roku 1235," *Historické štúdie* 18 (1973), pp. 57–60. Ľubomír Juck, "Majetky hronskobeňadického opátstva do roku 1235," *Historické štúdie* 18 (1973), pp. 121–147. Thus, not only Transylvania lay beyond this Hungarian land, but also the territory on the north side of the Danube, that is Nitria.

upper Tisza River region belonged to Biharia. In this Anonymus conforms with the Hungarian chroniclers. Tétény's son was called Horka, and his grandson and great-grandson had the name Gyula. All three highest Hungarian titles (kende, gyula and horka) were also popular names. Their bearers were not necessarily holders of these titles.[23]

The princes of Transylvania had their seats in northern Transylvania, until Tétény's grandson Gyula I moved his seat to the south: *And this Gyula was a great and powerful prince, who discovered in Transylvania while hunting Alba Iulia (civitatem Albam), which had long ago been built by the Romans.*[24] The Roman fortress Apulum, which got the name Gyulafehérvár in Hungarian, that is Gyula's White Castle (today's Alba Iulia, Romania), became the new seat of the Princes of Transylvania.[25]

Gyula I visited Constantinople in 953, was baptised there and got the title *patrokios* from the emperor. The Constantinople patriarch ordained the monk Hierothes as Hungarian bishop and sent him along with Gyula to Transylvania. Hierotheos baptised Gyula's family and began to baptise his principality: *Hierotheos led many from barbarian delusion to Christianity. Gyula persevered in the faith, then undertook to never again invade into the Roman (= Byzantine) empire, did not forget even captured Christians, paid ransom for many and took*

---

23 Katalin Fehértói, *Árpád-kori kis személynévtár* (Budapest 1983), pp. 148–149. Katalin Fehértói, *Árpád-kori személynévtár (1000–1301)* (Budapest 2004), pp. 339–341, 368, 473. Gyula Kristó – Ferenc Makk – László Szegfű, Adatok "korai" helyneveink ismereéhez I, *Acta Universitatis Szegediensis de Attila József nominatae, Acta historica* 44 (Szeged 1973), pp. 56–57. Benkő, *Név*, p. 20, 98–101. Transylvania Princes Gyula I and Gyula II did not have the title of gyula, just as other bearers of this name in Hungary did not have the title of gyula. SRH I, p. 425. SRH II, pp. 492, 555. DHA I, ed. Györffy, no. 73/II, 86, pp. 218, 265. CDES I, ed. Marsina, no. 137, 139, 140, 143, 147, 152, 153, 154, 156, 168, 173, 175, 188, 190, 198, 204, 205, 206, 207, 208, 209, 213, 216, 220, 221, 223, 224, 226, 257, 263, 290, 294, 306, 307, 310, pp. 110, 111, 112, 114, 115, 121, 123, 124, 133, 136, 137, 143, 150, 156, 160, 161, 162, 163, 164, 165, 168, 171, 173, 175, 176, 177, 178, 193, 196, 212, 214, 223, 224, 225. Not even Horka, the father of Gyula I, had the title horka, because the horka was Kál and his son was Bulcsú. See chapter 10, note 10. The title gyula belonged to the Kabar princes. In 955 both of these titles had ceased to exist.

24 *Chron. Hung. comp. saec. XIV.* II 30, SRH I, pp. 290–291. Gyula Kristó assumes that southern Transylvania belonged to Bulgaria up to the beginning of the 11th century. Transylvanian princes had only northern Transylvania and were seated at Doboka Castle. Southern Transylvania was conquered from the Bulgarians only after year 1003. Kristó, "A 10. századi Erdély politikai történetéhez," pp. 30–34. The mentioned chronicler report contradicts this opinion, because Gyula I could not have gone hunting on Bulgarian land.

25 *Kurze Geschichte Siebenbürgens*, ed. Köpeczi, pp. 22–23, 28, 31, 33, 35, 40, 42–43, 49–50, 53, 59, 63, 87, 104, 106, 111, 122–124, 130, 132, 134, 135, 137, 142–143, 145–146, 151, 154–160, 163–169, 172–173. György Györffy, *Az Árpád-kori Magyarország történeti földrajza II* (Budapest 1987), pp. 143–158.

care that they were made free.[26] Prince Gyula I could now have the Church of St. Michael built in the seat of his Transylvania principality at Gyulafehérvár[27] (at which a regular bishopric originated in 1009), and it could now serve for Bishop Hierotheos.[28]

Unlike with other principalities, Anonymus knew not only the territorial range, but also the older history of Transylvania. Tetény and his successors could not fall into oblivion in Hungary, because Sarolt, mother of Saint Stephen, came from their line.[29] The unknown author of the Gesta Ungarorum vetera wrote the history of the Transylvanian princes approximately 100 years before Anonymus wrote it, with some differences,[30] from where it got into the entire Hungarian chroniclers' traditions. Transylvania is proof about the beginnings of Hungarian principalities as far back as in the period of Árpád or his closest successors.

4   Marosvár

South of Biharia and west of Transylvania lay the Marosvár Principality. On the north the basin of the lower Maros (Mureș) belonged to it, where its castle seat (*civitas Morisena, urbs Morisena, Moroswar*) lay; to the east it reached up to the Transylvania border and on the west to the lower Tisza. The southern border was the Danube from the mouth of the Tisza up to the Iron Gates. Anonymus invented the first Marosvár Prince Glad: *The territory, which is from the Maros River (Mors) up to castle Orsova (Vrscia), was reportedly occupied by a prince by the name of Glad, who marched as help for the Cumans from castle Vidin (Bundyn), and from his descendents came Achtum (Ohtum).*[31] In stories about the invented campaign of three Árpád commanders *against Prince*

---

26 Ioannes Skylitzes 5, *Az Árpád-kori magyar történet bizanci forrásai*, ed. Moravcsik, pp. 85–86.

27 Györffy, *ÁMF II*, pp. 155–156. Mező, *Patrocíniumok*, pp. 285–286. Géza Entz, *A gyulafehérvári székesegyház* (Budapest 1958). *Kurze Geschichte Siebenbürgens*, ed. Köpeczi, pp. 158–159.

28 The predecessor of the cathedral was a rotunda, the foundations of which archaeologists have dated to the last third of the 10th century. Entz, *A gyulafehérvári székesegyház*, pp. 55–56, 71–73, 75–77. Gervers-Molnár, *A középkori Magyarország rotundái*, p. 52, Fig. 35.

29 Mór Wertner, *Az Árpádok családi története* (Nagy-Becskereken 1892), pp. 25–27. Szabolcs de Vajay, "Großfürst Geysa von Ungarn. Familie und Verwandschaft," *Südostforschungen* 21 (München 1962), p. 50.

30 *Chron. Hung. comp. saec. XIV.* II 30, 63, 65, *SRH I*, pp. 290–291, 312, 314–315.

31 *Anonymi (P. magistri) Gesta Hungarorum* 11, *SRH I*, pp. 49–50.

Glad, who had an estate from the Maros (Morus) up to castle Haram (Horom),[32] Anonymus recorded in detail the territorial range of the Marosvár Principality: Commanders Sovárd, Kadocsa and Vajta *crossed the Tisza (Tysciam) in Kanjiža (in Kenesna) and proceeded along the Csesztreg River (Seztureg) ... From there they marched to the country Bega (ad partes Beguey) and remained there for two weeks, until they had subjugated all the residents of this country from the Maros (a Morisio) up to the Timiș River (Temes) ... In a battle on the Temes (Timiș)* River they defeated Prince Glad and *marched to the border of the Bulgarians (versus fines Bulgarorum) and set up a camp on the Ponjavica River (Ponoucea).* Glad, after the downfall of his army, fled *to the castle Kovin (Keuee),* which then surrendered to the Magyars without a fight. *From there the Magyars on a march conquered castle Orsova (Ursova) and spent a month there.*[33]

The invented Prince Glad was, according to Anonymus, a distant relative of the last and only Marosvár Prince Ajtony (before 1002–about 1028). Ajtony (Achtum, *Ohtum*) is also mentioned in the St. Gerard legend, which writes similarly as Anonymus did regarding the territorial range of his principality: *In those days there was one prince at Marosvár Castle by the name of Achtum (quidam princeps in urbe Morisena nomine Acthum), very powerful ... in Maros (in Morosio), settling in the landings of this river up to the Tisza (ad Ticiam) customs officials and guards and included everything under the customs ... This man was served by everything that he contained under his power, from the Körös River (Keres, Criș) up to Transylvania (ad partes Transilvanas) and up to Vidin and the Severin (in Budin ac Zoren).*[34]

The St. Gerard legend confirms that Anonymus did not invent the Marosvár Principality and its territorial range. It was equally old as neighbouring Biharia and Transylvania. From the whole of its long history, however, only the last Marosvár Prince Ajtony was known, whom Stephen I removed, and his principality was transformed into a castle county, which took without change the territorial range of the abolished principality.

5   Eger

In the north-west vicinity of Biharia lay another Hungarian principality, which Anonymus demarcates with the confluence of the Hornád and Sajó rivers on the east, the Zagyva River on the west and the castles Örsúr, Poroszló and Pata

---

32   *Anonymi (P. magistri) Gesta Hungarorum* 44, SRH I, p. 89.
33   *Anonymi (P. magistri) Gesta Hungarorum* 44, SRH I, pp. 89–91.
34   *Legenda maior Sancti Gerhardi episcopi* 8, SRH II, pp. 489–490.

at its north-eastern, south-eastern and north-western edges. According to Anonymus, it originally belonged to the realm of Prince Salan: *Prince Salan ... out of fear abdicated to Prince Árpád territory up to the Zagyva River (Zegeua), which was requested.*[35] The borders of this relinquished territory consisted in, aside from the mentioned Zagyva River, the Tisza from the mouth of the Sajó through the mouth of the Zagyva and the Bükk Mountains. Approximately in the middle of this territory stands Eger Castle, which is among the oldest and most important castles of medieval Hungary, at which a bishop had a seat perhaps from year 1009.[36] Just as the mentioned Bihar, Gyulafehérvár (Alba Iulia) and Marosvár (later Csanád) were princely seats long before the first bishops were based in them,[37] the episcopal castle at Eger was also originally a princely seat. The Princes of Eger could come only from the local Aba family. Testimony about the princely origin of the Aba line is the marriage of Samuel Aba with the sister of Hungarian King Stephen.[38] Stephen would hardly have married his sister to an Aba and hardly have made him a palatine, if Aba had not ranked among the most prominent of Hungarian princes. Anonymus writes the following about the ancient past and the oldest property of his family: *Prince Árpád gave Ed and Edumen extensive territories in the Matra Mountains, where later their grandson Pata (Pota) built a castle. King Samuel Aba, known for his piety, came from this line after a longer time.*[39]

The Eger Principality lay along both sides of the Eger River. It later encompassed the southern Borsod with castle Örsur, which did not belong to the oldest Borsod County,[40] and later Heves, which then could still not have belonged

---

35 *Anonymi (P. magistri) Gesta Hungarorum* 30, SRH I, p. 71.
36 DHA I, ed. Györffy, no. 10, pp. 60–61. Kovács, *Az egri egyházmegye története*, p. 25.
37 György Györffy, *Wirtschaft und Geselschaft der Ungarn um die Jahrtausendwende* (Budapest 1983), p. 12.
38 Hungarian magnates in 1041 *quendam comitem nomine Abam, sororium sancti regis Stephani et eum super se regem constituerunt. Chron. Hung. comp. saec. XIV.* II 72, SRH I, p. 325. Wertner, *Az Árpádok családi története*, pp. 102–111. Vajay, "Großfürst Geysa," pp. 46, 48–49, 78–79.
39 *Anonymi (P. magistri) Gesta Hungarorum* 32, SRH I, p. 73. Benkő, *Név*, pp. 36, 46–48. The Aba family also had property in the Hornád Basin. Anonymus has the oldest report about them and then a document from the 13th century. *Anonymi (P. magistri) Gesta Hungarorum* 17, SRH I, pp. 57–58. Branislav Varsik, *Osídlenie Košickej kotliny I* (Bratislava 1964), pp. 91–93.
40 In perhaps 1067 Count Peter (*Petrus dei gracia comes*) from the Aba line founded and endowed an abbey consecrated to the Virgin Mary in Százd (*monasterium Sancte Marie ... quod dicitur Zazty*) on the bank of the Tisza River in what was later southern Borsod. DHA I, ed. Györffy, no. 58, pp. 182–185. Györffy, ÁMF I, pp. 804–805. János Foltin, *A Zázty-i apátság* (Eger 1883). The abbey lay on the territory of the former Eger Principality, which under the rule of Stephen I became a castle county. See p. 390. Count Peter, a descendant (son or grandson) of Samuel Aba, was thus the Eger Count. The later southern Borsod,

to the later Újvár County.[41] The marriage of Samuel Aba with Stephen's sister, Samuel's title as palatine[42] and the founding of a bishopric in his Eger seat were the culmination of the good relations of the Aba and Árpád families.

6 Árpád's Principality

Between the Danube, the lower Tisza and the Zagyva rivers was the territory of another Hungarian principality. According to Anonymus *thus, the land which lay between the Tisza and the Danube (inter Thisciam et Danubium), reportedly was occupied by Kean (Keanus), the great prince of Bulgaria, the grandfather of Prince Salan, up to the border of the Russians and Poles, and he settled Slavs*

---

where the Százd Abbey stood, belonged to Peter's Eger County. Just as in later Heves, the Abas also had until the arrival of the Örsúrs a crucial position. The Örsúr line came to southern Borsod only in the 12th century. See chapter 20, note 15.

41 Újvár County did not yet exist in the period of Stephen I. Castle Újvár was only built by King Samuel Aba (1041–1044) and became a county castle only after the breakup of the large Borsod County. See pp. 521–523. Samuel Aba, or some of his ancestors, founded on the territory of his principality (then a castle county), in Abasár, on the southern edge of the Matra Hills, an abbey consecrated to the Virgin Mary, where Samuel Aba was buried: *Tandem sepelierunt corpus eius in proprio monasterio in Sarus. Chron. Hung. comp. saec. XIV.* II 76, SRH I, p. 332. Györffy, ÁMF III, p. 130. And the Abasár and Százd abbeys, which were founded by the oldest of the Abas, demarcate the range of Eger County (before then principality) on the territory of the later Heves (without Kemej) and the southern Borsod. Kemej, which lay on the opposite, left bank, of the Tisza and later belonged to the Heves seat, was still in 1219 an independent castle county: *Minister regis de villa Tivan et de villa Tót et tota provincia de Quemey. Regestrum Varadiense*, no. 226 (96), ed. Karácsonyi, Borovszky, p. 238. Kemej belonged originally to the Biharian Principality, which to the west reached up to the Tisza River, more exactly to one of the four Biharian counties, probably the oldest one, Szabolcs County. If it belonged to neighbouring Bihar County, like Békés, then after being separated from it, it would have remained to the archdeaconate of the Bihar diocese, just as Békés County remained with it, more exactly the Békés and Szeghalom archdeaconate. Kemej was archdeaconate of the Eger diocese just as Szabolcs, originally belonged to Szabolcs County. Regarding the Kemej archdeaconate, see Ortvay, MEF I, pp. 124–129, 174. Györffy, ÁMF III, pp. 45, 48–49, 57–59. Kovács, *Az egri egyházmegye*, pp. 37, 50–51. Kristó, *A vármegyék*, pp. 405–406. Regarding the Békés and Szeghalom archdeaconate, which lay in Békés County, see Ortvay, MEF II, pp. 599–606. Györffy, ÁMF I, pp. 494–497, 500–501. Kristó, *A vármegyék*, pp. 479–482. Kemej could not have been an independent castle county within the Biharian Principality, because this principality had only four castle counties. See pp. 303–304.

42 Samuel Aba was palatine up to year 1041, when he took the throne from Peter Orseolo and himself became king: *Alba comes pallacii, deiecto Petro, regalem coronam et aulam regiam sibi usurpavit. Legenda maior sancti Gerhardi episcopi* 14, SRH II, p. 500. Tibor Szőcs, *A nádori intézmény korai története 1000–1342* (Budapest 2014), pp. 25–31.

and Bulgarians there.[43] The invented princes Kean and Salan not only had the interfluvial land, which ended on the north with the Galga and Verőce basins in the southern Novohrad (Nógrád) and thus reached up to the ridge of the Cserhát Mountains (Novohrad Mountains),[44] but also had subjugated to them the distant Principality of Ung neighbouring on the north with Russian Galicia and the neighbouring Borsod Principality bordering with Poland.[45] The land east from the Zagyva, where the Principality of Eger originated, linked Salan's principality with Borsod and Ung. We don't have to doubt the existence of the four principalities, whose territories allegedly made up Salan's realm. However, Anonymus invented their unnatural combination into a single realm.

The principality lying between the Danube, Tisza and the Zagyva[46] is the same historical fact as the other reliably documented Hungarian principalities mentioned by Anonymus and other sources. It certainly did not belong to the invented Salan. If Hungarian territory to the east of the Zagyva and lower Tisza fell to the non-Árpád principalities of Biharia, Transylvania, Marosvár and Eger, then the main Hungarian Prince Árpád, after occupying the Tisza River region, could have kept only this area between the rivers.[47] The history of the Hungarian principalities began, according to Anonymus, long before the arrival of the Magyars. The individual Magyar commanders only conquered and occupied them. Because Árpád was the main Hungarian prince, his principality in the area between the rivers Danube, the lower Tisza and the Zagyva, belonged, according to Anonymus, to Salan, the most important and most powerful among all pre-Hungarian princes in the Carpathian Basin, invented by Anonymus.

According to Anonymus, Árpád first settled in a place, *where now stands the castle Bodrog.*[48] Later (after conquering north-eastern Transdanubia from the

---

43   *Anonymi (P. magistri) Gesta Hungarorum* 11 (*SRH I*), p. 48.
44   See pp. 410–415.
45   See pp. 355–356.
46   The seat of this principality was according to Anonymus Titel, near the mouth of the Tisza into the Danube: *Qui cum ad ducem Salanum pervenissant, in illo loco, qui dicitur Tetel ... in curia ducis. Anonymi (P. magistri) Gesta Hungarorum* 38, *SRH I*, p. 80. *Dux autem Salanus ... de Tetel ... equitare cepit. Anonymi (P. magistri) Gesta Hungarorum* 39, *SRH I*, p. 81. *Postea vero dux Arpad ... usque ad Titulum subiugando sibi populum. Anonymi (P. magistri) Gesta Hungarorum* 41, *SRH I*, p. 84.
47   There were no pre-Hungarian principalities in this area between the rivers before the arrival of the Magyars. In the 9th century, this area was *a wasteland (Westenne), which spread out between Carinthia and Bulgaria. Orosius* I/1, *MMFH III*, pp. 338, 340. Anonymus invented Salan's principality so that he could give a pre-Hungarian predecessor to Árpád's principality, like other Hungarian principalities.
48   *Anonymi (P. magistri) Gesta Hungarorum* 44, *SRH I*, p. 88.

Moravians) he lived in Óbuda (in Attila's place Etzilburg) and on the Danube island of Csepel, and they buried him in 907 in the vicinity of Óbuda.[49]

Another supra-tribal prince, Kurszán, also settled in Árpád's vicinity. According to Anonymus, Árpád *granted to Kende (Künd), the father of Kurszán (Cundunec patri Curzan), the land from the town of King Attila up to Százhalom (Centum Montes) and up to Diósd (Gyoyg), and to his son he gave one castle for the protection of his people. Then Kurszán commanded that this castle be named after him, and this name has not yet fallen out of memory still today.*[50] Kurszán's (Kusal's) castle in Óbuda is mentioned in documents from 1332, 1373 and 1485, and we can identify it with a Roman amphitheatre which in unsettled times also served as a fortress.[51] After Kusal's death in 904 the title of gyula lost importance, and the highest military leadership remained in Árpád's hands. Thus, dual rule ended, and Árpád and his descendants remained the highest prince and main military leader of all the Hungarian tribes: *They have, however, as the first chief (próté kefalé), a prince from the Árpád line according to the succession and two others, namely a gylas* (= gyula) *and a karchas* (= horka), *who perform the office of a judge, but also each tribe has a chief. It is necessary to know that the gyula and the horka are not personal names but are titles.*[52] Aside from the main prince, who had to be a descendant of Árpád, the Hungarian tribal federation thus had at its head *two others* who were *not from the Árpád line*. Each of the

---

49 Anonymi (P. magistri) Gesta Hungarorum 44, 52, SRH I, pp. 88–89, 106. György Györffy, "Systeme des résidences d'hiver et d'été chez les nomades et les chefs hongrois du Xe siecle," in *Archivum Eurasiae Medii Aevi* 1 (1975), pp. 54–68, 136. Györffy, *Pest-Buda kialakulása*, pp. 66–68. According to Hungarian chroniclers *Árpád together with other Magyars ... built on the hill Noe* (= Novaj) *close to Székesfehérvár a castle and this place is the first which Árpád selected in Pannonia. That's why St. King Stephen, who came from his line, also founded there the nearby castle seat of Székesfehérvár (civitas Alba). Chron. Hung. comp. saec. XIV.* 11 28, SRH I, p. 290. *ipse Arpad in loco illo fixit tabernacula, ubi modo Albana civitas est fundata. Illeque locus primus descensus extitit Arpad ducis. Simonis de Keza Gesta Hungarorum* 11 27, SRH I, p. 166. Gyula Kristó – Ferenc Makk – László Szekfű, *Adatok "korai" helyneveink ismeretéhez II, Acta Universitatis Szegediensis de Attila József nominatae, Acta Historica* 48 (1974), p. 33. Székesfehérvár was the main royal seat from the times of Stephen I up through Béla IV; therefore, chroniclers wanted to have Árpád's seat in it.

50 Anonymi (P. magistri) Gesta Hungarorum 46, SRH I, p. 95.

51 György Györffy, "Kurszán és Kurszán vára. A magyar fejedelemség kialakulása és Óbuda honfoglaláskori szerepe," *Budapest Régiségei* 15 (1955), pp. 9–34. György Györffy, *Pest-Buda kialakulása*, pp. 69–71. Benkő, *Név*, p. 17.

52 Constantine Porphyrogenitus, *De administrando imperio* 40, ed. Moravcsik, pp. 178–179. Konstantinos Porfyrogenetos, *De administrando imperio* 40, *Az Árpád-kori magyar történet bizánci forrásai*, ed. Moravcsik, pp. 48–49. MMFH III, p. 397.

three Hungarian dignitaries was from another tribe in order to ensure equal power in the Hungarian tribal federation.

On 4 July 907 in a battle on the banks of the Danube near today's Bratislava, the Magyars destroyed a large Bavarian army;[53] they took over the territory of the Eastern March up to the Enns River and occupied its easternmost part in Upper Pannonia.[54] The Árpáds certainly kept this territory, and with it the open road to the west. Just as in the area between the rivers Danube, Tisza and Zagyva, not even in northern Transdanubia does anyone ever mention non-Árpád principalities. At the end of 900 and in July 907 the Árpáds thus enlarged their own principality by the whole northern part of Transdanubia.

7   Bulcsú's Principality

Kál and Bulcsú's principality certainly comprised the territory of the whole Pannonian Principality conquered in July 900. Thus, it could balance the area of the other Hungarian principalities and could be a base for large campaigns into Byzantium, Italy and Germany.

If Hungarian territory in Pannonia reached all the way to the lower Sava on the south, that is if it spread out *between the Danube and the Sava*, as Constantine Porphyrogenitus wrote,[55] then Kál and Bulcsú's principality certainly also included the adjacent area between the lower Drava and the lower Sava, that is today's eastern Slavonia (without Sirmium, which belonged until 1018 to the Bulgarians and then Byzantium.)[56] Only Hungarian chroniclers described the location of Bulcsú's principality. Anonymus does not mention it at all.

53   *Annales Iuvavenses maximi* ad a. 907, *MMFH I*, p. 115. Vajay, *Der Eintritt*, pp. 41–43. Wolfram, *Die Geburt*, p. 308.
54   See chapter 11, note 20.
55   Constantine Porphyrogenitus, *De administrando imperio* 42, ed. Moravcsik, pp. 182–183. Konstantinos Porfyrogenetos, *De administrando imperio* 42, *Az Árpád-kori magyar történet bizánci forrásai*, ed. Moravcsik, p. 50. *MMFH III*, p. 401. If Bulcsú also attacked in a south-easterly direction, to Byzantium (see chapter 10, note 7), then his principality could have reached all to the lower Sava. This territory, later the castle counties of Vukovar (Valkó) and Požega (Pozsega), belonged from 1009 to the Pécs diocese. *DHA I*, ed. Györffy, no. 9/I, II, pp. 54–59. Tivadar Ortvay, *A pécsi egyházmegye alapítása és első határai történet-topografi ai tanulmány* (Budapest 1890). Just as later Pécs diocese, Bulcsú's principality also lay on both banks of the lower Drava and touched the lower flow of the Sava.
56   Géza Fehér, "A bolgár egyház kísérletei és hazánkban," *Századok* 61 (1927), no. 1, pp. 3–4.

8   Árpád's Successors

Árpád's oldest son, Tarhos, became his successor and together with horka Kál sacked Italy.[57] Their descendents also proceeded together. In 948 Tarhos's grandson Tormás together with horka Bulcsú received baptism in Constantinople. At that time neither Tormás's grandfather Tarhos nor even his father Tevel were still alive: *It is necessary to know that Tevel* (Tevelis) *died, and it is his son Tormás* (Termatzous) *who came here recently as friend* (filos) *with Bulcsú* (Boultzous), *third prince and karchas of Turkey* (= Hungary).[58] The principality of the oldest of Árpád's sons, Tarhos, which his son Teveli later inherited and then his grandson Tormás,[59] lay to the south of Árpád's territory in the eastern vicinity of Kál's and Bulcsú's principality. From there it was equally close to Byzantium as from southern Transdanubia. Tarhos and Tormás were probably based in Kalocsa, which, like other episcopal seats, was originally a princely seat.[60] The territory of the later Kalocsa diocese belonged to their principality. The position of their principality in southern Hungary was crucial for an alliance with the similarly positioned Kál's and Bulcsú's principality.

Like other Hungarian principalities, Stephen I also transformed the Kalocsa principality into a castle county, from which the smaller counties, Bács (already mentioned in 1071)[61] and Bodrog (mentioned in 1135) were detached.[62] The remnant Kalocsa County, like the neighbouring Szigetfő County, detached from Vác County, became a part of the Transdanubia Fejér County. The original

---

57   See note 69, see chapter 10, note 41.
58   Constantine Porphyrogenitus, *De administrando imperio* 40, ed. Moravcsik, pp. 178–179. Konstantinos Porfyrogenetos, *De administrando imperio* 40, *Az Árpád-kori magyar történet bizánci forrásai*, ed. Moravcsik, p. 49. *MMFH III*, p. 398. Bulcsú then got from the emperor the title *patrikios*. *Ioannes Skylitzes* 5, *Az Árpád-kori magyar történet bizánci forrásai*, ed. Moravcsik, p. 85.
59   Tarhos behaved similarly as Bulcsú; thus, he had a principality similar to that of Bulcsú.
60   Györffy, *Wirtschaft und Gesellschaft*, p. 12.
61   *comes Vid cum Bachiensibus militibus eos invasisset*. *Chron. Hung. comp. saec. XIV.* II 105, SRH I, p. 371. Györffy, *ÁMF I*, p. 210. Kristó, *A vármegyék*, pp. 453–456. Count Vid is also on the list of witnesses at the end of the document from 1055: + *Signum Irnei comitis*. + *Signum Viti comitis*. And documents from: *comes Erney, comes Wydus*. DHA I, ed. Györffy, no. 43/I, II, 58, pp. 152, 156, 185. Counts Erney and Vid recorded alongside one another in both documents are certainly the same Counts Erney and Vid who in 1071–1074 battled together on the side of King Solomon at the siege of Belgrade and then against the appanaged princes Géza and Ladislas. Vid was the Bács count already in 1055. Bács County thus originated even before 1055.
62   *Lamberto comite Budrugiensi*. Györffy, *ÁMF I*, p. 711. Kristó, *A vármegyék*, pp. 451–453.

Fejér County did not reach beyond the Danube, because its eastern border was identical with the Danube border of the Veszprém diocese.[63]

The oldest documents on the expansion of Fejér by the territories of Kalocsa and Szigetfő are from 1211, 1229, 1238 and 1239.[64] Before Fejér exceeded its original border on the Danube, the remnant Kalocsa and Szigetfő had to be for at least a little time independent castle counties, so that within their borders equal archdeaconates could originate which remained a part of the Kalocsa and Vác dioceses.[65] The remaining counties, Kalocsa and Vác, expired in a similar way. Vác County sometime in the second half of the 12th century fell to neighbouring Nógrád (Novohrad)[66] and Kalocsa County became a part of neighbouring Fejér County.

Constantine Porphyrogenitus also mentions other Árpád sons and grandsons: *It is necessary to know that the grand prince of Turkey Árpád had four sons: the first Tarhos (Tarkatzous), the second Üllő (Ielech), the third Jutas (Iototzas) and the fourth Zoltán (Zaltas). It is necessary to know that the first of Árpád's sons, Tarhos, had a son named Teveli (Tevelis); the second son Üllő had a son Ezellő (Ezelech); the third son Jutas had a son Fajsz (Phalitzis), the current prince; and the fourth son Zoltán had a son Taksony (Taxis).*[67] This family tree has a simple structure; it is undoubtedly simplified and incomplete. It is hardly imaginable that all four of Árpád's sons had only one son each. Ultimately, the author of these lines convicts himself of incompleteness, when he continues: *It is necessary to know that all of Árpád's sons died, but his grandsons Fajsz (Phalis) and Tasi (Tasis) and their cousin Taksony (Taxis) are alive.*[68] Jutas thus had not only

---

63   See pp. 389–390.
64   The villages lying in this territory, Lodorffölde in 1211, Csakal 1229, Pereg 1238, Csaur, Inám and Ordas in 1239, then belonged to Fejér County. Györffy, *ÁMF II*, pp. 420, 426, 434, 435.
65   Ortvay, *MEF I*, pp. 112–113, 337. From 1251 we know Kalocsa Archdeacon Elias and from 1292 and 1298 Kalocsa Archdeacon Thomas. Györffy, *ÁMF II*, pp. 428–429. In 1278 Magister Nicholas was the archdeacon in Szigetfő. Györffy, *ÁMF II*, p. 441. See chapter 15, notes 111, 112.
66   See pp. 410–415.
67   Constantine Porphyrogenitus, *De administrando imperio* 40, ed. Moravcsik, pp. 178–179. Konstantinos Porfyrogenetos, *De administrando imperio* 40, *Az Árpád-kori magyar történet bizánci forrásai*, ed. Moravcsik, p. 49. *MMFH III*, pp. 397–398.
68   Constantine Porphyrogenitus, *De administrando imperio* 40, ed. Moravcsik, pp. 178–179. Konstantinos Porfyrogenetos, *De administrando imperio* 40, *Az Árpád-kori magyar történet bizánci forrásai*, ed. Gy. Moravcsik, p. 49. *MMFH III*, p. 398. Aside from Árpád's mentioned three grandsons and great-grandson Tormas, other great-grandsons of Árpád could have lived, the sons of late Tevel and Ezellő, or the still living Fajzs, whom Constantine Porphyrogenitus may not have known about. One of them (born perhaps after year 948) was Zerind, the future Somogy prince, Koppány's father. See note 79, see chapter 14, note 91.

a son Fajsz (*Phalis, Phalitzis*) but also Tas, although he is not mentioned in the previous recitation of Árpád's posterity. Constantine Porphyrogenitus put into this simplified family tree only those Árpáds who became princes. The brothers Tarhos, Üllő, Jutas and Zoltán (Zsolt) divided their father's possessions into four parts. Four principalities originated, which after the death of the four sons did not break apart, because only one of their sons took over rule of them.

The four brothers divided Árpád's holding in northern Transdanubia and in the area between the rivers Danube, Tisza and Zagyva into approximately equal parts. The oldest brother Tarhos, who after his father's death became one of his main successors, that is the prince of all of Hungary, got the southern area between the Danube and the Tisza. The youngest, 13-year-old Zoltán (* 894), who after Tarhos's death also became the main Hungarian prince,[69]

---

69 In the nearly 50-year period from the death of Prince Árpád until the succession of Prince Taksony, Anonymus mentioned only one main Hungarian Prince, Zoltán, who was Árpád's son and Taksony's father. He is silent about the others. When Árpád died in 907, his youngest son Zoltán was only 13 years old: *Post hec anno dominice incarnationis DCCCCVII. dux Arpad migravit de hoc seculo ... Et successit ei filius suus Zulta ... Transactis quibusdam temporibus dux Zulta cum esset XIII-cim annorum, omnes primates regni sui communi consilio et pari voluntate quosdam rectores regni sub duce prefecerunt ... Anonymi (P. magistri) Gesta Hungarorum* 52–53, SRH I, pp. 106–107. If the minor Zoltán had 3 older brothers, then he hardly acquired rule over the whole of the Hungarian tribal federation immediately after his father's death. Árpád's immediate successor was his oldest son Tarhos, whom Anonymus left out, just as he left out Jutas's son Fajsz, who was the main Hungarian prince from approximately 947–955 (see note 73); therefore, Tarhos and Fajsz were not direct ancestors of Saint Stephen and his father Géza. Anonymus removed at least two princes and thus created a direct ancestoral line always from father to son, from Árpád through Zoltán, Taksony, Géza to Saint Stephen and thus shifted the principle of primogeniture valid at his ties to the oldest Hungarian history. He thus cleansed Stephen's succession after Géza, who according to the law then valid belonged to his older relative Koppány. Tarhos and Fajsz are not mentioned even in the Hungarian chronicles. Even the Saint Stephen legends consider Géza as the fourth Hungarian prince after Árpád: *Erat tunc princeps quartus ab illo, qui ingressionis Hungarorum in Pannoniam ... nomine Geiza. Legenda maior S. Stephani regis* 2, SRH II, p. 378. *Legenda S. Stephani regis ab Hartvico episcopo conscripta* 2, SRH II, p. 403. The first of both Hungarian *reges*, who in the years 921–922 as allies of Italian king and emperor Berengar plundered the territory of his antagonists in Italy, Durszak is identical with Tarhos. Géza Nagy, "Trónöröklés az Arpádok alatt," *Turul* 32 (1914), pp. 23–25. Dezső Pais, "Szempontok Árpád-kori személy neveink vizsgálatához," in *Névtudományi vizsgálatok. A Magyar nyelvtudományi társaság névtudományi konferenciája 1958, Pais Dezső közreműködésével* ed. Mikesy Sándor (Budapest 1960), pp. 93–98. Károly Czeglédy, "Nyugati türk eredetű méltóságnevek Termacsu, barsbeg, jebu, bagatur," in *Névtudományi vizsgálatok*, pp. 119–125. Vajay, *Der Eintritt*, pp. 64–65. György Györffy, "A honfoglaló magyarok települési rendjéről," *Archaeologiai Értesítő* 97 (1970), p. 217. MT I/1, pp. 654, 663–664. Lajos Ligeti, "Régi török eredetű neveink," *Magyar Nyelv* 75 (1979), pp. 259–264. Gyula Kristó, "Árpád fejedelemutódai," *Acta Universitatis Szegediensis de Attila József nominatae. Acta Historica* 84 (1987), pp. 11–21.

inherited north-eastern Transdanubia, conquered from the Moravians. His descendants, his grandson Géza and great-grandson Stephen, were also based on this territory, in Esztergom and Székesfehérvár, and their wives Sarolt and Gisela in Veszprém.[70] The rest of Árpád's holdings went to the other two brothers, Üllő and Jutas. One of them got the land between the Danube and Zagyva rivers, that is the territory of the later Vác diocese, and the other got the land between the lower Rába and the lower Enns, conquered from the Bavarians after the victory near Bratislava.[71] Zoltán died in perhaps 947,[72] and his son Taksony did not become the main Hungarian prince, but instead Jutas's son Fajsz, who was then the oldest living Árpád.[73]

9   Battle on the Lech River

In July 955 the Magyars invaded Bavaria and Swabia. An army of some 12,000, led by commanders Bulcsú, Lehel and Súr, flooded into both German principalities. By early August Lehel was plundering southern German territory and Bulcsú began to besiege Augsburg, lying near the Lech River. Until the arrival of the royal army, this city was defended by Bishop Ulrich and a brave garrison force. German King Otto I was at that time held up in Saxony suppressing a rebellion of the Slavs along the Elbe River and his eastern neighbour. Otto

---

70   Györffy, *ÁMF II*, pp. 237–238, 363–364. Györffy, *István király*, pp. 74, 97–98, 102, 112, 116, 153, 158, 195, 244, 316–317, 321, 326–327, 350, 352, 355, 381–382, 384–385, 388–389, 464. Györffy, *König Stephan*, pp. 69, 89, 94, 99, 123, 132, 173, 179, 182, 184, 191, 194, 196, 202.

71   See chapter 11, note 20.

72   According to Anonymus, in the last three years of Zoltán's life his son Taksony ruled on his behalf. *Anonymi (P. magistri) Gesta Hungarorum* 57, SRH I, p. 114. That's why the Magyar campaign into Italy in the last year year of Zoltán's life in was led by his son Taksony: *Per idem tempus Taxis, Hungarorum rex, magno cum exercitu in Italiam venit. Liutprandi Antapadosis* V 33, ed. Pertz, p. 153. When Constantine Porphyrogenitus wrote in 948 his report on the Magyars, none of Árpád's sons, and thus not even Prince Zoltán, was still alive, and of his grandsons only Fajsz, Tas and Zoltán's son Taksony were still alive. From the living grandsons, he mentions only Tormás. See note 58.

73   According to the report of Constantine Porphygenitus from 948 *Jutas had a son Fajsz, the current prince.* See note 67. Fajsz's father Jutas was older than Taksony's father Zoltán. Therefore, even Fajsz, who himself had a still younger brother, was obviously older than Taksony. And obviously he was older that than all of his nephews, of which Constantine Porphygenitus mentions only Tormás. Tormás, as follows from the report on the Magyar visit to Constantinople in 948 (see note 58), remained behind in his importance even under the non-Árpád Prince Bulcsú; therefore, he could not have become the main Hungarian prince. If Fajsz got preference over the experienced Taksony in the choice of a main prince, then only because he was the older of the two.

assembled an army from all corners of his realm and hurried against the enemies. On 8 August 955 he neared the besieged city, and on 10 August he ordered his army into battle. He led 8 armies, each of them with a thousand riders. At the head he put three Bavarian armies with their Duke Henry I. Behind him stood Conrad, Duke of Lorraine, who led the Frankish army, and Otto I with his forces. In the third line were two Swabian armies with Duke Burchard II. A thousand selected and well-armed Bohemian riders, sent to Germany by their Prince Boleslav I, remained fully at the back as backup forces. The Magyars crossed the river, went around Otto's advancing army and surprised and defeated the Bohemians and then the Swabian armies. Duke Conrad the Red then turned the course of the battle sharply when he stopped the enemy and freed the captives. Immediately after, Otto struck. The attack of his heavy cavalry scattered the Magyars. Still on that same day the Germans destroyed the Magyar camp. Lehel's forces did not take part in this battle; however, they did not avoid annihilation. The Bohemians destroyed them, and they captured Lehel himself. Nearly all the Magyar fighters fell in battle or while on the run. The three captured commanders, Bulcsú, Lehel and Súr, were hanged on the gallows.[74]

Lehel's presence at the battle is testimony that a great many Magyars from Nitria took part in the campaigns. Since they did not survive the defeat near Augsburg, Magyar riding forces in Slovakia remained significantly decimated. Bohemian Prince Boleslaus, as an ally of the main victor Otto I, also contributed to the defeat of the Magyars in 955.[75] Since Boleslaus's large realm stretched all the way to Kraków,[76] he could immediately take advantage of the weakened Magyar power in Slovakia and at the expense of neighbouring Nitria acquired its northern territory, mentioned in a document of the Prague bishopric as the *Province of Váh*.[77]

---

[74] Widukindi Rerum gestarum Saxonicarum III 44, recognovit Georgius Waitz, Scriptores rerum Germanicarum in usum scholarum ex Monumentis Germaniae historicis recusi (Hannoverae 1882), pp. 71–73. Václav Novotný, *České dějiny I/1. Od najstarších dob do smrti knížete Oldřicha* (Praha 1912), pp. 558–563. Gyula Kristó: *Az augsburgi csata* (Budapest 1985), pp. 81–111. *MT I/1*, pp. 689–701.

[75] Novotný, *České dějiny I/1*, pp. 561–563.

[76] Ján Steinhübel, "Svätý Vojtech a Uhorsko," in *Svatý Vojtěch, Čechové a Evropa, Mezinárodní sympozium uspořádané Českou křesťanskou akademií a Historickým ústavem Akademie věd ČR 19.–20. listopadu 1997 v Praze*, ed. Dušan Třeštík, Josef Žemlička (Praha 1998), pp. 124, 129. Steinhübel, Kapitoly, pp. 104–105, 108–112, 133–134, 140–141.

[77] DHA I, ed. Györffy, no. 83, p. 245.

10 The Rise of the Árpáds

Árpád Prince Fajsz did not take part in the wars of 955. The friendly Aba family also certainly avoided the war together with the Árpáds. The power of Gyula I in Transylvania and Ajtony's ancestors in Marosvár also remained untouched. The powerful semi-independent principalities also further remained nearly independent from the main Árpád prince.[78]

With the death of Bulcsú in 955 the title of horka ended, and his principality was divided among several of the Árpáds. Among the small Árpád principalities which in the years 955–997 lay in southern Transdanubia, we know the Somogy Principality. Somogy Prince Zerind *already during the life of Prince Géza, father of Saint Stephen, had a principality*.[79] If his son Koppány aspired after Géza's death for princely power over Hungary, then he and his father Zerind had to belong among the descendants of Árpád.[80] The Somogy Principality, lying between the southern shore of Lake Balaton and the Hungary-Croatia border on the Drava River,[81] took up only a part of Bulcsú's extinct principality. We can assume other Árpád principalities similar to the Somogy Principality on the Zala River, on the upper Rába (later the castle counties of Kolon and Vasvár) and on the territory of the later Pécs diocese (castle counties Tolna, Baranya, Požega and Vukovar).

In addition to warriors from Lehel's Nitria and Bulcsú's south Transdanubia, Súr's soldiers also marched to Germany in 955. If we exclude Nitria and Transdanubia, as well as all non-aligned parts of Hungary, then Árpád's principalities in northern Transdanubia and in the area between the rivers Danube and Tisza, as well as the Marosvár, Transylvania and Eger principalities, then we are only left with Biharia, from which Súr and his fighters could have come.[82] Súr was thus a Kabar prince. The Kabars were, according to the nearly

---

78 *Eratque iste Gyula dux magnus et potens*. Chron. Hung. comp. saec. XIV. II 30, SRH I, p. 290. *In diebus illis erat quidam princeps in urbe Morisena, nomine Acthum, potens valde ... Unde procedebat in multitudine armatorum, regem autem minime reputabat*. Legenda maior S. Gerhardi episcopi 8, SRH II, pp. 489–490.
79 *Erat autem Cupan filius Calvi Zyrind, qui etiam vivente Geycha duce, patre Sancti Stephani regis ducatum tenebat*. Chron. Hung. comp. saec. XIV. II 64, SRH I, p. 313.
80 See chapter 14, note 91.
81 Slavonia, which lay south of the Drava, then belonged to Croatia. Ladislas I connected it to Hungary in 1091. See pp. 469–470.
82 György Györffy looks for Súr's seat on the territory of the Bratislava seat. MT I/1, p. 694. In the Bratislava seat, we know the villages of Hrubý Šúr, Malý Šúr, Valtov Šúr, Veľké Šúrovce and Zemianske Šúrovce. Jenő Házi, *Pozsony vármegye középkori földrajza* (Pozsony 2000), pp. 324–330. The names of these villages, however, don't come from a personal name. The word *šúry* was used for wet, inundated alder forests in long strips under the eastern slopes

contemporary testimony of Constantine Porphyrogenitus, the strongest and most courageous of all the Hungarian tribes. They were the first to attack in battles.[83] Therefore, the non-participation of the Kabars in the great campaign of 955 is unthinkable. The defeat on the Lechfeld was thorough, because the military power of the most aggressive Hungarian tribe was destroyed.

In 955 Bulcsú, Lehel and Súr died, and they left no successors behind them. Southern Transdanubia, Nitria and Biharia remained without princes and most of their soldiers. With the death of Súr and Bulcsú their family lines ended and with them the titles gyula and horka. The Árpáds, who did not take part in this war, preserved their military power, and this was crucial for their ascendancy. The Árpáds ruled all of Transdanubia, Nitria and Biharia and with them acquired a crucial predominance in Hungary. When Taksony's son Géza (in perhaps 967) married Sarolt from Transylvania,[84] the Árpád domain reached all the way to the Transylvania borders. Géza's son Stephen I subjugated Transylvania in 1003[85] and Marosvár in 1028[86] and did so without having to first subjugate Biharia.

11 Nitria after the Death of Prince Lehel

In August 955 one Bohemian army battled against the Magyars at Lechfeld and the other fought against them to the east: *And the Bohemians led another war with them* (= with the Magyars), *in which their king by the name of Lehel was captured, when his army was destroyed.*[87] On the command of victorious

---

of the Little Carpathian Mountains. They were destroyed in the 20th century by land improvement schemes. Only one large *šúr* was protected, near Jur, and thus a general naming of this type of forest remained the present-day nature reserve Jurský Šúr. Jozef Ľudovít Holuby, "Svätojurský šúr na Slovensku," *Věda přírodní* 7 (1926), pp. 112–116. Michal Lukniš et al., *Slovensko. Príroda* (Bratislava 1972), pp. 386, 834–835. Pavel Dvořák, "V mĺkvom náručí šúrov," in Pavel Dvořák, *Odkryté dejiny* (*Predveká Bratislava*) (Bratislava 1978), pp. 136–151. A *šúr* was also in the village lands of Modra and Rača. Evidence of this is in the land names *šúr* in Modra and in Rača. Vladimír Horváth, *Bratislavský topografický lexikon* (Bratislava 1990), p. 288. Darina Lehotská, *Dejiny Modry 1158–1958* (Bratislava 1961), p. 178. Kristó – Makk – Szegfű, *Adatok I*, pp. 75–76.

83 See note 12.
84 See chapter 14, notes 9, 10. Taksony had, aside from Géza, aso a younger son Michael: *Porro Toxun genuit Geycham et Michaelem. Chron. Hung. comp. saec. XIV.* 11 63, SRH I, pp. 311.
85 See chapter 15, notes 15, 16.
86 See chapter 15, note 45.
87 *Otto rex cum Agarenis pugnabat in festivitate s. Laurentii ... Et aliud bellum cum eis gerebatur a Poemanis, ubi comprehensus est rex illorum nomine Lele, extincto exercitu eius. Annales Sangalenses maiores* ad a. 955. Gombos, *Catalogus I*, p. 199. Hynek Bulín, "Počátky

German King Otto I, Lehel, together with Bulcsú and Súr, was hanged on the gallows in Regensburg.[88] Since Lehel was the Nitrian Prince, his death and the destruction of his army weakened Hungarian power in Nitria, which could have strengthened the position of small domestic princes. With the death of Lehel, Nitria temporarily lost a common prince, and its four small principalities (Little Nitria, Váh, Hont and Borsod) ceased to be connected by the rule of a common head prince. The combative Bohemian Prince Boleslaus I took advantage of the weakened Hungarian military power in neighbouring Nitria by intervening into its territory and obtaining two of its small principalities.

Boleslaus connected the small principality, which a document of the Prague bishopric mentions as the *province of Váh*, to Kraków, which belonged to his realm. The Váh Principality covered the northern Váh River region, which includes the Liptov, Orava, Turiec regions and the northern half of the later Trenčín seat. The mentioned road from Kraków through Orava and the Turiec region to Nitra connected it with neighbouring Kraków.[89] The names of the villages called Vážany in Moravia probably date from these times.[90] Just as Břetislav I resettled the Hedčani from Poland to Bohemia in 1039,[91] Boleslaus I or Boleslaus II could have resettled some Vážany residents from the small Váh Principality to Moravia.

Not only did Kraków get a secondary territorial attachment, but Moravia did, too. Vojtech's (Adalbert's) Prague (previously Moravian) diocese reached *up to the river which is called the Váh*. The Váh, however, in no case was the eastern border of Moravia. The *Dagome iudex*, too, names Olomouc (*Alemure*) as the border point of Polish territory, which Mieszko I sometime in the years

---

    česko-veletského přátelství. Dvě kapitoly z dějin vztahů západoslovanských v 10. století," *Vznik a počátky Slovanů* III (1960), pp. 55–58.
88   *Widukindi Rerum gestarum Saxonicarum* III 44, rec. Waitz, pp. 71–73. Novotný, *České dějiny I/1*, pp. 558–563. *MT I/1*, pp. 689–701.
89   *provintiaque, cui Uuag nomen est. DHA I*, ed. Györffy, no. 83, p. 245. Dušan Třeštík doubts the connection of the Váh province with Krakow: *this is evidently about the Váh province tending more (through Olšava gate) to Moravia than to Krakow*. Třeštík, "Veliké město", p. 50. His doubt is baseless. The Váh province covered only the northern Váh regions. It ended at the gorge of the Váh between Považská Bystrica and Púchov. The valley of the Váh south of this gorge, that is the Trenčín Valley, from which the road heading through the Vlársky pass (the Olšava Gate) to neighbouring Moravia, no longer belonged to the Váh. See pp. 352–353. Steinhübel, "Svätý Vojtech a Uhorsko," pp. 125–126, 129–130. Steinhübel, *Kapitoly*, pp. 112–113.
90   Chaloupecký, *Staré Slovensko*, pp. 186–187. Ladislav Hosák, "Moravské a slezské místní jméno jako historický pramen," *Acta Universitatis Palackianae Olomoucensis. Historica* 3 (1962), pp. 152, 153.
91   *Cosmae Pragensis Chronica Boemorum* II 2, ed. Bretholz, pp. 83–84.

989–990 handed over to papal protection,[92] but Olomouc did not lie directly on the border. Just as the southern border of Mieszko's Poland did not go through Olomouc, but north of Olomouc through the Jeseníky Mountains, so not even the eastern border of Moravia reached up to the Váh, but only along the ridge of the White Carpathian Mountains. The Váh was not the border, nor were the rivers Hron, Slaná (Sajó), Maros and Szamos, by which Hungarian Anonymus demarcated the ancient Hungarian principalities, border rivers. The border was up to the watershed which was sometimes formed by the nearby mountains.[93] Svätopluk's realm, according to Cosmas, reached to the north *up to the Oder* and to the east *to the Hron River*.[94] The Oder and the Hron, however, were not the borders of Svätopluk's realm, but flowed through its territory. If the Prague (previously the Moravian) bishopric reached *up to the river which is called the Váh*, then it reached to Nitria, through which the Váh flowed. From the viewpoint of Moravia, the Váh was the dominant river of neighbouring Nitria. The Váh was a large river, which the traveler from Moravia to the Nitrian interior could not avoid and had to laboriously cross. That's why the Váh River was predominant in the minds of Moravians and Bohemians in relation to Nitria, more precisely, in relation to one of its four small principalities.

Hungarian Anonymus wrote that *the country which lies between the Váh and the Hron, from the Danube up to the Morava River, was subdued by one Bohemian prince and he turned it into one principality*. The little principality with its centre in Nitra was defined by the rivers Váh, Hron, Danube and Morava. Its southern border was the Danube and on the north it extended as far as Trenčín.[95] This Little Nitria endured up to the time of Stephen I.[96]

If Vojtech's Prague diocese and thus also the realm of Bohemian Princes Boleslaus I and Boleslaus II reached *up to the river which is called the Váh*, that is up to Little Nitria, then the *prince of the Bohemians*, mentioned by Anonymus, who subjugated this Little Nitria and connected it to his realm, was certainly

---

92   *Darowizna Gniezna*. MPH I, ed. Bielowski, pp. 148–149. Łowmiański, *Początki Polski V*, pp. 607–610. Labuda, *Studia II*, pp. 240–263. Labuda, *Mieszko I*, pp. 177–195. Steinhübel, *Kapitoly*, p. 143.
93   See note 8, see chapter 14, note 149.
94   *Cosmae Pragensis Chronica Boemorum* I 14, ad a. 894, ed. Bretholz, pp. 32–33. MMFH I, p. 199.
95   *Anonymi (P. magistri) Gesta Hungarorum* 33–37, SRH I, pp. 74–80.
96   See pp. 403–406. The fact that Anonymus did not invent the territorial range of Little Nitria is indirectly documented for us by Cosmas. *Cosmae Chronica Bohemorum* I 14 ad a. retholz, pp. 32–33. MMFH I, p. 199. The Hron was not the eastern border of Svätopluk's realm, as is mentioned by Cosmas, and not even the eastern border of the whole of the Nitrian Principality, but only of Little Nitria, which in the time of Hungarian Prince Géza and briefly also his son Stephen was administered by Prince Poznan. See pp. 349–352.

Boleslaus I. This undoubtedly occurred in 955, when he triumphed over Prince Lehel, who up to then ruled in Nitria, captured him and destroyed his military.

The document of the Prague bishopric mentions the Váh twice, first as a province and then as a river. Behind these two different expressions hide two different territories.[97] The Váh province (the northern Váh River region) was subjugated to Kraków and thus to the Kraków bishop. Little Nitria (southwestern Slovakia), through which a part of the central and the entire lower Váh flowed, was claimed by the Moravian bishop. When the Prague bishop took over both dioceses (probably in 986), the territory of both of them fell to the Prague bishop, one via Moravia and the other via Kraków.

[97] Gerard Labuda saw the two different statements about the Váh in the document of the Prague bishopric as one and the same territory. Therefore, he erroneously stretched the Váh province over the whole of western Slovakia and rejected its membership to Krakow. Labuda, *Studia II*, pp. 228–239.

CHAPTER 14

Nitria in the Emerging Árpád State

1   The Road to Preslavets

A trade route which passed from Prague and headed to Praslavets in Bulgaria passed across Hungary. Prague, which grew rich from the long-distance trade, was also visited by merchants from Hungary: *The city of Prague is built from stone and limestone and is the richest country for goods. Russians and Slavs with goods arrive here from Kraków. And from the country of the Turks (l-Atráki = Hungarians) Muslims, Jews and Turks also with goods and trade scales, and they export from them slaves, tin and various pelts.*[1] Preslavets was the goal of wealth merchant caravans from Byzantium, Hungary, Bohemia and Russia: *All wealth is gathered here, from Greek gold, coverings, wines and various fruits from Bohemia then and silver and horses from Hungary and pelts and wax, honey and slaves from Russia.*[2]

The road to Preslavets served not only for long-distance trade, but was also a military route. Magyar units which took part in Bulgaria-Byzantium and Russia-Byzantium wars marched along it. In 965 Emperor Nikephoros II Phokas expelled Bulgarian emissaries who had come to Constantinople for the regular tribute, as a result of which Bulgarian Tsar (emperor) Peter had Byzantine provinces plundered by Hungarian units.[3] The Byzantine emperor requested help from Russian Prince Sviatoslav I of Kiev. In the summer of 968 Sviatoslav defeated the Bulgarians and then conquered a portion of Bulgarian territory, from the Danube delta up to Silistra, and settled in wealthy Preslavets.[4] In 969 Bulgaria broke up into two parts. The Russians battled with Byzantine forces over eastern Bulgaria, with a seat in Preslav, and western Bulgaria, with a seat in Serdika, became independent under rule of the four

---

1 *Ibráhím ibn Ja'kúb* 6, MMFH III, p. 413. Dmitrij Mishin, "Ibrahim ibn-Ya'qub At-Turtushi's account of the Slavs from the middle of the tenth century," in *Annual of medieval studies at the CEU* 1994–1995, edited by Mary Beth L. Davis and Marcell Sebők (Budapest 1996), pp. 184–199.
2 *Latopis Nestora* 34, year 6477 (969), MPH I, ed. Bielowski, p. 609.
3 Ioannes Skylitzes 6, *Az Árpád-kori magyar történet bizánci forrásai*, ed. Moravcsik, p. 86.
4 Ioannes Skylitzes 6, *Az Árpád-kori magyar történet bizánci forrásai*, ed. Moravcsik, p. 86. Lev Diakon, *Istorija* V 1–2, perevod M. M. Kopylenko, stat'ja M. J. Sjuzjumov, komentarij M. J. Sjuzjumov, S. A. Ivanov (Moskva 1988), p. 44. *Latopis Nestora* 32, year 6475 (968), MPH I, ed. Bielowski, p. 607. I. G. Konovalova – V. B. Perchavko, *Drevnjaja Rus i nižneje Podunavje* (Moskva 2000), pp. 53–69.

sons of Count Nicholas, called the Cometopuli.[5] Hungarian forces, which in the spring of 970 came to the aid of Sviatoslav, certainly returned along the mentioned road: *The Russians and their Prince Sviatoslav ... together with the subjugated Bulgarians and joined in among the allies the Pechenegs and Turks* (= Hungarians) *living to the West in Pannonia.*[6] Sviatoslav and his allies crossed the Balkan Mountains, conquered Plovdiv and devastated the whole of Thrace. In a bloody battle near Arcadiopolis (today Lüleburgaz) Sviatoslav, together with his troops of Hungarians and Pechenegs, suffered a heavy defeat.[7] Emperor John I Tzimiskes conquered Preslav in 971, captured Bulgarian Tsar Boris II and ruled over north-eastern part of Bulgaria.[8]

2   Géza and Sarolt

The trade route from Prague to Preslavets passed through Árpád territory from the Bohemian border up to the border of Biharia and could not have gone around the princely seats of Nitra, Esztergom and Bihar. At the Meszes Gates, however, it left Árpád territory and continued through Gyula's Transylvania. The Árpáds wanted as best they could to control the wealth, that is the *silver and horses*, as well as the *slaves, tin and various pelts*, which flowed along this road. Therefore, Taksony married his oldest son Géza (*around 947–950), probably in 967, with Sarolt, the younger daughter of neighbouring Transylvanian Prince Gyula I.[9]

Gyula's daughter was uncommonly beautiful: *He also had a very pretty daughter by the name of Sarolt, about whose beauty the provincial princes had*

---

[5] Panajotov, *Srednovekovna bălgarska istorija*, pp. 119–120.
[6] *Ioannes Skylitzes* 7, *Az Árpád-kori magyar történet bizanci forrásai*, ed. Moravcsik, p. 86.
[7] *Ioannes Skylitzes* 7, *Az Árpád-kori magyar történet bizanci forrásai*, ed. Moravcsik, pp. 86–87.
[8] Panajotov, *Srednovekovna bălgarska istorija*, pp. 120–121.
[9] Vajay, "Großfürst Geysa," pp. 49–50, 67. Géza, *who was now growing old and felt that his bodily end was approaching* (qui cum iam senesceret, resolutionemque sui corporis imminere sentiret) *married off his son*, and in 997 he died *full days* (plenus dierum), that is, in a higher age. *Legenda minor S. Stephani regis* 2, SRH II, p. 394. *Legenda maior S. Stephani regis* 5, SRH II, p. 381. If Taksony was born in 931, as Anonymus writes, then Géza, as the older of the two sons, could have been born sometime in the years 947–950 and lived to 50 or nearly 50 years. *Anonymi (P. magistri) Gesta Hungarorum* 55, SRH I, p. 111. Szabolcs de Vajay places Géza's birth in the years 940–945, which, however, contests the year in which, according to Anonymus, his father was born. Vajay, "Großfürst Geysa," p. 45. In the last years of Taksony's life Géza was already an adult who was capable of marrying and occupying the princely seat. If, after his father's death, perhaps in 971, he became the primary Hungarian prince, he was certainly older than the other then living Árpád, Somogy Prince Zerind. Géza's much older cousin Tormás, who in 948 visited Constantinople, was no longer living at that point.

very long spoken about, until finally Prince Géza ... took Sarolt as his lawful wife.[10] Even Thietmar, Bishop in Merseburg (1009–1018), heard of Géza's beautiful wife and wrote into his chronicle the name which the Hungarian Slavs had given to her: *Beleknegini, this is a pretty lady (pulchra domina) Slavic named (Sclavonicae dicta).*[11] And Thietmar also mentions Sarolt's brother Gyula II under the Slavic name Prokuj (*Procui*).[12]

If Géza married in perhaps 967, then he was already an adult and capable of princely rule. As the aspirant to the Hungarian princely seat, he certainly got a princely grant from his father, because this was the most certain way of securing the Hungarian princely seat for the expected successor.[13] A wedding with a Transylvanian bride indicates to us which of the two Árpád subordinate principalities, whether Biharia or Nitria, Géza's father Taksony granted to him. Biharia lay in the surroundings of Transylvania. Shortly before the wedding with Sarolt, Géza reached adulthood and became the prince of Biharia.[14]

Hungarian Prince Taksony, still before his death, could also assign a princely grant to his younger son Michael (* around 950–955). If Géza got Biharia, then

10 *Chron. Hung. comp. saec. XIV.* II 30, SRH I, p. 291. Perhaps in year 969 the oldest daughter was born to them, who in 985 married Boleslaw the Brave. Vajay, "Großfürst Geysa," pp. 48, 49, 68.

11 *Thietmari Chronicon* IX (VIII) 4, rec. Kurze, p. 241. *Thietmari Chronicon* VIII 4, cur. Trillmich, pp. 444–445. Thietmar also mentions a similar Slavic name of a mountain peak on the property of Margrave Gero: *Fit conventus in Belegori, quod pulcher mons dicitur, in Geronis predio marchionis. Thietmari Chronicon* VI 56 (38), rec. Kurze, p. 167. *Thietmari Chronicon* VI 56, cur. Trillmich, pp. 304–305. The peak *Belegori* is today Belgern, near Torgau, Germany. Jerzy Nalepa, "Biala Góra," in *Słownik starożytności słowiańskich 1* (Wrocław – Warszawa – Kraków 1961), pp. 110–111. Heinrich Kunstmann, "Zwei rätselhafte Namen der frühen Árpádendynastie. Beleknegini und Besprim," *Ungarn-Jahrbuch* 28 (2005–2007), pp. 17–20. László Szekfű has already pointed out the identifying of Sarolt with Beleknegini, though Miklós Halmágyi has doubts about it. László Szekfű: "Sarolta," in Középkori kritikus kérdései, ed. János Horváth, György Székely, (Budapest 1974), pp. 239–251. Miklós Halmágyi, "Beleknegini-Sarolt és társnői. Nőalakok Merseburgi Thietmar krónikájában," Acta Universitatis Szegediensis, Acta Historica 132 (2011), pp. 21–36.

12 See pp. 385–387. Even Géza had two names. Thietmar mentions Géza's other name Deviux. *Thietmari Chronicon* IX (VIII) 4, rec. Kurze, p. 241. *Thietmari Chronicon* VIII 4, cur. Trillmich, pp. 444–445. Károly Cseglédy, "Géza nevünk eredete," *Magyar Nyelv* 52 (1956), pp. 325–333. Róna-Tas, *A honfoglaló magyar nép*, p. 179.

13 In this way Prince Géza at the end of his rule changed the custom, according to which, after the death of a Hungarian prince the oldest living Árpád would be the successor. Perhaps two years before his death he gave the Nitrian Principality to his son Stephen and named him as his successor. Koppány, who was older than Stephen and wanted to claim his right, was unable to obtain superiority over Stephen, who could depend on Nitria. See pp. 341–344.

14 Géza first became an appanaged prince and only after got married, just like his son Stephen did later. See notes 85, 87.

Michael could have claimed Nitria. His father had already assigned Nitria to Michael, because Géza, who later forcibly removed his brother from Nitria, would hardly have left it to him. Since the most significant part of Nitria was from 955 under Přemyslid power, Michael had to be satisfied at the beginning with only part of it and the hope to look to the future to fully apply his claim.

3   The Baptising of Hungary

After Taksony's death († perhaps in 971) Géza inherited the highest rule and settled in Esztergom.[15] His wife Sarolt, just like the wives of subsequent Hungarian kings,[16] chose Veszprém as her seat. In 972 Hungarian Prince Géza turned to Emperor Otto I with a request for missionaries. The emperor had one of the monks, Bruno (Prunwart), from the abbey in St. Gallen ordained as the missionary bishop. Bruno stood at the head of the mission in Passau, which Passau bishop Pilgrim outfitted, and was provided for according to the emperor's wishes. Still in 972 Bruno came to Hungary and baptised Prince Géza, his younger brother and perhaps 5-thousand from among the distinguished Hungarians.[17] Among the first baptised were certainly lesser Árpád princes, among them the Somogy prince, who upon baptism took the name Severinus (Szörény, *Zerind*). We don't know his pagan name.[18]

---

15   Géza had a princely palace built at Esztergom Castle, in which his son Stephen was later born and grew up. *Legenda minor Sancti Stephani regis* 2. *Legenda Sancti Stephani regis ab Hartvico episcopo conscripta* 4, SRH II, pp. 394, 407. Györffy, *ÁMF II*, p. 237. László Zolnay, *A középkori Esztergom* (Budapest 1983), pp. 52–54, 64–74. See note 21.

16   Gutheil, *Az Árpád-kori Veszprém*, pp. 39, 41, 52, 53, 58–75, 86–105, 109–111.

17   Györffy, *István király*, pp. 67–78. MT I/1, pp. 727–732. Györffy, *König Stephan*, pp. 61–76. CDES I, ed. Marsina, no. 44, pp. 41–43.

18   See notes 90, 91. The village Szörénd in the seat Krassó in the years 1323, 1353 and 1363 was mentioned as *Zeurini, Zeurind* and *Zeurend*. Györffy, *ÁMF III*, p. 496. The village Szörény (Szörém) in the Pest seat is mentioned in 1312 as *Zeurem*. György Györffy, *Az Árpád-kori Magyarország történeti földrajza IV* (Budapest 1998), p. 558. Szörény (Szörém) lay in the Pilis seat, mentioned in 1258 as *Zewrem* and 1271 as *Zeurimi*. Györffy, *ÁMF IV*, p. 576. The St. Gerard legend mentions the castle and town of Turnu-Severin (Hungarian Szörény, in today's Romania) on the lower Danube as *Zoren*. *Legenda maior Sancti Gerhardi episcopi* 8, SRH II, p. 490. See chapter 12, note 5. The name of this castle is also mentioned in the Chronicon Pictum in the form *Zeurim* and in various manuscripts as *Zewren, Zewrin, Zeuryn, Sceurim* and *Zeurym*. *Chron. Hung. comp. saec. XIV.* 11 209, SRH I, p. 497. The German written chronicle of Heinrich von Mügeln states *Zebrun, purg Zebrün, zerung* and in other manuscripts also as *zebrin, zebrym, zeuerey, tzewrym, zevrin, sebrin, zeurin, zewrym, zebrin, zebrim, zeuerin* and *zeuereyn*. *Chronicon Henrici de Mügeln* 72, SRH II, p. 220. For other documents on the various forms of the name Severinus in Hungary, see Kristó – Makk – Szekfű, *Adatok I*, pp. 48–49. The name of Koppány's father, Zerind,

The small remnants of Great Moravian and Carolingian Christianity in Hungary at that time obviously endured, testimony of which is the continuity of the patrocinium of St. Emmeram in Nitra from Pribina's times[19] and the remnants of the foundations of the pre-Hungarian (probably Great Moravia) rotunda of St. George in Veszprém. They, however, were not the crucial basis for new Hungarian Christianity. Pilgrim, in a letter to the pope in 973, mentions the plentiful Christians in Géza's Hungary; those, however *were brought here from all ends of the world as captives.*[20]

Just as Magyar-Turkish bilingualism, mentioned by Constantine Porphyrogenitus, once ruled during their stay in Etelköz, in the Carpathian Basin Hungarian-Slavonic bilingualism was expanded, after which some 1300–1600 words of Slavic origin remained in Hungarian;[21] thus, perhaps five-times more than Turkish. The Passau missionaries did not have to struggle with a completely foreign Hungarian and spread the new faith in Hungary in the Slavonic language, which they had long known. Therefore, Passau Bishop Pilgrim deemed Hungary as a Slavic province: *Thus, it happened that soon the whole nation of the Hungarians is willing to accept the holy faith; however, still other Slavic provinces are ready to give themselves to the faith.*[22] The Magyars, who for two generations now had been settled among the Slavs and had accepted baptism together with them, understood their language and also learned the Slavic names of Christian feasts and Slavic religious and ecclesiastical terminology from the Bavarian missionaries.[23]

Undoubtedly, on the occasion of baptism, Hungarian Prince Géza had the Church of St. Stephen the Martyr built and consecrated at his princely seat in Esztergom.[24] Favourable relations for the renovation of the Church of

---

was used in Hungary in the form of the Christian name Severinus. Zerind and his son Koppány were thus Christians, as well as Géza, Michael and Stephen.

19 See pp. 120–124. Mező, *Patrocíniumok*, p. 73. The Romanesque Church of the Most Holy Saviour at Bratislava Castle stood on the foundations of its Great Moravian predecessor, which could have also been consecrated to the Most Holy Saviour. Mező, *Patrocíniumok*, p. 394. Štefanovičová, *Bratislavský hrad*, pp. 57–84.

20 CDES I, ed. Marsina, n. 44, pg. 42.

21 Pavel Bujnák, "Obrátenie Maďarov na vieru kresťanskú," in *Ríša Veľkomoravská*, ed. Stanislav, pp. 377–409. István Kniezsa, *A magyar nyelv szláv jövevényszavai I/1–2* (Budapest 1955).

22 *Factum est ergo, ut pene cuncta Ungrorum natio sit prona ad percipiendum fidem sanctam, sed et alie Sclavorum provintie ad credendum prompte.* CDES I, ed. Marsina, no. 44, p. 42.

23 Bujnák, "Obrátenie Maďarov," pp. 383–395.

24 According to the later testimony of a canonical visitation of the Esztergom Castle provost at the Church of St. Stephen from 1397 *dictam ecclesiam esse fundatam ante tempora Beati regis Stephani, scilicet per dominum Geyzam regem, patrem eiusdem, qui construxit etiam castrum Strigoniense. Monumenta ecclesie Strigoniensis I*, edidit Ferdinandus Knauz

St. Emmeram in Nitra and the Church of the Most Holy Saviour in Bratislava occurred in 955. The construction or renovation of the churches at the most important castles was essential for a country that had accepted baptism.

4   The Veszprém Bishopric

According to Saxon chronicler Thietmar, Prince Géza, even after receiving baptism, sacrificed to the pagan gods and for this was reproached *from his bishop (ab antistite suo)*.[25] His son, Stephen I, immediately after the defeat of Koppány's rebellion in 997, fulfilled the promise that he made to St. Martin, that he would gift to him the consecrated Pannonhalma Abbey, if he helped him to victory. He gave the ecclesiastical tithe from the whole of Somogy County, which he had taken from the authority of the Veszprém bishopric, to Pannonhalma Abbey. Five years later, in 1002, this decision is recorded by a donation document.[26] Thus, the Veszprém bishopric had to originate still before Koppány's rebellion, that is in the period of Prince Géza.[27] Its beginnings may be associated with the arrival of Bruno's mission to Hungary in 972 and with the wave of new bishoprics on the eastern borders of the realm of Otto I that occurred then. The Veszprém bishopric thus originated earlier as a Hungarian

---

(Strigonii 1874), no. 1, p. 30. Antal Pór, "Az Esztergom-várbeli Szent István első vértanuról nevezett prépostság története," in *A Szent-István-társulat tudományos és irodalmi osztályának felolvasó üléseiből* (Budapest 1909), p. 105. Györffy, *ÁMF II*, p. 237. Györffy, *István király*, pp. 68–71, 97. Mező, *Patrocíniumok*, pp. 125–126. Zolnay, *A középkori Esztergom*, pp. 64, 68, 73.

25   *Hic Deo omnipotenti vanisque deorum illusionibus immolans, cum ab antistite suo ob hoc accusaretur, divitem se et ad haec facienda satis potentem affirmavit. Thietmari Chronicon* IX (VIII) 4, rec. Kurze, p. 241. *Thietmari Chronicon* VIII 4, cur. W. Trillmich, pp. 444–445. Géza's *antistisis* was the bishop. If he had been only a common priest, then he hardly could have reproached his prince. And such that it was known about abroad, and Saxon chronicler Thietmar could write about it. According to György Györffy, this was Géza's bishop Bruno, whom he identifies with later first Esztergom Archbishop Domonkos. Györffy, *István király*, p. 76.

26   *supranominati comitatus decimationem ... quod in prediis eorum excresceret, ne parrochiano episcopo pertinere videretur, sed magis abbati eiusdem monasterii ... absque ulla mora subiugarem.... Et ne adhuc aecclesia Sancti Michaelis vacua esse videretur, vel episcopus parrochianus iniurias querimonia sue in collectione decimationis pateretur ...* The mentioned *aecclesia Sancti Michaelis* is the Veszprém bishopric, the episcopal cathedral of which is consecrated to St. Michael. On the edge of the document is a note from the 13th century *contra episcopos Vesprimienses quod nichil de decimis Symigiensibus vel etiam occasione earum debent a nobis exigere*. DHA I, ed. Györffy, no. 5/I, II, pp. 25–41.

27   Kristó, *A vármegyék*, pp. 239–241.

ecclesiastical province, just as the Poznań (Posen) bishopric arose in 968,[28] that is long before the establishment of the Polish ecclesiastical province. The oldest Hungarian and Polish bishopric didn't arise on the site of later archbishoprics, in the princely seats of Esztergom and Gniezno, but in Veszprém and Poznań.

Thanks to the Christians concentrated around St. George, whose rotunda had remained there from the times of Great Moravia,[29] Veszprém could have been very attractive for Géza's wife Sarolt, who was born and raised in the Christian family of Prince Gyula I. Perhaps that was why she selected it as her seat.[30] And it was obviously the energetic Sarolt who stood in the background of Géza's decision to settle the missionary bishop in Veszprém. Therefore, the Veszprém bishopric and later the bishopric's temple were consecrated to the Archangel Michael, who had accompanied and protected Sarolt since her birth.[31] Sarolt wanted to have her own favourite saint in Veszprém, just as Pribina's Bavarian wife had done in Nitra long before.

In 976 the Prague bishopric originated[32] and at this time also the Moravian bishopric.[33] The forward position of the Moravian bishopric in the near vicinity of Hungary gave it the opportunity and sufficient stimulus for similar missionary work as Pilgrim had performed. Just as the Passau bishop concentrated on his missionary interest in Géza's principality in Transdanubia, his Moravian colleague could take an interest in neighbouring Nitria. After the closing of

---

28   Labuda, *Studia nad początkami państwa polskiego II*, pp. 426–474. Stanisław Trawkowski, "Początki kosciola w Polsce za panowania Mieszka I.," in *Polska Mieszka I*. (Poznań 1993), pp. 51–72.

29   See p. 178.

30   See pp. 176–177.

31   St. Michael in Veszprém is also mentioned in the Pannonhalma document. Stephen I, immediately after the defeat of Koppány in 997, excluded from the authority of the Veszprém bishopric, mentioned as *aecclesia Sancti Michaelis*, the tithe from the territory of the Somogy County and gave it to the Pannonhalma Abbey. See note 23. Mező, *Patrocíniumok*, pp. 304–307. Construction on the bishopric cathedral in Veszprém was not initiated by princess Sarolt but by Queen Gisela. Gutheil, *Az Árpád-kori Veszprém*, pp. 58–66. Even though it was Gisela who began construction on the cathedral, it was Sarolt who took care of the consecration of the bishopric and thus also the future Cathedral of the Archangel Michael, and undoubtedly at its origin. Even the cathedrals in Vác and Pécs began being built only approximately 40 and 70 years after the establishment of both bishoprics. See note 237.

32   Novotný, *České dějiny I/1*, pp. 583–588. Dušan Třeštík, "Sv. Vojtěch a formování střední Evropy," in *Svatý Vojtěch, Čechové a Evropa*, ed. Třeštík, Žemlička, pp. 85–88. Steinhübel, *Kapitoly*, pp. 129–130.

33   *Iudicium archiepiscopi Mogutiensis*, MMFH IV, pp. 127–128. Steinhübel, *Kapitoly*, pp. 130–133.

the Nitrian bishopric and its subjugation to clerical organization, the Moravian bishop could then feel authorised to work on renewal of the local Christianity. The Moravian bishopric, however, did not last long, and after its expiry, Prague Bishop Vojtech took over not only its diocese territory[34] but also inherited its missionary activities in Hungary.

Missionary Bishop Hierotheos and his successor Theophylaktos, who were subject to the Constantinople patriarch, had been working in Transylvania since 953.[35] The operating of various Christian missions in Hungary ended only after the establishment of the Hungarian ecclesiastical province, with the Esztergom archbishop at its head.

5 Hungarian-Bulgarian Alliance and Michael's Bulgarian Wife

Géza took the name Stephen at his baptism[36] and his younger brother the name Michael.[37] We don't know what Michael's pagan name was. Géza obviously kept Biharia directly under his direct control, so that he further had a direct connection with Transylvania, from where his wife had come. Transdanubia and Biharia, both under his rule, directly neighboured with all the peripheral Hungarian principalities, and he could thus intervene in them to prevent their becoming independent.

Hungary's anti-Byzantine policy continued after the fall of Preslav through an alliance with the Cometopuli, the sons of Count Nicholas, who at the beginning of 969 tore away his western part from Bulgaria and created a second Bulgarian state. The two oldest brothers, David and Moses, were based in Macedonia, a younger brother Aaron in Sredets and the youngest Samuel in Vidin.[38] On 23 March 973 a dozen of Géza's emissaries came to Quedlinburg together with two Bulgarian emissaries.[39] The common approach and alliance of the Bulgarians and the Hungarians was confirmed by a political wedding.

---

34 Třeštík, "Sv. Vojtěch a formování střední Evropy," p. 88.
35 See note 23. An inscription on a lead Byzantine seal from the 11th century contains a mention about Theophylaktos, bishop of the Turks, that is the Hungarians. Az Árpád-kori magyar történet bizánci forrásai, ed. Moravcsik, p. 253.
36 László Gyula, "Die Anfänge der ungarischen Münzprägung," Annales Universitatis Scientiarum Budapestiniensis de Rolando Eötvös nominatae. Sectio historica IV (Budapest 1962), pp. 39–43.
37 See chapter 13, note 84.
38 Panajotov, Srednovekovna bălgarska istorija, p. 122.
39 Annales Hildesheimenses ad a. 973, contulit cum Codice Parisiensi Georgius Waitz. Scriptores rerum Germanicarum in usum scholarum ex Monumentis Germaniae historicis recusi (Hannoverae 1878), p. 23. Annales Altahenses maiores ad a. 973,

Géza's younger brother at his baptism in 972 took the name Michael, favoured in Bulgaria since 866, when then Bulgarian Khagan (later prince) Boris accepted along with baptism this very name.[40] Bulgarian prince and later Tsar Simeon (895–927) also gave the name Michael to his own oldest son.[41] If Géza's younger brother took the name Michael, which had great weight in Bulgaria, then he fulfilled the wish of his Bulgarian wife, with whom he had married only shortly before, perhaps in 971 or 972. The Bulgarian princess of name unkown to us thus made a likeness of her husband to the first Christian monarch of the Bulgarians.

The Bulgarian origin of Michael's wife is also evident in the names of his two sons: *Michael thus sired Ladislas the Bald and Vazul.*[42] Basilios, originally an imperial title, became a favourite Greek personal name and in the Slavic form Vasilij also with the neighbouring Bulgarians. The name Ladislas (László) is the Hungarian form of the name Vladislav. We know the names Vasilij and Vladislav from the Aaron family. Aaron's son, the only one saved from the Aaron family, was called Ivan Vladislav, and he became the last Tsar (1015–1018) of the Western Bulgarian realm. One of his grandsons was named Vasilij.[43] Therefore, Michael's wife and the mother of both of his sons Ladislas and Vazul could have come from the family of the four brothers of the Cometopuli.[44] Michael's Bulgarian wife, as well as Géza's Sarolt, were already Christians from birth, and they convinced their new pagan husbands rapidly and energetically[45] on the usefulness of baptism.

---

      recognovit Edmundus L. B. ab Oefele. Scriptores rerum Germanicarum in usum scholarum ex Monumentis Germaniae historicis recusi (Hannoverae 1890), p. 11.

40   See chapter 8, note 20.

41   Zlatarski, *Istorija na bălgarskata dăržava I/2*, p. 320. Panajotov, *Srednovekovna bălgarska istorija*, p. 101.

42   *Michael vero genuit Calvum Ladizlaum et Vazul.* Chron. Hung. comp. saec. XIV. II 63, SRH I, p. 311.

43   Moravcsik, *Byzantinoturcica* 2, pp. 89–90. Wincenty Swoboda, "Dynastie bulgarskie," in *Słownik starożytnosci słowiańskich 1*, p. 424–tab. 4, p. 426.

44   Györffy, *István király*, pp. 90–91. Györffy, *König Stephan*, p. 88. MT I/I, p. 740.

45   Bruno of Querfurt and Thietmar recall Sarolt's fiery nature. According to Bruno, Géza's wife *ruled the whole country through her husband's hand and what belonged to her husband she herself ruled alone.* Géza and along with him the whole of Hungary received baptism in 972, that is immediately after he became a prince. It was undoubtedly Sarolt, who was already a Christian, who oversaw the later baptising of Hungary. She was extraordinarily energetic and certainly did not stand in her husband's shadow. According to Bruno *Christianity commenced under her rule.* Bruno z Querfurtu, *Život svatého Vojtěcha. Legenda Nascitur purpureus flos* XXIIIa (Praha 1996), translation Marie Kyralová, pp. 92–93. *Thietmari Chronicon* IX (VIII) 4, rec. Kurze, p. 241. *Thietmari Chronicon* VIII 4, cur. W. Trillmich, pp. 444–445. And Michael's Bulgarian wife, if she came from the brothers of

Among the four brothers of the Cometopuli, it must have been Samuel, based in Vidin, which is very near to Hungary, who had the greatest interest in an alliance and good relations with Hungary. Evidence of this is also the later wedding of his son with Géza's daughter. Obviously, it is this son of Samuel, the son-in-law of Géza, whom after the origin of an independent western Bulgarian state, that is at the latest in January 969 and evidently still before the common appearance of Hungarian and Bulgarian emissaries in Quedlinburg, we can consider as proof of the Hungarian-Bulgarian alliance; that is, before 23 March 973, he negotiated an alliance with Hungary and the wedding of his relative (most likely his sister) with Géza's brother Michael. The alliance with Hungary then reliably covered from the north Aaron and Samuel's offensive in north-eastern Bulgaria in the spring of 976.[46]

The Hungarian-Bulgarian alliance also continued in the subsequent years, because Samuel's son Gabriel Radomir in year 986 (or shortly before then) married Géza's daughter (born around 973). In 988, although she was pregnant, he banished her and married the beautiful Irene, whom he had captured in 986 in Larissa.[47] Samuel was then, after the victory over emperor Basil II at the Ihtiman pass (also called the Gate of Trajan) on 17 August 986,[48] at the peak of power and felt secure. He didn't need Hungarian help. Therefore, his son could banish his Árpád wife in 988.

In 986, thus at the same time that as Gabriel Radomir married a Hungarian princess, Prince Géza married off his oldest daughter (* born around 969) to Boleslaw the Brave, son of Polish Prince Mieszko. Boleslaw's marriage, however, did not last long. In 987 Boleslaw banished Géza's daughter. The son she was expecting from this marriage was born in 987 after her return to Hungary, and she gave him the Slavic name Bezprym.[49]

---

the Cometopuli, thus could have also had a stormy nature, like the mentioned brothers. Her Balkan origin and the turbid family relations in which she grew up certainly influenced her. She, too, was a Christian, like Sarolt. Thus, both had the same interest in the rapid baptising of Hungary. Michael's wife, obviously with the same resolve, took care of the spreading of Christianity above all in Michael's Nitria.

46   Panajotov, *Srednovekovna bălgarska istorija*, p. 122.
47   *Michael pótlásai* 1, 2, *Az Árpád-kori magyar történet bizánci forrásai*, ed. Moravcsik, pp. 97–98. Fehér, *A bolgár egyház kísérletei*, pp. 7–11. Vajay, *Großfürst Geysa*, pp. 46–47, 49, 68.
48   Panajotov, *Srednovekovna bălgarska istorija*, p. 123.
49   *et tunc ab Ungaria sumpsit uxorem, de qua habuit filium, Besprim nomine, similiter expellens eam*. *Thietmari Chronicon* IV 58 (37), rec. Kurze, p. 96. *Thietmari Chronicon* IV 58, cur. Trillmich, pp. 174–175. Wertner, *Az Árpádok családi története*, pp. 33–35. Vajay, *Großfürst Geysa*, pp. 48, 58, 69, 73, 88–89. Jasiński, *Rodowód pierwszych Piastów*, pp. 85–86. Kunstmann, "Zwei rätselhafte Namen," pp. 20–28.

6   The Little Nitria and Váh Principalities Again in Hungarian Nitria

In 987 the Saxons marched against the Slavic Luticians. Polish Prince Mieszko I did not join his Saxon allies,[50] because he began a war against Bohemian Prince Boleslaus II, which lasted up to year 990: *In that time Mieszko and Boleslaus became enemies, and greatly harmed one another.*[51] The war began with a Polish attack on Kraków. Mieszko *immediately took over by means of deceit Kraków Castle, and he had all the Bohemians captured there slaughtered by the sword.*[52] Along with Kraków he took over the whole of the Krakówia (Kraków country),[53] whose administration he handed over to his son, his prospective successor Boleslaw the Brave.[54]

Bohemian chronicler Cosmas dated the loss of Kraków as year 999. According to Cosmas it was Boleslaus III, who *did not hold the conquered border*. Only when Boleslaus II died on 7 February 999 and his son Boleslaus III became the Prince of Bohemia, did Mieszko attack. If Cosmas put into the mouth of the dying Boleslaus II a speech in which he warns his son against grievances which *narrow the borders of this country, which I expanded to the mountains beyond Kraków, which are called the Tatras,*[55] then he could not have dated the loss of Kraków correctly to year 987.[56] His favourite Boleslaus II had to have kept his realm unreduced.

Not only did Kraków have a Bohemian military garrison, which in 987 opposed the attackers, but Nitra did as well. A former notary of Hungarian King Béla III of unknown name, whom for simplicity we call Anonymus, broadly mentions the campaign of three of Árpád's commanders, Sovárd, Kadocsa and Huba, *against the regions of the Bohemians up to Nitra Castle (versus fines*

---

50   *Ann. Hildesheim.* ad a. 987, cont. Waitz, p. 24. *Ann. Altah. maior.* ad a. 987, rec. Oefele, p. 15. *Ann. Qued.* ad a. 987, ed. Pertz, p. 67. *Thietmari Chronicon* IV 18 (12), rec. Kurze, p. 74. *Thietmari Chronicon* IV 18, cur. Trillmich, pg. 134–135.

51   *Thietmari Chronicon* IV 11 (9), rec. Kurze, pp. 70–71. *Thietmari Chronicon* IV 11, cur. Trillmich, pp. 126–127. Łowmiański, *Początki Polski V*, p. 571.

52   *Nam dux Poloniensis Mesco quo non fuit alter dolosior homo mox urbem Kracov abstulit dolo, omnibus quos ibi invenit Boemis extinctis gladio. Cosmae Pragensis Chronica Boemorum* I 34, ed. Bretholz, p. 60.

53   Steinhübel, *Kapitoly*, pp. 140–141.

54   Labuda, *Studia nad początkami państwa polskiego II*, pp. 255–258, 288–293. Labuda, *Mieszko I*, pp. 174–176, 188–190.

55   *Cosmae Pragensis Chronica Boemorum* I 33, ed. Bretholz, pp. 59–60.

56   Gerard Labuda puts the conquering of Krakow by Mieszko I up to year 989. Labuda, *Studia nad początkami państwa polskiego II*, pp. 167–211, 257–260, 264–293, 306–308. Gerard Labuda, *Mieszko II król polski (1025–1034). Czasy przełomu w dziejach państwa polskiego* (Kraków 1992), p. 23. Gerard Labuda, "Czeskie chrześcijaństwo na Śląsku i w Małopolsce w X i XI wieku," in *Chrystianizacja Polski południowej* (Kraków 1994), pp. 76–80, 144–145. Labuda, *Kraków biskupi przed rokiem 1000*, pp. 76–80. Labuda, *Mieszko I*, pp. 172–176.

Boemorum usque ad castrum Nitra). First, they reportedly took the Gemer and Novohrad regions without opposition and met with the first opposition only at the Hron River, where they had to conquer Varád (Tekovský Hrádok). Then *Sovárd (Zuard), Kadocsa (Cadusa) and Huba (Huba)* sent scouts to Nitra, who *saw that the inhabitants of that province, Slavs and Bohemians (Sclavos et Boemos), standing in their way, supported by the prince of the Bohemians. After the death of King Attila, the prince of the Bohemians had taken for himself the land which lies between the Váh and the Hron, from the Danube to the Morava River and made it one principality (unum ducatum).* At that time Zubur was made prince of Nitria by the grace of the prince of the Bohemians. After arrival of the Hungarian military to Nitria a battle broke out by the swollen river. *And when they had battled each other for a long time, the Hungarians killed many of the Bohemians and Slavs (ex Boemis et Sclauis) with arrow shots.* On the fourth day *the Bohemians and all the Nitrian Slavs (Boemi et omnes Nytrienses Sclaui)* had to retreat behind the ramparts of Nitra. Zubur covered the retreat of his soldiers and, wounded by Kadocsa's spear, fell into Hungarian hands. The Hungarians conquered Nitra in a bloody battle and in anger hanged Zubur on a hill, which then got his name. They then subjugated the inhabitants of the entire country. The Hungarians occupied the castles at Šintava, Hlohovec, Trenčín, Beckov and Bana and penetrated up to the Morava River, where they set the Hungarian border. Sovárd, Kadocsa and Huba delivered captives taken from Nitria *(de partibus Nytrie)* to Árpád. Prince Árpád settled them in different places outside of their country, in order to not damage *his faithful, living in the regions of Nitra (in confinio Nitrie).* And he happily made Huba the *Count of Nitra and other castles (comitem Nitriensem et aliorum castrorum).*[57]

Anonymus's detailed description of the conquering of Nitra and Little Nitria by the Hungarian army has only very limited historical value. It is full of anachronisms, invented details and purely literary images, exactly as with the descriptions of conquering of other castles and territories. The image of the castle system in Anonymus's work belongs to the 11th and 12th centuries, and the origin of the Nitrian Principality and the beginning of Zubur's rule immediately after Attila's death[58] and Zubur's end in the time of Árpád are

---

57 *Anonymi (P. magistri) Gesta Hungarorum* 33–37, SRH I, pp. 74–80. Peter Ratkoš puts the Bohemian presence in Nitra mentioned by Anonymus to the times of Bohemian Prince Boleslaus I and Boleslaus II (to years 956–998). Peter Ratkoš, "Podmanenie Slovenska Maďarmi," in *O počiatkoch slovenských dejín*, ed. Peter Ratkoš (Bratislava 1965), p. 153.

58 Equally anachronistically Anonymus writes about the origin of the Bulgarian estate in the area between the Danube and Tisza rivers with the upper Tisza region after the death of Attila. *Anonymi (P. magistri) Gesta Hungarorum* 11, 12, SRH I, pp. 48–51. And Svätopluk according to Simon of Kéza began to rule in Pannonia just 10 years after Attila's death. *Simonis de Keza Gesta Hungarorum* I 23, SRH I, p. 163.

also evident anachronisms. Anonymus didn't know the name of the Prince of Nitra, whom he left to die ignominiously. Therefore, he helped himself to the name of the local dominant feature, as was his habit when writing his work.[59] However, Anonymus did have knowledge of the old nations on Hungarian territory, which in the roughest groundplan corresponded to ancient history. If he wrote that once a long time ago the Carpathian Basin was settled or ruled by the Romans,[60] Huns[61] and Bulgars,[62] and if he also mentioned the rule of a Moravian prince (*Morout* and *Menumorout*) in Biharia,[63] then in the main he was not incorrect. We have significant realms reliably documented on the territory of the later Kingdom of Hungary: Roman, Hun, Bulgarian and Great Moravian. The Bohemian presence in Nitria belongs to this reliable historical context. Thus, Anonymus didn't invent a Bohemian presence in Nitra.

Anonymus mentioned among the conquerers of Nitrian commander Huba and his son Szemere (*prudens Zemera*).[64] Property of the family Szemere in the period of Anonymus (around 1200) lay *along the Žitava up to the Turčok forest*,[65] thus, near Esztergom, where Anonymus worked. Anonymus, as a former Esztergom provost,[66] could very well have known the Šintava Count Szemere mentioned in a royal document from 1177 (*Zemere, comes de Simtei*)[67] and transferred his name and the beginning of his family into an ancient and very glorious past.

The Sovárd line, whose ancestors according to Anonymus took part in the conquering of Nitria, really did live at the beginning of the 10th century. Magyar commander Szalárd (*Salardus*) attacked Italy in 924 with his horsemen brigades.[68] Simon of Kéza by mistake put this Italian campaign of

---

59 Aside from Zubur also the name Laborec, Salan, Gelou. *Anonymi (P. magistri) Gesta Hungarorum* 12, 13, 14, 16, 19, 24, 25, 26, 27, 30, 38, 41, 42, SRH I, pp. 51, 52, 53, 54, 56, 57, 59, 65, 67, 68, 69, 71, 80, 81, 82, 86.

60 *Anonymi (P. magistri) Gesta Hungarorum* 1, 11, 46, 48, 49, SRH I, pp. 35, 36, 48, 94, 97–99.

61 *Anonymi (P. magistri) Gesta Hungarorum* 1, 11, 12, 14, 19, 46, 50, SRH I, pp. 35, 48, 51, 53, 59, 94, 95, 101.

62 *Anonymi (P. magistri) Gesta Hungarorum* 11, 12, 14, 39, 41, 42, SRH I, pp. 48, 51, 53, 54, 81–83, 86.

63 *Anonymi (P. magistri) Gesta Hungarorum* 11, 19, 20, 22, 28, 50–52, SRH I, pp. 49, 59–62, 64, 70, 101–106.

64 Huba, a quo prudens Zemera descendit. *Anonymi (P. magistri) Gesta Hungarorum* 33, SRH I, p. 75.

65 *Anonymi (P. magistri) Gesta Hungarorum* 37, SRH I, p. 80.

66 György Györffy, "Az Árpád-kori magyar krónikák," *Századok* 127 (1993), no. 3–4, p. 392.

67 CDES I, ed. Marsina, no. 93, p. 89. János, Karácsonyi, *A magyar nemzetségek a XIV. század közepéig III* (Budapest 1901), pp. 57–58. Györffy, *Krónikáink*, pp. 112–113.

68 Liudprandi *Antapodosis* III 2, ed. Pertz, p. 74. Györffy, *Krónikáink*, p. 140. The name Salard/Szovárd (*Zuard*) comes from the tribal name *Sábartoi*. Györffy, *Krónikáink*, pp. 31–34, 58, 87, 98.

Sovárd (*Zoard*) into Attila's times and into Hun history[69] in the first part of his chronicle, which chroniclers of the 14th century then used.[70] At the time of Anonymus one of the most significant ancestors of this line of this magnate family, one Vécs, was alive. Since he ranked among the most important magnates in the Esztergom County, Anonymus wrote that his ancestors, the brothers Sovárd and Kadocsa, were cousins of Árpád himself, and he crowned them with many glorious acts. A later genealogical tradition of this family or a Hungarian chronicler who drew from it derived Sovárd's line from Magyar chieftain Lehel.[71] Evidently only because both had operated on the same territory, in Nitria. However, Lehel died only in 955 and therefore could not have been an ancestor of Sovárd, who was already alive in 924. This incorrect genealogical data, which is in conflict with the older genealogical tradition of the Sovárds processed by Anonymus, may come from the 13th century. Its author is either Magister Ákos, or the Szovárds themselves embellished their origin with the figure of chieftain Lehel, and Magister Ákos only took this genealogical mistake into his chronicle.

Two reports on two Hungarian occupations of Nitria, a brief chronicler's and the extensive one of Anonymus, captured two different and rather distant events in terms of time. The first played out in 920 and the second only in 987. But they were so similar that with the passage of a long time they began to partially blend with one another. And so both reports have several common elements: *Messiani et Boemi* = *Sclavi et Boemi*, *in partibus Nittriae* = *de partibus Nytrie*, *Zuard* = *Zuardu*, *Golgocha* = *Colgoucy*.

Hlohovec (*Colgoucy*) was one of those castles on the territory of the Nitrian Principality, which Szovárd, Kadocsa and Huba seized according to Anonymus. Magister Ákos ascribed the expulsion of the *Nitrians and Bohemians* from Hlohovec (*Golgocha*) to Lehel, which in Ákos's period enriched Szovárd's genealogy.

The Bohemian garrison force in Nitra that Anonymus wrote about ended the same as the garrison force in Kraków that Cosmas mentions. When Polish Prince Mieszko took over Kraków, *he had all the Bohemians he captured there slaughtered by the sword*. The Hungarians conquered Nitra, which was defended by *Bohemians and all Slavic Nitrians*, and they *spilled there the blood of many antagonists.*[72] From the reports of Cosmas and Anonymus it follows that Nitra and Kraków were defended by Bohemians and that they lost both

---

69 Simonis de Keza Gesta Hungarorum I 17, SRH I, p. 160.
70 Chron. Hung. comp. saec. XIV. I 17, SRH I, p. 274.
71 Anonymi (P. magistri) Gesta Hungarorum 7, 33–37, 44, 45, SRH I, pp. 41, 74–80, 89–93. Györffy, Krónikaink, pp. 14, 26, 31–34, 58, 87, 97, 98, 101, 105–106, 108, 118–119, 139–143. Chron. Hung. comp. saec. XIV. II 32, SRH I, pp. 291–292. MMFH I, pp. 310–311.
72 Anonymi (P. magistri) Gesta Hungarorum 37, SRH I, p. 78.

of these important castles in bloody battles. This similarity is testimony to the fact that Nitra had a small Bohemian garrison force at the same time in which Kraków had one. These were soldiers placed and held there by Bohemian Princes Boleslaus I and Boleslaus II.

The *Nytrienses Sclaui*, who according to Anonymus defended Nitra together with the Bohemians, are literally the *Nitrian Slavs*, that is Nitrians which are Slavic, that is Slavic Nitrians.[73] The Hungarian chronicler called these Slavs of Nitria *Messiani*.[74]

When Polish Duke Mieszko I attacked and conquered Kraków in 987, Krakowia lost on its southern edge the small Váh Principality, which until then, together with Kraków, belonged to the Přemyslids. Géza's younger brother Michael could have taken part in this Polish-Bohemian war. With the fall of Kraków into Mieszko's hands, Michael could have obtained two small principalities, Nitria and the Váh, which then were again connected with the small Hont and Borsod principalities. And so the Nitrian Principality renewed its territorial integrity under Hungarian rule. Thus, Michael became the first Árpád Prince in Nitria.[75] Prince Michael (*dux Michael*)[76] ruled in Nitria in the years 971/987–perhaps 995.

Biharia and Nitria, which the Árpáds added to their territory in years 955 and 987, respectfully, did not cease to exist and became Árpád subordinate principalities. The two principalities formed a third of Hungary (*tertia pars regni*), with which Hungarian kings up to the early 12th century satisfied the desire to rule of their maturing successors and other members of the Árpád line.[77] They thus had a significant territorial range and bordered one another. This great expansion of Árpád domain is associated with the transferring of their princely seat to the Esztergom seat,[78] which lay approximately in the centre of all the Árpád territories.

---

[73] In August and September 1074 the *Nitrians* (*Nitrienses*) were prepared and commenced defending the main castle of the Nitrian Principality against the deposed Hungarian King Solomon and against his allies, the German King Henry IV, who marched through Nitria with a large army. *Chron. Hung. comp. saec. XIV.* 127–128, *SRH I*, pp. 180–181.

[74] *Simonis de Keza Gesta Hungarorum* II 32, *SRH I*, pp. 166–167. *MMFH I*, pp. 279–280. *Chron. Hung. comp. saec. XIV.* II 32, *SRH I*, pp. 291–292. *MMFH I*, pp. 310–311.

[75] Szabolcs de Vajay wrote about Michael as the Prince of Nitria; however, in line with Anonymus, he defines Nitria only in south-western Slovakia between the Morava and Hron rivers. Vajay, *Großfürst Geysa*, pp. 54–56, 64–66, 68.

[76] See note 169.

[77] *Chron. Hung. comp. saec. XIV.* II 88, *SRH I*, pp. 344–345.

[78] See note 15.

7 Princes Michael and Stephen

Saxon chronicler Thietmar described Géza as a cruel ruler who killed many when in a rage.[79] Even the Saint Stephen legend recalls a bloody act of Hungarian Prince Géza. The legend doesn't mention in more detail the heavy sin, after which Géza remained with *hands stained with human blood* (*manus pollutas humano sanguine*) and because of which he could not carry out his great plans, but his son Stephen did carry them out. The image of the father of the future sainted king could not be blemished. It recalls the *suppression of rebels*, as well as *eradication of idolatrous customs*, which could not be avoided without the spilling of blood, but it understands them as a great credit and not as an unforgiveable fault.[80] It is thus impossible to see in them the origin of Géza's bloody tarnishing.

Very similar words characterize the murder that occurred on 28 September 935 in Stará Boleslav. The victim was Bohemian Prince Wenceslaus, and the murderer was his brother Boleslaus. St. Wenceslaus legends tell of Boleslaus's bloody hands: *He did not recoil to stain his hands even even by fratricide ... He did not recoil at bloodshed, did not shy away from fratricide; the opposite, he impatiently dashed after the torturing of his brother.*[81] Wenceslaus did not raise a weapon in his defence, and he said to Boleslaus: *but let not my hands be besmeared in your blood* (*sed apsit, ut meas in tuo cruore inquinem manus*).[82] Wenceslaus didn't want *to stain his own right hand* (*suam in hostis sanguine polluere dextram*) in enemy (= in his brother's) *blood.*[83] The St. Wencesluas legends don't leave us

---

79   *Huius pater erat Deuvix nomine, admodum crudelis et multos ob subitum furorem suum occidens. Thietmari Chronicon* IX (VIII) 4, rec. Kurze, p. 241. *Thietmari Chronicon* VIII 4, cur. Trillmich, pp. 442–443.

80   *Cumque nimium esset sollicitus de rebellibus domandis et ritibus sacrilegis destruendis ... Non tibi consessum est, quod meditaris, quia manus pollutas humano sanguine gestas. Legenda maior S. Stephani regis* 3, SRH *II*, p. 379. Thietmar reproached Géza's wife for killing a man in anger and had advice for her: That stained hand (*Manus haec polluta*) should rather touch a spindle. *Thietmari Chronicon* IX (VIII) 4, rec. Kurze, p. 241. *Thietmari Chronicon* VIII 4, cur. Trillmich, pp. 444–445.

81   *Legenda "Oportet nos fratres"* 17, 20, in *Život a umučení sv. Václava. Legenda "Oportet nos fratres". Řeč o jeho přenesení*, translation Antonín Stříž (Praha 1929). *Umučení svatého Václava* (*Oportet nos fratres*) 17, 20, *Nejstarší legendy přemyslovských Čech*, ed. Oldřich Králík (Praha 1969), pp. 177, 179.

82   *Vavřince, mnicha sv. Benedikta, Utrpění sv. Václava* 10, translation Josef Truhlář, *Fontes rerum Bohemicarum I. Prameny dějin českých I* (v Praze 1873), p. 177. *Laurentius montecasinský* 10, *Nejstarší legendy přemyslovských Čech*, ed. Králík, p. 97.

83   *Vavřince, mnicha sv. Benedikta, Utrpění sv. Václava* 11, translation Truhlář, FRB *I*, p. 178. *Laurentius montecasinský* 11, *Nejstarší legendy přemyslovských Čech*, ed. Králík, p. 97.

any doubts about what is hidden behind such words. But who did Géza have on his conscience? Was he, too, a fratricide like Boleslaus 60 years earlier?

If Géza wanted to ensure the Hungarian princely seat in Esztergom for his son Stephen, he had to have removed Michael, who after Géza's death, as the oldest living Árpád would have had the first claim to it. He couldn't leave him to rule in Nitria, which was a good starting point for ruling Esztergom and the whole of Géza's territory. As soon as Stephen, perhaps two years before Géza's death, reached the threshold of adulthood, Géza removed his younger brother[84] and handed over rule in Nitra to his perhaps 16-year-old son.[85] Only then could Géza call a diet, which consented to Stephen's succession: *His father called the magnates of Hungary (Ungarie primatibus) with retinue status (cum ordine sequenti) and according to the decision of a general diet (per*

---

84   That's why in the battles over the Hungarian princely seat after Géza's death and with other events no one ever mentions Michael.

85   According to the Hungarian chroniclers, Géza's son Stephen was born in the year *nongentesimo sexagesimo nono*, that is 969. *Chron. Hung. comp. saec. XIV.* II 63, SRH I, p. 312. According to Simon of Kéza, he was born in 967. *Simonis de Keza Gesta Hungarorum* II 43, SRH I, p. 172. In 997 he thus began to rule as a 28- to 30-year-old. Stephen I himself in his deed of donation for the Pannonhalma Abbey in 1002, however, mentions that he had to take up accession to his father's seat as a boy (*in puericia mea*) to face a rebellion. DHA I, ed. Györffy, no. 5/II, p. 39. Stephen's young age upon accession to the Hungarian princely seat is emphasized by all three Saint Stephen legends, and even Hungarian chroniclers: *qui transvadata pueritia, postquam primum gradum adolescentie transcedit ... Regno denique Pannonico beati iuvenis nutu adtendente. Legenda maior S. Stephani regis* 5, SRH II, p. 381. *Stephanus adhuc puer ... in regni solium laudabiliter provectus ... pueritie annis floreret. Legenda minor S. Stephani regis* 2, SRH II, p. 394. *Stephanus adhuc adolescens ... in patris solium laudabiliter provectus ... adolescentie annis floreret. Legenda S. Stephani regis ab Hartvico episcopo conscripta* 5, SRH II, p. 407. *Stephanus ... in adolescentia sua contra Cupan ducem ... gessit bellum gloriosum. Chron. Hung. comp. saec. XIV.* II 64, SRH I, pp. 312–313. Later Polish chroniclers are perhaps closer to the truth, when they write about the birth of King Stephen occurring in 975. Szabolcs de Vajay also leans towards this year. Vajay, *Großfürst Geysa*, pp. 47–49, 68, 76–77. Even the age of 22 years, however, seems high for a boy or immature youth. Therefore, we may together with György Györffy shift Stephen's birth up to year 980. György Györffy, "Der Aufstand von Koppány," *Studia Turcica* (1971), pp. 203–204. Györffy, *István király*, pp. 112, 114. Györffy, *König Stephan*, pp. 94, 96. MT I/1, pp. 745, 747. Therefore, none of the known Hungarian chronicles contain the correct year of Stephen's birth; the mistaken year of birth could have already been preserved in the Gesta Ungarorum vetera from the time of King Coloman. Their author probably mistakenly wrote *nongentesimo sexagesimo nono* in place of the correct year *nongentesimo septuagesimo nono* or DCCCCLXIX instead of the correct DCCCCLXXIX. Stephen was most probably born in 979. Nándor Knauz has already addressed this opinion. MES I, ed. Knauz, no. 1, 2, pp. 30–32.

communis consilium colloquii) *determined that after him his son Stephen will rule the people, and for confirmation of this he requested an oath from each of them.*[86] Shortly after, in 996, Stephen married 10-year-old Gisela, the daughter of Bavarian Duke Henry II, whom he brought to his princely court in Nitra.[87]

8 Koppány's Rebellion

Stephen's relationship to Nitria is clear from the events of 997. In that year his father Géza died.[88] Stephen, who until then was based in Nitra, certainly was by the side of his dying father in Esztergom. He came not only to accompany him on his final journey but also prepared to occupy the Esztergom princely seat, according to his father's will. Hardly had the old prince taken his last breath, however, when his son was surprised by a rebellion of Somogy Prince Koppány. The principality that Koppány inherited from his father Zerind was a large one. It covered the territory of the later Somogy County, which reached from Lake Balaton to the Drava River. Other Transdanubian princes and many pagans also rebelled against Stephen; however: *The pagan people* (plebs gentilis), *refusing to kneel under the yoke of the Christian faith, tried with their princes* (cum principibus suis) *to free themselves from its dominion.*[89] A Hungarian chronicler wrote: *Saint King Stephen once led, a long time ago in his youth, a glorious war against Koppány, a courageous and powerful prince. Koppány, however, was the son of Zerind the Bald* (Cupan filius Calvi Zyrind), *who also after the life of Prince Géza, the father of Saint King Stephen, held the principality* (ducatum tenebat). *When, however, Prince Géza died, Koppány wanted to shackle the mother of Saint King Stephen by incestuous marriage to himself, kill Saint Stephen and*

---

86   *Legenda maior S. Stephani regis* 5, SRH II, p. 381.
87   Györffy, *István király*, pp. 115–116. Györffy, *König Stephan*, p. 95. MT I/1, pp. 746–749. Just as Géza married as the Biharian Prince as roughly an 18-year-old, his son Stephen married as the Nitrian Prince as a 16- or 17-year-old. Just as Zoltán in 947 sent his 16-year-old son Taksony to Italy with a military campaign (see chapter 13, note 72), so Géza made his 16-year-old son Stephen the Prince of Nitria. This step was to ensure for both of them succession after their father. Only Stephen was successful. Taksony had to back away after his father's death before the authorised claim of his older cousin Fajsz and wait for his opportunity only after Fajsz's death.
88   *Legenda maior S. Stephani regis* 5, SRH II, p. 381. *Legenda S. Stephani regis ab Hartvico episcopo conscripta* 4, SRH II, p. 407. Vajay, "Großfürst Geysa," pp. 45, 67, 72.
89   *Legenda maior S. Stephani regis* 6, SRH II, p. 381. *Legenda S. Stephani regis ab Hartvico episcopo conscripta* 6, SRH II, p. 408.

subjugate his principality under his own power. He was the Prince of Somogy (dux Symigiensis).[90]

In order for Koppány's claim to the Hungarian princely seat to be authorised, he must have been of the Árpád line.[91] At the same time he had to be in close blood relation with Stephen's mother Sarolt, because the chronicler accused him of an attempt at an incestuous marriage. What was the family relationship of Koppány to Sarolt? Written sources offer us only one possibility. Koppány's father Zerind must have had as his wife Sarolt's older sister Karold, whom Anonymus mentions.[92] Koppány was thus Sarolt's nephew. The church could label a marriage with a mother's sister on the basis of a Biblical prohibition[93] as incestuous.

Koppány and his followers didn't wait until Stephen peacefully took his father's princely seat in Esztergom. They immediately *took up arms against him. They then began to devastate his castles, plunder his court, haul away property, kill servants and silence the others, and laugh at the* (future) *king*.[94] Koppány wanted to obtain Sarolt; thus, he had to conquer her seat at Veszprém Castle. The defence of Veszprém held off the rebels and thus allowed Stephen to gather his forces. Stephen called his magnates (*proceribus suis*) to the princely court in Esztergom and *in the presence of princes, namely Poznan, Hont, Ort (astantibus ducibus, videlicet Poznano, Cuntio, Orzio), also Lord Dominik the* (future) *archbishop*, he asked for the help of St. Martin and promised that he will gift to

---

90 Chron. Hung. comp. saec. XIV. 11 64, SRH I, pp. 312–313. György Szabados, *Magyar államalapítások a IX–XI. században. Előtanulmány a korai magyar állam történelmének* fordulópontjairól (Szeged 2011), pp. 240–243.

91 Koppány had to be not only an Árpád but was also older than his relative Stephen (see note 85). Only thus could he obtain the support of other princes and seriously threaten Stephen's succession. The malice of both Árpád princes could have had a longer family tradition. If in 947 Fajsz became the main Hungarian prince and not Taksony, despite the fact that Taksony in the last years of his father's life was already performing the authority of the highest prince, and if after Fajsz's death no one from his family became the main prince, but the competitive Taksony instead, then we have before us a rivalry of two Árpád branches, which could have climaxed with Koppány's rebellion against Stephen. Koppány's father Zerind could be the son of former Hungarian Prince Fajsz or his younger brother Tas. If after the extinction of Bulcsú's principality, Zerind got the part of its territory with its centre in Somogy, and formerly Fajsz's principality, then he certainly was not Fajsz's primary heir. Zerind's son Koppány, however, in 997 ended up in the rebellion of the oldest living Árpád and just as once his grandfather or great-uncle Fajsz claimed his right. For varying opinions about Koppány's Árpád origin, see Szabados, *Magyar államalapítások*, pp. 243–264.

92 *Geula genuit duas filias, quarum una vocabatur Caroldu et altera Saroltu. Anonymi (P. magistri) Gesta Hungarorum* 27, SRH I, p. 69.

93 Leviticus 18, 13.

94 *Legenda minor S. Stephani regis* 3, SRH II, p. 395.

him a consecrated abbey on the Pannonian hill (Pannonhalma).[95] The fortified military camp where Stephen's army assembled lay not far from Esztergom, on the lower Hron, in Bíňa,[96] on the safe territory of the Nitrian Principality. Stephen, certainly before the eyes of his advancing army, *was near the Hron River (ad amnem Goron) for the first time girded with a sword*; more precisely, these were *Hont and Poznan, who according to German custom put the sword on* (the future) *Saint King Stephen at the Hron River (in flumine Goron)*. Stephen immediately afterwards set both princes as his own bodyguards and decarled Swabian knight Vencelin as the commander of the whole of his army.[97]

Poznan and Hont put the belt on young Stephen with the sword, not, however, *according to German custom*, as the chronicler wrote. Poznan certainly and Hont probably were not German knights;[98] therefore, they could not have introduced a German custom into Hungary. And furthermore, since there was no such a custom even in Germany itself.[99] Prince Hont was settled in Castle

---

95 DHA I, ed. Györffy, no. 5/II, pp. 39–40.
96 Alojz Habovštiak, "K otázke datovania hradiska v Bíni," *Slovenská archeológia* 14 (1966), no. 2, pp. 439–486. *Významné slovanské náleziská na Slovensku*, ed. Chropovský, pp. 21–25. *Pramene I/1*, ed. Bialeková, pp. 243–246. Turčan et al., *Archeologické pamiatky*, pp. 88–93. Turčan, *Veľkomoravské hradiská*, pp. 10–15.
97 *Chron. Hung. comp. saec. XIV.* 11, 40, 41, 64, SRH I, pp. 297, 313–314. *Legenda minor S. Stephani regis* 3, SRH II, p. 395. Györffy, "Der Aufstand von Koppány," pp. 175–211. Györffy, *István király*, pp. 116–121. Györffy, *König Stephan*, pp. 99–104. MT I/1, pp. 748–753.
98 Testimony to this is the number of Slavic name in families of people in the Hont-Poznan line. Ján Lukačka, *Formovanie vyššej šľachty na západnom Slovensku* (Bratislava 2002), pp. 22, 30–32. See notes 126, 148.
99 György Györffy considers the putting of the sword on Stephen in the Hron River by Hont and Poznan as a later addition of Magister Ákos in the 13th century. According to Györffy Stephen did not camp by the Hron but everything played out in Esztergom. See note 97. László Veszprémy, relying on Zoltán Tóth, showed that putting the sword on a German king, duke or prince could not be done by his vassal, as Stephen was belted in 997 according to the Hungarian chronicler, and we don't have any record of this ceremony in Germany in the period from 936–1065. He therefore considers the putting of the sword on Stephen according to German custom as a late insertion into the chronicler's text, which is not based on truth. László Veszprémy, "Szent István felövezéséről," *Hadtörténelmi Közlemények* 102 (1989), no. 1, pp. 3–13. Magister Ákos supplemented the text of the old Gesta Hungarorum from the time of Coloman under the rule of Stephen V (1270–1272) with chapters on the old Magyar commanders, on the origin of the oldest Magyar noble lines, and modified and supplemented their contents and added them in the period from 1162–1272. See p. 169. Magister Ákos did not acknowledge even one noble line in Hungary as being of domestic Slavic origin. In his opinion Poznan and Hont had the same origin as Vencelin, and the Ják line came from him, that is it was Bavarian: *Descendit quoque de Bauaria Vecellinus videlicet de Wazunburg ... Ex istis Jako nascitur principium et origo. Adierunt etiam istis diebus Hunt et Paznan, qui Sanctum Stephanum regem in flumine Goron gladio Theutonico more accinxerunt. Istorum namque generatio ab istis nominibus distare non videtur ... Qui quidem temporis in processu Vngaris per contractus matrimoniorum*

Hont.[100] If he had come to Nitria as a foreigner, then he would certainly have adopted customs valid in Nitria. And even if not, the applying of a foreign custom would hardly have convinced Poznan and Stephen, who were not foreigners. Stephen had his sword put on by two small princes from Nitria according to an old Slavic custom valid in Nitria as early as in the Great Moravia period, when the military belt (*pojasъ*) was the sign of warriors, and members of the retinue and magnates wore it imitating the prince.[101] Stephen was 17 or 18 years old at that time[102] and was heading into open war for the first time in his life. This was not done without a ceremonial first putting on of the sword (*primitus accintus est gladio*). Vencelin and Ort, who were not at home in Nitria, could not perform this ceremony.

Stephen marched against the rebels, who were then besieging Veszprém. In a battle that took place between Veszprém and Várpalota Stephen's military triumphed. Koppány fell in combat with Vencelin. Stephen ordered the quartering of Koppány's dead body and hung the pieces on the gates of Esztergom, Veszprém and Győr and sent one part all the way up to Transylvania,[103] that is to Gyulafehérvár (Alba Iulia), the seat of Transylvanian Prince Gyula I. He then took up his inheritance after his father and left the Nitrian Principality unoccupied. He abolished the Somogy principality and transformed it into a castle county, which he put into the ecclesiastical administration of the Pannonhalma Abbey.[104] Stephen undoubtedly appointed Vencelin, the leader of his military and main victor over Koppány, as the first Count of Somogy County.[105]

---

sunt immixti. Chron. Hung. comp. saec. XIV. II 40, 41, SRH I, pp. 312–313. Simon of Kéza made two brothers from them who came from Swabia: *Post haec venit Hunt et Pazman, duo fratres carnales milites coridati orti de Svevia. Simonis de Keza Gesta Hungarorum. De nobilibus advenis*, SRH I, pp. 188–189. Magister Ákos invented not only the German origin of Poznan and Hont, which was wiped away only by the mixed marriages of them and their descendants, but it was certainly he who first labelled Stephen's girding by the sword as *Theutonico more*, or a German custom.

100   See note 145.
101   Lubomír E. Havlík, "Velká Morava v kontextu evropských a obecných dějin," in Poulík, – Chropovský, et al., *Velká Morava a počátky československé státnosti*, p. 201. Petr Sommer, "Duchovní svět raně středověké české laické společnosti," in *Svatý Vojtěch, Čechové a Evropa*, ed. Třeštík, Žemlička, pp. 144–145.
102   See note 85.
103   See note 97. Szabados, *Magyar államalapítások*, pp. 264–279.
104   A Pannonhalma document from year 1002 already mentions Somogy County: *comitatu qoudam nomine Sumigiense*. DHA I, ed. Györffy, no. 5/II, p. 39. Kristó, *A vármegyek*, pp. 254–260. Kristó, "Néhány vármegye kialakulásának kérdéséhez," pp. 470–473. Attila Zsoldos, "Somogy megye kialakulásáról," in *Szent István és az államalapítás*, ed. László Veszprémy (Budapest 2002), pp. 431–439.
105   A Hungarian chronicler mentions Vencelin's title as count: *Welinus comes. Chron. Hung. comp. saec. XIV.* II. 64, SRH I, p. 313, Vencelin, victor over Somogy Prince Koppány, could have been only the Somogy count. Perhaps 30 years later Stephen sent his army, then led

9   The First Castle County in Transdanubia

The oldest castle counties – Visegrád, Fejér (Székesfehérvár), Veszprém[106] and Győr[107] – originated in the central part of Árpád's domain in north-eastern

---

by his nephew Csanád, against the Marosvár Prince Ajtony. Ajtony suffered defeat and fell in battle. Stephen transformed Ajtony's principality into a castle county and named leader of the victorious royal army Csanád as its first count. See chapter 15, note 45. He did the same after the defeat of other disobedient princes Gyula II and Zombor in southern and northern Transylvania in 1003. See chapter 15, notes 13, 14, 15, 16, 17, 18.

106   DHA I, ed. Györffy, no. 8, pp. 49–53. Kristó, *A vármegyék*, pp. 239–247, 251–254. Kristó, "Néhány vármegye kialakulásának kérdéséhez," pp. 477–483. Györffy, *ÁMF II*, pp. 321–344, 363–365. Györffy, *ÁMF IV*, pp. 583–593, 705–706. Attila Zsoldos, "Somogy és Visegrád megye korai története, valamint a 'várelemek spontán expanziója'," in *Szent István és az államalapítás*, ed. Veszprémy, pp. 471–477. The first known Fejér (Székesfehérvár) count was Thomas, mentioned in 1108: *Thomas Albensis comes*. DHA I, ed. Györffy, no. 130, p. 357. The first known Veszprém count was Tomaj, mentioned in 1037. DHA I, ed. Györffy, no. 26, p. 119. CDES I, ed. Marsina, no. 52, p. 50. In 1277 Visegrád count Dominic is mentioned: *Dominici comitis de Wysagrad*. *Codex diplom. Arpadianus continuatus. Árpádkori új okmánytár IX*, edidit Gustav Wenzel (Pest 1871), no. 129, p. 189. Castle Veszprém has a name derived from the Slavic personal name Bezpriem. Stanislav, *Slovenský juh v stredoveku I*, pp. 74–75. Stanislav, *Slovenský juh v stredoveku II*, pp. 569–571. Castle Veszprém already bore this name in 997, when Koppány besieged it: *urbem, que vulgo Bresprem vocatur obsederant*. And when after his defeat a part of his dismantled body hung at its gate: *Ipsum vero Cupan Beatus Stephanus in quatuor partes fecit mactari: primam partem misit in portam Strigoniensem, secundam in Vespriniensem ... Legenda minor S. Stephani regis* 3, SRH II, 395. *Chron. Hung. comp. saec. XIV*. II 64, SRH I, pp. 313–314. Already then this was the seat of the oldest Hungarian bishopric and one of the oldest castle counties. See note 108. Stephen's nephew Bezprim, born in 987, thus could not have been the first Veszprém count, by which Veszprém would have taken its name, as György Györffy thought. Györffy, "A magyar nemzet ségtől a vármegyéig," p. 589. Györffy, *István király*, pp. 88, 176, 231, 283. György Györffy, "Kontakty Polski i Węgier w dobie tworzenia sie obu państw," *Kwartalnik Historiczny* 95 (1988), no. 4. pp. 8–9. MT I/1, pp. 807–808. For criticism of Györffy's opinion on this subject, see also Vajay, "Großfürst Geysa," pp. 88–89. Kristó, *A vármegyék*, pp. 240–241.

107   We know the first known Győr count Kornel from year 1177: *Cornelius comes Geuriensis*. Györffy, *ÁMF II*, p. 590. Castle Győr had to be the seat of a castle county already in August 1009. Then King Stephen met with a papal nuntius *in civitate Jauriana*, so that there with his participation as well as the presence of Hungarian bishops, administrators and other important honoraries he could decide on the establishing of other Hungarian bishoprics, among them also certainly the Győr bishopric. DHA I, ed. Györffy, no. 9/I, pp. 54–58. Győr was certainly a castle county from 997, when one part of the torn body of Koppány was hung from its gate: *Ipsum vero Cupan Beatus Stephanus in quatuor partes fecit mactari: primam partem misit in portam Strigoniensem, secundam in Vespriniensem, tertiam in Iauriensem, quartam autem in Erdelw. Chron. Hung. comp. saec. XIV*. II 64, SRH I, pp. 313–314. Stephen hung pieces of him at the most important castles, two of which were princely seats (Esztergom, Gyulafehérvár) and all four (that is Veszprém and Győr) the seats of castle counties. All four castles became bishopric seats. Kristó, *A vármegék*, pp. 262–267. Györffy, *ÁMF II*, pp. 563–576, 589–600.

Transdanubia perhaps still under the rule of Prince Géza.[108] In 997 Somogy became a castle county and together with it all of the Transdanubia principality, which had joined in Koppány's rebellion. If Koppány and his allies penetrated up to Veszprém and forced Stephen to pull back into Slovakia and there assemble his army, then they ruled the larger portion of Transdanubia. On this rebel territory Stephen immediately after his victory organized in 997, in addition to Somogy County, Kolon County, mentioned in a document for the Veszprém bishopric from 1009,[109] and Tolna, Baranya, Požega and Vukovar counties, which in August 1009 he assigned to the Pécs bishopric.[110] Stephen I certainly did not leave out from this reorganization even the remnant of Transdanubia on the western borders of Hungary, important for defence of the state. He established there the Moson,[111] Sopron[112] and Vasvár counties,[113] which together with the older Győr County he assigned in 1009 to the Győr bishopric.[114]

---

108 At the latest from the baptism of Géza and his family in 972 we can consider Hungary as a state like neighbouring Bohemia, Poland and the extinct Great Moravia from the baptism of the Přemyslids (perhaps in 883), the Piasts (in 966) and the Mojmírs (in 831). Géza's immediate domain in north-eastern Transdanubia with the seat in Esztergom already had a state organization, similarly as central Bohemia with Prague in the period of the oldest Přemyslids and the principality of the Poles with the castles Hniezdno and Poznan under the rule of Mieszko I. Stephen I installed this organization in the whole of Hungary, just as Boleslaus I in all of Bohemia. Jiří Sláma, "K počátkům hradské organizace v Čechách," in *Typologie raně feudálních slovanských států*, pp. 175–190. Jiří Sláma, *Střední Čechy v raném středověku III. Archeologie a počátky přemyslovského státu* (Praha 1988). Třeštík, *Počátky*, pp. 437–438. Josef Žemlička, *Čechy v době knížecí (1034–1198)* (Praha 1997), pp. 35–37. Henryk Łowmiański, *Początki Polski V* (Warszawa 1973), pp. 441–621. Géza still called a general diet (see note 86), but he was not dependent on it. Decisions were made on his will, as the Saint Stephen legends and Thietmar recall.

109 *DHA I*, ed. Györffy, no. 8, p. 52. József Holub, *Zala megye története a középkorban I* (Pécs 1929). Kristó, *A vármegyék*, pp. 247–251. Kristó, "Nehány vármegye kialakulásának kérdéséhez," pp. 483–484.

110 *DHA I*, ed. Györffy, no. 9, p. 58. Kristó, *A vármegyék*, pp. 283–305. Kristó, "Nehány vármegye kialakulásának kérdéséhez," pp. 476–477. Györffy, *ÁMF I*, pp. 247–268, 279–281. Fedeles – Koszta, *Pécs*, pp. 39–41.

111 In 1199 *Poth comite de Musuni* is mentioned. *Codex diplomaticus patrius hungaricus. Hazai okmánytár II*, kiadják Imre Nagy, Iván Páur, Károly Ráth, Dezső Véghely (Győrött 1865), no. 1, p. 2. Kristó, *A vármegyék*, pp. 267–268. Györffy, *ÁMF IV*, pp. 133–142, 160–168.

112 In 1071, at the siege of Belgrade by Hungarian King Solomon, the first known Sopron count, called John, battled with his county army: *super agmina Suproniensium, quorum rector erat Ian nomine. Chron. Hung. comp. saec. XIV.* II. 105, p. 371. Kristó, *A vármegyék*, pp. 268–273, 276–280.

113 In 1108 this was *Vgudi Vvasuariensis comes. DHA I*, ed. Györffy, no. 130, p. 357. Kristó, *A vármegyék*, pp. 273–283.

114 Ortvay, *MEF I*, pp. 313–323. See pp. 389–390.

If Stephen I in 1009 divided the territory of Transdanubia among three dioceses, then he certainly did so justly, giving the three the same number of castle counties. If the Veszprém diocese got 4 counties,[115] then the neighbouring Győr and Pécs dioceses each got 4 as well. Thus, Pécs diocese from 1009 had the counties Baranya, Tolna, Vukovar and Požega,[116] and the Győr diocese had counties Győr, Moson, Sopron and Vasvár. Episcopal authority over Somogy County belonged from 997 to Pannonhalma Abbey. At the end of the 10th century, there were 13 castle counties in Transdanubia.

In 997 the custom of securing a successor to the throne by granting him a principality proved to be a good one. The Nitrian Principality gave Stephen the whip hand over the rebels. As the Prince of Nitria he was stronger than any antagonist or insurgent, because not one, however strong and significant the antagonist's subordinate and incoming Hungarian prince, had available such a large and important principality as was then Nitria.

10   Small Principalities

Géza's principality in Transdanubia, as well as Michael's, later briefly Stephen's Nitrian Principality, were made up of several smaller principalities. According to Hungarian chroniclers, in Géza's time, in addition to the Árpád princes (primary and subordinate), there lived in Hungary also smaller princes (*provinciales duces*).[117] Koppány, Poznan, Hont, Ort, Gyula, Zombor, Ajtony, Samuel Aba and others were small princes, more or less, or only very loosely subjugated to Árpád princes Géza and Stephen (earlier Michael). Whether this was the main Árpád prince, seated in Esztergom, or an appanaged small prince, the Hungarian chroniclers and older documents label them the same, as *dux*. Great Moravia also had such a two-level princely subordination. The Přemyslid prince also had several smaller Bohemian princes beneath him.[118]

---

115   DHA I, ed. Györffy, no. 8, p. 52.
116   Gyula Kristó assumes that the Baranya castle county at the time of origin of the Pécs bishopric reached to the south all the way to the Sava, and that castle counties Požega and Vukovar were separated from this later. Kristó, *A vármegyek*, pp. 294–305. If the Pécs diocese had 4 castle counties from year 1009, then not only county Baranya and Tolna, but also Vukovar and Požega must have already existed. Anonymus recalls Požega and Vukovar castles (*castrum Posaga et castrum Vlcou*) together with Zagreb and in a completely different place than Baranya (*castrum Borona*). Anonymi (*P. magistri*) Gesta Hungarorum 43, 47, SRH I, pp. 87–88, 96.
117   Chron. Hung. comp. saec. XIV. II 30, SRH I, p. 291.
118   Sláma, "K počátkům hradské organizace v Čechách," pp. 182–186. Třeštík, *Počátky*, pp. 350–351. Lysý, "Druhostupňové kniežatá," pp. 123–127.

Poznan's principality and Hont's principality, lying in Stephen's Nitria, and Ort's principality, the location of which we are still trying to determine, were similar to Koppány's in Transdanubia or Aba's under the Matra, Gyula's and Zombor's in Transylvania or Ajtony's in lower Maros. Koppány was obviously only one of several small Árpád princes on the territory of Géza's principality. Árpád's great-grandsons and great-great grandsons with their offspring had to have the same territorial share as Koppány, who was one of them. Therefore, in addition to the small Somogy Principality, other small principalities subjugated to the main Árpád principality lay in Transdanubia and in the area between the Danube and the Tisza rivers. In 997 some of them took the side of the rebels.

Kalocsa and Vác were also seats of small principalities and later castle counties; therefore, the bishoprics which Stephen I later established there,[119] like other bishoprics had to rest on the authority of the king (Esztergom), a prince (Bihar) or an important count (Esztergom, Bihar, Veszprém, Győr, Vác), sometimes also a relative or near-relative with King Stephen (Eger, Gyulafehérvár, Csanád).[120]

The entire territory of the later Vác diocese, which was bordered on the west by the Danube, on the east by the middle and lower flow of the Zagyva and on the north by the ridge of the Cserhát Mountains, had to belong to the Vác Principality.[121] The southern part of the area between the Danube and the Tisza rivers, where the later Kalocsa diocese was later situated,[122] belonged to the principality of Kalocsa. We can also look for another principality or other principalities in the area between the Kalocsa and Somogy principalities, that is on the territory of the later Pécs diocese.

Princes Taksony and Géza had in their immediate power only that part of Transdanubia which was defined by the castles at Esztergom, Veszprém and Győr, lying on its edges. He hung three parts of Koppány's quartered body in 997 as a threat to neighbouring principalities, whose territory began not far from their ramparts. Stephen sent the fourth part of Koppány's body all the way to Transylvania, thus the most distant end of Hungary, by which he clearly expressed his claim to the entire country.

---

119 See notes 236, 237, see chapter 13, note 60.
120 See notes 232, 233, 235, 241, see chapter 15, notes 24, 32, 37, 46, 49, 53.
121 Ortvay, *MEF I*, pp. 106–113. Károly Emmanuel Csáky, *A váczi egyházmegye történeti névtára I* (Váczon 1915), pp. 7–9, 111–212.
122 Ortvay, *MEF I*, pp. 336–337.

11 Little Nitria

When Stephen made the promise to St. Martin in the presence of the three princes and the future Esztergom archbishop, the first in order named and thus the most important among them was Prince Poznan. According to the position of the oldest Poznan properties,[123] we have to look for Poznan's principality in south-western Slovakia. The whole of south-western Slovakia was the territory of a principality with its centre in Nitra, which Anonymus delimits by the rivers Váh, Hron, Danube and Morava and labels it as a *ducatus* and *provincia*. According to Anonymus, its southern border was the Danube and on the north it reached up beyond Trenčín.[124] Anonymus could have at least partially reliable knowledge of this Little Nitria, because it endured up to Stephen's age. The fact that he did not invent its territorial range is documented indirectly for us by Cosmas.[125] The Hron was not the eastern edge of Svätopluk's realm, as Cosmas states, and wasn't the eastern border of the Nitrian Principality, as Anonymus writes, but of Little Nitria, which in the time of Prince Géza and subordinate Prince Michael and briefly also Stephen could have been administered by Prince Poznan.[126]

The Poznans were patrons of Zobor Abbey.[127] The abbey owned a large amount of land spread over the extensive territory of south-western Slovakia,

---

123 Ján Lukačka, "Úloha šľachty slovanského pôvodu pri stabilizácii uhorského včasnofeudálneho štátu," in *Typologie raně feudálních slovanských států*, p. 192. Ján Lukačka, "Najstaršie nitrianske šľachtické rody," in *Najstaršie rody na Slovensku. Zborník príspevkov zo sympózia o najstarších rodoch na Slovensku 4.-6. októbra 1993 v Častej-Papierničke*, (Bratislava 1994), pp. 102–108. Lukačka, "Formovanie vyššej šľachty na západnom Slovensku,", pp. 26–30. Györffy, *ÁMF I*, pp. 419–420. Györffy, *ÁMF II*, pp. 210, 212, 215, 572–573. Györffy, *ÁMF IV*, pp. 336–337.

124 *Anonymi (P. magistri) Gesta Hungarorum* 33–37, *SRH I*, pp. 74–80. Poznan, prince of Little Nitria, could have been based in Nitra together with then Nitria prince Stephen, because two or three high dignitaries sometimes were seated in the most important Hungarian castles alongside one another. King Stephen I had his seat in Esztergom together with the archbishop and later also with the count, while in Veszprém were seated a Hungarian princess, then the queen, together with a bishop and a count. A king and a count were seated at Székesfehérvár. An Árpád appanaged prince, a bishop and a count were based in Bihar. And in several other castles bishops were based together with a count.

125 *Cosmae Chronica Bohemorum* I 14 ad a. 894, *MMFH I*, p. 201.

126 Juraj Hodál, "Pôvod, sídla a hodnosť predkov rodu Hunt-Pázmany," *Historický sborník. Časopis historického odboru MS* IV (Turčiansky sv. Martin 1946) no. 2, pp. 141–143, 157–163. Lukačka, *Úloha šľachty*, pp. 191–200. Lukačka, *Formovanie vyššej šľachty*, pp. 21–22, 25–27, 118–119.

127 Lukačka, "Úloha šľachty," p. 194. Lukačka, *Formovanie vyššej šľachty*, pp. 28–29.

which is written in the Zobor document from 1113.[128] The document, however, doesn't mention its donors. If many of the abbey properties neighboured immediately with properties of the Poznans, then those abbey properties that neighboured with the Poznan properties could have also originally been Poznan, and the unknown donor coming from this line sometime in the 10th century split them off of his extensive lands and donated them to the abbey.[129] The Poznans then, already in the time of Géza and his son Stephen I, had influence *with huge and extensive interited properties*[130] They thus had plenty to dispense. With the exception of one village in the upper Turiec region[131] the properties of Zobor Abbey (recorded in the mentioned Zobor document from 1113) did not continue on the territory of south-western Slovakia. To the north they reached up beyond Trenčín and to the Upper Nitra, to the south they touched the Danube,[132] but they did not cross it. They respected the range of Poznan's Little Nitria, as we know from Anonymus's description. Poznan, thanks to the extensive property, also had *threats of weapons* available, that is military units, which in 997 were crucial in the victory of Stephen I over the rebels.[133] This was the basis of Poznan's princely power.[134]

---

128   DHA I, ed. Györffy, no. 142/I, pp. 393–396. CDES I, ed. Marsina, no. 69, pp. 65–67. Richard Marsina, "Štúdie k slovenskému diplomatáru. K problematike najstarších zoborských listín," *Sborník Filozofickej fakulty Univerzity Komenského* 14 (1963), pp. 150–157. Györffy, ÁMF I, p. 419. Györffy, ÁMF II, p. 572. Györffy, ÁMF IV, pp. 335–336.

129   See note 127.

130   Chron. Hung. comp. saec. XIV. II 41, SRH I, p. 297.

131   [In] *Turc villa est quedam Sancti Ypoliti, cuius est terminus in villa Wescan abies et quercus; alter terminus est in quodam [... terci]us terminus est in villa Turc.* DHA I, ed. Györffy, no. 142/I, pp. 394–395. CDES I, ed. Marsina, no. 69, p. 66. Marsina, "Štúdie k slovenskému diplomatáru. K problematike najstarších zoborských listín," pp. 154, 157.

132   See chapter 15, note 90.

133   *Prince Géza and his son Saint Stephen ... turned on the opponents of Christianity* not only *with the help of God*, but also *with threats of weapons (armorum terroribus)*, whereby *they relied on the help* of the small princes Poznan and Hont. From the events of 997 it is clear that this was above all military help. A Hungarian chronicler knew (*is demonstrable evident even in the present*, that is in the time when this chronicler wrote his work), that the Poznan (as well as the Hont) line is distinguished *by vast and extensive inherited property (latis et amplis hereditatibus)* and that he had them already in the time of Géza and Stephen. However, the Hungarian chronicler only invented the fact that *Prince Géza and his son for their services* gifted this property to Poznan, just as he invented the German origin of Poznan and his arrival to Hungary in the time of Duke Géza. Chron. Hung. comp. saec. XIV. 41, 64. SRH I, pp. 297, 312–314.

134   And leading men of the Bohemian Munics (*de gente Muncia*) and Teptics (*de gente Tepca*) lines were *especially powerful with weapons, useful by loyalty, courageous in battle with excellent wealth (armis potentiores, fide meliores, milicia fortiores et divitiis eminentiores)*.

The Poznans could have already been small princes in Great Moravian Nitria. They could have survived the end of the Great Moravian state and remained Christians. In the time of rule of Hungarian Prince Géza the Poznans only renovated Zobor Abbey, just as later (in 1019) Hungarian King Stephen I renewed the abbey of St. Hadrian, which had stood in Zalavár (Blatengrad, Mosaburg) since 852.[135] The Poznans renovated and endowed Zobor Abbey, became its patrons and supported the Árpáds in spreading Christianity in Hungary.

Other Hungarian princes also had large properties and numerous military units. Marosvár Prince Ajtony owned pasturage with vast horse farms and livestock and *further farmsteads and yards* (*allodia et curias*). With such great wealth he could keep a strong army. Ajtony's army (*exercitus Achtum*) had *many soldiers* (*multitudine militum*),[136] and thus Ajtony could have withstood royal power for a long period. Just as Poznan richly gifted and obviously also renewed Zobor Abbey from his vast properties, Ajtony immediately after baptism in 1003 established and necessarily must have also richly endowed a Greek monastery in Marosvár consecrated to John the Baptist.[137]

Anonymus writes about both principalities, distant from one another at opposite ends of Hungary, almost equally. He records Ajtony's (in Anonymus also Glad's) principality by the rivers Maros, Tisza, Csesztreg, Temes (Timiş) and Ponjavica and the castles Haram, Kovin and Orsova (to the legend of which he also adds Marosvár)[138] and Poznan's (in Anonymus Zubur's) principality is circumscribed by the rivers Danube, Váh, Hron and Morava and the castles

---

The Vršov family (*Wrisovici*) also belonged to this most powerful Bohemian line. *Cosmae Pragensis Chronica Boemorum* I 42, ad a. 1037, ed. Bretholz, pp. 78–79. Martin Wihoda, "Kníže a jeho věrní. Kosmas o světě předáků a urozených," in *Šlechta, moc a reprezentace ve středověku, ed.* Martin Nodl, Martin Wihoda, *Colloquia mediaevalia Pragensia* 9 (2007), pp. 17–29. Petr Kopal, "Neznámy známy rod. Pokus o genealogii Vršovců," *Sborník archívních prací* 51 (2001), pp. 3–84. Petr Kopal, "Kosmovi d'áblové. Vršovsko – přemyslovský antagonismus ve světle biblických a legendárních citátů, motivů a symbolů," *Mediaevalia historica Bohemica* 8 (2001), pp. 7–41. Třeštík, "Počátky českého politického myšlení," pp. 406, 423, 431–432.

135   *DHA I*, ed. Györffy, no. 14, 17, pp. 86–92, 98–102. *Annales Posonienses* ad a. 1019, *SRH I*, p. 125. *Conversio*, ed. Wolfram, pp. 54–55, 135. *MMFH III*, pp. 314–315. The Abbey of St. Hadrian in Blatengrad is mentioned in a document forged around 977, which claims to be from 885. *MMFH III*, Diplomata 110, p. 125. Endre Tóth, "Szent Adorján és Zalavár," *Századok* 133 (1999), no. 1, pp. 3–40. Ritoók, "The Benedictine Monastery of Zala/Zalavár," pp. 19–47. Ágnes Ritoók, "The decline of a central place in the Middle Ages," in *"Castellum, Civitas, Urbs"*, ed. Heinrich-Tamáska, Herold, Straub, Vida, pp. 103–111.

136   *Legenda maior S. Gerardi episcopi* 8, *SRH II*, pp. 489–491.

137   *Legenda maior S. Gerardi episcopi* 8, *SRH II*, p. 490.

138   *Legenda maior S. Gerardi episcopi* 8, *SRH II*, p. 489. See chapter 13, notes 31, 32, 33, 34.

Nitra, Várad, Šintava, Hlohovec, Bana, Beckov and Trenčín.[139] At the beginning of their history Anonymus posits the invented Glad and Zubur; he also knows, however, the real Ajtony. The analogy of both principalities is further filled in for us by the Hungarian chronicles and legends, by the name of actual princes Ajtony and Poznan, reports on their holdings, princely forces and abbeys, which were established near their princely seats. The little Nitrian Principality was thus the same historical fact as the Marosvár Principality at the opposite end of Hungary. Anonymus's reports on both principalities are equally reliable.

12   Váh

North of Poznan's Little Nitria lay another small principality mentioned in a document of the Prague bishopric as the *Váh province (provintia Uuag)*.[140] As follows from its naming after the Váh, it lay along the Váh River, more precisely on the upper part, and on the norther part of the middle Váh, which no longer belonged to its southern neighbour. Thus the Liptov, Orava, Turiec and the northern half of the later Trenčín seat belonged to it.[141] At the time of origin of the Prague bishopric (in 976)[142] this northern principality, together with its neighbouring Krakówia, was subjugated to the Bohemian Přemyslids. After the conquering of Kraków by Polish Prince Mieszko I in 987[143] it again fell to Nitria.

---

139   See note 124.
140   *DHA I*. ed. Györffy, no. 83, p. 245. Richard Marsina, "Štúdie k slovenskému diplomatáru I," *Historické štúdie* 16 (1971), pp. 98–104. Labuda, *Studia nad początkami państwa polskiego II*, pp. 228–239.
141   Trenčín, Anonymus writes, belonged to Little Nitria, because it could not have belonged to the Váh province. To seek the centre of the Váh province in Trenčín on the basis of apparent identification of the Váh province with the castellan *Trecen*, as Józef Widajewicz and after him Erik Fügedi and Richard Marsina did, is a mistake. Józef Widajewicz, *Kraków i Poważe w dokumencie biskupstwa praskiego z 1086 roku* (Poznań 1938), pp. 35–47. Józef Widajewicz, *Panstwo Wislan* (Kraków 1947), pp. 119–124. Erik Fügedi, "Kirchliche Topographie und Siedlungsverhältnisse im Mittelalter in der Slowakei," *Studia Slavica Academiae scientiarum Hungaricae* v (1959), no. 3–4, pp. 366–367. Richard Marsina, "Nitrianske biskupstvo a jeho biskupi od 9. do polovice 13. storočia," *Historický časopis* 41 (1993), no, 5, pp. 535–536. The castellan *Trecen*, which according to a papal bull from 1155 belonged to the Wrocław diocese, did not lie along the Váh, but in lower Silesia and the castle *Trecen* itself is identical with the castle Ryczyn (in 1245 *Rechen*, 1342 *Drecen*) on the middle Odre, south of Wrocław. Labuda, *Studia nad początkami państwa polskiego II*, pp. 215–227, 237–239.
142   See note 32.
143   Steinhübel, *Kapitoly*, pp. 140–141.

Anonymus's description of Hungary ends in the north with Trenčín, Zvolen, the Tatras and the Salt Castle at Solivar (*castrum Salis*).[144] Anonymus thus knew in the north the territories of the later Šariš, Spiš and Zvolen seats and only the southern part of the later Trenčín seat. He doesn't mention the land to the north of the gorge between Púchov and Považská Bystrica, to the north of the Low Tatra Mountains and west of the High Tatra Mountains. There where Anonymus's telling ends is exactly where the document of the Prague bishopric continues. If we put the information from both sources on a map, we find out that the first is a continuation of the second. They respect one another, and with the exception of the Tatras (*Tritri, Turtur*), which both sources consider as border mountains, they don't overlap at all. They respect the clearly defined border, from which to the north lay Polish (before then Přemyslid) Kraków and the Váh province and south of it Hungary, without the Váh province. Not only the document of the Prague bishopric, but also Anonymus (aside from other information) rests on knowledge of the situation in the 2nd half of the 10th century.

13 Hont

The seat of Prince Hont was undoubtedly castle Hont,[145] which was built at the turn of the 10th to the 11th century.[146] If we take into consideration the position of the oldest lands that belonged to his family in the middle Ipeľ River region and in the valley of the Rimava,[147] and the territorial range of both preceding principalities, with which the size of Hont's principality must have been comparable, then a principality with it centre on Hont Castle had to cover a much greater territory than the later Hont seat. To the west, where it bordered with Poznan's Little Nitria, it could have touched or approach the Hron and from the north it was certainly divided from the Váh Principality by the Low Tatras. Thus, the later Zvolen, Novohrad (without the territory of the Vác

---

144   *Anonymi (P. magistri) Gesta Hungarorum* 17, 18, 34, 37, SRH I, pp. 58, 59, 76, 79.
145   István Bakács, *Hont vármegye Mohács előtt* (Budapest 1971), pp. 46–47. Gyula Nováky – György Sándorfi – Zsuzsa Miklós, *A Börzsöny hegység őskori és középkori várai* (Budapest 1979), pp. 29–41. Erik Fügedi, *Castle and society in medieval Hungary (1000–1437)* (Budapest 1986), pp. 19, 26, 27, 32, 33.
146   Maxim Mordovin, "Archeologický výskum komitátneho Hontianskeho hradu," *Acta historica Neosoliensia* 16 (2013), Vol. 1–2, pp. 6–37.
147   János Karacsonyi, *A magyar nemzetségek a XIV. század közepéig* (Budapest 1900, reprint 1995), pp. 639–656. Bakács, *Hont vármegye*, p. 299. Lukačka, "Úloha šľachty," pp. 193–194. Györffy, ÁMF III, pp. 157, 161, 164.

archdeaconate south of the Cserhát ridge) and Malohont (Little Hont) could have belonged to the Hont principality.

If prince Hont gave his name to a newly built castle and thus to the entire principality administered from it, then he could not have belonged to a domestic princely line. If Hont inherited his principality and castle from his ancestors, then he would have kept his old name. Where the original princely castle stood and what name it had and what the entire principality administered from it was called, we cannot say today. When Stephen became an appanaged prince, he removed the unreliable local prince and in his place put a reliable follower Hont, who was of domestic Hungarian origin or came to Stephen's princely court in Nitra in the train of Gisela in 996.[148]

14   Borsod

In Anonymus's telling Prince Salan, after conquering of the Ung principality by the Magyars, abandoned the other part of his realm to Árpád voluntarily: *He abandoned to him the territory up to the river Slaná/Sajó (Souyoy) along with its inhabitants*.[149] Since the abandoned territory bordered with the lost Principality of Ung, whose western border was made up of the Zemplín and Slanské hills,[150] and reached up to the Slaná/Sajó valley, then the basin of the Hornád River also belonged to it. Salan's realm reached, according to

---

148   Prince Hont could be of domestic Hungarian origin; testimony of this could be the spreading of this name (Hunt, Hont, Hontus, Hunche, Hunta, Hunda, Huned, Onth, Ontus, Onda, Chunt) in Hungary. Hodál, "Pôvod, sídla a hodnosť predkov rodu Hunt-Pázmány," pp. 152–156. Fehértói, *Árpád-kori kis személynévtár*, pp. 160, 162, 259, 362. Györffy, *ÁMF I*, pp. 422, 697, 699, 701. Kristó – Makk – Szegfű, *Adatok I*, p. 80. Kristó – Makk – Szegfű, *Adatok II*, p. 22. It could also be foreign, because Hunt is an old Anglo-Saxon name. *The Oxford English Dictionary, being a corrected reissue with an introduction, supplement, and bibliography of a new english dictionary on historical principles founded mainly on the materials collected by The Philological Society, volume V* (Oxford 1933, reprinted 1966), pp. 460–461.

149   Anonymi (P. magistri) *Gesta Hungarorum* 16, *SRH I*, p. 57. If Salan abandoned to Árpád the territory *up to the river Slaná/Sajó (usque ad fluvium Souyoy)*, then this does not mean that the Slaná/Sajó was the border of the abandoned territory, but that it took up the entire basin of the Slaná/Sajó, that is the enter Gemer region. Not even the lower Hron was the eastern border of Zubur's principality, and the lower Maros was not the northern border of Ajtony's principality, as Anonymus wrote, because both banks of the mentioned rivers belonged to these principalities. The Maros and Szamos rivers were not the borders of Biharia, as could follow from Anonymus's description. See chapter 13, notes 8, 10.

150   The ridge of the Zemplín and Slanské hills was later the western border of the Zemplín, which originally belonged to the Ung Principality. See chapter 13, note 2.

Anonymus, *up to the borders of Russians and the Poles (usque ad confinium Ruthenorum et Polonorum)*.[151] It reached there by means of both lost territories, from Salan's principality unnaturally shifted far away to the north-east. If the northern border of the Ung Principality was identical with the northern border of the later castle counties of Zemplín, Ung and Boržava, which bordered with Russian Galicia, then the northern border to Salan's abandoned territory in the basins of the Hornád and Sajó had to be identical with the northern border of the later Šariš and Spiš regions, which border Poland.

According to Anonymus, Árpád and his warriors *marched from castle Ung* and came to the territory which Salan abandoned: *They pitched camp beyond the mountain Tarcal (Turzol), on a field alongside the Takta River (Tucota) as far as the mountain Szerencs (Zereuche) ... they remained there for many days, until they had subjugated all the towns in the surroundings up to the river Slaná/Sajó (Souyou) and to the Salt Castle (ad Castrum Salis)*. Then a Magyar warrior Tarcal (*Turzol*) got from Árpád a *vast territory at the foot of the mountains, where the Bodrog (Budrug) flows into the Tisza (Tysciam), and in that place he built an earthen castle, which is today called Himesudvar (Hymusudvor)*. Then *after common counsel and on the appeal of all the inhabitants Bors, son of Bönger (Borsu, filius Bunger), was sent with a strong force to the land of the Poles to view the borders of the kingdom and to reinforce them with obstacles as far as the Tatra (Turtur) Mountains, and he built in a suitable place a castle to defend the kingdom. Bors, upon getting permission, went forth and having by good luck gathered many of the villagers and built a castle beside the Bodva (Buldua) river that is called by that people Borsod, because it was small. Bors, having taken the sons of the inhabitants as hostages, built boundary markers and returned through the Tatra (Turtur) Mountains to Prince Árpád. There was great joy in the court of the prince at his return. The prince then in his mercy as a reward appointed Bors as count in that castle and gave him complete responsibility for that country.*[152]

The oldest Borsod County, the beginning of which Anonymus erroneously put into the time of Árpád, reached from Szerencs and its surroundings up to the basins of the Slaná/Sajó, Hornád and Poprad rivers and to the surroundings of the Salt Castle (Solivar), to the Tatras and to the Hungary-Poland border. This Borsod County did not transgress the Bükk Mountains to the south. According to Anonymus, Prince Árpád *gave to Böngér, father of Bors, a large*

---

151 *Anonymi (P. magistri) Gesta Hungarorum* 11, SRH I, p. 48.
152 *Anonymi (P. magistri) Gesta Hungarorum* 17, 18, SRH I, pp. 57–59. *Prince Zoltán (Zsolt) ... set the border of the Hungarian kingdom ... from the side of the Poles up to the Tatra (Turtur) mountains, just as Bönger's son Bors first made the border of the kingdom. Anonymi (P. magistri) Gesta Hungarorum* 57, SRH I, p. 114. Benkő, *Név*, p. 52.

territory from the Tapolcsa River up to the Sajó, which is now called Miskolc, and in addition gave him a castle, which is called Győr. His son united this castle with his own castle, which is called Borsod, into one county.[153]

Count Bors did not live in Árpád's period as Anonymus writes, because then the castle counties headed by a count (ispán/župan) did not yet exist, but only in the time of King Stephen, who was their founder.[154] Even the oldest Borsod County, like other large counties (Csanád, Transylvanian Fehér, Doboka, Ung, Somogy), took up the territorial range of the preceding principalities. On the south, in the Bükk Mountains and near the confluence of the Sajó with the Tisza, this Borsod Principality (later castle county) bordered with the Eger Principality, and on the Tisza River between the mouth of the Sajó and the mouth of the Bodrog, it bordered with Szabolcs, and on the east the Zemplín and Slanské hills divided it from the Ung Principality (later a county). Its northern border was identical with the eastern half of the Hungary-Poland border reaching from the common Šariš-Zemplín and Poland-Galicia-Hungary interface (on the peak Pásiky in the Low Beskyds) up to the Tatras. To the west it bordered with the Hont and Váh principalities. Thus, it took up the northern part of the Borsod seat, the surroundings of the Szerencs (later a part of the Zemplín), Abov, Šariš, Turňa, Spiš and Gemer regions.

After deposing the old princes, such as Koppány, Gyula II, Zombor and Ajtony, King Stephen put his counts in their place, for example the foreigner Vencelin (in 997),[155] Stephen's relatives Zoltán (Zsolt) and Doboka (in 1003) and Doboka's son Csanád (perhaps in 1028).[156] The counts were based in the old princely castles; thus, there was no need to build new county castles. And several other princely castles, some of which were named after the prince seated in them, for example, Zombor and Gyulafehérvár (Alba Iulia), received after abolition of the principalities a new name, according to the first count placed in them by the king, for example Bars (Tekov), Doboka (previously Zombor) and Csanád (originally Marosvár). And Borsod Castle and the entire castle county associated with it got its name from the first administrator, Bors. The original name of the old principality expired, and we don't even know the

---

153 *Ibi etiam dux dedit Bungernec patri Borsu terram magnam a fluvio Topulucea usque ad fluvium Souyou, que nunc vocatur Miscoucy, et dedit ei castrum, quod dicitur Geuru, et illud castrum filius suus Borsu cum suo castro, quod dicitur Borsod, unum fecit comitatum.* Anonymi (P. magistri) Gesta Hungarorum 31, SRH I, p. 72.

154 Györffy, *ÁMF I*, p. 737. Mária Wolf, "Előzetes jelentés a borsodi földvár ásatárol (1987–1990)," in *A nyíregyházi Jósa András múzeum évkönyve* 30–32, 1987–1989 (Nyíregyháza 1992), p. 393.

155 See note 105.

156 See chapter 15, notes 17, 18, 45.

names of the princes to whom this eastern part of Nitria was subjugated before Bors's arrival.

If Bors and Hont gave their castle seats and also their entire principality their name, then these newly named castles and principalities were not inherited from their ancestors. Appanaged Prince Stephen, after arrival in Nitria in 995, certainly deposed the local small princes loyal to the removed Michael. He then put Hont and Bors in their places. Bors was thus not only the first Borsod count but also the last Borsod prince.

Borsod Castle stood on a hill which rises 15 metres above the wetlands of the Bodva River. Its ramparts enclose a smallish area of only 1.7 ha. According to the findings of archaeologists, they were built at the turn of the 10th to the 11th century. Before then this was only an unfortified settlement, which in the mid-10th century was destroyed by fire.[157] Thus, it was Prince Bors, who immediately after taking over rule of this principality, sought out and built a new princely seat and gave it and the entire principality his name. We do not know where it stood or what the old princely castle was called.

The territory which, according to Anonymus, Árpád gave to Bors's father Bönger, lay where the property of the Miškov family lay,[158] who had in this eastern principality a similar role as the Honts had in the neighbouring Hont principality. Therefore, we can consider Bors the last Borsod prince and the first count as the oldest known member of the family.[159] Count Bors, the son of

---

157 Wolf, "Előzetes jelentés a borsodi földvár ásatárol (1987–1990)," pp. 393–442. Mária Wolf, "Die Gespanschaftsburg von Borsod," *Acta Archaeologica Academiae Scientiarum Hungaricae* 48 (1996), pp. 209–240. Mária Wolf, "A borsodi ispánsági vár templomai Ecclesia baptismalis, ecclesia parochialis," *A Borsodi Tájház Közleményi* 17–18 (2005), pp. 3–18. Mária Wolf, *A borsodi földvár. Egy államalapításkori megyeszékhelyünk* (Edelény 2008). Gyula Nováki, "A borsodi földvár sánca." *A Hermann Ottó Múzeum Évkönyve* 30–31 (Miskolc 1993), pp. 125–145. Veronika Szilágyi – György Szakmány – Mária Wolf – Tamás Weiszburg, "10. századi kerámiák archeometriai vizsgálata Edelény, északkelet-Magyarország," *Archeometriai Műhely* 1 (2004), pp. 34–39. Peter Tajkov, *Sakrálna architektúra 11.–13. storočia na juhovýchodnom Slovensku*, (Košice 2012), pp. 136–137, 247.

158 The oldest property of the family Miškov lay in northern Borsod and in the upper Slaná/Sajó Basin. Karácsonyi, *A magyar nemzetségek*, pp. 822–825, 827–830. Györffy, *ÁMF I*, pp. 739, 745–746, 788–790, 792, 796, 801, 803, 809–810, 813, 816. Györffy, *ÁMF II*, pp. 468, 470–471, 473. CDES 2, ed. Marsina, no. 130, pp. 85–88.

159 Borša, son of Olen (*Borsa filius Olen*), was in the retinue of Břetislav, son of Bohemian King Vratislaus. In 1091 Borša together with two of Břetislav's warriors, murdered the royal adviser Zderad. *Cosmae Pragensis Chronica Boemorum* II 44 ad a. 1091, ed. Bretholz, p. 150. Borša was a Bohemian soldier and his name was Slavic. Therefore, the first Borsod count Bors (*Borsu*), who had this same Slavic name, was a Slav and his family could have been of Slavic origin. Regarding the Slavic origin of the Miškov family, see János Karácsonyi, *Magyar nemzetségek a XIV. század középeig II* (Budapest 1901), p. 364. Lukačka, *Formovanie vyššej šľachty*, pp. 21–22. Bönger, whom Anonymus mentions as Bors's father, may be invented, as is Zubur, Glad, Laborec and Salan.

Ban Dominic from the Miškov family, was a contemporary of Anonymus. Both magnates Dominic and Bors were related to Béla III and certainly visited his royal court. Béla's royal notary could thus have known their family tradition and drawn on it for his work.[160]

We can check the reliability of Anonymus's reports on the territorial range of the Hungarian principalities that Stephen I transformed into castle counties, according to the reports of other sources. Not only Anonymus, but Cosmas, too, mentioned the Hron River as a border. The eastern border of Little Nitria did not lay precisely on the Hron. We can identify it with the border dividing the later Tekov County from Hont County, which ran, with some deviations, along the Sikenica River up to its mouth into the Hron. And the northern border of the Marosvár Principality did not go exactly along the Maros, as Anonymus writes, but more to the north, along the basins of the Maros and Körös. Transylvania, Biharia and Ung also have invented princes. But we can consider the territorial range of these principalities as real, just as Anonymus described them, because it is confirmed in the reports of other chroniclers. We find the small Váh Principality recorded by a document of the Prague bishopric only as a negative imprint in Anonymus. Borsod County (previously principality), bordered on the south with the Bükk Mountains and the Tisza, on the north by the Tatra Mountains and the Hungary-Poland border, on the east by the western border of the Ung Principality in the Zemplín and Slanské hills and on the Ondava Mountains, and on the west with territories of principalities of Váh and Hont, unknown to Anonymus; we have in this the oldest territorial range documented only in Anonymus. We need not doubt this large range of the Borsod Principality, because Anonymus's reports on the existence and territorial extent of the old pre-county principalities are reliable.

---

160   In 1128 a portion of the magnates, unhappy with the rule of Stephen II, took advantage of his very serious illness and prepared two candidates for the choice of a new king, Ivan and Borša. Count Borša (*Bors vero comes*) was, according to his name, from the Miškov line. He lived at the royal court and was thus a count of the court. The king, however, unexpectedly got healthy and punished the conspirators. He had Ivan decapitated and Borša fled in shame to Byzantium. *Chron. Hung. Comp. saec. XIV.* II 158, SRH I, p. 444. Lajosné Fertály, *Miskolc az Árpádok korában* (Miskolc 1928), pp. 10, 18. MT I/2, pp. 1185–1186. Another from the Miškov line, who was also named Borsa, was Count Borsa, son of banus Dominic, who around 1240 died without an heir (*absque successore*). Thus, one branch of the Miškov family died out and its property went to the king. CDES 2, ed. Marsina, no. 130, pp. 86–87. Fertály, *Miskolc*, p. 13. His father Dominic established and endowed in 1194 on the southern edge of Sopron County an abbey called Borsmonostra. *Árpád-kori oklevelek 1001–1196*, főszerkesztő György Györffy (Budapest 1997), no. 50, p. 99. Karacsónyi, *A magyar nemzetség*, pp. 821–822. Imre Szentpétery, *A Borsmonostori apátság árpádkori oklevelei* (Budapest 1916), pp. 7–25, 109–110.

15   Vác

Three princes helped Stephen I suppress Koppány's rebellion: Poznan, Hont and Ort. Ort's principality lay, similarly as Poznan's and Hont's, at a safe distance from the area ruled by Koppány and his Transdanubian allies. At the same time these three allied princes must have neighboured one another. The armies of the three princes came to Stephen's military camp in Bíňa from three sides: from Nitra, from Hont and from Ort's princely seats. The position of their common gathering point on the lower Hron was not accidental. It had to lie at least about the same distance between the three princely seats from which the military help arrived. Nitra and Hont were approximately the same distance from Bíňa, and it is at this same distance from Bíňa we need to look for Ort's princely castle. The only major castle that lay approximately at the same distance from Bíňa as Nitra and Hont, was Vác. Like other bishopric seats, Vác had to be a princely seat long before establishment of the Vác bishopric. The road from Hont and Vác to Bíňa was a bit shorter than from Nitra. The army coming from Hont and Vác, however, had to cross two rivers, the Ipeľ and the Hron, and thus time of march from all three castles to Stephen's military camp could have been approximately the same. Prince Ort was thus settled in Vác. The Vác Principality bordered the Hont principality and had the same safe position on the same side of the Danube as both of its allies.

Ort had to be from the Árpád line, one of Árpád's great-great-grandchildren, because the Vác Principality belong to the oldest Árpád territory. If Ort and Koppány battled against one another, then they obviously came from different branches of the Árpád line. If Koppány was Jutas's great-grandson,[161] then Ort, could not have belonged to the Tarhos or Zoltán branches, because the Vác Principality did not belong to Tarhos or Zoltán; he could have been the only distant descendant, more exactly the great-grandson of Üllő. The first Prince in Vác could thus have been Árpád's son Üllő.

16   The Family of Prince Michael

The history of Árpád Nitria begins with the story of Michael's family. Duke Michael had sons Ladislas the Bald and Vazul and grandsons Domoslav, Levente, Andrew and Béla. Vazul was a cousin of Stephen I. If the Annales

---

161   See note 91.

Altahenses consider Vazul as Stephen's nephew (*filium fratris sui*),[162] then he was significantly younger than Stephen. If Stephen was born in 979[163] and Vazul's sons were still in 1031 only *parvuli*,[164] that is young (born in the span of years 1012–1020), then Vazul could have been born around 990 and married around 1010. He was thus at least 10 years younger than Stephen and gave the impression of being Stephen's nephew, and at the same time he was in terms of age, more like his sons.

Michael was born approximately between 950–955;[165] his son Vazul was thus about 35–40 years younger. If Vazul was older than his brother Ladislas,[166] then the age difference between Michael and his oldest son would be too great, and the age difference between father and a second son was larger still. If Ladislas was born before Vazul,[167] then he very rightly falls into the long-time gap between father Michael and second-born son Vazul. A difference of 35–40 years between father and an oldest son is in those time uncommon and unreasonable, but if this is the difference between a father and a second son, then it is understandable. Thus, those Hungarian chroniclers who consider Ladislas as the older of the two brothers are correct.[168]

Not only Vazul, but also Ladislas the Bald had to be younger than Stephen, because otherwise they would have been the same barrier for Stephen's succession as for Vazul's father Michael, and Géza would not have spared him, as he did not spare Michael. If Ladislas was younger than Stephen (* 979) and at the same time proportional to the age of his father (* 950–955) and the time of his father's marriage (perhaps 971 or 972),[169] then he was born approximately

---

162   See chapter 16, note 14. He similarly imprecisely speaks about Stephen's nephew *fratruelis* in 1042, although this was a more distant relative.
163   See note 85.
164   See chapter 16, note 14.
165   Géza's younger brother got the Christian name Michael undoubtedly upon baptism. If Géza and Michael received baptism in 972, then Michael was already then married with a Bulgarian princess, thanks to whom (acknowledged in neighbouring Bulgaria) he got the name. If Michael was younger than his brother Géza (* 947–950) and married around 971, at the latest 972, then he could have been born sometime in the years 950–955.
166   Vazul was according to today's predominate opinion older than Ladislas. Péter Váczy: "A Vazul-hagyomány középkori kútfőinkben," *Levéltári Közlemények* 18–19 (1940–1941), pp. 312–313. Bálint Hóman, *Geschichte des ungarischen Mittelalters I* (Berlin 1940), p. 235. *MT I/1*, p. 751.
167   Vajay, "Großfürst Geysa," pp. 66, 100.
168   *Michael vero genuit Calvum Ladizlaum et Vazul. Chron. Hung. comp. saec. XIV.* II 63, SRH I, p. 311. *Michael vero genuit Calvum Latislaum et Wazul. Chronicon Posoniense* 44, SRH II, p. 35.
169   See p. 205.

in 980, when his father was not yet 30 years old and had then been married 8 years with the Bulgarian princess.

Vazul was the father of three sons, two of whom (Andrew and Béla) became kings and ancestors of all the subsequent Hungarian kings. Vazul was thus more significant than his brother Ladislas. Therefore, some Hungarian chroniclers put him as being older than Ladislas.[170] Similarly, Andrew and Béla were more significant than their oldest brother Levente.[171] Therefore, all Hungarian chroniclers when naming Vazul's sons, name Levente in the last position, as if he were the youngest.[172] From Levente they made the third, just as from Ladislas they made the second. The lost Gesta Ungarorum vetera from the end of the 11th century named Michael's sons in the real order, first Ladislas and second Vazul. Even their continuers kept this correct order in the 12th century and after them even some of the later Hungarian chroniclers.[173]

Hungarian kings Andrew I (1046–1060) and Béla I (1060–1063) were Vazul's sons. If Vazul's fatherhood is recorded in the Annales Altahenses[174] and the St. Gerard legend,[175] then this was generally known at the time of canonization of Bishop Gerard (in 1083) and at the time of writing the Annales Altahenses (perhaps 10 years earlier). Therefore, the mentioned, only much later Gesta Ungarorum vetera, must have also recorded it.

A Hungarian chronicler recalled Vazul's *youthful devilry and madness*.[176] This characteristic is not related to the time of his imprisonment by Stephen I, as this follows from the chronicler's telling, because then he had already been an adult for some time and had two growing sons. This relates to the time of his youth, when he concluded a pagan marriage, from which his three sons were born.[177] The oldest of them, Levente, remained a pagan up to his death

---

170 *Dux iste Michael habuit duos filios. Primus fuit dux Wazul, secundus fuit dux Ladizlaus Calvus. Chronicon Zagrabiense cum textu Chronici Varadiensis collatum* 1, SRH I, p. 206. *Mihal vero, frater Geichae genuit Wazul et Zar Ladislaum. Symonis de Keza Gesta Hungarorum* II 43, 44, SRH I, pp. 172–173. Vajay, "Großfürst Geysa," pp. 66, 69, 100.

171 See chapter 16, note 74.

172 All sources consider Levente as the youngest of Vazul's sons. *Simonis de Keza Gesta Hungarorum* II 44, 52, SRH I, p. 173, 177. *Chronicon Zagrabiense* 1, SRH I, p. 206. *Chron. Hung. comp. saec. XIV.* II 29, 69, 78, 81, 82, 83, 84, 85, SRH I, pp. 290, 321, 334, 336, 337, 338, 339, 341, 342. *Chronicon Posoniense* 51, *Chronicon Monacense* 32, 37, 39, *Legenda S. Gerhardi episcopi* 15, SRH II, pp. 38, 67, 70, 71, 72, 501.

173 See note 168.

174 See chapter 16, note 14.

175 *post filios Wazul: Endre, Bela et Levente, qui erant de genere sancti regis Stephani. Legenda maior sancti Gerhardi episcopi* 15, SRH II, p. 501.

176 *iuvenilem lasciviam et stultitiam. Chron. Hung. comp. saec. XIV.* II 69, SRH I, p. 320.

177 *Chron. Hung. comp. saec. XIV.* II 87, SRH I, p. 344. József Gerics, "Quaedam puella de genere Tatun. Philologisches und Rechtsgeschichtliches zur Untersuchung einer

in 1047.[178] The name of Vazul's wife, *Tatun*, is Turkish. It arose from the title Katun (*catun*) for the wife of a khagan,[179] exactly as from the Greek emperor title basileos originated the personal name Basileos and Vasilij or from the title gyula and horka the Hungarian personal names. This is testimony about her origin. In Somogy County lay the village Tátony mentioned in 1275 as *Thatun*.[180] The name Tatun, recorded by a Hungarian chronicler, in his and obviously in Vazul's age was pronounced with an initial T. The change K > T is thus not a written error, but an older change in the pronunciation of what was already then a personal name.[181]

The foreign Turkish name of Vazul's wife and the paganism of his family are testimony that Vazul lived a longer time in the pagan and Turkish environment. The only pagan and Turkish neighbours of Hungary were the Pechenegs, who settled beyond the eastern borders of Hungary in later Wallachia and Moldovia and in the adjacent steppes (from the Eastern Carpathians and the lower Danube to the Don).[182] Vazul's grandfather Taksony also had a Pecheneg wife.[183] The Pecheneg Khagan Cselgü offered to Vazul's grandson, the deposed Hungarian King Solomon, marriage to his daughter.[184] And Vazul, with respect to his princely origin, could have found a wife in the family of a Pecheneg Khagan. How did Vazul get to the Pechenegs? Did he, too, flee from Hungary as Solomon would 90 years later?

17   The Fleeing of Michael's Sons

After Michael's violent death, which his brother, Hungarian Prince Géza, had on his conscience, Michael's sons Ladislas the Bald and Vazul could not remain

---

Chronikenstelle," *Annales Universitatis Scientiarum Budapestinensis de Rolando Eötvös nominatae, sectio Historica* IX (1967), pp. 3–30.

178   *Chron. Hung. comp. saec. XIV.* II 86, SRH I, p. 344.
179   György Györffy, "Török női méltóságnév, a magyar kútfőkben," *Magyar Nyelv* 49 (1953), no. 1–2, pp. 109–111. Gerics, "Quaedam puella," pp. 4–6. Pohl, *Die Awaren*, pp. 305–306.
180   Gerics, "Quaedam puella," p. 5. Dezső Csánki, *Magyarország történelmi földrajza a Hunyadiak korában II* (Budapest 1894), p. 65.
181   Gerics, "Quaedam puella," p. 5.
182   Constantine Porphyrogenitus, *De administrando imperio* 37, ed. Moravcsik, pp. 166–171. Konstantinos Porfyrogenetos, *De administrando imperio* 37, in *Az Árpád-kori magyar történet bizánci forrásai*, ed. Moravcsik, pp. 40–42. György Györffy, "Sur la question de l'établissement des Petchénégues en Europe," *Acta Orientalia Academiae Scientiarum Hungaricae* 25 (1972), pp. 283–292.
183   *tunc dux Zulta duxit filio Tocsun uxorem de terra Cumanorum*. Anonymi (P. magistri) *Gesta Hungarorum* 57, SRH I, p. 114.
184   *Chron. Hung. comp. saec. XIV.* II 134, SRH I, p. 408.

at home but had to seek protection and aid abroad. Ladislas headed to Russia, where he got married,[185] and Vazul, still a child, obviously accompanied him. Ladislav, with respect to his princely origin, probably found a wife in the family of then Prince of Kiev (Khagan), Vladimir the Great (978–1015).

Ladislas married some time in the years 995–1000. His son Domoslav (also called Bonuslav)[186] could have been born to Ladislas and his Russian wife around the year 1000 or in one of the following years and died in 1048.[187] He was thus older than Vazul's sons.

Since *Vladimir ... lived in peace with the surrounding princes ... and with Stephen's Hungary ... and there was peace and love between them*,[188] both brothers did not find help against Stephen in Russia. Ladislas benefited from growing Poland-Hungary tension and thus departed to Polish Prince Boleslaw the Brave. After the death of Bohemian Prince Boleslaus II († 7 February 999) Boleslaw the Brave took over *the whole of Moravia (totam Moraviam)*.[189] He occupied Moravian castles with Polish brigades[190] and turned his attention to neighbouring Nitria.

It was at that point that Vazul could have left his brother and headed off to the Pechenegs, who were settled from the lower Danube and the eastern Carpathians to the River Don,[191] that is on the territory of ancient Scythia, about which the Hungarian chroniclers showed great interest.[192] Here he mar-

---

185 *Calvi Ladislai, qui uxorem de Ruthenia dicitur accepisse*. Chron. Hung. comp. saec. XIV. II 87, SRH I, p. 344.
186 The Zagreb and Varadiense chronicles contain a report on this: *Dux autem Ladizlaus ... habuit filium, qui vocatus est Bonuzlo*. Chronicon Zagrabiense 1, SRH I, p. 206. *Dux autem Ladislas Calvus ... habuit filium, qui Domyzlo vocatur*. Chronicon Waradiense 1, Mór Wertner, *Az Árpádok családi története* (Nagy-Becskeren 1892), p. 590.
187 See chapter 16, notes 85, 86, 87.
188 *Latopis Nestora* 45, year 6504 (996), MPH I, ed. Bielowski, pp. 672–673.
189 *post obitum secundi Bolezlai ... totam Moraviam vi obtinuerant Polonii*. Cosmae Pragensis Chronica Boemorum I 40, ed. Bretholz, p. 75. MMFH I, p. 202.
190 See chapter 15, note 74. Boleslaw the Brave, immediately after suppressing the Bohemians from Moravia, had a castle built in Přerov. Čeněk Staňa, "Pronikání Boleslava II. na Brněnsko ve světle archeologických objevů," in *Přemyslovský stát kolem roku 1000*, ed. Polanský, Sláma, Třeštík, pp. 197, 207–208.
191 Constantine Porphyrogenitus, *De administrando imperio* 37, ed. Moravcsik, pp. 166–171. Konstantinos Porfyrogenetos, De administrando imperio 37. In: Az Árpád-kori magyar történet forrásai, ed. Moravcsik, pg. 40–42. Györffy, "Sur la question," pp. 283–292.
192 Anonymus has a detailed description of Scythia, to which are added the original settlements of the Magyars and part of the Russian territory, who took it (directly or mediated) from Regino. *Anonymi (P. magistri) Gesta Hungarorum* 1, SRH I, pp. 34–37. *Reginonis abbatis Prumiensis Chronicon* ad a. 889, rec. Kurze, pp. 131–133. Gyula Kristó, "Ősi epikánk és az Árpád-kori íráshagyomány," Ethnographia 81 (1970), pp. 113–135. Even Simon of Kéza, who recalled the Scythian origin of Levente's Andrew and Béla, describes Scythia in great detail. *Simonis de Keza Gesta Hungarorum* 6, SRH I, pp. 145–146. Chronicles from the

ried and leaned toward paganism.[193] With respect to the period of the birth of his sons, he married around year 1010. According to Simon of Kéza, Vazul's sons were *coming from Scythia (de Scitia oriundi)*,[194] which shows their Pecheneg origin from their mother's side. The oldest of them could have been born among the Pechenegs, that is on the territory of the ancient Scythians. If all three of Vazul's sons in 1031, when they fled from Hungary, belonged among the *parvulos*,[195] then the oldest of them, Levente, was a *parvulus*, too. He was then only a little bit older than second-born Andrew.[196] He was thus born sometime in the years 1012–1014.

18   A Falsified Genealogy

Vazul could not have concluded a Christian wedding with a pagan woman among pagans; therefore, his three sons came *not from a proper marriage (non de vero thoro)*.[197] Hungarian kings, beginning with Andrew I, come from the pagan marriage of Prince Vazul, whom Saint Stephen had cruelly mutilated.

14th century have the same description of Scythia as Simon of Kéza. *Chron. Hung. comp. saec. XIV.* I 5, SRH I, pp. 250–252. *Chronicon Posoniense* 4, SRH II, pp. 15–17. If the mentioned Hungarian chronicles contain the same description of Scythia, then they must have taken it from their common source, the Gesta Ungarorum vetera from the times of Coloman.

193   See pp. 419, 432–433.
194   See note 199. This data is a monument to the parenthood of Vazul and Tatun and is in conflict with the constructed fatherhood of Ladislas the Bald. It is found in the original text of the Gesta Ungarorum vetera. Magister Ákos and the only a little bit younger Simon of Kéza, who took it from him, were inconsistent with a change of the original text. Chroniclers of the 14th century left out this information, whereby they removed this contradiction.
195   See chapter 16, note 14.
196   The younger Andrew was born approximately in 1015–1016. See pp. 237–238.
197   See notes 199, 200. According to György Györffy, Vazul's wife and the mother of his three sons was from the family of a Bulgarian monarch. György Györffy, "Egy krónika magyarázatához," *Történelmi Szemle* 9 (1966), pp. 29–30. The high-born and socially high-ranked Bulgarian woman would, however, have to be a Christian, and he could not have lived with her in an inappropriate marriage, as with a pagan. According to József Gerics Vazul's wife was from the domestic Hungarian Tátony line, which could have have from Somogy County, where a village with this same name lies. József Gerics, "A Tátony nemzetségről. Adalékok egy krónika értelmezéséhez," *Történelmi Szemle* 9 (1966), no. 1, pp. 1–2, 19. Gerics, "Quaedam puella," pp. 3–30. László Szégfű identified Vazul's wife with the legendary Emese and put her as the daughter of the Pecheneg Thonuzob, mentioned by Anonymus. László Szégfű, "A Thonuzoba monda," *A Juhász Gyula Tanárképző Főiskola Tudományos Közleményei* (Szeged 1974), pp. 275–288. János Bollók repudiates Szégfű's opinion on the family relation of Vazul with Thonuzoba. János Bollók, "A Thonuzoba-legenda történelmi hitele," *Századok* 113 (1979), no. 1, pp. 97–107.

This origin was for the ruling Árpáds exceptionally inappropriate; therefore, a false genealogy of the first Hungarian kings originated, which displaced Vazul from the direct family line. Later Hungarian chroniclers, beginning with Anonymus,[198] persuade us that Andrew, Béla and Levente were the sons of Vazul's brother Ladislas the Bald and his Russian wife. And Simon of Kéza put Andrew, Béla and Levente as the sons of Ladislas the Bald, whom he considered as the younger of Michael's two sons.[199] The Chronicon Pictum (and the Buda Chronicle with it), which most fully preserved the text of the Gesta Ungarorum vetera, including its continuations, has Michael's sons in the correct order;[200] however, it also accepted the mentioned changed paternity.[201]

Under the rule of Géza II (1141–1162), an unknown chronicler transcribed and modified the Gesta Ungarorum vetera, containing Hungarian history up to 1095, and with its continuation, reaching to 1127, and then completed it up to year 1152. In his chronicler's continuation he wrote about the rule of Béla II and Géza II, who had to face the claim of Boris, son of Euphemia, Coloman's second wife. King Coloman caught Euphemia in an infidelity and sent her back to her father. Her son Boris, who was then born to her, declared himself as Coloman's son, though his origin was uncertain. If the chronicler emphasized Boris's doubtful origin,[202] then he had to remove any doubts about the full purity of the family tree of Hungarian kings. He had to deny that Andrew I and Béla II come from Vazul's *non de vero thoro*, and make them the sons of Vazul's brother Ladislas the Bald.[203]

Not everyone accepted this change of parentage, however, and not even the Gesta Ungarorum vetera included it; thus, a later chronicler, who took on the mentioned changed parentage, had to come to terms with this controversy. Simon of Kéza adopted this controversy: *Some, however, say that these brothers are the offspring of Prince Vazul from one girl from the Tatun line, not coming from a proper marriage, and with such mixing they would have acquired nobility from*

---

[198] *usque ad tempora Andree regis filii calvi Ladizlay.* Anonymi (P. magistri) Gesta Hungarorum 15, SRH I, p. 55.

[199] *Convocatis igitur ad se Andrea, Bela et Luenta, filiis Zarladislai.* Simonis de Keza Gesta Hungarorum II 44, SRH I, p. 173.

[200] See chapter 14, note 168.

[201] *Convocatis itaque filiis Calvi Ladizlai patrui sui, scilicet Andrea, Beela et Leuenta.* Chron. Hung. comp. saec. XIV. II 69, SRH I, p. 321.

[202] *Quia vero Hungari semper fluctuant iniuria, sicut mare salsum, filii namque Leviatan per nuncios invitabant Borith adulterum, ut veniret et eorum adiutorio regnum sibi vendicaret, credentes ipsum esse filium regis Colomani ... Proceres autem Hungariae vocati sunt ad colloquendum cum rege. Interrogavit autem eos rex, si scirent Borichium adulterum esse vel filium regis Colomani?* Chron. Hung. comp. saec. XIV. II 161, SRH I, pp. 447–448.

[203] Váczy, "A Vazul-hagyomány," pp. 333–338.

Tatun. This is certainly a knavish fable, because they were really from a high-born family and coming from Scythia; therefore, they were the sons of that Ladislas the Bald.[204] With small deviations, the Buda Chronicle and Chronicon Pictum also have this text: *Some say that these brothers were the sons of Prince Vazul from one girl from the Tatun line and not from a proper marriage and for this connection they would get nobility from the Tatun. This is a false and very poor fable, because they were really from a high-born family, because they were the sons of that Ladislas the Bald, who took his wife from Russia. The three brothers were born from this marriage.*[205] If Simon of Kéza and chronicles from the 14th century contain this controversy, then it must have already been in the lost chronicle which Magister Ákos wrote under the rule of Stephen V (1270–1272), which was their common source.[206] Magister Ákos aimed it against the older chronicles and against his contemporaries, who acknowledged the real origin of Hungarian kings from Vazul. In the Buda Chronicle and the Chronicon Pictum this controversy was also aimed against the authors of the Zagreb and the Várad chronicles (both from the 14th century), which further and correctly considered Vazul as the father of Levente, Andrew and Béla and Ladislas the Bald as the father of Bonuslav (Domoslav).[207] They error, however, as does Simon of Kéza, in the birth order of Michael's sons.

---

204   *Quidam autem istos fratres ex duce Wazul progenitos asseverant ex quadam virgine de genere Tatun, non de vero thoro oriundos, et pro tali missitalia illos de Tatun nobilitatem invenisse. Frivolum pro certo est et pessime enarratum. Absque hoc namque nobiles sunt et de Scitia oriundi, quia isti sunt filii Zarladislai.* Simonis de Keza Gesta Hungarorum II 55, SRH I, p. 178.

205   *Tradunt quidam istos tres fratres filios fuisse Vazul ducis ex quadam puella de genere Tatun et non de vero thoro ortos esse, et ob hanc coniunctionem illos de Tatun nobilitatem accepisse. Falsum pro certo est et pessime enaratum. Absque hoc namque sunt nobiles, quia isti filii sunt Calvi Ladizlai, qui uxorem de Ruthenia dicitur accepisse, ex qua tres isti fratres generantur.* Chron. Hung. comp. saec. XIV. II 87, SRH I, p. 344.

206   The chronicler who in the 12th century first attributed to Andrew, Béla and Levente as their father not Vazul but their uncle Ladislas (see note 203), did not at the same time also write an anti-Vazul polemic known from Simon of Kéza and from the 14th century chroniclers. See notes 204, 205. The controversy which refutes Vazul's fatherhood comes most probably from the 13th century. Györffy, "Egy krónikahely," p. 26. Gerics, "A Tátony nemzetségről," p. 4. Gerics, "Quaedam puella," pp. 3, 6–11. Tatun was not *from the Tatun line*. Tatun was her personal name, and the label *de genere* was added by Magister Ákos. Györffy, "Az Árpád-kori magyar krónikák," p. 404.

207   *Iste dux Wazul habuit tres [filios. Primus fuit dux Andreas, postea] factus rex. Secundus fuit dux Bela ... infra apparebunt. Tertius fuit dux L[euente. Dux autem Ladizlaus, de] quo supra, habuit filium, qui vocatus est [Bonuzlo.]* Chronicon Zagrabiense 1, SRH I, p. 206. *Post hec adeptus est coronam Andreas dux, filius Wazul ...* Chronicon Zagrabiense 5, SRH I, p. 208. *cum Bela duce filio Wazul ...* Chronicon Zagrabiense 6, SRH I, p. 208. *Post hec regnavit Bela dictus Begon, filius secundus Wazul, de quo supra.* Chronicon Zagrabiense 7, SRH I, p. 208.

19 Astrik-Anastasius and Radla-Sebastian

At the beginning of Stephen's rule Abbot Astrik, called Anastasius within his order, who was originally a monk at the Abbey of St. Boniface and St. Alexis on the Aventine in Rome, came to Hungary.[208] In the spring of 990 Vojtech/Adalbert, who had given up the title of Prague bishop, also entered this abbey.[209] In 992 Anastasius came together with 12 monks and with Vojtech to Bohemia and became the first abbot of the Břevnov Monastery.[210] The second departure of bishop Vojtech from Bohemia at the end of 994[211] and the murder of the Slavniks at the end of 995[212] unfavourably affected the monastery, which was closely associated with Vojtech and the Slavniks. The Břevnov monks, together with their abbot Anastasius, departed for Poland, where they took refuge with the oldest of the Slavniks, Soběslav,[213] and where they again met with Vojtech, who had come there in the winter of 996/997.[214] Astrik became the first abbot of the abbey *ad Mestrys* (Międzyrzecz, west of Poznan), which Vojtech then founded for him and his monks.[215]

---

[208] *Przibiconis de Radenin dicti Pulkavae Chronicon Bohemiae* 24, *Fontes rerum Bohemicarum*, Tomus V, pořádaním Josefa Emlera (v Praze 1893), p. 30. *Přibíka z Radenína, řečeného Pulkava, Kronika česká* 24, translation Jana Zachová, *Kroniky doby Karla IV* (Praha 1987), pp. 288–289. Rostislav Nový – Jiří Sláma – Jana Zachová, *Slavníkovci ve středověkém písemníctví* (Praha 1987), p. 347. See note 210. The Hartvik legend mentions the identification of Astrik with Anastasius: *eundem Ascricum presulem, qui alio nomine Anastasius dictus est. Legenda sancti Stepahni regis ab Hartvico episcopo conscripta* 9, SRH II, p. 412.

[209] *Johanni Canaparii Vita et passio sancti Adalberti martiris* 16, MPH I, ed. Bielowski, pp. 171–172. *Brunoni Querfurtensi Passio sancti Adalberti episcopi et martyris* 13–14, MPH I, ed. Bielowski, pp. 200–202. *Cosmae Pragensis Chronica Boemorum* I 29, 30, ed. Bretholz, pp. 52–55. *Pulkava* 24, translation Zachová, pp. 287–288. Novotný, *České dějiny I/1*, pp. 631–633.

[210] *Codex diplomaticus et epistolaris regni Bohemiae I*, ed. Gustavus Friedrich (Pragae 1904–1907), no. 37, p. 43, no. 38, pp. 43–46. *Pulkava* 24, 25, translation Zachová, pp. 288–290. Novotný, *České dějiny I/1*, pp. 634–637.

[211] *Canaparius* 20, 22, MPH I, ed. Bielowski, pp. 175–177. *Bruno* 17, MPH I, ed. Bielowski, pp. 203–205. *Pulkava* 24, translation Zachová, pp. 288, 290. Novotný, *České dějiny I/1*, pp. 637–641, 651–652.

[212] *Canaparius* 25, MPH I. ed. Bielowski, p. 178. *Bruno* 21, MPH I, ed. Bielowski, pp. 208–210. *Cosmae Pragensis Chronica Boemorum* I 29, ed. Bretholz, p. 53. *Pulkava* 24, translation Zachová, p. 290. Novotný, *České dějiny I/1*, pp. 646–651.

[213] *Canaparius* 25, MPH I, ed. Bielowski, p. 179. *Bruno* 21, MPH I, ed. A. Bielowski, p. 209. Novotný, *České dějiny I/1*, pp. 646–647, 650–651.

[214] *Canaparius* 26, MPH I, ed. Bielowski, pp. 179–180. *Bruno* 22, MPH I, ed. Bielowski, p. 210. *Passio sancti Adalperti martiris* 2, 3, MPH I, ed. Bielowski, p. 154. Novotný, *České dějiny I/1*, pp. 653–656.

[215] *Saxonica tellure in brevi recedens in Polaniam regionem cursum direxit, et ad Mestris locum divertes coenobium ibi construxit, monachosque quamplures congregans Aschricumque abbatem eos ad regendum constituit. Passio sancti Adalperti martiris* 3, MPH I, ed. Bielowski,

Vojtech's tutor and very close friend, the cleric Radla, survived the murders in Libice. He departed the destroyed Libice for Hungary, where he was received by Prince Géza,[216] who, though he had the reputation as a cruel person, was *however, merciful and generous to foreigners and especially to Christians*. Géza, certainly at the beginning of his rule, when he invited Bavarian missionaries to the country, *issued, aside from this command, that the blessing of hospitality and protection be shown to all Christians wanting to come to his country; he permitted clerics and monks to appear before him ... he enjoyed and freely desired to hear them*.[217]

And Géza's son and successor Stephen invited foreign missionaries after the victory over Koppány in 997. Thus, *many priests and clerics* as well as *abbots and monks* came to Hungary. Then Astrik and his pupils left the Polish Międzyrzecz and headed for Hungary. He settled down *at the foothills of the Iron Mountains* in Pécsvárad, where later the Abbey of St. Benedict originated.[218] Radla, Astrik

---

p. 154. On an incursion against Poland in September 1005 German King Henry II came *ad abbaciam, quee Mezerici dicitur* and here celebrated the holiday of St. Maurice. *Thietmari Merseburgensis episcopi Chronicon* VI 27, cur. Trillmich, pp. 270–271. Gerard Labuda, "Ein europäisches Itinerar seiner Zeit: Die Lebensstationen Adalberts," in *Adalbert von Prag-Brückenbauer zwischen dem Osten und Westen Europas*, ed. H. H. Hennix. *Schriften der Adalbert-Stiftung* 4, (Baden-Baden 1997), p. 70.

216 After arriving in Hungary, Radla remained at Géza's princely court. Vojtech sent a letter to Géza and his wife from Poland, asking them to send Radla to him, and in the following letter he asked Radla himself to come to him. Radla, however, did not want to leave and remained in Hungary. *Bruno* 15, 21, 23, *MPH I*, ed. Bielowski, pp. 202, 210, 211. Vincent Múcska assumes that simultaneously with Radla, Břevnov Abbot Anastasius also left for Hungary. He rejects the identification of Anastasius with Astrik and assumes that in Hungary Anastasius became the Abbot of Pannonhalma Abbey. Vincent Múcska, "About the First Hungarian Bishoprics," in *East Central Europe at the Turn of the 1st and 2nd Millennia. Acta historica Posoniensia* II (Bratislava 2002), p. 127. Vincent Múcska, "O prvých uhorských biskupstvách," *Historický časopis* 51 (2003), no. 1, pp. 19–20.

217 *Legenda maior sancti Stephani regis* 2, SRH II, p. 379. *Legenda sancti Stepahni regis ab Hartvico episcopo conscripta* 2, SRH II, pp. 403–404.

218 *Inde multi presbiteri et clerici ... relictis sedibus propriis elegerunt peregrinari; abbates et monachi nichil proprium habere cupientes sub tam religiosissimi principis patrocinio regulariter vivere desiseraverunt. Inter quos vite religiosus Ascricus pater cum suis discipulis advenit ... Aescricus abbas cum suis honorifice susceptus, ad radicem Montis Ferrei cenobium sub titulo sancti patris Benedicti construxit, ubi usque hodie congregata monasterialis disciplina regulari pollens ... Legenda maior sancti Stephani regis* 7, SRH II, pp. 382–383. *Legenda sancti Stephani regis ab Hartvico episcopo conscripta* 7, SRH II, pp. 410–411. The foundation deed of the abbey in Pécsvárad, dated to year 1015, mentions Astrik as the first Pécsvárad abbot and the Kalocsa archbishop: *monasterium Sancte Dei Genitricis Marie et Sancti Benedicti ad radicem Montis Ferrei diligenter construximus ... in ipso die consecracionis dicti monasterii per ministerium domini Ascrici Colocensis archiepiscopi et primi abbatis prescripti monasterii ... DHA I*, ed. Györffy, no. 12, pp. 67–72, 80. Although the document

and other foreigners came to Hungary from various countries. No one had to send them there. They knew that in the services of a Hungarian prince they could distinguish themselves more than if they remained at home. This was a great opportunity for them, and they wanted to take advantage of it.[219]

    is a forgery, Astrik and his monks could have lived there after their arrival in Hungary. György Györffy, "Zu den Anfängen der ungarischen Kirchenorganisation auf Grund neuer Quellenkritischer Ergebnisse," *Archivum historiae pontificiae* 7 (1969), pp. 100–101. On 4 April 1001 in Ravenna, at a great gathering of ecclesiastical representatives in the presence of Pope Sylvester II and Holy Roman Emperor Otto III, was also *Anastasius abbas monasterii Sancte Marie Sclavanensis provincie*. *DHA I*, ed. Györffy, no. 3, pp. 20–21. Václav Chaloupecký and György Györffy identified Abbot Anastasius, who was in Ravenna in April 1001, with Astrik-Anastasius. According to Václav Chaloupecký Anastasius, although he departed for Hungary, was further abbot of the Břevnov monastery up to 1002, when he became the Pannonhalma abbot. Chaloupecký, "Radla-Anastasius," pp. 216–217. According to György Györffy, abbot Anastasius was abbot of a Polish monastery in the Miedzyrzecze region and in the services of King Stephen left to Ravenna, where then the Holy Roman Emperor was staying with the pope, and he got there the foundation deed for the Esztergom archbishopric. Györffy, "Zu den Anfängen," pp. 85, 101–102, 105–108. *DHA I*, ed. Györffy, no. 4, pp. 22–24. *Sclavonia* was a very common name even for Croatia. György Györffy, "Szlavónia kialakulásának oklevélkritikai vizsgálata," *Leveltári Közlemények* 41 (1970), pp. 223–240. György Györffy, "Die Nordwestgrenze des byzantinischen Reiches im XI. Jahrhundert und die Ausbildung des 'ducatus Sclavoniae'," in "Mélanges offerts á Szabolcs de Vajay," (Braga – Livraria – Cruz 1971), pp. 295–313. István Elter, "Magyarország Idrísí földrajzi művében (1154)." *Acta Universitatis Szegediensis de Attila József nominatae. Acta Historica* 82 (1985), pp. 53–63. Croatia lay much closer to Ravenna than Poland or any other Slavic country to which the label *Sclavaniensis provincia* may relate. Therefore, the Abbot Anastasius came in April 1001 to Ravenna most probably from Croatia and had nothing in common with Hungary. He could not have been identical with the Astrik-Anastasius who brought the foundation deed for a Hungarian bishopric and with the royal crown to Stephen from Rome just a year before.

219 Monks, abbots and priests arrived to Stephen's Hungary from various countries, similarly as to Bohemia for St. Wenceslaus: *Thus, in that period many priests from Bavaria and from Swabia, hearing news of him, rushed to him with the relics of the saints and books.* (*In tempore autem illo multi sacerdotes de provincia Bavariorum et de Svevia audientes famam eo confluebant cum reliquiis sanctorum et libris ad eum*). *Život sv. Václava*, translation Josef Truhlář, *FRB I*, p. 185. *Crescente fide* 5, translation Jaroslav Ludvíkovský, in *Na úsvitu křesťanství. Z naší literární tvorby doby románské v století IX.–XIII.*, ed. Václav Chaloupecký (Praha 1942), pp. 81–82. Prince Wenceslas took good care of the foreign priests: *He established churches in all the castles very well and he beautifully assigned the servants of God from many nations in them. Charvátskohlaholská redakce původní legendy o sv. Václavu, Text Novljanský*, ed. Josef Vajs, *Sborník staroslovanských literárních památek o sv. Václavu a sv. Lidmile*, ed. Vajs, pp. 38–39. Miloš Weingard, *Rekonstruovaný text I. staroslověnské legendy o sv. Václavu* 30, *Svatováclavský sborník I. Kníže Václav Svatý a jeho doba*, ed. Karel Guth, Jan Kapras, Antonín Novák, Karel Stloukal (Praha 1934), pp. 976–977, 989–990. *První staroslovanská legenda o sv. Václavu* 3, translation Josef Vašica, in *Na úsvitu křesťanství*, ed. Chaloupecký, p. 70. Under the rule of Mojmír I and Rastislav missionaries

Astrik-Anastasius became Stephen's advisor and distinguished himself in his diplomatic services. Stephen *on the advice and with the consent of Abbot Anastasius* endowed the Pannonhalma Abbey,[220] the abbot of which (perhaps already then) was the Rasina mentioned in the St. Gerard legend.[221]

Another of Vojtech's friends, Radla, who came to Hungary perhaps two years before Astrik, took the order name of Sebastian.[222] Not only did Vojtech very

---

also came from various countries to the Moravians. Prince Rastislav sent a report about this to the Byzantine emperor: *And look, many Christian teachers from Wallachia and from Greece and from Germany came to us and they teach us variously.* ŽM 5, MMFH II, p. 144. Třeštík, *Vznik*, pp. 128, 180. Even Salzburg bishop (from 798 archbishop) Arno *from all sides (undique) ordaining priests and sending them to Slavic territories, that is the lands of Carinthia and also Lower Pannonia. Conversio* 7, ed. Wolfram, pp. 46–47.

220   Stephen, after the defeat of Koppány's rebellion in 997 *on the advice and with the consent of Abbot Anastasius* endowed the abbey at Pannonhalm: *nos interventu, consilio et consensu domini Anastasii abbatis <de> monasterio sancti Martini in monte supra Pannoniam sito ... talem concessimus libertatem, qualem detinet monasterium sancti Benedicti in Monte Cassino ... consiliante domno Anastasio prescripto abbate et iugiter adiuvante, confortari et laurenti sumus.* DHA I, ed. Györffy, no. 5, p. 39. The preposition *de* requires an ablative; however, the following word *monasterio ... concessimus* is in the dative. If we leave out this preposition, the grammatical issue falls away and the meaning of the sentence is clarified. From this it follows that a later forger added the preposition *de* to the cited sentence in the Pannonhalma document, and he thus made from abbot Anastasius the Pannonhalma abbot. Györffy, "Zu den Anfängen," pp. 93–94. Györffy, "Der Aufstand von Koppány," pp. 188–189. Györffy, "István király," pp. 140–144, 180. Györffy's statement that Stephen I could not have endowed the abbey *interventu, consilio et consensu* of its own abbot, but only a foreign abbot is doubted by József Gerics, who convincingly demonstrated that Stephen I could have endowed the abbey on the advice of its own abbot. Therefore, he considers Abbot Anastasius as abbot of Pannonhalma. József Gerics, *Egyház, állam és gondolkodás Magyarországon a középkorban* (Budapest 1995), pp. 28–36. Stephen, however, could have gotten the advice of another person, who had close relations to the abbey or to its abbot and at the same time belonged among Stephen's confidants and could have been the intermediary for the Pannanhalma Abbot. Abbot Anastasius was not the Pannanhalma Abbot, as the later forger and more recently József Gerics thought, but was identified with the Pécsvárad (before then the Břevnov and Miedzyrzecze) abbot Astrikom-Anastasius, whose advice and consent was important for Stephen could not have been lacking even when endowing the most important abbey in Hungary.

221   *Legenda sancti Gerhardi episcopi* 3–4, SRH II, pp. 483–486. György Györffy identified Radla with Pannonhalma Abbot Rasin. Györffy, "Zu den Anfängen," p. 94. Györffy, *István király*, pp. 181, 296. Györffy, *König Stephan*, pp. 125–126. MT I/1, pp. 771–772. Eszter Szőnyi – Péter Tomka, "Pannonhalma környékének története a bencének megjelenéséig," in *Mons Sacer 996–1996. Pannonhalma 1000 éve I*, ed. Imre Takács (Pannonhalma 1996), pp. 38–46. Géza Érszegi, "Szent István pannonhalmi oklevele," in *Mons Sacer 996–1996. Pannonhalma 1000 éve I*, ed. Takács, pp. 47–89. Gábor Thoroczkay, "Szent István pannonhalmi oklevelének historiográfiája," in *Mons Sacer 996–1996. Pannonhalma 1000 éve I*, ed. Takács, pp. 90–109.

222   Györffy, *István király*, pp. 61, 79–80, 120, 132, 139–140, 181–182, 241, 266, 335. Györffy, *König Stephan*, pp. 57, 109, 113, 125–126, 131, 156. MT I/1, pp. 726, 757, 771–772, 777, 800. If Radla was

much love Radla, but he was also a favourite of Géza's and Stephen's princely and then royal courts,[223] where he lived from year 995. He enjoyed exceptional favour above all with Stephen himself.[224]

20 Archbishopric and the Royal Crown

When Emperor Otto III in January and February of 1000 set off from Italy to Poland in order to establish an archbishopric there, with the consent of the pope, he remained for perhaps three weeks in Regensburg.[225] The emperor's long stay in Regensburg could have had several reasons. Perhaps he was approached there by a Hungarian embassy, which Astrik could have led there. Through him Stephen I negotiated with the emperor about the establishing of Hungarian bishoprics and about a royal crown.[226]

In March of 1000 Emperor Otto III visited Gniezno, where over the grave of St. Adalbert of Prague (also called St. Vojtech) he established an archbishopric, to which he subjugated the newly formed bishoprics in Kołobrzeg, Kraków and Wrocław. Vojtech's brother Radim (Gaudencius), whom the pope had already ordained as archbishop the year before in Rome, became the first Gniezno archbishop.[227] According to old and still valid rules, three bishops could ordain a fourth; therefore, a church province with four bishops was, in the case of

---

identical with the monk and future archbishop Sebastián, who died in 1007 (see note 112), then he could not be identical with the Pannonhalma Abbot Rasin, who lived still in the period when St. Gerard came to Hungary, that is in 1015 or sometime after. See chapter 15, note 47.

223 *he was with the monks, and as is said those who at that time knew him, beautiful and good.* Brunone Querfurtensi Passio sancti Adalberti episcopi et martyris 15, 21, 23, MPH I, ed. Bielowski, pp. 202, 210, 211.

224 *There was a monk by the name of Sebastian, a man of praiseworthy life and devout saintliness in the service of God. The worthy king loved him exceptionally, because he who was more godly was nicer for him.* Legenda sancti Stephani regis ab Hartvico episcopo conscripta 11, SRH II, p. 416.

225 On 17 January 1000 Otto III was still in Staffelsee; he came to Regensburg on about 20 January and on 6 February gave out two donations there. Around 10 February he was already in Meissen. *Regesta imperii II. Band: Sächsisches Haus (919–1024), 3. Abteilung: Die Regesten des Kaisserreiches unter Otto III.* (980 [983]–1002), 2. Lieferung 988–1002, nach Johann Friedrich Böhmer neubearbeitet von Mathilde Uhlirz (Graz – Köln 1957), no. 1341–1349b, pp. 740–744. Strzelczyk, Jerzy: Zjazd gnieznienski, Poznań 2000, pg. 27–28.

226 Nový – Sáma – Zachová, *Slavníkovci*, pp. 69–70.

227 Thietmari Chronicon IV 45, rec. Kurze, pp. 89–90. Thietmari Chronicon IV 45, cur. Trillmich, pp. 162–163. Galli Chronicon I 6, MPH I, ed. Bielowski, pp. 400–401. Cosmae Pragensis Chronica Boemorum I 34, ad a. 999, ed. Bretholz, p. 60. Regesta imperii II. Band, 3. Abteilung, 2. Lieferung, ed. Uhlirz, no. 1328b, 1349c–1350/1a, pp. 732, 744–749. Třeštík, "Sv. Vojtěch a formování střední Evropy," pp. 95–96. Strzelczyk, *Zjazd gnieznienski*, pp. 34–99.

the death of one of them, capable of ordaining a successor.[228] Otto, therefore, established in Poland an archbishopric and three bishoprics. That's why even the Great Moravian church got in the summer of 899 an archbishop and three bishops.[229] The Hungarian and Polish churches had at the beginning a completely parallel development, and so Stephen I achieved with the emperor in 1000 exactly what Boleslaw the Brave in that same year got for Poland, that is an archbishopric and three bishoprics.[230]

Stephen I established the Esztergom archbishopric while still a prince, that is before his royal coronation (which took place on 1 January 1001): *Servant of God, the most Christian prince (princeps) ... divided the provinces into ten bishoprics and with the written consent of successor of the apostles on the Roman seat determined the Esztergom church, to be in the future the metropolis and teacher of the others.*[231] Stephen appointed Dominic, the current missionary bishop in Veszprém, as the first Esztergom archbishop (1000–1002);[232] he had three years earlier stood by Stephen in the battle against Koppány.[233] He appointed Stephen, mentioned in 1009, as the new Veszprém bishop,[234] or earlier some predecessor of Stephen still unknown to us. Abbot Astrik became the first

---

228 Múcska, "About the First Hungarian Bishoprics," pp. 125–126. Múcska, "O prvých uhorských biskupstváh," pp. 14–16.
229 *MMFH III*, pp. 233–234. *CDES I*, ed. Marsina, no. 39, pp. 32–33. Steinhübel, "Štyri veľkomoravské biskupstvá," pp. 21–39.
230 According to Béla Kovács, the Esztergom archdiocese already had at the time of its origin four dioceses: Esztergom, Veszprém, Kalocsa and Eger. Béla Kovács, *Az egri egyházmegye története 1596-ig* (Eger 1987), pp. 25–26. And according to László Koszta the Hungarian ecclesiastical province had at the beginning four dioceses: Veszprém, Esztergom, Győr and Transylvania. László Koszta, "A keresztény egyházszervezet kialakulása," in *Árpád elött és után*, ed. Gyula Kristó, Ferenc Makk, (Szeged 1996), pp. 107–111. László Koszta, "A váci püspökség alapítasa," *Századok* 135 (2001), no. 2, p. 365. László Koszta, *A kalocsai érseki tartomány kialakulása* (Pécs 2013). Vincent Múcska very convincingly proffered the four oldest Hungarian bishoprics. In his opinion Stephen I simultaneously with the Esztergom bishopric established bishoprics in Veszprém, Kalocsa and in Vác. Múcska, "About the First Hungarian Bishoprics," pp. 125–126. Múcska, "O prvých uhorských biskupstváh," pp. 15–17.
231 *Legenda maior sancti Stephani regis* 8, SRH II, p. 383. *Legenda sancti Stephani regis ab Hartvico episcopo conscripta* 8, SRH II, pp. 411–412.
232 *DHA I*, ed. Györffy, no. 5/II, pp. 39, 41. Györffy, "Zu den Anfängen," pp. 94–96. Györffy, *István király*, pp. 76, 116, 119, 150–151, 158, 177–178, 181, 250, 267. Györffy, *König Stephan*, pp. 114, 126, 145–146, 157. *MT I/1*, pp. 731, 733, 761, 772, 792, 801. Missionary bishop Bruno-Domonkos, based in Veszprém, left Veszprém at the end of year 1000 and went to Esztergom. The first Kalocsa bishop Astrik, after the death of Domonkos's successor Sebastian in 1007, likewise left from Kalocsa and became the third Esztergom archbishop.
233 *DHA I*, ed. Györffy, no. 5/II, p. 39.
234 *DHA I*, ed. Györffy, no. 8, pp. 49–53.

Kalocsa bishop (1000–1007): *The wise prince (dux), knowing then the faith of the mentioned Astrik, decorated with the title of bishop and the infula, with the canonical choice promoted him and entrusted to him the station of the Kalocsa bishopric.*[235]

Vác became the seat of the fourth bishopric,[236] and exactly like Kalocsa, it lay on the eastern bank of the Danube. Prince Ort, who three years before fought on Stephen's side against Koppány, was seated in Vác. Stephen I, obviously when he established the Vác bishopric, kept his loyal Ort even closer to him. Thus, a small prince became a castle count and his Vác Principality became a castle county.[237]

Only Transdanubia, without Somogy County, which Stephen assigned under the ecclesiastical administration of the Pannonhalma Abbey, remained to the Veszprém bishopric, which from a missionary bishopric became a regular one. Nitria became the Esztergom diocese.[238] The Kalocsa and Vác bishoprics reached from the eastern bank of the Danube up to the Tisza River region.

Esztergom, Veszprém, Kalocsa and Vác lay on territory which Stephen had in year 1000 directly and safely under his power. This was the oldest Árpád territory, which had belonged directly to Prince Árpád and his successors.

The new and still unconsecrated bishoprics had to be confirmed by the emperor and the pope.[239] Therefore, Stephen sent the newly nominated Kalocsa bishop Astrik to Rome: *In the fourth year after his father's death* (that is, in 1000)

---

235   *Legenda sancti Stephani regis ab Hartvico episcopo conscripta* 8, SRH II, p. 412. According to László Koszta, the bishopric in Kalocsa originated only in 1009. Koszta, *A kalocsai érseki tartomány kialakulása.*
236   The opinion of Vincent Múcska that the Vác bishopric belonged among the four oldest Hungarian bishoprics established by Hungarian King Stephen I is convincing. See note 230. Géza I had the bishopric cathedral, consecrated to the Virgin Mary, built in Vác immediately after his coronation in 1074. *Chron. Hung. comp. saec. XIV.* II 124, SRH I, pp. 394–395. The building of this cathedral in 1074 is the oldest documentation on the existence of the Vác bishopric. Géza, however, did not establish the Vác bishopric. Indeed, King Peter Orseolo, who had the bishopric cathedral of St. Peter built in Pécs, was also not at the same time the founder of the Pécs bishopric. *Simonis de Keza Gesta Hungarorum* 53. SRH I, p. 178. *Chron. Hung. comp. saec. XIV.* II 85, SRH I, p. 343. Both bishoprics were founded in years 1000 and 1009 by Stephen I.
237   See p. 359. See chapter 15, note 78.
238   The Esztergom diocese belonged among the 9 Nitrian counties: Bratislava, Trenčín, Nitra, Komárno, Esztergom, Tekov, Hont, Novohrad (Nógrad) and Borsod. See pp. 408–411, 413–415, 520–521, 524–525. The Esztergom diocese to the south and east bordered from year 1000 with the Veszprém and Vác diocese and from 1009 also with the Győr and Eger diocese.
239   Múcska, "About the First Hungarian Bishoprics," p. 124. Múcska, "O prvých uhorských biskupstvách," p. 13.

he sent ... Bishop Astrik, who was otherwise called Anastasius, to the threshold of the blessed apostles; he was to request of the successor of St. Peter, the apostolic prince, to generously bless the young Christianity originating in Pannonia, to declare the Esztergom church by his deed as the seat of an archbishop and to give his blessing to the other dioceses and confirm them and also that he deign his power to strengthen the granting of the royal crown.[240]

The decision of the emperor and the pope regarding Hungary was taken at some common meetings in Rome; therefore, Astrik came there to meet them. From the beginning of January up to late summer of 1000 Otto III was not in Rome. Pope Sylvester II welcomed Otto III in Rome shortly before the middle of August. Another short stay of Otto III in Rome is shown to us by his donation from 7 October. Only after 1 November 1000 did the emperor settled in Rome for a longer time and spend Christmas there. In February of the following year, Otto was surprised by a Roman rebellion. The last written documented date of the emperor's stay in Rome is 15 February 1001. He had to flee from the besieged imperial residence on Aventine. Perhaps two weeks after fleeing Rome, he departed, accompanied by Sylvester II, from its vicinity. On 7 March he was in Perugia and on 25 March in Ravenna.[241]

Astrik set off for Rome when he could meet with not only the pope but also the emperor, because the emperor and the pope had to agree together on Stephen's requests. Astrik was in Rome even before Stephen's royal coronation. If we add to this the time he needed to return to Hungary, then he came to Rome and shortly left from it in November, or perhaps at the beginning of December of 1000. Astrik got the foundation document for the Esztergom archbishopric and other Hungarian bishoprics and the royal crown for Stephen at one time, during one visit to Rome, as is stated in the Saint Stephen legends.[242] After Astrik's return to Hungary, the Esztergom archbishopric and the three bishoprics that Stephen had organized even before Astrik's departure for Rome began to operate. Only after 1 January 1001 could the Hungarian duke be crowned by his archbishop and bishops.[243] Even according to Thietmar, who emphasizes the emperor's participation in the origin of the Hungarian ecclesiastical provinces and the granting of a royal crown, Stephen first organized the bishoprics and only after received the royal crown: *From the grace and on the initiative of*

---

240 *Legenda sancti Stephani regis ab Hartvico episcopo conscripta* 9, SRH II, pp. 412–413.
241 *Regesta imperii II. Band, 3. Abteilung, 2. Lieferung,* ed. Uhlirz, no. 1339–1402, pp. 739–790.
242 *Legenda maior sancti Stephani regis* 8, 9, SRH II, pp. 383–384. *Legenda sancti Stephani regis ab Hartvico episcopo conscripta* 9, SRH II, pp. 412–414.
243 Györffy, "Zu den Anfängen," p. 102. Györffy, *István király,* pp. 148–149. MT I/1, p. 761. DHA I, ed. Györffy, no. 1, pp. 17–18. Zsoldos, *The Legacy,* pp. 41–49.

Emperor Otto III, Vajk (= Stephen), *son-in-law of Henry, Duke of Bavaria, founding episcopal seats, received the blessing and the crown.*[244]

21   Preslava

King Stephen immediately after his coronation had the first Hungarian coins minted. These were silver denar with the legend PRESLAVVA CIV.[245] The first Hungarian mint thus worked at castle Preslava, today's Bratislava. The Annales Altahenses mention this castle under the name *Preslavvaspurch*.[246] The German purch and Latin CIV (civitas) have the same meaning: they mean castle. The legend +SPHANVS REX on the other side of this denar (the letter N, S are reversed) indicates the first Hungarian King Stephen (Stephanus, with the letters TE left out).[247]

The name of the castle Preslava began with the letter P, just like the names of Russian castles Pereslavľ (north-east of Moscow), Perejaslavľ (on the Dnieper,

---

244   *Thietmari Chronicon* IV 59 (38), rec. Kurze, p. 97. *Thietmari Chronicon* IV 59, cur. Trillmich, pp. 174–175. Thietmar emphasizes the emperor's participation in the decision to establish a Hungarian ecclesiastical province and to send a royal crown to Stephen. Vincent Múcska, "Uhorsko na ceste ku kresťanskej monarchii," in *Proměna středovýchodní Evropy raného a vrcholného středověku. Mocenské souvislosti a paralely*, ed. Libor Jan (Brno 2010), pp. 109–111.

245   Jonsson Kenneth, "The earliest Hungarian Coignage," in *Commentationes Numismaticae 1988. Festgabe für Gert und Vera Hatz* (Hamburg 1988), pp. 95–102. István Gedai, "Az első magyar pénzek időrendi kérdéséhez," *Századok* 122 (1988), no. 4, pp. 694–696. István Gedai, "Preslavva Civ(itas)," in *Numismatiska meddelanden 37. Festskrift till Lars O. Lagerqvist* (Stockholm 1989), pp. 95–102. László Kovács, *A kora Árpád-kori magyar pénzverésről. Érmetani és régészeti tanulmányok a Kárpát-medence I. (Szent) István és (Vak) Béla uralkodása közötti időszakának (1000–1141) érméiről. Varia Archaeologica Hungarica 7* (Budapest 1997), pp. 61–73, 79–80, 200, 237, 244–245.

246   *Cum enim urbem Preslavvaspurch, in finibus utriusque regni sitam ... Annales Altahenses maiores* ad a. 1052, rec. Oefele, p. 48. The daughter of Kiev Prince Svatopluk II, who in 1104 set off for Nitria and Bihar Prince Álmos, was named Predslava. *Latopis Nestora* 86, year 6612 (1104), *MPH I*, ed. Bielowski, p. 814. Wertner, *Az Árpádok családi története*, pp. 250–252.

247   In the portrait of Stephen I on a Hungarian coronation cloak is the inscription SEPHANVS REX, in which the letter T is missing. Györffy, *István király*, picture 19. Endre Tóth, "István és Gizella miseruhája," *Századok* 131 (1997), no. 1, pp. 17, 32. Katalin E. Nagy, Enikő Sipos, Ernő Marosi, "The picture fields of the mantle (1–43). Fragments of the embroidered band," in *The Coronation Mantle of the Hungarian Kings*, edited by István Bardoly (Budapest 2005), pp. 158–159. Saint Stephen the first martyr, depicted on this same cloak, however, has his name written error-free: STEPHANVS. Nagy, Sipos, Marosi, *The picture fields*, pp. 160–161.

south-east of Kiev), Peremyšľ (on the Oka River) and anther Peremyšľ (on the San River, today Przemyśl). Bulgarian Preslav also had such a name.[248]

The mint master of King Stephen, who worked directly at Preslava Castle, knew well the name of this castle from everyday hearing and correctly engraved it into the coin stamping tool. A monk who lived in the Altach monastery recorded the events of Hungarian history reliably and in detail. Thus, he well knew Hungary and with it also its significant border castle, to which a road led from his monastery directly down the Danube, and he wrote the name of the castle correctly. All other foreigners, separated by a larger distance from Preslava Castle, mutilated its Slavic name or took the already mutilated form, wrote it and thus left it for us.[249] Therefore, we need not doubt that both the mint master and the monk who recorded the name of the castle the same, recorded it exactly as it sounded in their time.

Castles, towns and other settlement that got their name after their princely founder, or another important nobleman, have it in the masculine form (although the family itself was sometimes changed to the feminine), for example, Bohemian Boleslav,[250] Vraclav (originally Vratislav), Čáslav, Radim, Vlastislav,

---

[248] The castle thus did not take its name from Braslav, as was assumed and is still often assumed, especially by linguists. Ján Stanislav, "Bratislava – Prešporok – Pressburg – Pozsony (Pôvod stredovekej Bratislavy. Vysvetlenie mien)," in *Slovanská Bratislava I. Sborník príspevkov k dejinám hl. mesta Bratislavy*, red. A. Fiala (Bratislava 1948), pp. 22–46. Rudolf Krajčovič, *Živé kroniky slovenských dejín skryté v názvoch obcí a miest* (Bratislava 2005), pp. 73–74. Matúš Kučera also advocates the improbable opinion about Braslav, which supposedly gave in the 9th century his name to then Bratislava. Kučera, Matúš Kučera, "O pôvode názvu Bratislavy," in *Bitka pri Bratislave v roku 907 a jej význam pre vývoj stredného Podunajska*, ed. Štefanovičová, Hulínek, pp. 53–63. Daniel Rapant assumed that the castle got its name after Svatoplukov's third son, who was said to be called Předěslav. Daniel Rapant, "Traja synovia Svätoplukovi," *Elán* 11 (jún 1940), pp. 2–4. Bratislava Castle, however, originated and thus also got its name much later than the assumed Svatoplukov's third son actually lived.

[249] Various mutilated forms of this name, recorded by more distant reporters, see János Melich, "Die Namen von Pressburg," *Zeitschrift für slawische Philologie* 3 (1926), pp. 212–313. Ján Stanislav, "Bratislava – Prešporok – Pressburg – Pozsony," pp. 22, 30–31.

[250] Václav Flajšhaus, "Osoby a místa v legendách svatováclavských," in *Svatováclavský sborník I. Kníže Václav Svatý a jeho doba*, redigovali Karel Guth, Jan Kapras, Antonín Novák, Karel Stloukal (Praha 1934), p. 824. Miloš Weingart, "První česko-církevněslovanská legenda o svatém Václavu," in *Svatováclavský sborník I*, ed. Guth, Kapras, Novák, Stloukal, pp. 910–911, 970, 979, 991. Aleksandr Ivanovič Rogov – Emilie Bláhová – Václav Konzal, *Staroslověnské legendy českého původu. Nejstarší kapitoly z dějin česko-ruských kulturních vztahů* (Praha 1976), pp. 70–71, 73, 96–97, 118, 121, 138, 308, 314.

Soběslav, Jaroměř, Moravian Spytihněv,[251] Silesian Vratislav (Wrocław),[252] Bulgarian Radomir (south-west from Sofia) and Preslav.[253] In Kievan Rus' this was Perejaslavl' Russkij (on the Dnieper, south-east of Kiev), Pereslavl' (north-east of Moscow), Izjaslavl' (on the Horyn River), Izjaslavl' (south-east of Smolensk), Izjaslavl' (north-west from Minsk), Mstislavl' (at the confluence of the Ostier and Vechra, east of Mogilev), Mstislavl' (south of Smolensk), Boguslavl' (on the Ros River, south of Kiev), Jaroslavl' (on the Volga, north-east of Rostov), Jaroslavl' (on the San River, today Jarosław in Poland), Roslavl' (on the Ostier River), Vladimir on the Klyazma, Volodymyr-Volynsky (on the Bug River), Glebl' (east of Kiev), Radomysl' (on the Teteriv River, west of Kiev), Peremyšl' (on the Oka River), Peremyšl' (on the San River, today Przemyśl), Vasilev, Svjatopolk (close to Jurjev).[254] In Hungary they got their name after the local prince or the first count of Veszprém Castle (originally Bezpriem), Hont, Borsod, Doboka (before then Zombor), Csanád and Szolnok.

Masculine names that became the names of castles and towns sometimes took a feminine ending –a. The antique cities of Alexandria, Antiochia, Roma,

---

251 Michal Lutovský – Zdeněk Petráň, *Slavníkovci. Mýtus českého dějepisectví* (Praha 2004), pp. 84–86. Kateřina Sučková – Roman Abušinov, *Staroslovanské hrady. Slovanská hradiště v Čechách, na Moravě a ve Slezsku* (Příbram 2005), pp. 42, 115, 170, 232, 233, 265, 287, 330, 358.

252 *Thietmari Chronicon* IV 45, VIII (VII) 64 (47), rec. Kurze, pp. 90, 231. *Thietmari Chronicon* IV 45, VII 64, cur. Trillmich, pp. 162–163, 424–425. *Galli Chronicon* II 8, III 10, 15, *MPH I*, ed. Bielowski, pp. 434, 469, 471.

253 Constantine Porphyrogenitus, *De administrando imperio* 32, 40, ed. Moravcsik, pp. 158–159, 176–177. Konstantinos Porfyrogennétos, *De administrando imperio* 32, 40, *MMFH III*, pp. 394–395. S. Vaklinov, *Formirane na starobălgarskata kultura. VI–IX vek* (Sofija 1977), pp. 124–127, 176–177, 180–227. I. G. Konovalova – V. B. Perchavko, *Drevnjaja Rus i nižneje Podunavje* (Moskva 2000), pp. 53–68.

254 *Latopis Nestora* 21, year 6415 (907), 27, year 6453 (945), 38, year 981 (6489), 42, year 6496 (988), 45, year 6501 (993), year 6504 (996), 58, year 6562 (1054–1055), 59, year 6562 (1055), 66, year 6580 (1072), 70, year 6586 (1079), 71, year 6592 (1084), 72, year 6595 (1087), 73, year 6598 (1090), 74, year 6599 (1091), 76, year 6601 (1093), 77, year 6602 (1094), 78, year 6603 (1095), 79, year 6604 (1096), 82, year 6605 (1097), 83, year 6606 (1098), year 6607 (1099), 6608 (1100), 85, year 6611 (1103), 86, year 6613 (1105), 87, year 6615 (1107), 89, year 6618 (1110), 92, year 6621 (1113), 93, year 6621 (1113), *MPH I*, ed. Bielowski, pp. 573, 574, 590–591, 624, 656–657, 668, 670, 671, 710, 711, 730, 753, 754, 755, 756, 757–758, 760, 765–767, 775, 777, 779, 789, 802–806, 807–808, 811, 815, 816, 819, 833, 834. *Nauka Monomacha*, *MPH I*, ed. Bielowski, pp. 874–877. Boris Dmitrijevič Grekov, *Kyjevská Rus* (Praha 1953), pp. 18, 91, 135, 222, 224, 230, 262, 297, 298, 332, 373, 405, 419, 429, 430, 480, 482, 425, 499, 500–503, 519, 521, 522, 523. Boris Aleksandrovič Rybakov, *Kyjevskaja Rus i russkije knjažestva XII–XIII vv.* (Moskva 1993), pp. 61–66, 71, 333–334, 453, 459–460, 471, 488–489, 500, 509–511, 519, 521, 525, 547–549, 551, 556, 558, 564. In 1095 *Svjatopolk then commanded to establish a fortified town in the Vitičevsky hills and named it after him as Svjatopolk. Latopis Nestora* 78, year 6603 (1095), *MPH I*, ed. Bielowski, p. 777.

Caesarea and Augusta have names with a feminine end -a. However, they got their names not after women but after significant rulers and commanders: Alexandros, Antiochos, Romulus, Caesar and Augustus. The names of the ancient and then Bavarian town of Regina (today's Regensburg) also has an -a ending, which is derived from the name of the Reganus River (today's Regen). The name Regina or Ratisbona (antique Castra Regina, today's Regensburg) we read in inscriptions REGINA CIVITAS and RATISPONA CIV[ITAS] on coins of Bavarian Duke Henry II (955–976, 985–995).[255] The name Augusta (antique Augusta Vindelicorum, today's Augsburg) we read in the inscription AVGVSTA CIVI[TAS] on the coins of Augsburg Bishops Henry I (973–982), Liudolf (987–996), Siegfried I (1000–1006) and Bruno (1006–1029)[256] and the name Mogoncia (antique Mogontiacum, todays Mainz) in the inscription MOGONCIA CIVIT[AS] on the coins of Emperor Otto II (973–983).[257] Prague, originally Praga,[258] got its name from the Vltava terrace.[259] Pragъ, which is grammatically masculine, took the feminine ending of –a. Thus, the name Praga originated for the castle, which stood out on the Vltava terrace. The coins of Bohemian Prince Boleslaus I (935–972) and his successors have the legend PRAGA CIVITAS.[260]

---

255 István Gedai, *A magyar pénzverés kezdete* (Budapest 1986), picture 4, 11. Zdeněk Petráň, *První české mince* (Praha 1998), p. 55. *Europas Mitte um 1000. Beiträge zur Geschichte, Kunst und Archäologie, Band 1*, ed. ed. Alfried Wieczorek, Hans-Martin Hinz (Stuttgart 2000), p. 189.
256 Gedai, *A magyar pénzverés kezdete*, pp. 42–43, picture 5. *Europas Mitte um 1000*), p. 268.
257 Petráň, *První české mince*, p. 153.
258 In 929 Henry I *Pragam adiit cum omni exercitu, Boemiorum urbem*. Widukindi Rerum gestarum Saxonicarum libri tres I 35, rec. Waitz, p. 29. Miloš Weingart, "První českocírkevněslovanská legenda o svatém Václavu. Rozbor filologický," in *Svatováclavský sborník I*, ed. Guth, Kapras, Novák, Stloukal, pp. 894–895, 946, 948, 969–970, 979, 983, 991, 993, 1008, 1013, 1074. Rogov, – Bláhová – Konzal, *Staroslověnské legendy*, pp. 71, 73, 98, 121, 138, 274, 284–285, 293, 302, 308, 314.
259 The Dnieper also had river terraces (*porogy*). *Latopis Nestora* 36, year 6479 (970), 6480 (971), 43, year 6496 (988), *MPH I*, ed. Bielowski, pp. 616, 662. Constantine Porphyrogenitus also recorded the Slavic names of seven Dnieper terraces: *Essupi, Ostrovuniprag, Gelandri, Niejasyt, Vulniprag, Veruci, Naprezi*. Constantine Porphyrogenitus, *De administrando imperio* 9, ed. Moravcsik, pp. 56–63. Konstantinos Porfyrogennétos, *De administrando imperio* 9, *MPH I*, ed. Bielowski I, pp. 16–19. Prague (Praga) could have a name from the parched hill called Pragъ, on which it originated. Antonín Profous, "Co znamená jméno Praha," *Věstník ministerstva vnitra ČSR* 8 (1926), pp. 325–331, 369–376. This assumption, however, is less probable. Not only did Czech Praha get its name after a river terrace, but also Prahovo in Serbia, which lies on the bank of the Danube near the Bulgarian border.
260 Petráň, *První české mince*, pp. 55, 62, 64, 96–99. *Europas Mitte, Katalog*, ed. Wieczorek, Hinz, p. 290.

Castle Preslava, although it had a feminine ending (–a) in its name, did not take its name from a woman called Preslava, but after an important, however, today unknown man who was called Preslav.[261] The name Preslav was favoured in Slovakia during the time of Árpád. Zvolen count Miko issued a document in 1246 in which he described the border of the territory Ban, donated by Béla IV to the former count, lying between the villages Nemce and Zabrod, labelled *under our bailiff Preslav (pristaldo vice nostri Preslao comite)*.[262] In 1252 *count Prejaslav, son of Prednej (comes Preyazlaus, filius Predney)*, got the land Krňa from King Béla IV.[263] After the death of the mentioned *count Preslav (Preslai comitis)*, Ludince, which *Preslav (Preslaus)* owned, fell to his wife and daughters.[264]

The small number of coins (we know of only three of them) that bear the name of the castle Preslava is testimony that Stephen's Bratislava mint worked for only a very short time.

---

261 For the various (mutilated by the writers) forms of the name Preslav in Hungary, especially in Slovakia, see Katalin Fehértói, *Árpád-kori személynévtár (1000–1301)* (Budapest 2004), pp. 652–654.
262 CDES 2, ed. Marsina, no. 233, p. 162.
263 Györffy, *ÁMF III*, p. 207.
264 CDES 2, ed. Marsina, no. 468, p. 324. *Pramene k dejinám Slovenska a Slovákov III. V kráľovstve svätého Štefana*, výber, preklad a komentáre Richard Marsina (Bratislava 2003), no. 90, p. 193.

CHAPTER 15

Between Hungary and Poland (1001–1029)

1   A Polish Incursion into Nitria and Prince Ladislas

Abbot and later Bishop Astrik obtained for Hungary a royal crown that the pope had originally had made for a Polish prince. Stephen literally pulled it out from under the nose of Boleslaw the Brave.[1] The Polish response to this was not long in coming. According to Polish chronicler Gallus Anonymus, Boleslaw the Brave *fully overpowered the Hungarians in battle and subjugated their entire territory up to the Danube to his own rule*.[2] Nitria, as in 997, was also this time loyal to Stephen and put up opposition to Boleslaw. Boleslaw the Brave *in battle overpowered* (*in certamine superavit*) the Nitrian Hungarians; that is he had to break their opposition. This opposition was obviously led by princes Poznan, Hont and Bors, who were loyal to Hungarian King Stephen.

The Wielkopolska (Great Polish) Chronicle names several Slavic princes who recognized Polish supremacy, among them also Árpád Prince Ladislas (*Wladislaus*) and his country demarcated by the rivers Tisza, Danube and Morava.[3] Thus, Michael's son Ladislas the Bald, with the aid of the powerful Polish monarch, obtained his father's former Nitrian Principality and recognized Polish supremacy.

Immediately after the king's coronation (1 January 1001), which intensified Hungarian-Polish relations, Stephen still managed to have his royal denar minted in Bratislava. In the war that followed, however, he lost Nitria. And since its southern border ran along the Danube, he also lost Bratislava with it. Then, after one or two months duration, Stephen's Bratislava mint ceased to operate. We can in this way account for the very small number of these denars that are still preserved.

---

1   *Legenda sancti Stephani regis ab Hartvico episcopo conscripta* 9, SRH II, pp. 413–414. František Hrušovský, "Boleslav Chrabrý a Slovensko," in *Sborník na počesť Jozefa Škultétyho* (Turčiansky sv. Martin 1933), pp. 460–461.
2   *Numquid non ipse Hungaros frequentius in certamine superavit, totamque terram eorum usque Danubium suo dominio mancipavit. Galli Chronicon* I 6, MPH I, ed. Bielowski, p. 399.
3   *Wladislai pars Ungariae, que inter fluvios Czissam, Danubium et Moravam constitit. Boguphali II episcopi Posnaniensis Chronicon Poloniae, cum continuatione Basconis custodis Posnaniensis* 8, *Monumenta Poloniae historica II*, edidit August Bielowski (Warszawa 1961), p. 479. Peter Ratkoš, "Podmanenie Slovenska Maďarmi," in *O počiatkoch slovenských dejín*, ed. Ratkoš, pp. 154–155, 160.

2 Report on the Borders of the Nitrian Principality

The southern and eastern borders of the Nitrian Principality, loosely connected to Poland, are very exactly described in the *Hungarian-Polish Chronicle*: *Because the border of the Poles reached to the bank of the Danube to Esztergom Castle. From there they went to Eger Castle, then to the river called the Tisza; receding, they wended along the river which is called the Cepla* (= Topľa), *up to Salis Castle* (= the Salt Castle of Solivar, near Prešov) *and here between the Hungarians, Russians and Poles they had their end*.[4]

The Nitrian Principality was approximately equally large as today's Slovakia. To the east the Zemplín, separated by the ridge of the Zemplín and a Slanské hills, did not belong to it; to the south, however, it took up part of today's northern Hungary up to the Cserhát and Bükk Mountains and the flooded Tisza between the mouth of the Sajó and the mouth of the Bodrog rivers.[5] Moson,

---

[4] *Nam termini Polonorum ad litus Danubii ad civitatem Strigoniensem terminabantur. Deinde in Agriensem civitatem ibant, demum in fluvium, qui Tizia nominatur, candentes, regirabant iuxta fluvium, qui Cepla nuncupatur usque ad castrum Salis ibique inter Ungaros, Ruthenos et Polonos finem dabant.* Chronicon Hungarico-Polonicum 7, SRH II, pp. 310–311. Branislav Varsik, "Kde ležal Castrum Salis (Soľný hrad)?," in Branislav Varsik, *Zo slovenského stredoveku* (Bratislava 1972), pp. 65–86. Branislav Varsik, "K vzniku a pôvodu názvu rieky Tople," in Varsik, *Zo slovenského stredoveku*, pp. 175–196. Lubomír Havlík considers these borders as the border of the eastern part of old Moravia. Havlík, "Územní rozsah," pp. 23, 37–38, 72. Lubomír Havlík, "K otázce hranice jižní Moravy v době Boleslava Chrabrého. Příspěvek k česko-polským vztahům na počátku 11. století," in *Studia z dziejów polskich i czechosłowackich 1* (Wrocław 1960), pp. 75, 88–89. Ryszard Grzesik, "Przebieg granicy polsko-węgierskiej we wczesnym średniowieczu w swietle Kroniky węgiersko-polskiej," *Studia Historiczne* 41 (1998), no. 2, pp. 147–166. Martin Homza, "Hranice Nitrianskeho vojvodstva (kniežatstva) v poľských kronikách," in *Nitra v slovenských dejinách*, ed. Richard Marsina (Martin 2002), pp. 65–78.

[5] The territorial range of Nitria, mainly in an eastern direction, is not an easy question to answer. Written sources offer us three possibilities. Anonymus limited it only to south-western Slovakia with the eastern border at the Hron River. The Hungarian-Polish Chronicle, as well as several Polish chroniclers, give us the possibility of identifying the border of Nitria with the borders of the extensive territory between the Morava, Danube and Tisza rivers, which Boleslaw the Brave occupied at the beginning of the 11th century at the expense of Hungary. If we accept the opinion that the Esztergom diocese, which according to sources from the 13th and 14th centuries ended on the east with the Spiš and Turňa archdeaconates, copied at the time of its origin the range of the Nitrian Principality, then we get a third, kind of middle possibility. Advocates of this opinion rely on the very uncertain assumption that the well-known range of the Esztergom diocese from the 14th century (together with the Nitra diocese set aside perhaps in 1110) was the same as in the 11th century. Václav Chaloupecký, *Staré Slovensko* (Bratislava 1923), pp. 26, 116–117. Václav Chaloupecký, "Slovenské diecéze a tak rečená apoštolská práva," *Bratislava, Učená společnost Šafaříkova* 2 (1928), p. 5. Richard Marsina, "Nitrianske biskupstvo," pp. 534–535, 541. Richard Marsina, "Začiatky cirkevnej organizácie na Slovensku (Od prelomu 8./9. až do začiatku 11. storočia)," *Slovenská archivistika* 30

Győr, Esztergom, Visegrád, Vác, Eger, Szabolcs and Zemplín all became border castles and ended up near the northern border of Stephen's reduced Hungary.

The *Hungarian-Polish Chronicle* took approximately half of its text from the Hartvik legend. The unknown author combined the selected and nearly copied word-for-word part of this Saint Stephen's legend with the remote (in terms of time) incursions of Hun King Attila (*Aquila*), supplemented by a legend of St. Ursula and Attila's victory over the Slavs and Croats, the unreality of which contrasts with the overall reliability of the Hartvik legend; the unknown author also added some very arbitrarily processed Hungarian history, beginning with Prince Géza (*Yesse*) and ending with the rule of Ladislas I, which he took from the now unpreserved Gesta Ungarorum vetera.[6]

In an equally old, if not older and at least as reliable source as was Hartvik's legend, there were also reports on the borders of the still then existing Nitrian Principality, which reached up to Esztergom, on the founding of the Esztergom cathedral by Saint Stephen and its consecration to St. Adalbert, on the temporary appending of Nitria to Poland and on the Esztergom peace between Boleslaw (according to the chronicler Mieszko) and Stephen. These reports, which make up the first half of the 7th chapter of the Hungarian-Polish Chronicle, cannot deny their Esztergom origin. The author of the Hungarian-Polish Chronicle knew these Esztergom records directly from the archbishop or another Esztergom archive or had in hand an unknown edition of the Gesta Ungarorum vetera supplemented with these Esztergom reports.[7] Because they described the border of the Nitrian Principality in detail, they had to have originated still before its extinction, that is in the 11th, or at the latest the beginning of the 12th century. We thus know about the incursion of Boleslaw the Brave from two old, reliable sources independent of one another, from Poland and Hungary.

(1995), no. 2, pp. 125–126. If we accept any of these three possibilities, then we must convincingly reject the other two.

6 Raimund Friedrich Kaindl, "Studien zu den ungarischen Geschichtsquellen III. Ueber die ungarisch-polnische Chronik," *Archiv für österreichische Geschichte* 82 (1895), pp. 589–625. Hrušovský, "Boleslav Chrabrý a Slovensko," pp. 470–476. Ryszard Grzesik, *Kronika węgiersko-polska. Z dziejów polsko-węgierskich kontaktów kulturalnych w średniowieczu* (Poznań 1999). Martin Homza, *Mulieres suadentes. Presviedčajúce ženy. Štúdie z dejín ženskej panovníckej svätosti v strednej a vo východnej Európe v 10.–13. storočí* (Bratislava 2002), pp. 144–158. Martin Homza, *Uhorsko-poľská kronika. Nedocenený prameň k dejinám strednej Európy* (Bratislava 2009).

7 Raimund Friedrich Kaindl, "Studien zu den ungarischen Geschichtsquellen VI. Spuren von Graner Geschichtsaufzeichnungen," *Archiv für österreichische Geschichte* 84 (1898), pp. 523–543. Grzesik, *Kronika węgiersko-polska*, pp. 51–53.

3 The Esztergom Peace

As the Hungarian-Polish Chronicle states *After the passing of three months from his* (= Stephen's) *coronation* (*Tribus vero post coronationis sue mensibus elapsis*), that is at the end of March or beginning of April 1001, both sides began to negotiate through their delegations. Boleslaw the Brave offered Stephen peace. Then Stephen proposed to Boleslaw a meeting at the Hungarian-Polish borders.[8] Boleslaw accepted this proposal: *When he assembled all of his army, he came to the king before Esztergom and here at the borders of Poland and Hungary he set up his tents ... On the next day, when the sun rose, they went out at the same time and received a kiss of peace and with hands held they came to Esztergom cathedral, which was then newly built in veneration of St. Adalbert the Martyr, apostle of the Poles and Hungarians ... When everything was thus happily fulfilled, the entire Polish army from the larger to the smaller was given remuneration and the prince received gifts. After this, however, they bid each other farewell. The prince of the Poles departed for the Salt Castle* (*in castrum Salis*) *and king of the Hungarians hurried off to his own pleasant Székesfehérvár.*[9] At this meeting Stephen acquiesced with the rule of Ladislas the Bald in Nitria.

---

[8] According to the Hungarian-Polish Chronicle, Krakow Bishop Lambert came to Stephen with Boleslaw's peace offering. Stephen agreed and through Esztergom Archbishop Astrik and his commander Aba (*Alba*) invited Boleslaw to Esztergom: *accedens ad ipsum Lambertus presul civitatis Cracovie licentiam petiit atque de corroboratione pacis et amicitie ad memoriam reduxit. Cum que sine mora presulem Strigoniensem Astriquum et principem militie Albam nomine ad avunculum suum Meschonem ducem Polonie transmisit, rogans ipsum, ut cum magnatibus suis in terminis Polonie et Ungarie conveniret.* Chron. Hungarico-Polonicum 7, SRH II, p. 310. Future Esztergom Archbishop Astrik worked in the diplomatic services of King Stephen and could have also taken part in the Poland-Hungary peace negotiations in 1001. The Hungarian chronicler naturally assumed that a high church dignitary could have been at the head of the Polish delegation just as at the head of the Hungarian delegation. Because he didn't know the contemporary Polish bishops, he helped himself with the name of later Krakow Bishop Lambert Sula (1082–1101). If some of the Polish bishops stood at the head of Boleslaw's peace delegation, then this was most likely the Krakow bishop, whose seat was closest to Hungary. The Krakow bishop at that time, however, was not Lambert, but Popo. Grzesik, *Kronika węgiersko-polska*, pp. 152–153. Aba was a palatine. See chapter 13, note 42. The Hungarian-Polish Chronicle recalls that he was the head of Stephen's army, that is a commander.

[9] *Qui congregato omni exercitu suo ad regem ante Strigonium venit ibique in terminis Polonie et Ungarie tentoria sua fixit ... Crastina autem die, orto iam sole conveniunt simul et osculum pacis acceperunt, simulque complexu manibus ad kathedralem ecclesiam Strigoniensem, que tunc in honorem sancti martyris Adalberti, Polonorum et Ungarorum apostoli novo opere fabricabatur, pervenerunt ... Hiis itaque feliciter completis, omnis Polonorum exercitus a maiori usque ad minorem muneribus replentur, duci vero dona offeruntur. Post hec separantur, dux Polonorum in castrum Salis porrexit, rex vero Ungarorum in Albam civitatem suam dilectam properavit.*

4   The Polish Attack on the Saxon March and Peace in Merseburg

After the assassination of the Meissen Margrave Eckard I on 30 April 1002, Boleslaw the Brave managed a similar, very rapid attack on Lusatia, Milcenia and the Meissen March up to the White Elster and lower Saale rivers.[10] Henry II, who on 7 June 1002 became the new German king, was willing to negotiate. Boleslaw the Brave, who took possession of the territory of the Saxon March, came to him on 24 July in the border town of Merseburg, lying on the west bank of the Saale River near the mouth of the White Elster, where both in the following days came to a compromise. Boleslaw kept Lusatia and Milcenia. The brother of the murdered Eckard, Boleslaw's successor and brother-in-law (labelled by Thietmar as Boleslaw's *frater*) Gunzelin of Kuckenburg, Henry's rival for the royal crown, got the Meissen March. The rest of the territory taken by the Poles from the borders of Gunzelin's march to the Moldava River up to the White Elster and to the lower Saale went to the sons of murdered Margrave Eckard and Gunzelin's nephews Hermann and Eckard. The younger Eckard II became the Merseburg margrave and the older Hermann settled somewhere in Eckard's and Gunzelin's vicinity.[11]

Boleslaw's rapid taking of the old Sorbian territory up to the White Elster and the lower Saale and the following peace negotiations with Henry II in the border town of Merseburg were very much like Boleslaw's rapid occupying of Nitria up to the Danube and subsequent meeting with Stephen I in the border town of Esztergom. Even the installing of Ladislas the Bald as the prince of Nitria was certainly the same compromise as the installing of Gunzelin as the Meissen margrave. The events in the south of Boleslaw's realm are thus not a later invention of Polish chroniclers and the unknown Hungarian author of the

---

Chron. Hungarico-Polonicum 7, SRH II, pp. 310–312. Erika Repaská, *Štruktúrno-obsahová analýza stretnutia kráľa Uhorska s kráľom Poľska z Uhorsko-poľskej kroniky* (*diplomová práca*) (Bratislava 2002).

10   *Hac elatus prosperitate Bolizlaus omnes regiones illius terminos usque ad Elstram fluvium preoccupavit presidiisque suimet munit*. Thietmari Chronicon V 9–10 (6), rec. Kurze, pp. 111–113. Thietmari Chronicon V 9–10, cur. Trillmich, pp. 202–205. According to Gallus Anonymus, Boleslaw stopped at the river Saale, which in a short time became the border of his realm: *Indomitos vero Saxones tanta virtute edomuit, quod in flumine Salae in medio terrae eorum meta ferrea fines Poloniae terminavit*. Galli Chronicon I 6, MPH I, ed. Bielowski, pp. 399–400.

11   Thietmari Chronicon V 10 (6), 15 (9), 18 (10), rec. Kurze, pp. 113, 115–116, 117. Thietmari Chronicon V 10, 15, 18, cur. Trillmich, pp. 202–205, 208–209, 210–213. Gerard Labuda, *Mieszko II król polski, 1025–1034. Czasy przełomu w dziejach państva Polskiego* (Kraków 1992), pp. 31–35.

Polish-Hungarian Chronicle, just as contemporary Saxon chronicler Thietmar did not invent similar events in the Saxon border area.

Nearly three months passed from Boleslaw's attack against the Saxon border marches to the peace of Merseburg; therefore Henry II, occupied by the coronation and the securing of support in various parts of Germany, could not devote immediate attention to the Saxony border occupied by the Poles. Hungarian King Stephen I at the time of Boleslaw's attack against Nitria had no other such cares. The peace negotiations of Boleslaw with Stephen could have therefore immediately followed the taking over of Nitria by the Poles, which must have been at least as fast as the seizing of the Saxon March a year later. If both sides began to negotiate three months after Stephen's coronation, which took place on 1 January 1001,[12] that is at the turn of March to April 1001, then the preceding war played out most probably in March and they concluded the Esztergom peace in April 1001.

5 Prokuj

In 1003 King Stephen sent his army against Transylvanian Prince Gyula II, whom Thietmar mentions under the Slavic name Prokuj (*Procui*).[13] He was Stephen's uncle (*avinculus regis Pannonici*),[14] the brother of his mother Sarolt, and he was based in Gyulafehérvár (Alba Iulia). Stephen deposed and took Gyula captive, along with his wife and two sons.[15] At the same time he deposed

---

12   See chapter 14, note 231.
13   *Thietmari Chronicon* IX (VIII) 4 (3), rec. Kurze, p. 241. *Thietmari Chronicon* VIII 3, ed. Trillmich, pp. 442–443.
14   See notes 13, 15.
15   *Stephanus rex Ungaricus super avunculum suum Iulum regem cum exercitu venit, quem cum adprehendisset cum uxore ac duobus eius filiis, regnum vi ad christianismum compulit.* Ann. Altah. maior. ad a. 1003, rec. Oefele, p. 16. *Tandem cum Gyula Hungaris in Pannonia habitantibus infestus esset et multipliciter agravatus, per Sanctum Stephanum regem in Pannoniam est deductus. Non tamen iste Gyula capitaneus, sed ab illo tertius.* Chron. Hung. comp. saec. XIV. II 30, SRH I, p. 291. *Porro Beatus Stephanus ... famosum et lucrosum bellum gessit contra avunculum suum nomine Gyulam, qui tunc temporis totius Ultra Siluam regni gubernacula possidebat. Anno itaque Domini M° II° beatus rex Stephanus cepit Gyulam ducem cum uxore et duobus filiis suis et in Hungariam transmisit. Hoc autem ideo fecit, quia sepissime amonitus a beato rege Stephano nec ad fidem Christi conversus, nec ab inferenda Hungaris iniuria conquevit. Universum vero regnum eius latissimum et opulentissimum monarchie Hungarie adiuxit. Dicitur autem regnum illud Hungarice Erdeelw.* Chron. Hung. comp. saec. XIV. II 65, SRH I, pp. 314–315. *Sanctus namque rex Stephanus ... Iula avunculo suo cum uxore et duobus filiis de Septem Castris in Hungariam adducto, et adiuncto Septem Castra Pannoniae.* Simonis de Keza Gesta Hungarorum II 43, SRH I, p. 172. Zumbor

Gyula's brother Zombor, who in the like-named castle administered the northern part of Transylvania.[16] On the territory of both brothers he established two large castle counties and handed over their administration to his relatives Zoltán and Doboka. Zoltán became the first count in the southern Fehér County with its seat at Gyulafehérvár.[17] The northern county with a seat at Zombor Castle got its new name after the first count Doboka (Dăbîca).[18]

Gyula (Prokuj) gained his freedom and entered into the services of Boleslaw the Brave. Boleslaw had a *kind of castle* (*quandam urbem*) on the borders of his realm with Hungary (*in confinio regni suimet et Ungrorum sitam*) and made Prokuj its custodian (*custos*).[19] Since Prokuj's castle lay directly on the border of Boleslaw's realm and the Kingdom of Hungary, which was then formed by the Danube, we can with all certainly identify it with Bratislava.[20] Bratislava, then called Preslava, was already a major border fortress in the time of Great Moravia and had maintained this role even in the centuries that followed. In 1001 it ended up at the interface of Poland, Hungary and the Eastern March.

    vero genuit minorem Geulam patrem Bue et Bucne, tempore cuius sanctus rex Stephanus subiugavit sibi terram Ultrasilvanam et ipsum Geulam vinctum in Hungariam duxit et per omnes dies vite sue carceratum tenuit eo, quod in fide esset vanus et noluit esse Christianus et multa contraria faciebat sancto regi Stephano, quamvis fuisset ex cognatione matris sue. Anonymi (P. magistri) Gesta Hungarorum 27, SRH I, p. 69. Györffy, *ÁMF II*, pp. 105, 143–144. Györffy, *István király*, pp. 163–171. *MT I/1*, pp. 764–766. *Erdély története I*. ed. László Makkai, András Mócsy (Budapest 1986), pp. 282–283. Györffy, *König Stephan*, p. 118. *Kurze Geschichte Siebenburgens*, ed. Köpeczi, p. 124.

16   Györffy, *István király*, pp. 170–171, 199. Györffy, *König Stephan*, p. 118.

17   *locavit ibi unum proavum suum nomine Zoltan, qui postea hereditavit illas partes Transiluanas et ideo vulgariter sic dici solet: Erdeelui Zoltan. Chron. Hung. comp. saec. XIV.* II 66, SRH I, pp. 315–316. Györffy, *István király*, p. 171. Györffy, *ÁMF II*, pp. 105, 144. Györffy, *König Stephan*, p. 118. *Erdély története I*, ed. Makkai, Mócsi, p. 285. Kristó, *A vármegyek*, pp. 497–501. *Kurze Geschichte Siebenbürgens*, ed. Köpeczy, p. 151.

18   Doboka was the father of Count Csanád, who 25 years later triumphed over Ajtony, Prince of Marosvár. See note 45. Csanád was the nephew of King Stephen: *Sunad filius Dobuca nepos regis*. Anonymi (P. magistri) Gesta Hungarorum 11, SRH I, p. 50. Györffy, *István király*, pp. 163, 170–171, 174, 199, 231–232. Györffy, *ÁMF II*, pp. 45–48, 66–67, 105. Györffy, *König Stephan*, pp. 118, 121. Kristó, *A vármegyék*, pp. 483–486. *Erdély története I*, ed. Makkai, Mócsy, p. 281. *Kurze Geschichte Siebenbürgens*, ed. Köpeczy, pp. 142–143.

19   See note 13.

20   Václav Chaloupecký identified Prokuj's border castle with the Salt Castle (*castrum Salis*), which after Boleslaw the Brave's taking over of Nitria also ended up near the borders of Boleslaw's realm and Stephen's Hungary. Chaloupecký, *Staré Slovensko*, pp. 59, 104–105. Bratislava, jutting into the centre of the southern border of Boleslaw's realm, had much greater strategic value for Boleslaw than the Salt Castle; therefore, he gave it and not the Salt Castle to Prokuj, who well knew the Hungarian relations, to guard Bratislava.

Boleslaw the Brave could not overlook its exposed position. Gyula thus became a border guard of Ladislas's Nitria.

Saxon chronicler Thietmar did not know that Prokuj had ruled in Transylvania. He knew only that he *from his settlements (a suis sedibus) ... was banished (expulsus)* by King Stephen. Prokuj, that is Gyula II, was according to the testimony of the Hungarian chronicles and the Annales Altahenses banished only once, and that was from Transylvania. Thietmar, however, related Prokuj's banishment to *some castle*, which Boleslaw the Brave relinquished to him. From this it follows that Stephen banished Prokuj two times. Prokuj somehow got out of Stephen's captivity, but *he could not free his wife from captivity*. Stephen, however, *because he spared the defeated*, soon released his wife (obviously, with his sons, too). And so, thanks to Stephen, *he received her as a gift*. Stephen's successes as a sovereign were said to be a reward for his mercifulness: *and therefore in the above-mentioned castle (in civitate superius memorata), as in others (castles), God permitted him other victories*. From Prokuj's one expulsion Thietmar mistakenly made two. The second expulsion Stephen supposedly did *the same as before (ut modo, antea)* the first. Since the second time he was to have banished Prokuj from a castle which Boleslaw the Brave had put into his administration, Thietmar evaluated this as an *unfortunate matter (infortunio res)* that happened to Boleslaw.[21]

6 Other Castle Counties and Bishoprics

After Dominik's death, Sebastian (1002–1007) became the archbishop of Esztergom.[22] For three years (1003–1006) he was blind and Kalocsa Bishop Astrik represented him in the archbishop's office. Astrik had to get a *pallium*

---

21 See note 13.
22 *Legenda sancti Stephani regis ab Hartvico episcopo conscripta* 11, SRH II, pp. 416–417. *Hae sunt nominatae ville in dedicatione aecclesie ab archiepiscopo Sebastiano et a comite Ceba.* DHA I, ed. Györffy, no. 5/II, p. 41. The Pannonhalma document issued in July or August of 1002 mentions the first Esztergom archbishop Dominic: *Dominicus archiepiscopus vicecancerarius fecit.* DHA I, ed. Györffy, no. 5, p. 41. His successor Sebastian thus could have become archbishop the earliest only in the second half of 1002, and during his time in office he was blind for three years. He died only after regaining his health, probably in 1007, because in this year Astrik-Anastasius, who was on 1 November 1007 at a synod in Frankfurt, was already archbishop. See note 25. For dating and diplomatic analysis of the Pannonhalma document, see DHA I, ed. Györffy, p. 26, note 1. Imre Szentpétery, "Szent István király oklevelei," in *Szent István emlékkönyv*, ed. Jusztinián Serédi (Budapest 1938), pp. 145–185. Györffy, "Zu den Anfängen," pp. 87–97. György Györffy, "Der Aufstand von Koppány," in *Studia Turcica* (Budapest 1971), pp. 183–189. Richard Marsina, "Štúdie k

from the pope in order to stand in for the archbishop. When Sebastian's sight returned, and he again took over the administration of the Esztergom archbishopric, Astrik returned to Kalocsa. He also returned *with the pallium* (*cum pallio*), which remained to him. Sebastian died soon after,[23] and Astrik-Anastasius, who already had an archbishop's pallium, became the third Esztergom archbishop (1007–1036).[24]

---

slovenskému diplomatáru I. Druhá časť: Obdobie od r. 1000 do r. 1235," *Historické štúdie* 18 (1973), pp. 29–33.

[23] Archbishop Sebastian was blind for three years; thus, he became archbishop at the earliest in 1004 and died at the latest in 1007 (before 1 November). See note 22. Since he was not blind up to his death, because he died only after his sight had returned, we must seek the beginning of this three-year's blindness in some of the preceding years and the beginning of his time as archbishop a bit earlier, at the earliest, however, in 1002. See note 25. If he became blind after some time in the archbishop's office and his sight returned to him before death, then he could have been archbishop from 1002–1007. From this he was blind from approximately 1003–1006 and was represented by Kalocsa Bishop Astrik. The second Esztergom archbishop, Sebastian, inspired by the king's generosity and certainly before going blind and being represented by Astrik, donated several villages to the Pannonhalma monastery. This donation, written in a supplement at the end of the Pannonhalma document, is testimony that Sebastian certainly did not go blind immediately after taking the office. *DHA I*, ed. Györffy, no. 5, p. 41. Therefore, some time must have passed between Sebastian's being ordained as archbishop and his going blind, for him to become familiar not only with the office and with the property relations of the archbishopric, but to also carry out the mentioned extensive donation. Sebastian, therefore, could have become Esztergom archbishop as early as 1002, more specifically sometime in its second half.

[24] *Cum his dei servus princeps Christianissimus ... Strigoniensem ecclesiam metropolim et magistram per consensum et subscriptionem Romane sedis apostolici ceterarum fore constituens. Cum iam dictum venerabilem Ascricum abbatem pontificalis dignitatis infula decoratum, electione canonica prefecit. Legenda maior sancti Stephani regis* 8, SRH II, pg. 383. *presul Strigoniensis civitatis, Astriquus nomine ad papam pervenit ... Mox presul Ungarorum Astriquus ... Chron. Hungarico-Polonicum* 6, 7, SRH II, pp. 308–311. Astrik was the Esztergom archbishop; however, he was not the first, as it would seem from the telling of the larger Saint Stephen legend and the Hungarian-Polish Chronicle. Astrik's exceptional merits and long time (1007–1036) as archbishop overshadowed both previous and more briefly serving archbishops, Dominic and Sebastian. Astrik's name, therefore, in the form *érsek* in Hungarian still today indicates an archbishop. Györffy, *István király*, p. 182. The Hartvik legend mentions Astrik as the first Kalocsa bishop and his representing the Esztergom archbishop. *Legenda sancti Stephani regis ab Hartvico episcopo conscripta* 8, 11, SRH II, pp. 411–412, 416–417. Astrik, who was first abbot in the Polish Miedzyrzecze, was later ordained as archbishop in Sobotín (*archiepiscopus ad Sobottin*). *Passio sancti Adalberti martiris* 3, MPH I, ed. Bielowski, p. 154. Nový – Sláma – Zachová, *Slavníkovci*, p. 190. Sobotín is Esztergom. Chaloupecký, "Radla," pp. 217–218. Györffy, *István király*, pp. 97, 153, 335.

In the autumn of 1007 Esztergom Archbishop Astrik-Anastasius was present at a synod of the imperial bishops in Frankfurt.[25] On 6 May 1012 he consecrated the altar in the newly built cathedral in Bamberg.[26] Around 1030 he received the monk Arnold from the Abbey of St. Emmeram in Regensburg, who was visiting Hungary.[27] Esztergom Archbishop Astrik-Anastasius died on 12 November 1036.[28]

On 23 August 1009 with the consent of the pope and in the presence of the papal nuntius, Hungarian bishops,[29] counts and other important persons, King Stephen issued a document in Győr, by which he established the bishopric in Pécs and exactly defined the borders of its diocese. He appointed Bonipert (1009–1036) as the first bishop of Pécs.[30] At this important gathering in Győr King Stephen could have also established the Győr bishopric. However, its foundation document has not been preserved.

By establishing the Győr and Pécs bishoprics King Stephen limited the area of the Veszprém diocese to the territory of 4 castle counties: Veszprém, Fejér, Visegrád and Kolon. The Veszprém diocese, reduced by the founding of the new dioceses, did not cross the Danube to the east, because on the east bank

---

25 On 1 November 1007 he signed as + *Anastasius* + *Ungrorum archiepiscopus interfui et subscripsi*. DHA I, ed. Györffy, no. 6, pp. 42–43.

26 *Altare ante criptam consecravit Aschericus Ungarorum archiepiscopus in honorem sanctorum confessorum Hylarii, Remigii, Vedasti*. Dedicatio ecclesiae sancti Petri Bambergensis. Albinus Franciscus Gombos, *Catalogus fontium historiae Hungaricae aevo ducum et regum ex stirpe Arpad descendentium ab anno Christi DCCC usque ad annum MCCCI. II* (Budapestini 1937), p. 842.

27 *cursu prosperato tertia die advehebar Pannoniae solo, qua me Anastasius archiepiscopus ... suscepit humanius*. De miraculis sancti Emmerami. *Monumenta ecclesiae Strigoniensis I*, edidit Ferdinandus Knauz (Strigonii 1874), no. 15, p. 42. Gombos, *Catalogus I*, pp. 308–309. If a Hungarian archbishop welcomed a monk arriving to Hungary from Regensburg, then this was the Esztergom archbishop. Arnold, arriving to Hungary, could not have bypassed the closer Esztergom in order to be welcomed by the more distant Kalocsa archbishop or still only a bishop.

28 *Strigoniae in Hungaria deposito sancti Anastasii episcopi et confessoris magnae sanctitatis viri*. MES I, ed. Knauz, no. 17, pp. 42–43. Györffy, "Zu den Anfängen," p. 109.

29 The bishops of the already existing Hungarian bishoprics must have been present in Győr, that is Esztergom archbishop Astrik-Anastasius, Veszprém bishop Stephen, an unkown Kalocsa bishop, an unknown Vác bishop and the recently ordained unknown Győr bishop and at the same time with him the ordained Pécs bishop Bonipert and the unknown bishops of Eger and Transylvania.

30 DHA I, ed. Györffy, no. 9/I, II, pp. 54–59. Tivadar Ortvay, *A pécsi egyházmegye alapítása és első határai történettopografiai tanulmány* (Budapest 1890). Tivadar Ortvay, *Magyarország egyházi földleírása a XIV. század elején a pápai tizedjegyzékek alapján feltüntetve I* (Budapest 1891), pp. 214–282. Fedeles – Koszta, *Pécs*, pp. 22–46.

of the Danube since year 1000 lay the Vác diocese.[31] King Stephen thus issued a document for this reduced Veszprém diocese in 1009. The Veszprém bishop was or had just then become Stephen.[32] The Győr bishopric, similarly as neighbouring Veszprém, got four castle counties from the king. These were Győr, Moson, Sopron and Vasvár. The bishoprics in Veszprém, Pécs and Győr (with the exception of Somogy County, which got into the ecclesiastical administration of the Pannonhalma Abbot), shared all the Transdanubian counties.

In this time King Stephen married off his younger sister to Samuel Aba[33] and made his new brother-in-law a palatine.[34] He attached him closer to himself, and thus a small prince became a count and his Eger Principality a castle county. In 1041 Hungarian magnates selected as king *a count by the name of Aba (quemdam comitem nomine Abam)*.[35] Samuel Aba was thus no longer a prince but a count, more exactly the highest court count, or palatine (*comes palatii*) and perhaps still also a castle count in Eger County.

After the origin of the castle counties in Transylvania, Eger and Biharia, there was no longer a barrier to placing bishoprics in the eastern part of Hungary, too. Papal legate Azzo, who was present in 1009 at the establishing of the new Hungarian bishoprics, visited and with great success baptized the Black Hungarians, that is Kabars and Székelys in Biharia and Transylvania. Bruno of Querfurt, who learned of this, notified Emperor Henry II in that same year.[36] Azzo visited these eastern ends of Stephen's state not only due to the Black Hungarians, but undoubtedly was also present for the founding of the Eger and Transylvanian bishoprics. Thus, King Stephen established the Eger[37] and Transylvania bishoprics in the same year as the bishopric in Győr and Pécs. The Eger diocese included not only Eger County but also the whole of Biharia.[38]

---

31 See chapter 14, note 237. For the territorial range of the Vác diocese, see Ortvay, MEF I, pp. 106–113.
32 DHA I, ed. Györffy, no. 8, pp. 49–53.
33 See chapter 13, note 38.
34 *Alba comes palatii. Legenda maior sancti Gerhardi episcopi* 14, SRH II, p. 500.
35 *Chron. Hung. comp. saec. XIV.* II 72, SRH I, p. 325. See chapter 13, note 38. The descendants of Samuel Aba were also Eger counts. Around 1067 Peter from the Aba line was the Eger count. See chapter 13, note 40.
36 DHA I, ed. Györffy, no. 7, p. 46. György Györffy and Gyula Kristó identify Bruno of Querfurt with Astrik's pupil St. Boniface. Györffy, *István király*, pp. 78–81, 141–142, 161, 172–173, 187–188. Györffy, *König Stephan*, pp. 117, 120–121, 123, 131. MT I/1, pg. 763, 767, 777. Gyula Kristó, *Írások szent Istvánról és koráról* (Szeged 2000), pp. 79–87.
37 DHA I, ed. Györffy, no. 10, pp. 60–61.
38 *Kurze Geschichte Siebenbürgens*, ed. Köpeczi pp. 145–146. The remainder of this large range of the Eger diocese to the south-east was archdeacon Zsomboly (later called Pankota) on the southern bank of the White Körös, which after later division of the Bihar diocese remained a remote enclave of the Eger diocese on the southern border of Biharia. The

The dioceses founded by Stephen I fully respected the division of Hungary into castle counties. Stephen divided the Transdanubian counties among the Veszprém, Pécs and Győr dioceses.[39] The borders of these three dioceses, like the other Hungarian dioceses established by Stephen, were thus the borders of the assigned counties. Other dioceses had equally clear borders as those of the Pécs and Veszprém diocese,[40] as did all the castle counties, small principalities and both subordinated principalities, which were their political and territorial basis.

In the years 997–1009 Stephen expanded his immediate power from a small territory bound between the castles of Esztergom, Veszprém and Győr, which he inherited from his father, first to all of Transdanubia and from there also to Transylvania. He subjugated and abolished other Hungarian principalities and transformed them or divided them into castle counties. In 1009, when Stephen I established the new bishoprics, his state had a solid county organization, outside of which the Nitria and Marosvár principalities remained for another 20 years.

---

northern bank of the White Körös belonged to the Kölesér archdeaconate, which reached up to Black Körös in the north and belonged to the Bihar (Varadín) diocese. Ortvay, *MEF I*, pp. 116, 129–131, 175–177. Tivadar Ortvay, *Magyarország egyházi földleirása a XIV. század elején a pápai tizedjegyzékek alapján feltüntetve II* (Budapest 1892), pp. 517, 585–599. Györffy, *ÁMF I*, pp. 574–576, 583–589. Kovács, *Az egri egyházmegye története 1596-ig*, pp. 25–26, 48–49. Kristó, *A vármegyék*, pp. 470–475, 478–480. Both mentioned archdeacons originated in the southern part of Bihar County even before Zaránd County was detached from it sometime between 1203–1214. See chapter 13, note 18. The northern border of the new Zaránd County, to which the whole upper basin of the White Körös belonged, transected the territory of the older Köles-ér archdeaconate, the northern part of which remained to Bihar County and the southern part of which went to Zaránd County.

39   The remaining 4 Transdanubian counties, Győr, Moson, Sopron and Vasvár, had to be assigned to the Győr diocese.

40   In 1009 the king set the exact borders of the Pécs diocese: *Primum terminum ... secundum ... tercium ... quartum ... DHA I*, ed. Györffy, no. 9/1, p. 58. Likewise clearly *cum ... terminis et finitibus* he also defined the Veszprém diocese. *DHA I*, ed. Györffy, no. 8, p. 52. According to Ibrahim ibn Yaqub, the realm of Bohemian Prince Boleslaus I, to whom Krakówia belonged, bordered with Hungary. See chapter 14, note 1. The Prague bishopric in the period of its origin, and thus also the then Přemyslid state, reached to the upper Bug and to the upper Dniester and bordered Hungary in the Tatra Mountains. Györffy, *István király*, pp. 84, 86. Györffy, *König Stephan*, pp. 79, 83. Ján Steinhübel, "Svätý Vojtech a Uhorsko," in *Svatý Vojtěch Čechové a Evropa*, ed. Třeštík – Žemlička, pp. 124, 129, note 16. Steinhübel, *Kapitoly*, pp. 108–116. See chapter 14, notes 29, 140. The border on the main Carpathian ridge was the old border of Nitria with the Vistulia (Krakówia). All the states that were attached to this territory, that is including Hungary and Poland, inherited it.

7 The End of Ajtony's Principality and the Origin of the Csanád Bishopric

Byzantine Emperor Basil II began his largest attack against the Bulgarians in 999. In the autumn of 1002, he began a siege of Vidin and made an alliance with Marosvár Prince Ajtony. Ajtony's castles Kovin, Haram and Orsova ruled over the northern bank of the lower Danube between the mouth of the Tisza and the Iron Gates. Byzantine boats, advancing against the Bulgarians, could safely pass up river beneath their ramparts. In 1003 the Byzantine army conquered the Bulgarian town of Vidin after an 8-month siege.[41] Ajtony visited the victorious emperor in the conquered town and received baptism by his hand. Shortly after, he established in Marosvár an Eastern Orthodox monastery dedicated to John the Baptist.[42] Ajtony was the last of several Hungarian princes to receive Byzantine baptism. Smaller Hungarian princes Bulcsú, Tormás (in 948), Gyula I (in 953) and Ajtony (in 1003) at the peak of their power defected from the main Árpád prince. Their principalities formed a wide and contiguous band of temporary Byzantine influence in southern Hungary.

At the end of 1003 Bruno of Querfurt (St. Bruno, also known as Boniface) set forth from Regensburg down the Danube to Hungary. In the following year he floated to the *Black Hungarians (Nigris Ungris)*, sent there by King Stephen: *He was sent by the blessed king to preach in the lower ends of Hungary (in inferiores Ungariae partes); there he was struck in the throat by a sword*. Bruno survived the injury, and in this same year of 1004 he became a missionary archbishop and again in some of the following years (probably on the way to the Pechenegs in 1007) returned to the Black Hungarians.[43] In 1009 papal legate Azzo visited and baptised the Black Hungarians.[44] Perhaps he also came to Ajtony's principality, which was among the Black Hungarians and where Bruno's mission had worked twice without greater success.

Ajtony seized the lower course of the Maros River, whereby he threatened Stephen's alliance with Transylvania. When he began to exact *in the ports of the rivers up to the Tisza* a duty from royal boats loaded with Transylvanian salt,

---

41 *Legenda maior sancti Gerhardi episcopi* 8, SRH II, pp. 489–490. Anonymus mentions the castles Kovin, Haram and Orsova. See pp. 191–192. *Kurze Geschichte Siebenbürgens*, ed. Köpeczi, pp. 124–125.
42 *Legenda maior sancti Gerhardi episcopi* 8, SRH II, p. 490.
43 *Legenda maior sancti Stephani regis* 7, SRH II, p. 382. *Legenda sancti Stephani regis ab Hartvico episcopo conscripta* 7, SRH II, p. 410. DHA I, ed. Györffy, no. 7, pp. 44–48. Györffy, *István király*, pp. 172–173. *Erdély története I*, ed. Makkai – Mócsy, pp. 280, 284. MT I/I, pp. 767–768. Györffy, *König Stephan*, pp. 120–121.
44 See note 36.

Stephen grew angry and in perhaps year 1028 he sent his army against Ajtony. He handed over his command to Doboka's son Csanád. Csanád and his soldiers *crossed the Tisza (transissent Ticiam)* and swept into Ajtony's principality. In the first battle, not far from Marosvár, Ajtony was victorious and Csanád pulled his forces back to the Tisza. On the next day Ajtony suffered a crucial defeat on the field Nagyósz (*Nageuz*) and fell in battle. Csanád's victorious soldiers, *crossed the Tisza (transeuntes Ticiam) and returned to the king*. The Marosvár Principality became another castle county, and King Stephen named as its first count the commander of the victorious royal army and his relative Csanád: *From this day on this castle (urbs) will not be called Maros (Morisena), but castle Csanád (urbs Chanadina). Because you defeated my enemy in its centre, may you be the count of that province (comes illius provincie) and you will call it after yourself, let it be called Csanád province (provincia Chanadiensis) for the whole of posterity*. Count Csanád then established at Oroszlány an Abbey of St. George and resettled monks from Ajtony's Abbey of St. John the Baptist there.[45]

In 1030 King Stephen established the Csanád bishopric, whose diocese covered the whole of Csanád County.[46] The monk Gerhard (Gellért, 1030–1046) became the first Csanád bishop according to the king's wishes.

8   Stephen's Son Emeric

Gerhard came from Venice and was brought to Hungary by Pannonhalma Abbot Rasina (perhaps around 1015). King Stephen entrusted the raising of his only son and successor, Emeric, to Gerhard. After several years his educational role ended, and for another 7 years he was a recluse in Bakonybél, from where the king recalled him as bishop.[47] If we subtract the 7 years of Gerhard's reclusive life from 1030, the year in which Gerhard became a bishop, then we get to

---

45   *Legenda maior sancti Gerhardi episcopi* 8, 9, SRH II, pp. 490–493. *Anonymi (P. magistri) Gesta Hungarorum* 11, 44, pp. 50, 89. *Erdély története I*, ed. Makkai, Mócsy, p. 284. *Kurze Geschichte Siebenbürgens*, ed. Köpeczi, pp. 125–126.

46   *Gerardus episcopus ordinatur. Annales Posonienses* ad a. 1030, SRH I, p. 125. *Legenda maior sancti Gerhardi episcopi* 9, SRH II, pp. 492–493. Gerhard's diocese covered the whole of Csanád County: *Cumque vir Dei totam provinciam Chanadiensem ad fidem Christi convertisset. Legenda maior sancti Gerhardi episcopi* 14, SRH II, p. 500. Ortvay, MEF II, pp. 353–357.

47   *Annales Posonienses* ad a. 1030, SRH I, p. 125. *Chron. Hung. comp. saec. XIV.* II 83, SRH I, p. 341. *Legenda maior sancti Stephani regis* 12, SRH II, p. 388. *Legenda sancti Stephani regis ab Hartvico episcopo conscripta* 14, SRH II, p. 422. *Legenda minor sancti Gerhardi episcopi* 1–3, SRH II, pp. 471–473. *Legenda maior sancti Gerhardi episcopi* 1–7, 9, SRH II, pp. 480–489, 492–494.

year 1023, in which Emeric's education ended. Emeric was born in 1007 and in 1023 turned 16 years old. This was the age at which he no longer needed a mentor and could become a prince.[48] King Stephen then didn't have Nitria under his power, so he could assign only Biharia to his son.

9   The Bihar Bishopric and the Kalocsa Archbishopric

Simultaneously with the Csanád bishopric Stephen also established a bishopric in Emeric's princely seat in Bihar.[49] However, he could not subordinate the whole of Biharia to the Bihar bishop, because then only a small part of Eger County would be left to the Eger bishop. Therefore, he limited the Bihar diocese, which he detached from Eger, to only one of the four Biharian counties: Bihar County itself. And he didn't even give all of this to it.[50] The southern bank of the upper flow of the White Körös (later archdeaconate Zsomboly, later called Pankota) remained as a remote enclave of the Eger bishopric on the southern edge of Biharia.[51] The first Bihar bishop could have been Bishop Budli, who in September 1046 together with first Csanád Bishop Gerhard and with Bishops Bystrík and Beneta and with Count Szolnok fell into the hands of pagan rebels, who killed them all, with the exception of Beneta.[52]

---

48   *Inclitus dux Hemericus ... a beato Stephano, primo rege Ungarie exortus. Legenda sancti Emerici ducis,* SRH II, p. 449. Emeric was born in 1007 and died in 1031 as a 24-year-old. Györffy, *István király,* p. 374.

49   Györffy, *István király,* p. 327. László Koszta, "A bihari püspökség alapítása," in *Nagyvárad és Bihar a korai középkorban,* pp. 41–80.

50   *Monumenta Vaticana Hungariae historiam regni Hungariae illustrantia, series I., tomus I. Rationes collectorum pontifi corum in Hungaria* (Budapest 2000), pp. 41–90. Ortvay, MEF II, pp. 495–606. Györffy, ÁMF I, pp. 575–576. The position of Archdeaconate Zsomboly (Pankota, today Pâncota) on the White Körös is testimony that the oldest Eger diocese reached up to the basin of the White Körös, and the whole of Biharia belonged to it. King Stephen thus detached the Bihar diocese from Eger, whereby he left the small territory on the White Körös to the Eger bishop, separated from it by the territory of the Bihar diocese. The Bihar diocese could thus not have been established concurrently with the Eger diocese in 1009 but only later, because it was detached from the Eger diocese.

51   *Mon. Vat I/1,* pp. 332–333, 350–351, 366. Ortvay, MEF I, pp. 116, 118–120, 129–131, 175–177. Ortvay, MEF II, pp. 517, 585–599. Györffy, ÁMF I, pp. 574–576, 583–589. Kovács, *Az egri egyházmegye története 1596-ig,* pp. 27–28, 48–49. Kristó, *A vármegyék,* pp. 470–475, 478–480.

52   *Ann. Altah. maior.* ad a. 1046. rec. Oefele, p. 43. *Chron. Hung. comp. saec. XIV.* II 82–85, SRH I, pp. 337–343. *Simonis de Keza Gesta Hungarorum* II 53, SRH I, pp. 53–54. *Legenda maior sancti Gerhardi episcopi* 15, SRH II, pp. 501–503. Bishop Budli was the founder of the family from which the brothers Klement and Saul, mentioned in the Varadin register, came: *Dato igitur termino, adduxit ... Clementem cum fratre suo Saul, de genere episcopi Budlu ... et alios. Regestrum Varadinense examinum ferri candentis ordine*

Evidently, on the occasion of establishment of two new bishoprics in 1030 King Stephen had the Kalocsa bishopric elevated to an archbishopric and connected the Kalocsa, Csanád, Bihar and Transylvanian dioceses to its new ecclesiastical province.[53] The new archdiocese, which covered the whole south-eastern half of Hungary, got an archbishop and three bishops subordinated to him and thus became self-sufficient for ordaining its own bishops, as the Esztergom archdiocese had 30 years before.

King Stephen always established several bishoprics at the same time. In year 1000 he established the Kalocsa and Vác bishoprics together with the Esztergom archbishopric and transformed the old Veszprém missionary bishopric into a regular one. In 1009 he founded bishoprics in Győr, Pécs, Eger and Transylvania. In 1030 he established bishoprics in Csanád and in Bihar. At the same time he had the Kalocsa bishopric elevated to an archbishopric and subordinated both newly established bishoprics and the older Transylvanian bishopric to it.

---

chronologico digestum descripta effigie editionis a. 1550 illustratum sumptibusque capituli Varadinensis lat. rit., curis et laboribus Joannis Karácsonyi et Samuelis Borovsky editum (Budapest 1903), no. 97 (323), pp. 187–189. All participants in the dispute mentioned in the list of the Varadin register belonged to Castle Bihar, and the villages in which they lived were in Bihar County, belonging to the Bihar diocese. Nearly all of the witnesses, among whom were also Clement and Saul, were from there. Györffy, *ÁMF I*, pp. 594, 602–603, 607, 620–621, 679. Bishop Budli (*Budlu*), an ancient ancestor of Clement and Saul, was therefore the Bihar bishop. The name Budli, derived from the Italian Baduil, betrays his Italian origin. *Kurze Geschichte Siebenbürgens*, ed. Köpeczi, p. 139. Budli and Gerhard, who in 1030 became bishops of two simultaneously established and neighbouring bishoprics, came from Italy.

53   Ortvay, *MEF I*, 327–336. The first known Kalocsa bishop is George (*Georgius Colocinensis archiepiscopus de Ungaria advenerat*), who in October 1050 met in Lorraine with Pope Leo IX and asked him to convince Emperor Henry III to let peace be made with Hungary. *Miracula Sancti Gerardi episcopi Tulliensis auctore Widrico abbate Tullensi ad elevationem sancti Gerhardi*, ad a. 1050, Gombos, *Catalogus II*, p. 1641. Kalocsa Archbishop George (*Georgio Colocensis ecclesiae Vngrorum archiepiscopo*) is also mentioned in a document of Pope Leo IX from 11 January 1051. *DHA I*, ed. Györffy, no. 38, pp. 138–139. The Kalocsa archbishopric could not have originated before Bihar was detached from the Eger diocese, which fell to the Kalocsa archdiocese, because the border between the Bihar and Eger dioceses became the border between the Kalocsa and Esztergom archdioceses. The Kalocsa bishop could have been elevated to an archbishop only after the origin of the Csanád and Bihar bishoprics in 1030, so that together with the older Transylvanian bishopric they could form a self-administering ecclesiastical province with an archbishop and three subordinate bishops. The establishing of the Csanád and Bihar bishoprics in 1030 was the most suitable opportunity for elevating the Kalocsa bishopric to the second Hungarian archbishopric.

Stephen I placed bishops into the most important castles in his state. The Esztergom archbishop was settled directly in an Árpád castle, and the Veszprém and Győr bishops resided in the oldest county castles. These three castles, at which parts of Koppány's quartered body were hung in 997, marked the centre of the state itself and were directly subjected to princes Géza and Stephen. Pécs was not a castle county, but it had, similarly as Veszprém and Nitra, the tradition of an old Christian centre, which King Stephen did not want to pass over. He certainly very gladly connected and thus gave preference to Pécs over the nearby county castle at Baranya. In the centre of the bishopric castle was also a *cella trichora* (a three-apse burial chapel), which further recalled Sopianae (the Roman name for Pécs).[54] Stephen placed the non-Pannonian bishoprics into old princely castles at Kalocsa, Vác, Eger, Gyulafehérvár, Csanád and Bihar, which he had previously made the seats of castle counties.

10 Prince Vazul

The position of Ladislas's Nitria differed significantly from neighbouring Moravia, which accepted Polish forces. Nitria had its own prince from the domestic Árpád line. Its dependence on the Polish prince could have been very loose and limited to a mutual alliance. In the Polish-German wars (1002–1018) the Moravians fought on the side of Boleslaw the Brave against the Bohemians and the Bavarians, allies of Emperor Henry II.[55] Not even Nitria avoided Boleslaw's wars. In July and August of 1018 a force of 500 Hungarian warriors (*ex Ungariis quingenti ... viri*) marched in a large Polish excursion against Kiev.[56] His Nitria ally and probably not Hungarian King Stephen sent them to help Boleslaw the Brave. Let us not be mistaken that Thietmar labelled these soldiers as Hungarians. Even Gallus Anonymus considered the *whole of their territory to the Danube,* that is Nitria, which temporarily ended up under Polish influence, as a land of Hungarians. It's clear that we cannot simply identify the Hungarians in Thietmar's and Gallus's reports, whom Boleslaw the Brave defeated in 1001 and who marched against Kiev with him in 1018, as Magyars, because the Hungarians in Nitria were mainly Slavs. And after all, if this northern part of Stephen's kingdom was dependent on Poland, an alliance of Stephen

---

54 See chapter 6, note 61.
55 *Thietmari Chronicon* VIII (VII) 57 (42), 61(44), rec. Kurze, pp. 228, 230. *Thietmari Chronicon* VII 57, 61, cur. Trillmich, pp. 418–419, 422–423. Metoděj Zemek, *Moravsko-uherská hranice v 10. až 13. století* (Brno 1972), pp. 26–27.
56 *Thietmari Chronicon* IX (VIII) 32, rec. Kurze, p. 258. *Thietmari Chronicon* VIII 32, cur. Trillmich, p. 474.

with Boleslaw the Brave was hardly possible. The Nitrian prince in 1018 had to meet his obligations as an ally, however. Hungarians also fought over Kiev. These were not, however, soldiers of the Hungarian king but of the Prince of Nitria.

Nitrian Prince Ladislas died before his brother Vazul; therefore, after the death of Stephen's son Emeric and after Vazul's blinding in Nitra, we no longer hear anything about him. In 1031, unlike Vazul, he no longer stood in the path of Stephen's successor Peter.[57] If Ladislas had still been alive, then he would have been the legal successor to the Hungarian crown, which Stephen reserved for a foreigner: his nephew Peter Orseolo. Ladislas the Bald could have died in war as an ally of Boleslaw the Brave. Vazul became his successor in Nitria.

Vazul became the Prince of Nitria at a time when Ladislas's son Domoslav was still a child and could not succeed to the princely seat after his father. If Ladislas married sometime between 995–1000, then Domoslav (who was the son of Ladislas and his Russian wife but did not have to be their first child) was born around 1000 or soon after. He could have become prince no sooner than as a 15- to 16-year old (just like Stephen in 995 and Emeric in 1023), that is around 1015, or a bit later. Ladislas thus must have died several years before the mentioned campaign in Kiev, when Domoslav was not yet capable of taking over the princely seat, thus at the latest about 1015 or a bit before.

The Wielkopolska (Great Polish) Chronicle mentions Prince Ladislas and is silent about Vazul. Ladislas's rule in Nitria was thus for Poland more significant than Vazul's. If Ladislas overshadowed his brother in the memory of the Poles, then he could not have ruled only briefly, and he certainly took part in the Poland-German wars as Boleslaw's ally. And he could have lost his life in one of these wars. This happened perhaps in 1015, when Boleslaw the Brave defended against a large incursion of Henry II.[58]

Vazul's military aid to Poland had to be incomparably smaller than that of Ladislas. It was probably limited to only the brigade of some 500 soldiers, which marched with Boleslaw's army to Kiev in 1018. Boleslaw the Brave and his son Mieszko II lived the following ten years in peace with their neighbours and didn't need any military help from the Prince of Nitria.

Boleslaw the Brave appointed his protégé to Nitra, but he did not have to fully detach Nitria from Hungary. Stephen I could have further considered Nitria as a part of his own kingdom. Ultimately, a prince ruled there from the same family as his own. However, for a longer time (1001–1029) he had to come

---

57 Vajay, "Großfürst Geysa," p. 66.
58 *Thietmari Chronicon* VIII (VII) 16 (11) – 23 (15), rec. Kurze, pp. 202–207. *Thietmari Chronicon* VII 16–23, cur. Trillmich, pp. 368–379. Labuda, *Mieszko II*, pp. 52–59.

to terms with the Polish orientation of the Nitrian princes and with the loosening of its connection with the Hungarian kingdom. The position of Ladislas's and Vazul's Nitria towards Boleslaw the Brave was similar to the position of Vladivoj's Bohemians, whom Boleslaw did not formally link to his realm, but where was able to exert his influence through Prince Vladivoj (1002–1003), whom he himself helped to appoint in Prague.[59]

If Vazul wanted to take over the Nitrian Principality, which was a Christian country, and after his brother's death rule there, moderately dependent on a Christian monarch, Polish Prince Boleslas the Brave,[60] then he could not have openly rejected Christianity. After their return to Nitra, Vazul's children, at least those born to him in Nitria, could not avoid being baptised. This, however, remained only a formality, and Vazul and his family further gave preference to paganism.[61]

Vazul's second-born son was born in approximately 1015, or a bit later, and at his baptism got the name Andrew, which was in Hungary naturalized only in the first half of the 11th century. Among the witnesses to a royal donation from 1055 was also one Count Andrew.[62] As a count, he was certainly of mature or older age. He could only have been a bit younger or approximately the same age, if not older than King Andrew I. One *Endre*, one of the bravest defenders of Bratislava Castle in 1052, could have been at least several years younger.[63] In the middle of a field between two villages somewhere in the Tisza River region one *Andreas iudex* dug a hole, which in 1075 became the border of a property donated by Géza I to the abbey in Hronský Beňadik.[64] We can assume that this Andrew was born and got his name still in the first half of the 11th century. A contemporary of Vazul's son Andrew was Bishop Andrew, whose former

---

59   *Thietmari Chronicon* IV 57 (36), V 23 (15), 29 (18), rec. Kurze, pp. 95–96, 120, 123–124. *Thietmari Chronicon* IV 57, V 23, 29, cur. Trillmich, pp. 172–175, 216–219, 222–225. Novotný, *České dějiny I/1*, pp. 671–675, 747.

60   Hungarian King Stephen could have considered Ladislas's and then Vazul's Nitria at least formally as a component of his own kingdom, because princes ruled there from the same Árpád line as he himself. However, he had to come to terms with their dependence on the more powerful Polish monarch.

61   See chapter 16, notes 11, 80. If in Hungary they considered Vazul's marriage as illegitimate, then Vazul's wife Tatun was unbaptised.

62   + *Signum Andree comitis*. DHA I, ed. Györffy, no. 43/I, p. 152.

63   *Chron. Hung. comp. saec. XIV.* II 89, SRH I, pp. 346–347.

64   *inter villam Sancti Benedicti et villam Albensium*. DHA I, ed. Györffy, no. 73/II, p. 217. CDES I, ed. Marsina, no. 58, p. 57. And this Andrew was born and got his name still in the first half of the 11th century.

properties are mentioned in 1082 and 1086. An Andrew could have been the Veszprém bishop in the years 1046–1071.[65]

At the time of the birth of Vazul's second son, the anchorite Svorad had left Poland (*de terra Poloniensium*) and settled in neighbouring Nitria (*in Nitriensi territorio*). In the Benedictine Abbey of St. Hyppolytus on Zobor he was received by Abbot Philippe, from whom he received the monastic name of Andrew.[66] Zobor Abbey was older, very important and then the only abbey in all of the Nitrian Principality. Since it lay in the surroundings of Nitra Castle, its abbot was certainly an important cleric in the surroundings of the Nitrian Principality. Zobor Abbot Philippe gave the name Andrew not only to the anchorite Svorad, but it could also have been him who baptised and gave this name to Vazul's middle son. Thus, Vazul's son most probably received baptism and with it the name Andrew in Nitra.[67] Vazul was undoubtedly already the Prince of Nitria at that time (around 1015).

---

65 Among the lands that Veszprém bishop John got in 1082 from Ladislas I were also properties *in villa Endered* and *in altera villa Endered* (Balatonendréd in Somogy County). *DHA I*, ed. Györffy, no. 81, pp. 236–237, 239. Both villages belonged to the former Bishop Andrew, and the Bakonybél Abbey had a property in one of them (*villa, que dicitur Andree episcopi*) in 1086. Bishop Andrew also had not far from Veszprém a furnace for burning limestone, which became a border point (*ad fornacem calcis Andree presulis*) of the property that Canon Martin donated to this abbey. The mentioned Bishop Andrew (*Andreas episcopus*) also donated 12 properties *in Felduuar* (Balatonföldvár in Somogy County) to Bakonybél Abbey. *DHA I*, ed. Györffy, no. 84/I, p. 252, no. 84/II, pp. 259, 260. Based on the position of the named properties, we can consider Andrew to be the Veszprém bishop, a predecessor of Veszprém Bishop Frank (1071–perhaps 1081), who was the immediate predecessor of the already mentioned Bishop John. Veszprém bishop John could have acquired two of Andrew's villages, because he was his successor. Andrew could have been the successor (not, however, the immediate one) of Veszprém Bishop Stephen, mentioned in 1009. Stephen's immediate successor and Andrew's immediate predecessor could have been Bishop Modest, mentioned as a witness to a donation of Stephen I for the Bakonybél Abbey from 1019. *DHA I*, ed. Györffy, no. 14, pp. 90–91. *Annales Posonienses* ad a. 1047, *SRH I*, p. 125. See note 78. *Korai magyar történeti lexikon (9–14. század)*, főszerkesztő Gyula Kristó (Budapest 1994), pp. 728–729. If Bishop Modest from 1019 is the same as Bishop Modest, who died in 1046, then his (perhaps immediate) successor Andrew could have been the Veszprém bishop from 1046–1071. We thus have a list of five Veszprém bishops: Stephen (before 1009–before 1019), Modest (before 1019–1046), Andrew (1046–1071), Frank (1071–perhaps 1081) and John (perhaps 1081–through 1082).

66 *Legenda sancti Zoerardi et Benedicti* 1, *SRH II*, p. 357. Ryszard Grzesik, "Polski święty na Słowacji – Andrzej Świerad," *Nasza Przeszłość* 92 (1999), pp. 461–479.

67 Andrew could not have received baptism and with it this Christian name after his arrival to Russia, as Bálint Hóman and more recently Kazimierz Jasiński have assumed. Hóman, *Geschichte I*, pp. 235, 255. Kazimierz Jasiński, "Filiacja Adelajdy, żony księcia czeskiego Wratysława II," *Rocznik polskiego towarzystwa heraldycznego* nowej serii tom 1 (12) (1993), p. 8. Andrew concluded a Christian wedding with a wife of German origin (see chapter 16,

The youngest of Vazul's sons, who with all certainly was born in his father's princely court in Nitra, got the Slavic name Belo (Hungarian Béla).[68] He could not have gotten this Slavic name among the Pechenegs, nor his baptismal name Adalbert,[69] which is testimony of the veneration in Nitria to a new Hungarian and Polish saint, the recent Prague Bishop Vojtech (Adalbert).

Andrew and Béla were born when their father was already the Prince of Nitria. As the sons of a prince, they had a higher-born origin than their older brother Levente, who was born to Vazul while he was in exile among the Pechenegs. And that's why chroniclers, with the naming of all three brothers,

---

note 23); therefore, he received baptism long before arriving in Russia. In addition, veneration of St. Andrew in Russian only began in the 1080s. Only in 1086 did Kiev Prince Vsevolod I (1076–1093) have the first Russian temple consecrated to the Apostle Andrew in Kiev. Only later did members of the Rurik dynasty accept this name. In 1102 Pereiaslav Prince Vladimir Monomakh (1094–1113, later Kiev Grand Prince 1113–1125) was born the eighth and youngest son, who got the name Andrew and became the Volyn (Vladimir) prince (1119–1135). In 1112 a second son was born to the later Rostov-Suzdal Prince Yuri Dolgoruky (1132–1157, from year 1154 Kiev Grand Prince) to whom he gave the name Andrew. This was later Vladimir-Suzdal Prince Andrei Bogolyubsky (Andrew the Pious) (1154–1174, from 1169 the Kiev Grand Prince). *Latopis Nestora* 71, year 6594 (1086), 84 year 6610 (1102), *MPH I*, ed. Bielowski, pp. 755, 810. Márta Font, *Magyarok a Kijevi Évkönyvben* (Szeged 1996), pp. 40–41, 44–45, 50–51, 114–115, 120–121, 126–129, 132–133, 148–149, 158–159, 162–165, 176–181, 216–217, 210–211, 220–223. Jan Blahoslav Lášek, *Počátky křesťanství u východních Slovanů* (Praha 1997), pp. 107–115. The mentioned Hungarian Andrews were born and got their names as early as in the 1st half of the 11th century. See notes 62, 63, 64, 65, 66. The name Andrew was thus already naturalized in Hungary in the first decades of the 11th century, which is much earlier than in Russia. Perhaps in the 1050s Andrew established an abbey near Visegrád. This was one of several Hungarian abbeys of the Eastern Rite. *Vita S. Gerhardi episcopi* 15, *SRH II*, p. 503. Györffy, *ÁMF IV*, pp. 705–712. King Andrew had this abbey consecrated to his personal patron. The St. Andrew patronage of Visegrád abbey cannot associate with the arrival of Andrew's second wife Anastasia, the daughter of Kiev Prince Yaroslav the Wise, to Hungary, because veneration for St. Andrew only spread later in Russia.

68 Belo (Béla) is a name of Slavic origin with the meaning *white*, like the names Belenig, Beli, Beluš and Belya. Fehértói, *Árpád-kori kis személynévtár*, pp. 45–46. Fehértói, *Árpád-kori személynévtár*, pp. 104–108. Like castles and towns with the name Belehrad (Belgrad), which means White Castle. *Słownik starożytności słowiańskich I* (Wrocław – Warszawa – Kraków 1961), pp. 101–102, 111–112, 118. For other improbable opinions, see Wertner, *Az Árpádok családi története*, p. 137. György Györffy considers the origin of this name from the Turkish word *bojla*. Györffy, *Tanulmányok a magyar állam eredetéről*, p. 81.

69 Béla's baptismal name Adalbert is mentioned in a document of Palatine Rado from 4 June 1057: *ego Rado palatinus licencia piissimi regis Andree eiusque fratris Adalberti invictissimi ducis … Rogavi eciam graciam dominorum meorum gloriosissimi Andree regis et optimi ducis Adalberti ego Rado palatinus … Ego autem Andreas rex et frater meus, dux Adalbertus dilectus*. *DHA I*, ed. Györffy, no. 46, pp. 161–162.

put his name at the end, as if he were the youngest. He was the least important of them.

11 The End of Polish Influence in Nitria and the Imprisonment of Vazul

Boleslaw the Brave died in 1025 shortly after being crowned the Polish king.[70] For several years after his death, Poland was a strong state, to which Lusatia and Milcenia were subjected on the west, Moravia and Nitria on the south and the Červen (Czerwień) Castles region to the east. In January 1028 Polish King Mieszko II desolated Saxony.[71] The retaliatory campaign of Emperor Conrad II in the summer of 1029, linked to the failed siege of Bautzen, kept the Polish army occupied in the west.[72] Then Bohemian Prince Oldřich, as an ally of the emperor, attacked Moravia.[73] Mieszko II, busy with the German attack, could not aid the Polish forces at the Moravian castles. Oldřich, *dislodging the Poles from all the castles, many of whom were taken prisoner, bound always by the hundred in lines, he had sold to Hungary and beyond.*[74]

Along with Moravia, Nitria was at the same time also experiencing eventful moments. Nitrian Prince Vazul remained without Polish help. Stephen took over Nitria and imprisoned his cousin Vazul directly in Nitra.[75]

---

70 Labuda, *Mieszko II*, pp. 66–67.
71 Labuda, *Mieszko II*, pp. 67–71.
72 Labuda, *Mieszko II*, pp. 74–75.
73 Novotný, *České dějiny* I/1, pp. 723–726. Labuda, *Mieszko II*, pp. 59, 71–77. Barbara Krzemieńska defends the dating of Bohemian rule over Moravia to year 1019 and does so despite the convincing arguments of Gerard Labuda on behalf of year 1029. Barbara Krzemieńska, "Politický vzestup českého státu za knížete Oldřicha (1012–1034)," *Československý časopis historický* 25 (1977), no. 2, pp. 249–250. Barbara Krzemieńska, *Břetislav I. Čechy a střední Evropa v prvé polovině 11. století* (Praha 1999), pp. 76–87. B. Krzemieńska starts from Třeštík's dating of the wedding of Oldřich and Božena, parents of Břetislav I, to year 1002. Třeštík, *Počátky*, pp. 461–463. Therefore, she defends Cosmas's unreliable dating of the kidnapping of Judith, daughter of Henry of Schweinfurt, by the young (perhaps 18-year-old) Moravian Prince Břetislav, to year 1021 and sets the preceding attaching of Moravia to Bohemia to year 1019. Krzemieńska, *Břetislav I.*, pp. 109–115. Most recently and convincingly Miroslav Lysý doubted the opinion of Dušan Třeštík and Barbara Krzemieńská about the time of Břetislav's birth and the year of attaching Moravia to the Bohemians that follows from it. Miroslav Lysý, "Politika českého kniežaťa Břetislava I. voči Uhorsku," *Historický časopis* 52 (2004), no. 3, pp. 452–455. Wihoda, *Morava v době knížecí*, pp. 109, 110, 119–121, 169. Steinhübel, *Kapitoly*, p. 147.
74 *Cosmae Pragensis Chronica Boemorum* I 40, ed. Bretholz, p. 75. *MMFH* I, pp. 201–202.
75 *Chron. Hung. comp. saec. XIV.* II 69, 78–81, *SRH* I, pp. 320–321, 334–337.

12   Prince Emeric and His *Sclavonia*

According to the unknown author of the Hungarian-Polish Chronicle, King Attila (mentioned as *Aquila*) subjugated the old Slavic territory called *Sclavonia* and gave it a new name: *Ungaria*.[76] The chronicler, who did not deny his own Slavic viewpoint on the oldest Hungarian history, even after, although only exceptionally (in the 1st, 3rd and 13th chapter of his chronicle), used the name *Sclavonia* as a second name for Hungary.[77]

Sclavonia, however, was the name not only for the whole of Hungary but also for the principality over which Stephen's son Emeric ruled: *Henricus nobilis dux Sclavonie*.[78] This was that part of the great pre-Hungarian Slavinia, which remained Slavic even after the fabled victory of King Attila over the Slavs. Emeric thus ruled in the old Slavic principality, which belonged to Hungary, but the name *Ungaria* did not do it justice. If Emeric was the *dux Sclavonie*, then it is clear which of the two Hungarian principalities the chronicler had in mind. He was certainly not thinking about Kabar Biharia, but he considered Emeric as the Prince of Nitria. He had reliable knowledge of Slavic Nitria; indeed, he left an exact description of its borders.[79] The mention of Emeric's Slavinia is in the 9th chapter of the Hungarian-Polish Chronicle, that is outside of the 1st, 3rd and 13th chapters, where *Sclavonia* is the second name for all of Hungary. If the chronicler named Emeric's principality *Sclavonia* in this particular place in his work, then he wasn't thinking about the whole of Hungary but had in mind the one of the two Hungarian principalities to which this name

---

76   Nora Verešová, "Sklavínia v historických prameňoch zo 6.–14. storočia. Prehľad koncepcií," *Historický zborník* 18 (2008), no. 1, pp. 132–133. Homza, *Uhorsko-poľská kronika*, pp. 41–43.

77   In the 1st, 3rd and 13th chapters of the Hungarian-Polish Chronicle *Sclavonia* and *Ungaria* are identical. In the 1st chapter *in omnes regiones large proveniens ... ad orientalem regionem Ungarorum usque diffusum est ... non in propria regione, in aliena, que Sclavonia nominatur*. *Chron. Hungarico-Polonicum* 1, SRH II, p. 299. The 3rd chapter tells of the fabled victory of Attila over the Croats and Slavs, who killed his King Kazimír. This same *Sclavonia* is here identical with Slavic territory which Attila conquered in this war and called *Ungaria*: *regem Kazimirum, qui in Sclavonie et Chrowacie partibus ... in terminos Chrvacie et Sclavonie inter fluvios Savam et Dravam ibique occurrerunt ei principes Chrwacie et Sclavonie ... Sclavi et Chrwati ... uxores Sclavas et Chrwatas ... a principe Sclavorum ... Rex vero Sclavonie et Chrwacie ... Columan, qui accepit uxorem de Chrvacia*. Attila's grandson *Bela ... movens se venit in terram suam Sclavoniam, quam atavus suus Ungariam appellavit*. *Chron. Hungarico-Polonicum* 3, SRH II, pp. 302–304. And finally in the conclusion of the last 13th chapter is a mention of Solomon, who ruled in Slavinia: *Remansit autem dux Ladislas in Galiciua, Salomon vero frater eius Sclavoniam regebat*. *Chron. Hungarico-Polonicum* 13, SRH II, p. 320. If Solomon was the Hungarian king (1063–1074), then the Slavinia in which he reigned was Hungary.

78   *Chron. Hungarico-Polonicum* 9, SRH II, p. 315.

79   See note 4.

fit, but which in Emeric's period really was called by that name. Emeric's Nitria was thus Slavinia within Hungary, that is it was Slovakia.

The recalled reference in the Hungarian-Polish chronicle about Prince Emeric belongs to the period after the deposing and imprisoning of Prince Vazul. So that after Vazul was deposed, Emeric (1029–1031) became the Nitrian Prince. The fact that from 1023 he was also the Biharian Prince was either of no interest to or unknown by the chronicler, who observed Hungary through Slavic eyes.

When Stephen's father Géza at the beginning of his rule took up residence in Esztergom and brought the centre of the state to north-eastern Transdanubia, adjacent and powerful Nitria became the more suitable starting point for succession to the throne than distant Biharia. Stephen himself began as the Nitrian Prince. In 997 he managed to rule Transdanubia from Nitria and to gain his inheritance from his father. If he wanted to secure the throne for his son, then he had to grant Nitria to him.

13 Castle Counties in Nitria and Their First Counts

The exchange of power in Nitria had to be consistent. Stephen could not be satisfied with only deposing Vazul and putting Emeric in his place. In order to fully exert his will in this part of the Hungarian Kingdom, too, and to imprison his cousin and safely guard him in his former princely seat, he had to remove from Nitra and from all of Nitria those still loyal to Vazul. He had to break down the entire background that served Vazul and before then his brother Ladislas the Bald for 28 years. First of all, he had to change the administration of the principalities. It was then that former small princes Hont and Borsa could have returned to Nitria, as well as the descendants of Poznan. They were loyal to King Stephen; therefore, they could not remain in Nitria after the attack of Boleslaw the Brave and after the deposing of his protégé Ladislas the Bald in 1001. In 1029 their former principalities, on the will of the king, became castle counties, and they became their first counts.

Immediately after taking over Nitria, King Stephen endowed Zobor Abbey. He gave it a third of all toll revenues and fees from all the trade in Nitra, in the part Dvory (*Doardi*), called *Baba*, at the fords over the Váh and in Trenčín. The sons of Nitrian count Bukven, Deda and Gečä in year 1111 are also testimony about Stephen's donations.[80] If both brothers at the time of their testimony

---

80 *DHA I*, ed. Györffy, no. 138/I, II, pp. 382–385. *CDES I*, ed. Marsina, no. 68, pp. 63–64. Richard Marsina, "Štúdie k slovenskému diplomatáru. K problematike najstarších zoborských

had lived in Nitra for more than 80 years,[81] they came there in 1029, when King Stephen acquired Nitria (1111 − 1029 = 82 = more than 80). They didn't come there alone, but together with their father Bukven, whom King Stephen then made the Nitrian count.

Four small principalities (Nitra, Váh, Hont and Borsod) covered exactly the entire territory and held the borders of Michael's, Stephen's, Ladislas's and Vazul's Nitrian Principality. King Stephen could have abolished these principalities only after getting Nitria out from under Polish dependence in 1029. In 1037 former princes Ort and Hont were already counts.[82] A document from 1037, which mentions former prince Hont already as count, dates the extinction of the four small principalities on Nitria territory to before that year. It certainly happened immediately after its renewed attachment to Hungary in 1029, just as in Somogy, Transylvania and in Marosvár, which Stephen I immediately after subjugating in years 997, 1003 and 1028 transformed into castle counties. Stephen I certainly did not delay in this very suitable opportunity in Nitria.

Prince Poznan was certainly not alive at that time. The king divided his former principality, which covered the whole of south-western Slovakia, into smaller castle counties. In 1029 we can look for the beginning of the Bratislava, Nitra, Trenčín, Komárno, Tekov and Esztergom counties. At that time the small

---

listín," *Sborník Filozofickej fakulty Univerzity Komenského* 14 (1963), pp. 135–141. *Dejiny Nitry*, ed. Fusek, Zemene, pp. 116, 127–129. Lukačka, *Formovanie vyššej šľachty*, p. 31.

81 *Deda et Cace, qui ambo filii Buquen, eiusdem civitatis Nitrie olim comitis fuerunt. Hi duo, Deda videlicet et Cace, qui ambo filii Buquen, comitis, octoginta annis et eo amplius in civitate Nitrie vixerant iam, cum hec facta esset discusio.* DHA I, ed. Györffy, no. 138/I, p. 383. CDES I, ed. Marsina, no. 68, p. 63.

82 *Vrzyo, Chuncio, Thomoyno comitibus.* DHA I, ed. Györffy, no. 26, p. 119. CDES I, ed. Marsina, no. 52, p. 50. Counts Ort and Hont appear together as witnesses of Stephen's donation for the Bakonybél Abbey. They are thus identical with the princes Ort and Hont who together battled on the side of Stephen I in 997. The third count, Tomaj (*Thomoyno*), was probably the Veszprém count, because the endowed abbey lay in Veszprém county. Bakonybél Abbey lay in the Veszprém diocese; therefore, another witness, Bishop Modest, could have been the Veszprém bishop. In 1019 Bishop Modest together with Pécs Bishop Bonipert took part in the founding and endowing of Zalavár Abbey by King Stephen I. DHA I, ed. Györffy, no. 14, pp. 90–91. And this abbey lay in Veszprém County; therefore, we can consider Modest on the basis of this document to be the Veszprém bishop. Just as Bishop Modest was probably the Veszprém bishop, then Count Tomaj could have been the Veszprém count. A donation letter for an abbey in Bzovík from year 1135 mentions Count Hont. The abbey then acquired, aside from other properties, also *predium iuxta Danubium, quod sanctus rex Stephanus condam comiti Hunt dedit ad pascenda animalia.* CDES I, ed. Marsina, no. 74, p. 71. If Hont and Ort were still alive in 1037, then 40 years before, when they battled against Koppány's rebellion, they were still young men who had become princes only shortly before then. Hont could have become the Hont prince probably in association with Stephen's arrival to Nitria in about 995 or came as a foreigner in the train of Stephen's wife Gisela in 996.

Váh Principality to the north of Nitria ceased to exist. After its breaking up, Trenčín County acquired the Žilina region in the north. The Liptov was attached to Hont County. Turiec and Orava fell to Nitra County. Testimony to the large extent of the Hont and Nitra counties is the range of the Nitra[83] and Hont archdeaconate.[84] The Rajčianka Valley also belonged to the Nitra archdeaconate.[85]

Princes Hont, Ort and Samuel Aba were loyal to Stephen I. Therefore, they could remain in their places even after the transformation of the principalities into castle counties. They became their first counts. Poznan also belonged among these princes loyal to Stephen. He, however, did not live to see the transformation and segmenting of his principality into several castle counties in 1029. King Stephen was bound to Poznan for his services, could not forget his loyalty, just as he did not forget the loyalty of Hont, Ort and Samuel Aba. Therefore, he could not appoint as the first Nitrian count a completely new person, as he did after the defeat of Koppány, Gyula II, Ajtony and other disobedient princes. He had to value the service of the now dead prince and could not leave out his heirs when filling the newly established county town in Nitra. The first Nitrian count thus had to be one of Poznan's descendants. Therefore, the first Nitrian count Bukven, who was resident in Poznan's former princely seat, was with all certainty his son. Since Nitra was the seat not only first of Poznan's principality and then Nitra County, but further also a subordinate principality, it was the most important castle in Slovakia; thus, Bukven had to be the most important and therefore the oldest of Poznan's sons. The Poznans, who were frequently Nitra counts, greatly favoured the name Bukven.[86]

The Sebes mentioned in the Annales Altahenses as *marchio*, that is the border count, could have been Poznan's ancestor.[87] Even the name Sebes was a favourite among the Poznans (later Hont-Poznans); but they didn't name their

---

83 *Rationes Jacobi Berengarii et Raimundi de Bonafato collectorum decimarum sexennalium in regno Hungariae 1332–1337*, in *Monumenta Vaticana historiam regni Hungariae illustrantia I/1* (Budapest 1887), pp. 183–187, 189, 192, 194–197, 222, 225, 230–231. Ortvay, MEF I, pp. 19–25. Fügedi, "Kirchliche Topographie," pp. 373, 378–379, 390. Kristó, *A vármegyék*, pp. 347–349, 380–381.

84 Ortvay, MEF I, pp. 29–35, 48–50. Fügedi, *Kirchliche Topographie* pp. 372, 373, 379–380, 385. Kristó, *A vármegyék*, pp. 374–384.

85 *In archidiaconatu Nitriensi ... [Paulus sacerdos ecclesie Sancti Ladislai de Raya] iuratus dixit benefi cium non ultra [marcam et mediam, solvit VIII] grossos. Mon. Vat. I/1*, p. 184.

86 János Karácsonyi, *A magyar nemzetségek a XIV. század közepéig* (Budapest 1900, reprint 1995), p. 670. Mór Wertner, *Die Grafen von St. Georgien und Bözing* (Wien 1891), p. 11. Hodál, "Pôvod, sídla a hodnosť predkov Hunt-Pázmány," pp. 159–160, 163. Lukačka, "Formovanie vyššej šľachty," pp. 37–41, 45, 60–61.

87 *Schebis marchio Ungarie eodem anno est defunctus. Ann. Altah. maior.* ad a 1039, ed. Oefele, p. 23.

sons with it as often as the name Bukven.[88] Because Bukven was then the Nitrian count, Sebes could have been a count in another border county that originated after the segmenting of Poznan's Little Nitria in 1029, in Bratislava County. Bukven and Sebes came from the family of Prince Poznan, and as a family loyal to Stephen it certainly had to leave Nitria in 1001 and could have returned in 1029. If Bukven and his family could only return to Nitra in 1029, then Stephen could have taken over Nitria only in that year.

Thanks to the forward position of his county and mainly his castle seat on the border of the Bavarian Eastern March, the first Bratislava Count Sebes (1029–1039) could have been very well known in Bavaria, and when he died in 1039, the unknown author of the Annales Altahenses did not forget to record it. Bratislava Count Sebes thus took over the place which had been previously held by Prokuj. Other descendants and relatives of Poznan could have only become counts in the other castle counties which in 1029 were split off from Little Nitria.

14   The Territorial Range of the Nitrian Principality

The territorial range of medieval kingdoms, principalities, dukedoms, counties, border marches and various permanently or temporarily connected and lost territories is a closely followed side of history. The greatest attention belongs to the oldest, original territorial range, namely those historical countries whose historical-legal continuity endures still today. The territorial range of the Nitrian Principality is found only in several doubtful reports, which tell of its temporary subjugation by Polish Prince Boleslaw the Brave at the beginning of the 11th century. If we compare it with the territorial ground plan of older castle counties, then we get the long-lost contours, which very naturally divided Nitria from the other Hungarian territories and which we can place very exactly on a map of the world back then.

Bratislava County and its corresponding Bratislava archdeaconate were delimited on the south by the Danube.[89] Csilizköz, lying on the north side of the Danube, originally did not belong to Győr County. Properties of Bratislava

---

[88]   Karácsonyi, *A magyar nemzetiségek*, pp. 665–672. Lukačka, *Formovanie vyššej šľachty*, pp. 30, 36–37.

[89]   Fügedi, "Kirchliche Topographie," pp. 373, 376–378, 383–384. Kristó, *A vármegyék*, pp. 339–345. Ján Steinhübel, "Bratislavský komitát," *Historický časopis* 60 (2012), no. 2, pp. 191–214. Ján Steinhüel, "The County of Bratislava," *Historický časopis* 61 (2013), Supplement, pg. 3–28.

Castle, as well as Poznan and Zobor property in Csilizköz[90] correspond to the northern orientation of this territory. This was originally a part of Poznan's small Nitrian Principality and then, at some unknown time, of Bratislava County.[91] The original size of the other counties on the Danube, Komárno and Esztergom, are determined for us by the older known area of the Komárno and Esztergom archdeaconate. Esztergom Archbishop Martyrius set in 1156 the collection of a church tithe in 70 villages in four archdeaconates on the territory of the Esztergom diocese: in Esztergom, Nitra, Tekov and Hont.[92] A part of the territory to the east of the later Komárno seat, with the villages Močola, Virt, Kürt and Teleki; the southern part of the Tekov with the villages Malás, Veľký Šalov (today Tekovské Lužany), Vdol and Svodov; and from the named villages only Farná and Keszi lay in the Esztergom seat itself, belonged to the Esztergom archdeaconate (*In parrochia Stigranensi*).[93] All 10 named

[90] In 1252 Csiližká Radvaň was the property of Bratislava Castle (*ville Roduan populorum castri Posoniensis*) and Medveďov (*cum villa Medve castri Posoniensis*). A part of the Radvaň lands belonged to Zobor Abbey: *terre ville Rodoan, que est abbatis de Zvbur. Codex diplomaticus et epistolaris Slovaciae* 2, ad edendum praeparavit Richard Marsina (Bratislava 1987), no. 400, p. 281. Györffy, *ÁMF II*, pp. 571–572, 607, 608, 621. In Pataš (Pastúchy) near the Csiliz River in 1270 lived Bratislava castellans: *terra agasonum ... Potos cum stagno suo Chelch ... super aquam Chelch ... castrenses castri Posoniensis ... seorsum super aquam.* Györffy, *ÁMF II*, p. 615. In 1277 Count Pamlen from Sap (Palkovičovo), the Komárno castellan and soldier of the banate, and Bratislava, Nitra and Komárno Count Thomas got from the king abandoned land Tunig belonging to Bratislava Castle: *quandam terram castri nostri Posoniensis Tunyg vocatam in comitatu Jauriensi existentem vacuam et habitatoribus destitutam, vicinam et contiguam terre sue hereditarie Zup ... predictam terram Tunyg cum omnibus suis pertinentiis ... quibus eandem quidam castrensis castri Posoniensis Buhte nomine nosscitur. Az Árpád-házi királyok okleveleinek kritikai jegyzéke II/2–3*, ed. Imre Szentpétery, Iván Borsa (Budapest 1961), no. 2813, pp. 194–195. Györffy, *ÁMF II*, pp. 624, 640. Kľúčovec and the neighbouring Negyven belonged in 1251 and 1252 to Hlohovec Castle. *CDES* 2, ed. Marsina, no. 370, pg. 257, no. 400, pp. 280–281. Györffy, *ÁMF II*, pp. 606–607. Kristó, *A vármegyék*, p. 265.

[91] Baloň, lying in the middle of Csilizköz, was in 1252 the property of the Győr chapter: *villa Bolon, que est ecclesie beate Virginis Iauriensis. CDES* 2, ed. Marsina, no. 400, p. 281. Györffy, *ÁMF II*, p. 580. In 1269, however, it still belonged to Bratislava County: *Ceterum possessionem Balun dictam in comitatu Posoniensi. Codex diplom. Arpadianus continuatus. Árpádkori új okmánytár VIII*, ed. Gusztáv Wenzel (Pest 1870), no. 168, p. 247. Györffy, *ÁMF II*, p. 580. Pataš (Pastúchy) and with it the whole of Csilizköz belonged originally to the Bratislava archdeaconate, and thus also to Bratislava County. *Mon. Vat. I/1*, pp. 202–203. Györffy, *ÁMF II*, pp. 576, 615. Györffy, *ÁMF III*, pp. 386–387.

[92] *CDES 1*, ed. Marsina, no. 81, pp. 78–79. Fügedi, "Kirchliche Topographie," pp. 374–375.

[93] *In parrochia Stigranensi, quoniam prope est et archiepiscopus ibi sepius conversatur, X tantum villas concessi, ubi Vranus et Sarar decimat. Ouarum meliores IIIIor sunt hee: Mosula, Malos, Furnod, Surlou; mediocres sunt Vdol, Kurt, ubi ovilia domini sunt; Wrt; inferiores sunt Scuodov, Teluki, Kesceu predium Zachei episcopi. CDES 1*, ed. Marsina, no. 81, p. 79. István

villages lay on the north side of the Danube. The southern border of the Esztergom archdeaconate and the castle counties corresponding to it was thus the Danube. And according to a papal tithe register from years 1332–1337, the Esztergom archdeaconate (*archidyaconatus Sancti Georgii*) lay on the northern side of the Danube. Its territorial range, however, was reduced on behalf of the neighbouring Komárno and Tekov archdeaconates, and with the exception of Esztergom itself (*Strigonio*), with several parishes and with neighbouring priories of Szent Tamás (*ecclesie Sancti Thome martiris de Promontorio Strigoniensi*) and Szentgyörgymező (*prepositus ecclesie Sancti Georgii Strigoniensis*), only the over the Danube part of the Esztergom seat with the parishes Farná (*Feruet*), Kamenín (*Quemen*), Kamenné Ďarmoty (*Annat ~ Armati*), Gbelce (*Bultuc ~ Gbulenti*), Búč (*Bulcsú*), Svodín (*Segimo*), Kvetná (*Chegi*), Nána (*Vana ~ Nana*), Mužla (*Musla*), another Svodín (*Sedino*) and Kohúty (*Kmot ~ Kacti*, today Štúrovo) further belonged to it.[94]

The papal tithe register from 1332–1337 emphatically tells that *The Komárno archdeaconate is over the Danube* (*Kamariensis est archidyaconatus ultra Danubium*) and its position only on the northern side of the Danube is also confirmed by the number of its parishes: Semerovo (*Toue[re] ~ Cemere*), Nasvad (*Vaskan ~ Naswoti*), Imeľ (*Hemen ~ Emew*), Lék (*Lak*), Bajč (*Boyg*), Iža (*Isa*), Aňala (*Anka ~ Anla*), Vámos (*Wamus*), Dvory nad Žitavou (*Hot Vorti, Hotvort*), Moč (*Mas*), Komárno (*Kamara*), Lél (*Lahal*), Sokolce (*Sakalas*), Kameničná (*Sacalas*) and Tôň (*Con*).[95]

Esztergom and Komárno counties lay originally only on the north side of the Danube, because the southern bank of the Danube belonged to Győr and Visegrád County. Visegrád County is already mentioned in a document for the Veszprém bishopric from 1009 as one of the four castle counties (Veszprém, Fejér, Kolon and Visegrád), which based on the decision of Stephen I made up the territory of the Veszprém diocese.[96] Later, neighbouring Esztergom, Komárno and Fejér sliced off a part of Visegrád County. The small remainder

---

Kniezsa, "Az esztergomi káptalan 1156-évi dézsmajegyzékének helységei," *Századok* 73 (1939), no. 1, pp. 169–172, 186–187.

94   *Mon. Vat.* I/1, pp. 187, 194, 216, 218, 219, 224–225, 231–232. Ortvay, MEF I, pp. 5–7. Györffy, ÁMF II, pp. 220–221, 229, 245, 255, 271, 273, 283, 289, 290, 293, 294, 295, 297, 301, 313. Kristó, *A vármegyék*, pp. 333–336.

95   *Mon. Vat.* I/1, pp. 183, 186, 188, 201, 217, 218, 234, 240. Ortvay, MEF I, pp. 17–19. György Györffy, *Az Árpád-kori Magyarország történeti földrajza III* (Budapest 1987), pp. 400–401, 403, 406, 423, 424, 436, 437, 441, 443, 451, 458, 461. Kristó, *A vármegyék*, pp. 336–339.

96   DHA I, ed. Györffy, no. 8, p. 52. Kristó, *A vármegyék*, p. 251. Zsoldos, "Visegrád," pp. 1–17.

of Visegrád County became Pilis County, mentioned for the first time in 1225.[97] Pilis County later brought its seat from Visegrád to Buda Castle (in today's Budapest). The Visegrád archdeaconate, however, was not affected by this division; it only changed its seat. The archdeacon first moved (probably at the time of the mentioned territorial changes) to Szentendre (where it was based until 1332) and then to Buda.[98] According to the papal tithe register of 1332–1337 to the Buda archdeaconate belonged Buda,[99] the Buda surroundings (*Suburbio Budensi*), Örs (*Vrs*), Sasad (*Sastiti*), Margitsziget (*Insula Budensi*), Szentendre (*Sancto Andrea ... est Budensis archidyaconatus*), Visegrád (*Vissiegrad*), Dömös (*prepositus Demisiensis, prepositura Demisiensi*), Old Buda/Óbuda (*prepositus Antique Bude*), Kelenföld (*Sancti Gerardi de Buda*), Tetény (*Dechen, Tethin*), Keszi (*Kezin*), Csöt (*Chic, Chut*), Adony (*Odon*), Gercse (*Gerche, Kerche*), Berki (*Boroky, Berky*), Epöl (*Epel*), Héreg (*Herecy*), Telki (*Teliki, Telky*), Bajót (*Beyod*), Nyergesújfalu (*Nova Villa*), Haláp (*Halab*), Neszmély (*Nezmel*), Piszke (*Pizke*), Barok (*Barchy*), Csamaszombata (*Chama Zumbata, Chamaburnata*), Zsámbék (*Zambuch, Sambok*), Perbál (*Prebor, Probor*), Dág (*Dag*), Iváncs (*Ivanch*), Csolnok (*Cholnuch, Cholnus*), Sáp (*Sap*), Bánhida (*Banchida*), Érd (*Erd*), Horhi (*Horky*), Szigetmonostor (*Monasterio*), Jenő (*Yeneu*), Piszke (*Pizke*), Kele, Kalász (*Kaluz*), Basztély (*Boztich*), Diód (*Gyod*), Torbágy (*Curbag*), Bot (*Bath*), Tolma

---

[97] *Petro comite Pilisiensi. Codex diplom. Arpadianus continuatus. Árpádkori új okmánytár XI*, ed. Gusztáv Wenzel (Budapest 1873), no. 120, pg. 183. Kristó, *A vármegyék*, pp. 252–254. Györffy, *ÁMF IV*, pp. 583, 692. Zsoldos, "Visegrád," pp. 17–21.

[98] *Archidiacono de Sancto Andrea* mentioned in 1226. *Vetera monumenta historica Hungariam sacram illustrantia maximam partem nondum edita ex tabulariis vaticanis de prompta collecta ac serie chronologica deposita ab Augustino Theiner. Tomus primus: Ab Honorio pp. III. usque ad Clementem pp. VI. 1216–1352* (Romae – Parisiis – Vindobonae 1859), no. 143, p. 69. Kristó, *A vármegyék*, pp. 251–252. Documents from years 1240, 1267, 1272, 1290, 1297, 1298, 1310, 1311, 1314, 1318, 1232 and the papal register from 1320 mention the archdeaconate of Szentendre. Györffy, *ÁMF IV*, pp. 696–697. *Mon. Vat. I/1*, p. 22. According to the papal tithe register from years 1332–1337, the seat of this archdeaconate was already Buda: *Item Paulus de Sancto Andrea iuratus [de credulitate, extirmavit] suum beneficium ad tres marcas, [et est Budensis archidiaconatus et] Vesprimiensis episcopatus, solvit decimam. Mon. Vat. I/1*, p. 183. *Incipit solutio decime papalis Wesprimiensis ecclesie scilicet anni secundi et tertii et quarti. Et primo de archidyaconatu Budensi. Mon. Vat. I/1*, p. 373. *Nota, solutio secundianni dominorum de capitulo Wesprimiensis ecclesie. Primo Nicolaus archidyaconus Simigiensis ... Item Budensis de archidyaconatu suo solvit II. marcas grossorum cum pondere Budensi. Mon. Vat. I/1*, p. 383. *Nota regestrum pro debitis papalibus anni tertii. Primo de archidyaconatu Budensi. Mon. Vat. I/1*, p. 384. *Item Budensis primo solvit LVI grossos. Mon. Vat. I/1*, p. 394. *Nota de solutionibus registrum pro dobitis papalibus anni quarti. Primo de archidiaconatu Budensi. Mon. Vat. I/1*, p. 395. Györffy, *ÁMF IV*, p. 614. See note 100.

[99] *Mon. Vat. I/1*, pp. 400, 401, 402, 403, 404, 406. Györffy, *ÁMF IV*, p. 614.

(*Tolma*), Úrsap (*Orsap*) and Mogyorós (*Monoreus*).[100] According to the position of the named parishes, aside from Pilis seat, the whole south of Esztergom, the south-east part of the Komárno and north-eastern edge of the Fejér seat also belonged to the Buda archdeaconate, which maintained the range of the expired Visegrád County. Visegrád County was bordered on the north and east by the Danube, on the west by the Által-ér River, the Vértes Mountains and on the south-west reached up to the valley of the Váli-víz River.

The south-western part of the later Komárno seat, lying south of the Danube and west of the Által-ér River, did not belong to the older Komárno County nor even to Visegrád County. Since it belonged to the Győr bishopric and the Győr archdeaconate,[101] it belonged to Győr County.

Not even Hont County maintained the whole territory of the extinct Hont principality. On the north it acquired the Liptov; to the south-east, however, it lost the upper and middle Ipeľ River region, where Novohrad County originated. In 1107 Prince Álmos donated to the Dömös Abbey, in addition to other property on the territory of Nitria, also five slaves (Stephen, Sokol, Kenesu, Seznete and his brother) *in civitate Naugrad*.[102] Novohrad (Nógrad) Castle and with it all of Novohrad County thus belonged with all certainty to the Nitrian Principality. The first known Novohrad Count Slaviz (*Slauiz comes Novogradensis*) is mentioned in 1108.[103] We have the first report about the Novohrad archdeacon, which had ecclesiastical care over the entire territory subjugated to Novohrad Castle, from 1252.[104] The southern border of Nitria separated two castle counties from one another, Novohrad from Vác and the two archdeaconates corresponding to them, Novohrad, which belonged to the

---

100 *Mon. Vat. I/1*, pp. 182, 183, 195, 197, 198, 199, 217, 219, 373, 374, 383, 384–385, 400, 401, Ortvay, *MEF I*, pp. 286–289. Györffy, *ÁMF II*, pp. 221, 225, 226, 232, 233, 236, 292, 300, 306, 307, 316, 342–344, 345, 349, 359, 389. Györffy, *ÁMF III*, pp. 392, 395, 400–401, 406, 420, 444, 460. Györffy, *ÁMF IV*, pp. 566, 567, 568, 569, 570, 572–573, 577, 578, 584, 592–593, 614, 626, 628, 631, 640, 641, 642, 652, 677, 688, 689, 695, 697, 701, 702, 714. Kristó, *A vármegyék*, p. 252.

101 Later, perhaps after connection to the Komárno seat, this most northern part of the Győr diocese separated from the Győr archdeaconate and became the second Komárno archdeaconate, which unlike the older same-named neighbour on the north side of the Danube remained a part of the Győr diocese. Ortvay, *MEF I*, pp. 316–319. Györffy, *ÁMF III*, pp. 392, 395, 400. Kristó, *A vármegyék*, pp. 263–265.

102 *CDES I*, ed. Marsina, no. 77, p. 74.

103 *DHA I*, ed. Györffy, no. 130, p. 357. For Novohrad County, see Kristó, *A vármegyek*, pp. 430–431. Kristó, "Néhány vármegye kialakulásának kérdéséhez," pp. 469–470.

104 *Nicolai archidiaconi de Neugrad. Codex diplomaticus patrius hungaricus. Hazai okmánytár VI*, ed. Arnold Ipoly, Imre Nagy, Dezső Véghely (Budapest 1876), no. 46, p. 66. After 1254 *Octomaro archidiacono Nogradiensi ... Strigoniensis diocesis*, after 1291 *Johannes archidiaconus Nougrad*, 1296 *archidiaconus Newgrad*, 1318 *Jacobus archidiaconus Neugrad*. Györffy, *ÁMF IV*, pp. 277–278.

Esztergom archdiocese, from Vác, which belonged to the Vác diocese. Both dioceses originated under Stephen I; they therefore had to respect the county division of Stephen's state. Therefore, we can also consider their mutual border in the Cserhát Mountains and on the upper Zagyva as the border of two castle counties, the northern Novohrad and the southern Vác counties.

The oldest Vác County, before then a principality, was covered by the territory of the Vác diocese.[105] Vác Prince Ort, who in 997 together with Poznan and Hont battled on Stephen's side, is mentioned in 1037 as a count.[106] In that time Hont and Poznan's descendants Bukven and Sebes were also counts. After the death of the first Vác Count Ort (after 1037) the smaller castle counties Szolnok, Csongrád, Pest and Szigetfő were detached from Vác County. Szolnok County, first mentioned in 1134,[107] got the name of its first Count, Szolnok (*Zonuc comes*), who in 1046 together with four bishops went to welcome the arriving Vazul's sons Levente and Andrew.[108] We have the first report of Csongrád County from year 1075,[109] about Pest County only from year 1255.[110] If in 1278 the archdeaconate Szigetfő is mentioned,[111] then a castle county also existed with it, which later became a part of Fejér.[112] In the borders of these smaller counties, separated from the large Vác County, the archdeaconates Vác (first

---

[105] See chapter 14, note 121. In this way Ort's Vác Principality could in its range approximately match two other allied principalities of Poznan and Hont, as well as other Hungarian principalities. In 1000 Vác County became the territory of the Vác diocese.

[106] See note 78.

[107] *Euzidinus comes de Saunic.* CDES I, ed. Marsina, no. 73, p. 70. Kristó, *A vármegyek*, pp. 434–440. Kristó, "Néhány vármegye kialakulásának kérdéséhez," pp. 475–476.

[108] *Chron. Hung. comp. saec. XIV.* II 83, SRH I, p. 339. *Zonug comes. Legenda S. Gerhardi episcopi maior* 15, SRH II, pp. 501–503. *Principum etiam unus, Zaunic nomine, omnibus modis cruciatus, ex hac luce migravit, quia priorem fidem recolens, nunc fidem Petro servare voluit.* Ann. Altah. maiores ad a. 1046, rec. Oefele, p. 43. Györffy, *István király*, pp. 331.

[109] *deinde partes dividuntur inter comitatum Cernigradensium et episcopatum Sancte Marie Wacensis.* DHA I, ed. Györffy, no. 73/II, p. 216. CDES I, ed. Marsina, no. 58, p. 56. Györffy, ÁMF I, pp. 881–889, 893–894. Kristó, *A vármegyék*, pp. 440–442.

[110] *Terram Kezw, sitam in comitatu Pestiensi. Codex diplom. Arpadianus continuatus. Árpádkori új okmánytár VII*, ed. Gusztáv Wenzel (Pest 1869), no. 274, p. 385, no. 274, p. 385. Györffy, ÁMF IV, pp. 527, 540. Kristó, *A vármegyék*, pp. 433–434.

[111] *magistro Nicolao de Zigetfey archidiaconibus. Codex diplomaticus Arpadianus. Árpádkori oklevelek 1095–1301 I*, ed. Ference Kubinyi (Pest 1867), no. 128, p. 108. Ortvay, MEF I, pp. 112–113.

[112] The territory of the former counties Szigetfő and the remnants of Kalocsa fell to the Solt seat (*ad sedem Solt* in 1325), which was one of the so-called processus (sub-counties or districts) of the Fejér seat. Györffy, ÁMF II, pp. 326, 329, 335, 337, 340, 342, 344, 437, 441. Kristó, *A vármegyék*, pp. 245–246.

mentioned in 1236),[113] Pest (1226),[114] Szigetfő (1278),[115] Csongrád (1271)[116] and Szolnok originated,[117] belonging to the Vác diocese.

After the detachment of Pest County (perhaps sometime in the second half of the 12th century) Vác County shrunk to a small territory on the southern slopes of the Cserhát Mountains, the basins of the Galga and Verőce, and was merged with Novohrad County. The reduced Vác County could have been connected with Novohrad County only after the extinction of the Nitrian Principality, that is after the extinction of the borders between these principalities and the royal part of Hungary in the Cserhát Mountains and on the upper Zagyva. Both parts created together Novohrad County even before the end of the 12th century. According to Anonymus, who wrote his work around year 1200, Árpád allegedly sent a military campaign *to subjugate the peoples of Gemer and Novohrad castles*. Árpád's commanders and their warriors, after returning from Gemer, *came up to the peak Bolhad* (the peak Szanda in the Cserhát Mountains), *from where passing to the territory of Novohrad Castle (per partes castri Nougrad), they came up to the Galga River. When they departed from there, they retreated along the bank of the Danube and crossing the Verőce River, camped by the Ipeľ River ... Then all the Slavs (Sclaui), inhabitants of this country, who first subjected themselves to Prince Salan, out of fear facing them voluntarily subjugated themselves.*[118] Anonymus's telling of the events of Árpád's period is nearly all untrue, but the geography of Anonymus's work, corresponding to the period in which he lived and wrote, is for us very interesting. Anonymus's Novohrad is defined only on the southern part, formerly in the reduced Vác County. Since Anonymus labelled it as Novohrad, a part of Novohrad County, it safely already was. Anonymus's Magyars did not cross the Cserhát Mountains. The peak Bolhad, to which they went, lay on the border of both parts of the enlarged Novohrad County.[119] Árpád's soldiers marched through the Galga and

---

113 In 1236 there is mention of *Ozyas archidiaconus Waciensis*, in 1237 *Jancka archidiaconus*, 1271 *Farkasio archidiacono Vachyensi*, 1278 *magistro Farkasio Waciensi ... archidiaconibus*, 1281 *Farkasio Waciensi*, 1295 *Oliverio archidiacono Wachiensi* and 1303 *Oliverio Wachiensi ... archidiaconis*. Györffy, *ÁMF IV*, pp. 311–312. Csáky, *A váczi egyházmegye I*, pp. 111–212.

114 *archidiacono Pestiensi ... Waciensis diocesis*. Györffy, *ÁMF IV*, p. 538. Ortvay, *MEF I*, pp. 110–111.

115 See note 111.

116 *Nicolao Chongradiensi archydiaconis. ÁÚO VIII*, ed. Wenzel, no. 246, p. 366. Györffy, *ÁMF I*, pp. 888–889, 893. Ortvay, *MEF I*, pp. 109–110.

117 Ortvay, *MEF I*, pp. 107–109.

118 *Anonymi (P. magistri) Gesta Hungarorum* 33, *SRH I*, pp. 74–75.

119 In 1255 a congregation of Novohrad, Hont and Gemer nobles arrived in Vác: *congregacionem in Wacia tribus comitatibus, videlicet Neugradiensi, Huntensi et Gumuriensi. Monumenta ecclesiae Strigoniensis I*, ed. Ferdinandus Knauz (Strigonii 1874), no. 553,

Verőce basins, that is south from the Cserhát Mountains, and without comment they also left Novohrad Castle itself, lying on the northern side of this mountain range, and hurried to cross the Ipeľ at its mouth into the Danube. Anonymus thus completely left the original Novohrad County, lying north of the Cserhát Mountains, out of his telling, just as he left out neighbouring Hont.

Southern Novohrad, in the basins of the Galga and Verőce, that is somewhere in the already reduced Vác County, also belonged on the north to the principality in the area between the Danube, Zagyva and lower Tisza rivers, which Anonymus ascribed to the invented Prince Salan. And this is testimony on the originally different territorial political orientation of the northern and southern parts of the later Novohrad seat, mutually separated by the ridge of the Cserhát Mountains.

In the years 1266, 1274 and 1279 Novohrad was still a county castle.[120] In this time Philippe (1263–1278), the Vác bishop and chancellor of Queen Elizabeth, was the Novohrad Count.[121] In 1284 it already belonged to Vác bishop Thomas (1278–1289).[122] This means that Bishop Thomas, who could have also been the Novohrad count, just as his predecessor Philippe, came into ownership of this castle sometime in the years 1279–1284. Only then did the Vác archdeaconate and with it also the Vác diocese get the small strip to the north of the Cserhát Mountains with the old county castle.

The papal tithe register from years 1332–1337 writes about the Novohrad archdeaconate (*De archidiaconatu Nigradiensi, De archidiaconatu Neugradiensi,*

---

p. 423. Former Vác County was thus already with complete certainty a part of Novohrad County.

[120] In 1266 the younger King Stephen dislodged Kuncsej and Jób, sons of Bartholomew of Berényi *a iobagionatu castri regii Neogradiensis*. HO VI, ed. Ipolyi, Nagy, Véghely, no. 96, p. 143. Novohrad is mentioned as a royal castle in 1274. HO VI, ed. Ipolyi, Nagy, Véghely, no. 141, p. 199. Elemér Vácz, "Nógrádvára történetéhez," in *Emlékkönyv Domanovszky Sándor* (Budapest 1937), p. 593. *Nógrádmegye története 896–1849, 1. kötet*, ed. Sándor Balogh (Salgótarján 1972), pp. 63–64. Still in 1279 Ladislas IV considered Novohrad as his royal castle: *castri nostri Nogradiensis. Az Árpád-házi királyok okleveleinek II/2–3*, ed. Szentpétery, Borsa, no. 3004, p. 249.

[121] In 1272 *Philippo Waciensi [episcopo], aule domine regine karissime matris nostre cancellario, comite Neugradinensi. ÁÚO IX*, ed. Wenzel, no. 1, p. 2. The Vác bishop, Novohrad Count Philippe, also arranged a donation from Queen Elizabeth from year 1273: *Datum per manus venerabilis patri Philippi episcopi Wachiensis aule nostri cancellarii, comiti Neugradiensis, fidelis nostri. Dl 33850*. Additional documents from years 1272–1274 also mention Vác bishop Philippe, who was Elizabeth's chancellor and Novohrad Count. Györffy, ÁMF IV, p. 278.

[122] On 1 May 1284 *Thomas ... episcopus Wachyensis, aule regie cancellarius ... hospites nostri de villa Neugradiensi ad montem loci eiusdem se transtulerunt, castrum ibidem et alias munitiones de permissione maiestatis regie ... pro augmentacione iurium episcopalium construentes,... eisdem hospitibus libertatem duximus concedendam*. DF 250220.

est archidyaconatus Neugradiensis, est Neugradiensis) with the parishes Salgó (*Sarro*), Nemti (*Henthi*), Tarján (*Tarian*), Nagyfa (*Vatfa*), Pôtor (*Sancti Petri*), Capola ~ Tarpola, Szügy (*Syug*), Hugyag (*Hudioch*), Balassagyarmat (*Germat*), Endrefalva (*Villandre*), Keresztúr (*Sancte Crucis*), Rimóc (*Ymog ~ Rimog*), Danca (*Dausa*), Ozdín (*Vsgra*), Terbelovce (*Terbedes ~ Terbeded*), Veľká nad Ipľom (*Villique*), Gerge (*Gerege*), Ság (*Saca*), Panické Dravce (*Deuout ~ Darouci*), Tarnóc (*Tarnouc*), Litke (*Luque ~ Luce*), Vrbovka (*Vatbo ~ Vorbo*), Szécsény (*Sypchen*), Strehová (*Strigonio*), Chrťany (*Archian*), Szakalmonostor (*Sac*), Lučenec (*Butens ~ Luceus*), Tomášovce (*Thomas Sancti Martini*), Dráh (*Dia ~ Dra*), Magyarnándor (*Vandor ~ Nandor*), Galša (*Agualsa*), Breznička (*Bersensa*), Fiľakovo (*Silec*), Karancslapujtő (*Lapot*), Marcal (*Morsol ~ Marsal*), Halič (*Gald ~ Galg*), Mašková (*Most*), Szentgál (*Sancto Gallo*), Šavoľ (*Sauli*), Karancskeszi (*Quesi*), Érsekvadkert (*Votquet ~ Votiquerti*), Varsány (*Bochtan ~ Boyschan*), Čeláre (*Cheylar*), Ludány (*Ludan*), Turečky (*Turci*), Senné (*Sinhua*), Strháre (*Straguar*), Kutasó (*Crursa*), Bárkány (*Mauhan ~ Banhan*), Nógrádmegyer (*Meget*), Mátraverebély (*Verep*), Ľuboreč (*Borsa*), Slatinka (*Salanania ~ Solanama*) and Šiator (*Sacra*).[123] Properties of the Esztergom archbishop lay on this territory.[124]

The papal register notes in the Vác archdeaconate the parishes (*Sancta Katherina ... est archidyaconatus Vacensis*), Nagymaros (*Moro, Morosis prope Vissegrad ultra Danubium*), Verőce (*Vetisza ~ Verutza*), Vác (*Vaciensis, Vacia, Vaxsia*), Némedy (*Neuig*) and Nádasd (*Nadast*).[125] In this archdeaconate properties of the Vác bishop are distributed,[126] which after the donation of Novohrad

---

123 Mon. Vat. I/1, p. 188, 192, 224, 227–229, 230–231. Ortvay, MEF I, pp. 36–42. Györffy, ÁMF IV, pp. 223–224, 228–229, 231, 233, 234, 235, 236–237, 238–239, 241–242, 243, 245–247, 248–249, 252, 257–258, 265, 266–272, 273, 274, 283, 289, 290–291, 292, 294–295, 297, 298, 299, 300, 302–304, 306, 308, 315–316, 317, 318–319, 320. Kristó, *A vármegyék*, pp. 430–431.

124 Györffy, ÁMF IV, p. 220.

125 Mon. Vat. I/1, pp. 183, 198, 218, 219, 220, 224, 254–255, 259–260, 342, 404. Ortvay, MEF I, p. 113. Györffy, ÁMF IV, pp. 223–224, 272–273, 275, 276, 299, 312, 315, 319–320. Kristó, *A vármegyék*, pp. 429–431. The papal tithe register from 1332–1337 mentions among the archdeaconates of the Vác diocese also the Novohrad archdeaconate with the Némedy parish: *Dyocesis Waciensis ... archidiaconatus Neugradiensis. Item Symon sacerdos de Neuig iuratus*. Mon. Vat. I/1, pp. 254–255. Since the Vác archdeaconate in which Némedy lay belonged to Novohrad County, it began being called the Novohrad archdeaconate, just like its northern neighbour. The Vác archdeaconate was transformed into the Novohrad archdeaconate only gradually, testimony of which is the mentioned papal register, which uses both names. This transformation is certainly also associated with the affiliation of Novohrad Castle and with its nearest surroundings to the Vác diocese and to the Vác archdeaconate around year 1280. See note 122. Komárno County also included two Komárno archdeaconates, one belonging to Esztergom and the other to the Győr diocese. See note 101.

126 Györffy, ÁMF IV, p. 220.

Castle to the Vác bishop by Béla IV around 1280 were expanded by the properties of the donated castle on the north side of the Cserhát Mountains. With this decision the border of the Vác archdeaconate was shifted to the northern edge of the acquired properties of Novohrad Castle. And the property relations of both high church dignitaries respected the archdeaconate, the diocese and the former county border, which before it shifted a bit north, around 1280, was also the old border of the Nitrian Principality.

Just as with the castle counties in western Slovakia, King Stephen could have established Borsod County to the east only after the complete re-attachment of Nitrian Principality to Hungary in 1029. Its first count, Borsa, took over the entire area of the abolished small principality, exactly as the other large castle counties in the other ends of Stephen's Hungary. According to Anonymus's description, the oldest Borsod County stretched from the Tisza between the mouth of the Bodrog and the mouth of the Sajó and the Bükk Mountains to the basin of the Sajó, Hornád and Poprad, to the Tatras and to the Hungary-Poland border.[127]

The territorial outlines of castle counties on the territory of the Nitrian Principality, which originated with the transformation and division of four old principalities (Nitra, Váh, Hont and Borsod), exactly followed the whole length of its border just as the Hungarian-Polish Chronicle describes them. The southern border ran along the Danube, then along the ridge of the Cserhát Mountains and the upper flow of the Zagyva, from there across the Heves-Borsod uplands and the Bükk Mountains to the confluence of the Sajó with the Hornád. The southern border of Nitria ended at the bend of the Tisza River near Szerencs Castle, between the mouth of the Sajó and the mouth of the Bodrog. The eastern border corresponded to the interface of the Abaújvár (to which the beginning of the Šariš region belonged) and the Zemplín, which was formed by the ridge of the Zemplín hills and the Slanské hills, the Topľa River between Hanušovce and Giraltovce, then crossed the Ondava Upland, and near Stropkov crossed the Ondava River and stretched along its feeder the Chotčianka up to the mountain Klin on the Hungary-Poland border. From there only perhaps 15 km further to the east lay the peak Pásiky, at which the borders of Hungary, Russia and Poland met. The Zemplín and Slanské hills are a very significant barrier in the east of Slovakia, beyond them lies only the Zemplín plain, widely open to the Tisza River region.

The old Slavic principalities were originally tribal territories, which already in the period of Slavic settlement had to be sufficiently large to support one large tribe, naturally segmented and significantly cut off from all the

---

127 See pp. 215–216.

neighbours and as easy as possible to defend. The historically stable principalities were able to survive the extinction of tribal organization and the origin of a state, the alternating of independence and foreign rule, connection to a larger state and later ethnic changes. Even the imperial dukedoms of Bavaria, Swabia, Thuringia, Saxony, Frisia, Francia, Lorraine, Burgundy in their territorial range were stable from the 5th and 6th centuries as the tribal territories of the Bavarians, Alamans, Thurings, Saxons, Frisians, Franks and Burgundians and did not change it up to the mid-12th century. Territorial stability of historical principalities and dukedoms is typical for proto-medieval Europe. Therefore, we can consider the territorial range of the Nitrian Principality as we know it from the beginning of the 11th century as stable for the entire period of its long history.

CHAPTER 16

The Escape and Return of Four Árpáds (1029–1048)

1   The Attack of Moravian Prince Břetislav on Nitria

After the conquering of Moravia by the Bohemians in 1029, Oldřich's son Břetislav became the prince of the Moravians.[1] Břetislav was unhappy with Hungary's occupation of Nitria; therefore, in June of 1030 he joined Emperor Conrad II's campaign against Hungary.

Conrad advanced with a large army south of the Danube. The road was full of intrigues. The emperor got to the narrow passage between the Danubian arms on the north and the Moson wetlands to the south, which on the east were closed by Győr Castle. There he stopped and began to quickly draw back. Hungarian King Stephen pursued him up to the Eastern March and occupied Vienna.[2] The Moravian prince invaded Slovakia and was successful there: *In this year Prince Břetislav caused a great defeat to the Hungarians and plundered their lands up to Esztergom Castle.*[3] The starting point of Břetislav's campaign was Moravia: *In this year Prince Břetislav caused a great defeat of the Hungarians, marching from Moravia and up to Esztergom he ravaged their land.*[4]

---

1   Novotný, *České dějiny I/1*, pp. 723–726. Labuda, *Mieszko II*, pp. 71–75.
2   Ann. Altah. maior. ad a. 1030, rec. Oefele, p. 18. *Wiponis Gesta Chuonradi II. imperatoris* 26, curavit Werner Trillmich. Quellen des 9. und 11. Jahrhunderts zur Geschichte der Hamburgischen Kirche und des Reiches (Berlin 1961), pp. 582–585. *Herimanni Aug. Chronicon* ad a. 1030, ed. Buchner, pp. 664–666. *Annales Hildesheimenses* ad a. 1030, contulit Georgius Waitz, Scriptores rerum Germanicarum in usum scholarum ex Monumentis Germaniae historicis recusi (Hannoverae 1878), p. 35. Novotný, *České dějiny I/1*, pp. 727–728. Albin Ferenc Gombos, "Szent István háborúja II. Konrád római-német császárral 1030-ban," in *Szent István Emlékkönyv*, ed. Serédi, pp. 299–324. Hóman, *Geschichte I*, pp. 247–248. Györffy, *István király*, pp. 309–315.
3   *Hoc anno dux Braciżlaus magna cede prostravit Ungaros et terram eorum usque ad urbem Strigoniam devastavit.* Cosmae Pragensis Chronica Boemorum I 41, ad a. 1030, ed. Bretholz, p. 76.
4   *Hoc anno dux Braciżlaus magna cede Ungaros stravit, procedens de Moravia et usque ad Strigoniam terram illorum vastavit.* Annales Gradicenses et Opatowicenses ad a. 1029, Fontes rerum Bohemicarum II/1, ed. Josef Emler (Praha 1874), p. 389. Gombos, *Catalogus I*, pp. 135–136. Barbara Krzemieńska tried to show that Břetislav marched to Hungary only in the following year of 1031 and did so independently of Conrad. Krzemieńska, *Politický vzestup*, pp. 251–271. Krzemieńska, *Břetislav I.*, pp. 145–152. Břetislav marched to Hungary in the same year in which Prague Bishop Hizzo died. If Hizzo died in 1030, then we have to date Břetislav's campaign to 1030. Miroslav Lysý, "Základná charakteristika východnej politiky Konráda II.

If Břetislav, *marching from Moravia*, advanced *up to Esztergom*, then he marched along the Bohemian Road.⁵ If he set off along the Bohemian Road, then he crossed the border at the Morava River near Holíč, marched to Šaštín and through the Bukovský pass in the Little Carpathians and came to Šintava, where he crossed to the other side of the Váh River. Then he came to the Nitra River, which he crossed near Nyárhíd (near today's Nové Zamky) and stopped on the Slovak bank of the Danube before Esztergom. Somewhere on this road *Prince Břetislav caused a great defeat of the Hungarians*. The emperor's defeat on the opposite bank of the Danube, however, prevented the Moravian prince from taking advantage of his victory in Slovakia. Nitria remained a firm part of Hungary.

In the spring of 1031 Stephen negotiated peace with the emperor's son and Bavarian Duke Henry in Vienna. Stephen returned Vienna to him; he could, however, at the expense of the Eastern March, keep the right bank of the lower flow of the Moravia (Moravian fields) and the territory between the Leitha and Fischa rivers.⁶

2   The Death of Emeric and the Blinding of Vazul

It seemed that peaceful times had finally come. After Stephen's death the royal crown was to pass to the head of his son.⁷ But Prince Emeric (*dux Hemericus*), to whom Stephen secured succession to the throne, unexpectedly died on 2 September 1031, succumbing to a hunting injury inflicted by a raging

---

(1024–1039)," *Medea* 6 (2003), pp. 56–60. Lysý, "Politika českého knížaťa Břetislava I. voči Uhorsku," pp. 455–457.

5   The path of the Bohemian Road is mentioned in a document which Hungarian King Charles I issued at Hungarian Visegrád in 1336. *Codex juris municipalis Regni Bohemiae. Tomus I. Privilegia civitatum Pragensium. Sbírka pramenů práva městského Království českého. Díl I. Privilegia měst pražských*, ed. Jaromír Čelakovský (v Praze 1886), no. 27, pp. 44–47. *Pramene k dejinám Slovenska a Slovákov IV. Pod vládou anjouovských kráľov*, ed. Blanka Brezováková, Ján Lukačka, Vincent Sedlák, Július Sopko (Bratislava 2002), no. 28, pp. 108–110. Štefan Janšák, "Česká cesta – najstarší spoj Slovenska s českými krajmi," *Vlastivedný časopis* 10 (1961), pp. 83–87. Štefan Janšák, "Z minulosti dopravných spojov na Slovensku," *Geografický časopis* 16 (1964), no. 1, pp. 13–29.

6   *Herimanni Aug. Chronicon ad* a. 1031, cur. Buchner, pp. 666–667. Heide Dienst, "Werden und Entwicklung der babenbergischen Mark," in *Österreich im Hochmittelalter (907–1246)*, ed. von der Kommission für die Geschichte Österreichs bei der Österreichischen Akademie der Wissenschaften (Wien 1991), p. 80. See note 49.

7   *Chron. Hung. comp. saec. XIV.* II 69, SRH I, p. 319. *Legenda maior S. Stephani regis* 15, SRH II, p. 391. *Legenda S. Stephani regis ab Hartvico episcopo conscripta* 19, SRH II, pp. 427–428.

wild boar.[8] The probable place of Emeric's death is marked by Hegyközszentimre Abbey (Sîntimreu), which originated in Emeric's honour after his canonization in 1083.[9] It lies on the edge of the Biharian Mountains, in medieval times called Igfon. The local forests in the 11th century were hunting grounds for the Biharian princes.[10]

After Emeric's death, Vazul remained the entitled claimant to the Hungarian throne, and his royal cousin had him imprisoned in Nitra. However, Stephen didn't like Vazul and his family's inclination towards paganism: *Sadness and grief weighed upon him primarily because among his blood relatives there was no one suitable to preserve the kingdom in the Christian faith after his death. The Hungarian nation namely preferred to lean toward paganism by custom than towards the Christian faith.*[11] Therefore, Stephen passed over the authorised claims of five living Árpáds and summoned from Venice his 20-year-old n ephew Peter Orseolo, whose father Otto Orseolo (the Venetian doge 1030–1031) had died in 1031, and named him as his successor.[12] Stephen's cousin Vazul, who *did not agree with this*,[13] became the victim of court intrigue and ended lamentably. The Annales Altahenses emphasize that Stephen ordered this: *King Stephen of blessed memory, his (= Peter's) uncle, when his son died during the life of his father, because he did not have another son, he adopted and named him as the successor to the kingdom. He blinded the son of his brother, the more entitled successor, because he did not agree with this, and he sent his young sons (parvulos) into exile (exilio relegavit).*[14]

The Hungarian chronicler denied Stephen's crucial share in Vazul's tragedy: *He rapidly sent a message to Buda, Egiruch's son, to bring his cousin Vazul from the Nitra prison, whom the king had locked up for his young devilry and madness, and thus he gave him the opportunity to get better. He wanted to appoint him*

---

8   Et Heinricus, Stephani regis filius, dux Ruizorum, in venatione ab apro discissus, periit flebiliter mortuus. Ann. Hildesh. ad a. 1031, cont. Waitz, p. 36. *Annales Posonienses* ad a. 1031, SRH I, p. 125. *Legenda maior S. Stephani regis* 15, SRH II, p. 391. *Legenda S. Stephani regis ab Hartvico episcopo conscripta* 19, SRH II, p. 428. Wertner, *Az Árpádok családi története*, pp. 58–61. Vajay, "Großfürst Geysa," pp. 59–60, 92–94. *Chron. Hung. comp. saec. XIV.* II 69, SRH I, p. 319. *Kurze Geschichte Siebenbürgens*, ed. Köpeczi, p. 138.

9   Györffy, ÁMF I, p. 667. Györffy, *István király*, pp. 374–375. Györffy, *König Stephan*, pp. 198–200. MT I/1, pp. 831–832.

10 *Chron. Hung. comp. saec. XIV.* II 14, 15, SRH I, pp. 380, 381.

11 *Chron. Hung. comp. saec. XIV.* II 69, SRH I, pp. 319–320.

12 See notes 14, 17, 18. Wertner, *Az Árpádok családi története*, pp. 61–102.

13 *hoc non consensit.* Ann. Altah. maior. ad a. 1041, rec. Oefele, p. 24.

14 Ann. Altah. maior. ad a. 1041, rec. Oefele, p. 24. According to Szabolcs de Vajay, Vazul's sons fled at the time of Vazul's imprisonment, which he puts in year 1033, and they then blinded him in 1037. Vajay, "Großfürst Geysa," p. 101.

as king before his death. The chronicle ascribed Stephen's blame to the queen: *When Queen Gisela heard about this, she consulted with the criminal Buda and expeditiously sent Budo's son Sebes to the prison where Vazul was being held. Sebes thus overtook the royal message, gouged out Vazul's eyes, poured lead into his ears and fled to Bohemia. When the king's messenger arrived, he found Vazul without eyes and with wounds in his eyes he led him to the king.* The Hungarian chronicler also invented the king's powerlessness on seeing his cousin: *Upon sight of him, at his lamentable mutilation, tears poured from King Saint Stephen, but a serious illness did not permit him to deservedly punish the criminals.* Ultimately, the chronicler managed to present even the escape of Levente, Andrew and Béla as the result of Stephen's good heartedness: *He invited the sons of his cousin Ladislas the Bald* (correctly Vazul), *namely Andrew, Béla and Levente, and advised them to flee as rapidly as possible and thus to save their bodily life. They accepted the wise counsel of the blessed king and fled from evil and intrigues to Bohemia.*[15]

According to the mentioned testimony of the reliable Annales Altahenses, Stephen did not have in mind at all to hand over the throne to Vazul; he himself ordered the blinding of Vazul and the exiling of his sons. Sebes thus did not act on the command of Queen Gisela, but fulfilled the will of Stephen himself. Sebes's father Buda did not intrigue with the Queen but advised the king directly and was with all certainly identical with the king's messenger Buda, the son of Egiruch, whom Stephen sent to Nitra, not, however, to free Vazul and bring him to the royal court but with the order for his blinding. Two Budas did not live at the royal court, but only one, who was Egiruch's son and at the same time Sebes's father. The Hungarian chronicler, in order to defend Stephen's innocence, turned one person into two. Stephen's Buda was allegedly to free Vazul and Gisela's Buda came with the idea of blinding Vazul.

Vazul's three sons, Levente, Andrew and Béla, escaped *from evil and intrigue* to Bohemia. Under these circumstances, not even Domoslav, son of Ladislas the Bald, could remain in Hungary. He, too, together with his younger cousins had to seek refuge in Bohemian exile. So that nothing could seriously endanger Peter's succession, King Stephen named Peter as prince.[16]

---

15   *Chron. Hung. comp. saec. XIV.* II 69, SRH *I*, pp. 320–321. Simon of Kéza left out the name of both Budos and simplified the entire story. *Simonis de Keza Gesta Hungarorum* II 44, SRH *I*, p. 173. If Gisela should get the credit for presenting Peter as Stephen's successor (as Hungarian chroniclers try to convince us) and not Stephen, then we would with difficulty explain Peter's conduct towards her upon his taking over rule. This would be ingratitude too great and difficult to understand. See note 18.

16   *Petro videlicet sororis sue filio, quem in Venetia genitum ad se vocatum iam dudum exercitui suo prefecerat ducem. Legenda maior pg. Stephani regis* 16, SRH *II*, p. 392.

3   Árpád Exiles

Stephen died on 15 August 1038,[17] and Peter Orseolo inherited his kingdom. The new Hungarian king immediately at the beginning of his rule rid the widowed Queen Gisela of all political influence. The royal widow had for several years to live closed up in some castle, probably in Veszprém. Peter took hold of her properties, which she received as her dowry on the occasion of her wedding.[18] With his conduct he made enemies of Bavaria, from where Gisela came, as well as King Henry III (1039–1056, emperor from 1046), who in the years 1027–1039 and in 1047–1049 was the Bavarian duke. The open antagonism with the Bavarians began with a devastating invasion into the Eastern March at the end of year 1039.[19]

Bohemian Prince Břetislav I (1035–1055) also antagonised Henry III with an incursion into Poland in the summer of 1039.[20] Břetislav and Peter were probably already allies by then. The alliance with Peter enabled Břetislav to triumph over Henry in August of 1040. Břetislav could leave Moravia unprotected and concentrate on the defence of Bohemia, alongside Bohemian forces, the whole Moravian army, to which three Hungarian units were added. Three thousand Hungarian warriors together with the Moravians were concentrated on the defence of the Bohemian borders near Bílina Castle.[21]

If Břetislav wanted to be an ally of Hungarian King Peter, then he had to rid himself of all four Árpáds, who were Peters enemies. The Árpád exiles thus had to leave Bohemia in 1039. Where they went is revealed in the name of Andrew's only daughter Adelaide († 27 January 1062).[22] The German name of Andrew's daughter is testimony of the German origin of her mother, Andrew's

---

17   *Stephanus Ungrorum rex in die assumptionis sanctae Mariae terminum fecit carnalis vitae.* Ann. Altah. maior. ad. a. 1038, ed. Oefele, p. 23. *Chron. Hung. comp. saec. XIV.* II 70, SRH I, pp. 321–322. *Simonis de Keza Gesta Hungarorum* II 45, SRH I, p. 173. *Ipso anno Stephanus Ungariorum rex, cum ante plurimos annos se cum ante plurimos annos se cum tota gente sua ad Christi fidem convertisset ecclesiasque multas et episcopatus construxisset et in regnum suum probis mitissimus operam inpedisset, Petrum, sororis suae filium de Venetia natum, pro se regem constituens obiit.* Herimanni Aug. Chronicon ad a. 1038, cur. Buchner, pp. 672–673.

18   Ann. Altah. maior. ad a. 1041, rec. Oefele, p. 24.

19   Herimanni Aug. Chronicon ad a. 1039, cur. Buchner, pp. 672–673.

20   Krzemieńska, *Břetislav I.*, pp. 230–253.

21   Ann. Altah. maior. ad a. 1040, rec. Oefele, p. 23. Herimanni Aug. Chronicon, ad a. 1040, cur. Buchner, pp. 672–675. Ann. Hildesh. ad a. 1040, cont. Waitz, p. 45. *Cosmae Pragensis Chronica Boemorum* II 8–11, ed. Bretholz, pp. 93–99. Krzemieńska, *Břetislav I.*, pp. 254–289. Wihoda, *Morava v době knížecí*, p. 121.

22   *Cosmae Pragensis Chronica Boemorum* II 20, ed. Bretholz, p. 112.

first wife.²³ The four Árpáds who had to leave Bohemia thus went to Germany, where one of them, Andrew, found a bride.

Adelaide in 1056, or 1057, married subordinate Olomouc Prince Vratislaus (1055, 1058–1061, later Prince of Bohemia and King Vratislaus II 1061–1085–1092). Vratislaus fled from his brother Spytihněv II to Hungary and became Andrew's guest: *By coincidence this king had a single daughter by the name of Adelaide; she was already mature for marriage, very pretty, with hope awakening envy in many suitors. As soon as the guest saw her, he fell fatefully in love with her; the good king did not prevent this and after a short time gave her to him as his wife.*²⁴ If Adelaide, to whom the widowed Vratislaus fell in love in 1056, was *already mature for marriage* (*iam thoro maritali tempestiva*), thus she could have been 13–16 years old, which was then the average age for girls to be married. Adelaide thus could have been born in late 1039 and at the latest 1043.

4 Rebellion against King Peter

Hungarian King Peter occupied the county towns, courts and castles with foreigners, mainly Germans and Italians. He handed property over to them and showed no regard for the Hungarians. When he removed two bishops and fired several pagan-sympathizing dignitaries from the service of the royal court, dissatisfaction peaked. Palatine Samuel Aba, brother-in-law of Saint Stephen, stood at the head of the rebellion in September 1041.²⁵ Peter very rapidly lost the ground under his feet in Hungary. He could not expect any help from abroad, because his ally Břetislav had already several weeks before defended against the great force of Henry's army and capitulated at the end of September.²⁶ Peter Orseolo fled to his brother-in-law Adalbert, Margrave of the Eastern March, and from there, shortly after, under the protection of his former enemy Henry III.²⁷

---

23 Jasiński, "Filiacja," p. 10. Kazimierz Jasiński, "Česko-polské dynastické vztahy v raném středověku," *Dějiny a současnost* 2 (1999), p. 8.
24 *Cosmae Pragensis Chronica Boemorum* II 16, ed. Bretholz, p. 107.
25 *Ann. Altah. maior.* ad a. 1041, rec. Oefele, pp. 24–26. *Chron. Hung. comp. saec. XIV.* II 71–72, SRH I, pp. 323–326. Szőcs, *A nádori intézmény*, pp. 26, 27, 31.
26 *Ann. Altah. maior.* ad a. 1041, rec. Oefele, pp. 36–27. *Cosmae Pragensis Chronica Boemorum* II 12, ed. Bretholz, pp. 99–100. Krzemieńska, *Břetislav I.*, pp. 290–315.
27 *Herimanni Aug. Chronicon* ad a. 1041, 1042, cur. Buchner, pp. 674–675. *Ann. Altah. maior.* ad a. 1041, 1042, rec. Oefele, pp. 26, 29.

Buda and his son Sebes, who ten years before were the main instrument at the royal court for the removal of Vazul, did not survive the rebellion.[28] Sebes, Buda's son and Egiruch's grandson, whom the rebels executed in 1041, cannot be identical with the border (probably Bratislava) Count Sebes mentioned in the Annales Altahenses, because that one died in 1039.[29] Simon of Kéza labels the royal messenger Sebes (*nuncium nomine Sebus*) as a count (*comitem Sebus*).[30] Buda's son Sebes could not have been the other border count, the Nitrian count, because the Nitrian count at that time was Bukven.[31] If Sebes moved in the vicinity of the king and had influence on his decisions, then he was not a castle count but probably a significant court count.

The new Hungarian King, Samuel Aba (1041–1044), surrounded himself with Hungarian magnates, who helped him triumph over Peter Orseolo. The most important of them were Stojslav and Pezili. On their advice Samuel Aba cancelled several decrees of the deposed King Peter.[32]

After victory in Bohemia, Henry III turned his attention to Hungary. Therefore, Peter's request for assistance against Samuel Aba came in handy to him. In October he pardoned the humiliated Břetislav and concluded an alliance with him against Hungary,[33] which also affected the life of the Árpád exiles. When Henry took in Peter Orseolo, Peter's Árpád competitors could not remain in Henry's realm and had to return to Bohemia.

After concluding a German-Bohemian alliance against Samuel Aba in October 1041, the hope of a return to Hungary flashed before one of the four Árpáds, who was staying in Bohemia. Břetislav, with his new Hungarian policy, gave preference to the oldest, that is the most important of them politically, Domoslav, to whom he assigned a place in the prepared campaign to Hungary.

---

28 *Ann. Altah. maior.* ad a. 1041, rec. Oefele, p. 25. *Chron. Hung. comp. saec. XIV.* II 72, SRH I, p. 325. *Simonis de Keza Gesta Hungarorum* II 47, SRH I, p. 174.
29 See chapter 15, note 83.
30 *Kysla regina ... misit comitem Sebus. Simonis de Keza Gesta Hungarorum* II, 44, SRH I, pp. 405–406.
31 Péter Váczy considers Sebes from the Hermanni Altahensis annales and Sebes from the Hungarian chronicles as one person, although each of them died in a different year. Sebes was, in his opinion, the Nitrian count. Váczy, "A Vazul-hagyomány," pp. 314–315. See pp. 405–406.
32 *Ann. Altah. maior.* ad a. 1041, rec. Oefele, p. 26. A Hungarian chronicler mentions *tres de principibus regni*; the first was Viska, the second Stojslav and the third Pezili. *Chron. Hung. comp. saec. XIV.* II, 72, SRH I, p. 326. Viska, who is also here, stood in 1046 at the head of a campaign of the second rebellion against King Peter. See note 62.
33 *Ann. Altah. maior.* ad a. 1041, rec. Oefele, pp. 27–28. Krzemieńska, *Břetislav I.*, pp. 316–334.

Levente, Andrew and Béla, whom Břetislav left out of his Hungarian plans, departed Bohemia and went to Poland.[34]

5 A Nitrian Prince from the Aba Family?

The goodwill with which the German King Henry embraced Peter Orseolo provoked a Hungarian attack on the Eastern March and Carinthia in February 1042. The Hungarian army struck *from both sides of the Danube* (*ex utraque Danubii parte*) ..., while King Samuel marched *on the south side of the river* (*in meridiana fluvii plaga*) with *countless soldiers* and *commanded his prince* (*duci suo*) *on the north* (*in aquilonari*) *to do the same*.

The prince, subordinate to King Samuel, not only had a princely army, but also his *principality* (*ducatu*) available. If he was also with his army *on the north*, that is on the north side of the Danube, then he set off from Nitria. Thus, he was the Prince of Nitria. Since the appanaged princes were always from the same family as the kings, the Prince of Nitra, who in February 1042 led his army into battle, could have been from the same line as his king, that is from the Aba line.

In the middle of February both Hungarian armies crossed the border. Samuel's royal army came all the way to the Traisen River, where on 15 February, from early morning to evening, it marauded and took captives. They spent the night near Tulln and on the next day happily returned home. The northern army led by *this prince and his fellow fighters* (*tantu duci et suis conmilitonibus*) also had good fortune at the beginning. On that same day it plundered the northern side of the Austrian Danube and took many captives. Margrave of the Eastern March, Adalbert, with his son Liutpold, however, rapidly assembled 300 warriors and hurried after them. The Hungarians were divided into three groups. The first group was to carry the captives to Hungary, while the second and third were to fight the Bavarians. But the Bavarians broke through the second group, which attacked them directly, and caught up with the first, laden with plunder and captives. Only then did the third Hungarian group attack

---

34   *Interea Endre, Bela et Leuente, qui fugerant in Bohemiam, inde propter paupertatis necessitudinem transierunt in Poloniam et a Misca* (correctly Kazimír) *duce Polonie benigne sunt suscepti et honorati. Chron. Hung. comp. saec. XIV.* II 78, SRH I, p. 334. *Andreas, Bela et Luenta de Boemia in Poloniam transeuntes a Misca Polonorum duce amicabiliter sunt recepti. Simonis de Keza Gesta Hungarorum* II 52, SRH I, p. 177. Levente, Andrew and Béla left Bohemia together, because Břetislav chose Domoslav for his Hungarian plans. And Levente with Andrew left Poland later, because Polish Prince Casimir favoured Béla. See note 56.

them from behind. A battle broke out. The captives used the confusion and took over weapons and joined in with the battle. Since there were a great many of them, they were the decisive element. The Bavarians killed a great many Hungarians not only in this battle but also on the bank of the Morava River, over which they wanted to escape. *The prince (Dux) who led the Hungarians also fled and managed to cross the river on horseback.* Simultaneously with the attack on the Eastern March a third Hungarian army invaded the Carinthian March (the border march of the Carinthian Principality on the border with Hungary, later called the March of Styria, to which the basin of the Mur River belonged). In a battle near Ptuj, however, the Carinthians (*Carintani*), led by Gotefrid, Margrave of Carantania, triumphed over the Hungarians.

King Aba wanted to show the German king the force of his army. The show of force, however, didn't come off due to the failures of the Prince of Nitria. The furious king could not forgive him and had him blinded.[35] Thus ended probably the only non-Árpád appanaged prince, who very briefly (from the rebellion in the autumn of 1041 up to February 1042) ruled in Árpád Nitria.

6   Nine Castles

At the beginning of September 1042 a large German and Bohemian army crossed the border into Hungary. The Bohemian army was *worthy of a king*, that is very numerous. Henry listened to Břetislav's advice and marched with the whole army on the north side of the Danube.[36] After conquering Hainburg and Bratislava it *plundered the country (partem) north of the Danube*, marched

---

[35]   Ann. Altah. maior. ad a. 1042, rec. Oefele, pp. 29–31. Ann. Hildesh. IV 10, ad a. 1042, cont. Waitz, p. 45. *Herimanni Aug. Chronicon* ad a. 1042, cur. Buchner, pp. 674–675. *Chron. Hung. comp. saec. XIV.* II 73, SRH I, pp. 326–327. *Simonis de Keza Gesta Hungarorum* II 48, SRH I, pp. 174–175. Kristó, *A XI. századi hercegség*, pp. 57–58. A legion had 1000 soldiers. See chapter 17, note 98. The Bavarians who attacked the retreating Hungarians could have been more than the mentioned 300. But even despite this there were many more Hungarian soldiers. The significant disproportion of the small Bavarian and large Hungarian army was balanced by the confused Hungarian commanders, and especially the large number of Bavarian captives (*magnam quidem captivitatem ... multitudinem captivitatis*), who rebelled.

[36]   *Expeditio vero facta est in mense sequenti, coadunato exercitu ingenti, quibus divina misericordia prosperum cursum proficiscentibus et magnum honorem contulit pervenientibus. Pertransierunt etenim terram ex aquilonali parte Danubii fluminis suasu et consilio Bohemici ducis, qui tum inibi una affuerat cum copia, quae regem decuerat.* Ann. Altah. maior. ad a. 1042, rec. Oefele, p. 31. *Movit itaque expeditionem ingentem et consilio Baratzlai ducis Bohemorum ex aquilonari parte Danubii venit ad confinium Hungarie. Chron. Hung. comp. saec. XIV.* II 74, SRH I, p. 328. *Simonis de Keza Gesta Hungarorum* II 48, SRH I, p. 175.

up the Hron and twice defeated Hungarians attempting a counterattack.[37] The residents (*incolae*) of the castle counties lying north of the Danube were subjugated via their representatives (*missa legatione*) dispatched to Henry. With all resoluteness, however, they refused to accept Peter Orseolo, whom Henry had brought with him. The German king thus listened to the Bohemian prince: *The king there accepted the subjugation of nine castles (novem civitates), which on the request of Břetislav and with the consent of the inhabitants (consensu incolarum) he gave to the nephew of King Stephen (fratrueli Stephani regis), who came with this prince.*[38]

We know two important details about the castles which in September 1042 recognized the rule of an unknown Árpád. There were nine of them, and they lay north of the Danube. The mentioned castle inhabitants lived in their surroundings and were subjugated to the counts seated in them. A castle at which a castle count (*comes castri*) was based had its own count. The basic meaning of the Latin word *comitatus* is the escort, which surrounds a lord and

---

[37] *Heinricus quoque rex autumno Pannonias petens Heimenburg et Brezesburg evertit, septentrionalem Danubii partem, quia flumina australem et paludes munierant, usque ad Grana flumen vastavit seu in dedicionem; et pars exercitus bis numero Ungariis incursantibus congrediens, strages magnas effecit. Herimanni Aug. Chronicon* ad a. 1042, cur. Buchner, pp. 674–675. *Heinricus rex Pannoniam ingressus, duas populosissimas civitates evertit, plures deditione subiecit. Ann. Hildesh.* ad a. 1043, cont. Waitz, p. 45. *duae tamen earundem urbium, Baioaricae marchae proxime, ante adventum nostratium urbanorum ignibus sunt abstumtae. Ann. Altah. maior.* ad a. 1042, rec. Oefele, p. 32.

[38] *Incolae autem missa legatione promisere se, quicquid rex praeciperet, velle perfi cere, nisi tantum Petrum regem suum recipere, quod tamen rex summopere voluerat et propter quod eum secum adduxerat. Postquam etenim auxilium suum illi promisit, hoc in restituendo regno illi ostendere cupivit, sed sui adeo execrabantur, ut nullum se illum recepturos faterentur. Novem ibi civitates rex deditione cepit, quas rogatu Bratezlavi et consensu incolarum fratrueli Stephani regis, qui cum eodem duce advenerat, dedit. Ann. Altah. maior.* ad a. 1042, rec. Oefele, pp. 31–32. *Sed cum Petrum regem, quem secum ducebat, provinciales recipere nollent, alium quem petebant, ducem eis constituit; quem Ovo post discessum eius in Boemiam reppulit. Ann. Hildesh.* ad a. 1043, cont. Waitz, p. 45. *Et subactis partium illarum Ungariis, cum Petrum recipere nollent, quendam alium ex illis, apud Boemannos item exulantem ducem eis constituit; quem tamen Ovo statim post discessum regis resistere non valentem in Boemiam repulit. Herimanni Aug. Chronicon* ad a. 1042, cur. Buchner, pp. 674–675. *Legati vero Hungarorum promiserunt cesari, quod Hungari in omnibus starent ad mandatum eius, nisi quia Petrum in restarent ad mandatum eius, nisi quia Petrum in regem non susciperent, quod tamen cesar summo opere perficere affectabat. Obligatus enim erat Petro promissione, quod ei regnum restitueret. Hungari vero nullatenus consenserunt et missis muneribus, data quoque fide, quod captivos Teutonicorum abire permitterent. Chron. Hung. comp. saec. XIV.* II 74, SRH I, p. 328. *Simonis de Keza Gesta Hungarorum* II 48, SRH I, p. 175.

accompanies him. A castle county was thus everything that surrounded a castle and belonged to it.

To a castle belonged above all the castle countryside (*hradský vidiek*) with a steady surrounding perimeter, which the Slavs called a *medza*, or boundary. This *medza* (*mega*) was not only a border which defined the castle countryside but also became synonymous for the countryside itself. The Hungarians took the Slavic word *medza* (*hradská medza*, castle boundary), whereby they left its other, figurative meaning. Hungarian therefore had the word *megye* (*vármegye*) for a castle countryside. Since a castle was a seat of state power and administration, the castle countryside (*hradská medza, vármegye*) was also the basic territorial unit of the state, that is a province. A castle county was thus a castle district or castle province.

A castle was, in addition to this, also the centre of part of a large royal or princely property, with villages in which the castle inhabitants lived. The king or prince shared the revenues that came from it with the castle count (the Hungarian *ispán*). Not only were most of the villages of its countryside, or district, subjected to a castle, but villages scattered in other castle districts were, too. A castle county was thus also royal or princely property subjected to a castle, territorially connected in its own district and scattered outside of it. This was a castle ispanate (Hungarian – *várispanság*, Slovak – *hradské španstvo* or *hradská župa*).[39]

The inhabitants subjected to the nine castles were *provinciales*,[40] that is the inhabitants of the castle provinces (districts, countrysides) administered from the mentioned castles. The nine castle counties on the north side of the Danube, whose representatives stood together before Henry III, accepted the new *ducem*, or prince. Thus, together they made up one principality, undoubtedly the old Nitrian Principality, *which on the south was fortified by the river and swamps*,[41] that is the Danube border, which separated it from the rest of Hungarian territory. The Nitrian Principality thus at that time was divided into 9 castle provinces (districts, countrysides). These were Bratislava (then called Preslava), Nitra, Trenčín, Komárno, Tekov, Esztergom (without Esztergom Castle itself, which lay on the south side of the Danube), Hont, Novohrad and Borsod.[42]

---

39 Steinhübel, "Bratislavský komitát," pp. 191–193. Steinhübel, "The County of Bratislava," pp. 3–5.
40 A province is a castle county. Kristó, *A vármegyék*, pp. 29–31. *Provinciales* are thus inhabitants of a castle county, who were subjected to a castle county, that is castle inhabitants.
41 See note 37, 38.
42 See pp. 240, 242–246, 248.

The other castles on the territory of Nitria: Šintava, Hlohovec, Bana, Beckov and Šaštín did not have their own associated territories, that is a castle province (district, countryside); thus, they did not have even their own *provinciales*, whose representative in September 1042 accepted the rule of an unnamed Árpád. Villages belonging to the castles Šintava, Hlohovec, Bana and Beckov were scattered on the territories of other very distant counties lying outside of Nitria.[43] Their counts were not equal to other counts within the Nitrian Principality.[44] They were dependent on a Nitrian (the Beckov count obviously from Trenčín) count, on whose territory their castles lay. Nitra County stretched to the west *up to the Váh River ... up to the Morava River* (*usque ad fluvium Wag ... usque ad fluvium Moroa*). The Nitrian count was *the count of Nitra and other castles* (*comitem Nitriensem et aliorum castrorum*).[45] At negotiations with the German king and the Bohemian prince the Nitrian count represented its inhabitants and perhaps also the counts *of other castles*, that is the subjugated counts of Šintava, Hlohovec and Bana and the Trenčín count of the subjugated Beckov count, if these castles were already then the seats of the mentioned scattered counties headed by counts.

---

43 Györffy, *István király*, pg. 329. Györffy, *ÁMF IV*, pp. 347–350, 383–390, 455–456, 459–460. Kristó, *A vármegyek*, pp. 166, 353–369. Ján Lukačka, "Die Kontinuität der Besiedlung auf dem Gebiet des Komitates Nitra im 9–13. Jahrhundert," *Studia historica Slovaca* 18 (1994), pp. 139, 146, 148–151, 155–156.

44 The Šintava count is mentioned for the first time in 1177: *Zemere comes de Simtei*. CDES I, ed. Marsina, no. 93, p. 89. From year 1249 we have the first report on the Hlohovec county: *terram Manya sitam circa fluvium Sythwa in comitatu de Golguch ... exemptam a castro Golguch*. CDES 2, ed. Marsina, no. 320, pp. 223–224. The Hlohovec count, identical with Szolgagyőr, is first mentioned in years 1250 and 1251. In 1250 *Erne magister agazonum et comes de Zolgageuri*. In 1251 *Sudan officialis Erne magistri agasonum regalium, comitis de Galgouch*. Györffy, *ÁMF IV*, p. 384. We know County Bana for the first time from 1226: *Yner in parochia Albensi, ad comitatum de Bana pertinens*. In 1234 *Baya comitis Arquibana*. Györffy, *ÁMF IV*, p. 347. Beckov Count Michal, mentioned in 1244, was the son of (perhaps also Beckov) Count Aba: *Michael, comes de Bolunduch, filius Apa comitis*. CDES 2, ed. Marsina, no. 147, p. 98. Šaštín was probably not a county seat. Kristó, *A vármegyék*, pp. 365–369.

45 *Anonymi (P. magistri) Gesta Hungarorum* 37, SRH I, pp. 78–80. György Györffy looks for these nine castles only in south-western Slovakia: Šaštín, Borona, Šintava, Trenčín, Beckov, Bana, Hlohovec, Nitra and Tekov. Györffy, *István király*, pp. 329–330. MT I/1, pp. 839–840. Györffy, *ÁMF IV*, p. 333. If in 1074 two-thirds of the Hungarian Kingdom had 30 counties (in 1042 there was certainly fewer), then the mentioned 9 counties had to take up not only a part of south-west Slovakia, but the whole of Nitria, which together with 4 Biharia counties formed (approximately) a third of Hungary. *Chron. Hung. comp. saec. XIV.* II 88, 117, SRH I, pp. 345, 384. Szabolcs de Vajay, too, defines Nitria in compliance with Anonymus by the Morava and Hron rivers. Vajay, "Großfürst Geysa," pp. 54–56, 64–66, 68.

7 Prince Domoslav

Who was this *nephew* (fratruelis = nephew, more exactly brother's son) of Stephen, who came to Slovakia in Břetislav's retinue? The Herimann's Chronicle, the Annales Altahenses and the Hildesheim Annals, from where we draw reports on these events, do not mention his name at all.

King Stephen had no brothers; he had only two cousins, Ladislas the Bald and Vazul, who were no longer alive. The labelling of *fratruelis* thus belonged to one of their sons. These, however, were Stephen's more distant, second cousins. Only one of the Árpáds could have hoped for help from Břetislav; the others had to seek it elsewhere. If Vazul's three sons departed at that time to Poland, then Břetislav showed preference to their cousin Domoslav, who was the oldest of them and had the greatest right to take over rule of Hungary or over its conquered part.[46] Nitria wanted Domoslav as its prince; after all, he was the son of former Nitrian Prince Ladislas the Bald. The representatives of nine Nitrian counties thus put him forward as his successor. Břetislav supported their wishes, and Henrich eventually followed his advice.

According to later testimony of Bavarian chronicler Aventine, who in writing his chronicles in the 16th century used some sources now lost to us today, this new prince received 2000 Bavarian and Bohemian fighters from Henry and Břetislav.[47] Aventine's report appears to be very probable, but we can no longer verify it anywhere. Prince Domoslav, however, did not remain long in Nitria. After the departure of the victorious armies, Samuel Aba expelled him, and he had to flee back to Bohemia.[48]

8 The End of Samuela Aba

In August 1043 a new German campaign headed for Hungary. On the bank of the Rábca River, however, Aba and Henry came to an agreement. Henry

---

46 Mór Wertner, Szabolcs de Vajay, Peter Ratkoš and Richard Marsina have already identified the unknown Árpád whom the allies put in Nitria in 1042 as Domoslav. Wertner, *Az Árpádok családi története*, pp. 591–592. Vajay, "Großfürst Geysa," pp. 65–67, 99–100. Ratkoš, "Podmanenie," p. 161. Richard Marsina, "Údelné vojvodstvo na Slovensku," *Zborník Slovenského národného múzea* 81 (1987), *História* 27, p. 203. Bálint Hóman and György Györffy thought that this could have been Béla. Hóman, *Geschichte I*, p. 255. MT I/1, pp. 839–840. Janusz Bieniak, Kazimierz Jasiński and Gerard Labuda identified him as Andrew. Janusz Bieniak, *Państwo Mieclawa. Studium analityczne* (Warszawa 1963), p. 109. Jasiński, "Filiacja," pp. 6, 10. Labuda, *Mieszko II*, pp. 181–182.
47 Krzemieńska, *Břetislav I.*, p. 343.
48 See note 38.

recognized Aba as the Hungarian king and promised him that we would no longer support Peter's claim. Aba returned to him a wide strip of land west of the border rivers Leitha and Morava, which Stephen I had acquired 13 years before at the expense of the Eastern March. In addition to this, he had to release captives from the previous year's war and send Henry a large amount of gold and valuable materials.[49]

In February 1044 Samuel Aba learned of a conspiracy being prepared by Hungarian magnates. Under the pretence of an important council, he called some 50 conspirators to Csanád and had them all killed. A portion of Aba's opponents fled the country and asked the German king for help.[50] Because Aba did not properly satisfy any of the peace conditions he had committed himself to the previous year, Henry sent a campaign against him in the middle of June 1044. Prince Břetislav joined Henry with a Bohemian army. Peter Orseolo accompanied Henry, too. The allies avoided the traditional path through Moson and Győr, closed on the north by the arms of the Danube and from the south by the extensive swamps around the Neusiedler See lake, the lower Rába and the Rábca. They conquered the border towns of Sopron and Kapuvár and went around the mentioned swamps from the south. When crossing the Rábca River, near the village Menfő, not far from Győr, the Hungarian king stopped them in their tracks with a large army. The Hungarian defeat was hastened by a sudden storm bringing with it a cloud of fine dust that blinded the Hungarians immediately at the start of the battle. And it was completed by the betrayal of many Hungarian soldiers, who went over to Peter Orseolo's side.

---

49 *Tunc ... partem regni retradere, quae quondam Stephano data fuerat causa amiciaciae. Ann. Altah. maior.* ad a. 1043, rec. Oefele, p. 33. *Heinricus rex iterum Pannonias petens, ab Ovone, vix impetrante pactum, satisfactionem, obsides, munera, regnique usque ad Litaha flumen partem accipiens discessit. Herimanni Aug. Chronicon* ad a. 1043, cur. Buchner, pp. 676–677. Dienst, "Werden und Entwicklung," pp. 81–84. In 1043 Hungary also lost the territory between the Lafnitz River and Fischbach Alps, which the neighbouring Carinthian March acquired lying in the basin of the middle Mur (the basis of the later Steyr March). Up to 1043 the Fischbach Alps, then called *mons Predel*, the ridge of which divided the basin of the middle Mur from that of the upper Rába, formed the border between Hungary and the Carinthian March. Frietz Posch, "Siedlungsgeschichte der Oststeiermark." *Mitteilungen des Österreichischen Instituts für Geschichtsforschung* 13 (1941), no. 4, pp. 404, 446. Posch, "Die deutsch-ungarische Grenzentwicklung," pp. 126–139. Posch, "Die Anfänge der Steiermark," pp. 105–112. Samuel Aba not only relinquished the mentioned border territory but committed himself to paying a large ransom. *Ann. Altah. maior.* ad a. 1043, rec. Oefele, pp. 32–33. *Herimanni Aug. Chronicon* ad a. 1043, cur. Buchner, pp. 676–677. *Chron. Hung. comp. saec. XIV.* II 75, *SRH I*, pp. 328–329. *Simonis de Keza Gesta Hungarorum* II 48, *SRH I*, p. 175.

50 *Ann. Altah. maior.* ad a. 1044, rec. Oefele, pp. 34–35. *Chron. Hung. comp. saec. XIV.* II 75–76, *SRH I*, pp. 329–330. *Simonis de Keza Gesta Hungarorum* II 49–50, *SRH I*, pp. 175–176.

Samuel Aba lost his kingdom in the unhappy Battle of Menfő on 5 July 1044. Peter Orseolo, accompanying the German king, entered into Székesfehérvár and again became the Hungarian king (1044–1046). Samuel Aba did not get far on his escape. They caught up with him near the Tisza, put him before a mixed Hungarian-German court, and after delivering a verdict, executed him.[51]

The military defeat of the Hungarian king in a single open battle and the occupation of his seat at Székesfehérvár decided the struggle over the whole of Hungary. At this time the victorious German king had in his power not only the immediately occupied part of Transdanubia, but the entire kingdom was subjugated to him, which he could hand over to his protégé Peter Orseolo. There was no power organized in the country at the time which could have put up successful opposition. We could have followed a similar situation, although to a smaller measure, in September 1042 in Nitria. Henry and Břetislav did not have to pass with their entire army here and there over the entire territory of the principality and all of its remote ends. Given that they took over the most important part of the country, the area of Nitra, they ruled the entire principality and could stop their military march near the Hron. Not only were six occupied castle counties from Bratislava up to the Hron subjected to them (Bratislava, Trenčín, Nitra, Tekov, Komárno and Esztergom), but another three as well (Hont, Novohrad and Borsod), which the allied army did not enter, thus nine Nitria counties.[52]

Domoslav was an Árpád. Thanks to his legitimacy, not only did the territory occupied by the military in south-west Slovakia accept him, but all of Nitria. Domoslav's principality thus did not end at the Hron,[53] but further surpassed the length and width of Henry and Břetislav's military march.

---

51   Ann. Altah. maior. ad a. 1044, ed. Oefele, pp. 35–37. *Herimanni Aug. Chronicon* ad a. 1044, cur. Buchner, pp. 676–679. *Chron. Hung. comp. saec. XIV.* 11 76–77, SRH I, pp. 330–333. *Simonis de Keza Gesta Hungarorum* 11 50–51, SRH I, pp. 176–177.

52   By the end of September 1041 Břetislav I, under siege in Prague by Henry III, capitulated. At this time the whole of Bohemia and with Moravia were subjugated to Henry, not only that part of Bohemia which the German army passed through and plundered: *Quod ubi dux cognovit, insidias praeoccupavit, legatos ex animo supplices mittit, omnium familiarium purpuratorum auxilium ac opem implorat, ut liceret sese cum omni regno suisque dedere et gratiam caesaris, veluti ipsi suisque placeret, quaerere.* Břetislav committed to come after Henry to Regensburg *et omnis subiectionis humilitate caesari subditurum. Ann. Altah. maior.* ad a. 1041, rec. Oefele, p. 27. See note 23.

53   Henry III came to Prague with his army in September of 1041 and in September 1042 stopped the march of his military by the Hron and in July 1044 entered into Székesfehérvár. Bohemia and the whole Bohemian state, however, did not end in Prague; the Hron was not the eastern border of Nitria and Hungary did not reach only up to Székesfehérvár. Bohemian Prince Břetislav subjugated to the German king *along with his entire country* (*cum omni regno suisque*). See note 52. Peter Orseolo, installed by Henry, was recognized

9 Vazul's Sons in Poland, with the Pechenegs and in Russia

Béla distinguished himself in Poland in a battle with the Pomeranians. In battle with a selected Pomeranian he showed himself to be an experienced, very capable and strong fighter: *And when they fought armed with spears, Béla from his horse struck a Pomeranian with such virility (viriliter) that he could not move from his place, and he killed him with a sword.* After this victory, Polish Prince Casimir heaped great favour on Béla and gave him his sister as his wife.[54] Two sons were born to Béla in Poland (in the years 1044–1048): Géza and Ladislas.[55] If the Annales Altahenses mention three sons of Vazul at the time of their escape from Hungary in the autumn of 1031 as *parvulos*, then the youngest of them, Béla, was then still a child. If 12 or 13 years after he was already an experienced soldier, in full force and at a good age for marrying, then he could have been born around the year 1020, or a bit earlier, and upon arrival to Poland was approximately 25 years old. Andrew, with respect to the age of his younger brother and the time of his first wedding (between autumn 1041 and summer 1042) and with respect to the fact that in 1031 he still belonged among the *parvulos*, could have been born around approximately 1015, or a bit later. He was approximately 25 years old at the time of his first marriage.

Béla gained a similar position with Casimir that Břetislav gave to his cousin Domoslav in his own political plans in 1042. Thus, Béla's brothers ended up in Poland in the same situation that all three had got in before in Bohemia and for which they departed from Bohemia: *Andrew and Levente didn't like the fact that because of Béla they would end up as appendages with the Polish prince (quasi appendices degerent) and refused to remain in the prince's court only thanks to his name.*[56] Levente and Andrew thus set off together (perhaps in 1043) to the Pechenegs, where they had relatives on their mother's side. They

---

as the king of Hungary. See note 51. Likewise, all of Nitria and not only the small territory in the south-west of Slovakia accepted Domoslav as its prince, as is assumed by Szabolcs de Vajay and György Györffy. See note 45.

54   *Chron. Hung. comp. saec. XIV.* II 79, SRH *I*, pp. 334–335. *Simonis de Keza Gesta Hungarorum* II 52, SRH *I*, p. 177. The Pomeranians were allies of the Mazovians in the fight against Casimir. *Galli Chronicon* I 21, MPH *I*, ed. Bielowski, pp. 418–419. In 1046 Pomeranian Prince Siemomysl and Polish Casimir concluded peace in Merseburg, in the presence of German King Henry III and Bohemian Prince Břetislav. *Ann. Altah. maior.* ad a. 1046, rec. Oefele, p. 41.

55   *Bela vero dux ipse in Polonia duos genuit filios, quorum unus Geysa, alter autem Ladizlaus nomine avi sui est vocatus. Chron. Hung. comp. saec. XIV.* II 80, SRH *I*, p. 335.

56   *Chron. Hung. comp. saec. XIV.* II 80, SRH *I*, p. 336. *Simonis de Keza Gesta Hungarorum* II 52, SRH *I*, p. 177.

travelled by road through Volodymyr-Volynsky, lying on the western edge of Kiev Rus. Volodymyr-Volynsky was not yet then a princely seat;[57] therefore, no Volodymyr prince yet lived who would refuse to take in Andrew and Levente, as Hungarian chroniclers wrote.[58] Vazul's two sons did not take refuge in this castle or even stay there for very long. They hurried to the Pechenegs, where the help and protection of their relatives awaited them. Ultimately, however, they decided for the most powerful monarch in all of Eastern Europe – Kiev Prince Yaroslav the Wise. They left the Pechenegs and headed for Kiev, where they further awaited their opportunity.[59]

10   The Pagan Rebellion and the Return of the Árpáds to Hungary

Less than a year after the victory over Samuel Aba, Henry III again visited Székesfehérvár. On 26 May 1045 he received there a feudal oath from King

---

[57] The first Volyn appanaged prince was Igor (1054–1057), the youngest son of Kiev Prince Yaroslav the Wise. *Latopis Nestora* 59, year 6563 (1055), MPH I, ed. Bielowski, p. 711.

[58] *Endre et Leuente ... iverunt* (= venerunt) *ad regem Lodomerie, qui ipsos non recepit.* Chron. Hung. comp. saec. XIV. II 80, SRH I, p. 336. *Andreas et Luenta aegre forentes ... in Rutheniam transierunt. Et dum ibi a duce Lodomeriae propter Petrum regem suscepti non fuissent.* Simonis de Keza Gesta Hungarorum II 52, SRH I, p. 177. Gerics, *Legkorábi Gesta-szerkésztéseink*, pp. 22–28. Castle Volodymyr belonged to the realm of Yaroslav the Wise; therefore, Yaroslav had to himself decide on their non-acceptance. If Yaroslav the Wise only a bit later received Levente and Andrew in Kiev and in 1046 supported them against Peter Orseolo, then he could not have been agreed with Peter against him. He thus could not only about a year before then have decided on the non-acceptance of Vazul's sons at Volodymyr *because of King Peter (propter Petrum regem)*. If Levente and Andrew had wanted to remain in Russia, then they would have gone directly to Yaroslav the Wise in Kiev, as they did later. Thus, they only passed through Volhyn at the time in order to get as soon as possible to their Pecheneg relatives. About 80 years later, in 1123, Hungarian King Stephen II invaded Volodymyr and unsuccessfully sieged Volodymyr Castle. Chron. Hung. comp. saec. XIV. II 155, SRH I, pp. 437–439. Font, *Magyarok a Kijevi Évkönyvben*, pp. 50–53. A contemporary of Stephen II, the first continuer of the Gesta Ungarorum vetera, who read in their original text that Andrew and Levente passed on the road from Poland to the Pechenegs through Volodymyr, under the impression of this failed campaign supplemented the original chronicle text with a note that the Volodymyr prince did not want to accept both Árpád brothers, so that their antagonism was preserved. Another continuer also worked on and modified the Gesta Ungarorum vetera, which at the time of the rule of Stephen's successor Géza II changed Andrew, Béla and Levente's father in order to remove the argument suitable for excusing the doubtful origin of Boris, an unsuccessful aspirant to the Hungarian throne. See chapter 14, note 198.

[59] Chron. Hung. comp. saec. XIV. II 80, SRH I, p. 336. Simonis de Keza Gesta Hungarorum II 52, SRH I, p. 177.

Peter as a reward for the desired Hungarian throne.[60] In the following year Peter learned of a conspiracy being prepared by the magnates Viska (*Visca*), Bolya (*Bua*) and Bonyha (*Buhna*). Bolya and Bonyha were the sons of former Transylvanian Prince Gyula II, deposed in 1003 by King Stephen.[61] They were preparing the return of Vazul's sons to Hungary, and they paid for their boldness with their lives.[62] The response to Peter's cruel reprisal was another conspiracy of Hungarian magnates, who under the leadership of Csanád Bishop Gerard assembled in Csanád and on behalf of Hungary sent emissaries to Russia, in order to call Vazul's sons Levente and Andrew to return.[63]

Simultaneously with the conspiracy of the magnates, a large pagan rebellion broke out in the Tisza River region focused not only against King Peter but also against the church and foreigners. At the head of the rebellion was Vata (*Vatha*), who according to pagan custom wore three pigtails on his otherwise shaved head. The rebels, following their leader, joyfully threw off the Christianity forced on them. They still well remembered the faith of their forefathers, and many of them had not yet given it up.[64]

The influence of the heretical Bogomils also grew. Csanád Bishop Gerard had already openly reproached King Aba for tolerating paganism and heresy.[65] His diocese bordered directly with Bulgarian territory, from where the Bogomil preachers arrived. The basis of their teaching was the old Manichean and Gnostic ideas on the dualistic division of the world between good and evil, light and darkness, the soul and substance and God and the devil. The Bogomils believed that the devil had created the whole visible world. They rejected the Church, its hierarchy, rites and sacraments as well as the state and its institutions as the work of the devil.[66]

In September 1046 Levente and Andrew entered Hungary and headed down the Hornád. The rebelling pagans went against them. They penetrated into Nitria, to which the entire valley of the Hornád belonged, and they met with

60   *Ann. Altah. maior.* ad a. 1045, rec. Oefele, p. 40. *Chron. Hung. comp. saec. XIV.* II 78, SRH I, p. 334.
61   *Anonymi (P. magistri) Gesta Hungarorum* 27, SRH I, p. 69. See chapter 15, notes 13, 15.
62   *Chron. Hung. comp. saec. XIV.* II 81, SRH I, pp. 336–337.
63   *Ann. Altah. maior.* ad a. 1046, rec. Oefele, pp. 42–43. *Chron. Hung. comp. saec. XIV.* II 81, SRH I, p. 337. *Simonis de Keza Gesta Hungarorum* II 53, SRH I, pp. 177–178.
64   *Ann. Altah. maior.* ad a. 1046, rec. Oefele, p. 43. *Chron. Hung. comp. saec. XIV.* II 82, pp. 337–338. *Simonis de Keza Gesta Hungarorum* II 53, SRH I, p. 177. *Legenda S. Gerhardi episcopi* 15, SRH II, p. 501.
65   *Legenda S. Gerhardi episcopi* 14, SRH II, p. 500.
66   Steven Runciman, *Średniowieczny manicheizm* (Gdańsk 1996), pp. 66–94. Mircea Eliade, *Dejiny náboženských predstáv a ideí III* (Bratislava 1997), pp. 154–156.

the rebels near Abaújvár.[67] Abaújvár lay approximately halfway between the northern borders of Hungary, from beyond which both Árpád brothers arrived, and the northern edge of the rebel territory, from where the pagan brigades entered into the valley of the lower Hornád in order to go meet them. If Vata's pagans had also seized Nitria, then Vazul's sons would have already met them in the vicinity of the northern borders and not so deeply into the interior, halfway between its northern and southern borders. Nitria thus lay to the side of the pagan rebellion.

The pagan rebellion did not sweep through all of Hungary. The rebels took over the Tisza River region, including territory of the Csanád and Bihar diocese and Szolnok County. Csanád Bishop Gerard, Bihar Bishop Budli (Buldi, Budlu) and the first Szolnok Count Szolnok had to flee from the pagans. The leader of the Tisza River region pagans, Vata, was based in the centre of the rebellious territory, at Békes Castle (*Selus*).[68]

Near Abaújvár the rebels submitted their program to both Árpáds. They wanted to live according to pagan customs, to rid themselves of bishops and priests, to abolish the church and to return to the faith of their fathers. They were joined with both Árpáds by Levente's paganism, their distrust of foreigners and the battle against King Peter.[69]

At the time when Levente and Andrew passed through the Tisza River region and moved very quickly toward Pest, King Peter Orseolo blithely set off from the well-fortified Székesfehérvár and went to the northern side of the Danube to Nitria.[70] If he wanted to find help there against the Árpáds, then he certainly fared badly. Nitria did not join the pagan rebellion, but it did not want Peter Orseolo either, and after four years it again accepted the oldest living Árpád, Domoslav, as prince.[71]

Transdanubia also remained a Christian land. Therefore, bishops Gerard, Bystrík, Budli and Beneta and Count Szolnok, who fled the pagans, also took refuge *with many Christians* directly in Székesfehérvár. However, even

---

67 *Endre vero et Leuente ... Cum autem venissent ad Novum Castrum, quod rex Aba construxerat, ecce universa multitudo Hungarorum catervatim confluxit ad ipsos.* Chron. Hung. comp. saec. XIV. II 82, SRH I, p. 337.
68 See chapter 15, note 52.
69 The rebelling pagans *killed priests as well as laymen, who served the Catholic faith and demolished many churches. Then they turned against King Peter and killed all the Germans and Italians, primarily those who took the most various offices in Hungary.* Chron. Hung. comp. saec. XIV. II 82, SRH I, p. 338.
70 If Peter *crossed the Danube near Žitvatorok*, in order to get from there to Székesfehérvár, then he arrived from the north bank of the Danube. See note 72. Peter Orseolo was thus for brief time before then in Nitria.
71 See p. 439.

Hungarian Christians revolted against King Peter and the foreigners. Except that Peter came to Nitria and heard that Levente and Andrew were already in Pest and wanting to cross the Danube with the pagan rebels. He was aware of the danger to his royal seat. And so he *crossed the Danube near Žitvatorok* (*transivit Danubium in Sytiaten*) and hurried back to Székesfehérvár. The inhabitants, however, occupied the ramparts and towers, closed the gates and refused to let him enter.[72]

Bishops Gerard, Bystrík, Budli and Beneta and Count Szolnok wanted to welcome the two Árpáds with honour. They went safely from Székesfehérvár to the Danube. Upon crossing the river on 24 September 1046 between Buda and Pest, however, they fell into the hands of the pagans. Andrew at the last instance managed to save the life of only one of them, Bishop Beneta.

Vata's rebels, with whom Levente and Andrew also came, crossed the Danube at Pest and penetrated (just as they had earlier penetrated into Nitria in Abaújvár) into Transdanubia to Székesfehérvár, which opened its gates to them. Peter wanted to escape to Moson and from there to the Eastern March. The rebels, however, occupied all the escape routes and surrounded Peter in a courtyard in the village of Zámoly (*Zamur*) near Székesfehérvár. When the whole of Peter's retinue fell after three days in battle, the besiegers, despite Andrew's guarantee of Peter's safety, blinded him. The mutilated Peter died soon after.[73] In October 1046 the Árpáds had the entire kingdom under their power.

11 The End of the Triumvirate and the Ban on Pagan Rites

The Hungarian pagans who took over the Tisza River region certainly most favoured Levente, who remained a pagan to his death. As a pagan he couldn't take part in a Christian rite and accept a royal crown from the hands of a

---

72   *Chron. Hung. comp. saec. XIV.* II 82, SRH I, p. 339.

73   See chapter 15, note 52. Richard Marsina included a large polemic on whether Bishop Bystrík (*Beztricus*) was or was not the Nitra bishop. He came to the uncertain, but acceptable conclusion that Bystrík could have been the provost of the Nitra Chapter with an archdeacon's authority and at the same time could have had a bishop's ordination. Nitra then was not the seat of a bishopric and diocese, and Bystrík could not have been a bishop, only *ad personam*. Richard Marsina, "Vývoj cirkevnej organizácie na Slovensku do začiatku 12. storočia," in *XXVII. mikulovské sympozium 2002* (Brno 2003), pp. 94–95. Richard Marsina, "Obnovenie Nitrianskeho biskupstva na prelome 11. a 12. storočia," in *Kresťanstvo v dejinách Slovenska*, editor Mária Kohútová (Bratislava 2003), pp. 22–24.

bishop. He preferred to give up royal power on behalf of younger Andrew[74] and be satisfied with perhaps the Biharian Principality, where paganism was centred. Andrew, who was a *Catholicus*,[75] had the greatest support mainly in Transdanubia. Domoslav, who returned from neighbouring Bohemia, became the Prince of Nitria.[76] For a brief time three princes ruled in Hungary.[77]

At the beginning of 1047,[78] still during the life of his older brother, Andrew had himself crowned as Hungarian king in Székesfehérvár by the three bishops who survived the pagan rebellion.[79] *In a few days*, that is shortly after the coronation, Andrew's pagan brother died: *Levente thus in a few days died, if he had lived further and gotten power in the country, then Hungary would undoubtedly have fallen victim of pagan idolatry. And because Levente himself did not live a Catholic life, he was buried near the village Taksony (Toxun), on that side of the Danube, where, as is said (dicitur), his grandfather Taksony was buried according to pagan custom.*[80] Levente's death ended the brief three-part rule in Hungary.

Transdanubia and Nitria did not turn to paganism, although the Tisza River region pagans, accompanying Vazul's sons, penetrated their territory for a brief period. Thanks to Christian predominance, which Hungary could thank Nitria and Transdanubia for, Andrew, who since the end of September 1046 had been based in Székesfehérvár, freed himself from the beginning of dependence on pagans and could punish Peter's persecutors, guilty of his blinding and

---

74 In 1059 King Andrew met with his brother Béla in Várkony and offered him the royal crown. Béla, however, did not accept the offer out of fear and was satisfied with his own principality. Béla gave up the offered crown on behalf of Andrew's young son Solomon, just as Levente once gave up (*sicut sibi Leuente dederat*) on behalf of Andrew. *Chron. Hung. comp. saec. XIV.* II 92, SRH I, p. 355. After the victory of Peter Orseolo, Levente abandoned his right to the royal crown and left it to Andrew. If Levente had the primary claim to taking power in Hungary, then he was older than Andrew. Hóman, *Geschichte I*, p. 258. Sándor Tóth, "Levente és András," *Acta Universitatis Szegediensis de Attila József nominatae. Acta historica* 82 (Szeged 1985), pp. 33–34.
75 *Iste quidem rex Albus Andreas et Catholicus est vocatus. Chron. Hung. comp. saec. XIV.* II 88, SRH I, p. 344.
76 See notes 16, 86, 87.
77 Andrew up until his royal coronation and Levente until his death were, according to Hungarian chroniclers, *dux*. If Domoslav was the Nitrian Prince and Andrew the Hungarian Prince, then Levente could have been the Biharian Prince.
78 *Ann. Altah. maior.* ad a. 1046, rec. Oefele, p. 43. *Annales Posonienses* ad a. 1047, SRH I, p. 125. *Chron. Hung. comp. saec. XIV.* II 86, SRH I, pp. 343–344. *Simonis de Keza Gesta Hungarorum* II 57, SRH I, p. 178.
79 *Ann. Altah. maior.* ad a. 1046, rec. Oefele, p. 43. *Annales Posonienses* ad a. 1047, SRH I, p. 125. *Chron. Hung. comp. saec. XIV.* II 86, SRH I, pp. 343–344. *Simonis de Keza Gesta Hungarorum* II 57, SRH I, p. 178.
80 *Chron. Hung. comp. saec. XIV.* II 86, SRH I, p. 344.

subsequent death.[81] King Andrew, immediately after Levente's death, forbade pagan rituals, which he had to tolerate during the life of his pagan brother: *And so he ordered his entire nation under punishment by beheading to leave off pagan rite, which was permitted up to this time, to turn to the true faith in Christ and to live in everything according that law, which was given to them by St. King Stephen.*[82] Andrew I betrayed his own pagan followers, and thus ended the first great crisis of the Hungarian state.

In the middle of May 1047 German King Henry III returned from Italy to Germany. He stayed for several days in Augsburg and celebrated the Pentecost, which fell on 6 June, in Speyer, where he summoned the realm's dukes. He began to prepare a military campaign against Hungary in order to revenge Peter Orseolo. Henry's plans were thwarted by the rebellion of deposed Gottfried III (called the Bearded), who was the duke of Upper Lotharingia, and Count Baldwin V of Flanders, to whom also Dietrich IV, a margrave from Holland joined in. Then an emissary from King Andrew came to Speyer. Andrew notified Henry that he had accepted rule in Hungary only on the request of his subordinates; he apologized for the injuries suffered by Peter Orseolo, and he was willing to hand over to the emperor the guilty parties, whom he had not yet punished by death. In the end he offered the emperor a feudal oath (*suamque imperatori subiectionem*); he consented with payment of annual tribute and with the case of military aid, if Henry recognized him as Hungarian king. Andrew was willing in regard to these far-reaching concessions; therefore, Henry put off the campaign to Hungary. And since Duke Gottfried appeared through emissaries to be conciliatory, Henry in the autumn loaded the gathered army and sent it against Holland.[83] The danger of war with the emperor passed, and Andrew could forget about his promises.

Andrew's proposals in Speyer were similar to the concessions of Peter Orseolo to the German king in years 1044–1045.[84] If Andrew could send an emissary with such proposals to Speyer, then he no longer had to consider the opinions of his older brother or even the Hungarian pagans. In summer of 1047, when Andrew promised the emperor feudal dependence, his older brother was thus already dead and the ban on pagan rites was already in force in all of Hungary. Andrew thus stood up to his recent pagan allies before sending the

---

81 Andrew I wrote in the following year to Emperor Henry III regarding punishment of those guilty for Peter's blinding and death. See note 84.
82 *Chron. Hung. comp. saec. XIV.* II 86, SRH I, p. 344. *Legenda S. Gerhardi episcopi* 15, SRH II, p. 503.
83 *Herimanni Aug. Chronicon* ad a. 1047, cur. Buchner. pp. 684–687.
84 *Ann. Altah. maior.* ad a. 1044, 1045, rec. Oefele, pp. 34–35, 40. *Chron. Hung. comp. saec. XIV.* II 75–76, 78, SRH I, pp. 329–330, 334.

emissary to the emperor. Andrew's coronation, Levente's death and the ban on pagan rites, which Hungarian chroniclers date to year 1047, had to have played out from January to May 1047.

Andrew's cousin Domoslav was a good Christian,[85] and he undoubtedly supported the ban on pagan rites. Domoslav was then the oldest living Árpád; he thus had a claim which King Andrew had to recognize. We don't know whether he also shared in Peter's fall or if he returned to Hungary after Levente and Andrew's victory. He did not become king, however, because the younger Andrew fought for the highest power in September and October 1046. He was thus satisfied only with the Nitrian Principality, which he had once (four years before) ruled very briefly. Nitrian Prince Domoslav (*Damaslaus dux*, 1046–1048) endowed an abbey in Pécsvárad, in which he was buried. Géza II confirmed Domoslav's donation, which is the only proof of his princely title, in 1158.[86] Domoslav had to have died in 1048, because then King Andrew handed over the princely seat, certainly vacated, to his younger brother Béla.[87]

---

85 If Domoslav endowed the abbey and was buried there, then he was undoubtedly a convinced Christian. See note 86.
86 *DHA I*, ed. Györffy, no. 12, pp. 77–78, no. 76, p. 222.
87 *Chron. Hung. comp. saec. XIV.* II 88, *SRH I*, pp. 344–345. Vajay, "Großfürst Geysa," pp. 65–66, 70, 100.

CHAPTER 17

Kings against Princes, Princes against Kings (1048–1077)

1   Prince Béla

After the birth of daughter Adelaide,[1] Andrew could no longer have children with his first wife. He thus lost hope of having his own son and heir to the throne. After Levente's death and after the ban on pagan rituals, he summoned Béla from Poland: *Then when this King Andrew lost his brother, he sent to Poland for his second brother Béla and filled with love summoned him, so that he could say: 'Dear brother, we were together in sorrow and pain. Now I ask of you: Come to me as soon as possible so that we are again together in friendship and enjoy the fruits of the country together. Because I do not have a single heir, no brother aside from you, you will be my heir and successor in ruling.' Béla, affected by these words, came with his whole family to the king.*[2]

Béla as the future successor to the Hungarian throne got, according to the old and verified custom, a princely appanage: *Then the king and his brother Béla consulted and divided the country into three parts, two of which remained the property of the king and the third of which passed into ownership of the prince.*[3] Sixteen years later Béla's oldest son Géza, who in years 1063–1064 threatened King Solomon, got his *ducatus*. If Bishop Desiderius, who wanted to make peace between the two antagonists, advised Géza to leave to Solomon the kingdom and *be satisfied with the principality that his father first had,*[4] then Béla's princely appanage was identical with the later princely appanage

---

1   See pp. 421–422.
2   *Chron. Hung. comp. saec. XIV.* II 88, SRH I, pp. 344–345.
3   *Post hec autem rex et frater eius Bela habito consilio diviserunt regnum in tres partes, quarum due in proprietate regie potestatis manserunt, tertia vero pars in proprietatem ducis est collata.* *Chron. Hung. comp. saec. XIV.* II 88, SRH I, p. 345. The words *prima regni huius divisio* are a later addition to the original chronicler's text. Gerics, *Legkorábbi gesta-szerkésztéseink*, p. 83. These words do not mean that Andrew and Béla were the founders of the Nitria and Biharian principalities, that Nitria and Biharia originated only in 1048. They only wanted to say that the mutual wars of the king and princes, which divided Hungary into two enemy parts battling against one another, began only under the rule of Andrew and Prince Béla. Nitria and Biharia had their princes even before then, but the oldest Hungarian chronicler, who wrote at the end of the 11th century, didn't know them.
4   See note 56.

belonging to his son Géza.[5] Géza abdicated a portion of his princely third to his younger brother Ladislas.[6] If in the battle near Mogyoród (in March 1074) Géza led the Nitrian and his younger brother Ladislas the Biharian armies,[7] then Géza had Nitria and Ladislas had Biharia. Béla's princely appanage, identical with the appanages of his sons, thus had two principalities. The first principality was Nitria, where earlier his cousin Domoslav, his father Vazul,[8] his cousin Emeric,[9] his uncle Ladislas,[10] his second-degree uncle Stephen and grandfather Michael all ruled.[11] The second was the neighbouring Biharian principality, where Emeric, the already mentioned cousin of Béla,[12] and his great-uncle Géza ruled.[13]

If Nitria with its 9 castle counties[14] and Biharia with 4 castle counties[15] together made up the princely third, then the royal two-thirds of Hungary evidently had 26 castle counties, whose number grew to 30 in 1074.[16] Since Nitria also belonged to Béla's princely appanage, the preceding Prince of Nitra, Domoslav, was certainly no longer alive then. Andrew's words upon inviting his brother Béla to Hungary also confirm this: *I do not have a single heir, no brother aside from you.*[17] Domoslav thus died still before Andrew summoned Béla from Poland.

Andrew's first wife, who bore his daughter Adelaide and for some unknown reason could not have any more children, had to still be alive when Andrew, without hope for a legitimate son and heir to the throne, appointed his brother Béla as his successor. Andrew later concluded a second marriage with Anastasia, daughter of Kiev Prince Yaroslav the Wise.[18] In 1053, when Andrew's son Solomon was born,[19] he must have already been married to Anastasia. Therefore, we can consider year 1049, which is mentioned by later

---

5   Kristó, *A XI. századi hercegség története*, pp. 60–64.
6   See notes 70, 71, 73, 80, 81.
7   See note 81.
8   See pp. 396–401, 425–429, 432, 435–439.
9   See 402.
10 See pp. 380, 383, 384, 396–397.
11 See pp. 326–327, 331–333, 338–341.
12 See pp. 393–394.
13 See pp. 326–327.
14 See pp. 425, 428.
15 See pp. 303–304.
16 See note 76.
17 See note 89.
18 *Duxit autem sibi uxorem filiam ducis Ruthenorum, de qua genuit Salomonem et David.* Chron. Hung. comp. saec. XIV. 11 88, SRH I, p. 345. Wertner, *Az Árpádok családi története*, pg. 117–123. Jasiński, "Filiacja Adelajdy," pp. 3–11.
19 See note 28.

Polish chronicler Jan Dlugosz, as the most probable time of the wedding.[20] Andrew was a widower certainly for only a very short time. Getting married again was politically astute, especially if such a bride as Anastasia was in the offing. Andrew most probably became a widower in the same year he remarried, that is 1049, or at the end of the previous year. If Andrew had known that he would marry a second time and thus gain hope for a legitimate son and heir, then he would not have promised succession to Béla. Béla thus returned to Hungary only after Levente's death (in the 1st half of 1047) and still during the life of Andrew's first wife (who died at the latest and most probably in 1049), that is between 1047–1049, most likely in 1048. Nitrian Prince Domoslav must have died then, because his principality, now certainly vacated, went to his younger cousin Béla.

Nitra Castle got a new rampart in the time of Prince Béla. The massive earthen-wooden rampart of chamber construction, as many as 21 metres wide at the base (rampart III), which was built in the mid-11th century, encircled the entire castle hill, just as the extinct Great Moravian rampart had.[21]

Béla got his princely third *into property* (*in proprietas*) and was thus the sovereign owner of his land. Not only does the mentioned chronicler's report testify to this, but also the princely half-denar with the legend +BELA DVX on

---

20   *Accepit autem prefatus Andreas rex principis Russiae filiam nomine Anastasiam, ex qua nati sunt ei duo filii, videlicet Salomon et David. Joannis Dlugosii Annales seu cronicae incliti Regni Poloniae II*, ad a. 1049 (Warszawa 1969), p. 61.

21   In the remains of the old Great Moravian ramparts (rampart I), in the southernmost, most accessible edge of the Nitra castle hill, an unfinished rampart (rampart II) grew in the 1030s or early 1040s, resembling the Great Moravian one. In the mid-11th century it was covered by a massive and wide rampart (rampart III), which encircled the entire castle hill and differed from the two previous ones. Moson, Sopron, Győr, Borsod, Abaújvár, Zemplín, Szabolcs, Doboka and Cluj-Napoca all got similar fortifications. Kiev and other castles of Kiev Rus also had a wide chamber rampart fortified in the 1030s by Prince Yaroslav the Wise. These could have been the model for the builders of the Hungarian castles. The massive Nitra rampart (rampart III) was burned, and at the end of the 11th or beginning of the 12th century it was replaced by a stone walled rampart, completed with crenellations, 200 to 330 cm wide, with support pillars on the interior side. This Roman-style rampart, which protected the castle up to the 15th century, had a stone gate on the southwestern base (at the site of today's county house). Peter Bednár, "Die Entwicklung der Befestigung der Nitraer Burg im 9.–12. Jahrhundert," in *Frühmittelalterlicher Burgenbau in Mittel- und Osteuropa*, ed. Joachim Henning, Alexander Ruttkay (Bonn 1998), p. 380. Bednár, *Nitriansky hrad v 9.–13. storočí. Autoreferát dizertácie*, pp. 13–18. *Dejiny Nitry*, ed. Fusek, Zemene, pp. 134–137. Peter Bednár, Marián Samuel, "Entwicklung der Befestigung der Nitraer Burg im 11. Jahrhundert," *Slovenská archeológia* 49 (2001), no. 2, pp. 301–342. Peter Bednár, Marián Samuel, "Nitriansky hrad na prelome tisícročí," in *Slovensko vo včasnom stredoveku*, ed. Ruttkay, Ruttkay, Šalkovský (Nitra 2002), pp. 152–155. Bednár – Šimkovic, "Opevnenie Nitrianskeho hradu," pp. 140–150.

the front and +PANNONIA on the reverse side. Today we know 417 coins of Prince Béla, 34 of them found on Slovak territory. If we add to these 34 coins the single coin found in the village Piliny in the Hungarian Ipeľ River region and two from the village of Tiszalúc on the Takta stream (north of the confluence of the Tisza and the Sajó rivers), then we today have a total of 37 known coins of Prince Béla directly from the territory of the Nitrian Principality. Béla's princely coins did not achieve the quality of those of Stephen I, because they had 25% less silver in them. They were of higher quality than Andrew's however, which each year were exchanged for new ones with less silver content. Prince Béla did not reduce the share of silver in his coins.[22]

Andrew and Béla lived for several years in the best agreement and together defended the country against German attacks. Already at the beginning of 1050 Regensburg Bishop Gebhard invaded Hungary, despoiled the western border area and left with rich quarry. The Hungarian army immediately afterwards marauded the neighbouring territory of the Eastern March and burned down Hainburg Castle, which had been recently rebuilt by German King Henry III. The repeated Hungarian attacks in the summer and autumn of 1050 were supposed to prevent the renewal of Hainburg, which Henry commanded in July of that year.[23]

In September of 1051 Henry III invaded Hungary. His ally, Bohemian Prince Břetislav I, marched together with Carinthian Duke Welf through Béla's principality. German boats floated down the Danube loaded with food, led by Regensburg Bishop Gebhard. Henry's large army proceeded from Styria on the right-hand bank of the upper Rába, along the Zala and Lake Balaton in the direction of Székesfehérvár. Prince Béla came to help King Andrew. The brothers avoided open battle. They burned the land through which the emperor marched, chased off the livestock and resettled the inhabitants. The emperor's

---

[22] Jozef Hlinka – Štefan Kazimír – Eva Kolníková, *Peniaze v našich dejinách* (Bratislava 1976), pp. 140–141, 165–166, 170. Jozef Hlinka, "Nálezy mincí na Slovensku z 11. až začiatku 14. storočia a ich historicko-numizmatická analýza," *Slovenská numizmatika* 10 (1989), pp. 157, 160–161. Ján Hunka, "New Notions about the 11th–14th Centuries related to the Territory of Slovakia," *Actes du XIe Congres International de Numismatique organisé a l' occasion di 150e anniversaire de la Société Royale de Numismatique de Belgique Bruxelles, 8–13 septembre 1991*, Volume III (Louvain-la-Neuve 1993), pp. 196–198. Ján Hunka, "Mincovníctvo uhorských vojvodov v druhej polovici 11. storočia," *Slovenská numizmatika* 14 (1996), pp. 63–84. Ján Hunka, "Vojvodská mincovňa z 11. storočia v Nitre," in *Nitra v slovenských dejinách*, ed. Marsina, pp. 169–180. *Dejiny Nitry*, ed. Fusek – Zemene, pp. 124–125. Kovács, *A kora Árpád-kori magyar pénzverésről*, pp. 104–107, 111–112, 131–133, 199–200, 202, 205, 207, 209, 210, 212, 213–215, 223–224, 245–247, 279, 282, 289–290.
[23] *Herimanni Aug. Chronicon* ad a. 1050, cur. Buchner, pp. 690–693. *Ann. Altah. maior.* ad a. 1050, rec. Oefele, p. 46.

soldiers went hungry, and in rainy weather they were decimated by nighttime traps and assaults of the Hungarians and Pechenegs. In October they came all the way to the Vértes Hills. In the meantime Bishop Gebhard reached Győr and sent a letter to the emperor in which he asked where he should wait for him. Hungarian watches, however, captured the bishop's emissary. King Andrew had a forged letter written and sent, which ordered Gebhard to destroy the boats with stores and to rapidly return to Regensburg. After the retreat of the deceived bishop, Henry ended up in a hopeless situation. Andrew and Béla, however, after agreement on 25 October, allowed him a free return by the shortest route to Hainburg, and they even supplied him with a great deal of food.[24]

In July 1052 the emperor again crossed the Hungarian border, this time without Břetislav. At the end of July he began to siege Bratislava. He set up siege engines against the ramparts but the defenders of the castle, among whom Vojtech, Andrew, Vilungard, Uros and Martin stood out in their heroism, repelled all the attacks and had no intention at all of surrendering. Even Pope Leo IX came to Henry's military camp under Bratislava Castle in August in order to broker peace. In September, when the siege had lasted 8 weeks, one of the Bratislavans, an excellent swimmer named Zothmund, in the night drilled holes in all the emperor's boats anchored in the Danube and sunk them. Henry III had to pull back without success.[25] At the imperial diet in Trebur in 1053 emissaries of King Andrew made peace with the emperor.[26]

In 1054 Bohemian Prince Břetislav prepared an independent campaign to Hungary. In the unusual time of winter at the end of 1054, he ordered the army to assemble and await him at Chrudim Castle in eastern Bohemia. The campaign never took place, however. On 10 January 1055 Prince Břetislav succumbed to a serious illness, which suddenly affected him at Chrudim. Thus ended the last of Břetislav's efforts to exert his influence in Nitria.[27]

King Andrew and Prince Béla ruled and defended Hungary together. Military operations in Transdanubia in 1051, aimed against the approaching German

---

24 *Herimanni Aug. Chronicon* ad a. 1051, cur. Buchner, pp. 694–697. *Ann. Altah. maior.* ad a. 1051, rec. Oefele, p. 47. *Chron. Hung. comp. saec. XIV.* II 90, SRH I, pp. 347–351. *Simonis de Keza Gesta Hungarorum* II 57, SRH I, pp. 178–179. DHA I, ed. Györffy, no. 39, 40, 42, pp. 140, 141, 144.
25 *Herimanni Aug. Chronicon* ad a. 1052, cur. Buchner, pp. 698–701. *Ann. Altah. maior.* ad a. 1052, rec. Oefele, p. 48. *Chron. Hung. comp. saec. XIV.* II 89, SRH I, pp. 346–347.
26 *Herimanni Aug. Chronicon* ad a. 1053, cur. Buchner, pp. 704–707. *Ann. Altah. maior.* ad a. 1053, rec. Oefele, p. 49.
27 *Cosmae Pragensis Chronica Boemorum* II 13, ed. Bretholz, pp. 101–103. Krzemieńska, *Břetislav I.*, pp. 370–371.

army, were commanded by both brothers in tandem. The emperor, to prevent a complete defeat, *sent to King Andrew and Prince Béla, requesting to conclude peace.* Both brothers concluded peace with the emperor: *And so King Andrew and Prince Béla ... concluded peace with the emperor.*[28] A dated document, by which Andrew established and endowed the Abbey of St. Anian in Tihany, speaks of the common rule of both brothers: *In year ... 1055, happily ruling by the mentioned most victorious monarch* (= Andrew), *in the ninth year of his rule and with him the most noble Prince B* (= Béla).[29] And judge Sarchas (perhaps in 1056) wrote of the castellans and royal servants in Hungary *in the time of King Andrew and Prince Béla.*[30] Palatine Rado in a testament from 4 June 1057 left his property to the to the Pécs bishop, to the abbey in Pécsvárád and his wife Lucia *with the permission of the most blessed King Andrew and his brother Adalbert* (= Béla), *the most unconquerable prince.*[31]

Béla was Andrew's co-ruler for ten years (1048–1058). He advised him to co-decide about all the most important things and to lead the war together with him. He had already distinguished himself as a warrior during his Polish exile. And in the end even Hungary could rely on the military arts of the *most unconquerable prince (invictissimi ducis).*[32]

2 Dispute and War of Prince Béla with King Andrew

In 1053 Andrew's son Solomon was born to him and later a son David. Andrew's illegitimate son George could have been older. Andrew had him with a concubine, whom he evidently found during the time of infertility of his first wife.[33]

In September 1058 Andrew I met with the new German king, Henry IV (1056–1105, from 1084 Emperor) and with Margrave of the Eastern March,

---

28 *Chron. Hung. comp. saec. XIV.* II 90, SRH I, pp. 349–350. *Simonis de Keza Gesta Hungarorum* II 57, SRH I, pp. 178–179.
29 *Feliciter regnante prefato victoriosissimo principe anno regni sui VIIII et cum eo nobilissimo duce B.* DHA I, ed. Györffy, no. 43/1, p. 152.
30 *A tempore regis Andree et ducis Bele.* DHA I, ed. Györffy, no. 45, pp. 158–159.
31 *Licencia piissimi regis Andree eiusque fratris Adalberti invictissimi ducis.* DHA I, ed. Györffy, no. 46, p. 161.
32 See note 31.
33 *Duxit autem sibi uxorem filiam ducis Ruthenorum, de qua genuit Salomonem et David. De concubina autem, quam habuit de villa Moroth, genuit Georgium. Chron. Hung. comp. saec. XIV.* II 88, SRH I, p. 345. Andrew I, in the 12th year of his rule, had his 5-year old son Solomon crowned as king. *Chron. Hung. comp. saec. XIV.* II 91, SRH I, 352. If 1055 was the 9th year of King Andrew's rule (see note 29), then the 12th year of Andrew's reign was 1058. If Solomon was in 1058 a five-year-old child, then he was born in 1053.

Ernest (1055–1075) on the Austrian bank of the Morava River. They concluded peace and engaged Andrew's 5-year-old son Solomon to Henry's 11-year-old sister Judith.[34] Shortly after Andrew was affected by a stroke, so that from then on he had to be carried around. In that same year King Andrew broke the promise he made to his younger brother and had his young son Solomon crowned to ensure him the Hungarian throne. The coronation ceremony was held in Székesfehérvár. The song *Be the lord to your brothers* sounded out in the cathedral. Its words, taken from the Old Testament (Gen 27, 29), deeply offended Prince Béla, who was present. Solomon, a small child, became his lord.[35]

Disappointed and offended, Béla had no intention of giving up his claim to the throne. He relied on the fact that his brother was now old and ill, and Solomon would long still be a minor. Andrew knew that Solomon as a child would be unable to rule Hungary against the will of Prince Béla. In 1059 both brothers met in the village of Várkony near the Tisza (south of Szolnok). Still before Béla's arrival Andrew put the crown and a sword out on a purple carpet. When Béla entered, Andrew rose up from his bed and explained to his brother that Solomon's coronation was a condition of the wedding with Henry's sister Judith, and that the wedding should ensure peace and good relations with neighbouring Germany. In the end he gave him a choice: *You have free will, however. If you want the kingdom, take the crown; if the principality, take the sword. What remains goes to my son. The crown is however, according to right, certainly yours.* In the room with Andrew waited two hired assassins, who were to murder Béla if he took the crown. Prince Béla, however, had learned of the danger from Nicholas, one of the royal courtiers, and therefore he chose the sword.[36] Thus, he escaped a certain death and fled with his whole family to Poland, to his brother-in-law Boleslaw II the Bold (1058–1080, from 1076 king).[37] The dispute of the two brothers was to be decided by war.

In the autumn of 1060 Béla attacked Hungary with three units of the Polish army. Andrew immediately sent his family to Mödling Castle in Austria, the seat of Margrave Ernest. A large German army led by Naumburg-Zeitz Bishop

---

34 *Ann. Altah. maior.* ad a. 1058, rec. Oefele, pp. 54–55. *Chron. Hung. comp. saec. XIV.* II 91, SRH I, p. 351. *Simonis de Keza Gesta Hungarorum* II 57, SRH I, p. 179.

35 *Chron. Hung. comp. saec. XIV.* II 91, SRH I, pp. 351–353. *Simonis de Keza Gesta Hungarorum* II 58, SRH I, p. 180. *Annales Posonienses* ad a. 1055, 1057, SRH I, p. 125. The dating of Solomon's coronation by the Bratislava Annals to year 1057 is erroneous, just as the dating of many other events in these annals. Like the preceding death of Emperor Henry III, it has erroneously in 1055 instead of 1056, and the subsequent coronation of Solomon was not done in 1057 but a year later, in 1058.

36 *Chron. Hung. comp. saec. XIV.* II 92, SRH I, pp. 353–355.

37 *Chron. Hung. comp. saec. XIV.* II 93, SRH I, pp. 355–356.

Eppo, Meissen Margrave Wilhelm IV from Weimar-Orlamünde, Count Poto from Altenburg and Margrave of the Eastern March, Ernest, marched to his assistance.[38] Béla knew about the numerical superiority of Andrew's military, but he had no intention of avoiding battle. He moved rapidly to the Tisza, where a decisive battle took place. Just as fortune began to lean toward Béla's side, many of Andrew's soldier ran over to his side. Béla triumphed, and the seriously injured Andrew, together with Margrave Wilhelm and Count Poto were unable to flee to Germany. Béla soldiers caught them before the gates of the Moson Castle. Andrew died soon after at the royal court in Zirc in the Bakon Forest.[39] They buried him in the Abbey of St. Anian in Tihany on the shore of Lake Balaton, which he had founded five years earlier together with Béla. On 6 December 1060 Hungarian Bishops in Székesfehérvár crowned Béla as the new Hungarian king.[40]

3   King Béla I

Béla I (1060–1063) sent out emissaries in 1061 on all sides to announce in all of Hungary his royal will to call a great gathering of people. Two older and articulate representatives from each community were to come to Székesfehérvár to expand the royal council. The king wanted at the assembly to submit important decisions about taxes, payment of old debts, the prices of goods, the value of coins, market days and other reform measures, which should elevate the economy of a country disabled by war. However, not only did invited representatives come to Székesfehérvár, but also an unknown number of unhappy peasants, servants and communal people wanting back the old pagan times. The king, bishops and magnates feared their attack. They closed the ramparts of Székesfehérvár and kept watch on the rebels, who incited the assembled people and reproached the Christian faith. The rebels submitted their requests

---

38   Bohemian Prince Spytihněv II also wanted to support Andrew. Polish Prince Boleslaw II crossed the Bohemian border and attacked Hradec near Opava. He thus busied Spytihněv, who could not march together with the German army to Hungary to help King Andrew. *Galli Chronicon* I 22, MPH I, ed. Bielowski, p. 419. Václav Novotný, *České dějiny* I/2. *Od Břetislava I. do Přemysla I.* (Praha 1913), pp. 108–111.
39   Ann. Altah. maior. ad a. 1060, rec. Oefele, pp. 56–57. *Chron. Hung. comp. saec. XIV.* II 93, SRH I, pp. 356–357. *Simonis de Keza Gesta Hungarorum* II 58, SRH I, p. 180. Béla could hardly have launched into battle with three Polish divisions against Andrew's royal army, reinforced by a large German army. While Andrew assembled his soldiers and waited for help from Germany, Béla could assemble his princely military from Nitria and Biharia. Hóman, *Geschichte des ungarischen Mittelalters I*, p. 268.
40   *Chron. Hung. comp. saec. XIV.* II 94, SRH I, p. 358.

to the king: *Allow us to live by the pagan custom of our fathers, to stone the bishops, to tear the bowels of the priests, to strangle the clerics, to hang the collectors of the tithe, to demolish the churches, to break the bells.* The king set aside three days to think things over. In the meantime he secretly called in the army, which on the third day scattered the surprised rebels. They killed several of them and imprisoned or beat others.[41]

Paganism had a robust life in Hungary. Vata's son Janus (*Ianus*), who remained faithful to the paganism of his father, gathered around himself many conjurers, augurs and diviners and with their arts they gained the favour with their lords. Among them was the conjurer Rashdi, whom King Béla imprisoned and who died in prison.[42] Evidence on the great appeal and long survival of the old paganism is found in the royal order against witches, against pagan rites and against neglecting to honour Christian holidays and burials.[43]

King Béla had to have made the mentioned important decision even without a large gathering of people. He had quality silver coins minted, such that 40 Hungarian denars had the value of one Byzantine solidus. He set a fixed price for goods at the market and shifted market days from Sunday to Saturday. He lowered taxes, abolished some fees and recovered old debts.[44]

King Béla wanted to obtain as many allies and friends as possible at home and abroad. Therefore, he didn't touch the properties of Solomon's followers, who fled after him to Germany to prepare for Béla's downfall. Several of them in the end returned home and joined with the king. Béla didn't even punish those who had earlier fought against him on the side of King Andrew.[45] He released both captured German leaders, Wilhelm and Poto. He eventually engaged Margrave Wilhelm to his oldest daughter Sophia († 18. 6. 1095). Since Wilhelm died soon after, Sophia (in 1062) married with his close relative, Carniola and Istrian Margrave Ulric (1054–1070).[46]

In August 1063 German King Henry IV began to assemble a large military campaign aimed at installing his brother-in-law Solomon on the Hungarian

---

41 *Chron. Hung. comp. saec. XIV.* II 95, SRH I, pp. 359–360.
42 *Chron. Hung. comp. saec. XIV.* II 82, SRH I, p. 338. József Gerics, *Egyház, állam és gondolkodás Magyarországon a középkorban* (Budapest 1995), pp. 133–136.
43 *Sancti Stephani decretorum liber primus* XXXIII. *Sancti Ladislai regis decretorum liber primus* XXII, XXV. *Colomanni regis decretorum liber primus* LVII. *A szent István, szent László és Kálmán korabeli törvények és zsinati határozatok forrásai. Függelék: A törvények szövege,* ed. Levente Závodszky (Budapest 1904), pp. 151, 161, 162, 191. Györffy, *Wirtschaft und Gesellschaft,* Anhang, pp. 273, 283, 284, 313.
44 *Chron. Hung. comp. saec. XIV.* II 94, SRH I, p. 358. *Simonis de Keza Gesta Hungarorum* II 59, SRH I, p. 180.
45 *Chron. Hung. comp. saec. XIV.* II 94, SRH I, p. 359.
46 Wertner, *Az Árpádok családi története,* pp. 144–156.

throne. Béla wanted to avoid war, and through emissaries he proposed to Henry that he hand over the throne to Solomon and keep his former principality. He offered his oldest son Géza as a hostage. Since the proposal wasn't accepted, he commanded the western border to be barricaded, castles to be reinforced and the army assembled. He tarried at the court in Dömös, where he suffered serious injuries when the construction beneath the throne collapsed. Despite this fact, he marched out against the advancing German army. On the journey, however, he died as a result of the injuries. He was buried in the Benedictine Abbey in Szekszárd, which he had established himself two years before.[47]

4 Princes Géza and Ladislas

King Béla I died on 11 September 1063. Immediately after, German King Henry IV invaded Hungary with a large army and installed Andrew's son Solomon on the empty throne in Székesfehérvár.[48] Béla's three sons, Géza, Ladislas and Lampert, fled to Poland.[49] Géza requested help from his uncle, Polish Prince Boleslaw II the Bold.

Henry IV departed Hungary on 27 September 1063. Shortly after the departure of the German king, Boleslaw the Bold invaded Hungary:[50] *Then he set off for Hungary, wanting to renew the borders of the Polish kingdom to the*

---

47   *Bel autem, qui Salomonem de regno expulerat ... quemadmodum regem dominum suum, paratus esset suscipere eique servire, ea tamen lege, si se permitteret ducatum illum, quem habuerat sub eius patre. Et ut omnem tolleret nostratibus suspicionem, huius pacti filium suum obsidem promisit se transmissurum ad regem.* Ann. Altah. maior. ad a. 1063, rec. Oefele, pp. 62–63. Chron. Hung. comp. saec. XIV. II 96, SRH I, p. 360. *Simonis de Keza Gesta Hungarorum* II 59, SRH I, p. 180.

48   Ann. Altah. maior. ad a. 1063, rec. Oefele, pp. 63–64. Chron. Hung. comp. saec. XIV. II 97, SRH I, pp. 361–362.

49   Géza fled to Poland *cum duobus fratribus adolescentibus.* Chron. Hung. comp. saec. XIV. II 97, SRH I, p. 361. If Géza's brothers Ladislas and Lampert were in September 1063 still *youth* (*adolescentibus*), then the older Ladislas, who was born at the time of Béla's Polish exile, thus at the latest in 1048, could have been at least 15 and at most 18 years old and the younger Lampert, who was born only after Béla's return to Hungary, could have been very young, at the most 15 years old, or still even a child. *Bela vero dux ipse in Polonia duos genuit filios, quorum unus Geysa, alter autem Ladislas nomine avi sui est vocatus.* Chron. Hung. comp. saec. XIV. II 80, SRH I, p. 335. *Porro dux Bela in Polonia genuit liberos Geysam et Ladiziaum, in Hungaria autem genuit Lampertum et filias.* Chron. Hung. comp. saec. XIV. II 88, SRH I, p. 345. And Stephen *in adolescentia sua*; he was probably 18 years old when he defeated Koppány. Chron. Hung. comp. saec. XIV. II 64, SRH I, pg. 312–313. See chapter 14, note 85.

50   See note 52, 53.

rivers *Danube, Tisza and Morava*.[51] Solomon suffered a defeat and fled to the strongly fortified Moson Castle on the western border of the kingdom.[52] After Boleslaw's victory, he had no choice: *King Solomon, admitting defeat, not only left off battle, but he also surrendered to him the part of his kingdom lying between the mentioned rivers, considering himself fortunate that he can remain in the second part beyond the Danube.*[53]

The Wielkopolska (Great Polish) Chronicle mentions two parts of Hungary, divided by the Danube. The first part of Hungary defined by the Danube, Tisza and Moravia, that is the Nitrian Principality, which Solomon had to surrender,[54] the Polish prince did not retain it for himself. He handed it over to his ally and nephew Géza.

Solomon feared Prince Géza and the strong Polish army. Therefore, he remained closed inside Moson Castle, close to German border, from beyond which he could expect aid.[55] Peace was brokered by Bishop Desiderius, who urged Géza to acknowledge Solomon as king and be satisfied with the princely third that once belonged to his father Béla.[56] Prince Géza took the bishop at his word, and on 20 January 1064 in Győr he made peace with Solomon. Solomon remained king and Géza as prince.[57] Prince Géza kept only Nitria under his

---

51 See note 53.
52 *Rex autem Salomon, tamquam novus et necdum in regno roboratus, timens ne forte Geysa cum exercitu Polonico super eum irrueret, paulisper retrocessit cum suis et in castro Musun munitissimo tuta statione resedit.* Chron. Hung. comp. saec. XIV. II 97, SRH I, p. 362.
53 *Post hoc Hungariam adiit, volens metas regni Poloniae in Danubio, Czyssawa et Morawa fluviis habere. Cui Salamon rex Hungarorum cum suo exercitu in montanis Russiae et Hungariae, ad suum regnum volens prohibere ingressum, occurit. Sed plurimis de suo exercitu in eisdem concludendo. Et cernens sibi et suae genti imminere periculum pacem praecatur, centum milia auri talenta off erens Boleslao, ut ab impugnatione sui desistat. Cui rex Boleslaus respondit: 'Polonos, inquit, non aurum habere, sed aurum habentibus imperare delectat; turpius enim, ait vinci pretio, quam proelio.' Victum itaque rex Salamon se cognoscens, tam bello quam parte sui regni, inter fluvios praedictos consistente, cessit; felicem se reputans, in alia parte regni, ultra Danubium, posse manere.* Boguphali II episcopi Posnaniensis Chronicon Poloniae, cum continuatione Basconis custodis Posnaniensis 13, MPH II, ed. Bielowski, pp. 486–487.
54 The Danube, Tisza and Morava had formed the southern border of Nitria since 1001, when it was ruled by Polish Prince Boleslaw the Brave. Thus, the territorial range of the Nitrian Principality did not change at all over a long period. It was stable in the borders we know from the Hungarian-Polish chronicle.
55 Chron. Hung. comp. saec. XIV. II 97, SRH I, p. 362.
56 *Maxime autem Desiderius episcopus delinitivis … animam Geyse ducis, ut Salomoni quamvis iuniori regnum cum pace redderet et ipse ducatum, quem pater eius prius habuerat pacifice teneret.* Chron. Hung. comp. saec. XIV. II 97, SRH I, p. 362.
57 Chron. Hung. comp. saec. XIV. II 97, SRH I, pp. 362–363. Kristó, *A XI. századi hercegség története*, pp. 62–63.

direct rule and installed his younger brother Ladislas in Biharia.[58] The youngest of the brothers, Lambert, probably still a minor, remained at Géza's princely court.[59]

Géza, who settled in Nitra, honoured the memory of the Zobor anchorites Svorad and Benedict. In April 1064 Géza visited Pécs, where he celebrated Easter together with Solomon.[60] On this occasion he visited Pécs bishop Maurus and asked him for half of the chain which the anchorite Svorad reportedly had ingrown to his body as an expression of penance and private self-torment. Maurus had acquired this chain from Zobor Abbot Philippe immediately after Svorad's death: *I got half of this chain from the abbot and I have cherished it until today. However, I couldn't deny the request of the most Christian Prince Géza (ducis christianissimi Gayse), who beseechingly requested it from me.*[61]

Bishop Maurus had heard about the life of both anchorites while he was still a young monk at the abbey in Pannonhalma, directly from Svorad's pupil Benedict and Zobor Abbot Philippe. Géza's veneration and exceptional interest were for Maurus an immediate stimulus for writing the legends of Svorad and Benedict. He immediately began to write the legend after Géza's visit; therefore, the gifting of the chain is mentioned in it as a current event.[62]

Prince Géza had minted, probably in Nitra, a half-denar coin which had, in comparison with the royal coins, a high silver content. Géza did not change the quality of the princely coin. Géza's half-denars have on the averse side the inscription +DVX MVGNAS, that is Prince Magnus, which was Géza's second name. On the reverse side they have the other name for Hungary +PANONAI, that is Pannonia, similarly as other Hungarian coins from the 11th century. Today we know of 1929 pieces of Géza's princely half-denars, which is several times more than the mentioned half-denars of Prince Béla. If we add one coin from the village Tiszalúc to the 1907 of Géza's princely coins found in Slovakia, we then have 1908 of these coins directly from the territory of the Nitrian Principality. A treasure trove found in Dolné Chlebany lying north of Nitra contained 1569 coins of Prince Géza. Thus far, only 21 of Géza's princely coins have

---

58 Among the witnesses of the donation of Count Peter for the Százd Abbey perhaps from year 1067 were princes Magnus (that is Géza) and Ladislas: *Tandem ego Petrus rogavi regem cum duce Magno et cum duce Ladizlao ... testimonio aliquorum nominibus atestari feci: rex Salamon, dux Magnus, dux Ladizlaus ...* DHA I, ed. Györffy, no. 58, p. 185. See notes 70, 71, 73, 80, 81.

59 Lampert was still a minor in 1064. See note 49. Lampert stayed by Géza, who in 1073 sent him to Poland for military aid. *Chron. Hung. comp. saec. XIV.* II 114, SRH I, p. 380.

60 *Chron. Hung. comp. saec. XIV.* II 97, SRH I, pp. 362–363.

61 *Legenda SS. Zoerardi et Benedicti* 3, SRH II, pp. 360–361.

62 *Legenda SS. Zoerardi et Benedicti* 1, SRH II, pp. 357–358.

been found outside of Nitria, which contrasts with the situation of coins of Béla, the majority of which were found outside the territory of his principality. King Solomon obviously banned the use of the more quality coins of his adversary on his own territory. Biharian Prince Ladislas did not mint any coins.[63]

Géza married at the beginning of his princely rule. His first wife[64] became the mother of Coloman and Álmos and four daughters whose names are unknown.[65] Géza's other sister Euphemia († 2 April 1111) married (around 1066) Olomouc appanaged Prince Otto I the Fair (1061–1087, before then the Znojmo Prince 1055, 1058–1061).[66] Géza's third sister Helena (Lepa, † after 1091) became the wife (sometime between 1063–1066) of Ban Demetrius Zvonimir, who administered the Croatian counties of Gacka, Lika and Krbava (from 1075–1089 he was the Croatian king).[67]

King Solomon led the defence of the country and military campaigns beyond its borders together with Prince Géza for several years, just as King Andrew and Prince Béla once had. In 1066 Géza's brother-in-law Demeter Zvonimír sent emissaries *to king Solomon and Prince Géza* with a request for help in the battle against Venetian Doge Domenico Contarini (1041–1069), who in 1062 attacked and conquered the Croatian coastal town of Zadar. *Thus the king and the prince, assembling the army, marched to Dalmatia*; they used the rebellion of Zadar inhabitants and reconquered the town from the Venetians.[68]

---

63 Hlinka – Kazimír – Kolníková, *Peniaze*, pp. 140–141, 165–166, 170–171. Hlinka, "Nálezy mincí," pp. 157, 160–161. Hunka, "New Notions," pp. 196–198. Hunka, "Mincovníctvo uhorských vojvodov," pp. 63, 66–84. Hunka, "Vojvodská mincovňa," pp. 169–180. *Dejiny Nitry*, ed. Fusek, Zemene, pp. 124–125. Kovács, *A kora Árpád-kori magyar pénzverésről*, pp. 124–126, 130–139, 199–200, 202, 205, 208, 209, 210, 212, 215, 224–226, 231, 246–247, 282, 284, 289–290, 307.

64 Géza's first wife could have been Sophia from the family of Count Arnold. Arnold's County Looz (today Borgloon between St. Truiden and Bassenge in modern Belgium) was one of several small counties which originated in the 10th century on the territory of the Lotharingian Kingdom. Wertner, *Az Árpádok családi története*, p. 592.

65 Both sons and all daughters were born to Géza at the time when he was still a prince, that is before his royal coronation, which took place in the second half of March 1074: *Dux autem Geysa genuit Colomanum et Almum ac filias. Chron. Hung. comp. saec. XIV.* II 100, SRH I, pg. 365.

66 Wertner, *Az Árpádok családi története*, pp. 167–168. According to Barbara Krzemieńska, Euphemia was the daughter of Andrew I and was born shortly after the wedding of his sister Adelaide in 1056 or 1057. Barbara Krzemieńska, *Moravští Přemyslovci ve znojemské rotundě* (Ostrava 1985), p. 24.

67 Wertner, *Az Árpádok családi története*, pp. 160–167. Klaić, *Povijest Hrvata*, pp. 350, 360–361, 377–378. MT I/1, pp. 874–875.

68 *Chron. Hung. comp. saec. XIV.* II 99, SRH I, pp. 363–364. DHA I, ed. Györffy, no. 50/II, pp. 170–171. MT I/1, pp. 874–875. Klaić, *Povijest Hrvata*, pp. 378–381.

In 1067 the Bohemians attacked Trenčín and took a great many captives and livestock. King Solomon and Prince Géza, each with his own army, together invaded in response to Moravia; they plundered an extensive area and returned with a number of captives to Hungary.[69]

In 1068 the Pechenegs crossed the Hungarian border into the Eastern Carpathians, passed through northern Transylvania and through the Meszes pass and invaded Ladislas's Biharia, where they pillaged it up to Bihar itself before heading back with many captives and a large amount of livestock. King Solomon and princes Géza and Ladislas assembled an army and hurried through the Meszes pass to Doboka Castle in northern Transylvania, where they awaited the Pechenegs. In a battle under Kerlés Mountain (Chiraleș), they defeated them, killing many of them and freeing their captives.[70]

In 1071 the Pechenegs invaded Hungary from the south. With the permission of Byzantine leader of Belgrade they crossed the Sava, marauded in Hungarian Sirmium and retreated with a wealth of plunder and captives: *Thus the king and the prince accused Belgrade of the crime of betrayal ... and therefore they went with assembled armies in Slankamen, where after a meeting they decided that it was necessary to surround the treacherous Belgrade and conquer it.* Near Slankamen, not far from the southern borders of Hungary, aside from the royal army, to which the county army of Bács Count Vid and Sopron Count John belonged, a princely army under the leadership of Géza gathered. A trip over the river followed: *Then the order came from the king and the prince, that the whole Hungarian army cross river Sava as quickly as possible.* A portion of the Hungarian boats were burned by the Byzantines, but the Hungarian soldiers, thanks to the great many boats, forced their way across the Sava: *Then the king and the prince crossed the Sava on Monday and in the morning aligned their ranks and with their many forces, with their platoons armed with shields completely surrounded the city.* Both Géza and Ladislas took part in the siege of Belgrade. The Byzantine garrison requested help from the Pechenegs, who defeated Count Vid and his Bácsian soldiers. Count John with the Sopron army, however, bravely defended. He killed many Pechenegs, *and did so before the king and the prince had risen from breakfast with their army.* After three months of the siege and battles before the city ramparts, the city was overpowered by a fire that had been set by one captured Hungarian girl. The Byzantine garrison force pulled back into the castle and the leader Niketas began to negotiate. Niketas surrendered the castle in exchange for free departure. Carrying a silver icon, he went out with most of the inhabitants and with the military garrison

---

69 Chron. Hung. comp. saec. XIV. II 101, SRH I, p. 365.
70 Chron. Hung. comp. saec. XIV. II 102–103, SRH I, pp. 366–369.

to meet Prince Géza, who had the reputation for being merciful. Therefore, they subjected themselves to him and accepted his protection. Only a few surrendered to Solomon, *because he was known to be unkind and to listen to the very bad counsel of Count Vid.* The offended Solomon was unable to hide his anger. A distrust developed between the king and the prince, and it deepened upon the dividing up of the spoils. The king wanted to divide up not only the gathered treasure and captives but also those who for coming out of the castle were given the promise of free departure and accepted Géza's protection. Géza did not agree with this perfidy, thus angering Solomon. Ultimately, only the pirated goods were divided. Solomon, on the advice of Vid, Bishop Frank, Bugar's son Radovan and Count Elias (who was Vid's son-in-law) divided the valuables into four parts among Géza, all the soldiers, Vid and Elias. Géza, who as a prince had a claim to a full third of the plunder, thus only received a quarter.[71]

Byzantine Emperor Michael VII Dukas (1071–1078) soon heard of Géza's magnanimity and through emissaries made peace and friendship with him. He wanted nothing to do with King Solomon. Géza had all of his captives set free and even released the castle garrison force being held. Solomon's anger grew, and Count Vid continued to instigate him to exile Géza as soon as possible and to seize his principality, emphasizing that *a king has more soldiers than a prince*. Vid fostered Solomon's hatred of Géza with the words: *Just as two sharp swords cannot be put into one scabbard, then not even you can rule together in this kingdom.* The king hid is intentions at the beginning, feigned friendship and let Géza leave for his principality.[72]

The following year, 1072, the king appealed to both princes for a campaign against Byzantium. Géza and Ladislas were wary, because they knew the intentions of the king, who wanted to capture them. Ladislas remained on Biharian territory, in the Nyír region, with half of the princely military and was prepared to intervene, if anything were to happen to his brother in the king's presence. Solomon and Géza crossed the Danube and together marched against the

---

71   *Chron. Hung, comp. saec. XIV.* II 104–109, SRH I, pp. 369–375. *The Pechenegs ... swiftly threw themselvs at the divisions of Sopron inhabitants* (*super agmina Suproniensium*), *whose leader was a count by the name of John. Chron. Hung. comp. saec. XIV.* II 105, SRH I, p. 371. Sopron Count John led the Sopron County army, which had several castle divisions (*agmina*); therefore, aside from Sopron Castle, the castles Kapuvár, Babót and Locsmánd also belonged to Sopron County. See note 83. Kristó, *A vármegyék*, pp. 268–273, 276–280. Attila Zsoldos, "Confinium és marchia. Az Árpád-kori határvédelem néhány intézményéről," *Századok* 134 (2000), no. 1, pp. 101–102, 115. If each of these castles had its own castle district, then it also had a military division. Sopron County had 3 archdeaconates: Sopron, Locsmánd and Rábaköz. Ortvay, MEF I, pp. 318–322. The castle districts of Kapuvár and Babót belonged to the Rábaköz archdeaconate.

72   *Chron. Hung. comp. saec. XIV.* II 110, SRH I, p. 376.

Byzantine city of Niš. Solomon this time had to give up on his original intention. After receipt of a large ransom from the inhabitants of Niš, the king and the prince returned to Hungary.

Near Kovin (on the northern bank of the Danube, east of Belgrade) Géza with his army separated from the king, and he met with his brother Ladislas in Biharia. Here they discussed how to further face the king's intrigues. On his brother's advice, Ladislas left Bihar for Russia with a request for help. The mutual tension so ratcheted up that Solomon and Géza assembled armies against one another. After longer discussions through emissaries they ultimately decided on a meeting in Esztergom. The king and the prince wanted to avoid an open clash, so they agreed and selected only eight attendants from bishops and magnates, who went with them to Esztergom. From there they crossed over to a nearby island in the middle of the Danube. The meeting of the two antagonists thus took place directly on the Danube border of the princely part of Hungary. After mutual reproaches and apologies and after long debates, in the end they made peace and left the border island. Géza returned to Nitria and Solomon to Székesfehérvár. Afterwards, the guarantors of the ceasefire were exchanged. The king sent Counts Vid and Ernej to the Nitrian prince and got the Bihar bishop and Count Vata from him.

In 1073 both sides were openly preparing for war. The German army came to Solomon's aid. In November they concluded a ceasefire valid from 11 November 1073 to 24 April 1074 and returned the mentioned captives.[73] Solomon spent Christmas 1073 in Ikevár (near Vasvár). Immediately after the holidays, he left for Zalavár, where Count Vid and Carinthian Duke Markward (1073–1077), head of the auxiliary German army in Hungary, proposed that he ignore the ceasefire and that together they strike at Géza, who was then staying in Biharia while his brother Ladislas sought help in Russia and their other brother Lampert in Poland. In January 1074 Solomon came to the abbey in Szekszárd and in nearby Kösztölc broke military camp. Géza was just then hunting in the Igfon mountains, which divided Biharia from Transylvania. Count Vid and with him other trusted advisers recommended to the king that while Géza's brothers were still seeking aid abroad he strike Géza rapidly, on that very night, capture him and blind him. They assumed that without Géza, Ladislas and Lampert would not have the courage to attack Solomon and would no longer return to Hungary. Vid, who wanted to be an appanaged prince, proposed to Solomon: *And give the principality (ducatum) to me and thus reinforce your crown.*

---

73   *Chron. Hung. comp. saec. XIV.* 11 111–113, SRH I, pp. 377–379. DHA I, ed. Györffy, no. 64, p. 191.

The abbot of the Szekszárd Abbey, Willerm, loyal to Prince Géza, secretly overheard everything and immediately sent a letter to him. But Géza's false advisers Petrud, Szolnok and Bykas, who were secretly allied with Vid and were prepared to betray Géza, after the arrival of Willerm's messenger and after reading the letter, accused the abbot of lying. In the meantime Ladislas returned, but without any Russian soldiers. Because Géza could not expect help even from Poland, he immediately sent Ladislas to Moravia, to his brother-in-law, Olomouc Prince Otto, and continued his hunting trip. Abbot Willerm on the next morning inconspicuously eavesdropped again on the secret royal meeting with Count Vid. He immediately sat on a horse and in time woke up Géza and told him of Solomon's advancing army. Géza immediately gathered the Biharian army and wanted to quickly march after his brother Ladislas to Moravia. However, when he wanted to cross the frozen Tisza in Kemej, Solomon stood in his way.[74]

Leaders of the princely army, Petrud and Bykas, who previously had given Géza false advice, secretly promised Solomon that they would betray Géza and come over to his side with the princely army, if he left them their current (certainly counts) title. Solomon agreed *and then came against the prince over the frozen Tisza.*[75]

Géza had only 4 Biharian military units from the 4 castle counties that made up Biharia. Solomon had a large numbers balance, because he led 30 units from 30 castle counties of the royal part of Hungary, with which he attacked Géza. Petrud and Bykas with three units treacherously abandoned Géza at the crucial moment. Only one unit remained to Géza. Despite this, he set forth into battle against the large force that surrounded him.[76] The traitors with lifted shield as a conventional signal that their king not follow them, set off to escape. The royal soldiers, however, did not know of the secret agreement and did not understand the sign of the traitors and took them on. The three traitorous units, who were not expecting an attack, met their death on 26 February 1074 in a battle near Kemej. Only a few Biharian soldiers were saved by fleeing.[77]

---

74   Chron. Hung. comp. saec. XIV. II 114–116, SRH I, pp. 379–383.
75   Chron. Hung. comp. saec. XIV. II 117, SRH I, p. 383. Vid and Erney, who advised King Solomon, were counts. Therefore, Petrud, Szolnok and Bykas, who advised the prince, were also counts. They betrayed Géza, because they wanted to remain *in their stations* (*in dignitatibus*), that is in positions as counts.
76   *Principes autem Geyse, Petrud et Bykas in ipso prelio cum tribus agminibus castrorum verterunt sa ad Salomonem, sicut sibi promiserant. Dux vero Geysa, quamvis maxima parte exercitus sui esset destitutus, non tamen abhorruit uno tantum agmine stipatus contra triginta Salomonis agmina sevissimum prelium committere.* Chron. Hung. comp. saec. XIV. II 117, SRH I, p. 384.
77   Chron. Hung. comp. saec. XIV. II 117, 118, SRH I, pp. 384, 385–386.

Géza, seeing a lost battle and the destruction of most of his army, had to retreat. Near Kota he crossed the frozen Tisza and left Biharia, which fell into Solomon's hands. Immediately after crossing the Tisza he sent his chaplain George the Black to Ladislas, who had returned from Moravia, where he obtained military help, and began to assemble the army on the territory of Géza's Nitrian Principality. Géza sent his cleric and scribe Ivanka to Lampert in Poland. By the shortest route he galloped to the north-west to Nitria, where Olomouc Prince Otto awaited him with a Moravian army and Ladislas with Nitrian forces.[78] Géza handed over the remainder of the Biharian army to Ladislas and himself stood at the head of the Nitrian army.

King Solomon was held up with securing Biharia, and when he crossed the Tisza in Kota, he heard about the meeting of Géza with Ladislas and Otto. Count Ernej in vain discouraged him from war. The king followed Vid's advice and set off against the princes and on 12 March camped in Rákos not far from Pest.[79] The princely army left the military camp on the territory of Nitria

---

[78] Chron. Hung. comp. saec. XIV. II 117, SRH I, pp. 384–385. Géza met with Ladislas still on the territory of Nitria and not in Vác, as is mentioned by the chronicler; therefore, they passed to Vác only after Géza's departure. See note 80.

[79] Chron. Hung. comp. saec. XIV. II 119, SRH I, pp. 386–387. If exactly two weeks passed between Solomon's victory near Kemej on Thursday 26 February and his arrival to Rákos on Thursday 12 March, then Solomon was certainly held up by securing Biharia, which fell into his hands after the victory. The crossing over the Tisza *in Cothoyd* or *in Thoroyd*, through which Géza and Solomon passed in 1074, was near the mouth of the Kotaér stream on the left bank of the Tisza not far from Tiszafüred. It is identical with the ford at Abád, where Pecheneg warrior Thonuzoba owned property: *Prince Taksony gave to him land for living in the Kemej country (in partibus Kemey) up to the Tisza, there where there is now the ford at Abád (portus Obad).* Anonymi (P. magistri) Gesta Hungarorum 57, SRH I, pp. 116–117. This property belonged to the Tomaj family, which took its origin from Thonuzoba. Györffy, ÁMF III, pp. 45, 54, 64–65. Gyula Pauler, Dezső Pais and György Györffy looked for him there. Pauler, *A magyar nemzet története I*, pp. 124, 435. Dezső Pais, "Cotoyd. (Egy XI. századi tiszai átkelő nevéhez)," *Magyar Nyelv* 56 (1960), pp. 111–112. MT I/1, pp. 878, 881. Some researchers identify the place where Géza and Solomon crossed over the Tisza, with the Tokaj. Györffy, "Török női méltóságnév," p. 110. Györffy, "A magyar nemzetségtől a vármegyéig," p. 50. Györffy, *Tanulmányok a magyar állam eredetéről*, p. 39. Benkő, *Név*, pp. 162–168. György Györffy changed his old opinion. MT I/1, pp. 878, 881. The Cumans, who in 1091 invaded Hungary, crossed over the Tisza *in Thocoyd*. Cuman Khagan Kapolcs first plundered Transylvania, from where he *invaded Biharia (venit ad Byhor)*, where he remained with his Cumans several days by the Omsó-ér River (*Vmsoer*). Then *in Thocoyd* he crossed the Tisza and divided his army into three parts. Two divisions plundered the Homok (*Sabulum*) region in the area between the Danube and the lower Tisza, and the third part marched down the Tisza up to Becsej. Ultimately King Ladislas defeated them near Temesvár (Timişoara). Chron. Hung. comp. saec. XIV. II 137, SRH I, pp. 412–414.

and crossed its southern border. It first entered Vác[80] and then set up camp in Cinkota near Pest. Between the two military camps stood the peak Mogyoród. On the next morning both armies were determined to launch into one another. However, a thick fog prevented the battle.

On the third morning, on 14 March 1074, Solomon with his army crossed over the Mogyoród peak and stood before the marshalled army of three principalities. In an effort to give the impression of a large superiority of numbers, Solomon brought with him the baggage carriers and ordered them to stand on the slope in order to appear as a guard unit. However, he didn't evoke any fear in the princes. In the midst of the Biharian army (*in medio siquidem bihoriensi agmine*), which made up the left flank, stood Ladislas. Géza, who led the Nitrian army (*in nitriensi agmine*), took the middle, and Otto with the Moravians stood on the right flank. In addition to this, the marshalled reserves waited on both sides. Géza and Ladislas correctly guessed Solomon's intention to first attack Géza, over whom he had recently triumphed. Thus, they exchanged their ensignias and banners (*signa sua cum vexillo*), so that Solomon would make an error. Count Vid led the first attack. He fell on Prince Otto on the right flank. Solomon most of all wanted to destroy Géza's army, so he attacked on the left flank, where he saw Géza's insignia (*signa Geyse*). However, as soon as he recognized Ladislas, he turned and returned the attack on the Nitrian army in the middle. Ladislas struck Solomon's flank and afterwards Géza also attacked him. In the meantime royal Count Vid fell in battle, and the Moravians destroyed his army. King Solomon quickly lost the battle. Nearly all of the king's soldiers died in the battle, among them Count Ernej.

If the Cumans marched from Transylvania through Biharia alongside the Omsó-ér River (the right inflow of the Berettyó/Barcău River), then they got to the inter-river region of the lower Tisza and the Danube through Kota in Kemej and not through the Tokaj. In Kota he had his highbred court (*curia*) and the very brave Biharian warrior Peter, who went into battle in shining armor, in a gilded helmet and on a dark brown horse. A warrior of King Solomon, Opos, killed this *militem ducis nomine Petrum audacissimum* in a fight immediately at the start of the battle near Kemej. Solomon, who crossed the river here, also stopped in Peter's court in Kota, which his son inherited. If Peter, who was a warrior in the Biharian princely army, settled on the left bank of the Tisza in Kota, then Biharia reached up to this river crossing. Thus, the whole of Kemej, which later (after the extinction of the Biharian Principality and the neighbouring Eger County) belonged to him, became a small castle county. Ultimately he attacked the Heves seat. The Tisza formed the western border of Biharia. See chapter 13, notes 7, 41.

80 *Sed et duces Geysa, Ladizlaus et Ottho ac totus exercitus Hungarorum, qui erant cum eis, descenderunt circa Vaciam. Chron. Hung. comp. saec. XIV.* II 119, SRH I, p. 387.

Ladislas found the dead Vid on the battlefield and harangued to him: *Well, I wonder when you were not from a family of princes, why did you want a principality (ducatum), not even from posterity* (the king's), *why did you want the crown? Now I see how a heart that desired a principality lies stabbed with a spear, and the head which wanted the crown, cloven by a sword.* Ladislas's reproaches were authorised because Count Vid had endangered the succession order, according to which only someone from the Árpád line could become prince and then could become a king. Ladislas knew that in the case of Solomon's victory Vid would have become a prince, and thus after the death of the childless Solomon and his likewise childless brother David he would have had an open path to the royal crown. If a victorious Solomon had handed over only Biharia to Vid, because he would have had to satisfy his brother David with Nitria, even then it would have guaranteed him access to the royal throne. After Solomon's death David would have inherited the kingdom, and Vid would have gotten Nitria, and after David's death the royal crown would rest on Vid's head. This would have been the end of Árpád rule in Hungary.

Solomon rapidly retreated from the battlefield with the rest of the soldiers, crossed the Danube near Szigetfő and followed by the princely army fled to Moson, where his wife Judith and mother Anastasia awaited him.[81] He closed himself up in the border castles of Moson and Bratislava, which he previously had reinforced, and asked his brother-in-law, Emperor Henry IV for help.[82] Both Árpád princes entered into Székesfehérvár. They then placed garrison forces in Kapuvár, Babót, Székesfehérvár and other important castles of the kingdom part of Hungary and dissolved the rest of the army.[83]

---

[81] *Chron. Hung. comp. saec. XIV.* II 120–122, SRH I, pp. 388–393. The singular number *in ... bihoriensi agmine* and *in nitriensi agmine* as well as *agmen Geyse* and *ad agmen Ladizlai* doesn't mean that Géza and Ladislas had only one county division. They could have hardly stood against the royal army and its allies with such a small army. The mentioned *agmen* did not have to be only one county division, but sometimes also an entire army made up of several county divisions. Ladislas's Biharian *agmen* was a whole army: *Prince Ladislas moved before his army (ante exercitum suum), borne on a rearing horse, encouraging his own and give them courage.* Solomon attacked *the divisions of Prince Géza (super agmina ducis Geyse)*, and Géza's *agmen* were thus *agmina*. The meaning of the word *agmen* is not in medieval sources precisely set. Pavel Choc, *S mečem a štítem. České raně feudální vojenství* (Praha 1967), p. 93.

[82] *Chron. Hung. comp. saec. XIV.* II 123, SRH I, pp. 393–394. *Simonis de Keza Gesta Hungarorum* II 60, SRH I, pp. 180–181.

[83] *Porro duces Geysa et Ladislaus cum exercitu Albam veniunt. Deinde Castrum porte, Bobuth et Albam ac alia castra fortissimorum militum presidio munientes dimissoque exercitu habitabant in Hungaria. Chron. Hung. comp. saec. XIV.* II 124, SRH I, p. 394.

5 Princes Ladislas and Lampert

Shortly after the victory over Solomon *on the urging of the Hungarians Prince Géza Magnus accepted the royal crown*.[84] Because the royal crown was in the hands of Solomon, Géza had to be crowned with a golden diadem, which he received as a gift from Byzantine Emperor Michael VII Dukas. This diadem, called the Greek Crown (corona graeca), forms the lower part today of the well-known Hungarian royal crown. It has a rich enamel embellishment. In the front, above the forehead, is the figure of the throning of Christ and around the perimeter of the headband are the Archangels Michael and Gabriel and Sts. George, Demeter, Cosmas and Damian. Completely in the back is a trio of monarchs. Depicted right in the middle, as Christ's earthly antipole, is Byzantine Emperor Michael VII Dukas (1071–1078) and along the sides beneath him his younger brother and co-ruler Constantine Porphyrogenitus and Hungarian King Géza I with the inscription *Geovitzas pistos králes Tourkias* (*Géza faithful king of Turkia*).[85]

Géza became king *and gave the principality to his brother Ladislas*.[86] Ladislas was from 1064 the Biharian prince; therefore, the principality which he got from Géza in 1074 was the Nitrian Principality. Thus, from 1074 the entire princely third of Hungary was subjugated to Ladislas. The foundation document of the St. Benedictine Abbey was issued by *Magnus, also called Géza, first prince of the Hungarians* (*Hungarorum dux*), *later, by the grace of God, consecrated king, son of King Béla ... in the presence of Prince Ladislas* (*Ladizlao duce*), *my nicest brother*.[87] The youngest of the brothers, Lampert (*Lampertus dux*),[88] who was then already an adult[89] and capable of princely rule, also became a prince. The older Ladislas, according to custom, left Biharia to the younger Lampert from his princely third and kept the Nitrian Principality for himself.

The conquered Solomon remained in the three border counties. Solomon got these three castle counties exactly and justly according to the principle of 2:1, according to which Hungary should be divided into a kingdom and a princely part. Géza I released two counties, Moson and Sopron, to Solomon

---

84   Chron. Hung. comp. saec. XIV. II 124, SRH I, p. 394.
85   *Az Árpád-kori magyar történet bizanci forrásai* XLI C, ed. Moravcsik, pp. 254–255. Éva Kovács – Zsuzsa Lovag, *Die ungarischen Krönungsinsignien* (Békéscsaba 1988), pp. 8–9, 18–43. Györffy, "A magyar nemzetségtől a vármegyéig," pp. 51–53. Avenarius, *Byzantská kultúra*, p. 116. Avenarius, *Die byzantinische Kultur*, p. 127.
86   *Ducatumque dedit fratri suo Ladizlao. Chron. Hung. comp. saec. XIV.* II 129, SRH I, p. 401.
87   DHA I, ed. Györffy, no. 73/II, pp. 213, 218. CDES I, ed. Marsina, no. 58, pg. 54, 58.
88   DHA I, ed. Györffy, no. 88, pp. 268, no. 106, p. 309. *Ann. Poson.* ad a. 1097, SRH I, p. 126.
89   See notes 49, 59.

from his royal two-thirds, and Solomon got one county, Bratislava, at the expense of Ladislas's princely third. However, Géza got the eastern part of Sopron County with Kapuvár and Babót, and filled these castles with his soldiers.[90]

Solomon acknowledged the feudal suzerainty of German King Henry IV and gifted him with property on the territory of his Moson and Sopron counties. From this property Henry donated on 26 November 1074 to Freising Bishop Ellenhard 100 homesteads in the villages *Ascherichesbrugge, Chuningesbrunnen, Nowendorf, Hasilowe* between the Leitha River and Neusiedler Lake, with the exception of hunting in the Leitha Mountains (*in Litahaberge*) under the condition that he and his representatives will care for the reinforcing of Moson and other castles on Solomon's territory, which were occupied by Henry's forces.[91]

At the beginning of spring 1074 *the Pechenegs unanimously turned with a request to King Géza that if he grant them freedom, they will fully suppress the attacks of King Solomon, so that he dare not even go out from Moson and Bratislava to agitate Hungary*. Solomon, despite the cowardliness of the helping German army, which was led by Margrave Ernest, triumphed at the time of the great fast over the Pechenegs.[92] Solomon, *battling King Géza and his brothers*, then took away his family and brought property to the Admont Abbey in Styria.[93] If Solomon in April 1074 feared not only Géza, but also his brothers, then Géza's brothers Ladislas and Lampert where then already subordinate princes and had their own princely armies.

After the return to Moson, Solomon set his mind on assembling an army in this castle and attacking his cousins. Because he could not triumph alone, he asked the German king for help.[94] In August 1074 Solomon finally got the impatiently expected help. German King Henry IV crossed the Hungarian border *with a large army* and marched through what is now Slovakia. German boats, loaded with large amounts of foodstuffs, floated down the Danube. Solomon waited in Šintava for the military forces from three castle counties that remained in his power. Henry came to the Váh and near Šintava crossed to the other bank. After the arrival of the German army, Solomon stood at the front of three castle units (*acceptis tribus agminibus*), which had just then arrived to him at Šintava, and together with a smaller German force rapidly entered into Nitra.

---

90   See notes 71, 83.
91   DHA I, ed. Györffy, no. 69, pp. 196–197.
92   *Chron. Hung. comp. saec. XIV.* II 125, SRH I, pp. 395–397.
93   *Chron. Hung. comp. saec. XIV.* II 126, SRH I, p. 397. *Simonis de Keza Gesta Hungarorum* II 61, SRH I, p. 181.
94   *Chron. Hung. comp. saec. XIV.* II 126, SRH I, pp. 397–398. *Simonis de Keza Gesta Hungarorum* II 61, SRH I, p. 181.

Soldiers of Bratislava County, who now served Solomon together with the Moson and Sopron soldiers, were marching into battle against those with whom just five months before had defeated their current leader Solomon. Still in March 1074, they had belonged to this same Nitrian princely army as soldiers from other castle counties of the Nitrian Principality, prepared in August and September of this same year to defend Nitra.

Solomon did not embark on a siege. He tested the force and determination of the defenders of Nitra in smaller skirmishes before the castle gate: *The enthusiastic youth set forth into battle, once these retreated, then those, and they long wrestled without injuries.* Up to the measuring of forces before the Nitra ramparts, which he avoided without more serious injuries, Solomon's soldier Opos, known for his strength and courage from previous battles, unexpectedly burst forward: *The soldier Opos, selected among the thousands, sitting on his horse, burst towards the castle gate and defeated one of the fighters. The Nitrians (Nitrienses), however, indignant by the death of their fellow, shrilly wailing, fell on Opos and killed his horse with a spear. He, however, bravely resisted them, got away unscathed.* Solomon was convinced that Nitra was being defended by numerous and resolute soldiers and with this finding he returned to Henry, who remained near the Váh. An auxiliary German unit also returned with Solomon: *The returning Germans then spoke to the emperor* (correctly to the king) *about Opos's courage and his unbelievable capabilities in battle. The emperor* (correctly, the king), *then summoned him, lavished him with great praise and thanked him with flattering words. And he asked Solomon, whether Géza and Ladislas have so many good soldiers? Solomon, meaning to praise the Hungarians, impetuously answered: There are many, it's said, many still even better. The emperor then said: If that is the case, fighting with such soldiers you won't get your kingdom back.* The king did not ask about the soldiers of Prince Lampert; therefore, Lampert, as the Biharian prince, was also subjugated with his soldiers to the Nitrian Prince Ladislas. Henry, preferring to avoid Nitra, where Ladislas's Nitrian army was concentrated, marched from Šintava further up to Vác. However, his closest advisor, Aquilean patriarch Sieghard, and the German dukes secretly bribed by King Géza, discouraged him from another trip. Henry had the boats destroyed and returned to Germany.[95]

In August and September 1074 King Géza I and Prince Ladislas together battled with enemies, just as in September and October 1051 King Andrew I and Prince Béla and the same as King Solomon and Prince Géza did in years 1066, 1067, 1068, 1071 and 1072.

---

[95] *Chron. Hung. comp. saec. XIV.* II 127–128, SRH I, pp. 398–400. *Simonis de Keza Gesta Hungarorum* II 60, SRH I, pp. 180–181.

After the departure of the German army in September 1074, the disappointed Solomon went back to Bratislava (*in Poson*). Bratislava belonged to the Nitrian Principality; therefore, Nitrian Prince Ladislas wanted to dislodge Soloman from it: *Prince Ladislas, however, laid siege to Bratislava Castle (castrum Poson) for many days, but Solomon's soldiers came out of the castle and set into battle with Ladislas's soldiers. Often, however, Solomon and Ladislas came out, changing their signs (*signa*), battling as soldiers. It happened, however, that Ladislas came to the castle during an afternoon rest. Solomon then saw him arriving, changing his armour to an unknown armour. He came out to him, but not even Ladislas knew him. Solomon's soldiers, sitting in the castle, observed them. And Solomon regarded Ladislas only as a regular soldier, and therefore went out to battle with him.* The battle under the ramparts of Bratislava recalled the recent duel before the Nitra castle gate. The antagonists spared each other in mutual battles and Prince Ladislas himself was magnanimous to the defenders of Bratislava: *Solomon's soldiers, however, compelled by the anxiety, came to Ladislas. He with truly princely magnanimity and most gracious generosity encouraged them and allowed them to freely return to their lord.*[96]

King Géza (*králs Oyggías*) married Synadené, who came from an important Byzantine family allied with the imperial family. Her father Theodulos Synadenos was brother-in-law of the future Byzantine emperor Nikephors III Botaneiates (1078–1081). Synadené, obviously young like her brother, lost her standing in Hungary after Géza's death and returned to Byzantium.[97] Nikephors III wanted Theodulo's young son Synaden to be made emperor after his own death, which would increase the standing of his sister in Hungary.[98]

Not only the German king refused to recognize Géza's royal coronation, but so did the pope. Pope Gregor VII sent on 17 March 1074 a letter *to Géza, prince of the Hungarians* (*Geuse duci Vngarorum*),[99] and another two letters on 23 March and 17 April 1075 addressed likewise *to Géza, prince of the Hungarians* (*Geuse Ungarie duci*).[100] He further considered Solomon as the Hungarian king, although he sharply reproached him that he gave the Hungarian kingdom,

---

96   Chron. Hung. comp. saec. XIV. 11 129–130, SRH I, pp. 400–402.
97   Johannes Scylitzes continuatus. *Az Árpád-kori magyar történet bizánci forrásai*, ed. Moravcsik, p. 96. Géza married Synadené only as king, that is sometime in the years 1074–1077 and had no children with her. Géza had all 6 of his children while still a prince, that is from his first marriage. See note 65. If Synadené was Géza's only wife and the mother of his children, then she would have certainly remained in Hungary after his death.
98   Anna Comnena, *Alexiás seu Alexiadis libri XV*, lib. II. Anna Komnena, *Paměti byzantské princezny*, kniha druhá, II 1, translation Růžena Dostálová (Praha 1996), p. 59.
99   DHA I, ed. Györffy, no. 65, p. 191, no. 66, pp. 192–193.
100 DHA I, ed. Györffy, no. 71, pp. 200–201, no. 72, pp. 202–203.

which was a papal fief, to the benefit of the German realm and his antagonist in battle over investiture, Henry IV.[101] The pope asked Géza to make peace with Solomon.

At the end of 1076 Géza I began to negotiate with Solomon about a peace treaty. In the end he was resolved to give up the royal crown. On Christmas 1076 before Kalocsa archbishop Desiderius and other bishops and abbots he *promised that he will return the kingdom to Solomon and affirm peace in such a way that he according to law hold the crown together with a third of the country, which belonged to his principality. Solomon then as a crowned king will have the two-thirds he previously held.* However, the peace negotiations were suspended on 25 April 1077 due to Géza's death.[102]

---

101   *DHA I*, ed. Györffy, no. 67, pp. 193, no. 68, pp. 194–195, no. 70, pp. 198–199.

102   *Chron. Hung. comp. saec. XIV.* II 130, *SRH I*, pp. 402–403. *Simonis de Keza Gesta Hungarorum* II 62, *SRH I*, p. 182. *DHA I*, ed. Györffy, no. 74, p. 219.

CHAPTER 18

The Last Princes (1077–1108)

1   Princes Lampert and David

Under the rule of Hungarian King Ladislas I (1077–1095) the two princes Lampert and David divided up the princely third of Hungary. Lampert, his younger brother and reliable ally against King Solomon, was closer to Ladislas than his cousin David. In addition, Lampert had already been the Biharian prince since 1074,[1] and he thus had a higher standing than David, who was younger[2] and had got a principality only in 1077.[3] Lampert, therefore, of the two appanage principalities certainly received the more important Nitria, which Ladislas freed up for him upon his own rise to the Hungarian throne. David had to be satisfied with the less important Biharia and thus with a subordinate position to Lampert. Evidence of this is in the order of the names of both princes in the list of 11 witnesses at the end of a foundation document of Ladisals I for the Abbey of St. Giles in Somogy from 1091: *The issuer of this command: King Ladislas. Witnesses who were with him: Prince Lampert, his brother, Prince David, his cousin, Yaroslav, son of king of the Russians, son-in-law of the same* …[4] The first witness was Lampert; thus he was more important than David, who was second in the sequence. Lampert thus had the more important Nitria, and David had Biharia, subjugated to it.

The more important position of Lampert was also demonstrated with the foundation of the Titel Chapter. King Ladislas, as co-founder of the chapter, invited only one of the two princes – Lampert. He did not have to invite both

---

1   Lampert was born only after the return of his brother Béla to Hungary, that is between years 1048–1063. When in 1073 he sought in Poland military aid for his brothers Géza and Ladislas, he was already an adult and politically experienced or at least was collecting his first political experience. *Chron. Hung. comp. saec. XIV.* II 114, SRH I, p. 380.
2   Prince David was the brother of deposed King Solomon. Solomon was born in 1053 and the younger David at the earliest in the following year of 1054. Their father, Andrew I, conceived David certainly before the stroke which afflicted him in the autumn of 1058. Since Andrew with his second wife and mother of both of his son did not have a daughter, David could have been born shortly after Solomon, that is around 1055. Lampert was thus older than David.
3   Up to 1077 the brothers Ladislas and Lampert divided up the princely third, which had two parts. See pp. 460–464. Thus, there was no place in it for David.
4   *Dator istius precepti: rex Latisclauus. Testes, qui cum eo fuerunt: dux Lambertus frater eius, dux Dauid consobrinus eius, Gerazclauus filius regis Rutenorum gener ipsius* … DHA I, ed. Györffy, no. 88, p. 268.

princes, because Lampert represented not only his own Nitria but also the entire princely third, including David's subordinated Biharia. The foundation and donation document of King Ladislas and Prince Lampert (*sanctissimorum regis Ladislay et ducis Lamperty*) contained, according to verbal testimony of chapter administrator Phillippe from 1347, the names and borders of 7 donated villages near the Maros (Mureș) River in the Arad county.[5]

In addition to his own principality, David also had property near the Danube in Bodrog County. Since they lay outside of Biharia, he got them still before he became the Biharian prince. His brother Solomon, or possibly his father Andrew, had gifted them to him, so that he had something to live on before he had a principality. Shortly before his death *David, the venerable prince (David venerabilis dux)*, with the permission of King Ladislas, donated these properties to the Abbey of St. Anian in Tihany: *In Aranyán (In Aureo Loco) he donated 5 settlements (mansiones) and land with three farmsteads and five fishponds, namely Budig, Eurim, Weimir, Plas, Strisin*. In addition to this, *this prince (dux) himself* permitted that fish caught in the Danube on Sunday that would fill one small basket belonged to the abbot under the condition that the abbot or his representative must be present at the removal of one such basketful from the water.[6]

2   Deposed Solomon

Ladislas's cousin, deposed Hungarian King Solomon, who did not give up his claim to the Hungarian throne and held a small territory near the border with Germany, was the brother-in-law and protégé of German King Henry IV. In 1078 Ladislas joined on the side of Henry's antagonist, Swabian duke and German anti-King Rudolf, and married his daughter Adelaide.[7] Thus, he clearly stood in the camp of Henry's adversaries, to which also Pope Gregory VII belonged.

Ladislas I, just as Géza I before him, counted on the possibility that he would have to abandon the throne to Solomon: *And he always opposed in his mind to be properly crowned and to have the crown, because, if there could be a*

---

5   DHA I, ed. Györffy, no. 106, p. 309. Györffy, ÁMF I, pp. 240–241. The Titel Chapter got 7 villages near the Maros (Mureș) River in Arad County.
6   DHA I, ed. Györffy, no. 86, pp. 264–265, no. 96, pp. 278, 284–285. David, perhaps at the wishes of the abbot, gave this donation to King Ladislas to consent to, write and seal, in order to give it greater esteem. Similarly, the Bohemian prince approved of the donation of the Moravian princes at the same time or additionally. Thus, he better secured the new property for this mostly ecclesiastical institution. Žemlička, *Čechy v době knížecí*, pp. 349–350.
7   Wertner, *Az Árpádok családi története*, pp. 193–205.

firm peace between them, he would return the kingdom to Solomon and he himself would retain the principality (ducatum).[8] In the winter, at the beginning of 1079, Ladislas conquered Moson Castle from Solomon.[9] Solomon's ally Henry burst into Hungary in the spring, but he had to return without success.[10]

In 1080 Ladislas concluded peace with Solomon. He left him only Bratislava and did not concede the division of the kingdom with him: *Ladislas ... in the fourth year of his reign made peace with Solomon, giving him a pension sufficient for a king's expenses. However, magnates of the kingdom, guardedly warning against the cataclysmic of future military dangers, did not permit the kingdom to be divided with Solomon, so that the previous damage not occur again.*[11] The unhappy Solomon engineered a conspiracy which, however, did not remain secret. Ladislas imprisoned Solomon at Visegrád, but he still recognized the agreement: *If Solomon were to return, he really would return the kingdom to him and take the principality (ducatum).*[12]

The imprisoned king, however, rapidly began to sink. His own wife Judith left him, departing to her brother Henry IV in Regensburg. Solomon lived in a castle tower for two years (1081–1083). On the occasion of canonization of King Stephen I in August Ladislas released Solomon.[13] Solomon visited his wife Judith in Regensburg and in vain requested reconciliation.[14] With the loss of his wife, he also lost any hope for German help, and angry, he set off through Poland and Galicia to Moldova, where he was welcomed by Pecheneg Khagan Chelgü: *He promised him that if he helped him against Ladislas, he would hand over Transylvania to him and take his daughter as his wife. Prince Kutesk* (= Chelgü), *seduced by false hope, bursting with a great many Cumans* (= Pechenegs) *into Hungary, marched up to the province of the castles of Užhorod and Boržava (usque in provinciam castrorum Vng et Borsua).* King Ladislas, however, sent Chelgü and Solomon in 1085 on the run. Many Pechenegs fell

---

8   Chron. Hung. comp. saec. XIV. 11 131, SRH I, pp. 404–405.
9   MT I/2, p. 896. Györffy, ÁMF IV, p. 167.
10 Lechner, Die Babenberger, pp. 111–112.
11 Chron. Hung. comp. saec. XIV. 11 133, SRH I, p. 407. If Solomon had only Bratislava in 1080 (*Porro Salomon erat in Poson*), then he had to have lost Moson in the previous year. The German invasion into Hungary in the spring of 1079 was a response of Solomon's ally Henry IV to Ladislas's occupying of Moson.
12 Chron. Hung. comp. saec. XIV. 11 133, SRH I, pp. 407–408.
13 Chron. Hung. comp. saec. XIV. 11 134, SRH I, pg. 408. Legenda sancti Stephani regis ab Hartvico episcopo conscripta 24, SRH II, pp. 433–435.
14 Bernoldus Monachus s. Blasii sive Bernoldus Constantiensis, Chronicon ad a. 1083, 1084. Gombos, Catalogus I, p. 413. Wertner, Az Árpádok családi története, p. 132.

in the battle.[15] In 1087 Solomon took part in a Pecheneg campaign against Byzantium and died in an unsuccessful battle.[16] The following year Solomon's widow, Judith, married Polish Prince Wladyslaw I Herman.[17]

Ladislas, through his emissaries, who in 1087 came to the imperial diet in Speyer, supported adversaries of Emperor Henry IV, who stood on the side of the deposed Pope Gregory VII, and offered him the help of 20-thousand Hungarian soldiers.[18] In May 1090 Queen Adelaide,[19] who linked Ladislas with her father Rudolpf of Swabia († 1080) and other adversaries of Henry IV, died. With the deaths of Solomon and Adelaide the reasons for antagonism between Ladislas and Henry came to an end.

3 Ladislas and Álmos in Croatia

In 1089 Croatian King Demetrius Zvonimír, whose wife was Ladislas's sister Helena, died. Demetrius died without children, and Ladislas, as the brother of Queen Helena, made his claim on his inheritance.[20] Demetrius's successor, Stephen II (1089–1091), who was the last Croatian king from the Trpimírovič family, died some time in the first months of 1091,[21] and Croatian Queen Helena (Lepa), widow of the previous King Demetrius Zvonimír and threatened by internal infighting, summoned her brother Ladislas to Croatia.[22] Hungarian King Ladislas acted quickly. In the spring of 1091 he subjugated Croatia, entering into Biograd na Moru and installing his younger nephew Álmos as the

---

15 Chron. Hung. comp. saec. XIV. II 134, SRH I, p. 408. Marek Meško, "Pečenežsko-byzantské dobrodružstvo uhorského kráľa Šalamúna (1083–1087)," Konštantínove listy 4 (2011), pp. 79–84.
16 Anna Comnena, Alexiás seu Alexiadis libri XV, lib. VII. Anna Komnene, Alexias, Az Árpád-kori magyar történet bizanci forrásai, ed. Moravcsik, pp. 103–105. Gombos, Catalogus I, pp. 82–85. Anna Komnena, Paměti byzantské princezny, kniha sedmá, I 1–2, translation Dostálová, pp. 201–202. Chron. Hung. comp. saec. XIV. II 134–136, SRH I, pp. 409–411. According to Hungarian chronicles Solomon was buried in the Istrian town of Pula. Chronicon Zagrabiense 6, SRH I, p. 208. Chron. Hung. comp. saec. XIV. II 136, SRH I, p. 411. MT I/2, pp. 928–929. Meško, "Pečenežsko-byzantské dobrodružstvo," pp. 84–93.
17 Galli Chronicon II 1, MPH I, ed. Bielowski, p. 429. Wertner, Az Árpádok családi története, p. 133. Jasiński, Rodowód pierwszych Piastów, pp. 168–170, 173–175.
18 Bernoldus Constantiensis, Chronicon ad a. 1087, Gombos, Catalogus I, p. 413.
19 Wertner, Az Árpádok családi története, pp. 197, 205.
20 Chron. Hung. comp. saec. XIV. II 132, SRH I, p. 406. Wertner, Az Árpádok családi története, pp. 164–167. Klaić, Povijest Hrvata, pp. 486–489.
21 Klaić, Povijest Hrvata, pp. 489–491.
22 Chron. Hung. comp. saec. XIV. II 132, SRH I, p. 406.

Croatian king.[23] King Ladislas did not want his older nephew Coloman to rule in Croatia and later in Hungary, as he, *was namely repulsive bodily from the outside, but underhanded and docile, bristly, hairy, half-blind, hunchbacked, lame and stuttering.*[24]

With the invasion in Croatia Ladislas made an enemy of Pope Urban II (1088–1099), because Croatia had been a papal fief since the autumn of 1075, when the papal legate crowned Demetrius Zvonimír.[25] Ladislas abandoned the existing orientation on the pope, and passed to the side of anti-Pope Clement III (1080–1100) and became an ally of German King Henry IV.[26]

Still in summer of 1091 Ladislas was with his army *in Slavonia*, that is in Croatia,[27] from where he had to return in order to stop the Cumans, who then were regularly invading Hungary. After the departure of the Hungarian army,

---

23 *Anno incarnacionis Jesu Christi nostri Domini millesimo XCI, Kyri Alexio Constantinopoleos imperante, tempore, quo Uladdislau Pannoniorum rex Chroacie invadens regnum domnum Almum, suum nepotem illo statuit regem, Jaderensi vero cathedre domino Andrea venerabiliter presulante neque Drago, domni Prestancii episcopi nepote iam tercio priorante.* DHA I, ed. Györffy, no. 92, pp. 273–274. Klaić, *Povijest Hrvata*, pp. 491–494. Tamás Körmendi, "Szent László és Horvátország," in *Nagyvárad és Bihar a korai középkorban*, pp. 81–100. Tamás Körmendi, "Szent László horvátországi háborújáról. Az 1091. évi hadjárat történetének forráskritikai vizsgálata," *Századok* 149, 2015, no. 2, pp. 443–477.

24 Chron. Hung. comp. saec. XIV. II 143, SRH I, p. 421.

25 Klaić, *Povijest Hrvata*, pp. 384–388.

26 Klaić, *Povijest Hrvata*, pp. 494–495.

27 *Rex autem Ladizlaus cum suis in Sclavonia fuerat.* Chron. Hung. comp. saec. XIV. II 137, SRH I, p. 412. Slavonia was originally the wholly Slavic territory from the Drava River to the Adriatic Sea, which belonged to the Croatian kingdom. In the 12th century a ban, a representative of the king, administered Slavonia (Croatia), an important Hungarian or Croatian magnate, sometimes a relative of the king, and from the 2nd half of the 12th century often also a prince (*dux*), usually from the Árpád family, to whom the ban was subjugated. In the 13th century Slavonia was narrowed to only the north-eastern part with Zagreb, separated from Croatia. In the 13th century the king (at the beginning only sometimes and from 1272 regularly) installed two bans, one for Slavonia and the second for Croatia and Dalmatia. The Slavonia ban was based in Zagreb and the Croatian ban in Knin. Klaić, *Povijest Hrvata*, pp. 314–325. Györffy, "Szlavónia," pp. 223–240. Györffy, "Die Nordwestgrenze," pp. 295–313. Pál Engel, *Magyarország világi archontológiája 1301–1457 I.* (Budapest 1996), pp. 16–27. According to György Györffy and other historians, the territory between the Drava and the Kapela Uplands never belonged to Croatia but from the 10th century belonged to Hungary and was a part of Somogy County. Györffy, "Szlavónia," pp. 223–226, 229–230, 237. Györffy, "Die Nordwestgrenze," pp. 295–299, 302–304. Kristó, *A vármegyék*, pp. 259–260. If Somogy Castle had several properties in Slavonia, then this doesn't mean that its castle district reached all the way there. The property of a castle county (várispanság) was often also outside the castle's own district (vármegye), on the territory of neighbouring and more distant castle districts. See chapter 16, note 43. Somogy Castle could also have acquired its property in Slavonia after 1091.

the Croats called on King Peter Svačič (1091–1097), who under the rule of King Demetrius Zvonimir was the Croatian ban.[28] Ladislas kept only the Sava River region of Slavonia lying between the Drava River and the Kapela Uplands, which had belonged to Croatia from the times of rule of Tomislav (before 914– up to 928),[29] and he connected it to Hungary.[30] All that remained to Álmos was the empty title of Croatian king.

4 The Cuman Incursion and Foreign Campaigns of King Ladislas

On 29 April 1091 the Cumans, in an alliance with the Byzantine army, triumphed over the Pechenegs in a large battle near Levounion (near the mouth of the Maritsa River). Immediately after, they ruled Pecheneg settlements in

---

28   Klaić, "Povijest Hrvata," pp. 507–512.
29   Klaić, "Povijest Hrvata," pp. 275–279, 304, 314, 333, 348.
30   The subjugating of Slavonia by Hungarian King Ladislas is mentioned in two completely different sources from the 13th century, one Hungarian and one Croatian. In a falsified document of Andrew II, which confirms the right of the Zagreb bishop and reports up to year 1217, we read: *cum ... venissemus ad Zagrabiensem episcopatum ac monasterium Zagrabiense a sancto Latislao rege ... predecessore nostro constructum, qui terram Sclavonie sive banatum ... corone Ungarie subiugavit, qui eciam in eodem banatu episcopatum instituit et monasterium in honorem Sancti Regis Stephani construxit ... DHA I*, ed. Györffy, np. 85b, p. 262. Györffy, "Szlavónia," pp. 231–233. Györffy, "Die Nordwestgrenze," pp. 304–307. The mention of a document on the subjugation of Slavonia by Ladislas we can take equally seriously as the undoubtedly truthful mention of Ladislas as the founder of the Zagreb bishopric, even though both references are embedded in an untrustworthy context. Split Archdeacon Thomas also wrote about the subjugation of Slavonia and Croatia by Hungarian King Ladislas: *His ergo Vladisclauus rex inductus consiliis, absque mora, coadunato exercitu copioso, uenit et occupauit totam terram a Drauo fluuio usque ad alpes, que dicuntur ferree nullo obice resistente. Post hec transivit alpes et cepit impugnare munitiones et castra multaque prelia comitare cum gentibus Chroatie. Sed cum alter alteri non ferret auxilium, essentque diuisi ab inuicem, facilem, uictoriam rex potuit optinere. Nec tamen usque ad maritimas regiones peruenit, sed audiens, quod quedam gens sui regni fines intrauerat, in Hungaria repedauit.* Thomas Spalatensis archidiaconus, *Historia Salonitana* 17, ed. Franjo Rački, Monumenta spectantia Historiam Slavorum meridionalium XXVI, Scriptores III (Zagrabiae 1894), p. 57. Gombos, *Catalogus III*, p. 2225. The Hungarian-Polish Chronicle mentions the victory of the Hungarian king, which it identifies with Attila, over the Slavs and Croats: *Movit autem inde se et exeritus suos et pertransivit Alpes Carintie et venit in terminos Chrvacie et Sclavonie inter fluvios Savam et Dravam: ibique occurrerunt ei principes Chrwacie et Sclavonie ... Cesi sunt autem Sclavi et Chrwati, alii fugerunt et alii in captivitatem ducti sunt. Chronicon Hungarico-polonicum* 3, SRH II, pp. 302–303. The *Sclavonia* in the 3rd chapter of the Hungarian-Polish Chronicle is not Croatian Slavonia but a second name for Hungary. See chapter 15, note 60. Ryszard Grzesik, *Kronika Węgiersko-polska. Przyczynek do dziejów polsko-węgierskich w średniowieczu* (Poznań 1994, manuscript), pp. 88–97. Klaić, *Povijest Hrvata*, pp. 488–489, 492–493, 499.

the Black Sea steppes from the Don up to the Eastern Carpathians and the lower Danube.[31] Only afterwards, that is sometime in the summer, did they attack Hungary. The Cumans invaded Hungary on the impulse of Russian Prince Vasilko (before 1091–1124), based in Terebovľ (today's Ternopil).[32] The Cuman khagan Kapolcs began to plunder Transylvania and from there invaded *into Biharia (ad Byhor)*, where he remained with his Cumans for several days near the Omsó-ér River. He then crossed the Tisza and divided his army into three parts. Two Cuman units plundered the region between the Danube and lower Tisza rivers, and the third unit marched down the lower Tisza to Bečej. Ultimately, King Ladislas defeated them near Timişoara, where they were to join with the other Cuman armies, which under the leadership of Ákos invaded along the lower Danube into Hungary. In a battle on the bank of the Danube, Ladislas also defeated Ákos's Cumans.[33]

In September 1091 Ladislas welcomed Břetislav, the son of Bohemian King Vratislaus II, and his cousin Adelaide, daughter of Andrew I, who had run away from Bohemia from fear of his father, accompanied by more than 2-thousand warriors and with all of his livestock and slaves. Břetislav remained in the Hungarian royal court, and his warriors settled on the territory of Nitria, not far from the Moravian border: *King Ladislas ... set his warriors beyond the settlement Bánov near Trenčín Castle*.[34] After the death of his father in January 1092 and his Uncle Conrad in September 1092, Břetislav returned to Bohemia and became the prince of Bohemia.[35]

In 1092 Ladislas marched to eastern Galicia against Terebovlyan Prince Vasilko, to get revenge for the Cuman invasion of the previous year.[36] In the second half of 1093 or in the following year 1094 Ladislas, on the appeal of Polish Prince Wladyslaw Herman (1079–1102), intervened against his antagonists in Poland and for three months laid siege to Kraków. The king marched against Kraków undoubtedly through Nitria and certainly chose the shortest and most traversable road, which led through Nitra, the Turiec and Orava regions. He didn't take the same way back, but from Poland he went into Moravia, from

---

31 Anna Comnena, *Alexiás seu Alexiadis libri XV*, lib. VIII. Gombos, *Catalogus I*, p. 85. Anna Komnena, *Paměti byzantské princezny*, kniha 8, IV–VI, translation Dostálová, pp. 237–244. *Dějiny Byzance*, ed. Bohumila Zástěrová (Praha 1992), p. 252.
32 See note 40.
33 *Chron. Hung. comp. saec. XIV.* II 137, SRH I, pp. 412–414. Körmendi, "Szent László horvátországi háborújáról," pp. 467–469.
34 *Cosmae Pragensis Chronica Boemorum* II 48, ed. Bretholz, p. 155. Novotný, *České dějiny I/2*, pp. 305–308.
35 *Cosmae Pragensis Chronica Boemorum* II 50, ed. Bretholz, pp. 157–158. Novotný, *České dějiny I/2*, pp. 354–355.
36 *Chron. Hung. comp. saec. XIV.* II 138, SRH I, pp. 414–415. Pauler, *A Magyar nemzet története I*, pp. 160, 448.

where he returned to Hungary with many captives,[37] and again he had to pass through Slovak territory.

5   The Zagreb Bishopric

Immediately after his return from Galicia, King Ladislas turned all of his attention to domestic relations, mainly on the Hungarian church. On 20 May 1092 he called a synod of Hungarian bishops, abbots and magnates to Szabolcs. The king enacted into law its resolutions, which were to organize ecclesiastical relations in Hungary.[38] Probably on this occasion *he established two bishoprics and richly endowed them*.[39] It was then that Várad (Oradea) and Zagreb became bishopric seats.

The Cumans, who in the summer of 1091 invaded Hungary, ravaged the old princely and bishopric seat of Bihar. Perhaps a year after the victory over the Cumans, King Ladislas brought the bishopric from the plundered Bihar to nearby Várad,[40] which he still so favoured that he had himself buried there. Probably at this time he also incorporated the newly connected area of Slavonia along the Sava River into the Hungarian church. The castle seat of Slavonic Savia and its old bishopric was Sisak. He subjected the Sisak bishop, mentioned in 928 together with other Croatian bishops, to the Split archbishop.[41] However, Ladislas I did not place the new bishopric in ancient

---

37   *Chron. Hung. comp. saec. XIV.* II 138, SRH I, p. 415. Chaloupecký, *Staré Slovensko*, pp. 89–90.
38   *Sancti Ladislai regis decretorum liber primus. A szent István, szent László és Kálmán korabeli törvények*, ed. Závodszky, p. 157.
39   *Legenda S. Ladislai regis* 5, SRH II, p. 519.
40   See note 48. The chronicler's reference regarding the Várad (Oradea) bishop in 1068 is a later interpolation and in 1072 a substitution for the Bihar bishop. *Chron. Hung. comp. saec. XIV.* II 103, 113, SRH I, pp. 368, 378–379. *Chronicon Posoniense* 54, SRH II, p. 39. Györffy, ÁMF I, pp. 681–688. Gerics, *Legkorábbi Gesta-szerkésztéseink*, pp. 84–88. Katalin Szende, "'Civitas opulentissima Varadiensis'. Püspöki székhely és városfejlődes a középkori Váradon," in *Nagyvárad és Bihar a korai középkorban*, pp. 101–128. Ladislas I, perhaps then, when he brought the bishopric from Bihar to Várad, also changed the seat of another Hungarian archbishopric, which he migrated from Kalocsa to the south to Bácsa Castle. The first Bács Archbishop, Fabián, then took part in establishing the Zagreb bishopric. DHA I, ed. Györffy, no. 85, p. 261. Meanwhile the transferring of the bishopric from plundered Bihar to Várad was permanent; the transferring of the archbishopric from Kalocsa to Bácsa was only temporary.
41   *Concilium Spalatense. Documenta historiae chroaticae periodum antiquam illustrantia*, collegit, digessit, explicuit Fr. Rački (Zagreb 1877), no. 150, pp. 194–195. MMFH IV, p. 126. Klaić, *Povijest Hrvata*, pp. 278–279.

Sisak, but in the new centre of Slavonia around the Sava River, in Zagreb, which lay halfway between Hungary and Croatian Biograd. Ladislas I subjugated the Zagreb bishopric to the Esztergom archbishop. The Slavonians were Slavs; therefore, Bohemian priest Duch, who as a Slav understood their language, became the first bishop of Zagreb.[42]

We know the foundation document from the Zagreb bishopric only from a later digest in a document from 1134, by which the Esztergom Archbishop Felicianus settled a dispute between the Zagreb bishopric and the people of Somogy County. According to its testimony, Ladislas I founded the bishopric in Zagreb at a time when Esztergom Archbishop Acha, Bács Archbishop Fabian, Veszprém Bishop Cosmas, Palatine Gyula and Somogy Count Grab were still alive.[43] Important among them for dating the origin of the Zagreb bishopric are Bishop Cosmas and Palatine Gyula, because their titles in 1091 and 1092 still belonged to their predecessors Altmar and Peter. In 1091 Veszprém Bishop Altmar and Palatine Peter, together with others, were witnesses present at the founding of the Abbey of St. Giles at Somogy Castle.[44] While Palatine Peter is mentioned for the first and last time in 1091, we find out more about Bishop Altmar one more time, on 25 August 1092.[45] Only after Peter's and Altmar's death (or after their departure) could Gyula become the new palatine and Cosmas the new Vezsprém bishop, again mentioned as bishop on 17 April 1093. Thus, when both were in their title as bishop and palatine could only have

---

42 See note 46. Klaić, *Povijest Hrvata*, p. 499. With selection of a bishop, whether he spoke the language that was spoken in the diocese was taken into consideration. In 1169, on the wishes of Bohemian Queen Judith, a foreigner, Magdeburg canon Fridrich was selected as the Prague bishop: *a distinguished and wealthy person from Saxony by the name of Fridrich, completely ignorant of the Bohemian language (ignarus omnino boemicae lingue), equally a relative of the queen, took the position. He achieved this more thanks to his relations than from a decision of the church, because they would have never selected a foreigner who doesn't know the language (nam sponte sua aduenam et linguae imperitum non eligerent).* Annales Gerlaci Milovicensis ad a. 1170, *Fontes rerum Bohemicarum II/2*, edidit Josef Emler (Praha 1875), p. 463.

43 Árpád-kori oklevelek 1001–1196, ed. Györffy, no. 14, pp. 49–50, 128–129. DHA I, ed. Györffy, no. 85, pp. 261, 263. Bálint Hóman, "A zágrabi püspökség alapítási éve," *Turul* 28 (1910), pp. 100–113. The Zagreb diocese got not only the Sava River region of Slavonia between the Drava River and the Kapela Uplands, but also a small territory at the expense of the neighbouring Veszprém diocese on the north bank of the Drava River, which became the Bekcsény Archdeaconate (a part of Zala Castle County) with its seat at Csesztreg. Ortvay, MEF II, pp. 670–768. Holub, *Zala megye I*, pp. 405–407, 410, 412. Kristó, *A vármegyék*, pp. 308–309.

44 *Almarus Uespremensis episcopus, comes palatinus Petrus*. DHA I, ed. Györffy, no. 88, p. 268.

45 *sub testimonio Althmari episcopi*. DHA I, ed. Györffy, no. 96, p. 285.

been after 25 August 1092, and only after then could they have been together in Zagreb for the ceremonial founding of the bishopric. King Ladislas thus founded the Zagreb bishopric at the earliest in the summer of 1092 and at the latest before his own death in the middle of summer 1095.[46] If in the last two years of his life he directed his attention on neighbouring Poland and Bohemia, then we can look for the origin of the bishopric in the years 1092–1093, with the greatest probability in the time in which Ladislas was resolving the relations in the Hungarian church, for which he called the Szabolcs synod, that is still in 1092 (after 25 August).

---

46 We take the opinion on the order Altmar – Cosmas and Peter – Gyula from Nada Klaić, who on the basis of this order dates the origin of the Zagreb bishopric approximately to year 1093. Klaić, *Povijest Hrvata*, pp. 499–500. Gyula Pauler dated the establishment of the Zagreb bishopric to 1094, which is also in conformity with this order. Pauler, *A magyar nemzet története I*, pp. 170–171. Bálint Hóman tried to demonstrate that Veszprém Bishop Cosmas and Palatine Gyula took their positions still before Veszprém Bishop Altmar, mentioned in years 1091 and 1092, and before Palatine Peter, mentioned in 1091. Therefore, he sought the origin of the Zagreb bishopric between years 1087–1090, thus even before Ladislas's campaign to Croatia. From this it then followed to him that Ladislas I did not attach the Sava River region of Slavonia to Hungary only in 1091, but that it belonged to Hungary long before then. György Györffy also accepted Hóman's opinion. Hóman, "A zágrabi püspökség," pp. 111–113. Györffy, "Szlavónia," pp. 223–240. Györffy, "Die Nordwestgrenze," pp. 295–313. *DHA I*, ed. Györffy, no. 85, pp. 261–263. György Györffy, in order to avoid conflicts which follow from reversed order of the mentioned dignitaries, shifted the dating of the other documents, in which Bishop Cosmas and Palatine Gyula are mentioned to year 1090 or even earlier. He puts the undated donation of Prince David, which mentions Bishop Cosmas and Palatine Gyula, to the years 1089–1090 or even earlier still. *DHA I*, ed. Györffy, no. 86, pp. 264–265. He doubts the dating of the document which Ladislas I issued on 17 April 1093 and with which he resolved the border dispute between the Kalocsa and Pécs dioceses, not because it is to some measure forged, but only because Bishop Cosmas is mentioned in it. *DHA I*, ed. Györffy, no. 98, pp. 288–290. Both documents could have then originated when Gyula became Palatine and Cosmas bishop, that is only after 25 August 1092. We do not have to doubt the dating of the falsified document of Ladislas to 17 April 1093. It is testimony that Bishop Altmar died sometime between 25 August 1092, when he is last mentioned, and 17 April 1093, when Cosmas was already Veszprém bishop. Thus, the order Altmar – Cosmas, which indirectly testifies about the correctness of the order Peter – Gyula, is correct. In this case not only does opinion on the founding of the Zagreb bishopric before Ladislas's campaign to Croatia fall, but also the opinion associated with it about the membership of the Sava River region of Slavonia being connected to Hungary already from the 10th century. In addition to this, settlements are lacking in the Sava River region of Slavonia which have names according to Magyar tribes. István Kniezsa, "Ungarns Völkerschaften im XI. Jahrhundert," in *Archivum Europae Centro-Orientalis IV* (Budapest 1938), pp. 376–386. István Herényi, *Magyarország nyugati végvidéke 800–1242* (Argumentum Kiadó 1999), pp. 29–36. At the time when settlement with Hungarian tribal names originated in Hungary, this territory had to lay beyond its borders.

6 The Death of Princes David and Lampert and King Ladislas

The most entitled aspirant to the Hungarian throne after Ladislas's death, according to the Hungarian succession order, was Nitrian Prince Lampert. Ladislas, who had no sons, certainly did acknowledge his claim. King Ladislas also thought about his own nephews. He granted Croatia to the younger Álmos, and he wanted to make a bishop of the older Coloman. He took care to have Coloman educated and prepared him for the office of the Eger bishop.[47] After the establishing of the Várad bishopric (in perhaps 1092), however, he changed his decision, and Coloman became the first Várad bishop: *This Coloman, as some say, was the Várad bishop, and only because his brothers died before him, he was permitted to rule.*[48]

We don't know about any of Coloman's brothers who would have died still under the rule of Ladislas I. It was Coloman's uncle Lampert and second degree uncle David, as appanaged princes and as older men, who had a greater claim to the Hungarian throne than both of Géza's sons. Their death opened the road to the royal throne for Coloman. Biharian Prince David, who did not survive King Ladislas, died sometime in the years 1092–1095. Like his older brother Solomon, he also died childless.[49] Nitrian Prince Lampert, who had the first claim to the royal crown after Ladislas, died in the same year as King Ladislas, that is in 1095, and while Ladislas was still alive. And thus succession fell to Géza's sons Coloman and Álmos.

After Lampert's death in 1095, Ladislas decided that Álmos will be the Hungarian king. Coloman, however, was never going to be happy with a bishopric and had no intention of leaving the kingdom to his younger brother. Therefore, he left Várad and fled to Poland, from where he returned only after Ladislas's death.[50]

At the end of his life, Ladislas *assembled his army and set off against the Bohemians due to the injustices committed on his nephew.*[51] This nephew of Ladislas could have been one of the sons of his sister Euphemia († 2 April 1111), who in approximately 1066 married Olomouc appanaged Prince Otto I the Fair (1061–1087, before then Znojmo Prince 1055, 1058–1061), either Svatopluk, or Otto the Black.[52] Ladislas wanted perhaps to help the older of the two

---

47 Chron. Hung. comp. saec. XIV. II 140, SRH I, pp. 419–420.
48 Chron. Hung. comp. saec. XIV. II 152, SRH I, pp. 432–433. DHA I, ed. Györffy, no. 95, pp. 276–277.
49 Chron. Hung. comp. saec. XIV. II 100, SRH I, p. 364.
50 Chron. Hung. comp. saec. XIV. II 140–142, SRH I, pp. 420–421.
51 Chron. Hung. comp. saec. XIV. II 140, SRH I, p. 419.
52 Wertner, Az Árpádok családi története, pp. 167–168.

sons, Svatopluk, who just then had become the Olomouc appanaged prince (1095–1107, later Bohemian prince 1107–1109) and could have on this occasion gotten into conflict with his cousin, Bohemian Prince Břetislav II (1092–1100). Ladislas proceeded through Slovakia, until he *reached the border of the Bohemians*, where he became seriously ill and had to turn back. The ill king again sent word to Coloman to return to Hungary and again confirmed Álmos as his successor.[53]

King Ladislas died on 29 July 1095.[54] After their uncle's death, the two brothers made an agreement. Coloman, whom the pope freed from his bishop's office,[55] became king (1095–1116). His younger brother Álmos received the Nitrian and Biharian Principalities (*et duci Almus ducatum plenarie concessit*).[56]

7   King Coloman and Prince Álmos Defeated the Crusaders

In 1096 Crusaders marched through Hungary. After a peaceful crossing of their forces, which in May 1096 were led by French Knight Walter Sans Avoir,[57] the Crusader army, led by French anchorite Peter the Hermit, marched through Hungary. They caused commotion in the southern border area of Hungary near Zemun and then on Byzantine territory.[58] The Crusaders who were led by Folkmar of Orleans left the Rhineland at the end of April. They passed through eastern Franconia, Saxony and Bohemia, where at the end of May they attacked Jews in Prague,[59] and then passed through Moravia and Slovakia. Along

---

53   *Chron. Hung. comp. saec. XIV.* II 140, SRH I, p. 419.
54   *Chron. Hung. comp. saec. XIV.* II 141, SRH I, p. 420.
55   *ideo summo pontifice cum eo dispensante regnare conpellitur. Chron. Hung. comp. saec. XIV.* II 152, SRH I, p. 432.
56   *Chron. Hung. comp. saec. XIV.* II 140, 142, SRH I, pp. 419–421.
57   Albertus Aquensis canonicus, *Historia Hierosolymitana seu Chronicon Hierosolymitanum de bello sacro* I 7–9. Gombos, *Catalogus I*, pp. 35–36.
58   Albertus Aquensis, *Historia Hierosolimitana* I, 8–11, 14, Gombos, *Catalogus I*, pp. 36–38. Ekkehardus Uraugiensis abbas, *Chronicon universale* ad a. 1096, Gombos, *Catalogus II*, p. 870. Guibertus abbas monasterii s. Mariae Novigenti, *Historia Hierosolymitana quae dicitur Gesta Dei per Francos* II, 4, 6, Gombos, *Catalogus II*, pp. 1096–1097. *Chron. Hung. comp. saec. XIV.* II 143, SRH I, pp. 421–422. Györffy, *ÁMF IV*, p. 161.
59   Ekkehardus Uraugiensis, *Chronicon universale* ad a. 1096, Gombos, *Catalogus II*, pp. 870–871. Ekkehardus Uraugiensis abbas, *Hierosolimita seu Libellus de opresione, liberatione ac restauratione sanctae Hierosolymitanae ecclesiae seu Libellus de expugnatione Hierosolymitana* 11, Gombos, *Catalogus II*, p. 873. Guilelmus Tyrius Archiepiscopus, cancellarius regis Amalrici, *Belli sacri historia libris XXIII comprehensa seu Historia rerum in partibus transmarinis gestarum seu Historia belli sacri verissima* I 19, Gombos, *Catalogus II*, pp. 1107–1108. *Cosmae Pragensis Chronica Boemorum* III 4, ed. Bretholz,

the entire route they looted and attacked Jewish communities. When 12,000 of Folkmar's Crusaders came in June to Nitra, the Nitrian army slaughtered some of them and captured others: *Folkmar's people marching through Bohemia, when they were near Nitra, the Pannonia Castle (aput Nitram, Pannonie civitatem), broken up by mischief, a portion died by the sword and a portion fell into captivity.*[60]

In June of 1096 near Székesfehérvár the Hungarians destroyed a 15-thousand strong Crusader army led by the priest Gottschalk.[61] Coloman refused to let another 14-thousand strong Crusader army into Hungary, led by Emich, Count of Leiningen. Coloman personally led the royal army in the Moson border area, the defence of which was as equally well prepared as the defence of Nitra. After 6 weeks of the siege, he ran into a surprising counter-attack. The majority of the Crusaders fell, and Emich fled to the Eastern March with the rest.[62]

For victory over Folkmar's Crusaders certainly the entire Nitrian and perhaps also the Biharian armies were needed. If in Transdanubia Coloman himself led the royal army in the battle against the Crusaders, then at the same time Nitrian and Biharian Prince Álmos evidently prepared the defence of Nitra against Folkmar. The defence of Nitra in June 1096 was at least as well prepared as in August 1074.[63] The entire princely army of Nitria could have been concentrated at Nitra Castle, which had an area of up to 8.6 hectares. In 1074 a large German army avoided Nitra, full of Ladislas's Nitrians, and 22 years

---

pp. 164–165. Novotný, *České dějiny I/2*, pp. 375–377. Steven Runciman, *Dzieje wypraw krzyżowych I* (Warszawa 1997), pp. 130–133.

[60] *Plebs Folcmarum per Boemiam sequens, cum aput Nitram, Pannonie civitatem, seditione concitata, partim ferro, partim captivitate disperisset, paucissimi qui supererant testantur, quod crucis signum super se celitus apparens ab imminenti eos nece liberasset.* Annalista Saxo, *Chronicon quo res gestae ab initio regni Francorum, 741–1139 enaratum* ad a. 1096, Gombos, *Catalogus I*, p. 223. Ekkehardus Uraugiensis, *Chronicon universale* ad a. 1096, Gombos, *Catalogus II*, p. 871. Györffy, *ÁMF IV*, p. 429.

[61] Albertus Aquensis, *Historia Hierosolymitana* I 24–25, Gombos, *Catalogus I*, pp. 38–39. Annalista Saxo, *Chronicon* ad a. 1096, Gombos, *Catalogus I*, pp. 223–224. Ekkehardus Uraugiensis, *Chronicon universale* ad a. 1096, Gombos, *Catalogus II*, p. 870. Guilelmus Tyrius, *Belli sacri historia* I 27–28, Gombos, *Catalogus II*, pp. 1108–1109. Györffy, *ÁMF II*, pp. 365, 626.

[62] Albertus Aquensis, *Historia Hierosolymitana* I 29–30, Gombos, *Catalogus I*, pp. 40–41. *Annales S. Disibodi sive Annales Disibodenbergenses* ad a. 1095 ac sequenti, id est 1096, Gombos, *Catalogus I*, p. 124. *Annales Magdeburgenses* ad a. 1096, Gombos, *Catalogus I*, p. 150. Annalista Saxo, *Chronicon* ad a. 1096, Gombos, *Catalogus I*, p. 224. Ekkehardus Uraugiensis, *Chronicon universale* ad a. 1096, Gombos, *Catalogus II*, pp. 870–871. Ekkehardus Uraugiensis, *Hierosolymita* 12, Gombos, *Catalogus II*, p. 873. Guilelmus Tyrius, *Belli sacri historia* I 29, Gombos, *Catalogus II*, pp. 1109–1110. Györffy, *ÁMF IV*, p. 161. Runciman, *Dzieje wypraw krzyżowych I*, pp. 133–134.

[63] See pp. 462–463.

later Folkmar's Crusaders suffered an overwhelming defeat at Nitra in an open battle with Álmos's princely army.

8   Coloman's and Álmos's Foreign Policy

The battle over investiture between the pope and the emperor further divided Hungary. King Coloman was a follower of Pope Urban II (1088–1099), and Prince Álmos stood on the side of his adversary, German King and Emperor Henry IV, and thus continued in the policy which his uncle Ladislas I initiated in 1092. The pope expressed great joy over Coloman's rule in a letter from 27 July 1096: *We felt indescribable joy upon hearing that Your Lordship by order of Almighty God began to rule the Hungarian land.*[64] In this same year, after the defeat of the Crusaders in Hungary, Henry IV sent a letter to *Álmos, celebrated prince and venerated friend,* in which he appealed to him to convince his brother Coloman to attack Bavarian Duke Welf IV (1070–1077, 1096–1101), a papal follower and Henry's enemy, who held in captivity relatives of the Salzburg anti-archbishop Berthold (1085–1106), installed by the emperor, and other of the emperor's followers.[65] Henry's appeal was unrealistic. Álmos certainly had no intention to get Coloman on the emperor's side. He well knew that he could not take this proposal to his brother.

At the beginning of 1097 Coloman defeated in the *Gozd* mountains (Gvozd, today the Velika Kapela), which formed the border between Slavonia and Croatia, Croatian King Peter, who died in the battle.[66] In this same year Byzantine Emperor Alexios II entrusted Venice, which he considered as his vassal, with the defence of the Dalmatian towns and islands.[67] Coloman acknowledged the claim of Venetian Doge Vitale I Michiel (1095–1102) to Dalmatia and Croatia and concluded an alliance with him.[68]

---

[64]   *DHA I*, ed. Györffy, no. 109, pp. 317–318.
[65]   *DHA I*, ed. Györffy, no. 112, pp. 322–323.
[66]   *Iste quoque in regnum Dalmatiae misso exercitu occidi fecit regem Petrum, qui Hungaris in montibus, qui Gozd dicitur, occurrens est devictus in montibus memoratis et occisus. Unde iidem montes usque hodie in Hungarico Patur Gozdia nominatur. Sedes enim huius regis et solium in Tenen* (= Knin) *erat civitate. Simonis de Keza Gesta Hungarorum* II 64, SRH I, p. 182. *Ipse Dalmacie regnum occiso suo rege Petro nominato in montibus Petergozdia Hungarie adiunxit. Chron. Hung. comp. saec. XIV.* II 152, SRH I, p. 433. Klaić, *Povijest Hrvata*, pp. 507–512.
[67]   Klaić, *Povijest Hrvata*, pp. 520–521.
[68]   *DHA I*, ed. Györffy, no. 115, p. 327. *Simonis de Keza Gesta Hungarorum* II 64, SRH I, pp. 182–183. *Chron. Hung. comp. saec. XIV.* II 152, SRH I, p. 433.

Immediately after the victory over Peter, Coloman (still in the spring of this same year) married the daughter of Norman-Sicilian Count Roger I, a most faithful papal ally. In 1101 sons Ladislas and Stephen were born to Coloman.[69]

The first rupture between Coloman and Álmos was the result of mutual suspicion of one another. In 1098 the armies of both adversaries met near Várkony on the Tisza. Coloman stood on the right bank of the river and Álmos on the left, in Biharia. The angry brothers had to reconcile, because both Hungarian armies refused to battle one another. Hungarian magnates proposed to Coloman and Álmos: *We see no reason for a battle, but if they like fighting, then let them fight one another alone, and he who triumphs we will recognize as our monarch.*[70]

At the beginning of May 1099 Coloman marched with 8-thousand soldiers at the request of Kiev Prince Sviatopolk against Prince Volodar in Peremyšľ (today Przemyśl (1092–1124) and Vasilko in Terebovľ (before 1091–1124), who in the battle at Rožňa defeated Sviatopolk and wanted to secede from Kiev. Coloman began to lay siege to Peremyšľ. Then Volhyn Prince David (1086–1097), whom Sviatopolk had exiled from Volhyn Volodymyr to Poland two years before, returned and led the Cumans. The Cumans attacked the Hungarian camp near Peremyšľ at night. Half of Coloman's army died in the battle and the subsequent retreat.[71]

In May 1099 Coloman came to Lučské pole, to the Olšava River, which then formed the Moravian-Hungarian border. Here he met with Bohemian Prince Břetislav II, with whom he concluded peace and friendship on 29 May. Břetislav then asked Esztergom Archbishop Serafin to ordain as a priest Herman, a candidate for the title of Bishop of Prague. Also, the future deacon of the Prague chapter and Bohemian chronicler Cosmas went together with Herman to be ordained in Esztergom.[72]

In the spring of 1102 Doge Vitale I Michiel died, and Coloman ceased to pay regard to the claims of Venice in Dalmatia. In 1102 he entered Croatia and had himself crowned King of Croatia and Dalmatia in Biograd.[73]

---

69   Chron. Hung. comp. saec. XIV. II 146, SRH I, p. 426. Wertner, *Az Árpádok családi története*, pp. 217–222, 226–228. Klaić, *Povijest Hrvata*, pp. 510–511.

70   Chron. Hung. comp. saec. XIV. II 144, SRH I, pp. 422–423.

71   Chron. Hung. comp. saec. XIV. II 145, SRH I, pp. 423–426. Latopis Nestora 82, year 6605 (1097), 83, year 6607 (1099), MPH I, ed. Bielowski, pp. 801–806. Annales Posonienses ad a. 1100, SRH I, p. 126.

72   *Cosmae Pragensis Chronica Boemorum* III 9, ed. Bretholz, p. 169. Třeštík, *Kosmova kronika*, pp. 42–43.

73   DHA I, ed. Györffy, no. 116, pp. 328–330. Thomas Spalatensis archidiaconus, *Historia Salonitana* 17, ed. Rački, p. 58. Gombos, *Catalogus III*, p. 2225. Klaić, *Povijest Hrvata*, pp. 513–517. MT I/2, p. 951.

On 11 August 1104 Álmos married Predslava, the daughter of Kiev Prince Sviatopolk II Izjaslavich (1093–1113).[74] Three children were born to Álmos and Predslava: Adelaide, Béla and Hedwig. The oldest, Adelaide, married Znojmo (1113/1115–1123 and future Bohemian 1125–1140) Prince Soběslav I. They wed shortly before Soběslav was deposed from Znojmo in March 1123, that is at the beginning of 1123 or earlier in 1122. Adelaide could have been born sometime in the years 1105–1107, and she died on 15 September 1140.[75] Béla was born in 1108, and in 1128 or 1129 he married Helena, daughter of Grand Count Uroš I of Raška. He died on 13 February 1141.[76] The youngest, Hedwig, married Margrave Adalbert III in 1132.[77] If she married 10 years later than Adelaide, then she could have been perhaps about 10 years younger.

9 Disputes of Álmos with Coloman

Álmos, as the Prince of Nitria, was according to old custom to inherit Coloman's royal throne. However, Coloman had two sons. Stephen was more capable than the equally old Ladislas, who died in 1112. Like his father, he, too, stood out with his intelligence. When Stephen ascended to the throne in 1116, *he was still a minor, his* (father's) *spirit was in his hands*,[78] that is, he inherited his wisdom from his father. Coloman decided to secure the kingdom early for Stephen. He did this in the usual way, having Stephen crowned as his co-ruler. This coronation of Stephen in 1105 could have been the reason for the new antagonism that arose between Coloman and Álmos. The coronation of the 4-year-old Stephen initiated a similar history as Andrew I started in 1058 with the coronation of his 5-year-old son Solomon. The claim of Prince Álmos to the Hungarian crown after Coloman's death was equally legitimate as the claim of Prince Béla a half-century before.[79]

Álmos felt aggrieved, and in the summer of 1105 he fled out of fear of Coloman to Passau, to Emperor Henry IV. The emperor, however, was occupied with the rebellion of his son Henry; therefore, he could not intervene in Hungary on Álmos's behalf. In 1106 Álmos returned to Hungary, but he did not

---

74 *Latopis Nestora* 86, year 6612 (1104), MPH I, ed. Bielowski, p. 814. Wertner, *Az Árpádok családi története*, pp. 250–252.
75 Wertner, *Az Árpádok családi története*, pp. 286–288.
76 Wertner, *Az Árpádok családi története*, pp. 295–297.
77 Wertner, *Az Árpádok családi története*, p. 293.
78 *Erat enim adhuc inpubes, sed spiritus eius in manibus eius. Chron. Hung. comp. saec. XIV.* II 153, SRH I, p. 434.
79 See pp. 440–447.

THE LAST PRINCES (1077–1108)   481

agree with the king. He then fled to Poland, to his brother-in-law Boleslaw III Wrymouth (1102–1138), *and returned to Hungary encouraged by the seditious orders of Poles and Hungarians and with their help*. With a Polish army and supported by domestic backers, Álmos penetrated up to Abaújvár. He occupied this castle, but after the arrival of Coloman and a brief siege, both brothers reconciled. Coloman then made peace with the Polish prince and an agreement on mutual military support. Thus, Álmos lost an ally.[80] In the following year Álmos set off on a pilgrimage to Jerusalem.[81]

Prince Álmos took care of the partial stone reconstruction of the wooden abbey at Szentjobb (today Sîniob) in Biharia, which had been founded (sometime between 1083–1093) by King Ladislas.[82] In addition, he founded and endowed two abbeys. On the eastern edge of Biharia, close to the Transylvanian borders, he established Meszes Abbey[83] and in the south of neighbouring Nitria the provostal in Dömös.[84] Dömös Abbey lay on right bank of the Danube, on the edge of the Pilis Mountains, that is outside the territory of his principality. However, it didn't get property in Transdanubia but in Nitria. Álmos's son, later Hungarian King Béla II, confirmed in 1138 his father's donation of abbey properties and with serfs and bondsmen with various obligations toward the abbey: fishermen, winegrowers, peasants in the extramural settlements of Novohrad (Nógrad) and in the villages Belá, Chľaba, Domaša, Tana, Čepeľ, Uten and Mocsola, which lay from the mouth of the Ipeľ up to Komárno, all on the north side of the Danube.[85] Álmos's subsequent donation also lay in Nitria. Prince Álmos donated a court in the village of Nenince (*Nena*) in Hont County to

---

80   Chron. Hung. comp. saec. XIV. II 147, SRH I, pp. 426–427. *Inde rediens Bolezlaus cum rege Ungarorum Colomanno, super reges universos suo tempore degentes litterali scientia erudito, diem et locum colloquii collocavit, ad quem rex Ungarorum venire, timens insidias, dubitavit. Erat enim Almus, Ungarorum dux, tunc temporis de Ungaria profugatus, et a duce Bolezlao hospitalitatis gratia sustentatus. Postea tamen aliis inter se legationibus transmandatis, insimul convenerunt, et invicem discesserunt, perpetuis fraternitatibus et amicitiis confirmatis.* Galli Chronicon II 29, MPH I, ed. Bielowski, p. 448.
81   Chron. Hung. comp. saec. XIV. II 147, SRH I, p. 427. Legenda sancti Emerici ducis 6, SRH II, p. 456.
82   Györffy, ÁMF I, pp. 668–669.
83   *monasterio Almi ducis in honore sancte Margarete in Meches constructo*. Árpád-kori oklevelek, ed. Györffy, no. 32, p. 72. Codex diplomaticus Transsylvaniae. Diplomata, epistolae et alia instrumenta litteraria res Transsylvanas illustrantia I. 1023–1300. Ad edendum in regestis praeparavit et introductione notisque illustravit Sigismundus Jakó (Budapestini 1997), no. 10, pp. 125–126.
84   *Dux autem construxit monasterium de Demes*. Chron. Hung. comp. saec. XIV. II 148, SRH I, p. 427. Györffy, ÁMF IV, pp. 583, 588–589, 629–631.
85   CDES 1, ed. Marsina, no. 77, pp. 74–75.

Count Lampert, whose offspring Prodsa died without heirs, so that King Béla II could in 1135 donate it to the Bzovik Abbey.[86]

In the summer of 1108 Álmos invited Coloman to a ceremonial consecration of the Dömös Abbey. Coloman, however, learned from his courtiers that during the celebration he was to be the victim of an attack being prepared by Álmos. In order to escape a real or imaginary ambush, which was to await him upon visiting the abbey, he strengthened his protection. The angry king wanted to capture the prince, but the bishops and several magnates convinced him that this was only enemy's gossiping about the prince. They stood up for Álmos and the two reconciled. The king and the prince confirmed their mutual peace with an oath. Then the king, as a sign of respect, assigned two ministerials (*iobagiones*) to the prince, and in peace they sent him hunting to the Bakon Forest. He secretly ordered both of Álmos's new guides to find out his intentions and to report to him so that he could prepare a scheme against him. When the prince came to the village Csór (*Chour*, in the Bakon Forest, west of Székesfehérvár), he released his falcon, which caught a crow: *Here the prince said to the ministerials: Whether that crow would promise the falcon that if he released him he would no longer caw? To this they replied that the falcon will not release the crow even on an oath, and he would not even allow the crow to make an oath, because it was an animal without reason.* Álmos thus expressed that he will never give up his claim to the royal crown, just as the crow will never stop cawing even if bound by an oath to do so. That same night the two ministerials notified the king of Álmos's words. The prince during the hunt distanced himself from his train and again fled to Passau.[87]

In Passau Álmos asked German King Henry V (1105–1125, from 1111 emperor) and the German dukes present regarding protection and help: *Álmos ..., bereft of things, as well as a principality (ducatu), by which he stood out among the Hungarians ..., came to King Henry and ... crying poverty, tried to impress on the magnates of the Roman empire for assuring and defence of his affairs.*[88] Álmos

---

86 *Quintum vero predium in villa Nena, quod Almus dux comiti Lamperto dedit, defuncto Prodsa cuius predium erat sine herede.* CDES I, ed. Marsina, no. 74, pp. 70–72.

87 *Chron. Hung. comp. saec. XIV.* II 148, SRH I, pp. 427–429. On 4 July 1108 Henry V was still in Goslar, where he issued a document for the Paulinzelle Abbey. Friedrich Hausmann, *Reichskanzlei und Hofkapelle unter Heinrich V. und Konrad III.* (Stuttgart 1956), pp. 16, 64. On 6 September 1108 Henry was already in Tulln. See note 92. If Henry was in Goslar on 4 July and in Tulln on 6 September, then in Passau, where Álmos came to him, he stayed some time in between, that is in the summer of 1108. The meeting of Coloman with Álmos in Dömös, the following Álmos's hunting trip in the Bakon Forest and Álmos's fleeing from the Balkon Forest to Passau played out through the summer of 1108.

88 Ekkehardus Uraugiensis, *Chronicon universale* ad a. 1108, Gombos, *Catalogus II*, p. 872.

had success with the German king.[89] Henry, who followed with displeasure Coloman's military advance in Dalmatia, close to the seaside borders of his own realm, very willingly complied with Álmos[90] and declared war against Coloman.[91]

On 6 September 1108 the German king was in Tulln, where he assembled a large military campaign.[92] The endangered Coloman turned to his Polish ally Boleslaw III Wrymouth and agreed with him on a common approach. If Henry were to attack Hungary, the Poles promised to attack Henry's Bohemian allies. If Henry attacked Poland, then the Hungarian king was to attack Henry's Bohemian allies.[93] Shortly after, in the middle of September 1108, Henry *set off with a massive army on behalf of Prince Álmos and came to the borders of Hungary*, where he began a siege of Bratislava.[94]

10   The Siege of Bratislava

On 29 September, in the military camp near Bratislava, Henry issued a donation for the Bamberg bishop. Witnesses to the donation were the most important participants in the campaign: the archbishop of Cologne, bishops from Münster, Halberstadt, Hildesheim, Naumburg, Regensburg, Freising, Passau, Eichstädt and Augsburg, Bavarian Duke Welf, Swabian Duke Frederick,

---

89 *Ottonis episcopi Frisigensis Chronica sive Historia de duabus civitatibus* VII 13, paraverat Adolf Hofmeister, curavit Walther Lammers (Berlin 1960), pp. 520–521. *Chronica Coloniensis* (*Annales maximi Coloniensis*) *cum continuationibus in Monasteri s. Pantaleonis scriptis aliisque historiae Coloniensis monumentis partim ex Monumentis Germaniae recusa* ad a. 1108, recensuit Georgius Waitz, Scriptores rerum Germanicarum in usum scholarum ex Monumentis Germaniae historicis recusi (Hannoverae 1880), p. 48.
90 Ekkehardus Uraugiensis, *Chronicon universale* ad a. 1108, Gombos, *Catalogus II*, p. 872.
91 *Ottonis episcopi Frisigensis Chronica* VII 13, par. Hofmeister, cur. Lammers, pp. 520–521.
92 Brunner, *Österreichische Geschichte 907–1156*, pp. 360, 485.
93 Coloman joined with Boleslaw III Wrymouth against the Bohemians and Germans in September 1108. DHA I, ed. Györffy, no. 132, pp. 360–361. *Galli Chronicon* II 46, MPH I, p. 457.
94 *Chron. Hung. comp. saec. XIV.* II 150, SRH I, pp. 429–430. The Hungarian chronicler mistakenly dated Henry's campaign against Hungary. Instead of the correct year of M°C°VIII° he wrote the incorrect date of M°C°XIII° (instead of the correct number V he mistakenly wrote an X). All foreign chroniclers have the correct year of 1108. Ekkehardus Uraugiensis, *Chronicon universale* ad a. 1108, Gombos, *Catalogus II*, p. 872. *Annales S. Disibodi* ad a. 1108, Gombos, *Catalogus I*, p. 124. Annalista Saxo, *Chronicon*, Gombos, *Catalogus I*, pp. 224–225. *Ottonis episcopi Frisigensis Chronica* VII 13, par. Hofmeister, cur. Lammers, pp. 520–521. *Chronica regia Coloniensis* ad a. 1108, rec. Waitz, p. 48. *Annales Hildesheimenses* ad a. 1108, cont. Waitz, p. 58. *Galli Chronicon* II 45, MPH I, ed. Bielowski, p. 457.

Margrave Liutpold of the Eastern March, Dietbold of Nordgau and Engelberd of Istria, Counts Wiprecht of Groitzsch, Hermann of Winzenburg, Louis of Thuringia, Berengar of Sulzbach, Otto of Habsburg, Friedrich of Tengling, Adalbert of Bogen, Otto of Regensburg, Gottfried of Calwa and others.[95]

While Henry laid siege to Bratislava, Bohemian Prince Svatopluk, together with his younger brother, Olomouc Prince Otto II the Black, sacked Slovak territory up the Váh, from its mouth in the Danube up to Trenčín in the north, and they didn't miss even a number of properties belonging to Zobor Abbey lying there. He captured the watch and spies that Coloman had sent and commanded that they be blinded or have their noses cut off.[96] He then joined Henry in his camp beneath Bratislava. Then Coloman sent more than a thousand selected Hungarian warriors, who hid in the swamps and ambushed the unwatchful besiegers of Bratislava. Prince Svatopluk, however, discovered their place of cover and surprised them; he killed or captured them and took them to be tortured, and he left only a few of them to live for a large ransom. Then, still in September, Coloman's ally, Polish Prince Boleslaw Wrymouth, attacked Bohemia, accompanied by deposed Bohemian Prince Bořivoj II, and plundered there for three days. He then rapidly returned and hurtled through all of Poland to the north to deflect an invasion of the Pomeranians. Svatopluk was furious, but he could not revenge the Polish attack immediately, because the hopeless siege of Bratislava lasted still another month. Only then did Svatopluk, without having achieved any significant success, pull back from Hungary, and on 26 October he was back in Bohemia.[97]

After Svatopluk's departure, Henry also ended the war. The position of Henry's army beneath Bratislava was also threatened by the swollen waters of the Danube and the rising water of the surrounding swamps. Henry, *after a dour and fruitless siege of Bratislava (castri Bresburg)*,[98] reconciled with the failure of his campaign and by the end of October began to retreat.[99] Just before then King Henry reconciled King Coloman with Prince Álmos.[100] On 4 November Henry was already back in Passau.[101]

---

95 *DHA I*, ed. Györffy, no. 134, p. 363.
96 *Cosmae Pragensis Chronica Boemorum* III 25, ed. Bretholz, p. 188. *DHA I*, ed. Györffy, no. 142/I, p. 392. *CDES I*, ed. Marsina, no. 69, pp. 64–65. Richard Marsina, "Štúdie k slovenskému diplomatáru. K problematike najstarších zoborských listín," *Sborník Filozofickej fakulty Univerzity Komenského* 14 (1963), p. 147.
97 *Cosmae Pragensis Chronica Boemorum* III 22, ed. Bretholz, pp. 188–190.
98 Ekkehardus Uraugiensis, *Chronicon universale* ad a. 1108, Gombos, *Catalogus II*, p. 872.
99 *Ottonis episcopi Frisigensis Chronica* VII 13, par. Hofmeister, cur. Lammers, pp. 520–521.
100 *Chron. Hung. comp. saec. XIV.* II 150, *SRH I*, p. 430.
101 Henry confirmed the donation of Eppon of Windberg for the Abbey of St. Florian in Passau on 4 November 1108. *DHA I*, ed. Györffy, no. 135, p. 364.

11 The Blinding of Álmos

Bohemian Prince Svatopluk immediately on the day following his return to Prague ordered the execution of Mutina, whom he accused of treason because he did not handle the defense of Bohemia against the recent incursions of the Poles. Together with him he also had the Vršovci family killed, whom he furiously despised.[102] Equally rapid as Svatopluk and without regard to the peace conditions, the angry Coloman also took action. After the departure of the German king from Hungary, Coloman decided to remove Álmos with finality; therefore, he did not return his principality to him.

In the autumn of 1108 the antagonism between the two Árpád brothers reached a peak. Henry and Svatopluk's campaign into Hungary was the worse thing that Álmos could have done to Coloman. At the end of October Coloman, before the German king, pretended to reconcile with Álmos, and only when Henry was beyond the Hungarian borders, he took his revenge on Álmos without hesitation: *Confirming the peace, however, the king nevertheless captured only the prince and his son, young Béla, and had them blinded. He also gave orders that the infant Béla should be castrated. But the man who was instructed to blind them feared God and the sterility of the royal line, and therefore he castrated a dog and brought its testicles to the King. Among the nobles of the country he also had Uros, Vata and Paul blinded.*[103] This act was not only on the conscience of King Coloman but also some counts, *on whose advise to have the prince and his son blinded, who was torn from the womb of his mother.* The Hungarian chronicle named three of them: Mark, son of Simon, Jakov, son of Achilles, and Benedict, son of Boto.[104]

Álmos's son Béla, whom *they took from the womb of his mother*, lost his sight before he could even speak. They blinded him *very young (infantulum)*. He could have only been a few months old, perhaps half a year at the time. If Álmos's son Béla was only several months old and not yet speaking at the end of October (or the beginning of November) 1108, when they blinded him, he must have been born in that same year. Coloman sent the blinded Álmos to the monastery at Dömös.[105]

Shortly after Henry's departure from Hungary Coloman got revenge on Svatopluk, too. When he pillaged Svatopluk's country, he certainly didn't leave

---

102 *Cosmae Pragensis Chronica Boemorum* III 22–24, ed. Bretholz, pp. 188–193. *Galli Chron.* II 46, MPH I, ed. Bielowski, p. 457. Annalista Saxo, *Chronicon* ad a. 1108, Gombos, *Catalogus I*, p. 225.
103 *Chron. Hung. comp. saec. XIV.* II 150, SRH I, p. 430.
104 *Chron. Hung. comp. saec. XIV.* II 142, 151, SRH I, pp. 421, 431.
105 *Chron. Hung. comp. saec. XIV.* II 150, SRH I, p. 430.

the dangerous Álmos behind him and certainly he harmed him still before leaving Hungary. When Coloman ravaged Moravia at the beginning of November, Álmos and Béla had already been blinded. Coloman thus had Álmos and Béla blinded shortly after the departure of Henry's campaign and before he himself invaded Moravia.[106]

[106] In 1113, the date given by the Hungarian chronicler for Henry's campaign into Hungary and thus also the blinding of Álmos and Béla, which followed immediately after Henry marched back from Hungary, is erroneous. See note 94. The chronicler also mistakenly put Coloman's death in 1114. Gyula Pauler considered the difference of one year, which should have passed between Álmos's blinding and Coloman's death, as correct. Therefore, he modified not only the year of Coloman's death from the incorrect 1114 to the correct 1116, but he also shifted the dating of Álmos's blinding by two years from the incorrect year of 1113 to the even more incorrect 1115. Pauler, *A magyar nemzet története I*, p. 224. In 1115 Béla was already 7 years old; therefore, he was not a toddler then and *torn from his mother's womb*. The antagonism of Coloman and Álmos reached its climax in the autumn of 1108. Why would Coloman wait until 1115 for his revenge, when the antagonsim climaxed in 1108?

CHAPTER 19

Árpád Nitria – Hungarian and Slavic

1   Nitria and Hungary

Árpád Hungary was a Magyar-Slavic state. To what extent did Hungary and primarily Nitria belong to the Slavic world? Did contemporaries perceive Árpád Nitria differently from the rest of the Hungarian state?

In 1003 Hungarian King Stephen deposed and took captive Transylvanian Prince Gyula II: *Ultimately, when Gyula was an enemy and several times meddlesome to the Hungarians living in Pannonia, he was taken by King Saint Stephen to Pannonia (in Pannoniam).*[1] In another place the Hungarian chronicler again repeats: *Saint King Stephen captured Prince Gyula with his wife and his two sons and sent them to Hungary (in Hungariam).*[2] Simon of Kéza writes the same: *Namely, Saint King Stephen ... captured his uncle Gyula with his wife and his two sons and brought them from Transylvania to Hungary (de Septem Castris in Hungariam) and connected Transylvania to Pannonia.*[3] In 1085 the Pechenegs marched through northern Transylvania and *broke through the barriers near the upper part of the Meszes Gates, rushed into Hungary and mercilessly despoiled the whole province of Nyírség up to Bihar Castle.*[4]

Gyula got to Hungary only after leaving Transylvania, and the Pechenegs entered into Hungary only after crossing the Transylvania-Biharia border at the Meszes Gates. Thus, Hungary existed in a narrow sense of the word, of which Biharia was a part but Transylvania was not. The natural mountain border, the marginal position and historical and ethnic differences ensured for Transylvania the position of an attached country, different from the rest of Hungary, even after Gyula was deposed.

A donation for Hronský Beňadik Abbey from 1075 mentions extensive abbey properties, first on the north side of the Danube and then in the Tisza River region. The properties in the Tisza River region were *in Meler, Sapi, Pelu, Sagi, Alpar, Chonu et Fizeg*. The villages Millér and Pelli were in the Szolnok county; Sáp, Ság, Alpár and Csany in the Csongrád county; and Füzegy was on the

---

[1] *Chron. Hung. comp. saec. XIV.* II 30, SRH I, p. 291.
[2] *Chron. Hung. comp. saec. XIV.* II 65, SRH I, pp. 314–315.
[3] *Simonis de Keza Gesta Hungarorum* II 43, SRH I, p. 172.
[4] *Superiori parte porte Mezes ruptis indaginibus in Hungariam totamque provinciam Nyr usque civitatem Byhor crudeliter depredantes. Chron. Hung. comp. saec. XIV.* II 102, SRH I, p. 366.

middle flow of the Zagyva in southern Novohrad (Nógrad). From the viewpoint of the abbey, which lay in the territory of Nitria and prepared this document, and from the viewpoint of its founder and donor, Hungarian King Géza I, who until recently was the Prince of Nitria, the mentioned Tisza River region properties lay *in Hungary (in Hungaria)*. Thus, not only did Transylvania lay outside of this actual Hungary, but so did the territory to the north of the Danube, that is Nitria.[5]

Nitrian Prince Géza, his brother Ladislas, and their ally Olomouc Prince Otto I left a military camp on the territory of Nitria before mid-March 1074 and came through Vác and Cinkota to Mogyoród, where on 14 March they destroyed the army of Hungarian King Solomon: *Then Princes Géza and Ladislas with their armies entered into Székesfehérvár ... they settled in Hungary.*[6] Nitria, from where the princes departed before the battle, thus did not belong to actual Hungary, in which the victorious princes settled. However, Biharia, which fell into Solomon's hands after the battle near Kemej at the end of February 1074, did belong to this actual Hungary.

2   Nitria and Biharia

Of the two Hungarian principalities, Nitria was more important than Biharia. Nitrian Prince Géza was older than his brother, Biharian Prince Ladislas. When in 1074 Géza became king, Ladislas got the Nitrian Principality, and the youngest brother Lampert became the Prince of Biharia. The older of the two appanaged princes had Nitria, and Biharia was left to the younger, who remained subordinate. The older of the two princes, and at the same time of the entire princely third, was the Nitrian Prince. That's why Nitrian Prince Géza, in addition to the Nitrian army, also had command over the army of the entire princely third, that is including Ladislas's Biharian army. Likewise, when Ladislas

---

5 *DHA I*, ed. Györffy, no. 73/II, p. 218. *CDES I*, ed. Marsina, no. 58, p. 57. Richard Marsina, "Štúdie k slovenskému diplomatáru 1. Druhá časť: Obdobie od roku 1000 do roku 1235," *Historické štúdie* 18 (1973), pp. 57–60. Ľubomír Juck, "Majetky hronskobeňadického opátstva do roku 1235," *Historické štúdie* 18 (1973), pp. 121–147. Thus, there was a difference between Hungary as a whole and actual or narrower Hungary, to which Nitria and Transylvania did not belong. From the taking over of Moravia by the Bohemians in 1029 there was a similar difference between the whole Bohemian state and the Bohemians. The feeling of differentness of Slovak territory from the rest of Hungary remained even after the extinction of the Nitrian Principality. Peter Ratkoš, "Otázky vývoja slovenskej národnosti do začiatku 17. storočia," *Historický časopis* 20 (1972), no. 1, pp. 39–40, 49–50.

6 *Porro duces Geysa et Ladizlaus cum exercitu Albam veniunt ... habitabant in Hungaria.* Chron. Hung. comp. saec. XIV. II 124, *SRH I*, p. 394.

became the Nitrian Prince, his brother, Biharian Prince Lampert, was subordinate to him. The Biharian princes remained in the shadow of the Nitrian princes, to whom the Hungarian chroniclers devoted much greater attention.

Princes Béla and Géza minted coins. Béla ruled in Nitria and in Biharia. Géza was only the Prince of Nitria. Géza's younger brother, Biharian Prince Ladislas, did not mint coins. The minting of princely coins is thus a clear connection with Béla and Géza's rule in Nitria. Princely coins were minted by the older and more important of the two princes. Ladislas, who ruled in Nitria for only three years, did not continue in minting coins.

3   The Nitrians

The *inhabitants (incolae)* of Nitria were *provincionales*, that is residents of the nine Nitria provinces (castle counties), which in September 1042 through *sent representatives (missa legatione)* negotiated with German King Henry III. Mainly their highest representatives, that is the castle counts, appeared before the victorious German king. Henry on the advice of his Bohemian ally Břetislav I satisfied their request and consented that the Árpád Domoslav, who came to Nitria along with Břetislav, become the new Prince of Nitria.[7]

The free inhabitants of the Nitrian Principality, that is the castle inhabitants of the nine counties of Nitria, selected from among themselves the soldiers of the princely army. The prince assembled his army undoubtedly the same as the king: *If sometimes the king wanted to lead an army, all without opposition go as one body. The peasants who live in the villages, however, they supply nine of ten or also seven of eight (novem decimum, vel etiam septem octavum), or less, as is needed, with all the equipment for war, others remain home to plough the fields.* In addition to the equipped castle armies, the kings and princes are surrounded by a retinue of professional warriors: *Those, however, who are from the military retinue (de militum ordine), presume to remain at home only in a very serious case.*[8]

---

[7] See pp. 257–258. In 1042 9 Nitria counts accepted Domoslav as the Prince of Nitra, just as in 1102 12 Croatian counts received Hungarian King Coloman as the Croatian king. *XII nobiles sapienciores de XII tribubus Chrouacie* had the title *comes*, that is count. Thomas Spalatensis archidiaconus, *Historia Salonitana* 17, ed. Rački, p. 58. Gombos, *Catalogus III*, p. 2225.

[8] *Ottonis episcopi Frisigensis et Rahewini Gesta Frederici seu rectius Cronica*, ed. Franz-Josef Schmale (Berlin 1965), pp. 194–195. Kučera, *Slovensko po páde Veľkej Moravy*, pp. 362–364. One of the decrees which Coloman issued around year 1100 differentiated the castle counties, more exactly castle districts (provinces) royal and princely. A prince had *in mega ducis* the same rights as a king had *in mega regis*. A prince equally as a king had a prepared military

The 15-thousand strong Hungarian army, which at the beginning of July 1167 marched against Byzantium, was made up of one unit of the royal elite forces and 36 castle units.[9] Hungary then had 72 castle counties; thus half of the Hungarian military went into the battle. If the royal heavy cavalry was only several hundred in numbers, then each of the 36 castle counties had to send to the 15-thousand strong army an average of 400 soldiers or a few less. If one castle unit in 1167 had about 400 soldiers, then a century before, with a somewhat smaller number of inhabitants and with the various sizes and populations of the castle counties, it could have had some 300 to 400 soldiers.[10] If one castle county could equip 300 to 400 armed men for war, then the 9 Nitria counties could put together approximately 3-thousand soldiers. If this was approximately one-tenth to one-eighth of the battle capabilities of the Nitria inhabitants who fought and ploughed the fields because they were peasants and soldiers both, then after calculating those who could not set off for war, or work in the fields, that is children, women, minors and the elderly, as well as non-free men without military obligations, then Árpád Nitria could have had a population of approximately 200-thousand inhabitants.[11]

---

horse in each of his own castle counties. This *megalis equus exercitualis*, mentioned in another of Coloman's decrees, belonged to the four military horses, which each castle county bred and on the command of the king sent to war. *Colomanni regis decretorum liber primus* XII, XXXVI. *A Szent István, Szent László és Kálmán korabeli törvények és zsinati határozatok forrásai (Függelék: a törvények szövege)*, írta Levente Zavodszky (Budapest 1904), pp. 185, 188. Kristó, *A XI. századi hercegség*, pp. 83–84. Kučera, *Slovensko po páde Vel'kej Moravy*, p. 121.

9   Ioannes Kinnamos 29, in *Az Árpád-kori magyar történet bizánci forrásai*, ed. Moravcsik, p. 242.

10 Kristó, *A vármegyék*, pp. 159–160, 204–205. Attila Zsoldos, *A szent király szabadjai. Fejezetek a várjobbágyság történetéből* (Budapest 1999), pp. 48, 103. The Nitrian prince had *ten legions*, with which in February 1042 he crossed the Hungarian border and attacked the Eastern March: *Hostium autem, ut comperimus, decem legiones fuerunt, quae in tres partes divisae sunt*. *Ann. Altah. maior.* ad a. 1042, rec. Oefele, p. 30. See pp. 424–425, see chapter 16, note 35. The Nitrian princely army could not have had up to ten thousand soldiers, because we cannot understand legions in this case as large army units with thousands of soldiers but divisions with 300 to 400 soldiers. These were military divisions of 9 Nitria counties and one division of the princely elite cavalry unit.

11 3-thousand × 10 = 30-thousand battle capable. 30-thousand × 3 = 90-thousand men, boys and older men. 90-thousand × 2 = 180-thousand men, women and children and elderly. If we count non-free men, without military obligations, then we get approximately 200-thousand inhabitants of Nitria. This was perhaps a fifth of the inhabitants of Hungary, because in the 11th century Hungary had about 1 million people. György Györffy, "Magyarország népessége a honfoglalástól a XIV. század közepéig," in *Magyarország történeti demográfiája*, ed. József Kovacsics (Budapest 1963), pp. 45–62. The estimate of György Györffy very well corresponds with the 43 castle counties which Hungary had in the

If the soldiers from the entire territory of the Nitrian Principality, from all of its castle counties, served *in the Nitrian army (in nitriensi agmine)*,[12] then all the residents who lived *on Nitrian territory (in nitriensi territorio)*,[13] from which they were conscripted, we can calmly name Nitrians, and we are entitled to assume that they really had such a name.[14]

The Nitrians (Nitrienses), who in August and September of 1074 were prepared to defend the main castle of their principality not only against the deposed Hungarian King Solomon,[15] but also against his ally, German King Henry IV, who marched *with a large army* through Nitria,[16] they could not have come only from Nitra itself or among the castle residents of Nitra County, but they certainly came to Nitra from other castle counties of the Nitrian Principality. These were the same Nitrian soldiers with which Prince Géza in March of this same year, together with Ladilsas's Biharians and Otto's Moravians, defeated King Solomon, and whose descendants in June 1096 destroyed Folkmar's Crusader army near Nitra.

4   Moesia and the Moesians

Hungarian King Ladislas I was according to the intitulation of his own document from 1091 not only king of the Hungarians, but also of Moesia: *L[adislas]*

---

second half of the 11th century. Moravia had in the mid-11th century about 230-thousand and Bohemia about 450-thousand inhabitants. Žemlička, *Čechy v době knížecí*, p. 18.

12   *Chron. Hung. comp. saec. XIV.* II 121, SRH I, p. 389. See p. 458.
13   *Legenda SS. Zoerardi et Benedicti* 1, SRH II, p. 357. See chapter 15, note 49.
14   During the siege of Belgrade in 1071 *Count Vid with his Bács soldiers (comes Vid cum Bachiensibus militibus eos)* also fought. In the battle with the Pechenegs beneath Belgrade *divisions of Sopronians, led by a count by the name of John (agmina Suproniensium, quorum rector erat comes Ian nomine)*, were recorded. He *(Hic)*, however, *courageously overpowered the attack of the Pechenegs and did so with the Sopronians (cum Supruniensibus). Chron. Hung. comp. saec. XIV.* II 105, SRH I, pp. 370–371. Bács Count Vid bragged: *The Bohemian* (= Moravian) *army certainly ... I with the Bácsians (ego cum Bachiensibus) very nearly met the danger of death. Chron. Hung. comp. saec. XIV.* II 119, SRH I, p. 386. Immediately at the beginning of the battle near Mogyoród, however, *Count Vid and the Bácsians (comes Vid et Bachienses)* were destroyed by the Moravians *(a Bohemis). Chron. Hung. comp. saec. XIV.* II 121, SRH I, p. 390. If Vid's Bács soldiers were *Bachienses* that is Bácsians and John's Sopron soldiers were *Supronienses*, that is Sopronians, then Géza's Nitrian army must have been *Nitrienses*, that is Nitrians. The fact that later Nitria was not only one county like Bács and Sopron, but a principality, further differentiates it historically and ethnically from the rest of Hungary.
15   See chapter 17, note 95.
16   See chapter 17, note 95.

Ungrorum ac Messie Dei gr[acia] rex. At the conclusion of this document three countries are mentioned in which he ruled, and among them again is Moesia: *in Ungaria et Messia et Sclauonia.*[17]

Moesia was also known in the older Passau tradition, as evidenced by Piligrim's three letters from the 970s. *Mesia*, on which Passau Bishop Piligrim (970–991) made a claim, was indicated as a former Great Moravian territory.[18] In the mid-13th century two works on the history of the Passau bishopric, the *Historia episcoporum Pataviensium et ducum Bavariae* and the *Historia Laureacensis*, write about Western Moesia (*Mesiae occidentales*), including, aside from Moravia and Bohemia, also the western part of Hungary south of the Drava River and east up the Tisza River.[19]

Hungarian chronicles again recall the Moesians, who together with other Pannonian nations remained after Attila's death in Pannonia, that is on the territory of later Hungary, and came under the rule of Svätopluk: *When the sons of Attila nearly died in the Krumhelt battle with the Scythian nation, Pannonia remained for ten years without a king, and the Slavs, Greeks, Germans, Moesians (Messiani) remained in it and the Vlachs, who served Attila during his life as his serfs, migrated in. Then Svatopluk, son of Morot, a former prince in Polonia* (=Pannonia), *who after subjugation of Bactria ruled the Bulgarians and the Moesians (Messiani), similarly seizing to rule after the eradication of the Huns in Pannonia.*[20] The chronicler's Moesians settled in Nitria, where Árpád's commander Lehel found them: *Lehel was then the leader of the sixth army. He originally lived around Hlohovec, expelled the Moesians and the Bohemians (Messianis et Boemis), and settled in the end more often in the Nitrian lands (in partibus Nitriae).*[21]

The Hungarian chronicler wrote about the Moesians as about one of the nations of former Pannonia, that is Hungary. If he put them *in partibus Nittriae*, that is into Nitria, where the mentioned Hlohovec lay, he could thus only have

17   *DHA I*, ed. Györffy, no. 91, pp. 271–272.
18   *MMFH III*, Epistolae 113, 122, 131, pp. 246–250, 254–259, 273–278. *CDES I*, ed. Marsina, no. 4, 44, 45, pp. 6, 42, 45. Havlík, *Moesie*, pp. 8–9.
19   Havlík, *Moesie*, p. 8.
20   *Simonis de Keza Gesta Hungarorum* I 23, *SRH I*, p. 163. *Chron. Hung. comp. saec. XIV.* I 23, *SRH I*, pp. 280–281. *MMFH I*, pp. 277–278.
21   *Simonis de Keza Gesta Hungarorum* II 32, *SRH I*, pp. 166–167. *MMFH I*, pp. 279–280.
    A later Hungarian chronicler, who in the 14th century took and modified an older chronicler's text, mistakenly identified the Moesians with the Bohemians: *Messianos scilicet Bohemicos. Chron. Hung. comp. saec. XIV.* II 32, *SRH I*, pp. 291–292. *MMFH I*, pp. 279–280.

been labelling the Slavic Nitrians with this name. He did not put their allies the Bohemians into the list of domestic Pannonian nations, because he correctly considered them to be foreigners. The Moesians in the Hungarian chronicles are thus a domestic nation that settled on the territory of Nitria long before the arrival of the Magyars.

The Moesians, identical with the Slavic Nitrians, that is with the Slovaks, locate Ladislas's Moesia in Slovakia and identify it with Nitria. Moesia, in the intitulation of Ladislas I, again dates the chronicler's references to the Moesians to the period of his rule, that is to the 11th century. Nitria and the Nitrians thus in the period of origin of the old Hungarian Gesta at the end of the 11th century were not lost under the general name Pannonia and Pannonians for Hungary and the Hungarians, but together with the standing of Nitria as a special principality lying outside of Hungary itself, they had a particular name for it. Moesia, identified with Nitria, was the country of the Moesians, that is the Nitrians.

The labelling of nations with second names of ancient origin was an old and widespread custom: Czechs – Bohemians (Bohemi, Bohemani); Bavarians – Noricans; Germans – Germani; Hungarians – Pannonians; Pechenegs – Schythians. It is thus understandable, if in the 11th century the Nitrians were also called the *Messiani* (Moesians) and their country *Messia* (Moesia). After the extinction of the Nitrian Principality, the name Moesians ceased being used and was forgotten very quickly. That's why a hundred years later Anonymus did not call the residents of the Nitrian Principality (*de partibus Nitriae*) together with the allied Bohemians the *Messiani et Boemi*, but gave preference for the naming *Sclavi et Boemi*, that is the Slavs (Slovaks) and the Bohemians.[22]

Slavonia (*Sclavonia*), that is a Slavic country, which the chronicler's report on the events of 1091 and Ladislas's document from this same year both mention,[23] was the whole Croatian kingdom from the Adriatic Sea up to the Drava River, which King Ladislas had then seized.[24] Ladislas's document from 1091 mentions Slavonia as a country that belongs to King Ladislas and like Moesia lay outside of actual Hungary. Ladislas's royal intitulation in the introduction of this letter does not include Slavonia, and in the list of three of Ladislas's countries it is after Moesia. Moesia, that is Nitria, was thus more significant for the Hungarian king than the newly attached Slavonia, that is Croatia.

---

22   *Anonymi (P. magistri) Gesta Hungarorum* 33–37, SRH I, pp. 74–80.
23   See note 17, see chapter 18, note 27.
24   See chapter 18, note 27.

5 Árpád Nitria and Přemyslid Moravia, the Nitrians and the Moravians

Árpád Nitria was similar to Přemyslid Moravia in many ways. Cosmas clearly differentiated Moravia from Bohemia, sometimes even the Moravian army from the Bohemian army, and he at least sometimes called the appanaged princes the Princes of Moravia. Bohemian Prince Břetislav I in August of 1040 handed over *all the cohorts which were from Moravia (tote cohorti, que fuit de Moravia)*, and with the auxiliary Hungarian army under the command of Prkoš, the administrator of Castle Bílina.[25] In May of 1082 Leopold II, Margrave of the Eastern March, antagonized *diarcham Moravie*, that is the ruler of half of Moravia, Brno and Znojmo Prince Conrad, and did so to a such measure that open war broke out. Conrad's brothers, Bohemian Prince Vratislaus II and Olomouc Prince Otto I the Fair also took part in the wars: *Prince Vratislaus marched with the Bohemians and together with the Germans who were from the Regensberg bishopric, from the other side joined Otto and Conrad with all of his own, who are warriors for all of Moravia (cum suis omnibus, qui sunt in tota Moravia militibus)*.[26] In 1087 Olomouc Prince Otto I died. Cosmas on this occasion called him the *Prince of Moravia*, because he had to differentiate him from Bohemian Prince Vratislaus II: *In that year, on 9 June, died Otto, prince of Moravia (dux Moravie), brother of Vratislaus, prince of Bohemia.*[27] When Hungarian King Coloman in November 1108 *invaded Moravia (invasisse Moraviam)*, Bohemian Prince Svatopluk *immediately took both the army of the Bohemians and the Moravians (utrumque exercitum Boemie atque Moravie)*, in order to lead them into battle.[28] After the death of Bohemian Prince Svatopluk, who was the victim of an attack on 21 September 1109, the proposal for the selection of his brother, Olomouc Prince Otto II the Black as the new Bohemian prince sounded out in Svatopluk's military camp. *All who were from Moravia (universi, qui erant de Moravia)* wanted Otto as the Bohemian prince, namely *without the consent of the Bohemians and the bishop*. Otto was not successful in Prague, because the old vow still applied by which *all Bohemians* two years before, when they elected Prince Svatopluk, were bound that Svatopluk's successor would be his cousin Vladislas.[29] At the end of 1123 Bohemian Prince Vladislas I and Olomouc Prince Otto II the Black *thus from Bohemia as well as*

---

25 *Cosmae Pragensis Chronica Boemorum* II 11, ed. Bretholz, pp. 98–99.
26 *Cosmae Pragensis Chronica Boemorum* II 35, ed. Bretholz, pp. 131–133.
27 *Cosmae Pragensis Chronica Boemorum* II 37, ed. Bretholz, p. 140.
28 *Cosmae Pragensis Chronica Boemorum* III 25, ed. Bretholz, pp. 194.
29 *Cosmae Pragensis Chronica Boemorum* III 27, ed. Bretholz, pp. 196–197.

from Moravia, taking the army (tam Boemie quam Moravie coadunato exercitu), rushed into the Margravate of Meissen.[30]

The Annals of Hradisko and Opatovice and three of Cosmas's continuers, that is Vyšehrad canon, a Sázava monk and Milevsko Abbot Jarloch, unlike Cosmas, did mention the Moravians. The Annals of Hradisko and Opatovice mention that the *Bohemians with the Moravians (Boemienses cum Moraviensibus)* invaded Poland in 1133. The *Moravians (Moravienses)* then attacked the Polish castle Koźle.[31] The Vyšehrad canon wrote that Poland was *often adversely plundered by the Bohemians, as well as the Moravians (a Bohemis nec non Moravis),* and in 1134 it was again sacked *by both mentioned armies, that is the Bohemians and the Moravians (utrisque supradictis ab exercitibus, Bohemis videlicet et Moravis).*[32] In 1142 the antagonism between Bohemian Prince Vladislas II and Znojmo Prince Conrad escalated into war: *... a mad quarrel broke out among the Bohemians, which divided them ... into two sides: the better and nobler side went for Conrad, the Moravian prince, but the lower and the younger remained by Vladislas.* Then, when part of Vladislas's Bohemian warriors ran over to Conrad, *the Moravians with the turncoat Bohemians (Moravienses cum profugis Bohemis) suddenly rebelled against Vladislas and his brothers Děpold and Jindřich and sent them with their whole army on the run.... Here the Bohemians, seeing the Moravians (Bohemi videntes Moravos) gaining predominance ..., sent everyone on the run ...*[33] The Sázava monk also recorded this event: *Count Načerat and other Bohemian leaders ganged up on Prince Vladislas and allied with the Moravians (et uniti Moraviensibus) and with great force hostilely attacked the Bohemians.*[34] The defeat of Bohemian Prince Vladislas *from the Moravians (a Moravicis)* in 1042 is also recalled by the Annals of Hradisko and Opatovice.[35] At that time a papal legate, Cardinal Guido, was visiting the Bohemian lands in order to negotiate peace between the battling sides. In 1143 Guido wrote to the pope that *the Moravians (Morauienses),* with whom he had met, *are under the Bohemian prince.*[36] Olomouc Prince Oldřich in 1174 endowed the Olomouc bishopric as *prince of the Moravians (dei gratia*

---

30   Cosmae Pragensis Chronica Boemorum III 53, ed. Bretholz, pp. 225–227.
31   Annales Gradicenses et Opatowicenses ad a. 1133, FRB II/1, ed. Emler, p. 395. Wihoda, Morava v době knížecí, pp. 203–204.
32   Canonici Wissegradensis continuatio Cosmae ad a. 1134, FRB II/1, ed. Emler, p. 217.
33   Canonici Wissegradensis continuatio Cosmae ad a. 1142, FRB II/1, ed. Emler, p. 235.
34   Monachi Sazawiensis continuatio Cosmae ad a. 1142, FRB II/1, ed. Emler, p. 261.
35   Annales Gradicenses et Opatowicenses ad a. 1142, FRB II/1, ed. Emler, p. 397.
36   Moravienses enim, qui tunc sunt sub duce Boemico. CDB I, ed. Friedrich, no. 135, p. 137. Wihoda, Morava v době knížecí, pp. 188–192, 199, 253, 257.

Morauorum dux).³⁷ Jarloch wrote that Bohemian Prince Soběslav and Znojmo Prince Conrad in 1176 *assembled all the people bound to their rule, namely the Bohemians and the Moravians (Bohemos scilicet et Morauos), high-bred and low-bred, warriors and peasants* and invaded Austria with them.³⁸

And Cosmas's contemporary, Polish chronicler Gallus Anonymus, wrote not only about Moravia and Moravian Prince Svatopluk but also about the Moravians. In the spring of 1103 Polish Prince Boleslaw III responded to the invasion of Olomouc Prince Svatopluk into Silesia from the start of the year and rushed two times into Moravia. The Polish army in March attacked *into Moravia (in Moraviam)* and pillaged it. *Moravian Prince Svatopluk (Swatopolc dux Moraviensis)* attacked the Poles, who carried away a wealth of quarry. *The Poles (Poloni)*, seeing that the *Moravians (Moravienses)* were resolved to fight, launched into a bloody battle with them. In the battle *Moravian Prince Svatopluk* in particular stood out. So many soldiers fell on both sides *that not even the Moravians (Moravienses) had a happy victory, and the Poles showed no signs of shame*. Shortly after Boleslaw himself invaded Moravia. He didn't cause any greater damage, however, because the population of the countryside hid with their livestock inside a fortress. He was not attacked *by the Bohemians and Moravians (Bohemis et Moraviensibus), although assembled*, and he returned to Poland. *The Moravians (Moravienses)* did not launch into open battle with the Polish army even on the journey back.³⁹ Five years later war again erupted for the Poles *with the Moravians (cum Moravis)*, who occupied the Polish border castle Ratibor. In the autumn of 1108 *the Moravians (Moravienses)* marched against the neighbouring Polish Koźle castle. The Polish army, which wanted to conquer Ratibor, met with the advancing enemies. In a sharp battle *with the Moravians (cum Moraviensibus)* the Poles triumphed. Many *Moravians (Moravienses)* fell in the battle, and Ratibor again got back into Polish hands.⁴⁰

Saxon chronicler Adam of Bremen knew that the rivers Oder and Elbe arose *in the deepest forest of the Moravians (in profundissimo saltu Marahorum)* and described the place of the Moravians between other nations: *The Moravians are a tribe of Slavs (Marahi sunt populi Sclavorum), who are to the east of the Bohemians and around whom they have from this side the Pomeranians and Poles, from the other side the Hungarians and the very cruel nation of the Pechenegs,*

---

37 *CDB I*, ed. Friedrich, no. 270, p. 238. Wihoda, *Morava v době knížecí*, p. 223.
38 *Boemos et Morauos, nobiles et ignobiles, milites et rusticos. Annales Gerlaci Milovicensis* ad a. 1176, *FRB II/2*, ed. Emler, p. 471. Wihoda, *Morava v době knížecí*, pp. 226, 257.
39 *Galli Chronicon* II 26, *MPH I*, ed. Bielowski, pp. 445–446.
40 *Galli Chronicon* II 45, *MPH I*, ed. Bielowski, p. 457.

who live by eating human flesh.[41] And another Saxon chronicler, Helmold, and Russian chronicler Nestor clearly differentiated the Moravians from the neighbouring Bohemians and from other Slavic nations.[42]

For Adam of Bremen, Helmold, Gallus Anonymus, Nestor, the author of the Annals of Hradisko and Opatovice, the canon of Vyšehrad, the monk of Sázava and Jarloch, the Moravians, even after the joining of Moravia to Bohemia, were still the Moravians. For Hungarian and Austrian chroniclers the Moravians were Bohemians. Bohemian chronicler Cosmas stood approximately halfway between both positions. He knew Moravia well, but never clearly mentioned the Moravians.

Nitria differed from the rest of Hungary approximately as much Moravia differed from Bohemia. In the years 1040[43] and 1074[44] an army of Nitrians fought completely divided from the Hungarian royal army, just as an army of Moravians battled in 1030,[45] 1040,[46] 1074,[47] 1103[48] and 1108[49] without the Bohemians. The Nitrian and Moravian princes also minted their own coins.[50] Moravia had its own Moravian bishopric, renewed in 1063,[51] while Nitria was a diocese of the Esztergom archbishopric,[52] which was originally a diocese of the extinct Nitria bishopric.[53] In Moravia lived Moravians and in Nitria the Nitrians.

Moravia, unlike Nitria, was not a single principality. The Přemyslids had the smallest state in Central Europe. All the Přemyslid appanaged princes, therefore, had to fit into little Moravia, which Břetislav I divided into two halves and

---

41 *Magistri Adam Bremensis Gesta Hammaburgensis ecclesiae Pontificum* II 22, Schol. 17, cur. Trillmich, pp. 254–255. *MMFH I*, p. 167.
42 See notes 58, 62.
43 See note 25.
44 See p. 458.
45 See pp. 417–418
46 See note 25.
47 See note 44.
48 See note 35.
49 See note 36.
50 Jan Šmerda, *Denáry české a moravské. Katalóg mincí českého státu od X. století do počátku XIII. Století* (Brno 1996), pp. 17–20, 96–125.
51 Novotný, *České dějiny I/2*, pp. 120–123. Žemlička, *Čechy v době knížecí*, pp. 98–99.
52 See pp. 520–521, 524–525.
53 Marsina, "Nitrianske biskupstvo," pp. 534–535. Marsina, "Začiatky cirkevnej organizácie na Slovensku," pp. 125–126. Richard Marsina, "O Nitrianskom biskupstve (Prečo nebolo obnovené biskupstvo v Nitre hneď začiatkom 11. storočia?)," in *Szomszédaink közöt Kelet-Európában. Emlékkönyv Niederhauser Emil 70. születésnapjára* (Budapest 1993), p. 29.

the western half further into two quarters.⁵⁴ Hungary was perhaps three-times larger than the Bohemian state. It was so large that it was not necessary to divide Nitria. The exact opposite occurred. In order for the princely appanage to achieve the required third, Nitria was connected with neighbouring Biharia.

6 The Slavs and Slavic Nitria

If Győr Bishop Hartvik wrote in his Saint Stephen legend that Stephen I *subjugated many nations (gentes) with God's help*,⁵⁵ then it was clear to him that Hungary from its origin was a multinational state. One of these Hungarian nations was also the Nitrians, who were counted both abroad and at home as Slavs or even considered as a component of a Slavic nation.

Merseburg Bishop Thietmar knew already at the beginning of the 11th century that Slavic languages were also spoken in Hungary. We can rely fully on his testimony, because he understood the Slavonic language quite well and his chronicle is a reliable source. He noticed that Hungarian Slavs did not always accept Hungarian or Tukish names of members of the Hungarian noble families and preferred to call them by a cogent Slavic name. Sarolt, wife of Hungarian Prince Géza, was *named in Slavic (Sclavonicae dicta)* Beleknegini, that is the Pretty Princess. They referred to her brother Gyula II, who after his departure from Transylvania in 1003 ended up directly among them in Nitria, as Prokuj.⁵⁶

---

54 *Cosmae Pragensis Chronica Boemorum* II 15, ed. Bretholz, p. 105. Novotný, *České dějiny* I/2, pp. 73, 79–80. Žemlička, *Čechy v době knížecí*, pp. 73–74, 110, 347–358.
55 *Legenda S. Stephani regis ab Hartvico episcopo conscripta* 9, SRH II, p. 414.
56 *Thietmari Chronicon* IX (VIII) 4 (3), rec. Kurze, p. 241. *Thietmari Chronicon* VIII 3, cur. Trillmich, pp. 442–445. Thietmar, Adam of Bremen and Helmold mention the Slavic language several times. Since Mereseburg Bishop Boso (968–970) had in his diocese many Slavs, *Sclavonica scripserat verba et eos kirieleison cantare rogavit exponens eis huius utilitatem. Thietmari Chronicon* II 37 (23), rec. Kurze, p. 42. *Thietmari Chronicon* II 37, cur. Trillmich, pp. 74–75. Emperor Otto I (973–983) had a soldier Henry, *qui Sclavonice Zolunta vocatur. Thietmari Chronicon* III 21 (12), rec. Kurze, p. 61. *Thietmari Chronicon* III 21, cur. Trillmich, pp. 108–109. The wife of Polish Prince Mieszko I was *Dobrawa enim Sclavonice dicebatur, quod Teutonico sermone Bona interpretatur. Thietmari Chronicon* IV 55 (35), rec. Kurze, p. 94. *Thietmari Chronicon* IV 55, cur. Trillmich, pp. 170–171. German King Henry II in September 1005 unfolded his tents on the bank of the river, *qui Pober* (= Bobrava) *dicitur Sclavonice, Castor Latine. Thietmari Chronicon* VI 26 (19), rec. Kurze, pp. 149. *Thietmari Chronicon* VI 26, cur. Trillmich, pp. 270–271. Impending Merseburg Bishop Thietmar on the road to Merseburg in September 1009 stopped at his court in Eisdorf, not far from Lützen: *Primoque ad curtem meam, Sclavonice Malacin dictam, Teutonice autem Egisvillam. Thietmari Chronicon* VI 42 (29) rec. Kurze, p. 159. *Thietmari Chronicon* VI 42,

A century later Russian chronicler Nestor wrote how the *Slavic nation* spread and split into several nations. First among them he mentioned the Danubian Slavs: *After a longer time the Slavs settled along the Danube, where Hungary and Bulgaria are now located.* He then writes about their history: *The Vlachs attacked the Danubian Slavs and settled among them.*[57] The Vlachs were replaced by the Magyars: *The Hungarians ... coming from the east, burst in through the large mountains which are called the Hungarian Mountains and they began to attack the Vlachs and Slavs living here. Because the Slavs settled here first. And the Vlachs took Slavic land. Then the Hungarians chased away the Vlachs and advanced through this country and settled here among the Slavs, subjugating them. And from these time the country was called Hungary.* The Russian chronicler again mentions the individual Slavic nations, with the Hungarian Slavs in first place, then the Moravians, the Bohemians, the Poles and the Russians, and he understands them as one Slavic nations with a common Slavic language: *There was one Slavic nation: the Slavs who settled along the Danube, whom the Hungarians took over, and the Moravians, the Bohemians and the Lachovians*

cur. Trillmich, pp. 290–291. Obotrite Prince Gottschalk (1043–1066) also wanted to use the Slavonic language during the spreading of Christianity in his country: *ut oblitus ordinis sui frequenter in ecclesia sermonem exhortacionis ad populum fecerit, ea, quae mystice ab episcopis dicebantur vel presbyteris, ipse cupiens Sclavanicis verbis reddere planiora.* Magistri Adam Hammaburgensis ecclesiae Pontificum III 20, cur. Trillmich, pp. 352–353. And according to Helmold, the Obotrites spoke a Slavic language: *Est autem Aldenburg* (= Oldenburg), *ea quae Slavica lingua Starigard, hoc est antiqua civitas, dicitur, sita in terra Wagirorum, in occiduis partibus Balthici maris, et est terminus Slaviae.* Helmoldi presbyteri Bozoviensis Cronica Slavorum I 12, recognovit Bernhard Schmeidler. Scriptores rerum Germanicarum in usum scholarum ex Monumentis Germaniae historicis separatim editi (Hannoverae et Lipsiae 1909), p. 23. In 1075 the Saxon Bards occupied Plön Castle (*castrum Plunense*) belonging to the Obotrite Vagers. On the next day, however, Obotrite Prince Kruk surrounded the castle with a large army. The Saxons of Holstein, Stormar and Dithmarschen, settled in the neighbouring Nordalbingia, marched to the aid of the surrounded Bard: *And when they came to the river, which is called the Suale* (today the Schwale) *and divided the Saxons from the Slavs, the first sent a man knowledgeable in the Slavic language (Slavicae linguae), so that he knew what the Slavs were doing and how they will begin with conquering the castle.* Helmoldi presbyteri Bozoviensis Cronica Slavorum I 25, rec. Schmeidler, pp. 49–50. Adolf II, Count of Nordalbingia, was a *wise man, very experienced in divine and human affairs. Because aside from speaking in the Latin and German language he was only a little bit less knowledgeable of the Slavic language (linguae Slavicae).* Helmoldi presbyteri Bozoviensis Cronica Slavorum I 49, rec. Schmeidler, p. 98. Adolf II, who in 1143 began to build the city of Lubek (= Lübeck), established an abbey in its vicinity, more precisely *in proximo oppido, quod Slavice Cuzalina, Teutonice Hagerestorp* (= Högersdorf) *dicitur.* Helmoldi presbyteri Bozoviensis Cronica Slavorum I 58, rec. Schmeidler, p. 113.

57   *Latopis Nestora* 3, MPH I, ed. Bielowski, p. 553. MMFH I, pp. 188–189.

and Poles, who are now called the Russians.[58] The Hungarian Slavs, that is the *Slavs who settled along the Danube, whom the Hungarians took over* and which were the same nation as the Moravians, Bohemians, Poles and Russians, could have been in Nestor's time only the Nitrians. Other Hungarian Slavs did not have a special principality, such as Nitria, that is a framework in which they could feel and be considered as an individual nation comparable with the Moravians, Bohemians, Poles and Russians.

Nestor's contemporary, Polish chronicler Gallus Anonymus, also knew about the Hungarian Slavs. He first mentioned Hungary as the southern neighbour of Poland: *If we then go from the north, Poland is the northern part of Slavinia (Sclavoniae), as neighbours it has from the east Russia, from the south Hungary, from the south-west Moravia and Bohemia, and from the west Denmark and Saxony.*[59] If, according to the Polish chronicler *Poland is the northern part of Slavinia*, then the southern part of this Slavinia is Nitria, belonging to Hungary. Aside from Nitria, obviously, the other Slavic states neighbouring with Poland named by the Polish chronicler also belonged to Slavonia. Russia was the eastern part, Moravia and Bohemia the south-west part of Slavinia. Then Gallus Anonymus described the whole range of Slavinia and also included Hungary in it: *The Slavic land (terra Sclavonica) ... stretches from the Sarmatians, who are also called the Gets, up to Denmark and Saxony, from Thrace then through Hungary (per Ungariam) occupied once by the Huns, who are also called the Hungarians, continuing through Carinthia (per Carinthiam), stretching to Bavaria; however, to the south along the Mediterranean Sea, beginning from Epirus through Dalmatia, Croatia and Istria, it is bordered by the ends of the Adriatic Sea, there where Venice and Aquileia lie, it is divided from Italy.*[60] Gallus Anonymus doesn't doubt that Hungary, although occupied by Magyars, is a Slavic country, just like neighbouring Carinthia and a larger part of the Balkan peninsula. The northern part of Hungary, that is Nitria, was the nearest to the Poles. Slavic Nitria evokes in the Polish chronicler the impression of Slavic Hungary, just as with other foreign chroniclers, who observed Hungary from the north-east, north or north-west, that is from the same or a similar direction as Gallus Anonymus.

Adam of Bremen, in his history of the Hamburg archbishopric, which he wrote in the 1070s, described Slavinia thus: *Slavinia (Sclavania), that is the vastest province of Germania ..., is ten-times larger than our Saxony, especially*

---

58 *Latopis Nestora* 18 (year 6406 = 898), MPH I, ed. Bielowski, pp. 568–569. MMFH I, pp. 190–193.
59 *Galli Chronicon* Prohemium, MPH I, ed. Bielowski, p. 394.
60 *Galli Chronicon* Prohemium, MPH I, ed. A. Bielowski, p. 395.

if Bohemia and those who are beyond the Oder, the Poles, who do not differ in appearance or even language, counted as a part of Slavinia ... Its breadth from north to south is from the river Elbe up to the Scythian (= Black) *Sea. But its length is such that its beginning is from our Hamburg region and is spread to the east the the endless large spaces up to Bavaria, Hungary and Greece* [Byzantium] (*usque in Beguariam, Ungriam et Greciam*). He then names in detail the *many tribes of Slavs (populi Sclavorum multi)*.[61] Slavinia reached *up to Bavaria, Hungary and Greece*; therefore, as this follows the similar descriptions of Gallus Anonymus and Nestor, the Slavic parts of these countries, that is Bavarian Carinthia, Hungarian Nitria and the larger part of the Balkan provinces of the Byzantine Empire, are included in it. The range of Slavinia in Adam of Bremen agrees with the range of Slavinia of the mentioned Polish and Russian chroniclers.

Helmold, in the first chapter of his Slavic chronicle, which is a century younger than the work of Adam of Bremen, named the Slavs, and he did not forget about Hungary: *Many are thus Slavic tribes (Slavorum igitur populi multi) living on the coast of the Baltic Sea ..., but the south shore is inhabited by nations of Slavs (Slavorum incolunt nationes), from which from the east are first the Russians, then the Poles, having from the north the Prussians, from the south the Bohemians and those who are called the Moravians or the Carinthians and also the Serbs. When you count Hungary into Slavinia (in partem Slavaniae), as some want to, because they do not differ neither in appearance nor in language, the range of the Slavic tongue (Slavicae linguae) grows so much that it is hardly possible to count.*[62]

According to Helmold, Hungary *does not differ even in appearance or language* from the Slavic countries; therefore, it can be considered as a part of Slavinia. According to Adam of Bremen and Helmold, the Slavs had the same appearance, but the main the common sign of the Slavs was, as Thietmar and Nestor also said, the common Slavic language.

At the turn of the 12th to 13th centuries, Hungarian Anonymus wrote about the Slavs in Nitria. The Nitrian Slavs (or the Slavic Nitrians) differed directly from the Bohemians (*Sclavi et Boemi* and *Boemi et omnes Nytrienses Sclavi*) and indirectly from the Poles, whom he names together with the Bohemians (*Boemy vel Polony*) in a different place in his work.[63] He thus indirectly differentiated them from any other Slavs. These were the Slavic Nitrians, that is the Slovaks, who by their number and range of settled territory significantly exceeded the

---

61   *Magistri Adam Bremensis Gesta Hammaburgensis ecclesiae Pontificum* II 21, cur. Trillmich, pp. 250–253.
62   *Helmoldi presbyteri Bozoviensis Cronica Slavorum* I 1, rec. Schmeidler, p. 5. MMFH I, p. 255.
63   *Anonymi (P. magistri) Gesta Hungarorum* 34–37, SRH I, pp. 76–78.

Magyars in the southern margin of Nitria.[64] According to Thietmar, Nestor, Gallus Anonymus, Adam of Bremen, Helmold and ultimately even Hungarian Anonymus, this part of Hungary was a Slavic country. The Magyars who lived on the southern edge of Nitria thus did not interfere in the Slavic character of this country, and since they were subjected to the Nitrian Prince and served in the Nitrian army the same as the Nitrian Slavs, they, too, were Nitrians.

Prague Bishop Adalbert in 997 undertook a missionary trip to the Prussians: *Here St. Adalbert, on the question of who he is, from whence he came and why he came here, replied in a moderate voice thus: I'm a native-born Slav (Sum nativitate Sclavus), by the name of Adalbert, a monk by profession, once a bishop by title, now an apostle in your service.*[65] Adalbert thus, in addition to being Bohemian, felt himself also to be a Slav, and he clearly gave preference to his broader identity toward remote foreigners. Great Moravian Prince Rastislav thought the same way when in a letter to the Byzantine emperor he labelled himself and his nation as *we Slavs.*[66] The Slavs, even though they were divided into many tribes and nations and formed several states, further considered themselves as one *Slavic nation.*

Nestor, Adam of Bremen and Helmold characterize the *Slavic nation* by a common Slavic language: *They are not differentiated even ... by the language,* as Adam of Bremen and Helmold wrote;[67] *they had only one Slavic language,* as Nestor emphasized.[68] And Nestor clearly differentiated various Finno-Ugric and Baltic tribes from the Slavs according to the language: *And these are other nations ... these have their own language.*[69] Slavic tribes and nations,

---

64   Richard Marsina, "O osídlení Slovenska od 11. do polovice 13. storočia," in *Slovenský ľud po rozpade Veľkomoravskej ríše, Historické štúdie* 27 (1984), no. 2, pp. 53–55. Hanuliak, "Gräberfelder der slawischen Population," pp. 282–287. Mária Vondráková, "Feststellungsmöglichkeiten der Antropologie über die Ethnizität der Populationen aus Gräberfeldern der sog. Bijelo-Brdo-Kultur," in *Ethnische und kulturelle Verhältnisse an der mittleren Donau vom 6. bis zum 11. Jahrhundert*, ed. Bialeková, Zábojník, pp. 409–420. The important inhabitants of Nitra mentioned in the Zobor Document from year 1111 have either Slavic and German or traditional Christian and untraditional (then fashionable) antique names. Not one of the names is Hungarian. See note 37. Ján Stanislav, *Dejiny slovenského jazyka III* (Bratislava 1957), pp. 97–100. Magyar settlements, which were limited in Nitria to its southern edge, did not reach up to Nitra itself.

65   *Johanni Canaparii Vita et passio sancti Adalberti martiris* 28, MPH I, ed. Bielowski, p. 181.

66   ŽM V, MMFH II, p. 144.

67   See notes 61, 62.

68   *Latopis Nestora* 20, MPH I, ed. Bielowski, p. 571.

69   *Latopis Nestora* 7, MPH I, ed. Bielowski, p. 557. Nestor has a common expression, *jązykъ*, for the concept of nation and language, as do the Life of Constantine and the Life of Methodius. The first Slavic legend about St. Wenceslaus tells of foreign priests *from all nations (otъ vsьchъ jazykъ)*, whom Bohemian Prince Wenceslaus put into churches at

among them the Slavs of Hungary, that is mainly the Slovaks, according to Thietmar spoke *Slavic (Sclavonicae)*.[70] And that is why the first Hungarian King Stephen I recommended to his son and other successors to acknowledge in the Hungarian Kingdom *varied languages and customs*,[71] among them undoubtedly the Slavic language.

In August of 1040 three legions came to the aide of Bohemian Prince Břetislav from Hungary (*tribus legionibus que fuerant misse in auxilium de Ungaria*).[72] A thousand soldiers made up a single legion;[73] thus, the auxiliary Hungarian army had 3-thousand soldiers. This was only a part of the army that Hungary could put together. It certainly came from that part of Hungary which was closest to the Bohemians, that is Nitria. The 3-thousand soldiers correspond to the number which the 9 Nitrian county castles could have put together. If the

---

his castles, as it is *in the large natio**ns (vъ velicъchъ jazycъchъ*). *Ruské redakce původní staroslov. Legendy o sv. Václavu. Text Vostokovský*, ed. N. J. Serebrjanskij, in *Sborník staroslovanských literárních památek o sv. Václavu a sv. Lidmile*, ed. Vajs, p. 16. Miloš Weingart, *Rekonstruovaný text I. staroslověnské legendy o sv. Václavu* 30, in *Svatováclavský sborník I*, ed. Guth, Kapras, Novák, Stloukal, pp. 976–977, 989–990. *Jązykъ* then and still today indicates speech in all Slavic language. This word originally had a second meaning, namely with the Greek *etnos* and with the Latin *gens*, Mareš, František Václav Mareš: *Cyrilometodějská tradice a slavistika*, Praha 2000, pp. 226–227. And in the oldest Bohemian written verse chronicle from the beginning of the 14th century, ascribed to Dalimil, the word *jazyk* means not only language but also nation. *Nejstarší česká rýmovaná kronika tak rečeného Dalimila*, předmluva, kap. 1, 2, 4, 57, 67, 70, 74, 92, 104, doplněk 7, připravili Bohuslav Havránek, a Jiří Daňhelka, poznámky Zdeněk Kristen (Praha 1958), pp. 16, 18, 19, 20, 24, 103, 118, 123, 128, 150, 166, 177. This word also acquired another meaning. Already in Ostromír's Gospel Book from the 1050s and in a liturgical menology (mineja) from 1096 *jazykъ* and *jazyčnyj* have the meaning pagan and paganistic. Izmail Ivanovič Sreznevskij, "Materialy dľa slovarja drevnerusskogo jazyka," (Sankt Peterburg 1903), p. 1649. In Russian *jazyčnik* still today means pagan. The meaning of Latin *gens* has likewise changed. One of the laws of St. Ladislas *On pagan rites* (*De ritu gentilium*) is testimony that to the original meaning of this word nation or tribe the meaning pagan was added: *Quicumque ritu gentilium iuxta puteos sacrificaverint, vel ad arbores et fontes et lapides oblaciones obtulerint, reatum suum bove luant. Sancti Ladislai regis decretorum liber primus* XXII. *A Szent István, Szent László és Kálmán korabeli törvények és zsinati határozatok forrásai*, ed. Zavodszky, p. 73. The word *narodъ*, as we know from the Life of Methodius, originally indicated a large crowd of gathered people of various origin and social standing, in which there could be *strangers and natives*. *ŽM* 17, MMFH II, p. 162. Later it took on the original meaning of the words *jązykъ* and *gens*. Ján Steinhübel, "Veľká Morava a slovanský svet," *Monumentorum tutela* 28 (2018), pp. 10–12.

70 See note 56.
71 *diversas linguas et consuetudines*. Libellus de institutione morum VI, SRH II, p. 625.
72 See note 25.
73 Choc, *S mečem a štítem*, pp. 63–65, 75–76, 93–97, 426.

9 Nitrian castle brigades made up 3 legions, then the brigades of 3 castle counties belonged to each of these legions.

The Nitrians could easily converse with their Slavic neighbours. The common Slavic language certainly eased the common approach of Nitrians and Moravians in the defence of Bohemia. The Moravians and Nitrians who took over the common defensive position near the Bohemian borders and the Bílina administrator Prkoš, who led both armies, didn't have the difficulties which a different language could have caused them.

7 Nitrians and Hungarians, Moravians and Bohemians

The Nitrians, who in the battle near Mogyoród, from the castle soldiers up to the castle counts, surrounded Prince Géza, were Hungarians, just like the soldiers of Hungarian King Solomon. Count Ernej expressed this very precisely when he discouraged Solomon from an attack against the princes: *I don't want you to fight against your brothers and that soldiers kill one another, a son his father or a father his son*.[74] The soldiers who in August 1074 were concentrated behind the ramparts of Nitra to defend against Solomon, who with his soldiers were found beneath the Nitra Castle ramparts, and against a large German army waiting in nearby Šintava, were Nitrians and at the same time Hungarians.[75] These Nitrians were those Hungarians who in 1001, loyal to Hungarian King Stephen I, defended Nitria against an attack of Boleslaw the Brave.[76] Likewise, they had stood on Stephen's side in 997 in the fight against Koppány.[77]

Nitrian Princes Béla and Géza did not have the name of their principality minted on their coins, but the other name of Hungary PANNONIA (PANONAI),[78] like the Hungarian kings Peter Orseolo, Samuel Aba, Andrew I, Béla I, Solomon, Géza I and Ladislas I.[79] Prince Béla and his successors were *princes of Hungary (duces Hungarie)*.[80] Nitrian Prince Géza labelled himself *prince of the Hungarians (Hungarorum dux)*,[81] and for Polish chronicler

---

74 *Chron. Hung. comp. saec. XIV.* II 119, *SRH I*, p. 387.
75 See pp. 462–463.
76 See p. 380.
77 See pp. 342–344.
78 See pp. 442–443, 451–452.
79 Lajos Huszár, *Münzkatalog Ungarn von 1000 bis heute* (Budapest 1979), no. 6, 7, 9, 11, 12, 14, 16, 17, 18, 19, 20, 21, pp. 32, 34–35. Kovács, *A kora Árpád-kori magyar pénzverésről*, pp. 95–99, 99, 101, 107, 108, 110, 113–117, 119, 124, 125, 128, 129, 141, 157, 159, 213, 215, 222, 237–246, 263–266, 268–271.
80 *Chron. Hung. comp. saec. XIV.* II 88, *SRH I*, p. 345.
81 *DHA I*, ed. Györffy, no. 73/II, pp. 213, 218. *CDES I*, ed. Marsina, no. 58, pp. 54, 58.

Gallus Anonymus the last Nitrian and Biharian Prince Álmos was *prince of the Hungarians* (*Ungarorum dux*),[82] just as Prince Otto, who ruled in his Olomouc grant in Moravia, was according to a Hungarian chronicler *prince of the Bohemians* (*dux Bohemorum*).[83]

Géza's and Ladislas's princely army was an *army of Hungarians* (*exercitus Hungarorum*).[84] Géza's Nitrians, like Ladislas's Biharians, were thus at the same time, and for the Hungarian chronicler mainly Hungarians, and the Moravian warriors of Olomouc Prince Otto were at the same time *Bohemians* (*Bohemis*)[85] and made up a *Bohemian army* (*Bohemicum agmen*).[86]

Not only the Hungarian chronicler, but also Bohemian chronicler Cosmas, made no distinction between the Moravians and the Bohemians. Cosmas wrote about the Bohemians, Hungarians, Poles, Pomeranians, Danes, Germans, Bavarians, Swabians, Franks, Saxons, Carinthians, Obotrites, Luticians, Milcenians, Slavs and Jews. But not once did he mention Moravians, though he clearly distinguished Moravia from Bohemia. Cosmas wrote about Moravia but not the Moravians,[87] because he considered them to be Bohemians, just as the Hungarian chronicler considered the Nitrians, whom he mentioned only once, to be Hungarians.

8   Principality

The Slavs were governed by princes. They called them къназь, that is *kъnęzъ* or *kъnjazъ* (Ѧ = ę, ja), and Latin chronicles, legends, documents and letters as *dux*

---

82   *Galli Chronicon* II 29, MPH I, ed. Bielowski, p. 448.
83   *Chron. Hung. comp. saec. XIV.* II 115, 122, SRH I, pp. 381, 393. According to Hungarian chronicle tradition, Otto ruled *in Bohemiam, in partes Bohemie*. *Chron. Hung. comp. saec. XIV.* II 115, 116, SRH I, pp. 381, 382. In 1067 King Solomon and Prince Géza plundered in Moravia. The Hungarian chronicler, however, writes about the plundering of Bohemia: *Rex autem et dux ... Bohemiam invaserunt ... Hungari fere totam Bohemiam igne ac gladio vastaverunt*. And he labelled the captured Moravians as Bohemians: *Rex itaque et dux ... cum maxima preda captivorum Bohemorum in Hungariam gaudentes sunt reversi*. *Chron. Hung. comp. saec. XIV.* II 101, SRH I, p. 365. The Zobor Document from 1113, which was compiled by the Zobor abbot and was likely prepared by the Nitra Chapter, however, mentions Otto as prince of the Moravians: *sedicione autem Athe ducis Morauiensium*. DHA I, ed. Györffy, no. 142/I, p. 392. CDES I, ed. Marsina, no. 69, p. 65.
84   *Chron. Hung. comp. saec. XIV.* II 119, SRH I, p. 387.
85   *Chron. Hung. comp. saec. XIV.* II 121, SRH I, p. 390.
86   *Chron. Hung. comp. saec. XIV.* II 119, SRH I, p. 386.
87   Josef Žemlička, "'Moravané' v časném středověku," *Český časopis historický* 90 (1992), no. 1, pp. 17–32. Žemlička, *Čechy v době knížecí*, pp. 353–354.

and sometimes as *princeps*, and did so without regard for their sovereignty.[88] Ibn Churdádbih, who lived in the caliph court in Baghdad, perhaps in year 846 wrote that *the ruler of the Slavs is called a qnáz*.[89] Rastislav was a *moravskyj knʌzь* (*Moravian prince*) and consulted with his *knʌzi*, that is with his smaller, subordinate princes.[90] Prince (*dux*) Svätopluk together with his subordinate princes (*cum principibus suis*) swore an oath in 884 to Emperor Charles the Fat.[91] Kocel was the *knʌzь panoneskъ*, that is the Pannonian prince,[92] and they knew him also by his residential castle as *knjʌza Blatьnska kostelʌ* (*prince of Blatengrad*).[93] Therefore, even his father Pribina, from whom he inherited the Pannonian Principality, mentioned in 860 as *dux*,[94] was a *prince*. The Bohemians and neighbouring Sorbs also had princes: *Blessed Ľudmila was from the Sorbian country, the daughter of a Sorbian prince* (*knʌzʌ serbьskago*). *She was married to a Bohemian prince* (*za češьskago knʌzʌ*) *by the name of Bořivoj*.[95] According to the Second Slavic legend about St. Wenceslaus, Bořivoj's son Spytihněv had *administration of a principality* (*knʌžiʌ stroj*) *under imperial supremacy*.[96] After Spytihněv, Vrastislaus ascended *to the princely seat* (*na knʌženie stola*),[97] and after him Wenceslaus took over *princely rule and was installed on the seat to the princely dignity* (*na stolь knʌžestvia čestj*).[98]

According to the First Slavic legend about St. Wenceslaus *there was in Bohemia one prince* (*knez*) *by the name of Vratislaus*. When Vratislaus died, *prince* (*kъnezь*) *Wenceslau ruled*.[99] The mentioned *prince* (*kъnjazь*) *Vratislaus* invited

---

88   Łowmiański, *Początki Polski IV*, pp. 108–128. Boroń, *Kniaziowie*, pp. 55–99. Vykypěl, *Studie k šlechtickým titulům*, pp. 128–133.

89   *Kitábu l-masáliki wa-l-mamáliki li-bni Churdádbiha* 1, MMFH *III*, p. 326. Paulíny, *Arabské správy o Slovanoch*, p. 90.

90   *ŽK* 14, MMFH *II*, p. 98. In the Life of Methodius Rastislav is *knʌzь slovьnьskъ*. *ŽM* 5, MMFH *II*, p. 143. Even Methodius's adhortation *Reproaching rulers* says: That's why each prince (*knʌzь*) is obligated ... MMFH *IV*, p. 201.

91   See chapter 9, notes 48, 55.

92   *ŽK* 15, MMFH *II*, p. 105.

93   *Čr'norizca Chrabra Skazanije o pismenech* 9, MMFH *III*, p. 371.

94   See chapter 6, notes 14, 82.

95   *Proložní legendy o sv. Lidmile a o sv. Václavu*, ed. N. J. Serebrjanskij, in *Sborník staroslovanských literárních památek o sv. Václavu a sv. Lidmile*, ed. Vajs, p. 64.

96   *Druhá staroslověnská legenda o sv. Václavu. Legenda Nikolského* 2, ed. Vašica, in *Sborník staroslovanských literárních památek o sv. Václavu a sv. Lidmile*, ed. Vajs, p. 89.

97   *Druhá staroslověnská legenda o sv. Václavu. Legenda Nikolského* 3, ed. Vašica, in *Sborník staroslovanských literárních památek o sv. Václavu a sv. Lidmile*, ed. Vajs, p. 89.

98   *Druhá staroslověnská legenda o sv. Václavu. Legenda Nikolského* 4, ed. Vašica, in *Sborník staroslovanských literárních památek o sv. Václavu a sv. Lidmile*, ed. Vajs, p. 91.

99   *Chorvátskohlaholská redakce původní legendy o sv. Václavu. Text Novljanský*, ed. J. Vajs, in *Sborník staroslovanských literárních památek o sv. Václavu a sv. Lidmile*, ed, Vajs, pp. 36, 37, 40, 43. *Žitije Vęceslava* (*I. redakce charvátsko-hlaholská*), MMFH *II*, p. 181.

to the tonsuring of his son Wenceslaus, in addition to the bishop also *princes* (*knʌzi ini*),[100] more specifically *princes* (*knʌzi*), *who were then in his area*,[101] that is under his power. When *Prince Vratislaus* (*Vorotislavъ knʌzъ*) died, *they put Prince Wenceslaus* (*knʌzʌ Vʌčeslava*) *on the hereditary seat*.[102] Wenceslaus married off his sisters *to various principalities* (*v rozna knʌženьja*).[103]

In the Czech language Chronicle of Dalimil from the beginning of the 14th century the Moravian Přemyslids were always *kněz* (*prince*) and *kniežatá* (*princes*), just as their superior Bohemian Přemyslids: *pro kněze moravského* (*for the Moravian prince*), *Bořivoje, kněze moravského* (*Bořivoj, prince of Moravia*), *kněz Bořivoj* (*prince Bořivoj*), *Ottu, kněze moravského* (*Otto, prince of Moravia*), *Otta, kněz moravský ... křičě na své Moravany* (*Otto, prince of Moravia ... cried for his Moravians*), *Morava svých kniežat zbyla* (*Moravia was for its princes*), *moravský kněz* (*Moravian prince*), *kněz moravský* (*prince of Moravia*), *Morava tu kniežat odstúpila a od toho času českým kniežatóm slúžila* (*she left the Moravian principality and from this time served the Bohemian princes*).[104]

Princes also ruled on the territory of Poland. Around year 875 *a pagan prince* (*knʌzъ*), *very powerful, sitting on the Vistula* (*vъ Vislъ*), had to subjugate himself to Svätopluk.[105] According to Dalimil, Mieszko II was *kněz polský* (*a Polish prince*).[106] Dalimil also names small Polish principalities that in the years 1291–1292 were seized by future Bohemian King Wenceslaus II: *Kněžstva*

---

100   *Ruské redakce původní staroslov. Legendy o sv. Václavu. Text Vostokovský*, ed. N. J. Serebrjanskij, in *Sborník staroslovanských literárních památek o sv. Václavu a sv. Lidmile*, ed. Vajs, p. 14. *Žitije Vęceslava* (*II. redakce vostokovská*), MMFH II, p. 182.

101   *Ruské redakce původní staroslov. Legendy o sv. Václavu. Text Minejní*, ed. N. J. Serebrjanskij, in *Sborník staroslovanských literárních památek o sv. Václavu a sv. Lidmile*, ed. Vajs, p. 21. *Žitije Veceslava* (*III. redakce minejní*), MMFH II, p. 183.

102   *Ruské redakce původní staroslov. Legendy o sv. Václavu. Text Vostokovský*, ed. Serebrjanskij, in *Sborník staroslovanských literárních památek o sv. Václavu a sv. Lidmile*, ed. Vajs, p. 15. V tom čase umrel knieža Vratislav (Vratislavъ knʌzъ). I posadili knieža Václava (knʌzʌ Vʌčeslava) na stolec jeho otca Vratislava. *Ruské redakce původní staroslov. Legendy o sv. Václavu. Text Minejní*, ed. N. J. Serebrjanskij, in *Sborník staroslovanských literárních památek o sv. Václavu a sv. Lidmile*, ed. Vajs, p. 21.

103   *Ruské redakce původní staroslov. Legendy o sv. Václavu. Text Vostokovský*, ed. Serebrjanskij, in *Sborník staroslovanských literárních památek o sv. Václavu a sv. Lidmile*, ed. Vajs, p. 15. v razna knʌžia. *Ruské redakce původní staroslov. Legendy o sv. Václavu. Text Minejní*, ed. Serebrjanskij, in *Sborník staroslovanských literárních památek o sv. Václavu a sv. Lidmile*, ed. Vajs, p. 22.

104   *Nejstarší česká rýmovaná kronika tak řečeného Dalimila*, kap. 50, 53, 55, 59, 60, 62, 70, 73, ed. Havránek, Daňhelka, Kristen, pp. 90, 95, 97, 105, 107, 110, 122, 123, 127. Žemlička, *Čechy v době knížecí*, pp. 329–330, 350–357.

105   ŽM II, MMFH II, p. 156.

106   *Nejstarší česká rýmovaná kronika tak řečeného Dalimila*, kap. 33, 35, 37, ed. Havránek, Daňhelka, Kristen, pp. 65, 66, 69, 71.

krakovského, pak Kališe a kněžstva pomořanského a králevstvie poznaňského (*The principalities of Krakow, then Kalisz, and the principality of Pomeranian and the kingdom of Poznan*). In 1292 he also conquered Sieradz, where *kněz siraský* (*Prince of Sieradz*) ruled.[107] The Danish Duke of Schleswig (1120–1131) and Obodrite prince (1129–1131) Canute Lavard said that *Sclavia*, that is the Slavic territory on the east side of the lower Elbe, where he ruled, did not have a king but a prince (*knese*).[108] Jazko, who under Polish suzerainty ruled the Spreevans (1150–1176), was a prince. The coins that he had minted at his seat in Köpenick, have the legend IAKZA.COPTNIK.CNE[Z] or IAC[ZA] K[N]ES.[109]

As Nestor and other Russian chroniclers testify, *kъnjazi*, that is princes, also ruled the eastern Slavs, first tribal, then Russian from the Rurik line. The main Russian prince was seated in Kiev and appanage princes in other important castles. The dukes had their *kъnjaženija*, that is their principalities.[110] In 912 Russian messengers came to the Byzantine emperor *from Oleg, a great Russian prince* (*velikago kъnjazja rusьkago*), *and from others who are under his hand, pure and great princes* (*velikych kъnjazь*) *and his great boyars.*[111] In 945 Russian messengers came to the Byzantine emperor *from Igor, a great Russian prince* (*velikago kъnjazja rusьkago*), *and from other princes* (*kъnjažija*) *and from other people of the Russian land.*[112] Russian Prince Vladimir the Great (972–1015) *had twelve sons ... And he made all of them princes in various lands ... Thus that poor Sviatopolk he made prince in Pinsk, Yaroslav in Novgorod, Boris in Rostov and Gleb in Murom.*[113] In 1066 Kherson emissary Kotopan addressed the Tmutarakan Prince Rastislav: *Prince* (*kъnaže*), *I wish to drink a toast to you.*[114] Polotsk Prince Všeslav Brjačislavič (1044–1101) issued grants to small

---

107   *Nejstarší česká rýmovaná kronika tak řečeného Dalimila*, kap. 94, ed. Havránek, Daňhelka, Kristen, p. 154. Jerzy Dowiat, *Polska państwem średniowiecznej Europy* (Warszawa 1968), pp. 223–252.

108   *Sclavia enim nec regem habuit, nec michi comissa me regem vocavit. Usuali quidem locucione cause dignitatis vel reverencie knese quemlibet vocare consuevit, hoc est dominus. Vita altera Kanuti ducis* 5. Łowmiański, *Początky Polski IV*, p. 120.

109   Herbert Ludat, *Slawen und Deutsche im Mittelalter. Ausgewählte Aufsätze zu Fragen ihrer politischen, sozialen und kulturellen Beziehungen* (Köln – Wien 1982), pp. 70–76, 82–83. Kazimierz Mysliński, *Polska wobec Słowian polabskich do końca wieku XII* (Lublin 1993), pp. 184–204, 209, 211–213.

110   Boris Dmitrijevič Grekov, *Kyjevská Rus* (Praha 1953), pp. 290–313. Boris Alexandrovič Rybakov, *Kijevskaja Rus i russkije knjažestva XII–XIII vv.* (Moskva 1993), pp. 256, 327–329.

111   *Latopis Nestora* 22, year 6420 (912), MPH I, ed. Bielowski, p. 575.

112   *Latopis Nestora* 27, year 6453 (945), MPH I, ed. Bielowski, pp. 588–589.

113   *Vyprávění o svatých mučenícich Borisovi a Glebovi a o jejich utrpení i jejich pochvala*, in *Písemníctví ruského středověku. Od křtu Vladimíra Velikého po Dmitrije Donského*, translation Emilie Bláhová, Zoe Hauptová a Václav Konzal (Praha 1989), pp. 62–63.

114   *Latopis Nestora* 61, year 6574 (1066), MPH I, ed. Bielowski, p. 714.

principalities: *The celebrated prince (кnѧзь) judged people, handed out castles to princes (кnѧzemъ)*.[115] Ingvar's sons ruled in the Ryazan Principality and in 1237 allied together against Batu Khan: *When Ryazan Grand Prince (velikij knjazь) Yuriy Ingvarevich learned that he will not get help from Grand Prince (velikago knjazja) Georgiy Vsevolodovich of Vladimír, he rapidly sent messengers to his brothers: to Prince (po knjazja) David Ingvarevich of Murom, to Prince (po knjazja) Gleb Ingvarevich of Kolomna, to Prince (po knjazja) Oleg the Fair, to Vsevolod of Pronsk and other princes (po pročii knjazi)*.[116]

Princes also ruled the southern Slavs. Boris and Simeon, who ruled the Bulgarians, had the Slavic title *kniez*[117] up to year 920, when Simeon declared himself as Tsar. Presian, son of the last Tsar of the Western Bulgarian realm of Ivan Vladislav, lived in the Zemplín at the end of his life. In 1060 or 1061 he died, and after him a burial marker with the name and title *kъnѧzь* remained in Michalovce after him.[118] The Serbs had several principalities in the Central Balkan. In one of them, in Chlm, a prince (*knezь*) Andrew ruled, who in perhaps 1234 made an alliance with Dubrovník.[119]

And the Slavic Nitrians addressed all of their princes, from Pribina and his predecessors up through Álmos, as well as their appanaged princes, such as Poznan and Hont, as prince and their lands spoken of as a *knѧženьje* (principality), as with all the surrounding Slavic principalities.

A prince could hand over his army to a duke (*voivode*), or commander.[120] Slavic voivodes were not from a princely line and their position was not

---

115   Boris Alexandrovič Rybakov, *Petr Borislavič. Poisk autora "Slova o polku Igoreve"* (Moskva 1991), p. 37.
116   *Povesť o razorenii Rjazani Batyem v 1237 godu*, in Alexandr Nikitič Kožin, *Literaturnyj jazyk Kijevskoj Rusi* (Moskva 1981), pp. 143, 146, 152, 154–155. *Povesť o zničení Riazane chánom Batuom*, in *Slovo o pluku Igorovom a ďalšie staroruské historické povesti*, translation Helena Križanová-Brindzová, pp. 41, 43, 48, 49–50.
117   *Poznámka Konstantina Prěslavského k překladu díla Athanasije Alexandrijského*, MMFH III, p. 363. *Čŕnorizca Chrabra Skazanije o pismenech* 9, MMFH III, p. 371.
118   Ľubor Matejko, "Niekoľko poznámok k náhrobnému nápisu kniežaťa Presiana v Michalovciach," *Slovanské štúdie* 2 (1992), pp. 136–147. Ľubor Matejko, "Some remarks on the interpretation of Slavonic written sources," in *Acta historica Posoniensia* II (2002), pp. 83–87.
119   *Codex diplomaticus regni Croatiae, Dalmatiae et Slavoniae II*, collegit et degessit T. Smičiklas (Zagrabiae 1904), no. 374, p. 432, no. 488, p. 559.
120   Grekov, *Kyjevská Rus*, pp. 204, 315, 349–350. Łowmiański, *Początki Polski IV*, pp. 119–122. Alexander Gieysztor, "Urzad wojewodzinski we wczesnych państwach słowiańskich w IX–XI w.," *Archeologia Polski* 16 (1971), pp. 317–325. Richard Marsina proposed labeling as commanders all appanaged princes despite the fact that their participants considered them as princes and called them prince. Richard Marsina, "Politický vývoj na Slovensku od 10. do začiatku 14. storočia," *Slovenská numizmatika* 10 (1989), p. 111. Marsina, "Svätopluk,

heritable. Russian Prince Igor (913–945) had a duke Svenald (*vojevoda bě svěnalьdъ*), who also served his son Sviatoslav (945–972) and grandson Yaropolk (972–980). Prince Sviatoslav had two dukes (voivodes), Svenald and Pretich. Duke (*voivoda*) Pretich with an army of Severans, who settled opposite Kiev, on the left bank of the Dniepr, saved Kiev from the Pechenegs in 968. The Pecheneg khagan asked him: *And are you a prince (kъnazь)?* Pretich replied: *I'm his man, and I came as a guard and behind me is an innumerable army with a prince (s kъnazěmь)*. Duke Svenald replaced Duke Blud, who in 980 betrayed his Prince Yaropolk (*vъ Bludu, vojevodě Jaroplъčju*) and secretly came to his brother Vladimir. In 984, on the command of Prince Vladimir, his Duke Wolf's Tail (*vojevoda Vlъčij Chvostъ*) marched against Radimichs and in the battle on the Píščena River defeated them. Budy was the guardian and duke of Prince Yaroslav the Wise (*I bě u Jaroslava krъmilьcь i vojevoda imenьmь Budy*). In 1018 he marched with him against Polish Prince Boleslaw the Brave and fell in the battle near the Bug River. Vyshata, who was the son of Novogorod Duke Ostromir, served Prince Yaroslav the Wise. In 1043 *Yaroslav sent the son of Vladimir to the Greeks and gave him a large army and entrusted a dukeship to Vyshata (vojevodьstvo porǫči Vyšatě), the father of Yan.* Yaroslav's other duke, Ivan Tvorimirich (*Ivanъ Tvorimiričь, vojevoda Jaroslaslavlь*), was also in this princely army. In 1064 Yaroslav's grandson Rastislav escaped together with Vyshata, the son of Novogorod duke Ostromir (*Vyšata, synъ Ostromirь vojevody novogorodьskogo*) to Tmutakaran. Duke Kosnyachek (*na vojevodu na Kosnjačьka*), mentioned in 1068, served Russian Prince Izyaslav.[121]

>   legenda a skutočnosť," pp. 155–165. Determining who was a duke (voivode) and who was a prince only according to his dependence and independence is an artificial template, which language sources reject. Sources in this case clearly tell about princes and not voivodes. The measure of independence could change even during the rule of one prince, but his title didn't have to because of this. And in the end not even a king had to always be an unambiguously sovereign ruler, as R. Marsina judges. The sons of Frankish king, later Emperor Charlemagne, were kings: Louis the Pious was the Aquitainean king (781–814) and Pepin the Italian king (781–810), despite the fact that they were not independent. Should we refer to them as dukes (voivodes) because of this? Even Aquitainean King Pepin I (814–838) and his brother, Bavarian King Louis the German (826–840), were subjugated to their father, Frankish King and Emperor Louis the Pious (814–840). We could find several such examples within Carolingian family alone. If a king could be subjugated to another king, then why couldn't a prince be subjugated to a prince? Do we need to differentiate them by the titles which they themselves didn't bear? Like-sounding titles don't have to have the same meaning. And not only in the past, but often still today. Therefore, it is enough if we understand their fine shades of meaning just as contemporaries did and that we not alter them.
> 121 *Latopis Nestora* 29, year 6453 (945), 30, year 6454 (946), 33, year 6476 (968), 36, year 6479 (971), year 6480 (972), 37, year 6483 (975), year 6485 (977), 38, year 6488 (980), 40, year

The Nikonov Chronicle names Russian princes, large and small, and their dukes, who in 1237 battled with the Tatars: *Ryazan Grand Prince Yuriy Ingvarevich (knjazь velikij Jurьi Inъgvorovičъ) and his brother Prince Oleg Ingvarevich (knjazь Olegъ Inъgvorovičъ) and the Murom and Pronsk princes (muromskije i pronskije knjazi) ... Then the Tatars marched on Kolomna. Grand Prince Yuriiy Vsevolodovich (knjazь že velikij Jurьi Vsevolodičъ) sent against him his son Prince Vsevolod from Vladimir (knjazja Vsevoloda iz Volodimerja) and with him Prince Roman Ingvarevich of Ryazan (knjazь Romanъ Ingvorovičъ Rjazanskij) with his army; Grand Prince Yuriy sent his duke Yerem Glebovich (vojevodu svojego Jeremnja Glъboviča) forward as a vanguard ... The Tartars ... killed Prince Roman Ingvarevich of Ryazan and killed Vsevolod Yurjevich's Duke Yerem Glebovich (vojevodu Jeremnja Glъboviča) ... The Tartars ... conquered Moscow and killed Duke Filip Nyanko (vojevodu ichъ Filipa Njanka) ... Grand Prince Yuriy Vsevolodovich ... held the place himself in Vladimir together with the bishop Princes Vsevolod and Mstislav and his duke Peter Oslyadyukovich (vojevodu svojego Petra Osljadjukoviča) and ... the Grand Prince expected his brothers Prince Yaroslav Vsevolodovich and Prince Sviatoslav Vsevolodovich with their armies and himself began to gather the army and Žiroslav Mikhaylovich named dukeship (vojevodstvo prikaza Žiroslavu Michajlovičju) ... Yuriy ... commanded his voivode to arm the people and to prepare for battle ... The Vladimir residents then with their princes and duke Peter Oslyadyukovich (Volodimerci že so knjazi svojimi i vojevodoju Petrom Osljadjukovičemъ) closed the city.*[122]

And the Great Moravian prince had a duke (voivode) who could represent him. Svätopluk's representative had the title *župan* (count). According to contemporary Arab reports on the Slavs, Svätopluk is *more esteemed than a župan (swt.dž) and the župan (swb.dž = súbandž) is his representative.*[123] Svätopluk's representative was the highest among the župans; he was a duke, to whom the prince could hand over leadership of his army. According to the Law of the Court *thus if God grants victory, the prince (knѧzju) may take a sixth part.* The duke rewarded counts from his share; therefore *the princely share (knѧža častь) is sufficient for the župans (žjupanomъ).* If some warriors distinguished themselves in a battle, then *let the prince or duke (knѧzь ili vojevoda) occurring*

6492 (984), 49, year 6526 (1018), 56, year 6551 (1043), 60, year 6572 (1064), 63, year 6576 (1068), MPH I, ed. Bielowski, pp. 597, 600, 608–609, 615–617, 619–621, 626, 691, 702–703, 712, 719.

122 *Ruskaja Lѣtopisь po Nikonovu spisku izdannaja pod smotreniemъ Imperatorskoj akademii nauk. Čast' vtoraja do 1237 goda,* (Vъ Sankt Peterburgѣ 1768 goda), pp. 371–373.

123 *Kitábu l-a'láki n-náfísati li-bni Rusta* 2, MMFH III, p. 347. Pauliny, *Arabské správy o Slovanoch,* p. 99.

there add (for them) *from the mentioned princely share* (*uroka kn*ᴀ*ža*).[124] The duke, that is the highest count, was fully subjugated to the prince and leading an army only loaned to him by the prince. A duke did not have his own army. Counts therefore got a reward and the bravest soldiers got extra, not from the duke but from the princely share.

Svatopluk, who ruled in Nitria during the time of Prince Rastislav, had an army and came from this same princely family as Rastislav, was thus a prince and not a duke (voivode). His younger son Svatopluk II, who also had the Nitria appanage and the Nitrian army, with which he revolted against his brother, was also a prince. Likewise, too, the Přemyslids, who had their territory in Moravia and a Moravian army, and the Árpáds, who had territory in Nitria and in Biharia and with them also the Nitrian and Biharian armies, were princes and not dukes (voivodes). From the princely lineages of the Mojmírs, Přemyslids, Obotrites, Piasts, Ruriks and Árpáds came princes, whether main or subordinated (appanaged) princes. A prince chose a duke from among his favourites outside of the princely line.

The first known Bohemian duke (voivode) was the heroic Tyr, who was *after the prince, second in power* (*post ducem secundus imperio*). The prince commanded him, *to sit on the lord's horse and go in his place before the warriors on the battlefield.*[125] The Hungarian-Polish Chronicle mentions how Hungarian King Stephen I in 1001 sent to the Polish prince *the army of a duke named Aba* (*principem militie Albam nomine*).[126] Stephen's brother-in-law, Samuel Aba, was thus Stephen's duke (voivode). He was second after the king.

In Hungary, Poland and Bohemia there was a duke (voivode) and a palatine.[127] Samuel Aba was the first known Hungarian palatine.[128] Palatine Setiech (1080–1100) was a duke (*militiae princeps*) of Polish Prince Wladyslaw Herman (1079–1102).[129] When Setiech rebelled, Prince Wladyslaw expelled him from Poland. Then *he did not appoint in his court any palatine or representative of a palatine* (*nullum tamen in curia sua palatinum vel palatini vicarium praefedit*) ... *And thus he ruled his homeland alone, without a palatine* (*sine palatio*

---

124 ZSL 3, *MMFH IV*, pp. 180–181. Counts (*žjupani*) are also mentioned in other places in this law book. ZSL 20, *MMFH IV*, p. 191.

125 *Cosmae Pragensis Chronica Boemorum* I 12, ed. Bretholz, pp. 26–28. Łowmiański, *Początki Polski IV*, p. 122.

126 *Chronicon Hungarico-Polonicum* 7, SRH II, p. 311.

127 Łowmiański, *Początki Polski IV*, pp. 121–122.

128 *Alba comes pallacii. Legenda maior sancti Gerhardi episcopi* 14, SRH II, p. 500. Angelika Herucová, "Arpádovskí palatíni vo vybraných naratívnych prameňoch," *Historické štúdie* 49 (2015), pp. 231–232, 236.

129 *Galli Chronicon* II 1, *MPH I*, ed. Bielowski, p. 429. Jerzy Dowiat, *Polska – państwem średniowiecznej Europy* (Warszawa 1968), pp. 187, 189–191, 196.

comite).¹³⁰ Under the rule of Boleslaw III Wrymouth (1107–1138) Skarbimír from the family Adbank (1107–1117, 1121–asi 1131) was the Polish palatine (*comes Polonie palatinus*),¹³¹ and he was replaced by Peter Vlastovic (1117–1121, perhaps 1131–1146).¹³² The Polish palatine, who was at the same time a duke (voivode), had an important position up to the end of the 12th century.¹³³ And in Bohemia a palatine was a duke (voivode) and a representative of the prince. Kojata, the son of Všebor, mentioned in 1061 and 1068, *was the first in the palace of the prince* (*primus erat in palatio ducis*), that is *the palatine* (*palatinus comes*).¹³⁴ Another Bohemian palatine was Vacek, mentioned in 1105. In 1111 Prince Vladislas, on the appeal of his mother and the Bishop of Prague *as well as Palatine Vacek* (*palatino comite*), reconciled with his brother Soběslav. In 1113 Prince Soběslav had Vacek killed and the title of palatine ceased to exist in Bohemia.¹³⁵

Dukes (voivodes) only exceptionally belonged to governing dynasties. The son of Hungarian King Stephen I belonged among these exceptions. Emeric, who was not only the prince in Biharia and in Nitria, but also *duke of the Russians* (*dux Ruizorum*, that is of the Russian retinue in the royal services.¹³⁶ After Emeric's death in 1031, King Stephen *appointed as duke of his army* (*exercitui suo prefecerat ducem*) his nephew Peter Orseolo,¹³⁷ whom he saw as his successor. Peter obtained such a strong position in the state and no one could threaten his succession. Samuel Aba remained only the palatine. The title duke (voivode) was in Hungary separated from the title of palatine. The palatine remained in the royal court, while the duke (vajda, *voievoda*) got from the king administration of Transylvania, which thus became a dukedom.¹³⁸

130   *Galli Chronicon* II 21, MPH I, ed. Bielowski, p. 443.
131   Galli Chronicon II 30, 31, 33, III epilog, 1, 23, MPH I, ed. A. Bielowski, pg. 445, 448, 476. Dowiat, *Polska*, pp. 195–196, 204, 230.
132   Marian Plezia, *Palatyn Piotr Włostowic. Sylwetka z dziejów Śląska w XII wieku* (Łódź 1947). Dowiat, *Polska*, pp. 156, 207, 220, 227, 230, 233.
133   Herucová, *Arpádovskí palatíni*, p. 231.
134   *Cosmae Pragensis Chronica Boemorum* II 19, 23, 24, ad a. 1061, 1068, ed. Bretholz, pp. 111, 115, 117.
135   *Cosmae Pragensis Chronica Boemorum* III 22, 27, 30, 32, 34, 37, 39, ad a. 1108, 1109, 1110, 1111, 1113, ed. Bretholz, pp. 189–190, 196–197, 200, 203, 205, 209, 211. Žemlička, *Čechy v době knížecí*, pp. 184, 469.
136   See chapter 16, note 8. Györffy, *István király*, pp. 313–314. Györffy, *König Stephan*, p. 199.
137   See chapter 16, note 16.
138   The first known Transylvanian voivode was Merkur, mentioned in years 1111 and 1113. *Mercurius princeps Ultrasilvanus*. DHA I, ed. Györffy, no. 138/I, II, pp. 383, 385, no. 141/I, p. 396. CDES I, ed. Marsina, no. 68, p. 64, no. 69, p. 67. Györffy: ÁMF II, pp. 97–99, 105, 143–158. *Erdély története I*, ed. Makkai, Mócsy, pp. 285–286, 313–315, 319–323, 341–346. *Kurze Geschichte Siebenburgens*, ed. Köpeczi, pp. 151, 192–204, 210–213.

9 Nitrian Princes and Hungarian Kings

In Nitria, unlike Piast, Rurik and partially also the Přemyslid appanages, the heritable rule of an indirect Árpád princely line did not arise, which would naturalize it and distance it from the kingdom part of Hungary. The Nitrian and Moravian principalities, unlike subordinated appanaged principalities in Poland and in Russia, never battled over the tearing away of Nitria from Hungary and Moravia from Bohemia, because the Nitrian princes wanted to become Hungarian kings and Moravian princes wanted to occupy the Bohemian princely seat in Prague. An exact process applied in occupying the kingdom and both princely titles in Hungary. After the death of the Hungarian King, the Prince of Nitria became the new king, and his subordinate Biharian Prince occupied the princely seat in Nitria and Biharia went to the next Árpád in line. This ladder, although not always complete[139] and interrupted by Solomon's coronation, prevented the origin of indirect dynasty of the Nitrian princes with a separatist program. Thanks to the partial heritability of the Moravian appanaged principalities, it differed from Bohemia more significantly than Nitria from the rest of Hungary. The expectancy of Moravian princes on the Bohemian princely seat in Prague, however, prevented the breaking away of Moravia from Bohemia.[140]

Nitrians were Hungarians to the measure to which Nitria was a part of Hungary and they were different than other Hungarians to the measure Nitria differed from the rest of Hungary. This certainly applied also for Moravia and Moravians in relation to Bohemia and the Bohemians.

---

139   Only Ladislas, who was the first Biharian Prince (1064–1074), then Nitrian Prince (1074–1077) and ultimately Hungarian King (1077–1095), passed through this entire sequence. With other Árpád princes this sequence is incomplete.
140   Žemlička, *Čechy v době knížecí*, pp. 330, 348–351, 354.

CHAPTER 20

The End of the Nitrian Principality (1108–1110)

1   The Zobor Documents

The German and Bohemian attack against Hungary in September and October of 1108, which the last Nitrian and Biharian prince Álmos instigated, backfired. At the beginning of November 1108, when German King Henry was already in Bavaria and blind Álmos sat powerlessly in Dömös Abbey, Hungarian King Coloman invaded Moravia as a form of retribution. Bohemian Prince Svatopluk hurried with his army to beat back the Hungarian attack, but he was wounded in the eye on a nighttime ride, and on 12 November 1108 he had to cancel the campaign.[1]

On 14 February 1109 Svatopluk with his younger brother, Olomouc Prince Otto II the Black (1107–1110, 1113–1125, in years 1123–1125 he was also the Brno prince), again invaded Slovakia: *Suddenly he invaded Nitra Castle with his army and would have attacked it, if the garrison force which is always on guard there had not closed the gate. Thus, they plundered and burned the area beneath the castle, and when they returned, they met multitudes of refugees who were fleeing on wagons and horses to the mentioned castle. They gathered them all like sheafs in the fields, burned their villages, scourged the entire country, and with a huge quarry of livestock and other property, they returned happily to their homes.*[2]

War events in years 1108 and 1109 afflicted Zobor Abbey. Lieges living on the ravaged abbey lands used the restless times and began to declare themselves as free men and refused to fulfill their obligations toward the abbey.[3] In addition to this, royal tax collectors, called *kalízi*, the centurion Prkoš, his assistant Etej and their partners Mark and Magiug, began to doubt the right of the abbey to a third of the market toll and fees from all the trading in Nitra, in the Courts, at the crossing of the Váh River and in Trenčín, which Stephen I had donated to the abbey.

The dispute of Zobor Abbot Gaufred with the tax collectors was ended by witness testimonies and oaths which were made *in this castle Nitra (in eadem*

---

[1] *Cosmae Pragensis Chronica Boemorum* III 25, ed. Bretholz, pp. 193–194. Annalista Saxo, *Chronicon* ad a. 1108, Gombos, *Catalogus I*, p. 225.
[2] *Cosmae Pragensis Chronica Boemorum* III 26, ed. Bretholz, pp. 194–195. Annalista Saxo, *Chronicon* ad a. 1108, Gombos, *Catalogus I*, pp. 225–226.
[3] DHA I, ed. Györffy, no. 142/I, pp. 392–393. CDES I, ed. Marsina, no. 69, p. 65.

civitate Nitrie). Testifying on behalf of the abbey were *optimates XII Nitrienses*, that is twelve exceptionally dignified inhabitants of Nitra, *whose memory undoubtedly stretched through the times since the days of the blessed King* (Stephen) *to the time of the above-mentioned dispute.* Among them, immediately in first and second place, were two former and long-time Nitrian counts, and after them went the sons of the first Nitrian count, who was no longer alive: *From them the first, by the name of Una, was for many years the count of this Nitra Castle; however the second, too, by the name Bača, was also for many years the Nitra count. The third and fourth, Deda and Gečä, were both sons of Bukven, once the count of Nitra Castle. These two, Deda and Gečä, sons of Count Bukven, had lived in Nitra Castle for eighty years now and furthermore, when this dispute took place.* Others among these dozen witnesses were Penet, Sejun, Martin (son of Mark), Petre, Kup, Zbyša, Figa and the judge Peregrin. Because the dispute was about fees for trading in Nitra, the mentioned Peregrin could have been the Nitra market judge. King Coloman appointed Batona, another resident of Nitra, as bailiff, that is his own trustee during the investigation of the entire dispute. Batona, as the royal bailiff, ensured that the mentioned 12 witnesses in the Church of St. Emmeram, and Andrew and Benedict at Nitra Castle, confirmed by an oath to the present Esztergom Archbishop Laurentius the heritable right of the abbey to the mentioned tolls and fees. Then, in order to remove all doubts, 11 younger witnesses, who unlike the previous 12 could not recall the times Saint Stephen, swore in this same church that they knew and testified to the rights that the abbey had before the origin of this dispute. The first among them was *Moses, at this time count of this castle* (*Moyses eiusdem civitatis tempore illo comes*). Together with Moses the following also took an oath: Lambert, the dean of the Nitra Chapter; the grammarian Willerm, probably director of the chapter school; presbyter Laurentius; presbyter Godefrid; and five canons: Martin, son of presbyter Matthew, Nicholas, son of Pestrej, Hector, son of Ulfod, and Daniel and Poško. The last witness was Yaroslav, son of the mentioned Batona. The dispute ended with the victory of the Zobor abbot. The document which confirmed all the rights of Zobor Abbey doubted by the tax collectors was issued in 1111 (before 1 September), probably by the Nitria Chapter and was sealed by the Zagreb Bishop Manases.[4]

Moses was the Nitrian count only to the time, *when this dispute took place.* All the others in the group of younger witnesses had their titles not only

---

4   DHA I, ed. Györffy, no. 138/I, pp. 382–383, 138/II, pp. 384–385. CDES I, ed. Marsina, no. 68, pp. 63–64. Béla Kossányi, "A kalizok vallása," in *Emlékkönyv Domanovszky Sándor* (Budapest 1937), pp. 355–368. Marsina, "Štúdie k slovenskému diplomatáru. K problematike najstarších zoborských listín," pp. 135–161. *Dejiny Nitry*, ed. Fusek, Zemene, pp. 127–129.

tempore illo like Moses, but also later in the time of writing the document (before 1 September 1111). Moses was no longer the count at that time. He lived further as a former count, just as his predecessors Bača and Una.

So that no one could further doubt the right of Zobor Abbey or its property, the abbot needed to obtain a complete list of the properties confirmed by the king. Against his lieges, *who very confidently declared their freedom*, Abbot Gaufred relied on the testimony of the magnates Cosmas and Moses (*regnique principies Cosmam et Moysem*). After hearing Cosmas's and Moses's testimony, King Coloman appointed two bailiffs, *Ceva, the vice-count of Count Moses* (*Ceuam curialem comitem comitis Moysi*), *and the second by the name of Batona, confirmed these by marking the borders of all the properties of the abbot of St. Hippolytus*. Batona, also mentioned as a bailiff confirmed by the king in the dispute with the tax collectors, was an inhabitant of Nitra. Therefore, his second bailiff, Ceva, was an inhabitant of Nitra; that is he was the Nitra vice-count, and his superior, Count Moses, who ranked among the leading magnates of the kingdom, was Count of Nitra, this same Count Moses who is mentioned in the first Zobor document. Therefore, Moses lost his title of count before the issuing of the first Zobor document (before 1 September 1111), and the decision on the dispute with the lieges of the abbey written only in 1113 in the second Zobor document had to have fallen into the time when Moses was still count, that is at the same time as the decision on the dispute with the tax collectors written in 1111 in the first Zobor document.

Zobor Abbey owned, aside from Zobor itself, on which it lay, 21 villages and 13 smaller properties (parts of villages and various lands) scattered over the extensive territory of south-western Slovakia. Going around them could have taken Ceva and Batona two years and shifted the issuing of the second Zobor document, which is actually a catalogue of this massive amount of property, up to year 1113. Zobor Abbot Gaufred (*Godefridus*) compiled it himself, and it was probably prepared by the Nitra Chapter and on the command of the king, stamped by Zagreb Bishop Manases.[5]

---

[5] See chapter 14, note 128, see chapter 20, note 3. Regarding the two-year gap between the writing of the two Zobor documents, see Marsina, "Štúdie k slovenskému diplomatáru. K problematike najstarších zoborských listín," pp. 147–148. Cosmas came from the Poznan family (*Cosma de genere Paznan*). In 1123 he marched in the campaign of Hungarian King Stephen II to Russia. During the siege of castle Vladimir, on behalf of other magnates and soldiers who were on the campaign, he refused obedience, rejected the ill-considered attack on this castle and compelled the king to return to Hungary. *Chron. Hung. comp. saec. XIV.* II 155, SRH I, pp. 437–439. Not only did Cosmas come from the Poznan line, but perhaps also Count Moses, too. Both could have been grandsons of Count Bukven and sons of Bukven's sons Deda and Geča. Lukačka, *Formovanie*, pp. 30–32. A bishop was required to know the language that was spoken in his diocese. Manases's predecessor Duch was Bohemian. He thus could speak the

The Zobor documents name the first four Nitra counts. These were Bukven (from 1029), Una (around the mid-11th century), Bača (perhaps in the last quarter of the 11th century) and Moses (before 1 September 1111). If the Zobor abbot no long required testimony of another county or his descendants, if this dispute no longer was relevant, then we can with complete certainty assume that Nitra County did not have several counts in this period. And furthermore, if two them, Una and Bača, were counts for long years (*multis annis*), then the period of 82 years (1029–1111) for all four counts is not at all too long a time. The list of them is thus complete.

2　The Nitra Bishopric

Nitrian Count Moses (*Nitriensis comes nomine Moyses*) got into a dispute with Pannonhalma Abbey, when he wanted to take abbey land near the Váh (perhaps in today's Šaľa). Then the king ordered Nitra Bishop Gervasius (*domno Geruasio eiusdem loci episcopo*) to judge the dispute and determine the border of the abbey property. Esztergom Archbishop Laurentius is mentioned in the record which the abbey made about Gervasius's decision.[6] Since Laurentius was archbishop in the years 1105–1116 and Moses at the time of preparing the first Zobor document (before 1 September 1111) was no longer count, we must place the mentioned event into the period 1105–summer of 1111. Gervasius thus became bishop no later than in the summer of 1111.

King Coloman ordered the judgements of God (ordeals) to be held only in the seats of the bishops, in larger provostals and also in Bratislava and in Nitra (*necnon Posanii et Nitrie*).[7] Thus, Nitra at the time of issuing of Coloman's laws, around the year 1100, was still not a bishopric seat. Gervasius thus became the Nitra bishop in approximately the first decade of the 12th century.

The renewal of the perhaps two-hundred years extinct Nitrian bishopric, just as the founding of other Hungarian bishoprics and the division of their

---

　　　Slavic language, which he could also use in the Zagreb diocese. See chapter 18, note 42. If Manases was bishop in Zagreb, then he must have been able to speak the Slavic language. If King Coloman commanded Manases to stamp the Zobor document, then evidently because he knew about the situation in Zobor Abbey and understood it. If Zobor Abbey was close to Manases and if he spoke the Slavic language, then he probably came from Slovak territory and was a Slovak.
6　*DHA I*, ed. Györffy, no. 137, p. 381. *CDES I*, ed. Marsina, no. 66, p. 62. See note 4.
7　*Colomanni regis decretorum liber primus* XXII. *A szent István, szent László és Kálman korabeli törvények*, ed. Závodszky, p. 186. Györffy, *Wirtschaft und Geselschaft*, p. 308.

dioceses, was in the authority of the king.[8] While Prince Álmos sat and ruled in Nitra, King Coloman could only contemplate the founding of a bishopric there. He could hardly undertake to set up a bishopric seat in Álmos's principality, because he could not cooperate with his enemy brother. And he could not at all name his man as bishop there, whom Álmos would not bear in his vicinity. Coloman renewed or re-established the Nitra bishopric only after the removal of Álmos from Nitra and after the end of the wars, which in the autumn of 1108 and in February 1109 endangered Nitra itself. At the latest, however, in the summer of 1111, when Gervasius was certainly already the bishop, thus, most probably in the peaceful year of 1110. The king thus established the Nitra bishopric perhaps two years after the deposing of the last Nitrian prince.

Esztergom Archbishop Laurentius was unwilling to relinquish the larger part of his own diocesal territory or even that of the Nitra archdeaconate itself on behalf of the newly established Nitra bishopric. He relinquished only the marginal Trenčín County with the Trenčín Castle archdeaconate and Nitra itself.[9]

3 The End and Territorial Breakup of Nitria

The oldest Hungarian chronicler, who wrote his Gesta Ungarorum vetera in the first years of Coloman's rule, sought in the appanaged principality the reason for pointless internal wars: *The dividing of the country occurred because of many breaches and disputes between the Hungarian princes and kings*.[10] These were thus unwanted, and it was necessary to remove them. Thus, the

---

8 The founders of the Hungarian bishoprics were Hungarian Kings Stephen I and Ladislas I. To reduce or increase the territory of the diocese was in the authority of the king. On 19 February 1299 Andrew III detached the Maramaros (Maramureș) seat from Transylvania diocese and attached it to the neighbouring Eger diocese. The dispute between the Transylvanian and Eger bishops over Maramaros did not end; therefore, on 10 August 1299 and 6 January 1300 the king had to again decide. Maramaros in the end remained to the Eger bishop. *Codex diplomaticus Hungariae ecclesiasticus ac civilis VI/2*, studio et opera Georgii Fejér (Budae 1830), pp. 192–194, 287–290. *Codex diplomaticus Transsylvaniae. Diplomata, epistolae et alia instrumenta litteraria res Transsylvanas illustrantia I. 1023–1300*. Ad edendum in regestis praeparavit et introductione notisque illustravit Sigismundus Jakó (Budapestini 1997), no. 575, 581, 592, pp. 323–324, 325, 341. Ortvay, *MEF I*, pp. 146–147, 202–203. Györffy, *ÁMF IV*, p. 124.

9 Fügedi, *Kirchliche Topographie*, pp. 366–368. Marsina, "Nitrianske biskupstvo," pp. 536–541. Marsina, "Vývoj cirkevnej organizácie," pp. 95–97. Marsina, "Obnovenie," pp. 24–26. Marián Róbert Zemene, "Územie Nitrianskej diecézy za feudalizmu," *Slovenská archivistika* 15 (1980), no. 2, pp. 137–141.

10 *Chron. Hung. comp. saec. XIV.* II 88, *SRH I*, p. 345.

chronicler was probably a former chaplain and scribe of King Ladislas I and later (perhaps Veszprém) Bishop Koppány.[11] In this opinion, he undoubtedly agreed with King Coloman, whom he accompanied for the last time on a campaign to Russia in April of 1099.[12] Coloman was *cunning* (*astutus*), and he managed to do what not one king had done since the times of Stephen I and Samuel Aba. He removed a prince. He wasn't satisfied, however, only with deposing and restraining Álmos, but he also abolished the principality itself and began to break apart its territory.

The eastern border of the Esztergom diocese, as we know from 13th and 14th century sources,[13] cut across the territory of the large Borsod County, which made up the eastern part of the Nitrian Principality, and according to Anonymus's description reached from the Tisza between the mouth of the Bodrog and the mouth of the Sajó and from the Bükk Mountains on the south to the Tatras and to the Hungary-Poland border on the north and to the Zemplín and Slanské hills and the Ondava Mountains in the east. The basins of the Sajó, the Hornád and the Poprad belonged to it. Between this large range of the oldest Borsod County and also the eastern range of the Nitrian Principality and the known range of the Esztergom diocese, which in the east ended by the later archdeaconates Spiš, Turňa and Gemer, is thus an apparent dispute.

According to the decision of Stephen I from year 1009, the Veszprém and Pécs dioceses, and thus also the neighbouring Győr diocese, copied the borders of castle counties from which they were made up. In 1030 King Stephen organized the Csanád bishopric, to which he assigned the whole of Csanád County. The border of Csanád County thus also became the borders of the Csanád diocese. Equally, the oldest Esztergom diocese had to respect the existing borders of Nitria, which was its diocesal territory. Thus, the whole large Borsod County had to belong to the east of it. The Esztergom diocesal borders, known from 13th- and 14th-century sources, did not respect the borders of the large Borsod County at all and cut across its territory. Thus, they could only have arisen after the extinction and territorial breakup of Nitria and after the breaking apart of its easternmost castle county. And the borders of other Hungarian dioceses, as we know them from sources in the 13th and 14th centuries, only partially correspond to their older borders, which founder Stephen determined for them. Therefore, even the range of the Esztegom diocese, known mainly from papal

---

11   *DHA I*, Györffy, no. 85, 88, 96, 151, pp. 261, 263, 268, 285, 412. Kállay, "Kopán krónikája," pp. 21–23. Györffy, "Az Árpád-kori magyar krónikák," pp. 393–394. See chapter 12, notes 25, 26.
12   See chapter 12, note 26, see chapter 18, note 71.
13   Ortvay, *MEF I*, pp. 1–61. Fügedi, *Kirchliche Topographie*, pp. 363–400.

tithe registers from the years 1332–1337, do not match the range that it had in the 11th century, when its borders overlapped with the borders of the Nitrian Principality.

Újvár County is mentioned for the first time in 1138.[14] Újvár and other castle counties were thus detached from great Borsod even before this year. At the latest, simultaneously with Újvár, Szerencz Castle was detached from Borsod with a small territory on the north bank of the Tisza, between the mouth of the Sajó and the mouth of the Bodrog, and connected with the territory of the Zemplín, which was detached from the large neighbouring Ung County. The seat of this new county was alternately on both sides of Szerencs and the Zemplín; therefore in the 13th and 14th centuries we come across a double-naming of it.[15]

---

14 *Mathei comitis Nove Civitatis*. CDES 1, ed. Marsina, no. 77, p. 75. King Samuel Aba (1041–1044) founded Újvár Castle (Nova Civitas, Novum Castrum, from the mid-13th century Abaújvár) on the right bank of the middle Hornád: *ad Novum Castrum, quod rex Aba construxerat. Chron. Hung. comp. saec. XIV.* II 81, SRH 1, 337. The older castle, lying on the opposite bank of the Hornád, then got the name Old Castle (Starý hrad, Óvár, Nagyóvár), in 1255 *Ouwar* and in 1317 *Nagyowar*. CDES 2, ed. Marsina, np. 466, p. 323. *Codex diplom. hungaricus Andegavensis. Anjoukori okmánytár I*, szerkesztette Imre Nagy (Budapest 1878) no. 381, p. 422. Györffy, ÁMF I, p. 126. Branislav Varsik, "Starý a Nový Hrad pri Hornáde v Abaujskej župe," *Historický sborník SAVU* IX (1951), pp. 59–64. Branislav Varsik, *Osídlenie Košickej kotliny I*, pp. 53–56, 85, 87. The New Castle (Újvár), founded by King Aba, was not the seat of a castle county at the beginning, just as the adjacent and the older Old Castle (Óvár) was not, or to the north the advanced Salt Castle (Salis). These castles lay on the territory of Borsod County. Újvár became a castle county only after the breaking up of large Borsod.

15 Szerencs County is mentioned only rarely. In 1217 *decimas parochie Sceremchi. Vetera monumenta historica Hungariam sacram illustrantia I*, ed. Theiner, no. IX, p. 6. In 1275 *in parochia Zerench villas Bezeg, Hyduegi et Zamthou usque fluvium Oronas. Codex diplomaticus Hungariae ecclesiasticus ac civilis* V/2, studio et opera Georgii Fejér (Budae 1829), p. 304. Györffy, ÁMF I, p. 142. In 1317 *decimas quarundam villarum in comitatibus de Wiuuar, Borsod, Vng et Zerempech ... Et in comitatu de Zerempech decimas villarum Pyud Kereztura, Kyusfalud, Zegey et Krthbenye vocatarum, cum aliis villis ad eundem comitatum pertinentibus usque fluvium Aranys, qui alio nomine Mezespatak appellatur. Regesta diplomatica nec non epistolaria Slovaciae* 2, ad edendum praeparavit Vincent Sedlák (Bratislava 1987), no. 282, p. 139. The position of Szerencs County (with the villages Bodrogkeresztúr, Bodrogkisfalud, Bodrogszegi and Kétbénye) between the counties Abov, Borsod and Ung, is testimony that this is actually Zemplín County, which had the name sometimes also according to Szerencs Castle. In 1319 *decimas quarundam villarum in comitatibus Abuüuar, Borsod, Zerempich et Vngh habitarum ... et in comitatu de Zerepnich decimas villarum Pyndkeretura, Kyusfalud, Zeged et Ketbeny usque fluvium Oranyas, quod alio nomine Mezespatak vocatur*. RDES 2, ed. Sedlák, no. 443, p. 210. Zemplín County is mentioned, starting with Zemplín vice-count Aladár in 1220, very often: *Olodarus, curialis comes de Zemlun*. CDES 1, ed. Marsina, no. 244, p. 188.

In the north Turňa[16] and the Spiš were divided from Borsod[17] and in the west the Gemer.[18] Simultaneously with the breaking up of Borsod, neighbouring Eger County also expired, because the reduced Borsod got its eastern part, the territory on the south side of the Bükk Mountains with Öršúr Castle.[19] The

---

16   In 1198 *praedium Torna* is mentioned. Györffy *ÁMF I*, p. 740. Kristó, *A vármegyék*, pp. 389–393.
17   In 1209 Bamberg Bishop Ekbert sold *terram quandam, in Chypus supra Poprad* to Spiš provost Adolf and his sister. *CDES I*, ed. Marsina, no. 154, p. 122. Kristó, *A vármegyék*, pp. 393–395. Michal Slivka, *Pohľady do stredovekých dejín Slovenska (Res intrincesus lectae)* (Martin 2013), pp. 84–85.
18   Anonymus considered the basin of the Sajó, that is the territory of the later Gemer region, as a part of the older Borsod. *Anonymi (P. magistri) Gesta Hungarorum* 16, SRH I, p. 57. See pp. 354–356. In another place Anonymus takes into consideration the situation of his period, when Gemer County, *populum de castro Gumur et Nougrad ... ad partes castri Gumur*, already existed and in conflict with the preceding statement places its oldest existence back to the period of Árpád. *Anonymi (P. magistri) Gesta Hungarorum* 33, SRH I, pp. 74–75. Kristó, *A vármegyék*, pp. 386–390.
19   Anonymus describes the territory of Öršúr Castle, which lay on the southern edge of the Bükk Mountains: *Regarding Öršúr Castle and the Eger River. Then from there Árpád and his soldiers marched and went as far as the Nyárad River and set up camp by the watery streams, beginning with the place that now which bears the name Kács. There Árpád also gave a large territory to Ócsád, father of Öršúr. Öršúr (Ursuur) here later built by the spring of this river a castle, which is called Öršúr. From here Prince Árpád then marched with his people up to the Eger River, where they resided in the huts a larger number of days. The mountain on which the prince built the huts from branches and leaves they called Szíhalom and their castles rose from the Ostoros River up to the castle Poroszló*. *Anonymi (P. magistri) Gesta Hungarorum* 32, SRH I, pp. 72–73. According to Anonymus, the territory of Öršúr between the Bükk Mountains, the Eger and Tisza rivers and the mouth of the Sajó did not originally belong to Borsod. According to Hungarian chroniclers, Örs was one of the captains of Árpád's army: *The seventh captain was named Örs (Vrs). His family had its seat near Sajó (Seyo)*. *Chron. Hung. comp. saec. XIV.* II 34, SRH I, p. 292. However, the captain of the fourth (army) was named Örs (Vrs); it is said that he built his tents by the river Sajó (Soio). *Simonis de Keza Gesta Hungarorum* II 30, SRH I, p. 166. Benkő, *Név*, pp. 16, 52–53. In 1194 Béla III, under the authority of Borsod Castle, detached the territory of Péla: *quandam aliam terram in concambium nomine Pel a iurisdiccione castri Borsod exemptam*, lying in the south of Borsod by the Tisza River. *ÁÚO XI*, ed. Wenzel, no. 37, p. 56. Györffy, *ÁMF I*, p. 801. In 1248, under the authority of Borsod Castle, Béla IV detached *villam Cherep ... in comitatu Borsod existentem*, that is the village Cserép lying on the southern edge of the Bükk Mountains. *Codex diplomaticus Hungariae ecclesiasticus ac civilis IV/2*, studio et opera Georgii Fejér (Budae 1829), pp. 17–18. Györffy, *ÁMF I*, pp. 767–768. Therefore, the territory between the Bükk Mountains and the rivers Tisza and Eger with castle Öršúr, where the villages Pély and Cserép lay, in 1194 certainly belonged to Borsod. The difference of northern and southern Borsod is also emphasized by the position of Borsod Castle lands and the position of the oldest properties of the Eger bishop, confirmed by Béla IV in 1261. The majority of the lands belonging to Borsod Castle lay in northern Borsod, concentrated mainly around the castle. The Eger Bishop had here only the village Borsodszirák

newly created Újvár castle county got its western part with the castle Heves.[20] Eger ceased being a castle county and remained only a bishopric seat.[21]

According to the Wielkopolska (Greater Polish) Chronicle, the Spiš belonged to Poland up to 1113. In 1113 Polish King Boleslaw III reportedly gave the Spiš castellany as a dowry for his daughter, who married Boris, the son of Hungarian King Coloman.[22] However, the Polish chronicler invented the story about how Poland lost the Spiš region. The year 1113, to which it dates it,

---

(*villa Zyrakh prope fluvium Harnad*). In southern Borsod only 3 castle properties lay; however, the Eger bishop owned 9 villages here: Felsőtárkány, Alsótárkány, Szöllöske, Szihalom, Harsány, Tiszakürt, Hejöpapi, Ároktő and Keresztespüspőki. *Az Árpád-házi királyok okleveleinek kritikai jegyzéke II/1*, szerkesztette Imre Szentpétery (Budapest 1943), no. 2123, pp. 120–122. Györffy, *ÁMF I*, pp. 745–746, 775, 784, 799, 807–808, 809. Kovács, *Az egri egyházmegye története 1596-ig*, pp. 27, 29, 128–131. The Miškov (Miskolcz) family had properties in the original northern Borsod. See chapter 14, note 158. In the later attached southern, Örsúr part of Borsod lay properties of the family Örsúr. Györffy, *ÁMF I*, pp. 739–746, 751, 758–759, 768–769, 772–773, 776, 778–779, 785, 787, 791–792, 794–795, 797–798, 802–804, 814–815, 817. Unlike the Abov family, we don't have any reliable proof on the presence of the Örsúrs in southern Borsod in the 11th century. The Örsúr family could have come to southern Borsod only in the 12th century. Karácsonyi, *A magyar nemzetségek*, pp. 876–887. Györffy, *Krónikaink*, pp. 107, 116–117.

20 Just as the territory of Castle Zaránd (see chapter 13, note 18) still belonged to Bihar County even under the rule of King Emeric (1196–1204), Heves then already belonged to the oldest Újvár County, which, however, originated perhaps a century later as Bihar County: *Hic quoque Henricus rex duas partes tributorum totius comitatus Byhoriensis tam circa Byhar quam circa Zarand et partem suam tributi, quod in comitatu Novi castri tam circa ipsum Novum castrum quam circa Hewes et in comitatu de Bebes tam in villis quam in foris exigitur, donavit ecclesie nostre Waradiensi, in duabus partibus episcopo et in tertia parte nobis, prout in privilegio eiusdem confirmato per Belam quartum, Stephanum, Ladislaum, Karolum et Lodovicum reges continetur. Chronicom Waradiense* 16, SRH I, p. 211. King Emeric made this donation in 1203, and other Hungarian kings confirmed it several times: *privilegium regis Henrici, anno Domini millesimo ducentesimo tertio confectum alienatis et combustis ... rex Bela per privilegium suum, confirmans ipsum privilegium Henrici regis, ita inquiens, quod cum propter devastationem, que per Tartaros culpis nostris exigentibus accidit ... privilegia ecclesie nostre Waradiensis super donationibus eidem ecclesie factis ... et solum quoddam privilegium regis Henrici pie recordationis illesium remansisset, donationes quasdam continens, Chronicom Waradiense*, SRH I, p. 204. *Codex diplom. hungaricus Andegavensis. Anjoukori okmánytár IV*, szerkesztette Imre Nagy (Budapest 1884), no. 175, p. 292. Kristó, *A vármegyék*, pp. 401, 473–474.

21 Just as the remnant Kalocsa County, after the detaching of Bác and Bodrog County, merged with neighbouring Fejér and the remnant Vác County after the detaching of the castle counties Szolnok, Csongrád, Szigetfő and Pest was attached to neighbouring Novohrad (Nógrád), thus Eger County ended when its territory was divided into the newly created Újvár and the remnant Borsod County. Kalocsa, Vác and Eger ceased to be county castles and remained only as bishopric seats.

22 *Et sic castellania de Spis a Polonis alienata, per Hungaros usque ad praesens fraudulenter detenda occupatur. Boguphali Chronicon Poloniae* 27, MPH II, ed. Bielowski, p. 508.

however, may be genuine. It was at this time that the Spiš could have become a castle county. Perhaps then the oldest stone ramparts were already being built at Spiš Castle and sometime about a century later the massive, stone residential tower.[23] The Spiš and at the same time the Turňa and Gemer castle counties, as well as Szerencs (Zemplín) and Ujvár, could thus have been detached from Borsod by King Coloman immediately after the abolishing of the Nitrian Principality in years 1110–1113.

The breakup of large Borsod was accompanied by the expanding of the Eger and the reduction of the Esztergom diocese. Turňa, Gemer and Spiš (together with the north-western part of the Šariš on the upper Torysa) remained to the Esztergom diocese. The Eger diocese acquired the residual Borsod, Szerencs and Újvár counties, because their newly connected parts Öršúr, Zemplín and Heves even before then belonged to the Eger diocese. The oldest proof on the affiliation of Újvár and Borsod (and thus also Szerencs) to the Eger diocese is the list of the archdeacons of the Eger diocese as witnesses in the conclusion of the document on the Eger Chapter from 1245. The witnesses were the Újvár, Boržava (Borsova), Szabolcs and Borsod archdeacons.[24] A document of the Eger Chapter from 1247 again mentions the Újvár archdeacon.[25] A document of the Eger Chapter from 1249 has in a list of witnesses the Eger provost and the archdeacons of Újvár, Boržava, Zsomboly, Szabolcs, Borsod and Kemej.[26] Stephen V, at a royal gathering in Hajóhalm and in Heves in 1271, had the old concessions of the Eger bishopric written down. Stephen's document names all the castle counties, ten of which belong to the Eger bishop. All the named counties belonged to the Eger diocese and Újvár and Borsod are also among them.[27] The borders *from the Körös up to the Zagyva River and to the Spiš forest,*

---

23   Andrej Fiala – Adrián Vallašek – Gabriel Lukáč, *Spišský hrad* (Martin 1988), pp. 30–35. Slivka, *Pohľady*, pp. 79–80, 95–96.
24   *Magistro Leustacio, Farkasio, Laurentio, Ladislao archidiaconis.* CDES I, ed. Marsina, no. 206 A, p. 141.
25   *Presentibus Leustasio, Novi castri archidiacono.* CDES I, ed. Marsina, no. 283, p. 199.
26   *Nicolao preposito, magistro Leustachio Noui castri, Farcasio de Bursua, Iacobo de Sumbun, Urbano de Zobolch, Ladizlao de Borsod, Iohanne de Kemey archidiaconis.* CDES I, ed. Marsina, no. 342, p. 239. Other documents of the Eger Chapter from years 1252, 1256, 1257 also have such a list of archdeacons of the Eger diocese. CDES I, ed. Marsina, no. 413, 533, 539, 587, pp. 289, 369, 374, 407.
27   *Az Árpád-házi királyok okleveleinek kritikai jegyzéke II/1*, ed. Szentpétery, no. 2124, pp. 124–125. In 1261 Béla IV renewed the old rights of the Eger bishop to property donated by the founder of the bishopric, Stephen I, Ladislas I and other Hungarian kings, whose donation documents were destroyed during the Mongol incursions. Most of the bishopric's property lay in Heves and in southern Borsod. The Eger bishop had in Heves, in addition to Eger itself, 33 villages and in southern Borsod 9 villages. Only 3 villages belonged to it on the territories attached to its diocese from the broken up large Borsod County:

which circumscribed the Eger diocese, are mentioned by Anonymus as the range of one of the Árpád invasions.[28] The shifting of the Esztergom-Eger diocese border, which we can safely date before 1245 and according to Anonymus even before 1200, is associated with the division of large Borsod County before 1138, probably back in the time of the abolishing of the Nitrian Principality and its territorial breakup.

In 1110 King Coloman reduced the range of the Esztergom diocese. In the north-west he detached the Little Nitria diocese from it and perhaps at the same time reduced the Esztergom diocese in the east, when the newly originated Szerencs (Zemplín), Újvár and small Borsod County were added to the Eger diocese; therefore, their new parts, Zemplín (before then a part of Ung County), Heves and Örsúr (until then they made up Eger County), already belonged to the Eger diocese. This occurred two years after the deposing of Álmos, the last appanaged prince.

Changes of the county and diocese borders is linked with the abolishing and territorial breakup of the Nitrian Principality, which remained unoccupied after the deposing and blinding of Álmos. King Coloman deposed the last Prince of Nitria in 1108 and two years later abolished and broke apart the principality itself. At the same time, he reduced the Esztergom diocese, which until then had served its ecclesiastical administration and covered it territorially. Croatia, Slavonia and Transylvania remained for future candidates to the Hungarian throne.

Borsodszirák (*villa Zyrakh prope fluvium Harnad*) in northern Borsod, Sajóhídvéh (*villa Hyduege cum Mechtheluk*) in Szerencs territory and Hejce in the Abov (*Heyche in comitatu Abawyuar adiacentes*). The Eger bishop had fewer properties in more distant counties of its diocese and on the territories of the Vác, Várad and Veszprém dioceses. *Az Árpád-házi királyok kritikai jegyzéke II/1*, ed. Szentpétery, no. 2123, pp. 120–124. Kovács, *Az egri egyházmegye története 1596-ig*, pp. 27, 29, 128–130. See note 12.

28   Hinc vero dux Arpad et sui egressi venerunt ... et subiugaverunt sibi omnes habitatores terre a Grisio usque ad silvam Zepus. Anonymi (P. magistri) Gesta Hungarorum 32, SRH I, p. 73.

CONCLUSION

Nitria and Slovakia

1   The Arrival of the Slavs into World History

The great migration of nations put all of Europe into motion. What didn't move, however, were some of the old, long-tested borders determined by large natural barriers, such as the Alps, the Carpathians and the Sudeten ridges, or the middle and lower flow of the Danube and some of its tributaries. Initially, these borders divided the old Roman provinces and tribal territories from one another and then later new barbarian realms. Stable historical areas changed their ethnic content, though they preserved the old territorial outlines, sometimes even the ancient name, or even an old centre.

The former Roman province Noricum mediterraneum (Landlocked Noricum), Dalmatia (the western part) and Savia, lying in the eastern Alps and in the western Balkan, became the territory of the later principalities of Carantania, Savia and Croatia. The old Boiohaemum, bordered by the ridges of the Sudeten Mountains, gave territorial basis of Bohemia. The Nitrian Principality inherited the territory of the broken up Suebia, which covered the northwestern part of the Carpathian basin.

Slavic tribes occupied these former Roman and Germanic territories in two waves. The first Slavic wave came to the territory lying north and north-west of the middle Danube, which the Suebs (formerly the Quads), Marcomans and several other Germanic tribes vacated, from beneath the Carpathians, and the second wave came from Avar Pannonia. Other Slavic waves which flooded Roman and Byzantine provinces in the central and western Balkan and in the eastern Alps came from the territory of the Avar Khaganate. The Slavs thus inherited a part of the historical world and settled in its old outlines.

The Slavs who occupied Hunimund's Suebia, subverted in 470 by the Ostrogoths, joined in the years 548–552 with the neighbouring Gepids against distant Byzantium. *An unprecedented number* or *a large number* of their horse and foot soldiers invaded the Byzantium provinces in the Balkan and were able to defeat the stronger Byzantium army. Only a large and strong tribe (*gens*), to which belonged extensive territory, could gain respect among the powerful German neighbours of the Gepids and Longobards and undertake extensive campaigns to Byzantium and to distant Italy. The Slavs who occupied the entire former kingdom of Hunimund were thus not yet scattered into small divided groups, but were one large and militarily well-organized tribe. One tribal centre concluded an alliance of this Slavic tribe with the Gepids and Ostrogoths and assembled a large military campaign.

The Avars took over the Gepid realm in the Tisza River region and the Longobard realm in Pannonia in years 567–568 and brought with them, and subsequently later attracted, other Slavs. The Slavs, who in 623 rebelled against Avar rule, departed the hotbed of rebellion in Pannonia, moved to the eastern Alps, the west and central Balkan, to Bohemia, on the Elbe and middle Oder, where they established new Slavic principalities. Samo, who led a portion of the rebels, handed the Avars several defeats and was able to unite the new tribal principalities on the middle Danube together into one realm. Some more distant principalities, Dervan's Sorbia and Bohemia, were allied with Samo's realm. After the disintegration of Samo's realm, the Slavic principalities which originated around the perimeter of Avar Pannonia had to recognize Avar (Savia, Carniola, Nitria, Moravia) or Bavarian (Carantania) sovereignty.

2 Pribina's and Mojmír's Nitria

Frankish campaigns in years 791–803 and Slavic attacks in 805–811 disrupted the Avar realm. In 805 the Nitrian Principality also jolted Avar rule. The last independent prince of the Nitrians, Pribina, ruled for only 6 years (before 828–833). If we examine more closely the exiling of Pribina by Moravian Prince Mojmír in 833 and everything that developed up to the end of the 9th century, then a rectangle of relations, in which Pribina and his princely family line was dangerous opposition to the Moravian Mojmírs, comes to the forefront:

```
M    ×   833   ×   861   ×   883 – 884   ×   P          M    Mojmírs
*        ×                                   *          P    Pribinas
                                             828
*        870 – 871                           *          W    Wilhelms
             ×                               853
*                                            *          A    Aribs
883 –        882 – 884             883 –
– 884                              –884      ×   antagonism
*                ×
899 –                      893               *   friendship
– 901                                             and alliance
*                              ×     *
A    ×   865   ×   882 – 884   ×   893   ×   W
```

Without the independence of Pribina's Nitrian Principality towards Mojmír's Moravia up to the fateful year of 833, the position of Pribina and his followers in this rectangle would be incomprehensible. Likewise, the origin of Moravian-Nitrian dualism in the Great Moravian state would be inexplicable.

In 880 Nitra became the seat of a bishop. The Nitrian bishopric is clear evidence of the continuing importance of Nitra as the centre of Nitria,[1] one of the two Great Moravian principalities. That's why we have to look for the seat of appanaged Prince Svatopluk I (perhaps 853–871), as well as that of his son Svätopluk II (894–899) in Nitra.

When Great Moravian Prince Svatopluk died in 894, nearly the entire Carpathian basin belonged to his realm. His successors did not hold onto this great legacy. A Magyar attack in 906 ended the rule of the Mojmírs. The dynasty which for 73 years united Nitria with Moravia ended, and the paths of the two principalities divided.

3 Nitria and Hungary

In the years 906–920 Nitria belonged to a wide anti-Saxon alliance, along with the Moravians, Bohemians, Glomucians, Hevellians and Magyars, and in 914 also the Bavarians. In 920 this alliance broke apart. One of the Hungarian chieftains, Tas, took over Nitria and afterwards his son Lehel inherited it. After Lehel's death in 955 and after removal of the short-term (955–987) Přemyslid dominance over the south-western and north-western parts of Nitria (over its Little Nitria and Váh principalities), Nitria became an internal dynastic appanage of the Árpáds. In the period of Hungarian Prince Géza, his younger brother Michael ruled in Nitria (971/987–perhaps 995) and after him Géza's son Stephen (perhaps 995–997), who from there got to his father's princely seat in Esztergom.

The Hungarian state grew, and its stability was founded on the geopolitical logic of the Carpathian Basin. Its natural centripetal tendency also pulled the Nitrian Principality, lying on its north-west, to the centre of the new state. In the dark periods between the end of the state of one, Svatopluk's, and the origin of the state of another, Stephen's, Nitria was one of several Hungarian principalities. The founder of the unified Hungarian kingdom, Stephen I, in order to create a new state in the Carpathian Basin had to destroy these principalities. Nitria, however, due to its historical stability, survived the hard unification force of the first Hungarian king.

---

1 Steinhübel, "Slovanský 'gens' a jeho stred," pp. 142, 155–159.

The Princes of Nitria had the first claim on the Hungarian throne. However, as soon as they became Hungarian kings, this rule made them feel uncomfortable. Hungarian kings didn't want to hand over, or only with difficulty handed over, their rule to brothers or cousins who were Princes of Nitria, because they wanted their own sons to sit on the throne after their death. Hungarian Prince Géza had *hands stained with human blood*, because he violently rid himself of his younger brother Michael and put his own son Stephen on the throne as his successor. The Princes of Nitria Ladislas the Bald (1001–perhaps 1015) and Vazul (perhaps 1015–1029), sons of Michael, opposed King Stephen from neighbouring Poland. Stephen I wanted to hand over the Hungarian throne to his own son Emeric, and then after Emeric's premature death, to his nephew Peter Orseolo; therefore, he imprisoned Vazul and then had him blinded. Emeric was the prince of Nitria for only two years (1029–1031).

Hungarian King Stephen I resolved the question of succession in the same way as his father Géza. Nitrian Princes Michael and Vazul were victims of the founders of the Hungarian state. Michael's four grandsons, however, demonstrated their capabilities, and it was they and their descendants who continued the work of the sainted founder. After Stephen's death, the Hungarian kingdom managed to overcome all the confusion of a pagan rebellion, the long-lasting battle over royal power and wars with the neighbouring German empire. Hungary thus issued clear testimony about its own capability to succeed.[2] Nitria was an obvious and permanent part of it. The rule of a non-Árpád prince in Nitra, who perhaps came from the Aba line, didn't last even a half-year (1041–1042). In September 1042 the Nitrians requested the Árpád Domoslav as their prince. Thus, they clearly linked their own fate with the Árpád dynasty and the Hungarian state.

After the death of Nitrian Prince Domoslav (1042, 1046–1048), King Andrew I agreed with his brother Béla on the sharing of power between the king and the prince or the princes according to the principle of 2:1. Since Nitria itself did not achieve the required third of the state, Nitrian princes became at the same time Biharian princes or the Biharian princes were subordinate to them.

The co-rule of King Andrew and Prince Béla (1048–1060) lasted only a few years. Andrew I, upon installing his minor son Solomon, got into a war with Béla and lost. King Solomon again led a war with Béla's sons, Prince Géza (1063–1074) and Ladislas (1074–1077) and also lost. Perhaps only Nitrian Prince Lampert (1077–1095) ruled peacefully. And this is obviously only because his royal brother, Ladislas I, did not have any sons. Hungarian kings looked on the principality as on a constrained concession to their brothers and cousins, a

---

2   Kučera, *Slovensko po páde Veľkej Moravy*, p. 350.

threat to the stability of their royal power and the largest obstacle for the succession of their sons. Until in the end King Coloman, in order to ensure the crown for his son Stephen, not only deposed and blinded his brother Prince Álmos (1095–1108) and his young son, but he wiped the Nitrian Principality completely off the map of the contemporary world. He and his successors broke apart its castle system and thus wiped away its borders and disrupted its territory.

The Nitrian prince became the Hungarian king almost every time. That's why no indirect Árpád line of the Nitrian princes could originate, which would settle in Nitria and consider it as their direct heritable principality, just as there were in Russian and Polish appanages. Hungarian Nitria thus did not have its own princely dynasty, which would have had an interest in its further duration. In 1108, the rule of the Árpád appanaged princes ended and perhaps two years after so did the entire history of the Nitrian Principality.

4 Nitrians – Hungarians – Slavs – Slovaks

Medieval people perceived and felt their tribe or nation mainly in opposition to other tribes and nations, that is in the contrast of us and them. This common self-perception wasn't simple, because it reflected the entire history of development of a tribe and nation. Pribina's and later Svätopluk's Nitravians were not only Nitravians (then later Nitrians), but also Slavs and temporarily (from 833–906) even Moravians. When Nitria became a part of Hungary, the Nitrians, mentioned by Hungarian chroniclers as *Nitrienses* or *Nytrienses Sclavi*, were at the same time Nitrians, Hungarians and Slavs. And now the fact that they were Nitrians and Hungarians meant they differed from the Slavs in the neighbouring Slavic states, from whom they were divided by the Hungarian state border or Hungarian territory, as well as their different history. Since they were Nitrians, they differed from other Hungarian Slavs, and as Slavs they differed from the Magyars. They were thus a nation different from all the neighbouring nations.

After the dissolution of the Nitrian Principality, they ceased being Nitrians. However, they further remained not only Hungarians but also Slavs; thus, they principally differed from the Magyars, who were only Hungarians. If Simon of Kéza wrote that *one father and one mother conceived all the Hungarians*,[3] then he did not count the Hungarian Slavs in this, because he could not consider

---

3 *unus pater et una mater omnes Hungaros procreaverit*. Simonis de Keza Gesta Hungarorum I 7, SRH I, p. 148.

such a common origin of Slavs and Magyars. The chronicler considered only the pure Magyars, those who once came from Scythia: *Hungary namely had one hundred and eight pure families and no more.*[4] This *pure Hungary (pura Hungaria)* was a national ideal of the Hungarian chronicler, to which later migrants *from all external nations* did not belong,[5] and certainly not the old settled Slavs.

For the Slavs who lived with the non-Slavic Magyars in one state and needed to differentiate themselves from them, it was enough if they used the originally widespread Slavic-wide naming of the Slavs, that is the *Slovieni* or *Sloveni*. Therefore, they adopted it, and it became their own national name. That is how this name acquired, in addition from its Slavic-wide meaning, a different, narrowed and pure national content.[6] Therefore, the people who lived or came from Slovak territory and were labelled, at first only on rare occasion and from the 13th century more commonly, as *Sclavus*, *Sclavi*, *Slavus*, *Slavi*, *Tóth*, *Winde*, *Wende*, *Wenden* and exceptionally also as *Slovyenyn* and *Slowyenyny* and from the beginning of the 15th century also *Slowak*, we can then consider as Slovaks, as they ended up in a common state with the non-Slavic Magyars.[7]

---

4   *Centum enim et octo generationes pura tenet Hungaria et non plures. Simonis de Keza Gesta Hungarorum* I 6, SRH *I*, pp. 145–146. *Cum pura Hungaria plures tribus vel progenies non habeat quam generationes centum et octo. Simonis de Keza Gesta Hungarorum* II 76, SRH *I*, p. 187.

5   *Ex omni extera natione. Simonis de Keza Gesta Hungarorum* II 94, SRH *I*, p. 192.

6   Slovieni or Sloveni could not be a narrower tribal name of the inhabitants of Nitria in the 9th century, because they lacked the ability to differentiate between them and the Moravians, with whom they lived in a common state and who were also Slavs, or Slovieni, as it were. The name *Slovieni* could not more closely characterize and differentiate the Great Moravian Nitrians, because the Slovieni were all who lived in Great Moravian and in Svatopluk's large realm. Třeštík, *Vznik*, p. 288. In 906 Nitria lost the common state with the likewise Slavic Moravia and ended up in sharp contrast with the non-Slavic Magyars. Only then did the Slavic character of Nitria became a contrast and thus also characteristic and suitable for naming the territory and the nation.

7   Peter Ratkoš, "Postavenie slovenskej národnosti v stredovekom Uhorsku," in *Slováci a ich národný vývin. Sborník materiálov z V. sjazdu slovenských historikov v Banskej Bystrici* (Bratislava 1969), pp. 16–26. Ratkoš, "Otázky vývoja," pp. 34–35, 37–39, 42–44, 46–59. Branislav Varsik, "K sociálnym a národnostným bojom v mestách na Slovensku v stredoveku," in *Slováci a ich národný vývin*, pp. 44, 51–52, 57–70. Varsik, *Zo slovenského stredoveku*, pp. 306, 314, 317, 323–332, 336–341. Branislav Varsik, "O vzniku a rozvoji slovenskej národnosti v stredoveku" in Branislav Varsik: *Kontinuita medzi veľkomoravskými Slovienmi a stredovekými severouhorskými Slovanmi (Slovákmi). Výber štúdií a článkov z rokov 1969–1992* (Bratislava 1994), pp. 14–24. Branislav Varsik, "Vznik názvu Slovák vo svetle historických dokladov," in Varsik, *Kontinuita*, pp. 271–279. František Šmahel, *Idea národa v husitských Čechách* (Praha 2000), pp. 208–212. Miloš Marek, "Slovanské etnonymá v toponymii stredovekého Uhorska," *Studia historica Tyrnaviensia* 3 (2003), pp. 65–87. Magyars and Slovaks lived alongside one another, often in common villages. People who lived on extensive properties of the abbey in Hronský

5 Slovakia

Slavinia, which included all the Slavic or at least western Slavic countries,[8] was the antipole of Germania, that is the Eastern Frankish and later the German empire. The Slavs, however, were not only the antipole of the Germans but also of smaller nations and tribes that belonged to the German realm, that is the Saxons and Bavarians, or they had their own states, that is Latins, Magyars and Greeks. These neighboured with the Slavs and included them or wanted to include them into their states and drew them into their territory. Therefore, any small Slavic territory which belonged, either actually or only according to a unilateral formal claim, to a non-Slavic state was called Slavinia and without regard to whether it had, didn't have or had lost its own old tribal name. Everywhere there was a Slav/non-Slav contrast, and the Slavic pole of this contrast had the name Slavinia, Slavonia or Slovenia.

Saxony, Bavaria, Venice, Byzantium and Hungary had within their borders or in the immediate vicinity to which they made a claim Slavic territory, that is their own Slavinia. Bavarian Slavinia was Carinthia and the Eastern March.[9] Saxon Slavinia (*Sclavania*) was the territory of the Slavic Sorbs, Luticians and Obotrites, divided among the Saxon eastern marches.[10] The Slavic antipole of the coastal and islands of Dalmatia, which was Roman and first belonged to the Byzantine Empire and then to Venice, was Croatia, which they called

---

Beňadik belonged to various nations. A document of Andrew II from year 1217 differentiates the Saxons, Magyars and Slovaks: *quatenus cuiuscumque nationis homines, Saxones videlicet, Hungarii, Sclaui seu alii ad terram monasterii sancti Benedicti de Goron.* CDES I, ed. Marsina, no. 227, p. 179. In Sebechleby lived Magyars, Slovaks and Germans, who are mentioned in a document of Andrew II from 1233: *quod cum hospites Teothonici in villa Zebehleb commorantes ... Ab aliis vero, qui sunt, vel erunt citra fontem, sive sint Hungari, sive Sclavi, seu Teothonici ...* CDES I, ed. Marsina, no. 417, 422, pp. 304–305, 307–308. Ratkoš, "Postavenie," p. 26. Ratkoš, "Otázky vývoja," p. 39. See chapter 12, notes 55, 56.

8   See pp. 498–501.
9   See chapter 4, note 33, 34.
10 Adam of Bremen tells of a divided Slavinia along the Elbe between the Saxon border bishoprics: *The whole of Slavinia (tota Sclavania) is subjugated to the Magdeburg (arch)bishop up to the Pena River. Five of the subjugated bishoprics, of which Merseburg and Zeitz lie on the Saale River, Meissen thus on the Elbe, and Brandenburg and Havelberg are further inland. The sixth bishopric of Slavinia is Oldenburg. Therefore, closer to us, the emperor subjugated it to the Hamburg archbishopric. Magistri Adam Bremensis Gesta Hammaburgensis ecclesiae Pontificum* II 16, cur. Trillmich, pp. 244–247. Not only Adam of Bremen, but other Saxon chroniclers wrote in many instances of Slavinia along the Elbe River subjugated to the Saxon margrave and the bishop.

Slavonia. In the 13th century the meaning of this name narrowed only to its part along the Sava River, which abutted Hungary.[11]

Large Slavinia thus had on its edges small Slavinias, which were (real or only claimed) a part of neighbouring non-Slavic states. Since the Slavs called themselves *Slovieni* or *Sloveni*, each country was called Slovenia after them. Slovenia (Slovenija) and Slovakia today still have this old name.

Hungary was also characterised by this Slavic–non-Slavic contrast. Saxon and Polish chroniclers of the 11th and 12th centuries counted Hungary as part of a large Slavinia.[12] The later author of the Hungarian-Polish Chronicle likewise perceived Hungary as Slavic. He called it not only *Ungaria*, but also *Sclavonia*.[13] In addition to this, Hungary also had within its borders a smaller country with the name *Sclavonia*, that is Slovenia. This was old Nitria, which in 1029 became Emeric's princely appanage. The son of Hungarian King Stephen I, Emeric was *dux Sclavonie*, that is, the prince of Slavonia. They thus called Árpád Nitria Slovenia, that is Slovakia, and the chronicler also knew the borders that divided this Slavic, or more exactly Slovak principality from the rest of Hungary, and very precisely described them. Its non-Slavic antipole was the smaller or internal Hungary, without Nitria and Transylvania, mentioned in years 1003, 1074, 1075 and 1085 and called the same *Ungaria*.[14] In the 11th century HUNGARY = Slovakia + Hungary + Transylvania. Árpád Nitria contrasted with the rest of Hungary; therefore, it had a second name, which represented this contrast. This was Slovenia (*Sclavonia*), that is Slovakia.

Nitria at the beginning of the 12th century ceased to exist, but the Slovak-Hungarian contrast remained and with it also Slovakia, although without the borders, which up to then divided it from the rest of Hungary. Reports from the following centuries tell clearly that the feeling of differentness of Slovakia from the rest of Hungary remained even after the extinction of the principality. Anyone in Slovakia who went south, went *towards Hungary* (*versus Hungariam*), that is, to the Magyar territory in the Hungarian interior. The land of the settlement Korytník in the Spiš in 1297 reached up to the road, *which goes towards Hungary*.[15] From 1331 the Hnilec River divided a disputed forest between Matthew, son of Count Jekkel of Hnilec, and the Abbey of Letanovce. The abbey got part of the forest *from this side of the Hnilec River*

---

11   See chapter 14, note 218, chapter 18, note 27.
12   See pp. 498–501.
13   See chapter 15, notes 86, 87.
14   See chapter 19, notes 1, 2, 3, 4, 5, 6.
15   *CDH VI*, 2, ed. Fejér, pp. 75–79. *Codex diplomaticus Hungariae ecclesiasticus ac civilis VIII*, 5, studio et opera Georgii Fejér (Budae 1835), no. 157, p. 280.

towards Hungary, that is from the south side,[16] thus again in the direction towards the interior, that is Magyar Hungary.

Ulrich of Richenthal in his Chronicle of the Council of Constance mentioned Slovakia several times. He wrote that Duke Stibor, who in 1417 attended the Council of Constance, had properties to which he included also the towns and castles in Trenčín, Beckov, Uherský Brod, Holíč, Skalica and Hlohovec, *in the Slovak countries between Moravia and Poland (in Windeshen landen zwischen Merhern und Boland), on the river which is called the Váh (Vag).*[17] To the Council of Constance also came Tekov Count Peter Čech (the Czech) from Šarovce *settled in the Slovak lands (in Windeschen landen).*[18] In February 1417 *the esteemed archbishop of Esztergom from Hungary (ertzbischoff von Granensis ausser Ungerland), whose bishopric and suffragens lay in the Slovak lands (in Windeschen landen),* came to Constance.[19] Emperor and Hungarian King Sigismund of Luxembourg, who in May 1418 left Constance, set off through southern Germany to Passau. In January 1419 he left Passau *and went to Bohemia and to Moravia (gen Beham und gen Mernher) and then to Slovakia (in Windenland) and then to Pressburg (gen Pressburg) and from there to Wroclaw.*[20] In the coat-of-arms part of the Chronicle of the Council of Constance (in the 193rd letter) Peter Čech *from Slovakia (ausser Windenland)* also has his own coat-of-arms. Other high-standing figures present at the council, whose coats-of-arms adorn this page of the chronicle, were *from Moravia (aus Mährerrn)*

---

16 *Codex diplomaticus Hungariae ecclesiasticus ac civilis VIII, 3,* studio et opera Georgii Fejér (Budae 1832), no. 249, pp. 555. Ratkoš, "Postavenie," pp. 14–15. Ratkoš, "Otázky vývoja," pp. 39–40.

17 Ulrich Richental, *Kostnická kronika* 54, ed. Mária Papsonová, František Šmahel, Daniela Dvořáková (Budmerice 2009), pp. 50–51, 56–57, 110. [See the latest digitalized edition *Ulrich Richental, Die Chronik des Konzils von Konstanz,* ed. Thomas Martin Buck (= MGH Digitale Editionen 1). MGH, München 2019; https://edition.mgh.de/001/html/]. *Prvý cisár na uhorskom tróne. Pramene k dejinám Slovenska a Slovákov 5,* translations Július Bartl, Daniela Dvořáková, Ján Lukačka, Tomáš Lukačka, Július Sopko (Bratislava 2001), p. 294.

18 Ulrich Richental, *Kostnická kronika* 55, ed. Papsonová, Šmahel, Dvořáková, pp. 48–50, 111.

19 Ulrich Richental, *Kostnická kronika* 203, ed. Papsonová, Šmahel, Dvořáková, pp. 56–57, 209. Ulrich's statement on the suffragan bishops of the Esztergom archbishop is inexact. The only suffragan of the Esztergom Archbishop whose diocese lay in Slovakia was the Nitrian Bishop. Only a smaller part of the diocese of the Eger suffragan reached into Slovakia. The diocese of other such suffragans lay outside of Slovakia. The Esztergom Archbishop was *ausser Ungerland*, that is *from Hungary*; his archdiocese took up approximately half of Hungary. His own diocese was much smaller and spread out *in Windeschen landen*, that is in that part of Hungary which was then called Slovakia.

20 Ulrich Richental, *Kostnická kronika* 316, ed. Papsonová, Šmahel, Dvořáková, pp. 57, 289–290. If the above-mentioned *Ungerland* was Hungary, then *Windenland* was Slovakia.

and *from Saxony* (*aus Sachssen*).[21] If chronicler Ulrich knew that Peter Čech is *from Slovakia* and the diocese of Esztergom Archbishop John Kanizsai lies *in the Slovak regions*, then Slovakia was for both high-standing figures and subsequently also for the foreign chronicler a land as obvious as Bohemia, Moravia, Poland, Saxony and other lands from which other figures present at the council came. Ulrich of Richenthal acquired a good idea of Slovakia. He knew that it lay between Moravia and Poland and that the whole of the Esztergom diocese belonged to it. And he named it in association with historical lands of Europe at that time. Jakub Ziegler, who in 1511 stayed in Leipzig, also had the same idea of Slovakia. He wrote that roads from Moravia lead to Silesia, to Poland and *to Slovakia* (*in Sclavoniam*) *by the Carpathian Mountains, which are also in Hungary*.[22] Domestic and foreign experts on Hungarian relations were able, even after the extinction of the Nitrian Principality, to differentiate the Slovak territory in northern Hungary from the Magyar territory in the south and to clearly designate this distinction.

The Nitrian Principality is the historical beginning of Slovakia. It stabilized the nation, which then survived its extinction. This nation was the Slavic Nitrians (originally the Nitravians), who from the time they ended up in Hungary, had the name Sloveni, later Slovaks, and the territory in which they lived got the name Slovenia, that is Slovakia. The Nitrian Principality laid the national, territorial and historical foundations of Slovakia.

---

21 In the 193rd letter (*Das CLXXXXIII blat*) of the Chronicle of the Council of Constance are six coats-of-arms. The owner of the first coat-of-arms is *Stech Peter von Schara ausser Windenland herre zu Toppelscham*, the second *Herr Peeter von Stramscz aus Mährerrn* and the third *Wilhalm Schenck von Sydaw aus Sachssen*. The fourth coat-of-arms has no owner written on it. The bearer of the fifth coat-of-arms is *Johannes von Waldaw aus Sachssen* and the sixth is *Hainrich von Rapellstein Steÿer herr*. Ulrich Richental, *Kostnická kronika*, ed. Papsonová, Šmahel, Dvořáková, pp. 56–57, 128.

22 Ratkoš, "Postavenie," pp. 15–16. Ratkoš, "Otázky vývoja," pp. 49–50. "The General orders of Banská Bystrica" in the German version of 1608 contains the words: *deutsch[er] oder windischer Nation*. The Slovak version has these words in Slovak: *budto Nemezkeho a neb Slowenskeho Narodu*. And in the other place there are similar words: Narodt budto Nemeczky y Slowensky. Ján Doruľa, O *slovensko-nemeckom spolunažívaní v 16. – 18. storočí* (Bratislava 2014), pp. 304, 305, 307. "The accounting book of Banská Bystrica" per annum 1651 contains the following words in German: *Windischen Herrn Geistlichen*. In the Slovak version it reads: *panom Slowenskim Kazatelom*. Doruľa, O *slovensko-nemeckom spolunažívaní*, pp. 220, 221. From this it is clear that in the mentioned official books windisch = Slovak, windischer Nation = Slovak nation.

Maps

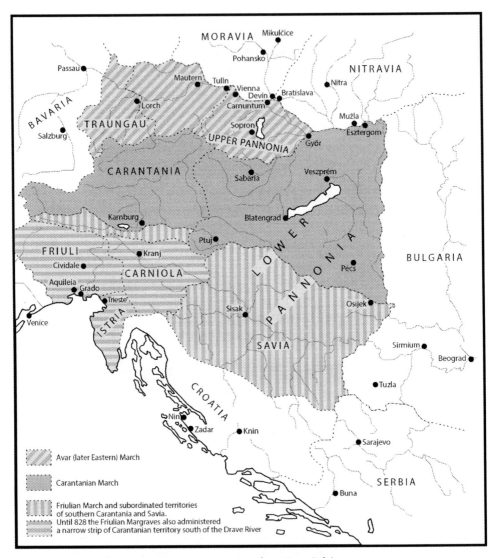

MAP 1   Division of Pannonia among Franconian Marches – Peter Rybár

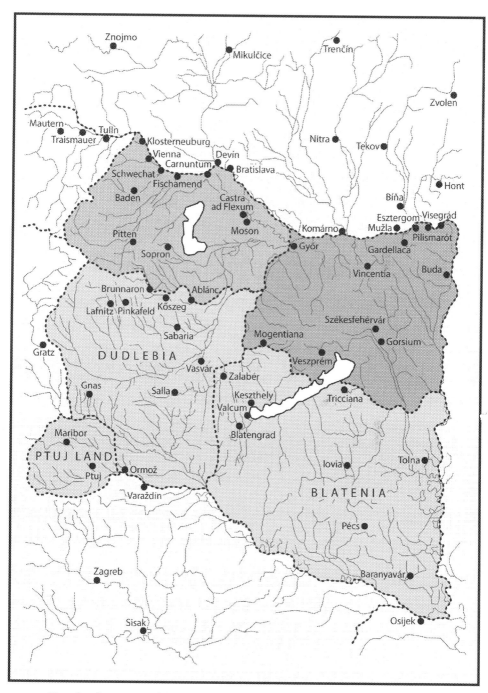

MAP 2 Transdanubia – Peter Rybár

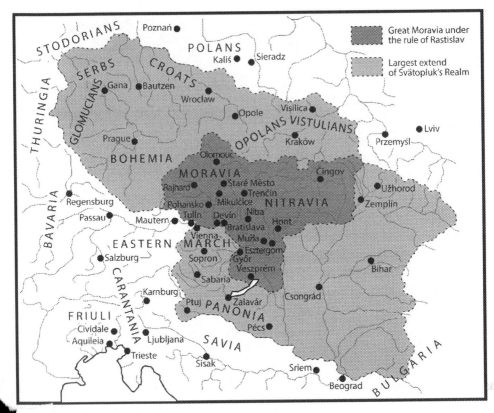

Great Moravia – Peter Rybár

MAP 4   Kingdom of Hungary – Peter Rybár

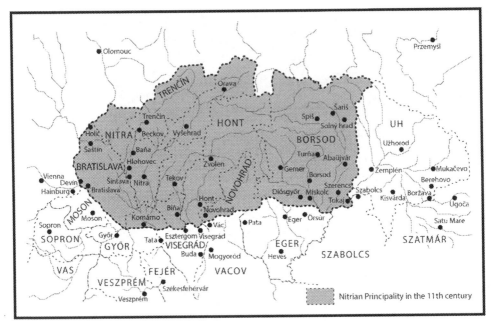

MAP 5   The Nitrian Principality – Peter Rybár

Bibliography

Primary Sources

Adam Brémsky. *Činy biskupů hamburského kostela. Velká kronika evropského severu*, trans. Libuše Hrabová. Praha 2009.

Ammiani Marcellini Rerum gestarum libri qui supersunt, recensuit Carolus Upson Clark. Berolini 1910–1915.

Ammianus Marcellinus. *Rímske dejiny*, trans. Daniel Škoviera. Bratislava 1988.

Ammianus Marcellinus. *Soumrak Římské říše*, trans. Josef Češka. Praha 1975.

An Anglo-Saxon Reader, edited by Alfred J. Wyatt. Cambridge 1947.

Anna Komnena. *Paměti byzantské princezny*, trans. Růžena Dostálová. Praha 1996.

Annales Admuntenses, edidit Wilhelmus von Wattenbach. Monumenta Germaniae historica, Scriptores 9. Hannoverae 1851.

Annales Alamannici, edidit Georgius Heinricus Pertz. Monumenta Germaniae historica, Scriptores I. Hannoverae et Lipsiae 1826.

Annales Altahenses maiores, recognovit Edmundus L. B. ab Oefele. Scriptores rerum Germanicarum in usum scholarum ex Monumentis Germaniae historicis recusi. Hannoverae 1890.

Annales Bertiniani, recensuit Georgius Waitz. Scriptores rerum Germanicarum in usum scholarum ex Monumentis Germaniae historicis recusi. Hannoverae 1883.

Annales Bertiniani, curavit Reinholdus Rau. Quellen zur karolingischen Reichsgeschichte, 2. Teil, neu bearbeitet von Reinhold Rau. Ausgewählte Quellen zur deutschen Geschichte des Mittelalters, herausgegeben von Rudolf Buchner, Band 6. Berlin 1966.

Annales Fuldenses, post editionem G. H. Pertzii recognovit Fridericus Kurze. Scriptores rerum Germanicarum in usum scholarum ex Monumentis Germaniae historicis recusi. Hannoverae 1891.

Annales Hildesheimenses, contulit cum Codice Parisiensi Georgius Waitz. Scriptores rerum Germanicarum in usum scholarum ex Monumentis Germaniae historicis recusi. Hannoverae 1878.

Annales Iuvavenses maiores, edidit Georgius Heinricus Pertz. Monumenta Germaniae historica, Scriptores I. Hannoverae et Lipsiae 1826, pp. 87–88.

Annales Iuvavenses maiores, edidit Harry Bresslau. Monumenta Germaniae historica, Scriptores XXX 2, Lipsiae 1934, pp. 727–744.

Annales Iuvavenses maximi et Continuationes, edidit Harry Bresslau. Monumenta Germaniae historica, Scriptores XXX 2. Lipsiae 1934, pp. 727–744.

Annales Iuvavenses minores, edidit Georgius Heinricus Pertz. Monumenta Germaniae historica, Scriptores I. Hannoverae et Lipsiae 1826, pp. 88–89.

Annales Iuvavenses minores, edidit Harry Bresslau. Monumenta Germaniae historica, Scriptores XXX 2. Lipsiae 1934, pp. 727-744.

Annales Laureshamenses, edidit Georgius Heinricus Pertz. Monumenta Germaniae historica, Scriptores I. Hannoverae et Lipsiae 1826.

Annales Mettenses priores, primum recognovit B. de Simson. Scriptores rerum Germanicarum in usum scholarum ex Monumentis Germaniae historicis separatim editi. Hannoverae et Lipsiae 1905.

Annales Moissiacenses, edidit Georgius Heinricus Pertz. Monumenta Germaniae historica, Scriptores I. Hannoverae et Lipsiae 1826.

Annales regni Francorum inde ab a. 741. usque ad a. 829. qui dicuntur Annales Laurissenses maiores et Einhardi, post editionem G. H. Pertzii recognovit Fridericus Kurze. Scriptores rerum Germanicarum in usum scholarum ex Monumentis Germaniae historicis separatim editi. Hannoverae 1895.

Annales regni Francorum, curavit Reinholdus Rau. Quellen zur karolingischen Reichsgeschichte, 1. Teil, neu bearbeitet von Reinhold Rau. Ausgewählte Quellen zur deutschen Geschichte des Mittelalters, ed. Rudolf Buchner, Band 5. Berlin 1955, pp. 1-155.

Annales sancti Emmerami Ratisponensis maiores, edidit Georgius Heinricus Pertz. Monumenta Germaniae historica, Scriptores I. Hannoverae et Lipsiae 1826.

Annales sancti Emmerami Ratisponensis maiores, edidit Harry Bresslau. Monumenta Germaniae historica, Scriptores XXX, 2. Hannoverae 1934, pp. 727-744.

Anonymi Vita Hludovici imperatoris, curavit Reinholdus Rau. Quellen zur karolingischen Reichsgeschichte, 1. Teil, neu bearbeitet von Reinhold Rau. Ausgewählte Quellen zur deutschen Geschichte des Mittelalters, ed. Rudolf Buchner, Band 5. Berlin 1955, pp. 257-381.

Antické písemné prameny k dějinám střední Evropy, ed. and trans. Dagmar Bartoňková and Irena Radová. Praha 2010.

Antika v dokumentech II. Řím, ed. Julie Nováková and Jan Pečírka. Praha 1961.

Árpád-kori oklevelek 1001-1196, ed. György Györffy. Budapest 1997.

A szent István, szent László és Kálman korabeli törvények és zsinati határozatok forrásai. Függelék: A törvények szövege, írta Levente Závodszky. Budapest 1904.

Az Árpád-házi királyok okleveleinek kritikai jegyzéke II/1, ed. Imre Szentpétery. Budapest 1943.

Az Árpád-házi királyok okleveleinek kritikai jegyzéke II/2-3, Szentpétery Imre kéziratának felhasználásával ed. Borsa Iván, Budapest 1961.

Az Árpád-kori magyar történet bizanci forrásai, összegyűjtötte, fordította, bevezetéssel és jegyzetekkel ellátta Gyula Moravcsik, Budapest 1988.

Beda Ctihodný. *Církevní dějiny národa Anglů*, trans. Jaromír Kincl, Magdalena Moravová. Praha 2008.

BIBLIOGRAPHY

Beowulf and the fight at Finnsburg, edited by Fr. Klaeber. Boston – New York – Chicago – Atlanta – San Francisco – Dallas – London 1941.

Beowulf. Ein altenglisches Heldenepos, ed. Martin Lehnert. Leipzig 1986.

Béowulf, trans. Jan Čermák. Praha 2003.

Bizánci források az Árpád-kori magyar történelemhez összegyűjtötte, fordította, bevezetéssel ellátta Terézia Olajos. Szeged 2014.

Böhmer, Johann Friedrich. *Regesta imperii I. Die Regesten des Kaiserreichs unter den Karolingern 751–918*, neubearbeitet von Engelbert Mühlbacher, vollendet von Johann Lechner. 1. Band, III. Abteilung. Innsbruck 1908.

Bruno z Querfurtu. *Život svatého Vojtěcha. Legenda Nascitur purpureus flos*, trans. Marie Kyralová. Praha 1996.

Cassii Dioni Cocceiani Historiarum Romanarum quae supersunt, edidit Ursulus Philippus Boissevain. Berolini 1955.

Chaloupecký, Václav. *Prameny X. století legendy Kristiánovi o svatém Václavu a svaté Ludmile. Svatováclavský sborník. Na památku 1000. výročí smrti knížete Václava Svatého*. Praha 1939.

Chronica regia Coloniensis (Annales maximi Coloniensis) cum continuationibus in Monasteri s. Pantaleonis scriptis aliisque historiae Coloniensis monumentis partim ex Monumentis Germaniae recusa, recensuit Georgius Waitz. Scriptores rerum Germanicarum in usum scholarum ex Monumentis Germaniae historicis recusi. Hannoverae 1880.

Chronicarum quae dicuntur Fredegarii Scholastici libri IV cum continuationibus. Fredegarii et aliorum Chronica inde ab anno Christi quingentesimo usque ad annum millesimum et quingentesimum. Scriptorum rerum Merovingicarum tomus II. Fredegarii et aliorum chronica. Vitae sanctorum, edidit Bruno Krusch. Monumenta Germaniae historica, Scriptores rerum Merovingicarum. Hannoverae 1888.

Chronicon Moissiacense, edidit Georgius Heinricus Pertz. Monumenta Germaniae historica, Scriptores I. Hannoverae 1826, pp. 280–313.

Chronicon Moissiacense, edidit Georgius Heinricus Pertz. Monumenta Germaniae historica, Scriptores II. Hannoverae 1829, pp. 257–259.

Codex diplomaticus Arpadianus. Árpádkori oklevelek 1095–1301 I, edidit Ferencz Kubinyi. Pest 1867.

Codex diplom. Arpadianus continuatus. Árpádkori új okmánytár IX, edidit Gusztáv Wenzel. Pest 1871.

Codex diplom. Arpadianus continuatus. Árpádkori új okmánytár VII, edidit Gusztáv Wenzel. Pest 1869.

Codex diplom. Arpadianus continuatus. Árpádkori új okmánytár VIII, edidit Gusztáv Wenzel. Pest 1870.

Codex diplom. Arpadianus continuatus. Árpádkori új okmánytár XI, edidit Gusztáv Wenzel. Budapest 1873.

Codex diplomaticus et epistolaris regni Bohemiae I, edidit Gustavus Friedrich. Pragae 1904-1907.

Codex diplomaticus et epistolaris Slovaciae 1, ad edendum praeparavit Richard Marsina. Bratislavae 1971.

Codex diplomaticus et epistolaris Slovaciae 2, ad edendum praeparavit Richard Marsina. Bratislavae 1987.

Codex diplomaticus Hungariae ecclesiasticus ac civilis I, studio et opera Georgii Fejér. Budae 1829.

Codex diplomaticus Hungariae ecclesiasticus ac civilis IV/2, studio et opera Georgii Fejér. Budae 1829.

Codex diplomaticus Hungariae ecclesiasticus ac civilis V/2, studio et opera Georgii Fejér. Budae 1829.

Codex diplomaticus Hungariae ecclesiasticus ac civilis VI/2, studio et opera Georgii Fejér. Budae 1830.

Codex diplomaticus Hungariae ecclesiasticus ac civilis VIII/3, studio et opera Georgii Fejér. Budae 1832.

Codex diplomaticus Hungariae ecclesiasticus ac civilis VIII/5, studio et opera Georgii Fejér. Budae 1835.

Codex diplomaticus patrius hungaricus. Hazai okmánytár II, ed. Imre Nagy, Iván Páur, Károly Ráth, Dezső Véghely. Győrött 1865.

Codex diplomaticus patrius hungaricus. Hazai okmánytár VI, ed. Arnold Ipoly, Imre Nagy, Dezső Véghely. Budapest 1876.

Codex diplomaticus regni Croatiae, Dalmatiae et Slavoniae II, collegit et degessit T. Smičiklas. Zagrabiae 1904.

Codex diplomaticus Transsylvaniae. Diplomata, epistolae et alia instrumenta litteraria res Transsylvanas illustrantia I. 1023-1300. Ad edendum in regestis praeparavit et introductione notisque illustravit Sigismundus Jakó. Budapestini 1997.

Codex diplom. hungaricus Andegavensis. Anjoukori okmánytár I, ed. Imre Nagy. Budapest 1878.

Codex diplom. hungaricus Andegavensis. Anjoukori okmánytár IV, ed. Imre Nagy. Budapest 1884.

Codex juris municipalis Regni Bohemiae. Tomus I. Privilegia civitatum Pragensium. Sbírka pramenů práva městského Království českého. Díl I. Privilegia měst pražských, ed. Jaromír Čelakovský. V Praze 1886.

Constantine Porphyrogenitus De administrando imperio, edidit Gyula Moravcsik, anglice vertit R. J. H. Jenkins. Washington 1967.

Conversio Bagoariorum et Carantanorum, edidit Milko Kos. Razprave znanstvenega društva v Ljubljani 11, Historični odsek 3. V Ljubljani 1936.

Conversio Bagoariorum et Carantanorum. Das Weißbuch der Salzburger Kirche über die erfolgreiche Mission in Karantanien und Pannonien, ed. Herwig Wolfram. Wien – Köln – Graz 1979.

Conversio Bagoariorum et Carantanorum. Das Weißbuch der Salzburger Kirche über die erfolgreiche Mission in Karantanien und Pannonien. Herausgegeben, übersetzt kommentiert und um die Epistola Theotmari wie um Gesammelte Schriften zum Thema ed. Herwig Wolfram. Ljubljana/Laibach 2012.

Cosmae Pragensis Chronica Boemorum. Die Chronik der Böhmen des Cosmas von Prag, ed. Bertold Bretholz. Monumenta Germaniae historica, Scriptores rerum Germanicarum nova series, tomus II. Berolini 1923.

Darés Fryžský. *Pád Tróje.* In Homérští hrdinové ve vzpomínkách věků, trans. Eva Kamínková, Praha 1977, s. 129–162.

Das altfranzösische Rolandslied, ed. Edmund Stengel. Heilbronn 1878.

Dějiny Sovětského svazu a československo-sovětských vztahů v dokumentech I. Od nejstarších dob do konce XVIII. století, ed. Dimitr Krandžalov, František Hejl, Jaroslav Vávra. Praha 1963.

Dětmar z Merseburgu. *Kronika,* trans. Bořek Neškudla, versed by Jakub Žytek. Praha 2008.

Die Bussordnungen der abendländischen Kirche nebst einer rechtsgeschichtlichen Einleitung, ed. F. W. H. Wasserschleben. Halle 1851.

Die Edda. Göttersagen, Heldensagen und Spruchweisheiten der Germanen. Nach der Handschrift des Brynjolfur Sveinsson in der Übertragung von Karl Simrock. Berlin 1987.

Die Traditionen des Hochstifts Freising, Band I, ed. Theodor Bitterauf. Quellen und Erörterungen zur bayerischen Geschichte, Neue Folge 4. München 1908.

Die Traditionen des Hochstifts Regensburg und des Klosters S. Emmeram, ed. Josef Widemann. Quellen und Erörterungen zur bayerischen Geschichte, Neue Folge 8. München 1943.

Diplomata Hungariae antiquissima I, ed. Georgius Györffy. Budapestini 1992.

Documenta historiae chroaticae periodum antiquam illustrantia, collegit Fr. Rački. Zagrabiae 1877.

Documenta historiae chroaticae periodum antiquam illustrantia, collegit, digessit, explicuit Fr. Rački. Zagrabiae 1877.

Edda. Bohatýrske písně, trans. Emil Walter. Praha 1942.

Einhardi Vita Karoli Magni, edidit Georgius Heinricus Pertz. Monumenta Germaniae historica, Scriptores II. Hannoverae et Lipsiae 1829, pp. 426–463.

Einhardi Vita Karoli Magni. Einhard Leben Karls des Grossen, curavit Reinholdus Rau. Quellen zur karolingischen Reichsgeschichte, 1. Teil, neu bearbeitet von Reinhold

Rau. Ausgewählte Quellen zur deutschen Geschichte des Mittelalters, Band 5, ed. Rudolf Buchner. Darmstadt 1980, pp. 157–211.

Einhardus. ... *a neuniknout budoucímu věku. Vita Caroli Magni*, trans. Petr Daniš. Praha 1999.

Epistolae variorum Carolo Magno regnante scriptae, edidit Ernst Dümmler. Monumenta Germaniae Historica, Epistolae IV. Berolini 1895.

Eugippius. *Das Leben des heiligen Severin*. Einführung, trans. and ed. Rudolf Noll. Berlin 1963.

Eutropii Breviarium ab urbe condita cum versionibus Graecis et Pauli Landolfique additamentis, recensuit et adnotavit Hans Droysen. Monumenta Germaniae historica, Auctorum antiquissimorum, Tom II. Berolini 1879.

Font, Márta. *Magyarok a Kijevi Évkönyvben*. Szeged 1996.

Fontes rerum Bohemicarum I/2, edidit Josef Kolář. Praha 1872.

Fontes rerum Bohemicarum II/1, edidit Josef Emler. Praha 1874.

Fontes rerum Bohemicarum II/2, edidit Josef Emler. Praha 1875.

Gallus Anonymus. *Kronika a činy polských knížat a vládců*, trans. Josef Förster. Praha 2009.

Geoffrey of Monmouth. *The history of the Kings of Britain*, translated with an introduction by Lewis Thorpe. Nottingham 1976.

Geographi latini minores, collegit, recensuit, prologomenis instruxit Alexander Riese. Heilbronnae 1878.

Gesta sancti Hrodberti confessoris, edidit W. Levison. Monumenta Germaniae historica, Scriptores rerum Merovingicarum Tomus VI. Passiones vitaeque sanctorum aevi Merovingici. Ediderunt B. Krusch et W. Levison. Hannoverae et Lipsiae 1913, pp. 157–162.

Gombos, Albinus Franciscus. *Catalogus fontium historiae Hungaricae aevo ducum et regum ex stirpe Arpad descendentium ab anno Christi DCCC usque ad annum MCCCI. Tomus I, II, III*. Budapestini 1937, 1937, 1938.

Gregorii episcopi Turonensis Historiarum libri decem. Post Brunnonem Krusch hoc opus edendum curavit Rudolfus Buchner. Ausgewählte Quellen zur deutschen Geschichte des Mittelalters. Berlin 1967.

Griechische und lateinische Quellen zur Frühgeschichte Mitteleuropas bis zur Mitte des 1. Jahrtausends u. Z., ed. Joachim Herrmann. *1. Teil: von Homer bis Plutarch*. Berlin 1988.

Helmoldi presbyteri Bozoviensis Cronica Slavorum, recognovit Bernhardus Schmeidler. Scriptores rerum Germanicarum in usum scholarum ex Monumentis Germaniae historicis separatim editi. Hannoverae et Lipsiae 1909.

Helmold z Bosau. *Kronika Slovanů*, trans. Jan Zdychinec. Praha 2012.

Herimanni Augiensis Chronicon, curavit Rudolf Buchner. Quellen des 9. und 11. Jahrhunderts zur Geschichte der Hamburgischen Kirche und des Reiches. Berlin 1961, pp. 615–707.

Herrmann, Erwin. *Slawisch-germanische Beziehungen im südostdeutschen Raum von der Spätantike bis zum Ungarnsturm. Ein Quellenbuch mit Erläuterungen.* Veröffentlichungen des Collegium Carolinum 17. München 1965.

Historia Langobardorum codicis Gothani, edidit Georgius Waitz. Monumenta Germaniae historica, Scriptores rerum Langobardicarum et Italicarum saec. VI–IX ex Monumentis Germaniae historicis recusi. Hannoverae 1878, pp. 7–11.

Historici Graeci Minores, edidit Ludovicus Dindorfius. Vol. II. Memander Protector et Agathias. Lipsiae 1871.

Hrochová, Věra. *Křížové výpravy ve světle soudobých kronik.* Praha 1982.

Ibn Fadlan's Reisebericht, ed. Ahmed Zeki Velidî Togan. *Archiv für die Kunde des Morgenlandes* 24, 1939, no. 3.

Isidor ze Sevilly. *Etymologiae IX,* trans. Irena Zachová, ed. Irena Zachová and Hana Šedinová. Praha 1998.

Izbornik. Povesti drevnej Rusi, ed. Lev Alexandrovič Dmitrijev, Nataľja Vladimirovna Ponyrko, introd. D. S. Lichačev. Moskva 1987.

Joannis Dlugosii Annales seu cronicae incliti Regni Poloniae. Warszawa 1969.

Johannis abbatis Victoriensis Liber certarum historiarum, Liber I. Rec. D, edidit Fedor Schneider. Scriptores rerum Germanicarum in usum scholarum ex Monumentis Germaniae historicis separatim editi. Hannoverae et Lipsiae 1909.

Jordanes. *De origine actibusque Getharum. O proischožděnii i dejaniach getov. Getica,* edidit Elena Česlavovna Skržinskaja. Moskva 1960.

Jordanes. *Gótske dějiny / Římske dějiny,* trans. Stanislav Doležal. Praha 2012.

Abú al-Hasan al-Kisáí. *Kniha o počiatku a konci a rozprávania o prorokoch. Islamské mýty a legendy,* trans. Ján Paulíny. Bratislava 1980.

Korán, trans. Ivan Hrbek. Praha 1991.

Kosmas. *Kronika Čechů,* trans. Karel Hrdina, Marie Bláhová, Magdalena Moravová. Praha 2011.

Kosmograph von Ravenna. Eine Erdschreibung um das Jahr 700, ed. Joseph Schnetz, Itineraria Romana II. Leipzig 1940.

Krahwinkler, Harald. *... in loco qui dicitur Riziano ... Zbor v Rižani pri Kopru leta 804. Die Versammlung in Rižana / Risano bei Koper/Capodistra im Jahre 804.* Koper 2004.

Kristiánova legenda. Život a umučení svatého Václava a jeho báby svaté Ludmily. Legenda Christiani. Vita et passio sancti Wenceslai et sancte Ludmile ave eius, edidit Jaroslav Ludvíkovský. Praha 1978.

Kronika anonymného notára kráľa Bela Gesta Hungarorum, trans. Vincent Múcska. Budmerice 2000.

Kronika Thietmara, trans. Marian Zygmunt Jedlicki. Kraków 2005.

Kroniky stredovekého Slovenska. Stredoveké Slovensko očami kráľovských a mestských kronikárov, trans. Július Sopko. Budmerice 1995.

La Cronaca Veneziana del Diacono Giovanni. Cronache Veneziane antichissime pubblicate a cura di Giovanni Monticolo. Volume I. Roma 1890, pp. 57–171.

Lamperti monachi Hersfeldensis annales, editionis quam paraverat Oswald Holder-Egger, textum denuo imprimendum curavit Wolfgang Dietrich Fritz, neu übersetzt von Adolf Schmidt, erläutert von Wolfgang Dietrich Fritz. Augewählte Quellen zur deutschen Geschichte des Mittelalters VII, ed. Rudolf Buchner. Berlin 1957.

Legendy a kroniky koruny uherské, trans. Dagmar Bartoňková a Jana Nechutová, ed. Richard Pražák. Praha 1988.

Legendy stredovekého Slovenska. Ideály stredovekého človeka očami cirkevných spisovateľov, trans. Richard Marsina, Július Sopko, Oľga Vaneková. Budmerice 1997.

Lev Diakon. *Istorija*, trans. M. M. Kopylenko, ed. M. J. Sjuzjumov, comm. M. J. Sjuzjumov, S. A. Ivanov. Moskva 1988.

Lewicka-Rajewska, Urszula. *Arabskie opisanie Słowian. Źródła do dziejów średniowiecznej kultury*. Wrocław 2004.

Literární památky epochy velkomoravské 863–885, trans. Josef Vašica. Praha 1960.

Liudprandi Antapodosis. Liudprandi episcopi Cremonensis opera omnia ex Monumentis Germaniae historicis, fecit Georgius Heinricus Pertz. Hannoverae 1839.

Liudprandi Antapodosis, edidit Joseph Becker. Scriptores rerum Germanicarum in usum scholarum ex Monumentis Germaniae historicis recusi. Hannoverae et Lipsiae 1915.

Magistri Adam Bremensis Gesta Hammaburgensis ecclesiae pontificum. Quellen des 9. und 11. Jahrhunderts zur Geschichte der Hamburgischen Kirche und des Reiches, curavit Werner Trillmich. Berlin 1961.

Magnae Moraviae fontes historici I. Annales et chronicae, curaverunt Dagmar Bartoňková, David Kalhous, Jiří K. Kroupa, Zdeněk Měřínský, Anna Žáková. Praha 2019.

Magnae Moraviae fontes historici II. Textus biographici, hagiographici, liturgici, curaverunt Dagmar Bartoňková, Lubomír Havlík, Jaroslav Ludvíkovský, Zdeněk Masařík, Radoslav Večerka. Brno 1967.

Magnae Moraviae fontes historici III. Diplomata, epistolae, textus historici varii, curaverunt Dagmar Bartoňková, Lubomír Havlík, Jaroslav Ludvíkovský, Radoslav Večerka. Brno 1969.

Magnae Moraviae fontes historici IV. Leges, textus iuridici, suplementa, curaverunt Dagmar Bartoňková, Karel Kaderka, Lubomír Havlík, Jaroslav Ludvíkovský, Josef Vašica, Radoslav Večerka. Brno 1971.

Abu l-Hasan ʿAlí al-Masʿúdí. *Rýžoviště zlata a doly drahokamů*, trans. Ivan Hrbek. Praha 1983.

Mauricii Strategicon. Das Strategikon des Maurikios, Einführung, Edition und Indices von George T. Dennis, übersetzt von Ernst Gamillscheg. Corpus Fontium Historiae Byzantinae, Series Vindobonensis 17. Wien 1981.

Milevský letopis. Zápisky Vincencia, Jarlocha a Ansberta, trans. Anna Kernbach, ed. Magdalena Moravová. Praha 2012.

Monumenta ecclesiae Strigoniensis I, edidit Ferdinandus Knauz. Strigonii 1874.

Monumenta Germaniae historica, Diplomata regum Germaniae ex stirpe Karolinorum 3. Die Urkunden Arnolfs, ed. Paul Kehr. Berlin 1940.

Monumenta historica ducatus Carinthiae I. Die Gurker Geschichtsquellen 864–1232, ed. August von Jaksch. Klagenfurt 1896.

Monumenta historica ducatus Carinthiae III. Die kärtner Geschichtsquellen 811–1202, ed. August von Jaksch. Klagenfurt 1904.

Monumenta Poloniae historica I, II, edidit August Bielowski. Warszawa 1960, 1961.

Monumenta Vaticana Hungariae historiam regni Hungariae illustrantia, series I., tomus 1. *Rationes collectorum pontificorum in Hungaria.* Budapest 2000.

Na úsvitu křesťanství. Z naší literární tvorby doby románské v století IX.–XIII. Ed. Václav Chaloupecký. Praha 1942.

Nejstarší česká rýmovaná kronika tak řečeného Dalimila, ed. Bohuslav Havránek a Jiří Daňhelka, Zdeněk Kristen. Praha 1958.

Nejstarší legendy přemyslovských Čech, ed. Oldřich Králik. Praha 1969.

Nestorův letopis ruský, trans. Karel Jaromír Erben. Praha 1940.

Nový, Rostislav – Sláma, Jiří – Zachová, Jana. *Slavníkovci ve středověkém písemníctví.* Praha 1987.

Olajos, Teréz. *A IX. századi avar történelem görög nyelvű forrásai.* Szeged 2001.

O początkach narodu Longobardów (Origo gentis Langobardorum), trans. Artur Foryt. Sandomierz 2012.

Origo gentis Langobardorum, edidit Georgius Waitz. Scriptores rerum Langobardicarum et Italicarum saec. VI–IX ex Monumentis Germaniae historicis recusi. Hannoverae 1878, pp. 1–6.

Ottonis episcopi Frisigensis Chronica sive Historia de duabus civitatibus, paraverat Adolf Hofmeister, curavit Walther Lammers. Berlin 1960.

Ottonis episcopi Frisigensis et Rahewini Gesta Frederici seu rectius Cronica. edidit Franz-Josef Schmale. Berlin 1965.

Pauli Historia Langobardorum, edentibus Ludwig Bethmann et Georgius Waitz. Monumenta Germaniae historica, Scriptores rerum Langobardicarum et Italicarum saec. VI–IX ex Monumentis Germaniae historicis recusi. Hannoverae 1878, pp. 12–187.

Paulíny, Ján. *Arabské správy o Slovanoch (9.–12. storočie).* Bratislava 1999.

Písemníctví ruského středověku. Od křtu Vladimíra Velikého po Dmitrije Donského. Výbor textů 11.–14. století, trans. Emilie Bláhová, Zoe Hauptová and Václav Konzal. Praha 1989.

Píseň o Nibelunzích, trans. Jindřich Pokorný. Praha 1974.

Píseň o Rolandovi, trans. Jiří Pelikán. Praha 1987.

Pokračovatelé Kosmovi, trans. Karel Hrdina, Václav Vladivoj Tomek and Marie Bláhová. Praha 1974.

Pramene k dejinám Slovenska a Slovákov I. Územie Slovenska pred príchodom Slovanov, ed. Pavol Valachovič. Bratislava 1998.

Pramene k dejinám Slovenska a Slovákov III. V kráľovstve svätého Štefana. Vznik uhorského štátu a čas arpádovských kráľov, trans. and ed. Richard Marsina. Bratislava 2003.

Pramene k dejinám Slovenska a Slovákov V. Prvý cisár na uhorskom tróne. trans. Július Bartl, Daniela Dvořáková, Ján Lukačka, Tomáš Lukačka, Július Sopko. Bratislava 2001.

Pramene k dejinám Veľkej Moravy, ed. Peter Ratkoš. Bratislava 1968.

Přibíka z Radenína, řečeného Pulkava Kronika česká, trans. Jana Zachová. Kroniky doby Karla IV. Praha 1987, pp. 272–438.

Priručnik izvora hrvatske historije I/1, ed. Ferdo Šišić. Zagreb 1914.

Procopios. *De bello Gothico*, addenda et corrigenda adiecit Gerhard Wirth. Procopii Caesariensis Opera omnia II, recensuit Jacob Haury. Leipzig 1963.

Prokopios z Kaisareie. *Válka s Góty*, trans. Pavel Beneš. Praha 1985.

Regesta diplomatica nec non epistolaria Slovaciae 2, ad edendum praeparavit Vincent Sedlák. Bratislavae 1987.

Regesta imperii II. Band: Sächsisches Haus (919–1024), 3. Abteilung: Die Regesten des Kaisserreiches unter Otto III. (980 [983]–1002), 2. Lieferung 988–1002, nach Johann Friedrich Böhmer neu bearbeitet von Mathilde Uhlirz. Graz – Köln 1957.

Regesten und Urkunden der ersten Karolinger II, ed. Theodor Sickel. Wien 1867.

Regestrum Varadinense examinum ferri candentis ordine chronologico digestum descripta effigie editionis a. 1550 illustratum sumptibusque capituli Varadinensis lat. rit. curis et laboribus Joannis Karácsonyi et Samuelis Borovsky editum. Budapest 1903.

Reginonis abbatis Prumiensis Chronicon cum continuatione Treverensi. recognovit Fridericus Kurze. Scriptores rerum Germanicarum in usum scholarum ex Monumentis Germaniae historicis recusi. Hannoverae 1890.

Reindel, Kurt. *Die bayerischen Liutpoldinger 893–989. Sammlung und Erläuterung der Quellen*. Quellen und Erörterungen zur bayerischen Geschichte. Herausgegeben von Kommision für bayerische Landesgeschichte bei der Bayerischen Akademie der Wissenschaft. Neue Folge 11. München 1953.

Řeroř z Toursu. *O boji králů a údělu spravedlivých. Kronika Franků. Dějiny v deseti knihách*, trans. Jaromír Kincl. Praha 1986.

Rimberti Vita Anskarii, curaverunt Werner Trillmich et Rudolf Buchner. Quellen des 9. und 11. Jahrhunderts zur Geschichte der Hamburgischen Kirche und des Reiches, neu übertragen von Werner Trillmich. Berlin 1961, pp. 3–136.

Rogov, Aleksandr Ivanovič – Bláhová, Emilie – Konzal, Václav. *Staroslověnské legendy českého původu. Nejstarší kapitoly z dějin česko-ruských kulturních vztahů*. Praha 1976.

Ruotgeri Vita Brunonis archiepiscopi Colonensis in usum scholarum ex Monumentis Germaniae historicis recudi, fecit Georgius Heinricus Pertz. Scriptores rerum Germanicarum in usum scholarum ex Monumentis Germaniae historicis recudi fecit Georgius Heinricus Pertz. Hannoverae 1841.

Sborník staroslovanských literárních památek o sv. Václavu a sv. Lidmile, ed. Josef Vajs. Praha 1929.

Scriptores rerum Hungaricarum tempore ducum regumque stirpis Arpadianae gestarum I, II, edendo operi praefuit Emericus Szentpétery. Budapest 1937, 1938.

Slovensko na úsvite dejín, ed. Daniel Škoviera. Bratislava 1977.

Slovo o pluku Igorovom a ďalšie staroruské historické povesti, trans. Helena Križanová-Brindzová. Bratislava 1986.

Snorri Sturluson. *Edda, Sága o Ynglinzích*, trans. Helena Kadečková. Praha 1988, 2003.

Szádeczky-Kardoss, Samu. *Az avar történelem forrásai 557-tól 806-ig*. Budapest 1998.

Theofylaktos Simokattes. *Na přelomu věků*, trans. Václav Bahník. Praha 1986.

Theofýlaktos Simokáttes. *Oikoymeniké istoría*. Teofilakt Simokatta Historia powszechna, trans. Anna Kotłowska, Łukasz Różycki. Poznań 2016.

Thietmari Merseburgensis episcopi Chronicon, post editionem Ioh. M. Lappenbergii recognovit Fridericus Kurze. Scriptores rerum Germanicarum in usum scholarum ex Monumentis Germaniae historicis recusi. Hannoverae 1889.

Thietmari Merseburgensis episcopi Chronicon, curavit Werner Trillmich. Ausgewählte Quellen zur deutsche Geschichte des Mittelalters, Band 9, ed. Rudolf Buchner. Berlin 1960.

Thomas Spalatensis archidiaconus. *Historia Salonitana*, digessit Franjo Rački. Monumenta spectantia Historiam Slavorum meridionalium XXVI, Scriptores III. Zagrabiae 1894.

Ulrich Richental. *Kostnická kronika*, ed. Mária Papsonová, František Šmahel, Daniela Dvořáková. Budmerice 2009.

Urkundenbuch des Burgenlandes und der angrenzenden Gebiete der Komitate Wieselburg, Ödenburg und Eisenburg. Band 1: Die Urkunden von 808 bis 1270, ed. Hans Wagner. Graz – Köln 1955.

Urkundenbuch des Burgenlandes und der angrenzenden Gebiete der Komitate Wieselburg, Ödenburg und Eisenburg. Band 2: Die Urkunden von 1271 bis 1301, ed. Irmtraut Lindeck-Pozza. Graz – Köln 1965.

Urkundenbuch des Herzogthums Steiermark. Band I: 798–1192, bearbeitet von Joseph von Zahn. Graz 1875.

Urkundenbuch des Herzogthums Steiermark. Band II: 1192–1246, ed. Joseph von Zahn. Graz 1879.

Urkundenbuch des Landes ob der Enns I, II, herausgegeben vom Verwaltungs-Ausschuss des Museums Francisco-Carolinum zu Linz. Wien 1853, 1856.

Vetera monumenta historica Hungariam sacram illustrantia maximam partem nondum edita ex tabulariis vaticanis de prompta collecta ac serie chronologica deposita ab Augustino Theiner. Tomus primus: Ab Honorio pp. III. usque ad Clementem pp. VI. 1216–1352. Romae – Parisiis – Vindobonae 1859.

Vita Anskarii auctore Rimberto, accedit Vita Rimberti, recensuit Georgius Waitz. Scriptores rerum Germanicarum in usum scholarum ex Monumentis Germaniae historicis recusi. Hannoverae 1884.

Vyprávění o minulých letech aneb Nestorův letopis ruský. Nejstarší staroruská kronika, trans. Michal Téra. Červený Kostelec 2014.

Warnlieder. Band I: Kriemhilt und Meister Kuonrat. Band II: Hildebrand, Dietrich, Kudrun, ed. Henrik Becker. Leipzig 1953.

Weingart, Miloš. *Rekonstruovaný text I. staroslověnské legendy o sv. Václavu*. In Svatováclavský sborník I. Praha 1934, pp. 973–998.

Widukindi Rerum gestarum Saxonicarum libri tres, recognovit Georgius Waitz. Scriptores rerum Germanicarum in usum scholarum ex Monumentis Germaniae historicis recusi. Hannoverae 1882.

Wipo. *Gesta Chuonradi II. imperatoris; Annales Sangallenses maiores; Chronicon Herimanni Augiensis; Chronicon Suevicum universale. Wiponis opera*, ed. Harry Bresslau. Scriptores rerum Germanicarum in usum scholarum ex Monumentis Germaniae historicis separatim editi. Hannoverae et Lipsiae 1915.

Wiponis Gesta Chuonradi II. imperatoris, curavit Werner Trillmich. Quellen des 9. und 11. Jahrhunderts zur Geschichte der Hamburgischen Kirche und des Reiches. Berlin 1961, pp. 505–613.

Źródła arabskie do dziejów Słowiańszczyzny I, ed. Tadeusz Lewicki. Wrocław – Kraków 1956.

Żywot św. Stefana króla Węgier czyli Kronika węgiersko-polska, trans. and ed. Ryszard Grzesik. Warszawa 2003.

Secondary Literature

Adler, Horst. "Das 'feld' bei Paulus Diaconus." *Archeologia Austriaca*, Beiheft 14, Teil 2 (1976), pp. 256–282.

A Kárpát-medence, a magyarság és Bizánc, ed. Teréz Olajos, Szeged 2014.

Alföldi, András. "A tarchan méltóságnév eredete." *Magyar Nyelv* 28 (1932) 7–8, pp. 205–220.

Alföldi, Andreas. "Zur historischen Bestimmung der Awarenfunde." *Eurasia septentrionalis antiqua* 9 (1934), pp. 285–307.

Alföldi, Andreas. "The central danubian provinces." *Cambridge ancient history* 11 (1936), pp. 540–554.

Alföldi, Andreas. "Das römische Pannonien." *Das Altertum* 9 (1963), pp. 142–157.

Alimov, Denis Eugenevič. "Politija Borny. Gentes i Herrschaft v Dalmacii v pervoj četverti IX veka." *Peterburgskije slavjanskije i balkanskije issledovanija* (2011) N° 1 (9), pp. 101–142.

Alimov, Denis Evgenevič. *Etnogenez chorvatov. Formirovanie chorvatskoj etnopolitičeskoj obščnosti v VII–IX vv.* Sankt-Peterburg 2016.

Államalapítás, társadalom, müvelödés, ed. Gyula Kristó, Budapest 2001.

Allgemeine deutsche Biographie, 9. Band. Leipzig 1879.

Amon, Karl. "Eigenkirche und salzburger Mission." In *Veröffentlichungen des Steiermarkischen Landesarchiv 12. Siedlung, Macht und Wirtschaft, Festschrift Fritz Posch zum 70. Geburtstag*, ed. Gerhard Pferschy, Graz 1981, pp. 319–333.

Anderson, George K. "Staroanglická a středoanglická literatura od počátků až do roku 1485." In *Dějiny anglické literatury I*, ed. Hardin Craig. Praha 1963, pp. 17–196.

von Ankershofen, Gottlieb. *Handbuch der Geschichte des Herzogthumes Kärnten im Mittelalter bis zur Vereinigung mit den österreichischen Fürstentümern II. Band, 1. Heft 476–1122.* Klagenfurt 1851.

Antoljak, Stjepan. "Hrvati u Karantaniji. Prilog seobi Hrvata iz Dalmacije u prekosavske krajeve u 7. stoljecu." *Godišen zbornik na Filozofskiot fakultet na Univerzitetot vo Skopje, Istorisko-filološki oddel* 9 (1956), pp. 15–38.

Antoljak, Stjepan. "Miscellanea medievalia Jugoslavica." *I Slovenica, Godišen zbornik* 20 (1968), pp. 113–118.

Appelt, Heinrich. "Kaisertum, Königtum, Landesherrschaft, Gesamelte Studien zur mittelalterlichen Verfassungsgeschichte." *Mitteilungen des Instituts für österreichische Geschichtsforschung*. Ergänzungsband 28 (1988), pp. 7–361.

Arbman, Holger. *Vikingové*. Praha 1969.

Archeologická topografia Bratislavy, ed. Belo Polla, Adrián Vallašek. Bratislava 1991.

Assman, Jan. *Kultura a pamět'. Písmo, vzpomínka a politická identita v rozvinutých kulturách starověku*. Praha 2001.

Atlas Slovenskej socialistickej republiky. Bratislava 1982.

Avenarius, Alexander. "Prabulhari v prameňoch 6.–7. storočia." *Slovanské štúdie* 8 (1966), pp. 185–204.

Avenarius, Alexander. "K otázke polohy a vzniku Samovej ríše." *Historické štúdie* 13 (1968), pp. 177–200.

Avenarius, Alexander. "K problematike avarsko-slovanského vzťahu na dolnom Dunaji v 6.–7. storočí." *Slovanské štúdie* 11 (1971), pp. 223–244.

Avenarius, Alexander. "Byzantská a západoslovanská zložka v Povesti vremennych let." *Slovanské štúdie* 14 (1973), pp. 165–186.

Avenarius, Alexander. *Die Awaren in Europa.* Amsterdam – Bratislava 1974.

Avenarius, Alexander. "Slovania v severozápadnom pomedzí Avarského kaganátu." In *Zborník prác Ľudmile Kraskovskej (k životnému jubileu)*, ed. Etela Studeníková, Lev Zachar. Bratislava 1984, pp. 151–158.

Avenarius, Alexander. "Stepné národy v Európe: charakter a vývoj avarskej spoločnosti." *Historický časopis* 36 (1988) no. 2, pp. 145–158.

Avenarius, Alexander. "Začiatky Slovanov na strednom Dunaji. Autochtonistická teória vo svetle súčasného bádania." *Historický časopis* 40 (1992) no. 1, pp. 1–16.

Avenarius, Alexander. *Byzantská kultúra v slovanskom prostredí v VI.–XII. storočí. K problému recepcie a transformácie.* Bratislava 1992.

Avenarius, Alexander. *Die byzantinische Kultur und die Slawen. Zum Problem der Rezeption und Transformation (6. bis 12. Jahrhundert).* Veröffentlichungen des Instituts für österreichische Geschichtsforschung, Band 35. Wien – München 2000.

Avenarius, Alexander. "Samova ríša a Slovensko: súčasný stav poznania." In *Nitra v slovenských dejinách*, ed. Richard Marsina, pp. 41–44.

Awaren in Europa. Schätze eines asiatischen Reitervolkes, 6.–8. Jahrhundert. Ausstellungskatalog. Frankfurt/Main 1985.

Baán, István. "The Foundation of the Archbishopric of Kalocsa: The Byzantine Origin of the second Archdiocese in Hungary." In *Early Christianity in Central and East Europe*, ed. Przemysław Urbańczyk. Warszawa 1997, pp. 67–73.

Bača, Róbert – Turčan, Vladimír. "Bronzové pozlátené nákončie z Bojnej I." In *Bojná. Hospodárske a politické centrum Nitrianskeho kniežatstva.* ed. Karol Pieta, Alexander Ruttkay, Matej Ruttkay, pp. 167–172.

Bagi, Dániel. *Gallus Anonymus és Magyarország. A Geszta magyar adatai, forrásai, mintái, valamint a szerző történetszemlélete a latin Kelet-Közép-Európa 12. század eleji latin nyelvű történetírásának tükrében.* Budapest 2005.

Bagi, Dániel. *Królowie węgierscy w Kronice Galla Anonima.* Kraków 2008.

Bakács, István. *Hont vármegye Mohács elött.* Budapest 1971.

Bakay, Kornél. "Az avarkori időrendjéről. Újabb avar temetők a Balaton környékén." *Somogyi Múzeumok Közleményei* 1 (1973), pp. 5–86.

Barb, Alphons. "Spuren alter Eisengewinnung im heutigen Burgenland." *Wiener praehistorische Zeitschrift* 24 (1937), pp. 113–157.

Barford, Paul. "Pochopit neznáme: Archeologie a šíření slovanských jazyků." In *"Neslované" o počátcích Slovanů*, ed. Przemysław Urbańczyk, pp. 63–88.

Barkóczi, László. "A 6th century cemetery from Keszthely-Fenékpuszta." *Acta Archaeologica Academiae Scientiarum Hungaricae* 20 (1968), pp. 275–311.

Barkóczi, László – Soproni, Sándor. *Die römischen Inschriften Ungarns 3. Lieferung.* Budapest 1981.

Bárta, Juraj. "Pohrebište zo staršej doby hradištnej v Dol. Krškanoch pri Nitre." *Archeologické rozhledy* 5 (1953), pp. 167–171, 190–191.

Bartha, Antal. *Hungarian society in the 9th and 10th centuries*. Budapest 1975.

Bartha, Antal. *A magyar nép őstörténete*. Budapest 1988.

Bartlett, Robert. "Od pohanství ke křesťanství ve středověké Evropě." In *Christianizace a utváření křesťanské monarchie*, ed. Nora Berendová, pp. 57–83.

Bartoš, František M. "Kníže Václav Svatý u Vidukinda." In *Svatováclavský sborník I. Kníže Václav Svatý a jeho doba*, ed. K. Guth, J. Kapras, A. Novák, K. Stloukal, pp. 833–841.

Baš, Franjo. "Mali grad v Ptuju." *Zgodovinski časopis* 4 (1950), pp. 127–150.

Baxa, Peter. "Die Kirche St. Margarethen und andere Fundplätze des 9.–10. Jahrhunderts auf der Flur 'Za jazerom pri sv. Margite' von Kopčany." In *Frühmittelalterliche Kirchen als archäologische und historische Quelle*, ed. Lumír Poláček, Jana Maříková-Kubková, pp. 135–148.

Baxa, Peter – Maříková-Kubková, Jana. "Die älteste Phase der Kirche St. Georg in Kostoľany pod Tríbečom." In *Frühmittelalterliche Kirchen als archäologische und historische Quelle*, ed. Lumír Poláček, Jana Maříková-Kubková, pp. 149–160.

Bednár, Peter. "Die Nitraer Burg im 9.–12. Jahrhundert." In *Frühmittelalterliche Burgen Mitteleuropas bis zum Ende des 12. Jahrhunderts. 4. Castrumbene-Konferenz, 10–13. Oktober 1994*, Visegrad 1994, pp. 18–19.

Bednár, Peter. "Nitriansky hrad v 9. storočí." *Pamiatky a múzeá* 3 (1995), pp. 65–67.

Bednár, Peter. "Zisťovací výskum na južnom nádvorí Nitrianskeho hradu." *AVANS v r. 1993*, Nitra 1995, pp. 31–33.

Bednár, Peter. "Siedma sezóna výskumu Nitrianskeho hradu." *AVANS v r. 1994*, Nitra, 1996, pp. 29–31.

Bednár, Peter. "Nitriansky hrad v 9. storočí a jeho význam v sídliskovej štruktúre veľkomoravskej Nitry." In *Svätopluk 894–1994*, ed. Richard Marsina, Alexander Ruttkay, pp. 19–32.

Bednár, Peter. *Nitriansky hrad v 9. až 13. storočí. Autoreferát dizertácie na získanie vedeckej hodnosti kandidáta historických vied*, Nitra 1998.

Bednár, Peter. "Die Entwicklung der Befestigung der Nitraer Burg im 9.–12. Jahrhundert." In *Frühmittelalterlicher Burgenbau in Mittel- und Osteuropa*, ed. Joachim Henning, Alexander Tivadar Ruttkay, Bonn 1998, pp. 371–382.

Bednár, Peter. "Sídlisková štruktúra Nitry v 9. storočí." In *Velká Morava mezi východem a západem. Sborník příspěvků z mezinárodní vědecké konference Uherské Hradiště, Staré Město 28. 9.–1. 10. 1999*, ed. Luděk Galuška, Pavel Kouřil, Zdeněk Měřínsky, Spisy Archeologického ústavu AV ČR Brno 17, 2001, pp. 29–39.

Bednár, Peter. "Nitra v 9. storočí. K problematike lokalizácie kniežacieho sídla a Pribinovho kostola." In *Nitra v slovenských dejinách*, ed. Richard Marsina, Martin 2002, pp. 88–98.

Bednár, Peter. "Nitriansky hrad v 9. storočí." In *Bojná. Hospodárske a politické centrum Nitrianskeho kniežatstva*, ed. Karol Pieta, Alexander Ruttkay, Matej Ruttkay, pp. 205–216.

Bednár, Peter. "Počiatky Nitrianskeho hradu." In *Kolíska kresťanstva*, ed. Viliam Judák, Peter Bednár, Jozef Medvecký, pp. 114–121.

Bednár, Peter. "Palác a vnútorná zástavba." In *Kolíska kresťanstva*, ed. Viliam Judák, Peter Bednár, Jozef Medvecký, pp. 174–183.

Bednár, Peter. "Nitra v časoch pôsobenia sv. Konštantína-Cyrila a sv. Metoda." In *Bratia, ktorí menili svet – Konštantín a Metod. Príspevky z konferencie*, ed. Branislav Panis, Matej Ruttkay, Vladimír Turčan, pp. 145–156.

Bednár, Peter – Poláková, Zuzana. "Katedrála sv. Emeráma." In *Kolíska kresťanstva*, ed. Viliam Judák, Peter Bednár, Jozef Medvecký, pp. 184–207.

Bednár, Peter – Samuel, Marián. "Entwicklung der Befestigung der Nitraer Burg im 11. Jahrhundert." *Slovenská archeológia* 49 (2001), no. 2, pp. 301–342.

Bednár, Peter – Samuel, Marián. "Nitriansky hrad na prelome tisícročí." In *Slovensko vo včasnom stredoveku*, ed. Alexander Ruttkay, Matej Ruttkay, Peter Šalkovský, pp. 149–155.

Bednár, Peter – Šimkovic, Michal. "Opevnenie Nitrianskeho hradu." In *Kolíska kresťanstva*, ed. Viliam Judák, Peter Bednár, Jozef Medvecký, pp. 134–161.

Bednár, Peter – Staník, Ivan. "Archeologický a stavebno-historický výskum národnej kultúrnej pamiatky Nitra – Hrad." *AVANS v r. 1991*, Nitra, 1992, pp. 21–22.

Bednár, Peter – Staník, Ivan. "Archeologický a stavebno-historický výskum Nitrianskeho hradu v rokoch 1988–1991." In *Nitra. Príspevky k najstarším dejinám mesta*, Nitra 1993, pp. 127–141.

Beljak Pažinová, Noémi – Beljak, Ján. "Fortifikácie na sútoku Hrona a Slatiny." In *Hradiská – svedkovia dávnych čias II. Zborník odborných prispevkov o hradiskách a ich obyvateľoch*, ed. Peter Jenčík, Zuzana Staneková, pp. 9–28.

Beňko, Ján. *Starý Turiec*. Martin 1996.

Benkő, Loránd. *Név és történelem. Tanulmányok az Árpád-korról*, Budapest 1998.

Beranová, Magdaléna. *Zemědělství starých Slovanů*. Praha 1980.

Berendová, Nora, Laszlovsky, József, Szakács, Bela Zsolt. "Království uherské." In *Christianizace a utváření křesťanské monarchie*, ed. Nora Berendová, pp. 314–362.

Béreš, Július. "Výsledky doterajšieho výskumu slovanského hradiska v Šarišských Sokolovciach." *Nové obzory* 16 (1974), pp. 113–131.

Béreš, Július – Šalkovský, Peter. "Výskum slovanského hradiska v Spišských Tomášovciach." *AVANS v r. 1977*, Nitra 1978, pp. 36–38.

Béreš, Július – Staššíková-Štukovská, Danica. "Výskum slovanského hradiska v Spišských Tomášovciach." *AVANS v r. 1978*, Nitra 1980, pp. 42–46.

Bertels, Klaus. "Carantania. Beobachtungen zur politisch-geographischen Terminologie und zur Geschichte des Landes und seiner Bevölkerung im frühen Mittelalter." *Carinthia I*, 177 (1987), pp. 87–196.

Bialeková, Darina. "Nové včasnoslovanské nálezy na juhozápadnom Slovensku." *Slovenská archeológia* 10 (1962), no. 1, pp. 97–148.

Bialeková, Darina. "Výskum slovanského hradiska v Pobedime v rokoch 1959–1962." *Archeologické rozhledy* 15 (1963), pp. 316, 349–364, 369–372.

Bialeková, Darina. "Výskum slovanského hradiska v Pobedime roku 1964." *Archeologické rozhledy* 17 (1965), pp. 516, 530–538.

Bialeková, Darina. "Výskum slovanského hradiska v Pobedime, okres Trenčín." *Archeologické rozhledy* 24 (1972), pp. 121–129.

Bialeková, Darina. "Archeologický výskum a prieskum v Pobedime v roku 1975." *AVANS v r. 1975*, Nitra 1976, pp. 43–46.

Bialeková, Darina. "Pobedim. Slovanské hradisko a sídliská z 9. storočia." In *III. medzinárodný kongres slovanskej archeológie, Bratislava 7.–14. september 1975*, Nitra 1975.

Bialeková, Darina. "Sporen von slawischen Fundplätzen in Pobedim (Typologie und Datierung)." *Slovenská archeológia* 25 (1977) no. 1, pp. 103–160.

Bialeková, Darina. "Výskum a rekonštrukcia fortifikácie na slovanskom hradisku v Pobedime." *Slovenská archeológia* 26 (1978) no. 1, pp. 149–177.

Bialeková, Darina. "Zur Datierung archäologischer Quellen vom Ende des 8. bis Mitte des 9. Jh. im nördlichen Teil des Karpatenbeckens." In *Ethnische und kulturelle Verhältnisse an der mittleren Donau vom 6. bis zum 11. Jahrhundert*, ed. Darina Bialeková, Jozef Zábojník, pp. 249–256.

Bialeková, Darina. "Das Gebiet der Slowakei vom Zusammenbruch des awarischen Kaganats bis zur Entstehung Großmährens." In *Central Europe in 8th–10th Centuries. International Scientific Conference, Bratislava October 2–4, 1995*, ed. Dušan Čaplovič, Ján Doruľa, pp. 31–39.

Bialeková, Darina. "Zur Bautechnik der Befestigungsmauer des Burgwalls in Pobedim, Bezirk Trenčín." In *Frühmittelalterlicher Burgenbau in Mittel- und Osteuropa*, ed. Joachim Henning, Alexander Ruttkay, pp. 383–390.

Bialeková, Darina – Chropovský, Bohuslav. "Umeleckohistorický rozbor nákončia z Nitry." In *Nitra v slovenských dejinách*, ed. Richard Marsina, pp. 99–112.

Bialeková, Darina – Pieta, Karol. "Zisťovací výskum v Hradci, okres Prievidza." *Slovenská archeológia* 12 (1964), no. 3, pp. 447–466.

Bič, Miloš. "Ze světa starého zákona II." Praha 1989.

Bieniak, Janusz. "Państwo Miecława. Studium analityczne." Warszawa 2012.

Bitka pri Bratislave v roku 907 a jej význam pre vývoj stredného Podunajska. ed. Tatiana Štefanovičová, Drahoslav Hulínek, Bratislava 2008.

Bláha, Josef. "Předběžná zpráva o objevu předvelkomoravského ústředí v Olomouci." *Archaeologia historica* 13 (1988), pp. 155–170.

Bláha, Josef. "Archeologické poznatky vývoju a významu Olomouce v období Velkomoravské říše." In *Velká Morava mezi východem a západem. Sborník příspěvků z mezinárodní konference Uherské Hradiště, Staré Město 28. 9.–1. 10. 1999*, ed. Luděk Galuška, Pavel Kouřil, Zdeněk Měřínsky, Spisy Archeologického ústavu AV ČR Brno 17 (2001), pp. 41–68.

Bláha, Josef. "Komunikace, topografie a importy ve středověku a raném novověku (7.–17. století) na území města Olomouce." *Archaeologia historica* 23 (1998), pp. 133–159.

Bláha, Josef. "Topografie a otázka kontinuity raně středověkého ústředí v Olomouci." In *Přemyslovský stát kolem roku 1000. Na paměť knížete Boleslava II. († 7. února 999)*, ed. Luboš Polanský, Jiří Sláma, Dušan Třeštík, pp. 179–196.

Bláhová, Marie. "Terminologie sídlišť v pramenech doby merovejské. Exkurs: Několik poznámek k problematice Fredegarova castrum Wogastisburc." *Z pomocných věd historických IV, Acta Universitatis Carolinae, Philologica et Historica* 5 (1980), pp. 39–44.

Bláhová, Marie – Frolík, Jan – Profantová, Naďa. *Velké dějiny zemí Koruny české I. Do roku 1197*. Praha 1999.

von Bogyay, Thomas. "Mosapurc und Zalavár, Eine Auswertung der archäologischen Funde der schriftlichen Quellen." *Südost-Forschungen* 14, (1955), pp. 349–405.

von Bogyay, Thomas. "Die Kirchenorte der Conversio Bagoariorum et Carantanorum, Methoden und Möglichkeiten ihrer Lokalisierung." *Südost-Forschungen* 19 (1960), pp. 52–70.

von Bogyay, Thomas. "Kontinuitätsprobleme im karolingischen Unterpannonien, Methodios Wirken in Mosapurc im Lichte der Quellen und Funde." *Das östliche Mitteleuropa in Geschichte und Gegenwart*, Abb. 2, Wiesbaden 1966.

von Bogyay, Thomas. "Die Salzburger Mission in Pannonien aus der Sicht der Archäologie und der Namenkunde, Salzburg und die Slawenmission." *Zum 1100. Todestag des hl. Methodius. Beiträge des internationalen Symposions von 20. bis 22. September 1985 in Salzburg*, ed. Heinz Dopsch, Salzburg 1986, pp. 273–290.

Bojná. Hospodárske a politické centrum Nitrianskeho kniežatstva, ed. Karol Pieta, Alexander Ruttkay, Matej Ruttkay, Nitra 2007.

Bojná 2. Nové výsledky výskumov včasnostredovekých hradísk, ed. Karol Pieta, Zbigniew Robak, Nitra 2015.

Bollók, János. "A Thonuzoba-legenda történelmi hitele." *Századok* 113 (1979), no. 1, pp. 97–107.

Bollók, János. "Még egyszer Thonuzobáról. Válasz Szegfű Lászlónak." *Századok* 116 (1982), no. 5, pp. 1078–1090.

Bóna, István. "Beiträge zu den ethnischen Verhältnissen des 6.–7. Jahrhunderts in Westungarn." *Alba Regia* 2–3 (1961–1962), pp. 49–68.

Bóna, István. "'Cundpald fecit'. Der Kelch von Petöháza und die Anfänge der bairisch-fränkischen Awarenmission in Pannonien." *Acta Archaeologica Academiae Scientiarum Hungungaricae* 18 (1966), pp. 279–325.

Bóna, István. *Der Anbruch des Mittelalters. Gepiden und Langobarden im Karpatenbekken*. Budapest 1976.

Bóna, István. *Die Awaren. Ein asiatisches Reitervolk an der Mittleren Donau. In: Awaren in Europa. Schätze eines asiatischen Reitervolkes, 6.–8. Jahrhundert. Ausstellungskatalog.* Frankfurt/Main 1985, pp. 5–19.

Bóna, István. "Az 'Erdelyi emberek'. A gótok Erdélyben." In *Erdély története I*, ed. László Makkai, András Mócsy. Budapest 1986, pp. 108–134.

Bóna, István. "A hunok." In *Erdély története I*, ed. László Makkai, András Mócsy, pp. 134–137.

Bóna, István. "A gepidák királysága." In *Erdély története I*, ed. László Makkai, András Mócsy, pp. 138–159.

Bóna, István. "Az Avar uralom századai." In *Erdély története I*, ed. László Makkai, András Mócsy, pp. 159–177.

Bóna, István. "A népvándorláskor és a korai középkor története Magyarországon." In *Magyarország története I/1*, ed. György Székely, pp. 265–373.

Bóna, István. "'Die Waldmenschen'. Die Goten in Siebenbürgen." In *Kurze Geschichte Siebenbürgens*, ed. Béla Köpeczi, pp. 66–77.

Bóna, István. "Die Hunen." In *Kurze Geschichte Siebenbürgens*, ed. Béla Köpeczi, s. 78–80.

Bóna, István. "Das Königreich der Gepiden (455–567)." In *Kurze Geschichte Siebenbürgens*, ed. Béla Köpeczi, pp. 80–90.

Bóna, István. "Die Awarenzeit." In *Kurze Geschichte Siebenbürgens*, ed. von Béla Köpeczi, pp. 90–97.

Bóna, István. "Ungarns Völker im 5. und 6. Jahrhundert. Eine historisch-archäologische Zusammenschau." In *Germanen, Hunen und Awaren. Schätze der Völkerwanderungszeit. Die Archäologie des 5. und 6. Jahrhunderts an der mittleren Donau und der östlich-merowingische Reihengräberkreis*, ed. Wilfried Menghin, Tobias Springer, Egon Wamers, pp. 116–130.

Bóna, István. *Das Hunnenreich*. Budapest 1991.

Bóna, István. *A magyarok és Európa a 9–10. században*. Budapest 2000.

Bóna, István – Cseh, János – Nagy, Margit – Tomka, Péter – Tóth, Ágnes. *Hunok – Gepidák – Langobardok. Történeti régészeti tézisek és címszavak*. Szeged 1993.

Borhy, László – Kuzmová, Klára – Rajtár, Ján – Számadó, Emese. *Kelemantia – Brigetio. Po stopách Rimanov na Dunaji*. Iža 2001.

Boroń, Piotr. *Słowiańskie wiece plemienne*. Katowice, 1999.
Boroń, Piotr. *Wiece słowiańskie a decyzja o przyjęciu chrześcijaństwa – możliwości poznawcze*. In: *Pohanstvo a kresťanstvo (zborník z konferencie usporiadanej 5.–6. II. 2003 v Banskej Bystrici)*, ed. Rastislav Kožiak, Jaroslav Nemeš, pp. 95–102.
Boroń, Piotr. *Kniazowie, królowie, carowie ... Tytuły i nazwy władców słowiańskich we wczesnym średniowieczu*. Katowice 2010.
Botek, Andrej. *Veľkomoravské kostoly na Slovensku a odraz ich tradície v neskoršom období*. Bratislava 2014.
Botoš, I. "Tekst Povesti o razorenii Rjazani Batyem po Volokolamskomu spisku XVI veka (No 523)." *Studia Slavica Academiae Scientiarum Hungaricae* 6 (1961) 1–4, pp. 23–73.
Božilov, Ivan A. "Kăm chronologijata na bălgaro-madžarskata vojna pri car Simeon (894–896 g.)." *Voennoistoričeski sbornik* 40 (1971) no. 6, pp. 20–33.
Bradács, Gábor. "'*Heinricus filius Stephani, qui tantis miraculis claruit.*' Szent Imre herceg a középkori európai történeirásban." *Történeti tanulmányok* 14, (Debrecen 2007), pp. 51–72.
Brather, Sebastian. "Byli slovanští přistehovalci jednotnou skupinou, nebo se regionálně odlišovali?" In *"Neslované" o počátcích Slovanů*, ed. Przemysław Urbańczyk, pp. 41–62.
Bratia, ktorí menili svet – Konštantín a Metod. Príspevky z konferencie, ed. Branislav Panis, Matej Ruttkay, Vladimír Turčan. Bratislava 2012.
Bratislavský hrad, dejiny, výskum a obnova. Kolektívna monografia prednášok z konferencie konanej v dňoch 22.–23. 9. 2014 na Bratislavskom hrade v rámci -projektu Európskej únie Danube Limes Brand, ed. Margaréta Musilová, Peter Barta, Angelika Herucová. Bratislava 2014.
Brent, Peter. *Sága Vikingov*. Bratislava 1982.
Brezinová, Gertrúda – Samuel, Marián. "Osídlenie hradného kopca v praveku a včasnej dobe dejinnej." In *Kolíska kresťanstva*, ed. Viliam Judák, Peter Bednár, Jozef Medvecký, pp. 96–113.
Brezováková, Blanka. "K pojmom gens a natio v písomných prameňoch v anjouovskom období." In *Studia historica Tyrnaviensia IV. Národnosti v minulosti Slovenska. K životnému jubileu prof. PhDr. Vincenta Sedláka, CSc.*, ed. Marta Dobrotková, Vladimír Rábik. Trnava 2006, pp. 77–98.
ten Brink, Bernhard. *Geschichte der Englischen Litteratur I*. Straßburg 1899.
Brønsted, Johannes. *Vikingové. Sága tří staletí*. Praha 1967.
Brunner, Karl. "Der fränkische Fürstentitel im neunten und zehnten Jahrhundert." In. *Intitulatio II. Lateinische Herrscher- und Fürstentitel im neunten und zehnten Jahrhundert*, ed. Herwig Wolfram. Mitteilungen des Instituts für österreichische Geschichtsforschung, Ergänzunsband 24 (1973), pp. 179–340.

Brunner, Karl. *Der österreichische Donauraum zur Zeit der Magyarherrschaft*. In: *Österreich im Hochmittelalter (907–1246)*. Ed. Kommision für die Geschichte Österreichs der Österreichischen Akademie der Wissenschaften. Wien 1991, pp. 54–61.

Brunner, Karl. *Österreichische Geschichte 907–1156. Herzogtümer und Marken. Von Ungarnsturm bis ins 12. Jahrhundert*. Wien 1994.

Bubeník, Josef. "K raně středověkému osídlení severozápadních Čech, jeho strukturám a centrům." *Studia mediaevalia Pragensia* 1 (1988), pp. 51–62.

Bubeník, Josef. "Die Besiedlung des südöstlichen Vorfeldes des Berges Rubin in der Burgwallzeit und ihre Chronologie. Ausgrabung in den Jahren 1984–1991." *Památky archeologické* 88 (1997), pp. 56–106.

Bubeník, Josef. "Hradiště Rubín u Podbořan v severozápadních Čechách v raném středověku." In *Na prahu poznání českých dějin. Sborník prací k poctě Jiřího Slámy. Studia mediaevalia Pragensia* 7 (2006), pp. 21–37.

Budinský-Krička, Vojtech. "Pohrebisko z neskorej doby avarskej v Žitavskej Tôni na Slovensku." *Slovenská archeológia* 4 (1956), no. 1, pp. 5–131.

Budinský-Krička, Vojtech. "Slovanské osídlenie na severovýchodnom Slovensku." *Slovenská archeológia* 9 (1961), no. 1–2, pp. 359–360.

Budinský-Krička, Vojtech. "Pokusný výskum na slovanskom hradisku v Šarišských Sokolovciach, okres Prešov." *Nové obzory* 9 (1967), pp. 164–185.

Budinský-Krička, Vojtech. "Slovanské hradisko v Kusíne." *Nové obzory* 25 (1983), pp. 97–109.

Budinský-Krička, Vojtech – Fettich, Nándor. *Das altungarische Fürstengrab von Zemplín*. Bratislava 1973.

Bujnák, Pavel. "Obrátenie Maďarov na vieru kresťanskú." In *Ríša Veľkomoravská. Sborník vedeckých prác*, ed. Ján Stanislav, pp. 377–409.

Bulat, Mirko. "Neki nalazi ranog srednjeg vijeka iz Osijeka." *Starohrvatska Prosvjeta* 3 (1968), no. 10, pp. 11–21.

Bulín, Hynek. "Podunajští 'Abodriti'. Příspěvek k dějinám podunajských Slovanů v 9. století." In *Slovanské historické studie* 3 (1960), pp. 5–44.

Bulín, Hynek. "Aux origines des formations étatiques des Slaves du moyen Danube au IXe siècle." In *Europe aux IXe–XIe siècles*. Varsovie 1968, pp. 149–204.

Burger, Alice Sz. – Fülep, Ferenc. *Die römischen Inschriften Ungarns 4. Lieferung*. Budapest 1984.

Burg – Vorburg – Suburbium. Zur Problematik der Nebenareale frühmittelalterlicher Zentren. Internationale Tagungen in Mikulčice VII, ed. Ivana Boháčová, Lumír Poláček. Brno 2008.

Bystrický, Peter. "Politická situácia strednej Európy po rozpade ríše Hunov." *Historický časopis* 49 (2001), no. 2, pp. 201–222.

Bystrický, Peter. "Slovanské a bulharské vpády na Balkán do roku 559." *Historický časopis* 51 (2003), no. 3, pp. 385–402.

Bystrický, Peter. *Sťahovanie národov (454–568). Ostrogóti, Gepidi, Longobardi a Slovania*. Bratislava 2008.

Bystrický, Peter. "Kolektívna pamäť, ústna tradícia a longobardské dejiny." In *Historocké štúdie. Medzi antikou a stredovekom. Rímska a germánska spoločnosť v barbarských zákonníkoch*, ed. Miroslav Daniš, Pavol Valachovič, *Acta historica Posoniensia* 13 (2010), pp. 23–41.

Bystrický, Peter. "Samova ríša a prepožičiavanie vlády cudzincom." In *Slovenské dejiny v dejinách Európy. Vybrané kapitoly*, ed. Dušan Kováč. Bratislava 2015, pp. 242–261.

Bystrický, Peter. "Historické pozadie germánskych piesní a ság." In *Od symbolu k slovu. Podoby stredovekej komunikácie*, ed. Miriam Hlavačková, pp. 233–256.

Byzantská kultúra a Slovensko. Zborník štúdií. Zborník Slovenského národného múzea. Archeológia supplementum 2, ed. Vladimír Turčan. Bratislava 2007.

Cankova-Petkova, Genoveva. "L'état bulgare, les Slaves et Byzance." In *Rapports du IIIe Congrés International d'Archéologie Slave, Bratislava 7–14 septembre 1975, Tome 2*, ed. Bohuslav Chropovský, pp. 73–77.

von Carnap-Bornheim, Claus. "Freund oder Feind? Überlegungen und Thesen zum König von Mušov." In *Gentes, Reges und Rom. Auseinandersetzung – Anerkennung – Anpassung*, ed. Jan Bouzek, Herwig Friesinger, Karol Pieta, Balázs Komoróczy. Spisy Archeologického ústavu AV ČR Brno 16 (2000), pp. 59–65.

"Castellum, civitas, urbs". Zentren und Eliten im frühmittelalterlichen Ostmitteleuropa. Centres and Elites in Early Medieval East-Central Europe, ed. Orsolya Heinrich-Tamáska, Hajnalka Herold, Péter Straub, Tivadar Vida, *Castellum Pannonicum Pelsonense* 6, Budapest – Leipzig – Keszthely – Rahden/Westf. 2015.

Cendelín, Dušan. "Kosmas k roku 1116. Interpretace historické události v reflexii krajiny moravsko-slovenského pomezí." *Historická geografie* 37 (2011), no. 1, pp. 7–48.

Central Europe in 8th–10th Centuries. International Scientific Conference, Bratislava October 2–4, 1995, ed. Dušan Čaplovič, Ján Doruľa. Bratislava 1997.

Chaloupecký, Václav. "Sv. Svorád." *Prúdy* 6 (1922), pp. 544–553.

Chaloupecký, Václav. *Staré Slovensko*. Bratislava 1923.

Chaloupecký, Václav. "Radla-Anastázius, druh Vojtěchův, organizátor uherské církve. Několik kritických poznámek." *Bratislava, časopis Učenej společnosti Šafaříkovy* 1 (1927), no. 2, pp. 210–228.

Chaloupecký, Václav. "Slovenské dioeceze a tak rečená apoštolská práva." *Bratislava, Učená společnost Šafaříkova* 2 (1928), pp. 1–70.

Choc, Pavel. *S mečem a štítem. České raně feudální vojenství*. Praha 1967.

Chorvátová, Hana. "Horizonty byzantsko-orientálneho šperku na tzv. veľkomoravských pohrebiskách." In *Byzantská kultúra a Slovensko. Zborník Slovenského* národného múzea Archeológia supplementum 2, ed. Vladimír Turčan. Bratislava 2007, pp. 83–101.

Chorvátová, Hana. "Untergang und Neuanfang – zur Christianisierung im Einflussbereich des frühmittelalterlichen mährischen Fürstentums auf dem Gebiet der heutigen Slowakei anhand archäologischen Quellen." *Centrum medievistických studií Akademie vied ČR a Univerzity Karlovy* 2012, pp. 240–260.

Chorvátová, Hana. "Móda šperku na hradiskách?" In *Hradiská – svedkovia dávnych čias. Zborník odborných príspevkov o hradiskách a ich obyvateľoch*, ed. Peter Jenčík, Víťazoslav Struhár, pp. 201–216.

Christentum in Pannonien im ersten Jahrtausend. Internationale Tagung im Balaton Museum in Keszthely vom 6. bis 9. November 2000, ed. Robert Müller. Zalai Múzeum 11, Zalaegerszeg, 2002.

Christianizace českých zemí ve středoevropské perspektivě, ed. Libor Jan. Brno 2011.

Christianizace a utváření křesťanské monarchie. Skandinávie, střední Evropa a Rus v období 10.–12. století, ed. Nora Berendová. Praha 2013.

Chropovský, Bohuslav. "Nálezy keramiky pražského typu v Nitre." *Sborník prací Filosofické fakulty Brněnské university* 20 (E 16). Brno 1971, pp. 147–149.

Chropovský, Bohuslav. "Príspevok k problematike cirkevnej architektúry a počiatkom kresťanstva na Slovensku." *Ochrana pamiatok* 8 (1972), pp. 173–208.

Chropovský, Bohuslav. "Pohrebisko z 9.–10. storočia pod Zoborom." *Slovenská archeológia* 26 (1978), no. 1, pp. 99–126.

Chropovský, Bohuslav. "Pokračovanie výskumu v Spišských Tomášovciach." *AVANS v r. 1984*. Nitra 1985, pp. 100–101.

Chropovský, Bohuslav. "Včasnoslovanský a predveľkomoravský vývoj na území Československa." In Poulík, Josef – Chropovský, Bohuslav a kolektiv. *Velká Morava a počátky československé státnosti*, pp. 81–106.

Chropovský, Bohuslav. "Slovensko v protohistorickom období." In *Dejiny Slovenska I*. Bratislava 1986, pp. 41–74.

Chropovský, Bohuslav – Fusek, Gabriel. "Výsledky výskumov na stavenisku športového areálu v Nitre." *Študijné zvesti Archeologického ústavu SAV* 24 (1988), pp. 153–154.

Cibulka, Josef. "Pribina a jeho kostol v Nitre." In *Ríša Veľkomoravská. Sborník vedeckých prác*, ed. Ján Stanislav, pp. 25–52.

Cibulka, Josef. *Velkomoravský kostel v Modré u Velehradu a začátky křesťanství na Moravě*. Monumenta Archeologica VII. Praha 1958.

Cognitioni gestorum. Studia z dziejów średniowiecza dedykowane profesorovi Jerzemu Strzelczykovi, ed. Darius A. Sikorski, Andrzej M. Wyrwa. Poznań – Warszawa 2006.

Csáky, Károly Emmanuel. *A váczi egyházmegye történeti névtára I*. Váczon 1915.

Csallányi, Dezső. *Archäologische Denkmäler der Awarenzeit in Mitteleuropa*. Budapest 1956.

Csallányi, Dezső. *Archäologische Denkmäler der Gepiden im Mitteldonaubecken (454–568 u. Z.)*. Budapest 1961.

Csánki, Dezső. *Magyarország történelmi földrajza a Hunyadiak korában II*. Budapest 1894.

Csánki, Dezső. *Magyarország történelmi földrajza a Hunyadiak korában III*. Budapest 1897.

Cseglédy, Károly. "Géza nevünk eredete." *Magyar Nyelv* 52 (1956), pp. 325–333.

Csendes, Peter. *Die Strassen Niederösterreichs im Früh- und Hochmittelalter*. Dissertationen der Universität Wien 33. Wien 1969.

Csóka, J. Lajos. *Szent Benedek fiainak világtörténete különös tekintettel Magyarországra I*. Budapest 1969.

Csütörtöky, Jozef. "Nové poznatky k ikonografii pozlátených medených plakiet z Bojnej a hypotetická rekonštrukcia ich aplikácie." In *Bojná 2. Nové výsledky výskumov včasnostredovekých hradísk*. ed. Karol Pieta, Zbigniew Robak, pp. 115–138.

Curta, Florin. *The Making of the Slavs. History and Archaeology of the Lower Danube Region, c. 500–700*. Cambridge 2001.

Curta, Florin. "Utváření Slovanů. Návrat ke slovanské etnogenezi." In *"Neslované" o počátcích Slovanů*, ed. Przemysław Urbańczyk, pp. 21–40.

Czeglédy, Károly. "Géza nevünk eredete." *Magyar Nyelv* 52 (1956), s. 325–333.

Czeglédy, Károly. "Nyugati türk eredetű méltóságnevek Termacsu, barsbeg, jebu, bagatur." In *Névtudományi vizsgálatok. A magyar nyelvtudományi társaság névtudományi konferenciája 1958*, ed. Pais Dezső, Mikesy Sándor. Budapest 1960, pp. 119–125.

Czeglédy, Károly. "Új arab forrás a magyarok 942 évi spanyolországi kalandozásáról." *Magyar Nyelv* 75 (1979), no. 3, pp. 273–282.

Czeglédy, Károly. "Még egyszer a magyarok 942 évi spanyolországi kalandozásáról." *Magyar Nyelv* 77 (1981), no. 4, pp. 419–423.

Czeglédy, Károly. *Magyar őstörténeti tanulmányok*. Budapest Oriental Reprints, Series A 2. Budapest 1985.

Čáp, Pavel – Dresler, Petr – Macháček, Jiří – Přichystalová, Renáta. "Großmährische Kirchen in Pohansko bei Břeclav." In *Frühmittelalterliche Kirchen als archäologische und historische Quelle*, ed. Lumír Poláček, Jana Maříková-Kubková, pp. 187–204.

Čaplovič, Dušan. "Výsledky výskumu hradiska v Zemplíne." *AVANS v r. 1984*. Nitra 1985, pp. 75–77.

Čaplovič, Dušan. *Včasnostredoveké osídlenie Slovenska*. Bratislava 1998.

Čaplovič, Pavol. "Sídlisko z doby rímskej a slovanskej na Ostrej Skale nad Vyšným Kubínom." *AVANS v r. 1975*. Nitra 1976, pp. 78–82.

Čaplovič, Pavol. "Osídlenie Ostrej Skaly nad Vyšným Kubínom." *AVANS v r. 1977*. Nitra 1978, pp. 72–73.

Čaplovič, Pavol. *Orava v praveku, vo včasnej dobe dejinnej a na začiatku stredoveku*. Martin 1987.

České země v raném středověku, ed. Petr Sommer. Praha 2006.
Čilinská, Zlata. "Slovansko-avarské pohrebisko v Žitavskej Tôni." *Slovenská archeológia* 11 (1963), no. 1, pp. 87–120.
Čilinská, Zlata. "Sociálno-ekonomická problematika vo svetle pohrebísk juhozápadného Slovenska zo 7.–8. stor." In *O počiatkoch slovenských dejín*, ed. Peter Ratkoš, pp. 36–54.
Čilinská, Zlata. *Frühmittelalterliches Gräberfeld in Želovce*. Bratislava 1973.
Čilinská, Zlata. "Zur Frage des Samo-Reiches." In *Rapports du IIIe Congrés International d'Archéologie Slave, Bratislava 7–14 septembre 1975, Tome 2*, ed. Bohuslav Chropovský. Bratislava 1980, pp. 79–86.
Čilinská, Zlata. "Dve pohrebiská z 8.–9. storočia v Komárne." *Slovenská archeológia* 30 (1982), no. 2, pp. 347–393.
Čilinská, Zlata. "K otázke príchodu Antov na stredný Dunaj." *Sborník prací Filosofické fakulty Brněnské university* E 34–35 (1989–1990), pp. 19–25.
Čilinská, Zlata. *Slovania a Avarský kaganát. Výpoveď staroslovanského pohrebiska v Želovciach*. Bratislava 1992.
Čižmář, Miloš. "Langobardský sídlištní objekt z Podolí, okr. Brno-venkov. K problematice langobardských sídlišť na Moravě." *Archeologické rozhledy* 49 (1997), pp. 634–642.
Čižmář, Miloš. *Encyklopedie hradišť na Moravě a ve Slezsku s leteckými záběry hradišť Miroslava Bálky*. Praha 2004.
Dąbrowski, Jan. "Studia nad początkami państwa polskiego." *Rocznik Krakówski* 34 (1957–1959), pp. 3–59.
Daicoviciu, Hadrian. *Dákové*. Praha 1973.
Daim, Falko. "Pilgeramulette und Frauenschmuck? Zu den Scheibenfibeln der frühen Keszthely-Kultur." In *Christentum in Pannonien im ersten Jahrtausend. Internationale Tagung im Balaton Museum in Keszthely vom 6. bis 9. November 2000*, ed. Robert Müller. Zalai Múzeum 11 (2002), pp. 113–132.
Dávne dejiny Nitry a okolia vo svetle najnovších archeologických nálezov. Zborník z konferencie konanej pri príležitosti Dňa Nitranov 2. júla 2005, ed. Matej Ruttkay. Nitra 2005.
Dejiny Nitry. Od najstarších čias po súčasnosť, ed. Gabriel Fusek a Marián Róbert Zemene. Nitra 1998.
Dejiny Slovenska I. Bratislava 1986.
Dekan, Ján. "K problémom slovanského osídlenia na Slovensku." *Historica Slavaca* VI–VII (1948–1949), pp. 55–82.
Dekan, Ján. "Výskum na Devíne v roku 1950." *Archeologické rozhledy* 3 (1951), pp. 164–168.
Dekan, Ján. *Začiatky slovenských dejín a Ríša veľkomoravská. Slovenské dejiny II*. Bratislava 1951.

Dekan, Ján. "Vývoj a stav archeologického výskumu doby predveľkomoravskej." *Slovenská archeológia* 19 (1971), no. 2, pp. 559–580.
Dekan, Ján. *Veľká Morava*. Bratislava 1976.
Dercsényi, Dezső. "L'église de Pribina á Zalavár." *Etudes Slaves Roumaines* I (1948), pp. 85–100.
Deržavin, N. S. *Slovania v dávnej minulosti. Kultúrnohistorický náčrt*. Bratislava 1950.
Dějiny Byzance, ed. Bohumila Zástěrová. Praha 1992.
Dějiny hutníctví železa v Československu I, ed. Jaroslav Purš. Praha 1984.
Dějiny politického myšlení II/1. Politické myšlení raného křesťanství a středověku, ed. Vilém Herold, Ivan Müller, Aleš Havlíček. Praha 2011.
Dějiny ve věku nejistot. Sborník k příležitosti 70. narozenin Dušana Třeštíka, ed. Jan Klápště, Eva Plešková, Josef Žemlička. Praha 2003.
Die Bayern und ihre Nachbarn. Berichte des Symposions der Kommision für Frühmittelalterforschung 25. bis 28. Oktober 1982, Stift Zwettl, Niederösterreich, Teil I, ed. Herwig Wolfram, Andreas Schwarcz, Dph 179 (1985).
Die frühmittelalterliche Elite bei den Völkern des östlichen Mitteleuropas (mit einem speciellen Blick auf die großmährische Problematik). Materialien der internationalen Fachkonferenz Mikulčice 25.–26. 5. 2004, ed. Pavel Kouřil. Spisy Archeologického ústavu AV ČR Brno 25. Brno 2005.
Die Germanen. Geschichte und Kultur der germanische Stämme in Mitteleuropa. Ein Handbuch in zwei Bänder, ed. Bruno Krüger. *Band 1: Von den Anfängen bis zum 2. Jahrhundert unserer Zeitrechnung. Band 2: Die Stämme und Stammesverbände in der Zeit vom 3. Jahrhundert bis zur Herausbildung der politischen Vorherrschaft der Franken*. Berlin 1983.
Dienst, Heide. "Werden und Entwicklung der babenbergischen Mark." In *Österreich im Hochmittelalter (907–1246)*, ed. der Kommission für die Geschichte Österreichs bei der Österreichischen Akademie der Wissenschaften. Wien 1991, pp. 63–102.
Dieseberger, Maximilian. "Baiern, das Ostfränkische Reich und die Ungarn bis zur Schlacht von Pressburg 862–907." In *Schicksalsjahr 907. Die Schlacht bei Pressburg und das frühmittelalterliche Niederösterreich*, ed. Roman Zehetmayer, pp. 31–43.
Dimitz, August. *Geschichte Krains von der ältesten Zeit bis auf das Jahr 1813. Mit besonderer Rücksicht auf Culturentwicklung. Erster Theil: Von der Urzeit bis zum Tode Kaiser Friedrichs III. (1493)*. Laibach 1874.
Dittrich, Zdeněk R. *Christianity in Great-Moravia. Bijdragen van het Instituut voor middeleeuwse Geschiedenis der Rijksuniversiteit te Utrecht 33*. Groningen 1962.
Dobiáš, Josef. *Dějiny československého území před vystoupením Slovanů*. Praha 1964.
Dobrev, Petr. *Prabălgarite. Proizchod, ezik, kultura*. Sofija 1991.
Domanovszki, Sándor. *Kézai Simon mester krónikája*. Budapest 1906.

Dopsch, Heinz. "Passau als Zentrum der Slawenmission. Ein Beitrag zur Frage des 'Grossmährischen Reiches'." *Südostdeutsches Archiv* 28–29 (1985), pp. 5–28.

Dopsch, Heinz. "Zwischen Salzburg, Byzanz und Rom. Zur Missionierung Pannoniens im 9. Jahrhundert." In *Christentum in Pannonien im ersten Jahrtausend. Internationale Tagung im Balaton Museum in Keszthely vom 6. bis 9. November 2000*, ed. Robert Müller. Zalai Múzeum 11 (2002), pp. 267–294.

Dorica, Jozef. "Predrománska Rotunda sv. Juraja pri Nitrianskej Blatnici vo svetle reštaurátorského výskumu a reštaurovania a jej nové zaradenie v kontexte najstarších sakrálnych stavieb na Slovensku." In *Bojná 2. Nové výsledky výskumov včasnostredovekých hradísk*, ed. Karol Pieta, Zbigniew Robak, pp. 281–296.

Doruľa, Ján. *O slovensko-nemeckom spolunažívaní v 16. – 18. storočí*. Bratislava 2014.

Dowiat, Jerzy. *Polska – państwem średniowiecznej Europy*. Warszawa 1968.

Drahošová, Viera. "Podbranč – Starý hrad." *Záhorie* IV (1995), no. 4, pp. 18–19.

Dralle, Lothar. "Zur Vorgeschichte und Hintergründen der Ostpolitik Heinrichs I." In *Europa Slavica – Europa Orientalis*, ed. Klaus-Detlev Grothusen, Klaus Zernack, pp. 99–126.

Dresler, Petr – Macháček, Jiří – Přichystalová, Renáta. "Die Vorburgen des frühmittelalterlichen Zentralortes in Pohansko bei Břeclav." In *Burg – Vorburg – Suburbium. Zur Problematik der Nebenareale frühmittelalterlicher Zentren*. ed. Ivana Boháčová, Lumír Poláček, pp. 229–270.

Dresler, Petr – Přichystalová, Renáta. "Břeclav – Pohansko. Veľkomoravské hradisko." *Historická revue* 25 (2014), no. 12, pp. 45–50.

Droberjar, Eduard. *Věk barbarů. České země a stěhování národů z ohledu archeologie*. Praha – Litomyšl 2005.

Dušek, Sigrid. "Veľkomoravské pohrebisko v Smoleniciach." *Slovenská archeológia* 27 (1979) no. 3, pp. 365–374.

Dušek, Sigrid. "Ostroha s háčikmi zo Smoleníc." In *Zborník prác Ľudmile Kraskovskej (k životnému jubileu)*, ed. Etela Studeníková, Lev Zachar. Bratislava 1984, pp. 159–162.

Dümmler, Ernst. "Über die südöstlichen Marken des Fränkischen Reiches unter den Karolingern (795–907)." *Archiv für Kunde österreichischer Geschichtsquellen* 10 (1853), pp. 1–85.

Dümmler, Ernst. *Geschichte des Ostfränkischen Reiches I, II, III*. Leipzig, 1862, 1865, 1888.

Dvorník, František. "Byzancia a Veľká Morava." In *Ríša Veľkomoravská. Sborník vedeckých prác*, ed. Ján Stanislav, pp. 101–161.

Dvorník, František. "Metodova diecéza a boj o Illyricum." In *Ríša Veľkomoravská. Sborník vedeckých prác*, ed. Ján Stanislav, pp. 162–225.

Dvorník, František. *Byzantské misie u Slovanů*. Praha 1970.

Dvorník, František. *Zrod střední a východní Evropy. Mezi Byzancí a Římem*. Praha 1999.

Dvořák, Pavel. "V mĺkvom náručí šúrov." In Dvořák, Pavel. *Odkryté dejiny (Predveká Bratislava).* Bratislava 1978, pp. 136–151.

Eckhardt, Sándor. "Micolt". *Magyar Nyelv* 26 (1930), no. 5–6, pp. 167–170.

Egy elfeledett diadal. A 907. évi pozsonyi csata, ed. Béla Gyula Torma, László Veszprémy. Budapest 2008.

Eichenberger, Thomas. *Patria. Studien zur Bedeutung des Wortes im Mittelalter (6.–12. Jh.),* Nationes 9. Sigmaringen 1991.

Eichert, Stefan. "Kirchen des 8. bis 10. Jahrhunderts in Kärnten und ihre Bedeutung für die Archäologie der Karantanen." In *Frühmittelalterliche Kirchen als archäologische und historische Quelle,* ed. Lumír Poláček, Jana Maříková, Kubková, pp. 219–232.

Eichert, Stefan. "Zentralisierungsprozesse bei den frühmittelalterlichen Karantanen." In *Zentralisierungsprozesse und Herrschaftsbildung im frühmittelalterlichen Ostmitteleuropa,* ed. Przemyslaw Sikora, pp. 13–60.

Eisner, Jan. *Devínska Nová Ves. Slovanské pohřebiště.* Bratislava 1952.

Eisner, Jan. "Slované a Maďaři v archeologii." *Slavia antiqua* 7 (1960), pp. 189–*210.

Eliade, Mircea. *Dejiny náboženských predstáv a ideí III.* Bratislava 1997.

Eliade, Mircea. *Mýtus o věčném návratu. Archetypy a opakování.* Praha 2003.

Elschek, Kristián. "Rímsko-germánska vidiecka usadlosť s kúpeľom v Bratislave-Dúbravke." *Pamiatky a múzeá* (2000), no. 3, pp. 27–29.

Elter, István. "Néhány megjegyzés Ibn Ḥayyānnak a magyarok 942. évi spanyolországi kalandozásáról szóló tudósításához." *Magyar Nyelv* 77 (1981), no. 4, pp. 413–419.

Elter, István. "Magyarország Idrísí földrajzi művében (1154)." *Acta Universitatis Szegediensis de Attila József nominatae. Acta Historica* 82 (1985), pp. 53–63.

Elter, István. "A magyar kalandozáskor arab forrásai." In *A honfoglaláskor írott forrásai,* ed. László Kovács, László Veszprémy. Budapest 1996, pp. 173–180.

Elter, István. *Ibn Ḥayyān a kalandozó Magyarokról.* Szeged 2009.

Emlékkönyv Domanovszky Sándor születése hatvanadik fordulójának ünnepére 1937 május 27. Budapest 1937.

Encyklopédia archeológie. Bratislava 1986.

Engel, Pál. *Magyarország világi archontológiája 1301–1457 I, II.* Budapest 1996.

Entz, Géza. *A gyulafehérvári székesegyház.* Budapest 1958.

Erb, Ewald. *Geschichte der deutschen Literatur I/1,2, von den Anfängen bis 1160.* Berlin 1982.

Erdély története I, ed. László Makkai, András Mócsy. Budapest 1986.

Erdélyi, István. *Die Kunst der Awaren.* Budapest 1966.

Erläuterungen zum historischen Atlas der österreichischen Alpenländer, ed. der Kaiserliche Akademie der Wissenschaften in Wien. I. Abteilung: Die Landgerichtskarte, 4. Teil: Kärnten, Krain, Görz und Istrien von August von Jaksch, Martin Wutte, Anton Kaspret und Anton Mell, 1. Heft: Kärnten, Görz und Gradisca. Wien 1914.

Erläuterungen zum historischen Atlas der österreichischen Alpenländer, ed. Kaiserliche Akademie der Wissenschaften in Wien. I. Abteilung: Die Landgerichtskarte, 1. Teil: Salzburg, Oberösterreich, Steiermark von Eduard Richter, Anton Mell, Julius Strnadt, Hans Pirchegger. Zweite Ausgabe. Wien 1917.

Erläuterungen zum historischen Atlas der österreichischen Alpenländer, ed. der Akademie der Wissenschaften in Wien. I. Abteilung: Die Langerichtskarte, 3. Teil: Tirol und Voralberg von Otto Stolz, Hans von Voltelini, Josef Zösmair, *2. Heft: Das Welsche Südtirol.* Wien 1919.

Erläuterungen zum historischen Atlas der österreichischen Alpenländer, ed. Akademie der Wissenschaften in Wien. I. Abteilung: Die Landgerichtskarte, 4. Teil: Kärnten, Krain, Görz und Istrien von August von Jaksch, Martin Wutte, Ludmil Hauptmann, Anton Mell und Hans Pirchegger, *2. Heft: Kärnten (Nachtrag), Krain und Istrien.* Wien 1929.

Érszégi, Géza. "Szent István pannonhalmi oklevele." In *Mons Sacer 996–1996. Pannonhalma 1000 éve I.* ed. Imre Takács, pp. 47–89.

Ethnische und kulturelle Verhältnisse an der mittleren Donau vom 6. bis zum 11. Jahrhundert. Symposium Nitra 6. bis 10. November 1994. ed. Darina Bialeková, Jozef Zábojník. Bratislava 1996.

Europa Slavica – Europa Orientalis. Festschift für Herbert Ludat zum 70. Geburtstag, ed. Klaus-Detlev Grothusen, Klaus Zernack. Berlin 1980.

Europas Mitte um 1000. Beiträge zur Geschichte, Kunst und Archäologie, Band 1, 2, ed. Alfried Wieczorek, Hans-Martin Hinz. Stuttgart 2000.

Europas Mitte um 1000. Katalog, ed. Alfried Wieczorek, Hans-Martin Hinz. Stuttgart 2000.

Farkaš, Zdeněk. "Ojedinelé nálezy zo Svätého Jura." *AVANS v r. 1993.* Nitra 1995, p. 40.

Farkaš, Zdeněk. "Zisťovací výskum v Modre, poloha Zámčisko." *Zborník Slovenského národného múzea* 95 (2001) *Archeológia* 11, pp. 135–168.

Fedeles, Tamás – Koszta, László. *Pécs (Fünfkirchen). Das Bistum und die Bischofsstadt im Mittelalter.* Wien 2011.

Fehér, Géza. "A bolgár egyház kísérletei és hazánkban." *Századok* 61 (1927), no. 1, pp. 1–20.

Fehértoi, Katalin. *Árpád-kori kis személynévtár.* Budapest 1983.

Fehértoi, Katalin. *Árpád-kori személynévtár (1000–1301).* Budapest 2004.

Fertály, Lajosné. *Miskolc az Árpádok korában.* Miskolc 1928.

Fettich, Nandor. "Der Fund von Čadjavica." *Vjesnik Hrvatskoga arheološkoga društva nova serije sveska* 22–23 (1941–1942), pp. 55–61.

Fettich, Nandor. *Das awarenzeitliche Gräberfeld von Pilismarót-Basaharc.* Budapest 1965.

Fiala, Andrej – Vallašek, Adrián – Lukáč, Gabriel. *Spišský hrad.* Martin 1988.

Fiedler, Uwe. "Die Slawen im Bulgarenreich und im Awarenkhaganat. Versuch eines Vergleichs." In *Ethnische und kulturelle Verhältnisse an der mittleren Donau vom 6. bis zum 11. Jahrhundert. Symposium Nitra 6. bis 10. November 1994*, ed. Darina Bialeková, Jozef Zábojník, pp. 195-214.

Filip, Jan. *Keltové ve střední Evropě*. Praha 1956.

Fitz, Jenő. *Gorsium*. Székesfehérvár 1983.

Fitz, Jenő – Császár, László – Papp, Imre. *Székesfehérvár*. Budapest 1966.

Flajšhans, Václav. "Osoby a místa v legendách svatováclavských." In *Svatováclavský sborník I. Kníže Václav Svatý a jeho doba*, ed. Karel Guth, Jan Kapras, Antonín Novák, Karel Stloukal, pp. 819-832.

Florja, Boris Nikolajevič. "Skazanie o preloženii knig na slovjanskij jazyk. Istočniki, vremja i mesto napisanija." *Byzantinoslavica* 46 (1985), pp. 121-130.

Florja, Boris Nikolajevič. "Prinjatie christianstva v Velikoj Moravii, Čechii i Poľše." In *Prinjatie christianstva narodami Centraľnoj i Jugo-Vostočnoj Evropy i kreščenie Rusi*, ed. Gennadij G. Litavrin, pp. 122-158.

Fodor, István. "Altungarn, Bulgarotürken und Ostslawen in Südrußland." *Archeologische Beiträge. Acta Antiqua et Archaeologica* 20 (Szeged 1977), pp. 7-64.

Fodor, István. "On Magyar-Bulgar-Turkish Contacts." In *Chuvash Studies*, ed. András Róna-Tas. Budapest 1982, pp. 45-81.

Fodor, István. "Zur Problematik der Ankunft der Ungarn im Karpatenbecken und ihrer Fortlaufenden Besiedlung." In *Interaktionen der mitteleuropäischen Slawen und anderen Ethnika im 6.-10. Jahrhundert. Symposium Nové Vozokany 3.-7. Oktober 1983*, ed. Peter Šalkovský, pp. 97-104.

Foltin, János. *A Zázty-i apátság*. Eger 1883.

Font, Márta. "Krone und Schwert. die Anerkennung des Herrschaftsrechts in Mittel- und Osteuropa." In *East Central Europe at the Turn of the 1st and 2nd Millennia*, ed. Vincent Múcska. *Acta historica Posoniensia* 2 (Bratislava 2002), pp. 9-36.

Források a korai magyar történelem ismeretéhez, ed. András Róna-Tas. Budapest 2001.

Fottová, Eva – Henning, Joachim – Ruttkay, Matej. "Archeologický výskum včasnostredovekého hradiska v Majcichove." In *Bojná. Hospodárske a politické centrum Nitrianskeho kniežatstva*, ed. Karol Pieta, Alexander Ruttkay, Matej Ruttkay, pp. 217-236.

Frinta, Antonín. "Wogastisburg." *Slavia* 32 (1963), no. 4, pp. 528-531.

Frühmittelalterliche Burgenbau in Mittel- und Osteuropa, ed. Joachim Henning, Alexander Tivadar Ruttkay. Bonn 1998.

Frühmittelalterliche Kirchen als archäologische und historische Quelle, ed. Lumír Poláček, Jana Maříková-Kubková. Internationale Tagungen in Mikulčice, Band VIII. Brno 2010.

Frühmittelalterliche Machtzentren in Mitteleuropa. Mährjährige Grabungen und ihre Auswertung. Symposion Mikulčice 5.–9. September 1994, ed. Čeněk Staňa, Lumír Poláček. Brno 1996.

Fusek, Gabriel. "Včasnostredoveké sídlisko v Nitre na Mikovom dvore." Slovenská archeológia 39 (1991), pp. 289–330.

Fusek, Gabriel. "Archeologické doklady k najstaršiemu slovanskému osídleniu Slovenska." Slavica Slovaca 28 (1993), no. 1–2, pp. 30–35.

Fusek, Gabriel. Slovensko vo včasnoslovanskom období. Nitra 1994.

Fusek, Gabriel. "Der Bestattunsritus und die materielle Kultur der Slawen im 6.–8. Jh. in der Südwestslowakei." In Ethnische und kulturelle Verhältnisse an der mittleren Donau vom 6. bis zum 11. Jahrhundert, ed. Darina Bialeková, Jozef Zábojník, pp. 37–49.

Fusek, Gabriel. "Poznámky k výskumu neopevnených veľkomoravských sídlisk v Nitre." In Svätopluk 894–1994, ed. Richard Marsina, Alexander Ruttkay, pp. 47–52.

Fusek, Gabriel. "Pôvodné alebo prisťahované obyvateľstvo? Príspevok k vypovedacím možnostiam archeologických prameňov o počiatkoch slovanského osídlenia Slovenska." In Historická Olomouc 12. Sborník příspěvků ze sympózia Historická Olomouc XII., zaměřeného k problematice zakladatelských mýtů a mýtů "počátků" ve světle kritiky pramenů, Muzeum umění Olomouc – sál Beseda, 6.–7. října 1998, ed. Josef Bláha. Olomouc 2001, pp. 71–89.

Fusek, Gabriel. "Príchod prvých Slovanov do Nitry." In Nitra v slovenských dejinách, ed. Richard Marsina. Martin 2002, pp. 79–87.

Fusek, Gabriel. "Včasnoslovanské obdobie." In Slovensko vo včasnom stredoveku, ed. Alexander Ruttkay, Matej Ruttkay, Peter Šalkovský. Nitra 2002, pp. 23–27.

Fusek, Gabriel. "Osídlenie Nitry v 10. storočí. Kontinuita alebo diskontinuita?" In Bitka pri Bratislave v roku 907 a jej význam pre vývoj stredného Podunajska, ed. Tatiana Štefanovičová, Drahoslav Hulínek, pp. 295–304.

Fusek, Gabriel. "Die Nebemareale in der Struktur der großmährischen Burgstadt von Nitra." In Burg – Vorburg – Suburbium. Zur Problematik der Nebenareale frühmittelalterlicher Zentren, ed. Ivana Boháčová, Lumír Poláček, pp. 271–290.

Fusek, Gabriel. "Hradisko Veľký vrch v Divinke." In Hradiská – svedkovia dávnych čias. Zborník odborných príspevkov o hradiskách a ich obyvateľoch, ed. Peter Jenčík, Víťazoslav Struhár, pp. 147–161, 262–263, 268.

Fusek, Gabriel. "Eine karolingische Prunkschnalle von Nitra-Šindolka, Grab F246." In Zwischen Byzanz und der Steppe. Archäologische und historische Studien. Festschrift für Csanád Bálint zum 70. Geburtstag, ed. Ádám Bollók, Gergely Csiky and Tivadar Vida, pp. 623–629.

Fusek, Gabriel – Zábojník, Jozef. "Príspevok do diskusie o počiatkoch slovanského osídlenia Slovenska." Slovenská archeológia 51 (2003), no. 2, pp. 319–340.

Fügedi, Erik. "Kirchliche Topographie und Siedlungsverhältnisse im Mittelalter in der Slowakei." *Studia Slavica Academiae scientiarum Hungaricae* V (1959), no. 3–4, pp. 363–400.

Fügedi, Erik. *Castle and society in medieval Hungary (1000–1437)*. Budapest 1986.

Fülep, Ferenc. "Neuere Ausgrabungen in der Cella trichora von Pécs." *Acta Archaeologica Academiae Scientiarum Hungaricae* 11 (1959), pp. 399–417.

Fülep, Ferenc. *Sopianae. Die Stadt Pécs zur Römerzeit*. Budapest 1975.

Fülep, Ferenc. *Sopianae*. Budapest 1984.

Gábler, Dénes. "Győr a rómaiak korában." In *Győr. Várostörténeti tanulmányok*. Győr, 1971, pp. 19–48.

Galuška, Luděk. *Uherské Hradiště – Sady. Křesťanské centrum Říše velkomoravské*. Brno 1996.

Galuška, Luděk. "K problematice nejstaršího slovanského osídlení východní Moravy." *Pravěk, Nová řada* 10 (2000), pp. 119–132.

Galuška, Luděk. "O otrocích na Velké Moravě a okovech ze starého Města." In *Dějiny ve věku nejistot*, ed. Jan Klápště, Eva Plešková, Josef Žemlička, pp. 75–86.

Galuška, Luděk. "Bylo povědomí o Svatoplukově Moravě, Veligradu a Metodějově arcibiskupství na Moravě 10.–12. století skutečně věcí neznámou?" In *Od knížat ke králům. Sborník u příležitosti 60. narozenin Josefa Žemličky*, ed. Eva Doležalová, Robert Šimůnek. Praha 2007, pp. 50–62.

Galuška, Luděk. "Die großmährische Siedlungsagglomeration Staré Město – Uherské Hradiště und das Problem ihrer Gliederung anhand der Befestigungen." In *Burg – Vorburg – Suburbium. Zur Problematik der Nebenareale frühmittelalterlicher Zentren*, ed. Ivana Boháčová, Lumír Poláček, pp. 169–178.

Galuška, Luděk. "Kirchliche Architektur des großmährischen Veligrad und die Besiedlung des Machtzentrums. Funktion und Lage einzelner Bauten im Rahmen der Siedlungsstruktur der frühmittelalterlichen Agglomeration Staré Město – Uherské Hradiště." In *Frühmittelalterliche Kirchen als archäologische und historische Quelle*, ed. Lumír Poláček, Jana Maříková-Kubková, pp. 161–186.

Galuška, Luděk. "Veligrad Veľkej Moravy. Sídelná aglomerácia Staré Město – Uherské Hradiště." *Historická revue* 25 (2014), no. 12, pp. 39–44.

Gams, Pius Bonifacius. *Series episcoporum ecclesiae catholicae quorquot innotuerunt a beato Petro apostolo*. Leipzig 1931.

Garam, Éva Sz. "A böcsi későavarkori lelet és köre." *Archaeologiai Értesítő* 108 (1981), no. 1, pp. 34–51.

Gáspár, Dorottya. "Donatio Iustiniani." In *Christentum in Pannonien im ersten Jahrtausend. Internationale Tagung im Balaton Museum in Keszthely vom 6. bis 9. November 2000*, ed. Robert Müller. Zalai Múzeum 11 (2002), pp. 79–83.

Gassner, Verena – Groh, Stefan – Jilek, Sonja – Kaltenberger, Alice – Pietsch, Wolfgang – Sauer, Roman – Stiglitz, Herma – Zabehlicky, Heinrich. *Das Kastell Mautern – Favianis. Der römische Limes in Österreich*, Heft 39. Wien 2000.

Gedai, István. *A magyar pénzverés kezdete*. Budapest 1986.

Gedai, István. "Az első magyar pénzek időrendi kérdéséhez." *Századok* 122 (1988), no. 4, pp. 694–696.

Gedai, István. "Preslavva Civ(itas)." In *Numismatiska meddelanden 37. Festskrift till Lars O. Lagerqvist*. Stockholm 1989. pp. 95–102.

Genser, Kurt. *Der österreichische Donaulimes in der Römerzeit. Der römische Limes in Österreich*, Heft 33. Wien 1986.

Gerics, József. "Adalékok a Kézai Krónika problémainak megoldásához." *Annales Universitatis Scientiarum Budapestinensis*, Sectio Historica 1 (1957), pp. 106–134.

Gerics, József. *Legkorábbi Gesta-szerkésztéseink keletkezésrendjének problémái*. Budapest 1961.

Gerics, József. "A Tátony nemzetségről. Adalékok egy krónika értelmezéséhez." *Történelmi Szemle* 9 (1966), no. 1, pp. 1–23.

Gerics, József. "Quaedam puella de genere Tatun. Philologisches und Rechtsgeschichtliches zur Untersuchung einer Chronikenstelle." *Annales Universitatis Scientiarum Budapestinensis de Rolando Eötvös nominatae, sectio Historica* 9 (1967), pp. 3–30.

Gerics, József. *A korai rendiség Európaban és Magyarországon*. Budapest 1987.

Gerics, József. *Egyház, állam és gondolkodás Magyarországon a középkorban*. Budapest 1995.

Germanen, Hunen und Awaren. Schätze der Völkerwanderungszeit. Die Archäologie des 5. und 6. Jahrhunderts an der mittleren Donau und der östlich-merowingische Reihengräberkreis, ed. Wilfried Menghin, Tobias Springer, Egon Wamers. Nürnberg 1987.

Gervers-Molnár, Vera. *A középkori Magyarország rotundái*. Budapest 1972.

Geuenich, Dieter – Keller, Hagen. "Alamannen, Alamanien, alamanisch im frühen Mittelalter. Möglichkeiten und Schwierigkeiten des Historikers beim Versuch der Eingrenzung." In *Die Bayern und ihre Nachbarn. Berichte des Symposions der Kommission für Frühmittelalterforschung 25. bis 28. Oktober 1982, Stift Zwettl, Niederösterreich, 1. Teil*, ed. Herwig Wolfram, Andreas Schwarcz, Dph 179 (1985), pp. 135–157.

Gieysztor, Alexander. "Urzad wojewodziński we wczesnych państwach słowiańskich w IX–XI w." *Archeologia Polski* 16 (1971), no. 1–2, pp. 317–325.

Gjuzelev, Vasil Todorov. *Knjaz Boris Părvi*. Sofija 1969.

Glaser, Franz. "Die Bildmotive der Scheibenfibeln aus Keszthely." In *Christentum in Pannonien im ersten Jahrtausend. Internationale Tagung im Balaton Museum in Keszthely vom 6. bis 9. November 2000*, ed. Robert Müller. *Zalai Múzeum* 11 (2002), pp. 145–152.

Glaser, Franz. "Teurnia – civitas Tiburnia." In *"Castellum, civitas, urbs"*, ed. Orsolya Heinrich-Tamáska, Hajnalka Herold, Péter Straub, Tivadar Vida, pp. 11–26.

Godlowski, Kazimierz. *Pierwotne siedziby Słowian. Wybór pism pod redakcja Michala Parczewskiego*. Kraków 2000.

Goetz, Hans-Werner. "Regnum. Zum politischen Denken der Karolingerzeit." In *Zeitschrift für Rechtsgeschichte*. Germanische Abteilung 104 (1987), pp. 110–147.

Golden, Peter Benjamin. *Khazar Studies. An Historico-Philological Inquiry into the Origins of the Khazars I*. Budapest 1980.

Golema, Martin. *Stredoveká literatúra a indoeurópske mytologické dedičstvo. Prítomnosť trojfunkčnej indoeurópskej ideológie v literatúre, mytológii a folklóre stredovekých Slovanov*. Banská Bystrica 2006.

Gombocz, Zoltán. "Árpádkori török személyneveink VII." *Magyar Nyelv* 11 (1915), no. 10, pp. 433–439.

Gombos, F. Albin. "Szent István háborúja II. Konrád római-német császárrál 1030-ban." In *Szent István Emlékkönyv, ed. Jusztinián Serédi*. Budapest, 1938, reprint 1988, pp. 299–324.

Gömöri, János. *Castrum Supron. Sopron váraés környéke az Árpad-korban*. Sopron 2002.

Görich, Knut. "Eine Wende im Osten: Heinrich II. und Boleslaw Chrobry." In *Otto III. – Heinrich II. Eine Wende?* ed. B. Schneidmüller, Stefan Weinfurter. Sigmaringen 1997, pp. 95–167.

Graf, Andreas. *Übersicht der antiken Geographie Pannoniens. Dissertationes Pannonicae Musei nationalis hungarici* I 5. Budapest 1936.

Grafenauer, Bogo. "Nekaj vprašaj iz dobe naseljevanja južnih Slovanov." *Zgodovinski časopis* 4 (1950), pp. 23–126.

Grafenauer, Bogo. "Vprašenje konce Koclejeve vlade v spodnji Pannoniji." *Zgodovinski časopis* 6–7 (1952–1953), pp. 171–188.

Grafenauer, Bogo. "Prilog kritici izvještaja Konstantina Porfirogenita o doseljenju Hrvata." *Historijski zbornik* 5 (1952), pp. 1–56.

Grafenauer, Bogo. *Ustoličevanje koroških vojvod in država karantanskih Slovencev*. Slovenska akademija znanosti in umetnosti, Razred za zgodovinske in družbene vede, Dela 7. Ljubljana 1952.

Grafenauer, Bogo. "Hrvati u Karantaniji." *Historijski zbornik* 11–12 (1958–1959), pp. 207–231.

Grafenauer, Bogo. "Deset let proučevania koroških vojvod, kosezov in država karantanskih Slovencev." *Zgodovinski časopis* 16 (1962), pp. 176–210.

Grafenauer, Bogo. "Razvoj in struktura države karantanskih Slovanov od VII. do IX. stoletja." *Jugoslovenski istorijski časopis* 3 (1963), pp. 19–30.

Grafenauer, Bogo. *Zgodovina slovenskega naroda I, II*. Ljubljana 1964, 1965.

Grafenauer, Bogo. "Grossmähren, Unterpannonien und Karantanien." In *Das Grossmährische Reich. Tagung der wissenschaftlichen Konferenz des Archäologischen Instituts der Tschechoslowakischen Akademie der Wissenschaft Brno – Nitra 1.–4. X. 1963*. Praha 1966, pp. 377–389.

Grafenauer, Bogo. "Ustoličevanie koroških vojvod in vojvodski prestol." *Zgodovinski časopis* 24 (1970), pp. 112–122.
Grafenauer, Bogo. *Die Kärnter Herzogseinsetzung*. Aus dem Slowenischen übersetzt von Doris Debenjak. Ljubljana 2016.
Grant, Michael. *Židé v římském světě*. Praha 2003.
Graus, František. "Rex – dux Moraviae." In *Sborník prací filosofické fakulty Brněnské university, Řada historická* IX, C 7 (1960), pp. 181–190.
Graus, František. "Říše velkomoravská, její postavení v současné Evropě a vnitřní struktura." In *Konferencia o Veľkej Morave a Byzantskej misii, Brno – Nitra 1.–4. X. 1963 (referáty)*. Nitra 1963, pp. 5–74.
Graus, František. "Raně středověké družiny a jejich význam při vzniku státu ve střední Evropě." *Československý časopis historický* 1 (1965), no. 1, pp. 1–18.
Graus, František. "Böhmen zwischen Bayern und Sachsen." *Historica* 17 (1969), pp. 5–42.
Graus, František. *Die Nationenbildung der Westslawen im Mittelalter*. Sigmaringen 1980.
Grekov, Boris Dmitrijevič. *Kyjevská Rus*. Praha 1953.
Grenze und Differenz im früher Mittelalter, ed. Walter Pohl, Helmut Reimitz. Wien 2000.
Grzesik, Ryszard. *Kronika Węgiersko-polska. Przyczynek do dziejów polsko-węgierskich w średniowieczu*. Poznań 1994 (rukopis).
Grzesik, Ryszard. "Przebieg granicy polsko-węgierskiej we wczesnym średniowieczu w swietle Kroniki węgiersko-polskiej." *Studia Historyczne* 41 (1998), no. 2, pp. 147–166.
Grzesik, Ryszard. *Kronika węgiersko-polska. Z dziejów polsko-węgierskich kontaktów kulturalnych w średniowieczu*. Poznań 1999.
Grzesik, Ryszard. "Polski swiety na Slowacji – Andrzej Swierad." *"Nasza Przeszłość"* 92 (1999), pp. 461–479.
Gutheil, Jenő. *Az Árpád-kori Veszprém*. Veszprém 1977.
Gyoni, Mátyás. "A Kievi ősévkönyv volochjai." *Századok* 123 (1989), no. 3–4. pp. 298–342.
Györffy, György. *Krónikáink és a magyar őstörténet*. Budapest 1948.
Györffy, György. "Török női méltóságnév a magyar kútfőkben." *Magyar Nyelv* 49 (1953), no. 1–2, pp. 109–111.
Györffy, György. "Kurszán és Kurszán vára. A magyar fejedelemség kialakulása és Óbuda honfoglaláskori szerepe." *Budapest Régiségei* 15 (1955), pp. 9–34.
Györffy, György. "A magyar nemzetségtől a vármegyéig, a törzstől az országig." *Századok* 92 (1958), no. 1–4, pp. 12–87, 549–552, 565–615, 950–952.
Györffy, György. *Tanulmányok a magyar állam eredetéről*. Budapest 1959.
Györffy, György. "Magyarország népessége a honfoglalástól a XIV. század közepéig." In *Magyarország történeti demográfiája*, ed. József Kovacsics. Budapest 1963, pp. 45–62.
Györffy, György. "Die Erinnerung an das Grossmährische Fürstentum in der mittelalterlichen Überlieferung Ungarns." *Acta Archaeologica Academiae Scientiarum Hungaricae* 17 (1965), s. 41–45.

Györffy, György. "Formation d'états au IXe siècle suivant les 'Gesta Hungarorum' du notaire anonyme." *Nouvelles études historiques publiées á l'occasion du XIIe Congrés International des Sciences Historiques par la Commission Nationale des Historiens Hongrois I.* Budapest 1965, pp. 27–53.

Györffy, György. "Egy krónikahely magyarázatához." *Történelmi Szemle* 9 (1966), no. 1, pp. 25–35.

Györffy, György. *Az Árpád-kori Magyarország törtéteti földrajza I, II, III, IV.* Budapest 1966, 1987, 1987, 1998.

Györffy, György. "Zu den Anfängen der ungarischen Kirchenorganisation auf Grund neuer Quellenkritischer Ergebnisse." *Archivum historiae pontificiae* 7, 1969, pp. 79–113.

Györffy, György. "A honfoglaló magyarok települési rendjeről." *Archaeologiai Értesitő* 97 (1970), pp. 191–242.

Györffy, György. "Szlavónia kialakulásának oklevélkritikai vizsgálata." *Levéltári Közlemények* 41 (1970), no. 2, pp. 223–240.

Györffy, György. "Der Aufstand von Koppány." *Studia Turcica* 1971, pp. 175–211.

Györffy, György. "Die Nordwestgrenze des byzantinischen Reiches im XI. Jh. und die Ausbildung des 'ducatus Sclavoniae'." In *Mélanges offerts á Szabolcs de Vajay.* Braga – Livraria – Cruz 1971, pp. 295–313.

Györffy, György. "Az Árpád-kori szolgálónépek kérdéséhez." *Történelmi Szemle* 15 (1972), no. 3-4, pp. 261–320.

Györffy, György. "Sur la question de l'établissement des Petchénégues en Europe." *Acta Orientalia Academiae Scientiarum Hungaricae* 25 (1972), pp. 283–292.

Györffy, György. "Systéme des résidences d'hiver et d'été chez les nomades et les chefs hongrois du Xe siècle." In *Archivum Eurasiae Medii Aevi* 1 (1975), pp. 42–136.

Györffy, György. "Die Entstehung der ungarischen Burgorganization." *Acta Achaeologica Scientiarum Hungaricae* 28 (1976), pp. 323–358.

Györffy, György. *István király és műve.* Budapest 1977.

Györffy, György. "Arpad. Persönlichkeit und historische Rolle." *Acta Antiqua Scientiarum Hungaricae* 26 (1978), pp. 115–136.

Györffy, György. "A 942. évi magyar vezérnévsor kérdéséhez." *Magyar Nyelv* 76 (1980), no. 3, pp. 308–317.

Györffy, György. "Új arab forrás a magyarok 942. évi kalandozásáról." *Magyar Nyelv* 77 (1981), no. 4, pp. 511–512.

Györffy, György. *Wirtschaft und Gesellschaft der Ungarn um die Jahrtausendwende.* Budapest 1983.

Györffy, György. "Die Kanzleien der Arpaden-Dukate." In *Münchner Beiträge zur Mediävistik und Renaissance-Forschung* 35 (1984), ed. Gabriel Silagi, pp. 325–335.

Györffy, György. "Honfoglalás és megtelepedés. A kalandozások kora. Államszervezés." In *Magyarország története I/1–2*. Budapest 1987, pp. 575–650, 651–716, 717–834.
Györffy, György. *Anonymus. Rejtély avagy történeti forrás? Válogatott tanulmányok.* Budapest 1988.
Györffy, György. *König Stephan der Heilige*. Budapest 1988.
Györffy, György. "Kontakty Polski i Węgier w dobie tworzenia sie obu państw." *Kwartalnik Historiczny* 95 (1988), no. 4. pp. 5–19.
Györffy, György. *A magyarság keleti elemei*. Budapest 1990.
Györffy, György. "Az Árpád-kori magyar krónikák." *Századok* 127 (1993), no. 3–4. pp. 391–412.
Györffy, György. *Krónikáink és a magyar őstörténet. Régi kérdések – új válaszok.* Budapest 1993.
Györffy, György. "Dual kingship and the seven chieftains of the Hungarians in the era of the conquest and the raids." *Acta Orientalia Academiae Scientiarum Hungariae* 47 (1994), no. 1–2, pp. 87–104.
Györffy, György. *Pest-Buda kialakulása. Budapest története a honfoglalástól az Árpádkor végi székvárossá alakulásig.* Budapest 1997.
Györffy, György. *Święty Stefan I król Węgier i jego dzieło*. Warszawa 2003.
Gyula, László. *Die Anfänge der ungarischen Münzprägung. Annales Universitatis Scientiarum Budapestiniensis de Rolando Eötvös nominatae. Sectio historica IV*. Budapest 1962.
Gyula, László. "Über das landnahmezeitliche Häuptlingsgrab von Zemplín." In *Rapports du IIIe Congrés International d'Archéologie Slave, Bratislava 7–14 septembre 1975, Tome 1*, ed. Bohuslav Chropovský, pp. 477–485.
Gyürky, Katalin H. "Die St.-Georgs-Kapelle in der Burg von Veszprém." *Acta Archaeologica Academiae Scientiarum Hungaricae* 15 (1963), pp. 340–408.
Habovštiak, Alojz. "K otázke datovania hradiska v Bíni." *Slovenská archeológia* 14 (1966), no. 2, pp. 439–486.
Habovštiak, Alojz. "Burgwälle im mittleren Grantal in der Slowakei." In *Rapports du IIIe Congrés International d'Archéologie Slave, Bratislava 7–14 septembre 1975, Tome 1*, ed. Bohuslav Chropovský, pp. 359–365.
Habovštiak, Alojz – Juck, Ľubomír. "Starý Tekov v praveku a stredoveku." *Vlastivedný časopis* 23 (1974), pp. 168–178.
Hajmási, P. Erika. "Szombathely középkori várának kutatástörténete és a külső várfal nyomvonalának meghatározása néhány ponton." *Savaria* 20 (1991), no. 1, s. 39–51.
Hajnóczi, J. Gyula. *Pannónia római romjai*. Budapest 1987.
Halmágyi, Miklós. "Beleknegini-Sarolt és társnői. Nőalakok Merseburgi Thietmar krónikájában." *Acta Universitatis Szegediensis, Acta Historica* 132 (2011), pp. 21–36.
Hanuliak, Milan. "Gräberfelder der slawischen Population im 10. Jahrhundert im Gebiet der Westslowakei." *Slovenská archeológia* 40 (1992), no. 2, pp. 243–308.

Hanuliak, Milan. "Methodik der Bearbeitung der Keramikkollektion aus Mužľa-Čenkov und ihre Ergebnisse." In *Slawische Keramik in Mitteleuropa vom 8. bis zum 11. Jahrhundert – Terminologie und Beschreibung. Internationale Tagungen in Mikulčice 2*, ed. H. Brachmann, Falko Daim, Lumír Poláček, Čeněk Staňa, J. Tejral. Brno 1995, pp. 39–50.

Hanuliak, Milan. "Hroby a ich svedectvo k dejinám Nitry v 9.–12. storočí." In *Nitra v slovenských dejinách*, ed. Richard Marsina. Martin 2002, pp. 113–124.

Hanuliak, Milan. "Opevnené sídlisko v Mužle – Čenkove." In *Hradiská – svedkovia dávnych čias. Zborník odborných príspevkov o hradiskách a ich obyvateľoch*, ed. Peter Jenčík, Víťazoslav Struhár, pp. 163–173, 267, 270–271.

Hanuliak, Milan. "Opevnené sídlisko v Mužle – Čenkove." In *Bojná 2. Nové výsledky výskumov včasnostredovekých hradísk*, ed. Karol Pieta, Zbigniew Robak, pp. 205–217.

Hanuliak, Milan – Kuzma, Ivan – Šalkovský, Peter. *Mužla – Čenkov I. Osídlenie z 9.–12. storočia*. Nitra 1993.

Hardt, Matthias. "Die Donau als Verkehrs- und Kommunikationsweg zwischen der ostfränkischen Residenz Regensburg und den Zentren an der mittleren Donau im 9. Jahrhundert." In *Flüsse und Flusstäler als Wirtschafts- und Kommunikationswege*, ed. Stephan Freund, Mathias Hardt, Petra Wiegel. Bonn 2007, pp. 103–120.

Harvát, Matej. "... iactitant se magnitudine pecuniae. Otázka platobných prostriedkov na mojmírovskej Morave," in *Acta historica Neosoliensia* 22, 2019, no. 1, pp. 4–28.

Hasenöhrl, Victor. "Deutschlands südöstliche Marken im 10., 11. und 12. Jahrhundert." *Archiv für österreichische Geschichte* 82 (1895), pp. 419–562.

Hattenhauer, Hans. *Evropské dějiny práva*. Praha 1998.

Hauck, Albert. *Kirchengeschichte Deutschlands I, II, III*. Leipzig 1922, 1935, 1936.

Hauptmann, Ljudmil. "Politische Umwälzungen unter den Slovenen vom Ende des sechsten Jahrhunderts bis zur Mitte des neuenten." *Mitteilungen des österreichischen Instituts für Geschichtsforschung* 36 (1915), pp. 229–287.

Hauptmann, Ljudmil. "Mejna grofija Spodnjepanonska." *Rozprave Znanstvenega Društva za humanistične vede 1*. Ljubljana 1923, pp. 311–357.

Hauptmann, Ljudmil. "Karantanska Hrvatska." In *Zbornik kralja Tomislava*. Zagreb 1925, pp. 297–317.

Hauptmann, Ljudmil. *Staroslovenska družba in obred na knežjem kamnu*. Ljubljana 1954.

Hausmann, Friedrich. *Reichskanzlei und Hofkapelle unter Heinrich V. und Konrad III*. Stuttgart 1956.

Havlík, Lubomír. "Územní rozsah Velkomoravské říše v době posledních let vlády krále Svatopluka. K problematice vzájemných vztahů středoevropských Slovanů v 9. století." In *Príspevky k medzislovanským vzťahom v československých dejinách. Slovanské štúdie* 3 (1960), pp. 9–79.

Havlík, Lubomír. "K otázce hranice jižní Moravy v době Boleslava Chrabrého. Příspěvek k česko-polským vztahům na počátku 11. století." In *Studia z dziejów polskich i czechoslowackich* 1. Wrocław 1960, pp. 73–91.

Havlík, Lubomír. "K otázce karolínske kolonizace a slovanského osídlení Dolních Rakous v 9. století." *Slovanské historické studie* 3 (1960), pp. 45–82.

Havlík, Lubomír. "Tři kapitoly z nejstarších česko-polských vztahů." *Slovanské historické studie* 4 (1961), pp. 5–86.

Havlík, Lubomír. "Velká Morava a Franská říše. K otázce vzájemných politických vztahů." *Historické štúdie* 8 (1963), pp. 129–180.

Havlík, Lubomír. *Staří Slované v rakouskem Podunají v době od 6. do 12. století. Rozpravy ČSAV*, ročník 73, sešit 9. Praha 1963.

Havlík, Lubomír. "Slované v anglosaské chorografii Alfréda Velikého." *Vznik a počátky Slovanů* 5 (1964), pp. 53–85.

Havlík, Lubomír. *Slované ve Východní marce v 9.–11. století. Slavia Antiqua* 11 (1964).

Havlík, Lubomír. *Velká Morava a středoevropští Slované*. Praha 1964.

Havlík, Lubomír. "O politických osudech a zahraničních vztazích státu a říše Moravanů." In *O počiatkoch slovenských dejín*, ed. Peter Ratkoš, pp. 104–140.

Havlík, Lubomír. "Moravské a české tradice v uherských kronikách." *Slovanský přehled* 55 (1969), pp. 337–343.

Havlík, Lubomír E. "Panonie ve světle franských pramenů s novějším řešením některých otázek." *Slavia Antiqua* 17 (1970), pp. 1–36.

Havlík, Lubomír E. "Moesie a listy pasovského biskupa Pilgrima." *Jižní Morava* 8 (1972), pp. 7–20.

Havlík, Lubomír E. "Dukljanská kronika a Dalmatská legenda." Praha 1976.

Havlík, Lubomír E. *Morava v 9.–10. století. K problematice politického postavení, sociální a vládní struktury a organizace*. Praha 1978.

Havlík, Lubomír. "Moravská společnost a stát v 9. století." *Slavia antiqua* 27 (1980), pp. 1–42.

Havlík, Lubomír E. "The Character of the Early Feudal Society of Slavic States." In *Rapports du IIIe Congrés International d'Archéologie Slave, Bratislava 7–14 septembre 1975, Tome 2*, ed. Bohuslav Chropovský. Bratislava 1980, pp. 133–148.

Havlík, Lubomír E. "Velká Morava v kontextu evropských a obecných dějín." In Poulík, Josef – Chropovský, Bohuslav et al. *Velká Morava a počátky československé státnosti*, s. 187–214.

Havlík, Lubomír E. "Slované a Maďaři ve středním Podunají v IX.–X. století." In *Současný stav a úkoly československé hungaristiky*. Brno 1985, pp. 65–81.

Havlík, Lubomír E. *Slovanské státní útvary raného středověku. Politické postavení a vládní organizace státních útvarů ve východní, střední a jihovýchodní Evropě od 8. do 11. století*. Praha 1987.

Havlík, Lubomír E. "Bulgaria and Moravia between Byzantium, the Franks and Rome." *Paleobulgarica* 13 (1989), no. 1, pp. 5-20.

Havlík, Lubomír E. *Mähren und die Ungarn am Ende des 9. und am Anfang des 10. Jahrhunderts, Baiern, Ungarn und Slawen im Donauraum.* Linz 1991, pp. 105-120.

Havlík, Lubomír E. *Kronika o Velké Moravě.* Brno 1993.

Havlík, Lubomír E. *Svatopluk Veliký, král Moravanů a Slovanů.* Brno 1994.

Hägermann, Dieter. *Karel Veliký. Vládce Západu.* Praha 2002.

Heckenast, Gusztáv - Nováki, Gyula - Vastagh, Gábor - Zoltay, Endre. *A Magyarországi vaskohászat története a korai középkorban. A honfoglalástól a XIII. század közepéig.* Budapest 1968.

Heinrich-Tamaska, Orsolya. "Die spätrömische Innenbefestigung von Keszthely-Fenékpuszta. Innere Chronologie und funktioneller Wandel." In *Keszthely-Fenékpuszta im Kontext spätantiker Kontinuitätsforschung zwischen Noricum und Moesia. Castellum Pannonicum Pelsonense Vol. 2*, ed. Orsolya Heinrich-Tamáska, pp. 653-702.

Hennig, Joachim - Ruttkay, Matej - Pieta, Karol - Heussner, Karl-Uwe. "Bojná a datovanie hradísk Nitrianskeho kniežatstva. Prínos prírodovedných metód k archeologickému výskumu." In *Bojná 2. Nové výsledky výskumov včasnostredovekých hradísk*, ed. Karol Pieta, Zbigniew Robak, pp. 335-345.

Herényi, István. *Magyarország nyugati végvidéke 800-1242.* Argumentum Kiadó 1999.

Herrmann, Joachim. "Zur Gründungsgeschichte des Erzbistum Hamburg." *Mitteilungen des Instituts für österreichische Geschichtsforschung* 33 (1912), pp. 201-271.

Herucová, Angelika. "Arpádovskí palatíni vo vybraných naratívnych prameňoch." *Historické štúdie* 49 (2015), pp. 227-239.

Historija narodaJugoslavije I. Zagreb 1953.

Hladík, Marek. "Zur Frage der heidnischen Kultstätte in 'Těšický les' im Suburbium des Burgwals von Mikulčice." In *Frühmittelalterliche Kirchen als archäologische und historische Quelle*, ed. Lumír Poláček, Jana Maříková-Kubková, pp. 101-122.

Hlawitschka, Eduard. "Die Verbreitung des Namens Zwentibold in frühdeutscher Zeit." In *Personengeschichtliche Beobachtungen und Erwägungen. Festschrift für Herbert Kolb zu seinem 65. Geburtstag.* Bern - Frankfurt am Main - New York - Paris 1989, pp. 264-292.

Hlinka, Jozef. "Die bisherigen Erkenntnisse über die Münze BRESLAVVA CIVITAS." In *Rapports du IIIe Congrés International d'Archéologie Slave, Bratislava 7-14 septembre 1975, Tome 1*, ed. Bohuslav Chropovský, pp. 375-384.

Hlinka, Jozef. "Nálezy mincí na Slovensku z 11. až začiatku 14. storočia a ich historicko-numizmatická analýza." *Slovenská numizmatika* 10 (1989), pp. 153-164.

Hlinka, Jozef - Kazimír, Štefan - Kolníková, Eva. *Peniaze v našich dejinách.* Bratislava 1976.

Hodál, Juraj. "Pôvod, sídla a hodnosť predkov rodu Hunt-Pázmány." *Historický sborník, časopis historického odboru MS* 4 (Turčiansky sv. Martin 1946), no. 2, s. 136–164.

Hoffiller, Viktor. "Starohrvatsko groblje u Velikoj Gorici." *Vjesnik Hrvatskoga arheološkoga društva nove serije* sveska 10 (1908–1909), pp. 120–134.

Hoffmann, Hartmut. "Böhmen und das deutsche Reich im hohen Mittelalter." *Jahrbuch für Geschichte Mittel- und Ostdeutschlands* 18 (1969), pp. 1–62.

Holub, József. *Zala megye története a középkorban I. A megyei és egyházi közigazgatás története.* Pécs 1929.

Holuby, Jozef Ludovít. "Svätojurský šúr na Slovensku." *Věda přírodní* 7 (1926), pp. 112–116.

Hóman, Bálint. "A zágrabi püspökség alapitási éve." *Turul* 28 (1910), pp. 100–113.

Hóman, Bálint. *A Szent László-kori Gesta Ungarorum és XII.–XIII. századi leszármazói.* Budapest 1925.

Hóman, Bálint. "Szkitia leírása a Gesta Ungarorumban." *Magyar Könyvszemle* 1930, pp. 243–263.

Hóman, Bálint. *Geschichte des ungarischen Mittelalters I.* Berlin 1940.

Hóman, Bálint. *A magyar hún-hagyomány és hún-monda.* Máriabesnyő – Gödöllő 2010.

Homza, Martin. "Hranice Nitrianskeho vojvodstva (kniežatstva) v poľských kronikách." In *Nitra v slovenských dejinách*, ed. Richard Marsina, pp. 65–78.

Homza, Martin. *Mulieres suadentes. Presviedčajúce ženy. Štúdie z dejín ženskej panovníckej svätosti v strednej a vo východnej Európe v 10.–13. storočí.* Bratislava 2002.

Homza, Martin. *Uhorsko-poľská kronika. Nedocenený prameň k dejinám strednej Európy.* Bratislava 2009.

Homza, Martin. *O kráľovskom titule Svätopluka I. († 894). Historický časopis* 61 (2013), no. 4, pp. 655–669.

Homza, Martin. "K argumentácii o kráľovskom titule Svätopluka I. († 894)." In Homza, Martin et al. *Svätopluk v európskom písomníctve*, pp. 142–161.

Homza, Martin. "Stredoveké korene svätoplukovskej tradície u Slovákov (čierna a biela svätoplukovská legenda)." In Homza, Martin et al. *Svätopluk v európskom písomníctve*, pp. 48–141.

Homza, Martin et al. *Svätopluk v európskom písomníctve. Štúdie z dejín svätoplukovskej legendy.* Bratislava 2013.

Horvat, Anđela. "O Sisku u starohrvatsko doba na temelju pisanih izvora i arheoloških nalaza." *Starohrvatska prosvjeta* 3 (1954), no. 2, pp. 93–104.

Horváth, János. *Árpád-kori latin nyelvű irodalmunk stílusproblémái.* Budapest 1954.

Horváth, János. "A hun történet és szerzője," *Irodalomtörténeti Közlemények* 67 (1963), pp. 446–476.

Horváth, Tibor. "Az üllői és kiskörösi avar temető." *Archaeologia Hungarica* 19 (1935), pp. 9–128.

Horváth, Vladimír. *Bratislavský topografický lexikon.* Bratislava 1990.

Hosák, Ladislav. "Moravské a slezské místní jméno jako historický pramen." *Acta Universitatis Palackianae Olomoucensis. Historica* 3 (1962), pp. 141–182.

Hošek, Radoslav. "Zum römischen castellum Mušov." In *Gentes, Reges und Rom. Auseinandersetzung – Anerkennung – Anpassung. Festschrift für Jaroslaw Tejral zum 65. Geburtstag*, ed. Jan Bouzek, Herwig Friesinger, Karol Pieta, Balázs Komoróczy. Spisy Archeologického ústavu AV ČR Brno 16 (2000), pp. 77–78.

Hošek, Radoslav. "Die Römer in Nordmähren." In *Zwischen Rom und dem Barbaricum. Festschrift für Titus Kolník zum 70. Geburtstag*, ed. Klára Kuzmová, Karol Pieta, Ján Rajtár. Nitra 2002, pp. 127–128.

Hradiská – svedkovia dávnych čias. Zborník odborných príspevkov o hradiskách a ich obyvateľoch, zostavovatelia Peter Jenčík, Víťazoslav Struhár. Dolná Mariková 2015.

Hradiská – svedkovia dávnych čias II. Zborník odborných prispevkov o hradiskách a ich obyvateľoch, zostavovatelia Peter Jenčík, Zuzana Staneková. Dolná Mariková 2019.

Hrubant, László. *Az Erdélyi egyházmegye a XIV-ik század elején. Mérték 1 : 600000*. Photolitographie und Schnellpressendruck des k. k. militärgeographischen Instituts in Wien, 1888.

Hrubý, Vilém. *Staré Město. Velkomoravský Velehrad*. Praha 1965.

Hrušovský, František. "Boleslav Chrabrý a Slovensko." In *Sborník na počesť Jozefa Škultétyho*. Turčiansky sv. Martin 1933, pp. 454–482.

Huber, Michael. "Tiburnia – Liburnia – Lurn: Philologische Beobachtungen zu einem alten Namensproblem." In *"Castellum, civitas, urbs"*, ed. Orsolya Heinrich-Tamáska, Hajnalka Herold, Péter Straub, Tivadar Vida, pp. 27–34.

Hudáček, Pavol. *Castrum Salis. Severné pohraničie Uhorska okolo roku 1000*. Bratislava 2016.

Hudáček, Pavol. "*Civitas, urbs, grad, castellum* a *castrum* v stredovekých prameňoch. K otázke označovania hradov a pevností v Uhorsku do konca 12. storočia." In Dvořáková, Daniela a kol. *Stredoveké hrady na Slovensku. Život, kultúra, spoločnosť*. Bratislava, 2017, pp. 63–98, 429–430.

Hulínek, Drahoslav. "Prví rímski legionári na Slovensku. Rimania na Devínskom hrade." *Historická revue* 26 (2015), no. 6, pp. 23–28.

Hulínek, Drahoslav – Čajka, Michal. "Včasnostredoveké hradiská na Orave v kontexte hradísk na strednom a západnom Slovensku." *Slovenská archeológia* 52 (2004), no. 1, pp. 70–120.

Hummer, Hans J. "The fluidity of barbarian Identity: the Ethnogenesis of Alemanni and Suebi, AD 200–500." *Early Medieval Europe* 7 (1998), no. 1, pp. 1–27.

Hunka, Ján. "New Notions about the 11th–14th Centuries related to the Territory of Slovakia." *Actes du XIe Congres International de Numismatique organisé a l' occasion di 150e anniversaire de la Société Royale de Numismatique de Belgique Bruxelles, 8–13 septembre 1991*. Volume III, Louvain-la-Neuve 1993, pp. 196–198.

Hunka, Ján. "Mincovníctvo uhorských vojvodov v druhej polovici 11. storočia." *Slovenská numizmatika* 14 (1996), pp. 63–84.

Hunka, Ján. "Počiatky stredovekého mincovníctva na Slovensku." In *Slovensko vo včasnom stredoveku*, ed. Alexander Ruttkay, Matej Ruttkay, Peter Šalkovský. Nitra 2002, pp. 189–194.

Hunka, Ján. "Vojvodská mincovňa z 11. storočia v Nitre." In *Nitra v slovenských dejinách*, ed. Richard Marsina. Martin 2002, pp. 169–180.

Hurbanič, Martin. "Obliehanie Konštantínopolu roku 626 v byzantskej historiografii I. História a legenda avarského útoku na Konštantinopol roku 626 v Chronografii Theofana Homologéta." *Byzantinoslovaca* I (2006), pp. 52–85.

Hurbanič, Martin. "Avarské vojsko počas obliehania Konštantínopola." *Vojenská história* 11 (2007), no. 3, pp. 16–38.

Hurbanič, Martin. "Byzancia a Avarský kaganát v rokoch 623–624." *Historický časopis* 55 (2007), no. 2, pp. 229–248.

Hurbanič, Martin. "Historické súvislosti a príčiny avarského útoku na Konštantinopol roku 626." *Vojenská história* 12 (2008), no. 3, pp. 3–23.

Hurbanič, Martin. *Posledná vojna antiky. Avarský útok na Konštantínopol roku 626 v historických súvislostiach*. Prešov 2009.

Hurbanič, Martin. *História a mýtus. Avarský útok na Konštantínopol roku 626 v legendách*. Prešov, 2010.

Hurbanič, Martin. "Vpády Avarov na balkánske územia Východorímskej ríše v rokoch 582–626." *Historický časopis* 63 (2015), no. 3, pp. 387–404.

Hurbanič, Martin. *Konstantinopol 626. Poslední bitva antiky*. Praha 2016.

Huszár, Lajos. *Münzkatalog Ungarn von 1000 bis heute*. Budapest 1979.

Hýbl, František. *Dějiny národa bulharského I*. Praha 1930.

Illáš, Martin. "Predrománsky kostol na Devíne." *Historický zborník* 21 (2011), no. 1, pp. 19–39.

Interaktionen der mitteleuropäischen Slawen und anderen Ethnika im 6.–10. Jahrhundert. Symposium Nové Vozokany 3.–7. Oktober 1983, ed. Peter Šalkovský. Nitra 1984.

Irmscher, Johannes. "Die Slawen und das Justinianische Reich." In *Rapports du IIIe Congrès International d'Archéologie Slave, Bratislava 7–14 septembre 1975, Tome 2*, ed. Bohuslav Chropovský, pp. 157–169.

Ivaniček, Franjo. *Staroslavenska nekropola u Ptuju*. Slovenska akademija znanosti in umetnosti, Razred za zgodovinske in družbene vede, Dela 5 (1951).

Ivanov, Sergej Arkaďjevič. *Byzantské misie aneb je možné udělat z "barbara" křesťana?* Červený kostelec 2012.

Jakliński, Michal. *Hunovie. Historia i tradycja*. Sandomierz 2011.

von Jaksch, August. "Fredegar und die Conversio Carantanorum (Ingo)." *Mitteilungen des österreichischen Instituts für Geschichtsforschung* 41 (1926), pp. 44–45.

von Jaksch, August. *Geschichte Kärntens bis 1335 I, II*. Klagenfurt 1928, 1929.

Jakubčinová, Miriam. "Ostrohy s háčikmi z Bojnej." In *Bojná 2. Nové výsledky výskumov včasnostredovekých hradísk*, ed. Karol Pieta, Zbigniew Robak, pp. 91–107.

Jakubčinová, Miriam – Vangľová, Terézia. "Príspevok k vnútornej zástavbe hradiska Bojná I – Valy." In *Bojná 2. Nové výsledky výskumov včasnostredovekých hradísk*, ed. Karol Pieta, Zbigniew Robak, pp. 63–89.

Jan, Libor. "Počátky moravského křesťanství a církevní správa do doby husitské." In *XXVII. Mikulovské sympozium 2002*. Brno 2003, pp. 7–20.

Jan, Libor. "O smysl příběhu bratří Konstantina a Metoděje." In *Christianizace českých zemí ve středoevropské perspektivě*, ed. Libor Jan, pp. 100–115.

Jan, Libor. "Stará Morava mezi Východem a Západem." In *Svatý Prokop, Čechy a střední Evropa*, ed. Petr Sommer, pp. 251–264.

Jan, Libor. "Strukturelle Veränderungen – zwischen Altmähren und dem frühpřemyslidischen Staat." In *Die frühmittelalterliche Elite bei den Völkern des östlichen Mitteleuropas*, ed. Pavel Kouřil, pp. 19–24.

Janošík, Jiří – Pieta, Karol. "Nález zvona na hradisku z 9. storočia v Bojnej." In *Bojná. Hospodárske a politické centrum Nitrianskeho kniežatstva*, ed. Karol Pieta, Alexander Ruttkay, Matej Ruttkay, pp. 121–158.

Janšák, Štefan. "Česká cesta – najstarší spoj Slovenska s českými krajmi." *Vlastivedný časopis* 10 (1961), pp. 83–87.

Janšák, Štefan. "Z minulosti dopravných spojov na Slovensku." *Geografický časopis* 16 (1964), no. 1, pp. 13–29.

Jasiński, Kazimierz. *Rodowód pierwszych Piastów*. Warszawa – Wrocław 1992.

Jasiński, Kazimierz. "Filiacja Adelajdy, zony księcia czeskiego Wratyslawa II," *Rocznik polskiego towarzystwa heraldycunego nowej serii* tom 1/12 (1993), pp. 3–11.

Jasiński, Kazimierz. "Česko-polské dynastické vztahy v raném středověku." *Dějiny a současnost* 2 (1999), pp. 6–10.

Javorský, František. "Výsledky archeologického výskumu v Slovenskom raji." *AVANS v r. 1976*. Nitra 1977, pp. 153–166.

Javorský, František. "Výskumy a prieskumy výskumnej expedície v okrese Spišská Nová Ves." *AVANS v r. 1977*. Nitra 1978, pp. 103–120.

Javorský, František. "Záchranný výskum na hradisku I v Smižanoch." *AVANS v r. 1978*. Nitra 1980, pp. 131–135.

Jelínková, Dagmar. "Morava v časně slovanském období." In *Staroslovanská Morava*, ed. Bohuslav Klíma. Brno 2000, pp. 42–54.

Johannes de Thurocz Chronica Hungarorum II, Commentarii 1, Ab initiis usque ad annum 1301, composuit Elemér Mályusz, adiuvante Julio Kristó. Budapest 1988.

Juck, Ľubomír. "Majetky hronskobeňadického opátstva do roku 1235." *Historické štúdie* 18 (1973), pp. 121–156.

Justová, Jarmila. *Dolnorakouské Podunají v raném středověku. Slovanská archeologie k jeho osídlení v 6.–11. století.* Praha 1990.

Kaindl, Raimund Friedrich. *Beiträge zur älteren ungarischen Geschichte.* Wien 1893.

Kaindl, Raimund Friedrich. "Studien zu den ungarischen Geschichtsquellen III. Ueber die ungarisch-polnische Chronik." *Archiv für österreichische Geschichte* 82 (1895), pp. 589–625.

Kaindl, Raimund Friedrich. "Studien zu den ungarischen Geschichtsquellen VI. Spuren von Graner Geschichtsaufzeichnungen." *Archiv für österreichische Geschichte* 84 (1898), pp. 523–543.

Kalhous, David. "Christian und Großmähren." In *Die frühmittelalterliche Elite bei den Völkern des östlichen Mitteleuropas*, ed Pavel Kouřil, pp. 25–34.

Kalhous, David. "Hroby, kostely, kultura a texty." In *Pád Velké Moravy aneb Kto byl pohřben v hrobu 153 na Pohansku u Břeclavi*, ed. Jiří Macháček, Martin Wihoda, pp. 166–189.

Kalhous, David. "Státnost v Kristiánově legendě? K roli tradice při formování přemyslovského státu." In *Stát, státnost a rituály přemyslovského věku. Problémy, názory, otázky*, ed. Martin Wihoda, Demeter Malaťák, pp. 135–153.

Kállay, Ubul. "Kopán krónikája." *Turul* 33 (1915), pp. 21–25.

Kandler, Manfred – Vetters, Hermann. *Der römische Limes in Österreich, Ein Führer.* Wien 1989.

Karácsonyi, János. *A magyar nemzetségek a XIV. század közepéig.* Budapest, 1900, 1901, (reprint 1995).

Kardaras, Georgios Th. *To Byzantio kai oi Abaroi.* Athhna 2010.

Karolínska kultúra a Slovensko. Štúdie. Zborník Slovenského národného múzea. Archeológia supplementum 4, ed. Vladimír Turčan. Bratislava 2011.

Karpf, Kurt. "Kirchen in Karantanien vor und nach Einführung der Grafschaftsverfassung (828)." In *Frühmittelalterliche Kirchen als archäologische und historische Quelle*, ed. Lumír Poláček, Jana Maříková-Kubková, pp. 233–242.

Kasparek, M. U. "Fränkische Gräber aus Neutra, Slowakei." *Karpaten-Jahrbuch* 7. München 1956.

Katičić, Radoslav. "Die Ethnogenesen in der Avaria." In *Typen der Ethnogenese unter besonderer Berücksichtigung der Bayer, Teil I.* ed. Herwig Wolfram, Walter Pohl, pp. 125–128.

Katičić, Radoslav. "Die Anfänge des kroatischen Staates." In *Die Bayern und ihre Nachbarn. Berichte des Symposions der Kommission für Frühmittelalterforschung 25. bis 28. Oktober 1982, Stift Zwettl, Niederösterreich, 1. Teil*, ed. Herwig Wolfram, Andreas Schwarcz. Dph 179, 1985, pp. 299–312.

Kavánová, Blanka. *Slovanské ostruhy na území Československa. Studie Archeologického ústavu ČSAV* 4 (1976), no. 3.

Kavánová, Blanka. "Slovanské pohřebiště v Mutěnicích, okr. Hodonín." *Archeologické rozhledy* 34 (1982), no. 5, pp. 504–522.

Kejř, Jiří. "Wogastisburg – burgum?" *Československý časopis historický* 21 (1973), no. 3, pp. 399–410.

Kelemina, Jakob. "Nekaj o Dulebih na Slovenskem." *Časopis za zgodovino in narodopisje* 20 (1925), pp. 144–154.

Kelemina, Jakob. "Nove dulebske študije," *Časopis za zgodovino in narodopisje* 21 (1926), pp. 57–75.

Keller, Erwin – Bierbrauer, Volker. "Beiträge zum awarenzeitlichen Gräberfeld von Devínska Nová Ves." *Slovenská archeológia* 13 (1965), no. 2, pp. 377–397.

Kenneth, Jonsson. "The earliest Hungarian Coignage." In *Commentationes Numismaticae 1988. Festgabe für Gert und Vera Hatz*. Hamburg 1988, pp. 95–102.

Keszthely-Fenékpuszta im Kontext spätantiker Kontinuitätsforschung zwischen Noricum und Moesia. Castellum Pannonicum Pelsonense. Band II, ed. Orsolya Heinrich-Tamáska. Budapest – Leipzig – Kesthely – Rahden/Westf. 2011.

Kiss, Attila. "A tüskevári római telep 1961–1063 évi feltárása." *Veszprém megyei múzeumok közleményei* 6 (1967), p. 37.

Kiss, Attila. "Keszthely kultúra a Pannónia Római kontinuitás kérdésében." *Archaeologiai Értesítő* 95 (1968), pp. 93–101.

Kiss, Attila. "Skiren im Karpatenbecken, ihre Wohnsitze und ihre materielle Hinterlassenschaft." *Acta Archaeologica Academiae Scientiarium Hungaricae* 35 (1983), pp. 95–131.

Kiss, Attila. "Zur Frage der Kontinuität bzw. Diskontinuität des awarischen Khaganats (567–796). Wieviel Khaganate der Awaren hat es gegeben?" In *Ethnische und kulturelle Verhältnisse an der mittleren Donau vom 6. bis 10. Jahrhundert*, ed. Darina Bialeková, Jozef Zábojník, pp. 83–98.

Kiss, Gábor. "Die Entstehung und Anwendung des Keszthely-Kultur-Begriffs aus forschungsgeschichtlicher Sicht." In *Keszthely-Fenékpuszta im Kontext spätantiker Kontinuitätsforschung zwischen Noricum und Moesia. Castellum Pannonicum Pelsonense Vol. 2*, ed. Orsolya Heinrich-Tamáska, pp. 491–508.

Klaić, Nada. *Povijest Hrvata u ranom srednjem vijeku*. Zagreb 1971.

Klaić, Vjekoslav. *Slavonija od X. do XIII. stoljeca. Razpravica što ju je povodom spisa "Die Entstehung Croatiens" od F. Pesty-a*. Zagreb 1882.

Klaić, Vjekoslav. *Povijest Hrvata od najstarijih vremena do svršetka XIX stolječa I*. Zagreb 1972.

Klanica, Zdeněk. *Předvelkomoravské pohřebiště v Dolních Dunajovicích*. Praha 1972.

Klanica, Zdeněk. "Die südmährischen Slawen und andere Ethnika im archäologischen Material des 6.–8. Jahrhunderts." In *Interaktionen der mitteleuropäischen Slawen und anderen Ethnika im 6.–10. Jahrhundert. Symposium Nové Vozokany 3.–7. Oktober 1983*, ed. Peter Šalkovský, pp. 139–150.

Klanica, Zdeněk. "Náboženství a kult, jejich odraz v archeologických pramenech." In Poulík, Josef – Chropovský, Bohuslav a kolektív. *Velká Morava a počátky československé státnosti*, pp. 107–140.

Klanica, Zdeněk. *Počátky slovanského osídlení našich zemí*. Praha 1986.

Klanica, Zdeněk. "Zur Periodisierung vorgroßmährischer Funde aus Mikulčice." In *Studien zum Burgwall von Mikulčice. Band 1*, ed. Falko Daim, Lumír Poláček. Brno, 1995, pp. 379–469.

Klanica, Zdeněk. "Vom Awarenfall zum Untergang Großmährens." In *Central Europe in 8th–10th Centuries*, ed. Dušan Čaplovič, Ján Doruľa, pp. 40–45.

Klanica, Zdeněk. "Zur Struktur des frühmittelalterlichen Zentrum in Mikulčice." In *Burg – Vorburg – Suburbium. Zur Problematik der Nebenareale frühmittelalterlicher Zentren*, ed. Ivana Boháčová, Lumír Poláček, pp. 213–227.

Klaniczay, Gábor. "A Szent László – kultusz kialakulása." In *Nagyvárad és Bihar a korai középkorban. Tanulmányok Biharország történetéről*, I, pp. 7–39.

Klebel, Ernst. "Die Ostgrenze des Karolingischen Reiches." *Jahrbuch für Landeskunde von Niederösterreich* 21 (1928), pp. 348–380.

Klebel, Ernst. "Der Einbau Karantaniens in das ostfränkische und deutsche Reich." *Carinthia* I 150, 1960, pp. 663–692.

Klemenc, Josip. *Ptujski grad v kasni antiky*. Ljubljana 1950.

Klíma, Bohuslav. "Archeologický výskum MU na velkomoravském výšinném Hradišti sv. Hypolita ve Znojmě." In *Velká Morava mezi východem a západem. Sborník příspěvků z mezinárodní konference Uherské Hradiště, Staré Město 28. 9.–1. 10. 1999*, ed. Luděk Galuška, Pavel Kouřil, Zdeněk Měřínsky, *Spisy Archeologického ústavu AV ČR Brno* 17 (2001), pp. 229–240.

Klíma, Bohuslav. "Objev části velkomoravského pohřebiště pod středověkým až novověkým hřbitovem u kostela sv. Hypolita ve Znojmě-Hradišti." In *Zborník na počesť Dariny Bialekovej*, ed. Gabriel Fusek, pp. 179–190.

Kniezsa, István. "Ungarns Völkerschaften im XI. Jahrhundert." In *Archivum Europae Centro-Orientalis IV*. Budapest 1938, pp. 241–411.

Kniezsa, István. "Az esztergomi káptalan 1156. évi dézsmajegyzékének helységei." *Századok* 73 (1939), no. 1, pp. 167–187.

Kniezsa, István. *A magyar nyelv szláv jövevényszavai I/1–2*. Budapest 1955.

Kniezsa, István. "Charakteristik der slowakischen Ortsnamen in Ungarn." *Studia Slavica* 9 (1963), pp. 27–44.

Knific, Timotej. "Carniola in the early Middle Ages." *Balcanoslavica* 5 (1976), pp. 111–121.

Kolíska kresťanstva na Slovensku. Nitriansky hrad a Katedrála sv. Emeráma v premenách času, ed. Viliam Judák, Peter Bednár, Jozef Medvecký. Bratislava 2011.

Kollányi, Ferenc. "Visitatio capituli E. M. Strigoniensis anno 1397." *Történelmi Tár* 1901, pp. 71–106, 239–272.

Kollautz, Arnulf. *Denkmäler byzantinischen Christentums aus der Awarenzeit der Donauländer.* Amsterdam 1970.

Kollautz, Arnulf. "Nestors Quelle über die Unterdrückung der Duleben durch die Obri (Awaren)." *Die Welt der Slawen* 27, Neue Folge 6 (1982), pp. 307–320.

Koller, Heinrich. "Der 'mons Comagenus'." *Mitteilungen des Instituts für Österreichische Geschichtsforschung* 71 (1963), pp. 237–245.

Koller, Heinrich. "Fluß und Ort 'Peinihhaa'." *Burgenländische Heimatblat* 26 (1964), pp. 61–70.

Kolník, Titus. "Ausgrabungen auf der römischen Stattion in Milanovce in den Jahren 1956–1957." In *Limes Romanus Konferenz Nitra*, ed. Anton Točík. Bratislava 1959, pp. 27–48.

Kolník, Titus. "Prehľad a stav bádania o dobe rímskej a sťahovaní národov." *Slovenská archeológia* 19 (1971) no. 2, pp. 499–558.

Kolník, Titus. "Cífer-Pác. Stanica z mladšej doby rímskej." In *III. medzinárodný kongres slovanskej archeológie, Bratislava 7.–14. september 1975*. Nitra 1975.

Kolník, Titus. "Doba rímska a doba sťahovania národov." *Slovenská archeológia* 28 (1980), no. 1, pp. 197–212.

Kolník, Titus. "Römische Stationen im slowakischen Abschnitt des nordpannonischen Limesvorlandes." *Archeologické rozhledy* 38 (1986), pp. 314–434, 467–474.

Kolník, Titus. "Bola v Nitre rímska stanica?" In *Nitra. Príspevky k najstarším dejinám mesta.* Nitra 1993, pp. 94–95.

Kolník, Titus. "Cífer-Pác – záhada na pokračovanie. Germánska rezidencia alebo rímska vojenská stanica?" *Pamiatky a múzeá* (2000), no. 3, pp. 41–44.

Kolník, Titus. "Kontakty raného kresťanstva s územiami strednej Európy vo svetle archeologických a historických prameňov." *Studia archaeologica slovaca mediaevalia* 3–4 (2000–2001), pp. 51–92.

Komatina, Predrag. "The Slavs of the Mid-Danube Basin and the Bulgarian Expansion in the first Half of the 9th Century." In *Zbornik radova Vizantološkog instituta* 47 (2010), pp. 55–82.

Komoróczy, Balázs. "Das römische temporäre Lager in Modřice (Bez. Brno-venkov)." In *Zwischen Rom und dem Barbaricum. Festschrift für Titus Kolník zum 70. Geburtstag*, ed. Klára Kuzmová, Karol Pieta, Ján Rajtár. Nitra 2002, pp. 129–135.

Konovalova, I. G. – Perchavko, V. B. *Drevnjaja Rus i nižneje Podunavje.* Moskva 2000.

Kopal, Petr. "Kosmovi ďáblové. Vršovsko-přemyslovský antagonismus ve světle biblických a legendárních citátů, motivů a symbolů." *Mediaevalia historica Bohemica* 8 (2001), pp. 7–41.

Kopal, Petr. "Neznámy známy rod. Pokus o genealogii Vršovců." *Sborník archívních prací* 51 (2001), pp. 3–84.

Koperski, Andrzej. "Cmentarzysko staromadziarskie w Przemyślu." *Prace i Materiały Muzeumu Archeologocznego i Etnograficznego w Łodźi* 29 (1982), pp. 261–267.

Koperski, Andrzej – Parczewski, Michal. "Das althungarische Reitergrab von Przemyśl (Südpolen)." *Acta Archaeologica Academiae Scientiarum Hungaricae* 30 (1978), pp. 213–231.

Koperski, Andrzej – Parczewski, Michal. "Wczesnośredniowieczny grób Węgra-koczownika z Przemyśla." *Acta Archaeologica Carpatica* 18 (1978), pp. 151–199.

Korai magyar történeti lexikon (9–14. század), ed. Gyula Kristó. Budapest 1994.

Korošec, Josip. *Slovansko svetišče na ptujskem gradu*. Slovenska akademija znanosti in umetnosti, Razred za zgodovinske in zemljepisne vede, za filozofijo in filologijo. Dela 6 (1948).

Korošec, Josip. *Staroslovansko grobišče na Ptujskem gradu*. Slovenska akademija znanosti in umetnosti, Razred za zgodovinske in družbene vede. Dela 1 (1950).

Kos, Luděk. "Raně středověké fortifikace s čelní kamennou plentou ve střední Evropě." *Studia mediævalia Pragensia* 11 (2012), pp. 117–175.

Kos, Milko. "K histórii kniežaťa Pribinu a jeho doby." In *Ríša Veľkomoravská. Sborník vedeckých prác*, ed. Ján Stanislav, pp. 53–64.

Kos, Milko. *Zgodovina Slovencev od naselitve do konca petnajstega stoletja*. Ljubljana 1955.

Kossányi, Béla. "A kalizok vallása." In *Emlékkönyv Domanovszky Sándor*. Budapest 1937, pp. 355–368.

Koszta, László. "A keresztény egyházszervezet kialakulása." In *Árpád előtt és után*, ed. Gyula Kristó, Ferenc Makk. Szeged 1996, pp. 105–118.

Koszta, László. "A váci püspökség alapítasa." *Századok* 135 (2001), no. 2, s. 363–375.

Koszta, László. "Egyház- és államszervezés." In *Államalapítás, társadalom, művelődés*, ed. Gyula Kristó. Budapest 2001, pp. 65–74.

Koszta, László. "A nyitrai püspökség létrejötte," *Századok* 143 (2009), no. 2, s. 257–318.

Koszta, László. *A kalocsai érseki tartomány kialakulása*. Pécs 2013.

Koszta, László. "A bihari püspökség alapítása." In *Nagyvárad és Bihar a korai középkorban. Tanulmányok Biharország történetéről* 1, pp. 41–80.

Kouřil, Pavel. "Staří Maďaři a Morava z pohledu archeologie." In *Dějiny ve věku nejistot. Sborník k příležitosti 70. narozenin Dušana Třeštíka*, ed. Jan Klápště, Eva Plešková, Josef Žemlička, pp. 110–146.

Kouřil, Pavel. "Archeologické doklady nomádského vlivu a zásahu na území Moravy v závěru 9. a v 10. století." In *Bitka pri Bratislave v roku 907*, ed. Tatiana Štefanovičová, Drahoslav Hulínek, pp. 113–134.

Kouřil, Pavel et al. *Cyrilometodějská misie a Evropa 1150 let od příchodu soluňských bratří na Velkou Moravu*. Brno 2014.

Kouřil, Pavel et al. *The Cyril and Methodius Mission and Europe. 1150 Since the Arrival of the Thessaloniki Brothers in Great Moravia*. Brno 2014.

Kouřil, Pavel. "Staří Maďaři a jejich podíl na kolapsu a pádu Velké Moravy aneb Spojenci, sousedé, nepřátelé." In *Pád Velké Moravy aneb Kto byl pohřben v hrobu 153 na Pohansku u Břeclavi*, ed. Jiří Macháček, Martin Wihoda, pp. 102–143.

Kovács, Béla. *Az egri egyházmegye története 1596-ig*. Eger 1987.

Kovács, É. – Lovag, Zs. *Die ungarischen Krönungsinsignien*. Békéscsaba 1988.

Kovács, László. *Münzen aus der ungarischen Landnahmezeit. Archäologische Untersuchung der arabischen, byzantinischen, westeuropäischen und römischen Münzen aus dem Karpatenbecken des 10. Jahrhunderts, Fontes Archaeologici Hungariae*. Budapest 1989.

Kovács, László. *A kora Árpád-kori magyar pénzverésről. Érmetani és régészeti tanulmányok a Kárpát-medence I. (Szent) István és (Vak) Béla uralkodása közötti időszakának (1000–1141) érméiről. Varia Archaeologica Hungarica 7*. Budapest 1997.

Kovács, László. "Szent István pénzverése." In *Államalapítás, társadalom, művelődés*, ed. Gyula Kristó. Budapest 2001, pp. 93–100.

Kováč, Dušan et al. *Slovenské dejiny v dejinách Európy. Vybrané kapitoly*. Bratislava 2015.

Kováčová, Lucia – Kovár, Branislav – Milo, Peter. "Hradisko Pružina – Mesciská a jeho okolie." In *Hradiská – svedkovia dávnych čias. Zborník odborných príspevkov o hradiskách a ich obyvateľoch*, redaktor a zostavovateľ Peter Jenčík, Víťazoslav Struhár s. 175–185, 264–265, 268.

Kovrig, Ilona. "Megjegyzések a Keszthely kultúra kérdéséhez." *Archaeologiai Értesítő* 87 (1960), pp. 136–168.

Kovrig, Ilona. "Újabb kutatások a keszthely avarkori temetőben." *Archaeologiai Értesítő* 87 (1960), pp. 136–168.

Kožiak, Rastislav. "Cyrilometodské kresťanstvo v Malopoľsku vo svetle najnovších výskumov." *Ročenka Katedry dejín FHPV PU* 2003, pp. 9–23.

Kožiak, Rastislav. "Christianizácia Avarov a Slovanov na strednom Dunaji. Príbeh svätcov-misionárov, svätá vojna alebo kultúrny šok?" In *Svätec a jeho funkcie v spoločnosti I*, ed. Rastislav Kožiak, Jaroslav Nemeš. Bratislava 2006, pp. 121–147.

Kožiak, Rastislav. "*Coversio Gentum* a christianizácia vo včasnom stredoveku." In *Ružomberský historický zborník I*. ed. P. Zmátlo. Ružomberok 2007, pp. 83–106.

Kožin, Alexandr Nikitič. *Literaturnyj jazyk Kijevskoj Rusi*. Moskva 1981.

König, Tomáš. "Nitrianski Slovania a zánik Veľkej Moravy." In *Od Bachórza do Światowida ze Zbrucza. Tworzenie się słowiańskiej Europy w ujęciu źródłoznawczym. Księga jubileuszowa Profesora Michała Parczewskiego*, ed. Barbara Chudzińska, Michal Wojenka, Marcin Wołoszyn. Kraków-Rzeszów 2016, pp. 181–191.

König, Tomáš. "The Great Moravian territory of Nitra. Cultural manifestations, territorial scope and the ethnic and social-political identity of its population." *Muzeológia a kultúrne dedičstvo* 5, 2017, no. 2, pp. 9–28.

König, Tomáš et al. *Nitra-Mlyny. Stredoveké osídlenie kotliny*. Bratislava 2014.

Körmendi, Tamás. "Szent László horvátországi háborújáról. Az 1091. évi hadjárat történetének forráskritikai vizsgálata." *Századok* 149 (2015), no. 2, pp. 443–477.

Körmendi, Tamás. "Szent László és Horvátország." In *Nagyvárad és Bihar a korai középkorban. Tanulmányok Biharország történetéről* 1, pp. 81–100.

Középkori kritikus kérdései, ed. János Horváth, György Székely. Budapest 1974.

K problematike osídlenia stredodunajskej oblasti vo včasnom stredoveku, ed. Zlata Čilinská. Nitra 1991.

Krahwinkler, Harald. *Friaul im Frühmittelalter. Geschichte einer Region vom Ende des fünften bis zum Ende des zehnten Jahrhunderts. Veröffentlichungen des Instituts für Österreichische Geschichtsforschung, Band 30*. Wien – Köln – Weimar 1992.

Krajčovič, Rudolf. *Náčrt dejín slovenského jazyka*. Bratislava 1971.

Krajčovič, Rudolf. *Živé kroniky slovenských dejín skryté v názvoch obcí a miest*. Bratislava 2005.

Kralčák, Ľubomír. "K výkladu neznámeho textu na plakete z Bojnej." *Slavica slovaca* 49 (2014), no. 1, pp. 3–10.

Krandžalov, Dimitr. "Vznik bulharského státu a národa na Balkánskem poloostrově." *Slavia antiqua* 16 (1969), pp. 1–32.

Kraskovská, Ľudmila. "Nálezy z doby sťahovania národov na západnom Slovensku." *Archeologické rozhledy* 15 (1963), pp. 693–700, 709.

Kraskovská, Ľudmila. "Hroby z doby sťahovania národov pri Devínskom Jazere." *Archeologické rozhledy* 20 (1968), pp. 209–212.

Kraskovská, Ľudmila. *Slovansko-avarské pohrebisko pri Záhorskej Bystrici*. Bratislava 1972.

Krautschick, Stefan. "Die Familie der Könige in Spätantike und Frühmittelalter." In *Das Reich und die Barbaren*, ed. Evangelos K. Chrysos, Andreas Schwarcz. Veröffentlichungen des Instituts für österreichische Geschitsforschung, Band 29. Wien – Köln 1989, pp. 109–142.

Kristó, Gyula. "Anjou-kori krónikáink." *Századok* 101 (1967), no. 4, pp. 457–504.

Kristó, Gyula. *A történeti és politikai gondolkodás elemeinek fejlödése krónikairodalmunkban*. Budapest 1968.

Kristó, Gyula. "Az Exordia Scythica, Regino és a magyar krónikák." *Filológiai Közlöny* 16 (1970), pp. 106–115.

Kristó, Gyula. "Ősi epikánk és az Árpád-kori íráshagyomány." *Ethnographia* 81 (1970), pp. 113–135.

Kristó, Gyula. *A XI. századi hercegség története Magyarországon*, Budapest 1974.

Kristó, Gyula. *Levedi törzssövetségétől Szent István államáig. Elvek és utak*. Budapest 1980.
Kristó, Gyula. "Az Árpád-dinasztia szentjei és legendáik." In Kristó, Gyula. *Tanulmányok az Árpád-korról*, pp. 359-368.
Kristó, Gyula. *Tanulmányok az Árpád-korról*. Budapest 1983.
Kristó, Gyula. *Az augsburgi csata*. Budapest 1985.
Kristó, Gyula. *Az Árpád-kor háborúi*. Budapest 1986.
Kristó, Gyula. "A Képes Krónika szerzője és szövege." In *Képes Krónika*. Budapest 1986, pp. 459-516.
Kristó, Gyula. "Árpád fejedelemutódai." *Acta Univesitatis Szegediensis de Attila József nominatae. Acta Historica* 84 (1987), pp. 11-21.
Kristó, Gyula. *A vármegyek kialakulása Magyarországon*. Budapest 1988.
Kristó, Gyula. "A 10. századi Erdély politikai történetéhez." *Századok* 122 (1988), no. 1-2, pp. 3-35.
Kristó, Gyula. *A magyar állam megszületése*. Szeged 1995.
Kristó, Gyula. *A magyar nemzet megszületése*. Szeged 1997.
Kristó, Gyula. *Írások szent Istvánról és koráról*. Szeged 2000.
Kristó, Gyula. "Magyarország népei Szent István korában." *Századok* 134 (2000), no. 1, pp. 3-44.
Kristó, Gyula. "Néhány vármegye kialakulásának kérdéséhez." *Századok* 136 (2002), no. 2, pp. 469-484.
Kristó, Gyula. *Nem magyar népek a középkori Magyarországon*. Budapest 2003.
Kristó, Gyula - Makk, Ferenc - Szegfű, László. *Adatok "korai" helyneveink ismertéhez I, Acta Universitatis Szegediensis de Attila József nominatae, Acta historica* 44. Szeged 1973.
Kristó, Gyula - Makk, Ferenc - Szegfű, László. *Adatok "korai" helyneveink ismeretéhez II, Acta Universitatis Szegediensis de Attila Jószef nominatae, Acta historica* 48. Szeged 1974.
Kronsteiner, Otto. *Die alpenslawischen Personennamen. Österreichische Namenforschung, Sonderreihe* 2 (1975).
Kronsteiner, Otto. "Gab es unter den Alpenslawen eine kroatische ethnische Gruppe?" *Österreichische Namenforschung* 6 (1978), pp. 137-157.
Krumbacher, Karl. *Geschichte der byzantinischen Literatur von Justinian bis zum Ende des Oströmischen Reichs*. München 1897.
Krzemieńska, Barbara. "Politický vzestup českého státu za knížete Oldřicha (1012-1034)." *Československý časopis historický* 25 (1977), no. 2, pp. 246-272.
Krzemieńska, Barbara. "Wann erfolgte der Anschluß Mährens an den böhmischen Staat?" *Historica* 19 (1980), pp. 195-243.
Krzemieńska, Barbara. *Moravští Přemyslovci ve znojemské rotundě*. Ostrava 1985.

Krzemieńska, Barbara. *Břetislav I. Čechy a střední Evropa v první polovině XI. století.* Praha 1999.

Krzemieńska, Barbara – Třeštík, Dušan. "Hospodářské základy raně středověkého státu ve střední Evropě (Čechy, Polsko, Uhry v 10.–11. století)." *Československý časopis historický* 27 (1979), no. 1, pp. 113–130.

Křížek, František. "Limes romanus na Žitném ostrově." *Bratislava, časopis pro výskum Slovenska a Podkarpatské Rusi* 10 (1936), no. 4, pp. 418–432.

Křížek, František. "Das Problem der römischen Grenzen am nordpannonischen Limes." In *Limes Romanus Konferenz Nitra*, ed. Anton Točík. Bratislava 1959, pp. 49–61.

Kubů, František – Zavřel, Petr. "Terénní průzkum starých komunikací na příkladu Zlaté stezky." *Archaeologia historica* 23 (1998), pp. 35–57.

Kučera, Matúš. "Problémy vzniku a vývoja feudalizmu na Slovensku." *Historický časopis* 22 (1974), no. 4, pp. 541–556.

Kučera, Matúš. *Slovensko po páde Veľkej Moravy (Štúdie o hospodárskom a sociálnom vývine v 9.–13. storočí).* Bratislava 1974.

Kučera, Matúš. "O historickom vedomí Slovákov v stredoveku," *Historický časopis* 25 (1977), no. 2, pp. 217–238.

Kučera, Matúš. "Typológia včasnostredovekého štátu na strednom Dunaji." *Československý časopis historický* 27 (1979), no. 6, pp. 856–883.

Kučera, Matúš. "Hutníctví železa na Slovensku v 10.–13. století." In *Dějiny hutníctví železa v Československu I*, ed. Jaroslav Purš, pp. 59–66.

Kučera, Matúš. "Veľká Morava a začiatky našich národných dejín." *Historický časopis* 33 (1985), no. 2, pp. 163–200.

Kučera, Matúš. "Veľká Morava a slovenské dejiny." In Poulík, Josef – Chropovský, Bohuslav et al. *Velká Morava a počátky československé státnosti*, pp. 245–272.

Kučera, Matúš. *Postavy veľkomoravskej histórie.* Martin 1986.

Kučera, Matúš. "O pôvode názvu Bratislavy." In *Bitka pri Bratislave v roku 907 a jej význam pre vývoj stredného Podunajska*, ed. Tatiana Štefanovičová, Drahoslav Hulínek, pp. 53–63.

Kučera, Matúš. *Kráľ Svätopluk (830?–846–894).* Martin 2010.

Kučerovská, Taťána. "Die Zahlungsmittel in Mähren im 9. und 10. Jahrhundert." In *Rapports du IIIe Congrés International d'Archéologie Slave, Bratislava 7–14 septembre 1975, Tome 2*, ed. Bohuslav Chropovský, pp. 211–229.

Kunstmann, Heinrich. "Zwei rätselhafte Namen der frühen Árpádendynastie. Beleknegini und Besprim." *Ungarn-Jahrbuch* 28 (2005–2007), pp. 17–28.

Kurze Geschichte Siebenbürgens, ed. Béla Köpeczi. Budapest 1990.

Kuskov, Vladimir Vladimirovič. *Istorija drevnerusskoj literatury.* Moskva 1988.

Kútnik Šmálov, Jozef. *Kresťanský stredovek Slovenska.* Bratislava 2005.

Kútnik Šmálov, Jozef. "Benediktíni na Slovensku v IX.–XI. storočí." In Kútnik Šmálov, Jozef. *Kresťanský stredovek Slovenska*, pp. 27–61.

Kuzmík, Jozef. *Slovník starovekých a stredovekých autorov, prameňov a knižných skriptorov so slovenskými vzťahmi*. Martin 1983.

Kuzmin, Apollon G. "Letopisnye izvestija o razorenii Rjazani Batyem." *Vestnik Moskovskogo universiteta* 1963, no. 2, pp. 55–70.

Kuzmová, Klára – Rajtár, Ján. "Rímsky kastel v Iži – hraničná pevnosť na Dunaji." In *Rímsky kastel v Iži. Výskum 1978–2008. Zborník príspevkov k 30. výročiu archeologického výskumu*, ed. Klára Kuzmová, Ján Rajtár, pp. 11–38.

Kuzsinsky, Bálint. "Solva." In *Emlékkönyv d^r gróf Klébelsberg Kuno negyszázados kultúrpolitikai működésének emlékére születésének ötvenedik évfordulóján*, ed. Lukinich Imre. Budapest 1925, pp. 107–119.

Labuda, Gerard. *Pierwsze państwo słowiańskie państwo Samona*. Poznań 1949.

Labuda, Gerard. *Fragmenty dziejów Słowiańscyzny zachódniej*. Poznań 1960.

Labuda, Gerard. "Kraków biskupi przed rokiem 1000. Przyczynek do dyskusji nad dziejami misji metodianskiej w Polsce." *Studia historyczne* 27 (1984), no. 3 (106), pp. 371–412.

Labuda, Gerard. "O najstarszej organizacji Kościóla w Polsce." *Przeglad powszechny* 6 (1984), pp. 373–396.

Labuda, Gerard. *Studia nad początkami państwa polskiego II*. Poznań 1988.

Labuda, Gerard. *Mieszko II król polski (1025–1034). Czasy przełomu w dziejach państwa polskiego*. Kraków 1992.

Labuda, Gerard. "Udział książat węgierskich w walkach polsko-pomorskich za Mieszka II czy za Kazimiera Odnowiciela?" In *Opuscula minora in memoriam Iosepho Spors*, 1993, pp. 65–73.

Labuda, Gerard. "Czeskie chrzescijaństwo na Śląsku i w Małopolsce w X i XI wieku." In *Christianizacja Polski południowej*. Kraków 1994, pp. 73–98.

Labuda, Gerard. "Ein europäisches Itinerar seiner Zeit: Die Lebensstationen Adalberts." In *Adalbert von Prag – Brückenbauer zwischen dem Osten und Westen Europas*, ed. H. H. Hennix. *Schriften der Adalbert-Stiftung* 4. Baden-Baden 1997, pp. 59–75.

Labuda, Gerard. "Aspekty polityczne i kościełne tzw. 'zjazdu gnieznienskiego' w roku 1000." In *Ziemie polskie w X wieku i ich znaczenie w kształtowaniu sie nowej mapy Europy*, ed. Henryk Samsonowicz. Kraków 2000, pp. 17–33.

Labuda, Gerard. *Mieszko I*. Wrocław – Warszawa – Kraków 2002.

Labuda, Gerard. *Fragmenty dziejów Słowiańszczyzny zachódniej*. Poznań 2002.

Labuda, Gerard. *Pierwsze wieki monarchii piastowskiej*. Poznań 2012.

Labuda, Gerard. *Studia nad początkami państwa polskiego I, II, III*. Wodzisław Śląski 2012.

Lamiová-Schmiedlová, Mária. "Römerzeitliche Siedlungskeramik in der Südostslowakei." *Slovenská archeológia* 17 (1969), no. 2, pp. 404–458.

Lamiová-Schmiedlová, Mária. "K otázke proveniencie mincí z doby rímskej na východnom Slovensku." *Slovenská numizmatika* 9 (1986), pp. 131–144.

László, Gyula. *Steppenvölker und Germanen*. Budapest 1970.

László, Gyula. "Inter Sabarium et Carnuntum ...". *Studia Slavica Academiae Scientiarum Hungaricae* 21 (1975), no. 1–4, pp. 139–157.

Lášek, Jan Blahoslav. *Počátky křesťanství u východních Slovanů*. Praha 1997.

Lauermann, Ernst. "Ein landnahmezeitliches Reitergrab aus Gnadendorf." *Archäologie Österreichs* 11 (2000), no. 2, pp. 34–35.

Lauermann, Ernst. "Ein frühungarischer Reiter aus Gnadendorf, Niederösterreich." In *Schicksalsjahr 907. Die Schlacht bei Pressburg und das frühmittelalterliche Niederösterreich. Katalog zur Ausstellung des Niederösterreichischen Landesarchivs*, ed. Roman Zehetmayer, pp. 92–98.

Lechner, Karl. *Die Babenberger, Markgrafen und Herzoge von Österreich 976–1246*. Wien – Köln – Weimar 1992.

Lehotská, Darina. *Dejiny Modry 1158–1958*. Bratislava 1961.

Lelkes, István. *Kőszeg*. Budapest 1960.

Lengyel, Alfréd. "A középkori Győr." In *Győr. Várostörténeti tanulmányok*. Győr 1971, pp. 79–108.

Leube, Achim. "Die Burgunden bis zum Untergang ihres Reiches an der oberen Rhône im Jahre 534." In. *Die Germanen 2*, ed. Bruno Krüger, pp. 373–376.

Lexikon des Mittelalters III. München – Zürich 1986.

Lexikon des Mittelalters IV. München – Zürich 1989.

Ligeti, Lajos. "A magyar nyelv török kapcsolatai és ami körulöttük van." *Magyar Nyelv* 72 (1976), no. 1, pp. 11–27.

Ligeti, Lajos. "Régi török eredetű neveink." *Magyar Nyelv* 75 (1979), no. 3, pp. 259–273.

Ligeti, Lajos. *A magyar nyelv török kapcsolatai a honfoglalás elött és az Árpád-korban*. Budapest 1986.

Limes Romanus Konferenz Nitra, ed. Anton Točík. Bratislava 1959.

Lippert, Andreas. "Awaren nach 800 in Niederösterreich?" *Jahrbuch für Landeskunde* 63 (1970), pp. 145–157.

Litavrin, Gennadij G. "Vvedenije christianstva v Bolgarii (IX–načalo X v.)." In *Prinjatije christianstva narodami Central'noj i Jugo-Vostočnoj Evropy i kreščenie Rusi*, ed. Gennadij G. Litavrin, pp. 30–57.

Lošek, Fritz. "Ethnische und politische Terminologie bei Iordanes und Einhard." In *Typen der Ethnogenese unter besonderer Berücksichtigung der Bayer, Teil I*, ed. Herwig Wolfram, Walter Pohl, pp. 147–152.

Lotter, Friedrich. "Die germanischen Stämmesverbände im Umkreis des Ostalpen-Mitteldonau-Raumes nach der literarischen Überlieferung zum Zeitalter Severins." In *Die Bayern und ihre Nachbarn. Berichte des Symposions der Kommission für*

Frühmittelalterforschung 25. bis 28. Oktober 1982, Stift Zwettl, Niederösterreich, Teil 1, ed. Herwig Wolfram, Andreas Schwarcz, Dph 179 (1985), pp. 29–59.

Ludat, Herbert. *Slaven und Deutsche im Mittelalter. Ausgewählte Aufsätze zu Fragen ihrer politischen, sozialen und kulturellen Beziehungen*. Köln – Wien 1982.

Lukáč, Gabriel. "K počiatkom stredovekého osídlenia Spiša (do konca 12. stor.)." *Archaeologia historica* 18 (1993), pp. 9–18.

Lukačka, Ján. "Úloha šľachty slovanského pôvodu pri stabilizácii uhorského včasnofeudálneho štátu." In *Typologie raně feudálních slovanských států*, pp. 191–200.

Lukačka, Ján. "Die Kontinuität der Besiedlung auf dem Gebiet des Komitates Nitra im 9–13. Jahrhundert." *Studia historica Slovaca* 18 (1994), pp. 129–178.

Lukačka, Ján. "Najstaršie nitrianske šľachtické rody." In *Najstaršie rody na Slovensku. Zborník príspevkov zo sympózia o najstarších rodoch na Slovensku 4.–6. októbra 1993 v Častej-Papierničke*. Bratislava 1994, pp. 102–110.

Lukačka, Ján. *Formovanie vyššej šľachty na západnom Slovensku*. Bratislava 2002.

Lukačka, Ján. "K problému kontinuity kresťanstva na území Slovenska v 10. storočí." *Studia historica Tyrnaviensia* 3 (2003), pp. 37–40.

Lukniš, Michal et al. *Slovensko. Príroda*. Bratislava 1972.

Lutovský, Michal. *Encyklopedie slovanské archeologie v Čechách, na Moravě a ve Slezsku*. Praha 2001.

Lutovský, Michal – Petráň, Zdeněk. *Slavníkovci. Mýtus českého dějepisectví*. Praha 2004.

Lutovský, Michal – Profantová, Naďa. *Sámova říše*. Praha 1995.

Lysá, Žofia. *Bratislava na ceste k privilégiu 1291. Štúdie k dejinám Bratislavy v 13. storočí*. Bratislava 2014.

Lysý, Miroslav. "Intervencie Nemeckej ríše do Uhorska v prospech kráľa Petra Orseola." *Medea* 5 (2001), pp. 32–47.

Lysý, Miroslav. "Základná charakteristika výbojnej politiky Konráda II. (1024–1039)." *Medea* 6 (2002), pp. 53–63.

Lysý, Miroslav. "Politika českého kniežaťa Břetislava I. (1035–1055) voči Uhorsku." *Historický časopis* 52 (2004), no. 3, pp. 451–468.

Lysý, Miroslav. "Nemecké výboje proti Uhorsku v 11. storočí." In *Vojenská história* 9 (2005), no. 2, pp. 22–44.

Lysý, Miroslav. "Druhostupňové kniežatá na Morave v 9. storočí." *Byzantinoslovaca* V (2014), pp. 123–127.

Lysý, Miroslav. *Moravania, Mojmírovci a Franská ríša. Štúdie k etnogenéze, politickým inštitúciám a ústavnemu zriadeniu na území Slovenska vo včasnom stredoveku*. Bratislava 2014.

Lysý, Miroslav. "'Ibique Legatos Zuentibaldi pacem petentes et fidelitatem promittentes suscepit.' Posolstvá včasného stredoveku ako prostriedok diplomacie." In *Od symbolu k slovu. Podoby stredovekej komunikácie*, ed. Miriam Hlavačková, pp. 17–28.

Łowmiański, Henryk. *Początki Polski. Z dziejów Słowian w I tysiącleciu n. e. I, II, III, IV, V, VI 1, VI 2.* Warszawa 1964, 1964, 1967, 1970, 1973, 1985.

Mácelová, Marta. "Príspevok k stredovekému osídleniu Zvolena," *Archaeologia historica* 14 (1989), pp. 171–180.

Mácelová, Marta. "K počiatkom osídlenia Zvolena v stredoveku." *Archaeologia historica* 18 (1993), pp. 69–74.

Mácelová, Marta. "Môťovský hrádok vo svetle archeologického výskumu." In *Zvolen 1243–2008. Zborník príspevkov z vedeckých konferencií*, ed. Júlia Ragačová, Pavol Maliniak. Zvolen 2008, pp. 25–27.

Mácelová, Marta. *Slovania vo Zvolenskej kotline.* Kraków 2013.

Madzar, Imre. "A hun krónika szerzője." *Történeti Szemle* 11 (1922), pp. 75–103.

Magyar, István Lórand. "'Quaestio bulgarica' (*A kereszténység felvétele Bulgáriában*)." *Századok* 116 (1982), no. 5, pp. 839–878.

Magyarország régészeti topográfiája 1, ed. László Gerevich. *Veszprém megye régészeti topográfiája*, ed. Károly Sági. *A keszthelyi és tapolcai járás*, írta Kornél Bakay – Nándor Kalicz – Károly Sági. Budapest 1966.

Magyarország régészeti topográfiája 2, ed. László Gerevich. *Veszprém megye régészeti topográfiája*, ed. István Éri. *A veszprémi járás*, írta István Éri – Márta Kelemen – Péter Németh – István Torma. Budapest 1969.

Magyarország története I. Előzmények és magyar történet 1242-ig, 1. kötét, ed. György Székely, Antal Bartha. Budapest 1987.

Magyarország története I. Előzmények és magyar történet 1242-ig, 2. kötét, ed. György Székely, Antal Bartha. Budapest 1987.

Magyarország történeti kronológiája I. A kezdetektől 1526-ig, ed. Kálmán Benda. Budapest 1986.

Makk, Ferenc. "Megjegyzések Salamon és I. Géza történetéhez." *Acta Universitatis Szegediensis de Attila József nominatae. Acta Historica* 84 (1987), pp. 31–44.

Mal, Josip. *Probleme aus der Frühgeschichte der Slowenen.* Ljubljana 1939.

Malory, Thomas. *Artušova smrť*, translation Eduard Castiglione. Bratislava 1979.

Malory, Thomas. *Artušova smrt*, translation Jan Caha. Praha 1997.

Mályusz, Elemér. *A Thuróczy-krónika és forrásai.* Budapest 1967.

Mályusz, Elemér. *Az V. István-kori Gesta.* Budapest 1971.

Marek, Miloš. "Slovanské etnonymá v toponymii stredovekého Uhorska." *Studia historica Tyrnaviensia* 3 (2003), pp. 65–87.

Marek, Miloš. *Cudzie etniká na stredovekom Slovensku.* Martin 2006.

Mareš, František Václav. *Cyrilometodějská tradice a slavistika.* Praha 2000.

Marosi, Arnold. "Volt-e Székesfehérvárott római telep?" *Századok* 69 (1935), pp. 266–269.

Marosi, Arnold. "Volt-e Székesfehérvárott római telep?" *Századok* 69 (1935), no. 1, pp. 266–269.

Marsina, Richard. "Tri štúdie zo slovenskej diplomatiky." *Historické štúdie* 3 (1957), pp. 276–302.

Marsina, Richard. "O počte a hustote obyvateľstva v Uhorsku do začiatku 14. storočia." *Historický časopis* 9 (1961), no. 4, pp. 617–632.

Marsina, Richard. "Štúdie k slovenskému diplomatáru. K problematike najstarších zoborských listín." *Historické štúdie* 7 (1961), pp. 201–220.

Marsina, Richard. "Štúdie k slovenskému diplomatáru. K problematike najstarších zoborských listín." *Sborník Filozofickej fakulty Univerzity Komenského* 14 (1963), pp. 135–170.

Marsina, Richard. "Uhorské kroniky a kronikári." *Historický časopis* 16 (1968), no. 3, pp. 426–431.

Marsina, Richard. "Povolenie slovanskej liturgie na Veľkej Morave." *Historický časopis* 18 (1970), no. 1, pp. 4–16.

Marsina, Richard. "Veľkomoravské deperditá." *Slovenská archivistika* 6 (1971), no. 1, pp. 18–44.

Marsina, Richard. "Štúdie k Slovenskému diplomatáru I." *Historické štúdie* 16 (1971), pp. 5–108.

Marsina, Richard. "Štúdie k Slovenskému diplomatáru I. Druhá časť: Obdobie od roku 1000 do roku 1235." *Historické štúdie* 18 (1973), pp. 5–119.

Marsina, Richard. "O osídlení Slovenska od 11. do polovice 13. storočia." In *Slovenský ľud po rozpade Veľkomoravskej ríše. Historické štúdie* 27 (1984), no. 2, pp. 39–59.

Marsina, Richard. "Stredoveké uhorské rozprávacie pramene a slovenské dejiny." *Zborník Slovenského národného múzea* 78 (1984), *História* 24, pp. 167–195.

Marsina, Richard. "Metodov boj." Bratislava 1985.

Marsina, Richard. "Údelné vojvodstvo na Slovensku." *Zborník Slovenského národného múzea* 81 (1987), *História* 27, pp. 199–212.

Marsina, Richard. "Kristianizácia Maďarov a Uhorska medzi východom a západom." *Historický časopis* 40 (1992), no. 4, pp. 409–421.

Marsina, Richard. "Nitrianske biskupstvo a jeho biskupi od 9. do polovice 13. storočia." *Historický časopis* 41 (1993), no. 5, pp. 529–542.

Marsina, Richard. "O Nitrianskom biskupstve (Prečo nebolo obnovené biskupstvo v Nitre hneď začiatkom 11. storočia?)." In *Szomszédaink közöt Kelet-Európában. Emlékkönyv Niederhauser Emil 70. születésnapjára.* Budapest 1993, pp. 27–32.

Marsina, Richard. "Začiatky cirkevnej organizácie na Slovensku (Od prelomu 8./9. až do začiatku 11. storočia)." *Slovenská archivistika* 30 (1995), no. 2, pp. 113–126.

Marsina, Richard. "Svätopluk, legenda a skutočnosť." In *Svätopluk 894–1994*, ed. Richard Marsina, Alexander Ruttkay. Nitra 1997, pp. 155–165.

Marsina, Richard. "Cirkevná organizácia na Veľkej Morave." In *Velká Morava mezi východem a západem. Sborník příspěvků z mezinárodní vědecké konference Uherské Hradiště, Staré Město 28. 9.–1. 10. 1999*, ed. Luděk Galuška, Pavel Kouřil, Zdeněk Měřínský. *Spisy Archeologického ústavu AV ČR Brno* 17 (2001), pp. 291–296.

Marsina, Richard. "Obnovenie Nitrianskeho biskupstva na prelome 11. a 12. storočia." In *Kresťanstvo v dejinách Slovenska*, ed. Mária Kohútová. Bratislava 2003, pp. 17–26.

Marsina, Richard. "Vývoj cirkevnej organizácie na Slovensku do začiatku 12. storočia." In *XXVII. Mikulovské sympózium 2002*, Brno (2003), pp. 91–100.

Matejko, Ľubor. "Niekoľko poznámok k náhrobnému nápisu kniežaťa Presiana v Michalovciach." *Slovanské štúdie* 2 (1992), pp. 136–147.

Matejko, Ľubor. "Some remarks on the interpretation of Slavonic written sources." In *East Central Europe at the Turn of the 1st and 2nd Millennia*, ed. Vincent Múcska. *Acta historica Posoniensia II* (2002), pp. 83–87.

Materialy dlja slovarja drevne-russkago jazyka po pismennym pamjatnikam, trud I. I. Sreznevkago. Tom 1. (A–K), Sankt Peterburg 1893. Tom 2. (Л–П), Sankt Peterburg 1902. Tom 3. (Р–Я), Sankt Peterburg 1912.

Mazuch, Marian. "Revidierte Interpretation der 'kreisförmigen heidnischen Kultstätte' im nördlichen Suburbium von Mikulčice." In *Frühmittelalterliche Kirchen als archäologische und historische Quelle*, ed. Lumír Poláček, Jana Maříková-Kubková, pp. 123–134.

Mazuch, Marian. "Výzkumy severního podhradí hradiště Valy u Mikulčic: k otázce násilného zániku velkomoravských mocenských center na počátku 10. věku." In *Mezi raným a vrcholním středověkem*, ed. Jiří Doležal, Martin Wihoda, pp. 137–159.

McCormick, Michael. *Narodziny Europy. Korzenie gospodarki europejskiej 300–900*. Warszawa 2007.

Megiser, Hieronymus. *Annales Carinthiae. Das ist Chronica des löblichen Ertzherzogthumbs Kharndten*. Leipzig 1612.

Meletinskij, Jeleazar Mojsejevič. *Proischožđenie geroičeskogo eposa*. Moskva 1963.

Meletinskij, Jeleazar Mojsejevič. *Poetika mýtu*. Bratislava 1989.

Melich, János. "Szvatopluk." *Magyar Nyelv* 18 (1922), no. 4–6, pp. 110–114.

Melich, János. "Pozsony magyar, német és tót nevéről." *Századok* 57–58 (1923–1924), pp. 695–713.

Melich, János. "Die Namen von Pressburg." *Zeitschrift für slawische Philologie* 3 (1926), pp. 212–313.

Melich, János. "Szepes és Poprád," *Magyar Nyelv* 25 (1929), no. 1–2, pp. 34–46.

Melik, Vasilij. "Vprašenje bitke pri Ljubljani v dobi madžarskih napadov." *Zgodovinski časopis* 6–7 (1952–1953), pp. 202–217.

Mencl, Václav. *Stredoveká architektúra na Slovensku. Kniha prvá: Stavebné umenie na Slovensku od najstarších čias až do konca doby románskej*. Praha – Prešov 1937.

Menghin, Wilfried. "Die Völkerwanderungszeit im Karpatenbecken." In *Germanen, Hunen und Awaren. Schätze der Völkerwanderungszeit*, ed. Wilfried Menghin, Tobias Springer, Egon Wamers, pp. 15–26.

Merhautová, Anežka – Třeštík, Dušan. *Románske umění v Čechách a na Moravě*. Praha 1983.

Mesterházy, Károly. "Die Landnehmenden ungarischen Stämme." *Acta Archaeologica Academiae Scientiarium Hungaricae* 30 (1978), pp. 313–347.

Meško, Marek. "Pečenežsko-byzantské dobrodružstvo uhorského kráľa Šalamúna (1083–1087)." *Konštantínove listy* 4 (2011), s. 77–94.

Meško, Marek. "Nová pravdepodobná príčina kumánskeho vpádu na byzantský Balkán roku 1095." *Byzantinoslovaca* v (2014), pp. 192–204.

Mezi raným a vrcholním středověkem. Pavlu Kouřilovi k šedesátým narozeninám přátelé, kolegové a žáci, ed. Jiří Doležal, Martin Wihoda. Brno 2012.

Mező, András. *Patrocíniumok a középkori Magyarországon*. Budapest 2003.

Měřínský, Zdeněk. "Die Zentren Großmährens." In *Velká Morava mezi východem a západem. Sborník příspěvků z mezinárodní vědecké konference Uherské Hradiště, Staré Město 28. 9.–1. 10. 1999*, ed. Luděk Galuška, Pavel Kouřil, Zdeněk Měřínsky, *Spisy Archeologického ústavu AV ČR Brno* 17 (2001), pp. 297–304.

Měřínský, Zdeněk. *České země od příchodu Slovanů po Velkou Moravu I, II*. Praha 2002, 2006.

Měřínský, Zdeněk. "Mikulčice – das Gräberfeld bei der IX. Kirche. Verlauf der Forschung und Fundschlage." In *Die frühmittelalterliche Elite bei den Völkern des östlichen Mitteleuropas*, ed. Pavel Kouřil, pp. 115–136.

Měřínský, Zdeněk – Zumpfe, Eva. "Obchodní cesty na jižní Moravě a v Dolním Rakousku do doby vrcholného středověku." *Archeologia historica* 23 (1998), pp. 173–181.

Michalík, Tomáš. "Počiatky Trenčianskeho hradu. Včasnostredoveké hradisko v Trenčíne." In *Hradiská – svedkovia dávnych čias II. Zborník odborných príspevkov o hradiskách a ich obyvateľoch*, ed. Peter Jenčík, Zuzana Staneková, pp. 155–164.

Michna, Pavel J. "K utváření raně středověké Moravy. Olomouc a historické Olomoucko v 9. až počátku 13. století." *Československý časopis historický* 30 (1982), no. 4, pp. 716–744.

Michna, Pavel J. – Pojsl, Miloslav. *Románský palác na olomouckém hradě. Archeologie a památková obnova*. Brno 1988.

Mihok, Ľubomír – Soláriková, Marta – Hollý, Alojz – Čilinská, Zlata. "Archeometalurgický výskum sečných zbraní z pohrebiska v Želovciach." In *K problematike osídlenia stredodunajskej oblasti vo včasnom stredoveku*, ed. Zlata Čilinská, pp. 67–101.

Mikkola, Jooseppi Julius. "Avarica." *Archiv für slavische Philologie* 41 (1927), pp. 158–160.

Mikkola, Jooseppi Julius. "Samo und sein Reich." *Archiv für slavische Philologie* 42 (1928), pp. 77–97.

Mikl-Curk, Iva. "Poetovio." *Das Altertum* 9 (1963), pp. 84–97.

Mináč, Vladimír. "O osídlení Bratislavskej brány v 7. a 8. storočí." *Zborník Slovenského národného múzea* 72 (1978) *História* 18, pp. 61–81.

Mishin, Dmitrij. "Ibrahim ibn-Ya'qub At-Turtushi's account of the Slavs from the middle of the tenth century." In *Annual of medieval studies at the CEU 1994–1995*, ed. Mary Beth L. Davis, Marcell Sebők. Budapest 1996, pp. 184–199.

Mitáček, Jiří. "'Campus Lucsco'. Proměny jedné otázky." In *Východní Morava v 10. až 14. století*, ed. Luděk Galuška, Pavel Kouřil, Jiří Mitáček. Brno 2008, pp. 155–167.

von Mitis, Oskar. "Die Herkunft des Ostmarkgrafen Wilhelm." *Mitteilungen des Instituts für österreichische Geschichtsforschung* 58 (1950), pp. 534–549.

Mittelalterliche nationes – neuzeitliche Nationen. Probleme der Nationenbildung in Europa, ed. Almut Bues, Rex Rexheuser. Deutsches Historisches Institut Warschau. Quellen und Studien, Band 2. Wiesbaden 1995.

Mitterauer, Michael. "Slawischer und bayrischer Adel am Ausgang der Karolingerzeit." *Carinthia* I 150 (1960), pp. 693–726.

Mitterauer, Michael. "Karolingische Markgrafen in Südosten, Fränkische Reichsaristokratie und bayerischer Stammesadel im österreichischen Raum." *Archiv für österreichische Geschichte* 123 (1963).

Mócsy, András. *Die spätrömische Festung und das Gräberfeld von Tokod*. Budapest 1981.

Mócsy, András. "A római kor." In *Magyarország története I/1*. Budapest 1987, pp. 199–264.

Modzelewski, Karol. *Barbarzyńska Europa*. Warszawa 2004.

Mokrý, Ladislav. "Hudobná problematika veľkomoravského obdobia." In *O počiatkoch slovenských dejín*, ed. Peter Ratkoš, pp. 277–290.

Mons Sacer 996–1996. Pannonhalma 1000 éve I, ed. Imre Takács. Pannonhalma 1996.

Mór, Wertner. *Az Árpádok családi története*. Nagy-Becskereken 1892.

Moravcsik, Gyula. *Byzantinoturcica. Sprachreste der Türkvölker in den byzantinischen Quellen 1, 2*. Budapest 1942, 1943.

Mordovin, Maxim. "Archeologický výskum komitátneho Hontianskeho hradu." *Acta historica Neosoliensia* 16 (2013), no. 1–2, pp. 6–37.

Moro, Gotbert. "Zur politischen Stellung Karantaniens im fränkischen und deutschen Reich." *Südost-Forschungen* 22 (1963), pp. 78–96.

Múcska, Vincent. "About the First Hungarian Bishoprics." In *East Central Europe at the Turn of the 1st and 2nd Millennia*, ed. Vincent Múcska. Acta historica Posoniensia 2. Bratislava 2002, pp. 119–139.

Múcska, Vincent. "O prvých uhorských biskupstvách." *Historický časopis* 51 (2003), no. 1, pp. 3–22.

Múcska, Vincent. "Uhorsko na ceste ku kresťanskej monarchii." In *Proměna středovýchodní Evropy raného a vrcholného středověku. Mocenské souvislosti a paralely*, ed. Libor Jan, pp. 97–116.

Musil, Jiří. "Römische Wehranlagen und Baumaterial nördlich der mittleren Donau." In *Gentes, Reges und Rom*, ed. Jan Bouzek, Herwig Friesinger, Karol Piet, Balázs Komoróczy. *Spisy Archeologického ústavu AV ČR Brno* 16 (2000), pp. 87–94.

Musilová, Margaréta. "Najnovšie objavy na Bratislavskom hrade. Stopy antického Ríma v Bratislave." *Historická revue* 26 (2015), no. 6, pp. 8–15.

Musilová, Margaréta – Minaroviech, Jana. "Hypotetická rekonštrukcia Rímskej stavby I a skladu amfor v Zimnej jazdiarni na Bratislavskom hrade." In *Bratislavský hrad, dejiny, výskum a obnova*, ed. Margaréta Musilová, Peter Barta, Angelika Herucová, pp. 72–95.

Müller, Ivan. "Barbarská království (500–750)." In *Dějiny politického myšlení II/1. Politické myšlení raného křesťanství a středověku*, ed. Ivan Müller, Vilém Herold, Aleš Havlíček, pp. 123–154.

Müller, Ivan. "Počátky politického myšlení na Západě (750–1050)." In *Dějiny politického myšlení II/1. Politické myšlení raného křesťanství a středověku*, ed. Ivan Müller, Vilém Herold, Aleš Havlíček, pp. 308–403.

Müller, Robert. "Neue Ausgrabungen in der Nähe von Zalavár." In *Interaktionen der mitteleuropäischen Slawen und anderen Ethnika im 6.–10. Jahrhundert*. Nitra 1984, pp. 185–188.

Müller, Robert. "Die Spätrömische Festung Valcum am Plattensee." In *Germanen, Hunen und Awaren. Schätze der Völkerwanderungszeit*, ed. Wilfried Menghin, Tobias Springer und Egon Wamers, pp. 270–273.

Müller, Robert. "Friedhöfe der Keszthely-Kultur." In *Germanen, Hunen und Awaren. Schätze der Völkerwanderungszeit*, ed. Wilfried Menghin, Tobias Springer und Egon Wamers, pp. 274–283.

Müller, Robert. "Karoling udvarház és temetője." In *Honfoglalás és régészet*. Budapest 1994, pp. 91–98.

Müller, Robert. "Über die Herkunft und das Ethnikum der Keszthely-Kultur." In *Ethnische und kulturelle Verhältnisse an der mittleren Donau vom 6. bis zum 11. Jahrhundert*, ed. Darina Bialeková, Jozef Zábojník, pp. 75–82.

Müller, Robert. "Die Umgebung des Zala Flusses im 8.–10. Jahrhundert." In *Central Europe in 8th–10th Centuries*, ed. Dušan Čaplovič, Ján Doruľa, pp. 74–80.

Müller, Robert. "Die Bevölkerung von Fenékpuszta in der Frühawarenzeit." In *Christentum in Pannonien im ersten Jahrtausend. Internationale Tagung im Balaton Museum in Keszthely vom 6. bis 9. November 2000*, ed. Robert Müller. *Zalai Múzeum* 11 (2002), pp. 93–101.

Mysliński, Kazimierz. *Polska wobec Słowian połabskich do konca wieku XII*. Lublin 1993.

Nagy, Géza. "Trónöröklés az Árpádok alatt." *Turul* 32 (1914), pp. 19–25.

Nagy, Katalin E., Sipos, Enikő, Marosi, Ernő. The picture fields of the mantle (1–43). Fragments of the embroidered band. In: The Coronation Mantle of the Hungarian Kings, edited by István Bardoly, s. 141–230.

Nagyvárad és Bihar a korai középkorban. Tanulmányok Biharország történetéről 1, Nagyvárad 2014.

Nalepa, Jerzy. "Biala Góra." In Słownik starożytnosci słowiańskich 1. Wrocław – Warszawa – Kraków 1961, pp. 110–111.

Nedev, Stefan T. "Razgromät na Nikifor I Genik prez 811 g." Voennoistoričeski sbornik 46 (1977), no. 1, pp. 115–127.

Németh, Péter. Borsova határvármegye kialakulása. A Kisvárdai Vármúzeum kiadványi 5. Debrecen 1975.

Németh, Péter. "Frühgepidische Gräberfunde an der oberen Theiss." In Germanen, Hunen und Awaren. Schätze der Völkerwanderungszeit. Die Archäologie des 5. und 6. Jahrhunderts an der mittleren Donau und der östlich-merowingische Reihengräberkreis, ed. Wilfried Menghin, Tobias Springer, Egon Wamers, pp. 219–222.

"Neslované" o počátcích Slovanů, ed. Przemysław Urbańczyk. Praha, 2011.

Nešporová, Tamara. "Druhá sezóna výskumu na Brezine." AVANS v r. 1987. Nitra 1988, pp. 118–119.

Nešporová, Tamara. "Hrad Trenčín v archeologických prameňoch." Pamiatky a múzeá 3 (1997), pp. 6–9.

Nevizánsky, Gabriel. "K významu a vypovedacej schopnosti mincí v staromaďarských hroboch." Slovenská numizmatika 6 (1980), pp. 121–130.

Nevizánsky, Gabriel. "Aktuálne problémy výskumu pamiatok staromaďarského etnika na území dnešného Slovenska." In Bitka pri Bratislave v roku 907 a jej význam pre vývoj stredného Podunajska, ed. Tatiana Štefanovičová, Drahoslav Hulínek, pp. 265–278.

Niederle, Lubor. Rukověť slovanských starožitností. Praha 1953.

Nitra. Príspevky k najstarším dejinám mesta, ed. Karol Pieta. Nitra 1993.

Nitra v slovenských dejinách, ed. Richard Marsina. Martin 2002.

Nógrádmegye története. 1. kötet 896–1849, ed. Sándor Balogh. Salgótarján, 1972.

Nótari, Támas. A salzburgi historiográfia kezdetei. Szeged 2007.

Nováki, Gyula. "Archäologische Denkmäler der Eisenverhüttung in Nordostungarn aus dem X.–XII. Jahrhundert." Acta Archaeologica Academiae Scientiarum Hungaricae 21 (1969), pp. 299–331.

Nováki, Gyula. "Die topographischen Eigentümlichkeiten der ungarischen Burgen im 10.–11. Jahrhundert am nördlichen Randgebiet der grossen Tiefebene." Acta Archaeologica Academiae Scientiarum Hungaricae 28 (1976), pp. 359–369.

Nováki, Gyula. "A borsodi földvár sánca." A Herman Ottó Múzeum Évkönyve 30–31. Miskolc 1993, pp. 125–145.

Nováki, Gyula – Sándorfi, Gyorgy – Miklós, Zsuzsa. *A Börzsöny hegység őskori és középkori várai*. Budapest 1979.

Novotný, Bohuslav. "Nové nálezy z doby sťahovania národov na Slovensku." *Zborník FFUK Musaica* 17 (1984), pp. 111–117.

Novotný, Bohuslav. *Slovom a mečom. Slovensko v rímskej dobe*. Martin 1995.

Novotný, Václav. *České dějiny I/1. Od nejstarších dob do smrti knížete Oldřicha*. Praha 1912.

Novotný, Václav. *České dějiny I/2. Od Břetislava I. do Přemysla I*. Praha 1913.

Od symbolu k slovu. Podoby stredovekej komunikácie, ed. Miriam Hlavačková. Bratislava 2016.

Odler, Martin. "Avarské sídliská v strednej Európe: problémová bilancia." *Studia mediævalia Pragensia* 11 (2012), pp. 17–96.

Oettinger, Karl. *Das Werden Wiens*. Wien 1951.

Oliva, Pavel. *Pannonia a počátky krize římskeho imperia*. Praha 1959.

Ondrouch, Vojtěch. *Limes romanus na Slovensku*. Bratislava 1938.

Ondrouch, Vojtěch. "Územie Československa v geografii Klaudia Ptolemaia." *Naša veda* 5 (1958), pp. 14–22.

O počiatkoch slovenských dejín. Sborník materiálov, ed. Peter Ratkoš. Bratislava 1965.

Ortvay, Tivadar. *A pécsi egyházmegye alapitása és elsö határai történet – topografiai tanulmány*. Budapest 1890.

Ortvay, Tivadar. *Magyarország egyházi földleirása a XIV. század elején a pápai tizedjegyzékek alapján feltüntetve I, II*. Budapest 1891, 1892.

Ortvay, Tivadar – Hrubant, László. *Az Erdélyi egyházmegye a XIV-ik század elején. Mérték 1 : 600 000. Photolitographie und Schnellpressendruck des k. k. militär-geographischen Instituts in Wien*. Wien 1888.

Österreich im Hochmittelalater (907–1246). Ed. Kommision für die Geschichte Österreichs der Österreichischen Akademie der Wissenschaften. Wien 1991.

Pád Velké Moravy aneb Kto byl pohřben v hrobu 153 na Pohansku u Břeclavi, ed. Jiří Macháček, Martin Wihoda. Praha 2016.

Pais, Dezső. "A gyula és a kündüh." *Magyar Nyelv* 27 (1931), no. 2, pp. 170–176.

Pais, Dezső. "Gyila, Julus." *Magyar Nyelv* 31 (1935), no. 1–2, pp. 53–54.

Pais, Dezső. "Cotoyd (Egy XI. századi tiszai átkelő nevéhez)." *Magyar Nyelv* 56 (1960), no. 2, pp. 111–112.

Pais, Dezső. "Szempontok Árpád-kori személy neveink vizsgálatához." In *Névtudományi vizsgálatok. A magyar nyelvtudományi társaság névtudományi konferenciája 1958, Pais Dezső közreműködésével ed. Mikesy Sándor*. Budapest 1960, pp. 93–105.

Palacký, František. *Dějiny národu českého w Čechách a w Moravě I/1. Od prvowěkosti až do roku 1125*. W Praze 1876.

Panajotov, Panajot. *Srednovekovna bălgarska istorija*. Gabrovo 1992.

Panic, Idzi. *Ostatnie lata Wielkich Moraw*. Katowice 2003.

Pannonia régészeti kézikönyve, ed. András Mócsy, Jenő Fitz. Budapest 1990.

Parczewski, Michal. *Początki ksztaltowania się polsko-ruskiej rubieży etnicznej w Karpatach. U źródel rozpadu Slowiańszczyzny na odlam wschodni i zachodni*. Kraków 1991.

Pauler, Gyula. *A magyar nemzet története az Árpád-házi királyok alatt I*. Budapest 1899.

Pauliny, Eugen. "Západoslovanské výpožičky v staromaďarskej lexike." In *O počiatkoch slovenských dejín*, ed. Peter Ratkoš, pp. 190–204.

Pauliny, Eugen. *Slovesnosť a kultúrny jazyk Veľkej Moravy*. Bratislava 1964.

Pekař, Josef. "Svatý Václav." In *Svatováclavský sborník. Na památku 1000. výročí smrti knížete Václava Svatého I. Kníže Václav Svatý a jeho doba*, ed. Karel Guth, Jan Kapras, Antonín Novák, Karel Stloukal, pp. 9–101.

Pelikán, Oldřich. *Slovensko a rímske impérium*. Bratislava 1960.

Perényi, József. "Vývoj maďarského 'národného povedomia' v 11.–13. storočí." *Historický časopis* 20 (1972), no. 1, pp. 1–17.

Peške, Lubomír. "Osteologické nálezy z langobardského sídliště v Podolí (okr. Brno-venkov)." *Archeologické rozhledy* 49 (1997), pp. 643–644.

Petráň, Zdeněk. *První české mince*. Praha 1998.

Petrov, Aleksej Leonidovič. *Příspěvky k historické demografii Slovenska v 18.–19. století*. Praha 1928, pp. 238–304.

Petrov, Petăr Ch. "Za godinata na nalagane christinstvoto v Bălgarija." *Izvestija na Instytut za bălgarskata istorija* 14–15 (1964), pp. 569–589.

Petrov, Petăr Ch. *Obrazuvane na bălgarskata dăržava*. Sofija 1981.

Pieta, Karol. "Die Slowakei im 5. Jahrhundert." In *Germanen, Hunen und Awaren. Schätze der Völkerwanderungszeit*, ed. Wilfried Menghin, Tobias Springer, Egon Wamers, pp. 385–417.

Pieta, Karol. "Spätswebische Siedlungs- und Grabfunde." In *Germanen, Hunen und Awaren. Schätze der Völkerwanderungszeit*, ed. Wilfried Menghin, Tobias Springer, Egon Wamers, pp. 407–410.

Pieta, Karol. "Osídlenie z doby rímskej a sťahovania národov v Nitre." In *Nitra. Príspevky k najstarším dejinám mesta*, ed. Karol Pieta. Nitra 1993, pp. 74–93.

Pieta, Karol. "Osídlenie Slovenska v dobe sťahovania národov." In *Slovensko vo včasnom stredoveku*, ed. Alexander Ruttkay, Matej Ruttkay, Peter Šalkovský. Nitra 2002, pp. 11–22.

Pieta, Karol. "Hradiská Bojná II a Bojná III." In *Bojná. Hospodárske a politické centrum Nitrianskeho kniežatstva*, ed. Karol Pieta, Alexander Ruttkay, Matej Ruttkay, pp. 173–190.

Pieta, Karol. "Včasnostredoveké mocenské centrum Bojná – výskumy v rokoch 2007–2013." In *Bojná 2. Nové výsledky výskumov včasnostredovekých hradísk*, ed. Karol Pieta, Zbigniew Robak, pp. 9–49.

Pieta, Karol – Plachá, Veronika. "Nové objavy na rímskom Devíne." *Pamiatky a múzeá* 2000, no. 3, pp. 6–9.

Pieta, Karol – Ruttkay, Alexander. "Bojná – mocenské a christianizačné centrum Nitrianskeho kniežatstva. Predbežná správa." In *Bojná. Hospodárske a politické centrum Nitrianskeho kniežatstva*, ed. Karol Pieta, Alexander Ruttkay, Matej Ruttkay, pp. 21–70.

Pieta, Karol – Ruttkay, Matej. "Germanische Siedlung aus dem 4. und 5. Jh. in Nitra – Párovské Háje und Problem der Siedlungskontinuität." In *Neue Beiträge zur Erforschung der Spätantike im mittleren Donauraum*. Brno 1997, pp. 145–164.

Pirchegger, Hans. "Karantanien und Unterpannonien zur Karolingerzeit." *Mitteilungen des österreichischen Institust für Geschichtsforschng* 33 (1912), pp. 272–319.

Plachá, Veronika – Hlavicová, Jana. "Devín v 9. storočí." In *Svätopluk 894–1994*, ed. Richard Marsina, Alexander Ruttkay, pp. 167–174.

Plachá, Veronika – Hlavicová, Jana – Keller, Igor. *Slovanský Devín*. Bratislava 1990.

Plachá, Veronika – Pieta, Karol. "Römerzeitliche Besiedlung von Bratislava – Devín." *Archeologické rozhledy* 38 (1986), no. 4, pp. 339–357.

Pleiner, Radomír. "Die Eisenverhüttung in der 'Germania Magna' zur römischen Kaiserzeit," 45. *Bericht der Römisch-Germanischen Kommission 1964*. Berlin 1965, pp. 11–86.

Pleterski, Andrej. "Die karantanischen Slawen und die Nichtslawen." In *Interaktionen der mitteleuropäischen Slawen und anderen Ethnika im 6.–10. Jahrhundert*. Nitra 1984, pp. 199–204.

Pleterski, Andrej. "Mitska stvarnost koroških knežjich kamnov." *Zgodovinski časopis* 50, 1996, no. 4 (105), pp. 481–534.

Pleterski, Andrej. "Modestuskirchen und Conversio." In *Slovenija in sosednje dežele med antiko in karolinško dobo. Začetki slovenske etnogeneze I*, ed. Rajko Bratož. Ljubljana 2000, pp. 425–476.

Plezia, Marian. *Palatyn Piotr Włostowic. Sylwetka z dziejów Śląska w XII wieku*. Łódź 1947.

Plezia, Marian. "Ungarische Beziehungen des ältesten polnischen Chronisten." *Acta Antiqua* 7 (1959), pp. 285–295.

Póczy, Klára. *Scarbantia. A római kori Sopron*. Budapest 1977.

Pohanstvo a kresťanstvo. Zborník z konferencie usporiadanej 5.–6. II. 2003 v Banskej Bystrici, ed. Rastislav Kožiak, Jaroslav Nemeš. Bratislava 2004.

Pohl, Walter. *Die Awaren. Ein Steppenvolk in Mitteleuropa 567–822 n. Chr*. München 1988.

Pohl, Walter. "Die Langobarden in Pannonien und Justinians Gotenkrieg." In *Ethnische und kulturelle Verhältnisse an der mittleren Donau vom 6. bis zum 11. Jahrhundert*, ed. Darina Bialeková, Jozef Zábojník, pp. 27–35.

Pohl, Walter. "Počátky Slovanů – několik historických poznámek." In *"Neslované" o počátcích Slovanů*, ed. Przemysław Urbańczyk, pp. 11–20.

Poláček, Lumír. "Zur Erkenntnis der höchsten Eliten des großmährischen Mikulčice. Gräber mit beschlagenen Särgen." In *Die frühmittelalterliche Elite bei den Völkern des östlichen Mitteleuropas*, ed. Pavel Kouřil, pp. 137–156.

Poláček, Lumír. "Die Kirchen von Mikulčice aus siedlungsarchäologischer Sicht." In *Frühmittelalterliche Kirchen als archäologische und historische Quelle*, ed. Lumír Poláček, Jana Maříková-Kubková, pp. 31–56.

Poláček, Lumír. "Mikulčice 60 rokov po svojom objave." *Historická revue* 25 (2014), no. 12, pp. 32–38.

Polaschek, Erich. "Noricum." *Realencyklopädie der classischen Altertumwissenschaft* XVII, 11 (1936), pp. 971–1048.

Polek, Krzysztof. "The political and military relations between the Charlemagne's Frankish Empire and Avarian Khanate." In *Central Europe in the 8th–10th Centuries*, ed. Dušan Čaplovič, Ján Doruľa, pp. 46–52.

Polek, Krzysztof. "'Państwo Samona' w nowych badaniach archeologicznych i historicznych." In *Cognitioni gestorum. Studia z dziejów średniowiecza dedykowane profesorowi Jerzemu Strzelczykowi*, ed. Darius A. Sikorski, Andrzej M. Wyrwa, pp. 41–51.

Polišenský, Josef. *Dějiny Británie*. Praha 1982.

Pomfyová, Bibiana. "Die Interpretationsmöglichkeiten der Sakraltopographie in Mikulčice." In *Frühmittelalterliche Kirchen als archäologische und historische Quelle*, ed. Lumír Poláček, Jana Maříková-Kubková, pp. 87–100.

Popov, Vasil. "Chan Krum." *Voennoistoričeski sbornik* 51 (1982), no. 1, pp. 190–200.

Pór, Antal. "Az Esztergom-várbeli Szent István első vértanuról nevezett prépostság története." In *A Szent-István-társulat tudományos és irodalmi osztályának felolvasó üléseiből*, no. 74. Budapest 1909.

Posch, Fritz. "Siedlungsgeschichte der Oststeiermark." *Mitteilungen des Österreichischen Instituts für Geschichtsforschung* 13 (1941), no. 4, pp. 385–672.

Posch, Fritz. "Die detsch-ungarische Grenzentwicklung im 10. und 11. Jahrhundert auf dem Boden der heutigen Steiermark." *Südost-Forschungen* 22 (1963), pp. 126–139.

Posch, Fritz. "Die Anfänge der Steiermark." In *Österreich im Hochmittelalter (907–1246)*, ed. der Kommission für die Geschichte Österreichs bei der Österreichischen Akademie der Wissenschaften. Wien 1991, pp. 103–128.

Posch, Fritz. Die Dudleben in der Steiermark, Blätter für Heimatkunde 66, 1992, s. 21–25.

Poucha, Pavel. *Die Geheime Geschichte der Mongolen als Geschichtsquelle und Literaturdenkmal. Ein Beitrag zu ihrer Erklärung*, ČSAV Archiv orienální, supplementa IV. Praha 1956.

Poulík, Josef. *Mikulčice. Sídlo a pevnost knížat velkomoravských*. Praha 1975.

Poulík, Josef. "Svědectví výzkumů a pramenů archeologických o Velké Moravě." In Poulík, Josef – Chropovský, Bohuslav et al. *Velká Morava a počátky československé státnosti*, pp. 9–80.

Poulík, Josef. "K otázce vzniku předvelkomoravských hradišť." *Slovenská archeologia* 36 (1988), no. 1, pp. 189–216.

Poulík, Josef. "Zur Frage der Lokalisierung der 'ineffabilis munitio' und 'urbs antiqua Rastizi' nach den Fuldauer Annalen." In *Central Europe in the 8th–10th Centuries*, ed. Dušan Čaplovič, Ján Doruľa. Bratislava 1997, pp. 121–132.

Poulík, Josef – Chropovský, Bohuslav et al. *Velká Morava a počátky československé státnosti*. Praha – Bratislava 1985.

Pozdišovský, Štefan. *Zisťovací výskum na Čerešňovom sade v Trenčíne v roku 1957*. *Informačné správy okresného múzea v Trenčíne* 4 (1958), pp. 49–56.

Pramene k dejinám osídlenia Slovenska z konca 5. až z 13. storočia I/1,2, Bratislava, hlavné mesto SSR a Západoslovenský kraj, ed. Darina Bialeková. Nitra 1989.

Pramene k dejinám osídlenia Slovenska z konca 5. až z 13. storočia II, Stredoslovenský kraj, ed. Darina Bialeková. Nitra 1992.

Pramene k dejinám osídlenia Slovenska z konca 5. až z 13. storočia III, Východné Slovensko, ed. Július Bereš. Nitra 2008.

Pray, Georgius. *Dissertationes Historico-Criticae de Sanctis Salamone rege et Emerico duce Hungariae*. Posonii 1774.

Pray, Georgius. *Specimen hierarchiae Hungaricae complectens seriem chronologicam archiepiscoporum et episcoporum Hungariae I, II*. Posonii et Cassoviae 1776, 1779.

Pražák, Richard. "K dataci a typologickému zařazení legend o nejstarších uherských světcích 11. století." In *Slovenský ľud po rozpade Veľkomoravskej ríše, Historické štúdie* 27 (1984), no. 2, pp. 93–108.

Preidel, Helmut. "Zur Frage des Aufenthaltes von Awaren in den Sudetenländern." *Südostdeutsche Forschungen* 4 (1939), pp. 395–406.

Prinjatie christianstva narodami Centraľnoj i Jugo-Vostočnoj Evropy i kreščenie Rusi, otvetstvennyj redaktor Gennadij G. Litavrin. Moskva 1998.

Procházka, Rudolf. "Charakteristika opevňovacích konstrukcí předvelkomoravských a velkomoravských hradišť." In *Pravěké a slovanské osídlení Moravy. Sborník k 80. narozeninám Josefa Poulíka*. Brno 1990, pp. 283–306.

Procházka, Vladimír. "Organisace kultu a kmenové zřízení polabsko-pobaltských Slovanů." *Vznik a počátky Slovanů* II (1958), pp. 145–168.

Procházka, Vladimír. "Sněmovnictví a soudníctví polabsko-pobaltských Slovanů." *Vznik a počátky Slovanů* III (1960), pp. 83–122.

Procházka, Vladimír. "Župa a župan." *Slavia Antiqua* 15 (1968), pp. 1–59.

Profantová, Naďa. "K nálezům ostruh z konce 7.–9. stol. v Čechách." *Mediaevalia archaeologica Bohemica 1993*, Památky archeologické – Supplementum 2 (1994), pp. 60–85.

Profantová, Naďa. *Kněžna Ludmila. Vládkyně a světice, zakladatelka dynastie*. Praha 1996.

Profantová, Naďa. "Problém importů a rekonstrukce cest v 8.–9. století." *Archaeologia historica* 23 (1998), pp. 79–88.

Profantová, Naďa. "On the archaeological evidence for Bohemian elites of the 8th–9th century." In *Central Europe in the 8th–10th Centuries*, ed. Dušan Čaplovič, Ján Doruľa, pp. 105–114.

Profantová, Naďa. "Problém interpretace staromaďarských nálezů v Čechách." In *Bitka pri Bratislave v roku 907 a jej význam pre vývoj stredného Podunajska*, ed. Tatiana Štefanovičová, Drahoslav Hulínek, pp. 149–168.

Profantová, Naďa – Profant, Martin. "Archeologie a historie aneb 'jak vykopávať dějiny?" In *Dějiny ve věku nejistot. Sborník k příležitosti 70. narozenin Dušana Třeštíka*, ed. Jan Klápště, Eva Plešková, Josef Žemlička, pp. 239–250.

Profous, Antonín. "Co znamená jméno Praha." *Věstník ministerstva vnitra ČSR* 8 (1926), pp. 325–331, 369–376.

Proměna středovýchodní Evropy raného a vrcholného středověku. Mocenské souvislosti a paralely, ed. Libor Jan. Brno 2010.

Přemyslovci. Budování českého státu, ed. Petr Sommer, Dušan Třeštík, Josef Žemlička. Praha 2009.

Přemyslovský stát kolem roku 1000. Na pamäť knížete Boleslava II. (+ 7. února 999), ed. Luboš Polanský, Jiří Sláma, Dušan Třeštík. Praha 2000.

Radnóti, Aladár. "Une église du haut moyen age a Zalavár." *Études Slaves et Roumaines* I (1948), pp. 21–30.

Rajtár, Ján. "Limes romanus a rímske opevnenia na Slovensku." *Pamiatky a múzea* 1996, no. 3, pp. 18–23.

Rajtár, Ján. "Kastel v Iži – hraničná pevnosť na Dunaji." *Pamiatky a múzea* 2000, no. 3, pp. 34–38.

Rajtár, Ján. "Stĺp Marca Aurelia a archeologické doklady o rímskych výpravách proti Kvádom." In *Stĺp Marca Aurelia a stredné Podunajsko. Zborník Slovenského národného múzea, Archeológia supplementum* 8, ed. Vladimír Turčan. Bratislava 2014, pp. 113–115.

Rapant, Daniel. "Traja synovia Svätoplukovi." *Elán* 11 (jún 1940), pp. 2–4.

Rapant, Daniel. "Pribynov kostolík v Nitre." *Elán* 12 (november–december 1941), no. 3–4, pp. 18–21.

Rapant, Daniel. "Ešte raz o Pribynovom nitrianskom kostolíku." *Elán* 13 (marec 1943), no. 7, p. 5.

Rapant, Daniel. "Drobné štúdie k slovenskému stredoveku I. Provincia Wag." *Slovenská archivistika* 9 (1974), no. 1, pp. 47–53.

Rapports du IIIe Congrès International d'Archéologie Slave Bratislava 7–14 septembre 1975. Tome 1, ed. Bohuslav Chropovský. Bratislava 1979.

Rapports du IIIe Congrès International d'Archéologie Slave Bratislava 7–14 septembre 1975. Tome 2, ed. Bohuslav Chropovský. Bratislava 1980.

Rašev, Rašo. *Prabǎlgarite prez V–VII vek.* Sofija 2005.

Rásonyi Nagy, László – Pais, Dezső. "Kál és társai." *Magyar Nyelv* 25 (1929), no. 3–4, pp. 121–128.

Ratimorská, Priska. "Jazdecký hrob z 8. storočia v Komárne." *AVANS v r. 1978.* Nitra 1980, pp. 228–229.

Ratkoš, Peter. "K otázke hranice Veľkej Moravy a Bulharska." *Historický časopis* 3 (1955), no. 2, pp. 206–218.

Ratkoš, Peter. "Podmanenie Slovenska Maďarmi." In *O počiatkoch slovenských dejín*, ed. Peter Ratkoš, pp. 141–178.

Ratkoš, Peter. "Postavenie slovenskej národnosti v stredovekom Uhorsku." In *Slováci a ich národný vývin. Sborník materiálov z V. sjazdu slovenských historikov v Banskej Bystrici.* Bratislava 1969, pp. 7–40.

Ratkoš, Peter. "Christianizácia Veľkej Moravy pred misiou Cyrila a Metoda." *Historický časopis* 19 (1971), no. 1, pp. 71–83.

Ratkoš, Peter. "Otázky vývoja slovenskej národnosti do začiatku 17. stor." *Historický časopis* 20 (1972), no. 1, pp. 19–64.

Ratkoš, Peter. "Cenný prírastok k prameňom o Veľkej Morave." *Slovenská archivistika* 11 (1976), no. 2, pp. 178–179. *Slovenská archivistika* 15 (1980), no. 1, p. 210.

Ratkoš, Peter. "Anonymove Gesta Hungarorum a ich pramenná hodnota." *Historický časopis* 31 (1983), no. 6, pp. 825–870.

Ratkoš, Peter. "Vzťahy naddunajských Slovanov a starých Maďarov v rokoch 881–1018." *Historický časopis* 35 (1987), no. 6, pp. 801–818.

Ratkoš, Peter. *Slovensko v dobe veľkomoravskej.* Košice 1988.

Regna and Gentes. The Relationship between Late Antique and Early Medieval Peoples and Kingdoms in the Transformation of the Roman World, ed. Hans-Werner Goetz, Jörg Jarnut, Walter Pohl. Leiden – Boston 2003.

Reinecke, Paul. "Die archäologische Hinterlassenschaft der Awaren." *Germania* 12 (1928), no. 3, pp. 87–98.

Rejholcová, Mária. "K problematike severnej hranice výskytu tzv. belobrdských pohrebísk." *Slovenská archeológia* 30 (1982), no. 1, pp. 199–209.

Remiášová, Marta. "Zisťovací výskum na lokalite Vyšehrad." In *Horná Nitra* 6 (1974), pp. 236–244.

Remiášová, Marta. "Archeologický výskum na hradisku Vyšehrad." *AVANS v r. 1974.* Nitra 1975, pp. 91–92.

Remiášová, Marta. "Archeologický výskum na hradisku Vyšehrad v r. 1975." *AVANS v r. 1975*. Nitra 1976, pp. 189–190.

Remiášová, Marta. "Nové slovanské lokality na hornom Ponitrí." In *Horná Nitra* 8 (1978), pp. 73–87.

Remiášová, Marta. "Pokračovanie výskumu na lokalite Vyšehrad." *AVANS v r. 1976*. Nitra 1978, pp. 205–206.

Remiášová, Marta. "Hradisko Vyšehrad." In *Horná Nitra* 9 (1980), pp. 13–29.

Remiášová, Marta. "Pokračovanie výskumu hradiska Vyšehrad." *AVANS v r. 1978*. Nitra 1980, pp. 231–233.

Repaská, Erika. *Štruktúrno-obsahová analýza stretnutia kráľa Uhorska s kráľom Poľska z Uhorsko-poľskej kroniky* (diplomová práca). Bratislava 2002.

Richter, Gustav – Kohl, Horst. *Annalen der deutschen Geschichte im Mittelalter. Von Gründung des Fränkischen Reichs bis zum Untergang der Hohenstaufen. II. Abteilung: Annalen des Fränkischen Reichs im Zeitalter der Karolinger. 1. Hälfte: Vor der Thronbesteigung Pippins bis zum Tode Karls des Grossen*. Halle 1885.

Richter, Gustav – Kohl, Horst. *Annalen der deutschen Geschichte im Mittelalter. Von Gründung des Fränkischen Reichs bis zum Untergang der Hohenstaufen. II. Abteilung: Annalen des Fränkischen Reichs im Zeitalter der Karolinger. 2. Hälfte: Von der Thronbesteigung Ludwigs der Frommen bis zum Tode Ludwigs des Kindes, Konrad I. von Franken*. Halle 1887.

Richter, Gustav – Kohl, Horst. *Annalen der deutschen Geschichte im Mittelalter. Von Gründung des Fränkischen Reichs bis zum Untergang der Hohenstaufen. III. Abteilung: Annalen des Deutschen Reichs im Zeitalter der Ottonen und Salier. 1. Band: Von der Begründung des Deutsche Reichs durch Heinrich I. bis zur Machtenfaltung des Kaisertums unter Heinrich III*. Halle 1890.

Richter, Václav. "Die Anfänge der grossmährischen Architektur." In *Magna Moravia. Spisy University J. E. Purkyně v Brně, Filosofická fakulta 102*. Praha 1965, pp. 121–360.

Rímsky kastel v Iži. Výskum 1978–2008. Zborník príspevkov k 30. výročiu archeologického výskumu, ed. Klára Kuzmová, Ján Rajtár. Nitra 2010.

Ríša Veľkomoravská. Sborník vedeckých prác, ed. Ján Stanislav. Praha – Bratislava 1933.

Ritoók, Ágnes. "The Benedictine Monastery of Zala/Zalavár (Hungary)." *Kultúrne dejiny* 5 (2014), no. 1, pp. 19–47.

Ritoók, Ágnes. "The decline of a central place in the Middle Ages." In *"Castellum, civitas, Urbs". Zentren und Eliten in frühmittelalterlichen Ostmitteleuropa. Centres and Elites in Early Medieval East-Central Europe*, ed. Orsolya Heinrich-Tamáska, Hajnalka Herold, Péter Straub, Tivadar Vida, pp. 103–111.

Ritz, Otto. "Svätý Emmerám, patrón nitrianskeho kostola." In *Ríša Veľkomoravská. Sborník vedeckých prác*, ed. Ján Stanislav, pp. 71–100.

Robak, Zbigniew. "K otázke počiatkov včasnostredovekého osídlenia Bojnej." In *Bojná 2. Nové výsledky výskumov včasnostredovekých hradísk*, ed. Karol Pieta – Zbigniew Robak, pp. 51–62.

Robak, Zbigniew. "The Origins and the Collapse of the Blatnica-Mikulčice Paradigm." *Slovenská archeológia* 65 (2017), no. 1, pp. 99–162.

Ronin, Vladimir Karlovič. "Prinjatie christianstva v Karantanskom knjažestve." In *Prinjatie christianstva narodami Centraľnoj i Jugo-Vostočnoj Evropy i kreščenie Rusi*, ed. Gennadij G. Litavrin, pp. 104–121.

Róna-Tas, András. *A honfoglaló magyar nép. Bevezetés a korai történelem ismeretébe*. Budapest 1997.

Rosner, Gyula. "Ethnische Probleme im 8.–9. Jh. Südostpannonien." In *Rapports du IIIe Congrés International d'Archéologie Slave, Bratislava 7–14 septembre 1975, Tome 1*, ed. Bohuslav Chropovský, pp. 671–676.

Ross, James Bruce. "Two Neglected Paladins of Charlemagne, Erich of Friuli and Gerold of Bavaria." *Speculum* 20 (1945), pp. 212–235.

Runciman, Steven. *Średniowieczny manicheizm*. Gdansk 1996.

Runciman, Steven. *Dzieje wypraw krzyżowych 1, 2*. Warszawa 1997.

Ruttkay, Alexander. "Výskum včasnostredovekého opevneného sídla v Ducovom, okres Trnava." *Archeologické rozhledy* 24 (1972), pp. 130–139, 217–220.

Ruttkay, Alexander. "Ducové. Veľkomoravský veľmožský dvorec a včasnostredoveké pohrebisko." In *III. medzinárodný kongres slovanskej archeológie, Bratislava 7.–14. september 1975*. Nitra 1975.

Ruttkay, Alexander. "Osídlenie Piešťan–Banky v 11.–13. storočí." *AVANS v r. 1975*. Nitra 1976, pp. 197–200.

Ruttkay, Alexander. *Výsledky výskumu v Ducovom na Kostolci v rokoch 1968–1972 a 1975*. *AVANS v r. 1975*. Nitra, 1976, pp. 190–196.

Ruttkay, Alexander. "Problematika historického vývoja na území Slovenska v 10.–13. storočí z hľadiska archeologického bádania." In Poulík, Josef – Chropovský, Bohuslav. *Velká Morava a počátky československé státnosti*, pp. 141–185.

Ruttkay, Alexander. "Počiatky stredovekej Nitry." In *Slovensko a európsky juhovýchod*, ed. Alexander Avenarius, Zuzana Ševčíková. Bratislava 1999, pp. 299–324.

Ruttkay, Alexander. "Dvorce v 9.–13. storočí." In *Slovensko vo včasnom stredoveku*, ed. Alexander Ruttkay, Matej Ruttkay, Peter Šalkovský. Nitra 2002, pp. 135–147.

Ruttkay, Alexander. "Odraz politicko-spoločenského vývoja vo veľkomoravskom vojenstve a výzbroji." In *Slovensko vo včasnom stredoveku*, ed. Alexander Ruttkay, Matej Ruttkay, Peter Šalkovský. Nitra, 2002, pp. 105–121.

Ruttkay, Alexander. "Významné archeologické lokality z včasného stredoveku v oblasti Považského Inovca." In *Bojná. Hospodárske a politické centrum Nitrianskeho kniežatstva*, ed. Karol Pieta, Alexander Ruttkay, Matej Ruttkay, pp. 191–204.

Ruttkay, Alexander T. "Nitrianska Blatnica – The Origins and the Ninth–Sixteenth-Century History of the St. George Rotunda as Reflected in the Archeological Record." In *Zwischen Byzanz und der Steppe. Archäologische und historische Studien. Festschrift für Csanád Bálint zum 70. Geburtstag*, ed. Ádám Bollók, Gergely Csiky, Tivadar Vida, pp. 663–688.

Ruttkay, Alexander T. "Výskum Rotundy sv. Juraja v lesoch nad Nitrianskou Blatnicou a osídlenia mikroregiónu v 9.–13. storočí." In *Bojná 2. Nové výsledky výskumov včasnostredovekých hradísk*, ed. Karol Pieta, Zbigniew Robak, pp. 233–249.

Ruttkay, Alexander – Slivka, Michal. "Cirkevné inštitúcie a ich úloha v sídliskovom a hospodárskom vývoji Slovenska v stredoveku." *Archaeologia historica* 10 (1985), pp. 333–356.

Ruttkay, Matej. "Mocenské centrá Nitrianskeho kniežatstva." In *Bratia, ktorí menili svet*, ed. Branislav Panis, Matej Ruttkay, Vladimír Turčan, pp. 134–137.

Ruttkay, Matej. "Využitie leteckej prospekcie a skenovania pri výskume hradísk *a ich zázemia na západnom Slovensku." In *Bojná 2. Nové výsledky výskumov včasnostredovekých hradísk*, ed. Karol Pieta, Zbigniew Robak, pp. 297–333.

Ruttkay, Matej – Bednár, Peter. "Nitra. Významné mocenské centrum Veľkej Moravy." *Historická revue* 25 (2014), no. 12, pp. 51–57.

Ruttkayová, Jaroslava. "K problematike osídlenia severozápadného pomedzia Avarského kaganátu." In *K problematike osídlenia stredodunajskej oblasti vo včasnom stredoveku*, pp. 185–217.

Ruttkayová, Jaroslava. "Nitra a okolie v rímskej dobe." In *Dávne dejiny Nitry a okolia*, ed. Matej Ruttkay, pp. 45–54.

Rybakov, Boris Alexandrovič. *Petr Borislavič. Poisk avtora "Slova o polku Igoreve"*. Moskva 1991.

Rybakov, Boris Alexandrovič. *Kijevskaja Rus i russkije knjažestva XII–XIII vv.* Moskva 1993.

Sághy, Marianne. "Aspects de la christianisation des Hongrois aux IXe–X[e] siécles." In *Early Christianity in Central and East Europe*, ed. Przemysław Urbanczyk. Warszawa 1997, pp. 53–65.

Sági, Károly. "Die spätrömische Bevölkerung der Umgebung von Keszthely." *Acta Archaeologica Academiae Scientiarum Hungaricae* 12 (1960), pp. 187–256.

Sági, Károly. "Die zweite altchristliche Basilica von Fenékpuszta." *Acta Antiqua Academiae Scientiarum Hungaricae* 9 (1961), pp. 397–460.

Sági, Károly. "A Balaton szerepe Fenékpuszta, Keszthely és Zalavár IV–IX. századi történetének alakulásában." *Antik Tanulmányok* 15 (1968), pp. 15–46.

Sági, Károly. "Das Problem der pannonischen Romanisation im Spiegel der völkerwanderunszeitlichen Geschichte von Fénékpuszta." *Acta Antiqua Academiae Scientiarum Hungaricae* 18 (1970), pp. 147–196.

Sági, Károly. "Die Spätrömische Umgebung von Keszthely." *Acta Antiqua Academiae Scientiarum Hungaricae* 24 (1976), pp. 391–396.

Salamon, Ágnes. "Über die ethnischen und historischen Beziehungen des Gräberfeldes von Környe (VI. Jh.)." *Acta Archaeologica Academiae Scientiarum Hungaricae* 21 (1969), pp. 273–297.

Salamon, Ágnes – Erdélyi, István. *Das völkerwanderungszeitliche Gräberfeld von Környe.* Budapest 1971.

Saria, Balduin. "Pettau, Entstehung und Entwicklung einer Siedlung im deutsch-slowenischen Grenzraum." *Zeitschrift des Historischen Vereines für Steiermark*, Sonderband 10 (1965), pp. 5–38.

Sasinek, František Víťazoslav. *Dejiny drievnych národov na území terajšieho Uhorska.* Skalica 1867.

Schicksalsjahr 907. Die Schlacht bei Pressburg und das frühmittelalterliche Niederösterreich. Katalog zur Ausstellung des Niederösterreichischen Landesarchivs, ed. Roman Zehetmayer. St. Pölten 2007.

Schreiber, Hermann. *Die Vandalen. Siegeszug und Untergang eines germanischen Volkes.* Bern – München 1993.

Schrot, G. "Zur Colonia Claudia Savaria und ihrer Geschichte." *Das Altertum* 11 (1965), pp. 158–173.

Schulze, Hagen. *Stát a národ v evropských dějinách.* Praha 2003.

Schulze-Dörrllam, Mechthild. "Zur Interpretation der vergoldeten Kupferblechreliefs aus dem grossmährischen Burgwall Bojná I (Slowakei)." In *Zwischen Byzanz und der Steppe. Archäologische und historische Studien. Festschrift für Csanád Bálint zum 70. Geburtstag*, ed. Ádám Bollók, Gergely Csiky, Tivadar Vida, pp. 519–536.

Schütz, Joseph. "Die Slawen der Frühzeit zwischen Aquileja und Salzburg." In *Rapports du IIIe Congrés International d'Archéologie Slave, Bratislava 7–14 septembre 1975, Tome 2*, ed. Bohuslav Chropovský, pp. 393–397.

Schwarcz, Andreas. "Pannonien im 9. Jahrhundert und die Anfänge der direkten Beziehungen zwischen dem Ostfrankischen Reich und den Bulgaren." In *Grenze und Differenz in frühen Mittelalter*, ed. Walter Pohl, Helmut Reimitz, pp. 99–104.

Sedlák, Vincent. "Historicko-spoločenský vývin Slovanov v dunajsko-karpatskej oblasti (so zreteľom na predkov Slovákov)." *Slavica Slovaca* 27 (1992), no. 2, pp. 177–186.

Sieklicki, Jan. "Quidam Priwina. Z zagadnień kszałtowania się państwowości morawskiej w IX wieku." *Slavia Occidentalis* 22 (1962), pp. 115–146.

Sieklicki, Jan. "Privina exulatus", *Pamietnik Słowiański* 17 (1967), pp. 161–165.

Sláma, Jiří. "Svatojiřské kostely na raně středověkých hradištích v Čechách." *Archeologické rozhledy* 29 (1977), no. 2, pp. 269–280.

Sláma, Jiří. "K počátkům hradské organizace v Čechách." In *Typologie raně feudálních slovanských států*, pp. 175–190.

Sláma, Jiří. *Střední Čechy v raném středověku III. Archeologie a počátky přemyslovského státu*. Praha 1988.

Sláma, Jiří. "Vratislav I. a sv. Václav." *Archelogické rozhledy* 42 (1990), pp. 296–298.

Sláma, Jiří. "Vitislav (ui utizla)." In *Seminář a jeho hosté. Sborník prací k 60. narozeninám doc. dr. Rostislava Nového*, ed. Zdeněk Hojna, Jiří Pešek, Blanka Zilynská. Praha 1992, pp. 11–19.

Sláma, Jiří. "K údajnému moravskému původu knížete Bořivoje." In *Velká Morava mezi východem a západem. Sborník příspěvků z mezinárodní vědecké konference Uherské Hradiště, Staré Město 28. 9.–1. 10. 1999*. ed. Luděk Galuška, Pavel Kouřil, Zdeněk Měřínsky. *Spisy Archeologického ústavu AV ČR, Brno* 17 (2001), pp. 349–353.

Sláma, Jiří. "K problému historické interpretace archeologických výskumů staroslovanských hradišť v Čechách," *Archeologie ve středních Čechách* 5 (2001), svazek 2, pp. 533–535.

"Slawen in Pannonien." *Studia Slavica Academiae Scientiarum Hungaricae* 1 (1955), pp. 333–361.

Slivka, Michal. "Najstarší kláštor na Slovensku." *Historická revue* 2 (1991), no. 7, pp. 4–5.

Slivka, Michal. "Doterajšie poznatky z dejín a kultúry kresťanstva na Slovensku (4.–15. stor.)." *Studia archaeologica mediaevalia* 3–4 (2000–2001), pp. 17–50.

Slivka, Michal. *Pohľady do stredovekých dejín Slovenska (Res intrincesus lectae)*. Martin 2013.

Slovensko – dejiny. Bratislava 1971.

Slovensko a európsky juhovýchod. Medzikultúrne vzťahy a kontexty. Zborník k životnému jubileu Tatiany Štefanovičovej, ed. Alexander Avenarius, Zuzana Ševčíková. Bratislava 1999.

Slovensko vo včasnom stredoveku, ed. Alexander Ruttkay, Matej Ruttkay, Peter Šalkovský. *Archaeologica Slovaca monographiae. Studia Instituti archaeologici Nitriensis Academiae scientiarum Slovacae, tomus 7*, ed. Alexander Ruttkay. Nitra 2002.

Słownik starożytności słowiańskich I. Wrocław – Warszawa – Kraków 1961.

Słupecki, Leszek Paweł. "Ślęża, Radunia, Wieżyca. Miejsca kultu pogańskiego Słowian v średniowieczu." *Kwartalnik historyczny* 99 (1992), no. 2, pp. 3–15.

Snášil, Robert. "Specializovaná řemesla z ostrovního hradiska v Uherském Hradišti a jejich přínos pro další poznání společenské diferenciace 8.–9. století." In *13. Mikulovské sympozium*. Praha 1984, pp. 152–161.

Snášil, Robert. "Grad Morava." In *Velká Morava mezi východem a západem. Sborník příspěvků z mezinárodní vědecké konference Uherské Hradiště, Staré Město 28. 9.–1. 10. 1999*, ed. Luděk Galuška, Pavel Kouřil, Zdeněk Měřínský. *Spisy Archeologického ústavu AV ČR Brno* 17 (2001), pp. 355–364.

Sokolovský, Leon. *Grad – španstvo – stolica – župa. Príspevok k terminológii dejín správy. Slovenská archivistika* 16 (1981), no. 2, pp. 94–118.

Sommer, Petr. "Duchovní svět raně středověké české laické společnosti." In *Svatý Vojtěch, Čechové a Evropa*, ed. Dušan Třeštík, Josef Žemlička. Praha 1998, pp. 133–166.

Sommer, Petr – Třeštík, Dušan – Žemlička, Josef. "Čechy a Morava." In: *Christianizace a utváření křesťanské monarchie*, ed. Nora Berendová, pp. 219–261.

Soproni, Sándor. "Der spätrömische Limes zwischen Visegrád und Esztergom," in *Limes Romanus Konferenz Nitra*, ed. Anton Točík. Bratislava 1959, pp. 131–143.

Soproni, Sándor. *Der spätrömische Limes zwischen Esztergom und Szentendre. Das Verteidigungssystem der Provinz Valeria im 4. Jahrhundert*. Budapest 1978.

Soproni, Sándor. *Die letzten Jahrzehnte des pannonischen Limes, Münchner Beiträge zur Vor- und Frühgeschichte 38*. München 1985.

Sós, Ágnes Cs. "Wykopaliska w Zalavár." *Slavia Antiqua* 7 (1960), pp. 211–305.

Sós, Ágnes Cs. "Das frühmittelalterliche Gräberfeld von Keszthely-Fenékpuszta." *Acta Archaeologica Academiae Scientiarum Hungaricae* 13 (1961), pp. 247–305.

Sós, Ágnes Cs. "Die Ausgrabungen Géza Fehérs in Zalavár." *Archaeologia Hungarica* 41 (1963), pp. 42–68.

Sós, Ágnes Cs. "Über die Fragen des frühmittelalterlichen Kirchenbaues in Mosapurc-Zalavár." *Annales Institutis Slavici* 1/2. Wiesbaden 1966, pp. 68–86.

Sós, Ágnes Cs. "Bericht über die Ergebnisse der Ausgrabungen von Zalavár-Récéskút in den Jahren 1961–1963." *Acta Archaeologica Academiae Scientiarum Hungaricae* 21 (1969), pp. 51–103.

Sós, Ágnes Cs. *Die slawische Bevölkerung Westungarns im 9. Jahrhundert. Münchner Beiträge zur Vor- und Frühgeschichte 22*. München 1973.

Sós, Ágnes Cs. "Zalavár-Kövecses Ausgrabungen 1976–78." *Magyar Nemzeti Müzeum* 1984, pp. 13–26.

Sreznevskij, Izmail Ivanovič. *Materialy dľa slovarja drevnerusskogo jazyka*. Sankt Peterburg, 1903.

Staník, Ivan – Turčan, Vladimír. "Rímska stanica v Stupave." *Pamiatky a múzeá* 2000, no. 3, pp. 22–26.

Stanislav, Ján. "Pribinovi veľmoži." *Linguistica Slovaca* I–II, 1939–1940, pp. 118–150.

Stanislav, Ján. "Bratislava – Prešporok – Pressburg – Pozsony (Pôvod stredovekej Bratislavy. Vysvetlenie mien)." In *Slovanská Bratislava I. Sborník príspevkov k dejinám hl. mesta Bratislavy*, ed. A. Fiala. Bratislava 1948, pp. 22–46.

Stanislav, Ján. *Slovenský juh v stredoveku 1–2*. Turčiansky sv. Martin 1948.

Stanislav, Ján. *Dejiny slovenského jazyka I*. Bratislava 1956.

Staňa, Čeněk. "Diskusní příspěvky z Mezinárodního kongresu slovanské archeologie, Warszava 1965." *Přehled výzkumů Archeologického ústavu ČSAV*. Brno 1966, 1967, pp. 60–64.

Staňa, Čeněk. "Velkomoravské hradiště Staré Zámky u Líšně. Stavebný vývoj." In *Monumentorum tutela – ochrana pamiatok* 8 (1972), pp. 109–171.

Staňa, Čeněk. "Pustiměřský hrad." *Archaeologia historica* 18 (1993), pp. 181–197.
Staňa, Čeněk. "Archäologische Erforschung mährischer Höhenburgwälle." In *Frühmittelalterliche Machtzentren in Mitteleuropa. Mährjährige Grabungen und ihre Auswertung*, ed. Čeněk Staňa, Lumír Poláček, pp. 267–281.
Staňa, Čeněk. "Přerov – eine Burg des Bolesław Chrobry in Mähren." In *Frühmittelalterliche Burgenbau in Mittel- und Osteuropa*, ed. Joachim Henning, Alexander Tivadar Ruttkay, pp. 49–69.
Staňa, Čeněk. "Pronikání Boleslava II. na Brněnsko ve světle archeologických objevů." In *Přemyslovský stát kolem roku 1000*, ed. Luboš Polanský, Jiří Sláma, Dušan Třeštík, pp. 197–208.
Staššíková-Štukovská, Danica. "Zu manchen spezifischen Äußerungen des Bestattungsritus im Frühmittelalter." In *Ethnische und kulturelle Verhältnisse an der mittleren Donau vom 6. bis zum 11. Jahrhundert*, ed. Darina Bialeková, Jozef Zábojník, pp. 287–304.
Staššíková-Štukovská, Danica. "Vybrané nálezy z Boroviec a Břeclavi-Pohanska k otázke interakcii staromoravských a nitrianskych Slovanov." *Sborník prací Filozofické fakulty Brněnské univerzity* M 5 (2000), pp. 97–111.
Staššíková-Štukovská, Danica. "Odraz politicko-spoločenského vývoja v 10. storočí na pohrebiskách stredného Podunajska." In *Bitka pri Bratislave v roku 907 a jej význam pre vývoj stredného Podunajska*, ed. Tatiana Štefanovičová, Drahoslav Hulínek, pp. 279–293.
Staššíková-Štukovská, Danica – Šalkovský, Peter – Béreš, Július – Hajnalová, Eva – Hušťáková, Eva – Krempaská, Zuzana – Javorský, František. "Včasnostredoveké Hradisko I Spišské Tomášovce – Smižany – 1. etapa spracovania." *Zborník Slovenského národného múzea* 100 (2006). *Archeológia* 16, pp. 187–234.
Stát, státnost a rituály přemyslovského věku. Problémy, názory, otázky, ed. Martin Wihoda, Demeter Malaťák. Brno 2006.
Steblin-Kamenskij, Michail Ivanovič. *Svět islandských ság*. Praha 1975.
Steblin-Kamenskij, Michail Ivanovič. *Mýtus a jeho svět*. Praha 1984.
Stein, Frauke. "Awarisch-merowingische Beziehungen, ein Beitrag zur absoluten Chronologie der awarenzeitlichen Funde." *Študijné zvesti Archeologického ústavu SAV* 16 (1968), pp. 233–244.
Steinhauser, Walter. "Die Ortsnamen des Burgenlandes als siedlungsgeschichtliche Quelle." *Mitteilungen des Instituts für österreichische Geschichtsforschung* 45 (1931), pp. 281–321.
Steinhübel, Ján. "Štyri veľkomoravské biskupstvá." *Slovanské štúdie* 1 (1994), s. 21–39.
Steinhübel, Ján. *Veľkomoravské územie v severovýchodnom Zadunajsku*. Bratislava 1995.
Steinhübel, Ján. "Die Großmährischen Bistümer zur Zeit Mojmirs II." *Bohemia* 37 (1996), Heft 1, pp. 2–22.

Steinhübel, Ján. "Pôvod a najstaršie dejiny Nitrianskeho kniežatstva." *Historický časopis* 46 (1998), no. 3, pp. 369–416.
Steinhübel, Ján. "Svätý Vojtech a Uhorsko." In *Svatý Vojtěch, Čechové a Evropa*, ed. Dušan Třeštík, Josef Žemlička. Praha 1998, pp. 122–130.
Steinhübel, Ján. "Die Kirchenoganisation in Neutra um die Jahrtausendwende." *Bohemia* 40 (1999), Heft 1, pp. 65–78.
Steinhübel, Ján. "Vznik Uhorska a Nitrianske kniežatstvo." *Historický časopis* 47 (1999), no. 4, pp. 569–614.
Steinhübel, Ján. "Následníci Štefana I. v bojoch o uhorský trón." *Historický časopis* 48 (2000), no. 4, pp. 585–606.
Steinhübel, Ján. "Uhorské kráľovstvo a Nitrianske kniežatstvo za vlády Štefana I." *Historický časopis* 48 (2000), no. 1, pp. 3–34.
Steinhübel, Ján. "Uhorskí králi a nitrianske kniežatá v rokoch 1046–1077." *Historický časopis* 49 (2001), no. 3, pp. 393–414.
Steinhübel, Ján. "Arpádovské Nitriansko – uhorské a slovanské," *Historický časopis* 49 (2001), no. 4, pp. 585–598.
Steinhübel, Ján. "Zánik Nitrianskeho kniežatstva." *Historický časopis* 50 (2002), no. 385–406.
Steinhübel, Ján. "Nitra a Pribinovo kniežacie sídlo." In *Nitra v slovenských dejinách*, ed. Richard Marsina, pp. 50–55.
Steinhübel, Ján. "Das arpadianische Fürstentum Neutra und die Neutraer." In *East Central Europe at the Turn of 1st and 2nd Millennia*, ed. Vincent Múcska. Acta historica Posoniensia 2. Bratislava, 2002, pp. 97–100.
Steinhübel, Ján. "Kaganát a tudunát." *Studia historica Tyrnaviensia* 3 (2002), pp. 15–30.
Steinhübel, Ján. "Nitriansko a Slovensko. Odkedy môžeme hovoriť o Slovensku a Slovákoch." In *Zborník na počesť Dariny Bialekovej*, ed. Gabriel Fusek, pp. 357–362.
Steinhübel, Ján. "Veľká Morava a bavorské pohraničie v rokoch 871–901." *Byzatinoslovaca* I (2006), pp. 144–160.
Steinhübel, Ján. "Die Herrschaft der Ungarn über die Slowakei. Slawen, Ungarn, Baiern und Sachsen in den Jahren 896–921." In *Schicksalsjahr 907. Die Schlacht bei Pressburg und das frühmittelalterliche Niederösterreich. Katalog zur Ausstellung des Niederösterreichischen Landesarchivs*, ed. Roman Zehetmayer, pp. 57–65.
Steinhübel, Ján. "Maďari, Slovania, Bavori a Sasi v rokoch 896–933." In *Bitka pri Bratislave v roku 907 a jej význam pre vývoj stredného Podunajska*. ed. Tatiana Štefanovičová, Drahoslav Hulínek, pp. 39–51.
Steinhübel, Ján. "Praha, Krakov a Olomouc – tri hrady a tri časti ríše českých Boleslavov." In *Proměna středovýchodní Evropy raného a vrcholného středověku*, ed. Libor Jan, pp. 61–96.

Steinhübel, Ján. "Hont." In Urban, Peter et al. *Zlatá kniha Hontu*. Martin, 2010, pp. 26–40.

Steinhübel, Ján. "Ad rem. Rozhovor s historikom Jánom Steinhübelom." Zhovárali sa Miroslav Lysý, Katarína Nádaská a Daniela Rošková. *Medea – Studia mediaevalia et antiqua* XIV–XV (2010–2011), pp. 153–158.

Steinhübel, Ján. "Včasnostredoveký národ a jeho dejiny." In *Karolínska kultúra a Slovensko*, ed. Vladimír Turčan, pp. 105–115.

Steinhübel, Ján. "Das Christentum zwischen Großmähren und Ungarn. Frage der Kontinuität und Diskontinuität." In *Eastern Christianity, Judaism and Islam between the Death of Muhammad and Tamerlane (632–1405)*, ed. Marián Gálik, Martin Slobodník. Bratislava 2011, pp. 73–98.

Steinhübel, Ján. *Kapitoly z najstarších českých dejín 531–1004*. Kraków 2012.

Steinhübel, Ján. "Bratislavský komitát." *Historický časopis* 60 (2012), no. 2, pp. 191–214.

Steinhübel, Ján. "Moravania, Chorváti a Bulhari v plánoch pápežskej kúrie (860–880)." In *Bratia, ktorí menili svet – Konštantín a Metod. Príspevky z konferencie*, ed. Branislav Panis, Matej Ruttkay, Vladimír Turčan. Bratislava – Nitra 2012, pp. 157–174.

Steinhübel, Ján. "Bol alebo nebol Svätopluk kráľom?" *Historický časopis* 61 (2013), no. 4, pp. 671–696.

Steinhübel, Ján. "The County of Bratislava." *Historický časopis* 61 (2013), Supplement, pp. 3–28.

Steinhübel, Ján. "Methodius' Conflict with the Bavarian bishops." In Kouřil, Pavel et al. *The Cyril and Methodius Mission and Europe. 1150 Since the Arrival of the Thessaloniki Brothers in Great Moravia*. Brno 2014, pp. 228–233.

Steinhübel, Ján. "Metodov konflikt s bavorskými biskupmi." In Kouřil, Pavel et al. *Cyrilometodějská misie a Evropa. 1150 let od příchodu soluňských bratří na Velkou Moravu*. Brno 2014, pp. 220–225.

Steinhübel, Ján. "Slovanský 'gens' a jeho stred. Kniežací hrad, pohanská svätyňa, snem a trh." *Byzantinoslovaca* V (2014), pp. 142–159.

Steinhübel, Ján. "Slovanské 'gentes' a ich vladykovia, kniežatá a kagani od sťahovania národov po Svätopluka." In Kováč, Dušan et al. *Slovenské dejiny v dejinách Európy. Vybrané kapitoly*, Bratislava 2015, pp. 262–284.

Steinhübel, Ján. "Hrady a župani na Veľkej Morave, v Chorvátsku, v českých krajinách a v Uhorsku." In Dvořáková, Daniela et al. *Stredoveké hrady na Slovensku. Život, kultúra, spoločnosť*. Bratislava 2017, pp. 29–57, 429.

Steinhübel, Ján. "Hrady a podhradia, cesty a trhy. Od kupeckého podhradia k mestu." In Štefánik, Martin et al. *Stredoveké mesto a jeho obyvatelia*, pp. 189–206, 295.

Steinhübel, Ján. "Veľká Morava a slovanský svet." *Monumentorum tutela* 28 (2018), pp. 7–14.

Straub, Péter. "Eine frühchristliche Taubenfibel mit christlichem Symbol von Keszthely-Fenékpuszta." In *Christentum in Pannonien im ersten Jahrtausend. Internationale Tagung im Balaton Museum in Keszthely vom 6. bis 9. November 2000*, ed. Robert Müller, *Zalai Muzeum* 11 (2002), pp. 103–111.

Stred Európy okolo roku 1000. Historické, umeleckohistorické a archeologické štúdie a katalóg k výstave, ed. Alfried Wieczorek, Hans-Martin Hinz. Praha 2000.

Strzelczyk, Jerzy. "Gótok Közép – Európában." *Századok* 122 (1988), no. 5–6. pp. 753–768.

Strzelczyk, Jerzy. *Wandalowie i ich afrykanskie państwo*. Warszawa 1992.

Strzelczyk, Jerzy. *Zjazd gnieznienski*. Poznań 2000.

Strzelczyk, Jerzy. *Longobardowie. Ostatni z Wielkiej wędrówki ludów V–VIII wiek*. Warszawa 2014.

Studien zum Burgwall von Mikulčice. Band 1, ed. Falko Daim, Lumír Poláček. Brno 1995.

Stuppner, Alois. "Zur Kontinuität in der Spätantike am norisch-pannonischen Limes in Niederösterreich." In *Keszthely-Fenékpuszta im Kontext spätantiker Kontinuitätsforschung zwischen Noricum und Moesia. Castellum Pannonicum Pelsonense Vol. 2*, ed. Orsolya Heinrich-Tamáska, pp. 129–156.

Sučková, Kateřina – Abušinov, Roman. *Staroslovanské hrady. Slovanská hradiště v Čechách, na Moravě a ve Slezsku*. Příbram 2005.

Svatováclavský sborník I. Na památku 1000. výročí smrti knížete Václava Svatého I. Kníže Václav Svatý a jeho doba, ed. Karel Guth, Jan Kapras, Antonín Novák, Karel Stloukal, vydal Národní výbor pro oslavu svatováclavského tisíciletí. Praha 1934.

Svatý Vojtěch, Čechové a Evropa. Mezinárodní sympozium uspořádané Českou křesťanskou akademií a Historickým ústavem Akademie věd ČR 19.–20. listopadu 1997 v Praze, ed. Dušan Třeštík, Josef Žemlička. Praha 1998.

Svätopluk 894–1994. Materiály z konferencie organizovanej Archeologickým ústavom SAV v Nitre v spolupráci so Slovenskou historickou spoločnosťou pri SAV, Nitra 3.–6. október 1994, ed. Richard Marsina, Alexander Ruttkay. Nitra 1997.

Svetoň, Ján. *Slováci v Maďarsku, Príspevky k otázke štatistickej maďarizácie*. Bratislava 1942.

Svetoň, Ján. *Slováci v európskom zahraničí*. Bratislava 1943.

Svoboda, Bedřich. "K dějinám římskeho kastelu na Leányváru u Iže, okres Komárno." *Slovenská archeológia* 10 (1962), no. 2, pp. 397–424.

Swoboda, Erich. *Carnuntum, seine Geschichte und seine Denkmäler*. Wien 1953.

Swoboda, Wincenty. "Dynastie bulgarskie." In *Słownik starożytnosci słowiańskich 1*. Wrocław – Warszawa – Kraków 1961, pp. 424–426.

Szabados, György. *Magyar államalapítások a IX–XI. században. Előtanulmány a korai magyar állam történelmének fordulópontjairól*. Szeged 2011.

Szabó, Ádám – Heinrich-Tamáska, Orsolya. "Eine spätrömische Innenbefestigung in Környe." In *Keszthely-Fenékpuszta im Kontext spätantiker Kontinuitätsforschung* zwischen Noricum und Moesia. Castellum Pannonicum Pelsonense Vol. 2, ed. Orsolya Heinrich-Tamáska, pp. 47-60.

Szádeczky-Kardoss, Samu. *Az avar történelem forrásai 557-től 806-ig.* Budapest 1998.

Szegfű, László. "A Thonuzoba monda." *A Juhász Gyula Tanárképző Főiskola Tudományos Közleményei.* Szeged 1974, pp. 275-288.

Szegfű, László. "Megjegyzések Thonuzoba históriájahoz." *Századok* 116 (1982), no. 5, pp. 1060-1078.

Szekfű, László. "Sarolta." In *Középkori kritikus kérdései,* ed. János Horváth, György Székely, pp. 239-251.

Szende, Katalin. "'Civitas opulentissima Varadiensis'. Püspöki székhely és városfejlődes a középkori Váradon." In *Nagyvárad és Bihar a korai középkorban. Tanulmányok Biharország történetéről* 1, pp. 101-128.

Szent István Emlékkönyv, ed. Jusztinián Serédi. Budapest 1938, reprint 1988.

Szent István és az államalapítás, ed. László Veszprémy. Budapest 2002.

Szentpétery, Imre. *A Borsmonostori apátság árpádkori oklevelei,* Budapest 1916.

Szentpétery, Imre. "Szent István király oklevelei." In *Szent István Emlékkönyv,* ed. Jusztinián Serédi, pp. 145-185.

Szentpétery, József. "Eines awarenzeitlichen Gürtelbeschlagtyps (rechteckige Beschläge mit durchbrochenen Doppeldreieckmustern)." In *Interaktionen der mitteleuropäischen Slawen und andere Ethnika im 6.-10. Jahrhundert,* Nitra 1984, s. 239-254.

Szentpétery, József. "Cartographia avarica. Kartographische Bemerkungen von ADAM bis Bajan." In *Ethnische und kulturelle Verhältnisse an der mittleren Donau vom 6. bis zum 11. Jahrhundert, Symposium Nitra 6. bis 10. November 1994,* ed. Darina Bialeková, Jozef Zábojník, pp. 151-165.

Szilágyi, Veronika - Szakmány, György - Wolf, Mária - Weiszburg, Tamás. "10. századi kerámiák archeometriai vizsgálata Edelény, északkelet-Magyarország." *Archeometriai Műhely* 1 (2004), no. 1, pp. 34-39.

Szöcs, Tibor. *A nádori intézmény korai története 1000-1342.* Budapest 2014.

Szőke, Béla Miklós. "Zalavár." *Zalai Gyüjtemény* 6 (1976), pp. 69-103.

Szőke, Béla Miklós. "Christliche Denkmäler in Pannonien aus der Karolingarzeit." In *Christentum in Pannonien im ersten Jahrtausend. Internationale Tagung im Balaton Museum in Keszthely vom 6. bis 9. November 2000,* ed. Robert Müller. *Zalai Múzeum* 11 (2002), pp. 247-266.

Szőke, Béla Miklós. "Archäologische Angaben zu den ethnischen Verhältnissen Pannoniens am Anfang der Karolingerzeit." In *Zborník na počesť Dariny Bialekovej,* ed. Gabriel Fusek. Nitra 2004, pp. 371-382.

Szőke, Béla Miklós. "Eine Kirchenfamilie von Mosapurc/Zalavár (Ungarn). Neue Ergebnisse zur Kirchenarchäologie in Pannonien." In *Kirchenarchäologie heute.*

Fragestellungen – Methoden – Ergebnisse, ed. Niklot Krohn und Alemannisches Institut Freiburg im Breisgau e. V. Darmstadt 2010, pp. 561–585.

Szőke, Béla Miklós. "Mosaburg/Zalavár und Pannonien in der Karolingerzeit." *Antaeus* 31–32 (2010), pp. 9–52.

Szőke, Béla Miklós. "Beziehungen zwischen Keszthely-Fenékpuszta und *Mosaburg/ Zalavár* in der Karolingerzeit." In *Keszthely-Fenékpuszta im Kontext spätantiker Kontinuitätsforschung zwischen Noricum und Moesia. Castellum Pannonicum Pelsonense Vol. 2*, ed. Orsolya Heinrich-Tamáska. Budapest – Leipzig – Kesthely – Rahden Westf. 2011, pp. 509–540.

Szőke, Béla Miklós. *The Carolingian age in the Carpathian basin*. Budapest 2014.

Szőke, Béla Miklós – Éry, Kinga – Müller, Robert – Vándor, László. *Die Karolingerzeit im unteren Zalatal. Gräberfelder und Siedlungsreste von Garabonc I–II und Zalaszabar-Dezsösziget*. Budapest 1992.

Szőnyi, Eszter – Tomka, Péter. "Pannonhalma környékének története a bencének megjelenéséig." In *Mons Sacer 996–1996. Pannonhalma 1000 éve I*, ed. Imre Takács, pp. 38–46.

Szűcs, Jenő. "'Národnosť' a 'národné povedomie' v stredoveku. K vytváraniu jednotnej terminológie." *Historický časopis* 19 (1971), no. 4, pp. 495–547.

Szűcs, Jenő. *Nation und Geschichte. Studien*. Budapest 1981.

Szűcs, Jenő. "Sárospatak kezdetei és pataki erdőuradalom." *Történelmi Szemle* 35 (1993), no. 1–2, pp. 1–57.

Šafařík, Pavel Josef. *Slowanské starožitnosti. Oddil dějepisný*. W Praze 1837.

Šalkovský, Peter. "K vývoju a štruktúre slovanského osídlenia v hornatých oblastiach Slovenska." In *IV. medzinárodný kongres slovanskej archeológie, Sofia 15.–22. 9. 1980, zborník referátov ČSSR*. Nitra 1980, pp. 166–173.

Šalkovský, Peter. *Hradisko v Detve*. Nitra 1994.

Šalkovský, Peter. "Frühmittelalterlicher Burgwall bei Detva." *Slovenská archeológia* 42 (1994), no. 1, pp. 110–142.

Šalkovský, Peter. "Dávna pevnosť na Spiši. Slovanské hradisko v Slovenskom raji." *Historická revue* 7 (1996), no. 2, pp. 2–3.

Šalkovský, Peter. "Slovanské hradisko pri Detve – príspevok k rekonštrukcii dejín stredného Slovenska v 9.–11. storočí." In *Svätopluk 894–1994*, ed. Richard Marsina, Alexander Ruttkay, pp. 213–219.

Šalkovský, Peter. *Detva. Praveké a včasnohistorické hradisko k dávnym dejinám Slovenska. Archeologické pamätníky Slovenska 10*. Nitra 2009.

Šalkovský, Peter. "Hradiská na Pohroní." In *Slovensko vo včasnom stredoveku*, ed. Alexander Ruttkay, Matej Ruttkay, Peter Šalkovský, pp. 123–133.

Šalkovský, Peter. *Stredné Slovensko vo včasnom stredoveku*. Nitra 2011.

Šalkovský, Peter. "Počiatky, rozmach, premeny a zánik hradov západných Slovanov." *Byzantinoslovaca* v (2014), pp. 97–115.

Šalkovský, Peter. "Včasnostredoveké hradiská – hrady na Slovensku, Morave a v Čechách." In *Hradiská – svedkovia dávnych čias. Zborník odborných príspevkov o hradiskách a ich obyvateľoch*, ed. Peter Jenčík, Víťazoslav Struhár, pp. 83–100.

Šalkovský, Peter. "K územným 'zoskupeniam' slovanských hradov vo včasnom stredoveku." In *Hradiská – svedkovia dávnych čias II. Zborník odborných prispevkov o hradiskách a ich obyvateľov*, zostavovatelia Peter Jenčík, Zuzana Staneková. Dolná Mariková 2019, pp. 221–235.

Šedivý, Juraj. "Chápanie etník v nemeckých kronikách a obraz starých Maďarov na prelome 1. a 2. tisícročia." *Historický časopis* 44 (1996), no. 3, pp. 353–382.

Šimák, Josef Vítěslav. *Pronikání Němců do Čech kolonisací ve 13. a 14. století*. Praha 1938.

von Šišić, Ferdinand. *Geschichte der Kroaten I*. Zagreb 1917.

Škutová, Martina. "Neskoroantické cesty v Karpatskej kotline na príklade úseku z Itineraria Burdigalense." *Byzantinoslovaca* v (2014), pp. 11–26.

Šmahel, František. *Idea národa v husitských Čechách*. Praha 2000.

Šmalcelj, Marija. "Privlaka – 'Gole njive' (opčina Vinkovci) – nekropola 7–9 stoljeca – sistematska iskopavanja." *Arheološki Pregled* 15 (1973), pp. 117–119.

Šmerda, Jan. *Denáry české a moravské. Katalóg mincí českého státu od X. století do počátku XIII. století*. Brno 1996.

Šmilauer, Vladimír. *Vodopis starého Slovenska*. Praha – Bratislava 1932.

Štefan, Ivo. "Proč zanikla Velká Morava? Nový pohled na staré téma." *Dějiny a současnost* 2011, no. 3, pp. 41–42.

Štefan, Ivo. "Etnicita v raném středověku aneb pátrání po původu kabátu, který se už nenosí." In *"Neslované" o počátcích Slovanů*, ed. Przemysław Urbańczyk, pp. 103–110.

Štefan, Ivo. "Velká Morava, počátky přemyslovských Čech a problém kulturní změny." In *Pád Velké Moravy aneb Kto byl pohřben v hrobu 153 na Pohansku u Břeclavi*, ed. Jiří Macháček, Martin Wihoda, pp. 190–231.

Štefanovičová, Tatiana. *Bratislavský hrad v 9.–12. storočí*. Bratislava 1975.

Štefanovičová, Tatiana. "K niektorým otázkam stavebnej techniky a proveniencie veľkomoravskej architektúry." *Zborník Filozofickej fakulty Univerzity Komenského – Historica* 26 (1975), pp. 25–38.

Štefanovičová, Tatiana. *Osudy starých Slovanov*. Martin 1989.

Štefanovičová, Tatiana. "K problémom slovanského osídlenia Slovenska v 8.–10. stor. vo svetle archeologických nálezov." *Slovenský národopis* 38 (1990), no. 3, pp. 402–412.

Štefanovičová, Tatiana. "Neufunde aus der Bratislavaer Burg." In *Frühmittelalterlicher Burgenbau in Mittel- und Osteuropa*, ed. Joachim Henning, Alexander Tivadar Ruttkay, pp. 427–434.

Štefanovičová, Tatiana. "Osídlenie Nitry na prelome 9.–10. storočia a príchod Maďarov." In *Nitra v slovenských dejinách*, ed. Richard Marsina, pp. 125–139.

Štefanovičová, Tatiana. "Slovensko v 10. storočí." In *Bitka pri Bratislave v roku 907 a jej význam pre vývoj stredného Podunajska*, ed. Tatiana Štefanovičová, Drahoslav Hulínek, pp. 137–148.

Štefanovičová, Tatiana. "Blatnohrad. Osudy Pribinu a Koceľa po opustení Nitrianska." *Historická revue* 25 (2014), no. 12, pp. 72–76.

Štefanovičová, Tatiana et al. *Najstaršie dejiny Bratislavy*. Bratislava 1993.

Štefanovičová, Tatiana – Hennig, Joachim – Ruttkay, Matej. "Možnosti prezentácie veľkomoravských archeologických pamiatok na Bratislavskom hrade." In *Bojná. Hospodárske a politické centrum Nitrianskeho kniežatstva*, ed. Karol Pieta, Alexander Ruttkay, Matej Ruttkay, pp. 237–246.

Štih, Peter. "Priwina: slawischer Fürst oder fränkischer Graf?" In *Ethnogenese und Überlieferung. Angewandte Methoden der Frühmittelalterforschung*, ed. Karl Brunner, Brigitte Merta. Wien – München, 1994, pp. 209–222.

Štih, Peter. "Carniola, patria Sclavorum." *Österreichische Osthefte* 37 (1995), Heft 4, pp. 845–861.

Štih, Peter. "Salzburg, Ptuj in nastanek štajersko-madžarske meje v današnji Sloveniji." *Zgodovinski časopis* 50 (1996), no. 4 (105), pp. 535–544.

Štih, Peter. "Die Ostgrenze Italiens im Frühmittelalter." In *Grenze und Differenz im früher Mittelalter*, ed. Walter Pohl, Helmut Reimitz, pp. 19–37.

Štih, Peter. "Karantanci – zgodnjesrednjeveško ljudstvo med Vzhodom in Zahodom." *Zgodovinski časopis* 61 (2007) (135), no 1–2, pp. 47–58.

Štih, Peter. *The Middle Ages between the Eastern Alps and the Northern Adriatic. Select Papers on Slovene Historiography and Medieval History*. East Central and Eastern Europe in the Middle Ages 450–1450. General Editor Florin Curta. Leiden – Boston 2010.

Štrbáková, Ľubica. "Svätopluk Lotrinský († 900), krstný syn Svätopluka I., ako postava historická a hagiografická." In Homza, Martin et al. *Svätopluk v európskom písomníctve*, pp. 177–229.

Šušarin, Vladimir P. "Russko-vengerskije otnošenija v IX v." In *Meždunarodnyje svjazi Rosii do XVII v*. Moskva 1961, pp. 131–179.

Tabula Imperii Romani. Castra Regina, Vindobona, Carnuntum, M–33. ed. Pavel Oliva, Jan Burian, Zdenka Nemeškalová – Jiroudková, Jaroslav Tejral. Praha 1986.

Tajkov, Peter. *Sakrálna architektúra 11.–13. storočia na juhovýchodnom Slovensku*. Košice 2012.

Tejral, Jaroslav. "K langobardskému odkazu v archeologických pramenech na území Československa." *Slovenská archeológia* 23 (1975), no. 2, pp. 379–446.

Tejral, Jaroslav. "K otázce doby stěhování národů a počátků slovanského osídlení na Moravě." In *IV. medzinárodný kongres slovanskej archeológie, Sofia 15.–22. septembra 1980, zborník referátov ČSSR*. Nitra 1980, pp. 177–182.

Tejral, Jaroslav. *Morava na sklonku antiky*. Praha 1982.

Tejral, Jaroslav. "Probleme der Völkerwanderungszeit nördlich der mittleren Donau." In *Germanen, Hunen und Awaren. Schätze der Völkerwanderungszeit*, ed. Wilfried Menghin, Tobias Springer, Egon Wamers, pp. 351–367.

Tejral, Jaroslav. "Spätswebische Siedlungsfunde." In *Germanen, Hunen und Awaren. Schätze der Völkerwanderungszeit*, ed. Wilfried Menghin, Tobias Springer, Egon Wamers, pp. 368–369.

The Coronation Mantle of the Hungarian Kings, ed. István Bardoly. Budapest 2005.

The Oxford English dictionary being a corrected reissue with an introduction, supplement, and bibliography of a new English dictionary on historical principles founded mainly on the materials collected by The Philological Society, volume V. Oxford 1933, reprinted 1966.

Thomas, Edit Baja. "Die Romanität Pannoniens im 5. und 6. Jahrhundert." In *Germanen, Hunen und Awaren. Schätze der Völkerwanderungszeit*, ed. Wilfried Menghin, Tobias Springer, Egon Wamers, pp. 284–294.

Thomas, Edit Baja. *Römische Villen in Pannonien. Beiträge zur pannonischen Siedlungsgeschichte*. Budapest 1964.

Thoroczkay, Gábor. "Szent István pannonhalmi oklevelének historiográfiája." In *Mons Sacer 996–1996. Pannonhalma 1000 éve I*, ed. Imre Takács, pp. 90–109.

Thoroczkay, Gábor. "Az első magyarországi érsekek kérdéséhez." In *Tanulmányok a középkori magyar történelemről. Az I. Medievisztikai PhD-konferencia (Szeged, 1999. július 2.) előadásai*, ed. Sárolta Hommonai, Ferenc Piti, Ildikó Tóth. Szeged 1999, pp. 129–142.

Tibenský, Ján. "Funkcia cyrilometodskej a veľkomoravskej tradície v ideológii slovenskej národnosti." *Historický časopis* 40, 1992, no. 5, pp. 579–594.

Točík, Anton. "Slovania na strednom Dunaji v 5.–8. stor." In *O počiatkoch slovenských dejín*, ed. Peter Ratkoš, pp. 20–35.

Točík, Anton. *Slawisch-awarisches Gräberfeld in Holiare*. Bratislava 1968.

Točík, Anton. *Altmagyarische Gräberfelder in der Südwestslowakei*. Bratislava 1968.

Točík, Anton – Budinský-Krička, Vojtech. "Z archeologických zbierok na Slovensku." *Zborník Slovenského národného múzea* 81 (1987), *História* 27, pp. 63–93.

Tóth, Endre. "Zu den historischen Problemen der Stadt Savaria und ihrer Umgebung zwischen dem 4. bis 9. Jahrhundert." *Folia Archaeologica* 27 (1976), pp. 89–120.

Tóth, Endre. "Pannonia és Noricum közös határának a kialakulása." *Antik tanulmányok* 24 (1977), pp. 192–200.

Tóth, Endre. "Die karolingische Burg von Sabaria-Szombathely." *Folia Archaeologica* 29 (1978), pp. 151–182.

Tóth, Endre. "Megjegyzések Pannonia provincia kialakulásának kérdéséhez." *Archaeologiai Értesítő* 108 (1981), pp. 13–33.

Tóth, Endre. "Dacia római tartomány." In *Erdély története I. A kezdetektől 1606-ig*, ed. László Makkai, András Mócsy, pp. 46–106.

Tóth, Endre. "István és Gizella miseruhája." *Századok* 131 (1997), no. 1, pp. 3–74.

Tóth, Endre. "Szent Adorján és Zalavár." *Századok* 133 (1999), no. 1, pp. 3–40.

Tóth, Sándor. "Kabarok (Kavarok) a 9. századi magyar törzsszövetségben." *Századok* 118 (1984), no. 1, pp. 92–113.

Tóth, Sándor. "Levente és András." *Acta Universitatis Szegediensis de Attila József nominatae. Acta Historica* 82 (1985), pp. 31–36.

Tóth, Sándor. "A magyar fejedelmi méltóság öröklödése." *Acta Universitatis Szegediensis de Attila József nominatae. Acta Historica* 83 (1986), pp. 3–9.

Tóth, Sándor. "Kabarok és fekete magyarok." *Acta Universitatis Szegediensis de Attila József nominatae. Acta Historica* 84 (1987), pp. 23–29.

Tóth, Sándor László. "Az etelközi magyar-besenyő háború." *Századok* 122 (1988), no. 4, pp. 541–576.

Tóth, Sándor László. "A kavarok (kabarok) katonai és politikai szerepe." *Hadtörténelmi Közlemények* 126 (2013), no. 2, pp. 315–352.

Tóthová, Štefánia. "Výsledky archeologického výskumu na Beckovskom hrade." In *Archaeologia historica* 3 (1978), pp. 393–401.

Török, Sándor. "Mi volt a neve a három kabar törzsnek?" *Századok* 116 (1982), no. 5, pp. 986–1059.

Tősér, Márton. "Arab-bizánci harcok a IX. század második felében. A porsoni ütközet, 863. szeptember 3." *Hadtörténelmi Közlemények* 116 (2003), no. 2, pp. 505–534.

Trawkowski, Stanisław. "Początki kościóła w Polsce za panowania Mieszka I." In *Polska Mieszka I*. Poznań 1993, pp. 51–72.

Trugly, Alexander. "Pohrebisko z doby Avarskej ríše v Komárne – Robotníckej štvrti." *Spravodaj Oblastného podunajského múzea v Komárne* 2 (1982), pp. 5–48.

Trugly, Alexander. "Gräberfeld aus der Zeit des Awarischen Reiches bei der Schiffswert in Komárno." *Slovenská archeológia* 35 (1987), no. 2, pp. 251–344.

Trugly, Alexander. "Gräberfeld aus der Zeit des Awarischen Reiches bei der Schiffswert in Komárno II (1987–1989)." *Slovenská archeológia* 41 (1993), no. 2, pp. 191–237.

Třeštík, Dušan. *Kosmova kronika. Studie k počátkům českého dějepisectví a politického myšlení*. Praha 1968.

Třeštík, Dušan. "'Trh Moravanů' – ústřední trh staré Moravy." *Československý časopis historický* 21 (1973), no. 6, pp. 869–894.

BIBLIOGRAPHY

Třeštík, Dušan. "Bořivoj a Svatopluk – vznik českého státu a Velká Morava." In Poulík, Josef – Chropovský, Bohuslav et al. *Velká Morava a počátky československé státnosti*, pp. 273–301.

Třeštík, Dušan. "Pád Velké Moravy." In *Typologie raně feudálních slovanských států. Sborník příspěvků z mezinárodní konference k tématu "Vznik a rozvoj slovanských raně feudálních států a národností ve střední a jihovýchodní Evropě", konané ve dnech 18.–20. listopadu 1986 v Praze*, pp. 27–73.

Třeštík, Dušan. "Objevy ve Znojmě." *Československý časopis historický* 35 (1987), no. 4, pp. 548–576.

Třeštík, Dušan. "Mír a dobrý rok. Česká státní ideologie mezi křesťanstvím a pohanstvím." *Folia historica Bohemica* 12 (1988), pp. 23–45.

Třeštík, Dušan. "Vozniknovenie slavjanskich gosudarstv v srednem Podunave." In *Rannefeodaľnye gosudarstva i narodnosti (južnye i zapadnye slavjane VI–XII vv.)*. Moskva 1991, pp. 69–86.

Třeštík, Dušan. "Kdy zanikla Velká Morava?" *Studia mediaevalia Pragensia* 2 (1991), pp. 9–27.

Třeštík, Dušan. "Václav a Berengár. Politické pozadí postřižin sv. Václava roku 915." *Český časopis historický* 89 (1992), no. 5–6, pp. 641–661.

Třeštík, Dušan. "Křest českých knížat roku 845 a christianizace Slovanů." *Český časopis historický* 92 (1994), no. 3, pp. 423–459.

Třeštík, Dušan. "Moderne Nation, hochmittelalterliche politische Nation, frühmittelalterliche gens und unsere genetische Software. Der Fall Mitteleuropa." In *Mittelalterliche nationes – neuzeitliche Nationen. Probleme der Nationenbildung in Europa*, ed. Almut Bues, Rex Rexheuser, pp. 161–181.

Třeštík, Dušan. "Příchod prvních Slovanů do českých zemí v letech 510–530." *Český časopis historický* 94 (1996), no. 2, pp. 245–280.

Třeštík, Dušan. *Počátky Přemyslovců. Vstup Čechů do dějin (530–935)*. Praha 1997.

Třeštík, Dušan. "Sv. Vojtěch a formování střední Evropy." In *Svatý Vojtěch, Čechové a Evropa*, ed. Dušan Třeštík, Josef Žemlička, pp. 81–108.

Třeštík, Dušan. "Großmähren, Passau und die Ungarn um das Jahr 900. Zu den neuen Zweifeln an der Authentizität des Briefes der bayerischen Bischöfe an Papst Johann IX. aus dem Jahr 900." *Byzantinoslavica* 59 (1998), pp. 137–160.

Třeštík, Dušan. "Místo Velké Moravy v dějinách. Ke stavu a potřebám bádání o Velké Moravě." *Český časopis historický* 97 (1999), no. 4, pp. 689–727.

Třeštík, Dušan. *Mysliti dějiny*. Praha – Litomyšl 1999.

Třeštík, Dušan. "Vznik Velké Moravy. Moravané, Čechové a střední Evropa v letech 791–871." Praha 2001.

Třeštík, Dušan. *Mýty kmene Čechů (7.–10. století). Tři studie ke "starým pověstem českým"*. Praha 2003.

Třeštík, Dušan. "Počátky přemyslovské státnosti mezi křesťanstvím a pohanstvím." In *Stát, státnost a rituály přemyslovského věku. Problémy, názory, otázky*, ed. Martin Wihoda, Demeter Malaťák, pp. 25–46.

Třeštík, Dušan. "Od příchodu Slovanů k 'říši' českých Boleslavů." In *Přemyslovci*, ed. Petr Sommer, Dušan Třeštík, Josef Žemlička, pp. 61–63, 69–73, 77–96.

Třeštík, Dušan. "Gens Bohemanorum – kmen Čechů." In *Přemyslovci*, ed. Petr Sommer, Dušan Třeštík, Josef Žemlička, pp. 137–139, 144–148.

Třeštík, Dušan. "Přemyslovský mýtus a první čeští světci." In *Přemyslovci*, ed. Petr Sommer, Dušan Třeštík, Josef Žemlička, pp. 149–153, 157–161.

Třeštík, Dušan. "Idea státu a národa." In *Přemyslovci*, ed. Petr Sommer, Dušan Třeštík, Josef Žemlička, pp. 272–277, 281–286.

Třeštík, Dušan. "Počátky českého politického myšlení." In *Dějiny politického myšlení II/1. Politické myšlení raného křesťanství a středověku*, ed. Ivan Müller, Vilém Herold, Aleš Havlíček, pp. 404–446.

Turčan, Vladimír. "K otázke najstaršieho slovanského osídlenia juhozápadného Slovenska a vzťahu Slovanov a Avarov." *Zborník Slovenského národného múzea* 78 (1984), *História* 24, pp. 131–146.

Turčan, Vladimír. "Ďalšie slovanské nálezy zo Smoleníc-Molpíra." *Zborník Slovenského národného múzea* 88 (1994), *Archeológia* 4, pp. 75–84.

Turčan, Vladimír. "Nové nálezy ostrôh zo Smoleníc-Molpíra." *Zborník Slovenského národného múzea* 89 (1995), *Archeológia* 5, pp. 77–82.

Turčan, Vladimír. "Príspevok k poznaniu včasnostredovekého osídlenia Sv. Jura pri Bratislave." *Zborník Slovenského národného múzea* 94 (2000), *Archeológia* 10, pp. 123–136.

Turčan, Vladimír. "Rímske pamiatky na Slovensku." Bratislava 2000.

Turčan, Vladimír. "Old-Slavonic Sanctuaries in Czechia and Slovakia." *Studia mythologica slavica* 4 (2001), pp. 97–116.

Turčan, Vladimír. "Výšinné polohy v germánskej vojenskej stratégii na strednom Podunajsku v 1.–4. storočí." *Zborník Slovenského národného múzea* 95 (2001), *Archeológia* 11, pp. 105–110.

Turčan, Vladimír. "Nové včasnostredoveké nálezy z Oravy." In *Zborník na počesť Dariny Bialekovej*, ed. Gabriel Fusek, pp. 427–431.

Turčan, Vladimír. "Prvé staromaďarské nálezy z okolia Bratislavy." In *Bitka pri Bratislave v roku 907 a jej význam pre vývoj stredného Podunajska*, zostavili Tatiana Štefanovičová, Drahoslav Hulínek, pp. 305–311.

Turčan, Vladimír. "Depoty z Bojnej v zbierkach Archeologického múzea SNM." In *Bojná. Hospodárske a politické centrum Nitrianskeho kniežatstva*, ed. Karol Pieta, Alexander Ruttkay, Matej Ruttkay, pp. 159–166.

Turčan, Vladimír. "Severný Jadran – jeden z možných inšpiračných zdrojov umeleckého remesla stredodunajských Slovanov." In *Karolínska kultúra a Slovensko*, ed. Vladimír Turčan, pp. 123–128.

Turčan, Vladimír. "Depoty z Bojnej a včasnostredoveké hromadné nálezy železných predmetov uložené v zbierkach SNM – Archeologického múzea." *Zborník Slovenského národného múzea, archeológia*, supplementum 6. Bratislava 2012.

Turčan, Vladimír. "Pôvodné slovanské náboženstvo a kristianizácia stredodunajských Slovanov." In *Bratia, ktorí menili svet – Konštantín a Metod*, ed. Branislav Panis, Matej Ruttkay, Vladimír Turčan, pp. 71–78.

Turčan, Vladimír. "K geologickému a historickému pozadiu uloženia depotov v Bojnej." In *Bojná 2. Nové výsledky výskumov včasnostredovekých hradísk*, ed. Karol Pieta, Zbigniew Robak, pp. 109–113.

Turčan, Vladimír et al. *Archeologické pamiatky*. Bratislava 2009.

Turčan, Vladimír et al. *Veľkomoravské hradiská*. Bratislava 2012.

Turek, Rudolf. *Čechy na úsvitě dějin*. Praha 1963.

Turek, Rudolf. *Čechy v raném středověku*. Praha 1982.

Typen der Ethnogenese unter besonderer Berücksichtigung der Bayern, Teil 1. Berichte des Symposions der Kommission für Frühmittelalterforschung, 27. bis 30. Oktober 1986, Stift Zwettl, Niederösterreich, ed. Herwig Wolfram, Walter Pohl. Wien 1990.

Typologie raně feudálních slovanských států. Sborník příspěvků z mezinárodní konference k tématu "Vznik a rozvoj slovanských raně feudálních států a národností ve střední a jihovýchodní Evropě", konané ve dnech 18.–20. listopadu 1986 v Praze, Ústav československých a světových dějin ČSAV. Praha 1987.

Tyszkiewicz, Lech A. *Słowianie i Awarowie. Organizacja plemienna Słowian*. Wrocław 2009.

Ubl, Hannsjörg. *Der spätrömische Burgus von Zeiselmauer, Grabung und Restaurierung*. Studien zu den Militärgrenzen Roms II. Köln – Bonn 1977, pp. 251–262.

Uhrman, Iván. "Iulus rex. A gyula-dinasztia, a kabarok és Szent István Intelmei." *Hadtörténelmi Közlemények* 116 (2003), no. 2, pp. 267–344.

Uličný, Ferdinand. *Dejiny Slovenska v 11. až 13. storočí*. Bratislava 2013.

Urbańczyk, Przemysław. *Gordický uzel slovanství v Polsku*. In *"Neslované" o počátcích Slovanů*, ed. Przemysław Urbańczyk, pp. 89–102.

Urbańczyk, Przemysław – Rosik, Stanisław. "Polsko." In *Christianizace a utváření křesťanské monarchie*, ed. Nora Berendová, pp. 262–313.

Uzsoki, András. "A veszprémi püspökség szent Mihály patrocinium." In *Egyházak a változó világban. A nemzetközi egyháztörténeti konferencia előadásai, Esztergom 1991 május 29–31*, ed. István Bárdos, Margit Beke. Tatabánya 1992, pp. 87–89.

Vácz, Elemér. "Nógrádvára történetéhez." In *Emlékkönyv Domanovszky Sándor születése hatvanadik fordulójának ünnepére, 1937 május 27*. Budapest 1937, pp. 590–603.

Váczy, Péter. "A Vazul-hagyomány középkori kútföinkben." *Levéltári Közlemények* 18-19 (1940-1941), pp. 304-338.

Váczy, Péter. "Karolingische Kunst in Pannonien: Der Cundpald-Kelch. Évolution générale et dévelopements régionaux en l'histoire de l'art." *Actes du XXIIe Congrés international de l'histoire de l'art, Tome II*. Budapest 1972, pp. 303-335.

Váczy, Péter. *A magyar történelem korai századaiból*. Budapest 1994.

Vaillant, André - Lascaris, Michel. "L'date de l'conversion des Bulgares." *Revue des études* 13 (1933), pp. 5-15.

de Vajay, Szabolcs. "Großfürst Geysa von Ungarn. Familie und Verwandschaft." *Südostforschungen* 21. München 1962, pp. 45-101.

de Vajay, Szabolcs. *Der Eintritt des ungarischen Stämmebundes in die europäische Geschichte (862-933)*, Studia Hungarica 4, Mainz 1968.

de Vajay, Szabolcs. "Byzantinische Prinzessinen in Ungarn." *Ungarische Jahrbuch* 10 (1979), pp. 15-28.

Vaklinov, S. *Formirane na starobălgarskata kultura. VI-IX vek*. Sofija 1977.

Valachovič, Pavol. "Hospodárske a sociálne problémy miest v Panónii v 4.-5. storočí." *Historický časopis* 30 (1982), no. 3, pp. 376-394.

Vančo, Martin. "Figurálne motívy plakiet z Bojnej v kontexte veľkomoravského umenia." *Studia mediaevalia Pragensia* 9 (2010), pp. 111-152.

Vaněček, Václav. "Souvislost Velké Moravy se slovanským svazem Sámovým? (Ke vzniku státu na Moravě)." *Právněhistorické studie* 9 (1963), pp. 211-227.

Váňa, Zdeněk. "Maďaři a Slované ve světle archeologických nálezů X.-XII. století." *Slovenská archeológia* 2 (1954), no. 1, pp. 51-104.

Várady, László. *Das letzte Jahrhundert Pannoniens (376-476)*. Budapest 1969.

Varsik, Branislav. "Starý a Nový Hrad pri Hornáde v Abaujskej stolici." *Historický sborník SAVU* 9 (1951), pp. 54-76.

Varsik, Branislav. "Veľká stolica Nový hrad (novum Castrum, Újvár) a vznik Abovskej, Hevešskej a Šarišskej stolice." *Historické štúdie* 7 (1961), pp. 161-187.

Varsik, Branislav. *Osídlenie Košickej kotliny I*. Bratislava 1964.

Varsik, Branislav. "K sociálnym a národnostným bojom v mestách na Slovensku v stredoveku." In *Slováci a ich národný vývin*. Bratislava 1969, pp. 41-72.

Varsik, Branislav. *Zo slovenského stredoveku. Výber historických štúdií a článkov z rokov 1946-1968*. Bratislava 1972.

Varsik, Branislav. "Kde ležal Castrum Salis (Soľný hrad)?" In Varsik, Branislav. *Zo slovenského stredoveku*, pp. 65-86.

Varsik, Branislav. "K vzniku dnešného slovenského názvu Nitra." In Varsik, Branislav. *Zo slovenského stredoveku*, pp. 147-155.

Varsik, Branislav. "K vzniku a pôvodu názvu rieky Tople." In Varsik, Branislav. *Zo slovenského stredoveku*, pp. 175-196.

Varsik, Branislav. "K sociálnym a národnostným bojom v mestách na Slovensku v stredoveku." In Varsik, Branislav. *Zo slovenského stredoveku*, pp. 301–343.

Varsik, Branislav. *Z osídlenia západného a stredného Slovenska v stredoveku*. Bratislava 1984.

Varsik, Branislav. *Kontinuita medzi veľkomoravskými Slovienmi a stredovekými severouhorskými Slovanmi (Slovákmi). Výber štúdii a článkov z rokov 1969–1992*. Bratislava 1994.

Varsik, Branislav. O vzniku a rozvoji slovenskej národnosti v stredoveku. In Varsik, Branislav. *Kontinuita medzi veľkomoravskými Slovienmi a stredovekými severouhorskými Slovanmi (Slovákmi)*, pp. 11–46.

Varsik, Branislav. "Vznik názvu Slovák vo svetle historických dokladov." In Varsik, Branislav. *Kontinuita medzi veľkomoravskými Slovienmi a stredovekými severouhorskými Slovanmi (Slovákmi)*. pp. 271–279.

Varsik, Vladimír. "Život v rímskom štýle. Germánske panské sídlo v Cíferi-Páci." *Historická revue* 26 (2015), no. 6, pp. 48–53.

Vavák, Július. "Včasnostredoveké hrady na juhozápade Malých Karpát. Ich vznik, význam a úloha. Hradiská – svedkovia dávnych čias." *Zborník odborných príspevkov o hradiskách a ich obyvateľoch*, ed. Peter Jenčík, Víťazoslav Struhár, pp. 101–126.

Vavák, Július. *Pevnosť v Malých Karpatoch. Vznik, význam a úloha výšinného centra vo Svätom Jure*. Pezinok 2019.

Vavruš, Ján. "Hradisko a hrad v Trenčíne, jeho význam a postavenie v dejinnom vývoji." In *Slovensko a európsky juhovýchod. Medzikultúrne vzťahy a kontexty. Zborník k životnému jubileu Tatiany Štefanovičovej*, ed. Alexander Avenarius, Zuzana Ševčíková. Bratislava 1999, pp. 385–395.

Vavruš, Ján. *Nové pohľady na interpretáciu pohrebísk 10. storočia z juhozápadného Slovenska (dizertačná práca)*. Bratislava 2000.

Vavruš, Ján. "Prvá maďarská generácia v archeologických a písomných prameňoch." In *Bitka pri Bratislave v roku 907 a jej význam pre vývoj stredného Podunajska*, ed. Tatiana Štefanovičová, Drahoslav Hulínek, pp. 183–193.

Vavřínek, Vladimír. "Die Christianisation und Kirchenorganisation Grossmährens." *Historica* 7 (1963), pp. 5–56.

Vavřínek, Vladimír. *Cyril a Metoděj mezi Konstantinopolí a Římem*. Praha 2013.

Velká Morava mezi východem a západem. Sborník příspěvků z mezinárodní vědecké konference Uherské Hradiště, Staré Město 28. 9.–1. 10. 1999, ed. Luděk Galuška, Pavel Kouřil, Zdeněk Měřínský. *Spisy Archeologického ústavu AV ČR Brno* 17 (2001).

Verešová, Nora. "Sklavínia v historických prameňoch zo 6.–14. storočia. Prehľad koncepcií." *Historický zborník* 18 (2008), no. 1, pp. 124–143.

Verešová, Nora. "Povesť vremennych let a jej koncepcia Slovienskoj zemli." *Historia nova* 2 (2011), no. 1, pp. 12–20.

Veselovskij, Alexander Nikolajevič. *Historická poetika*. Bratislava 1992.
Veselý, Rudolf. "Politické myšlení v muslimských zemích." In *Dějiny politického myšlení II/1. Politické myšlení raného křesťanství a středověku*, ed. Ivan Müller, Vilém Herold, Aleš Havlíček, pp. 225–272.
Veszprémy, László. "Szent István felövezéséről." *Hadtörténelmi Közlemények* 102 (1989), no. 1, s. 3–13.
Veszprémy, László. "Hadszervezet Szent István korában." In *Államalapítás, társadalom, müvelödés*, ed. Kristó Gyula. Budapest 2001, pp. 31–41.
Veszprémy, László. "Mint békák a mocsárban. Püspökök gyűlése a Duna mellett 796-ban." *Aetas* 19 (2004), no. 2, pp. 53–71.
Veszprémy, László. "Eine wechselvolle Rezeptionsgeschichte. Die Pressburger Schlacht aus Sicht der Ungarn." In *Schicksalsjahr 907*, ed. Roman Zehetmayer, ed. 99–102.
Veszprémy, László. "Aventinus híradása a magyarok 907. évi győzelméről. Csata Pozsonynál." *Történelmi Szemle* 49 (2007), no. 1, pp. 1–17.
Veszprémy, László. "Boj pri Bratislave (907) v maďarskej historiografii." In *Bitka pri Bratislave v roku 907 a jej význam pre vývoj stredného Podunajska*, ed. Tatiana Štefanovičová, Drahoslav Hulínek, pp. 33–37.
Vida, Tivadar. "Heidnische und christliche Elemente der awarenzeitlichen Glaubenswelt, Amulette in der Awarenzeit." In *Christentum in Pannonien im ersten Jahrtausend. Internationale Tagung im Balaton Museum in Keszthely vom 6. bis 9. November 2000*, ed. Robert Müller. *Zalai Múzeum* 11 (2002), pp. 179–209.
Vinski–Gasparini, Ksenija – Ercegović, Slavenka. "Ranosrednjovjekovno groblje u Brodskom Drenovcu." *Vjesnik Arheološkog muzeja u Zagrebu* 3 (1958), no. 1, pp. 129–161.
Vinski, Zdenko. "O postojanju radionica nekita starohrvatskog doba u Sisku." *Vjesnik Arheološkog muzeja u Zagrebu* 3 (1970), no. 4, pp. 45–92.
Vlček, Emanuel. "Anthropologický materiál z období stěhování národů na Slovensku." *Slovenská archeológia* 5 (1957), no. 2, pp. 402–434.
Vlček, Emanuel. *Nejstarší Přemyslovci. Atlas kosterných pozůstatků prvních sedmi historicky známých generací Přemyslovců s podrobným komentářem a historickými poznámkami*. Praha 1997.
Vondráková, Mária. "Feststellungsmöglichkeiten der Antropologie über die Ethnizität der Populationen aus Gräberfeldern der sog. Bijelo-Brdo-Kultur." In *Ethnische und kulturelle Verhältnisse an der mittleren Donau vom 6. bis zum 11. Jahrhundert*, ed. Darina Bialeková, Josef Zábojník, pp. 409–420.
Voretzsch, Karl. *Einführung in das Studium der altfranzösischen Literatur im Anschluss an die Einführung in das Studium der altfranzösischen Sprache*. Halle 1925.
Vörös, Gabriella. "Spätsarmatische Siedlungen und Gräberfelder in der Tiefebene Südostungarns." In *Germanen, Hunen und Awaren. Schätze der Völkerwanderungszeit*, ed. Wilfried Menghin, Tobias Springer, Egon Wamers, pp. 133–148.

Vrtel, Andrej – Lesák, Branislav – Kováč, Jozef – Staník, Ivan. "Neskorolaténske osídlenie na nádvorí paláca Bratislavského hradu." In *Bratislavský hrad, dejiny, výskum a obnova*, ed. Margaréta Musilová, Peter Barta, Angelika Herucová, pp. 44–71.

Vykypěl, Bohumil. *Studie k šlechtickým titulům v germánskych, slovanských a baltských jazycích*. Praha 2011.

Vyvíjalová, Mária. "Bitka pri Bratislave roku 907. Príspevok ku kritickému prehodnoteniu prameňov." *Študijné zvesti Archeologického ústavu Slovenskej akadémie vied* 21 (1985), pp. 226–234.

Významné slovanské náleziská na Slovensku, ed. Bohuslav Chropovský. Bratislava 1978.

Wasilewski, Tadeusz. "Data chrztu Bulgarii." *Pamiętnik Słowiański* 18 (1968), pp. 115–129.

Wasilewski, Tadeusz. "Studia nad dziejami panowania cesarza Michala III. (842–867). Cz. II: Przewrót państwowy w 851/852 r. i ofenzywa w Azji Mniejszej przeciwko Arabom." *Przegląd Historyczny* 61 (1970), no. 4, pp. 369–373.

Wasilewski, Tadeusz. *Byzancium i Słowianie w IX wieku. Studium z dziejów stosunków politycznych i kulturalnych*. Warszawa, 1972.

Wasilewski, Tadeusz. "L'église de la Bulgarie danubienne en 863–1082." In *Early Christianity in Central and East Europe*, ed. Przemysław Urbanczyk. Warsawa, 1997, pp. 47–52.

Wasilewski, Tadeusz. *Bălgarija i Vizantija IX–XV vek*. Sofija 1997.

Weingart, Miloš. "První česko-církevněslovanská legenda o svatém Václavu." In *Svatováclavský sborník I. Kníže Václav Svatý a jeho doba*, ed. Karel Guth, Jan Kapras, Antonín Novák, Karel Stloukal, pp. 863–972.

Weingart, Miloš. "Pribina, Koceľ a Nitra v zrkadle prameňov doby cyrilometodejskej." In *Ríša Veľkomoravská. Sborník vedeckých prác*, ed. Ján Stanislav, pp. 319–353.

Weisz, Boglárka. "A 15. századi váradi vámper Árpad-kori gyökerei." In *Nagyvárad és Bihar a korai középkorban. Tanulmányok Biharország történetéről 1*, pp. 147–165.

Weller, Karl. "Die Nibelungenstrasse." *Zeitschrift für deutsches Altertum und deutsche Literatur* 70 (1933), pp. 49–66.

Wenskus, Reinhard. *Stammesbildung und Verfassung. Das Werden der frühmittelalterlichen gentes*. Köln – Graz 1961.

Wertner, Mór. *Die Grafen von St. Georgien und Bözing*. Wien 1891.

Wertner, Mór. *Az Árpádok családi története*. Nagy – Becskereken 1892.

Widajewicz, Józef. *Kraków i Poważe w dokumencie biskupstwa praskiego z 1086 roku*. Poznań 1938.

Widajewicz, Józef. *Państwo Wiślan*. Kraków 1947.

Wiesinger, Peter. "Antik-romanische Kontinuitäten im Donauraum von Ober- und Niederösterreich am Beispiel der Gewässer-, Berg-, und Siedlungsname." In *Typen der Ethnogenese unter besonderer Berücksichtigung der Bayern, Teil 1. Berichte des*

Symposions der Kommission für Frühmittelalterforschung, 27. bis 30. Oktober 1986, Stift Zwettl, Niederösterreich, ed. Herwig Wolfram, Walter Pohl, pp. 261–328.

Wihoda, Martin. "Die mährischen Eliten als Problem der Kontinuität (oder Diskontinuität?) der böhmischen Geschichte." In *Die frühmittelalterliche Elite bei den Völkern des östlichen Mitteleuropas*, ed. Pavel Kouřil, pp. 9–18.

Wihoda, Martin. "Morava v 10. století." In *České země v raném středověku*, ed. Petr Sommer, pp. 53–73.

Wihoda, Martin. *Morava v době knížecí 906–1197*. Praha, 2010.

Wihoda, Martin. Großmähren und seine Stellung in der Gechichte. In *Zentralisierungsprozesse und Herrschaftsbildung im frühmittelalterlichen Ostmitteleuropa*, ed. Przemyslaw Sikora, pp. 61–91.

Wihoda, Martin. "Druhý život mojmírovských knížat." In *Pád Velké Moravy aneb Kto byl pohřben v hrobu 153 na Pohansku u Břeclavi*, ed. Jiří Macháček, Martin Wihoda, pp. 144–165.

Wolf, Mária. "Előzetes jelentés a borsodi földvár ásatárol (1987–1990)." In *A nyíregyházi Jósa András múzeum évkönyve 30–32, 1987–1989*. Nyíregyháza 1992, pp. 393–442.

Wolf, Mária. "Die Gespanschaftsburg von Borsod." *Acta Archaeologica Academiae Scientiarum Hungaricae* 48 (1996), pp. 209–240.

Wolf, Mária. "A borsodi ispánsági vár templomai Ecclesia baptismalis, ecclesia parochialis," *A Borsodi Tájház Közleményi* 17.–18. füzet, 2005, pp. 3–18.

Wolf, Mária. *A borsodi földvár. Egy államalapításkori megyeszékhelyünk*. Edelény 2008.

Wolfram, Herwig. "Überlegungen zur politischen situation der Slawen im heutigen Oberösterreich (8.–10. Jahrhundert)." In *Baiern und Slawen in Oberösterreich. Probleme der Landnahme und Besiedung. Symposion 16. November 1978, redigiert von Kurt Holter. Schriftenreihe des OÖ. Musealvereins-Geselschaft für Landeskunde*. Band 10. Linz 1980, pp. 17–24.

Wolfram, Herwig. "Der Zeitpunkt der Einführung der Grafschaftsverfassung in Karantanien." In. *Siedlung, Macht und Wirtschaft. Festschrift Fritz Posch zum 70. Geburtstag*, ed. Gerhard Pferschy. *Veröffentlichungen des Steiermarkischen Landesarchiv* 12. Graz 1981, pp. 313–317.

Wolfram, Herwig. "Liudewit und Priwina (ein institutioneller Vergleich)." In *Interaktionen der mitteleuropäischen Slawen und anderen Ethnika im 6.–10. Jahrhundert*. Nitra 1984, pp. 291–296.

Wolfram, Herwig. *Die Geburt Mitteleuropas. Geschichte Österreichs vor seiner Entstehung 378–907*. Wien 1987.

Wolfram, Herwig. "Der Raum der Güssinger Herrschaft in der Karolingerzeit," *Wissenschaftliche Arbeiten aus dem Burgenland*, Heft 79, 1989, pp. 3–14.

Wolfram, Herwig. *Die Goten. Von den Anfängen bis zur Mitte des sechsten Jahrhunderts. Entwurf einer historischen Ethnographie*, München 1990.

Wolfram, Herwig. "Einleitung oder Überlegungen zur Origo Gentis." In *Typen der Ethnogenese unter besonderer Berücksochtigung der Bayern. Teil I*, ed. Herwig Wolfram, Walter Pohl, pp. 19–33.

Wolfram, Herwig. "Karantanija med vzhodom i zahodom. Obri, Bavarci in Langobardi v 8. in 9. stoletju." *Zgodovinski časopis* 45 (1991), no. 2, pp. 177–187.

Wolfram, Herwig. "Origo et religio. Ethnische Traditionen und Literatur in frühmittelalterlichen Quellen." In *Mittelalter – Annäherungen an eine fremde Zeit, ed. Wilfried Hartmann. Schriftenreihe der Universität Regensburg, Neue Folge*, Band 19 (1993), pp. 27–39.

Wolfram, Herwig. *Salzburg, Bayern, Österreich. Die Conversio Bagoariorum et Carantanorum und die Quellen ihrer Zeit. Mitteilungen des Instituts für österreichische Geschichtsforschung, Ergänzungsband 31*. Wien – München 1995.

Wolfram, Herwig. *Österreichische Geschichte 378–907. Grenzen und Räume. Geschichte Österreichs vor seiner Entstehung*. Wien 1995.

Wolfram, Herwig. "Historické pramene a poloha (Veľkej) Moravy." *Historický časopis* 43 (1995), no. 1, pp. 1–15.

Wolfram, Herwig. "The Bavarian Mission to Pannonia in the 9th century," in Pavel Kouřil et al., *The Cyril and Methodius Mission and Europe – 1150 Years Since the Arrival of the Thessaloniki Brothers in Great Moravia*. Brno 2014, pp. 28–33.

Wolters, Reinhard. *Římané v Germánii*. Praha 2002.

Zábojník, Jozef. "K výskytu predmetov západného pôvodu na pohrebiskách z obdobia Avarskej ríše v Dunajskej kotline." *Slovenská archeológia* 26 (1978), no. 1, pp. 193–214.

Zábojník, Jozef. "Zur Problematik des Waffenvorkommens auf Gräberfeldern aus der Zeit des Awarenreiches in den nordwestlichen Teilen des Karpatenbeckens." In. *Interaktionen der mitteleuropäischen Slawen und anderen Ethnika im 6.–10. Jahrhundert*. Nitra 1984, pp. 297–302.

Zábojník, Jozef. "Zur horizontalen Stratigraphie des Gräberfeldes in Radvaň nad Dunajom – Žitavská Tôň." *Slovenská archeológia* 33 (1985), no. 2, pp. 329–346.

Zábojník, Jozef. "Seriation von Gürtelbeschlaggarnituren aus dem Gebiet der Slowakei und Österreichs (Beitrag zur Chronologie der Zeit des Awarischen Kaganats)." In *K problematike osídlenia stredodunajskej oblasti vo včasnom stredoveku*, pp. 219–321.

Zábojník, Jozef. "Soziale Problematik der Gräberfelder des nördlichen und nordwestlichen Randgebietes des Awarischen Kaganats." *Slovenská archeológia* 43 (1995), no. 2, pp. 205–344.

Zábojník, Jozef. "Zum Vorkommen der Reitergräber auf Gräberfeldern aus der Zeit des Awarischen Kaganats." In *Ethnische und kulturelle Verhältnisse an der mittleren Donau vom 6. bis zum 11. Jahrhundert. Symposium Nitra 6. bis 10. November 1994*, ed. Darina Bialeková, Jozef Zábojník, pp. 179–193.

Zábojník, Jozef. "Das Awarische Kaganat und die Slawen an seiner nördlichen Peripherie (Probleme der Archäologischen Abgrenzung)." *Slovenská archeológia* 47 (1999), no. 1, pp. 153–173.

Zábojník, Jozef. "Materiálna kultúra nálezísk z obdobia Avarského kaganátu na Slovensku (Stav, možnosti a perspektívy štúdia)." In *Slovensko a európsky juhovýchod. Medzikultúrne vzťahy a kontexty. Zborník k životnému jubileu Tatiany Štefanovičovej*, ed. Alexander Avenárius, Zuzana Ševčíková, pp. 189–222.

Zábojník, Jozef. "Slovensko a Avarský kaganát." In *Slovensko vo včasnom stredoveku*, ed. Alexander Ruttkay, Matej Ruttkay, Peter Šalkovský, pp. 29–39.

Zábojník, Jozef. *Slovensko a Avarský kaganát*. Bratislava 2004.

Zábojník, Jozef. "Mikulčice – awarische Stadt?" In *Die frühmittelalterliche Elite bei den Völkern des östlichen Mitteleuropas*, ed. Pavel Kouřil, pp. 101–114.

Zábojník, Jozef. "Problematika včasného stredoveku na Slovensku." *Historický časopis* 58 (2010), no. 2, pp. 213–231.

Zábojník, Jozef – Béreš, Július. *Pohrebisko z obdobia avarského kaganátu vo Valalikoch-Všechsvätých*. Nitra 2016.

Záborský, Jonáš. *Dejiny kráľovstva uhorského od počiatku do časov Žigmundových*. Bratislava 2012 (manuscript 1875).

Zagiba, Franz. *Das Geistesleben der Slawen im frühen Mittelalter. Die Anfänge des slavischen Schrifttums auf dem Gebiete des östlichen Mitteleuropa vom 8. bis 10. Jahrhundert, Annales Instituti Slavici 7*. Wien – Köln – Graz 1971.

Zástěrová, Bohumila. "Avaři a Slované. K současnému stavu bádání o starším období avarských dějin a vztahů avarsko-slovanských." *Vznik a počátky Slovanů* II (1958), pp. 19–54.

Zástěrová, Bohumila. "Avaři a Dulebové v svědectví Povesti vremennych let." *Vznik a počátky Slovanů* III (1960), pp. 15–37.

Zavadil, Ondřej. "Dopis markrabího Ariba králi Arnulfovi." *Mediaevalia historica Bohemica* 11, 2007, pp. 7–21.

Zborník na počesť Dariny Bialekovej, ed. Gabriel Fusek. Nitra 2004.

Zbořil, J. "Ptolemaiova východná Germánia." *Historický sborník Matice slovenskej* 5 (1947), pp. 261–295.

Zehetmayer, Roman. "Rakouské Podunají kolem roku 900." In *Pád Velké Moravy aneb Kto byl pohřben v hrobu 153 na Pohansku u Břeclavi*, ed. Jiří Macháček, Martin Wihoda, pp. 73–101.

Zeller, Bernhard. "Baiern, das Ostfränkische Reich und die Ungarn zwischen der Niederlage bei Pressburg und dem Sieg auf dem Lechfeld bei Augsburg 907–955." In *Schicksalsjahr 907. Die Schlacht bei Pressburg und das frühmittelalterliche Niederösterreich. Katalog zur Ausstellung des Niederösterreichischen Landesarchivs*, ed. Roman Zehetmayer, pp. 45–56.

Zeman, Jiří. "Nejstarší slovanské osídlení Čech." *Památky archeologické* 67 (1976), pp. 115-235.

Zeman, Jiří. "K problematice časně slovanské kultury ve střední Evropě." *Památky archeologické* 70 (1979), pp. 113-130.

Zemek, Metoděj. *Moravsko-uherská hranice v 10. až 13. století.* Brno 1972.

Zemene, Marián Róbert. "Územie Nitrianskej diecézy za feudalizmu." *Slovenská archivistika* 15 (1980), no. 2, pp. 132-155.

Zentralisierungsprozesse und Herrschaftsbildung im frühmittelalterlichen Ostmitteleuropa, ed. Przemyslaw Sikora. Studien zur Archäologie Europas 23, ed. Joachim Henning, Felix Biermann, Jiří Macháček. Bonn 2014.

Zervan, Vratislav. "Úloha Pečenehov v kríze euroázijskej stepi v 9. stotočí na základe informácií Konštantína Porfyrogenneta." *Byzantinoslovaca* I (2006), pp. 161-174.

Zgodovina Slovencev. Ljubljana 1979.

Zibermayr, Ignaz. *Noricum, Baiern und Österreich. Lorch als Hauptstadt und die Einführung des Christentums.* München - Berlin 1944.

Zientara, Benedykt. *Swit narodów europejskich. Powstawanie swiadomosci narodowej na obszarze Europy pokarolinskej.* Warszawa 1996.

Zlatarski, Vasil Nikolov. *Istorija na bălgarskata dăržava prez srednite vekove* I/1,2. Sofija 1970, 1971.

Zlatarski, Vasil Nikolov. "Veľká Morava a Bulharsko v IX. storočí." In *Ríša Veľkomoravská. Sborník vedeckých prác*, ed. Ján Stanislav, pp. 275-288.

Zolnay, László. *A középkori Esztergom.* Budapest 1983.

Zsoldos, Attila. "Péter és Gurka (Gurcu) ispán nemzetsége." *Történelmi Szemle* 37 (1995), no. 3, pp. 345-351.

Zsoldos, Attila. "Visegrád vármegye és utódai." *Történelmi Szemle* 40 (1998), no. 1-2, pp. 1-32.

Zsoldos, Attila. *A szent király szabadjai. Fejezetek a várjobbágyság történetéből.* Budapest, 1999.

Zsoldos, Attila. "Confinium és marchia (Az Árpad-kori határvédelem néhány intézményéről)." *Századok* 134 (2000), no. 1, pp. 99-116.

Zsoldos, Attila. "Szent István vármegyéi." In *Államalapítás, társadalom, művelődés*, ed. Gyula Kristó. Budapest 2001, ed. 43-54.

Zsoldos, Attila. "Szent István vármegyéi." In *Szent István és az államalapítás*, ed. László Veszprémy, pp. 420-430.

Zsoldos, Attila. "Somogy megye kialakulásáról." In *Szent István és az államalapítás*, ed. László Veszprémy, pp. 431-439.

Zsoldos, Attila. "Somogy és Visegrád megye korai története, valamint a 'várelemek spontán expanziója'." In *Szent István és az államalapítás*, ed. László Veszprémy, pp. 471-477.

Zsoldos, Attila. "Somogy és Visegrád megye korai története, valamint a 'várelemek spontán expanziója'." *Századok* 136 (2002), no. 3, pp. 679–685.

Zsoldos, Attila. "Szepes megye kialakulása." *Történelmi Szemle* 44 (2002), no. 1–2, pp. 19–31.

Zsoldos, Attila. "Vznik Spišského komitátu." In *K stredovekým dejinám Spiša*, ed. Miroslav Števík. Stará Ľubovňa 2003, pp. 15–29.

Zsoldos, Attila. "The Origins of Szepes County." In *K stredovekým dejinám Spiša*, ed. Miroslav Števík. Stará Ľubovňa 2003, pp. 31–40.

Zsoldos, Attila. *The Legacy of Saint Stephen*. Budapest 2004.

Zsoldos, Attila. "Korai vármegyéink az újabb történeti kutatások fényében." *Castrum* 11 (2010), pp. 5–14.

Zsoldos, Attila. "Bihar megye korai története." In *Nagyvárad és Bihar a korai középkorban*, pp. 167–190.

Zvolen. Monografia k 750. výročiu obnovenia mestských práv, ed. Viera Vaníková. Zvolen 1993.

Zwischen Byzanz und der Steppe. Archäologische und historische Studien. Festschrift für Csanád Bálint zum 70. Geburtstag, ed. Ádám Bollók, Gergely Csiky, Tivadar Vida. Budapest 2016.

Żak, Jan. "Problematik der westlichen Ausbreitung der Westslawen zu Beginn des Frümittelalters (5./6.–7. Jh.)." In *Rapports du IIIe Congrés International d'Archéologie Slave, Bratislava 7–14 septembre 1975, Tome 1*, ed. Bohuslav Chropovský, pp. 917–939.

Žemlička, Josef. "'Moravané' v časném středověku." *Český časopis historický* 90 (1992), no. 1, pp. 17–32.

Žemlička, Josef. *Čechy v době knížecí (1034–1198)*. Praha 1997.

Žigo, Pavol. "Neznámy text na plakete z Bojnej." *Historický časopis* 62 (2014), no. 1, pp. 3–17.

Žirmunskij, Viktor Maximovič. *O hrdinském eposu (slovanském a středoasijském)*. Praha 1984.

Županič, Niko. "Etnička pripadnost moža Unguimerija v anonimni pesmi Hymnus de Pippini regis victoria Avarica in pojasnilo avarskih besed v njej." *Zbornik Filozofske fakultete Univerza v Ljubljani* 11. Ljubljana 1955, pp. 239–255.

Žužek, Aleš. "Naselitiv Slovanov v vzhodnoalpski prostor." *Zgodovinski časopis* 61 (2007), no. 3–4 (135), pp. 261–287.

Index of Names

Aaron, son of Bulgarian count Nicholas 331–333
Aba, see Samuel Aba
Abas, Aba family, Aba line 309, 310, 319, 348, 424, 529
Abd ar-Rahmán I, amir of Córdoba (756–788) 87
Abdaláh, son of Abd ar-Rahmán I 87
Abraham, Avar khagan (round 805) 93, 94, 96, 145
Acha, archbishop of Estergom (1087–round 1090) 473
Adalbert, see Vojtech
Adalbert III, margrave of Eastern March (1018–1055) 422, 424, 480
Adalbert of Bogen 484
Adalram, archbishop of Salzburg (821–836) 116, 117, 120, 123, 124, 140, 156, 183
Adalvín, archbishop of Salzburg (859–873) 153, 176
Adam, archbishop of Bremen, Saxon chronicler 496, 497, 500–502
Adelaide, daughter of Hungarian king Andrew I 421–422, 440, 441, 471
Adelaide, daughter of prince Álmos, wife of Bohemian prince Soběslav I 480
Adelaide, wife of Ladislav I 466, 468
Agilimund, Quadian prince (about 358) 7
Agilulf, Longobard king (520–616) 31
Aizo, courtier of Louis the Pious Francia king and emperor 87, 88
Ajtony (Achtum), prince of Marosvár (before 1002–about 1028) 307, 308, 319, 347, 348, 351, 352, 356, 392, 393, 405
Ákos, leader of Cumans 471
Ákos (magister Ákos), provost of Buda (1254–1272), Hungarian chronicler (1270–1272) 276–278, 290–293, 299, 337, 366
Alamanni (Alamans) 19, 21, 45, 53–55, 207, 230, 416
Alans 14, 15, 49
Alarich, Herulian king (about 469) 19
Alberic, margrave of Avar March and Carantanian March (after 806–before 818) 100, 101, 102

Alberic, chorbishop of Pasau (about 850) 145
Albgar, nephew of Unruoch 106
Albgar, leader of Bavarian army and Dudlebian count (since 828) 118, 119, 165, 168, 176
Albgis, frankish refugee (in 852) 132, 133, 184
Alboin, Longobard king (561–572) 30
Alciok (Alciocus), Bulgarian prince (before 631–after 671) 55–56
Alcuin of Nitra 217
Alderic (Adeleric), Basque 132
Alexander the Great, king of Macedonia 289, 290
Alexios II, Byzantine emperor (1180–1183) 478
Alfred the Great, Anglo-Saxon king (871–900) 85, 100, 104, 243
Álmos, father of Magyar prince Árpád 239, 300
Álmos, prince of Nitria and Biharia (1095–1108) 275, 410, 452, 468–470, 475–486, 505, 509, 515, 519, 520, 525, 530
Altfrid, archipresbyter of Blatengrad 153
Altman, bishop of Passau (1065–1091) 126
Altmar, bishop of Veszprém (about 1093) 473
Anartes 5, 6
Anastasia, wife of Andrew I, king of Hungary 441, 442, 459
Anastasios I, Byzantine emperor (491–518) 23
Anastasius, see Astrik
Andrew, prince of Chlm (around 1234) 509
Andrew I, king of Hungary (1046–1060) 291, 292, 359, 360, 364–366, 398, 400, 411, 420–422, 424, 432–449, 452, 462, 466, 471, 504, 529
Andrew, defender of Bratislava castle (in 1052) 398, 444
Andrew, count (in 1055) 398
Andrew, iudex (in 1075) 398
Andrew, bishop of Veszprém (1046–1071) 398–399
Angelarius, pupil of Methodius 214

Anonymus, Hungarian chronicler   243, 277, 278, 280–281, 283, 290, 292, 299–303, 305–313, 322, 334–337, 342, 349–358, 365, 412, 413, 415, 493, 501, 502, 525
Ansgar, archbishop of Hamburg (834–849–865)   118
Arabs   200
Arahari, son of Sarmatian king (about 358)   6, 7
Arathot, count of Upper Pannonia (about 877)   167
Ardagast, Slav leader (before pred 584– after 594)   32, 99
Ardarich, Gepidian king (about 454)   15
Arfrid, fief-tenant of archbishop Liupram   159
Aribo, margrave of Eastern March (871–po 909)   120, 136, 221, 228, 231, 233, 234, 237
Arioald, Longobard king (624–636)   54
Arnefrit (Warnefrit), son of Friulian duke Lupus   36, 73
Arno, bishop (785–798) and archbishop (798–836) of Salzburg   77, 79, 83–84, 85, 92, 124, 125
Arnold, count of Looz   452
Arnold, monk from the Abbey of Saint Emmeram in Regensburg (around 1030)   389
Arnulf, Carantanian margrave and Pannonian prince (876–887), East Francia king (887–899) and emperor (896–899)   133, 135, 142, 154, 212, 220–224, 226–234, 237, 244, 245, 247, 250, 257, 286
Arnulf, duke of Bavaria (907–937)   260–262, 266
Áron, Bulgarian komitopul   331–332
Árpád, Hungarian prince († 907)   147, 148, 239–243, 248, 257, 279–281, 284, 300–303, 307, 309, 311–317, 319, 334, 335, 337, 338, 340, 345, 354, 355, 357, 373, 412, 492, 525
Árpáds, Árpád line, Árpád family, Árpád dynasty   291, 310, 319, 320, 325, 327, 342, 347, 348, 359, 365, 392, 396, 412, 417, 419–423, 425, 426, 431, 433, 435, 436, 439, 459, 485, 494, 512, 514, 528–530, 533

Arthur, British king (about 500)   294–295, 299
Astrik (Anastázius), monk at the Abbey on the Aventine in Rome, abbot on the Pannonhalma abbey, bishop of Kalocsa (1000–1007) and archbishop of Esztergom (1007–1036)   367, 368, 370–374, 380, 387–389
Attila, Hun king († 453)   49, 147, 288–290, 312, 335, 337, 382, 402, 492
Atto, bishop of Freising (784–811)   79
Audoin, Longobard king (547–565)   26, 28, 29, 143
Audulf, margrave of the Bavarian Northern March (Nordgau) and prefekt of Bavaria (799–818)   90
Austrasians   45, 48, 52, 53, 55
Avars   30, 31, 32, 33, 34, 35, 41, 42, 43, 45, 48, 55–62, 66, 67, 70, 73, 74, 78–82, 85, 86, 91–99, 101, 111, 114, 128–130, 150, 151, 158, 164, 168, 527
Aventinus, Bavarian chronicler (16th c.)   233, 429
Azali, Pannonian tribe   146
Azzo, papal legate   390, 392

Babaj, Sarmatian king († 471)   19, 20
Bača, count of Nitra (about in the last quarter of the 11th c.)   516–518
Bajan, Avar khagan († perhaps 602)   31, 32
Baldric, margrave of Friuli (819–828)   106, 107, 114, 117, 118
Baldwin V, count of Flanders (1036–1067)   438
Basil I, Byzantine emperor (867–886)   235
Basil II, Byzantine emperor (976–1025)   333, 392
Batona, royal bailiff in Nitra (in 1111–1113)   516, 517
Batu Khan, khan of Tatars († 1242)   295–296, 509
Bavarians   31, 47, 49, 50, 74, 78, 85, 86, 127, 132, 135, 149, 152, 158, 159, 208, 209, 223, 230–234, 244, 248, 249, 252, 255, 257–261, 313, 317, 318, 368, 396, 416, 424, 425, 429, 493, 505, 528, 532
Beatus, Bavarian magnate   158
Béla I (Adalbert), prince of Nitria (1048–1060), king of Hungary (1060–1063)   291,

INDEX OF NAMES

292, 359, 361, 365, 366, 400, 420, 424, 432, 439–450, 452, 460, 462, 489, 504, 529
Béla II, king of Hungary (1131–1141)   169, 275, 276, 365, 480–482, 485, 486
Béla III, king of Hungary (1173–1196)   358
Béla IV, king of Hungary (1235–1270)   379
Beleknegini, another name of Sarolt   498
Benedikt, bishop (around 900), papal legate   246
Benedikt, son of Boto, Hungarian count (around 1108)   485
Benedikt, anchorite of Zobor   451
Beneta, bishop (around 1046)   394, 435, 436
Berengar, count of Toulouse (round 819)   133
Berengar I., king of Italy (888–924) and emperor (915–924)   244, 245, 261
Berengar II., king of Italy (950–963)   116
Berengar of Sulzbach   484
Bernhard, Italian king (813–817)   101
Berthold, bavarian count   222
Bernhard von Sponheim, margrave of Ptuj (1122–1147)   161–162
Berthold, Carantanian margrave (907–937), duke of Bavaria (937–947)   260
Berthold, anti-archbishop of Salzburg (1085–1106)   478
Bertric, count palatine   114
Beuka, Sarmatian king (†471)   19
Biharians, Biharian army   456–458, 477, 488, 491, 505, 512
Black Hungarians   390, 392
Blud, duke of Kiev prince (khagan) Yaropolk   510
Bobrans   213
Bogomils   434
Bohemians (Czechs), Bohemian army   34, 39, 42, 49, 55, 96, 101, 111, 112, 136, 185, 207, 211–213, 220, 223–226, 232, 237, 249, 252, 255–257, 259–263, 265, 266, 318, 320, 322, 334–338, 347, 396, 398, 417, 425, 429, 430, 453, 475, 476, 492–496, 499–501, 503–506, 514, 528
Boleslaus I, prince of Bohemia (935–972)   36, 237, 318, 321–323, 338–340, 378
Boleslaus II, prince of Bohemia (972–999)   36, 321, 322, 334, 338, 363

Boleslaw I the Brave, prince (992–1025) and king (1025) of Poland   333, 363, 372, 380, 382–387, 396–398, 401, 403, 406, 504, 510
Boleslaw II the Bold, prince (1058–1076) and king (1076–1080) of Poland   446, 449, 450
Boleslaw III Wrymouth, prince of Poland (1102–1138)   334, 481, 483, 484, 496, 513, 523
Bolya, Hungarian magnate   434
Bonipert, bishop of Pécs (1009–1036)   389
Bonyha, Hungarian magnate   434
Boris, prince of Rostov   508
Boris, son of Euphemia, Coloman's second wife   365, 523
Boris I, khagan (later prince) of Bulgaria (852–889)   183, 185, 200, 202–204, 235, 332, 509
Boris II, tsar of Bulgaria (970–974)   325
Borna, prince of Croatia (†821)   99, 105, 106, 107, 108, 109, 127, 129, 131, 143
Borsa, son of Bönger, prince and count of Borsod   355–358, 380, 403, 415
Borsa, count, son of bán Dominik
Borut, prince of Carantania (before 742–749)   74, 183
Bořivoj, prince of Bohemia (perhaps 872–888)   210–212, 223–226, 256, 506, 507
Bořivoj II, prince of Brno and Znojmo (1099–1100), prince of Bohemia (1101–1107, 1117–1120)   484, 507
Botond, Magyar hero   277–278, 290
Bönger, father of Borš   357
Branimír, prince of Croatia (879–892)   140
Braslav, prince of Savia (896–900)   134, 142, 154, 230, 244, 248, 257
Bruno of Querfurt (saint Bruno, also known as Boniface)   390, 392
Bruno (Prunwart), monk from the abbey Sankt Gallen, since 972 mission bishop on Hungaria   177, 327, 329
Bruno, bishop of Augsburg (1006–1029)   378
Břetislav I, prince of Moravia (1029–1035), and Bohemia (1035–1055)   321, 417, 418, 421–426, 429–432, 443, 444, 489, 494, 497, 503
Břetislav II, prince of Bohemia (1092–1100)   471, 476, 479

INDEX OF NAMES

Buda, Egiruch's son and father of Sebes 419, 420, 423
Budli, bishop of Bihar (1030–1046) 394, 435, 436
Budy, guardian and duke of Kiev prince (khagan) Yaroslaw the Wise 510
Bukven, count of Nitra (from 1029) 403–406, 411, 423, 516, 518
Bulcsú (Vérbulcsú), Magyar horka (†955), son of Kál 246, 247, 277, 313, 314, 317–321, 392
Bulgarians (Bulgars) 30, 55, 57, 70, 98, 99, 100, 112, 114–119, 127, 129, 136, 141, 151, 162, 164, 165, 173, 175, 176, 184, 185, 200–202, 205, 214, 221, 241, 280, 288, 300, 308, 311, 313, 324, 325, 331–333, 336, 392, 492, 509
Burchard, duke of Saxony and Thuringia (892–908) 253, 254
Burchard, bishop of Passau (903–915) 259
Burchard II, duke of Swabia (954–973) 262, 318
Burgundians 279, 294, 416
Bykas, count and adviser of prince Géza 456
Byrhtnoth, aeldorman of Essex 295
Bystrík, bishop (†1046) 394, 435, 436
Byzantines 143, 453, 470, 526

Cadolah I, margrave of Friuli (799–802) 90
Cadolah II, margrave of Friuli (802–819) 105, 106
Caesar 5
Canute Lavard, Obodrite prince (1129–1131) 508
Carantanians 31, 34, 36, 37, 38, 73, 74, 76, 79, 84, 100, 101, 102, 106, 107, 108, 111, 113, 114, 281
Carinthians 425, 501, 505
Carloman, margrave of Eastern and Carantanian march (856–863), Bavarian administartor (865–876), king of Bavaria (876–880) 81, 132, 136, 141, 166, 167, 196, 198–201, 204–209, 211, 220
Carloman, brother of Frankish king Pipin the Short 87
Carniolans (Carniolan Slavs) 58, 106, 107, 113, 114
Casimir I, Prince of Poland (1034–1058) 432

Ceva, vice-count and royal bailiff of Nitra (in 1111–1113) 517
Charlemagne (Charles the Great), Francia king (768–814) and emperor (800–814) 49, 50, 51, 53, 68–71, 78–82, 84–86, 89–93, 96–98, 101, 102, 104, 132, 141, 145, 168, 227
Charles II the Bald, West Francia king (840–877) and emperor (875–877) 51, 130, 139, 198, 200
Charles III the Fat, East Francia (876–887), West Francia king (885–888) and emperor (881–887) 207, 221, 223, 226–228, 236, 506
Chelgü (Cselgü, Kutesk), Pecheneg khagan 301, 362, 467
Chlotar II, Frankish king (584–628) 39
Chorso, duke of Toulouse (round 790) 132
Chrabr, monk 172
Chrodobert, leader of Alamannian army (about 631) 54, 55
Chuds 256
Cividale 73
Claffo, Longobard king (after 489–before 505), son of Gudeoch 22, 23
Claudius, emperor (41–54) 144, 170
Claudius Ptolemy 8
Clement (Kliment), Velika bishop, pupil of Methodius 142, 214
Clement III, anti-pope (1080–1100) 469
Coloman, king of Hungary (1095–1116) 271, 272, 274–276, 292, 365, 452, 469, 475–486, 494, 515–520, 523–525, 530
Cometopuli (David, Moses, Aaron, Samuel), sons of Bulgarian count Nicholas (komit Nikola) 325, 331–333
Commodus, emperor (180–192) 9
Conrad the Red, duke of Lorraine (944–953) 318
Conrad I, duke of Franconia and German king (911–918) 261
Conrad, prince of Brno and Znojmo (1055, 1061–1092), Bohemian prince (1092) 471, 494–496
Conrad II, German king (1024–1039) and emperor (1027–1039) 401, 417
Conrad III, German king (1138–1182) 162
Conrad II, prince of Znojmo (1123–1128, 1134– perhaps 1170) 495

INDEX OF NAMES

Constantine (Cyril), Byzantine missionary (†869) 40, 181, 235
Constantine II, emperor (337–361) 147
Constantine Porphyrogenitus, Byzantine emperor (913–959) 35, 36, 105, 214, 215, 217, 248, 269, 270, 280, 303, 313, 315, 316, 320, 328
Constantine Porphyrogenitus, brother and co-ruler of Byzantine emperor Michael VII Dukas 460
Constantine II, emperor (337–361) 7, 147
Cosmas, bishop of Veszprém (around 1085–perhaps 1093) 473
Cosmas, Prague chapter and Bohemian chronicler (†1125) 3, 211, 219, 270, 272, 285–287, 292, 295, 297, 299, 322, 334, 337, 349, 358, 494–496, 505
Cosmas, magnate (around 1111) 517
Cotins 5, 6, 13
Costobocs 5
Croat (*Chrobatos*), Croatian prince 35
Croats (Croatians) 34, 35, 36, 37, 38, 39, 40, 57, 92, 112, 127, 185, 220, 382, 470
Csanad, son of Doboka, count of Csanad (perhaps 1028) 356, 392, 393
Czechs, see Bohemians
Cumans (Polovtsi, Kipchak) 273, 307, 469–472, 479
Cunimund, Gepidian king (†567) 30
Cyrus, king of Persia 289
Čech 39
Čestibor, Sorbian prince (†858) 135

Dacians 5, 6
Dadosezans 213
Dagobert I, Frankish king (628–658) 44, 45, 48, 52–56
Dalimil, Bohemian chronicler 507
Dalmatians 105, 106
Danes 200, 251, 505
Daniel, bishop (around 900), papal legate 246
Daniel, canon of the Nitra chapter 516
David of Sasun, Armenian hero 299
David, son of Bulgarian count Nicholas 331
David, Prince of Biharia (1077–since 1095), son of Hungarian king Andrew I 445, 459, 465, 466, 475

David, Volyn prince (1086–1097) 479
David Ingvarevich, prince of Murom 509
Deda, son of Bukven, count of Nitra 403, 516
Demeter Zvonimir, ban and king of Croatia (1075–1089) 452, 468–470
Dervan, Sorb prince (round 631) 39, 42, 55, 527
Desiderius, bishof of Kalocsa (before 1064–after 1076) 440, 450, 464
Dietbold of Nordgau 484
Dietrich IV, margrave of Holland (1039–1049) 438
Diocletian, emperor (284–305) 144, 146
Doboka, count of Doboka (Dăbîca) county (since 1003) 356, 386, 393
Domenico Contareni, Venetian doge (1041–1069) 452
Dominic, magnate from the Miškov family, ban of Croatia 358
Dominic, presbyter of Blatengrad (from 850) 153, 157, 166
Dominic (Domonkos), missionary bishop in Veszprém, archibishof of Esztergom (1000–1002) 342, 372, 387
Domoslav (Bonuslav), prince of Nitria (1042, 1046–1048) 359, 363, 366, 396, 420, 423, 429, 431, 432, 435, 437, 439, 441, 442, 489, 529
Drahomíra, wife of Bohemian prince Vratislaus I 253, 266, 267
Dramagos, father in law of Savian prince Ljudevit 106, 107
Dudlebs 30, 42, 112, 164
Dukh (Duch), bishof of Zagreb (perhaps since 1093) 473
Dukljanin (pop Dukljanin), priest of Duklja, chronicler 187, 287

Eckard I, margrave of Meissen (985–1002) 384
Eckard II, margrave of Merseburg (since 1002) 384
Edgar, prince of Transdanubia 103, 104, 174, 176, 180
Edgar the Peaceful, Anglo-Saxon king (959–975) 174
Edika, Scirian king (†469) 19

Egino, count   253
Einhard, biographer of Charlemagne   93
Elemund, Gepidian king (till 546)   28
Elias, count   454
Elizabeth, queen of Hungary   413
Ellenhard, bishof of Freising (1052–1078)   461
Emeric (Saint Emeric), son of Hungarian king Stephen I, prince of Nitria (1029–1031)   178, 283, 393, 394, 397, 402, 403, 418, 419, 441, 513, 529, 533
Emich, count of Leiningen (around 1096)   477
Emmeram, Bavarian saint   120, 124, 128, 15
Engelberd of Istria   484
Engelschalk I, margrave of Eastern March (865–871)   133, 136, 207, 208, 221
Engelschalk II, son of Engelschalk I   230
Engilrada, wife of Traungau count Wilhelm I   121
Eppo, bishof of Zeitz-Naumburg (1045–1078)   446–447
Eravisci, Celtic tribe in Pannonia   147
Erik, margrave of Friuli (†799)   81, 82, 85, 86, 89, 92
Erkenbald, bishop of Eichstädt (884–916)   259
Ermperht, priest   153, 172
Ernej, count (†1074)   455, 457, 458, 504
Ernest, margrave of Eastern march (1055–1075)   445–447, 461
Ernest, Dudlebian count (before 877)   167, 168
Ernest, margrave of Bavarian Northern march (till 861)   184, 198
Etej, assistant of royal tax collector Prkoš   515
Euphemia, Coloman's second wife   365
Euphemia, (†1111), sister of Hungarian king Géza I, wife of Olomouc prince Otto I the Fair   452, 475
Excalibur, sword   295
Ezellő, son of Üllő   315

Fabian, archbishop of Bács (1089–round 1090)   473

Fajsz (Fali, Falichi), Hungarian prince (perhaps 947–perhaps 955), son of Jutas   315–317, 319
Fastida, Gepidian king (round 271)   6
Felicianus, archbishop of Esztergom (1027–1039)   473
Ferdulf, duke of Friuli (about 700)   58
Feva (Feletheus), Rugian king (before 476–488)   22
Figa, dignified inhabitant of Nitra   516
Filip Nyanko, duke of Moscow prince   511
Flaccitheus, Rugijan king (about 454)   16
Folkmar of Orleans, leader of crusaders   476–478, 491
Fortunatus, patriarch of Grado (perhabs 802–about 826)   108, 143
Fragiled, Sarmatian prince (about 358)   7
Frank, bishop of Veszprém (1071–1081)   454
Franks   45, 49, 50, 51, 53, 89, 90, 129, 133, 141, 185, 207, 210, 230, 260, 262, 416, 505
Fredegar, Frankish chronicler   32
Frederick (Friedrich), count of Tengling   484
Frederick, duke of Swabia (1079–1105)   483
Frisians   49, 50, 80, 416
Friulians   107

Gabriel Radomir, son of bulgarian tsar Samuel   333
Gallus Anonymus, Polish chronicler   380, 396, 496, 497, 500–502, 505
Gardízí, Persian historian (middle 12th c.)   240
Garsando, brother of Warin of Auvergne (round 819)   133
Gaufred, abbot of Zobor (beginning 12th c.)   515, 517
Gebhard III, bishop of Regensburg (1036–1060)   443, 444
Gečä, son of Nitrian count Bukven   403, 516
Gelou, Valachian prince of Transylvania   305
Geoffrey of Monmouth, bishop of Flintshire and Westminster, English chronicler (in the mid 12th century)   295
George, illegitimate son of Andrew I   445
George the Black, chaplain   457
Georgiy Vsevolodovich, grand prince of Vladimir (1212–1216, 1219–1236)   509

INDEX OF NAMES 645

Gepids   6, 14, 15, 17, 18, 19, 21, 22, 24–30, 32, 42, 135, 136, 137, 526, 527
Gerhard (Gerard, Gellért), bishop of Csanád (1030–1046)   361, 393, 394, 434–436
Germanus, commander of Byzantine forces in 550   27
Germans, German army   280, 288, 289, 294, 318, 422, 444, 446, 449, 455, 461–463, 477, 492–494, 504, 505, 532
Gerold I, Bavarian prefekt and margrave of Avar and Carantanian March (788–799)   78, 79, 84, 85, 89, 90, 100, 101, 102
Gerold II, margrave of Avar and Carantanian March (before 826–828)   101, 114, 117, 118, 120
Gervasius, bishop of Nitra (perhaps since 1100)   518, 519
Gets   500
Géza, prince of Hungary (asi 971–997)   146, 177, 317, 319, 320, 325–333, 338–341, 346–351, 360, 362, 368, 371, 382, 396, 498, 528, 529
Géza I Magnus, prince of Nitria (1063–1074), king of Hungary (1074–1077)   432, 440, 441, 449–458, 460–464, 466, 475, 488, 489, 491, 504, 505, 529
Géza II, king of Hungary (1141–1162)   365
Gisela, sister of Arnulf, perhaps second wife of Svätopluk I   233
Gisela, wife of Hungary king Stephen I   317, 341, 354, 419–421
Glad, prince of Marosvár   307, 308, 351, 352
Gleb, prince of Murom   508
Gleb Ingvarevich, prince of Kolomna   509
Glomucians   250–253, 257, 259, 267, 268, 528
Godefrid, presbyter of the Nitra chapter   516
Goths   136, 137
Gotefrid, Carinthian margrave (1040–1055)   425
Gotofrid, Carantanian margrave (before 818–up to 823)   100, 101, 102, 108
Gorazd (Cacatius), prince of Carantania (749–752), son of Borut   74, 75, 183
Goteram, margrave of Avar and Carantanian March (799–802)   90, 100, 101, 102

Gottfried (Gotofrid), margrave of Avar and Carantanian March (before 818–up to 823)   100–101, 102, 108
Gottfried the Bearded, duke of Upper Lotharingia (1044–1045) and of Lower Lorraine (1065–1070)   438
Gottfried, count of Calw   484
Gottshalk, priest in Crusader army (in 1096)   477
Gozwin, count of Ptuj (around 874)   123, 144, 160, 163
Grab, count of Somogy (1087–round 1090)   473
Greeks   100, 288, 289, 324, 492, 532
Gregory IV, pope (827–844)   130
Gregory VII, pope (1073 - 1085)   463, 466, 468
Gregory of Tours, Frankish chronicler   138
Grimoald, Longobard king (662–671)   58, 73
Gudeoch, Longobard king (about 489)   22
Guduscans   105, 107
Guido, cardinal (around 1143)   495
Gunther, king of Burgundians   279, 294
Gunzelín of Kuckenburg, brother in law of Boleslaw the Brave   384
Gundakar, margrave of Carantania (863–865)   201, 207
Gundbat, deacon   154
Gunther, king of Burgundians   279, 294
Gunther, fief-tenant of archbishop Liupram   159
Gyula I, prince of Transylvania (about 950–about 970)   177, 306, 307, 319, 325, 330, 344, 347, 392
Gyula II (Prokuj), prince of Transylvania (about 970–1033)   326, 347, 348, 356, 385–387, 405, 406, 433, 487, 498
Gyula, palatine (1075–perhaps 1093)   473

Hadrian (Adrian) II (857–872), pope   110, 186
Hartvik, bishop of Győr (about 1100)   498
Hasdings   5, 7, 13
Hedvig, daughter of prince Álmos, wife of margrawe Adalbert III   480
Hector, son of Ulfod, canon of the Nitra chapter   516

Helena Lepa, (†after 1091), sister of
  Hungarian king Géza I, wife of ban
  Demetrius Zvonimír   452, 468
Helena, (†1141), wife of Béla II, daughter of
  Uroš I, grand count of Raška   480
Helmold, Saxon chronicler   497, 501, 502
Helmwin, leader of Bavarian army and count
  of Ptuj (from 828)   118, 119, 162–163, 176
Henry, leader of forces of Louis, son of Louis
  the German in 866   207
Henry I the Fowler, Saxon duke (912–936)
  and German king (919–936)   140,
  250–253, 262, 266–268
Henry I, bishop of Augsburg (973–982)   378
Henry I, duke of Bavaria (945–955) and
  Carantania (948–955, 983/985–989)
  161, 318
Henry II, duke of Bavaria (955–976, 985–995)
  and Carantania (955–976, 989–995)
  341, 375, 378
Henry II, German king (1002–1024) and
  emperor (1014–1024)   383, 385, 390,
  396, 397
Henry III, Bavarian duke (1027–1039,
  1047–1049), German king (1039–1056)
  and emperor (1046–1056)   171, 418,
  421–427, 429–431, 433, 438, 443, 444,
  446, 489
Henry IV, German king (1056–1105) and
  emperor (1084–1105)   448, 449, 459–464,
  466–469, 478, 480, 491
Henry V, German king (1105–1125) and
  emperor (1111–1125)   482–486, 515
Heraclius (Herakleios), Byzantine emperor
  (610–640)   35, 38
Herman, bishop of Prag (1099–1122)   479
Hermann, count of Winzenburg   484
Hermann, son of Meissen margrave Eckhart I
  (985–1002)   384
Heruls   15, 16, 17, 19, 22, 23, 24, 40, 42, 150
Hierotheos, missionary bishop of
  Transylvania (since 853)   306, 307, 331
Hildigis (†552), son of Risiulf   25, 26, 27,
  28, 29
Hishám I, amir of Córdoba (788–796)   87
Hitto, abbot in Abbey of Saint Emmeram in
  Regensburg (around 883)   169–170

Hont, prince and count of Hont   342,
  343, 347, 348, 353–354, 357, 359, 380,
  403–405, 411, 509
Horka, Hungarian prince of Transylvania
  (2 quarter 10 c.), Tetény's son   241, 306
Hostivít, father of Bořivoj   211
Hotimir (Chotimír), prince of Carantania
  (752–769), nephew of Borut   74–76, 183
Hrodgaud, duke of Friuli (†776)   78, 79
Huba, Árpád's commander   334–337
Hungarians (Hungari, Ungari, Ungri),
  Hungarian army   206, 239, 259, 273, 312,
  313, 320, 324, 325, 327, 328, 331, 333, 335,
  337, 380, 381, 383, 396, 397, 417–419,
  422, 424–427, 430, 444, 453, 460, 462,
  463, 469, 477, 479, 481, 482, 484, 487,
  490–494, 496, 499, 500, 503–505, 514,
  530
Hunimund, Suebian king (before 454–470)
  14, 19, 21, 526
Huns   1, 14, 15, 17, 49, 136, 137, 150, 276, 277,
  279, 288, 293, 294, 297, 336, 492, 500
Hunt, Prince and later count of Hont (before
  997–after 1037)   342–344, 347, 353, 354,
  357–359, 380, 403–405, 411, 509
Hunvulf (Hunulf), son of Scirian king
  Edika   19

Ibn Churdádbih, Arab scholar   506
Ibn Rustah (Ibn Rust), Persian scholar   195,
  236, 240, 269
Igor, Russian prince (khagan) of Kiev
  (913–945)   508, 510
Ingo, missionary in Carantania   77
Ingomer (Unguimeri), in 796 appealed to the
  Avar khagan   82
Ingvar (Igor) I, prince of Ryazan (1219–1235)
  509
Irene, wife of Gabriel Radomir   333
Isaac, Izauki, Avar khagan (about 811)
  96–97
Isaac, Erinbert's soldier, owned fief near
  Pinka   163
Isangrim, Bavarian magnate   158
Isanrich, margrave of Eastern march
  (899–901)   221, 234, 247, 249
Italians   422

INDEX OF NAMES

Ivan Tvorimirich, duke of Kiev prince (khagan) Yaroslaw the Wise (around 1043)   510
Ivan Vladislav, tsar of Bulgaria (1015–1018)   332, 509
Ivanka, scribe   457
Izyaslav, prince of Kiev (1054–1068, 1069–1073)   510

Jakov, son of Achilles, Hungarian count (around 1108)   485
Jakub Ziegler, in 1511 stayed in Leipzig   535
Jarloch, abbot of Milevsko, Bohemian chronicler   495–497
Janus, son of Vata   448
Jazko, prince of Spreevans (1150–1176)   508
Jeleg, see Üllő
Jenő   239
Jews   324, 476–477, 505
John I Tzimiskes, Byzantine emperor (969–976)   325
John VIII, pope (872–882)   211, 215
John, archbishop (around 900), papal legate   246
John I Tzimiskes, Byzantine emperor (969–976)   325
John Dlugosz, Polish chronicler   442
John, count of Sopron (about 1071)   453
John Kanizsai, archbishop of Esztergom   535
John the Deacon, Venetian chronicler   140
Jordanes, Gothic historian   1
Judith, wife of Louis the Pious   130
Judith, wife of Solomon, king of Hungary   446, 459, 467, 468
Justinian, Byzantine emperor (527–526)   26, 27, 28, 143
Jutas (Jutocha), third son of Árpád   315–317, 359

Kabars   239–242, 248, 303, 304, 319–320, 390
Kadocsa, Árpád's commander   308, 334–335, 337
Kál (Bogat), Hungarian horka   247, 248, 257, 313, 314
Kapolcs, Cuman khagan (round 1092)   471
Karolda, sister of Sarolt   342
Kean, Bulgarian prince, grandfather of prince Salan   310, 311

Kende (Kund), father of Kurszán   312
Kér   239
Keszi   239
Khazars   239, 240
Kocel, Panonian prince (861–pred 876), son of Pribina   85, 121, 122, 123, 128, 138, 139, 142, 152–154, 156–160, 163, 165, 169, 171–173, 176, 178, 180, 186, 211, 212, 222, 257, 506
Kojata, son of Všebor, Bohemian palatine (mentioned in 1061 and 1068)   513
Koppány, prince of Somogy (†997), son of Zerind   319, 329, 341–344, 346–348, 356, 359, 368, 372, 373, 396, 405, 504
Koppány, chaplain and scribe of king Ladislaus I, later bishop (perhaps Veszprém). Hungarian chronicler   275, 519–520
Kosnyachek, duke (around 1068) of Kijev prince (khagan) Izjaslav   510
Kotopan, Kherson emissary (in 1066)   508
Kriemhild (Krumhelt)   280, 286, 288, 492
Krivichians   256
Krum, Bulgarian khagan (802–814)   98, 141
Kunigunde, wife of Bernhard von Sponheim, sister of Styrian margrave Leopold the Strong   162
Kup, dignified inhabitant of Nitra   516
Kurszán (Kuszal), Kabar prince and Hungarian gyula (†904)   148, 240, 242, 248, 249, 303, 312
Kutrigurs   27, 30, 55
Kürt–Gyarmat   239
Kyros, king of Persia   289

Laborec, prince of Ung   300–301, 305
Lachovians   499
Ladislas, prince of Croatia (since 821)   108
Ladislas I (Saint Ladislas), prince of Biharia (1064–1074) and Nitria (1074–1077), king of Hungary (1077–1095)   272–274, 301, 382, 432, 441, 449, 451–463, 465–476, 478, 479, 481, 488, 489, 491, 493, 504, 505, 520, 529
Ladislas IV, king of Hungary (1272–1290)   277
Ladislas the Bald, prince of Nitria (1001–perhaps 1015)   291, 332, 359–363,

365, 366, 380, 383, 384, 387, 396–398, 403, 404, 420, 429, 529
Ladislas, son of Hungarian king Kálman (†1112)   480
Lambert, dean of the Nitra chapter (around 1111)   516
Lampert, prince of Biharia (1074–1077) and of Nitria (1077–1095)   449, 451, 455, 457, 460–462, 465, 466, 475, 488, 489, 529
Lampert, emperor (894–898)   245
Lampert, count of Hont   481
Latins   532
Laurentius, archbishop of Esztergom (1105/1106–1116)   516, 518, 519
Laurentius, presbyter of the Nitra chapter   516
Lehel (Lél), Árpád's commander and Hungarian prince in Nitria (†955), son of Tas   263, 264, 277, 278, 290, 317–318, 320, 321, 323, 337, 492, 528
Leo I, Byzantine emperor (457–474)   19
Leo V, Byzantine emperor (813–820)   105, 106
Leo VI the Wise, Byzantine emperor (886–912)   242
Leo IX, pope (1048–1054)   444
Leopold the Strong, Styrian margrave (1122–1129)   162
Leopold II, margrave of Eastern march (1079–1096)   494
Levedi   239
Levente (†1047), son of Vazul   291, 359, 361, 364–366, 400, 411, 420, 424, 432–440, 442
Lindolf, Bavarian magnate   158
Linones   197
Liudolf, bishop of Augsburg (987–996)   378
Liudprand, bishop of Cremona (961–972)   269, 270, 287
Liupram, archbishop of Salzburg (836–859)   152, 153, 159
Liutpold, margrave of Nordgau and Eastern march (893–907)   231, 233, 247, 254, 257, 258, 260
Liutpold III, margrave of Eastern march (1096–1136)   424, 484
Ljudemysl, uncle of Borna   105, 109

Ljudevit (Louis), prince of Savia (before 818–822)   99, 105, 106, 108, 109, 129, 131, 139, 143, 173
Longobards   22–32, 40–42, 44, 45, 53, 54, 55, 60, 85, 86, 92, 143, 150, 526
Lorio, owned fief near Lafnitz   163
Lothair, emperor (840–855), son of Louis the Pious   130, 139
Louis II the German, king of Bavaria (826–840), East Francia king (840–876), son of Louis the Pious   45, 86, 100, 101, 111, 117–122, 124, 130, 135, 138, 139, 141, 153, 154, 159, 165, 166, 167, 173, 175, 176, 183–185, 188, 196, 198–207, 211, 212, 220, 236
Louis IV the Child, East Francia king (900–911)   249
Louis the Pious, Aquitanian king (781–814), Francia king and emperor (814–840)   52, 99, 101, 102, 104, 105, 106, 111, 114, 115, 116, 126, 129, 130, 132, 133, 182, 211
Louis, count of Thuringia, son of Louis the German   207, 484
Louis III the Junior, East Francia king (876–882)   206, 207
Louis VII, French king (1137–1180)   52
Lucia, wife of palatine Rado   445
Ludmila, wife of Bořivoj   225, 266, 506
Lupus Centulli, Basque (round 819)   133, 134
Lupus (Lupo), duke of Friuli (†664)   36, 58, 73
Lusatians   213, 267
Luticians   267, 334, 505, 532

Madalvin, chorbishop of Passau (around 903)   259
Magiug, partner of royal tax collector Prkoš   515
Magnus, see Géza I   434
Magyars   134, 136, 178–180, 200, 206, 214, 230, 231, 239–268, 273, 277–285, 292–294, 296, 298–300, 302, 308, 311, 313, 317, 318, 320, 328, 354, 396, 412, 493, 499–502, 528, 530–532
Malamir, Bulgarian khagan (831–836)   129
Manas, Kirgizian hero   299

INDEX OF NAMES

Manasses, bishop of Zagreb (round 1111) 516, 517
Marcianus, emperor (450–457) 16
Marcomanni (Marcomans) 5, 6, 8, 13, 526
Marcus Aurelius, emperor (161–180) 6, 10
Mark, son of Simon, Hungarian count (around 1108) 485
Mark, partner of royal tax collector Prkoš 515
Marko, Serbian hero 299
Markwart, Carinthian duke (1073–1077) 160, 455
Martin, son of presbyter Matthew, canon of the Nitra chapter 516
Martin, defender of Bratislava castle (in 1052) 444
Martin, son of Mark, dignified inhabitant of Nitra 516
Martin, son of presbyter Matthew, canon of the Nitra chapter 516
Martyrius, archbishop of Esztergom (1151–1157) 407
Matthew, son of count Jekkel 533
Maurus, bishop of Pécs (about 1036–about 1075) 451
Meginfred, highest chamberlain, commander of Frizian army (in 623) 49, 50, 80
Megingoz, son of Wilhelm II 222
Megyer 239
Menandros, Byzantine historian 30
Menumorout, Biharian prince, grandson of Morout (Moravec) 280, 281, 302, 305, 336
Messians 263, 288, 289, 337, 338
Methodius, Byzantine missionary and archbishop of Moravia (869–885) 40, 104, 110, 140, 181, 186, 195, 210, 212, 213, 217, 219, 224, 235, 236, 238
Michael, prince of Nitria (971/987–perhaps 995) 177, 326, 327, 331–333, 338–340, 347, 349, 357, 359, 360, 362, 365, 366, 380, 404, 441, 528, 529
Michael I, Byzantine emperor (811–820) 93
Michael III, Byzantine emperor (842–867) 186, 202, 203
Michael VII Dukas, Byzantine emperor (1071–1078) 454, 460
Micolt, Bactrian princess 289

Mieszko I, prince of Poland (around 960–992) 321–323, 334, 337, 338, 352
Mieszko II, king (1025–1031) and prince (1131–1034) of Poland 397, 401, 507
Miko, Zvolen count (in 1246) 379
Milcens (Milcenians) 213, 267, 505
Miloš Kobilić, Serbian hero 299
Minigo, presbyter (around 860) 169
Miškov family 357–358
Modestus, chorbishop of Salzburg (before 757–about 763) 75, 76
Moesians 491–493
Mojmír I, prince of Great Moravia (833–846) 86, 109, 112, 127, 129–131, 134, 136, 137, 139, 181, 183, 217, 527, 528
Mojmír II, prince of Great Moravia (894–906) 136, 215, 231–234, 237, 247, 249, 254
Mojmírs (Mojmirids, Mojmír line) 222, 232, 233, 235, 237, 243, 244, 248, 250–256, 512, 528
Moravec (Morot, Marót), Pannonian ruler (prince) 283–285, 288, 292–294, 296–299, 492
Moravec (Morout), Biharian prince 280, 302, 336
Moravians (Moravian Slavs), Moravian army 34, 41, 62, 67, 81, 91, 94, 100, 111–114, 125–136, 152, 183, 185, 189, 195, 196, 198, 199, 202, 204, 205, 207, 208, 210–212, 215, 220, 222, 228–238, 242–245, 248–257, 259, 262, 265, 269, 281, 298, 312, 322, 396, 417, 421, 457, 458, 479, 491, 494–497, 499–501, 504, 505, 507, 512, 514, 528, 530
Moses, son of Bulgarian count Nicholas 331
Moses, count of Nitra (around 1105–around 1110) 516–518
Muslims 324
Mutimír, Serbian prince of Raška (872–891) 212
Mutina from the Vršovci family 485
Muzzili, Bavarian magnate 158

Načerat, Bohemian count (around 1142) 495
Nasr ibn Ahmed, Samanid amir (914–943) 264
Naum, pupil of Methodius 110, 214

Nennius, English chronicler 295
Nestor, Russian chronicler 34, 39, 113, 265, 279, 497–502, 508
Nibelungs 286, 294, 299
Nicholas, Bulgarian count (komit Nikola) 325, 331
Nicholas I, pope (858–867) 201
Nicholas, royal courtier (around 1059) 446
Nicholas, son of Pestrej, canon of the Nitra chapter 516
Nikeforos, emissary of the Byzantine emperor 105, 106
Nikeforos I, Byzantine emperor (802–811) 92
Nikeforos II, Phokas, Byzantine emperor (963–969) 324
Nikeforos III, Bataneiates, Byzantine emperor (1078–1081) 463
Niketas Skleros, Byzantine leader 242
Niketas, Byzantine chief of Belgrade (till 1071) 453
Nitrians (originally the Nitravians), Nitrian Slavs, Nitrian army 93, 94, 111–114, 128, 129, 256, 257, 262, 263, 335, 337, 338, 457, 458, 462, 477, 489–494, 497, 498, 500–502, 504, 505, 509, 512, 514, 516, 527, 529, 530, 535
Nother II, bishop of Verona (before 915–928) 261
Nyék 239

Obotrites 106, 111, 112, 133, 184, 200, 267, 505, 508, 512, 532
Obri (Avars) 164
Odilo, duke of Bavaria (737–748) 74
Odoacer, see Odovakar
Odolric, Dudlebian count (around 860) 167, 168, 172
Odovakar (Odoacer), son of Skirian king Edika 19, 22
Olaf I Tryggvesson, king of Norway (996–1000) 295
Oldřich, Bohemian prince (1012–1033, 1034) 401, 417
Oldřich, prince of Olomouc (1173–1177) 495
Oleg, Russian prince (khagan) of Novgorod and Kiev (879–882–912) 508
Oleg the Fair 509
Oleg Ingvarevich, brother of Ryazan grand prince Yuriy Ingvarevich 511

Omar, amir of Meletine 200
Omurtag, Bulgarian khagan (814–831) 99, 114, 116, 119, 129, 141
Onegavon, Bulgarian tarkhan 99
Onogurs 239, 240
Opolans 213
Opos, soldier of Hungarian king Solomon 462
Ort, prince and count of Vác (before 997–after 1037) 342, 344, 347, 348, 359, 373, 404, 405, 411
Orosius 85, 104
Osians 5, 6, 13
Ostrogotha, son of Gepidian king Elemund 28
Ostrogoths 14, 15, 16, 17, 18, 19, 21, 22, 29, 150, 526, 527
Ostromir, duke of Novgorod 510
Otachar, Bavarian magnate 158
Otakar, count of Leoben 175
Otto, Saxon duke (880–912) 250
Otto I, German king (936–973) and emperor (962–973) 317–318, 321, 327, 329
Otto I the Fair, prince of Znojmo (1055, 1058–1061) and Olomouc (1061–1087) 452, 456–458, 475, 488, 494, 505
Otto II the Black, prince of Olomouc (1107–1110, 1113–1125) and Brno (1123–1125) 475, 484, 494, 505, 507, 515
Otto II, German king and emperor (973–983) 160, 378
Otto III, German king (983–1002) and emperor (996–1002) 371, 372, 374, 375
Otto Orseolo, Venetian doge (1030–1031) 419
Otto of Habsburg 484
Otto of Regensburg 484
Ottokar II (V), Styrian margrave (1129–1164) 162, 175
Otto Orseolo, Venetian doge (1030–1031) 419

Pabo, leader of Bavarian army, Blatenian count (828–about 840) 118, 119, 173, 176
Pabo, Carantanian count (till 861) 136, 141, 166, 198
Pabo, son of Engelschalk 222
Paldmund, Bavarian magnate 158
Pannonians 134–136, 493, 494

INDEX OF NAMES

Paul, pope (757–767) 92
Paulino, patriarch of Aquilea (776–802) 83, 91
Paulus Orosius, priest of Bracara, scholar and historian (1th half 5th c.) 100
Paul the Deacon, Longobard chronicler (8th c.) 113
Paul, Hungarian noble (around 1108) 485
Pavel, archipresbyter of Bohemia 266
Pechenegs 136, 239, 242, 271, 273, 301, 305, 325, 362–364, 392, 400, 432, 433, 444, 453, 461, 467, 468, 470, 487, 493, 496, 510
Pemmo, duke of Friuli (about 720–perhaps 738) 58
Penet, dignified inhabitant of Nitra 516
Pepin, king of Aquitania (814–838), son of Louis the Pious 130
Pepin, king of Italy (781–810), son of Charlemagne 71, 72, 80–83, 85, 86, 91, 95, 124
Peregrin, dignified inhabitant and market judge of Nitra 516
Peter, Bulgarian tsar (927–970) 324
Peter Čech (the Czech) from Šarovce, count of Tekov 534, 535
Peter Orseolo, king of Hungary (1038–1041, 1044–1046) 397, 419–424, 426, 430, 431, 434–436, 438, 439, 504, 513, 529
Peter Oslyadyukovich (+1238), duke of Vladimir grand prince Yuriy II Vsevolodovich 511
Peter Svačič, king of Croatia (1091–1097) 470, 478, 479
Peter the Hermit, French anchorite 476
Peter, Hungarian palatine (before 1091– perhaps since 1093) 473
Peter Vlastovic, Polish palatine (1117–1121, perhaps 1131–1146) 513
Petre, dignified inhabitant of Nitra 516
Petronas, Byzantine strategist 200
Petrud, leader of army and adviser of prince Géza 456
Pezili, Hungarian magnate 423
Philippe, abbot from Zobor 399, 451
Philippe, administrator of Titel chapter (around 1347) 466
Philippe, bishop of Vác (1263–1278) and count of Novohrad 413

Photios, patriarch of Constantinople (860–867, 877–886) 202, 203
Piasts 512, 514
Piligrim, bishop of Passau (971–991) 216, 217, 327, 328, 330, 492
Pliny the Elder (Gaius Plinius Secundus) 110
Poles, Polish army 310, 355, 363, 381, 383–385, 396, 397, 401, 446, 450, 481, 483, 485, 496, 499–501, 505
Pomeranians 432, 452, 484, 496, 505
Porga, prince of Croatia 35
Poško, canon of the Nitra chapter 516
Poto, count of Altenburg (round 1060) 447, 448
Poznan, prince of Little Nitria (since 997–1001) 342–344, 347–352, 359, 380, 403–407, 411, 509
Poznans 349–351
Predslava, daughter of Kiev prince Sviatopolk II, wife of Almos 480
Presian I, Bulgarian khagan (836–852) 141
Presian, son of Bulgarian tsar Ivan Vladislav 509
Preslav, name in Slovakia in time of Árpád 379
Pretich, duke of Kiev prince Sviatoslav 510
Pribina, prince of Nitria (before 828–833) and Pannonia (round 840–861) 85, 109–112, 116, 120–123, 127, 128, 130–132, 134–143, 149–159, 165, 171–174, 178, 181–184, 198, 199, 215, 222, 257, 328, 330, 506, 509, 527, 528, 530
Pribislav, prince of Transdanubia (do 827) 103, 104, 174, 175
Prkoš, centurion, royal tax collector 515
Prkoš, administrator of castle Bílina 494, 504
Prodsa, offspring of count Lampert 482
Prokopios, Byzantine historian 29
Prokuj, another name of Transylvanian prince Gyula II 385–387
Prussians 501, 502
Přemyslids 210, 232, 237, 256, 327, 338, 347, 352, 353, 494, 497, 507, 512, 514, 528

Quadi (Quads) 5, 6, 7, 8, 9, 11, 12, 13, 14, 16, 17, 526

Rachwin, count of Ptuj (before 980–after 985) 160, 161, 163
Radim (Gaudencius), archbishop of Gniezno (1000–1006) 371
Radimichs 510
Radla, see Sebastián
Rado, Hungarian palatine (around 1057) 445
Radovan, son Bugar 454
Radulf, duke of Thuringia (about 631) 48
Raptus, king of Hasdings 5
Rashdi, conjurer 448
Rasina, abbot of Pannonhalma (perhaps arount 1015) 370, 393
Rastislav, prince of Great Moravia (846–870) 86, 183–188, 198 - 202, 204–208, 215, 217, 222, 235, 236, 502, 506, 512
Rastislav, prince of Tmutakaran (1064–1066) 508, 510
Ratbod, margrave of Eastern and Carantanian March (828–854) 118, 119, 120, 122, 132, 135, 136, 138, 139, 141, 142, 159, 166, 184, 188, 198
Ratchis, duke of Friuli (asi 738–744) and Longobard king (744–749) 58
Ratimir, prince of Savia (till 838) 115, 119, 135, 137, 141
Rato, fief-tenant of archbishop Liupram 159
Raus, king of Hasdings 5
Reginger, owned fief near Gnasbach 163
Reginhar, bishop of Passau (818–838) 100–101, 124–126, 181
Regino, West Frankisch chronicler (†908) 142, 227, 228, 250, 251, 254, 269, 270, 287
Richard, Dudlebian count (before 844–857) 119, 120, 132, 166–168
Richard, bishop of Passau (899–903) 247
Rihpald, archiprebyster of Blatengrad (till 869) 153
Risiulf, nephew of Longobard king Wacho 25, 26
Rodulph, Herulian king (†508) 23
Roger I, Norman-Sicilian count 479
Roland 294
Roman Ingvarevich, grand prince of Ryazan 511
Romans 5, 6, 7, 8, 10, 11, 12, 13, 14, 16, 19, 22, 44, 46, 71, 136, 137, 143, 146, 150, 170, 336

Roxana, wife of Alexander the Great 289
Rudolf, duke of Swabia (1057–1079) and German king (1077–1080) 466, 468
Rudolf, bishop of Würzburg (892–907) 253
Rudolf II, king of Upper Burgundy (911–934), king of Italy (922–934), king of Burgundy (934–937) 262
Rugians 15, 16, 19, 22
Rumo, Sarmatian prince (round 358) 7
Ruodpert, margrave of Carantania (887–893), son of Wilhelm II 133, 226, 230–231
Ruotger, Benediktine monk from Cologne 251, 253
Rupert, bishop of Salzburg (before 696–715/716) 60
Rurik, Varangian ruler to Ladoga and Novgorod 256
Ruriks, Rurik line 508, 512, 514
Russians 256, 301, 310, 324, 355, 381, 456, 465, 499–501, 513
Ryazans 295

Salacho, count of Carniola (round 838) 135
Salan, Bulgarian prince 243, 300, 301, 309–311, 354, 355, 412, 413
Samo, Frankish merchant, Slav ruler (623–658) 39, 42, 44, 45, 47, 48, 52–56, 71, 73, 140, 527
Samuel, cometopul and tsar of Bulgaria (991–997–1014), son of Bulgarian count Nicholas 331–333
Samuel Aba, palatine and king (1041–1044) of Hungary 170, 309, 310, 347, 390, 405, 422–425, 429–431, 433, 434, 504, 512, 513, 520
Sandrat, priest 153, 172
Saracens 294
Sarchas, judge (perhaps in 1056) 445
Sarmatians 6, 7, 14, 17, 18, 20, 21, 22, 24, 500
Sarolt (Beleknegini), wife of Hungarian prince Géza 177, 307, 317, 325–327, 330, 332, 342, 385, 498
Saxons 49, 50, 79, 96, 133, 207, 220, 250–253, 255, 259, 260, 262, 267, 295, 334, 416, 505, 532
Scirs 15, 17, 18, 19, 21, 22, 24
Scythians 364, 492, 493

INDEX OF NAMES

Sebastian (Radla), archbishop of Esztergom (1002–1007)   367, 368, 370–371, 387
Sebes, border (probably Bratislava) count (†1039)   405, 406, 411, 423
Sebes, son of Buda and grandchild of Egiruch   419, 420, 423
Sejun, dignified inhabitant of Nitra   516
Semika (Cemicas), prince of Transdanubia (till 827)   103, 104, 174, 175
Semnoni   339
Serafin, archbishop of Esztergom (around 1095–1104)   270, 479
Serb, prince of Serbs   38, 39
Serbs   35, 36, 38, 39, 108, 141, 501, 509
Setiech, palatine and duke (1080–1100) of Polish prince Wladyslaw Herman   512
Seven lines   57
Severans   510
Sieghard, patriarch of Aquileja (1068–1077)   462
Siegfrid, bishop of Augsburg (1000–1006)   378
Sigismund of Luxembourg, king of Hungary (1387–1437) and emperor (1433–1437)   534
Silesians   213
Simeon, prince and later tsar of Bulgaria (895–927)   332, 509
Simon of Kéza, Hungarian chronicler (1282–1285)   263, 265, 276–279, 283, 284, 288–292, 299, 336, 364–366, 423, 487, 530
Sineus, brother of Rurik   256
Skarbimir from the family Adbank, polish palatine (1107–1117, 1121–perhaps 1131)   513
Slavitah, prince of Bohemia (till 857)   135, 136, 185
Slaviz, Novohrad count (around 1108)   410
Slavniks, Bohemian princely family   367
Slavomir, prince of Nitria (871)   81, 136, 208, 209
Slavomir, Obotrite prince (819–821)   133, 134, 137
Slovaks   286, 299, 493, 501, 503, 530, 531, 535
Sloviens of Novgorod   256
Soběslav, son of prince Slavník   367
Soběslav I, prince of Znojmo (1113/1115–1123) and Bohemia (1125–1140)   480, 496, 513

Solomon, king of Hungary (1063–1074)   271–273, 301, 303, 362, 440, 441, 445, 446, 448–468, 475, 488, 490, 504, 529
Sophia, daughter of Béla I (†1095)   448
Sorbs   34, 35, 42, 49, 55, 96, 111, 112, 198, 224, 232, 237, 250, 255, 506, 532
southern Obotrites (Predenecentes)   71, 99, 111, 114
Sovárd, Árpád's commander   308, 334–337
Sponheims   162
Spreevans   508
Spytihněv I, prince of Bohemia (895–915)   225, 226, 232, 253, 256, 506
Spytihněv II, prince of Bohemia (1055–1061)   422
Stephen, bishop of Veszprém (around 1009)   390
Stephen I (Saint Stephen), prince of Nitria (perhaps 995–997), Hungarian prince (997–1001) and king (1001–1038)   146, 178, 237, 273, 274, 301, 307, 309, 310, 314, 317, 319, 320, 322, 329, 339–344, 346–351, 354, 356–361, 363, 364, 368, 370–376, 379, 380, 382–385, 387, 389–397, 403–406, 411, 415, 417–422, 426, 429, 430, 434, 438, 441, 443, 467, 487, 498, 503, 504, 512, 513, 515, 516, 520, 528, 529
Stephen II, king of Croatia (1089–1091)   468
Stephen II, pope (752)   92
Stephen II, king of Hungary (1116–1131)   479, 480
Stephen V, king of Hungary (1270–1272)   276, 366, 524
Stibor, duke   534
Stodorans (Hevells, Hevelians)   252, 267, 528
Stojmir, prince of Transdanubia (do 827)   103, 104, 174, 175
Stojslav, Hungarian magnate   423
Suebs   5, 14, 15, 16, 17, 18, 19, 20, 21, 22, 49, 526
Sulajmán al-Kalbí, amir of Zaragoza   87
Súr, Hungarian (Kabar) prince (†955)   317–321
Svatopluk, prince of Olomouc (1095–1107), prince of Bohemia (1107–1109)   287, 475, 476, 484, 485, 494, 496, 507, 515

Svätopluk I, prince of Nitria (before 862–871), prince of Great Moravia (871–894)   81, 180, 186–189, 193, 195, 207–215, 219–224, 226–233, 235, 236, 238, 243, 249, 250, 256, 269–271, 279, 280, 283–290, 292, 293, 295–299, 322, 349, 492, 506, 511, 512, 528, 530
Svätopluk II, prince of Nitria (894–899)   136, 215, 232, 234, 237, 512, 528
Svätožízňa, Bohemian princess, wife of Svätopluk, prince of Great Moravia   210, 211, 233
Svenald, duke of Kiev prince Igor   510
Sviatopolk, prince of Pinsk   508
Sviatopolk II Izjaslavich, prince of Kiev (1093–1113)   479, 480
Sviatoslav I, prince of Kiev (945–972)   324, 325, 510
Sviatoslav Vsevolodovich, brother of Vladimir grand prince Yuriy II Vsevolodovich   511
Svorad, anchorite of Zobor   399, 451
Swabs (Swabians)   260, 261, 505
Swarnagal, presbyter of Blatengrad   153
Sylvester II, pope (999–1003)   374
Synadené, wife of Géza I, king of Hungary   463
Szalárd, Magyar commander (around 924)   336
Székelys   390
Szemere, son of Huba   336
Szemere family   336
Szemere, count of Šintava (around 1177)   336
Szolnok, count (†1046)   394, 411, 435, 436
Szolnok, count and adviser of prince Géza   456

Tacitus   110
Taksony, Hungarian prince (perhaps 955–perhaps 971), son of Zsolt   291, 315, 317, 320, 325–327, 348, 362, 437
Tarcal (Turzol), Magyar warrior   355
Tarhos (Tarkachu, Dursak), Hungarian prince (907–trough 922), Árpád's oldest son   247, 257, 314, 315, 316, 359
Tarján   239
Tas, Hungarian prince, son of Jutas   263, 264, 315, 316

Tassilo I, duke of Bavaria (591–609)   30
Tassilo III, duke of Bavaria (748–788)   76, 78, 79, 132, 182
Tatars   511
Tato, Longobard king (before 505–510), son of Claffo   23, 25
Tatun, wife of Nitrian prince Vazul   291, 362, 365, 366
Taurisci   170
Tetény (Tuhutum), Árpád's commander   305–307
Tetraxites (Crimean Goths)   27
Tevel, son of Tarhos   314
Theodemir (Thiudimer), Ostrogoth king (468/469–474)   16, 19, 22
Theodor, Avar kapkhan (†805)   82, 91, 94, 95, 96, 168
Theodorich, count, commander of the Saxons army (in 623)   49, 50, 80
Theodorich (Theudarichi) the Great, Ostrogoth king (474–526)   20, 22
Theodorich, chorbishop of Salzburg (798–after 821)   84, 104
Theodulos Synadenos, brother-in-law of Byzantine emperor Nikephoros III Botaneiates (1078–1081)   463
Theophylaktos, missionary bishop of Transylvania   331
Thietmar, bishop of Merseburg (1009–1018), Saxon chronicler   326, 329, 339, 374, 384, 385, 387, 396, 498, 501–503
Thietmar, archbishop of Salzburg (873–907)   160, 258, 339
Thomas, bishop of Vác (1278–1289)   413
Thuringians (Thurings)   55, 207, 253, 416
Thurisind, Gepidian king (546–560)   26–29
Tiberius, emperor (14–37)   145
Timochans   99, 106
Tomislav, prince of Croatia (before 914–up to 928)   470
Tormás (Termachu), son of Tevel, grandchild of Tarhos   314, 392
Totila, Ostrogoth king (541–552)   27, 29
Trajan, emperor (98–117)   146
Transiugitans   6
Trebovans   213
Trpimír I, prince of Croatia (845–864)   185

INDEX OF NAMES	655

Trpimírovič family   468
Truvor, brother of Rurik   256
Tugumir, Hevelian prince   140
Tuto, bishop of Regensburg (893–930)   259
Turks   162
Tyr, duke of Bohemia   512

Udo, bishop of Freising (906–907)   258
Ulric, margrave of Carniola and Istria (1054–1070)   448
Ulrich, bishop of Augsburg (923–973)   317
Ulrich of Richental, chronicler   534–535
Una, count of Nitra (around the mid-11th c.)   516–518
Unzat, Slav magnate (about 850)   157–158
Urban II, pope (1088–1099)   469, 478
Urolf, bishop of Passau (804–806)   126
Uroš, defender of Bratislava castle (in 1052)   444
Uroš I, grand count of Raška (†1141)   480
Uroš, Hungarian noble (around 1108)   485
Ursus, patriarch of Aquilea (802–807)   91
Usafer, Sarmatian prince (around 358)   6, 7
Usubu, Magyar commander   281
Utigurs   27, 30
Üllő (Jeleg), second son of Árpád   315, 316, 359

Vacek, Bohemian palatine (around 1105)   513
Vajk, see Stephen I
Vajta, Árpád's commander   308
Valachs   288, 300, 305
Valamer, Ostrogoth king (before 454–468/469)   16, 19
Valentinian I, emperor (364–375)   14, 44, 146
Valtunk, prince of Carantania (772–788)   77, 79, 102
Valuk, prince of Carantania (before 631–after 663)   36–37, 54
Vandals   5, 6, 7, 14, 15, 49
Varangians   256
Vasilko, prince of Terebovľ (before 1091–1124)   471, 479
Vata, leader of the Tisza river region pagan rebels (in 1046)   434–436, 448
Vata, count and bishop of Bihar   455
Vata, Hungarian noble (around 1108)   485

Vazul, prince of Nitria (perhaps 1015–1029)   291, 332, 359–366, 396–401, 403, 404, 411, 418–420, 429, 432–435, 441, 529
Vécs, magnate of family Sovárd   337
Velets (Luticians)   111, 267
Vencelin, Swabian knight (about 997) and count of Somogy   343, 344, 356
Vergilius, bishop of Salzburg (748–785)   75, 77, 84, 140
Venetians   452
Vesians   256
Vezzilo, count   221
Vid, count of Bács (†1074)   453–459
Vidimer, brother of Ostrogoth king Valamer (†473)   16, 22
Viduari, Kvadian king (about 358)   6, 7, 8, 13
Vikings   229, 230, 295
Vilungard, defender of Bratislava castle (in 1052)   444
Visigoths   14, 22
Vistrach, prince of Bohemia (perhaps from 846)   135, 185
Vistulians   213, 237
Vitale I Michiel, Venetian doge (1095–1102)   478, 479
Vitemir   157, 158
Vitrodor, son of king Viduari   7, 13
Visigoths   6, 14
Viska, Hungarian magnate   434
Vladislas I, prince of Bohemia (1109–1117, 1120–1125)   513
Vladovoj, prince of Bohemia (1002–1003)   398
Volodar, prince of Peremyšľ (1092–1124)   479
Vladimir (Volodymyr) the Great, Russian prince of Novgorod (972–977) and prince (khagan) of Kiev (978–1015)   363, 508, 510
Vladimir (Volodymyr), Bulgarian prince (889–893)   230
Vlachs   289, 492, 499
Vladislas I, prince of Bohemia (1109–1117, 1120–1125)   494
Vladislas II, prince of Bohemia (1140–1172)   495
Vojnomir, prince of Savia (around 796)   81, 85–89

Vojtech (Adalbert), Prague bishop
(983–989)   321, 322, 331, 367, 368, 370,
371, 400, 502
Vojtech, defender of Bratislava castle
(in 1052)   444
Volodar, prince of Peremyšľ (1092–1124)   479
Vratislaus I, prince of Bohemia (915–921)
225, 226, 232, 253, 256, 262, 265, 266,
422, 506, 507
Vratislaus II, prince of Olomouc (1055,
1058–1061), Bohemian prince (1061–1085)
and king (1085–1092)   422, 471, 494
Vršovci family   485
Vsevolod, prince of Pronsk (1217–1237)   509
Vsevolod Dimitriy Yuriyevich (†1238),
son of Vladimir grand prince Yuriy II
Vsevolodovich   511
Všeslav Brjačislavič, prince of Polotsk
(1044–1101)   508
Vyshata, duke (since 1043) of Kiev prince
(khagan) Yaroslav the Wise, son of
Novgorod duke Ostromir   510

Wacho, Longobard king (510–540)   25
Walter Sans Avoir, French knight   476
Walthari, Longobard king (540–547)   25, 26
Warin, count of Auvergne (round 819)   133
Wechtar, Friuian prince (663–671)   73
Welf IV, duke of Bavaria (1070–1077,
1096–1101)   478, 483
Welf, duke of Carinthia (1047–1055)   443
Wenceslaus (saint), prince of Bohemia
(921–935)   266, 339, 506, 507
Wenceslaus II, king of Bohemia
(1191–1192)   507
Werinhar (Warnar), margrave of Avar and
Carantanian March (802–after 806)   96,
100, 101, 102
Werinhar (Warnar), margrave of Eastern
March (863–865)   201, 206, 207
Werinhar, son of Engelshalk   221
White Croats   34, 213
Wiching, bishop of Nitra (880–891)   215–219
Wiedheri, Bavarian magnate   158
Wilhelm I, count of Traungau (821–853)
101, 121, 122, 123, 128, 130, 172, 207, 208

Wilhelm II, margrave of Eastern March
(865–871)   136, 206, 208, 221, 223
Wilhelm, brother of Engelschalk II   231
Wilhelm IV from Weimar-Orlamünde,
margrave of Meissen (1046–1062)
447, 448
Wilhelm, count of Savinja (about 980)   160
Wilhelms, Bavarian family   121, 123, 127, 133,
221–223, 229, 231
Willerm, gramarian, probably director of the
chapter school of Nitra (round 1111)   516
Willerm, abbot of Szekszárd (about 1074)
456
Wiprecht, count of Grojtzsch   484
Wladyslaw I Herman, prince of Poland
(1079–1102)   468, 471, 512
Wolf's Tail, duke of Kiev prince (khagan)
Vladimir (around 984)   510

Yaropolk, Russian prince (khagan) of Kiev
(972–980) and Novgorod (977–980)   510
Yaroslav, son of Batona   516
Yaroslav the Wise, Russian prince of
Novgorod and prince (khagan) of Kiev
(1012–1019–1054)   433, 441, 465, 508,
510
Yaroslav Vsevolodovich, brother of Vladimir
grand prince Yuriy II Vsevolodovich   511
Yerem Glebovich (+ 1237), duke of Vladimir
grand prince Yuriy II Vsevolodovich   511
Yuriy Ingvarevich, grand prince of Ryazan
(1235–1237)   295–296, 509, 511
Yuriy II Vsevolodovich, grand prince of
Vladimir (1218–1238)   511

Zacharias, bishop of Säben (–907)   258
Zacharias, pope (741–752)   92
Zbyša, dignified inhabitant of Nitra   516
Zdeslav, prince of Croatia (876–879)   140
Zerind (Szörény, Severinus), prince
of Somogy (2 half 10 c.), father of
Koppány   319, 327, 341, 342
Zinafer, Sarmatian prince (about 358)   7
Zizai, Sarmatian prince (about 358)   7
Zoltán, count in the Fehér county
(since 1003)   386

INDEX OF NAMES

Zoltán see Zsolt
Zombor (Zsombor), prince on northern part of Transylvania (about 970–1003), brother of Gyula II   347, 348, 356, 386
Zothmund, defender of Bratislava castle (in 1052)   444

Zubur, prince of Nitria   335, 351, 352
Zsolt (Zoltán), fourth son of Arpád, Hungarian prince (after 922–perhaps 947)   281, 315, 316, 356, 359
Žiroslav Mikhaylovich, duke of Vladimir grand prince Yuriy II Vsevolodovich   511

Index of Places

Aachen   51, 81, 97, 101, 105, 114, 116, 117, 130, 133
Abaújvár, Újvár, Abov (castle, county, archdeaconate)   5, 263, 310, 356, 415, 435, 436, 481, 521, 523–525
Ablanc (Abláncz)   156, 157, 165
Abov, see Abaújvár
Admont, abbey in Styria   461
Adrianopolis (Edirne)   27
Aelium Cetium   149
Aequinoctium (Fischamend)   145
Africa   289
Agasta (Aist)   46, 47
Aguntum   75
Aist   46, 49
Alamania   51
Albing   46
Alexandria   377
Alexandreid   286
Alpár   243
Alta Ripa (Tolna)   147
Amber Road   143, 145, 159, 164, 170
Antiochia   377
Aquileia   91, 107, 500
Aquileian patriarchat   84, 85, 91, 462
Aquincum (Óbuda)   14, 144, 147
Aquis (Baden)   145
Aquitaine   134
Arad (castle, county)   466
Aranyán   466
Arcadiopolis (Lüle-Burgas)   325
Arrabona (Győr)   145
Árpád's principality between the Danube, Tisza and the Zagyva rivers   310–313, 316, 348, 373
Aschach   121
Assyria   289
Asturis (Klosterneuburg)   145
Augsburg   260, 317, 318, 378, 438
Augsburg bishopric   378, 483
Augusta Vindelicorum (Augsburg)   378
Augustianis   149
Austrasia   48
Austria   496
Avalon, island   295

Avar khaganate, Avar realm, Avaria   30, 32, 42, 43, 54, 57, 58, 60, 61, 66, 68, 71, 72, 73, 78, 79, 80, 85, 98, 104, 130, 141, 174, 526, 527
Avar (later Eastern) March   70, 79, 81, 83, 84, 85, 89, 90, 95, 96, 97, 98, 100, 101, 102, 108, 111
Aventine, Abbey of saint Boniface and saint Alexis   367, 374

Babót   459, 461
Bacharnsdorf   149
Bács (castle, county)   214, 314, 453
Bács, archbishopric   472, 473
Bactria, see Bracta
Baghdad   506
Bakonybél abbey   282, 393
Bakonykoppány   282
Balassagyarmat   67
Balaton (Blatenian lake, Marsh lake)   34, 83, 144, 150, 152, 154, 173, 246, 319, 341, 443, 447
Bamberg   389
Bana   335, 352, 428
Banat   214
Bánhida   248, 283–288, 295, 297, 409
Bánov near Trenčín   471
Baranya (castle, county)   172, 281, 319, 346, 347, 396
Barca   67
Basaharc   285
Basel   252
Batavis (Passau)   46
Bautzen   401
Bavaria   31, 42, 50, 51, 53, 55, 60, 61, 75, 78, 79, 80, 84, 89, 90, 91, 94, 101, 102, 110, 116, 118, 119, 123, 127, 137, 141, 176, 178, 183, 185, 198–200, 206, 207, 220, 221, 223, 229–231, 244, 252, 260, 261, 266, 267, 317, 406, 416, 421, 501, 515, 532
Beckov   335, 352, 428, 534
Békés (castle, county)   304, 435
Belá   481
Belgrade (Beograd)   214, 453, 455
Beloozersk   256

INDEX OF PLACES

Bernolákovo 67
Bešeňov 67, 263
Bihar (castle, county)   280, 302–305, 309, 325, 348, 394, 453, 455, 472, 487
Biharia, Biharian principality   280, 292, 299, 302–308, 311, 319, 320, 325, 326, 331, 336, 338, 358, 390, 394, 402, 419, 437, 441, 451–457, 459, 460, 462, 465, 466, 471, 476, 481, 487–489, 498, 512–514
Bihar bishopric, diocese   304, 394–396, 435, 455, 472
Bijelo Brdo (near Osijek)   279
Bílina   421, 494, 504
Bíňa   343, 359
Biograd na Moru   468, 473, 479
Bischofshofen, monastery   74
Blatengrad (Mosaburg, Marsh castle, Zalavár)   139, 142, 143, 152–159, 171, 172, 222, 229, 506
Blatenia (Blatenland, Blatenian county)   171–174, 176, 229
Blatenian lake, see Balaton
Bodrog (castle, county)   311, 314, 466
Bodza   67
Boguslavľ (south of Kiev)   377
Bohemia (Boiohaemum)   34, 36, 46, 49, 50, 51, 52, 80, 112, 164, 210, 211, 223, 224, 226–229, 237, 238, 252, 262, 265, 266, 267, 321, 324, 325, 334, 367, 420–424, 429, 432, 437, 444, 471, 474, 476, 479, 484, 485, 492, 494–498, 500, 501, 504, 512–515, 526, 527, 534, 535
Bohemian road   418
Boioduria   46
Boiodurum (Pasov)   46
Boiohaemum   526
Bojná   65, 193
Boleslav (Stará Boleslav)   376
Bolia, River   19, 42
Bononia (Bonoštor)   7
Borsod (castle, principality, county, archdeaconate)   263, 309, 311, 321, 338, 354–358, 377, 404, 415, 427, 431, 520–522, 524, 525
Boržava, Borzsova (castle, county, archdeaconate)   300–302, 304, 355, 467, 524
Böcs   67

Bracta (Bactria)   286, 288, 289, 492
Bratislava, Preslava (castle, county, archdeaconate, provostal)   12, 67, 72, 182, 183, 190, 191, 205, 254, 257, 258, 260, 313, 317, 329, 375–380, 386, 404, 406, 407, 425, 427, 431, 444, 459–463, 467, 483, 484, 518, 534
Bremen   252
Brenna   140
Brent   244
Brigetio   6, 7, 8, 11, 14, 145
Britain   295
Brno   494, 515
Brunnaron (today Pilgersdorf or Lebenbrun)   157, 166
Břeclav-Pohansko   64
Břevnov monastery   367
Buda   179
Buda (castle, archdeaconate)   409, 410, 436
Buchenau   101
Bulgaria, Bulgarian khaganate   34, 57, 100, 141, 157, 172, 200, 201, 203, 204, 214, 215, 230, 242, 243, 248, 294, 310, 324, 325, 331–333, 434, 499
Burgundy   49, 252, 261, 294, 416
Byzantium, Byzantine empire   20, 21, 27–32, 92, 99, 105, 141, 201, 246, 273, 278, 306, 313, 314, 324, 392, 454, 463, 468, 476, 490, 501, 502, 526, 532
Bzovík, abbey   482

Caesarea   378
Carantania, Carantanian principality   30, 36, 38, 40, 42, 54, 55, 60, 61, 70, 73–75, 77, 79, 84, 85, 91, 100, 102, 103, 104, 107–109, 117, 118, 119, 140–142, 159–164, 166, 198, 201, 205, 207, 220, 223, 230, 249, 260, 261, 279, 281, 526, 527
Carantanian march   70, 79, 83, 84, 89, 90, 92, 95, 99, 100, 101, 102, 104, 107, 108, 111, 114, 119, 142, 162, 231
Carinthia, Carinthian duchy   424, 425, 455, 500, 501, 532
Carinthian march   425
Carniola   38, 40, 58, 59, 61, 70, 73, 74, 80, 81, 117, 118, 141, 161, 527

Carnuntum   11, 12, 44, 54, 70, 93, 95, 96, 145,
    164, 168, 170
Castra Regina (Regensburg)   46
Castra ad Herculem (Pilismarót)   146, 147,
    284–285
Catalaunian Plains   15
Cella   158
Chľaba   481
Chrudim   444
Chlm   509
Cinkota (near Pest)   458, 488
Cividale   73
Colmar   130
Cologne   52
Cologne archbishopric   483
Comagena   149
Comagenan Mount (Kaumberg)   124, 223,
    236
Constance   534
Constantinople   27, 28, 32, 43, 93, 186, 201,
    203, 204, 269, 278, 306, 314, 324, 331
Cremona   31
Croatia, Croatian principality, Croatian
    kingdom   38, 39, 40, 92, 105, 109, 131, 143,
    248, 468–470, 475, 478, 479, 500, 525,
    526, 532
Csanád, Cenad (castle, county)   348, 356,
    377, 393, 430, 520
Csanád bishopric, diocese   392–396, 434,
    435, 520
Csepel   34, 312
Csilizköz   406–409
Csongrád (castle, county, archedeaconate)
    411, 412, 487
Csór (Chour)   482
Čakajovce   263
Čáslav   376
Cataj   67
Čepeľ   481
Červen (Czerwień)   401
Červeník   263
Čierny Brod   67
Čingov (Hradisko I at the interface of Spišské
    Tomášovce and Smižany)   66, 194
Čingov (Hradisko II in Smižany)   194, 195

Dacia   6, 15, 99
Dalmatia   19, 27, 31, 35, 36, 38, 40, 57, 92, 105,
    107, 131, 452, 478, 479, 483, 500, 526, 532

Damascus   52
Denmark   500
Devín   44, 45, 47, 59, 61, 62, 67, 70, 71, 94, 182,
    189, 204–206, 236
Devínska Nová Ves   44, 60, 61, 64, 71
Dioclea, see Duklja
Divinka (near Žilina)   193
Doboka, Dăbîca (castle, county)   356, 377,
    453
Dobruja   57
Dolné Chlebany   451
Dolné Věstenice   64, 65
Dolní Dunajovice   67
Dolný Peter   263
Domaša   481
Dömös (abbey, court)   410, 449, 481, 482,
    485, 515
Dubrovník   509
Ducové   192
Dudleba (Dudleipin)   157, 163, 165, 169
Dudlebia (Dudlebland), Dudlebian
    principality, county   163–172, 174, 176, 229
Duklja   187–188
Dvory nad Žitavou   67, 403, 408

East Francia, East Francia kingdom,
    East Francia empire, Easter Frankish
    empire   86, 100, 112, 184, 185, 187, 201, 202,
    206, 212, 219, 226, 241, 243, 250, 294, 532
Eastern march (before Avar march)   118, 119,
    120, 136, 142, 149, 157, 166, 182–185, 196,
    204, 207, 208, 221, 223, 230, 231, 234,
    241, 249, 260, 313, 386, 406, 417, 418,
    421, 424, 425, 430, 436, 443, 445–447,
    477, 532
Edelány   67
Eger (castle, principality, county)   308–311,
    319, 356, 381, 382, 390, 394, 522–525
Eger chapter   524
Eger bishopric, diocese   274, 304, 310,
    394–396, 475, 524, 525
Egypt   289
Eichstädt bishopric   483
Emona (Ljubljana)   170
Epidamnos (Durres)   26
Eresburg   220
Erfurt   51
Essex   295

INDEX OF PLACES

Esztergom, Gran (castle, county, archdeaconate)   46, 146, 179, 270, 317, 325, 326, 328, 330, 336–338, 340–344, 347, 348, 381–385, 391, 404, 407, 408, 410, 417, 418, 427, 431, 455, 479, 528, 534
Esztergom archbishopric, archdiocese, diocese   330, 331, 349, 372–374, 387–389, 395, 396, 407, 411, 414, 473, 479, 497, 516, 518–520, 524, 525, 535
Etelköz   239, 241, 242, 328
Etzilburg (Attila's town)   148, 312

Favianis   149
Fehér (county with its seat at Gyulafehérvár, archdeaconate)   386, 356
Fejér (county with its seat at Székesfehérvár, archdeaconate)   314, 315, 345, 389, 408, 410, 411
Fenékpuszta, see Valcum
Flanders   438
Flavia Solva   76
Floriana (Csákvár)   148
Forchheim   51, 212, 227
Francia   416
Franconia   252, 260, 261, 476
Frankfurt an Main   51, 98, 112, 113, 114, 207, 389
Frankish realm, Frankish kingdom   42, 47, 48, 53, 55, 63, 69, 73, 74, 75, 96, 98, 99, 106, 112–115, 126, 129, 130, 132, 134, 135, 139, 141
Freising bishopric   154, 258, 461, 483
Frisia   416
Friuli   54, 58, 59, 60, 73, 79, 118, 161
Friulian march   78, 80, 83, 85, 86, 89, 90, 92, 107, 113, 117, 118
Fulda   51

Gacka (Croatian county)   452
Galicia, Galician principality   242, 244, 311, 355, 356, 457, 471, 472
Gardellaca (Tokod)   147
Gascony   133, 134
Gaul   22, 49
Gemer (castle, county, archdeaconate)   335, 356, 412, 520, 522, 524
Gepid realm   32, 527
Germania   532

Germany, German realm, German empire   246, 261, 313, 317, 319, 385, 422, 438, 447, 448, 462, 464, 466, 500, 529, 532, 534
Giraltovce   415
Glebl' (east of Kiev)   377
Gniezno   330, 371
Gorsium (Herculia, Tác-Fövenypuszta)   144, 148
Grado   108
Great Moravia   141, 143, 178, 180, 181, 185–187, 194, 195, 199, 201, 202, 205–207, 210, 213–217, 219, 221, 222, 226, 228, 230, 232–235, 237–239, 245, 248, 250, 255, 269, 280, 285, 286, 293, 297–299, 302, 328, 330, 344, 347, 351, 372, 442, 492, 528
Greece   501
Grunzvitigau   101, 118, 182
Guntio's castle   90
Győr (castle, county, archdeaconate)   146, 179, 344–348, 382, 389–391, 406, 408, 410, 417, 430, 444, 450
Győr bishopric, diocese   346, 347, 389, 390, 395, 396, 410, 520
Győr (Diósgyőr)   356
Győrszentmárton   148
Gyulafehérvár (Gyula's White castle, Alba Iulia)   177, 306, 307, 309, 344, 348, 356, 385, 396

Haibach   121
Hainburg   425, 443, 444
Hajóhalm   524
Halberstadt bishopric   483
Hallstadt   51
Hamburg   118, 500, 501
Hanušovce   415
Haram (castle, county)   308, 351, 392
Hedčani, villages in Bohemia   321
Hegyközszentimre abbey (Sîntimreu)   419
Hengstfeld   230
Herstal   99, 106
Herul realm   16–18, 22–24, 40, 42
Hevlín   67
Heves (castle, county)   309, 523–525
Hidegleloskerest   146, 147
Hildesheim bishopric   483

Himesudvar 355
Hircanian Forest 50, 51
Hlohovec 263, 264, 335, 337, 352, 428, 492, 534
Holiare 67
Holland 438
Holíč 418, 534
Hont (castle, principality, county, archdeaconate) 321, 338, 344, 353–354, 356, 358, 359, 377, 404, 405, 407, 410, 413, 415, 427, 431, 481
Horné Obdokovce 263
Horné Saliby 263
Hortobágy-Árkus 68
Hronský Beňadik abbey 398, 487
Hungary, Hungarian principality, Hungarian kingdom 34, 40, 52, 145, 170, 179, 214, 237, 238, 271–273, 277, 292, 299, 301, 305, 308, 314, 319, 320, 324, 326–333, 336, 338, 340, 346–348, 352, 353, 356, 362, 364, 367–369, 374, 376, 377, 380–383, 386, 389–392, 395, 397, 398, 401–404, 415, 417, 418, 422–425, 427, 429, 431–435, 437–439, 441–450, 453, 455, 456, 459–461, 463, 467, 469–473, 476–478, 480, 481, 483–488, 490–493, 497–504, 512–515, 519, 520, 528–535
Hun realm 42
Hurbanovo-Bohatá 263

Ihtiman pass (Gate of Trajan) 333
Igfon (Biharian mountains) 419
Ikevár, near Vasvár 455
Illyricum (Illyria) 26, 28, 201
Ingelheim 114, 117
Ingolstatt 102
Iovia (Alsóheténypuszta) 148, 150
Ireland 140
Iron gates 214, 307, 392
Isfahán 269
Istria 31, 78, 92, 93, 161, 500
Italy 22, 29, 31, 92, 117, 244, 246, 257, 313, 314, 336, 371, 438, 500, 526
Izborsk 256
Izjaslavľ (on the Horyn river) 377
Izjaslavľ (south-east of Smolensk) 377
Izjaslavľ (nord-west from Minsk) 377
Iža 263
Iža near Komárno, see Kelemantia

Jaroměř 377
Jaroslavľ (nord-east of Rostov) 377
Jaroslavľ (on the San river) 377
Jerusalem 481

Kaiserlautern 48
Kajar 282
Kalamárka (near Detva) 65–66, 194
Kalisz 508
Kalocsa (castle, principality, county) 173, 314, 315, 348
Kalocsa bishopric, dioceze, archbishopric, archdioceze 348, 373, 387, 388, 394–396, 464
Kanjiža 308
Kapuvár 430, 459, 461
Karnburg (Krnski grad, civitas Carantana) 118
Kechnec 67
Kelemantia (Iža near Komárno) 8, 13, 14
Kemajten 121
Kemej (castle, county, archdeaconate) 303, 456, 488, 524
Keszthely 150, 151
Kethellak 282
Khazar empire 239
Kherson 508
Kiev 34, 324, 396, 397, 433, 441, 479, 508, 510
Kiev Rus 433
Kisvárda 301, 304
Klátova Nová Ves 65
Koblenz 49
Kolomna 511
Kolon (castle, county) 319, 346, 389, 408
Kołobrzeg, bishopric 371
Komárno 34, 43, 48, 59, 66, 67, 70, 94, 95
Komárno (castle, county, archdeaconate) 71, 282, 407, 408, 410, 427, 431, 481
Korytník 533
Košúty 263
Kota 457
Kovin (Keve, castle, county) 308, 351, 392, 455
Koźle 495, 496
Köpenick 508
Környe, see Vincentia
Köszeg (Keisi) 157, 165, 166, 169
Köszegfalva 170
Kösztölc 455

INDEX OF PLACES 663

Közép-Szolnok (castle, county)   304
Kraków   213, 318, 321, 323, 324, 334, 337, 338, 352, 471
Krakówia (Kraków country)   334, 352, 338, 352, 353, 507–508
Kraków bishopric   323, 371
Kraszna (castle, county)   304
Krbava (Croatian county)   452
Krems   16, 60
Kremsmünster, Abbey of the Most Holy Saviour   101, 118, 167, 182
Krivín (in Rybník)   65
Krnski grad (Karnburg, civitas Carantana)   76, 118
Krupina   264
Kulmitzberg   242
Kundpoldesdorf   169

Ladenburg   52
Ladoga   256
Laodicea   162
Larissa   333
Laugaricio (Trenčín)   8
Lauriacum (Lorch)   149
Lech, Lechfeld   74, 276, 317, 320
Lemešany   67
Letanovce, abbey   533
Levedia   239
Levice   254
Levounion   273, 470
Libice   368
Liburnia (Teurnia, Tiburnia), Liburnian principality   75, 92, 93, 105
Lika (Croatian county)   452
Linz   248
Liptov (castle, county)   321, 352, 405, 410
Little Carantania   75, 76
Little (small) Nitria   322, 323, 334–335, 338, 349–352, 358, 405–407, 415, 525, 528
Ljubljana (Lajbach), see Emona
Lombardy   244–247
Longobard kingdom (in Italy)   78, 143
Longobard realm (in Pannonia)   527
Lorraine   252, 416
Lorch (Lauriacum)   22, 45, 49, 50, 54, 60, 79, 96, 149
Lower Altaich, abbey   153

Lower Pannonia   84, 95, 96, 97, 102, 104, 106, 115, 119, 120, 124, 142, 143, 147, 153, 163, 166, 168, 228
Lower Silesia   213
Lučenec   264
Lučské pole   479
Lusatia   35, 213, 384, 401
Luttraif   102

Macedonia   141, 331
Mainz   49, 50, 51, 132, 184, 378
Majcichov   192, 193
Malá Čalomija   67
Maldon   295
Malohont (Little Hont)   354
Maramaros, Maramureş (castle, county)   304
March of Friuli, see Friulian march
Marosvár (castle, principality, later Csanád castle, county)   307–309, 311, 319, 320, 352, 356, 358, 391–393, 404
Marosvár, monastery of John the Baptist   351, 392, 393
Mařín   188
Matsee, Abbey of Saint Michael   167
Mauer (near Amstetten)   149
Mauer (near Vienna)   149
Mauerbach (near Vienna)   149
Mautern   149, 234
Meissen march   384, 495
Menfő   291, 430, 431
Merseburg   384, 385
Meszes (Mezeş) gates   302, 303, 305, 325, 453, 487, 488
Meszes abbey   481
Metz   48, 49, 50, 52
Międzyrzecz, abbey   367, 368
Michaľany   264
Michalovce   509
Mikulčice   59, 62–65, 67, 184, 205, 207, 245, 250
Milcenia   384, 401
Miltenberg   52
Miskolc   356
Miskolc-Repülőtér   263
Miskolc (Vezér út)   67
Mistelbach   67
Močola   481

Moesia 7, 22, 57, 491–493
Mogoncia, Mogontiacum (Mainz) 378
Mogyoród 441, 458, 488, 504
Moldovia 273, 301, 362, 467
Molpír in Smolenice 65, 191
Mondsee, abbey 170
Moosburg 118
Morava castle (Mikulčice) 188
Moravia, Moravian Principality 5, 7, 16, 24, 29, 30, 34, 40, 41, 42, 44, 45, 57, 60–64, 67, 70, 74, 81, 85, 86, 91, 95, 97, 109–112, 126, 129–131, 134, 181, 184–186, 188, 207–211, 214, 215, 217, 224, 230, 234–237, 245, 246, 249–257, 262, 265, 269, 270, 321–323, 363, 396, 401, 417, 418, 421, 450, 453, 456, 457, 471, 476, 486, 492, 494–497, 500, 505, 507, 512, 514, 515, 527, 528, 534, 535
Moravian archbishopric, archdiocese 215, 217
Moravian bishopric, diocese 321, 323, 330, 331
Moravian fields 418
Moesia 22, 491–493
Mosaburg, see Blatengrad
Moscow 511
Moson (castle, county) 346, 347, 381, 390, 417, 430, 436, 447, 450, 459–462, 467, 477
Mount Badon 295
Mödling, castle 446
Mstislavľ (east of Mogilev) 377
Mstislavľ (south of Smolensk) 377
Mudroňovo 263
Mukačevo (Munkács) 300
Murom 511
Mursa (Osijek) 144, 173
Mursa lake 173
Musella (Kisárpás) 148
Mutěnice 64
Mužla 191, 408
Münster bishopic 483

Nagyósz 393
Nakléřovský pass 49
Naumburg bishopric 483
Nedao 15, 19, 42

Nenince 481
Nestelbach 169
Neštich in Svätý Jur 65, 191
Neuching 261
Neusiedler Lake 19, 430, 461
Nibelung road 48–53
Nieder Alteich (Altach) abbey 101, 376
Nin (Nona) 105
Niš 455
Nitra 8, 9, 10, 13, 14, 45, 48, 59, 63, 65, 66, 67, 264
Nitra (castle, county, archdeaconate, provostal) 112, 116, 120, 121, 123, 124, 126, 128, 134, 140, 141, 152, 182, 183, 189, 190, 191, 215–218, 222, 325, 328–330, 334, 335, 337, 340, 341, 349, 352, 359, 387, 396–401, 403–407, 419, 420, 423, 427, 428, 431, 442, 451, 455, 461, 462, 471, 477, 478, 491, 504, 515–519, 528, 529
Nitrava (Nitravia) 110, 111, 112, 114, 217
Nitria (Nitraland), Nitrian Principality 40, 41, 42, 44, 60, 61, 65–70, 71, 74, 85, 91, 95–97, 99, 100, 109, 110, 112, 114, 124–131, 134–136, 139–141, 146, 153, 181–183, 186–190, 199, 207–209, 215, 220, 222, 237, 255, 256, 257, 262–265, 270, 286, 292, 293, 295, 299, 318–324, 326, 327, 330, 335, 338, 340, 341, 343, 344, 347–349, 351, 352, 357, 359, 363, 380–385, 391, 394, 396–406, 410, 412, 415–418, 424, 425, 427–429, 431, 435–437, 439, 441, 443, 444, 450–452, 455, 457, 459–463, 465, 466, 471, 476, 477, 480, 481, 487–494, 497, 498, 500–504, 512–515, 519–521, 524–530, 533, 535
Nitrian bishopric, diocese 215–219, 234, 237, 331, 373, 497, 518–519
Nitra chapter 516, 517
Nógrad, see Novohrad
Nordgau (Bavarian Northern march) 90, 102, 231
Noricum 16, 22, 42, 76, 143, 170
Noricum mediteraneum (Landlocked Noricum) 26, 30, 36, 75, 526
Noricum ripense 22, 42, 60, 145, 149, 227
Nové Zámky 67

INDEX OF PLACES

Novohrad, Nógrad (castle, county, archdeaconate)   263, 311, 315, 335, 353, 410–415, 427, 431, 481, 488
Nuremberg   52
Nyárhíd, near Nové Zámky   418
Nyír (Nyírség)   302, 305, 454, 487

Oberrana   149
Obid   67
Óbuda   312, 409
Ohringen   52
Olomouc   189, 287, 321, 322, 457, 475, 494, 505, 515
Oltenia (Lesser Wallachia)   16
Omundesberg (Omuntesperch)   226, 227, 230, 231
Omundesdorf   227
Orava (castle, county)   321, 352, 405, 471
Orléans   49
Oroszlános (Orozlanus), abbey of saint George   393
Orsova   307, 308, 351, 392
Ortahu   154, 158, 176, 179
Ostrá Skala (in Vyšný Kubín)   66, 190, 191
Ostrogót realm   15–22
Otakareschirichun   174
Örsúr (castle)   308, 309, 522, 524, 525

Pác   12, 67
Paderborn   184
Pannonia   6, 7, 9, 14, 15, 16, 19, 21–24, 26, 30–32, 34, 35, 38, 39, 40–44, 48, 49, 51, 54, 55, 56, 58, 59, 60, 68–73, 80–86, 89, 91, 93, 94, 96–100, 102, 111, 114–116, 124, 125, 136, 140–144, 148–152, 158, 159, 162, 164, 170, 171, 174, 176, 178, 183, 213, 220–224, 227, 228, 230, 244–247, 252, 254, 257, 265, 273, 281, 283, 288, 289, 293, 297, 313, 325, 374, 443, 451, 477, 487, 492, 493, 504, 526, 527
Pannonian diocese   211, 212
Pannonian principality   122, 134, 142, 143, 154, 157, 158, 159, 171–174, 199, 211, 212, 222, 223, 228–231, 242, 244–246, 248, 313, 506
Pannonhalma, abbey   329, 343, 344, 347, 370, 373, 390, 393, 451, 518

Passau   49, 124, 181, 327, 480, 482, 484, 492, 534
Passau bishopric, Passau diocese   85, 95, 100, 124–126, 166, 181, 195, 202, 217, 327, 328, 330, 483, 492
Pata (castle, county)   308, 309
Pécs (Päťkostolie, Fünfkirchen)   149, 157, 172, 396, 445, 451
Pécs bishopric, diocese   149, 319, 346–348, 389–390, 395, 396, 451, 520
Pécsvárád, abbey of saint Benedict   368, 445
Perejaslavľ (on the Dnieper south-east of Kiev)   375–376, 377
Peremyšľ (on the Oka river)   376, 377
Peremyšľ (Przemyśl, on the San River)   376, 377, 379, 479
Pereslavľ (nord east of Moscow)   375, 377
Perschling   121
Pest   248
Pest (castle, county, archdeaconate)   411, 412, 435, 436, 457, 458
Perugia   374
Pförring   48, 49, 52, 53
Piliny-Leshegy   263, 443
Pilis   284–286, 290–293, 295, 297, 299
Pilis county (seat in Buda castle)   409, 410
Pilismarót   146, 284
Pinkava (Pinkafeld)   167, 169
Platting   48
Pliska   99
Plovdiv   325
Pobedim   65, 192, 193
Pocking   260
Podbranč   64, 188
Poetovio (Ptuj)   144, 170
Pohansko near Břeclav   62, 188, 250
Poland   238, 311, 321, 322, 330, 353, 356, 367, 368, 371, 372, 380–383, 386, 396, 397, 399, 415, 421, 423, 429, 432, 440, 441, 445, 446, 449, 455–457, 467, 471, 474, 475, 479, 481, 483, 484, 492, 495, 500, 507, 512, 514, 520, 523, 529, 530, 534, 535
Pomerania   432, 508
Pone Navata (Visegrád)   147
Poroszló   308
Potentia   280
Považská Bystrica   353

Povel near Olomouc   62, 63, 64, 189
Poznań (Posen)   330, 367, 508
Požega (castle, county)   319, 346, 347
Prague (Praha)   270, 324, 325, 371, 378, 398,
    476, 485, 494, 514
Prague bishopric, diocese   318, 321–323, 330,
    331, 352, 353, 358, 479, 502, 513
Premberg (Pfreimt)   51
Preslav   324, 325, 331, 376, 377
Preslava, see Bratislava
Preslavets (Perejaslavets)   324, 325
Prievidza-Hradec   191
Pronsk   511
Prša   67, 263
Przemyśl (Peremyšľ)   244, 479
Ptuj, Pettau, (castle, principality, county,
    marchia)   143, 144, 157, 159–164, 172, 174,
    176, 229, 425
Puchham   121
Púchov   353

Quadia   5, 6, 13, 14
Quartinaha   154
Quedlinburg   331, 333

Radim   376
Radkersburg   163
Radomír (in Bulgaria)   377
Radomysľ (west of Kiev)   377
Radvaň nad Dunajom   66
Raffelstetten   196, 249
Rajhrad   188
Rákoš near Pest   457
Raška   480
Ratibor, castle   496
Ratisbona (Regina)   378
Ravenna   374
Regensburg   46, 48–54, 79, 91, 119, 121, 139,
    183, 198, 230, 232, 234, 249, 261, 266, 321,
    371, 378, 392, 467
Regensburg, abbey of Saint Emmeram   169,
    389
Regensburg bishopric, diocese   154, 169, 170,
    178, 443, 444, 483, 494
Rennersdorf   121
Rhineland   476
Riade   268
Rimavská Sobota   264

Rjazaň (castle, principality)   511
Rome (Roma)   105, 201, 226, 373, 374, 377
Roman empire   532
Rotfeld (Field of Lies near Colmar)   130
Roding   119
Rosdorf   121
Roslavľ (on the Ostier river)   377
Rott   260
Rožňa   479
Rugiland   16, 22, 23, 30, 42, 45, 60
Ruginesfeld   154, 157, 163, 169, 176
Russia   276, 291, 324, 363, 366, 415, 432, 455,
    500, 508, 514, 520, 530
Ryazan, (castle, town, pricipality)   295–296
Říp   39, 220

Saarbrücken   48
Sabaria, Savaria, Szombathely,
    Steinamanger   14, 50, 60, 70, 80, 95, 96,
    144, 164, 167–170
Sabarian ford   169
Safenbach   169
Saint Emmeram abbey in Regensburg   95,
    121, 122, 123
Saint Gallen abbey   327
Saint Médard abbey in Soissons   130
Saint Pantaleon   46
Saint Pölten   149
Sajószentpéter   67
Salapiugin, see Zalabér
Salla   170
Salt castle (Salis, Solivar) near Prešov   353,
    355, 381, 383
Salzburg   75, 91, 92, 102, 104, 124, 138, 141,
    155, 174
Salzburg bishopric, archbishopric, Salzburg
    diocese   60, 75, 77, 83–85, 91, 95, 102, 110,
    120, 124, 125, 140, 142, 153, 155–157, 166,
    167, 169, 172, 179, 180, 211, 212, 229
Samarkand   264
Samos's realm   22, 41–44, 47, 48, 52–56, 59,
    61, 67, 71, 72, 527
Sár   282
Sarmatia   6
Saxony   36, 49, 80, 207, 250–255, 257, 261,
    267, 268, 317, 384, 385, 401, 416, 476,
    500, 528, 532, 535
Saxon marches (Saxony border)   384, 385

INDEX OF PLACES

Savia, Savian principality, principality of
  Sisak   35, 36, 38, 40, 42, 58, 59, 61, 70, 83,
    85, 86, 96, 105, 107, 114, 115, 119, 135,
    141–143, 157, 159, 172, 230, 472, 526, 527
Savinja   160, 161
Scarbantia (Sopron)   144, 145, 170
Schleswig   508
Schönering   121
Schönkirchen-Reysenhofene   67
Scythia   363, 364, 531
Seňa   5
Serbia   109, 279
Serdika   324
Sereď   263
Sibrik   147
Sicambria   280
Sieradz   508
Silesia   35, 496, 535
Silesian mount (Ślęża)   220
Silistra   324
Simmering   60
Singidunum (Belgrade)   20, 21,
Sirmium (Sriemska Mitrovica)   24, 70, 144,
    201, 214, 313, 453
Sisak (Siscia)   35, 86, 106, 107, 108, 129, 143,
    173, 472, 473
Skalica   534
Slankamen   453
Slavinia   402, 403, 500, 501, 532, 533
Slavonia   57, 70, 279, 313, 470, 472, 473, 478,
    493, 500, 525, 533
Slovakia   5, 23, 24, 29, 41, 42, 57, 66, 170,
    263, 270, 279, 318, 346, 349, 350, 381,
    403–405, 415, 417, 418, 429, 431, 443,
    451, 461, 472, 476, 484, 493, 515, 517, 526,
    531–535
Slovenija   533
Smižany   194, 195
Soběslav   377
Solva (Esztergom)   146, 147
Somlóvásárhely   148
Somogy, (castle, principality, county)   172,
    319, 327, 329, 341, 342, 344, 346, 348,
    356, 362, 373, 390, 404, 473
Somogy, abbey of saint Giles   465, 466, 473
Sopianae (Pécs)   148, 149, 396,
Sopron (castle, county)   164, 346, 347, 390,
    430, 453, 460–462

Sorbia   225, 255, 506, 527
Sóshartyán-Zúdótető   263
Spain   246
Speyer   438, 468
Spiš (castle, county)   353, 356, 520, 522–524,
    533
Split archbishops   472
Spytihněv (in Moravia)   377
Sredets   331
Sriem   24, 214, 313, 453
Stanacum   149
Stará Boleslav   339
Staré Město (Na Valách)   62, 189
Staré Zámky in Brno – Líšeň   62–64, 188,
    250
Starý Tekov   193
Strachotín   250
Stropkov   415
Strumingen   121
Styria   161, 443
Styrian march   425
Suebia   5, 17, 18, 24, 526
Svjatopolk (close to Jurjev)   377
Swabia   219, 252, 260, 261, 317, 416, 466
Szabols (castle, county, archdeaconate)   301,
    304, 382, 472, 524
Szamos   305
Szatmár, Satu-Mare (castle, county,
    archdeaconate)   302–304
Százhalom   312
Szécsény   67
Székesfehérvár, Stoličný Belehrad,
    Weissenburg, Alba Regia   148, 179, 317,
    383, 421, 431, 433, 435–437, 443, 446,
    447, 449, 455, 459, 488
Szekszárd, abbey   449, 455, 456
Szentendre   409
Szentjobb (Sîniob), abbey   481
Szerencs (castle, county)   301, 355, 356, 415,
    521, 524, 525
Szigetfő, (castle, county, archdeaconate)
    314, 315, 411, 412
Szob   67, 248, 283–285
Szob-Kiserdő   263
Szolnok (castle, county, archedeaconate)
    377, 411, 412, 435, 487
Šaľa   67, 518
Šariš (castle, county)   5, 353, 356, 415, 524

Šarišské Sokolovce (Hradová hura)   194
Šaštín   418, 428
Šebastovce   67
Šintava   335, 352, 418, 428, 461, 462, 504
Štúrovo   67

Taksony   437
Tana   481
Tarvisio   117
Tata   282, 286
Tátony (village in Somogy county)   362
Tatras, Tatra mountains   353, 355, 356, 358, 520
Tekov, Bars (castle, county, archdeaconate)   356, 358, 404, 407, 408, 427, 431, 534
Tekovský Hrádok (Várad)   335, 352
Temesvár (Timişoara)   471
Terebovľ (Tarnopoľ, Ternopil)   471, 479
Tersatto   92
Tetín   225
Teurnia (Tiburnia), see Liburnia
Thessaloniki   27
Thionville   96
Thrace   14, 26, 325, 500
Thuringia   31, 48, 49, 51, 55, 207, 224, 252–255, 268, 416
Tihany, Abbey of saint Anian   445, 447, 466
Tisza river region (area around the Tisza river, land along the Tisza)   5, 57, 58, 71, 82, 98, 99, 141, 184, 213, 217, 218, 237, 242–244, 247–249, 254, 255, 273, 279–281, 298, 306, 311, 415, 434–437, 487, 488, 527
Tiszalúc, village   443, 451
Titel, chapter   243, 465–466
Tmutokaraň   510
Tokaj   263
Tolna (castle, county)   147, 172, 319, 346, 347
Toperos   26
Trajan's bridge (near Turnu Severin)   214
Traismauer   128, 138, 149
Transdanubia   57, 83, 84, 102, 104, 112, 114–120, 124, 129, 136, 143, 162, 164, 172–176, 178–180, 199, 200, 206, 221, 223, 228, 230, 237, 245, 248, 257, 279, 281, 286, 290, 293, 294, 298, 299, 311, 313, 314, 316, 317, 319, 320, 330, 345–348, 359, 373, 390, 391, 431, 435–437, 444, 481

Transylvania   32, 57, 71, 141, 173, 214, 249, 273, 301, 302, 305–308, 311, 319, 325, 326, 331, 344, 348, 358, 385–387, 390–392, 404, 453, 455, 471, 481, 487, 488, 498, 513, 525
Transylvania (bishopric, diocese)   304, 331, 390, 395, 533
Traungau, Bavarian border county   78, 83, 120–123, 127, 182, 183, 234, 247
Trebur   444
Trenčianske Bohuslavice   65
Trenčín (castle, county)   8, 192, 321, 322, 335, 349, 350, 352, 353, 403, 404, 405, 427, 431, 453, 471, 484, 515, 519, 534
Trentino   161
Tricciana (Ságvár)   148, 150
Trier   50
Tulln   149, 202–205, 223, 424, 483
Tullnerfeld   23
Turiec (castle, county)   321, 352, 405, 471
Turňa (castle, county)   264, 356, 520, 522, 524
Turnu-Severín (Szörény)   214, 308
Tüskevár (perhaps antique Mogentiana)   148
Tvrdošovce   263

Ugoča, Ugocsa (castle, county)   300, 304
Uherské Hradiště (Ostrov svatáho Jiří)   62, 64, 189
Uherský Brod   524, 534
Újvár, see Abaújvár
Undrima   75
Ung, Ungvár, Užhorod (castle, principality, county)   300–304, 311, 354, 355, 356, 358, 467, 521, 525
Upper Burgundy   252, 261
Upper Lorraine, Upper Lotharingia   252, 438
Upper Silesia   213
Upper Pannonia   85, 94, 95, 98, 107, 114, 115, 117, 119, 120, 124, 125, 142, 145, 149, 164, 166–168, 174, 223, 228, 229, 231, 234, 249, 259, 281, 313
Uten   481

Vác (castle, principality, county, archdeaconate)   48, 314, 315, 348, 353, 359, 373, 382, 410–415, 457, 462, 488

INDEX OF PLACES

Vác bishopric, dioecese   315, 317, 348, 373, 390, 395, 396, 411–415
Váh (Wag), little principality   318, 321–323, 334, 338, 352–353, 356, 358, 404, 405, 415, 528
Valachia   362
Valcum (Fenékpuszta)   148, 150, 151
Valeria (Roman Pannonian provinces)   148, 149
Valaliky   67
Vandal kingdom   6
Várad (Oradea)   292, 366, 472, 475
Várad bishopric   275, 472, 475
Várad, see Tekovský Hrádok
Várkony, village near Tisza (south of Szolnok)   446, 479
Várpalota   344
Vasilev   377
Vasvár (Castrum Ferreum, Železný hrad, Eisenburg) Vas county   163, 170, 281, 319, 346, 347, 390
Vážany, village in Moravia   321
Velika   142
Veľké Kosihy   67
Veľké Kostoľany   263
Veľký Meder   67
Veľký Kýr   13, 263
Venice   27, 92, 245, 393, 419, 452, 478, 479, 500, 532
Verdun   139
Verona   161
Veszprém (castle, county, archdeaconate)   176, 178, 179, 281, 282, 283, 285, 286, 288, 290, 291, 293, 297, 299, 317, 326, 328, 330, 342, 344–346, 348, 377, 389, 408, 421
Veszprém bishopric, dioecese   176–177, 315, 329, 330, 346, 347, 372, 373, 389–391, 395, 396, 408, 520
Vidin   307, 308, 331, 333, 392
Vienna   22, 241, 417, 418
Vienna Woods   59, 60, 72, 80, 81, 94, 95, 100, 101, 118, 120, 124, 145, 221, 223, 227, 228, 231, 234, 247
Villach   117
Vincentia (Környe)   148, 150, 286
Vindobona (Vienna)   11, 145
Virt   67

Virunum   75, 76, 144
Visegrád (castle, county, archdeaconate)   147, 179, 345, 382, 389, 408, 409, 467
Vistulia (Vistulaland), Vistulian principality   191, 213, 214, 507
Vladimir on the Klyazma river   377, 511
Vladimir-Volynsky (Volodymyr-Volynsky, on the Bug river)   377, 433
Vlastislav   376
Vojnice   67, 263
Volhyn   479
Vraclav   376
Vukovar, Valkó (castle, county)   319, 346, 347
Vyšehrad (in Turiec)   191
Vyškovce   67

Wallachia   362
Wampaldi   154
Weimar-Orlamünde   447
West Francia   198
White Croatia   35
White Serbia   35, 39
Wildungsmauer (near Petronell)   149
Wimpfen   52
Wisitindorf (Ussitin)   157, 165, 169
Wogastisburg   45, 47, 48, 53, 54, 55
Worms   48, 49, 51, 52, 53, 130, 132, 221
Wrocław   377, 534
Wrocław bishopric   371
Würzburg   51, 52

Zadar   452
Zagreb   366, 472–474
Zagreb bishopric (dioceze)   472–474, 516, 517
Zala (county)   172
Zalabér, Salapiugin   153, 154, 155, 158
Zalavár   151, 455
Zalavár, abbey of saint Hadrian   351
Zámoly, village   436
Zaránd   304
Zeiselmauer   149
Zelená Hora near Vyškov   64, 188, 250
Zemianska Olča   263
Zemplín, Zemplén (castle, county, archdeaconate)   5, 263, 300, 301, 355, 356, 381, 382, 415, 509, 520, 521, 524, 525
Zemun   476

Zelená hora near Vyškov 62
Zilah, Zalău 302
Zirc, royal court 447
Znojmo 188, 494
Zobor hill 65, 219–220, 264, 270, 285, 292, 299
Zobor, abbey of saint Hyppolitus 219–220, 270, 349–351, 403, 407, 451, 484, 515–518
Zombor (castle, county) 356, 377
Zsomboly (later called Pankota, archdeaconate) 394, 524
Zvolen (castle, county) 353
Zvolen-Môťová 194
Želovce 67
Žilina 405
Žitavská Tôň 66
Žitvatorok 436

Printed in the United States
By Bookmasters